2012
PowerBoat Guide

Ed McKnew • Mark Parker

American Marine Publishing, Inc.

COVER PICTURES:

Sabre 42 Express, Top Center
Grand Banks 53 RPH, Lower Left
Regulator 32, Lower Right

PUBLISHED BY
American Marine Publishing, Inc.
www.powerboatguide.com
info@powerboatguide.com

ISBN-13: 978-1466283411

For information on advertising in the PowerBoat Guide,
contact Shari at 231-360-0827

Printed and bound in the United States of America.

Table of Contents

Introduction

Welcome to the 2012 PowerBoat Guide, the latest edition of what has become one of the best-selling publications in the marine industry. First published in 1989, the PowerBoat Guide was originally conceived as a reference handbook for yacht brokers and dealers. Within a few short years, however, the book found it's way into the public domain, and it has been an invaluable resource for hundreds — perhaps thousands — of boat buyers ever since. Produced by experienced yacht brokers, the PowerBoat Guide has stood the test of time with marine industry professionals across the country.

In making the selections for this year's edition, the editors have endeavoured to include those boats of the greatest potential interest to our readers. No effort has been made to include *all* models from *any* manufacturer, and there are many builders whose products we have not featured at all. Because we don't charge manufacturers to include their products in the PowerBoat Guide, we are able to make our selections without any outside pressure.

For ease of use, the book is divided into three sections: Motoryachts & Trawlers; Sportfishermen; and Cruisers & Sportboats. Models featured in each section are sorted by manufacturer name first, and then by size. Note that there are occassions where the same boat appears in two different sections — some models simply resist catagorization. In general, however, the sections are tightly drawn and easy to navigate.

About The Prices

Retail high-low values are provided for models built only after 1995. In the case of new or limited production models, we may choose not to offer price estimates due to lack of resale activity. The prices quoted in this book reflect the market conditions projected by our staff for the 2012 model year, a difficult task indeed considering the uncertainty of today's boating market.

Just as it is with cars, RVs, and homes, you get what you pay for. High-end yachts are nearly always the leaders when it comes to resale value. Trawlers and motoryachts — especially those from quality manufacturers — typically retain roughly 50% of their original purchase price after five years of ownership. Very high-end trawlers may retain 60–70% of their original value after five years if they're well equipped and maintained.

It is especially important to review the section "About These Prices" on page 529 before referencing the assigned values. And remember, no matter what the various price guides (including ours) might say, the fact remains that the only real value of a boat is what someone is willing to pay for it on a given day. *The prices in this book are provided as rough estimates only.* They are meant to be used as a starting point in determining a boat's actual value in a given market. Do not take them too literally.

Finding A Specific Model

If you don't find what you're looking for in a given section, be sure to check the index to make sure it isn't found elsewhere in the book. Keep in mind that the PowerBoat Guide covers boats between 27' and 80' in length built after 1985.

Companion CD Volume

Note that the 2012 PowerBoat Guide is available on CD or may be downloaded directly to your desktop. For details, please visit our website at www.powerboatguide.com.

* * * * * *

We sincerely hope you will find the information in the PowerBoat Guide to be useful, and we welcome any comments you might care to offer regarding the content or the character of this publication.

About the Authors

Ed McKnew

Ed McKnew began his career in the boating industry in 1979 when he purchased a small brokerage operation in Traverse City, MI. Moving to Texas in 1980, Ed continued to sell boats in Clear Lake until 1987 when he and partner Mark Parker published the first edition of the PowerBoat Guide. Ed has spent the past two decades serving as editor of the PowerBoat Guide while living in both Florida and northern Michigan. He has a bachelors degree in Business from Oakland University in Rochester, MI. He and his wife Shari live in Salem, Oregon.

Mark Parker

Mark Parker has been a yacht broker since 1982, first in Texas and, starting in 1990, in South Florida. Mark started his boating career as a mate, then a captain and managed to complete an education along the way with a BA in Marketing. Mark and Ed started writing the first PowerBoat Guide in 1987 and have worked together ever since to keep the publication up to date. Now closing in on three decades of full time yacht brokerage service, Mark spends his spare time in the Bahamas and touring on his motorcycle.

How to Use This Book

For the most part, the contents of this book are straightforward and easily understood. Before launching into the pages, however, we strongly suggest that you take a few moments and review the following points. Failure to do so is likely to result in some confusion and misunderstanding.

Pricing Information

Boat prices have been compiled from 1995, the base year for our calculations. Prices are not provided for models built before 1995 or for those models whose resale activity is insufficient to determine a reliable price range.

In the Price Schedule, six asterisks (******) indicate that we have insufficient data to render a value for a particular model year.

The *Retail High* is the average selling price of a clean, well-equipped and well-maintained boat with low-to-moderate engine hours. Boats with an exceptional equipment list, outstanding maintenance, or those with unusually low hours will usually sell at a figure higher than the published Retail High.

The *Retail Low* is the average selling price of a boat with below-average maintenance, poor equipment, high-time engines, or excessive wear. High-time boats in poor condition will generally sell for less than the published Retail Low.

Used boats located in the following markets are generally valued at 10–15 percent higher than published prices:

Great Lakes	+10–15%
Pacific Northwest	+10–15%
Inland Rivers & Lakes	+5–10%
California	+10–15%

The prices presented in this book reflect our best estimates of used boat prices for the model year 2012. They are intended for general use only and are not meant to represent exact market values.

Factory Specifications

The specifications listed for each model are self-explanatory although the following factors are noted:

Clearance refers to bridge clearance, or the height above the waterline to the highest point on the boat. Note that this is often a highly ambiguous piece of information since the manufacturer may or may not include such things as an arch, hardtop, or mast. Use this figure with caution.

Weight is a factory-provided specification that may or may not be accurate. Manufacturers differ in the way they compute this figure. For the most part, it refers to a dry boat with no gear.

NA means that information (or data) is not available.

Performance Data

Whenever possible, performance figures have been obtained from the manufacturer or a reliable dealer or broker. When such information was unavailable, the authors have relied upon their own research together with actual hands-on experience. The speeds are estimates and (in most cases) based on boats with average loads of fuel, water, options and gear.

All speeds are reported in knots. Readers in the Great Lakes or inland waterways may convert knots to miles-per-hour by multiplying a given figure by 1.14.

Cruising Speeds, Gas Engines
Unless otherwise noted, the cruising speed for gas-powered inboard (or stern drive) boats is calculated at 3,000–3,200 rpm.

Cruising Speeds, Diesel Engines
The cruising speeds for diesel-powered boats are calculated as follows:

Detroit (2-stroke) Diesels: about 200–250 rpm off the top rpm rating.

Other (4-stroke) Diesels: about 350–400 rpm off the manufacturer's maximum rpm rating.

Cruising Speeds, Outboard Engines
The cruising speeds for outboard-powered boats is generally figured at 4,000 rpm.

Useful Terms

Abaft—behind

Athwartships—at a right angle to the boat's length

Bulkhead—an upright partition separating compartments in a boat

Bulwark—a raised portion of the deck designed to serve as a barrier

Chine—the point at which the hullsides and the bottom of the boat come together

Coaming—vertical surface surrounding the cockpit

Cuddy—generally refers to the cabin of a small boat

Deadrise—the angle from the bottom of the hull (not the keel) to the chine

Deep-V Hull—a planing hull form with at least 18 degrees of deadrise at the transom and a fairly constant "V" bottom shape from stem to stern.

Displacement Hull—a hull designed to go through the water and not capable of planing speed

Forefoot—the underwater shape of the hull at the bow

Freeboard—the height of the sides of the hull above the waterline

gph—gallons per hour (of fuel consumption)

Gunwale (also gunnel)— the upper edge of the sheerline

Hull Speed—the maximum practical speed of a displacement hull. To calculate, take the square root of the LWL (waterline hull length) and multiply by 1.34.

Knot—one nautical mile per hour. To convert knots to statute mph, multiply by 1.14.

Modified-V Hull—a planing hull form with (generally) less than 18 degrees of transom deadrise

Nautical Mile—measurement used in salt water. A nautical mile is 6,076 feet.

Planing Speed—the point at which an accelerating hull rises onto the top of the water. To calculate a hull's planing speed, multiply the square root of the waterline length by 2.

Semi-Displacement Hull—a hull designed to operate economically at low speeds while still able to attain planing speed performance

Sheerline—the fore-and-aft line along the top edge of the hull

Sole—a nautical term for floor

Statute Mile—measurement used in fresh water. A statute mile equals 5,280 feet.

Tender—may refer to either (a) a dinghy, or (b) lack of hull stability.

Marine Surveyor Directory

ABYC ....American Boat & Yacht Council
IAMI ....International Assoc. of Marine Investigators
NAMS .... National Association of Marine Surveyors
NFPA.................................. National Fire Prevention Association
SAMS ....Society of Accredited Marine Surveyors
SNAME ....Society of Naval Architects & Marine Engineers

ALABAMA

James Dinges
AYS Marine
100 Ayreswood Dr.
Dothan, AL 36303
334-479-0570; Cell:256-603-1076
jdinges@hiwaay.net
SAMS, ABYC

Christopher Collier
C.E. Collier & Assoc., Inc.
PO Box 643
Coden, AL 36523-0643
251-873-4382; Cell:251-610-1546
cemarine1@aol.com
ABYC, NAMS, NFPA

Joseph "Tommy" Backe Jr.
Honor Marine Services
4108 Indian Hills Rd.
Decatur, AL 35603
256-566-4732
jtbacke@aol.com
SAMS, ABYC

Dennis Heine
Nautical Services, Inc
767 Wedgewood Dr.
Gulf Shores, AL 36542
251-979-2024
nsi@mchsi.com
SAMS

D.J. Smith
Port City Marine Surveyors
PO Box 190321
Mobile, AL 36619
251-661-5426; Cell:251-421-5426
masurveyor@aol.com
www.portcitymarineservices.com
ABYC, SAMS, NAMI, NFPA

Richard Schiehl
Schiehl & Associates LLC
6650 River Pl
Gulf Shores, AL 36542-2518
251-979-5912; Cell:251-979-5912
rschiehl@gulftel.com
www.alabamamarinesurveyor.com/
ABYC, NAMS, NAMI

ARKANSAS

John Linck
Linck Marine Surveying
600 Pine Forest Dr. Suite 4D
Maumelle, AR 72113
501-231-9350; Cell:501-231-9350
JELMarine@aol.com
www.Marinesurveyor.com/Linck
ABYC, SAMS

CALIFORNIA

Clark Barthol
Clark Barthol Marine Surveyors
27 Buccaneer St
Marina del Rey, CA 90292-5103
310-823-3350; Cell:310-823-3350
cbarms@aol.com
ABYC, NAMS, NFPA

Lyndon "Zeph" Despard
Donru Marine Services, LLC
413 Corral de Tierra Rd.
Salinas, CA 93908
831-484-9561; Cell:831-229-3238
zdespard@aol.com
SAMS, ABYC

Ron Grant
Grant Marine Surveys
31091 Paseo Valencia
San Juan Capistrano, CA 92675-2950
949-240-8353
vaimalu9@gmail.com
ABYC, SAMS

Thomas Prior
Priority Marine Survey & Consulting
PO Box 2927
Sausalito, CA 94965
415-459-4050; Cell:650-521-3907
tomprior1@aol.com
SAMS

Peggy Feakes
R.J. Whitfield & Associates
835 Yerba Buena Ave
Stockton, CA 95210
209-956-8488; Cell:209-406-9679
peggy@rjwsurvey.com
www.rjwsurvey.com
ABYC, SAMS, IAMI

Gary Beck
Yachtsman Marine Survey LLC
5318 E. 2nd St. #415
Long Beach, CA 90803
562-234-3585; Cell:562-234-3585
yachtsmanmarine@aol.com
www.vesselsurveyor.com
ABYC, SAMS, NFPA

COLORADO

James Beck
Columbine Marine Service
PO Box 3545
Breckenridge, CO 80424-3545
970-453-0350; Cell:970-393-2425
svptarmigan@earthlink.net
ABYC, SAMS

CONNECTICUT

Phillip Gaudreau
Allpoint Marine Services, LLC
11 Pettipaug Rd.
Haddam Neck, CT 06424
860-467-6956; Cell:860-638-7667
pgaudreau41@comcast.net
ABYC, SAMS, NFPA

William Stadel
George H. Stadel Jr. & Sons Inc.
1088 Shippan Ave

Stamford, CT 06902-7424
203-324-2610
bill.stadel@gmail.com
SAMS

Buddy Hitchcock
Hitchcock Marine Services
PO Box 612
Essex, CT 06426
860-767-7251; Cell:860-388-7886
buddy.hms@sbcglobal.net
SAMS, ABYC

Chris Nebel
Advanced Marine Surveyors
51 W. Lake Ave.
Guilford, CT 06437
203-623-0301
captainchris@thatboatguy.com
www.advancedmarinesurveyors.com
SAMS, ABYC, NFPA

James Curry
James M. Curry - Yacht Surveys
5 Pleasant Hill Lane
Clinton, CT 06413-2535
860-669-3119; Cell:860-834-1600
jcurry01@snet.net
ABYC, SAMS, NAMI

Blake Powell
JMS Naval Architects
34 Water St.
Mystic, CT 06355
860-536-0009; Cell:860-662-2014
blake@jmsnet.com
www.jmsnet.com
SAMS, ABYC, SNAME

Adrian & Kenneth Johnson
Johnson Marine Services
PO Box 271
West Mystic, CT 06388-0271
860-572-8866; Cell:860-235-2990
aj@johnsonmarineservices.com
www.johnsonmarineservices.com
ABYC, SAMS

FLORIDA

John Allinson II
Allinson Associates, Inc.
222 University Blvd N. #2
Jacksonville, FL 32211-7534
904-721-2177; Cell:904-721-2177
jna2@allinson.com
www.allinson.com
SAMS, ABYC, SNAME, NFPA

Malcom Elliott
Florida Nautical Surveyors
2727 NE 32nd St
Ft. Lauderdale, FL 33306-1507
954-630-2141; Cell:954-801-2140
fnsurveys@aol.com
www.floridanauticalsurveyors.com
ACMS

Arlen Leiner
AAC Marine Group, Inc.
2333 Knoll Ave N.
Palm Harbor, FL 34683
727-647-7112
captaleiner@gmail.com
www.aacmarinesurveyor.com
ABYC, SAMS, SNAME, NAMI, NFPA

Capt. Ronald W. Morgan
Accredited Marine Consultants, Inc.
313 Lake Cr. Suite 113
West Palm Beach, FL 33408-5227
561-845-1953
Capt_RWMorgan@Bellsouth.net
www.AccMarCon.Com
ABYC, SAMS, SNAME

Dewey Acker
Acker Marine Survey Co.
801 73rd St., Ocean
Marathon, FL 33050-5101
305-743-2397
ackermarinesurvey@att.net
www.ackermarinesurvey.com
ABYC, SAMS, NAMI

Johnny Smith
Anchor Marine Services, LLC
2720 Semoran Drive
Pensacola, FL 32503
850-982-5079; Cell:850-982-5079
marine.surveys@yahoo.com
www.anchormarineonline.com
ABYC, SAMS

Patrick Guckian
Aquarius Marine Systems
160 SE Duxbury Ave
Port St Lucie, FL 34983-2604
772-871-0364
aquariusmarinesy@bellsouth.net
www.aquariusmarinesytems.com
ABYC, SAMS, SNAME, IAME

William R. Potter
Bill Potter Marine Surveys
PO Box 560-532
Miami, FL 33256-0532

305-989-9100; Cell:305-989-9100
billpotter@ymail.com
www.billpottermarinesurveys.com
SAMS, NFPA, ABYC

Brian Galley
Brian Galley & Assoc
9423 S. Ocean Dr. #77
Jenson Beach, FL 34957
772-692-1893; Cell:772-932-4034
bgsurveyor@yahoo.com
www.mariensurveyor.com/galley
SAMS

Bryan Norman
Bryan Norman Marine Surveyor
PO Box 3812
St Augustine, FL 32085-3812
904-797-5880; Cell:904-347-3549
ibnorm63@msn.com
SAMS, ABYC

Charlie Lopez
C&K Marine
1614 Beach Pkwy Unit 104
Cape Coral, FL 33904
239-233-6116; Cell:507-261-5546
calkjl@gmail.com
SAMS

Airel Cabrera
Capt. Ariel & Associates
8915 SW 19 Street
Miami, FL 33165
Cell:305-431-6936
ariel@captainariel.com
www.captainariel.com
SAMS

Gary Flack
Capt. Gary Flack, Marine Surveyor
8360 144th Lane N.
Seminole, FL 33776-2802
727-398-2267
shipreg@aol.com
www.FlackMarineSurvey.com/
SAMS

Donald Eiler
Eiler Marine Enterprises
26153 Rampart Blvd
Punta Gorda, FL 33983-6216
941-624-5003; Cell:941-276-2523
swflsurveyor@gmail.com
www.eilermarine.com
SAMS, ABYC

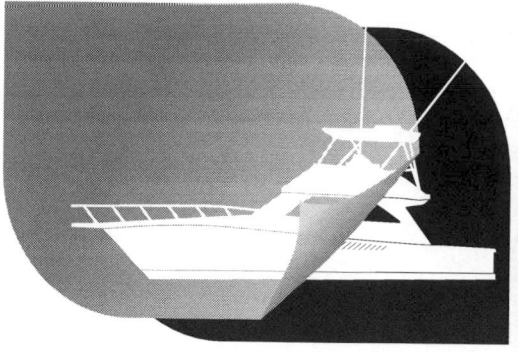 

–Surveyor Directory–

James Avery
Emerald Coast Marine Services
981 Hwy 98 E. Ste 3 Unit #224
Destin, FL 32541
850-582-9880; Cell:850-582-9880
averyjamesr@gmail.com
www.marinesurvey.org
ABYC, SAMS

David Ghidoni
Florida Keys Harbor Surveyors
10-B Hilton Haven Dr.
Key West, FL 33040
305-797-4325
kwtugcapt@comcast.net
www.keywestmarinesurveyor.com
SAMS, ABYC

Kerry Nikula
Florida Nautical Surveyors
618 NE 3rd St.
Dania Beach, FL 33304
954-630-2141; Cell:954-232-3416
kerrynikula@yahoo.com
www.floridanauticalsurveyors.com
ABYC

Rolland Freeman
Freeman & Company, Marine Survey
588 Bayview Dr.
Long Boat Key, FL 34228
941-383-2952; Cell:941-705-8800
freemanmarinesvy@aol.com
SAMS

Lou Gonzalez, A.M.S.
Global International Marine Surveyors
10773 NW 58th St. #530
Miami, FL 33178
305-718-9742; Cell:305-986-2563
globalmarsurvey@aol.com
SAMS

Robert R. Garay, AMS
Global Yacht & Ship Surveyors
6805 SW 89th Ct
Miami, FL 33173-2429
305-270-1553; Cell:305-986-3362
marinesurveys@gmail.com
SAMS

Van D. Kline
Gulf Coast Marine Survey
12635 115th St North
Largo, FL 33778-1809
727-588-0546; Cell:727-278-8162
vankline@yahoo.com

www.gulfcoastmarinesurvey.com
ABYC, SAMS

Arthur Whiting
Harden Marine Associates, Inc.
202 S. 22nd St. Ste 203
Tampa, FL 33605-6396
813-248-3505; Cell:813-361-8126
awhiting3@aol.com
ABYC, SAMS, SNAME

David Huffman
Huffman Marine Surveyors
2015 SW 25th Terrace
Ft. Lauderdale, FL 33312
954-205-3153; Cell:954-205-3153
dwhuffman@earthlink.net
www.huffmarinesurveyors.com
ABYC, NAMS

Matthew W. Jones
Jones Marine Surveyors Inc.
6131 SW 20th St.
Plantation, FL 33317-5226
954-791-6224
sylvia@jonesmarinesurveyors.com
www.JonesMarineSurveyors.com.
ABYC

Bill King
Kingsway Marine Surveyors
1151 James Ave
Marathon, FL 33050
305-965-3600; Cell:305-965-3600
bking@kingswaymarineent.com
www.kingswaymarineent.com
ABYC, NFPA

Kurt Merolla, CMS
Merolla Yacht & Boat Marine Surveyors, Inc.
2500 NE 48th Lane #504
Ft. Lauderdale, FL 33308
954-772-8090; Cell:954-401-5399
YotSurveyR@aol.com
www.YachtSurveyor.org
ABYC, SAMS, NAMS, SNAME, NFPA

Noel Miley
Miley Marine Surveying
1021 Twin Lakes Rd
Longwood, FL 32750-4537
877-897-4180; Cell:877-897-4180
info@floridamarinesurveyors.us
www.floridamarinesurveyors.us
ABYC, SAMS

Jonathan Howe
Nautical Services Group
2442 Marathon Lane
Ft. Lauderdale, FL 33312
954-584-5819; Cell:772-557-7563
nautserv@aol.com
www.marinesurveyor.com/nsg
ABYC, SAMS, NFPA

Paul DeBold
Paul J. DeBold, NAMS-CMS
1126 S. Federal Hwy
Ft. Lauderdale, FL 33316
954-524-8869
paul.debold@gmail.com
NAMS, ABYC

Scott Grabner
Power & Sail Marine Surveyors
PO Box 10685
Daytona Beach, FL 32120
Cell:386-631-2528
pwrsail@msn.com
www.powerandsailmarinesurveyors.com
ABYC, SAMS

Mark Rhodes
Rhodes Marine Surveyors & Consultants
10302 S. Federal Hwy Ste 285
Port St. Lucie, FL 34952-5605
772-398-0860; Cell:954-646-3760
marmarklhp@aol.com
ABYC, SAMS

T.J. Day
South East Fire & Marine
1749 SW 4th St.
Ft. Lauderdale, FL 33312-7539
954-527-1981; Cell:954-536-1981
sefmarine@aol.com
ABYC, SAMS, NFPA

Brian G. Stetler
Stetler Marine Surveys
15971 Mellen Lane
Jupiter, FL 33478
561-312-7544
bstetler@amarinesurveyor.com
www.amarinesurveyor.com
SAMS

–Surveyor Directory–

Capt. John Banister
Suenos Azules Marine Surveying &
Consulting
9910 Alt A1A Ste 702-214
Palm Beach Gardens, FL 33410
561-255-4139; Cell:561-255-4139
suenos.azules@yahoo.com
www.suenos.azules.com
SAMS, ABYC, NFPA, IAMI

Lee Taylor
Taylor Marine Surveying & Consulting, LLC
963C Woodland Estates Ave
Ruskin, FL 33570
813-500-9811; Cell:727-490-9811
taylormarinesurveying@yahoo.com
www.taylormarinesurveying.com
SAMS, ABYC

Richard F. Davis
The Marine Specialists
10001 Gulf Blvd.
Treasure Island, FL 33706
marspec@verizon.net
SAMS, ABYC, SNAME, NAMI, NFPA

Ron L. Smith
Tri-State Marine Services, Inc.
13509 Mallard Cove Blvd
Orlando, FL 32837
309-696-3241; Cell:309-696-3241
ronsmith2000@yahoo.com
SAMS, ABYC

Gordon Wright
Wright Way Marine Surveys
1017 Lewis Cove Road
Delray Beach, FL 33483-6512
561-927-0087; Cell:561-702-1027
gordonw95@gmail.com
ABYC, SAMS

GEORGIA

Charles Bullock
American Marine Surveyors
3446M Winder Hwy., Ste. PMB 326
Flowery Branch, GA 30542-3087
770-967-1883; Cell: 386-255-5169
amsur@mindspring.com

ILLINOIS

Rick Lenschow
Certified Marine Surveyors
716 Edward St
Sycamore, IL 60178-2011

866-627-7878; Cell:866-627-7878
rick@cmsurveyors.com
www.cmsurveyors.com
ABYC, SAMS, NAMI, NFPA

John Russell
Marine Specialists
PO Box 322
Winthrop Harbor, IL 60096
847-731-1400
expertinboats@aol.com
ABYC, NFPA

INDIANA

Timothy Dry
Captain Timothy Dry LLC
2715 Floral Trail
Long Beach, IN 46360
219-872-2286; Cell:219-871-9052
timdry@earthlink.net
SAMS, ABYC, NFPA

Buck Kittredge
Lake Effect Surveying & Consulting
801 Ivy St.
Chesterton, IN 46304-3227
219-926-5186; Cell:219-877-7982
sail4deck@comcast.net
ABYC, SAMS

KENTUCKY

Carl Ecklund
Captain's Marine
PO Box 593
Paducah, KY 42002
270-559-8031; Cell:270-559-8031
ecklundcs@cs.com
SAMS

Greg Weeter
Riverlands Marine Surveyors & Consultants, Inc.
935 Riverside Dr
Louisville, KY 40207-1036
502-897-9900
riverlandsmarine@insightbb.com
www.riverlandsmarine.com
ABYC, SAMS, NAMS

LOUISIANA

Hjalmar Breit
Breit Marine Surveying
8654 Pontchartrain Blvd Unit 3
New Orleans, LA 70124
504-283-2929; Cell:504-559-3075

hbreitiii@aol.com
NAMS

MAINE

Geordie King
King Marine LLC
26 Thunder Rock Rd.
Eliot, ME 03903
207-703-0569; Cell:207-337-8706
kinggeordie@comcast.net
ABYC, SAMS

MARYLAND

Derek Rhymes
All Boat & Yacht Inspections, LLC
PO Box 6188
Annapolis, MD 21401
410-268-4404; Cell:866-608-4404
derek@allboatsurveys.com
www.allboatsurveys.com
ABYC, NAMS, SAMS

Reno Panico
Atlantic Seaboard Marine Surveyors
2839 Cox Neck Rd.
Chester, MD 21619-2874
410-604-0432; Cell:301-807-7593
asmsrp@verizon.net
www.atlanticseaboardmarine.com
ABYC, SAMS, NFPA

Alan Gaidelis
Bayside Marine Surveying, Inc.
6903 Harewood Park Dr.
Middle River, MD 21220
410-335-3955
yachtinspector@aol.com
www.baysidemarinesurveying.com
ABYC, SAMS,

William Weyant
East Coast Marine Consulting
321 Tidewater Dr.
Havre de Grace, MD 21078
410-322-6701; Cell:410-322-6701
ECMarineComsulting@comcast.net
www.eastcoastmarineconsulting.com
ABYC, SAMS

Richard Levy
Independent Marine Survey, LLC
5715 Ross Neck Road
Cambridge, MD 21613
410-221-1108
labradog@dmv.com
ABYC, SAMS

–Surveyor Directory–

George Kastendike
J Ramsey Berry LLC
860 Washington Ave
Chestertown, MD 21620-0114
410-778-1143; Cell:410-708-3162
georgekastendike@jrbclaims.com
SAMS, ABYC

Michael Kaufman
Kaufman Design, Inc.
40 Boone Trail
Severna Park, MD 21146-4533
410-263-8900
kaufman99@aol.com
ABYC, NAMS, SNAME

Frank Pettolina
Pettolina Marine Surveying & Consulting LLC
9800 Mooringview Lane #14
Ocean City, MD 21842-9387
410-251-0575
surveyfp@yahoo.com
ABYC, SAMS

Harry Seemans
Quaker Neck Marine Surveying
7902 Quaker Neck Rd.
Bozman, MD 21612-0069
410-745-5452; Cell:410-829-3007
seemans@atlanticbb.net
www.quakerneck.com
ABYC, SAMS

MASSACHUSETTS

Bob Gallagher
Gallagher Marine Surveyors
6 Fosters Point
Beverly, MA 01915
978-807-2163; Cell:978-807-2163
captbgallagher@comcast.net
www.gallaghermarinesurveyors.com
ABYC, SAMS

George Gallup
Gallup Yacht Surveying
13 Sherman Terrace
Lynn, MA 01902-2743
781-598-5465
GallupYachtSurveying@gmail.com
www.gallupyachtsurveying.com
ABYC, SAMS

Patrick Goodrow
High Tech Marine Surveys
85 Humphrey St.
Marblehead, MA 01945

781-290-6782
goodrow@gmail.com
www.hightechmarinesurveys.com
ABYC, SAMS

Timothy Pitts
Ocean Way Technology, Inc.
PO Box 158
East Falmouth, MA 02536-4619
508-564-8680
tpitts@capecod.net
www.oceanwaytech.com
ABYC, SAMS, NMMA, ABYC

MICHIGAN

Melvin Surdel
A-1 Marine Surveying
PO Box 80 20 Wilderness Ridge Dr.
Douglas, MI 49406
708-259-6436; Cell:813-205-8711
ssn578688@aol.com
www.A1marinesurveying.com
ABYC, SNAME

Les Salliotte
Downriver Marine Surveyors
2304 18th St
Wyandotte, MI 48192-4140
734-516-1176; Cell:734-516-1176
lessalliotte@aol.com
www.downrivermarinesurveyors.com
ABYC, SAMS, BOATUS, NFPA

Dennis Parsons
Interstate Marine Survey
306 W. Spring St.
Port Austin, MI 48467
866-799-2628; Cell:248-761-2636
ims.boat@yahoo.com
ABYC, SAMS

Brent Strieter
Strieter Marine Survey
3750 East Burt Rd
Burt, MI 48417
989-624-9747; Cell:989-327-2597
brents@avci.net
SAMS

NEVADA

James Lang, AMS
Northstar Marine Survey
3215 S. Tenaya Way
Las Vegas, NV 89117
702-274-7780; Cell:702-274-7770

jlsearay@aol.com
SAMS, ABYC

NEW JERSEY

Jeff McDaniel
Advanced Marine Consulting
17 Ave D
Atlantic Highlands, NJ 07716
732-291-7400; Cell:732-768-0990
jeff@casemac.com
ABYC, SAMS, IAMI

Philip Topps
Bay Shore Marine Services, LLC
20 Davids Lane
Little Egg Harbor, NJ 08087
609-812-1535; Cell:201-390-4964
southerncross6@verizon.net
www.marinesurveyor.com/BayShore
SAMS

Robert Duane
Bob Duane Marine Services, Inc
819 Donna Dr
Pt Pleasant, NJ 08742-4503
732-295-5951; Cell:732-300-5705
bobduane@comcast.net
ABYC, SAMS

Bob Moro
Captain Moro, LLC
74 Skytop Rd.
Cedar Grove, NJ 07009
973-239-5821; Cell:973-390-4902
captbmoro@hotmail.com
ABYC, SAMS, SNAME

Bill Gross
Midatlantic Marine Consulting, LLC
39 Waterford Rd
Blue Anchor, NJ 08037-2327
609-321-5254
b-gross@comcast.net
www.midatlanticmarine.com/
ABYC, NAMS, SAMS, SNAME

Reinier VanDerHerp
RV Marine Surveying
126 Station Dr.
Forked River, NJ 08731
609-693-9005; Cell:609-618-8511
rvmarinesurveying@gmail.com
www.rvmarinesurveying.com
SAMS, NAMS, ABYC

–Surveyor Directory–

John Spencer
Spencer Marine Surveys
104 Longman St
Toms River, NJ 08753-2439
732-255-4700; Cell:732-267-6980
spencermarine@comcast.net
ABYC, SAMS

William Hymans
The Boat Doc Marine Surveys, LLC
260 Pennington Rocky Hill Rd
Pennington, NJ 08534-1817
609-730-1200; Cell:609-213-1882
billhymans@aol.com
www.theboatdocmarinesurveys.com
SAMS

NEW YORK

Alan Bartlett
Bartlett Marine Services
507 Malta Ave
Malta, NY 12020
Cell:518-859-8660
survey@bartlettmarine.net
www.bartlettmarine.net
SAMS, ABYC

Shawn Bartnett
Bartnett Marine Services, Inc.
52 Ontario St.
Honeoye Falls, NY 14472-1120
585-624-1380
bartmarser@aol.com
ABYC, NAMS, SNAME, NAMI, NFPA

Guy Falkenheimer
Coast Marine Services
23 Pine Hill Park
Valatie, NY 12184
518-449-3391; Cell:518-265-3605
capten1@msn.com
www.coastmarineservices.com
ABYC, SAMS, SNAME, NAMI, NFPA

Joseph Oldak
Farragut Marine Service Co.
192 Farragut Cir
New Rochelle, NY 10801-5739
914-589-0104; Cell:914-589-0104
marinesurveyor@farragutmarine.com
www.farragutmarine.com
SAMS, ABYC

Frank T. Abbey
Frank Abbey Marine Surveyor Inc.
PO Box 729
Massapequa Park, NY 11762-2343

516-236-1911; Cell:516-236-1911
fta102@yahoo.com
www.marinesurveyor-frankabbey.com
ABYC, ACMS

Charlie Gruetzner
Oceanis Marine Services, Inc.
1124 Main St.
Peekskill, NY 10566
914-737-0253; Cell:945-216-0497
charlie@oceanismarine.com
www.oceanismarine.com
ABYC, SAMS, SNAME, NAMI

David McClay
QBC Marine Services
57 Maple Ave
Northport, NY 11768-1937
631-757-9415; Cell:631-764-7842
dmcclay@optonline.net
www.marinesurveyor.com/qbc
SAMS, ABYC

Manuel Rebelo
Rebelo Surveyors
PO Box 1025
Greenwood Lake, NY 10925
845-595-6061; Cell:845-742-0355
captmanny@optonline.net
SAMS, ABYC

Gary Washienko
Sound Marine Survey
490 Bleeker Ave Apt 4J
Mamaroneck, NY 10543-4549
914-584-2086
info@soundmarinesurvey.com
www.soundmarinesurvey.com
SAMS

Peter Luciano
Stay New Yacht Service
50 Davinport Ave #2F
New Rochelle, NY 10805-3660
914-260-6092
sloopquest@aol.com
ABYC, SAMS, SNAME

NORTH CAROLINA

John Day
Day Yacht Services
2707 Homes Dr.
Morehead City, NC 28557
252-241-7287; Cell:252-241-7287
sday@ec.rr.com
www.dayyachtservices.com
SAMS

Lloyd Griffin III
Frigate Marine Surveyors
739 Riverside Ave
Elizabeth City, NC 27909
252-333-6105
lgriffin111@yahoo.com
www.frigatemarinesurveyors.com
ABYC, SAMS, ABYC

Robert Eldridge
R.J. Eldridge Marine Surveying
PO Box 15558
Wilmington, NC 28408-5558
Cell:910-232-8356
rjesurveys@bellsouth.net
SAMS, ABYC

OKLAHOMA

Thomas Benton
Marine Damage Consultants, LLC
PO Box 627
Ketchum, OK 74349-0627
918-782-1001; Cell:918-519-1972
tom.benton@marinesurveyor.com
www.marinesurveyor.com/benton
ABYC, SAMS, NAMS, IAMI

PENNSYLVANIA

William Mullin
Boatcheck Marine Surveyors
1051 Bolton Ct
Bensalem, PA 19020
215-327-9219; Cell:215-327-9219
wmullin@boatcheck.net
www.boatcheck.net
SAMS, ABYC

PUERTO RICO

Ciro Malatrasi
Marine Surveyor & Consultant
El Batey Street, 1#6
Fajardo, PR 00738
787-504-4066
ciromsurveys@yahoo.com
SAMS, ABYC

Carlos Suarez
Carlos Suarez & Associates
PO Box 141737
Arecibo, PR 00614-1737
787-879-1048
suarez.307@hotmail.com
SAMS

–Surveyor Directory–

RHODE ISLAND

James Cross
Jim Cross Certified Marine Surveyors
19 Nooseneck Hill Rd.
W. Greenwich, RI 02817
401-397-5040
jimcross@jimcross.net
www.jimcross.net
ACMS

Fredk C. Bieberbach,Jr., AMS
BRAVO MARINE ASSOCIATES
40 Union St.
Riverside, Rhode Island 02915
401-301-1733; Cell: 401-301-1733
bravomarine@cox.net
www.marinesurveyor.com/bravo
SAMS,ABYC, NFPA

SOUTH CAROLINA

Neil Haynes
Blue Water Surveys, Inc.
1739 Maybank Hwy #T
Charleston, SC 29412-2103
843-559-2857
nhaynes@boatsurveyor.com
www.boatsurveyor.com
ABYC, NAMS, SAMS, IAMI

David P. Hill
Carolina Yacht Services, Inc.
24 Nuffield Rd.
Charleston, SC 29407
843-571-5808
Cell:843-607-3834
uphilldph@knology.net
ABYC, SAMS, NFPA

Richard Newsome
Dana C. McLendon
PO Box 481
Isle of Palms, SC 29451-0481
843-886-3852; Cell:843-813-5210
dcmsurvey@bellsouth.net
ABYC, SAMS

Louis Harrison
Harrison Marine Services
3520 Johan Blvd
Johns Island, SC 29455-8917
843-559-3383; Cell:843-729-6490
harrisonimc@aol.com
ABYC, SAMS

John Peeples
Peeples Marine, Inc.
1090 Sea Eagle Watch
Charleston, SC 29412-8248
843-795-1673; Cell:803-261-7863
peeplesj@ieee.org
SAMS

TENNESSEE

Gary Wright
American Marine Specialists
2425 N. Shore Acres Rd
Soddy Daisy, TN 37379-7949
423-451-0128; Cell:423-400-0001
gr.wright@comcast.net
www.marinesurveyor-sams.com
SAMS, ABYC

Edward Fry
FRYCO
5420 Waddell Hollow Rd
Franklin, TN 37064-9422
615-591-8455; Cell:954-494-1557
edfry@frycoyachts.com
www.frycoyachts.com
ABYC, SNAME

Pete Hosemann
Hosemann Marine Services
396 Pleasant View Cr.
Jasper, TN 37347
423-653-3558
captpete@hosemannmarine.com
www.hosemannmarine.com
ABYC, NFPA

Stan Johnson
Riverport Marine Surveying, Inc.
286 Stonewall St
Memphis, TN 38112-5143
901-278-2161; Cell:901-485-2072
riverportms@aol.com
www.riverportms.com
ABYC, SAMS, NAMS

Jim T. McKay
Yacht Surveyors Inc.
153 Gordon Dr.
Ten Mile, TN 37880
865-376-2726; Cell:865-567-1623
sailboat@aol.com
www.yachtsurveyorsinc.com
SAMS, ABYC, NFPA

TEXAS

Dale Vandermolen
Aloha Marine Surveyors
3336 Floyd St
Corpus Christi, TX 78411-1461
361-855-3807; Cell:361-960-4674
alohasurv@msn.com

Kurtis Samples
Anchor Marine Consultants
1920 Abrams Pkwy #169
Dallas, TX 75214
Cell:214-796-4305
kkboat@airmail.net
ABYC, SAMS, IAMI

Adam R. Johnson
Johnson Marine Survey
17231 Blackhawk Blvd #1213
Friendswood, TX 77546
772-781-9398; Cell:772-631-4064
surveyoradam@gmail.com
SAMS, ABYC

Casey Auten
Professional Marine Surveyors
15812 Grove Crest Dr.
Frisco, TX 75035
972-556-2829; Cell:580-490-1660
autlake@gmail.com
www.professionalmarinesuveyors.com
ABYC, SAMS

Donald Neese
Subacuatica Marine Surveys
416 Blanco St.
San Marcos, TX 78666
512-353-7622
Cell:512-757-5723
neese.don@gmail.com
SAMS, ABYC

James G. Merritt
Tangent Development Co.
1715 Harliquin Run
Austin, TX 78758-6121
512-837-9170; Cell:512-731-5708
survrjim@austin.rr.com
ABYC, SAMS, SNAME, NAMI, NFPA

Marine Surveyor Directory

VERMONT

George Little
Tamarack Marine Surveys
82 Turquoise Dr
Colchester, VT 05446-6597
802-864-5214; Cell:802-233-5214
grayluders@yahoo.com
www.tamarackmarinesurveys.com
SAMS, ABYC, NFPA

VIRGINIA

Richard D. Milner, AMS
Dynamic Marine Surveys
8172 Shore Drive #101
Norfolk, VA 23518
757-418-4008; Cell:757-418-4008
rmilner12@hotmail.com
SAMS, ABYC, NFPA

WASHINGTON

Stephen Berg
Berg Marine Surveys
1004 Commercial Ave #354
Anacortes, WA 98221-4117
360-301-6879; Cell:360-301-6879
steve@bergmarinesurveys.com
www.bergmarinesurveys.com
SAMS, ABYC, NAMI

Thomas Laing
Commercial Marine Service
PO Box 33836
Seattle, WA 98133-0836
425-742-7424; Cell:206-660-4654
tommy@cmservice.us
NAMS, SNAME

Jay McEwen
Reisner, McEwen & Associates
5350 30th Ave NW
Seattle, WA 98107-5813
206-285-8194; Cell:206-371-6138
jaymcewen@msn.com
NAMS, ABYC

David Wilson
Wilson & Associates Marine Surveyors
9621 241st Pl SW
Edmonds, WA 98020-6511
206-396-6284; Cell:206-396-6284
wilson@marinesurveyor.com
www.marinesurveyor.com/wilson
SAMS, ABYC

WASHINGTON D.C.

Guy R. Nolan
Cascade Corporation
1000 Water St SW
Washington DC 20024-2425
571-344-1239; Cell:571-344-1239
cascadegrn@starpower.net
ABYC, SAMS, SNAME, NFPA

WISCONSIN

Chris Kelly
Chris Kelly & Associates, LLC
7528 Pershing Blvd B-135
Kenosha, WI 53142
800-299-3197
ckelly@chriskellyassociates.com
www.chriskellyassociates.com
AYBC, SAMS, SNAME, NAMI, NFPA

Michael R. Tock
Lakeshore Marine LLC
2622 Wilgus Ave
Sheboygan, WI 53081
920-452-3361
ticktock@bytehead.com
SAMS, ABYC

Richard E. Lawrence
Lawrence Marine Service Inc.
9746 Sheridan Rd
Pleasant Prairie, WI 53158-5403
262-694-5609
lawrencemarine@wi.rr.com
lawrencemarineserviceinc.vpweb.com
ABYC,

Gary Shorrel
Midwest Marine Surveyors, LLC
17428 99th Ave
Chippewa Falls, WI 54729-5367
715-828-5320
marine-surveyor@charter.net
www.marinesurveyor.com/midwest
SAMS, ABYC

CANADA

Kenneth W. Rorison
Kenneth R. Rorison Marine Surveyors Ltd.
11416 Sycamore Pl.
Sidney, BC V8L5L2
CANADA
250-655-3425; Cell:250-812-3351
krorison@shaw.ca
NAMS, ABYC, SNAME

Barry Goodyear
Ra Kon Marine Surveyors & Appraisers
1826 St. John's Rd.
Innisfil, ON L9S1T4
CANADA
705-431-9485; Cell:905-853-8100
bgoodyear@rakon.ca
www.rakon.ca
ABYC, NFPA

CAYMAN ISLANDS

Michael Pickthorne
Alpha Marine Surveyors
24 Warwick Dr.
George Town, Grand Cayman KY1-1103
CAYMAN ISLANDS
345-949-9210; Cell:345-916-1765
la1marine@candw.ky
www.a1marinecayman.com
ABYC, NAMS

Broker/Dealer Directory

ALABAMA

Bill Thompson
Bill Thompson Yacht Sales
31304 River Rd.
Orange Beach, AL 36561
251-979-6000
sales@billthompsonyachts.com
www.billthompsonyachts.com
Brokerage Sales

Erwin Marine Sales of Huntsville LLC
28601 US Hwy 431
Grant, AL 35747
256-582-6610
fcochran@erwinmarinesales.com
www.erwinmarinesales.com
New Boat Sales, Brokerage Sales,
Service Yard

Marine Group Emerald Coast LLC
PO Box 650
Orange Beach, AL 36561
251-981-9200; Cell:850-496-1172
www.marinegroupec.com
Brokerage

CALIFORNIA

Nancy Adair
Adair Yachts
PO Box 1418
Sunset Beach, CA 90742
562-592-6220; Cell:562-252-2167
Adairyachts@gmail.com
www.adairyachts.com
Brokerage

Nereus Dastur
Adventure Yacht Sales
13555 Fiji Way Ste A
Marina del Rey, CA 90292-6909
310-821-5883
nereus@denisonyachtsales.com
New Boat Sales, Brokerage Sales

Ardell Yacht & Ship Brokers
2101 W. Coast Hwy
Newport Beach, CA 92663-4712
949-642-5735

kay@ardell.com
www.ardell.com
Brokerage Sales

Marc Bay
Bay Yachts
3201 Marina Way Ste 101
National City, CA 91950
619-474-5500
marc@bayyachts.net
www.bayyachts.com
New Boat Sales, Brokerage Sales

CA Yacht Sales International
955 Harbor Island Dr. Ste 160
San Diego, CA 92101
619-291-2628
info@cayachtsales.com
www.CAyachtsales.com
New Boat Sales, Brokerage Sales

Dan Peter
Cabrillo Yacht Sales
5060 N. Harbor Dr. Ste 155
San Diego, CA 92106-2309
619-523-1745; Cell:619-200-1024
danpeter@cabrilloyachtsales.com
www.cabrilloyachts.com
New Boat Sales, Brokerage

Daniel R. Cornwell
Cays Yacht Sales, Inc.
550 Marina Pkwy # D-3
Chula Vista, CA 91910-4054
619-422-7376
drcatcays@hotmail.com
www.caysyachtsalesinc.com
Brokerage Sales

CFB Marine Group
1880 Harbor Island Dr. #F
San Diego, CA 92101
619-291-9300
john@cfbmarine.com

Chuck Hovey
Chuck Hovey Yachts
717 Lido Park Drive
Newport Beach, CA 92663-4461
949-675-8092

info@chuckhoveyyachts.com
www.chuckhoveyyachts.com
New Boat Sales, Brokerage Sales

Crow's Nest Yacht Sales
2801 W Coast Hwy Ste 260
Newport Beach, CA 92663-4029
949-574-7600
info_new@crowsnestyachts.com

Cruisers West
2353 Shelter Island Dr.
San Diego, CA 92106-3109
949-723-1098; Cell:949-274-1826
nbsales@cruiserswest.com
www.cruiserswestyachts.com
New Boat Sales, Brokerage, Service Yard

Tom Trainor
Delta Yacht Sales
11285 Crocker Grove Lane
Gold River, CA 95670
deltayachtsales@aol.com
www.deltayachtsales.net
Brokerage Sales

Dick Simon Yachts
3008 Vina Vial
San Clemente, CA 92673
949-533-6505
brokermark1@gmail.com

Nancy Dixon
Dixon Yachts International, Inc.
1001 W. 17th St. Ste N
Costa Mesa, CA
949-355-4898
hulltruth1@sbcglobal.net
www.yachtworld.com/dixonyachts
Brokerage Sales, Service Yard

Heritage Yacht Sales
231 N. Marina Dr.
Long Beach, CA 90803-4623
866-569-2248; Cell:310-995-9989
info@heritageyachts.com
www.heritageyachts.com
New Boat Sales, Brokerage

– Broker/Dealer Directory –

Art Henry
Mariners Group
19521 Pompano Lane Unit 108
Huntington Beach, CA 92648-2840
866-364-0677
art@marineryachtsales.com
www.marineryachtsales.com
Brokerage

Tari Soderling
Newport Coast Yachts
2801 West Coast Hwy Ste 270
Newport Beach, CA 92663-4089
888-4-1-YACHT
cme4yachts@aol.com
Brokerage Sales

Orange Coast Yachts
42 Dolphin Isle
Novato, CA 94949
501-523-2628
yachtcowboy@yahoo.com

Art Burnevik
Pacific Yacht Broker Inc.
24591 Del Prado Ste 201
Dana Point, CA 92629-2509
949-295-2984
art@pacificyachtbroker.com
www.yachtshopping.com
Brokerage Sales

RD Snyder Yachts, Inc
1551 Shelter Island Dr.
San Diego, CA 92106
619-224-2464
info@sandiegoyachts.com
www.sandiegoyachts.com
Brokerage Sales

Lou Mencuccini
South Mountain Yachts
10 Corniche Dr. #H
Monarch Beach, CA 92629
949-240-8198
lou@smyyachts.com
www.southmountainyachts.com
New Boat Sales, Brokerage Sales

Anita Mays
Valkyrie Yacht Sales
2461 Jamestown Ct.
Channel Islands Harbor, CA 93035
855-825-5974
anita@valkyrieyachts.com
www.valkyrieyachts.com
New Boat Sales, Brokerage Sales

Tom Yorath
Yorath Yachts
16400 Pacific Coast Hwy #107
Huntington Beach, CA 92649-1852
714-840-2373; Cell:714-264-3443
tomjr@yorathyachts.com
www.yorathyachts.com

CONNECTICUT

James Economou
Brewer Yacht Sales
56 Roseleah Dr.
Mystic, CT 06355
860-536-2293; Cell:860-536-6060
jeconomou@byy.com

Channing C. Moser
Chan Moser Yachts
123 Downs Ave
Stamford, CT 06902-7802
203-324-4479
cmoser@optonline.net
www.yachtworld.com/chanmoser
New Boat Sales, Brokerage Sales

Petzold's Marine
37 Indian Hill Ave
Portland, CT 06480-1123
860-342-1196
w.j.petzold@snet.net
www.petzolds.com
New Boat Sales, Brokerage Sales,
Service Yard

Rex Marine
144 Water St
S. Norwalk, CT 06854-3144
203-866-5555
yachtbroke@aol.com
www.rexmarine.com

FLORIDA

765 Yachts
1017 34th Dr. West
Palmetto, FL 34221
800-505-3920
greg.para@765Yachts.com

AAA Marine Service
17994 Anchor Dr
Jupiter, FL 33458-3366
561-818-9245
aaamarineservice@comcast.net

Roger Droukas
Admiral Yacht Sales Inc.
3024 Harbor Dr.
St. Augustine, FL 32084
904-814-7717
rdroukas@admiralyachtsales.net
www.admiralyachtsales.net
New Boat Sales, Brokerage Sales,
Service Yard

David A. Lash
Admiralty Yacht Sales
911 SE 6th Ave Ste 109
Delray Beach, FL 33483-5190
561-330-9095
dlash@admiraltyyacht.com
www.admiraltyyacht.com
Brokerage Sales

Roger Droukas
Admiralty Yacht Sales Inc.
3024 Harbor Drive
St. Augustine, FL 32084
904-814-7717
rdroukas@admiralyachtsales.net
www.admiralyachtsales.net
New Boat Sales, Brokerage Sales,
Service Yard

Andy Kniffin
AK Yachts
Davie, FL 33325
954-889-7330; Cell:954-292-0629
andy@akyachts.com
www.akyachts.com
Brokerage Sales

Allied Marine
1445 SE 16th St
Ft. Lauderdale, FL 33316-1712
954-462-5527

Rick Erisman
Atlantic Yacht Brokers
405 S. Federal Hwy Ste 200
Pompano Beach, FL 33062-6719
954-942-5210
aybyachts@hotmail.com
www.atlanticyachtbrokers.com

Atlantic Yacht & Ship
850 NE 3rd St #213
Dania Beach, FL 33004
954-921-1500
info@ayssales.com
www.atlanticyachtandship.com
New Boat Sales, Brokerage Sales,
Service Yard

– Broker/Dealer Directory –

David C. Lacz
Bartram & Brakenhoff
304 SE 20th St
Ft. Lauderdale, FL 33316-2851
954-779-7377
florida@bartbrak.com
www.bartbrak.com
New Boat Sales, Brokerage Sales

Jason Borden
Borden & Associates Yacht Sales
301 W. Atlantic Ave Ste 0-5
Delray Beach, FL 33444
561-644-0797
info@bordenyachts.com
www.bordenyachts.com
Brokerage Sales

Bradford Marine Yacht Sales
3051 State Rd. 84
Ft. Lauderdale, FL 33312
954-377-3900
info@bradford-marine.com
www.bradfordmarineyachtsales.com
Brokerage Sales, Service Yard

Cape Regal Yachts
1507 SE 47th Terrace
Cape Coral, FL 33904
239-699-3981; Cell:239-699-3981
bob@caperegal.com
www.caperegal.com

David Giannone
Complete Marine
800 S. Federal Hwy
Pompano Beach, FL 33062
954-567-2628
completeboat@aol.com
www.completeboat.com
New Boat Sales, Brokerage Sales,
Service Yard

Craig Leonard
Craig Leonard Sales
1301 River Reach Dr. #215
Ft. Lauderdale, FL 33315
954-650-1030
craiggleonard@gmail.com
www.lloydsyachtbrokers.com

Barry Lipoff
Crown International Yacht Sales
1751 Mound St. Ste 204
Sarasota, FL 34236
941-552-6713
barry@crownyachtsales.com

www.crownyachtsales.com
Brokerage Sales

David Walters
David Walters Yachts
1702 Cordova Road
Ft. Lauderdale, FL 33316
954-527-0664
sales@dwyfl.net
www.davidwaltersyachts.net
New Boat Sales, Brokerage Sales

Robert Denison
Denison Yacht Sales
401 SW 1st Ave #102
Ft. Lauderdale, FL 33301
888-339-2248
bob@denisonyachtsales.com
www.denisonyachtsales.com
New Boat Sales, Brokerage Sales,
Service Yard

Dennis Flandreau
Dennis Flandreau Yacht Sales
2929 NE 49th St. #8
Ft. Lauderdale, FL 33308
954-489-3665; Cell:954-531-3056
dflandreau@att.net
Brokerage Sales

Dwight Tracy & Friends
1515 SE 17th St. Ste A131
Ft. Lauderdale, FL 33316-1736
954-767-0007; Cell:954-325-3461
info@dtfyachts.com
www.dtfyachts.com
New Boat Sales, Brokerage

Howard Donhauser
DYB Charter & Yacht Sales
1514 Royal Palm Dr
Edgewater, FL 32132-2520
386-409-0854
howard-dybyachts@cfl.rr.com
www.dybyachts.com
Brokerage Sales

Capt. Bob Fillingham
Fillingham Yacht Sales
105 - 15th Ave SE
St. Petersburg, FL 33711
Cell:727-460-5687
captbob@fillinghamyachts.com
www.fillinghamyachts.com
Brokerage, Service Yard

Galati Yacht Sales
126 Harbor Blvd
Destin, FL 32541-7344
850-654-1575
jcovington@galatiyachts.com
www.galatiyachts.com
New Boat Sales, Brokerage, Service Yard

Gold Key Yacht Group
521 SE 9th Ave
Pompano Beach, FL 33060
954-764-7775
info@goldkeyyachts.com
www.yachtworld.com/goldkeyyachts

Lauran E. Lee
Gulf Coast Yacht Sales, Inc.
101 16th Ave S. Ste 1
St. Petersburg, FL 33701
727-896-0671
info@gcyachts.com
www.gcyachts.com
New Boat Sales, Brokerage Sales,
Service Yard

Capt. Rick Hill
Half Hitch Marine
57 Comares Ave
St. Augustine, FL 32080
904-449-4186
captrickhill@msn.com
www.halfhitchmarine.com
Brokerage Sales, Service Yard

HMY Yacht Sales
2640 S Bayshore Dr. Ste 1-103
Coconut Grove, FL 33133
305-856-8486
gmacaluso@hmy.com

James Barboni
HMY Yacht Sales
17125 Bay St
Jupiter, FL 33477-1211
561-252-5220
jbarboni@hmy.com
www.hmy.com
New Boat Sales, Brokerage Sales

Barton Holmes
Holmes & Owen Yacht Sales
3423 Lakeshore Blvd
Jacksonville, FL 32210
904-387-5432
sales@hoyachtsales.com
www.hoyachtsales.com
Brokerage Sales

– Broker/Dealer Directory –

Horizon Yachts Inc.
1212 US Hwy One Ste A
N. Palm Beach, FL 33408
561-346-5966
elise@horizonyachtusa.com

Island Yacht Sales
1555 SE 14th Ct
Deerfield Beach, FL 33441-7331
954-520-2222
repojay@bellsouth.net

Andrew Cilla
Luke Brown Yachts
1500 Cordova Rd. #200
Ft. Lauderdale, FL 33316-2190
954-525-6617
sales@lukebrown.com
www.lukebrown.com
New Boat Sales, Brokerage Sales

Linda Krantz
Luxury Yachts International
2495 Cat Cay Lane
Ft. Lauderdale, FL 33312-4751
954-584-1888; Cell:954-465-9775
linda@luxuryyachtsinternational.com
www.luxuryyachtsinternational.com
Brokerage

Marc A. Harris
Marcali Yachts
1401 Lee St Ste B
Ft. Meyers, FL 33901
239-275-3600
marc@teammarcali.com
www.marcaliyacht.com
Brokerage Sales, Service Yard

Mare Blue Yacht Brokerage
247 SW 8th St. #304
Miami, FL 33130
305-354-9600
brokerage@mareblue.com

Marina Yacht Brokers
3120 Matecumbe Key Rd
Punta Gorda, FL 33955-1964
941-575-8522; Cell:941-628-0140
jwiczek@nisswamarine.com
www.marinayachtbrokers.com

Lisa Heath
Marine Wholesalers
6419 Toulon Dr.
Boca Raton, FL 33433
561-368-0578

marinewholesaler@aol.com
www.floridamarinewholesalers.com

MarineMax
18167 US Highway 19 North
Clearwater, FL 33764-3510
727-536-2628; Cell:850-477-1112
mark.breton@marinemax.com

MarineMax
2550 S. Bayshore Dr. #1
Coconut Grove, FL 33133-4743
888-474-2940
ccg-brokerage@marinemax.com
www.marinemax.com
New Boat Sales, Brokerage Sales,
Service Yard

Ken Reda
MarineMax East, Inc.
2 Fishing Village Dr.
Key Largo, FL 33037
305-367-3969, ext.16320
ken.reda@marinemax.com
www.marinemax.com
New Boat Sales, Brokerage Sales,
Service Yard

JB Marshall
Marshall Marine Group Inc.
2402 N Riverside Dr
Pompano Beach, FL 33062-1231
954-786-8897
jb@marshallmarinegroup.com
www.marshallmarinegroup.com
New Boat Sales, Brokerage Sales,
Service Yard

Alexjandra "Alex" Acevedo
Merle Wood & Associates
888 East Las Olas Blvd 4th Fl
Ft. Lauderdale, FL 33301-2285
954-525-5111
aacevedo@merlewood.com
www.merlewood.com
New Boat Sales, Brokerage Sales

Richard Merritt
Merritt Yacht Brokers
2890 State Rd. 84 #105
Ft. Lauderdale, FL 33312
954-761-1300
ajlobster@gmail.com

Greg Wheble
Mynt Yacht Sales
1314 E. Las Olas Blvd #130
Ft. Lauderdale, FL 33301

954-401-2808
greg@myntyachts.com
www.myntyachts.com
Brokerage Sales

Pete Peterson
Naples Yacht Brokerage
PO Box 882
Naples, FL 34106
239-434-8338; Cell:239-777-4489
naplesyb@earthlink.net
www.naplesyachtbrokerage.com
Brokerage

Ron Brozic
National Liquidators
1915 SW 21st Ave
Ft. Lauderdale, FL 33312-3113
954-791-9601
rbrozic@natliq.com
www.yachtauctions.com

Shirley Nelle
Nio Group
13205 Gulf Blvd #C
Madeira Beach, FL 33708-2630
727-639-2862
niogroup@aol.com
www.NioGroupInc.com
Brokerage Sales

Nordhavn Yachts
600 NW Dixie Hwy
Stuart, FL 34994
772-223-6331
ted.robie@nordhavn.com

Peter Kehoe & Assoc.
101 N. Riverside Dr. Ste #123
Pompano Beach, FL 33062-5051
954-767-9880
peterkehoe@peterkehoe.com
www.peterkehoe.com

Frank Piedra
Phoenix Yacht Sales
PO Box 832047
Miami, FL 33283-2047
305-761-7797
pyssales@aol.com
www.yachtworld.com/phoenixyachtsales
Brokerage Sales, Service Yard

Rick Augusto
RA Marine Brokerage, Inc.
4617 SW 34th Terrace
Ft. Lauderdale, FL 33312

– Broker/Dealer Directory –

954-249-7565; Cell:954-249-7565
ramarine55@yahoo.com
www.ramarinebrokerage.com
Brokerage Sales, Service Yard

Rialto Harbor Docks
1901 Balsey Rd.
Alva, FL 33920-3604
239-728-9891
rialtoharbor@earthlink.net
www.rialtoharbor.com

Robert Christopher Yacht Sales
2504 SE 24th Ct.
Cape Coral, FL 33904
239-440-2464
corykcooper@hotmail.com
www.robertchristopheryacht.com

Robert J. Cury Yacht Sales
399 SE 18th Ct.
Ft. Lauderdale, FL 33316-2809
954-525-7484
rjcyachts@aol.com
www.rjcyachts.com
Brokerage

Ross Yacht Sales
500 Main St.
Dunedin, FL 34698
727-210-1800
rick@rossyachtsales.com
www.rossyachtsales.com
New Boat Sales, Brokerage

Sarasota Yacht & Ship
1306 Main St.
Sarasota, FL 34236-5614
941-365-9095
info@sarasotayacht.com
www.sarasotayacht.com
New Boat Sales, Brokerage, Service Yard

Bob Zarchen
Sparkman & Stephens
205 Cordova Rd. Suite 205
Ft. Lauderdale, FL 33316
954-524-4620
bobz@mindspring.com
www.sparkmanstephens.com
Brokerage Sales

Stuart Yacht Sales
4805 SE Dixie Hwy
Stuart, FL 34997
772-283-9400
sys@stuartyachtsales.com
www.stuartyachtsales.com

Suncoast Marine Management
8290 Bay Pines Blvd N
St. Petersburg, FL 33709-4002
727-384-2628
mark@suncoast-marine.com
www.suncoast-marine.com
Brokerage

Tropical Yacht Sales
328 Elliott Rd. SE
Ft. Walton Beach, FL 32548
866-448-1477
tropicalyachts@earthlink.net
www.tropicalyachtsales.com

John Pribik
United Yacht Sales
1100 Lee Wagner Blvd Suite 105
Ft. Lauderdale, FL
954-494-5956
jpribik@bellsouth.net
www.unitedyacht.com/johnpribik
Brokerage Sales

US Liquidators
2605 43rd St. N.
Tampa, FL 33605
813-627-0172
johna@usliquidatorsonline.com
www.usliquidatorsonline.com
Brokerage

Redfish Yacht Brokers
25096 Mario Ave
Punta Gorda, FL 33950
941-639-9400
redfishyacht@earthlink.net
www.redfishyacht.com
brokerage Sales

Mark Peck
Westport Yacht Sales
2957 State Rd. 84
Ft. Lauderdale, FL 33312-7702
954-224-1351
mpeck@westportyachtsales.com
www.westportyachts.com
New Boat Sales, Brokerage Sales

Phillip Purcell
Westport Yacht Sales
2957 State Rd. 84
Ft. Lauderdale, FL 33312-7702
954-316-6364
info@westportyachtsales.com
www.westportyachts.com
New Boat Sales, Brokerage Sales

David White
World Class Yacht Sales
1673 Oak Park Ct.
Tarpon Springs, FL 34689
727-945-7500
worldyachts@wcyachtsales.com
www.world-yachts.com
New Boat Sales, Brokerage

Worldwide Yacht Sales, Inc.
2101 Davie Blvd
Ft. Lauderdale, FL 33312
954-483-8765
bill@worldwideyachts.net
www.worldwideyachtsales.net

Worldwide Yacht Sales, Inc.
3501 Del Prado Blvd
Cape Coral, FL 33904
239-549-8683
info@worldwideyachts.net
www.worldwideyachts.net

Joe Egeberg
Yacht Brokers of Daytona
645 S Beach St
Daytona Beach, FL 32114-5007
386-253-6266
joe@daytonayachts.com
www.daytonayachts.com
New Boat Sales, Brokerage Sales, Service Yard

Dennis Matthews
Yacht Club Longboat Key Club Moorings
2630 Harbourside Dr
Longboat Key, FL 34228-4115
941-383-8383
dennis.matthews@longboatkeyclub.com
www.longboatkeyclub.com
Brokerage Sales, Service Yard

Matthew Lavin
Yacht Sales Consultants, Inc.
4561 SW Long Bay Dr.
Palm City, FL 34990-8810
772-463-2645
matt@yscinc.com
www.yscinc.com
Brokerage Sales

– Broker/Dealer Directory –

GEORGIA

Park Marine Boating Center
1989 Cobb Parkway N.
Kennesaw, GA 30152
770-919-2628
cbell@bestinboating.com
www.parkmarine.com
New Boat Sales, Brokerage, Service Yard

ILLINOIS

Larsen Marine Service
625 E Sea Horse Dr
Waukegan, IL 60085-2163
847-336-5456
les@larsenmarine.com
www.larsenmarine.com
New Boat Sales, Brokerage Sales,
Service Yard

Pier 11 Marina
826 E. 138th St.
Chicago, IL 60827
773-468-9605; Cell:773-468-1965
pier11marina@hotmail.com
www.pier11marina.com
New Boat Sales, Brokerage, Service Yard

Spring Brook Marina
PO Box 379
Seneca, IL 61360
815-357-8666
sales@springbrookmarina.com
www.springbrookmarina.com
New Boat Sales, Brokerage, Service Yard

Starved Rock Marina
PO Box 2460
Ottawa, IL 61350-7060
815-433-4218; Cell:815-228-1988
tom@starvedrockmarina.com
www.starvedrockmarina.com
New Boat Sales, Brokerage, Service Yard

J.Jeffrey Pierce
Windy City Yacht Brokerage
934 N. Branch St.
Chicago, IL 60642-4230
312-440-9500; Cell:630-240-0409
jeff@windycityyachts.com
www.windycityyachts.com
Brokerage

INDIANA

Kentuckiana Yacht Sales
700 E Market St
Jeffersonville, IN 47130-3975
812-282-7579
info@kys.com
www.kys.com
New Boat Sales, Brokerage, Service Yard

KENTUCKY

Bill Huffman
Green Turtle Bay Yacht Sales
PO Box 102
Grand Rivers, KY 42045
800-498-0428; Cell:270-205-0035
bhuffman@greenturtlebay.com
www.greenturtlebayyachtsales.com
Brokerage

Vebbie Griffith
Green Turtle Bay Yacht Sales
PO Box 102
Grand Rivers, KY 42045
800-498-0428; Cell:270-205-0293
vgriffith@greenturtlebay.com
www.greenturtlebayyachtsales.com
Brokerage

George East
Paradigm Yacht Sales
PO Box 1043
Louisville, KY 40059
502-292-0444
george@paradigmyachts.com

LOUISIANA

Charles Cyr
CYR Boat Works
3501 N. Causeway Blvd Ste 319
Metarie, LA 70002
504-338-3738
Cyrboatworks@cox.net

Michael Mayer
MG Mayer Yacht Services, Inc.
406 S. Roadway
New Orleans, LA 70124
504-282-1700; Cell:504-251-6565
mmayer@mayeryacht.com
www.mayeryacht.com
Brokerage, Service Yard

Gregory T. Whelton
Whelton Marine LLC

700 Mariner's Plaza Dr. Ste 703
Mandeville, LA 70448
888-258-2897
gtwhelton@yahoo.com
www.wheltonmarine.com
Brokerage Sales

MARYLAND

Paul Rosen
Annapolis Yacht Sales
7350 Edgewood Rd.
Annapolis, MD 21403
410-267-8181; Cell:410-703-7367
garth@annapolisyachtsales.com

Richard Nissen
Atlantic Yacht Works/C&C Charters
506 Kent Narrows Way N.
Grasonville, MD 21638
410-827-3300
rick@cccharters.com

Baltimore Boating Center
2015 Turkey Point Rd
Baltimore, MD 21221-1912
410-687-2000
brendaw@baltimoreboatingcenter.com

Eric Horst
Bayport Yachts
323 Piney Narrows Rd.
Chester, MD 21619
410-212-5264
eric@bayport.biz
www.bayport.biz
Brokerage Sales

Vicki Rasmussen
Integrity Yacht Sales
PO Box 479
Deale, MD 20751
301-261-5775
broker@integrityyachtsales.com

Doug Curtiss
Jarrett Bay Yacht Sales
4 Poplar Trail
Ocean City, MD 21811
443-497-2582
dcurtiss@jarrettbay.com
www.jarrettbayyachtsales.com
New Boat Sales, Brokerage Sales

Thomas Trainer
McDaniel Yacht Basin, Inc.
PO Box E

– Broker/Dealer Directory –

North East, MD 21901-0286
410-287-8121
yachtoffice@mcdanielyacht.com
www.mcdanielyacht.com
New Boat Sales, Brokerage Sales,
Service Yard

Mchael A. Sweeney
Mears Point Yacht Sales
428 Kent Narrows Way North
Grasonville, MD 21638-1022
Cell:410-382-6346
mike@mearspoint.com
www.mearspointyachtsales.com
Brokerage Sales

Dave Shields
Ocean Club Yacht Sales, Inc.
3030 A Kent Narrow Way S.
Grasonville, MD 21638
410-643-1111; Cell:410-829-0080
dave@oceanclubyachts.com

Sassafras Harbor Marina Yacht Sales
1 George St. Ste 300
Georgetown, MD 21930
888-221-5022
shmys@baybroadband.net
www.sassafrasharbormarina.com

MASSACHUSETTS

Jim Power
Allen Harbor Marine
335 Lower County Rd
Harwichport, MA 02646-0445
800-832-2467
info@allenharbor.com
www.allenharbor.com
New Boat Sales, Brokerage Sales,
Service Yard

American Marine & Boat Sales
58R Merrimac St.
Newburyport, MA 01950-3065
978-462-2323
rvorias@usedpowerboats.com
www.usedpowerboats.com
Brokerage

Dan O'Connell
Captain O'Connell Inc.
180 River St.
Fall River, MA 02720-1616
508-672-6303
captainoconnell@comcast.net
www.captoconnell.com
Brokerage, Service Yard

Gary Voller's Yacht Sales
56 Scranton Ave
Falmouth, MA 02540
508-540-5540
gvoller@garyvollersyachtsales.com

Paul Hegarty
Keepeh Yacht Brokers LLC
15 Pleasant St. Unit 21E
Harwich Port, MA 02646-1862
781-258-7238
paul@keepeh.com
www.keepeh.com

Niemiec Marine Inc.
173 Popes Island
New Bedford, MA 02740-7252
508-997-7390
bniemiec@niemiecmarine.com
www.niemiecmarine.com
New Boat Sales, Brokerage, Service Yard

John A. Crosby
Northeast Yacht Brokerage LLC
550 Pleasant St. Ste 105
Winthrop, MA 02152
617-207-5433
john@neyb.com
www.neyb.com
Brokerage Sales

Ron Cahoon
Onset Bay Marina & Yacht Sales
3 Green St.
Buzzards Bay, MA 02558
508-295-2300
ron@onsetbay.com
www.onsetbay.com

Peter Maryott
Oyster Harbors Marine
122 Bridge St
Osterville, MA 02655-2303
508-428-2017
jim@oysterharborsmarine.com
www.oysterharborsmarine.com

South Shore Dry Dock Marine
612 Plain St
Marshfield, MA 02050-2740
781-834-9790
ssdrydock@aol.com
www.southshoredrydock.com

Tern Harbor Marina
275 River St.
N. Weymouth, MA 02191-2239

781-337-1964; Cell:781-760-4157
knoonan@ternharbormarina.com
www.ternharbormarina.com/
New Boat Sales, Brokerage, Service Yard

MICHIGAN

Mike Sandmair
765 Yachts
1627 Sunningdale
Grosse Pointe Woods, MI 48236
586-291-6596
765mfs@gmail.com
765yachts.com
Brokerage Sales

Douglas Bergmann
Bergmann Marine
05953 Loeb Rd
Charlevoix, MI 49720-9562
231-547-3957
bergmann@freeway.net
www.bergmannmarine.com

David Klicki
Blue Lagoon Yacht Sales
41680 Conger Bay Dr.
Harrison Township, MI 48045
586-463-1020
boats@bluelagoonmarina.com
www.bluelagoonmarina.com
New Boat Sales, Brokerage Sales,
Service Yard

Josh Van Howe
Coral Gables Yachts LLC
430 W. 23rd St.
Holland, MI 49423-5901
616-928-1002
brokers@cgyacht.com
www.coralgablesyachts.com/
Brokerage Sales, Service Yard

Douglas Glendening
Glendening Yacht Sales
30675 N. River Rd.
Harrison Township, MI 48045
586-465-7833
doug@glendeningyachtsales.com
www.glendeningyachtsales.com
Brokerage Sales

– Broker/Dealer Directory –

Gary Kohout
Gregory Boat Company
9666 E Jefferson
Detroit, MI 48214-2993
313-823-1900
gary@gregoryboat.com
www.gregoryboat.com
Brokerage, Service Yard

Harborview Yacht Sales
12935 W Bayshore Dr #105
Traverse City, MI 49684-6214
231-933-5414
info@harborviewyachtsales.com
www.harborviewyachtsales.com
New Boat Sales, Brokerage

Irish Boat Shop
13000 Stover Rd
Charlevoix, MI 49720-9500
231-547-9967
jeffglenny@irishboatshop.com
www.irishboatshop.com

John Slaven
John B. Slaven, Inc.
31300 N. River Rd.
Harrison Town, MI 48045
586-463-0000
yachts@jbslaven.com
www.jbslaven.com

Bob Myers
Pier 1000 Marina
1000 Riverview Drive
Benton Harbor, MI 49022-5028
616-927-4471
chillout@pier1000.com
www.pier1000.com
Brokerage Sales, Service Yard

Mitch Jordan
Portside Yacht Brokers LLC
915 W Savidge St
Spring Lake, MI 49456-1626
616-850-7678; Cell:616-638-1600
mitchatpyb@sbcglobal.net
www.yachtworld.com/portsideyacht
Brokerage Sales

Eric Robinson
Starboard Yachts, Inc.
1111 Ottawa Beach Rd.
Holland, MI 49424
616-796-0505
erob@starboardyachts.com
www.starboardyachts.com
New Boat Sales, Brokerage Sales

Carl Knaack
SuperBrokers
13310 SW Bayshore Dr.
Traverse City, MI 49684
231-922-3002
superbro@superbrokers.com

Paul J. Zvonek
Temptation Yacht Sales, Inc.
49 Macomb Pl #14
Mt. Cemens, MI 48043
586-463-8060
paul@temptationyachtsales.com
www.temptationyachtsales.com
Brokerage Sales

Walstrom Marine
501 E. Bay St.
Harbor Springs, MI 49740-1607
231-526-2141
boats@walstrom.com
www.walstrom.com
New Boat Sales, Brokerage Sales,
Service Yard

MINNESOTA

Watergate Marina Boat Sales
2500 Crosby Farm Rd.
St. Paul, MN 55116-2691
651-695-3780; Cell:612-916-1171
jason@watergatemarina.net
www.watergatemarina.net
New Boat Sales, Brokerage, Service
Yard

Yacht Brokers Inc.
PO Box 732
Stillwater, MN 55082-0732
612-430-9703
yachtbrokers@yahoo.com
www.yachtbrokersinc.com
Brokerage

MISSOURI

Glencove Marina
PO Box 759
Lake Ozark, MO 65049
573-365-4001
Barb@GlencoveMarina.com

Jeffrey Clark
Ozark Yacht Brokers, Inc.
PO Box 40
Lake Ozark, MO 65049-0040
573-365-8100

sales@ozarkyachts.com
www.ozarkyachts.com
Brokerage

Safe Harbor Yacht Sales
6171 Highway V
St. Charles, MO 63301-5937
636-250-3500; Cell:314-409-8698
jim@safeharboryachts.com
www.safeharboryachts.com

NEVADA

Brent Thompson
Image Boats
1019 Armillaria St.
Henderson, NV 89011
866-593-5539
imageboats@gmail.com
www.ImageBoats.com/
Brokerage Sales

NEW HAMPSHIRE

Laurence Bussey
Northeast Yachts
189 Wentworth Rd.
Portsmouth, NH 03801-5624
603-433-3222
skipper@neyachts.com
www.neyachts.com
New Boat Sales, Brokerage Sales

NEW JERSEY

Mike Szegeski
Brightwater Yacht Brokers
311 Channel Dr.
Pt. Pleasant Beach, NJ 08742-2623
732-714-0500
brightwateryachts@comcast.net
www.brightwateryachts.com
Brokerage Sales

Cape May Marine
12 Falcon Ridge
Cape May, NJ 08204-1723
609-884-0262
cmmarine@yahoo.com

Holiday Harbor Yacht Sales
115 Admiral Way
Waretown, NJ 08758-1902
609-693-7188
hhys@verizon.net
www.holidayharboryachtsales.com
Brokerage

– Broker/Dealer Directory –

John Schachel
Prestige Yacht Sales
201 Union Ave
Brielle, NJ 08730
732-292-1500
prestyacht@aol.com
www.prestigeyachtsales.com
Brokerage Sales

Kevin McGettigan
Sandy Hook Yacht Sales
1410 Ocean Ave
Sea Bright, NJ 07760
732-530-5500; Cell:732-539-3250
kevinm@sandyhookyachts.com
www.sandyhookyachts.com
New Boat Sales, Brokerage Sales

Lou Piergross
South Jersey Yacht Sales
1231 Route 109
Cape May, NJ 08204-5215
609-884-1600
lpiergross@sjyachtsales.com
www.southjerseyyachtsales.com
New Boat Sales, Brokerage Sales

NEW YORK

David Devol
Bay Watch Yachts
86 Orchard Beach Blvd
Port Washington, NY 11050-1427
516-767-6970
baywatchs@aol.com
www.baywatchyachts.com
Brokerage Sales

Oakley Gentry
Blue Water Boat Brokers
201 Montauk Hwy Suite 7
Westhampton Beach, NY 11978
631-567-0545
sales@bluewaterboatbrokers.com
www.bluewaterboatbrokers.com
New Boat Sales, Brokerage Sales

Howard McMichael
McMichael Yacht Brokers
447 E Boston Post Rd
Mamaroneck, NY 10543-3739
914-381-5900
maryann@mcmyacht.com
www.mcmichaelyachtbrokers.com

Staten Island Yacht Sales
222 Mansion Ave

Staten Island, NY 10308-3409
718-984-7676
bonjornio@siyachts.com
www.siyachts.com

NORTH CAROLINA

Captain Steve Miller
Crystal Coast Boats
PO Box 2158
Beaufort, NC 28516
252-723-8187
captainsteve@ec.rr.com
www.crystalcoastboats.com
Brokerage Sales

Magnum Marine
335 S. Belvedere Dr.
Hampstead, NC 28443
910-250-6087; Cell:910-250-6087
gp163@aol.com
New Boat Sales, Brokerage

Neal Littman
Marina Management Services
208 Arendell St.
Morehead City, NC 28557
252-726-6862
littman@moreheadcityyachtbasin.com
www.moreheadcityyachtbasin.com
Brokerage

MarineMax
130 Short St.
Wrightsville Beach, NC 28480
910-256-8100
mike.knoll@marinemax.com

OHIO

Captain's Cove Marine
4670 Kellogg Ave
Cincinnati, OH 45226-2408
513-321-1111
MARC@CAPTAINSCOVEMARINE.COM
www.captainscovemarine.com

Rockey Piacentino
Catawba Moorings
2313 NE Catawba Rd
Port Clinton, OH 43452-3548
419-797-4775
cmi@cros.net
www.catawbamoorings.com
New Boat Sales, Brokerage Sales,
Service Yard

Marine Tech Concepts
145 SE Catawba Rd Ste A
Port Clinton, OH 43452
419-732-3355; Cell:419-552-0080
jeff@marinetechconcepts.com
www.marinetechconcepts.com
New Boat Sales, Brokerage, Service Yard

National Liquidators
5401 N. Marginal Rd.
Cleveland, OH 44114
216-391-1900
leonettid@natliq.com
www.yachtauctions.com
Brokerage, Service Yard

PTL Yacht Sales, LLC
2035 First St.
Sandusky, OH 44870
419-734-2900
jake3@coastalwave.net
www.ptlyachts.com

Tom Mack
South Shore Marine
1611 Sawmill Pkwy
Huron, OH 44839-2247
419-433-5798
tom@southshoremarine.com
www.southshoremarine.com
New Boat Sales, Brokerage Sales,
Service Yard

OREGON

Hayden Island Yacht Center
50 NE Tomahawk Island Dr
Portland, OR 97217-7934
503-289-4007; Cell:503-519-4234
rlaird6905@aol.com
New Boat Sales, Brokerage

Seaward Yacht Sales
303 NE Tomahawk Island Dr. Ste 2
Portland, OR 97217
503-224-2628; Cell:503-781-3638
motis@seawardyachtsales.com
www.seawardyachtsales.com

Sam Vercoe
Vercoe Yacht Sales
515 NE Tomahawk Island Dr
Portland, OR 97217-8000
503-735-3024
vercoeys@aol.com
www.vercoeyachtsales.com
New Boat Sales, Brokerage Sales,
Service Yard

– Broker/Dealer Directory –

PUERTO RICO

CFR Yacht Sales, Inc.
153 Ramon Powel St.
San Juan, PR 00908-0816
787-722-7088; Cell:787-360-3370
carlosluis@cfryachtsales.com
www.cfryachts.com
New Boat Sales, Brokerage

SOUTH CAROLINA

Edward James
Ashley Yachts LLC
3 Lockwood Dr Suite 302B
Charleston, SC 29401-1100
843-577-7222
info@ashleyyachts.com
www.ashleyyachts.com
Brokerage Sales

Berry-Boger Yacht Sales
PO Box 36
N. Myrtle Beach, SC 29597-0036
843-249-6167
jeff@bbyacht.com
www.bbyacht.com
Brokerage

John Douglas
Charleston Harbor Yacht Sales
24 Patriots Point Rd.
Mt. Pleasant, SC 29464
843-425-6888
john@charlestonharboryachtsales.com
www.charlestonharboryachtsales.com
Brokerage Sales

Doug Glendinning
Glendinning Marine Products
740 Century Cr.
Conway, SC 29526
843-399-6146x108
johng@glendinningprods.com
Brokerage Sales

TENNESSEE

Capt. Sam Evans
Captain's Choice
PO Box 351
Pickwick Dam, TN 38365
662-279-0303
captainschoiceofpickwick@gmail.com
www.captainschoiceofpickwick@com
Brokerage Sales

Erwin Marine Sales
3001 Kings Point Rd.
Chattanooga, TN 37343
423-622-1978
dunderwood@erwinmarinesales.com
www.erwinmarinesales.com
New Boat Sales, Brokerage Sales,
Service Yard

TEXAS

Rick Lemon
Cedar Mills Yacht Sales
500 Harbour View Rd.
Gordonville, TX 76245
903-523-4574
rick@cedarmills.com
www.cedarmills.com
Brokerage Sales, Service Yard

Jerry Mudd
Eriksen Marine
5975 Hiline Rd
Austin, TX 78734-1150
512-266-3493
mike@eriksenmarine.com
www.eriksenmarine.com/
Brokerage Sales, Service Yard

Pete Fox
Fox Yacht Sales
PO Box 772
Port Aransas, TX 78373-0772
361-749-4870
foxyachtsales@centurytel.net
www.foxyachtsales.com
New Boat Sales, Brokerage

Jay Bettis & Company
2509 Nasa Rd 1
Seabrook, TX 77586-3452
281-326-3333
info@jb-yachts.com
www.jb-yachts.com
New Boat Sales, Brokerage Sales

Lone Star Yacht Sales
1500 Marina Bay Dr. Bldg 125 #3380
Clear Lake Shores, TX 77565
281-334-3500
jhedges@lsyachts.com
www.lsyachts.com
New Boat Sales, Brokerage

Tommy Nolan
Texas Sportfishing Yacht Sales
South Shore Harbour Marina, Pier 15

League City, TX 77573
281-535-2628
txyachts@quikus.com
www.texassportfishingyachtsales.com
New Boat Sales, Brokerage Sales

VIRGINIA

Ryan White
Marine Concepts Yacht Sales
8172 Shore Dr.
Norfolk, VA 23518
757-313-8787
ryan@marineconcepts.net
www.marineconcepts.net
Brokerage Sales

Olversons Lodge Creek Marina
1161 Melrose Rd.
Lottsburg, VA 22511-2306
804-529-6868; Cell:804-512-6256
boatsales@olversonsmarina.com
www.olversonsmarina.com

D.A. Adams
Sea D.A. Yachts
2100 Marina Shores Dr Bldg 4 #108
Virginia Beach, VA 23451
757-434-5242
seadayachts@live.com
www.seadayachts.com
Brokerage Sales, Service Yard

WASHINGTON

Nick Ouilette
Bellingham Yachts
1801 Roeder Ave Ste 174
Bellingham, WA 98225-2258
877-31-09446
sales@bellinghamyachts.com
www.bellinghamyachts.com
New Boat Sales, Brokerage Sales,
Service Yard

Breakwater Marina Yacht Sales
5603 N Waterfront Dr
Tacoma, WA 98407-6536
253-752-6663
yachtsales@breakwatermarina.com
www.breakwatermarina.com
Brokerage, Marina, Service Yard

Classic Yachts Inc.
PO Box 98964
Des Moines, WA 98198-0964
206-824-1200; Cell:206-255-3469

– Broker/Dealer Directory –

sdwilkes@yahoo.com
www.classicyachtsinc.com
Brokerage

Crow's Nest Yacht Sales
809 Fairview Pl. N Ste 150
Seattle, WA 98109-4452
206-625-1580
dwood@crowsnestyachts.com
www.crowsnestcpy.com
Brokerage Sales

Van Draper
Elliott Bay Yacht Sales
2601 W Marina Place Ste D
Seattle, WA 98199-4331
206-285-9563
van@elliottbayyachtsales.com
www.elliottbayyachtsales.com
Brokerage Sales

Fraser Yachts
2292 W. Commodore Way #220
Seattle, WA 98199
206-382-9494; Cell:206-669-1197
seattle@fraseryachts.com

Cecilia O. Hebert
Hebert Yachts
1220 Westlake Ave North
Seattle, WA 98109
206-948-9198
cjordan@hebertyachts.com
www.yachtworld.com/hebertyachts
Brokerage Sales

Ted Grifin
Seattle Yachts
7001 Seaview Ave NW Suite 150
Seattle, WA 98117
206-789-8044
Ted@sasyachts.com
New Boat Sales, Brokerage Sales

WISCONSIN

Captain Jim's Yacht Sales
5017 Sheridan Rd
Kenosha, WI 53140
262-652-8866
captjimsyachts@aol.com
www.captjims.net
Brokerage, Service yard

Chicago Yacht Brokers
1117 N. Main St
Racine, WI 53402

262-637-9121
admin@chicagoyachtbrokers.com
www.chicagoyachtbrokers.com

Chuck Kotovic
Emerald Yacht & Ship
N60 W29709 Woodfield Rd.
Hartland, WI 53029
262-681-0600
chuck@emeraldyachtship.com
www.emeraldyachtship.com

Emerald Yacht-Ship Group
3107 Six Mile Rd. #3
Racine, WI 53402
262-681-0600; Cell:414-350-8505
sales@emeraldyachtship.com
www.emeraldyachtship.com
Brokerage

Tad Harvey
Harvey Yacht Sales
6018 Trillium Ln
Sturgeon Bay, WI 54235-9753
920-743-0980
tad@harveyyachtsales.com
www.harveyyachtsales.com
Brokerage Sales

Mark Derenne
North Beach Marine
1001 Michigan Blvd
Racine, WI 53402
414-651-3100
boats@northbeachmarine.com
www.northbeachmarine.com
New Boat Sales, Brokerage Sales,
Service Yard

Paul Gilling
South Bay Marine Sales, Inc.
101 Bay Beach Rd.
Green Bay, WI 54302
920-680-8550
pgilling@southbaymarina.com
www.southbaymarina.com
Brokerage Sales, Service Yard

CANADA

Richard Evans
Calibre Yacht Sales
415 West Esplanade
N. Vancouver, BC V7M1A6
CANADA
604-929-0651
richard@calibreyachts.com

www.calibreyachts.com/
Brokerage Sales

Custom Yacht Sales Ltd.
1955 Swartz Bay Rd.
Sidney, BC V8L3X9
CANADA
250-656-8771; Cell:250-727-1523
ghorne@customyachtsales.com
www.customyachtsales.com

Far Point Marine
1788 Emerson Ct
N. Vancouver, BC V7H2Y6
CANADA
604-209-2464
info@farpointmarine.com

Brent Leathwood
765 Yachts
6-2400 Dundas St. W. Suite 143
Mississauga, ON L5K2R8
CANADA
800-505-3920
info@765yachts.com
Brokerage Sales

Chris Sellner
C.A.S. Marine Power Ltd.
2564 Cedar Creek Rd.
Ayr/Cambraidge, ON N0B1E0
CANADA
519-623-2372
csellner@casmarine.com
www.casmarine.com/
New Boat Sales, Brokerage Sales,
Service Yard

Peter Solty
Crates Marine Port Credit
#1 Port Street East
Mississauga, ON L5G4N1
CANADA
416-802-9251; Cell:416-802-9251
petsol@msn.com
Brokerage Sales, New Boat Sales

P.G. (Greg) Heffering
Simcoe Yacht Sales
Unit 26 1111 Wilson Rd. North
Oshawa, ON L1G8C2
CANADA
905-576-8288
pghsimcoe@rogers.com
www.SimcoeYachts.com
Brokerage Sales

Section 1
Motoryachts & Trawlers

See index for complete list of models.

Trawlers & Motoryachts

Trawlers & Motoryachts

Albin 34 Aft Cabin

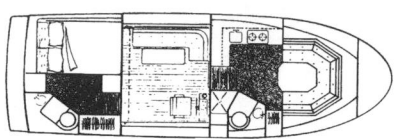

1987–92

Small aft-cabin trawler/cruiser with standard diesel power combines versatility, economy, simplicity. Generous 11'6" beam allows for roomy cabin layout with teak trim, lower helm, fore and aft heads, L-shaped galley, wraparound dinette. Large cabin windows provide panoramic views. Note twin deck doors, integral swim platform, extended flybridge with ample seating. Tiny aft deck is useful mostly for line-handling. Single 250hp Cummins diesel (or twin 157hp Isuzus) cruise at 12 knots with top speed of 15–16 knots.

Prices Not Provided for Pre-1995 Models

Length Overall	34'3"	Fuel	200 gals.
Length WL	30'6"	Water	70 gals.
Beam	11'6"	Waste	30 gals.
Draft	3'0"	Hull Type	Modified-V
Weight	16,500#	Deadrise Aft	NA

Albin 36 Express Trawler

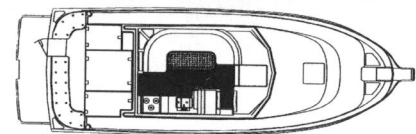

1999–2004

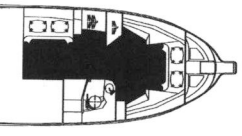

Handsome performance cruiser with trawler profile targets boaters looking for an affordable blend of speed, comfort, versatility. Space-efficient interior has guest stateroom to port with athwartships double berth extending under salon floor. U-shaped dinette can seat six. Good visibility from lower helm. Hardtop shades entire cockpit. Wide side decks are a plus. Reverse-slanted windshield reduces glare. Aft engine room uses V-drives to deliver the power. Cruise at 12 knots with single 450hp Cat diesel; 16–18 knots with twin 330hp Cummins.

See Page 512 For Value Estimates

Length w/Pulpit	37'5"	Clearance	11'10"
Hull Length	36'0"	Fuel	380 gals.
Beam	12'9"	Water	120 gals.
Draft	3'3"	Hull Type	Modified-V
Weight	18,000#	Deadrise Aft	12°

Albin 36 Trawler

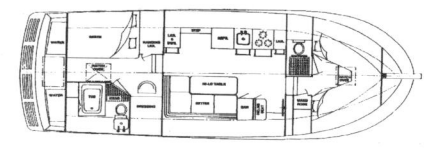

1978–93

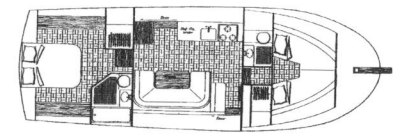

Classic Taiwan trawler with single-diesel power, traditional teak interior pairs sturdy construction with economical operation. Practical galley-up interior includes port and starboard deck doors, generous storage, teak parquet flooring, tub/shower in aft head. Flared bow keeps decks dry; full-length keel protects running gear from grounding. Lots of exterior bright work means lots of maintenance. Very popular boat—over 500 were built. Cruise at 7–8 knots with 120hp Lehman diesel; 9–10 knots with single 210hp Cummins.

Prices Not Provided for Pre-1995 Models

Length Overall	35'9"	Clearance	12'4"
Length WL	31'3"	Fuel	350 gals.
Beam	13'2"	Water	220 gals.
Draft	3'6"	Waste	40 gals.
Weight	18,500#	Hull Type	Semi-Disp.

Albin 37 Palm Beach

1985–89

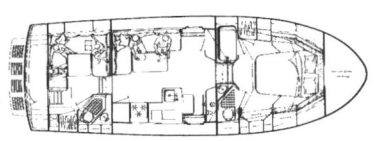

Compact cruiser with trawler profile and Hunt-designed hull pairs traditional styling with solid construction, untrawler-like performance. Galley-up layout with lower helm has owner's stateroom forward with centerline queen bed, ensuite head with separate stall shower. Versatile aft cabin features horse-shoe settee with center table that converts for guest accommodations, private head, engine room access, access to aft deck. Twin salon doors provide good deck access. Note transom door. Cruise economically at 14 knots with twin 210hp Cummins diesels.

Prices Not Provided for Pre-1995 Models

Length Overall	36'8"	Clearance	NA
Length WL	31'6"	Fuel	360 gals.
Beam	12'9"	Water	115 gals.
Draft	3'0"	Waste	30 gals.
Weight	16,000#	Hull Type	Modified-V

Albin 40 North Sea Cutter

2005–08

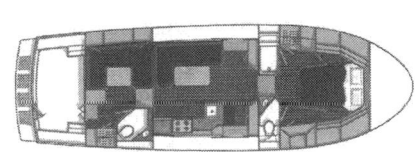

High-performance trawler combines unusual interior layout with traditional styling, good build quality. Open floorplan is arranged with owner's stateroom forward rather than aft. Versatile aft cabin with direct cockpit access, convertible U-shaped dinette can be used as a den/office or second state-room. Generous galley storage is a plus. Note twin salon deck doors, planked cabin sole, wide side decks, large cockpit. Well-constructed boat is built to last. Yanmar 370hp diesels cruise at 20 knots (24–26 knots top).

See Page 512 For Value Estimates

Length	39'6"	Fuel	500 gals.
Beam	13'0"	Water	200 gals.
Draft	4'0"	Waste	40 gals.
Weight	25,000#	Hull Type	Modified-V
Clearance	NA	Deadrise Aft	NA

Albin 40 Sundeck

1987–93

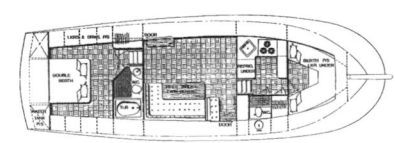

Conventional Taiwan-built trawler with full-beam aft cabin is sturdy, comfortable, economical to operate. Two-state-room, galley-down interior includes lower helm, fold-down serving counter, parquet flooring, port/starboard deck doors, excellent storage. Teak interior woodwork is finished to high Asian standards. Flybridge seats six. Wide side decks, roomy aft deck are a plus. Good range. Full-length keel protects props, rudders from grounding. Cruise at 10 knots with twin 135hp Lehman diesels; 12 knots with 210hp Cummins diesels.

Prices Not Provided for Pre-1995 Models

Length Overall	40'3"	Clearance	NA
Length WL	34'2"	Fuel	400 gals.
Beam	13'8"	Water	180 gals.
Draft	3'6"	Waste	50 gals.
Weight	26,000#	Hull Type	Semi-Disp.

Albin 40 Trawler

1987–93

Popular semi-displacement cruiser with classic trawler profile combines traditional teak interior with fuel-efficient operation. Galley-down layout with parquet flooring includes convertible salon settee, lower helm with sliding deck door, teak parquet flooring. Owner's stateroom has queen bed, large head with tub/shower. Flybridge with facing settees seats six. Note that her sistership, the Albin 40 Sundeck, is the same boat with full-beam aft deck, increased aft cabin dimensions. Cruise at 10 knots with 135hp Lehmans; 12 knots 210hp Cummins diesels.

Prices Not Provided for Pre-1995 Models

Length Overall	40'3"	Headroom	6'4"
Length WL	34'2"	Fuel	400 gals.
Beam	13'8"	Water	180 gals.
Draft	3'6"	Waste	50 gals.
Weight	26,000#	Hull Type	Semi-Disp.

Albin 43 Sundeck

1981–94

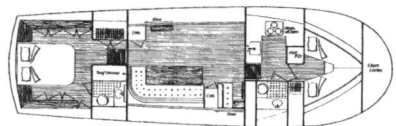

Two-stateroom Interior

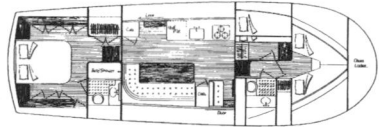

Optional three-stateroom Layout

Sturdy Taiwan trawler with full-beam aft stateroom makes the cut with cruising couples. Standard two-stateroom teak interior boasts lower helm, parquet flooring, twin salon deck doors, tub/shower in aft head. Note wide side decks, teak handrails, teak window frames, simulated lapstrake hull lines. Keel protects prop, running gear. Three-stateroom interior was optional. Salon lacks access door to aft deck—unusual in a trawler this size. Lehman 135hp diesels cruise at 8–9 knots; 210hp Cummins cruise at 12–14 knots.

Prices Not Provided for Pre-1995 Models

Length Overall	42'6"	Headroom	6'5"
Length WL	37'11"	Fuel	500 gals.
Beam	14'6"	Water	300 gals.
Draft	4'1"	Waste	60 gals.
Weight	30,000#	Hull Type	Semi-Disp.

Albin 43 Trawler

1979–94

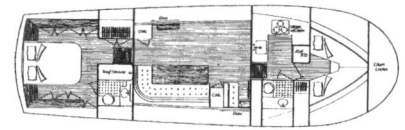

Two-stateroom Interior

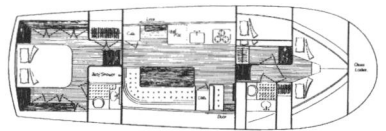

Optional three-stateroom layout

Traditional trunk-cabin trawler with walkaround decks targets buyers looking for interior comfort, cruising economy. Two-stateroom teak interior includes full lower helm, parquet flooring, twin salon deck doors, tub/shower in aft head. Note wide side decks, teak handrails, teak window frames, simulated lapstrake hull lines. Keel protects prop, running gear. Three-stateroom interior was optional. No rear salon door to aft deck—unusual in a trawler this size. Lehman 135hp diesels cruise at 8–9 knots; 210hp Cummins cruise at 12–14 knots.

Prices Not Provided for Pre-1995 Models

Length Overall	42'6"	Headroom	6'5"
Length WL	37'11"	Fuel	500 gals.
Beam	14'6"	Water	300 gals.
Draft	4'1"	Waste	60 gals.
Weight	30,000#	Hull Type	Semi-Disp.

Albin 48 North Sea Cutter

1983–89

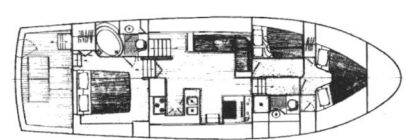

Handsome cockpit yacht with Hunt-designed hull blends durable construction with tasteful accommodations, impressive rough-water handling. Three-stateroom interior with galley up features standard lower helm, salon deck door, tub/shower in aft head, teak woodwork and cabinetry. Note cockpit access door in master stateroom. Additional highlights include cockpit lazarette, wide side decks with raised bulwarks, excellent storage. Volvo 307hp diesels cruise at 16–17 knots; Cat 375hp diesels cruise at 20+ knots.

Prices Not Provided for Pre-1995 Models

Length Overall	47'9"	Clearance	NA
Length WL	43'0"	Water	300 gals.
Beam	14'0"	Fuel	600 gals.
Draft	4'0"	Hull Type	Deep-V
Weight	31,000#	Deadrise Aft	24°

Albin 49 Tri-Cabin

1979–85

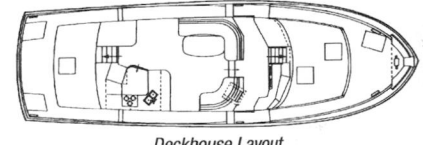

Deckhouse Layout

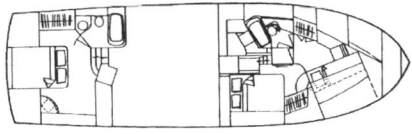

Stateroom Layout

Seaworthy long-range trawler with traditional trunk-cabin profile meets cruiser's need for comfort, security, economy. Features include full teak interior with parquet flooring, spacious salon with galley aft, three double staterooms, teak-over-fiberglass decks, large cockpit. Pilothouse staircase provides easy access to flybridge. Note bathtubs in both heads—very unusual. Bridge overhangs shade side decks. Plenty of exterior teak to maintain. Cruise at 8–10 knots with twin 135hp Lehman diesels. Range exceeds 700 nautical miles.

Prices Not Provided for Pre-1995 Models

Length Overall	48'4"	Clearance	13'6"
Length WL	43'0"	Fuel	620 gals.
Beam	15'1"	Water	320 gals.
Draft	3'8"	Waste	100 gals.
Weight	39,050#	Hull Type	Semi-Disp.

American Tug 34

2001–Current

Sought-after coastal cruiser with tug-like profile is fast, stable, loaded with practical features. Single-stateroom layout with full-beam salon is well suited for cruising couples. False stack creates unique raised area in forward salon overhead. Excellent helm visibility. Side decks are wide with raised bulwarks for added security. Full-length keel provides excellent directional stability. Updates in 2009 include raised cockpit, extended side rails, sliding pilothouse doors. Single Cummins 330hp diesel will cruise at 12–14 knots (about 16 knots top).

See Page 512 For Value Estimates

Length Overall	34'5"	Clearance	NA
Length WL	32'9"	Fuel	400 gals.
Beam	13'3"	Water	150 gals.
Draft	3'5"	Waste	45 gals.
Weight	20,000#	Hull Type	Semi-Disp.

Trawlers & Motoryachts

American Tug 41

2005–Current

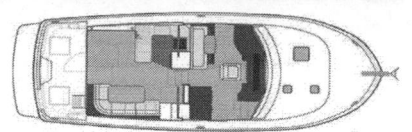

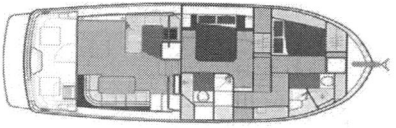

See Page 512 For Value Estimates

Stout pilothouse trawler with semi-displacement hull combines classic styling with solid construction, luxury-class accommodations. Wide beam results in roomy interior with two double staterooms, two full heads, full-beam salon with Ultraleather seating, U-shaped galley. Good visibility from raised pilothouse. Bow thruster is standard, flybridge is optional. Note underwater exhaust, deep cockpit. False stack creates unique raised area in forward salon overhead. Cruise at 12–14 knots with single 540hp Cummins diesel (about 16 knots top).49

Length Overall	45'6"	Clearance	16'0"
Hull Length	37'9"	Fuel	640 gals.
Beam	15'10"	Water	210 gals.
Draft	4'10"	Waste	60 gals.
Weight	30,000#	Hull Type	Semi-Disp.

Atlantic 37 Double Cabin

1982–92

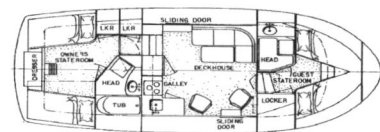

Prairie 36 Floorplan

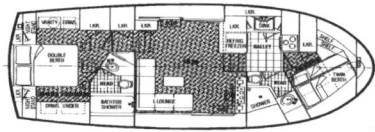

Atlantic 37 Layout

Prices Not Provided for Pre-1995 Models

Rebranded version of popular Prairie 36 Trawler (1979–81) earned an enviable reputation for quality construction, sea-kindly handling, strong resale values. Compact two-stateroom interior boasts stall showers in both heads—a real plus in a boat this size. Teak woodwork is finished to high standards. Port and starboard deck doors provide good deck access. Spacious engine room makes service easy. Keel protects prop and rudder. Cruise at 10 knots with twin 135hp diesels; 12 knots with twin 250hp diesels.

Length	36'7"	Headroom	6'5"
Beam	13'9"	Fuel	250 gals.
Draft	3'3"	Water	200 gals.
Weight	22,000#	Waste	30 gals.
Clearance, Mast	19'9"	Hull Type	Semi-Disp.

Atlantic 44 Motor Yacht

1977–92

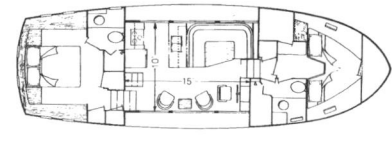

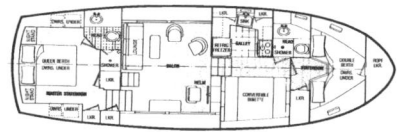

Prices Not Provided for Pre-1995 Models

Heavily built cruising yacht with classic Hargrave lines enjoys continued popularity of today's used-boat market. Several two-stateroom floorplans were offered over the years. Highlights include wide side decks, full teak interior, spacious engine room. Note generous freeboard. Early models came with mast and boom assembly. Very fuel efficient with small diesels. Remained in production for 15 years without major alterations—a long production run by any standard. Cruise at 8 knots with Lehman 135hp diesels; 14–15 knots with 300hp Cats.

Length Overall	43'8"	Clearance	13'8"
Length WL	38'6"	Water	240 gals.
Beam	14'0"	Fuel, Std.	320 gals.
Draft	3'5"	Fuel, Opt.	620 gals.
Weight	30,000#	Hull Type	Modified-V

Atlantic 47 Motor Yacht

1982–92

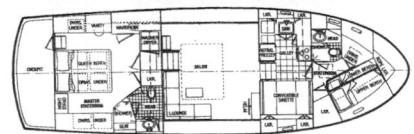

2-Stateroom Floorplan

3-Stateroom Floorplan

Prices Not Provided for Pre-1995 Models

Traditional Hargrave-designed motoryacht delivers time-tested blend of solid construction, spacious accommodations, comfortable ride. Available with choice of two- or three-stateroom floorplans—original three-cabin layout proved most popular. Lower helm position was standard. Note spacious aft deck dimensions, roomy master suite. Optional hard aft enclosure turned aft deck into fully enclosed second salon. Cat 375hp diesels cruise at 14–15 knots; 435hp GM diesels cruise at 16 knots. Originally marketed as the Prairie 46 LRC (1979–81).

Length	46'9"	Headroom	6'5"
Beam	16'0"	Fuel, Std.	400 gals.
Draft	3'9"	Fuel, Opt.	800 gals.
Weight	41,000#	Water	400 gals.
Clearance, Arch	18'0"	Hull Type	Modified-V

Azimut 39

1999–2005

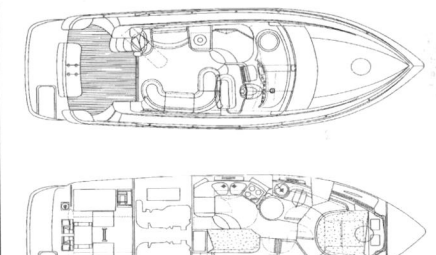

See Page 512 For Value Estimates

Polished Italian cruising yacht with striking profile offers impressive display of stylish design, interior craftsmanship. Luxurious two-stateroom interior with cherry accents, wraparound salon windows is finished to very high standards. Corner posts obstruct visibility from lower helm. Teak decks, teak cockpit sole, low profile radar arch, foredeck sun pad are standard. Tight engine room is typical of Mediterranean yachts. Note modest fuel capacity. Cat (or Cummins) 355hp diesels cruise at 26–28 knots (30+ knots top).

Length	39'10"	Water	132 gals.
Beam	13'3"	Clearance	12'0"
Draft	3'7"	Headroom	6'4"
Weight	22,000#	Hull Type	Modified-V
Fuel	264 gals.	Deadrise Aft	14.6°

Azimut 42

1999–2005

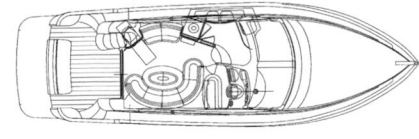

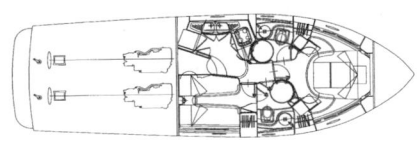

See Page 512 For Value Estimates

Sleek flybridge cruiser is Italian styling at its best in a midsize luxury yacht. Interior highlights include spacious salon, two full heads, sunken galley, large master stateroom. Lower helm lacks chart space; helm seat is not adjustable. Engine room, accessed from cockpit lazarette, is very tight. Note roomy cockpit with twin transom doors, well-placed handrails. Well-arranged bridge seats several guests in comfort. Meticulous craftsmanship, superb finish. Agile and quick, 390hp Cat diesels cruise at 28 knots (32–33 knots top).

Length	43'4"	Fuel	317 gals.
Beam	13'6"	Water	132 gals.
Draft	3'5"	Headroom	6'4"
Weight	24,000#	Hull Type	Deep-V
Clearance	14'6"	Deadrise Aft	17°

Trawlers & Motoryachts

Azimut 43 Flybridge

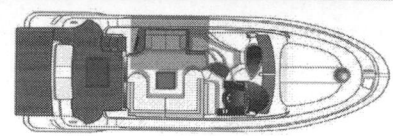

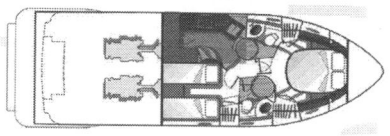

2007–Current

Italian-bred flybridge yacht with signature Azimut styling delivers imposing blend of full-time luxury, world-class construction. Handsome two-stateroom interior includes lavish main salon with tiered windows, deluxe master suite with generous storage, sunken galley with premium appliances. Enormous flybridge with sun pad can seat a small crowd. Additional features include extended swim platform, cockpit lounge seating, ergonomic lower helm position. Cummins 425hp diesels cruise at 24–25 knots (29 top). Cummins 480hp engines run a few knots faster.

See Page 512 For Value Estimates

Length	42'4"	Fuel	290 gals.
Beam	13'10"	Water	132 gals.
Draft	4'2"	Waste	40 gals.
Weight	30,000#	Hull Type	Deep-V
Clearance	NA	Deadrise Aft	21°

Azimut 43S

2007–Current

Italian thoroughbred with awesome Azimut styling was the first European yacht to incorporate Volvo IPS drives as standard equipment. Stunning open-plan interior with sunken galley, wraparound lounge seating takes comfort, luxury to unsurpassed levels. Design highlights include enormous power sunroof, hydraulic swim platform, tiered cabin windows. Triple hatches provide good (but not great) engine access. Volvo 370hp IPS diesels—small for a boat this size—cruise efficiently at 24–25 knots; later models with 435hp IPS drives cruise at 30 knots.

See Page 512 For Value Estimates

Length	43'10"	Fuel	290 gals.
Beam	13'10"	Water	132 gals.
Draft	3'9"	Waste	35 gals.
Weight	28,000#	Hull Type	Modified-V
Clearance	16'2"	Deadrise Aft	14°

Azimut 46

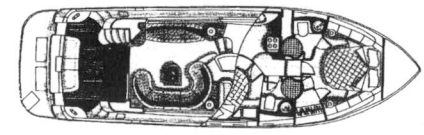

2-Stateroom Interior

1997–2004

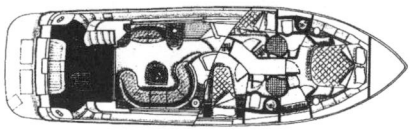

3-Stateroom Interior

Elegant styling, impeccable workmanship make this Med cruiser a modern classic. Choice of two- or three-stateroom interiors. Ultra-stylish salon is surrounded by vast amounts of window space, beautiful high-gloss cherry woodwork. Galley is set below salon level where it's hidden from view. Uncomfortable lower helm position. Engine room, accessed from cockpit lazarette, is a tight fit. Cat 435hp diesels cruise in low 20s (27–28 knots top); newer models with 505hp Cats top out at 30 knots. Very popular model—over 350 were sold.

See Page 512 For Value Estimates

Length	49'0"	Fuel	449 gals.
Beam	14'4"	Water	132 gals.
Draft	3'4"	Headroom	6'5"
Weight	27,000#	Hull Type	Deep-V
Clearance	NA	Deadrise Aft	18°

Azimut 50

2004–10

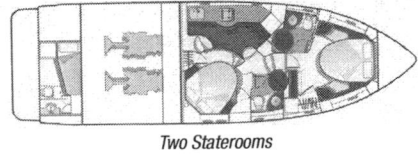

Two Staterooms

Three Staterooms

See Page 512 For Value Estimates

Leading-edge sportyacht with sweeping lines, distinctive shark-fin windows turns heads in every marina. Lavish two-stateroom interior (most 50-foot flybridge yachts have three) boasts exceptionally spacious salon. Lower helm is a work of art, but seating ergonomics are poor. Galley is big in the two-stateroom layout, small when optional third stateroom is added. Note large cockpit lazarette, extended swim platform, roomy engine compartment. A popular model, MAN 660hp—or Cat 715hp—diesels cruise at 28 knots (30+ knots top).

Length	52'6"	Headroom	6'6"
Beam	14'11"	Fuel	581 gals.
Draft	3'11"	Water	132 gals.
Weight	46,000#	Hull Type	Modified-V
Clearance	18'5"	Deadrise Aft	13°

Azimut 50/52

1996–2002

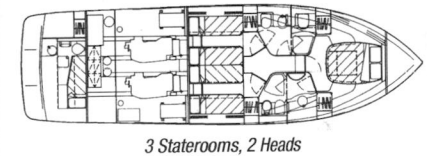

3 Staterooms, 2 Heads

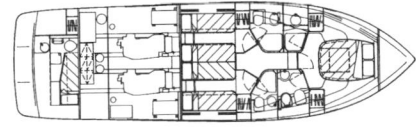

3 Staterooms, 3 Heads

See Page 512 For Value Estimates

Powerful sportyacht with elliptical windows, sharply raked profile combines speed, luxury, performance. Posh three-stateroom interior with two or three heads includes small crew cabin beneath cockpit. Unlike many Azimuts, galley is open to salon rather than sunken. Ultra-low railings surrounding flybridge provide very little security. Note underwater exhausts, power vent windows. Engine room is tight fit. Called Azimut 50 until 1998 when swim platform was extended. Cruise at 28 knots (low 30s top) with 660hp Cats.

Length	51'11"	Fuel	475 gals.
Beam	14'8"	Water	158 gals.
Draft	4'1"	Headroom	6'5"
Weight	38,000#	Hull Type	Deep-V
Clearance	NA	Deadrise Aft	18°

Azimut 54/58

1993–2001

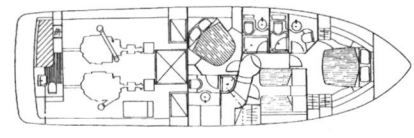

54 Layout

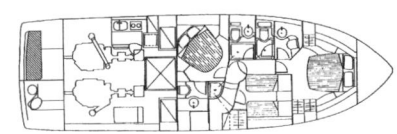

58 Layout

See Page 512 For Value Estimates

Distinctive flybridge yacht (called Azimut 54 until swim platform was extended in 1998) boasts timeless Italian styling, exceptional handling, lavish interior. Highlights include large cockpit with teak sole, aft crew quarters, twin transom walk-throughs to bathing platform. Spacious flybridge has two sun pads, wet bar, seating for a small crowd. Good engine access. Cruise at 23 knots with 600hp V-drive Cats (27–28 knots top); optional 765hp MTUs will cruise at a fast 28 knots (32–33 knots top). Over 150 were sold.

Length, 54	54'7"	Weight, 58	48,500#
Length, 58	57'8"	Fuel	688 gals.
Beam	15'1"	Water	238 gals.
Draft	4'1"	Hull Type	Deep-V
Weight, 54	44,092#	Deadrise Aft	18°

Trawlers & Motoryachts

Azimut 55

2001–05

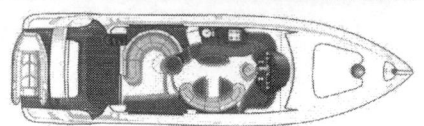

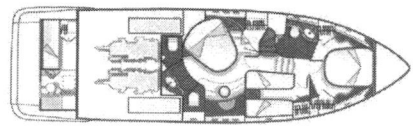

Italian masterwork is a modern blend of sophisticated Mediterranean styling, world-class yachting luxury. Huge salon with swivel tables, circular seating, central bar unit is far more spacious than other yachts in her class. (Few other aft-cockpit 55-footers have a full-beam owner's cabin.) Highlights include distinctive shark-fin styling, ergonomic lower helm, good engine room access. Aft crew quarters sleep a single adult. Extended swim platform can stow small tender. Cat 710hp engines cruise in the mid 20s (about 28 knots top).

See Page 512 For Value Estimates

Length	57'5"	Fuel	665 gals.
Beam	15'7"	Water	169 gals.
Draft	4'0"	Headroom	6'5"
Weight	44,600#	Hull Type	Deep-V
Clearance	16'2"	Deadrise Aft	16.6°

Azimut 62 Flybridge

2003–06

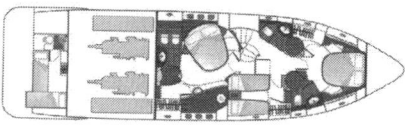

Beautifully styled luxury yacht introduced in 2003 raised the bar for sex appeal, big-boat performance. Expansive salon/dinette/helm area with posh furnishings, high-gloss cherry cabinetry dominates spacious three-stateroom interior. Highlights include opulent master suite with elliptical hull ports, well-executed lower helm, large flybridge with dinghy stowage. Note foredeck, flybridge sun pads. Large engine room—rare in a European yacht—is a plus. Cat 1,150hp diesels cruise at 28–30 knots (about 32 knots wide open).

See Page 512 For Value Estimates

Length	65'1"	Fuel	898 gals.
Beam	16'5"	Water	265 gals.
Draft	4'6"	Max Headroom	6'10"
Weight	60,400#	Hull Type	Deep-V
Clearance	19'9"	Deadrise Aft	17°

Azimut 68 Plus

2001–07

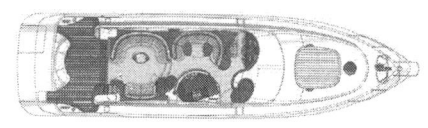

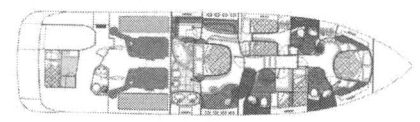

Luxury-class Med yacht with enormous owner's suite is sleek, fast, lavishly appointed. Stunning four-stateroom interior blends lacquered cherry woodwork, sweeping curves, posh furnishings. Full-beam master stateroom with vertical hull windows resembles small hotel suite. Each guest cabin has private en suite head. Engineroom, crew quarters are small. Party-time cockpit offers seating for eight. Note huge foredeck sun pad, big anchor locker with chainwash. Beautifully styled, impeccably detailed. MTU 1,150hp engines cruise at 26–28 knots (30+ knots top).

See Page 512 For Value Estimates

Length Overall	70'10"	Fuel	1,268 gals.
Beam	17'8"	Water	317 gals.
Draft	5'5"	Waste	66 gals.
Weight	80,000#	Hull Type	Modified-V
Clearance	23'6"	Deadrise Aft	16°

Azimut 75 Flybridge

2005–10

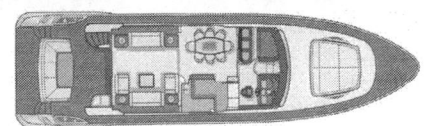

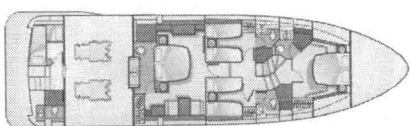

World-class flybridge yacht combines bold Italian styling with posh accommodations, impressive open-water performance. Extravagant four-stateroom interior boasts expansive salon with facing settees, formal dining area, sumptuous master suite, crew quarters aft. Sliding screens close wheelhouse off from salon; big windows provide panoramic outside views. Huge bridge offers pit-style seating, large sun pad. Cockpit lounge converts to sun pad. MAN 1,360hp engines cruise at 26 knots (28–30 knots top).

Insufficient Resale Data to Assign Values

Length	75'3"	Fuel	1,590 gals.
Beam	18'4"	Water	303 gals.
Draft	5'10"	Headroom	6'8"
Weight	100,000#	Hull Type	Modified-V
Clearance	NA	Deadrise Aft	15.3°

Azimut 78 Ultra

1994–98

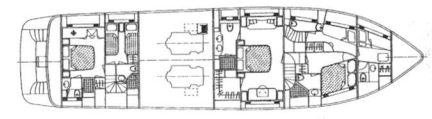

American Layout

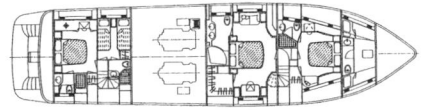

European Floorplan

Top-shelf luxury yacht set class standard in her day for extravagant accommodations, outstanding big-boat performance. Dramatic Italian styling was well ahead of competitive yachts of her era. Highlights include extremely spacious salon with formal dining area, cherrywood interior, transom garage, aft-deck dining table. Several floorplans available including four-stateroom layout with crew quarters. Note exceptionally wide flybridge. Cruise at 23 knots with 1,150hp MTUs, top speed of 26–27 knots. Over 45 were built.

Insufficient Resale Data to Assign Values

Length	78'0"	Fuel	1,546 gals.
Beam	19'5"	Water	412 gals.
Draft	5'8"	Headroom	6'6"
Weight	125,400#	Hull Type	Deep-V
Clearance	NA	Deadrise Aft	18°

Azimut 80 Carat

2001–Current

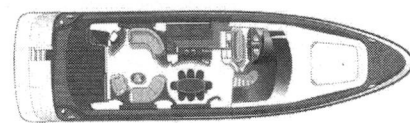

Deckhouse Layout

Lower Level Floorplan

Striking Med yacht makes good on Azimut promise of distinctive styling, elegant accommodations, outstanding performance. Lavish four-stateroom interior boasts richly appointed salon with facing settees, formal dining area, marble flooring, gourmet galley with granite counters. Twin transom garages push crew quarters forward of engine room resulting in slightly reduced stateroom dimensions compared with other 80-footers. Note spacious engine room with platform access. MTU 1,500hp V-drive diesels cruise at 28 knots (30+ top).

Insufficient Resale Data to Assign Values

Length	78'8"	Fuel	1,584 gals.
Beam	19'0"	Water	396 gals.
Draft	5'11"	Headroom	6'6"
Weight	114,000#	Hull Type	Modified-V
Clearance	NA	Deadrise Aft	13°

Trawlers & Motoryachts

Bayliner 3270/3288 Motor Yacht

1981–95

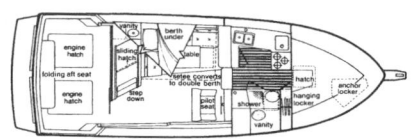

Best-selling flybridge sedan (called the 3270 MY in 1981–88; 3288 MY in 1989–95) was stylish, spacious, economical to operate. Innovative interior with teak trim boasts expansive salon with large cabin windows, raised dinette platform, full lower helm. Second stateroom beneath dinette is great for kids, okay for adults. Bow pulpit, transom door, swim platform were standard. Early models with 110hp Hino diesels cruise at 12 knots; later models with 150hp turbo Hinos cruise at 16–17 knots. Over 3,000 were sold.

See Page 513 For Value Estimates

Length Overall	32'1"	Fuel	200 gals.
Beam	11'6"	Water	65 gals.
Draft	2'11"	Waste	23 gals.
Weight	12,500#	Hull Type	Modified-V
Clearance	13'10"	Deadrise Aft	12°

Bayliner 3587 Motor Yacht

1995–99

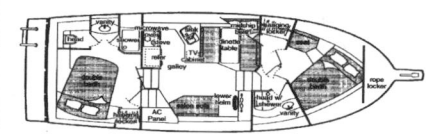

Contemporary aft-cabin motoryacht broke new ground for midsize cruisers with innovative three-stateroom interior. In addition to standard fore, aft staterooms, small midcabin sleeping area is located under salon dinette. Compact salon is arranged with galley aft, standard lower helm. Awkward three-door configuration provides access to forward head and staterooms. Engineroom is a tight fit. Hardtop was a popular option. MerCruiser 310hp gas inboards cruise at 18 knots and deliver 26–27 knots top.

See Page 513 For Value Estimates

Length Overall	37'3"	Fuel	220 gals.
Hull Length	34'8"	Water	77 gals.
Beam	13'1"	Waste	68 gals.
Draft	3'9"	Hull Type	Modified-V
Weight	22,000#	Deadrise Aft	10°

Bayliner 3688 Motor Yacht

1992–94

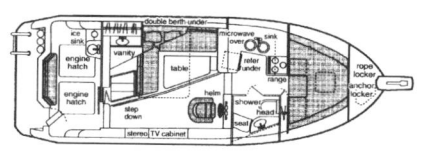

Rakish styling, low price, innovative interior set this early 1990s cruiser apart from the pack. Narrow staircase just inside salon door descends to private cabin with partial standing headroom, cabinet, and sink. Salon—with raised dinette, standard lower helm—is small for a 36-foot boat. Forward stateroom privacy is limited to just a curtain; absence of stall shower in head is notable. Bow pulpit, radar arch, transom door, fender rack were standard. Twin 200hp V-drive diesels cruise at 15 knots, top out at 17–18 knots.

Prices Not Provided for Pre-1995 Models

Length	36'1"	Fuel	250 gals.
Beam	12'2"	Water	96 gals.
Draft	2'11"	Waste	23 gals.
Weight	13,700#	Hull Type	Modified-V
Clearance	13'10"	Deadrise Aft	14°

Bayliner 3788 Motor Yacht

1996–99

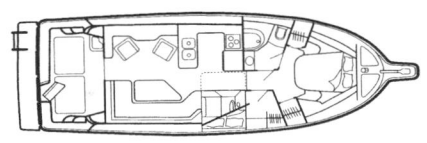

Popular 1990s flybridge cruiser offered crisp styling, family-friendly accommodations at affordable price. Spacious interior is arranged with salon-level galley, midcabin berth with hanging locker, bow stateroom with privacy door, head with tub/shower. Additional features include cockpit sink, roomy engine room, transom door, swim platform, radar arch, bow pulpit. MerCruiser 310hp gas inboards cruise at 18 knots (27–28 knots top); 250hp Cummins diesels cruise at 20 knots and top out at 23–24 knots. Updated 3788 model came out in 2001.

See Page 513 For Value Estimates

Length	38'6"	Water	100 gals.
Beam	13'4"	Waste	30 gals.
Draft	2'11"	Headroom	6'5"
Weight	20,000#	Hull Type	Modified-V
Fuel	250 gals.	Deadrise Aft	10°

Bayliner 3788 Motor Yacht

2001–02

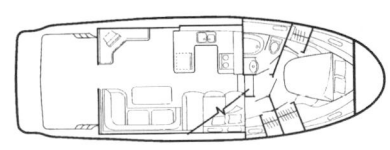

Updated version of the original Bayliner 3788 MY (above) with refined styling, updated interior made a good boat even better. Wide-open salon with dinette and galley forward offers lots of usable space, good overall finish. Both staterooms have double berths. Tub/shower is fitted in head compartment. Molded steps make bridge access easy and safe. Swim platform, transom door, radar arch were standard. MerCruiser 310hp gas inboards cruise at 17–18 knots; 330hp Cummins diesels cruise at 20 knots.

See Page 513 For Value Estimates

Length	39'4"	Water	125 gals.
Beam	13'7"	Waste	36 gals.
Draft	3'4"	Headroom	6'5"
Weight	22,274#	Hull Type	Modified-V
Fuel	300 gals.	Deadrise Aft	7.5°

Bayliner 3870/3888 Motor Yacht

1983–94

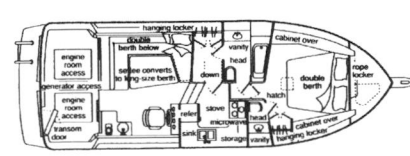

Super-popular diesel cruiser (called Bayliner 3870 MY in 1983–89) offered buyers remarkable comfort, economy at surprisingly affordable price. Boxy profile conceals expansive interior with innovative midcabin floorplan. Master stateroom is very spacious. Lower helm was standard. Fuel economy at cruise is an impressive 1 mpg. Engine room is tight. Over 1,000 were built during a decade of production. Early models with twin 135hp diesels cruise at 10 knots; later models with 210hp Hino diesels cruise at 16 knots.

Prices Not Provided for Pre-1995 Models

Length	38'2"	Fuel	304 gals.
Beam	13'5"	Water	80 gals.
Draft	3'2"	Waste	40 gals.
Weight	17,500#	Hull Type	Modified-V
Clearance	14'10"	Deadrise Aft	6°

Trawlers & Motoryachts

Bayliner 3988 Motor Yacht

1995–2002

Feature-rich motoryacht enjoys continued popularity thanks to spacious interior, affordable price. Two-stateroom, two-head floorplan includes standard lower helm station, spacious U-shaped galley, comfortable L-shaped settee. Large cabin windows provide excellent natural lighting. Note teak-and-holly galley floor, bathtub in starboard head, foredeck sun lounge. Cummins 250hp diesels cruise at 20 knots (23–24 knots top); Cummins 330hp Cummins engines cruise at 24 knots (high 20s top). One of the best selling boats in her class.

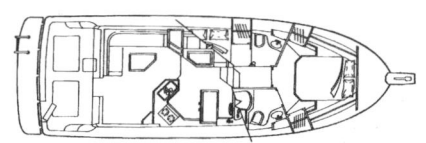

See Page 513 For Value Estimates

Length w/Pulpit	46'3"	Fuel	298 gals.
Hull Length	39'0"	Water	100 gals.
Beam	14'1"	Waste	36 gals.
Draft	3'3"	Hull Type	Modified-V
Weight	21,000#	Deadrise Aft	10°

Bayliner 4087 Cockpit MY

1997–2001

Cockpit version of Bayliner 3587 MY boasts sporty lines, innovative three-stateroom interior. In addition to roomy fore and aft staterooms, small midcabin is located under salon dinette. Compact salon is arranged with galley aft, standard lower helm. Note spacious aft deck with hardtop, wet bar. Flybridge seats four aft of helm. Bow pulpit, swim platform were standard; hardtop, radar arch were popular options. MerCruiser 310hp gas inboards cruise at 18 knots (26–27 knots top); Cummins 270hp diesels cruise at 20 knots.

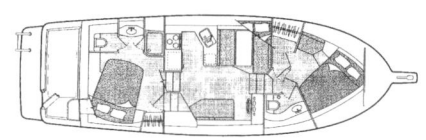

See Page 513 For Value Estimates

Length Overall	41'5"	Water	77 gals.
Beam	13'1"	Waste	68 gals.
Draft	3'9"	Clearance	15'5"
Weight	24,000#	Hull Type	Modified-V
Fuel	220 gals.	Deadrise Aft	10°

Bayliner 4387 Aft Cabin MY

1990–93

Affordable double-cabin motoryacht with roomy interior, large aft deck was considered a lot of boat for the money in her day. Two-stateroom floorplan is arranged with galley and dinette down, standard lower helm, salon entertainment center. Both staterooms have diagonal double berths to save space. Cheap interior furnishings, so-so fit and finish. Lightweight hull is a hard ride in a chop. Standard 330hp gas engines cruise at 16 knots (mid 20s top); 250hp Hino diesels cruise at 18–19 knots (about 24 knots top).

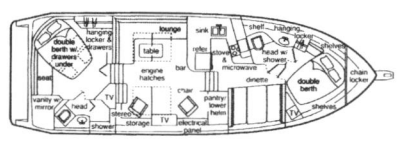

Prices Not Provided for Pre-1995 Models

Length	43'1"	Fuel	300 gals.
Beam	14'3"	Water	100 gals.
Draft	3'0"	Waste	74 gals.
Weight	20,000#	Hull Type	Modified-V
Clearance	13'6"	Deadrise Aft	14°

Bayliner 4388 Motor Yacht

1991–94

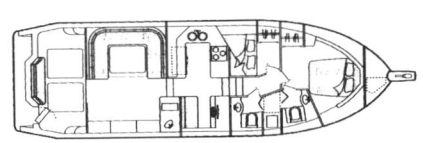

Low-priced 1990s flybridge yacht with spacious midcabin interior is well-suited to coastal cruising, dockside entertaining. Large salon offers full 360-degree visibility, extensive lounge seating, wet bar, lower helm station. Mid stateroom with partial standing headroom extends under galley. Note common shower stall between both heads. Transom door, shower, bench seat were standard in cockpit. Small fuel capacity limits cruising range. Twin Hino 250hp V-drive diesels cruise at 19 knots and (24–25 knots top).

Prices Not Provided for Pre-1995 Models

Length	43'1"	Fuel	300 gals.
Beam	14'3"	Water	100 gals.
Draft	3'0"	Waste	46 gals.
Weight	19,000#	Hull Type	Modified-V
Clearance	13'6"	Deadrise Aft	14°

Bayliner 4550/4588 Pilothouse MY

1984–93

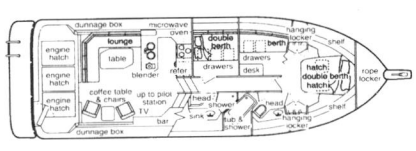

Popular all-weather pilothouse yacht introduced in 1984 remains the best-selling 45-foot yacht ever produced. Spacious layout includes two VIP staterooms, third stateroom/office adjacent to master suite, roomy salon/galley area, raised pilothouse with excellent helm visibility. Both heads share common tub/shower. Extended hardtop shelters cockpit where hatches provide access to compact engine room. Efficient Hino 220hp—or Hino 250hp—diesels cruise at 15 knots burning just over a gallon per mile. Nearly 400 were built.

Prices Not Provided for Pre-1995 Models

Length	45'4"	Fuel	444 gals.
Beam	14'11"	Water	200 gals.
Draft	3'0"	Waste	48 gals.
Weight	28,000#	Hull Type	Modified-V
Clearance	15'6"	Deadrise Aft	6°

Bayliner 4587 Cockpit MY

1994–95

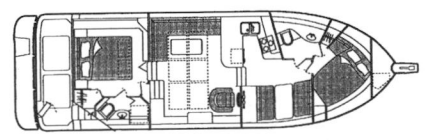

Cockpit version of Bayliner's 4387 Aft Cabin MY combined versatile deck plan with comfortable layout, economical operation. Prop pockets used on 4387 were eliminated and a spray rail was added for a drier ride, but in most other respects the two boats are very similar. Two-stateroom floorplan is arranged with the galley and dinette down. No shower stall in forward guest head. Large salon windows provide excellent lower helm visibility. Small engine room, modest fuel capacity. Hino 250hp diesels cruise at 18–19 knots (about 25 knots top).

See Page 513 For Value Estimates

Length	45'1"	Cockpit	NA
Beam	14'3"	Water	100 gals.
Draft	3'0"	Fuel	300 gals.
Weight	22,000#	Hull Type	Modified-V
Clearance	14'0"	Deadrise Aft	14°

Trawlers & Motoryachts

Trawlers & Motoryachts

Bayliner 4788 Pilothouse MY

1994–2002

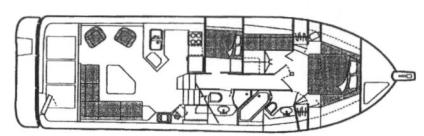

Slightly restyled, lengthened version of Bayliner 4550/4588 Pilothouse remains one of the most in-demand used models her size on the market. Efficient two-stateroom floorplan with third stateroom/dressing area is tough to beat. Increased hull length is seen in larger galley and salon dimensions. Excellent lower helm visibility; both heads share common tub/shower. Extended hardtop shelters cockpit. Early models with 315hp Hino diesels cruise at 18 knots; later models with 370hp Cummins diesels cruise at 20–21 knots.

See Page 513 For Value Estimates

Length w/Pulpit	54'0"	Fuel	444 gals.
Hull Length	47'4"	Water	200 gals.
Beam	15'1"	Waste	48 gals.
Draft	3'4"	Hull Type	Modified-V
Weight	29,990#	Deadrise Aft	6°

Bayliner 5288 Pilothouse MY

1999–2002

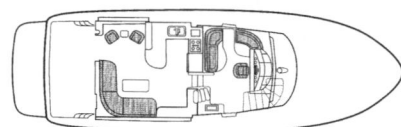

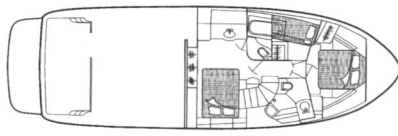

Handsome pilothouse yacht for all-weather cruising offered solid value at reasonable price. Highlights include fully cored hull, spacious three-stateroom layout with full-beam master, large cockpit, generous side decks. Open salon/galley is ideal for entertaining. Spacious flybridge can seat a small crowd. Additional highlights include washer/dryer in third stateroom, large engine room, underwater exhausts, dinghy davit, tub/shower in owner's head. Cruise at 20 knots with 600hp MANs (24–25 knots top).

See Page 513 For Value Estimates

Length w/Platform	56'0"	Fuel	700 gals.
Beam	16'3"	Water	200 gals.
Draft	4'10"	Waste	73 gals.
Weight	47,560#	Hull Type	Modified-V
Clearance	19'3"	Deadrise Aft	12°

Bayliner 5788 Motor Yacht

1997–2002

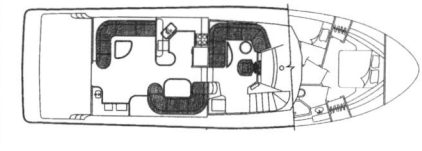

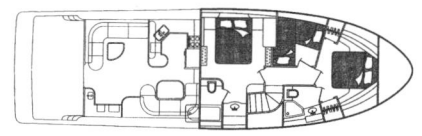

Feature-packed pilothouse yacht gets high marks for comfort, value. Spacious three-stateroom interior includes two big sleeping cabins, superb galley with plenty of workspace, full-beam salon. Owner's stateroom has walk-in wardrobe, home-size bath with tub/shower. Excellent visibility from both helm stations. Surprisingly good fit and finish considering the low price. Note huge salon windows, narrow side decks, pilothouse deck doors, spacious engine room. MAN 610hp diesels cruise at 20 knots (23–24 knots top).

See Page 513 For Value Estimates

Length	59'4"	Fuel	800 gals.
Beam	17'2"	Water	222 gals.
Draft	4'11"	Waste	76 gals.
Weight	49,000#	Hull Type	Modified-V
Clearance, Arch	19'7"	Deadrise Aft	10°

Beneteau 42 Swift Trawler

2004–09

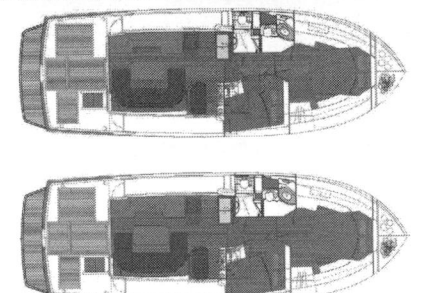

French-built cruiser with high-performance hull, Europa styling is fast, comfortable, easy on the eye. Well-appointed interior with varnished woodwork includes two double staterooms, two heads, two deck doors, convertible salon settee. Galley is small for a boat this size; salon storage is practically zilch. Excellent helm visibility. Teak decks, transom door, bow pulpit are standard. Note protected side decks, good engine access, hullside boarding gate. Early models had a single head. Yanmar 370hp diesels cruise at 18–20 knots (mid 20s top).

See Page 513 For Value Estimates

Length Overall	44'3"	Fuel	395 gals.
Length WL	37'5"	Water	169 gals.
Beam	13'11"	Waste	24 gals.
Draft	3'5"	Hull Type	Modified-V
Weight	22,000#	Deadrise Aft	12°

Bertram 42 Motor Yacht

1973–87

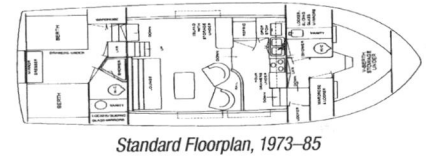

Standard Floorplan, 1973–85

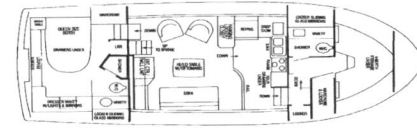

Double Berth Aft Layout, 1986–87

Prices Not Provided for Pre-1995 Models

Traditional flush-deck motoryacht introduced in 1973 gets high marks for build quality, ride comfort, lasting popularity. Unusual floorplan layout has mid-level galley forward, companionway to starboard. Teak interior replaced original mica woodwork in 1983; queen berth replaced the single beds in master stateroom in 1986. Excellent visibility from semi-enclosed lower helm. Note small, old-style flybridge. GM 335hp 6-71 diesels cruise at 16 knots (18–19 knots top); GM 435hp 6V71 diesels cruise at 20 knots (24 knots top).

Length	42'6"	Fuel	406 gals.
Beam	14'10"	Water	150 gals.
Draft	4'0"	Waste	60 gals.
Weight	39,000#	Hull Type	Deep-V
Clearance	17'11"	Deadrise Aft	17°

Bertram 46 Motor Yacht

1973–87

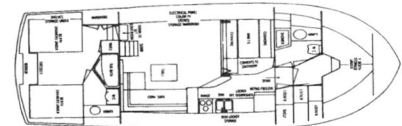

Twin Berths Aft, 1973–85

Double Berth Aft, 1986–87

Prices Not Provided for Pre-1995 Models

Traditional flush-deck motoryacht introduced in 1973 appealed to buyers with an eye for solid construction, roomy accommodations, exceptional seakeeping qualities. Built on proven deep-V hull used in production of original Bertram 46 Convertible. Two-stateroom interior features spacious salon with galley and dinette down, tub/shower in aft head. Good visibility from both helm positions. Note large aft deck, small flybridge. Cruise at 19–20 knots with 435hp 8V71 diesels; 22 knots with 570hp 8V92s offered after 1982.

Length	46'6"	Fuel	615 gals.
Beam	16'0"	Water	230 gals.
Draft	4'8"	Waste	50 gals.
Weight	45,600#	Hull Type	Deep-V
Clearance	18'8"	Deadrise Aft	19°

Trawlers & Motoryachts

Bertram 58 Motor Yacht

1976–86

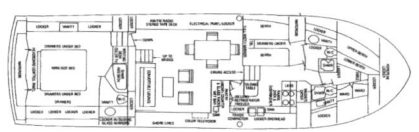

Distinctive flushdeck motoryacht built on Bertram's signature deep-V hull combines spacious accommodations with superior sea-keeping qualities. Original three-stateroom floorplan with home-size galley, huge master suite remained unchanged during her decade in production. Highlights include roomy aft deck, tub/shower in aft head, molded foredeck seating, wide side decks. Bridge is tiny compared with modern motoryachts. Good lower-helm visibility; excellent range. Standard GM 12V71 diesels cruise at 18 knots (21–22 knots top).

Prices Not Provided for Pre-1995 Models

Length	58'3"	Fuel	1,250 gals.
Beam	17'11"	Water	275 gals.
Draft	5'4"	Headroom	6'6"
Weight	87,500#	Hull Type	Modified-V
Clearance	18'0"	Deadrise Aft	15°

Bestway 50 Cockpit MY

1982–88

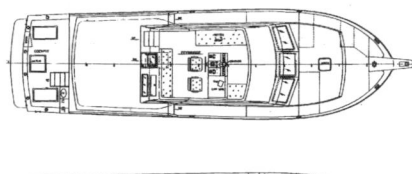

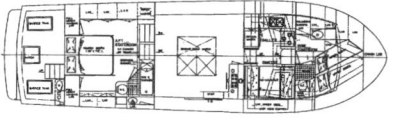

Popular 1980's cockpit yacht offered a winning blend of roomy accommodations, solid construction, competitive price. Expansive two-stateroom interior with solid teak cabinetry features spacious salon with standard lower helm, booth-style dinette, huge master suite. Covered aft deck is among the largest in her class. Cockpit came with transom door, in-floor storage boxes, sink. Wide side decks are a plus. Cruise at 8–9 knots with 235hp Lehman diesels; around 12 knots with 350hp Cat diesels.

Prices Not Provided for Pre-1995 Models

Length	52'6"	Fuel	780 gals.
Beam	14'6"	Water	262 gals.
Draft	3'6"	Waste	50 gals.
Weight	33,000#	Hull Type	Modified-V
Clearance	NA	Deadrise Aft	14°

Californian 34 LRC

1977–84

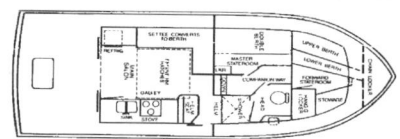

Two-stateroom Floorplan

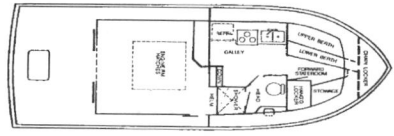

Single-Stateroom Floorplan

Popular sedan cruiser with trawler styling combined planing-speed performance with versatile deck layout, low-cost operation. Well-finished interior was available with single- or twin-stateroom floorplans, both with standard lower helm. Highlights include mahogany interior cabinetry, head with stall shower, wide side decks, roomy cockpit. Note that two-stateroom layouts are rare on a 34-footer. Perkins 85hp diesels cruise at 7 knots; optional 210hp Cat (or 200hp Perkins) diesels cruise at 16–18 knots (20+ knots wide open).

Prices Not Provided for Pre-1995 Models

Length	34'6"	Fuel	250 gals.
Beam	12'4"	Water	75 gals.
Draft	3'2"	Waste	30 gals.
Weight	18,000#	Hull Type	Modified-V
Clearance	10'8"	Deadrise Aft	NA

Californian 35 Motor Yacht

1985–87

Small aft-cabin motoryacht from 1980s was comfortable, stylish, built to last. Compact two-stateroom interior includes comfortable salon, galley and dinette down, stall shower in each head. Note twin double beds in aft stateroom. Additional features include integral bow pulpit, wide side decks, radar arch, swim platform. Lower helm, hardtop were optional. Above-average fit and finish. Standard gas engines cruise at 17–18 knots; optional 210hp Cat diesels cruise at 16 knots and reach 20 knots wide open.

Prices Not Provided for Pre-1995 Models

Length	34'11"	Water	75 gals.
Beam	12'4"	Fuel	270 gals.
Draft	3'2"	Waste	40 gals.
Weight	19,000#	Hull Type	Modified-V
Clearance	NA	Deadrise Aft	15°

Californian 38 LRC Sedan

1978–84

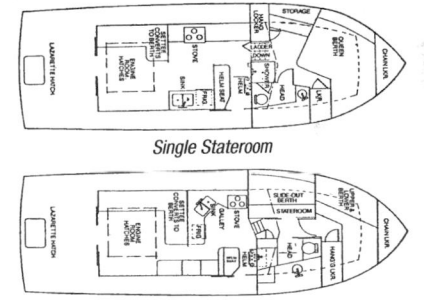

Single Stateroom

Two-Stateroom

This well-built sedan may look like a trawler on the outside, but her modified-V hull provides true planing-speed performance. Single- and twin-stateroom mahogany interiors were offered, both galley-up layouts with a convertible settee in the salon, lower helm with deck access door, large head with separate stall shower. Cockpit is big enough for fishing. Note wide side decks, teak bow pulpit. Small engine room. Good lower helm visibility. Cruise at 12 knots with twin 210hp Cat diesels; 19–20 knots with 300hp Cats.

Prices Not Provided for Pre-1995 Models

Length Overall	37'8"	Fuel	400 gals.
Length WL	36'6"	Water	100 gals.
Beam	13'0"	Waste	25 gals.
Draft	3'6"	Hull Type	Modified-V
Weight	28,000#	Deadrise Aft	NA

Californian 38 Motor Yacht

1983–87

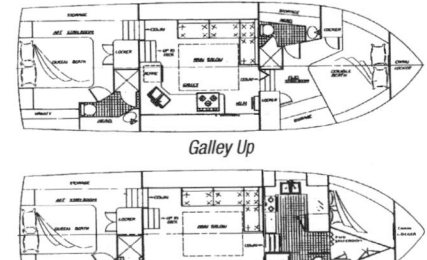

Galley Up

Galley Down

Handsome aft-cabin motoryacht with many appealing features has held her value well over the years. Highlights include dark mahogany interior paneling, lower helm station with deck door, upright refrigerator, stall showers in both heads. Large master stateroom for a 38-footer with vanity, generous stowage. Note spacious aft deck. Bow pulpit, radar arch, teak handrails, swim platform were standard. Hardtop was a popular option. Twin 210hp Cat diesels will cruise at 12 knots; 300hp turbo-Cats cruise at 18–20 knots.

Prices Not Provided for Pre-1995 Models

Length Overall	37'8"	Clearance	14'6"
Length WL	36'6"	Fuel	365 gals.
Beam	13'3"	Water	100 gals.
Draft	3'6"	Hull Type	Modified-V
Weight	28,000#	Deadrise Aft	NA

Californian 42 LRC

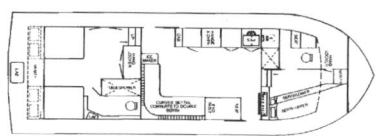

1975–84

Good-selling performance trawler (over 200 were built) combines solid construction with traditional styling, comfortable accommodations. Standard two-stateroom, galley-up mahogany interior with two full heads includes roomy aft cabin with two double beds and cockpit access door. Forward stateroom was offered with double berth or over/under bunks. Large cockpit is a plus. Note tub/shower in aft head. Slender hull is very fuel-efficient. Cruise at 10 knots with 185hp Perkins diesels; 12 knots with 210hp Cats.

Prices Not Provided for Pre-1995 Models

Length	41'8"	Fuel	500 gals.
Beam	13'8"	Water	175 gals.
Draft	3'4"	Waste	50 gals.
Weight	31,000#	Hull Type	Modified-V
Clearance	NA	Deadrise Aft	NA

Californian 42 Motor Yacht

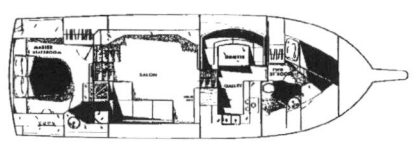

1986–87

Well-built flybridge yacht from mid 1980s still appeals to knowledgeable boaters with an eye for quality. Comfortable two-stateroom teak (or mahogany) interior features large salon with entertainment center, fully equipped galley, well-appointed master with dresser. Space for washer/dryer in forward stateroom. Lower helm was a popular option; big U-shaped dinette seats six. Wet bar, wing doors, hardtop, bow pulpit, swim platform were standard. Cruise at 16–18 knots with 375hp Cat diesels (around 20 knots top).

Prices Not Provided for Pre-1995 Models

Length w/Pulpit	45'8"	Fuel	400 gals.
Beam	15'2"	Water	190 gals.
Draft	4'3"	Waste	60 gals.
Weight	38,000#	Hull Type	Modified-V
Clearance	13'6"	Deadrise Aft	15°

Californian 43 Cockpit MY

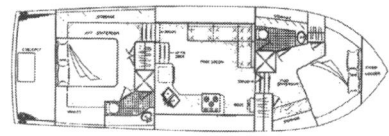

1983–87

Standard Floorplan

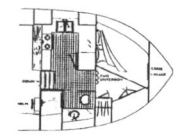

Optional Floorplan

Popular cockpit motoryacht received high marks in her day for quality construction, practical accommodations, versatile deck layout. Standard layout had galley up with huge forward stateroom; optional galley-down floorplan opens up salon at expense of smaller bow stateroom. Features include lower station with deck door, large master stateroom, spacious aft deck, full-beam bridge. Hardtop was a popular option. Cat 210 diesels cruise at 10 knots; 300hp Cats cruise at 14 knots (16–17 knots top).

Prices Not Provided for Pre-1995 Models

Length Overall	43'8"	Headroom	6'4"
Beam	13'3"	Fuel	400 gals.
Draft	3'6"	Water	140 gals.
Weight	32000#	Hull Type	Modified-V
Clearance	14'6"	Deadrise Aft	NA

California 45 Motor Yacht

1988–91

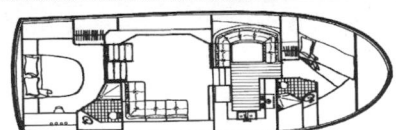

Over/Under Bunks Forward

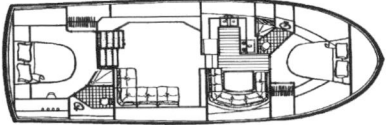

Island Berth Forward

Prices Not Provided for Pre-1995 Models

Late-model motoryacht came with full array of features, amenities at a reasonable price. Available with two floor-plan configurations: one with over/under berths in forward stateroom, the other with island double berth forward. Lower helm was optional; both heads have separate stall showers. Hardtop, aft-deck enclosure panels, bow pulpit were standard. Above-average fit and finish. Slender modified-V hull is easily driven, dry in a chop. Cruise at 16–18 knots with 375hp Cat diesels (about 20 knots top).

Length	45'0"	Fuel	400 gals.
Beam	15'2"	Water	190 gals.
Draft	4'0"	Waste	70 gals.
Weight	40,000#	Hull Type	Modified-V
Clearance, Arch	17'3"	Deadrise Aft	15°

Californian 48 Cockpit MY

1986–89

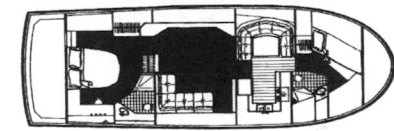

Over/Under Bunks Forward

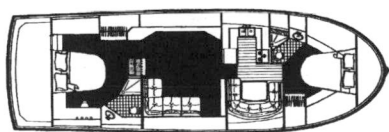

Island Berth Forward

Prices Not Provided for Pre-1995 Models

Quality construction, well-appointed accommodations, comfortable ride have kept this 1980s cockpit yacht popular on the used markets. Galley-down floorplan came with choice of forward stateroom configurations. Interior woodwork updated from walnut to teak in 1988. Cockpit has a transom door as well as door to aft stateroom—a convenience many cockpit yachts fail to provide. Hardtop, radar arch, swim platform, bow pulpit were standard. Twin 375hp Cat diesels will cruise at 16–17 knots (about 20 knots top).

Length	48'5"	Fuel	500 gals.
Beam	15'2"	Water	190 gals.
Draft	4'8"	Waste	70 gals.
Weight	41,000#	Hull Type	Modified-V
Clearance, Arch	16'3"	Deadrise Aft	15°

Californian 48 Motor Yacht

1985–91

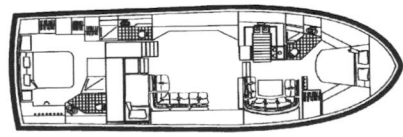

Prices Not Provided for Pre-1995 Models

Quality flush-deck yacht was one of Californian's most popular models in late 1980s. Big interior for a 48-footer—slide-out settee in small guest stateroom aft of salon converts into double berth; all three heads have separate stall showers. Relatively narrow beam results in modest salon dimensions. Huge afterdeck is a great entertainment center. Excellent ride; above-average fit and finish. Cruise at 15–16 knots with 375hp Cat diesels; 18 knots with 485hp GM 6-71s. Clean used models are always in demand.

Length	48'5"	Fuel	560 gals.
Beam	15'2"	Water	210 gals.
Draft	4'8"	Waste	165 gals.
Weight	43,000#	Hull Type	Modified-V
Clearance, Arch	17'3"	Deadrise Aft	15°

Trawlers & Motoryachts

Californian 52 Cockpit MY

89–91

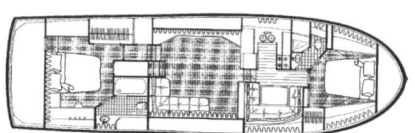

Good-looking motoryacht (essentially a Californian 45 MY with a cockpit) combines handsome lines with upscale accommodations. Interior highlights include handsome teak cabinetry, two large staterooms, full dinette, built-in washer/dryer, salon entertainment center, generous storage. Lower helm was optional. Cockpit has transom door, access door to master stateroom. Hardtop, radar arch were standard. Slender 15'2" beam is easily driven, surprisingly fuel efficient. Cruise at 15–16 knots with 375hp Cat diesels (about 18 knots top).

Prices Not Provided for Pre-1995 Models

Length Overall	51'11"	Fuel	747 gals.
Beam	15'2"	Water	185 gals.
Draft	4'5"	Waste	60 gals.
Weight	44,200#	Hull Type	Modified-V
Clearance, Arch	17'3"	Deadrise Aft	15°

Californian 55 Cockpit MY

1986–91

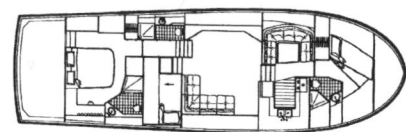

3-Stateroom, Over/Under Berths Forward

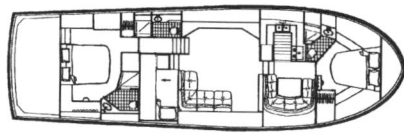

3-Stateroom, Island Berth Forward

Quality-built cockpit yacht is highly regarded by knowledgeable boaters for her classic profile, elegant accommodations, comfortable ride. Big interior for 55-footer—slide-out settee in small guest stateroom aft of salon converts into double berth; all three heads have separate stall showers. Relatively narrow beam results in modest salon dimensions. Large aft deck can seat a small crowd. Cruise at 18 knots with 485hp GM 6-71 diesels; 20+ knots with 550hp GM 6V92s. Popular boat—about 40 were built.

Prices Not Provided for Pre-1995 Models

Length Overall	54'6"	Fuel	650 gals.
Beam	15'2"	Water	210 gals.
Draft	4'3"	Waste	80 gals.
Weight	46,200#	Hull Type	Modified-V
Clearance, Arch	17'3"	Deadrise Aft	15°

Camano 28/31

1990–Current

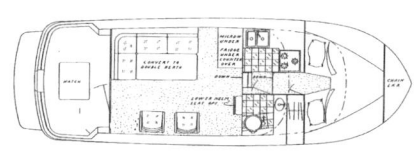

Popular Canadian cruiser (called Camano 28 in 1990–2002) is salty, efficient, surprisingly spacious. Highlights include large flybridge, well-crafted interior, wide side decks, roomy cockpit with transom door, good storage. Distinctive trolley-style windows provide panoramic outside views. Fuel capacity was increased in 2003. Bow thruster is standard. Full keel protects running gear against grounding. Bridge ladder is very steep. Single 150hp Volvo diesel will cruise at 12 knots (16–17 knots top); 200hp Volvo runs a little faster. Not inexpensive.

See Page 515 For Value Estimates

Length w/Pulpit	31'0"	Clearance	NA
Hull Length	28'0"	Fuel	100/133 gals.
Beam	10'6"	Water	77 gals.
Draft	3'3"	Waste	12 gals.
Weight	10,000#	Hull Type	Semi-Disp.

Camano 41

2006–Current

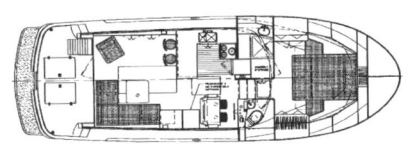

High-quality sedan with trawler-style profile combines comfortable accommodations with economical operation, good turn of speed. Spacious salon with big windows boasts leather seating, hardwood flooring, meticulous workmanship. Excellent lower-helm visibility. Note overhead salon grabrail. Topside features include very wide side decks, large cockpit, integral swim platform. Easily driven hull with prop-protecting keel is fuel efficient, stable. Bow thruster is standard. Cruise at 12 knots (15–16 top) with 440hp Yanmar diesel.

See Page 515 For Value Estimates

Length Overall	41'0"	Clearance	NA
Length WL	38'7"	Fuel	385 gals.
Beam	14'0"	Water	170 gals.
Draft	3'9"	Waste	42 gals.
Weight	28,000#	Hull Type	Semi-Disp.

Camargue 48 Yachtfish

1987–93

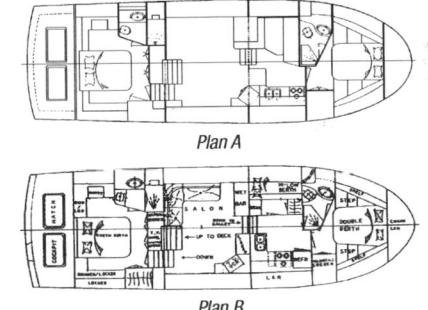

Plan A

Plan B

Good-selling Taiwan import received high marks for appealing styling, traditional teak interior, above-average finish. Standard interior plant with galley and dinette down boasts spacious salon, two roomy staterooms. (Optional three-stateroom layout eliminated the dinette.) Portside lower helm is cleverly concealed in an exquisite roll-top console. Note wide side decks, spacious engineroom. Modified-V hull has shallow keel for directional stability. Cruise at 18 knots with 375hp Cat diesels; 22 knots with 485hp GM diesels. About 50 were built.

Prices Not Provided for Pre-1995 Models

Length	47'11"	Fuel	540 gals.
Beam	15'5"	Water	210 gals.
Draft	3'6"	Headroom	6'5"
Weight	35,000#	Hull Type	Modified-V
Clearance, Arch	16'8"	Deadrise Aft	15°

Carver 28 Aft Cabin; 300 Aft Cabin

1991–94

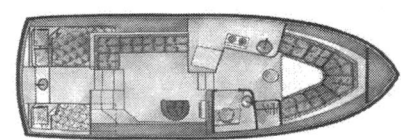

Maxi-volume family cruiser with wide beam (called the Carver 28 Aft Cabin in 1991–92; 300 Aft Cabin in 1993–94) offered big-boat comfort in modest 28-foot hull. Highlights include small aft stateroom with double and single berth, roomy salon with convertible settee, full galley, roomy head compartment. Lower helm was optional. Molded bow pulpit, swim platform, swim ladder were standard. Aft deck is small, side decks are narrow. Modified-V hull delivers stable ride. Cruise at 16 knots with twin 210hp gas engines (low 20s top).

Prices Not Provided for Pre-1995 Models

Length Overall	32'9"	Fuel	168 gals.
Beam	11'10"	Water	51 gals.
Draft	2'11"	Waste	20 gals.
Weight	12,600#	Hull Type	Modified-V
Clearance	NA	Deadrise Aft	16°

Carver 32 Aft Cabin

1983–90

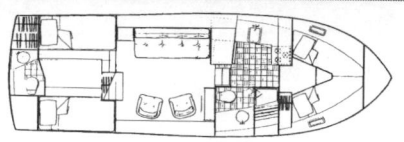

1983–89

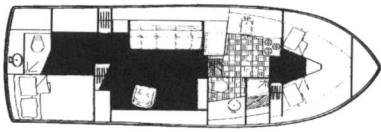

1990

Spacious double-cabin cruiser with boxy profile makes up in comfort whatever she lacks in sex appeal. Accommodations include two private staterooms, two heads, full-size galley, compact salon with convertible sofa, lower helm. Note limited stowage space. Small aft deck can accommodate a couple of folding chairs; flybridge offers seating for four. Aft stateroom was redesigned in 1990. Definitely a stiff ride when the waves pick up. Cruise at 16–18 knots with standard 270hp gas engines (mid 20s top).

Prices Not Provided for Pre-1995 Models

Length Overall	32'0"	Clearance	11'6"
Length WL	28'1"	Fuel	182 gals.
Beam	11'7"	Water	84 gals.
Draft	2'10"	Hull Type	Modified-V
Weight	12,000#	Deadrise Aft	10°

Carver 325/326 Aft Cabin

1995–2001

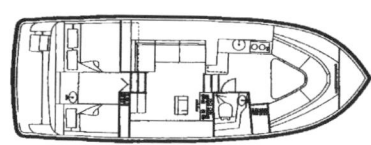

Popular aft-cabin cruiser (called 325 Aft Cabin in 1995–98; 326 Aft Cabin in 1999–2001) set class standards in her day for space-efficient floorplan. Galley-down interior includes roomy salon with standard lower helm, full galley, convertible dinette forward, small stateroom aft with vanity/sink. Note that double berth in aft cabin extends slightly below salon sole. Single head lacks stall shower. Integrated swim platform has handy storage locker. Cruise at 18 knots with twin 300hp inboard gas engines (25–26 knots top).

See Page 516 For Value Estimates

Length w/Pulpit	35'0"	Fuel	162 gals.
Hull Length	32'2"	Water	51 gals.
Beam	11'11"	Waste	20 gals.
Draft	2'11"	Hull Type	Modified-V
Weight	15,100#	Deadrise Aft	16°

Carver 33 Aft Cabin; 350 Aft Cabin

1991–94

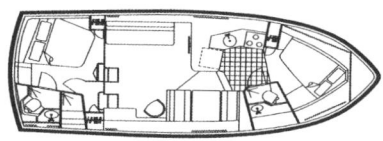

Full-bodied mini-motoryacht (called the Carver 33 Aft Cabin in 1991–92; 350 Aft Cabin in 1993–94) targeted 1990s boaters with an eye for value. Few other 33-footers can match her for interior volume. Highlights include double staterooms fore and aft, roomy salon with large windows, well-equipped galley with upright refrigerator, convertible booth dinette. Good engine room access, wide side decks are a plus. Hardtop, swim platform were standard. Twin 300hp gas inboards cruise at 16–18 knots (mid 20s top).

Prices Not Provided for Pre-1995 Models

Length	39'0"	Fuel	220 gals.
Beam	13'3"	Water	81 gals.
Draft	2'7"	Waste	36 gals.
Weight	16,600#	Hull Type	Modified-V
Clearance	NA	Deadrise Aft	11°

Carver 355/356 Motor Yacht

1995–2003

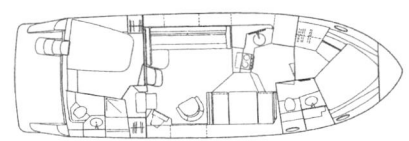

Updated version of Carver 33/350 MY (1991–94) with integrated transom, revised interior gets high marks for solid construction, common-sense accommodations. Expansive interior offers the amenities of a much larger boat. Highlights include two double staterooms, full dinette, well-appointed salon with built-in entertainment center. Note molded steps leading down to extended swim platform. Hardtop, radar arch, bow pulpit were standard; lower helm station was optional. Cruise at 16–18 knots with twin 320hp gas inboards (about 25 knots top).

See Page 516 For Value Estimates

Length w/Pulpit	41'2"	Fuel	318 gals.
Beam	13'3"	Water	70 gals.
Draft	3'3"	Waste	36 gals.
Weight	23,400#	Hull Type	Modified-V
Clearance, Arch	17'6"	Deadrise Aft	11°

Carver 36 Motor Yacht

2002–07

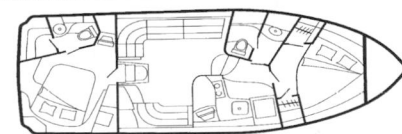

346 Interior (2002 Only)

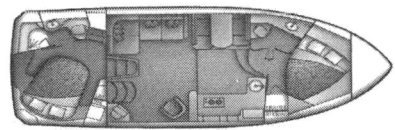

Standard Layout

Opulent condo-yacht (called Carver 346 MY in 2002; 366 MY in 2003–06; 37 MY in 2007) gives owners the space, amenities required for cruising or entertaining. Vast two-stateroom interior with full-width salon is enhanced by tiered cabin windows. Original floorplan was redesigned in 2003 to include dinette—a major improvement. Features include integrated transom with molded steps, wide side decks, spacious bridge with L-shaped lounge. Cruise at 18 knots with 385hp gas inboards; 20 knots with 310hp Volvo diesels.

See Page 516 For Value Estimates

Length	36'11"	Fuel	250 gals.
Beam	13'2"	Water	70 gals.
Draft	2'4"	Waste	36 gals.
Weight	21,800#	Hull Type	Modified-V
Headroom	6'6"	Deadrise Aft	16°

Carver 3607 Aft Cabin

1982–89

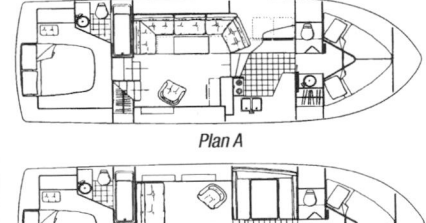

Plan A

Plan B

Prices Not Provided for Pre-1995 Models

Popular 1980s double-cabin cruiser offered impressive blend of solid construction, roomy accommodations, proven owner satisfaction. Interior is spacious for a 36-footer with good headroom, generous stowage. Plan A with extended salon sleeps eight; Plan B with booth-style dinette sleeps six. Lower helm, tub/shower in aft head were standard in both floorplans. Numerous opening ports permit good cabin ventilation. Wide side decks are a plus. Twin 350hp gas engines cruise at 16 knots (25–26 knots top).

Length Overall	35'7"	Clearance	11'9"
Length WL	31'4"	Fuel	240 gals.
Beam	12'6"	Water	109 gals.
Draft	3'2"	Hull Type	Modified-V
Weight	18,500#	Deadrise Aft	8°

Trawlers & Motoryachts

Carver 36 Aft Cabin; 370 Aft Cabin

1990–96

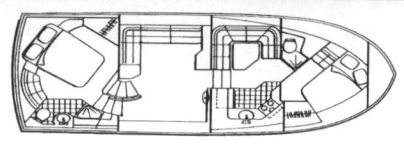

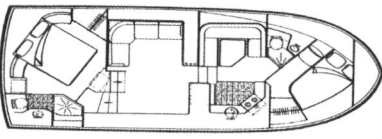

See Page 516 For Value Estimates

Compact motoryacht (called Carver 36 MY in 1990–92) offered buyers an impressive mix of comfort, amenities at a reasonable price. Space-efficient interior features two double staterooms, stall showers in both heads, full dinette, well-equipped galley. Flybridge seats up to six in comfort. Additional features include wide side decks, bow pulpit, radar arch, swim platform. Lower helm station, hardtop were popular options. Modified-V hull can handle a chop. Twin 300hp gas inboards cruise at 15–16 knots (mid 20s top).

Length w/Pulpit	41'3"
Hull Length	38'2"
Beam	13'10"
Draft	3'1"
Weight	18,500#
Clearance	15'0"
Fuel	240 gals.
Water	80 gals.
Hull Type	Modified-V
Deadrise Aft	19°

Carver 370/374 Voyager

1993–2002

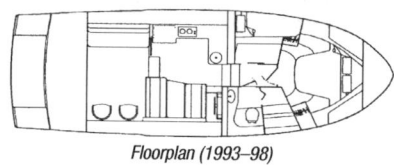

Floorplan (1993–98)

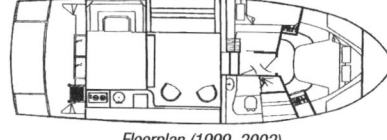

Floorplan (1999–2002)

See Page 516 For Value Estimates

Good-selling 1990s pilothouse yacht struck the right mix of price, comfort, performance. Original two-stateroom floorplan has galley and dinette forward in salon; revised layout in 1999 moved galley and dinette aft. Principal features include large owner's stateroom, double-entry head, spacious flybridge, wide side decks. Note small cockpit, side-dumping exhausts, standard radar arch. Twin 310hp inboard gas engines cruise at 16 knots (25 knots top); 330hp Cummins diesels cruise at 24 knots (high 20s top).

Length w/Pulpit	40'1"
Hull Length	37'1"
Beam	13'3"
Draft	3'8"
Weight	21,350#
Fuel	297 gals.
Water	83 gals.
Waste	35 gals.
Hull Type	Modified-V
Deadrise Aft	11°

Carver 38 Aft Cabin; 390 Aft Cabin

1987–95

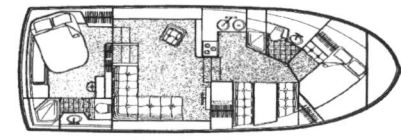

Lower Helm Floorplan

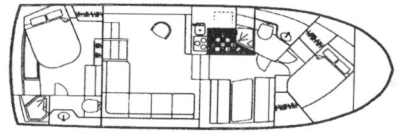

Without Lower Helm

See Page 516 For Value Estimates

Durable double-cabin cruiser mixed conservative styling with space-efficient layout, rugged construction. Offered with several floorplans during her production years, all with two double staterooms, full dinette, stall showers in both heads. Lower helm station was optional. Large interior results in small aft-deck platform. Relatively heavy boat is a handful for gas engines to push. Crusader 340hp gas engines cruise at 14–15 knots (low 20s top). Optional 375hp Cat—or 370hp Cummins—diesels cruise at 21 knots (25 knots top).

Length	42'6"
Beam	14'0"
Draft	3'4"
Weight	22,750#
Clearance	NA
Fuel	280 gals.
Water	91 gals.
Waste	75 gals.
Hull Type	Modified-V
Deadrise Aft	12°

Carver 396/39/40 Motor Yacht

2000–07

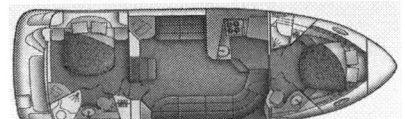

Standard Floorplan

Dinette Floorplan

See Page 516 For Value Estimates

Popular aft-cabin yacht (called the 396 MY in 2000–04; 39 MY in 2005–6; 40 MY in 2007) gets high marks for dramatic styling, cavernous interior. Full-beam salon—focal point of the entire boat—boasts nearly seven feet of headroom. Updated dinette floorplan introduced in 2003. Wing doors, hardtop were standard. Note small swim platform. Huge bridge features centerline helm, wraparound seating, wet bar. Twin 370hp gas engines cruise at a modest 14–15 knots; optional 370hp Cummins diesels cruise at 20 knots.

Length	40'7"	Fuel	330 gals.
Beam	13'11"	Water	90 gals.
Draft	3'6"	Waste	72 gals.
Weight	29,500#	Hull Type	Modified-V
Clearance	18'0"	Deadrise Aft	16°

Carver 390/400/404 Cockpit MY

1993–2003

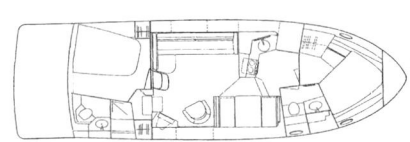

See Page 516 For Value Estimates

Late-model cockpit yacht (called 390 Cockpit MY in 1993–95; 400 CMY in 1996–98; 404 CMY in 1999–2003) offers market-proven mix of sturdy construction, upscale accommodations. Well-planned interior with light oak trim includes two heads, roomy galley, full dinette, double berths in both staterooms. Master suite has sliding glass door to cockpit. Note spiral cockpit stairs. Flybridge seats six around center helm. Engineroom is a tight fit. Standard gas engines cruise at 16 knots; optional 315hp Cummins diesels cruise at 20 knots.

Length	43'5"	Fuel	318 gals.
Beam	13'3"	Water	70 gals.
Draft	3'3"	Waste	36 gals.
Weight	24,300#	Hull Type	Modified-V
Clearance	NA	Deadrise Aft	11°

Carver 405/406 Aft Cabin MY

1997–2002

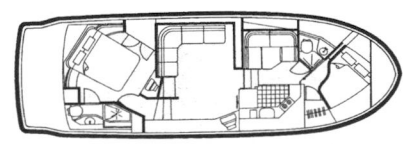

See Page 516 For Value Estimates

Conservative aft-cabin motoryacht (called Carver 405 in 1997–98; 406 in 1999–2001) offers enticing blend of space, comfort, value. Expansive galley-down interior boasts huge salon with L-shaped settee, full dinette, double berths in both staterooms. Large aft deck is surrounded with weather boards; swim platform has storage compartment for fins and scuba tanks. Note wide side decks, foredeck sun pad. Standard gas inboards cruise at 16 knots; optional 330hp Cummins diesels will cruise at 20–21 knots.

Length	42'3"	Fuel	342 gals.
Beam	13'10"	Water	70 gals.
Draft	3'3"	Waste	64 Gals.
Weight	27,900#	Hull Type	Modified-V
Clearance, Arch	17'2"	Deadrise Aft	20°

Trawlers & Motoryachts

Carver 41 Cockpit MY

2005–07

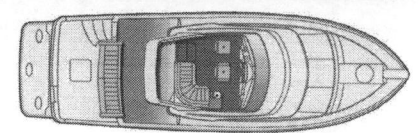

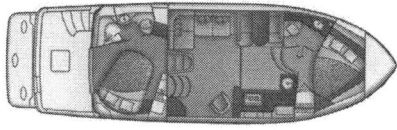

Polished cockpit yacht with sweeping lines makes the cut with boaters seeking European styling with American luxury, comfort. Full-beam salon boasts excellent natural lighting, easy-on-the-eye decor. Angled double berths in both staterooms make the most of available space. Sliding door in master stateroom opens to cockpit. Aft-deck wing doors provide protection from elements. Note molded cockpit steps, extended swim platform, well-arranged engineroom. Cruise in the mid 20s with 370hp Volvo diesels (26–27 knots top).

See Page 517 For Value Estimates

Length	42'11"	Fuel	360 gals.
Beam	13'5"	Water	70 gals.
Draft	2'7"	Waste	50 gals.
Weight	26,000#	Hull Type	Modified-V
Clearance	15'1"	Deadrise Aft	15°

Carver 410 Sport Sedan

2002–03

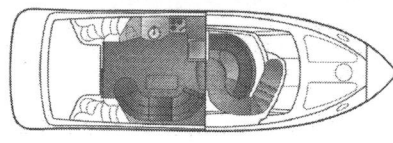

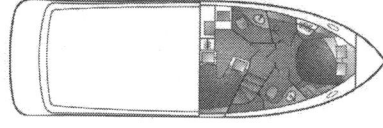

Maxi-volume sport sedan with signature Carver styling blends motoryacht luxury with sportyacht versatility. Wide-open salon is made possible by raising side decks to flybridge level. Guest quarters are positioned under dinette without sacrificing headroom or storage. Note split head/shower forward, Ultraleather seating, copious storage. Molded cockpit steps lead to bridge and portside side deck. Volvo 375hp gas engines cruise at 15 knots; 370hp Volvo diesels cruise at 18 knots (24–25 knots top). Not a big seller—only two years in production.

See Page 517 For Value Estimates

Length	46'4"	Fuel	400 gals.
Beam	13'11"	Water	95 gals.
Draft	2'8"	Waste	75 gals.
Weight	31,625#	Hull Type	Modified-V
Clearance, Arch	19'2"	Deadrise Aft	13°

Carver 42 Cockpit MY

1986–88

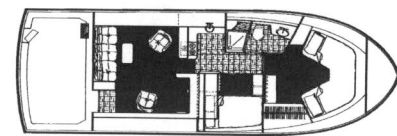

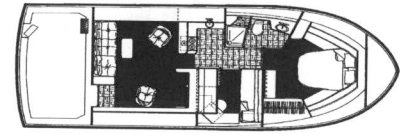

Sturdy flybridge sedan was the largest boat in Carver's fleet when she was introduced in 1986. While a two-stateroom floorplan was available, most were sold with dinette interior with single stateroom. Lower helm was a popular option. Cockpit is big enough for fishing; flybridge has a raised command console with overhead electronics box built into radar arch. Standard 350hp gas engines cruise at a sluggish 13–14 knots (low 20s top); optional Cat 375hp diesels cruise at 20 knots (23–24 knots wide open).

Prices Not Provided for Pre-1995 Models

Length	42'0"	Fuel	400 gals.
Beam	15'0"	Water	170 gals.
Draft	3'6"	Headroom	6'5"
Weight	23,150#	Hull Type	Modified-V
Clearance	16'6"	Deadrise Aft	12°

Carver 42 Mariner

2004–06

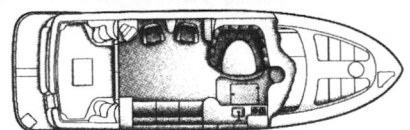

Super-spacious cruiser with large cockpit, extended swim platform delivers condo-size accommodations in a mid-size yacht. Expansive two-stateroom interior features cavernous full-beam salon with raised dinette, large step-down galley, island queen berth in forward stateroom. (Note big storage locker under galley sole.) Filler converts single berths in guest cabin into double. Huge flybridge has three helm chairs, wet bar, circular aft lounge. Volvo 370hp diesels cruise at 20 knots (24–25 knots top).

See Page 517 For Value Estimates

Length	44'5"	Fuel	400 gals.
Beam	13'11"	Water	95 gals.
Draft	32"	Waste	35 gals.
Weight	31,280#	Hull Type	Modified-V
Clearance, Arch	19'2"	Deadrise Aft	17°

Carver 42 Motor Yacht

1985–91

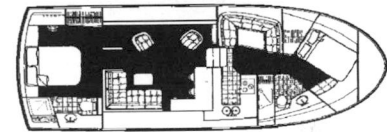

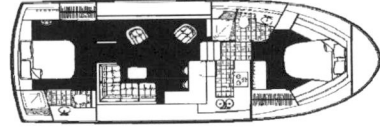

Durable aft-cabin motoryacht set class standards for popularity, value in the late 1980s. Space-efficient interior—available with or without dinette—features large owner's stateroom, expansive salon with serving counter, U-shaped galley down, stall showers in both heads. Most were sold with optional lower helm and hardtop. Big salon windows provide panoramic outside views. Flybridge seats six around centerline helm. Cruise at 13–14 knots with 300hp gas engine (20+ knots top). Cat 375hp diesels cruise at 20 knots (mid 20s top).

Prices Not Provided for Pre-1995 Models

Length	42'0"	Fuel	400 gals.
Beam	15'0"	Water	170 gals.
Draft	3'6"	Headroom	6'4"
Weight	23,600#	Hull Type	Modified-V
Clearance	20'0"	Deadrise Aft	12°

Carver 42/43 Super Sport

2006–Current

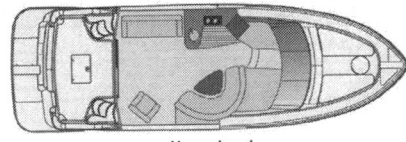

Upper Level

Lower Level

Feature-rich sport sedan with expansive, full-beam interior couples big-boat luxury with traditional Carver quality, value. Combined salon/galley/dinette with cherry paneling offers spacious accommodations with room for nonstop entertaining. Both staterooms feature queen berths—unusual in a boat this size. Note washer/dryer beneath galley sole, low galley counters. Party-time bridge can seat a small crowd. Bridge overhang shades large cockpit. Optional Volvo 370hp diesels with IPS drives cruise at 24 knots (about 28 knots top).

See Page 517 For Value Estimates

Length	43'7"	Fuel	400 gals.
Beam	13'11"	Water	90 gals.
Draft	3'10"	Waste	50 gals.
Weight	33,650#	Hull Type	Modified-V
Clearance, Arch	19'7"	Deadrise Aft	NA

Trawlers & Motoryachts

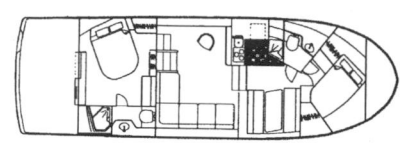

Carver 430 Cockpit MY

1991–97

Sturdy construction, luxury-class accommodations made this contemporary cockpit yacht a popular model in 1990s. Roomy galley-down interior has angled double berths in both staterooms, full dinette, wide-open salon with L-shaped sofa. Sliding door in master suite opens directly on cockpit. Additional features include wide side decks, bow pulpit, radar arch, transom door, extended swim platform. Standard gas engines cruise at a modest 14–15 knots; Cummins 330hp diesels cruise at 20 knots (22–23 knots top).

See Page 517 For Value Estimates

Length	47'10"	Fuel	390 gals.
Beam	14'0"	Water	91 gals.
Draft	3'4"	Waste	75 gals.
Weight	28,700#	Hull Type	Modified-V
Clearance	15'4"	Deadrise Aft	11°

Carver 43/47 Motor Yacht

2006–Current

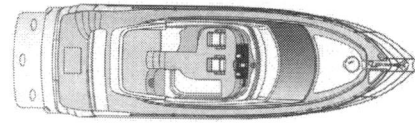

Gold-plated cockpit yacht (called the Carver 43 MY in 2006–07) gets high marks for deluxe accommodations, quality construction. Enormous full-beam salon with high-gloss cabinetry rivals many 50-footers for living space, luxury. Compact master stateroom features desk, washer/dryer, cockpit door. Note full-size refrigerator, faux-granite galley counters. Wing doors, bench seating are standard on aft deck. Cockpit opens to extended swim platform capable of stowing PWC. Yanmar 480hp diesels cruise at 20–22 knots.

See Page 517 For Value Estimates

Length w/Platform	49'2"	Fuel, Diesel	580 gals.
Beam	14'2"	Water	90 gals.
Draft	3'6"	Waste	75 gals.
Weight	35,811#	Hull Type	Modified-V
Fuel, Gas	400 gals.	Deadrise Aft	NA

Carver 440/445 Aft Cabin

1993–99

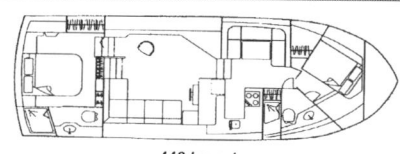

440 Layout

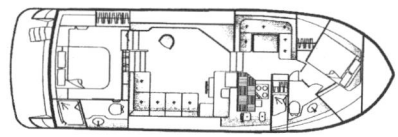

445 Layout

Conservative, broad-shouldered motoryacht from the late 1990s combines roomy interior with efficient space utilization, sturdy construction. Open-plan interior with expansive salon has galley and dinette down, double berths in both staterooms, built-in entertainment center. Relatively small aft deck for a 44-footer. Updated 445 model introduced in 1997 has integrated transom with molded steps. Among several gas or diesel engine options, twin 330hp Cummins diesels cruise at 17–18 knots (about 22 knots top).

See Page 517 For Value Estimates

Length	47'8"	Fuel	476 gals.
Beam	15'0"	Water	165 gals.
Draft	4'3"	Waste	80 gals.
Weight	32,000#	Hull Type	Modified-V
Clearance, Arch	18'9"	Deadrise Aft	14°

Carver 444 Cockpit MY

2001–06

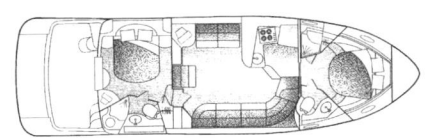

Lengthened version of Carver 396 MY gets extra fuel with added versatility of 60-square-foot cockpit. Spacious galley-down interior is arranged with double berths fore and aft, stall showers in both heads. Immense full-beam salon with curved Ultraleather sofa boasts nearly seven feet of headroom. Note absence of dinette. Huge bridge features center helm, wraparound seating, wet bar. Twin 370hp gas engines cruise at a modest 14–15 knots (mid 20s top); 370hp Cummins diesels cruise at 20 knots (22–23 knots top).

See Page 517 For Value Estimates

Length	46'6"	Fuel	404 gals.
Beam	13'11"	Water	90 gals.
Draft	3'6"	Waste	72 gals.
Weight	33,860#	Hull Type	Modified-V
Clearance, Arch	18'0"	Deadrise Aft	16°

Carver 450 Voyager

1999–2004

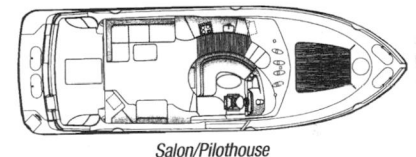

Salon/Pilothouse

Salon/Lower Level

Luxury pilothouse cruiser with innovative two-stateroom interior gets high marks for distinctive styling, state-of-the-art amenities. Open-plan salon with cherry trim, facing leather settees features elevated, helm-level dinette—a unique design that keeps guests close to the helmsman. Both double staterooms have full, en-suite heads. Note limited galley storage. Sliding glass doors open to partially shaded cockpit with engine room access hatch. Cummins 480hp diesels will cruise at 19–20 knots (low 20s top).

See Page 517 For Value Estimates

Length w/Platform	46'11"	Fuel	560 gals.
Beam	14'11"	Water	150 gals.
Draft	3'7"	Waste	80 gals.
Weight	39,600#	Hull Type	Modified-V
Clearance	16'8"	Deadrise Aft	15°

Carver 455/456 Aft Cabin MY

1996–2000

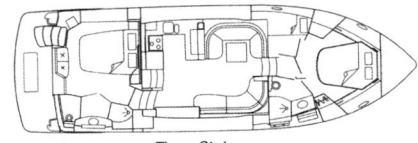

Three Staterooms

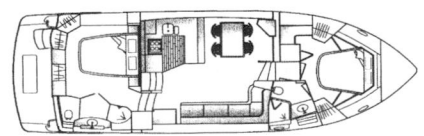

Two Staterooms

Rakish aft-cabin yacht (called Carver 455 in 1996–98, Carver 456 in 1999–2000) led the way in late 1990s for motoryacht value. Original three-stateroom layout is unusual—galley is aft in salon permitting enormous bow stateroom, concealed guest cabin. Conventional two-stateroom floorplan with salon dinette became available in 1998. Highlights include large engine room, transom staircase, side exhausts. Note tub/shower in forward head. Twin 315hp Cummins diesels cruise at 16 knots; 340hp Cats cruise at 18 knots.

See Page 517 For Value Estimates

Length	45'9"	Fuel	464 gals.
Beam	15'4"	Water	132 gals.
Draft	4'7"	Waste	80 gals.
Weight	35,000#	Hull Type	Modified-V
Clearance	18'9"	Deadrise Aft	14°

Trawlers & Motoryachts

Carver 460/46 Voyager

2003–Current

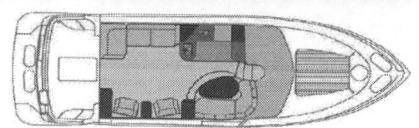

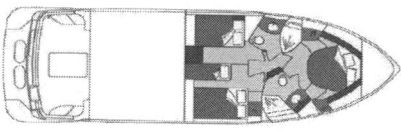

Revised version of popular 450 Voyager (1999–2004) replaced 450's inventive two-stateroom, lower-helm interior with three-stateroom layout with no lower helm. Highlights include cherrywood furnishings and cabinetry, spacious salon with premium leather sofas, gourmet galley with generous storage, well-appointed staterooms. Stylish bridge offers plenty of guest seating. Sliding glass doors open to partially shaded cockpit with engine room access hatch. Called 460 Voyager in 2003–04. Cummins 480hp diesels will cruise at 19–20 knots (low 20s top).

See Page 517 For Value Estimates

Length w/Platform	46'11"	Fuel	560 gals.
Beam	14'11"	Water	150 gals.
Draft	3'7"	Waste	80 gals.
Weight	39,600#	Hull Type	Modified-V
Clearance	16'8"	Deadrise Aft	15°

Carver 466 Motor Yacht

2001–07

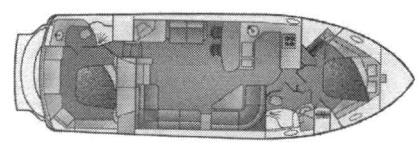

Spacious, well-bred cruising yacht with high-impact styling targets upscale buyers in search of world-class comforts. Enormous full-width salon rivals many 55-footers in size. Two-and-a-half-stateroom floorplan (note tiny berth under salon settee) is arranged with mid-level galley, breakfast bar, walkaround island beds in each stateroom, two full heads. Hardtop, wing doors enclose spacious aft deck. Roomy flybridge can seat eight. Excellent fit and finish. Twin 480hp Volvo diesels cruise at 20 knots and reach a top speed of 22–23 knots.

See Page 517 For Value Estimates

Length	46'11"	Fuel	480 gals.
Beam	14'11"	Water	130 gals.
Draft	3'7"	Waste	80 gals.
Weight	37,000#	Hull Type	Modified-V
Clearance	19'5"	Deadrise Aft	14°

Carver 500/504 Cockpit MY

1996–2000

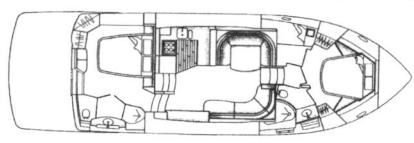

Three Staterooms

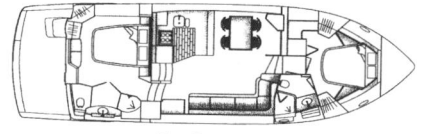

Two Staterooms

Luxury-class 50-footer (called the 500 CMY in 1996–98; 504 CMY in 1999–2000) was flagship of the Carver fleet in the mid 1990s. Spacious interior offered with two or three staterooms has the galley positioned aft in the salon—an unusual layout in a yacht of this type. Note aft-facing bed, cockpit access door in master stateroom. Large cockpit serves anglers and bathers alike. Additional features include tub in forward head, large engine room, molded cockpit steps, washer/dryer space, integral swim platform. Cummins 420hp diesels cruise at 20 knots.

See Page 517 For Value Estimates

Length	49'7"	Fuel	688 gals.
Beam	15'4"	Water	200/350 gals.
Draft	4'7"	Waste	80 gals.
Weight	43,100#	Hull Type	Modified-V
Clearance, Arch	18'9"	Deadrise Aft	14°

Trawlers & Motoryachts

Carver 506 Motor Yacht

2000–04

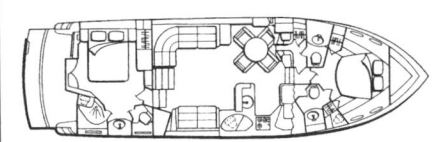

Garish floating condo with enormous, maxi-volume interior took showy styling to previously unimagined heights. Cavernous full-width salon with seven-foot headroom is made possible by raising the side decks to eye level. Three-stateroom, galley-down floorplan features formal dining area, three heads, salon seating for a small crowd. Note tiered salon windows, rich cherry woodwork, generous galley storage. Enclosed flybridge is rare in a yacht this size. Cummins 450hp diesels cruise at 17 knots (20+ top).

See Page 517 For Value Estimates

Length	51'7"	Fuel	510 gals.
Beam	15'4"	Water	158 gals.
Draft	4'6"	Waste	95 gals.
Weight	47,900#	Hull Type	Modified-V
Clearance	20'1"	Deadrise Aft	13°

Carver 52 Voyager

2007–Current

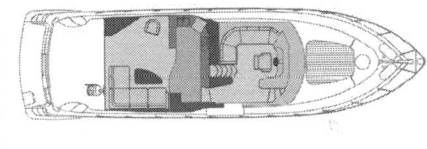

Executive-class flybridge yacht meets cruiser's needs for elegant entertaining, comfortable cruising. Spacious three-stateroom floorplan has combined salon/galley separated from pilothouse by galley bulkhead. (Most pilothouse yachts have salon/galley area open to lower helm.) Huge deckhouse windows, vertical ports in master suite provide good natural lighting. Pilothouse door is a plus, but engine room is tight. No rear visibility from lower helm. Bow, stern thrusters are standard. Volvo 575hp diesels cruise at 20–22 knots (high 20s top).

Insufficient Resale Data to Assign Values

Length	53'9"	Fuel	800 gals.
Beam	15'4"	Water	200 gals.
Draft	4'9"	Waste	100 gals.
Weight	48,500#	Hull Type	Modified-V
Clearance, Arch	19'0"	Deadrise Aft	13°

Carver 530 Voyager Pilothouse

1998–2005

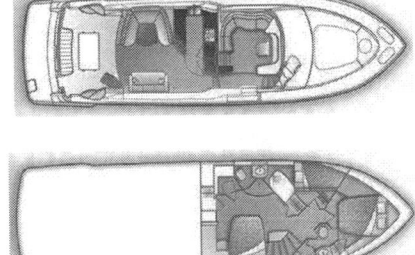

Top-selling pilothouse yacht took Carver styling, versatility to the next level. Opulent three-stateroom cherry interior features spacious salon with wraparound lounge, aircraft-style pilothouse with helm seat surrounded by guest seating, lavish full-beam owner's stateroom, luxurious VIP cabin. Note near 7' salon headroom, gourmet galley with hardwood flooring, inside bridge access. Extended flybridge with lounge seating can entertain a small crowd. Cruise at 16–17 knots (about 20 top) with Cummins 450hp diesels.

See Page 517 For Value Estimates

Length w/Platform	53'9"	Fuel	800 gals.
Beam	15'4"	Water	200 gals.
Draft	4'9"	Waste	100 gals.
Weight	48,500	Hull Type	Modified-V
Clearance, Arch	19'0"	Deadrise Aft	13°

Trawlers & Motoryachts

Trawlers & Motoryachts

Carver 564 Cockpit MY

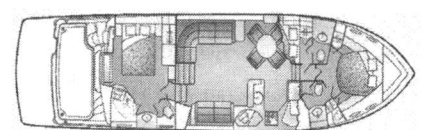

2002–06

Cockpit version of Carver's slab-sided 506 MY (2000–04) offers owners added versatility, additional range, slightly better profile. Cavernous full-width salon with nearly seven feet of headroom is made possible by raising the side decks to eye level. Three-stateroom, galley-down floorplan includes formal dining area, three heads, salon seating for a crowd. Wing doors, hardtop with retractable sunroof are standard. Cummins 450hp diesels will cruise at 17 knots; Volvo 675hp diesels cruise at 22 knots.

See Page 517 For Value Estimates

Length	59'2"	Fuel	646 gals.
Beam	15'4"	Water	158 gals.
Draft	4'6"	Waste	95 gals.
Weight	54,167#	Hull Type	Modified-V
Clearance, Arch	20'11"	Deadrise Aft	13°

Carver 570 Voyager PH; 56 Voyager Sedan

2001–Current

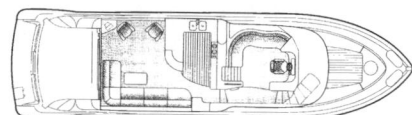

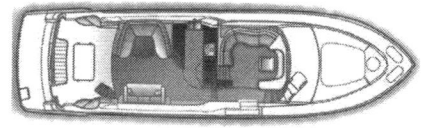

Enlarged version of best-selling 530 Voyager PH made an exceptional yacht even better. Luxurious three-stateroom interior features spacious salon with Ultraleather seating, raised pilothouse with helm seat surrounded by guest seating, lavish full-beam owner's stateroom. Note near 7' salon headroom, inside bridge access. Extended flybridge can entertain a small crowd. Cruise at 18 knots with Volvo 4800hp diesels; 24 knots with 675hp Volvos. Called the 570 Voyager PH in 2001–04; 57 Voyager PH in 2005–06; 56 Voyager Sedan 2007–09.

See Page 517 For Value Estimates

Length	59'2"	Fuel	800 gals.
Beam	15'4"	Water	200 gals.
Draft	4'9"	Waste	100 gals.
Weight	52,500#	Hull Type	Modified-V
Clearance, Arch	19'0"	Deadrise Aft	13°

CHB 34 Double Cabin

1972–85

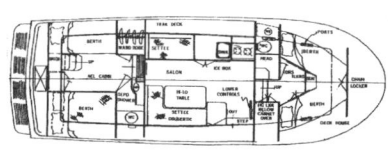

Classic family trawler enjoyed huge popularity in 1970s, 1980s thanks to low price, economical operation, rich teak interior. Compact-but-efficient layout with parquet flooring is comfortable for two, crowded for four. Storage space is at a premium, especially in galley. Built with plywood house before 1975. Decks were teak-planked until 1985 (a constant source of leaks); teak-over-fiberglass thereafter. Teak window frames eliminated in 1982. Over 1,600 built. Single 120hp or 135hp diesel cruises at 6–7 knots burning just 3 gallons per hour.

Prices Not Provided for Pre-1995 Models

Length Overall	33'6"	Clearance	NA
Length WL	30'3"	Fuel	300 gals.
Beam	11'9"	Water	85 gals.
Draft	3'6"	Waste	40 gals.
Weight	27,000#	Hull Type	Semi-Disp.

CHB 38 Trawler

1978–86

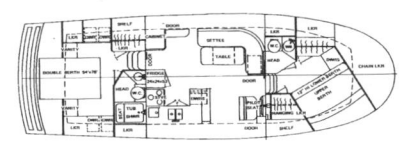

Vintage double-cabin trawler from well-regarded Taiwan builder delivers appealing mix of timeless style, economical operation. Several two-stateroom, galley-up teak interiors were offered over the years, all with parquet flooring, port/starboard deck doors, tub/shower in aft head. Teak decks, window frames and handrails were standard. Note fold-down mast, simulated lapstrake hull lines. Deep keel protects running gear. Above-average finish. Cruise at 7–8 knots with single 120hp Lehman diesel; 10+ knots with twin 120s.

Prices Not Provided for Pre-1995 Models

Length Overall	37'10"	Clearance	NA
Length WL	35'4"	Fuel	400 gals.
Beam	13'2"	Water	200 gals.
Draft	3'9"	Waste	40 gals.
Weight	21,000#	Hull Type	Semi-Disp.

CHB 42 Sundeck

1984–89

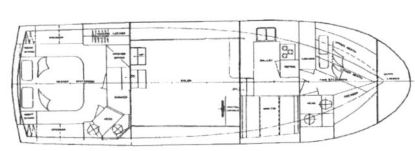

Appealing 1980s sundeck yacht with contemporary styling, traditional teak interior continues to enjoy strong buyer appeal. Standard twin-stateroom layout with galley and dinette down boasts roomy master suite with space for washer/dryer, teak parquet floors, standard lower helm. Topside highlights include covered aft deck with wet bar, wide side decks, flybridge seating for six. Also marketed as Present or Ponderosa 42. Among several engine options, twin 255 Lehman diesels cruise at 10–12 knots (about 14 knots top).

Prices Not Provided for Pre-1995 Models

Length Overall	41'10"	Clearance	16'4"
Length WL	38'0"	Fuel	450 gals.
Beam	13'8"	Water	200 gals.
Draft	3'6"	Waste	30 gals.
Weight	26,000#	Hull Type	Semi-Disp.

CHB 45 Pilothouse

1979–85

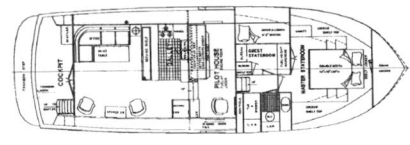

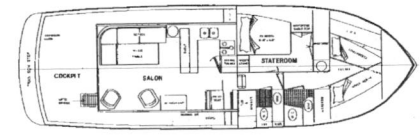

All-weather pilothouse trawler couples cruising comfort with liveaboard amenities. Spacious teak interior with split-level floorplan boasts expansive salon with U-shaped galley, parquet flooring, pilothouse watch berth, full-size head with tub/shower. Note spacious engine room, teak-over-fiberglass decks, cabintop and flybridge. Transom door make boarding easy. Deep keel protects running gear. Also marketed as Puget 45 Pilothouse. Standard 120hp Lehman diesels cruise at 8 knots; optional 235hp Volvos cruise at 10–12 knots.

Prices Not Provided for Pre-1995 Models

Length Overall	44'10"	Headroom	6'8"
Length WL	40'6"	Fuel	600 gals.
Beam	14'6"	Water	250 gals.
Draft	4'2"	Waste	40 gals.
Weight	30,000#	Hull Type	Semi-Disp.

Trawlers & Motoryachts

CHB 48 Seamaster MY

1983–89

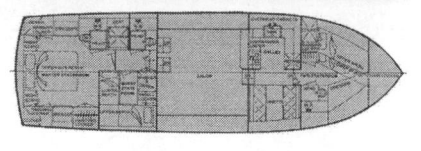

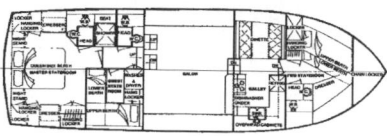

Heavily-built motoryacht with conservative lines, spacious three-stateroom interior offered 1980s buyers big-boat luxury at a competitive price. Highlights include full teak interior, expansive salon, booth-style dinette, luxurious owner stateroom, washer/dryer space in aft guest cabin. Both aft heads share common shower stall. Note huge aft deck with wing doors, wet bar. Basically a Taiwan knock-off of the Hatteras 48 MY (1981–84). Also marketed as Ponderosa 48. Cat 375hp diesels cruise at 12–14 knots (18 knots top).

Prices Not Provided for Pre-1995 Models

Length Overall	47'8"	Clearance	16'10"
Length WL	43'6"	Fuel	590 gals.
Beam	15'0"	Water	200 gals.
Draft	3'10"	Waste	75 gals.
Weight	39,000#	Hull Type	Semi-Disp.

Cheoy Lee 35 Sedan

1979–86

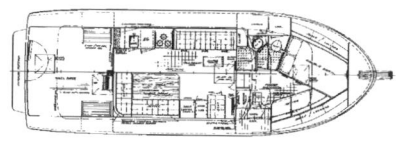

Heavily-built small trawler offers long-range coastal cruising for couples on a budget. Traditional teak interior boasts large salon with convertible L-shaped settee, roomy head with separate stall shower, large forward stateroom with double berth, lots of storage. Deckhouse galley is next to aft salon door where it's convenient to cockpit and flybridge. Note very wide side decks, folding mast, huge fuel capacity. Extended hardtop shelters cockpit. Deep keel protects running gear. Cruise at 7–8 knots with single 120hp Lehman diesel.

Prices Not Provided for Pre-1995 Models

Length Overall	34'11"	Clearance	NA
Length WL	32'6"	Fuel	650 gals.
Beam	12'0"	Water	210 gals.
Draft	3'7"	Waste	30 gals.
Weight	21,000#	Hull Type	Semi-Disp.

Cheoy Lee 40 Trawler

1973–86

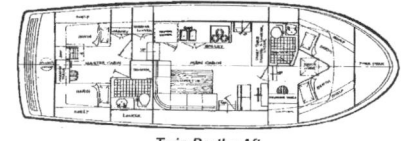

Twin Berths Aft

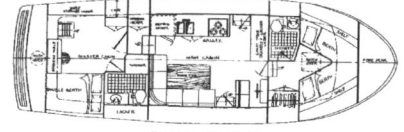

Double Berth Aft

Vintage Asian-built trawler with traditional trunk-cabin profile is seaworthy, economical, built to last. Generic teak interior originally had twin berths in aft stateroom; later models have double berth aft. Note convenient cockpit access door in aft stateroom. Well-finished engine room offers good service access. Mast and boom assembly, teak decks were standard. Full-length keel protects props and running gear from grounding. Cruising range exceeds 1,000 nautical miles. Twin 120hp Lehman diesels cruise efficiently at 7–8 knots.

Prices Not Provided for Pre-1995 Models

Length Overall	40'0"	Clearance	NA
Length WL	35'8"	Fuel	650 gals.
Beam	14'6"	Water	250 gals.
Draft	4'8"	Waste	40 gals.
Weight	38,000#	Hull Type	Semi-Disp.

Cheoy Lee 46 Trawler

1978–81

Deckhouse Plan

Lower Level Plan

Graceful Cheoy Lee trawler with handsome Europa styling is the smallest double-deck production yacht ever built. Three-stateroom interior with combined salon/galley includes private wheelhouse with flybridge access, aft master stateroom with private salon staircase, full-beam VIP guest cabin, walk-in engine room. Note protected side decks, cushioned bow seating. Teak-over-fiberglass decks were standard. Displacement hull is easy on the fuel. Twin 120hp Lehman diesels cruise at 8 knots with range of 800–850 miles.

Prices Not Provided for Pre-1995 Models

Length Overall	45'11"	Clearance	NA
Length WL	42'0"	Fuel	820 gals.
Beam	14'8"	Water	510 gals.
Draft	4'8"	Waste	70 gals.
Weight	49,200#	Hull Type	Displacement

Cheoy Lee 52 Efficient MY

1984–94

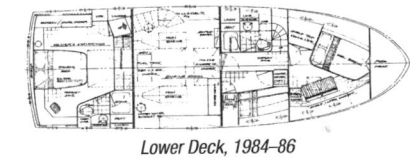

Lower Deck, 1984–86

Lower Deck, 1986–94

Sturdy cockpit yacht introduced in 1984 combined economical operation with practical layout, sea-kindly hull design. Interior highlights include expansive full-beam salon, deckhouse galley with home-size appliances, large master stateroom with private access. Inside bridge access is a plus. Floorplan update in 1986 added full-beam VIP stateroom. Small aft deck overlooks cockpit with transom door, swim platform. Among several engine options, twin 375hp Cat diesels cruise efficiently at 12–14 knots (about 18 knots top).

Prices Not Provided for Pre-1995 Models

Length Overall	51'11"	Clearance	16'1"
Length WL	47'6"	Fuel	1,000 gals.
Beam	15'6"	Water	450 gals.
Draft	4'2"	Waste	100 gals.
Weight	51,500#	Hull Type	Semi-Disp.

Cheoy Lee 55 Long Range MY

1977–86

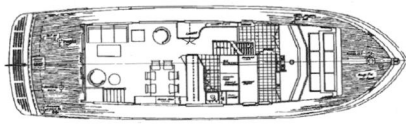

Standard Plan

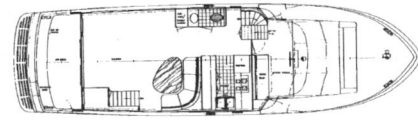

Wide Body Plan

Heavy displacement cruising yacht with transatlantic range travels the world in comfort, confidence. Highlights include expansive four-stateroom teak interior with deckhouse galley, three full heads, stand-up engine room, protected side decks, aft-deck wing doors, washer/dryer, teak-over-fiberglass decks. Note inside flybridge access, pilothouse watch berth, teak parquet flooring. Many of these yachts have been stabilized. Widebody model with extended, full-beam salon also available. Cruise at 8–9 knots with 210hp Cat diesels.

Prices Not Provided for Pre-1995 Models

Length Overall	55'0"	Clearance	NA
Length WL	50'0"	Fuel, Std.	2,700 gals.
Beam	17'2"	Water	450 gals.
Draft	5'4"	Waste	125 gals.
Weight	80,000#	Hull Type	Displacement

Trawlers & Motoryachts

Cheoy Lee 61 Long Range Cockpit MY

1983–2000

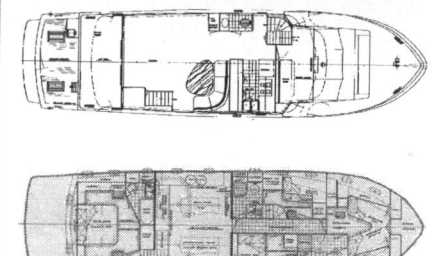

Cockpit version of Cheoy Lee 55 Long Range MY boasts revised four-stateroom interior, enhanced cruising versatility. Twin-deck layout has extended salon with home-size galley forward, private pilothouse with watch berth, opulent full-beam master suite with Jaquzzi tub and salon access, three full heads. Flybridge can be reached from pilothouse or aft-deck ladder. Note protected side decks, wing doors, teak decks. Also offered in Widebody version and unique aft engine room model. Cruise at 8–9 knots with 210hp Cat diesels.

Insufficient Resale Data to Assign Values

Length Overall	60'11"	Clearance	NA
Length WL	55'0"	Fuel, Std.	2,700 gals.
Beam	17'2"	Water	450 gals.
Draft	5'8"	Waste	125 gals.
Weight	90,000#	Hull Type	Displacement

Cheoy Lee 66 Long Range MY

1978–2003

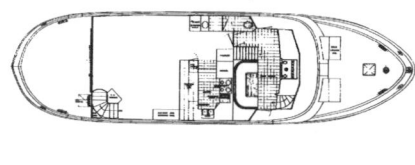
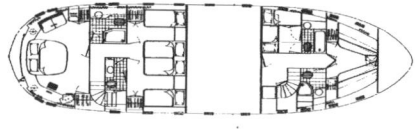

Iconic Cheoy Lee motoryacht with transoceanic range takes cruising adventure to the next level. Semicustom yacht was offered with several interior plans with four or five staterooms. Wide body model with full-beam salon (1987–2003) outsold standard version with walkaround deck. Highlights include king bed in master stateroom, walk-in engine room, private pilothouse, extended bridge with fake stack. Note wave-breaking Portuguese bridge, distinctive canoe stern. Cat 355hp diesels deliver 2,500-mile range at 9 knots.

Insufficient Resale Data to Assign Values

Length Overall	65'6"	Clearance	NA
Length WL	59'0"	Fuel	2,700 gals.
Beam	18'0"	Water	700 gals.
Draft	5'3"	Waste	250 gals.
Weight	87,000#	Hull Type	Displacement

Chris Craft 350 Catalina

1974–87

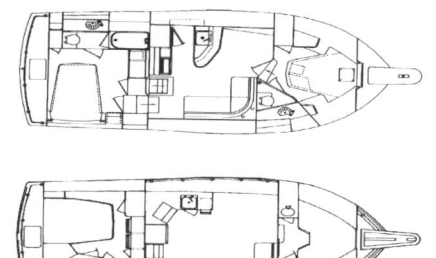

Iconic double-cabin cruiser was among best-selling Chris Craft models of her era. Expansive interior was offered in several configurations over the years, all with main-deck galley, large aft stateroom. Combined helm/aft deck area keeps skipper close to guests. Wide side decks make getting around easy. Additional features include molded foredeck seating, bow pulpit, swim platform, large engine room. Twin 235hp gas engines cruise at 14–15 knots and top out in the low 20s. Note fuel increase to 250 gallons in 1983.

Prices Not Provided for Pre-1995 Models

Length Overall	35'1"	Clearance	10'8"
Beam	13'1"	Fuel	180/250 gals.
Draft	2'10"	Water	55/100 gals.
Weight	17,229#	Hull Type	Modified-V
Headroom	6'4"	Deadrise Aft	NA

Trawlers & Motoryachts

Chris Craft 362 Catalina

1986–87

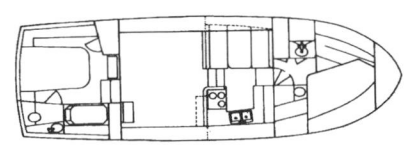

Roomy aft-cabin cruiser (originally built by Uniflite) combined contemporary 1980s styling with sturdy construction, comfortable ride. Practical galley-down floorplan features two double staterooms, U-shaped galley with upright refrigerator, convertible dinette, spacious salon. Lower helm was a popular option. Teak interior trim, bow pulpit, swim platform were standard. Modified-V hull can handle a chop with ease. Twin 270hp gas inboards cruise at 17–18 knots and reach a top speed of 25–26 knots.

Prices Not Provided for Pre-1995 Models

Length	36'0"	Fuel	250 gals.
Beam	12'4"	Water	100 gals.
Draft	2'7"	Headroom	6'4"
Weight	15,500#	Hull Type	Modified-V
Clearance	12'2"	Deadrise Aft	NA

Chris Craft 372 Catalina

1988–90

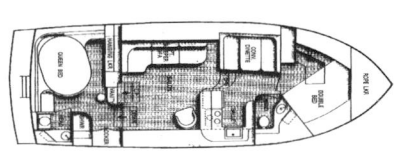

Contemporary aft-cabin cruising yacht appealed to entry-level buyers seeking liveaboard amenities at an affordable price. Beamy hull allows for unusually spacious accommodations for a 37-footer with full dinette, large U-shaped galley, wide-open salon. Both staterooms are on small side with angled berths to save space. Topside features include wide side decks, bow pulpit, swim platform, aft-deck wet bar. Hardtop was a popular option. Twin 270hp gas engines cruise at 16–17 knots (about 25 knots top).

Prices Not Provided for Pre-1995 Models

Length w/Pulpit	42'9"	Fuel	250 gals.
Hull Length	37'5"	Water	100 gals.
Beam	13'10"	Waste	18 gals.
Draft	2'9"	Hull Type	Modified-V
Weight	17,200#	Deadrise Aft	NA

Chris Craft 380 Corinthian

1978–86

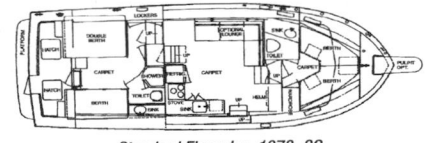

Standard Floorplan, 1978–82

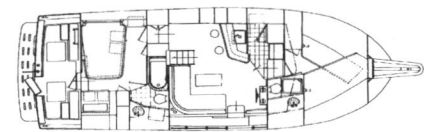

Standard Floorplan, 1983–85

Popular double-cabin cruiser with houseboat profile repays in versatility what she lacks in eye appeal. Very sociable topside seating has bridge just two steps up from afterdeck. Several two-stateroom floorplans were offered, all with salon, cockpit entry doors. Lower helm was a popular option. Wide side decks make getting around easy. Note thoughtful afterdeck safety railings. Cockpit transom door, bow pulpit, swim platform were standard. A stiff ride in a chop, twin gas inboards cruise at 15–16 knots (mid 20s top).

Prices Not Provided for Pre-1995 Models

Length Overall	38'0"	Clearance	12'2"
Length WL	33'6"	Fuel	400 gals.
Beam	14'0"	Water	65 gals.
Draft	3'0"	Hull Type	Modified-V
Weight	22,500#	Deadrise Aft	NA

Trawlers & Motoryachts

Chris Craft 381 Catalina

1980–89

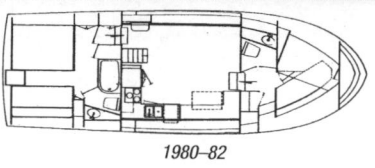

1980–82

1983–89

Enlarged version of best-selling Chris 350 Catalina has the interior space of many 45-footers. Innovative floorplan boasts huge salon with open galley, deck access door, two large staterooms, plenty of storage. Wide side decks provide secure access to cushioned bow seating. Express-style bridge/afterdeck area keeps skipper close to guests. Modified-V hull can be a stiff ride in a chop. Not the prettiest boat at the dock. Twin 330hp gas inboards cruise at 16–17 knots (low-to-mid 20s top).

Prices Not Provided for Pre-1995 Models

Length Overall	38'0"	Fuel	410 gals.
Beam	14'0"	Water	65 gals.
Draft	3'0"	Waste	75 gals.
Weight	21,600#	Hull Type	Modified-V
Clearance	11'7"	Deadrise Aft	NA

Chris Craft 410 Motor Yacht

1972–86

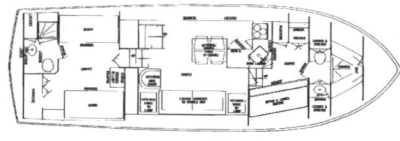

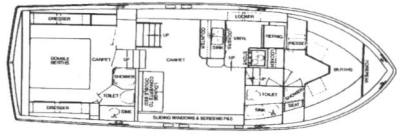

Classic flush-deck yacht introduced in 1972 became one of the best-selling motoryachts of her era. Highlights include spacious main salon, protected helm/aft-deck area, full walkaround decks, large engine room with good service access. Early models were mostly hardtops; later models have standard flybridge. Offered with many floorplans over the years; queen berth became standard in master stateroom in 1981. Note small fuel capacity. Cruise at 14–15 knots with gas engines; optional diesels deliver 18- to 20-knot cruising speed.

Prices Not Provided for Pre-1995 Models

Length	41'0"	Fuel	350 gals.
Beam	14'0"	Water	100 gals.
Draft	3'3"	Waste	40 gals.
Weight	26,565#	Hull Type	Modified-V
Clearance	15'10"	Deadrise Aft	NA

Chris Craft 425/426/427 Catalina

1985–90

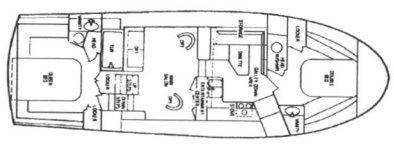

Updated version of earlier Uniflite 42 (1971–84) gave 1980s Chris Craft enthusiasts something to cheer about. Spacious galley-down interior includes double berths fore and aft, full dinette, large galley with upright refrigerator. Big aft deck is a plus. Called Chris Craft 425 Catalina in 1985; 426 Catalina in 1986; 427 Catalina in 1987–90. One of the better-riding small motoryachts of her era. Standard gas engines cruise at 17–18 knots (mid 20s top); optional Cat 375hp diesels cruise at 21–22 knots (24–25 top).

Prices Not Provided for Pre-1995 Models

Length Overall	42'0"	Fuel	400 gals.
Beam	14'9"	Water	160 gals.
Draft	3'6"	Waste	60 gals.
Weight	33,000#	Hull Type	Modified-V
Clearance	12'10"	Deadrise Aft	13°

Chris Craft 480 Catalina

1985–89

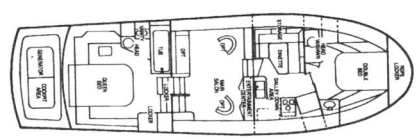

Popular double-cabin yacht from 1980s is basically a Chris 427 Catalina (1985–90) with six-foot cockpit extension. Spacious galley-down interior includes double berths fore and aft, full dinette, large galley with upright refrigerator. Note the tub in aft head. Cockpit is large enough for serious fishing. Flybridge was restyled in 1986. Modified-V hull is known for excellent seakeeping qualities, smooth ride. Standard gas engines cruise at 18 knots; optional 375hp Cat diesels cruise at 20 knots with a top speed in the mid 20s.

Prices Not Provided for Pre-1995 Models

Length	48'0"	Fuel	590 gals.
Beam	14'9"	Water	160 gals.
Draft	3'6"	Headroom	6'4"
Weight	34,000#	Hull Type	Modified-V
Clearance	12'10"	Deadrise Aft	13°

Chris Craft 500 Constellation MY

1985–90

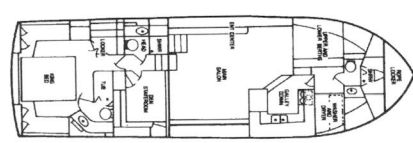

Handsome 50-footer originally built by Uniflite is basically a stretched version of the popular Pacemaker 46 Motor Yacht from the 1970s. Expansive three-stateroom interior in notable for wide-open salon, standard washer/dryer, unusual forepeak head compartment. Fully enclosed and paneled aft deck serves as second salon. Aft guest cabin doubles as den/office. Extended flybridge can seat a dozen guests. Note wide walkways. GM 550hp 6V92 diesels cruise at 16–17 knots and top out at close to 20 knots.

Prices Not Provided for Pre-1995 Models

Length	50'6"	Fuel	600 gals.
Beam	15'3"	Water	160 gals.
Draft	4'4"	Headroom	6'6"
Weight	54,000#	Hull Type	Modified-V
Clearance	17'1"	Deadrise Aft	4°

Chris Craft 501 Motor Yacht

1987–90

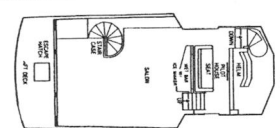

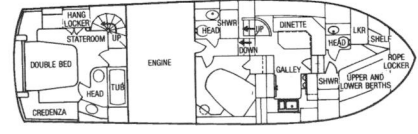

Contemporary twin-deck motoryacht with extended deckhouse salon offered Hatteras-style accommodations at a Chris Craft price. Spacious three-stateroom, three-head interior with home-sized galley, full-beam salon is huge for a 50-footer. Spiral salon staircase provides private entry to well-appointed master suite with king bed, full-size tub. Note inside bridge access, stand-up engine room, small aft deck for line handling. GM 550hp 6V92TA diesels cruise at 16 knots and reach a top speed of 18–19 knots.

Prices Not Provided for Pre-1995 Models

Length	50'8"	Fuel	778 gals.
Beam	15'5"	Water	260 gals.
Draft	4'6"	Cockpit	NA
Weight	49,000#	Hull Type	Modified-V
Clearance	NA	Deadrise Aft	4°

Cruisers 3650 Motor Yacht; 375 MY

1995–2005

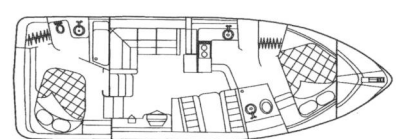

Popular aft-cabin cruiser (called 3650 Aft Cabin in 1995–99; 375 MY in 2000–05) delivered impressive mix of sporty-acht styling, balanced accommodations. Spacious salon with cherry joinery is wide open to galley and dinette. Compact staterooms have athwartships double berths to preserve space. Note tall salon headroom, tub in master head. Updates in 1999 included wing doors, aft-deck weather enclosure, molded bridge steps instead of ladder. Standard 370hp gas engines cruise at 18 knots (about 25 knots top).

See Page 519 For Value Estimates

Length	40'10"	Fuel	300 gals.
Beam	13'8"	Water	68 gals.
Draft	3'2"	Waste	55 gals.
Weight, Gas	20,000#	Hull Type	Modified-V
Weight, Diesel	21,500#	Deadrise Aft	11°

Cruisers 385/395 Motor Yacht

2006–08

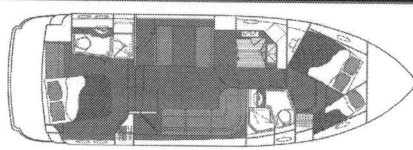

Standard Layout

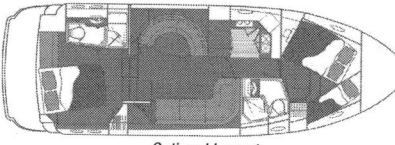

Optional Layout

Slightly over-styled flybridge yacht (called Cruisers 385 MY in 2006) makes good on promise of spacious accom-modations, brisk performance. Elegant twin-stateroom interior is offered with choice of facing or crescent-shaped di-nette. Overlapping elliptical windows provide excellent outside visibility. Topside highlights include acrylic wing doors, U-shaped bridge seating, extended swim platform with boarding steps. Note narrow side decks, good fit and finish. Standard 375hp gas inboards cruise at 25 knots (about 30 knots top).

See Page 519 For Value Estimates

Length	42'2"	Fuel	300 gals.
Beam	13'8"	Water	68 gals.
Draft	3'3"	Waste	51 gals.
Weight, Gas	23,500#	Hull Type	Modified-V
Weight, Diesel	25,000#	Deadrise Aft	16°

Cruisers 405/415 Express Motor Yacht

2003–Current

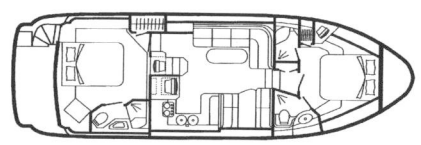

Versatile hardtop cruiser with tall-freeboard profile blends express-boat deck layout, motor-yacht accommodations. Well-furnished interior with combined salon/galley/dinette includes two large staterooms, generous storage. Hatch in salon floor provides access to spacious engine room. Note washer/dryer in master stateroom. Forward head is split with shower, toilet in separate compartments. Roomy aft deck features hard-top, wet bar, molded steps to swim platform. Cat 420hp diesels cruise in the low 20s (27–28 knots top).

See Page 519 For Value Estimates

Length	42'6"	Fuel	380 gals.
Beam	13'8"	Water	100 gals.
Draft	3'6"	Waste	70 gals.
Weight	31,000#	Hull Type	Modified-V
Clearance, Arch	14'0"	Deadrise Aft	16°

Cruisers 4280 Express Bridge

1988–94

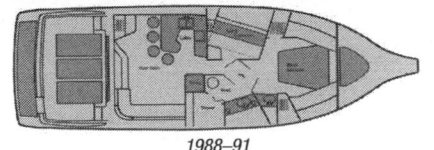

1988–91

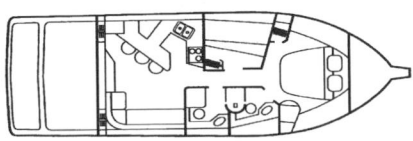

1992–94

Prices Not Provided for Pre-1995 Models

Maxi-volume cruiser with party-time accommodations delivers impressive comfort, versatility. Single-level interior (updated in 1992) features full-beam salon, two staterooms, open galley with serving counter. Massive flybridge can seat a small crowd. Bridge steps in cockpit are a nice touch. Fully cored hull has prop pockets to reduce draft and shaft angles. Cat 375hp diesels cruise at 20 knots (around 24 knots top). Note that Cruisers 4285 Express Bridge is same boat with more expansive single-stateroom interior.

Length	46'6"	Fuel	400 gals.
Beam	14'6"	Water	160 gals.
Draft	3'6"	Headroom	6'5"
Weight, Gas	23,700#	Hull Type	Modified-V
Weight, Diesel	25,200#	Deadrise Aft	16°

Cruisers 4450 Express MY

2000–03

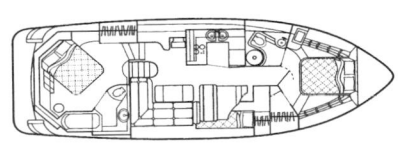

See Page 520 For Value Estimates

Innovative aft-cabin cruiser with open-deck layout combines express-boat styling, condo-style accommodations. Three-stateroom interior has salon, galley, slightly raised dinette on same level. Forward guest cabin with walk-in closet is nearly as large as owner's stateroom. Aft head includes whirlpool in addition to stall shower. Tiered helm and cockpit area keeps captain, passengers in close proximity. Extended swim platform can support PWC. Cruise at 18 knots with 420hp Cat diesels (23–24 knots top).

Length	45'6"	Fuel	500 gals.
Beam	15'4"	Water	140 gals.
Draft	3'3"	Waste	100 gals.
Weight	38,000#	Hull Type	Modified-V
Clearance, Arch	14'6"	Deadrise Aft	18°

Cruisers 447 Sport Sedan

2007–Current

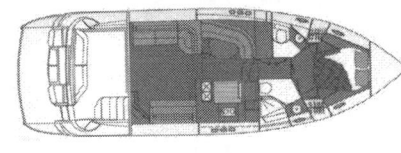

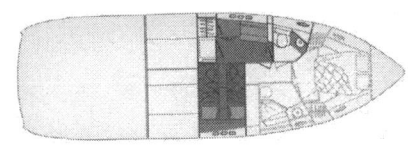

See Page 520 For Value Estimates

Feature-rich flybridge yacht meets cruiser's needs for on-the-water style, comfort, versatility. Expansive two-stateroom interior with two heads has split-level salon with galley and dinette forward, facing lounge seats aft. Storage compartment under salon is big enough for inflatables, bikes. Guest stateroom has space for washer/dryer. Big engine room is a plus. Note wraparound bridge windshield, aft sun lounge, fiberglass hardtop. Yanmar 480hp V-drive diesels cruise at 25–26 knots (about 30 knots top).

Length	45'2"	Fuel	375 gals.
Beam	14'6"	Water	100 gals.
Draft	3'10"	Waste	50 gals.
Weight	29,500#	Hull Type	Modified-V
Clearance	16'0"	Deadrise Aft	18°

Trawlers & Motoryachts

Cruisers 455 Express Motor Yacht

2004–Current

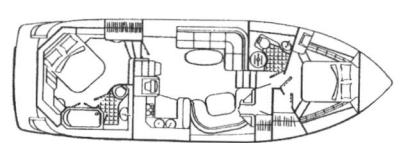

Updated version of Cruiser's 4450 Express MY (1998–2003) offers enticing mix of luxury accommodations, spirited performance. Posh three-stateroom interior has salon, galley, slightly raised dinette on same level. Forward guest cabin with walk-in closet is nearly as large as owner's stateroom; aft head includes whirlpool in addition to stall shower. Combined helm, cockpit area keeps captain, passengers in close proximity. Extended swim platform can support PWC. Cruise at 22 knots with 480hp Volvo diesels (28–29 knots top).

See Page 520 For Value Estimates

Length	45'6"	Fuel	500 gals.
Beam	15'4"	Water	140 gals.
Draft	3'3"	Waste	100 gals.
Weight	36,000#	Hull Type	Modified-V
Clearance, Hardtop	15'4"	Deadrise Aft	16°

Cruisers 497 Sport Sedan

2006–07

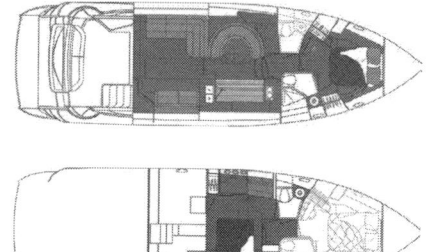

Rakish flybridge sedan (called 477 Sport Sedan in 2006) with semi-protected bridge took sportyacht comfort, styling to the next level. Luxurious midcabin interior with split-level salon, cherry cabinetry features two large staterooms, facing salon settees, huge galley with acres of counter space. Innovative bridge with hardtop, wet bar, full glass windshield offers good weather protection. Note spacious cockpit with molded bridge steps, extended swim platform. Volvo 575hp V-drive diesels cruise at 24–25 knots (30+ knots wide open).

See Page 520 For Value Estimates

Length	50'2"	Fuel	526 gals.
Beam	15'0"	Water	150 gals.
Draft	4'1"	Waste	75 gals.
Weight	39,500#	Hull Type	Modified-V
Headroom	6'6"	Deadrise Aft	18.5°

Cruisers 5000 Sedan Sport

1998–2003

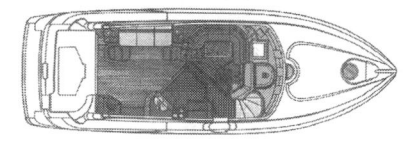

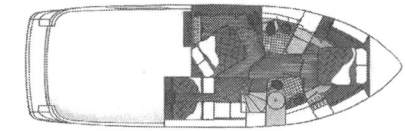

Well-mannered flybridge yacht with sleek profile, vast interior is ideal for liveaboards and cruisers alike. Wide-open salon is open to huge starboard-side galley, raised helm/dinette area forward. Inside bridge access is rare in a boat this size. Two of three staterooms have double berths; both heads have separate stall showers. Note rich cherrywood cabinetry, good engine room access. Fully cored hull has prop pockets to reduce draft and shaft angles. Volvo 480hp V-drive diesels cruise at 18 knots; 660hp Cats cruise 24–25 knots.

See Page 520 For Value Estimates

Length	49'6"	Fuel	600 gals.
Beam	15'6"	Water	150 gals.
Draft	3'5"	Waste	100 gals.
Weight	42,000#	Hull Type	Modified-V
Clearance, Arch	16'5"	Deadrise Aft	11°

CT 35 Trawler

1977–86

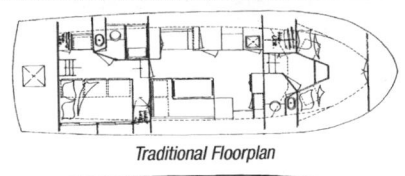

Traditional Floorplan

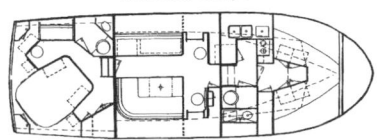

Sundeck Floorplan

Prices Not Provided for Pre-1995 Models

Well-built Taiwan trawler with traditional teak interior is easy on the eye, light on the wallet, inexpensive to run. Principal highlights include roomy master stateroom with cockpit access door, large salon with efficient galley area, very spacious engine room. Teak window frames—replaced with aluminum frames in later models—are prone to leaks. With plenty of exterior brightwork, this boat requires a fair amount of maintenance. Cruise at 7–8 knots with single 120hp diesel; 10 knots with twin 85hp diesels.

Length Overall	34'11"	Clearance	NA
Length WL	30'5"	Fuel	300 gals.
Beam	12'0"	Water	200 gals.
Draft	3'5"	Waste	60 gals.
Weight	19,800#	Hull Type	Semi-Disp.

DeFever 41 Trawler

1980–89

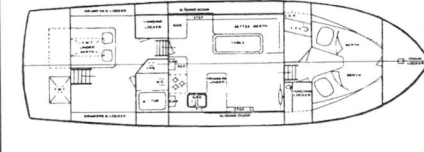

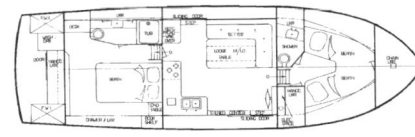

Prices Not Provided for Pre-1995 Models

Classic DeFever trawler popular in the 1980s combines traditional trunk-cabin styling with time-tested layout, economical operation. Highlights include roomy galley-up interior with teak woodwork, post/starboard salon doors, full walkaround decks, mast and boom assembly. Cabintop can stow small dinghy. Note teak decks, tub/shower in aft head, aft stateroom deck door, simulated lapstrake hull lines. Solid fiberglass hull has prop-protecting keel. Quality boat from a good Taiwan yard. Cruise at 7–8 knots with 135hp Lehman diesels.

Length Overall	40'7"	Clearance	NA
Length WL	34'7"	Fuel	400 gals.
Beam	14'2"	Water	250 gals.
Draft	4'0"	Waste	60 gals.
Weight	23,000#	Hull Type	Semi-Disp.

DeFever 44 Trawler

1981–2004

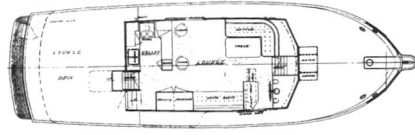

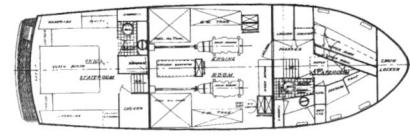

See Page 520 For Value Estimates

Heavily-built displacement trawler with covered aft deck remains among most popular DeFever designs ever produced. Expansive two-stateroom interior has galley aft in the salon—most galley-up trawlers have the galley forward. Master stateroom is huge with copious storage, space for washer/dryer. Walk-in engine room has near-standing headroom, built-in workbench. Note generous fuel, water capacities. Full-length keel protects running gear. Twin 135hp diesels cruise at 8 knots with range of 1,500+ miles.

Length Overall	43'9"	Clearance	NA
Length WL	38'6"	Fuel	900 gals.
Beam	14'9"	Water	350 gals.
Draft	4'7"	Waste	60 gals.
Weight	44,000#	Hull Type	Displacement

Trawlers & Motoryachts

DeFever 45 Pilothouse

2002–08

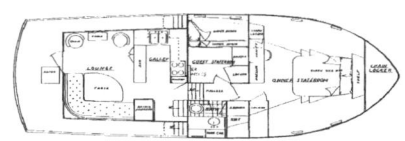

Well-crafted pilothouse trawler pairs signature DeFever styling with efficient deck layout, luxury-class amenities. Deluxe split-level interior boasts large master stateroom with desk/vanity, guest stateroom with engine room access, U-shaped galley with Corian counters, raised pilothouse with pilot berth. Note Portuguese bridge, wide, protected side decks. Washer/dryer space is provided in portside stateroom. Most boats this size have two heads. Twin John Deere 150hp diesels cruise efficiently at 8–10 knots (12 knots top).

See Page 520 For Value Estimates

Length Overall	45'0"	Fuel, Std.	500 gals.
Length WL	40'6"	Fuel, Opt.	700 gals.
Beam	15'0"	Water	250 gals.
Draft	3'10"	Waste	50 gals.
Weight	38,000#	Hull Type	Semi-Disp.

DeFever 47 POC Motor Yacht

1986–92

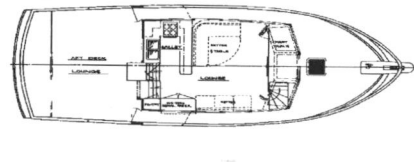

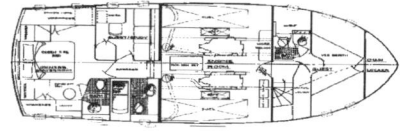

Appealing DeFever motoryacht with hard-enclosed aft deck provides extra space for cruising and liveaboard comfort. Standard galley-up interior includes three staterooms, three heads, walk-in engine room, salon/lounge with centerline helm. Second guest stateroom (aft of engine room) doubles as office/study. Main salon opens to small aft deck suitable for line handling. Combined double head aft shares common tub/shower. Semi-displacement hull is fully cored. Cat 210hp diesels cruise at 8 knots; 375hp Cats cruise at 12–14 knots.

Prices Not Provided for Pre-1995 Models

Length	46'10"	Headroom	6'5"
Beam	16'0"	Fuel	600 gals.
Draft	4'8"	Water	275 gals.
Weight	43,200#	Waste	60 gals.
Clearance	15'6"	Hull Type	Semi-Disp.

DeFever 48 Trawler

1978–92

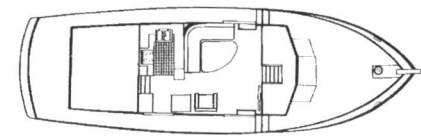

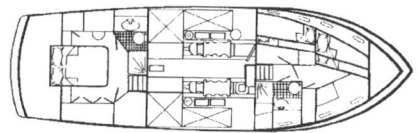

Long-range trawler yacht with Europa styling, near bullet-proof construction ranks among the best-selling DeFever designs ever produced. Comfortable three-stateroom interior features expansive salon with U-shaped galley aft, two full heads, spacious master suite. Salon has three deck doors—very unusual. Cavernous walk-in engine room includes sea chest, work bench. Note protected side decks. Popular model (over 200 built) is always in demand. Cruise at 8 knots with 135hp Lehman diesels, 14–15 knots with 375hp Cats.

Prices Not Provided for Pre-1995 Models

Length Overall	47'3"	Headroom	6'5"
Length WL	40'10"	Fuel	950 gals.
Beam	15'4"	Water	500 gals.
Draft	4'9"	Waste	100 gals.
Weight	50,000#	Hull Type	Semi-Disp.

DeFever 49 Cockpit MY

1994–2007

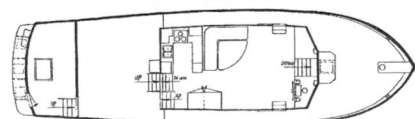

Main Deck Plan

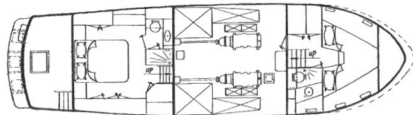

Lower Deck Plan

See Page 520 For Value Estimates

Cockpit version of popular DeFever 44 Trawler makes a good boat even better. Expansive two-stateroom interior is arranged with U-shaped galley aft in the salon—most galley-up trawlers have the galley forward. Master stateroom is huge with copious storage, space for washer/dryer. Walk-in engine room has near-standing headroom, built-in workbench. Cockpit with transom door serves anglers and cruisers alike. Full-length keel protects props and running gear. Twin 150hp John Deere diesels cruise at 8 knots with range of 1,500+ miles.

Length Overall	48'10"	Headroom	6'6"
Length WL	43'6"	Fuel	1,100 gals.
Beam	15'0"	Water	370 gals.
Draft	4'7"	Waste	90 gals.
Weight	53,900#	Hull Type	Displacement

DeFever 49 Pilothouse (Hard-Chine)

1978–90

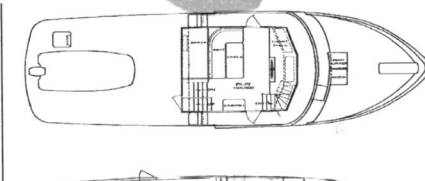

Prices Not Provided for Pre-1995 Models

Popular pilothouse yacht with hard-chined, semi-displacement hull is intended for long-range cruising in comfort, security. Split-level interior with combined salon/galley includes amidships master stateroom with queen bed, guest stateroom with upper/lower bunds, raised pilothouse with dinette and watch berth. Topside features include covered side decks, wave-breaking Portuguese bridge. Note that alternate DeFever 49 model with soft chines (built by CTF Marine) was also available. Cruise at 8 knots with 135hp diesels.

Length Overall	49'9"	Clearance	17'0"
Length WL	42'0"	Fuel	800 gals.
Beam	15'0"	Water	400 gals.
Draft	4'6"	Waste	70 gals.
Weight	50,000#	Hull Type	Semi-Disp.

DeFever 49 Pilothouse (Soft-Chine)

1977–2004

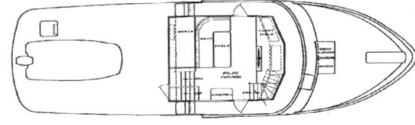

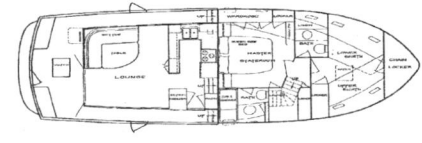

See Page 520 For Value Estimates

Classic DeFever design built with ship-like profile is intended for long-range cruising in comfort, security. Split-level interior with combined salon/galley includes amidships master stateroom with queen bed, guest stateroom with upper/lower bunks, raised pilothouse with dinette and watch berth. Note wave-breaking Portuguese bridge. Semi-displacement hull with rounded chines is easily driven, economical to operate. Alternate DeFever 49 model with hard chines (built by Sen Koh Marine) was also available. Cruise at 8 knots with 135hp diesels.

Length Overall	49'9"	Clearance	NA
Length WL	43'9"	Fuel	1,000 gals.
Beam	15'0"	Water	450 gals.
Draft	4'9"	Waste	70 gals.
Weight	50,000#	Hull Type	Semi-Disp.

Trawlers & Motoryachts

DeFever 52 Offshore Cruiser

1980–91

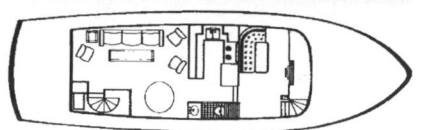

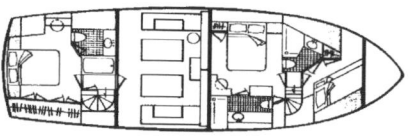

Heavy-weather displacement trawler with wide 16'8" beam couples beefy construction with spacious accommodations, long-range capability. Main deck level with U-shaped galley, extended salon with day head, is open from wheelhouse to cockpit. Pilothouse includes watch berth, deck doors, direct bridge access. Two of the three staterooms below are huge. Short foredeck adds to interior living space. Wide body version with full-width salon was also available. Cat 210hp diesels cruise at 8 knots with up to 2,000-mile range.

Prices Not Provided for Pre-1995 Models

Length Overall	51'7"	Clearance	NA
Length WL	45'5"	Fuel	1,500 gals.
Beam	16'8"	Water	500 gals.
Draft	4'9"	Waste	70 gals.
Weight	77,000#	Hull	Displacement

DeFever 53 POC

1986–89

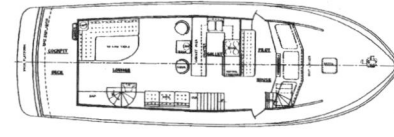

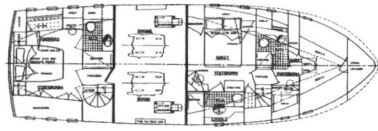

Spacious twin-deck motoryacht made good on DeFever promise of liveaboard comfort, cruising elegance. Three-stateroom floorplan boasts spacious master with private salon access, huge VIP cabin, three full heads, walk-in engine room. Expansive salon with home-size galley, separate dining area features inside bridge access—a convenience not always found in a yacht this size. Side decks are sheltered by bridge overhangs. Hull is fully cored to reduce weight. Twin 375hp Cat diesels cruise at 12 knots (15–16 top).

Prices Not Provided for Pre-1995 Models

Length	52'7"	Clearance	18'5"
Beam	16'6"	Fuel	1,000 gals.
Draft	4'8"	Water	400 gals.
Weight	55,000#	Waste	80 gals.
Headroom	6'6"	Hull Type	Semi-Disp.

DeFever 57 Yachtfish

1986–89

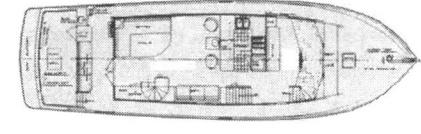

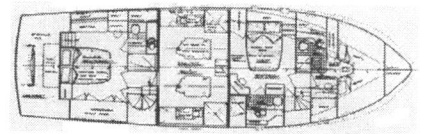

Cockpit version of popular DeFever 53 POC is ideally suited for extended coastal cruising in comfort, security. Three-stateroom floorplan boasts spacious master with private salon access, huge VIP cabin, three full heads, walk-in engine room. Expansive salon with home-size galley, separate dining area features inside bridge access—a convenience not always found in a yacht this size. Side decks are sheltered by bridge overhangs. Hull is fully cored to reduce weight. Twin 375hp Cat diesels cruise at 12 knots (15–16 top).

Prices Not Provided for Pre-1995 Models

Length	56'7"	Clearance	18'5"
Beam	16'6"	Fuel	1,200 gals.
Draft	4'8"	Water	400 gals.
Weight	60,000#	Waste	80 gals.
Headroom	6'6"	Hull Type	Semi-Disp.

Dyna 53 Yachtfisher

1988–92

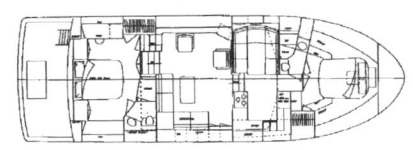

Cockpit version of popular Dyna 46 Sundeck added increased fuel capacity, greater user versatility. Galley-down floorplan permits very expansive salon with entertainment center, L-shaped settee. Lower helm was a popular option; big U-shaped dinette seats six. Note well-crafted interior teak cabinetry. Topside features include hardtop, radar arch, wing doors, wet bar, bow pulpit. Roomy cockpit with transom door is big enough for fishing, diving, swimming. Engineroom is a tight fit. GM 6V92 550hp diesels cruise at 16–18 knots (20+ knots top).

Prices Not Provided for Pre-1995 Models

Length	52'6"	Fuel	750 gals.
Beam	15'6"	Water	250 gals.
Draft	3'6"	Waste	40 gals.
Weight	38,000#	Hull Type	Modified-V
Clearance, Arch	15'6"	Deadrise Aft	14°

Eagle 32 Pilothouse Trawler

1985–98

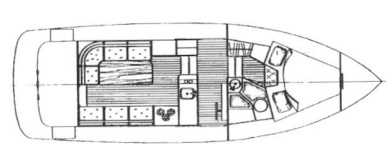

Salty displacement cruiser with tug-like profile offers impressive mix of personality, comfort, economy. Space-efficient teak interior boasts surprisingly roomy salon considering the wide side decks. Good helm visibility from raised pilothouse. Stateroom is small, but head has separate stall shower. Optional upper helm is concealed within false smokestack. Deep keel protects prop. Tremendous eye appeal. Used Eagle 32s are always in demand. Cruise at 7–8 knots with 600-mile range with single 135hp diesel.

See Page 520 For Value Estimates

Length Overall	32'0"	Headroom	6'4"
Length WL	28'0"	Fuel	168 gals.
Beam	11'6"	Water	125 gals.
Draft	3'4"	Waste	25 gals.
Weight	17,000#	Hull Type	Displacement

Eagle 40 Pilothouse Trawler

1994–2002

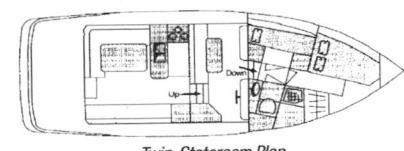

Twin-Stateroom Plan

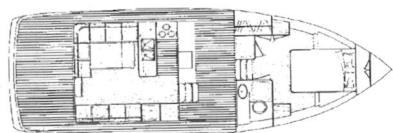

Single-Stateroom Plan

Seaworthy single-diesel trawler with full displacement hull targets seasoned buyers with an eye for quality. Handsome teak interior, available with one or two staterooms, features combined salon/galley with convertible settee, raised pilothouse with settee/watch berth, teak-planked flooring throughout. Note spacious engine room, wide side decks, functional mast and boom. Upper helm is concealed in false stack. Deep keel protects running gear. Excellent joinerwork, first-rate finish. Cruise at 8 knots with single Cummins diesel.

See Page 520 For Value Estimates

Length Overall	40'6"	Clearance	NA
Length WL	36'10"	Fuel	400 gals.
Beam	14'6"	Water	240 gals.
Draft	4'5"	Waste	40 gals.
Weight	28,000#	Hull Type	Displacement

Trawlers & Motoryachts

Trawlers & Motoryachts

Eagle 53 Pilothouse Trawler

2002–Current

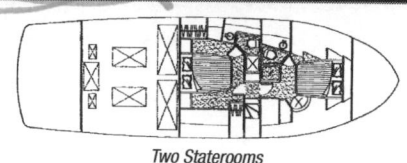

Two Staterooms

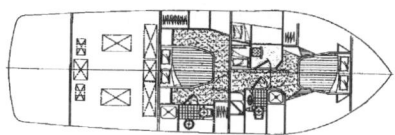

Three Staterooms

Insufficient Resale Data to Assign Values

Quality-built pilothouse yacht with classic lines is designed for extended coastal cruising in comfort, security. Available with two- or three-stateroom layouts (den/office can replace third stateroom) with teak-planked flooring throughout. Bridge overhangs protect side decks and cockpit. Large engine room is a plus. Note watertight pilothouse doors, wave-breaking Portuguese bridge. Semi-displacement hull has long, prop-protecting keel. Cruise at 14–15 knots with 450hp Cummins diesels (about 18 knots top).

Length Overall	53'3"	Headroom	6'6"
Length WL	44'9"	Fuel	830 gals.
Beam	15'9"	Water	250 gals.
Draft	4'0"	Waste	48 gals.
Weight	43,000#	Hull Type	Semi-Disp.

Endeavour TrawlerCat 36

1998–2005

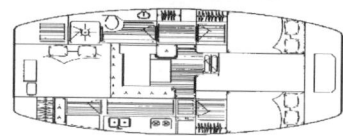

Original Layout

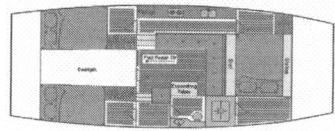

Revised Layout

See Page 521 For Value Estimates

Midsize catamaran trawler sold factory-direct is stable, comfortable, affordable. Highlights include roomy cockpit with standard hardtop. Original three-stateroom interior with double bed aft replaced in 2004 (2005?) with new floorplan with double forward. Comfortable salon overlooks expansive gourmet galley with copious storage in port hull. Teak-and-holly flooring is a nice touch. Note full-beam foredeck, opening front windshield. Wide side decks make getting around easy. Twin 150hp diesels cruise efficiently at 10–12 knots.

Length Overall	36'0"	Clearance	14'0"
Length WL	34'6"	Fuel	300 gals.
Beam	15'0"	Water	90 gals.
Draft	2'10"	Waste	30 gals.
Weight	16,000#	Hull Type	Catamaran

Endeavour TrawlerCat 44

2001–05

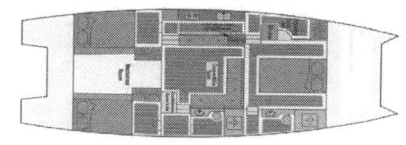

Galley Down

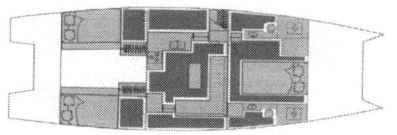

Galley Up

See Page 521 For Value Estimates

Roomy catamaran trawler appeals to cruisers attracted to multihull's seakindly handling, spacious foredeck, impressive economy. Available with galley-down or galley-up layout, both with twin aft staterooms, wide-open salon, two full heads. Topside features include full-beam foredeck, semi-enclosed lower helm, wide side decks, roomy cockpit with lazarette storage. Engines are located under aft-cabin berths; running gear is recessed for grounding protection. Yanmar 240hp diesels cruise at 14–15 knots at better than 1 mpg.

Length Overall	43'5"	Clearance	NA
Length WL	41'0"	Fuel	500 gals.
Beam	18'8"	Water	115 gals.
Draft	3'0"	Waste	50 gals.
Weight	22,800#	Hull Type	Catamaran

Fairline 43 Phantom

2000–04

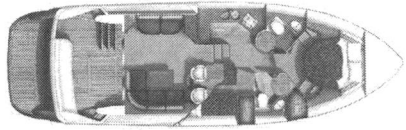

Executive-class flybridge yacht blends seductive styling with lush accommodations, nimble performance. Elegant two-stateroom interior with two full heads boasts facing salon settees, step-down galley with generous storage, high-gloss cherry woodwork. Twin-seat lower helm provides excellent fore, aft visibility. Roomy bridge offers three helm seats, wide sun pad. Note teak-laid cockpit, extended swim platform, electric cabin windows. Engineroom is a tight fit. A good performer, 480hp Volvo diesels cruise at 27 knots (31–32 knots top).

See Page 521 For Value Estimates

Length Overall	44'6"	Fuel	410 gals.
Hull Length	43'1"	Water	209 gals.
Beam	13'7"	Clearance	6'4"
Draft	3'6"	Hull Type	Deep-V
Weight	29,000#	Deadrise Aft	17°

Fairline 46 Phantom

1999–2005

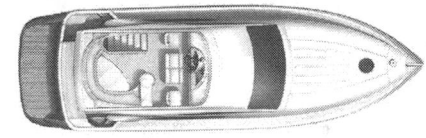

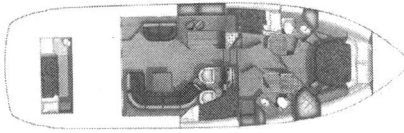

Med-inspired flybridge cruiser offers compelling blend of aggressive styling, spacious accommodations. Three-stateroom floorplan with comfortable salon is rare in a 46-footer; optional crew quarters brings total to four staterooms. Galley is on salon level rather than sunken as it is in many European yachts. Note high-gloss cherry joinery, teak cockpit sole, extended swim platform. Deep-V hull is noted as a good heavy weather performer. Popular model is always in demand. Volvo 480hp diesels cruise at 24 knots (28–29 knots top).

See Page 521 For Value Estimates

Length Overall	47'10"	Fuel	416 gals.
Hull Length	46'0"	Water	187 gals.
Beam	14'2"	Clearance	16'6"
Draft	3'8"	Hull	Deep-V
Weight	29,000#	Deadrise Aft	19°

Fairline 50 Phantom

2002–06

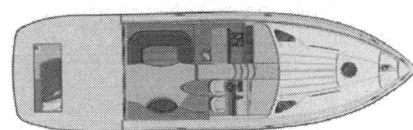

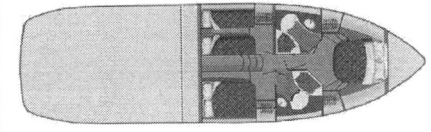

Sleek U.K. flybridge yacht blends world-class engineering with lavish accommodations, sportboat handling. Opulent three-stateroom, two-head interior boasts twin-seat lower helm, full-feature galley, high-gloss cherry woodwork, unique peninsular bar unit in salon. Hatch in cockpit sole opens to reveal cavernous storage area (or optional crew cabin). Note electric cabin windows, standard washer/dryer, pump room for air-conditioning units. Engineroom is tight; galley storage is minimal. Volvo 675hp diesels cruise at 25–26 knots (low 30s top).

See Page 521 For Value Estimates

Length	51'10"	Headroom	6'6"
Beam	14'9"	Fuel	523 gals.
Draft	3'11"	Water	148 gals.
Weight	34,000#	Hull Type	Deep-V
Clearance	17'0"	Deadrise Aft	18°

Trawlers & Motoryachts

Fairline 52 Squadron

1998–2002

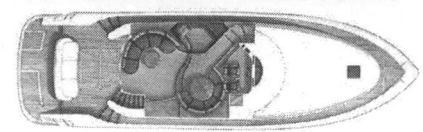

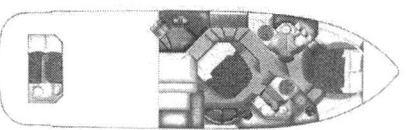

High-end European import with mini-megayacht styling, innovative layout was a bold departure from previous Fairline designs. Standard two-stateroom floorplan—most 52-footers have three staterooms—has rare cabin berth option located off galley. Highlights include spacious, open-plan salon with raised dinette forward, state-of-the-art lower helm, gourmet galley, extravagant master suite with laundry room. Oval flybridge design is completely unusual. Engineroom is a tight fit. Cat 600hp diesels cruise at 25 knots (30 knots top).

See Page 521 For Value Estimates

Length Overall	53'3"	Fuel	576 gals.
Hull Length	52'6"	Water	151 gals.
Beam	15'4"	Clearance	17'5"
Draft	3'8"	Hull	Deep-V
Weight	37,000#	Deadrise Aft	18°

Fairline 55 Squadron

1996–2004

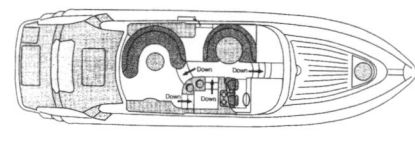

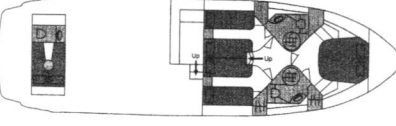

Acclaimed U.K. flybridge yacht matched signature Fairline reputation for big-boat luxury, performance, quality. Remarkably open interior features salon with semi-circular settee, sunken galley, elevated dinette, and lower helm. Note open-tread bridge stairs, large utility room behind galley door. Additional features include extended swim platform, curved salon doors, aft crew quarters, super-large flybridge. Engineroom is a tight fit. Volvo 600hp—or Cat 660hp—diesels cruise at 25–26 knots (30 knots top). Over 160 were built.

See Page 521 For Value Estimates

Length Overall	55'11"	Fuel	576 gals.
Hull Length	54'3"	Water	150 gals.
Beam	15'3"	Clearance	17'3"
Draft	3'8"	Hull Type	Deep-V
Weight	48,000#	Deadrise Aft	18.5°

Fairline 58 Squadron

2002–08

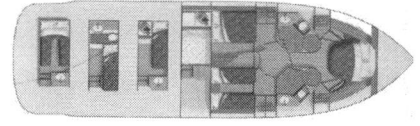

World-class motoryacht is a successful blend of modern European styling, sumptuous accommodations, impressive performance. Three-stateroom floorplan with unusually large heads is identical to earlier Squadron 55 (1999–2004) with opulent salon, sunken galley, elevated dining area forward, crew quarters aft. Note open-tread bridge stairs, large utility room behind galley door. Truly extraordinary bridge layout. Topside features include twin-pillar mast, teak decks, extended swim platform. Cruise at 28 knots with 800hp Cat diesels (low 30s top).

See Page 521 For Value Estimates

Length Overall	58'10"	Headroom	6'6"
Beam	16'0"	Fuel	721 gals.
Draft	4'4"	Water	247 gals.
Weight	44,000#	Hull Type	Deep-V
Clearance	19'9"	Deadrise Aft	18°

Fairline 59 Squadron

1996–99

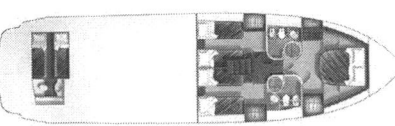

U.K. luxury yacht (called 56 Squadron until 1996 when extended swim platform was added) set 1990's standards for modern motoryacht styling, luxury-class accommodations. Well-appointed interior features split-level salon with open-plan galley, three double cabins forward, optional crew cabin aft. Note inside bridge access, huge storage room beneath galley floor. Large bridge with centerline helm seats ten. Cat or Volvo 600hp diesels cruise at 24 knots (26–27 knots top); optional 680hp MANs cruise at 26 knots (29 knots top).

See Page 521 For Value Estimates

Length Overall	59'9"	Fuel	720 gals.
Hull Length	57'10"	Water	160 gals.
Beam	15'6"	Clearance	18'5"
Draft	3'10"	Hull	Deep-V
Weight	49,200#	Deadrise Aft	18.5°

Fairline 62 Squadron

1999–2002

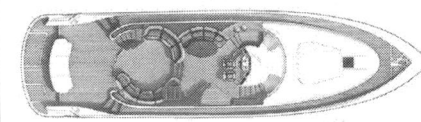

Bold Med-style cruising yacht (based on previous Fairline 52 Squadron) combined then-futuristic styling with avant-garde interior, premium build quality. Classy three-stateroom interior features spacious salon with facing curved sofas, ergonomically perfect lower helm, unique circular owner's stateroom, crew cabin aft. Oval-shaped flybridge with circular lounge, sun pad forward of helm, seats a small crowd. Note twin-pillar mast, teak-laid decks. Galley and engine room are small. Cat 800hp engines deliver top speed of nearly 30 knots.

See Page 521 For Value Estimates

Length Overall	64'5"	Fuel	991 gals.
Hull Length	63'1"	Water	265 gals.
Beam	16'5"	Clearance	18'10"
Draft	4'6"	Hull	Deep-V
Weight	62,700#	Deadrise Aft	18°

Fairline 65 Squadron

1995–2003

Seductive Euroyacht with striking profile made good on Fairline promise of cutting-edge design, deluxe accommodations. Extravagant four-stateroom, three-head interior includes well-appointed salon with leather seating, full-beam master suite with king bed, enormous master bath, polished cherry woodwork. Galley has pass-through to helm, washer/dryer closet. Note fore and aft crew cabins. Restyled in 1998 for a more streamlined profile. Popular model. Cruise at 25 knots with MAN 1,100hp engines (about 30 knots top).

See Page 521 For Value Estimates

Length Overall	66'10"	Clearance	NA
Hull Length	65'0"	Fuel	1,105 gals.
Beam	17'4"	Water	336 gals.
Draft	4'9"	Hull	Deep-V
Weight	71,680#	Deadrise Aft	19°

Trawlers & Motoryachts

Fairline 74 Squadron

2003–07

Largest Fairline ever combines iconic Med styling with world-class accommodations, state-of-the-art construction. Beautiful four-stateroom interior with sumptuous salon, formal dining area, enclosed galley, opulent owner's suite is designed to pamper and impress. Steel-and-glass salon door opens to spacious teak cockpit with tender garage, small crew cabin below. Note narrow cabin windows, stand-up engine room. Massive bridge includes grill, refrigerator, sun lounge. MAN 1,550hp engines cruise in the high 20s (30+ knots top).

See Page 521 For Value Estimates

Length Overall	74'5"	Fuel	1,556 gals.
Beam	18'8"	Water	333 gals.
Draft	5'3"	Waste	100 gals.
Weight	81,200#	Hull Type	Deep-V
Clearance	24'11"	Deadrise Aft	18°

Ferretti 680 Motor Yacht

1999–2005

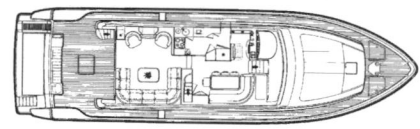

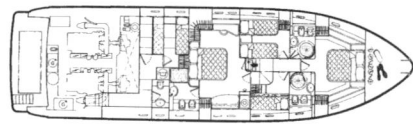

Acclaimed flybridge yacht introduced in 1999 confirmed Ferretti reputation for compelling styling, executive-class accommodations. Four-stateroom floorplan was standard but several alternate arrangements were also available. Interior highlights include opulent full-beam master suite, condo-size galley, dining table for eight, aft crew quarters. Huge flybridge offers every possible amenity. Note PWC storage in swim platform, hidden passerelle, teak decks. An excellent performer, twin 1,360hp V-drive MANs cruise at 27–28 knots and reach 30+ knots top.

Insufficient Resale Data to Assign Values

Length Overall	69'6"	Fuel	1,102 gals.
Hull Length	67'8"	Water	277 gals.
Beam	18'6"	Clearance	18'9"
Draft	5'8"	Hull Type	Modified-V
Weight	99,225#	Deadrise Aft	12°

Ferretti 72 Motor Yacht

1997–2002

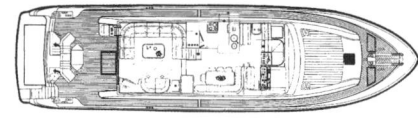

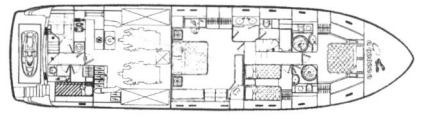

Richly appointed motoryacht matches world-class styling with unsurpassed luxury, powerful performance. Elegant cherrywood paneling, meticulously joined furniture grace salon and staterooms. Notable features include enclosed galley with deck door, formal dining area, extravagant full-beam master, crew quarters with berths for three. Swim platform serves as a garage for PWC. Additional features include teak decks, engine room work area, huge bridge with dinghy storage. MTU 1,150hp diesels cruise at a fast 28 knots (32–33 knots top).

Insufficient Resale Data to Assign Values

Length Overall	73'3"	Clearance	20'4"
Hull Length	72'3"	Fuel	1,321 gals.
Beam	18'0"	Water	264 gals.
Draft	5'8"	Hull Type	Modified-V
Weight	97,020#	Deadrise Aft	15.5°

Trawlers & Motoryachts

Fleming 55 Pilothouse

1986–Current

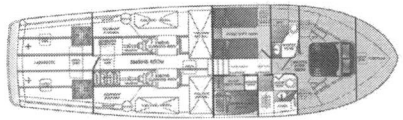

World-class pilothouse yacht built to exceptional standards makes the grade with owners demanding uncompromising quality. Highlights include full teak interior, three large staterooms, wave-breaking Portuguese bridge, protected side decks, spacious cockpit. Easily driven hull has long, prop-protecting keel. Excellent visibility from raised pilothouse. Note inside bridge access, flybridge pass-thru to galley, teak decks, large storage lazarette. A classic yacht with over 200 built. Cat 435hp—or Cummins 450hp—diesels cruise at 15–16 knots.

See Page 522 For Value Estimates

Length Overall	55'9"	Clearance, Arch	16'0"
Length WL	50'10"	Fuel	1,000 gals.
Beam	16'0"	Water	300 gals.
Draft	5'0"	Waste	100 gals.
Weight	66,000#	Hull Type	Semi-Disp.

Fleming 65 Pilothouse

2006–Current

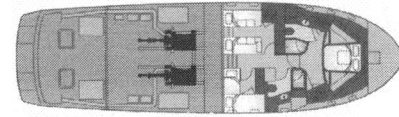

Highly regarded pilothouse yacht blends exceptional beauty with luxurious accommodations, unsurpassed build quality. Maxi-volume interior boasts spacious salon with integrated galley and dining area, raised pilothouse with day head and dinette, opulent master suite, two VIP guest cabins. Note protective Portuguese bridge, stand-up engine room, spacious cockpit, feature-packed flybridge with extended hardtop. This is as good as it gets in a long-range yacht. Cruise at 12–14 knots (18 top) with 800hp Cat diesels.

See Page 522 For Value Estimates

Length Overall	65'0"	Clearance, Arch	22'11"
Length WL	59'2"	Fuel	1,700 gals.
Beam	18'8"	Water	400 gals.
Draft	5'0"	Waste	100 gals.
Weight	108,000#	Hull Type	Semi-Disp.

Fleming 75 Pilothouse

2001–Current

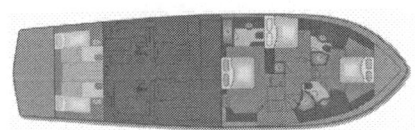

Sophisticated long-range cruising yacht combines traditional styling with world-class luxury, unsurpassed build quality. Handsome teak interior includes two en suite guest cabins, full-beam owner's cabin, spacious salon with galley, dinette forward. Note day head in pilothouse, posh crew cabin aft. Additional features include wide, well-protected side decks, huge engine room, bow thruster, underwater exhausts. Cat 800hp diesels offer a cruising range of 1,500 miles at 10 knots. Optional 1,400hp Cats cruise at 18 knots (20+ knots top).

See Page 522 For Value Estimates

Length Overall	75'0"	Clearance	NA
Length WL	68'10"	Fuel	3,000 gals.
Beam	21'5"	Water	500 gals.
Draft	5'3"	Headroom	6'6"
Weight	165,000#	Hull Type	Semi-Disp.

Trawlers & Motoryachts

Grand Alaskan 60/64 Pilothouse

1998–2006

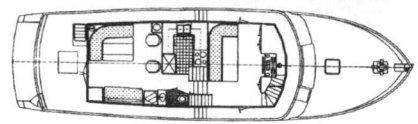

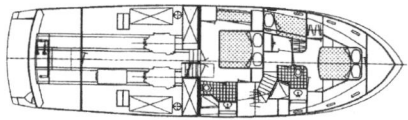

Popular pilothouse yacht with classic DeFever styling was designed for extended cruising in maximum comfort, security. Expansive three-stateroom teak interior includes midships master with private salon entry, VIP guest stateroom forward, home-size galley with breakfast bar, day head forward in salon. Stabilizers, granite counters, bow thruster are standard. Note Portuguese bridge, prop-protected keel. Alaskan 64 differs from 60 model in her enlarged salon, engine room and cockpit. Over 30 were built. Cruise at 12–14 knots with 715hp C-12 Cats.

Insufficient Resale Data to Assign Values

Length	64'0"	Fuel, Std.	1,300 gals.
Beam	17'2"	Water	400 gals.
Draft	4'9"	Waste	100 gals.
Weight	85,000#	Hull Type	Semi-Disp.
Clearance	NA	Deadrise Aft	NA

Grand Alaskan 65 Flushdeck

2001–Current

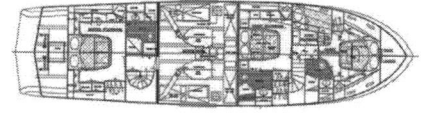

Handsome long-range motoryacht couples traditional pilothouse profile with elegant teak interior, seaworthy semi-displacement hull. Four-stateroom, three-head layout includes large pilothouse with dinette, gourmet galley with serving counter, spacious full-beam master, two VIP guest staterooms, deckhouse day head, stand-up engine room, covered side decks, fishing cockpit, large swim platform. Stabilizers, granite counters, bow thruster are standard. Note Portuguese bridge, expansive foredeck. Cruise at 12–14 knots with 660hp Cats.

Insufficient Resale Data to Assign Values

Length Overall	65'0"	Headroom	6'5"
Beam	17'2"	Fuel	1,300 gals.
Draft	4'9"	Water	300 gals.
Weight	80,000#	Waste	100 gals.
Clearance	NA	Hull Type	Semi-Disp.

Grand Banks 32 Sedan

1965–95

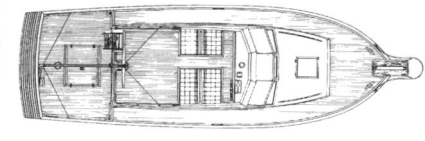

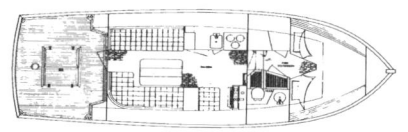

Polished sedan cruiser still commands admiration for her classic trawler profile, top-notch construction, great resale values. Single-stateroom interior with convertible salon settees, fully equipped galley is perfect for the cruising couple. Large engine room provides good service access. Cockpit is large enough for fishing. Superb fit and finish throughout. Wood construction until 1973. Long keel protects prop and rudder. Total of 861 were built. Cruise at 6–8 knots with single 120hp or 135hp Lehman diesel.

See Page 523 For Value Estimates

Length Overall	31'11"	Headroom	6'4"
Length WL	30'9"	Fuel	225/250 gals.
Beam	11'6"	Water	110 gals.
Draft	3'9"	Waste	30 gals.
Weight	17,000#	Hull Type	Semi-Disp.

Grand Banks 36 Classic

1965–2004

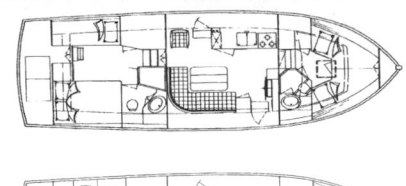

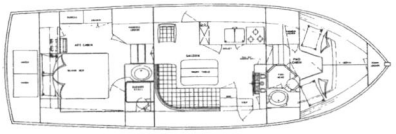

Highly regarded aft-cabin trawler enjoys lofty reputation for beauty, comfort, quality and seaworthiness. Several twin-stateroom interiors were offered over the years, all with solid teak woodwork, premium hardware, superb finish. Large aft stateroom has direct cockpit access. Keel protects prop and rudder. Updated in 1988 when 4 inches were added to beam. Wood construction until mid-1973. No production in 1997–99. Over 1,200 built. Cruise efficiently at 7–8 knots with single 135hp Lehman diesel; 10 knots with twins.

See Page 523 For Value Estimates

Length Overall	36'10"	Clearance, Mast	22'4"
Length WL	35'2"	Fuel	400 gals.
Beam	12'8"	Water	154 gals.
Draft	4'0"	Waste	40 gals.
Weight	26,000#	Hull Type	Semi-Disp.

Grand Banks 36 Europa

1988–98

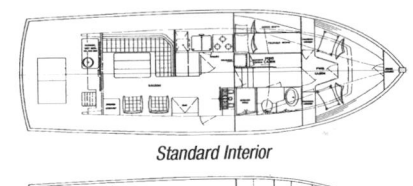

Standard Interior

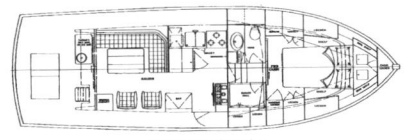

Alternate Interior

Handsome sedan trawler with classic Europa styling appeals to upscale cruisers who value nautical beauty, boat-building excellence. Highlights include elegant two-stateroom teak interior, protected side decks, extended hardtop, mast and boom, teak decks, bow pulpit, deep, prop-protecting keel. Single-stateroom layout with divided head was optional. The standard by which other sedan trawlers her size are measured. Single 135hp Lehman diesel will cruise at 7–8 knots; twin 210hp Cummins diesels cruise at 10–12 knots.

See Page 523 For Value Estimates

Length Overall	36'10"	Headroom	6'4"
Length WL	35'2"	Fuel	400 gals.
Beam	12'8"	Water	170/205 gals.
Draft	4'0"	Waste	40 gals.
Weight	27,000#	Hull Type	Semi-Disp.

Grand Banks 36 Motor Yacht

1995–98

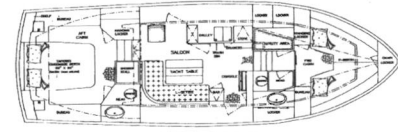

Standard Interior

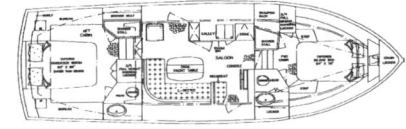

Alternate Interior

Distinctive cruising yacht combines iconic Grand Banks quality with timeless styling, roomy accommodations. Highlights include full teak interior, spacious owner stateroom, sliding deck access door, teak parquet flooring, meticulous engine room. Standard floorplan features utility area forward, opposite the head; alternate floorplan has separate stall shower in place of utility space, island bed forward. Note opening front windshield, generous galley storage. Wide side decks are a plus. Cruise at 12–14 knots with twin 210 Cummins diesels.

See Page 523 For Value Estimates

Length Overall	36'10"	Headroom	6'4"
Length WL	35'2"	Fuel	400 gals.
Beam	12'8"	Water	140 gals.
Draft	4'0"	Waste	40 gals.
Weight	27,000#	Hull Type	Semi-Disp.

Trawlers & Motoryachts

Grand Banks 36 Sedan

1986–96

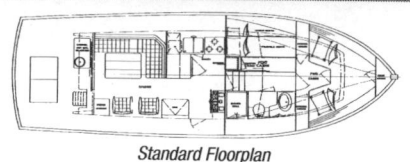

Standard Floorplan

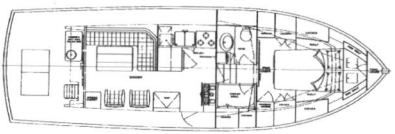

Alternate Floorplan

See Page 523 For Value Estimates

Elegant sedan cruiser with extended salon, spacious flybridge sets class standard for engineering, comfort, seakeeping qualities. Standard two-stateroom layout is a model of space utilization. Highlights include full teak interior, large U-shaped galley, lower helm deck door, head with separate stall shower, roomy engine compartment, wide side decks. Front windshield opens for ventilation. Long keel protects prop and rudder from damage. Single 135hp diesel will cruise at 8 knots; twin 210hp Cummins cruise at 12 knots.

Length Overall	36'10"	Headroom	6'4"
Length WL	35'2"	Fuel	400 gals.
Beam	12'8"	Water	205 gals.
Draft	4'0"	Waste	40 gals.
Weight	26,000#	Hull Type	Semi-Disp.

Grand Banks 41 Heritage EU

2009–Current

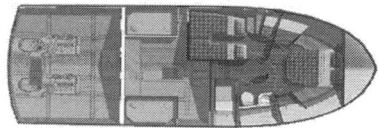

See Page 523 For Value Estimates

Handsome "fast trawler" with refined Europa profile, new hull form is the first Grand Banks model designed for Zeus pod drives. Well-appointed galley-up, two-stateroom interior features expansive salon with facing settees, lower helm with deck access door, huge head, teak-planked flooring throughout. Full-beam utility room beneath salon sole accommodates optional washer/dryer, workbench. Note cockpit engine room access. Keel protects pods from grounding. Cummins 425hp diesels cruise at 15–16 knots (20+ knots wide open).

Length Overall	41'4"	Clearance, Mast	19'4"
Length WL	37'11"	Fuel	500 gals.
Beam	15'8"	Water	195 gals.
Draft	3'9"	Waste	50 gals.
Weight	40,200#	Hull Type	Semi-Disp.

Grand Banks 42 Classic

1975–2004

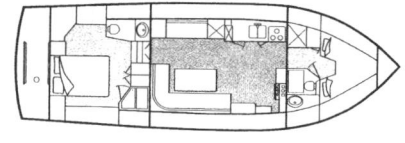

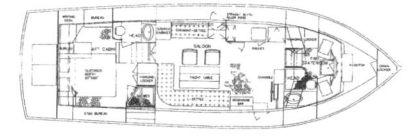

See Page 523 For Value Estimates

Iconic double-cabin trawler (over 1,500 were built) is easily the most successful trawler design ever produced. Several two-stateroom floorplans were offered over the years. Highlights include full teak interior, port/starboard salon doors, wide side decks, roomy flybridge, protected prop. Mahogany construction prior to 1973. Hull was widened, lengthened in 1992 for larger galley, bigger forward stateroom. Fine bow delivers superb head sea performance. Twin 210hp Cats cruise at 10 knots; 375hp Cats cruise at 14–15 knots.

Length Overall	42'7"/43'3"	Clearance, Mast	22'6"
Length WL	41'1"	Fuel	600 gals.
Beam	13'7"/14'1"	Water	271 gals.
Draft	4'2"	Waste	50 gals.
Weight	37,400#	Hull Type	Semi-Disp.

Grand Banks 42 Europa

1979–90; 96–04

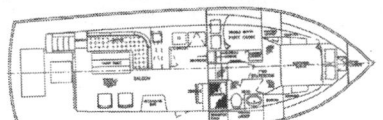

Standard Layout

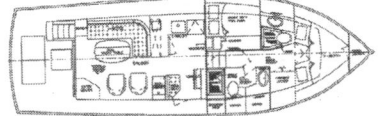

Optional Layout

Elegant sedan trawler blends Europa styling with top-quality construction, time-tested layout. Standard two-stateroom teak interior boasts big U-shaped galley galley, queen berth forward, stall showers in both heads. Cockpit and side decks are protected by bridge overhangs. Note teak decks, large cockpit lazarette, prop-protecting keel. Production discontinued in 1990, resumed in 1996 when hull was redesigned with wider beam. Among several engine choices, 210hp Cats cruise at 10 knots; 375hp Cats cruise at 14–15 knots.

See Page 524 For Value Estimates

Length Overall	43'3"	Clearance, Mast	22'9"
Beam (1979–90)	13'7"	Fuel	600 gals.
Beam (1996–2004)	14'1"	Water	278 gals.
Draft	4'2"	Waste	50 gals.
Weight	39,000#	Hull Type	Semi-Disp.

Grand Banks 42 Motor Yacht

1987–2004

Standard Floorplan

Optional Floorplan

Motoryacht version of GB 42 Classic combines enlarged master stateroom layout with full-beam afterdeck, standard three-stateroom floorplan. Highlights include full teak interior, port/starboard salon doors, wide side decks, fold-down mast, roomy flybridge, bow pulpit, protected prop. Note simulated lapstrake hull lines. Two-stateroom, galley down interior was optional. Note that hull redesign in 1992 increased width, length by several inches. Exemplary fit and finish. Twin 210hp Cats cruise at 10 knots; 375 Cats cruise at 14–15 knots.

See Page 524 For Value Estimates

Length Overall	42'7"/43'3"	Clearance, Mast	25'6"
Length WL	41'1"	Fuel	600 gals.
Beam	13'7"/14'1"	Water	237 gals.
Draft	4'2"	Waste	50 gals.
Weight	40,700#	Hull Type	Semi-Disp.

Grand Banks 43 Eastbay Flybridge

1998–2004

Standard Floorplan

Optional Layout

Gold-plated flybridge yacht (called Eastbay 40 until 1998 when cockpit was lengthened) with timeless Downeast styling delivers impressive blend of luxury, craftsmanship, performance. Elegant two-stateroom interior with lower helm, deluxe galley, features handcrafted teak cabinetry, top-quality hardware and furnishings. Spacious cockpit with transom door can entertain a small crowd. Note wide side decks. Twin 300hp Cat diesels cruise at 18–20 knots (about 22 knots top); 375hp Cats cruise at 22–24 knots (high 20s top).

See Page 524 For Value Estimates

Length	43'0"	Fuel	450 gals.
Beam	13'4"	Water	110 gals.
Draft	3'8"	Headroom	6'6"
Weight	31,970#	Hull Type	Deep-V
Clearance	16'6"	Deadrise Aft	18°

Trawlers & Motoryachts

Trawlers & Motoryachts

Grand Banks 46 Classic

1987–2007

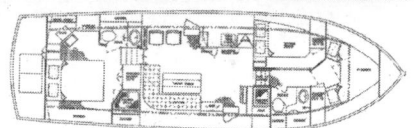

Standard Layout

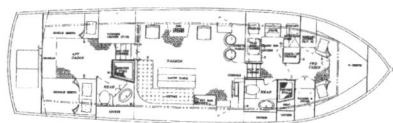

Optional Layout

See Page 524 For Value Estimates

Acclaimed long-range trawler introduced in 1987 makes good on promise of luxury-class accommodations, exceptional owner satisfaction. Three-stateroom interior was standard, two-stateroom layout was optional. Highlights include hand-crafted teak cabinetry, parquet flooring, large engine room, teak walkaround decks, fold-down mast, bow pulpit, simulated lapstrake hull. Tooling updated in 1988 (hull #43) to provide slightly wider side decks aft. The perfect cruising yacht. Twin Cat or Cummins diesels cruise at 12–14 knots.

Length Overall	47'1"	Clearance, Mast	23'7"
Length WL	44'10"	Fuel	630 gals.
Beam	14'9"	Water	300 gals.
Draft	4'5"	Waste	80 gals.
Weight	42,960#	Hull Type	Semi-Disp.

Grand Banks 46 Europa

1993–2008

Standard Floorplan

Optional Floorplan

See Page 524 For Value Estimates

Gold-plated cruising yacht combines sporty Europa styling with luxury-class amenities, unsurpassed quality. Well-appointed interior includes two comfortable staterooms, lower helm with deck door, generous storage, teak parquet flooring. Salon opens to covered cockpit with stairway to flybridge. Additional features include teak decks, extended hardtop, covered side decks, cockpit engine room access, protected running gear. Exemplary fit and finish. Cummins 210hp diesels cruise at 10 knots; 435hp Cats cruise at 12–14 knots.

Length Overall	47'1"	Clearance, Mast	21'5"
Length WL	44'10"	Fuel	630 gals.
Beam	14'9"	Water	276 gals.
Draft	4'5"	Waste	80 gals.
Weight	43,000#	Hull Type	Semi-Disp.

Grand Banks 46 Motor Yacht

1990–2001

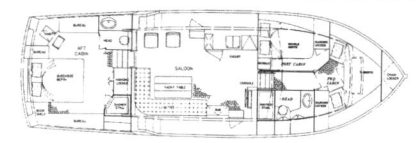

Standard Floorplan

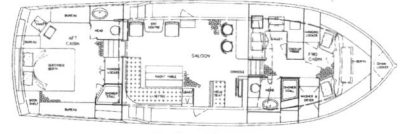

Optional Layout

See Page 524 For Value Estimates

Distinctive trawler-style motoryacht from 1990s offers luxury, comfort on a grand scale. Standard three-cabin interior has deckhouse galley; optional twin-cabin layout with galley down has expanded salon, optional washer/dryer forward. Note salon deck doors, huge full-beam master stateroom, solid teak woodwork. Large aft deck is enclosed by safety rails. Large engine room is a plus. Outstanding craftsmanship throughout. Twin 135hp Lehman diesels cruise at 8 knots; 375hp Cats cruise at 12–13 knots (about 16 knots top).

Length Overall	47'1"	Clearance, Mast	23'7"
Length WL	44'9"	Fuel	600 gals.
Beam	14'9"	Water	290 gals.
Draft	4'4"	Headroom	6'4"
Weight	39,000#	Hull Type	Semi-Disp.

Grand Banks 47 Eastbay Flybridge

2005–Current

Standard Floorplan

Optional Layout

See Page 524 For Value Estimates

Elegant Downeast flybridge yacht boasts top-drawer build quality with spacious accommodations, luxury amenities. Available with standard two-cabin layout or optional single-cabin floorplan with two heads, open-plan "office" with sofa bed in place of second stateroom. Highlights include Burmese teak interior, wide side decks, unique spiral bridge staircase, large cockpit with built-in seating. Note teak cockpit sole, fold-down radar mast, spacious engine room. Cruise at 25 knots (about 30 knots top) with 720hp Caterpillar diesels.

Length Overall	52'4"	Fuel	700 gals.
Length WL	43'3"	Water	206 gals.
Beam	15'0"	Waste	75 gals.
Draft	3'10"	Hull Type	Deep-V
Weight	47,900#	Deadrise Aft	18°

Grand Banks 47 Heritage Classic

2007–Current

Standard Layout

Optional Layout

See Page 524 For Value Estimates

Updated version of classic Grand Banks tri-cabin blends new high-performance hull with traditional trawler profile. Standard twin-stateroom interior features chart table/entertainment center with pop-up TV, step-down galley with granite counters, teak plank flooring. Roomy flybridge offers lounge seating around beautiful teak table. Note teak side decks, frameless windows, aft salon entry, spacious engine room, expanded lazarette. Three-stateroom interior also available. Cat 567hp diesels cruise at 16–18 knots (20+ knots top).

Length Overall	46'10"	Fuel	600 gals.
Length WL	44'1"	Water	260 gals.
Beam	15'9"	Waste	77 gals.
Draft	3'10"	Hull Type	Modified-V
Weight	52,333#	Deadrise Aft	18°

Grand Banks 47 Heritage Europa

2007–Current

Standard Layout

Optional Layout

See Page 524 For Value Estimates

Next-generation Europa built on modified-V hull combines planing-speed performance with graceful styling, signature Grand Bank's quality. Highlights include elegant teak interior with granite counters, teak-plank flooring throughout, extended aft-deck overhang, teak decks, protected side decks, frameless windows, flybridge stairway, meticulous engine room. Guest cabin can be configured as office. Space in second head for washer/dryer. Hull extends under swim platform. Cat 567hp diesels cruise at 16–17 knots (over 20 knots top).

Length Overall	46'10"	Fuel	600 gals.
Length WL	44'1"	Water	260 gals.
Beam	15'9"	Waste	77 gals.
Draft	3'10"	Hull Type	Modified-V
Weight	51,233#	Deadrise Aft	18°

Grand Banks 49 Classic

1980–97

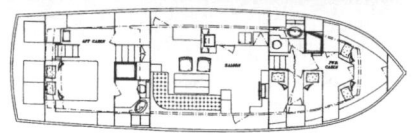

Standard Floorplan

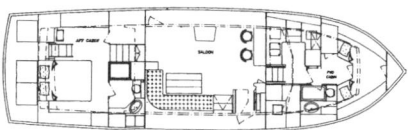

Optional Layout

See Page 524 For Value Estimates

Sought-after Grand Banks cruising yacht set class standards in her era for graceful trawler styling, world-class construction. Standard three-stateroom interior boasts spacious master with cockpit access door, teak parquet flooring, twin salon deck doors. Teak walkaround decks are broad, secure; standup engine room is spacious and carefully detailed. Note space in galley for washer/dryer. Popular model—about 125 were built. Early models with 120hp Lehman diesels cruise at 8 knots; later models with 210hp Cats cruise at 10–12 knots.

Length Overall	50'6"	Clearance, Mast	26'5"
Length WL	48'9"	Fuel	1,000 gals.
Beam	15'5"	Water	500 gals.
Draft	5'1"	Waste	60 gals.
Weight	60,000#	Hull Type	Semi-Disp.

Grand Banks 49 Motor Yacht

1986–99

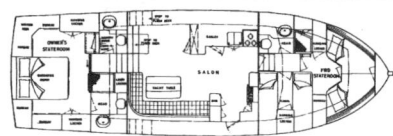

Standard Floorplan

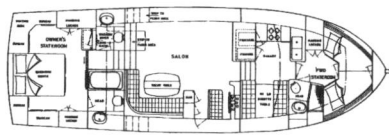

Optional Layout

See Page 524 For Value Estimates

Quintessential Grand Banks trawler yacht introduced in 1986 took motoryacht elegance, sophistication to the next level. Three-stateroom, galley-up interior was standard; optional twin-cabin layout with galley down has expanded salon. Highlights include spacious, full-beam master stateroom, expansive salon with parquet flooring, stand-up engine room. Large aft deck—enclosed by safety rail—has room for a small party. Wide side decks with high protective bulwarks are a plus. Cruise at 14 knots (18 top) with 375hp Cat diesels.

Length Overall	50'6"	Clearance	NA
Length WL	48'9"	Fuel	1,000 gals.
Beam	15'5"	Water	500 gals.
Draft	5'2"	Waste	60 gals.
Weight	60,000#	Hull Type	Semi-Disp.

Grand Banks 52 Europa

1998–2008

See Page 524 For Value Estimates

Luxury-class motoryacht was an evolutionary step up in size, comfort, for Grand Banks when introduced in 1998. Deluxe accommodations include home-size gourmet galley, open dinette, entertainment center, slide-away pilothouse privacy door, full-beam master suite. Expansive salon affords clear view from helm to aft deck. Optional lower-level layout has engine room forward, master stateroom aft. Note protected side decks, spacious flybridge. A graceful, gold-plated cruising yacht. Cat 660hp diesels cruise at 15 knots (18–19 knots top).

Length Overall	54'1"	Clearance, Mast	29'0"
Length WL	51'9"	Fuel	1,200 gals.
Beam	15'5"	Water	500 gals.
Draft	4'10"	Waste	56 gals.
Weight	58,000#	Hull Type	Semi-Disp.

Grand Banks 58 Classic

1990–2002

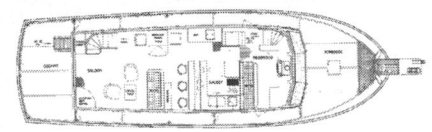

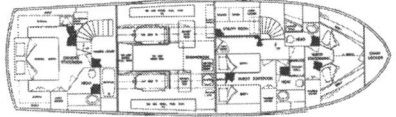

Stoutly built offshore yacht designed for extended cruising offers top-shelf construction, spacious interior, unsurpassed comforts. Lavish three-stateroom floorplan features full-beam master suite with private entry, wide-open salon, country-kitchen galley, enclosed pilothouse with centerline helm. Bridge overhangs shelter side decks and cockpit from weather. Note stand-up engine room, huge flybridge with dinghy storage, utility room with washer/dryer. At a 9-knot cruising speed, 375hp Cat diesels deliver a range of some 1,400 miles.

See Page 524 For Value Estimates

Length Overall	58'11"	Clearance	17'6"
Length WL	54'4"	Fuel	1,400 gals.
Beam	17'6"	Water	450 gals.
Draft	5'6"	Waste	80 gals.
Weight	100,000#	Hull Type	Semi-Disp.

Grand Banks 58 Eastbay Flybridge

Trawlers & Motoryachts

2004–07

Standard Layout

Optional Layout

Prestigious flybridge yacht with gorgeous Downeast styling sets class standard for cruising elegance. Opulent three-stateroom, galley-down interior boasts wide-open salon; optional galley-up layout provides fourth cabin that may also serve as an office. Highlights include lower-helm deck door, holding-plate refrigeration, stand-up engine room, wide side decks. Note curved bridge staircase, teak cockpit sole. Stidd helm seats, cockpit wet bar, bow thruster are standard. Cat 1,400hp diesels deliver a top speed of over 30 knots.

See Page 524 For Value Estimates

Length w/Platform	63'5"	Clearance	18'9"
Hull Length	58'8"	Fuel	1,175 gals.
Beam	17'8"	Water	280 gals.
Draft	5'4"	Hull Type	Deep-V
Weight	91,000#	Deadrise Aft	21°

Grand Banks 59 Aleutian RP

2007–Current

Sumptuous long-range cruiser delivers impressive mix of timeless style, aggressive performance, top-quality construction. Lavish teak interior with raised pilothouse sleeps six in two large double staterooms—including full-beam master—and one twin cabin. Topside features include hardtop, spacious flybridge with twin teak tables, protected side decks, teak decks, curved cockpit staircase. Note convenient pass-through between galley and flybridge. Cat C18 (1,000hp) diesels cruise at 20–22 knots (about 25 knots top).

See Page 524 For Value Estimates

Length Overall	58'7"	Fuel	1,400 gals.
Length WL	55'4"	Water	385 gals.
Beam	18'0"	Waste	110 gals.
Draft	5'4"	Hull Type	Modified-V
Weight	90,000#	Deadrise Aft	16°

Grand Banks 64 Aleutian RP

2002–07

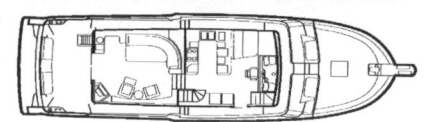

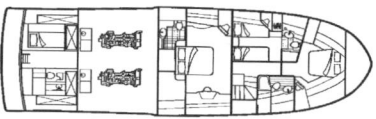

Original Grand Banks Aleutian model pairs impressive accommodations with graceful styling, luxury-class amenities. Raised pilothouse interior includes expansive main salon with entertainment center, huge U-shaped galley with Corian counters, opulent master stateroom with engine room access. Lazarette can house optional crew quarters. Note Portuguese bridge, watertight engine room bulkheads. A stately yacht built to very high standards. Modified-V hull with prop pockets will cruise at 18 knots with 800hp Cat diesels.

Insufficient Resale Data to Assign Values

Length Overall	64'4"	Fuel	2,200 gals.
Length WL	59'4"	Water	440 gals.
Beam	19'10"	Waste	150 gals.
Draft	5'6"	Hull Type	Modified-V
Weight	105,000#	Deadrise Aft	14°

Grand Banks 72 Aleutian

2006–Current

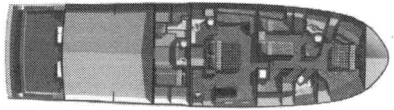

Cockpit version of Grand Banks 64 Aleutian combines cruising opulence with timeless styling, fuel-efficient operation. Basic configuration is same as the 64 Aleutian: three-stateroom interior with open-plan salon/pilothouse/galley is designed so that second guest cabin can be used as office. Engineroom is accessed from master stateroom or cockpit. Lazarette can house optional crew quarters. Note Portuguese bridge, generous fuel capacity, protected side decks. Fexas-designed hull with long keel, prop pockets will cruise at 18 knots with 1,015hp Cat diesels.

See Page 524 For Value Estimates

Length Overall	76'0"	Fuel	2,625 gals.
Length WL	64'5"	Water	350 gals.
Beam	19'10"	Waste	150 gals.
Draft	5'4"	Hull Type	Modified-V
Weight	111,000#	Deadrise Aft	14°

Great Harbour 37

1998–Current

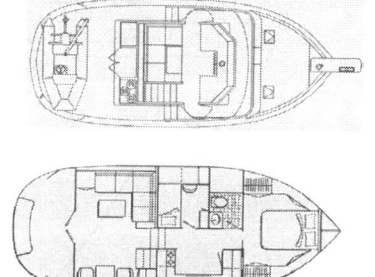

Maxi-volume liveaboard with ship-like profile targets coastal cruisers seeking true condo-style accommodations. Beamy, high-sided hull conceals tremendous interior volume with full-beam salon, home-size galley, two staterooms, covered aft cockpit, raised pilothouse with convertible settee and pilot berth. Note standard washer/dryer. Portuguese bridge surrounds pilothouse. Beachable! More small ship than boat. Designed for near-shore and coastal cruising. Cruise at an economical 7–8 knots with twin 56hp Yanmar diesels.

Insufficient Resale Data to Assign Values

Length Overll	36'10"	Clearance	14'8"
Length WL	36'1"	Fuel	500 gals.
Beam	15'10"	Water	300 gals.
Draft	2'10"	Waste	100 gals.
Weight	48,000#	Hull Type	Displacement

Gulfstar 44 Motor Yacht

1985–88

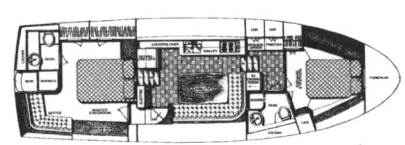

Roomy double-cabin motoryacht with fully enclosed after-deck delivers big-boat accommodations in a midsize hull. Early models have walkaround decks; later models (called 44 MK II) replace open aft deck of original models with fully enclosed, full-beam main salon. Highlights include quality teak interior joinery, washer/dryer, walk-in engine room with seawater intake chest. Note home-size galley/dinette, large aft stateroom with aft-facing bed. Twin 300hp Cat diesels cruise at 16 knots (19–20 knots top).

Prices Not Provided for Pre-1995 Models

Length Overall	43'9"	Clearance	17'0"
Length WL	39'1"	Fuel	400 gals.
Beam	15'0"	Water	200 gals.
Draft	3'6"	Hull Type	Modified-V
Weight	36,400#	Deadrise Aft	NA

Gulfstar 49 Motor Yacht

1984–87

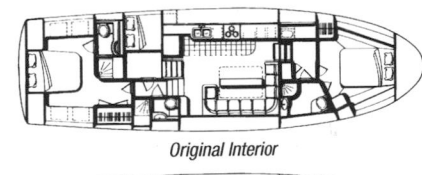

Original Interior

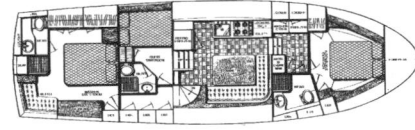

Alternate Interior

Updated version of Gulfstar 48 MY (1981–83) rivals bigger boats for liveaboard comforts, cruising amenities. Enclosed afterdeck serves as main salon, while mid-level deckhouse—the salon in most motoryachts—houses big country-kitchen galley. Laundry center was standard; small aft-deck platform is provided for line-handling. Additional features include teak interior joinery, spacious engine room (with seawater intake chest), bow pulpit. Perkins 350hp diesels cruise at 12 knots; 435hp GM 6-71s will cruise at 16–17 knots.

Prices Not Provided for Pre-1995 Models

Length Overall	49'0"	Clearance	17'0"
Length WL	44'4"	Fuel	675 gals.
Beam	15'1"	Water	370 gals.
Draft	3'10"	Hull Type	Semi-Disp.
Weight	42,000#	Deadrise Aft	NA

Hampton 580 Pilothouse

2008–Current

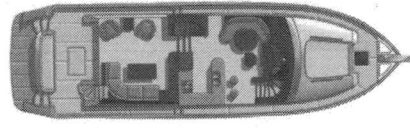

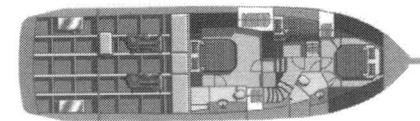

Full-bodied cruiser with modern pilothouse styling matches top-shelf construction with posh accommodations, impressive standard feature list. Highlights include expansive three-stateroom, two-head layout with open-galley design, high-gloss cherry woodwork, deluxe master suite with copious stowage, standup engine room with transom entry. Wheelhouse deck doors are a plus. Wesmar stabilizer, bow thruster, cockpit controls are standard. Note huge lazarette, bow anchor chute. Twin Cummins 715hp diesels cruise at 16 knots (20–21 knots top).

See Page 524 For Value Estimates

Length	59'10"	Fuel	900 gals.
Beam	17'3"	Water	250 gals.
Draft	4'8"	Waste	100 gals.
Weight	66,000#	Hull Type	Modified-V
Clearance	20'6"	Deadrise Aft	12°

Trawlers & Motoryachts

Hatteras 40 Motor Yacht

1986–97

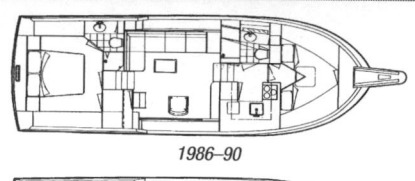

1986–90

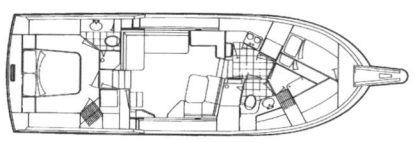

1989–97

See Page 525 For Value Estimates

Good-selling pocket motoryacht gets high marks for classic styling, comfortable accommodations, solid construction. Surprising amount of interior space for a 40-footer. Highlights include full-beam master stateroom, well-appointed salon, large aft deck. Excellent fit and finish. Flybridge redesigned in 1990 when helm was moved forward. Last of the "small" Hatteras motoryachts. Very popular model—over 120 were built. Cruise at 18 knots with Cat 340hp diesels (low 20s top).

Length	40'10"	Fuel	359 gals.
Beam	13'7"	Water	110 gals.
Draft	4'9"	Waste	60 gals.
Weight	38,000#	Hull Type	Modified-V
Clearance	15'9"	Deadrise Aft	14°

Hatteras 42 Cockpit MY

1993–97

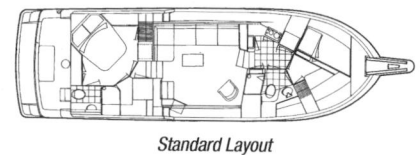

Standard Layout

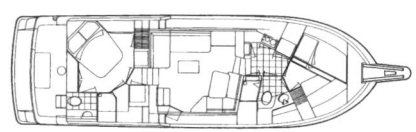

Dinette Layout

See Page 525 For Value Estimates

Enduring 1990s cockpit yacht gets high marks for sporty styling, spacious interior, quality construction. Offered with choice of interior plans—standard layout boasts wide-open salon; alternate floorplan has deckhouse dinette. Topside features include large aft deck, cockpit transom door, integrated swim platform. Hardtop, radar arch were popular options. Flybridge redesigned in 1990 when helm was moved forward. Engineroom is a tight fit. Cat 375hp diesels cruise at 18 knots (22–23 knots top).

Length	42'10"	Fuel	375 gals.
Beam	13'7"	Water	115 gals.
Draft	4'9"	Hull Type	Modified-V
Weight	41,000#	Headroom	6'5"
Clearance	15'9"	Deadrise Aft	NA

Hatteras 42 Long Range Cruiser

1976–85

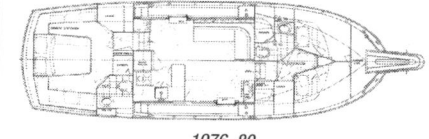

1976–80

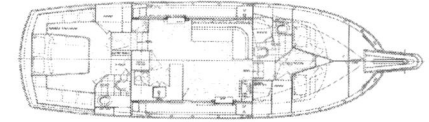

1981–85

Prices Not Provided for Pre-1995 Models

Heavy-weather Hatteras cruiser with full-displacement hull ranks among the best trawlers her size ever produced. Original model with walkaround decks, single beds in aft stateroom, was replaced in 1980 with sundeck (Mark II) model with full-beam afterdeck, queen bed in master. Highlights include teak interior woodwork, port/starboard salon deck doors, two full heads, big engine room, fold-down mast, bow pulpit. Total of 29 were built, used models are always in demand. Cruise efficiently at 8 knots with 140hp GM diesels.

Length Overall	42'6"	Clearance	13'6"
Length WL	38'0"	Fuel	700 gals.
Beam	14'6"	Water	220 gals.
Draft	3'10"	Waste	50 gals.
Weight	36,000#	Hull Type	Displacement

Trawlers & Motoryachts

Hatteras 43 Motor Yacht

1985–87

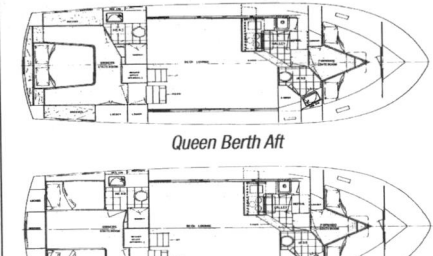

Queen Berth Aft

Twin Berths Aft

Prices Not Provided for Pre-1995 Models

Sporty 1980s motoryacht ranks among the smallest double-cabin designs ever produced by Hatteras. Highlights include comfortable—if not spacious—salon with wraparound windows, teak interior joinery, full-beam master stateroom with space for washer/dryer, large aft deck with wing doors. Hardtop and radar arch were standard. Note wide 12" side decks, teak handrails. First-rate fit and finish throughout. Standard 375hp Cat diesels cruise at 16 knots (20–21 knots top); optional GM 465hp 6-71s cruise at 17–18 knots (20+ knots top).

Length Overall	43'1"	Clearance	16'7"
Length WL	37'9"	Fuel	375 gals.
Beam	14'0"	Water	130 gals.
Draft	3'5"	Hull Type	Modified-V
Weight	34,500#	Deadrise Aft	NA

Hatteras 48 Cockpit Motor Yacht

1993–96

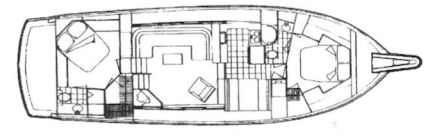

Standard Layout

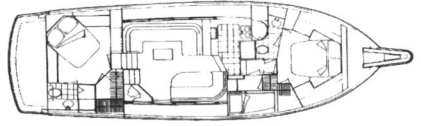

Optional Arrangement

See Page 525 For Value Estimates

Deluxe cruising yacht introduced in 1993 was class leader in styling, space, comfort. Wide 16-foot beam permits expansive floorplan with two double staterooms, expansive salon, choice of dinette or optional third stateroom. Large aft deck can accommodate a small crowd. Note roomy flybridge. Additional features include spacious engine room, standard washer/dryer, wide side decks, aft-deck hardtop. No transom door in cockpit. Twin 535hp GM diesels cruise at 18 knots (20+ knots wide open).

Length	48'11"	Fuel	667 gals.
Beam	16'0"	Water	170 gals.
Draft	5'6"	Waste	100 gals.
Weight	59,000#	Hull Type	Modified-V
Clearance	16'9"	Deadrise Aft	16°

Hatteras 48 Motor Yacht

1990–96

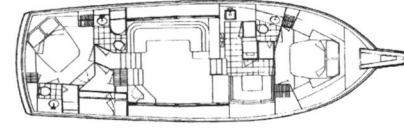

Standard Interior

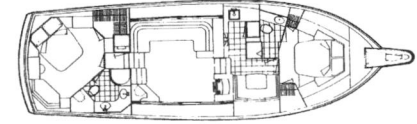

Alternate Layout

See Page 525 For Value Estimates

Conservative styling, luxurious accommodations made this heavily built motoryacht a popular model for Hatteras in early 1990s. Offered with several floorplans over the years—most were delivered with three-stateroom layout with dinette, galley down. Wraparound salon widows provide panoramic outside views. Notable features include large aft deck, roomy bridge, wide side decks. Hardtop, radar arch, bow pulpit were standard. GM 535hp diesels cruise at 16 knots (19 knots top); 720hp 8V92s cruise at 18–20 knots (low 20s top).

Length	48'9"	Fuel	764 gals.
Beam	16'0"	Water	170 gals.
Draft	5'3"	Headroom	6'6"
Weight	63,000#	Hull Type	Modified-V
Clearance	16'8"	Deadrise Aft	14°

Trawlers & Motoryachts

Hatteras 50 Sport Deck MY

1996–98

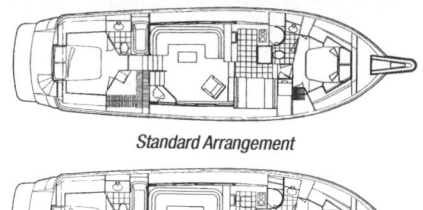

Standard Arrangement

Optional Arrangement

See Page 525 For Value Estimates

Quality-built motoryacht from one of America's premier builders suffered from conservative styling, expensive price. Lavish interior with expansive salon boasts large galley with home-sized appliances, spacious master stateroom with walk-in closet, optional third stateroom in lieu of dinette. Note tub in aft head. Topside highlights include huge aft deck, wide side decks, reverse transom with curved staircase, roomy flybridge. Poor aft helm visibility. Standard 535hp diesels cruise at 17 knots (low 20s top).

Length	50'10"	Fuel	622 gals.
Beam	16'0"	Water	170 gals.
Draft	5'6"	Headroom	6'6"
Weight	60,000#	Hull Type	Modified-V
Clearance	16'9"	Deadrise Aft	NA

Hatteras 52 Cockpit MY

1990–99

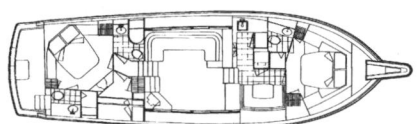

Standard Layout

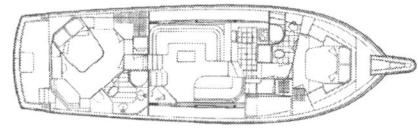

Optional Layout

See Page 525 For Value Estimates

Shapely 1990s cruising yacht provides still-impressive balance of motoryacht luxury, quality, comfort. Offered with several interiors over the years—standard three-stateroom layout boasts expansive salon with galley, dinette down; alternate floorplan offered enlarged master stateroom by moving second guest cabin forward. Spacious aft deck with hardtop, wing doors can entertain a small crowd. Note cockpit transom door, spacious engine room. Standard GM 720hp diesels cruise at 19–20 knots (about 23 knots top).

Length	52'11"	Fuel	994 gals.
Beam	16'0"	Water	170 gals.
Draft	5'2"	Headroom	6'6"
Weight	66,000#	Hull Type	Modified-V
Clearance	16'9"	Deadrise Aft	14°

Hatteras 52 Motor Yacht

1993–96

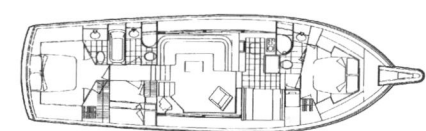

Standard Arrangement

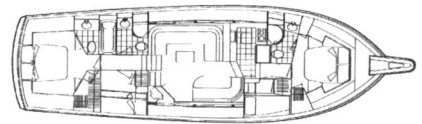

Optional Arrangement

See Page 525 For Value Estimates

Handsome 1990s motoryacht courted upscale buyers with a taste for luxury-class accommodations, signature Hatteras quality. Posh three-stateroom, three-head interior features queen berths fore and aft, tub in master stateroom, home-sized galley, standard washer/dryer. Huge aft deck could be fully enclosed and air-conditioned. Additional features include stand-up engine room (accessed via galley stairs), wide side decks, spacious flybridge. Standard 735hp GM diesels cruise at 18–19 knots (20+ knots wide open).

Length	52'9"	Fuel	994 gals.
Beam	16'0"	Water	170 gals.
Draft	5'2"	Headroom	6'6"
Weight	66,000#	Hull Type	Modified-V
Clearance	16'9"	Deadrise Aft	16°

Hatteras 53 Motor Yacht

1969–88

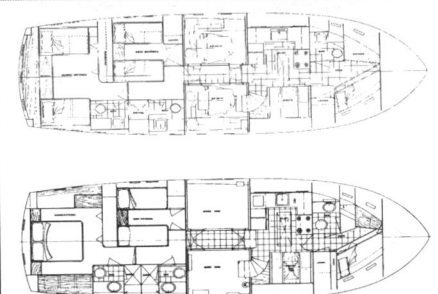

Acclaimed Hatteras cruising yacht with near 20-year production run left a sales, popularity legacy unsurpassed in motoryacht design. Spacious three-stateroom, three-head interior was long considered ideal in a yacht this size. Split-engineroom design became standard in many Hatteras motoryachts of her era. Flybridge updated in 1978; queen in master became standard in 1978. Total of 350 were built. Early models with GM 350hp diesels cruise at 12–13 knots. Later models with 435hp (or 450hp) GMs cruise at 16 knots.

Prices Not Provided for Pre-1995 Models

Length Overall	53'1"	Clearance	18'6"
Length WL	47'3"	Fuel	550/600/700 gals.
Beam	15'10"	Water	245 gals.
Draft	4'0"	Hull Type	Modified-V
Weight	55,000#	Deadrise Aft	NA

Hatteras 53 Extended Deckhouse MY

1983–88

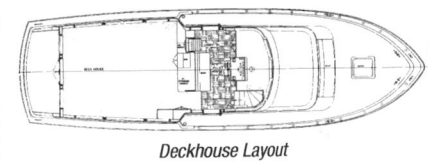

Deckhouse Layout

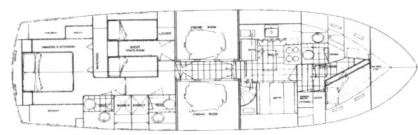

Lower Deck Arrangement

Handsome big-water motoryacht with classic Hatteras profile, executive-class amenities offered 1980's luxury on a grand scale. Spacious three-stateroom layout boasts huge full-beam salon, three full heads, home-sized galley with dinette opposite. Galley pass-through to salon is a nice touch. Split engine rooms provide easy access to motors, pumps. Small aft deck is perfect for line-handling. Many have been fitted with after-market stabilizers. Standard GM 465hp diesels cruise at 15 knots (18–19 knots top).

Prices Not Provided for Pre-1995 Models

Length	53'1"	Fuel	700 gals.
Beam	15'10"	Water	287 gals.
Draft	4'0"	Waste	150 gals.
Weight	57,000#	Hull Type	Modified-V
Clearance	17'2"	Deadrise Aft	NA

Hatteras 54 Extended Deckhouse MY

1989–92

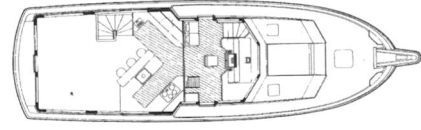

Deckhouse Arrangement

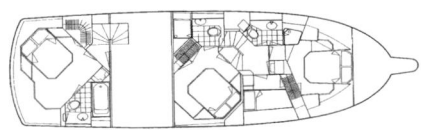

Lower Deck Floorplan

Muscular twin-deck motoryacht introduced in 1989 combined bold Hatteras styling with truly spacious accommodations. Innovative galley-up floorplan features enclosed wheelhouse, full-beam salon, three full heads. Remarkably, three of the 54's four staterooms boast walkaround queen beds. Note private salon access to master suite, tub in aft head. Additional features include foredeck sun lounge, small aft deck for line-handling, large flybridge, bow pulpit. GM 720hp engines cruise at 16 knots (about 20 knots top).

Prices Not Provided for Pre-1995 Models

Length	54'9"	Fuel	1,014 gals.
Beam	17'6"	Water	250 gals.
Draft	4'9"	Headroom	6'6"
Weight	76,000#	Hull Type	Modified-V
Clearance	20'11"	Deadrise Aft	NA

Hatteras 54 Motor Yacht

1985–88

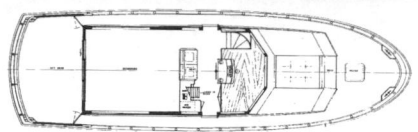

Deckhouse Arrangement

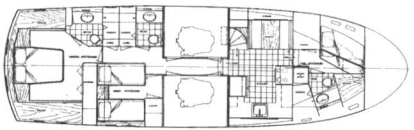

Lower Deck Layout

Stately 1980s motoryacht with "new look" Hatteras styling, wide 17'6" beam delivered big-boat luxury, comfort on a grand scale. Expansive galley-down, three-stateroom interior boasts three full heads. Lower helm (with deck access door) is open to salon. Split engine rooms provide easy access to motors. Semi-enclosed aft deck is huge for a yacht this size. Inside flybridge access is a plus. Fit and finish is as good as it gets in a production yacht of her era. GM 650hp diesels cruise at 15 knots; 720hp GMs cruise at 16–17 knots (20+ top).

Prices Not Provided for Pre-1995 Models

Length	54'9"	Fuel	800 gals.
Beam	17'6"	Water	250 gals.
Draft	4'2"	Headroom	6'4"
Weight	62,500#	Hull Type	Modified-V
Clearance	21'3"	Deadrise Aft	NA

Hatteras 56 Motor Yacht

1980–85

Maxi-volume 1980s motoryacht with signature Hatteras styling combines roomy twin-deck interior with top-shelf amenities, solid fiberglass construction. Three-stateroom, three-head floorplan with galley, dinette down rivals bigger boats for space and comfort. Wheelhouse is open to salon, providing near 360-degree helm visibility. Semi-enclosed aft deck is large enough for serious entertaining activities. Split engine rooms provide excellent service access. Cruise at 15–16 knots with 650hp Detroit diesels (about 18 knots top).

Prices Not Provided for Pre-1995 Models

Length	56'3"	Fuel	1,020 gals.
Beam	18'2"	Water	350 gals.
Draft	4'11"	Waste	NA
Weight	74,000#	Hull Type	Modified-V
Clearance	18'10"	Deadrise Aft	NA

Hatteras 58 Motor Yacht

1985–87

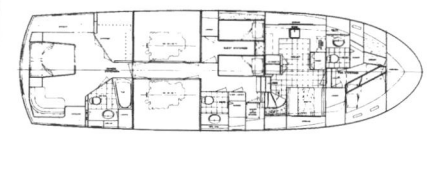

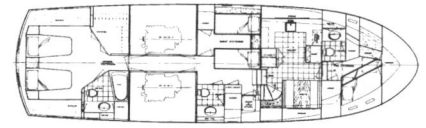

Heavily built motoryacht with signature Hatteras styling made good on company promise of executive-class accommodations, world-class quality. Wide 18'2" beam results in cavernous three-stateroom, galley-down interior with three full heads, laundry center. Expansive salon is open to helm; master suite is lavish in size, luxuries. Separate engine rooms was a Hatteras trademark in the 1980s. Huge flybridge seats a crowd. Bridge overhangs shelter side decks. GM 650hp diesels cruise at 16–17 knots (about 20 knots top).

Prices Not Provided for Pre-1995 Models

Length	58'9"	Fuel	1,030 gals.
Beam	18'2"	Water	350 gals.
Draft	4'11"	Headroom	6'5"
Weight	79,000#	Hull Type	Modified-V
Clearance	18'10"	Deadrise Aft	NA

Hatteras 60 Motor Yacht

1988–90

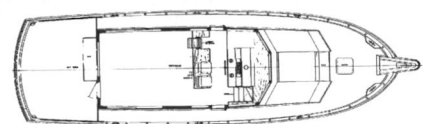

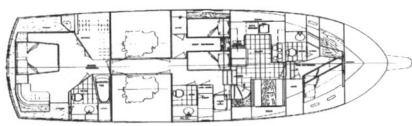

Updated version of earlier Hatteras 58 MY (1985–87) with new-look styling, inside bridge access made a good motoryacht even better. Wide 18'2" beam results in cavernous three-stateroom, galley-down interior with three full heads, laundry center. Expansive salon is open to helm; master suite is lavish in size, luxuries. Separate walk-in engine rooms were a Hatteras trademark in the 1980s. Flybridge is huge. Large aft deck can be fully enclosed. Standard 720hp 8V92s cruise at 17–18 knots and reach a top speed of 20+ knots.

Prices Not Provided for Pre-1995 Models

Length	60'9"	Fuel	1,033 gals.
Beam	18'2"	Water	335 gals.
Draft	5'0"	Headroom	6'5"
Weight	86,000#	Hull Type	Modified-V
Clearance	20'9"	Deadrise Aft	6°

Hatteras 60 Motor Yacht

2008–Current

Original Main Deck Layout

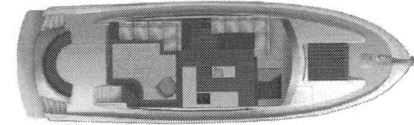

Revised Main Deck Layout

Supersize 60-foot motoryacht with enormous interior, huge engine room towers in size over European competitors of similar length. Original layout with large island galley, salon staircase to bridge was replaced in 2010 with more conventional plan offering additional entertainment space. Exceptional 6'8" headroom throughout. Full-beam owner suite defines opulence. Guest cabins lack portholes for outside view. Note cavernous forward deck lockers, very wide side decks, spacious flybridge. Cat 1,000hp V-drive diesels cruise at 20–22 knots (mid 20s top).

See Page 525 For Value Estimates

Length	60'11"	Fuel	1,175 gals.
Beam	18'2"	Water	250 gals.
Draft	4'6"	Headroom	100 gals.
Weight	94,000#	Hull Type	Modified-V
Clearance	15'0"	Deadrise Aft	5°

Hatteras 61 Cockpit MY

1981–85

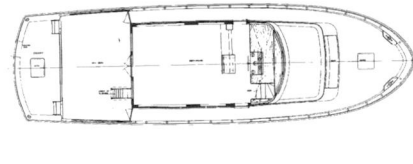

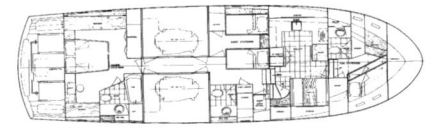

Stretched version of Hatteras 56 MY (1980–85) combines cockpit versatility with motoryacht comfort. Three-stateroom, three-head floorplan with galley, dinette down rivals bigger boats for space and comfort. Wheelhouse is open to salon providing good helm visibility. Semi-enclosed aft deck is large enough for serious entertaining; cockpit makes boarding easy. Split engine rooms—a Hatteras trademark—provide easy access to motors and pumps. Cruise at 15–16 knots with 650hp Detroit diesels (about 18 knots top).

Prices Not Provided for Pre-1995 Models

Length Overall	61'3"	Clearance	18'10"
Length WL	55'9"	Fuel	1,150 gals.
Beam	18'2"	Water	350 gals.
Draft	4'11"	Hull Type	Modified-V
Weight	85,000#	Deadrise Aft	NA

Hatteras 61 Motor Yacht

1981–85

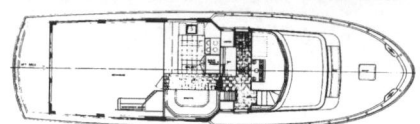

Deckhouse Layout

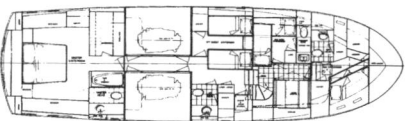

Queen Bed in Master

Classic twin-deck Hatteras motoryacht with full-beam salon combines spacious interior with top-shelf construction, sea-kindly hull. Galley-up, four-stateroom interior with enclosed pilothouse is tough to beat in a yacht this size. Extended salon rivals larger yachts for comfort, space. Highlights include second dinette on lower level, lavish master suite, separate engine rooms, huge flybridge. Note tub in aft head. Small aft deck is useful for line-handling. GM 650hp diesels cruise at 16–17 knots (about 20 knots top).

Prices Not Provided for Pre-1995 Models

Length Overall	61'3"	Clearance	18'10"
Length WL	55'9"	Fuel	1,150 gals.
Beam	18'2"	Water	350 gals.
Draft	4'11"	Hull Type	Modified-V
Weight	82,000#	Deadrise Aft	NA

Hatteras 63 Cockpit MY

1985–87

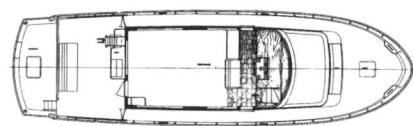

Deckhouse Layout

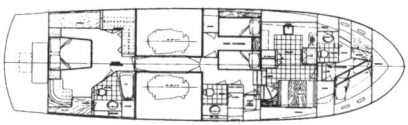

Queen Bed in Master

Heavily built cockpit yacht is basically a Hatteras 58 Motor Yacht (1985–87) with 5-foot cockpit addition. Wide 18'2" beam results in cavernous interior with three staterooms and heads, roomy aft deck, full walkaround decks. Expansive salon is completely open to helm. Master suite is lavish in size, luxury. Note laundry center, home-size galley appliances, separate walk-in engine rooms. GM 840hp diesels cruise at 18 knots and reach a top speed of 20+ knots. Only a few of these yachts were built.

Prices Not Provided for Pre-1995 Models

Length	63'8"	Fuel	1,170 gals.
Beam	18'2"	Water	375 gals.
Draft	4'11"	Headroom	6'4"
Weight	79,000#	Hull Type	Modified-V
Clearance	18'10"	Deadrise Aft	NA

Hatteras 63 Motor Yacht

1986–87

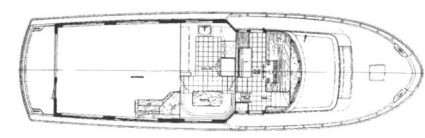

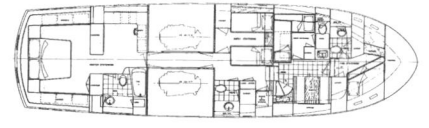

Luxury four-stateroom motoryacht with enormous full-beam salon, classic Hatteras styling rivals most condos for living space and comfort. Expansive interior features separate galley/dinette forward of salon, private wheelhouse, lavish master suite with dressing area, walk-in closets, full-size tub in aft head. Note second lower-level dinette, separate engine rooms, formal dining area in salon. Flybridge is huge. Small aft deck provides adequate space for line-handling. Cruise at 16–17 knots with standard 650hp GM diesels (about 20 knots top).

Prices Not Provided for Pre-1995 Models

Length	63'10"	Fuel	1,170 gals.
Beam	18'2"	Water	350 gals.
Draft	5'0"	Headroom	6'4"
Weight	92,000#	Hull Type	Modified-V
Clearance	21'3"	Deadrise Aft	NA

Hatteras 6300 Raised Pilothouse

2000–03

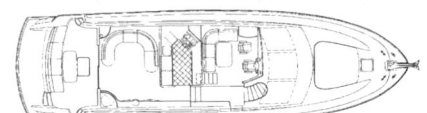

Upper Deck, Standard Layout

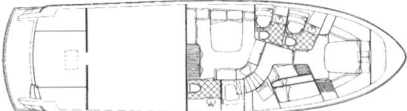

Lower Deck, Standard Layout

See Page 525 For Value Estimates

Modern pilothouse yacht introduced in 2000 took Hatteras styling in a whole new direction. Plush three-stateroom, three-head interior features huge galley open to salon, inside bridge access, raised pilothouse with centerline helm. With no obstructing bulkheads, visibility from lower helm is excellent in all directions. Topside features include massive flybridge with tender stowage, huge cockpit lazarette, walkaround decks, integral swim platform. No outside bridge access. Cat 1,400hp engines cruise at 25 knots (28–30 knots top).

Length	63'0"	Fuel	1,290 gals.
Beam	18'3"	Water	280 gals.
Draft	4'11"	Waste	100 gals.
Weight	115,000#	Hull Type	Modified-V
Clearance	18'10"	Deadrise Aft	1.5°

Hatteras 65 Long Range Cruiser

1981–86

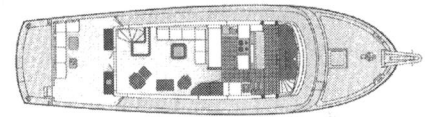

Standard Deckhouse Layout

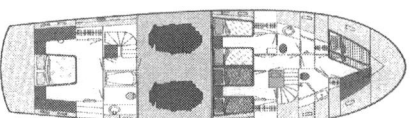

Standard Lower-Deck Floorplan

Prices Not Provided for Pre-1995 Models

Heavily built displacement cruiser from the 1980s took Hatteras-style comfort, security to new levels. Spacious four-stateroom interior features fully enclosed pilothouse, extravagant owner's suite with private salon access, full-beam engine room. Portuguese bridge protects against oncoming seas. Note deckhouse day head, home-size galley, wide side decks. Enclosed aft deck overlooks small cockpit with transom door. GM 6-71N diesels cruise at 8–10 knots with range of 2,000–2,500 nautical miles. Total of 13 were built.

Length Overall	65'0"	Clearance	18'9"
Length WL	58'8"	Fuel	2,625 gals.
Beam	17'11"	Water	455 gals.
Draft	4'10"	Waste	200 gals.
Weight	114,000#	Hull Type	Displacement

Hatteras 65 Motor Yacht

1988–96

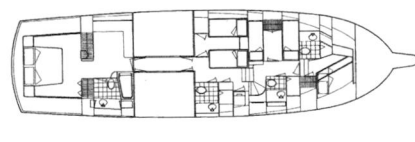

See Page 525 For Value Estimates

Classic Hatteras motoryacht proved popular with sophisticated owners seeking maxi-volume luxury, world-class accommodations. Original four-stateroom interior with separate engine rooms was joined in 1989 with revised four-stateroom layout with full-beam engine room, amidships VIP stateroom. Highlights include enclosed wheelhouse, lavish master suite, full-width salon, enormous flybridge, covered aft deck. Twin 870hp GM engines cruise at 17 knots (20 knots top); 1,075hp GMs cruise at 18–19 knots (low 20s top).

Length	65'10"	Fuel	1,170 gals.
Beam	18'2"	Water	350 gals.
Draft	5'5"	Headroom	6'6"
Weight	99,000#	Hull Type	Modified-V
Clearance	21'5"	Deadrise Aft	NA

Trawlers & Motoryachts

Hatteras 67 Cockpit MY

1988–91

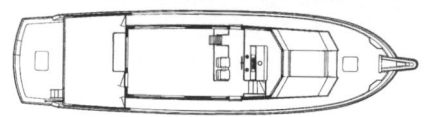

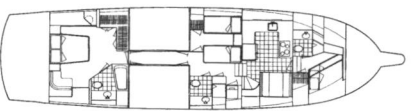

Graceful cockpit motoryacht combined the tasteful styling, top-shelf construction synonymous with the Hatteras name. Wide beam results in spacious interior with three staterooms and heads, protected aft deck, walkaround decks. Expansive salon is completely open to helm. Master suite is lavish in size, luxury. Note laundry center, home-size galley, separate engine rooms. Cockpit includes wide transom door. Standard 770hp (870hp in later models) GM diesels cruise at 17 knots (20+ top); optional 1,040 GMs boost top speed to about 25 knots.

Prices Not Provided for Pre-1995 Models

Length	67'8"	Fuel	1,170 gals.
Beam	18'2"	Water	375 gals.
Draft	5'1"	Headroom	6'4"
Weight	90,000#	Hull Type	Modified-V
Clearance	20'3"	Deadrise Aft	6°

Hatteras 70 Cockpit MY

1984–91

Standard Layout, 1988–91

Standard Layout, 1992–98

Popular cockpit motoryacht was among the most luxurious production models offered by Hatteras during the 1990s. Highlights include huge full-width salon, enclosed pilothouse, massive bridge. Originally designed with four-stateroom floorplan with twin engine rooms, new layout introduced in 1992 has full-width engine room, improved guest accommodations. Small aft deck overlooks roomy cockpit. GM 870hp engines cruise at 16–17 knots. Later models with 1,075hp GMs cruise at 19–20 knots. Over fifty were built.

Prices Not Provided for Pre-1995 Models

Length	70'10"	Fuel	1,596 gals.
Beam	18'2"	Water	345 gals.
Draft	5'6"	Headroom	6'7"
Weight	103,000#	Hull Type	Modified-V
Clearance	21'4"	Deadrise Aft	NA

Hatteras 70 Motor Yacht

1988–96

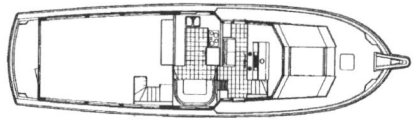

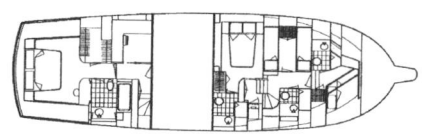

Lengthened version of popular Hatteras 65 MY (1988–96) with bigger salon, enlarged master stateroom takes motoryacht luxury to the next level. Semicustom interior features extended, full-beam salon, enormous master suite, up to four guest cabins. For owner privacy, galley and pilothouse are separate from salon. Walkaround version became available in 1990 but few were built. Note huge engine room, massive flybridge, small aft deck for line handling. GM 870hp diesels cruise at 18 knots; later models with 1,075hp GMs cruise at 19 knots.

Insufficient Resale Data to Assign Values

Length	70'11"	Fuel	1,596 gals.
Beam	18'2"	Water	251 gals.
Draft	5'6"	Headroom	6'4"
Weight	108,000#	Hull Type	Modified-V
Clearance	21'2"	Deadrise Aft	NA

Hatteras 70 Sport Deck MY

1995–98

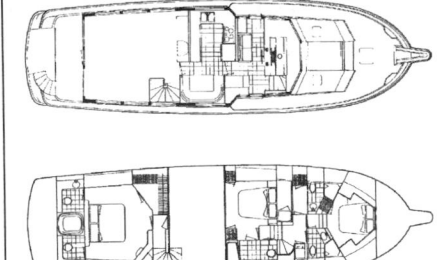

Sophisticated 1990s motoryacht is essentially a late-model Hatteras 65 MY (1988–96) with Eurostyle swim platform. Lavish four-stateroom, four-head interior boasts spacious full-beam salon, enormous master suite with his-and-her heads, opulent VIP stateroom amidships. Galley and pilothouse are separate from salon to insure privacy for owner and guests. Curved staircase descends from aft deck to swim platform. No lightweight, 1,100hp GM engines cruise at 18 knots (21–22 knots top). Cruising luxury on a grand scale.

Insufficient Resale Data to Assign Values

Length	70'10"	Water	460 gals.
Beam	18'2"	Clearance, Arch	21'4"
Draft	5'6"	Headroom	6'4"
Weight	103,000#	Hull Type	Modified-V
Fuel	1,596 gals.	Deadrise Aft	NA

Hatteras 72 Motor Yacht

2008–Current

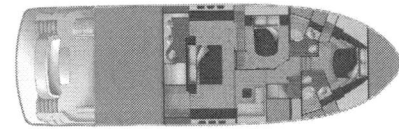

New-generation Hatteras motoryacht combines contemporary styling with world-class construction, luxury-class accommodations. Highlights include palatial main salon with optional sunken bar, roomy country kitchen with walk-in pantry, full-beam master suite with king-size bed, optional aft crew or VIP stateroom. Spacious flybridge can be accessed from aft deck or galley. Note huge engine room, wide side decks, recessed windlass. Forward sun pad converts into a seat. Cruise at 20 knots with Cat C32 (1,800hp) engines.

Insufficient Resale Data to Assign Values

Length	73'4"	Fuel	2,200 gals.
Beam	20'2"	Water	300 gals.
Draft	5'4"	Waste	350 gals.
Weight	160,000#	Hull Type	Modified-V
Clearance, Arch	21'4"	Deadrise Aft	NA

Hatteras 74 Cockpit MY

1996–99

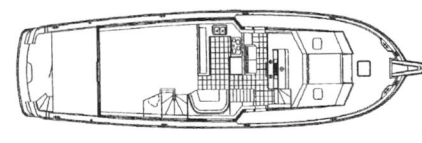

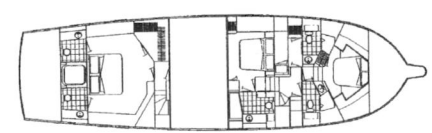

Heavily built cockpit yacht defined Hatteras concept of luxury, style in the 1990s. Four-stateroom interior boasts enormous owner's suite with his-and her heads, two full-featured VIP staterooms, full-width salon with formal dining area, protected aft deck. Several alternate lower-level layouts were offered (including en suite office in master stateroom). Note massive bridge, roomy cockpit with curved staircase. GM 1,100hp diesels cruise at 18 knots (20–21 knots top); optional 1,350hp Cats cruise at 22 knots (25–26 knots top).

Insufficient Resale Data to Assign Values

Length Overall	74'4"	Fuel	1,561 gals.
Beam	18'2"	Water	345 gals.
Draft	5'6"	Waste	215 gals.
Weight	106,000#	Hull Type	Modified-V
Clearance, Arch	21'2"	Deadrise Aft	3°

Trawlers & Motoryachts

Hatteras 74 Sport Deck MY

1996–99

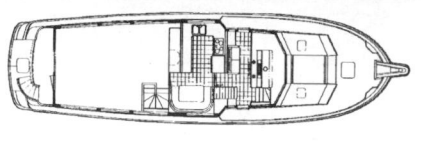

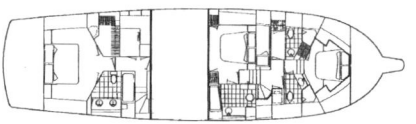

Leading-edge Hatteras motoryacht raised the bar for contemporary luxury, quality in the late 1990s. Four-stateroom interior boasts enormous owner's suite with his-and hers heads, two full-featured VIP staterooms, full-width salon with formal dining area, protected aft deck. Reverse transom design allows for "activity platform" in place of cockpit. Note huge walk-in engine room, roomy pilothouse. Detroit 1,100hp diesels cruise at 18 knots (20–21 knots top); optional 1,350hp Cats cruise at a respectable 22 knots (25–26 knots top).

Insufficient Resale Data to Assign Values

Length Overall	74'4"	Fuel	1,561 gals.
Beam	18'2"	Water	345 gals.
Draft	5'6"	Waste	215 gals.
Weight	110,000#	Hull Type	Modified-V
Clearance, Arch	21'4"	Deadrise Aft	3°

Heritage East/Nova 36 Sundeck

1985–Current

Enduring Asian import combines Old World craftsmanship with classic styling, small-boat economy. Traditional teak interior boasts roomy salon with full lower helm, double berths in both staterooms, generous storage, teak-and-holly cabin sole, good engine room access. Overhead salon grabrails are a thoughtful touch. Aft deck hardtop is a popular option. Large cabin windows let in plenty of natural lighting. Popular model has stood the test of time. Cruise efficiently at 8–10 knots with single 220hp Cummins diesel.

See Page 525 For Value Estimates

Length Overall	36'0"	Clearance	15'8"
Length WL	32'1"	Fuel	420 gals.
Beam	12'7"	Water	180 gals.
Draft	3'8"	Waste	60 gals.
Weight	23,000#	Hull Type	Semi-Disp.

Hi-Star Star 48 Sundeck

1986–92

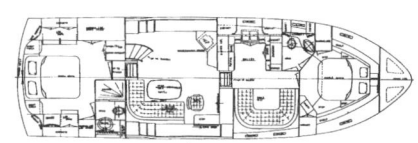

Popular Taiwan motoryacht introduced in 1986 earned considerable praise for above-average construction, spacious accommodations. Two-stateroom interior—many 48-footers have three—features home-size galley, big U-shaped dinette, two large en suite cabins. Forward head lacks separate stall shower. Topside features include roomy aft deck with hardtop, molded bow pulpit, wide side decks. Well-arranged engine room offers good access to motors. Standard 375hp Cats cruise 18–19 knots and reach about 22 knots top.

Prices Not Provided for Pre-1995 Models

Length Overall	47'9"	Clearance	13'6"
Length WL	41'3"	Fuel	500 gals.
Beam	15'2"	Water	250 gals.
Draft	3'10"	Hull Type	Modified-V
Weight	37,000#	Deadrise Aft	16°

Hi-Star Star 55 Yacht Fisherman

1986–92

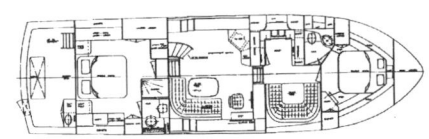

Well-regarded cockpit yacht with contemporary styling combined versatile accommodations with above-average construction. Spacious two-stateroom interior features home-size galley, U-shaped dinette, two large en suite cabins. Note quality teak cabin joinery. Large cockpit with sink, transom door is big enough for light-tackle fishing. Topside features include hardtop, molded bow pulpit, wide side decks, aft deck wet bar. Note well-finished engine room. Cat 375hp engines cruise 18–19 knots and reach 22 knots wide open.

Prices Not Provided for Pre-1995 Models

Length	54'9"	Fuel	500 gals.
Beam	15'2"	Water	250 gals.
Draft	4'1"	Headroom	6'4"
Weight	39,000#	Hull Type	Modified-V
Clearance	NA	Deadrise Aft	16°

Horizon 62 Motor Yacht

2003–06

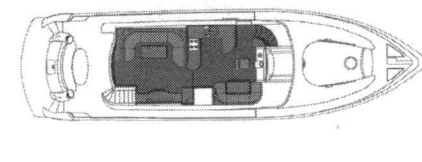

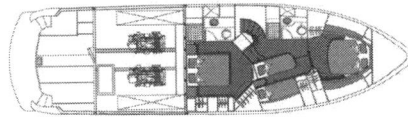

Quality built flybridge yacht combines graceful styling with executive-class accommodations, world-class engineering. Beautifully finished interior offers luxurious accommodations for six in three staterooms including lavish full-beam master. Spacious salon is dominated by 11-foot sofa, full entertainment center. Transom—with twin lighted staircases, crew-cabin door—resembles that of a 90-footer. Note large cockpit with curved bridge steps, roomy engine compartment. Cat 1,000hp diesels cruise at 20 knots (22–23 knots top).

Insufficient Resale Data to Assign Values

Length	64'3"	Fuel	1,000 gals.
Beam	17'4"	Water	350 gals.
Draft	5'7"	Waste	150 gals.
Weight	74,960#	Hull Type	Semi-Disp.
Clearance	18'5"	Deadrise Aft	12°

Horizon V68

2007–Current

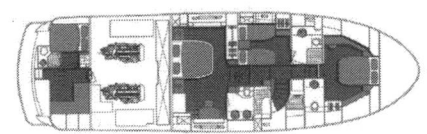

Stately mini-superyacht combines broad 20'6" beam with enormous interior, impressive feature list. Versatile four-stateroom, four-head layout includes crew quarters aft with double berth, full-beam master suite, open-plan salon/galley/dinette, roomy skylounge with dinette and day head. Stand-up engine room is a work of art. Seating area aft on bridge deck features barbecue, wet bar. Available with open or enclosed flybridge, with or without cockpit. Cruise at 16 knots (about 20 top) with 1,000hp Cat diesels.

Insufficient Resale Data to Assign Values

Length	71'8"	Fuel	1,400 gals.
Beam	20'6"	Water	360 gals.
Draft	5'6"	Waste	150 gals.
Weight	121,000#	Hull Type	Semi-Disp.
Clearance	26'3"	Deadrise Aft	12°

Trawlers & Motoryachts

Trawlers & Motoryachts

Horizon 70 Motor Yacht

1998–2003

Crew Cabin Forward

Crew Cabin Aft

Insufficient Resale Data to Assign Values

Eurostyle pilothouse yacht with megayacht interior matched superior finish with world-class amenities, competitive price. A semicustom yacht, several interior configurations were available. (Note that three-stateroom floorplans include crew quarters.) Principal features include high-gloss interior joinery, deep swim platform, wide side decks, spacious flybridge with dinghy, PWC storage. Walk-in engine room is cavernous compared with most European yachts. Cat 1,350hp engines cruise in the low 20s and top out at 27–28 knots.

Length	69'4"	Fuel	1,720 gals.
Beam	18'9"	Water	400 gals.
Draft	6'0"	Waste	150 gals.
Weight	96,100#	Hull Type	Semi-Disp.
Clearance	18'6"	Deadrise Aft	12°

Horizon 70/73 Motor Yacht

2004–09

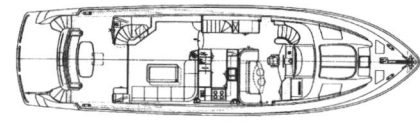

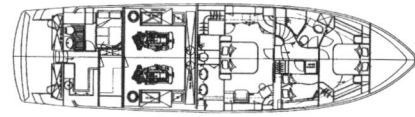

Insufficient Resale Data to Assign Values

World-class luxury yacht (marketed as second-generation Horizon 70 MY from 2004–06) combines gorgeous styling, sophisticated build quality, impressive performance. Elegant semicustom interior with mirrored salon ceiling, exquisite high-gloss cabinetry offers unsurpassed comfort, luxury. Twin transom staircases descend to swim platform with crew-cabin access door. Hardtop, bow/stern thrusters, teak decks are standard. Note huge flybridge, meticulous engine room. Cat 1,550hp diesels cruise at 21–22 knots.

Length	73'0"	Fuel	1,750 gals.
Beam	19'0"	Water	400 gals.
Draft	6'0"	Waste	200 gals.
Weight	99,200#	Hull Type	Semi-Disp.
Clearance	20'3"	Deadrise Aft	12°

Horizon V74

2007–Current

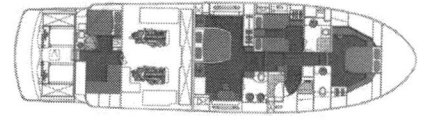

Insufficient Resale Data to Assign Values

Cockpit version of Horizon V68 Skylounge combines broad 20'6" beam with enormous interior, impressive feature list. Versatile four-stateroom, four-head layout includes crew quarters aft with double berth, full-beam master suite, open-plan salon/galley/dinette, roomy skylounge with dinette and day head. Stand-up engine room is a work of art. Seating area aft on bridge deck features barbecue, wet bar. Pilothouse access door, wide side decks make getting around easy. Cruise at 16 knots (about 20 top) with 1,000hp Cat C-18 diesels.

Length	76'6"	Fuel	1,680 gals.
Beam	20'6"	Water	360 gals.
Draft	6'0"	Waste	150 gals.
Weight	130,000#	Hull Type	Semi-Disp.
Clearance	26'3"	Deadrise Aft	12°

Horizon 76 Motor Yacht

2002–05

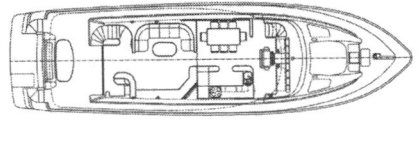
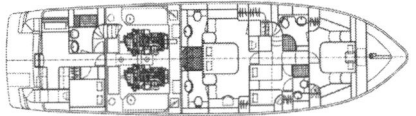

Semicustom motoryacht delivers impressive blend of sleek styling, lavish accommodations, state-of-the-art construction. Offered with several floorplan variations—standard three-stateroom layout with crew quarters is displayed here. Highlights include large pilothouse with home-size galley, formal dining area, twin transom staircases, wide side decks, spacious engine room. Enclosed Skylounge model converts flybridge into small salon with entertainment center, dinette. Cat 1,400hp diesels cruise at 20 knots (24–25 knots top). Over 25 were sold.

Insufficient Resale Data to Assign Values

Length Overall	76'0"	Fuel	1,930 gals.
Length WL	64'2"	Water	400 gals.
Beam	18'9"	Waste	100 gals.
Draft	6'0"	Hull Type	Semi-Disp.
Weight	106,500#	Deadrise Aft	12°

Hyundai 49 Motor Yacht

1988–94

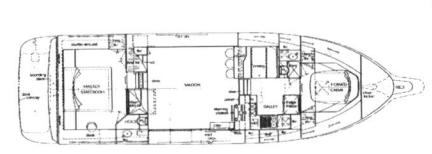

Korean-built motoryacht from 1980s (also called Elegant 49; Sonata 5300) was widely viewed as a lot of boat for the money. Roomy galley-down interior features two large staterooms, solid teak cabinetry, lower helm with deck access door. Wing doors, enclosure panels, wet bar were standard on the aft deck. Many of these boats were fitted with Jacuzzi in aft head. Large salon windows provide panoramic outside views. Note fully cored hull, wide side decks. Cruise at 16–18 knots with 375hp Cat diesels (20+ knots wide open).

Prices Not Provided for Pre-1995 Models

Length w/Pulpit	53'0"	Headroom	6'4"
Hull Length	48'6"	Fuel	700 gal.
Beam	15'8"	Water	300 gal.
Draft	3'6"	Hull Type	Modified-V
Weight	34,000#	Deadrise Aft	14°

Independence 45 Trawler

1985–2000

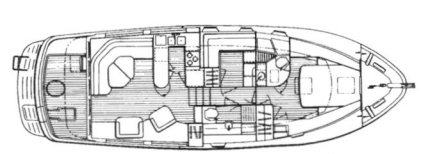

Sturdy pilothouse trawler combines handsome lines with sea-kindly hull, single-screw economy. Highlights include well-appointed interior with full-beam salon, roomy pilothouse, weather-tight doors, comfortable cockpit, large boat deck with room for dinghy stowage. Deep keel protects running gear from grounding. Imported from Taiwan by Hans Christian through 1995, production shifted to U.S.-based Cherubini starting with hull #19 in 1996. Cruise at 7–8 knots with single 135hp Lugger diesel; 10 knots with 355hp Cummins.

See Page 526 For Value Estimates

Length Overall	48'8"	Clearance	13'6"
Length WL	40'9"	Fuel	630 gals.
Beam	14'6"	Water	300 gals.
Draft	4'6"	Waste	80 gals.
Weight	38,000#	Hull	Semi-Disp.

Trawlers & Motoryachts

Island Gypsy 30 Sedan

1975–85

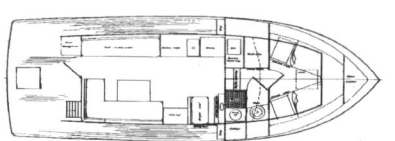

Pocket sedan trawler appeals to low-budget couples drawn to sporty styling, practical accommodations, fuel-efficient operation. Traditional teak interior with V-berths forward, convertible dinette and settee can sleep up to six. Highlights include lower helm station with sliding deck door, teak parquet flooring, teak bow pulpit, teak handrails, teak swim platform. Note wide side decks, simulated lapstrake hull. Fun to drive, easy to maintain, inexpensive to own. Cruise at 6–7 knots (burning just 2–3 gph) with standard 120hp Lehman diesel.

Prices Not Provided for Pre-1995 Models

Length Overall	30'0"	Clearance	12'0"
Length WL	27'9"	Fuel	250 gals.
Beam	11'6"	Water	120 gals.
Draft	3'8"	Waste	25 gals.
Weight	14,400#	Hull Type	Semi-Disp.

Island Gypsy 32 Europa

1989–2003

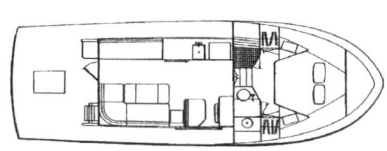

Handsome sedan trawler with distinctive styling ranks among the most popular small cruisers built by Island Gypsy over the years. Highlights include well-crafted teak interior with open salon, lower helm with deck access door, split head with separate stall shower, covered aft deck, protected side decks. Surprisingly roomy flybridge with facing settees seats several guests. Full-length keel protects running gear from grounding. Note small holding tank capacity. Cruise at 6–7 knots with single 135hp diesel; 8–9 knots with 210hp Cummins.

See Page 526 For Value Estimates

Length Overall	32'0"	Clearance	12'4"
Length WL	29'7"	Fuel	250 gals.
Beam	12'0"	Water	120 gals.
Draft	3'8"	Waste	15 gals.
Weight	16,400#	Hull Type	Semi-Disp.

Island Gypsy 32 Sedan

1981–96

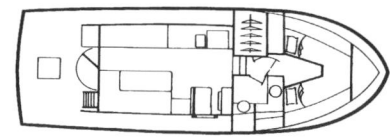

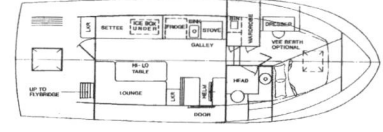

Salty sedan trawler with handsome profile, versatile layout appeals to cruising couples on a budget. Space-efficient teak interior boasts comfortable salon with facing settees, lower helm with deck access door, teak parquet flooring, complete galley with stove/oven. Teak-over-fiberglass decks, mast and boom assembly, teak hand rails were standard. Full-length keel protects running gear from grounding. Good lower helm visibility. Small holding tank capacity. Cruise at 7–8 knots with single 250hp Cummins diesel.

See Page 526 For Value Estimates

Length Overall	32'0"	Clearance	12'4"
Length WL	29'7"	Fuel	250 gals.
Beam	12'0"	Water	120 gals.
Draft	3'8"	Waste	15 gals.
Weight	16,400#	Hull Type	Semi-Disp.

Island Gypsy 36 Classic

1981–2002

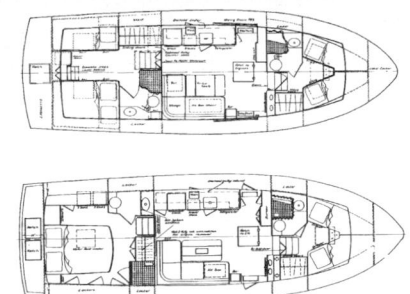

Popular double cabin trawler with signature Island Gypsy profile is built for coastal cruising in comfort, security. Several twin-stateroom floorplans were offered over the years. Highlights include teak interior woodwork, teak parquet flooring, standard lower helm, galley with stove/oven, port and starboard salon deck doors, full-size head with stall shower, teak-over-fiberglass decks, roomy flybridge with seating for six. Note simulated lapstrake hull lines. Cruise at 8 knots with single Cummins diesel; 10–12 knots with twins.

See Page 527 For Value Estimates

Length Overall	36'0"	Clearance	12'6"
Length WL	32'10"	Fuel	400 gals.
Beam	13'0"	Water	200 gals.
Draft	3'6"	Waste	50 gals.
Weight	27,000#	Hull Type	Semi-Disp.

Island Gypsy 36 Europa

1982–98

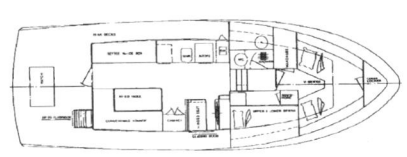

Sought-after Eurosedan combines classic trawler styling with top-shelf construction, fuel-efficient operation. Highlights include elegant teak interior with lower helm and two staterooms, covered aft deck, protected walkways, teak-over-fiberglass decks, semi-displacement hull with prop-protecting keel. Note large engine room, cockpit storage lazarette, simulated lapstrake hull lines. Excellent range with 450-gallon fuel capacity. Cruise at 8 knots with twin 135hp diesels; 10–12 knots with twin 210hp Cummins.

See Page 527 For Value Estimates

Length Overall	36'0"	Clearance	16'0"
Length WL	32'10"	Fuel	450 gals.
Beam	13'0"	Water	200 gals.
Draft	3'11"	Waste	40 gals.
Weight	25,520#	Hull Type	Semi-Disp.

Island Gypsy 36 Motor Yacht

1992–2002

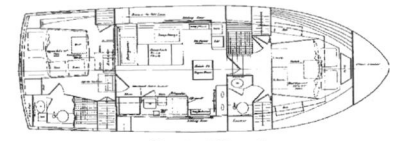

Standard Floorplan

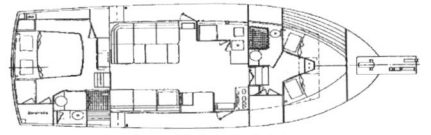

Three-Stateroom Interior

Stylish sundeck trawler makes good on Island Gypsy promise of solid construction, common-sense layout, proven owner satisfaction. Traditional teak interior features surprisingly spacious salon with facing settees, port/starboard deck doors, two full heads, choice of two or three staterooms. Large engine room provides good service access. Radar mast, bow pulpit, swim platform are standard. Salon dimensions rival many 40-footers. Cruise at 8 knots with twin 135hp Lehman diesels; 10–12 knots with 210hp Cummins.

See Page 527 For Value Estimates

Length Overall	36'0"	Clearance	12'6"
Length WL	32'10"	Fuel	400 gals.
Beam	13'0"	Water	200 gals.
Draft	3'11"	Headroom	6'4"
Weight	28,000#	Hull Type	Semi-Disp.

Trawlers & Motoryachts

Island Gypsy 40 Flush Aft Deck

1986–94

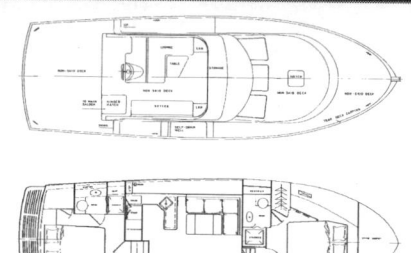

Durable sundeck cruiser offers an inviting mix of agile handling, quality construction, practical layout. Galley-up interior boasts full-beam master stateroom aft, large salon with dinette and lower helm, queen bed in forward stateroom, two full heads. Galley is positioned aft in salon, convenient to both aft deck and flybridge. Note well-crafted teak woodwork. Helm-aft flybridge layout is unusual—most motoryachts have the helm forward with guest seating aft. Twin 135hp diesels cruise at 8 knots. Cat 375hp diesels cruise at 18 knots.

Prices Not Provided for Pre-1995 Models

Length Overall	40'0"	Clearance	13'3"
Length WL	35'3"	Fuel	400 gals.
Beam	14'3"	Water	200 gals.
Draft	3'6"	Waste	60 gals.
Weight	33,500#	Hull Type	Semi-Disp.

Island Gypsy 44 Flush Aft Deck

1979–96

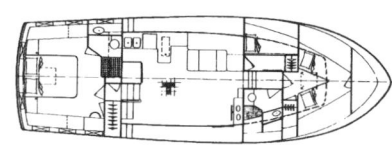

No-nonsense sundeck yacht combines a seaworthy hull design with tank-like construction, excellent range, and a very comfortable layout. Standard three-stateroom floorplan (most 44-footers have two) boasts expansive salon with convertible dinette and lower helm, full-beam master stateroom, two small guest cabins forward. Galley is aft in salon, convenient to aft deck and flybridge. Both heads have stall showers. Supernice interior joinerwork. Cruise at 12 knots with twin 275hp diesels (15 top); 16–17 knots with 375hp Cats (20 knots top).

See Page 527 For Value Estimates

Length Overall	44'3"	Clearance	13'7"
Length WL	38'9"	Fuel	800 gals.
Beam	15'4"	Water	400 gals.
Draft	4'3"	Waste	60 gals.
Weight	38,500#	Hull Type	Semi-Disp.

Island Gypsy 44 Motor Cruiser

1983–96

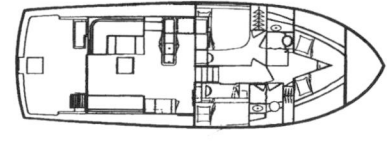

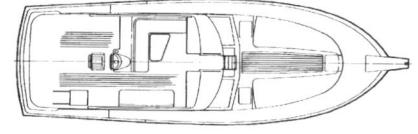

Sporty sedan cruiser delivers compelling mix of solid construction, excellent range, comfortable accommodations. Three-stateroom interior (most 44-footers have two) includes amidships master, roomy salon with galley forward, lower helm with deck access door. Unique fold-down stairwell in bridge coaming makes foredeck access easy. Flybridge layout with seating forward, helm aft is unusual. Note teak decks, cockpit transom door. Cruise at 12 knots with twin 275hp diesels; 16–17 knots with 375hp Cats.

See Page 527 For Value Estimates

Length Overall	44'3"	Clearance	13'7"
Length WL	38'9"	Fuel	720 gals.
Beam	15'4"	Water	320 gals.
Draft	4'3"	Waste	60 gals.
Weight	38,500#	Hull Type	Semi-Disp.

Island Gypsy 49 Classic

1988–94

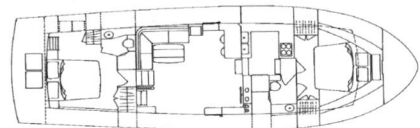

Two-Stateroom, Galley Down

Three-Stateroom, Galley Up

Prices Not Provided for Pre-1995 Models

Heavily-built motoryacht with classic trawler lines strikes a balance between cruising comfort, economical operation. Offered with choice or two- or three-stateroom interior plans, both with beautifully crafted Burmese teak joinery, port/starboard salon deck doors, teak-planked flooring, copious storage. Good lower-helm visibility. Topside features include teak walkaround deck, functional mast and boom, teak railings. Spacious flybridge can seat a small crowd. Excellent range at lower speeds. Cruise at 12–14 knots with twin 375hp Cats.

Length Overall	49'0"	Clearance	13'7"
Length WL	43'6"	Fuel	800 gals.
Beam	15'4"	Water	400 gals.
Draft	4'5"	Waste	80 gals.
Weight	38,000#	Hull Type	Semi-Disp.

Jefferson 37 Sundeck

1989–94

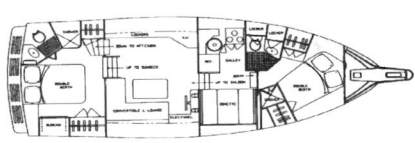

Prices Not Provided for Pre-1995 Models

Affordably priced 1990s import matched Jefferson claim of comfortable accommodations, durable construction. Low-deadrise hull with shallow keel boasts wide 14'5" beam. Two-stateroom interior with lower helm is notable for hand-rubbed teak cabinetry, spacious salon, double berths fore and aft—not bad for a 37-footer. Galley is on the small side and so is the aft deck. Note good-sized bridge. Hardtop, radar arch, bow pulpit, swim platform were standard. Twin 300hp Cummins diesels cruise at 18–19 knots (low 20s top).

Length Overall	36'10"	Clearance	15'7"
Length WL	32'6"	Fuel	350 gals.
Beam	14'5"	Water	120 gals.
Draft	3'0"	Hull Type	Modified-V
Weight	27,000#	Deadrise Aft	NA

Jefferson 42 Sundeck

1985–90

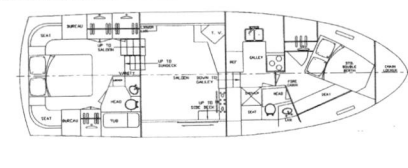

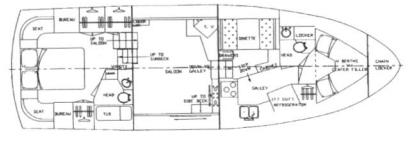

Prices Not Provided for Pre-1995 Models

Generic aft-cabin motoryacht with traditional lines combines roomy accommodations with economical operation, solid fiberglass construction. Several two-stateroom, galley-down floorplans were offered, all with full teak interior, tub/shower in aft head, standard lower helm. Highlights include large salon, full-width aft deck platform, roomy flybridge. Hardtop, radar arch, swim platform were standard. Low-deadrise hull incorporates long keel for directional stability. Cat 260hp diesels cruise at 15–16 knots (around 18 knots top).

Length Overall	41'8"	Clearance	NA
Length WL	37'8"	Fuel	350 gals.
Beam	14'3"	Water	200 gals.
Draft	3'7"	Hull Type	Modified-V
Weight	30,000#	Deadrise Aft	NA

Trawlers & Motoryachts

Jefferson 43 Marlago Sundeck

1990–2001

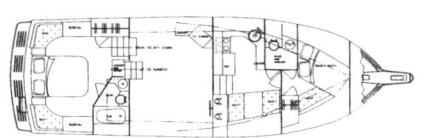

Appealing double-cabin cruiser offers an enduring blend of traditional styling, common-sense accommodations, affordable cost. Spacious two-stateroom, galley-down layout includes tub/shower in aft head, full dinette, standard lower helm. Expansive aft deck can entertain a small crowd. Note wide side decks, roomy bridge, large cabin windows. Most were sold with optional hardtop and radar arch. Low-deadrise hull with moderate beam, shallow keel delivers comfortable ride. Cruise at 20 knots with Cat 425hp diesels (low 20s top).

See Page 527 For Value Estimates

Length Overall	42'10"	Clearance	16'7"
Length WL	NA	Fuel	420 gals.
Beam	15'0"	Water	200 gals.
Draft	3'10"	Hull Type	Modified-V
Weight	31,000#	Deadrise Aft	NA

Jefferson 45 Motor Yacht

1984–88

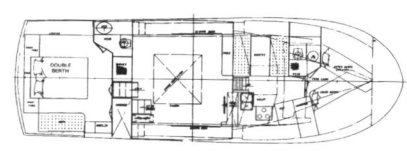

Generic Taiwan import from the 1980s hit the sweet spot with boaters seeking affordable motoryacht luxury. Expansive teak interior features spacious, open-plan salon with full lower helm, galley down with dinette opposite, large master staterooms. Note port, starboard deck access doors in salon. Roomy aft deck is large enough to entertain several guests. Radar arch, hardtop, swim platform, bow pulpit were standard. Perkins 200hp diesels cruise at 10–11 knots (14 knots top); 320hp Cats cruise at 16 knots (about 20 top).

Prices Not Provided for Pre-1995 Models

Length Overall	45'3"	Clearance	17'10"
Length WL	41'0"	Fuel	600 gals.
Beam	15'2"	Water	300 gals.
Draft	4'5"	Hull Type	Modified-V
Weight	41,000#	Deadrise Aft	NA

Jefferson 46 Sundeck

1986–90

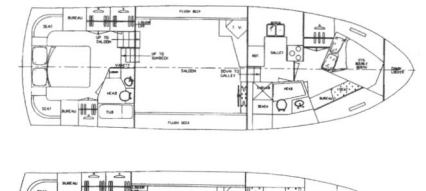

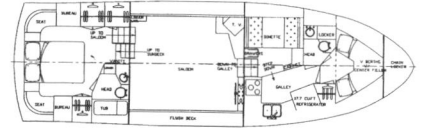

Feature-rich motoryacht from late 1990s was notable for conservative styling, competitive price. Several two-stateroom floorplans offered, all with galley down, standard lower helm. Solid teak paneling, teak parquet flooring highlight interior. Aft deck is big for a boat this size. Note wide side decks, spacious flybridge. Modest fuel capacity limits range. Swim platform, radar arch were standard. Slender modified-V hull delivers very comfortable ride. Cat 375hp diesels cruise at 18 knots (low 20s top).

Prices Not Provided for Pre-1995 Models

Length Overall	45'8"	Clearance	NA
Length WL	41'8"	Fuel	350 gals.
Beam	14'3"	Water	200 gals.
Draft	3'7"	Hull Type	Modified-V
Weight	43,000#	Deadrise Aft	NA

Jefferson 46 Marlago Sundeck

1990–2001

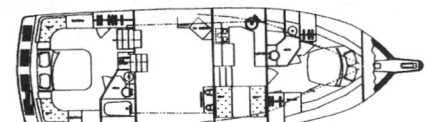

Galley-Down Interior

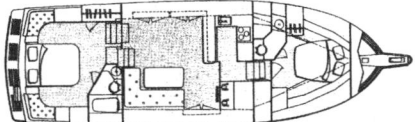

Galley-Up Interior

Contemporary aft-cabin motoryacht adhered to the Jefferson tradition of offering good value for the money. Standard galley-down interior has dinette opposite galley; alternate mid-galley layout has expanded salon with space forward for washer/dryer. Highlights include well-crafted teak cabinets, lower helm station, full-beam owner stateroom with settee seating, aft-deck wet bar, hardtop, radar arch. Cummins 315hp diesels cruise 15–16 knots (about 18 top); optional 430hp Volvo diesels cruise in the low 20s (mid 20s knots top).

See Page 527 For Value Estimates

Length Overall	45'10"	Clearance	11'7"
Length WL	NA	Fuel	420 gals.
Beam	15'0"	Water	200 gals.
Draft	3'10"	Hull Type	Modified-V
Weight	34,700#	Deadrise Aft	NA

Jefferson 50 Rivanna SE

2004–Current

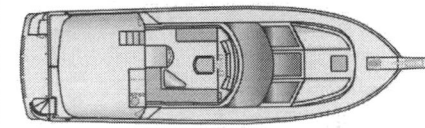

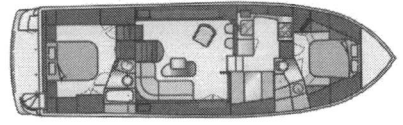

Sporty aft-cabin cruising yacht with integral swim platform gets high marks for styling, comfort, affordability. Standard two-stateroom, galley-down interior features spacious salon with wraparound windows, large master stateroom, generous storage. Teak cabinetry is expertly finished. Lower helm position is optional. Expansive aft deck with wet bar, wing doors can entertain small crowd. Note wide side decks, molded swim platform steps, bow pulpit. Cummins 480hp diesels cruise at 18 knots (low 20s top).

See Page 527 For Value Estimates

Length Overall	50'0"	Fuel	420 gals.
Beam	15'0"	Water	200 gals.
Draft	4'0"	Waste	60 gals.
Weight	37,700#	Hull Type	Modified-V
Clearance	12'10"	Deadrise Aft	12°

Jefferson 52 Marquessa

1989–2001

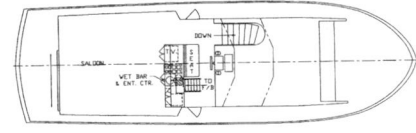

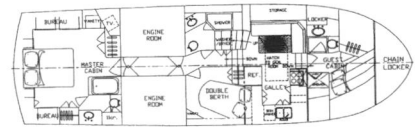

Twin-deck Jefferson motoryacht—similar in design to the Chris Craft 501 MY—combined bold styling with spacious accommodations, efficient deck plan. Three-stateroom, three-head interior with galley and dinette down boasts separate, walk-in engine rooms, large master with generous storage, deluxe owner's suite. Teak entertainment center separates lower helm from vast, full-beam salon. Small aft deck is useful for line-handling. Note wheelhouse deck doors, tub in aft head. GM 550hp diesels cruise at 15–16 knots (about 20 knots top).

See Page 527 For Value Estimates

Length Overall	52'5"	Fuel	700 gals.
Length WL	NA	Water	200 gals.
Beam	16'0"	Waste	45 gals.
Draft	4'0"	Hull Type	Modified-V
Weight	55,800#	Deadrise Aft	6°

Trawlers & Motoryachts

Jefferson 52 Monticello

1986–89

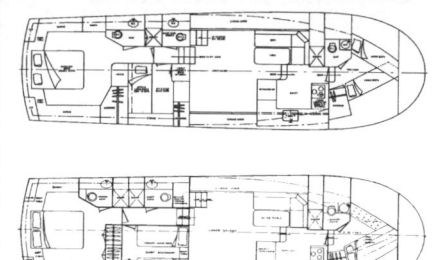

Affordable Taiwan import from late 1980s combined traditional flush-deck styling with spacious accommodations, solid construction. Three-stateroom interior features home-sized galley, expansive master suite, three full heads. Enclosed afterdeck/wheelhouse serves as main salon. Teak paneling and cabinetry are used throughout interior. Note molded bow seating. Wide side decks are a plus, but bridge is on the small side for a 52-footer. Twin Caterpillar 375hp diesels cruise at a sedate 14 knots (around 18 knots top).

Prices Not Provided for Pre-1995 Models

Length Overall	51'6"	Clearance	NA
Length WL	47'0"	Fuel	600 gals.
Beam	15'2"	Water	300 gals.
Draft	3'7"	Hull Type	Modified-V
Weight	45,000#	Deadrise Aft	NA

Jefferson 52 Pilothouse SE

2005–Current

Well-built pilothouse cruiser with distinctive Portuguese bridge meets class standards for space, comfort, affordability. Highlights include spacious pilothouse with L-shaped dinette, full-beam salon, covered aft deck, handcrafted teak interior woodwork. Combined salon/galley area benefits from large cabin windows; lazarette under aft deck provides access to well-arranged engine room. Note good lower-helm visibility, unique "boat deck" platform aft of bridge. Cummins 540hp engines cruise at 18 knots (low 20s top).

See Page 527 For Value Estimates

Length	51'7"	Fuel	680 gals.
Beam	15'0"	Water	200 gals.
Draft	4'0"	Waste	60 gals.
Weight	59,400#	Hull Type	Modified-V
Clearance	18'11"	Deadrise Aft	NA

Jefferson 52 Rivanna Cockpit MY

1994–1999

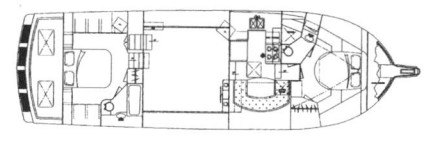

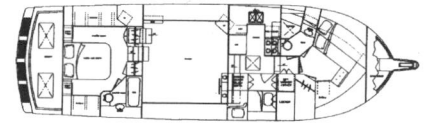

Popular 1990s cockpit yacht with seductive teak interior paired traditional Jefferson value with sporty styling, practical accommodations. Available with two or three staterooms, both with expansive salon, standard lower helm, home-size galley. Impressive list of standard equipment included hardtop, radar arch, bow pulpit, aft-deck wing doors, swim platform. Spacious engine room offers good outboard access to motors. Swim, dive, or fish from small cockpit. Cummins 450hp diesels cruise at 16 knots (around 20 knots top).

See Page 527 For Value Estimates

Length	52'4"	Headroom	6'5"
Beam	16'0"	Fuel	600 gals.
Draft	4'0"	Water	200 gals.
Weight	44,500#	Hull Type	Modified-V
Clearance, Arch	13'4"	Deadrise Aft	8°

Jefferson 56 Marquessa Cockpit MY

1991–2001

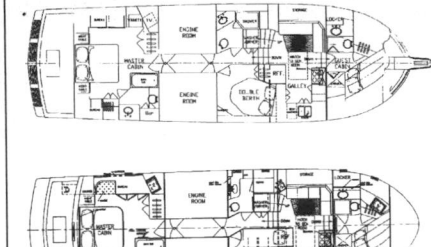

See Page 527 For Value Estimates

Roomy twin-deck cockpit yacht with full-beam salon took signature Jefferson value to the next level. Several three-stateroom, galley-down floorplans were available, all with lower helm open to salon and aft deck. Master suite is reached via corridor between separate walk-in engine rooms. Note port/starboard sliding deck doors, washer/dryer space in amidships head. Huge flybridge is accessed from salon only. Cockpit transom door makes boarding easy, convenient. GM 550hp diesels cruise at 14–15 knots (about 18 knots wide open).

Length	56'4"	Fuel	700 gals.
Beam	16'0"	Water	200 gals.
Draft	4'0"	Waste	45 gals.
Weight	57,500#	Hull Type	Modified-V
Clearance	19'6"	Deadrise Aft	6°

Jefferson 56 Rivanna Cockpit MY

1994–2009

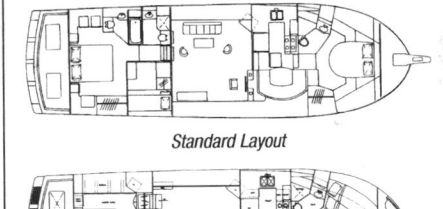

Standard Layout

Alternate Layout

See Page 527 For Value Estimates

Appealing cockpit motoryacht introduced in 1994 enhanced Jefferson reputation for graceful styling, versatile accommodations, exceptional value. Offered with several two- and three-stateroom interiors over the years, all with full-beam master suite, well-appointed salon with standard lower helm. Notable features include traditional teak interior, roomy aft deck with wet bar, good-size cockpit with transom door. Large engine room is a plus. Cat 600hp—or 635hp Cummins—diesels cruise at 18 knots and reach just over 20 knots top.

Length Overall	56'4"	Fuel	600 gals.
Beam	16'0"	Water	200 gals.
Draft	4'0"	Waste	45 gals.
Weight	47,000#	Hull Type	Modified-V
Clearance	16'5"	Deadrise Aft	6°

Jefferson 57 Pilothouse

2001–09

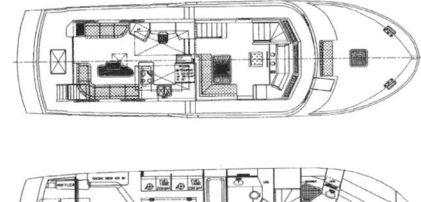

See Page 527 For Value Estimates

Heavily built pilothouse yacht was built for comfortable cruising in a wide range of conditions. Three-stateroom interior boasts expansive pilothouse with centerline helm, amidships master suite, VIP stateroom forward, home-sized galley. Note high-gloss teak joinery, protected decks, massive bridge, spacious engine room. Semi-displacement hull with hard aft chines has deep prop-protecting keel. Widebody version with full-beam salon also available. Cruise at 18–20 knots with 625hp Cummins diesels (low 20s top).

Length	57'5"	Headroom	6'6"
Beam	16'0"	Fuel	800 gals.
Draft	4'6"	Water	200 gals.
Weight	57,500#	Waste	75 gals.
Clearance	19'0"	Hull Type	Semi-Disp.

Trawlers & Motoryachts

Trawlers & Motoryachts

Jefferson 60 Marquessa MY

1987–89

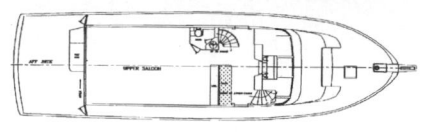

Main Deck

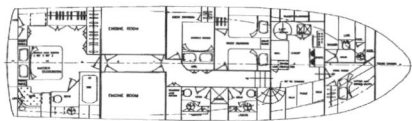

Lower Deck

Prices Not Provided for Pre-1995 Models

Taiwan-built motoryacht from late 1980s combined affordable price with spacious, total-teak interior, solid fiberglass construction. Several galley-down floorplans were offered, most with four staterooms, four heads. Extended salon with day head, staircase to flybridge, is completely open to lower helm. Note separate, walk-in engine rooms, tub in aft head. Topside features include enclosed aft deck with wing doors, protected side decks, large flybridge. GM 735hp diesels cruise at 15–16 knots (about 18 knots top).

Length	59'10"	Fuel	1,000 gals.
Beam	17'6"	Water	400 gals.
Draft	4'7"	Waste	45 gals.
Weight	88,000#	Hull Type	Semi-Disp.
Clearance, Arch	21'2"	Deadrise Aft	6°

Johnson 56/58 Motor Yacht

1992–2005

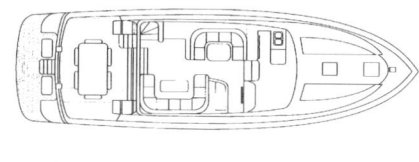

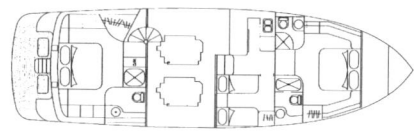

See Page 527 For Value Estimates

Rakish Taiwan sportyacht (called the High-Tech/Johnson 56 in 1992–99) with spacious twin-deck interior offered Eurostyle comfort, eye appeal at an attractive price. Standard three-stateroom floorplan includes three full heads, spacious salon with huge U-shaped sofa, step-down galley with dishwasher. Large aft deck—partially protected by bridge overhang—can accommodate a small crowd. Note foredeck sun pad, extended swim platform, wide side decks. Cruise at 20 knots (22–23 knots top) with GM 735hp diesels; 25 knots with 800hp Cats.

Length	58'0"	Fuel	1,000 gals.
Beam	16'0"	Water	200 gals.
Draft	4'10"	Waste	60 gals.
Weight	64,000#	Hull Type	Modified-V
Clearance	NA	Deadrise Aft	16°

Johnson 70 Motor Yacht

1996–2007

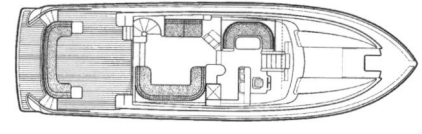

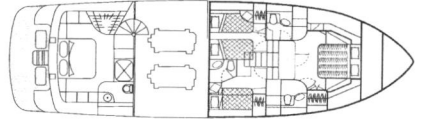

See Page 527 For Value Estimates

Spacious four-stateroom sportyacht with broad 19-foot beam made the cut with buyers attracted to lavish accommodations, Eurostyle performance, at an affordable price. Floorplan is unusual in that master suite is forward rather than amidships. Protected aft deck with twin transom staircases entertains a small crowd. Note standard lower helm, huge walk-in engine room. Available with open or enclosed flybridge. Bow thruster was standard. MTU 1,150hp diesels cruise at 20 knots; 1,400hp Cats cruise at 26 knots (30+ top).

Length Overall	70'0"	Clearance	20'6"
Length WL	58'6"	Fuel	1,600 gals.
Beam	19'0"	Water	350 gals.
Draft	5'2"	Hull Type	Modified-V
Weight	100,000#	Deadrise Aft	15°

Kha Shing 40 Sundeck

1980–86

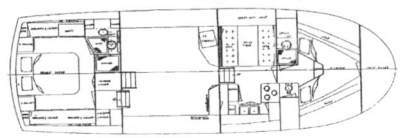

Two-Stateroom Layout

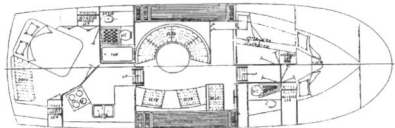

Alternate Three-Stateroom Layout

Prices Not Provided for Pre-1995 Models

Popular Taiwan cruiser with conservative lines gets high marks for quality teak interior, spacious accommodations, durable construction. Most were delivered with two-stateroom/dinette floorplan with lower helm. Highlights include well-crafted teak cabinetry, expansive salon with deck door, generous storage, big engine room. Hardtop was a popular option. Called Spindrift 40 on the West Coast; Vista or Southern Star 40 on East Coast. Over 120 sold. Cruise at 10–12 knots (around 15 knots top) with Volvo 165hp diesels.

Length Overall	39'6"	Clearance	15'1"
Length WL	34'0"	Fuel	300/340 gals.
Beam	14'0"	Water	200 gals.
Draft	3'7"	Waste	60 gals.
Weight	22,800#	Hull Type	Semi-Disp.

Krogen Manatee 36 Trawler

1984–92

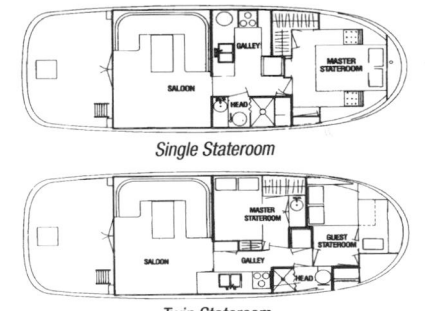

Single Stateroom

Twin Stateroom

Prices Not Provided for Pre-1995 Models

Unorthodox coastal cruiser from 1980s delivers more interior space, versatility than many 40-footers. Highlights include expansive full-beam salon, semi-enclosed flybridge, dinghy platform (rare on a 36-foot boat), weather-protected cockpit. Roomy single-stateroom floorplan proved far more popular than confining twin-cabin layout. Displacement hull with rounded transom, prop-protecting keel is fully cored. Range can exceed 1,000 miles. Cruise at 6–7 knots with 100hp Volvo diesel. Very popular boat—total of 99 were built.

Length Overall	36'4"	Clearance	14'0"
Length WL	34'0"	Fuel	280 gals.
Beam	13'8"	Water	300 gals.
Draft	3'2"	Waste	30 gals.
Weight	23,000#	Hull Type	Displacement

Krogen 39 Trawler

1998–Current

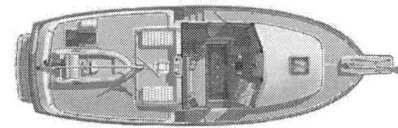

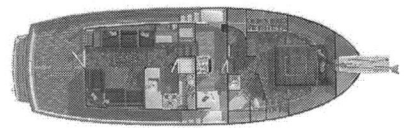

See Page 528 For Value Estimates

Muscular, quality-built pilothouse trawler—based on classic Krogen 42 hull—is built for big-water cruising in comfort, security. Beautifully finished interior features huge master stateroom forward, well-appointed salon, big U-shaped galley, raised pilothouse with fold-out berth. Walk-in engine room has built-in workbench. Good visibility from both helm positions. Extended hardtop can stow 10-foot dinghy; bridge overhangs shelter side decks and cockpit. Cruise at 7–8 knots with 121hp John Deere diesel. Range exceeds 2,500 miles.

Length Overall	43'8"	Ballast	2,000#
Length WL	36'8"	Fuel	700 gals.
Beam	14'3"	Water	300 gals.
Draft	4'3"	Waste	35 gals.
Weight	33,470#	Hull Type	Displacement

Trawlers & Motoryachts

Krogen 42 Trawler

1977–97

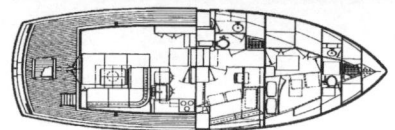

Standard Floorplan

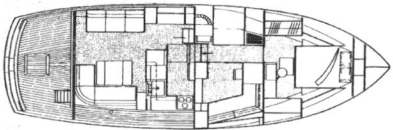

Widebody Layout

Classic Krogen trawler with full-displacement hull is widely praised for excellent seakeeping ability, efficient operation. Highlights include very tall freeboard, roomy cockpit, wide side decks, superb pilothouse visibility. Glass-over-plywood decks, superstructure upgraded to fiberglass in 1985 (hull #65); cored hull became solid fiberglass in 1995. Offered with one head or two. Widebody version with full-beam salon came out in 1989. Generator doubles as get-home engine. Range exceeds 2,000 miles. Total of 206 were built including five with twin engines.

See Page 528 For Value Estimates

Length Overall	42'4"	Ballast	2,500#
Length WL	39'2"	Fuel	700 gals.
Beam	15'0"	Water	360 gals.
Draft	4'7"	Waste	40 gals.
Weight	39,500#	Hull Type	Displacement

Krogen Silhouette 42

1987–91

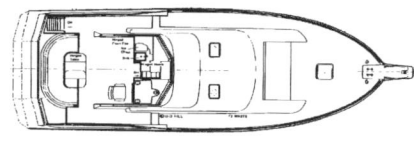

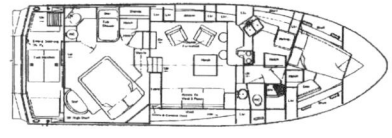

Distinctive coastal trawler built by Chien Hwa makes up in comfort, practicality whatever she lacks in sex appeal. Slightly awkward profile with semi-enclosed pilothouse conceals surprisingly spacious interior with two double staterooms, large salon with breakfast bar, home-sized galley, two full heads. Unique hydraulically operated stern gate drops to create a practically wide-open transom and swim platform. Note shaded lounge seating aft of helm, cushioned foredeck seating. Volvo 100hp diesels cruise at 7–8 knots. Total of 12 were built.

Prices Not Provided for Pre-1995 Models

Length Overall	41'10"	Clearance	NA
Length WL	37'6"	Fuel	400 gals.
Beam	14'6"	Water	150 gals.
Draft	3'2"	Cockpit	NA
Weight	28,000#	Hull Type	Modified-V

Krogen 44 Trawler

2004–Current

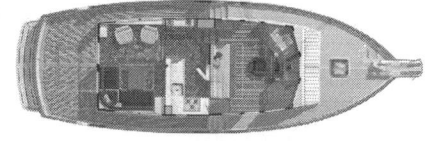

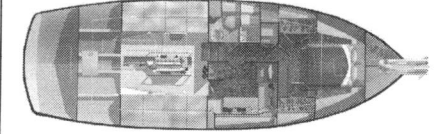

Iconic trawler yacht with distinctive pilothouse profile makes good on Krogen promise of long-range cruising in comfort, security. Twin-stateroom interior is similar to the old Krogen 42, but pilothouse is larger with space for fixed helm chair. Aft deck is larger as well with more entertaining space. Additional highlights include watertight aluminum doors and windows, protected walkways, meticulous engine room. Note desk in guest cabin. Offered in widebody or walkaround versions. Cruise at 7–8 knots with single 156hp John Deere diesel.

See Page 528 For Value Estimates

Length Overall	49'0"	Ballast	2,500#
Length WL	40'11"	Fuel	850 gals.
Beam	15'6"	Water	350 gals.
Draft	4'6"	Waste	52 gals.
Weight	43,140#	Hull Type	Displacement

Krogen 48 North Sea

1996–2008

Walkaround

Widebody

Graceful pilothouse trawler with ballasted, full-displacement hull offers leading-edge comfort, range, stability. Available with two- or three-stateroom interior, both with extensive teak joinery, parquet salon sole, galley with home-sized appliances. Optional widebody version increases salon space by eliminating port side deck. Cockpit and side decks are shaded by bridge overhangs. Extended flybridge can stow tender. Note galley access to large engine room. Single 210hp Cat diesel has range of about 2,000 miles at 8 knots. Over 50 built.

See Page 528 For Value Estimates

Length Overall	53'0"	Ballast	4,500
Length WL	45'5"	Fuel	1,000 gals.
Beam	16'8"	Water	400 gals.
Draft	5'0"	Waste	125 gals.
Weight	56,450#	Hull Type	Displacement

Krogen 48 Whaleback

1993–2003

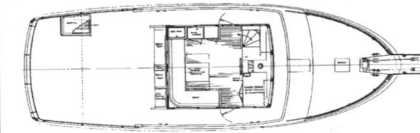

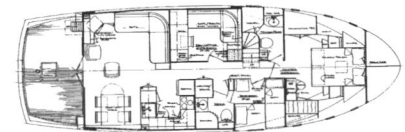

Sturdy full-displacement trawler exemplifies Krogen heritage of world-class engineering, quality construction, uncommon luxury. With wide 16'8" beam and no side decks, interior dimensions are extravagant for a boat this size. Single-level floorplan has three staterooms (one doubling as den), two full heads, expansive salon, large galley. Raised pilothouse with reverse windshield boasts 360-degree visibility, wet bar. Note protected walkway surrounding pilothouse. Cruising range with Cat 210hp engine is about 2,000 miles. Total of 30 were built.

See Page 528 For Value Estimates

Length Overall	48'5"	Ballast	4,500#
Length WL	45'5"	Fuel	1,020 gals.
Beam	16'8"	Water	540 gals.
Draft	5'0"	Waste	100 gals.
Weight	56,200#	Hull Type	Displacement

Krogen 54 Trawler

1987–89

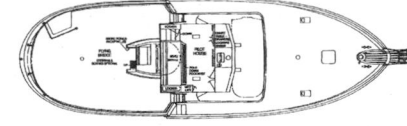

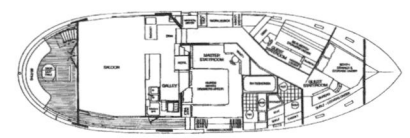

Heavy-weather trawler was designed for leisurely coastal cruising or extended ocean crossings. Built on ballasted, full-displacement hull with deep keel, rounded stern. Roomy three-stateroom interior features amidships master suite, spacious salon/galley, private wheelhouse with canted windows. Asymmetric layout lacks port side deck. Upper helm is tucked inside false funnel. Steadying sails dampen rolling motion common to displacement hulls. Cruising range of nearly 2,000 miles with single Lehman diesel. Eight were built.

Prices Not Provided for Pre-1995 Models

Length Overall	54'5"	Ballast	6,000#
Length WL	47'11"	Fuel	1,200 gals.
Beam	17'0"	Water	600 gals.
Draft	5'6"	Headroom	6'5"
Weight	67,800#	Hull Type	Displacement

Krogen 58 Trawler

2001–Current

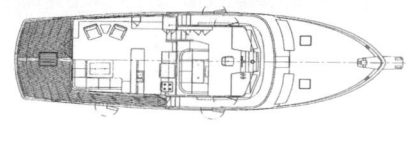

Feature-rich trawler with long-range capability travels the world in comfort, security. Built on full-displacement hull with long keel, twin prop-protecting skegs. Elegant cherrywood interior has master suite forward, guest staterooms aft with portside cabin doubling as office. Note engine room workbench, watertight doors. Reverse pilothouse windshield reduces glare. Asymmetric layout lacks port side deck. Portuguese bridge protects against breaking seas. Single 154hp diesel delivers impressive 2,000-mile range at 8 knots.

See Page 528 For Value Estimates

Length Overall	63'3"	Ballast	7,000#
Length WL	52'3"	Fuel	1,760 gals.
Beam	18'1"	Water	400 gals.
Draft	5'3"	Waste	100 gals.
Weight	96,830#	Hull Type	Displacement

Lagoon 43

2001–05

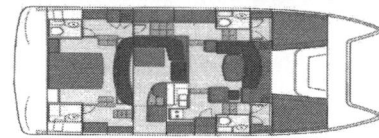

Three Staterooms

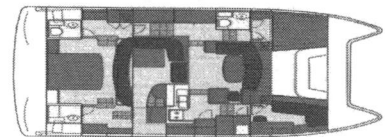

Two Staterooms

French-built catamaran trawler with mega-wide beam offers space, stability, economy unavailable in monohull yachts. Aft-cabin floorplan is unique: standard three-stateroom interior has guest cabins forward in each hull; optional two-stateroom layout has den/office in starboard hull. Lower-helm visibility is excellent thanks to panoramic salon windows. Expansive foredeck is perfect entertaining, sunning platform. Note small flybridge. Yanmar 250hp diesels cruise efficiently at 16–18 knots (about 20 knots top). Over 400 mile range.

See Page 528 For Value Estimates

Length Overall	42'9"	Headroom	6'3"
Length WL	39'1"	Fuel	412 gals.
Beam	21'1"	Water	206 gals.
Draft	3'11"	Waste	45 gals.
Weight	24,693#	Hull Type	Catamaran

Lazzara 68 Motor Yacht

2005–09

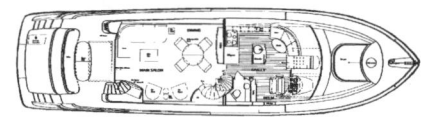

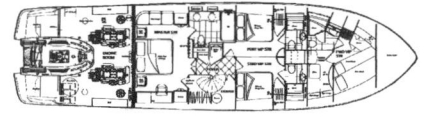

Seductive luxury yacht—smallest in the Lazzara fleet—combines European styling, performance in an all-American package. Lavish interior features full-beam master suite, three en suite VIP staterooms, spacious salon with formal dining area. Large country kitchen forward of salon includes day head, island counter top. Semi-enclosed bridge with huge sun pad, seating for 12 takes luxury to the next level. Megayacht-like transom garage has self-launching tender. Cat 1,000hp diesels cruise in the mid 20s (27–28 knots wide open).

See Page 528 For Value Estimates

Length	68'6"	Fuel	1,300 gals.
Beam	18'2"	Water	300 gals.
Draft	4'2"	Waste	100 gals.
Weight	104,000#	Hull Type	Modified-V
Clearance	22'8"	Deadrise Aft	12.5°

Lazzara 76 Motor Yacht

1993–2003

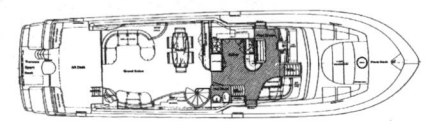

Sleek Eurostyle luxury yacht introduced in 1993 combines truly spacious accommodations, unsurpassed cruising comfort. Offered with walkaround decks or full-beam salon with no side decks. Interior highlights include condo-size galley, day head, lavish master suite, four guest cabins, den/office. Aft engine room permits expansive lower-level floorplan. Note transom garages, giant foredeck sun pad. Hull is fully cored to reduce weight. Cruise in the low 20s (about 25 knots top) with 1,150 MTU V-drive diesels.

Insufficient Resale Data to Assign Values

Length	76'11"	Water	350 gals.
Beam	19'1"	Waste	100 gals.
Draft	4'6"	Clearance, Arch	23'6"
Weight	94,000#	Hull Type	Modified-V
Fuel	1,750 gals.	Deadrise Aft	14°

Legacy 40 Sedan

1995–2006

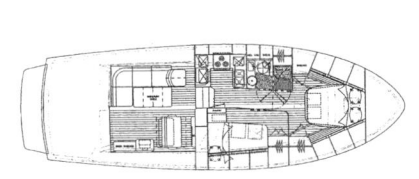

Purebred Downeast sedan introduced in 1995 was Legacy's first-ever powerboat model. Luxurious galley-down, two-stateroom floorplan boasts comfortable pilothouse/salon area with L-shaped settee, teak-and-holly sole, deck access doors. Wide side decks make getting around easy. Note attractive teak exterior trim. Shallow keel protects running gear in single-engine installations. Exceptional craftsmanship throughout. Single 420hp Cat diesel will cruise at 17–18 knots; twin 370hp Cummins cruise at 22–23 knots. Flybridge was optional.

Insufficient Resale Data to Assign Values

Length Overall	39'4"	Fuel	410 gals.
Length WL	36'0"	Water	120 gals.
Beam	13'7"	Waste	40 gals.
Draft	3'8"	Hull Type	Modified-V
Weight	22,000#	Deadrise Aft	17°

Lien Hwa 42 Motor Yacht

1983–94

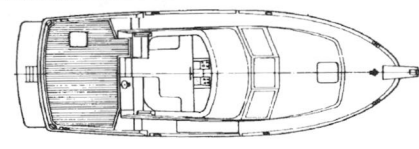

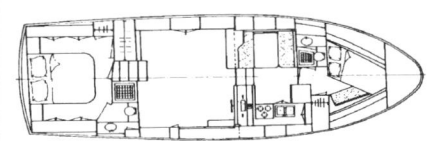

Contemporary aft cabin motoryacht (marketed as Vitesse, Vantare on the West Coast) compared well with class competitors in comfort, space, price. Traditional galley-down interior consists of roomy salon with entertainment center and lower helm, booth-style dinette, full-beam owner's stateroom with walkaround king bed. Additional features include lower helm deck door, copious storage, sundeck wet bar with ice-maker, hardtop, wing doors. Twin 275hp Lehman diesels cruise economically at 12 knots (15–16 top).

Prices Not Provided for Pre-1995 Models

Length	42'0"	Fuel	475 gals.
Beam	14'11"	Water	250 gals.
Draft	3'10"	Waste	40 gals.
Weight	28.600#	Headroom	Semi-Disp.
Clearance	NA	Hull Type	NA

Lien Hwa 47 Cockpit MY

1990–99

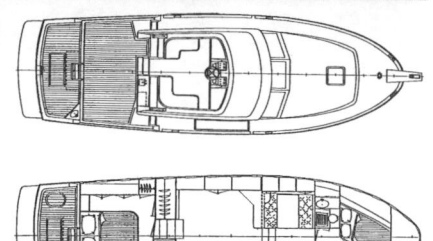

Popular Taiwan import from the 1990s (also marketed under Tradewinds, Vitesse nameplates) couples sharp styling with practical layout, solid construction. All-teak interior features roomy salon with lower helm position, U-shaped galley and dinette down. Note compact bow stateroom, absence of shower stall in forward head. Additional features include wide side decks, teak cockpit sole, hardtop, folding radar arch. Optional 375hp Cat (or 330hp Cummins) diesels cruise at 19–20 knots and reach a top speed of around 23 knots.

See Page 528 For Value Estimates

Length	45'11"	Fuel, Std.	540 gals.
Beam	14'11"	Fuel, Opt.	700 gals.
Draft	3'10"	Water	300 gals.
Weight	29,700#	Headroom	6'4"
Clearance	NA	Hull Type	Modified-V

Lord Nelson 37 Victory Tug

1982–89

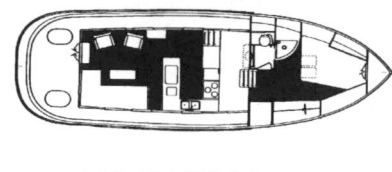

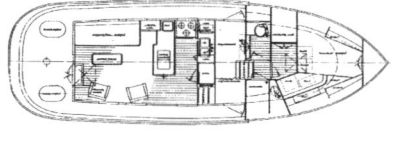

Popular coastal cruiser with bold workboat profile, ballasted keel is distinctive, secure, built to last. Single-stateroom interior boasts spacious salon with U-shaped galley forward, convertible settee aft. Raised pilothouse with Dutch doors gives helmsman superb outside views. Engine room is accessed via walk-in galley door or pilothouse hatches. Full teak interior is finished to high standards. Total of 76 were built. Cruise at 7 knots with 800- to 900-mile range with single 150hp Cummins diesel. Burns just 2 gph at 7 knots.

Prices Not Provided for Pre-1995 Models

Length Overall	36'11"	Clearance	12'6"
Length WL	33'4"	Fuel	250 gals.
Beam	13'2"	Water	185 gals.
Draft	3'6"	Waste	40 gals.
Weight	20,500#	Hull Type	Displacement

Mainship 34 Motor Yacht

1996–98

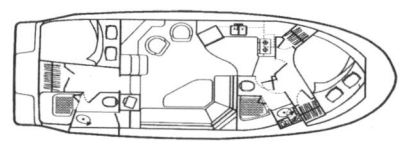

Tall-freeboard miniyacht with wide 13'8" beam packs big-boat accommodations in a midsize hull. Full-beam interior includes double berths in both staterooms, two full heads, cozy salon with convertible settee/dinette, mid-level galley with hardwood floor. Flybridge has bow walk-thru gate for deck access. Small aft deck has wet bar, hardtop. Note convenient port/starboard boarding gates, integral swim platform. Very popular model for Mainship. Twin 320hp gas inboards cruise at 15 knots (26–27 knots top).

See Page 529 For Value Estimates

Length w/Pulpit	36'5"	Fuel	300 gals.
Hull Length	34'6"	Water	70 gals.
Beam	13'8"	Waste	30 gals.
Draft	3'2"	Hull Type	Modified-V
Weight	18,500#	Deadrise Aft	16°

Mainship 34 Trawler

2005–09

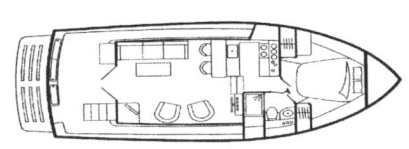

Stylish coastal cruiser with trawler profile is an impressive blend of looks, comfort, practicality. Roomy single-state-room interior with expansive salon, large head features attractive cherry joinery, huge salon windows. Side door opening to deck is a plus; wide side decks make getting around easy. Note engine room access hatch beneath bridge steps. Lower helm is optional. Cruise at 8 knots with single 240hp Yanmar diesel (12–13 knots top). Twin 315hp Yanmars reach 16–18 knots top, but range is limited.

See Page 529 For Value Estimates

Length w/Pulpit	38'10"	Headroom	6'4"
Beam	14'3"	Fuel	250 gals.
Draft	3'4"	Water	70 gals.
Weight	20,000#	Waste	34 gals.
Clearance	15'0"	Hull Type	Semi-Disp.

Mainship 350/390 Trawler

1996–2005

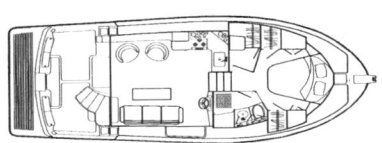

Popular sedan trawler (called Mainship 350 Trawler in 1996–98; 390 in 1999–2005) offered classic lines with well-planned layout, good turn of speed. Traditional teak interior features roomy salon with dinette/settee, lower helm door, opening salon windows, classy teak-and-holly sole. Molded bridge steps intrude into already-small cockpit. Transom door, radar mast, swim platform were standard; bow thruster was standard on single-engine boats. Cruise at 10–11 knots with single 300hp Cat; 14–15 knots with twin 230hp Yanmar diesels.

See Page 529 For Value Estimates

Length Overall	39'9"	Clearance	18'8"
Hull Length	34'9"	Fuel	300 gals.
Beam	14'2"	Water	130 gals.
Draft	3'8"	Waste	30 gals.
Weight	22,000#	Hull Type	Semi-Disp.

Mainship 36 Double Cabin

1984–89

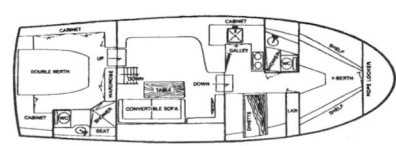

Conservative double-cabin cruiser from 1980s offered entry-level Mainship buyers a lot of boat for the money. Roomy interior with convertible salon sofa, convertible dinette can sleep as many as eight. Original teak interior was replaced with light oak joinery in 1985. Topside features include large aft deck platform, radar mast, swim platform. Easily driven hull designed for efficient low-speed operation runs well at higher speeds. Relatively small 270hp gas engines cruise at 14–15 knots (low 20s top).

Prices Not Provided for Pre-1995 Models

Length Overall	36'2"	Clearance	11'3"
Length WL	NA	Fuel	240 gals.
Beam	13'0"	Water	100 gals.
Draft	2'2"	Headroom	6'4"
Weight	20,000#	Hull Type	Semi-Disp.

Trawlers & Motoryachts

Trawlers & Motoryachts

Mainship 37 Motor Yacht

1995–98

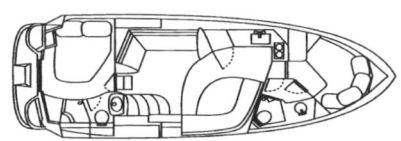

Portly aft-cabin cruising yacht from the late 1990s appealed to Mainship buyers seeking condo-size accommodations in a midsize boat. Truly expansive salon with built-in dinette, extraordinary headroom rivals many 45-footers for space, comfort. Oversized salon dimensions result in two very small staterooms. Gate in forward bridge coaming provides easy foredeck access. Note molded boarding steps on either side of aft deck. A heavy boat with lots of freeboard, twin 370hp gas inboards cruise at 14–15 knots (low 20s top).

See Page 529 For Value Estimates

Length w/Pulpit	39'6"	Fuel	300 gals.
Hull Length	37'9"	Water	100 gals.
Beam	13'5"	Clearance	13'6"
Draft	3'7"	Hull Type	Modified-V
Weight	21,000#	Deadrise Aft	17°

Mainship 395 Trawler

2010–Current

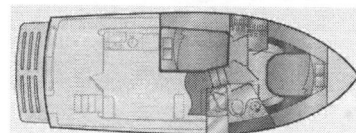
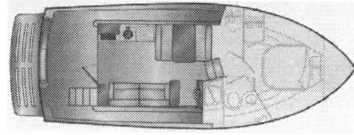

Handsome coastal cruiser with classic trawler lines delivers an impressive blend of space, comfort, affordability. Two-stateroom cherry interior boasts expansive salon with hardwood floors, large galley with Corian counter, 4-person dinette, compact lower helm with leaning post (no seat) and deck access door. Note secure side decks with raised bulwarks. Flybridge stairs lift for access to engine compartment. Bow/stern thrusters are standard. Cruise economically at 8 knots (14–15 top) with single 380hp Yanmar V-drive diesel.

Insufficient Resale Data to Assign Values

Length Overall	39'5"	Fuel	250 gals.
Hull Length	37'5"	Water	70 gals.
Beam	14'3"	Waste	35 gals.
Draft	3'3"	Hull Type	Modified-V
Weight	20,000#	Deadrise Aft	8°

Mainship 40 Double Cabin

1984–88

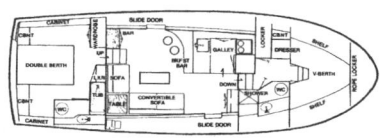

Roomy 1980s cruiser (often called Nantucket 40) offered motoryacht space, comfort at a budget-friendly price. Roomy salon boasts lower helm position, port and starboard deck doors, convertible sofa. Full-width aft stateroom includes double berth, excellent storage, tub/shower in adjoining head. Note that light oak woodwork replaced original teak joinery in 1985. Factory hardtop was never available. Bow pulpit, hinged radar mast, swim platform were standard. Cruise at 18 knots (high 20s top) with 350hp gas inboards.

Prices Not Provided for Pre-1995 Models

Length	40'0"	Fuel	300 gals.
Beam	14'0"	Water	140 gals.
Draft	3'4"	Headroom	6'4"
Weight	24,000#	Hull Type	Modified-V
Clearance	17'6"	Deadrise Aft	NA

Mainship 40 Trawler; 41 Expedition

2003–Current

2003–09 Interior

Revised Interior

See Page 529 For Value Estimates

Handsome sedan trawler (called the Mainship 40 Trawler until 2009) made good on promise of liveaboard comfort, cruising efficiency. Expansive interior with combined salon/galley/dinette features roomy master stateroom, compact guest cabin with single berths, large head with stall shower. Large flybridge has space for huge barbecue area with wet bar, and dinette. Additional features include washer/dryer, lower helm deck door, wide side decks, deep cockpit lazarette. Cruise efficiently at 10–12 knots with single 385hp Cat—or 370hp Cummins—diesel.

Length w/Pulpit	41'4"	Clearance	19'2"
Hull Length	38'4"	Fuel	300 gals.
Beam	14'2"	Water	130 gals.
Draft	3'8"	Waste	47 gals.
Weight	24,000#	Hull Type	Semi-Disp.

Mainship 41 Cockpit

1989–92

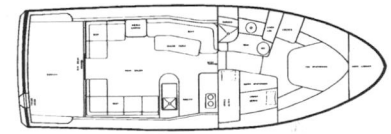
1989–1990

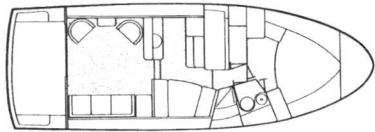
1991–92

Prices Not Provided for Pre-1995 Models

Well-built sedan appealed to entry-level buyers seeking big-boat comforts, amenities on a modest budget. Chief attraction is spacious salon with generous seating, built-in entertainment center. Original two-stateroom layout was completely revised in 1991. Guest stateroom is a tight fit. Cheap furnishings, plain decor leave much to be desired. Small windows restrict natural lighting in salon. Note very roomy bridge. Standard 320hp gas engines cruise at 15–16 knots (low 20s top); 375hp Cat diesels cruise at 20 knots (24–25 knots top).

Length	40'11"	Fuel	375 gals.
Beam	14'5"	Water	130 gals.
Draft	3'6"	Cockpit	75 sq. ft.
Weight	22,000#	Hull Type	Modified-V
Clearance	11'4"	Deadrise Aft	12°

Mainship 41 Grand Salon

1989–90

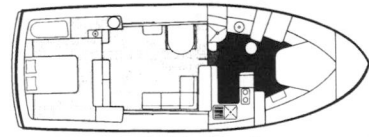
Double Cabin Floorplan

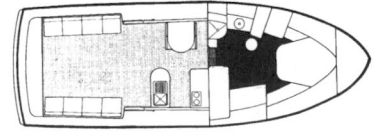
Grand Salon Layout

Prices Not Provided for Pre-1995 Models

Gaudy, slab-sided motoryacht with rectangular salon windows, maxi-volume interior may be the perfect floating condo. Two versions of the Mainship 41 were offered: Double Cabin model has master stateroom aft; Grand Salon features enormous, full-length salon stretching back to transom. Tiny cockpit is useful for line-handling; spacious bridge can accommodate several guests. Stiff ride in a chop. Standard 350hp gas engines cruise at 15 knots; optional Cat 375hp diesels cruise at 22 knots (mid 20s top). Note brief production run.

Length	40'11"	Fuel	375 gals.
Beam	14'5"	Water	130 gals.
Draft	3'6"	Headroom	6'5"
Weight	23,000#	Hull Type	Modified-V
Clearance	15'0"	Deadrise Aft	12°

Mainship 430 Aft Cabin Trawler

1999–2006

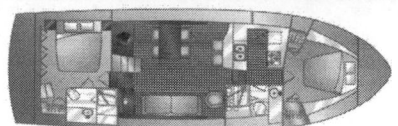

2-Stateroom Layout

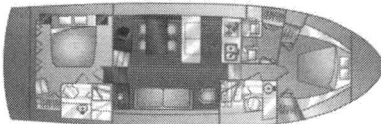

3-Stateroom Floorplan

See Page 530 For Value Estimates

Affordably priced aft-cabin cruiser combined spacious accommodations with traditional trawler styling, good turn of speed. Offered with several two- or three-stateroom interiors, all with two heads, athwartships double in aft cabin. Note teak interior joinery, cockpit door in aft cabin. Deep side decks provide secure fore-and-aft access; roomy bridge seats six to eight guests. Lower helm visibility is not great. Radar mast, transom door, bow pulpit were standard. Cruise at 14–16 knots with 370hp Cat diesels (about 20 knots top).

Length w/Pulpit	47'9"	Clearance	18'8"
Hull Length	43'0"	Fuel	500 gals.
Beam	15'6"	Water	250 gals.
Draft	3'8"	Waste	50 gals.
Weight	36,000#	Hull Type	Semi-Disp.

Mainship 43/45 Trawler

2006–Current

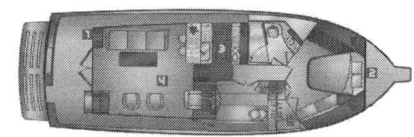

See Page 530 For Value Estimates

Blue-chip performance trawler (called Mainship 43 Trawler in 2006–07) with well-finished interior, user-friendly layout is a lot of boat for the money. Broad 15'6" beam provides spacious interior with two roomy staterooms, fully equipped galley, lower helm with deck door, cherrywood trim. Note tub/shower in head, two-section hanging locker in bow stateroom. Plenty of lounge/entertaining space on large bridge. Big fuel capacity provides excellent range. Cruise at 18 knots (low 20s top) with Yanmar 440hp V-drive diesels.

Length Overall	47'9"	Headroom	6'3"
Hull Length	43'0"	Fuel	777 gals.
Beam	15'6"	Water	200 gals.
Draft	3'8"	Waste	56 gals.
Weight	40,000#	Hull Type	Semi-Disp.

Mainship 47 Motor Yacht

1990–99

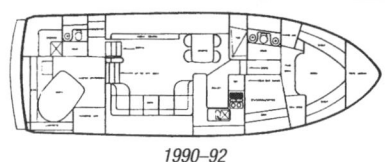

1990–92

1993–99

See Page 530 For Value Estimates

Durable 1990s motoryacht matched Mainship promise of space, comfort at an affordable price. Originally offered with three staterooms; alternate floorplan introduced in 1993 has two staterooms with galley, dining area aft in salon, small office/den forward. Salon is very spacious and so is the forward stateroom, but aft cabin is small for a boat this size. Utility room with washer/dryer, workbench is forward of engine room. Note foredeck sun lounge, underwater exhaust. Twin 485hp GM 6-71s cruise at 20 knots (23–25 knots top).

Length	46'10"	Fuel	600 gals.
Beam	15'5"	Water	200 gals.
Draft	3'10"	Waste	50 gals.
Weight	44,000#	Hull Type	Modified-V
Clearance	19'6"	Deadrise Aft	12°

Marine Trader 34 Double Cabin

1972–2001

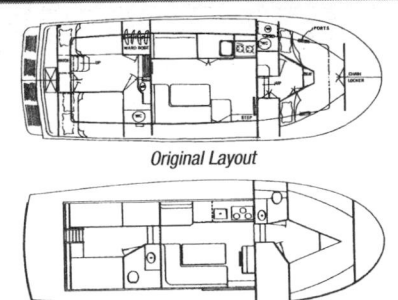

Original Layout

Late-Model Interior

See Page 530 For Value Estimates

Best-selling small trawler enjoyed great popularity in 1970s, 1980s thanks to low price, appealing teak interior, economical operation. Several floorplans were offered over the years, all with two heads, lower helm with deck door, compact galley. Built with plywood house prior to 1975, solid fiberglass thereafter. Decks were teak-planked until 1985—a constant source of leaks. Teak window frames were eliminated in 1992. Single 135hp diesel cruises at 6–7 knots (burning just 3 gph).

Length Overall	33'6"	Headroom	6'4"
Length WL	30'3"	Fuel	300 gals.
Beam	11'9"	Water	150 gals.
Draft	3'6"	Waste	40 gals.
Weight	17,000#	Hull Type	Semi-Disp.

Marine Trader 34 Sedan

1973–2001

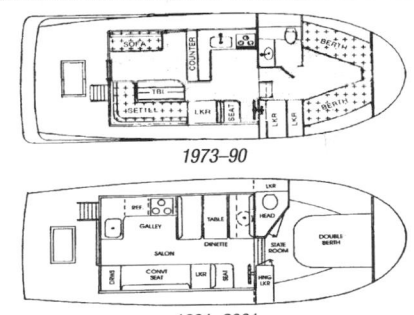

1973–90

1991–2001

See Page 530 For Value Estimates

Economical sedan cruiser with salty lines makes the grade with entry-level buyers on a budget. Highlights include full teak interior, lower helm station with sliding deck door, protected side decks, extended flybridge, spacious engine room, teak bow pulpit, teak cockpit sole, swim platform, mast and boom assembly. Early models were built with glass-over-plywood construction. Teak window frames (eliminated in 1995) often leak. So-so fit and finish. Cruise efficiently at 7 knots with single 120/135hp Lehman diesel; 10 knots with 210hp Cummins.

Length Overall	33'6"	Clearance	12'0"
Length WL	30'3"	Fuel	300 gals.
Beam	11'9"	Water	150 gals.
Draft	3'6"	Waste	40 gals.
Weight	19,600#	Hull Type	Semi-Disp.

Marine Trader 36 Double Cabin

1975–93

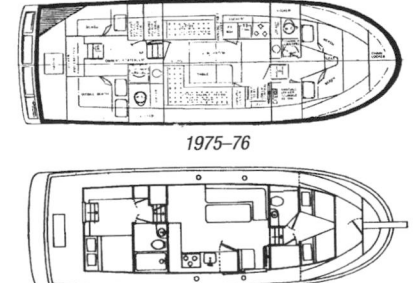

1975–76

1977–79

Prices Not Provided for Pre-1995 Models

Value-priced Taiwan import with classic trawler profile, traditional teak interior is ideally suited for the cruising couple. Originally designed with twin berths in aft stateroom; floorplan was rearranged in 1977 with double berth aft. Lower helm with teak deck door was standard. Note tub in aft head. Cockpit access door in aft stateroom is a plus. Additional features include folding mast, teak swim platform, teak decks. Teak window frames often leak. Called the 37 DC in 1978–79. Cruise at 6–7 knots with single Lehman diesel.

Length Overall	36'0"	Clearance	NA
Length WL	32'0"	Fuel	400 gals.
Beam	12'2"	Water	150 gals.
Draft	3'6"	Waste	40 gals.
Weight	21,000#	Hull Type	Semi-Disp.

Trawlers & Motoryachts

Marine Trader 36 Sedan

1975–93

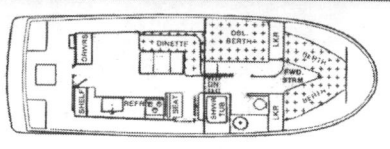

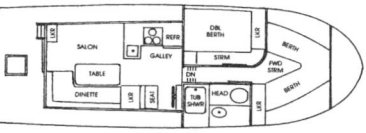

Durable sedan with classic trawler profile offers versatile layout with affordable price, low-cost operation. Galley-up teak interior with standard lower helm, convertible salon settee includes master stateroom with double berth to port, head with tub/shower, V-berths forward. Bridge overhangs protect decks and cockpit. Extended flybridge can stow a dinghy. Teak window frames are prone to leaks. Not-so-good workmanship and finish. Cruise at 7–8 knots with 120/135hp Lehman diesels.

Prices Not Provided for Pre-1995 Models

Length Overall	36'0"	Clearance	NA
Length WL	32'0"	Fuel	350 gals.
Beam	12'2"	Water	150 gals.
Draft	3'6"	Waste	50 gals.
Weight	21,000#	Hull Type	Semi-Disp.

Marine Trader 36 Sundeck

1985–94

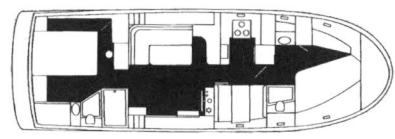

Popular sundeck trawler combines economical operation with family-friendly layout, traditional teak interior. Galley-down floorplan with booth-style dinette, convertible salon settee includes double berths in both staterooms, lower helm with deck access door, generous storage. Aft-deck hardtop, radar arch, teak swim platform, bow pulpit were standard. Good engine room access, wide walkways are a plus. Unimpressive fit and finish. Twin 135hp Lehman diesels (or single 210hp Cummins diesel) will cruise efficiently at 8 knots.

Prices Not Provided for Pre-1995 Models

Length Overall	36'0"	Clearance	NA
Length WL	32'0"	Fuel	350 gals.
Beam	12'2"	Water	150 gals.
Draft	3'6"	Waste	50 gals.
Weight	19,000#	Hull Type	Semi-Disp.

Marine Trader 38 Double Cabin

1980–2000

Galley Up

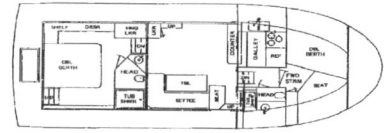

Galley Down

See Page 530 For Value Estimates

Generic double-cabin trawler offers timeless blend of traditional styling, common-sense accommodations, solid construction. Two-stateroom teak interior with lower helm, port/starboard salon doors was offered with galley down or up. Large master stateroom has cockpit access door—very useful. Topside features include teak decks, bow pulpit, teak handrails, folding mast. Note tub/shower in aft head, simulated lapstrake hull lines. Cruise at 7–8 knots with twin 135hp Lehman diesels or single 210hp Cummins.

Length Overall	38'0"	Clearance	NA
Length WL	34'8"	Fuel	300 gals.
Beam	12'10"	Water	250 gals.
Draft	4'0"	Waste	50 gals.
Weight	22,000#	Hull Type	Semi-Disp.

Trawlers & Motoryachts

Marine Trader 38 Sedan

1987–94

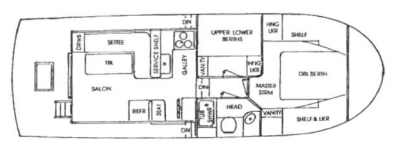

Semi-displacement sedan trawler appealed to entry-level cruisers for her handsome lines, low price, economical operation. Two-stateroom interior is arranged with salon galley, L-shaped dinette, lower helm with deck door, large master stateroom forward. Note handcrafted teak joinerwork, tub/shower in head. Bridge overhangs protect teak decks, cockpit. Extended flybridge can stow small dinghy. Additional features include teak swim platform, radar mast, deep side decks. Cruise at 8 knots with twin 135hp Lehman diesels.

Prices Not Provided for Pre-1995 Models

Length Overall	38'0"	Clearance	NA
Length WL	34'8"	Fuel	300 gals.
Beam	12'10"	Water	250 gals.
Draft	4'0"	Waste	50 gals.
Weight	22,000#	Hull Type	Semi-Disp.

Marine Trader 40 Double Cabin

1974–85

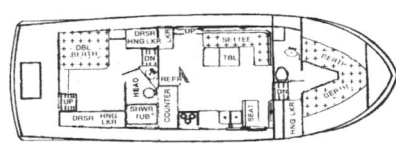

Traditional double-cabin trawler with total teak interior set class standards in her day for affordability, value. Twin-stateroom layout with salon galley includes lower helm, two salon deck doors, roomy master cabin with direct cockpit access door. Note tub/shower in aft head. Topside features include teak decks, folding mast, teak bow pulpit, teak swim platform. Plenty of exterior teak will keep owners busy. Note simulated lapstrake hull lines. Unimpressive fit and finish. Cruise efficiently at 7–8 knots with twin 120hp Lehman diesels.

Prices Not Provided for Pre-1995 Models

Length Overall	40'0"	Clearance	NA
Length WL	36'7"	Fuel	400 gals.
Beam	13'8"	Water	250 gals.
Draft	4'0"	Waste	50 gals.
Weight	30,000#	Hull Type	Semi-Disp.

Marine Trader 40 Sundeck

1983–2000

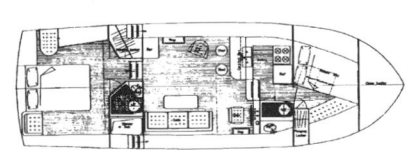

Appealing sundeck cruiser blends comfortable accommodations with conservative styling, fuel-efficient operation. Standard two-stateroom interior with galley down features convertible salon settee, breakfast bar, lower helm with deck door, walkaround queen in master, tub/shower in aft head. Full-width sundeck is big for a boat this size. Hardtop, radar arch, swim platform, bow pulpit were standard. Always a popular model. Note simulated lapstrake hull lines. Twin 135hp Lehman diesels cruise economically 7–8 knots.

See Page 530 For Value Estimates

Length Overall	39'4"	Clearance	NA
Length WL	36'5"	Fuel	350 gals.
Beam	12'11"	Water	250 gals.
Draft	4'0"	Waste	50 gals.
Weight	25,000#	Hull Type	Semi-Disp.

Trawlers & Motoryachts

Marine Trader 49 Pilothouse

1979–93

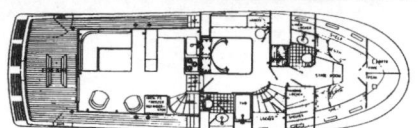

Standard Upper Deck

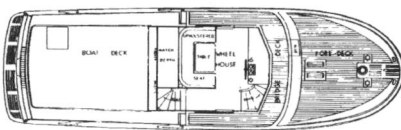

Standard Lower Deck

Prices Not Provided for Pre-1995 Models

Long-range pilothouse trawler introduced in 1979 delivered big-boat comfort, amenities at a super-competitive price. Spacious two-stateroom, two head floorplan offers U-shaped galley forward in salon, amidships master suite with tub/shower, pilothouse watch berth, inside bridge access. Note protected side decks, abundant outside teak. Prominent bow, wave-breaking Portuguese bridge can push through heavy seas. Fit and finish leaves a lot to be desired. Cruise at 8 knots with 135hp Lehman diesels; 10 knots with 165hp Perkins diesels.

Length	48'6"	Headroom	6'5"
Beam	15'0"	Fuel	700 gals.
Draft	4'6"	Water	375 gals.
Weight	46,000#	Waste	70 gals.
Clearance	NA	Hull Type	Semi-Disp.

Marine Trader 50 Motor Yacht

1979–93

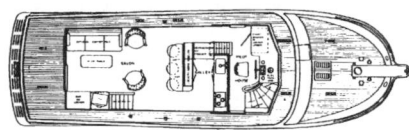

Main Deck, Standard Floorplan

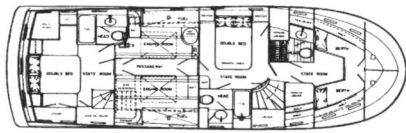

Lower Deck, Standard Floorplan

Prices Not Provided for Pre-1995 Models

Twin-deck motoryacht with classic trawler profile earned praise for solid construction, good seakeeping abilities, low price. Standard model has walkaround decks, covered aft deck. Widebody model introduced in 1985 has huge full-beam salon. Both versions share same three-stateroom floorplan with teak cabinetry and flooring, deckhouse galley with serving counter, wheelhouse deck doors. Separate walk-in engine rooms provide easy access to engines, pumps, etc. Cruise efficiently at 8–9 knots with standard 135hp Lehman diesels.

Length Overall	50'0"	Clearance	16'6"
Length WL	44'0"	Fuel	750 gals.
Beam	15'5"	Water	380 gals.
Draft	4'8"	Waste	80 gals.
Weight	46,000#	Hull	Displacement

Marlow 53 Explorer

2005–Current

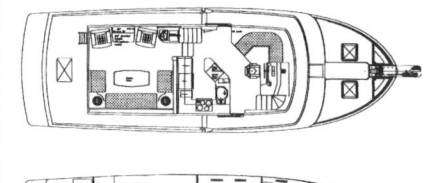

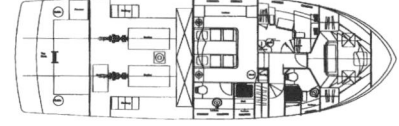

Insufficient Resale Data to Assign Values

Beautifully finished pilothouse yacht with full teak interior targets buyers with an eye for timeless styling, unabashed quality. Expansive three-stateroom layout with crew quarters aft includes spacious pilothouse with home-size galley, full-beam master suite, comfortable salon with indirect lighting. Portuguese bridge adds big-water security; standup engine room makes service easy. Note Burmese teak decks, cockpit controls, unusual twin-keel hull. Update in 2009 enlarged cockpit. Cat 700hp diesels cruise at 16 knots (20+ top).

Length	54'3"	Fuel	1,200 gals.
Beam	18'2"	Water	350 gals.
Draft	4'2"	Waste	120 gals.
Weight	59,000#	Hull Type	Semi-Disp.
Clearance	NA	Deadrise Aft	14°

Trawlers & Motoryachts

Marlow 57 Explorer

2005–Current

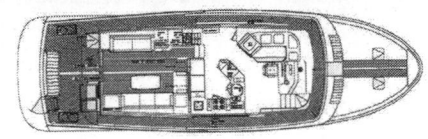

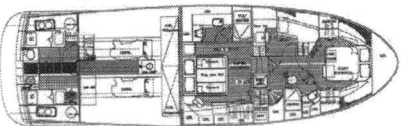

Striking pilothouse yacht with meticulous finish, Kevlar-reinforced hull takes cruising luxury to the next level. All-teak interior features expansive salon with panoramic windows, galley/dinette area forward, three private staterooms. Overhead grabrail in salon is a nice touch. Flybridge has space for dinghy aft of pilothouse. Note Portuguese bridge, protected side decks, extended swim platform. Engine room is very spacious. Distinctive twin-keel bottom allows this beamy yacht to reach 22 knots top with 700-hp Cat engines.

Insufficient Resale Data to Assign Values

Length Overall	62'2"	Fuel	1,200 gals.
Beam	18'2"	Water	300 gals.
Draft	4'2"	Waste	120 gals.
Weight	61,000#	Hull Type	Semi-Disp.
Clearance	NA	Deadrise Aft	14°

Marlow 61 Explorer

2005–Current

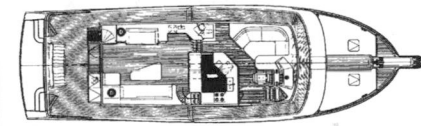

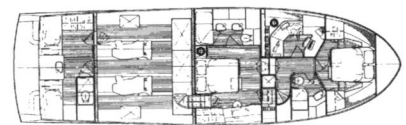

Handsome pilothouse cruiser with traditional styling makes good on promise of space, comfort, amenities. Highlights include gorgeous hardwood interior, aft crew quarters, Portuguese bridge, protected side decks. Space-efficient floorplan features expansive salon with built-in entertainment center, two roomy staterooms, private den/office. Engine room—reached from crew cabin—provides excellent service access. Lightweight Kevlar hull with twin-keel bottom will cruise at 12–14 knots (about 20 knots top) with 700hp Cat engines.

Insufficient Resale Data to Assign Values

Length	61'5"	Fuel	1,400 gals.
Beam	18'2"	Water	300 gals.
Draft	4'2"	Waste	150 gals.
Weight	77,000#	Hull Type	Semi-Disp.
Clearance	NA	Deadrise Aft	14°

Marlow 65 Explorer

2001–Current

Compelling long-range cruiser introduced in 2001 established Marlow's reputation for elegant design, practical accommodations. Traditional three-stateroom interior boasts varnished cherry (or teak) cabinetry, roomy salon with hardwood floor, country kitchen/pilothouse. Portuguese bridge fronts pilothouse; wide side decks are sheltered by bridge overhangs. Note fuel increase to 1,800 gallons in 2006. Unusual twin-keel hull protects running gear. Lugger 700hp diesels cruise at 12–14 knots (around 20 knots top).

Insufficient Resale Data to Assign Values

Length	65'10"	Fuel	1,400/1,800 gals.
Beam	18'4"	Water	400 gals.
Draft	4'5"	Waste	150 gals.
Weight	83,000#	Hull Type	Semi-Disp.
Clearance	18'0"	Deadrise Aft	14°

Trawlers & Motoryachts

Marlow 70 Explorer

2003–Current

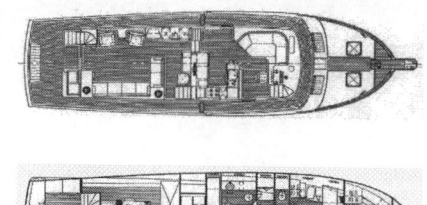

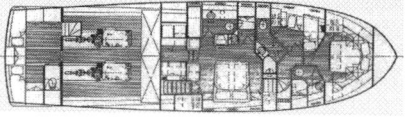

Good-selling luxury yacht is actually a Marlow 65 Explorer with a European transom — same interior layout, but a slightly longer yacht with a larger swim platform and a stairway to the aft deck. Spacious interior with high-gloss cabinetry boasts expansive salon/pilothouse, three large staterooms, walk-in engine room, crew quarters aft. Note wide side decks, Portuguese bridge, signature twin-keel hull design. A practical, versatile yacht perfect for extended cruising in comfort and security. Cruise at 22 knots (mid 20s top) with 1000hp Cat C18 diesels.

Insufficient Resale Data to Assign Values

Length	71'3"	Fuel	1,900 gals.
Beam	18'4"	Water	400 gals.
Draft	4'5"	Waste	150 gals.
Weight	85,000#	Hull Type	Semi-Disp.
Clearance	18'2"	Deadrise Aft	NA

Marlow 78 Explorer

2004–Current

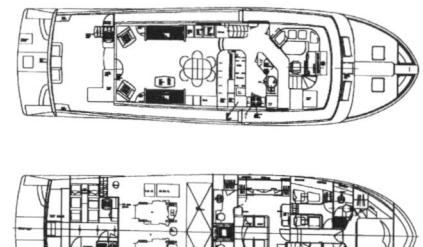

Heavily built pilothouse yacht with traditional styling combines high-tech construction, old-world craftsmanship. Highlights include ocean-crossing fuel capacity, protective Portuguese bridge, spacious cockpit, opulent interior with many luxurious features. Semicustom design is offered with several three-, four-stateroom layouts with crew quarters aft. Massive bridge can entertain a small crowd. Note that 78E (shown above) has integrated swim platform, 78C has conventional transom. Cat 1,500hp diesels cruise at 18–20 knots (mid 20s knots top).

Insufficient Resale Data to Assign Values

Length	78'2"	Fuel	3,000 gals.
Beam	20'4"	Water	550 gals.
Draft	4'10"	Waste	200 gals.
Weight	100,000#	Hull Type	Semi-Disp.
Clearance	18'2"	Deadrise Aft	NA

Marquis 55 LS

2007–Current

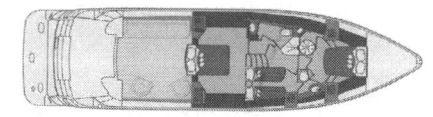

Head-turning pilothouse yacht (called the Marquis 560 since 2009) makes good on promise of luxury, style, performance. Stylish interior with split-level salon features elegant master suite with two walk-in wardrobes, third stateroom/office. Open galley and salon permit good aft visibility from lower helm. Watertight door in transom opens to spacious lazarette and engine room. Side decks are on the narrow side. Note roomy flybridge with pop-up helm display, distinctive hullside windows. Volvo 775hp diesels cruise in the low 20s (27–28 knots top).

See Page 530 For Value Estimates

Length	57'4"	Fuel	836 gals.
Beam	16'0"	Water	200 gals.
Draft	4'11"	Waste	100 gals.
Weight	62,000#	Hull Type	Modified-V
Clearance	18'5"	Deadrise Aft	14°

Trawlers & Motoryachts

Marquis 59 Pilothouse

2003–Current

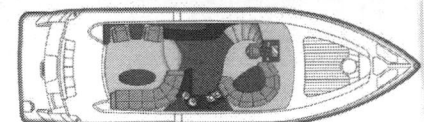

Main Deck Plan

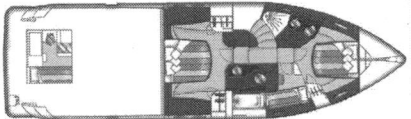

Lower Level Plan

Popular pilothouse sportyacht (called Marquis 600 after 2009) combines seductive European looks with American practicality. Opulent split-level salon stretches unbroken from sliding entryway doors to pilothouse windshield. Highlights include centerline lower helm with wraparound seating, huge galley with granite countertops, full-beam master stateroom with king bed. Curved staircase leads to huge flybridge with lounge seating, wet bar, davit. Note stand-up engine room. MAN 825hp diesels cruise in the low 20s (about 30 top).

See Page 530 For Value Estimates

w/Platform	59'6"	Fuel	800 gals.
Beam	16'6"	Water	200 gals.
Draft	5'5"	Waste	80 gals.
Weight	58,500#	Hull Type	Modified-V
Clearance, Arch	16'3"	Deadrise Aft	14°

Marquis 65 Pilothouse

2005–Current

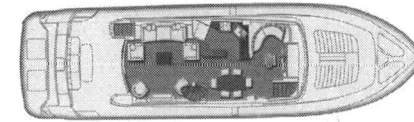

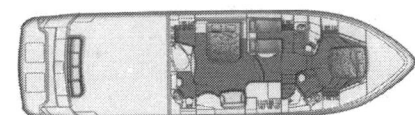

World-class pilothouse yacht (called the Marquis 690 after 2009) blends flashy Italian styling with posh accommodations, impressive performance. Interior highlights include near-perfect cherry joinery, opulent master suite with his-and-her bath, glass bridge staircase, formal dining area. Two-person crew quarters are aft of engine room with direct transom access. Extended hardtop ensures year-round entertaining. Hydraulic swim platform makes launching a tender easy. MTU 1,350hp V-drive diesels cruise at 24–26 knots (30+ top).

See Page 530 For Value Estimates

Length	69'11"	Fuel, Std/Opt	1,200 gals.
Beam	17'11"	Water	200 gals.
Draft	6'0"	Waste	153 gals.
Weight	94,000#	Hull Type	Modified-V
Clearance	24'5"	Deadrise Aft	13°

Maxum 4100 SCA

1997–2001

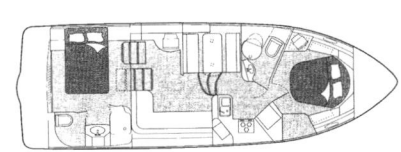

Competitively priced motoryacht with rakish styling matched Maxum promise of big-boat luxury, comfort at an affordable price. Spacious two-stateroom, twin-head interior—dominated by simple, plain-Jane decor—provides lots of entertaining space. Note large forward cabin, full-size galley with Corian counter. Topside features include wide side decks, foredeck sun pads, aft-deck wet bar, molded transom steps. Most were sold with optional hardtop. Cruise at 15 knots with standard gas engines; 20 knots with 370hp Cummins diesels.

See Page 531 For Value Estimates

Length	41'8"	Fuel	300 gals.
Beam	13'10"	Water	90 gals.
Draft	3'9"	Waste	76 gals.
Weight	30,000#	Hull Type	Modified-V
Clearance	18'2"	Deadrise Aft	10°

Trawlers & Motoryachts

Maxum 4100 SCB

1997–2001

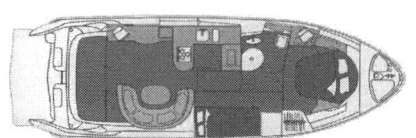

Value-priced flybridge yacht with generous 13'11" beam combined sexy European styling with liveaboard comfort, motoryacht versatility. Expansive wood-trimmed salon with wraparound windows features booth-style dinette, large galley, full entertainment center. Both staterooms share single double-entry head with separate stall shower. Note cockpit wet locker, flybridge wet bar, extended swim platform. Engine room is tight. Standard gas engines cruise at 15 knots; optional 370hp Cummins diesels cruise at 20 knots.

See Page 531 For Value Estimates

Length	42'2"	Fuel	380 gals.
Beam	13'11"	Water	100 gals.
Draft	3'9"	Waste	75 gals.
Weight	28,770#	Hull Type	Modified-V
Clearance	18'0"	Deadrise Aft	13°

Maxum 4600 SCB

1997–2001

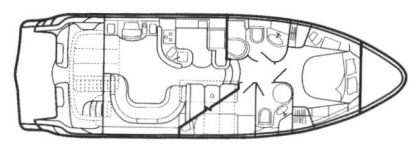

Handsome sedan yacht introduced in 1997 offered motoryacht space, luxury at budget-friendly price. Wide-open salon with cherry (or maple) cabinetry features large galley with conventional oven, raised dinette, huge U-shaped settee. Note roomy forward stateroom, large heads with stall showers. Extended flybridge includes wet bar, aft sun lounge. Wide swim platform can stow small inflatable or PWC. Cummins 370hp diesels cruise at 18 knots (20+ top); Cummins 450hp diesels cruise at 20 knots and reach a top speed of 23–24 knots.

See Page 531 For Value Estimates

Length	45'11"	Fuel	418 gals.
Beam	14'4"	Water	100 gals.
Draft	4'0"	Waste	75 gals.
Weight	30,400#	Hull Type	Modified-V
Clearance, Arch	14'2"	Deadrise Aft	9°

McKinna 47 Sedan/481 Sedan

1999–2006

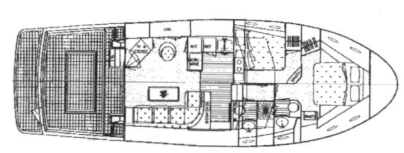

Appealing Taiwan-built sedan (called the 47 Sedan in 1999–2000; 481 Sedan in 2001–06) is stylish, roomy, built to last. Efficient galley-up floorplan with lower helm has two staterooms, both with queen-size berths and built-in vanities. Note maple cabinets, granite and marble counters, convenient pilothouse deck door. Both heads share a common shower stall. Excellent range with huge 700-gallon fuel capacity. Stout, heavily built yacht is capable of serious cruising. Cruise at 18–20 knots with 370hp Cummins diesels.

See Page 531 For Value Estimates

Length Overall	50'0"	Fuel	700 gals.
Beam	15'0"	Water	200 gals.
Draft	3'10"	Waste	40 gals.
Weight	29,700#	Hull Type	Modified-V
Clearance	19'6"	Deadrise Aft	18°

McKinna 48 Pilothouse

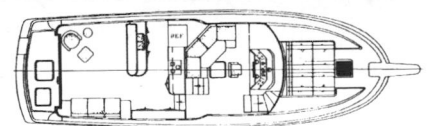

1996–2000

Heavily-built pilothouse yacht (built in Taiwan by Lien Hwa) blurs the line between full-feature cruising yacht, blue-chip liveaboard. Standard three-stateroom interior boasts amidships master suite, spacious full-beam salon, gourmet galley. Sliding glass doors open to roomy cockpit with transom door. Note exquisite teak interior joinery, teak parquet floors. Raised pilothouse has chart table, L-shaped settee, twin deck access doors. Flybridge can stow small dinghy. Cat 375hp diesels cruise at 17–18 knots (about 20 knots top).

See Page 531 For Value Estimates

Length w/Pulpit	54'3"	Fuel	825 gals.
Hull Length	47'10"	Water	250 gals.
Beam	15'5"	Headroom	6'4"
Draft	4'2"	Hull Type	Modified-V
Weight	44,500#	Deadrise Aft	18°

McKinna 57 Pilothouse

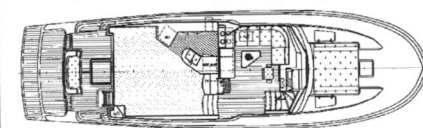

1997–2006

Salon Galley

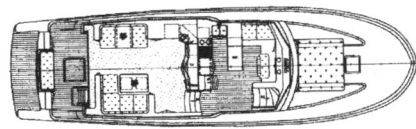

Pilothouse Galley

Luxury-class pilothouse yacht (built by Lien Hwa in Taiwan) with spacious three-stateroom interior couples quality construction with tasteful accommodations, excellent range. Highlights include sociable full-beam salon with galley forward, raised pilothouse with dinette and deck door, inside flybridge access, three heads with walk-in showers, extended swim platform with dual transom doors. Large cockpit has wet bar, barbecue, docking station, in-sole engine room entry. MAN 600hp diesels cruise in the low 20s (26–27 knots top).

See Page 531 For Value Estimates

Length Overall	62'0"	Fuel	850 gals.
Beam	15'5"	Water	270 gals.
Draft	4'2"	Headroom	6'5"
Weight	52,500#	Hull Type	Modified-V
Clearance	NA	Deadrise Aft	18°

Trawlers & Motoryachts

McKinna 65 Pilothouse

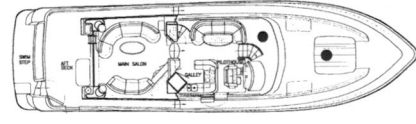

2000–05

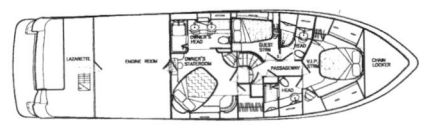

Executive-class pilothouse yacht matches sleek styling with top-shelf accommodations, world-class construction. Luxury-class interior is an impressive display of furniture-quality woodwork, designer furnishings. Lower helm, galley and dinette share space on pilothouse level. Expansive salon comes with leather upholstery, full entertainment center. Note inside-only bridge access. Additional features include teak-planked decks, extended swim platform, secure side decks. Engine room is a tight fit. Cruise at 20 knots with Cat 800hp diesels.

See Page 531 For Value Estimates

Length Overall	67'6"	Fuel	1,100 gals.
Beam	17'3"	Water	280 gals.
Draft	3'7"	Headroom	6'8"
Weight	70,000#	Hull Type	Modified-V
Clearance	NA	Deadrise Aft	NA

Trawlers & Motoryachts

Meridian 368 Motor Yacht

2005–08

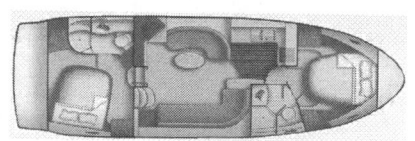

Well-conceived motoryacht with maxi-volume interior blurs the line between home-size liveaboard, deluxe coastal cruiser. Interior highlights include full-beam salon with facing settees, large galley with cherry cabinetry, two double staterooms with en suite heads. Tiered cabin windows provide panoramic outside views; picture window in master stateroom overlooks swim platform. Bow and stern thrusters, opening salon windows are standard. Twin 370hp gas engines cruise at 18–19 knots; 330hp Cummins diesels cruise in the mid 20s.

See Page 531 For Value Estimates

Length	37'8"	Fuel	250 gals.
Beam	13'7"	Water	90 gals.
Draft	3'6"	Waste	50 gals.
Weight	24,250#	Hull Type	Modified-V
Clearance	13'6"	Deadrise Aft	13°

Meridian 408 Motor Yacht

2003–08

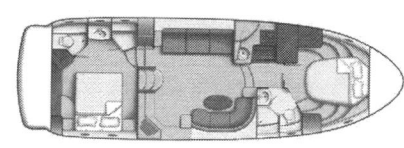

Maxi-volume motoryacht delivers the goods when it comes to amenities, comfort, versatility. Condo-style interior with huge salon, roomy staterooms rivals that of a small apartment. Tiered windows provide near 360-degree visibility. Split forward head saves space, adds convenience. Note classy cherrywood cabinets, hardwood galley sole. Topside features include molded swim-platform steps, large flybridge with wet bar. Fuel capacity is modest for a 40-footer. Cruise at 20 knots (mid 20s top) with Cummins 370hp diesels.

See Page 531 For Value Estimates

Length	42'2"	Fuel	330 gals.
Beam	14'4"	Water	90 gals.
Draft	3'10"	Waste	55 gals.
Weight	29,000#	Hull Type	Modified-V
Clearance	14'4"	Deadrise Aft	10°

Meridian 411 Sedan

2003–07

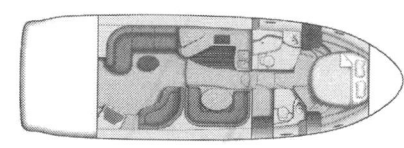

Competitively priced sedan with crisp styling, spacious interior was Meridian's best-selling model. Split-level salon has galley and dinette forward, facing settees and entertainment center aft. Hatch in salon floor provides access to engine room. Additional features include bridge seating for eight, extended swim platform, cherry interior cabinetry, radar arch. Single-stick control system with bow, stern thrusters makes docking easy. Lower helm was optional. Cruise at 22 knots with 370hp Cummins diesels (26–28 knots top). Over 300 were sold.

See Page 531 For Value Estimates

Length	46'0"	Fuel	400 gals.
Beam	14'2"	Water	150 gals.
Draft	3'9"	Waste	55 gals.
Weight	25,000#	Hull Type	Modified-V
Clearance	15'0"	Deadrise Aft	7°

Meridian 441 Sedan Bridge

2008–09

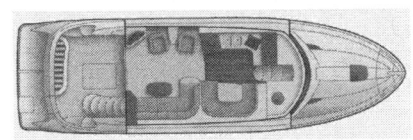

Updated version of popular Meridian 411 Sedan (2003–07) boasts new joystick docking system, enlarged salon, additional storage space. Luxurious cherry interior features well-appointed salon with curved settee, home-style galley with dinette opposite, three large staterooms with the master forward. Hullside windows provide midcabin sea view. Note tiered salon windows, huge utility room under salon sole. Large flybridge can seat a small crowd. Outboard engine access is a tight fit. Cummins 425hp V-drive diesels cruise at 22 knots.

See Page 531 For Value Estimates

Length	47'2"	Fuel	432 gals.
Beam	14'3"	Water	150 gals.
Draft	3'1"	Waste	55 gals.
Weight	31,233#	Hull Type	Modified-V
Clearance	NA	Deadrise Aft	7°

Meridian 459 Cockpit MY

2004–08

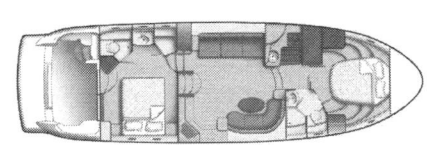

Stretched version of the Meridian 408 MY adds cockpit versatility to a proven motoryacht design. Huge interior with wide-open salon, tiered windows rivals larger yachts for living space, comfort. Highlights include cherry interior cabinetry, full-beam master suite with direct cockpit access, roomy guest stateroom with walkaround queen, space for washer/dryer. Aft deck is on the small side, but the cockpit (with extended swim platform) is large. Note modest fuel capacity. Cruise at 18 knots (low 20s top) with Cummins 370hp diesels.

See Page 531 For Value Estimates

Length	47'8"	Fuel	330 gals.
Beam	14'4"	Water	90 gals.
Draft	3'10"	Waste	55 gals.
Weight	30,700#	Hull Type	Modified-V
Clearance	14'4"	Deadrise Aft	10°

Meridian 490 Pilothouse

2004–08

Rebranded version of popular Bayliner 4788 Pilothouse (1994–2002) offers big-boat value in a handsome, well-appointed package. Versatile three-stateroom floorplan with cherry cabinets features roomy full-beam salon with full-service galley forward, raised pilothouse with flybridge access, two full heads. Third stateroom, accessed from master stateroom, has settee with hinged upper/lower berths allowing it to double as a dressing room. Engine room is a little tight. Cruise efficiently at 20 knots with standard Cummins 330hp diesels.

See Page 531 For Value Estimates

Length w/Pulpit	54'0"	Fuel	444 gals.
Beam	15'1"	Water	200 gals.
Draft	3'4"	Waste	48 gals.
Weight	29,990#	Hull Type	Modified-V
Clearance	18'2"	Deadrise Aft	NA

Trawlers & Motoryachts

Meridian 540 Pilothouse

2003–06

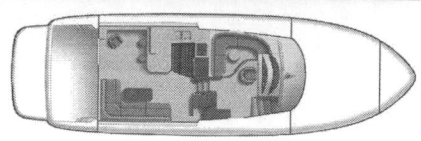

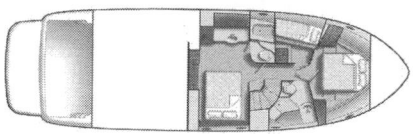

Well-bred pilothouse yacht offers levels of comfort, luxury usually associated with more expensive yachts. Luxury class interior with three private staterooms includes full-beam salon with entertainment center, U-shaped galley with hardwood floor, bathtub in master head, raised pilothouse with wraparound dinette. Engine room is accessed from cockpit door. Note underwater exhaust system, foredeck sun pad. Graceful lines incorporate the best in modern pilothouse styling. Cruise at 22–23 knots (mid 20s top) with 635hp Cummins diesels.

See Page 531 For Value Estimates

Length	56'9"	Fuel	700 gals.
Beam	16'3"	Water	200 gals.
Draft	4'10"	Waste	76 gals.
Weight	50,554#	Hull Type	Modified-V
Clearance	19'3"	Deadrise Aft	12°

Meridian 580 Pilothouse

2003–09

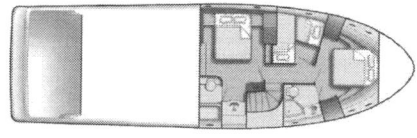

Restyled version of earlier Bayliner 5788 (1997–2002) offers appealing blend of modern pilothouse styling, deluxe amenities, luxury class accommodations. Appealing three-stateroom interior boasts home-size galley with faux granite counters, built-in dinette, salon entertainment center, well-appointed pilothouse, standard washer/dryer, tub in master head. Note stand-up engine room (with cockpit access), underwater exhaust system, foredeck sun lounge. Cummins 635hp diesels cruise at 18 knots (low 20s top).

See Page 531 For Value Estimates

Length	59'5"	Fuel	800 gals.
Beam	17'4"	Water	218 gals.
Draft	4'11"	Waste	74 gals.
Weight	59,920#	Hull Type	Modified-V
Clearance	19'7"	Deadrise Aft	10°

Monk 36 Trawler

1982–2007

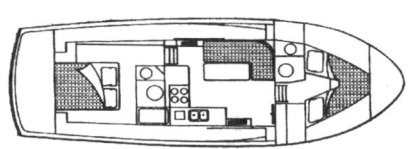

Graceful aft-cabin trawler offers solid mix of simplicity, comfort, seaworthiness. Comfortable galley-up interior with teak cabinetry, spacious master stateroom is mostly unchanged from original, although post-1992 models eliminated tub in aft head. Room for small dinghy on aft cabintop. Wide side decks are a plus. Built in Taiwan until 1991 when production was shifted to Canada. Over 250 built. Early models came with plenty of exterior teak trim. Single 120hp diesel will cruise at 7 knots; single 220hp will cruise at 9–10 knots.

See Page 532 For Value Estimates

Length Overall	36'0"	Clearance, Mast	17'11"
Length WL	33'0"	Fuel	320 gals.
Beam	13'0"	Water	120 gals.
Draft	4'0"	Waste	45 gals.
Weight	18,000#	Hull Type	Semi-Disp.

Nautique 42 Cockpit MY

1985–90

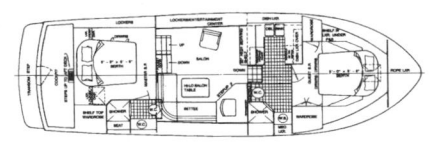

Well-regarded Taiwan import with traditional teak interior combines distinctive styling with roomy accommodations, solid construction. Offered with several floorplan layouts. Popular two-stateroom, galley-down plan includes expansive salon with serving counter, two full heads, lower helm station. Large cabin windows admit plenty of natural lighting. Additional highlights include cockpit transom door, radar arch, bow pulpit, swim platform. Cruise at 16–18 knots (just over 20 knots top) with 320hp Cat diesels.

Prices Not Provided for Pre-1995 Models

Length	41'10"	Fuel	350 gals.
Beam	13'5"	Water	150 gals.
Draft	3'4"	Waste	50 gals.
Weight	25,000#	Hull Type	Modified-V
Clearance	NA	Deadrise Aft	14°

Navigator 44 Classic

2002–07

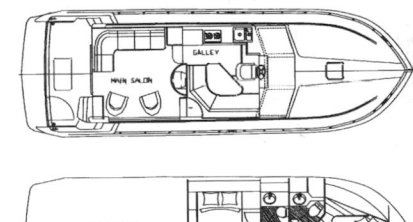

Value-priced cruising yacht with spacious pilothouse interior is well built, roomy, economical to operate. Two-stateroom layout is arranged with galley, dinette on pilothouse level, two steps up from salon. L-shaped sofa and clever centerline entertainment center dominate salon. Both staterooms have double berths, en suite heads. Note attractive cherrywood cabinetry, Corian counters, large flybridge. Good lower helm visibility, but no pilothouse deck door. Volvo 318hp diesels cruise at 18 knots and reach a top speed in the low 20s.

See Page 532 For Value Estimates

Length	44'0"	Headroom	6'5"
Beam	15'0"	Fuel	500 gals.
Draft	4'5"	Water	130 gals.
Weight	34,500#	Waste	70 gals.
Clearance	19'3"	Hull Type	Modified-V

Navigator 48 Classic

1997–2007

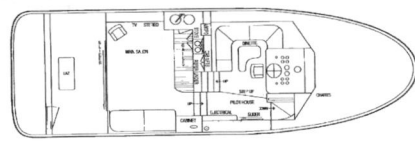

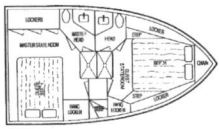

Smooth-running pilothouse cruiser combines sea-kindly hull with comfortable accommodations, all-weather versatility. Expansive twin-stateroom interior features well-appointed salon with U-shaped galley, raised pilothouse with wraparound dinette aft of centerline helm. Note bar seating in salon, stall showers in both heads. Cockpit hatch provides good access to engine room. Additional features include large bridge with dinghy/davit storage, radar arch, pilothouse deck door. Cruise at 16–17 knots with Volvo 318hp diesels (20+ top).

See Page 532 For Value Estimates

Length Overall	52'8"	Fuel	500 gals.
Beam	15'0"	Water	130 gals.
Draft	4'5"	Waste	70 gals.
Weight	37,000#	Hull Type	Modified-V
Clearance	NA	Deadrise Aft	15°

Navigator 50 Classic

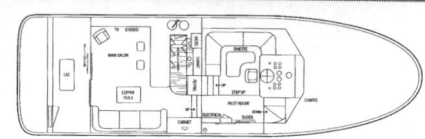

1993–2000

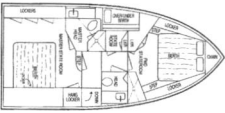

Versatile flybridge yacht combines affordable long-range cruising with practical layout, tasteful styling. Expansive twin-stateroom interior features well-appointed salon with U-shaped galley, raised pilothouse with wraparound dinette aft of centerline helm. Note bar seating in salon, stall showers in both heads. Cockpit hatch provides good access to engine room. Additional features include large bridge with dinghy/davit storage, radar arch, pilothouse deck door. Cruise at 16–18 knots with Volvo 340hp diesels (20+ top).

See Page 532 For Value Estimates

Length Overall	50'0"	Fuel	600 gals.
Beam	15'0"	Water	170 gals.
Draft	4'3"	Waste	70 gals.
Weight	38,000#	Hull Type	Modified-V
Headroom	6'6"	Deadrise Aft	15°

Navigator 53 Classic

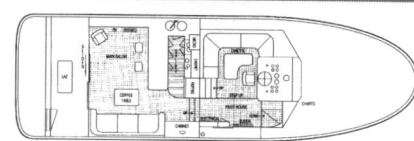

1995–2006

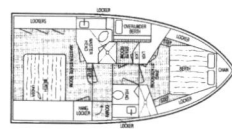

Popular pilothouse yacht combined signature Navigator value with handsome lines, common-sense layout. Open-plan interior features spacious full-beam salon with U-shaped galley forward, inside bridge access, three well-appointed staterooms, two full heads. Note attractive hardwood cabinets, pilothouse deck door. Huge cockpit is a plus, but lack of bridge ladder (or steps) is notable. Easily driven hull with modest 15-foot beam is more fuel efficient than most. Cruise at 16 knots with Volvo 370hp diesels (about 20 knots top).

See Page 532 For Value Estimates

Length Overall	53'0"	Fuel	600 gals.
Beam	15'0"	Water	170 gals.
Draft	4'6"	Waste	70 gals.
Weight	42,500#	Hull Type	Modified-V
Headroom	6'6"	Deadrise Aft	15°

Navigator 56 Classic

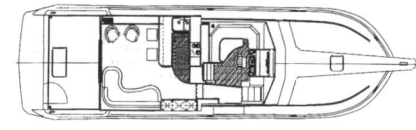

2000–05

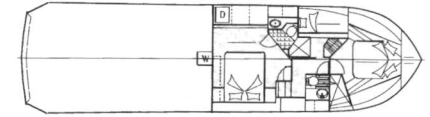

Handsome pilothouse yacht with graceful profile makes good on promise of comfortable accommodations, all-weather cruising ability. Roomy interior features expansive full-beam salon with galley forward, raised pilothouse with wraparound dinette and centerline helm. Note attractive maple and cherry woodwork, Corian galley counters, large cockpit. Engine room is reached via hatch in galley sole. Easily driven hull with slender 15-foot beam is fuel-efficient, stable in a chop. Volvo 370hp diesels cruise at 16–17 knots (around 20s knots top).

See Page 533 For Value Estimates

Length Overall	56'0"	Fuel	600 gals.
Beam	15'0"	Water	170 gals.
Draft	4'6"	Waste	40 gals.
Weight	45,500	Hull Type	Modified-V
Clearance	NA	Deadrise Aft	15°

Navigator 5600

1994–99

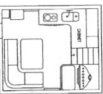

Stretched version of popular Navigator 5300 Pilothouse (1993–99) offers increased living space, greater versatility. Expansive three-stateroom interior features full-beam salon with entertainment center, wet bar, large windows. Raised pilothouse includes L-shaped galley area, dinette, sliding deck door. Note private salon access to master suite, large forward cabin with island berth. No cockpit bridge access. Volvo 430hp diesels cruise at 17–18 knots (20+ top). Replaced in 2001 with new (restyled) Navigator 56 Classic model.

See Page 533 For Value Estimates

Length Overall	56'0"	Fuel	600 gals.
Beam	15'0"	Water	200 gals.
Draft	5'6"	Waste	70 gals.
Weight	50,000#	Hull Type	Modified-V
Clearance	NA	Deadrise Aft	15°

Navigator 57 Rival

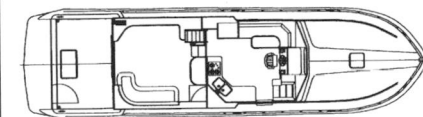

2003–07

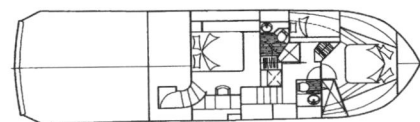

Sure-footed cruising yacht made good on Navigator promise of sturdy construction, practical accommodations. Highlights include full-beam salon with wet bar and entertainment center, extended pilothouse with open galley, three well-appointed staterooms, large cockpit with transom door. Note inside flybridge access, private entry to master suite. Steps from salon to pilothouse open to huge storage area below. Well-arranged engine room offers good service access. Cruise at 16 knots with Volvo 370hp diesels (about 20 knots top).

See Page 533 For Value Estimates

Length	57'0"	Fuel	750 gals.
Beam	15'0"	Water	200 gals.
Draft	4'7"	Waste	50 gals.
Weight	47,500#	Hull Type	Modified-V
Headroom	6'5"	Deadrise Aft	15°

Navigator 5800

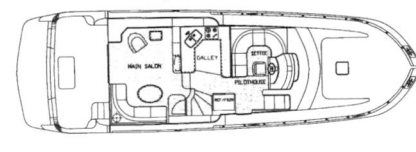

1999–2001

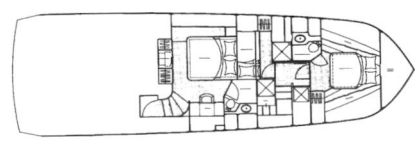

Value-priced pilothouse cruiser with broad 17'4" beam combines stylish exterior with spacious accommodations, versatile layout. Spacious, open-plan interior includes well-appointed salon with L-shaped sofa, home-size galley with generous storage, lower helm position with wraparound settee. Master suite is accessed from private salon staircase. Note inside/outside flybridge stairs, spacious engine room, large swim platform. GM 485hp diesels cruise at 18 knots (20+ top). New Navigator 5800 model with slender 15' beam came out in 2007.

See Page 533 For Value Estimates

Length Overall	58'0"	Fuel	800 gals.
Beam	17'4"	Water	200 gals.
Draft	4'9"	Waste	70 gals.
Weight	64,000#	Hull Type	Modified-V
Headroom	6'6"	Deadrise Aft	NA

Navigator 6100

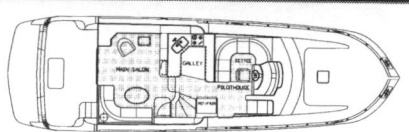

1999–2002

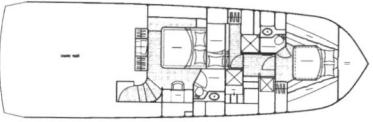

Sturdy pilothouse yacht provides an impressive blend of space, comfort, affordability. Spacious, open-plan interior features well-appointed salon with L-shaped sofa, home-size galley with generous storage, lower helm position with wraparound settee. Master suite is accessed from private salon staircase. Note inside/outside flybridge stairs, spacious engine room. Additional features include high-gloss cherry joinery, twin transom doors, stand-up engine room. Cruise at 18 knots with 700hp Volvo diesels (low 20s top).

See Page 533 For Value Estimates

Length Overall	61'6"	Fuel	800 gals.
Beam	17'4"	Water	200 gals.
Draft	4'9"	Waste	70 gals.
Weight	66,000#	Hull Type	Modified-V
Headroom	6'5"	Deadrise Aft	15°

Neptunus 56 Flybridge

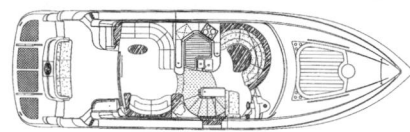

2001–07

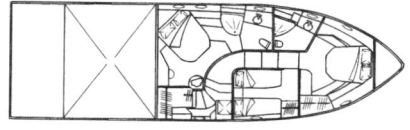

Stylish (perhaps overstyled?) deep-V motory-acht—from Canadian arm of Dutch builder Neptunus—combines strong performance with expansive interior, premium furnishings. Floorplan differs from most European designs in that staterooms are accessed from staircase opposite the galley rather than a forward passageway. Lower helm was standard. Cockpit is quite spacious with transom seating and engine room access hatch. Narrow side decks are the price for all the interior volume. Cruise at 25–26 knots with 800hp Cat V-drive diesels.

Insufficient Resale Data to Assign Values

Length	57'0"	Fuel	820 gals.
Beam	16'2"	Water	180 gals.
Draft	4'4"	Waste	110 gals.
Weight	52,000#	Hull Type	Deep-V
Clearance	16'7"	Deadrise Aft	19°

Nordhavn 35 Coastal Pilot

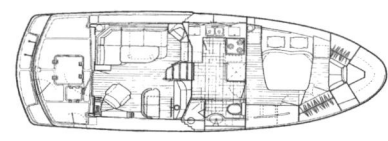

2001–05

Heavily built coastal trawler with feature-packed layout is ideally suited for the cruising couple. Single-stateroom, galley-down interior boasts well-appointed pilothouse with convertible settee, large master suite with copious storage, teak-planked flooring throughout. Note commercial-grade doors and windows, huge cockpit lazarette. Early models were overbuilt, heavy and slow; later models were built with prop pocket and lighter layup schedule. Total of 35 were built. Cruise at 10–12 knots with single 370hp Yanmar diesel.

See Page 533 For Value Estimates

Length Overall	35'4"	Clearance	NA
Length WL	33'4"	Fuel	590 gals.
Beam	13'2"	Water	165 gals.
Draft	3'6"	Waste	40 gals.
Weight	25,000#	Hull Type	Semi-Disp.

Nordhavn 40

1999–Current

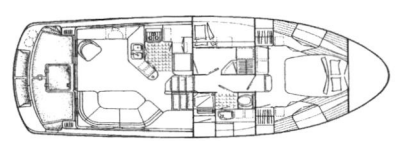

Seaworthy displacement trawler offers long-range cruising credentials second to none. Spacious interior with full-beam salon features raised pilothouse with fold-down helm seat, varnished teak cabinets, commercial-quality doors and windows, beautifully finished engine room. Raised foredeck with Portuguese bridge protects against heavy seas. Dry-stack exhaust, keel cooling system are standard. Auxiliary get-home engine is optional. Single 140hp diesel will cruise at 7 knots with a range of around 2,500 miles.

See Page 533 For Value Estimates

Length Overall	39'9"	Ballast	2,500#
Length WL	35'5"	Fuel	920 gals.
Beam	14'6"	Water	250 gals.
Draft	4'9"	Waste	70 gals.
Weight	50,000#	Hull Type	Displacement

Nordhavn 43

2004–Current

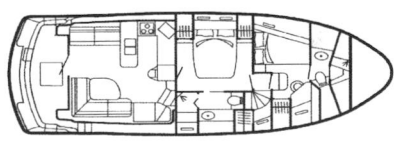

Ship-like trawler with towering profile appeals to oceangoing cruisers demanding world-class engineering, unrivaled build quality. Twin-stateroom interior has salon offset to port leaving single, starboard-side walkway from cockpit to bow. Full-beam master stateroom is amidships, guest stateroom has head forward, berth aft for maximum comfort. Note dry-stack exhaust system, pilothouse Dutch doors, 30hp back-up wing engine. Engine room is a work of art. Lugger 165hp diesel offers 2,500-mile cruising range at 7–8 knots.

Insufficient Resale Data to Assign Values

Length Overall	43'0"	Clearance, Mast	30'4"
Length WL	38'4"	Fuel	1,200 gals.
Beam	14'10"	Water	300 gals.
Draft	4'11"	Waste	50 gals.
Weight	54,540#	Hull Type	Displacement

Nordhavn 46

1989–2005

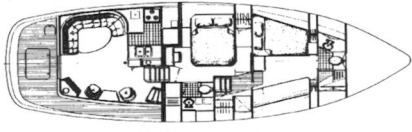

Standard Floorplan

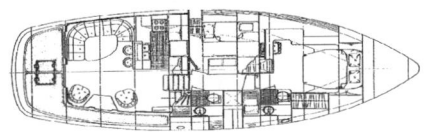

Alternate Floorplan

Compelling full-displacement trawler with classic pilothouse profile established Nordhavn reputation for engineering excellence, obsessive attention to detail. Standard interior features full-beam amidships master with private salon access; alternate floorplan has master stateroom forward. Salon is offset to port leaving single starboard walkway from cockpit to bow. Note wave-breaking Portuguese bridge, unique dry-stack exhaust system. Single 140hp diesel will cruise at 8 knots with a range of 1,800–2,000 miles. Over 80 were built.

See Page 533 For Value Estimates

Length Overall	45'9"	Ballast	4,800#
Length WL	38'4"	Fuel	1,000 gals.
Beam	15'5"	Waree	280 gals.
Draft	5'0"	Waste	50 gals.
Weight	60,000#	Hull Type	Displacement

Trawlers & Motoryachts

Nordhavn 47

2003–Current

Heavy-weather trawler with ballasted hull carries owners in safety, comfort anywhere in the world. Deluxe interior has salon offset to port leaving a single, starboard-side walkway from cockpit to bow. Master stateroom is amidships; guest stateroom has head forward, berth aft for maximum comfort. Note Portuguese bridge, office/nav station, auxiliary diesel, dry stack exhaust, keel cooler (to dissipate engine heat). Tall bow can punch through very heavy seas. Single 173hp Lugger diesel will cruise at 8 knots for nearly 3,000 miles.

See Page 533 For Value Estimates

Length Overall	51'0"	Ballast	6,000#
Length WL	43'4"	Fuel	1,450 gals.
Beam	16'1"	Water	400 gals.
Draft	5'6"	Waste	120 gals.
Weight	85,000#	Hull Type	Displacement

Nordhavn 50

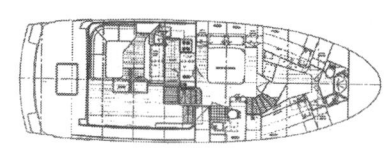

1997–2006

Oceangoing trawler with wide-body hull was built for heavy-weather cruising. Several layouts available—most have wide-body salon with single, starboard-side walkway. Two-stateroom interior boasts lavish amidships master (with engine room access), raised pilothouse with nav station, roomy guest cabin with head forward, opulent salon with well-equipped galley. Bulbous bow extension beneath waterline improves fuel efficiency, hull speed. Single 300hp Lugger diesel will cruise at 7–8 knots with 2,500-mile range.

See Page 533 For Value Estimates

Length Overall	51'2"	Ballast	6,600#
Length WL	44'2"	Fuel	1,320 gals.
Beam	16'0"	Water	260 gals.
Draft	5'2"	Waste	50 gals.
Weight	80,000#	Hull Type	Displacement

Nordhavn 55

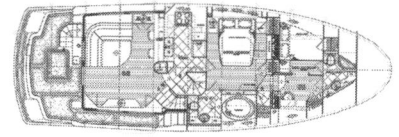

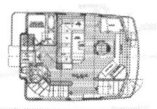

2005–Current

Stately ocean trawler with towering profile appeals to hard-core cruisers obsessed with quality, security. Maxi-volume interior boasts opulent master stateroom amidships, spacious guest cabin forward with office, spacious salon with breakfast bar, commercial-like pilothouse with private stateroom and head. Note quality teak woodwork, home-size galley appliances, bathtub in master head. High bow punches through heavy seas; dry exhaust eliminates need for through-hull. Range is nearly 3,000 miles at 8 knots with single 330hp diesel.

See Page 533 For Value Estimates

Length Overall	59'0"	Clearance, Mast	27'8"
Length WL	50'1"	Fuel	2,250 gals.
Beam	18'0"	Water	600 gals.
Draft	6'4"	Waste	120 gals.
Weight	124,500#	Hull Type	Displacement

Nordhavn 57

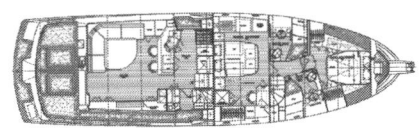

1999–2007

Big-water passagemaker with genuine ocean-crossing potential delivers top-shelf build quality, uncompromised cruising security. Luxurious three-stateroom interior boasts spacious salon with serving bar, day head, professional-level pilothouse, stand-up engine room. Galley deck door is a plus. Wide keel allows for stand-up engine room. Note Portuguese bridge, high protective bulwarks, dry exhaust. Wide side deck to starboard, narrow walkway to port. Single Lugger 340hp diesel delivers 3,000-mile-plus range at 8 knots.

See Page 533 For Value Estimates

Length Overall	57'6"	Clearance	21'0"
Length WL	52'8"	Fuel	2,000 gals.
Beam	17'7"	Water	300 gals.
Draft	6'8"	Waste	60 gals.
Weight	120,000#	Hull Type	Displacement

Nordhavn 62

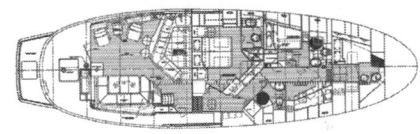

1995–Current

Gold-plated trawler yacht with ship-like appearance is designed for transoceanic voyages in style, safety, comfort. Maxi-beam interior has three double staterooms, home-size galley appliances, crew quarters forward. Enclosed pilothouse includes head, bunk beds. Note stand-up engine room, keel cooler, workshop, auxiliary back-up diesel, Portuguese bridge. Bulbous bow extension beneath waterline improves fuel efficiency, hull speed. Single 340hp Lugger diesel will cruise at 8–9 knots with 3,000-mile-plus range.

Insufficient Resale Data to Assign Values

Length Overall	62'8"	Ballast	10,000#
Length WL	55'6"	Fuel	2,652 gals.
Beam	19'4"	Water	525 gals.
Draft	6'10"	Waste	100 gals.
Weight	150,000#	Hull Type	Displacement

Nordhavn 64

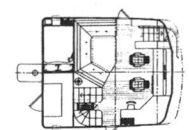

2006–Current

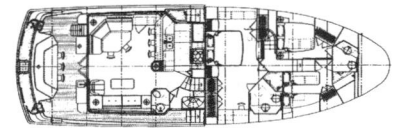

Elegant world cruiser with imposing profile combines long-range comfort, unsurpassed security. High bow, tall free-board result in very spacious interior with wide-open salon, full-beam master (with king bed), two guest staterooms forward. Wide, full protected side deck to starboard connects foredeck to aft cockpit. Commercial-like pilothouse offers superior visibility, double-size pilot berth. Detroit 400hp main engine delivers 3,000-mile cruising range at 8–9 knots. Lugger 105hp emergency engine will cruise at 4–5 knots.

Insufficient Resale Data to Assign Values

Length Overall	66'3"	Headroom	6'6"
Length WL	59'2"	Fuel	3,200 gals.
Beam	20'4"	Water	500 gals.
Draft	6'8"	Waste	150 gals.
Weight	176,000#	Hull Type	Displacement

Nordhavn 72

2005–Current

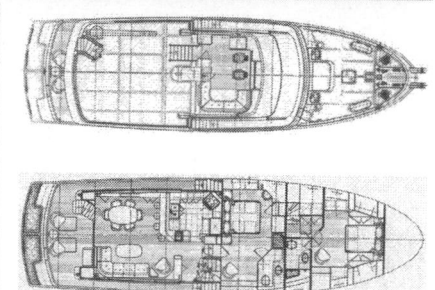

Ship-like world cruiser offers heightened levels of yachting quality, comfort, security. Broad 21-foot beam permits spacious four-cabin, four-head interior with expansive salon/dining area, spacious wheelhouse, opulent owner's suite. Massive Portuguese bridge protects pilothouse; prominent bow keeps decks dry when punching through heavy seas. Full-beam boat deck aft of bridge can stow 17-foot tender. Note commercial-grade doors and windows, meticulous fit and finish. Single GM 535hp delivers 3,000-mile-plus cruising range at 8–9 knots.

Insufficient Resale Data to Assign Values

Length Overall	72'3"	Clearance	NA
Length WL	65'0"	Headroom	6'6"
Beam	21'0"	Fuel	4,100 gals.
Draft	7'6"	Water	800 gals.
Weight	240,000#	Hull Type	Displacement

Nordic 26 Tug

1980–Current

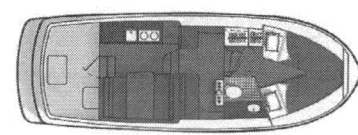

Iconic pocket cruiser with salty tugboat profile, wide 9'6" beam is super-economical to operate, secure in open water, built to last. Cozy interior with teak-planked flooring, large windows, features well-appointed salon with convertible dinette, fully-equipped galley, step-up pilothouse with two sliding deck doors, compact stateroom and head forward. Slightly redesigned "2-26" model introduced in 1995 has raked stack, wider catwalks. Out of production in 1997, reintroduced in 2009. Cruise at 6–7 knots with 100hp Yanmar diesel.

See Page 533 For Value Estimates

Length Overall	26'4"	Clearance	9'8"
Length WL	25'2"	Fuel	100 gals.
Beam	9'6"	Water	40 gals.
Draft	3'3"	Waste	20 gals.
Weight	7,500#	Hull Type	Semi-Disp.

Nordic 32 Tug

1986–Current

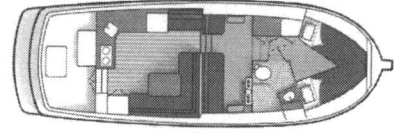
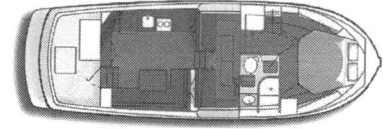

Iconic pilothouse cruiser with workboat lines delivers impressive blend of superior quality, deluxe accommodations, lasting value. Several cabin layouts offered over the years, all featuring full-beam salon with convertible dinette, teak cabinetry and flooring, raised pilothouse with 360-degree visibility. Updated 32+ model introduced in 2002 has island berth forward, enlarged head, integral swim platform. Revised prop-pocket hull introduced in 2008. Cruise at 12 knots with single 220hp Cummins diesel; 14 knots with 270hp Cummins.

See Page 533 For Value Estimates

Length Overall	34'2"	Headroom	6'4"
Beam	11'0"	Fuel	200 gals.
Draft	3'6"	Water	100 gals.
Weight	16,000#	Waste	30 gals.
Clearance	10'4"	Hull Type	Semi-Disp.

Trawlers & Motoryachts

Nordic 37 Tug

1998–Current

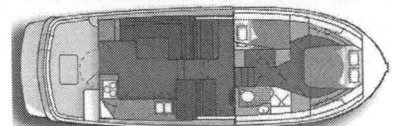

Two Staterooms

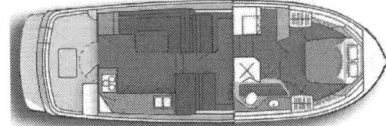

Single Stateroom

See Page 533 For Value Estimates

Legendary Nordic cruiser with classic workboat lines gets high marks for craftsmanship, comfort, seaworthiness. Stylish full-beam salon with solid teak cabinetry, convertible dinette, is open to wheelhouse and aft deck. Original two-stateroom interior was joined in 2003 with alternate single-stateroom layout with enlarged master stateroom and head. Note spacious engine room, integral swim platform. Flybridge has been a popular option in recent years. Cruise efficiently at 12–14 knots with single 330hp Cummins diesel.

Length Overall	39'2"	Clearance	12'4"
Length WL	37'4"	Fuel	320 gals.
Beam	12'11"	Water	144 gals.
Draft	4'4"	Waste	32 gals.
Weight	22,600#	Hull Type	Semi-Disp.

Nordic 42 Tug

1996–Current

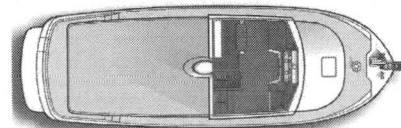

See Page 533 For Value Estimates

Stately pilothouse yacht with rugged tugboat styling is ideally suited for coastal cruising in comfort, security. Well-appointed teak interior features large salon with U-shaped galley, two roomy staterooms, laundry center under pilothouse steps. Forward stateroom is accessed from the wheelhouse in early models, salon in later models. Note wide side decks, roomy cockpit, spacious engine room. Fake cabintop stack houses a radar reflector. Flybridge is optional. Single 540hp Cummins diesel will cruise at 12 knots (15–16 knots top).

Length Overall	46'3"	Headroom	6'6"
Length WL	40'2"	Fuel	600 gals.
Beam	13'10"	Water	200 gals.
Draft	4'7"	Waste	50 gals.
Weight	31,400#	Hull Type	Semi-Disp.

Nordic 52/54 Tug

2004–Current

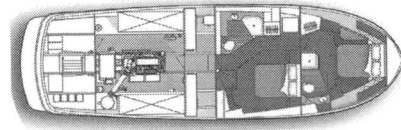

Two-Stateroom Interior

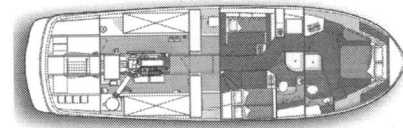

Three-Stateroom Interior

Insufficient Resale Data to Assign Values

Heavily built coastal trawler with signature Nordic Tug profile combines luxury-class accommodations with fuel-miserly operation. Elegant pilothouse interior is offered with two- and three-stateroom floorplans. Highlights include spacious pilothouse, enormous engine room, standard washer/dryer. Early hulls had twin engines; redesigned single-screw power became standard starting with hull #3. Marketed since 2009 as the Nordic 54. Cruise at 9–10 knots with single 670hp Cummins engine (about 15 knots top).

Length Overall	56'10"	Clearance, Mast	21'9"
Length WL	52'6"	Fuel	1,300 gals.
Beam	16'10"	Water	300 gals.
Draft	5'3"	Waste	130 gals.
Weight	60,000#	Hull Type	Semi-Disp.

Trawlers & Motoryachts

Nova 40 Sundeck

1984–91

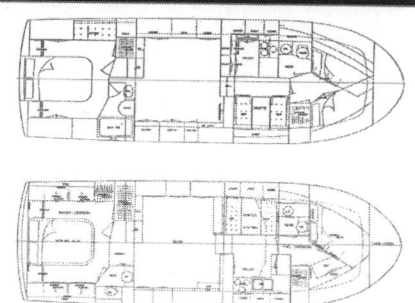

Traditional 1980s sundeck yacht with economical diesel power, full teak interior, is one part liveaboard, one part cruiser. Several galley-down floorplans were offered, all with large owner stateroom aft. Forward stateroom is best described as a tight fit. Most Nova 40s were delivered with lower helm. Covered aft deck has wet bar, wing doors. Solid fiberglass hull incorporates long, shallow keel for directional stability. Twin 135hp Lehmans cruise 8 knots; 165hp Volvos cruise at 9–10 knots (about 12 knots top).

Prices Not Provided for Pre-1995 Models

Length Overall	38'9"	Fuel	400 gals.
Hull Length	34'7"	Water	200 gals.
Beam	13'6"	Waste	40 gals.
Draft	3'7"	Headroom	6'4"
Weight, Approx.	28,000#	Hull Type	Semi-Disp.

Nova 42 Sundeck

1983–89

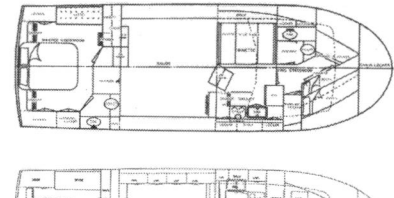

Strong-selling 1980s import is a proven trawler design marketed in the U.S. by several companies over the years. Roomy galley-down interior features large, full-beam master stateroom, expansive salon with standard lower helm, full-service galley, generous storage. Salon access door to sundeck is a nice touch. Teak decks, sundeck wet bar, hardtop were popular options. Semi-displacement hull has long, prop-protecting keel. Cruise at 8 knots with twin 135hp Perkins diesels; 10–12 knots with twin 200hp Perkins.

Prices Not Provided for Pre-1995 Models

Length Overall	41'9"	Clearance	NA
Hull Length	36'10"	Fuel	500 gals.
Beam	13'8"	Water	300 gals.
Draft	3'8"	Waste	50 gals.
Weight	26,000#	Hull Type	Semi-Disp.

Nova 44 Sundeck

1985–90

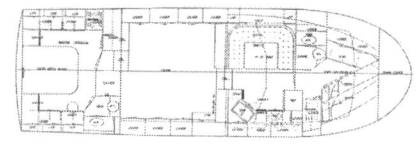

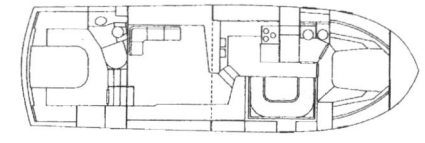

Stretched version of popular Nova 42 Sundeck made a good boat even better. Available with several two-stateroom interior plans, all with galley down and booth-style dinette. Highlights include full teak interior, full-beam owner's stateroom, spacious aft deck platform, large engine room. Note generous fuel, water capacities. Hardtop, radar arch, swim platform, bow pulpit were standard. Semi-displacement hull has long keel for prop protection. Cruise at 9–10 knots with twin 135hp Perkins diesels; 12–13 knots with 200hp Volvo diesels.

Prices Not Provided for Pre-1995 Models

Length Overall	43'5"	Clearance	19'0"
Hull Length	39'5"	Fuel	500 gals.
Beam	13'8"	Water	300 gals.
Draft	3'10"	Waste	50 gals.
Weight	24,400#	Hull Type	Semi-Disp.

Ocean 42 Sunliner

1981–85

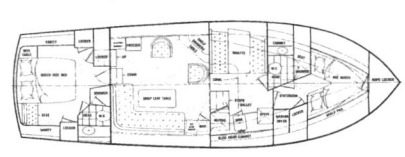

Double-cabin version of Oceans 42 Sportfisherman (1980–83) delivered motoryacht versatility, comfort at an affordable price. Generic galley-down interior with teak cabinets boasts spacious salon with L-shaped settee, full dinette, separate stall showers in both heads. Strong list of standard equipment included generator, garbage disposal, washer/dryer, vacuum system, instant hot water, microwave oven. Note compact engine room. Among several engine choices, GM 450hp 6-71 diesels cruise at 24–25 knots (high 20s top).

Prices Not Provided for Pre-1995 Models

Length Overall	42'0"	Clearance	12'0"
Length WL	38'0"	Fuel	480 gals.
Beam	14'4"	Water	100 gals.
Draft	3'6"	Hull Type	Modified-V
Weight	28,000#	Deadrise Aft	1.5°

Ocean 44 Motor Yacht

1992–99

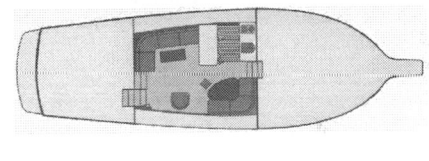

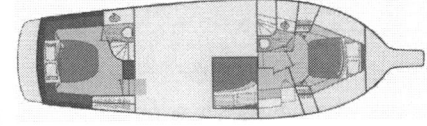

Popular Viking motoryacht set class standards in her day for sleek styling, leading-edge performance. Innovative three-stateroom floorplan boasts combined salon/galley/dinette, stall showers in both heads, guest stateroom under salon sole. Note teak interior joinerwork, designer-style decor. Protected aft deck with wet bar, wing doors can entertain several guests. Washer/dryer, central vacuum system, radar arch were standard. Engine room is a tight fit. Detroit 485hp 6-71 diesels cruise at 24 knots (27–28 knots top).

See Page 534 For Value Estimates

Length	44'0"	Max Headroom	6'6"
Beam	15'0"	Fuel	466 gals.
Draft	3'7"	Water	100 gals.
Weight	40,000#	Hull Type	Modified-V
Clearance	12'0"	Deadrise Aft	5°

Ocean 46 Sunliner

1983–86

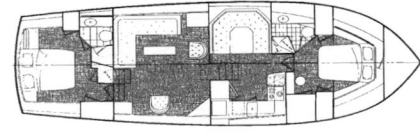

Plan A

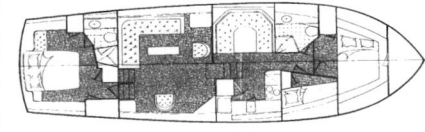

Plan B

Aft-cabin version of Ocean 46 SF (1983–85) made the cut with Ocean buyers looking for brisk convertible performance, luxury motoryacht amenities. Originally offered with twin-stateroom, galley-down interior, alternate three-stateroom layout became available in 1985. Notable features include teak interior cabinets, protected aft deck with wing doors, central vacuum system, washer/dryer, garbage disposal. A fast ride compared with most 1980s-era motoryachts, she'll cruise in the low 20s with standard GM 450hp 6-71 diesels (26–27 knots top).

Prices Not Provided for Pre-1995 Models

Length	46'0"	Fuel	480 gals.
Beam	15'2"	Water	150 gals.
Draft	3'6"	Headroom	6'3"
Weight	40,000#	Hull Type	Modified-V
Clearance	13'3"	Deadrise Aft	1.5°

Trawlers & Motoryachts

Ocean 48 Cockpit Motor Yacht

1993–99

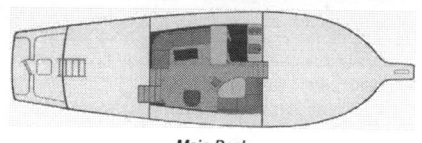

Main Deck

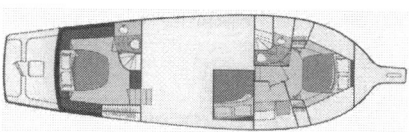

Lower Deck

See Page 534 For Value Estimates

Cockpit version of popular Ocean 44 MY (1992–99) combined rakish styling with roomy layout, sporty performance. Innovative three-stateroom floorplan boasts combined salon/galley/dinette, stall showers in both heads, guest stateroom under salon sole. Note teak interior joinerwork, designer-style decor. Protected aft deck with wet bar, wing doors can entertain several guests. Washer/dryer, central vacuum system, radar arch were standard. Engine room is a tight fit. Detroit 485hp 6-71 diesels cruise at 24 knots (27–28 knots top).

Length	48'0"	Max Headroom	6'6"
Beam	15'0"	Fuel	466 gals.
Draft	3'7"	Water	100 gals.
Weight	42,500#	Hull Type	Modified-V
Clearance	12'0"	Deadrise Aft	5°

Ocean 48 Motor Yacht

1989–94

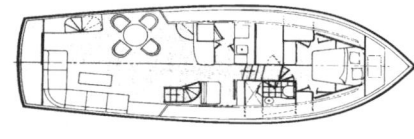

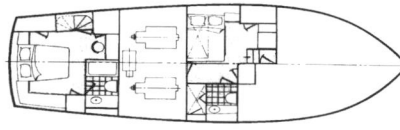

Prices Not Provided for Pre-1995 Models

Spacious twin-deck motoryacht introduced in 1989 gets high marks for maxi-volume interior space, good performance, signature Ocean value. Highlights include extended full-beam salon, gourmet galley with deck access door, inside bridge access, three double staterooms, three full heads. Large stand-up engine room is a plus. Note inside bridge access ladder, small aft deck (for line-handling). Central vacuum system, radar arch, bow pulpit were standard. Standard 485hp GM diesels cruise at 23–24 knots and top out in the high 20s.

Length	48'6"	Fuel	500 gals.
Beam	16'4"	Water	150 gals.
Draft	4'0"	Headroom	6'4"
Weight	51,000#	Hull Type	Modified-V
Clearance	14'10"	Deadrise Aft	7°

Ocean 53 Motor Yacht

1988–91

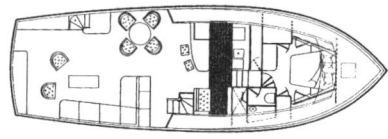

Deckhouse, Layout A

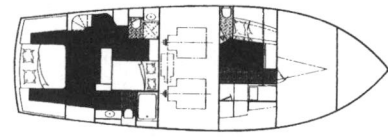

Lower Deck, Layout A

Prices Not Provided for Pre-1995 Models

Maxi-volume motoryacht with twin-deck floorplan offered luxury accommodations, good performance at reasonable price. Expansive four-stateroom interior—rare in a 53-footer—was offered with full-beam salon or shortened salon with semi-enclosed aft deck. Master stateroom has big king-size bed. Extended, full-beam flybridge has room for a small crowd. Note wheelhouse deck doors, inside flybridge access, spacious stand-up engine room. Twin 735hp Detroit diesels cruise at 24 knots (about 30 knots top).

Length	53'0"	Headroom	6'6"
Beam	17'2"	Fuel	750 gals.
Draft	4'6"	Water	300 gals.
Weight	64,000#	Hull Type	Modified-V
Clearance	16'0"	Deadrise Aft	8°

Ocean 55 Sunliner

1983–86

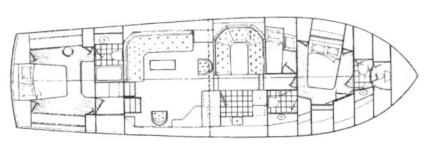

Well-appointed 1980's cruising yacht is basically an aft-cabin version of Ocean's hugely popular 55 SS (1981–90). Comfortable three-stateroom interior boasts large galley with home-size refrigerator, big U-shaped dinette, spacious master suite forward with built-in washer/dryer and unique forepeak head. Note aft-deck wing doors, enclosure panels. Hardtop can support weight of a small dinghy. Standard 600hp GM 8V92s cruise at 22 knots (about 25 knots top); optional 675hp 8V92s are a couple of knots faster.

Prices Not Provided for Pre-1995 Models

Length	55'8"	Fuel	750 gals.
Beam	16'4"	Water	200 gals.
Draft	4'4"	Headroom	6'4"
Weight	60,000#	Hull Type	Modified-V
Clearance	14'6"	Deadrise Aft	4°

Ocean 56 Cockpit MY

1990–91

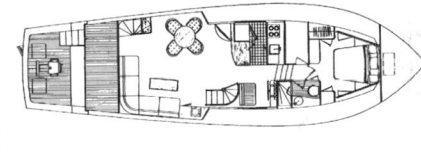

Versatile cruising yacht is basically an Ocean 48 MY (1989–94) with an 8-foot cockpit addition. Highlights include extended full-beam salon, gourmet galley with deck access door, three double staterooms, three full heads, stand-up engine room. Note inside bridge access, small aft deck (for line-handling), foredeck bench seating, private master stateroom access. Central vacuum system, radar arch, transom door were standard. Standard 485hp 6-71 diesels cruise at 22 knots and top out in the mid 20s. Only two years in production.

Prices Not Provided for Pre-1995 Models

Length	56'0"	Fuel	525 gals.
Beam	16'4"	Water	150 gals.
Draft	4'0"	Cockpit	80 sq. ft.
Weight	54,500#	Hull Type	Modified-V
Clearance	14'10"	Deadrise Aft	5°

Ocean 57 Odyssey

2004–Current

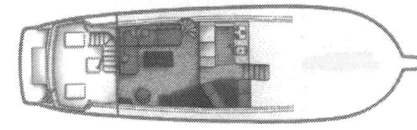

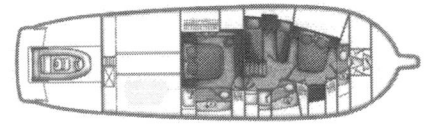

Luxurious cruising yacht is basically a repurposed Ocean 57 Super Sport with enclosed bridge, guest-friendly cockpit, transom garage. Lavish three-stateroom, three-head interior features elegant salon with direct bridge access, step-up galley and dinette, washer/dryer under companionway steps. Enclosed bridge includes custom helm chairs, refrigerator, TV/DVD. Note large engine room with cockpit access, flybridge afterdeck with full controls, cockpit boarding gates. Cat 1,015hp engines cruise in the mid 20s (30+ knots top).

See Page 534 For Value Estimates

Length Overall	63'8"	Headroom	6'5"
Beam	16'10"	Fuel	893 gals.
Draft	4'10"	Water	200 gals.
Weight	71,000#	Hull Type	Modified-V
Clearance	17'7"	Deadrise Aft	NA

Trawlers & Motoryachts

Trawlers & Motoryachts

Ocean 65 Odyssey

2003–Current

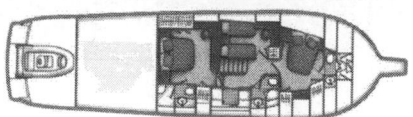

3 Staterooms

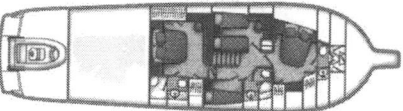

4 Staterooms

Insufficient Resale Data to Assign Values

Feature-rich cruising yacht is basically a reworked Ocean 62 Super Sport with enclosed bridge, roomy cockpit, storage garage for hard-bottom inflatable. Beautifully appointed teak interior boasts spacious salon, abundant storage, choice of three or four staterooms. Note side-by-side galley refrigeration, laundry room in three-stateroom layout. Spiral salon staircase provides access to enclosed bridge with entertainment center, aft sundeck with steering station. Cruise in the mid 20s with Cat 1,015hp diesels (33–35 knots top).

Length Overall	67'6"	Headroom	6'5"
Beam	17'5"	Fuel	1,100 gals.
Draft	5'0"	Water	350 gals.
Weight	87,000#	Hull Type	Modified-V
Clearance, Hardtop	18'1"	Deadrise Aft	12°

Ocean Alexander 38 Double Cabin

1984–87

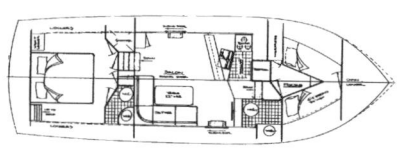

Handsome 1980s cruiser with traditional teak interior combined classic trawler styling with solid construction, economical operation. Well-finished interior boasts roomy salon with lower helm, two salon deck doors, generous storage. Aft stateroom boasts cockpit access door, divided head compartment with shower to port. Aft cabintop can stow small dinghy. Raised bulwarks enhance side deck security; flybridge has seating for four. Twin 135hp Lehman diesels cruise efficiently at 7–8 knots.

Prices Not Provided for Pre-1995 Models

Length Overall	38'4"	Headroom	6'4"
Beam	13'4"	Fuel	300 gals.
Draft	3'2"	Water	200 gals.
Weight	21,500#	Waste	30 gals.
Clearance	NA	Hull Type	Semi-Disp.

Ocean Alexander 390 Sundeck

1986–99

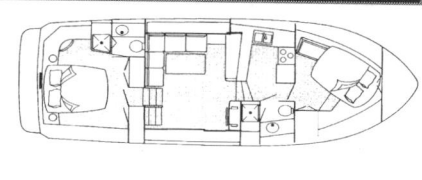

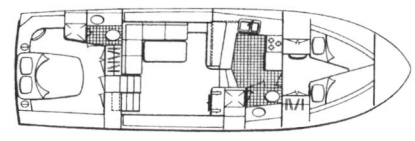

Popular Ed Monk design combined rakish styling with versatile layout, fuel-efficient operation. Well-appointed teak (or light ash) interior features expansive salon with serving counter, lower helm station, two double staterooms, separate stall showers in both heads. Note full-beam aft deck, wide side decks, standard swim platform. Most were sold with radar arch and hardtop. Offered with several diesel options over the years—cruising speeds range from 15–17 knots, top speeds are in the neighborhood of 20 knots.

See Page 533 For Value Estimates

Length	39'3"	Fuel	300 gals.
Beam	13'11"	Water	150 gals.
Draft	3'2"	Waste	18 gals.
Weight	24,800#	Hull Type	Modified-V
Clearance	14'0"	Deadrise Aft	12°

Ocean Alexander 40 Double Cabin

1980–89

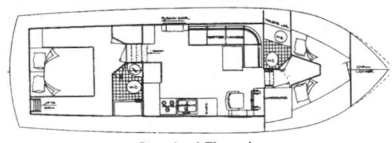

Standard Floorplan

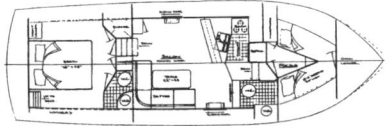

Alternate Floorplan

Graceful double-cabin trawler with full teak interior gets high marks for solid construction, practical layout, fuel-efficient operation. Tasteful two-stateroom interior—offered with galley up or down—features roomy salon with lower helm station, deck access door, teak parquet flooring. Cockpit access door in aft stateroom is a big plus. Note large engine room, wide side decks, roomy flybridge with L-shaped settee. Better gelcoat finish than most Asian imports of her era. Twin 120hp Lehman diesels will cruise efficiently at 7–8 knots.

Prices Not Provided for Pre-1995 Models

Length Overall	40'10"	Clearance	NA
Length WL	36'0"	Fuel	400 gals.
Beam	13'4"	Water	240 gals.
Draft	3'6"	Waste	50 gals.
Weight	22,500#	Hull Type	Semi-Disp.

Ocean Alexander 40 Sedan

1983–89

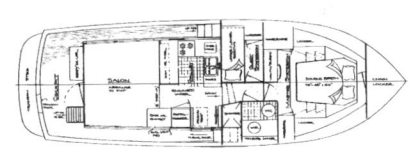

Versatile 1980s sedan combines classic trawler styling with solid construction, economical operation. Sedan-style layout with extended salon, small cockpit offers easy access to the water. Highlights include teak interior woodwork, home-sized galley, lower helm with sliding deck door, large forward stateroom with vanity. Expansive flybridge can seat several guests. Transom door, teak decks, teak swim platform were standard. Twin 135hp Lehman diesels will cruise at 8 knots (11–12 knots top). GM 260hp diesels cruise at 14 knots.

Prices Not Provided for Pre-1995 Models

Length	39'8"	Fuel	400 gals.
Beam	13'4"	Water	200 gals.
Draft	3'2"	Headroom	6'5"
Weight	22,500#	Hull Type	Semi-Disp.
Clearance	NA	Deadrise Aft	NA

Ocean Alexander 420 Sundeck

1987–99

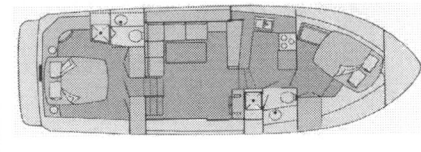

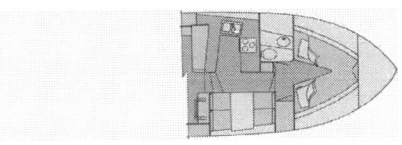

Classy cockpit yacht with sleek lines, quality construction became one of Alexander's more popular models. Features include well-appointed interior with large master stateroom, lower helm with deck door, roomy aft deck, commanding bridge with good helm visibility. Note wide side decks, large engine room. GM or Cummins 250hp diesels cruise at 15 knots (about 18 knots top); 350hp or 375hp Cats cruise at 20 knots (23–24 knots top). Note that Alexander 440 or 460 Sundeck are the same boats with extended cockpits.

See Page 533 For Value Estimates

Length, 420	42'3"	Fuel	300 gals.
Length, 440	43'9"	Water	150 gals.
Beam	13'11"	Waste	68 gals.
Draft	3'2"	Hull Type	Modified-V
Weight	27,000#	Deadrise Aft	NA

Trawlers & Motoryachts

Ocean Alexander 423 Classico

1993–2002

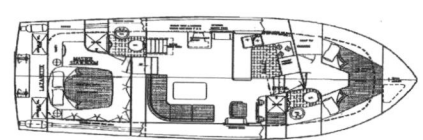

Handsome aft-cabin cruiser with walkaround decks offers comfort, performance in a timeless design. House is set well forward on foredeck to maximize salon and galley dimensions. Two-stateroom interior is arranged with V-berths forward, walkaround queen bed aft, spacious salon open to mid-level galley. Note twin salon deck doors, handcrafted teak joinerwork, roomy head with stall shower. Twin 220hp Cummins diesels cruise 11–12 knots (16 knots top); 420hp Cats cruise at 18 knot and reach a top speed of 22–23 knots.

See Page 533 For Value Estimates

Length	42'3"	Fuel	550 gals.
Beam	14'8"	Water	160 gals.
Draft	3'10"	Waste	60 gals.
Weight	34,200#	Hull Type	Modified-V
Clearance	NA	Deadrise Aft	10°

Ocean Alexander 426 Classico

1994–2002

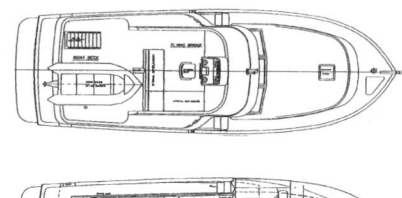

Graceful sedan-style cruiser enjoyed wide popularity in recent years thanks to spacious accommodations, leading-edge styling, solid construction. Standard galley-up interior with expansive teak joinery features two comfortable staterooms, roomy head with stall shower, lower helm with deck access door. Extended flybridge can accommodate an 11-foot inflatable. Heavily built hull incorporates shallow, prop-protecting keel, prop pockets to reduce draft. Cummins 220hp diesels cruise at 10–12 knots; 350hp Cats cruise at 16–17 knots.

See Page 533 For Value Estimates

Length	42'3"	Fuel	600 gals.
Beam	14'8"	Water	200 gals.
Draft	4'0"	Waste	60 gals.
Weight	35,000#	Hull Type	Modified-V
Clearance	12'8"	Deadrise Aft	10°

Ocean Alexander 430/460 Classico MKI

2000–06

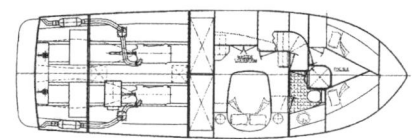

Single-Head Layout

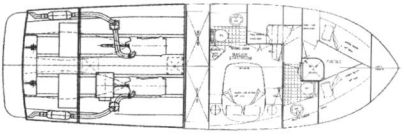

Two-Head Layout

Sturdy pilothouse trawler projects the ship-like image of a serious cruiser. Luxurious two-stateroom interior features impeccable teak cabinetry, full-beam salon with galley forward, raised pilothouse with excellent visibility. Gate in Portuguese bridge provides access to bow; steps on port side of pilothouse lead to cabintop where a dinghy can be stored. Flybridge is optional. Prop pockets in hull reduce draft. Cruise at 10 knots with 220hp Cummins diesels (13–14 top). Note that 460 Classico is same boat with larger cockpit.

See Page 533 For Value Estimates

Length, 460	45'8"	Weight, 460	42,500#
Length, 430	43'6"	Fuel	600 gals.
Beam	14'8"	Water	200 gals.
Draft	4'2"	Waste	60 gals.
Weight, 430	38,900#	Hull Type	Semi-Disp.

Ocean Alexander 450 Classico Sedan

2001–04

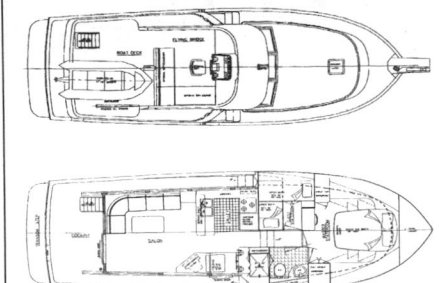

Sporty sedan yacht gets high marks for handsome styling, sea-kindly hull, tasteful accommodations. Practical two-stateroom interior boasts spacious master stateroom, large head compartment, teak-paneled salon with galley forward. Roomy cockpit, wide walkaround decks are valuable assets in any cruising yacht. Extended bridge can stow a small tender. Transom door, bow pulpit, hinged radar mast are standard. Twin 220hp Cummins diesels cruise at 8–10 knots and reach a top speed of about 13 knots.

See Page 533 For Value Estimates

Length	44'9"	Fuel	600 gals.
Beam	14'8"	Water	200 gals.
Draft	4'0"	Waste	40 gals.
Weight	36,900#	Headroom	6'4"
Clearance	NA	Hull Type	Semi-Disp.

Ocean Alexander 456 Classico

1992–2002

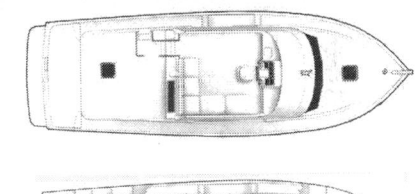

Traditional double-cabin cruising yacht with full walkaround decks delivers impressive blend of feature-rich accommodations, fuel-efficient operation. Comfortable galley-down floorplan boasts surprisingly spacious salon with serving counter, lower helm with deck access door, roomy master stateroom with vanity, two full heads. Teak joinery is finished to high standards. Note well-arranged engine room, step-down cockpit, hinged radar mast. No lightweight, 220hp Cummins diesels cruise at 10 knots (12–15 knots top).

See Page 534 For Value Estimates

Length	45'6"	Fuel	550 gals.
Beam	15'8"	Water	250 gals.
Draft	4'0"	Waste	40 gals.
Weight	40,000#	Headroom	6'3"
Clearance	12'9"	Hull Type	Semi-Disp.

Ocean Alexander 480 Sport Sedan

1993–2001

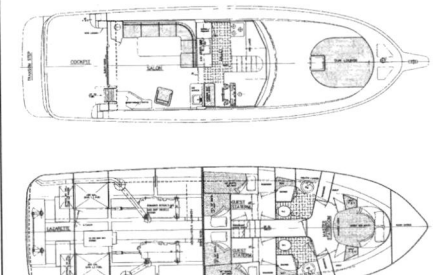

Rakish Mediterranean styling, classy accommodations set this 1990s cruiser apart from the competition. Richly paneled three-stateroom, two-head floorplan is arranged with galley and helm forward, one step up from spacious main salon. Sliding doors open salon to expansive cockpit with transom door. Note full teak interior, sunken foredeck sun pad, well-arranged engine room. Prop pockets reduce draft requirements. Twin 420hp Cat diesels—small engines indeed for a 48-footer—cruise at 22 knots (mid 20s top).

See Page 534 For Value Estimates

Length	48'6"	Fuel	500 gals.
Beam	15'6"	Water	180 gals.
Draft	2'9"	Waste	40 gals.
Weight	36,000#	Hull Type	Modified-V
Clearance	NA	Deadrise Aft	NA

Ocean Alexander 486 Classico

1993–2002

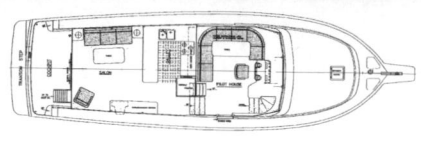

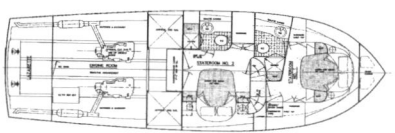

Luxury-class pilothouse yacht with wide beam, prop-protecting keel targets serious, quality-focused cruisers. Expansive interior features two large staterooms, both with walkaround queen beds. Salon is open to roomy U-shaped galley; visibility from raised pilothouse is excellent. Both heads have separate stall showers. Note protected side decks, washer/dryer in forward stateroom. Cat 420hp diesels cruise at 14–15 knots (around 18 knots top). A good-selling model for Ocean Alexander in the 1990s.

Insufficient Resale Data to Assign Values

Length, 486	48'0"	Clearance	NA
Length, 510	50'6"	Fuel	700 gals.
Beam	15'8"	Water	260 gals.
Draft	4'0"	Hull Type	Semi-Disp.
Weight	48,000#	Deadrise Aft	NA

Ocean Alexander 50 Pilothouse MK II

1985–90

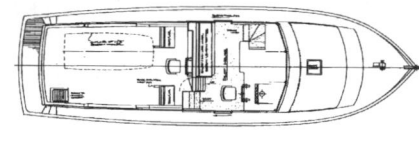

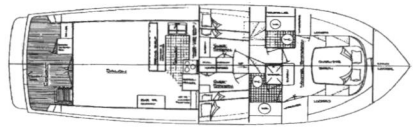

Updated version of original Alexander 50 Pilothouse (1978–85) has completely restyled exterior, updated floorplans. Interior highlights include enclosed pilothouse with watch berth, extended salon, home-sized galley, generous storage. Note that master stateroom is forward, guest staterooms are aft. Huge flybridge can entertain a small crowd. Engine room is a tight fit. Semi-displacement hull delivers secure open-water ride. Cat 375hp—or GM 400hp 6V53—diesels cruise at 16–17 knots (about 20 knots top).

Prices Not Provided for Pre-1995 Models

Length	50'0"	Fuel	600 gals.
Beam	15'6"	Water	220 gals.
Draft	4'6"	Headroom	6'5"
Weight	42,000#	Hull Type	Semi-Disp.
Clearance	NA	Deadrise Aft	NA

Ocean Alexander 51/53 Sedan

1989–98

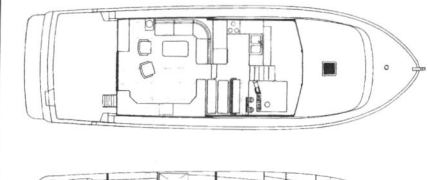

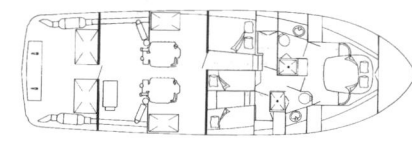

Rakish Eurostyle sedan gave 1990s Alexander buyers a compelling blend of style, comfort, amenities. Offered in two versions, the 51 Sedan (pictured above) has standard transom; 53 Sedan has a reverse transom that adds two extra feet to her length. Modern floorplan with master stateroom forward has galley, dinette on pilothouse level allowing expansive main salon. Note quality woodwork, excellent fit and finish. Early models with 400hp 6V53s cruise at 15 knots (18 top). Optional 735hp 8V92s cruise in the mid 20s (about 28 knots top).

See Page 534 For Value Estimates

Length, 51	51'1"	Clearance	12'6"
Length, 53	53'0"	Fuel	500 gals.
Beam	16'4"	Water	250 gals.
Draft	3'2"	Waste	60 gals.
Weight	45,500#	Hull Type	Modified-V

Ocean Alexander 520/540 Pilothouse

1990–2002

Three Staterooms

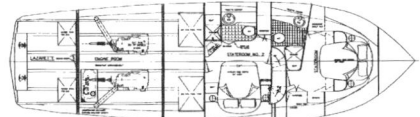

Two Staterooms

See Page 534 For Value Estimates

Taiwan-built pilothouse yacht from 1990s is classy, spacious, easy on the eye. (Note that Alexander 520 has standard transom; 540—pictured above—has Eurostyle transom.) Original three-stateroom interior with solid teak joinery has master suite forward; alternate two-stateroom layout (available in more recent models) has master stateroom amidships. Note very spacious engine room, wide side decks, large flybridge with dinghy platform. Cruise at 15–16 knots with 425hp Cat—or 440hp Yanmar—diesels (18 knots top).

Length	52'5"	Fuel	600 gals.
Beam	15'6"	Water	300 gals.
Draft	4'7"	Waste	40 gals.
Weight	41,500#	Headroom	6'4"
Clearance	14'0"	Hull Type	Modified-V

Ocean Alexander 548 Pilothouse

1996–2002

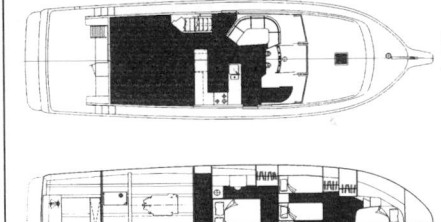

See Page 534 For Value Estimates

Striking 1990s pilothouse motoryacht combined sleek styling with spacious accommodations, first-rate workmanship. Good-running modified-V hull with prop pockets boasts unusually wide 17'6" beam. Highlights include three large staterooms, expansive raised pilothouse with galley and dinette, elegant salon, exceptionally large walk-in engine room. Two-stateroom layout was optional. Note exquisite interior woodwork. Flybridge can stow a 15-foot dinghy. Cruise at 18 knots with GM 485hp diesels; 20 knots with 660hp Cats.

Length	55'7"	Fuel	1,000 gals.
Beam	17'6"	Water	260 gals.
Draft	4'0"	Waste	80 gals.
Weight	52,000#	Headroom	6'5"
Clearance	NA	Hull Type	Modified-V

Ocean Alexander 58 Pilothouse

2004–09

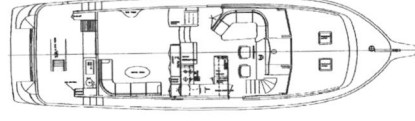

See Page 534 For Value Estimates

Classy pilothouse cruiser combines timeless Pacific Northwest styling with sea-kindly hull, elegant accommodations. Varnished teak interior includes full-beam master suite, expansive salon with full entertainment center, raised pilothouse with wraparound dinette and full-size galley. Pilothouse doors provide easy access to decks; teak-laid cockpit is large enough for swimming, diving, fishing. Note large cockpit lazarette. Semi-V hull has prop pockets, underwater exhausts. Cruise at 15 knots (18–20 top) with 700hp Cat diesels.

Length w/Pulpit	64'3"	Fuel	1,000 gals.
Beam	17'6"	Water	260 gals.
Draft	4'0"	Waste	100 gals.
Weight	69,500#	Hull Type	Modified-V
Clearance	NA	Deadrise Aft	NA

Trawlers & Motoryachts

Ocean Alexander 60 Pilothouse

1983–87

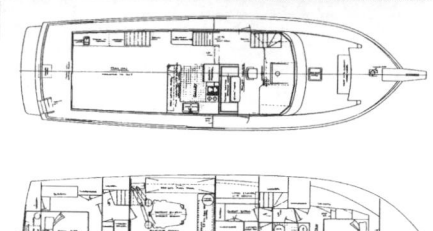

Sturdy long-range passagemaker from the 1980s combined classic pilothouse styling with top-shelf construction, executive-class accommodations. Twin-deck floorplan features three guest staterooms forward, full-beam master suite aft, combined salon/galley, raised pilothouse with centerline helm. Note convenient day head opposite galley. Bridge overhangs protect wide side decks. Transom staircase provides easy access to swim platform. GM 735hp 8V92s cruise at 15–16 knots (about 20 knots top).

Prices Not Provided for Pre-1995 Models

Length Overall	60'0"	Clearance	17'0"
Length WL	NA	Fuel	1,200 gals.
Beam	18'0"	Water	365 gals.
Draft	4'10"	Hull Type	Semi-Disp.
Weight	65,000#	Deadrise Aft	12°

Ocean Alexander 610 Pilothouse

1997–2003

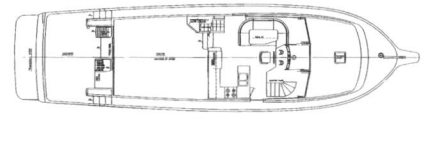

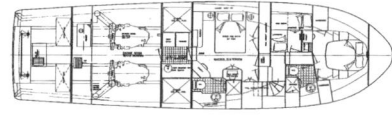

Sure-footed pilothouse yacht with handsome lines took Alexander luxury, quality to the next level. Spacious twin-deck floorplan includes opulent main salon, raised pilothouse with home-size galley and dinette, two double staterooms, two full heads. Second guest stateroom can be configured as office. Large engine room is accessed via cockpit stairs. Extended flybridge can seat a small crowd. Note large cockpit, underwater exhaust system. GM 735hp—or 660hp Cat—diesels cruise at 20 knots (22–23 knots top).

Insufficient Resale Data to Assign Values

Length	61'0"	Fuel	1,000 gals.
Beam	17'6"	Water	300 gals.
Draft	4'0"	Headroom	6'9"
Weight	69,300#	Hull Type	Modified-V
Clearance	NA	Deadrise Aft	NA

Ocean Alexander 64 Motor Yacht

2002–07

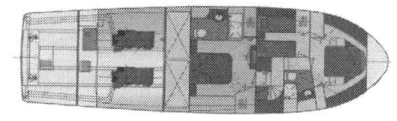

All-weather pilothouse yacht is loaded with luxury appointments experienced cruisers will appreciate. Lavish three-stateroom interior is an impressive blend of high-gloss woodwork, top-quality furnishings. Huge salon with sculpted ceiling, formal dining area rivals larger yachts for space, comfort. Gourmet galley includes dishwasher, granite counters. Additional features include stand-up engine room, extended bridge with dinghy storage, twin transom staircases. Cruise at 20 knots with 825hp MTU diesels (22–23 knots top).

See Page 534 For Value Estimates

Length	69'8"	Headroom	6'5"
Beam	17'6"	Fuel	1,500 gals.
Draft	4'0"	Water	300 gals.
Weight	73,500#	Waste	100 gals.
Clearance	NA	Hull Type	Modified-V

Offshore 48 Pilothouse

1999–2001

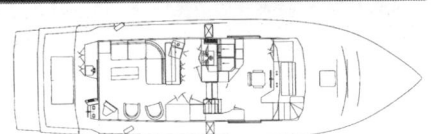
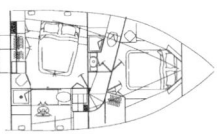

Popular Taiwan cruising yacht combines traditional lines with deluxe accommodations, proven owner satisfaction. Well-appointed teak interior with raised pilothouse, main-deck galley features two double staterooms, each with en suite head. Topside highlights include roomy flybridge with tender platform, full walkaround decks, cockpit transom door. Note large lazarette storage locker in cockpit sole. Low-deadrise hull with shallow keel delivers secure open-water ride. Cat 420hp diesels cruise at 16 knots (19–20 knots top).

See Page 535 For Value Estimates

Length	48'6"	Fuel	600 gals.
Beam	15'6"	Water	300 gals.
Draft	4'4"	Waste	50 gals.
Weight	47,000#	Hull Type	Modified-V
Clearance	NA	Deadrise Aft	11°

Offshore 48 Sedan

1987–2001

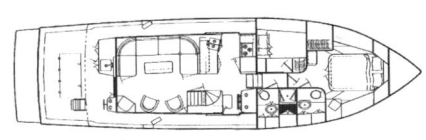

Well-bred sedan yacht introduced in 1987 delivered on Offshore promise of modern styling, comfortable accommodations. Upscale teak interior boasts roomy salon with U-shaped galley, standard lower helm, two large staterooms. Inside bridge access is rare in a boat this size. Note that both heads share common stall shower. Exterior highlights include big flybridge with tender platform, spacious cockpit, wide walkaround decks. Cat 375hp diesels cruise at 15–16 knots; later models with 420hp Cats cruise at 18–20 knots.

See Page 535 For Value Estimates

Length	48'6"	Fuel	600 gals.
Beam	15'6"	Water	300 gals.
Draft	3'6"	Waste	50 gals.
Weight	41,500#	Hull Type	Modified-V
Clearance	15'2"	Deadrise Aft	11°

Offshore 48 Yacht Fish

1985–99

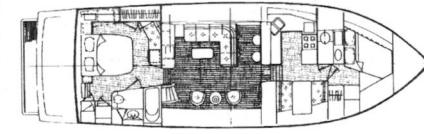
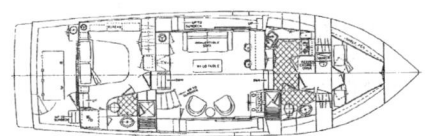

Sought-after cockpit yacht popular in late 1980s, 1990s delivered the right mix of style, comfort, price. Two-stateroom, galley-down floorplan with standard lower helm was available with or without dinette. Wide-open salon is big for a boat this size. Additional features include full teak interior, salon deck doors, cockpit door in aft cabin. Note wide side decks, washer/dryer in master stateroom. Swim, dive, fish from large cockpit. Cat 375hp diesels cruise at 16 knots (about 20 knots top); later models with 435hp Cats cruise at 18 knots.

See Page 535 For Value Estimates

Length	48'3"	Fuel	600 gals.
Beam	15'6"	Water	300 gals.
Draft	3'6"	Headroom	6'4"
Weight	41,000#	Hull Type	Modified-V
Clearance	15'2"	Deadrise Aft	11°

Trawlers & Motoryachts

Offshore 52/54 Pilothouse

1998–Current

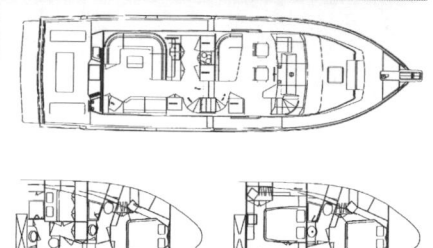

Popular pilothouse cruiser makes good on promise of up-scale accommodations, meticulous finish. Teak interior is offered with choice of two- or three-stateroom layouts, both with U-shaped galley forward in salon, raised pilothouse with stairway to bridge. Topside features include covered side decks, cockpit engine room access, large flybridge with dinghy storage. Note that Offshore 54 (pictured above) has integrated transom; 52 model has swim platform. Cummins 450hp diesels cruise at 14–15 knots; 660hp Cats cruise at 18 knots.

See Page 535 For Value Estimates

Length, 52	56'3"	Fuel	1,000 gals.
Length, 54	57'3"	Water	300 gals.
Beam	15'10"	Waste	70 gals.
Draft	4'1"	Hull Type	Modified-V
Weight	57,000#	Deadrise Aft	12°

Offshore 55/60 Pilothouse

1990–2004

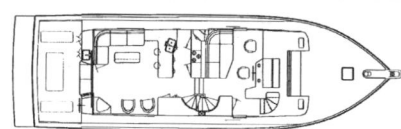

55 Pilothouse

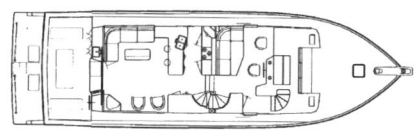

60 Pilothouse with Sport Deck

Versatile cruising yacht introduced in 1990 has well-earned reputation for quality, comfort, long-term value. Spacious three-stateroom interior boasts elegant amidships master suite, expansive salon, raised pilothouse with centerline helm, inside bridge access. Note solid teak cabinetry, concealed washer/dryer, protected side decks. Note that 55 Pilothouse (pictured above) has swim platform; 60 has integrated transom deck. Early models with 485hp Detroit 6-71s cruise at 16–17 knots; newer models with 660hp Cats cruise at 20 knots.

Insufficient Resale Data to Assign Values

Length, 55	55'0'	Weight, 60	63,000#
Length, 60	59'6"	Fuel, 55	700 gals.
Beam	16'10"	Fuel, 60	1,000 gals.
Draft	5'0"	Water	400 gals.
Weight, 55	61,500#	Hull Type	Modified-V

Offshore 58/62 Pilothouse

1994–Current

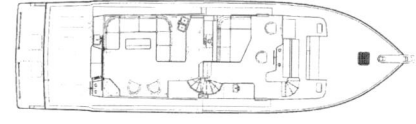

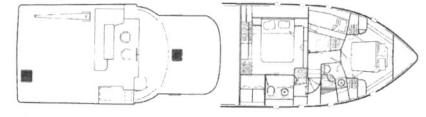

Handsome pilothouse yacht offers the space, comfort required for extended cruising. Expansive three-stateroom interior is arranged with galley forward of salon, raised pilothouse with centerline helm, twin deck doors. Luxurious full-beam master suite—with salon access—features king-size bed. Engine room is reached via cockpit hatch. Note protected side decks, huge bridge. Beamy, low-deadrise hull delivers stable open-water ride. Detroit 550hp diesels cruise at a modest 15 knots; later models with 800hp Cats cruise at 18 knots.

Insufficient Resale Data to Assign Values

Length, 58	58'0"	Fuel	1,000 gals.
Length, 62	62'6"	Water	400 gals.
Beam	16'10"	Waste	85 gals.
Draft	4'8"	Hull Type	Modified-V
Weight	65,000#	Deadrise Aft	12°

Outer Reef 65 Pilothouse

2007–Current

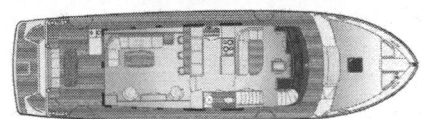

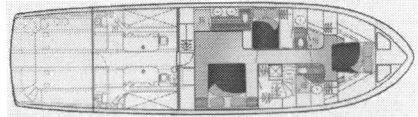

Premium quality, semicustom pilothouse yacht with broad 18'6" beam offers more interior volume, deck space than many larger cruising yachts. Standard layout provides three cabins including huge, full-beam master, roomy ensuite VIP forward, ensuite twin. Optional fourth stateroom/crew quarters with head is aft. Raised pilothouse offers commanding views from centerline helm. Full-beam flybridge features barbecue, two L-shaped lounges aft. Note deep, prop-protecting keel. Cruise at 12 knots (14–15 top) with Cat 503hp C-9 diesels.

Insufficient Resale Data to Assign Values

Length	65'0"	Fuel	2,000 gals.
Beam	18'6"	Water	400 gals.
Draft	5'0"	Waste	100 gals.
Weight	93,500#	Hull Type	Semi-Disp.
Clearance	NA	Deadrise Aft	NA

Pacific Mariner 65 Motor Yacht

1997–08

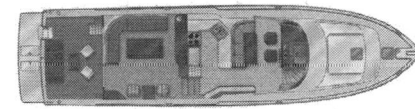

Feature-rich pilothouse yacht built in Washington State is one of the better big-boat values available. Sold as fully equipped, turnkey yacht with few options. Well-appointed interior features spacious salon with panoramic views, opulent full-beam master with king bed, extended pilothouse with centerline helm. Note galley deck door, aft crew quarters, tub in master head. Upgraded "SE" version introduced in 2003 incorporates many subtle design revisions. Cat 800hp—or MTU 825hp—diesels cruise at 20 knots (25–26 knots top). Over 50 built.

See Page 535 For Value Estimates

Length	64'11"	Water	285 gals.
Beam	17'3"	Waste	110 gals.
Draft	4'9"	Headroom	6'6"
Weight	69,000#	Hull Type	Modified-V
Fuel	1,100 gals.	Deadrise Aft	10°

Pacific Seacraft 38T Fast Trawler

1999–2002

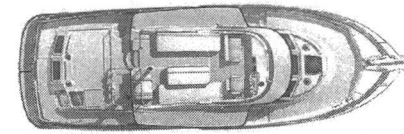

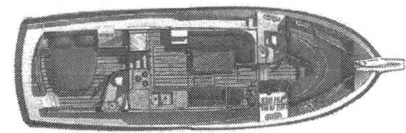

Top-quality performance trawler with handsome styling, superb finish is loaded with personality. Luxurious two-stateroom interior with teak trim features lower helm, salon deck doors, large cabin windows, roomy aft stateroom with cockpit door. Flybridge seats six to eight on facing settees. Space for dinghy storage on cabintop. Note deep bulwarks around side decks, fold-down radar mast, boarding gates in both gunwales. Exemplary fit and finish. Twin 350hp Cats cruise at 15–16 knots and reach a top speed of about 20 knots.

See Page 535 For Value Estimates

Length Overall	37'6"	Fuel	320 gals.
Length WL	33'6"	Water	240 gals.
Beam	13'2"	Waste	55 gals.
Draft	3'11"	Hull Type	Modified-V
Weight	27,000#	Deadrise Aft	14°

Trawlers & Motoryachts

Pacific Trawler 40

2000–03

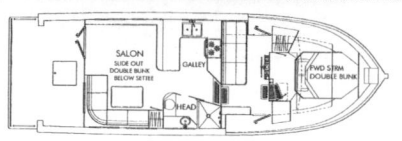

Open Transom

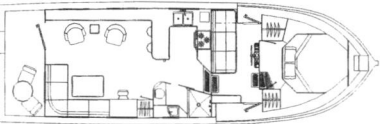

Closed Transom

See Page 535 For Value Estimates

Sturdy coastal trawler with tug-like profile combines live-aboard comfort, economical operation. First twelve were built with unique open transom with cockpit extending to end of swim platform; closed-transom model introduced in 2002 has conventional transom, slightly lengthened salon. Roomy aft-galley floorplan has head opposite galley rather than forward. Note excellent helm visibility, protected cockpit, mahogany cabin joinery, bow thruster. Single 330hp Cummins diesel will cruise at 10 knots (14–15 knots top).

Length Overall	39'10"	Fuel	465 gals.
Length WL	37'2"	Water	265 gals.
Beam	13'3"	Waste	50 gals.
Draft	4'2"	Clearance	12'6"
Weight	26,000#	Hull Type	Semi-Disp.

PDQ 34 Catamaran

2000–07

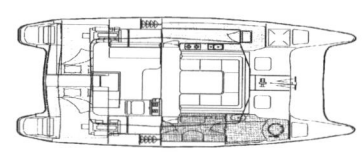

Strong-selling catamaran trawler from Canada matches great styling with outstanding economy, stable rough-water handling. Two-stateroom layout boasts huge salon with U-shaped lounge, lower helm. Galley is in portside hull; head is forward in starboard hull. Additional features include large windows, very wide side decks, roomy flybridge. Called the PDQ 32 until hulls were lengthened in 2003. Skeg protects props and rudders. Twin 75hp Yanmar diesels cruise at 13–14 knots burning 4 gallons per hour.

See Page 535 For Value Estimates

Length Overall	34'6"	Clearance	12'3"
Length WL	33'11"	Fuel	184 gals.
Beam	16'10"	Water	80 gals.
Draft	2'4"	Waste	38 gals.
Weight	12,000#	Hull Type	Catamaran

Pearson 38 Double Cabin

1988–91

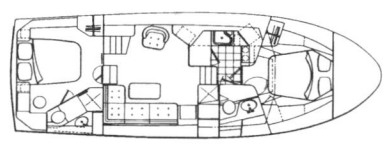

Deep-V cruiser introduced in 1988 received high marks for quality construction, exemplary fit and finish. Two-stateroom, galley-down interior is accented with satin-finished oak trim, high-end fabrics, premium furnishings. Both staterooms include walkaround double berths; both heads have separate stall showers. Additional features include well-arranged engine room, bow pulpit, wide side decks, swim platform. Standard 320hp gas engines cruise at 16 knots cruise; optional Cat 320hp diesels cruise at 20 knots.

Prices Not Provided for Pre-1995 Models

Length	37'9"	Fuel	300 gals.
Beam	13'10"	Water	100 gals.
Draft	3'9"	Headroom	6'4"
Weight	25,000#	Hull Type	Deep-V
Clearance	13'0"	Deadrise Aft	19°

Pilgrim 40

1983–89

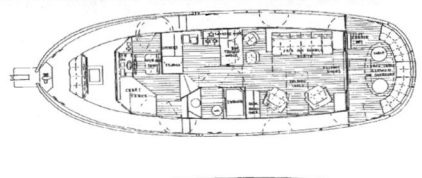

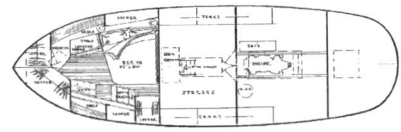

Tug-like Canadian cruiser with plumb bow, rounded stern is a genuine eye-catcher in a sea of look-alike trawlers. Well-appointed interior features roomy salon with mahogany trim, U-shaped galley with in-floor storage, large stateroom with copious storage. High bulwarks provide good side deck security. Extended flybridge with fake stack has space for a dinghy. Note trolly-car pilothouse windows, shaded fantail deck. Bow thruster was standard. Displacement hull will cruise at 8 knots (at 3 gph) with single 100hp diesel. Over 45 were built.

Prices Not Provided for Pre-1995 Models

Length Overall	40'0"	Clearance	22'0"
Length WL	NA	Fuel	142 gals.
Beam	14'0"	Water	240 gals.
Draft	3'6"	Headroom	6'4"
Weight	25,000#	Hull Type	Displacement

Present 38 Sundeck

1981–87

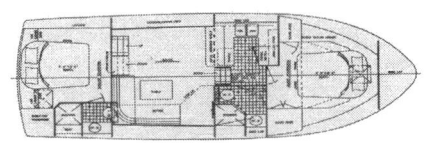

Sporty sundeck motoryacht (built by Nautique Marine in Taiwan) combines time-tested layout with solid construction, low-cost operation. Standard galley-down teak interior includes two double staterooms, each with en-suite head with separate stall shower. Salon with U-shaped settee is big for a 38-footer, but aft deck is smaller than most. Note serving counter overlooking galley. Big engine room is a plus. Above-average workmanship throughout. Cruise efficiently at 12–14 knots with twin 225hp Lehman diesels (about 16 knots top).

Prices Not Provided for Pre-1995 Models

Length Overall	38'2"	Clearance	17'6"
Beam	13'3"	Fuel	300 gals.
Draft	3'4"	Water	150 gals.
Weight	21,000#	Waste	35 gals.
Headroom	6'4"	Hull Type	Semi-Disp.

Present (CHB) 35 Sundeck

1982–87

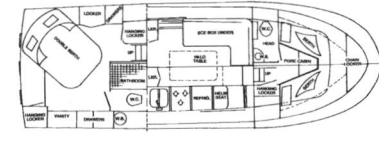

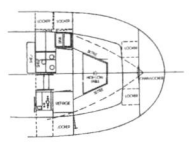

Popular double-cabin import (built by both CHB and Chien Hwa) combines timeless trawler profile with traditional teak interior, economical operation. Several floorplans were available, all with full-beam aft cabin, port/starboard salon deck doors, parquet flooring, lower helm with deck door. Surprisingly roomy aft deck. Flybridge seats four. Bow pulpit, swim platform, radar arch were standard. Keel protects running gear. Also marketed as the Ponderosa 35. Cruise at 7 knots with single 135hp diesel; 8–10 knots with twin 85hp diesels.

Prices Not Provided for Pre-1995 Models

Length Overall	34'5"	Clearance	NA
Length WL	31'6"	Fuel	300 gals.
Beam	12'0"	Water	200 gals.
Draft	4'2"	Waste	30 gals.
Weight	18,700#	Hull Type	Semi-Disp.

Present (CHB) 42 Sundeck

1984–89

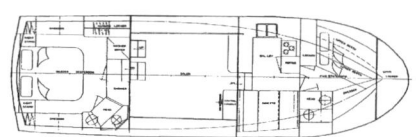

Appealing 1980s sundeck yacht with contemporary styling, traditional teak interior continues to enjoy strong buyer appeal. Standard twin-stateroom layout with galley and dinette down boasts roomy master suite with space for washer/dryer, teak parquet floors, standard lower helm. Topside highlights include covered aft deck with wet bar, wide side decks, flybridge seating for six. Also marketed as CHB or Ponderosa 42. Among several engine options, twin 255 Lehman diesels cruise at 10–12 knots (about 14 knots top).

Prices Not Provided for Pre-1995 Models

Length Overall	41'10"	Clearance	16'4"
Length WL	38'0"	Fuel	450 gals.
Beam	13'8"	Water	200 gals.
Draft	3'6"	Waste	30 gals.
Weight	26,000#	Hull Type	Semi-Disp.

Present (CHB) 46 Cockpit Motor Yacht

1984–88

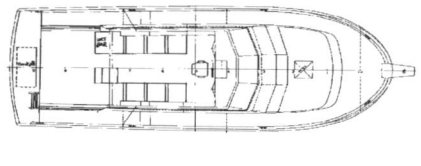

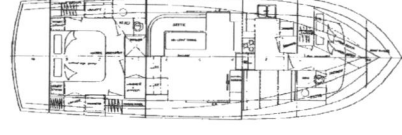

Handsome cockpit yacht (built by CHB; designed by Ed Monk) made good on promise of cruising luxury, economical operation. Twin-stateroom layout with galley, dinette down, lower helm with sliding deck door, boasts well-appointed master suite with space for washer/dryer. Covered aft deck came standard with wing doors, wet bar. Roomy flybridge seats eight in comfort. Long keel protects running gear. Better range than most motoryachts her size. Cruise at 10 knots with Perkins 200hp diesels; 12 knots with 250hp Perkins.

Prices Not Provided for Pre-1995 Models

Length Overall	46'3"	Headroom	6'4"
Beam	14'6"	Fuel	600 gals.
Draft	3'10"	Water	265 gals.
Weight	26,000#	Waste	50 gals.
Clearance	NA	Hull Type	Semi-Disp.

President 35 Double Cabin

1987–92

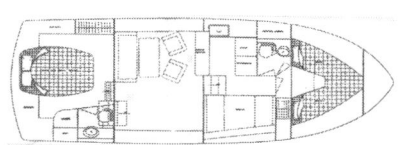

Roomy double-cabin cruiser with broad 12'10" beam combined solid fiberglass construction with affordable price, economical operation. Offered with several interior layouts over the years, all with rich teak joinery, comfortable salon with wraparound windows. Lower helm was optional. Storage—while not plentiful—is adequate for most weekend getaways. Tall freeboard results in somewhat top-heavy appearance. Hardtop, radar arch were standard. Twin 225hp Lehman diesels cruise at 15 knots and reach a top speed of around 18 knots.

Prices Not Provided for Pre-1995 Models

Length	34'5"	Headroom	6'4"
Beam	12'10"	Fuel	250 gals.
Draft	3'1"	Water	100 gals.
Weight	18,700#	Hull Type	Modified-V
Clearance	11'7"	Deadrise Aft	NA

President 37 Double Cabin

1986–88

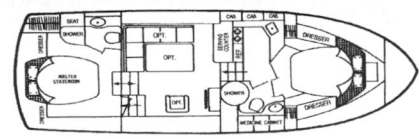

Sturdy Taiwan import with full teak interior offers a timeless mix of contemporary styling, solid fiberglass construction, economical operation. Several two-stateroom floorplans were available with the dinette layout being the most popular. Lower helm was not standard. Big cabin windows offer panoramic outside views. Note teak-and-holly cabin sole. Most were sold with hard-top and radar arch. Modified-V hull incorporates shallow keel for directional stability. Twin 275hp diesels cruise at 15 knots; optional 300hp Cummins diesels cruise at 20 knots.

Prices Not Provided for Pre-1995 Models

Length	36'6"	Headroom	6'3"
Beam	12'10"	Fuel	300 gals.
Draft	3'2"	Water	100 gals.
Weight	20,400#	Waste	40 gals.
Clearance	11'6"	Hull Type	Modified-V

President 41 Double Cabin

1982–87

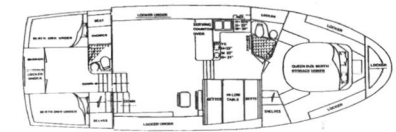

Twin Beds in Master

Double Berth in Master

Popular Taiwan import with full teak interior, modest price became one of the best-selling boats of her type during the 1980s. Offered with two- or three-stateroom layouts, all with large forward staterooms, booth-style dinette, standard lower helm. Good cabin storage. One of the more efficient boats of her type. Over 120 were built making this President's best-selling model during the 1980s. Twin 120/135hp Lehman diesels provide 8-knot cruising speed. Larger 225hp Lehmans cruise at 12 knots (15–16 knots top).

Prices Not Provided for Pre-1995 Models

Length Overall	40'6"	Clearance	NA
Length WL	35'10"	Fuel	420 gals.
Beam	13'5"	Water	120 gals.
Draft	2'10"	Hull Type	Modified-V
Weight	22,500#	Deadrise Aft	14°

President 43 Double Cabin

1984–88

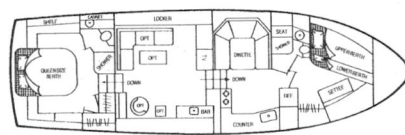

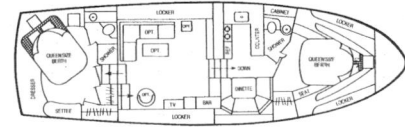

Value-priced motoryacht imported during late 1980s combined lavish teak interior with traditional lines, economical operation. Twin-stateroom floorplan with galley/dinette down is notable for expansive salon, generous storage. Lower helm was optional. Teak-laid aft deck came standard with hard-top, wet bar. Additional features include large engine room, wide side decks, radar arch, bow pulpit, teak swim platform. Twin 275hp Lehmans cruise at 15 knots and reach a top speed of 17–18 knots. A total of 42 were built.

Prices Not Provided for Pre-1995 Models

Length Overall	42'6"	Clearance	12'4"
Length WL	37'10"	Fuel	420 gals.
Beam	13'10"	Water	120 gals.
Draft	3'2"	Hull Type	Modified-V
Weight	28,000#	Deadrise Aft	NA

Trawlers & Motoryachts

PT 35 Sundeck

1984–90

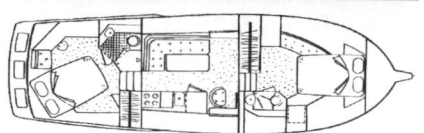

Galley Up Layout

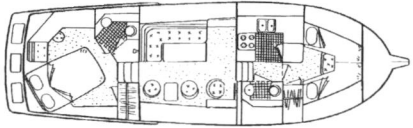

Galley Down Layout

Generic 1980s Taiwan cruiser made good on promise of solid construction, affordable price. Available with two floorplans: galley-up layout features huge forward stateroom; galley-down arrangement opens up salon with increased seating possibilities. Standard features included teak interior joinery, lower helm, salon deck doors. Note roomy full-beam afterdeck. Solid fiberglass hull has shallow keel for directional stability. Single 200hp Perkins will cruise efficiently at 8–9 knots. Twin-diesel models can reach 18–20 knots top.

Prices Not Provided for Pre-1995 Models

Length Overall	35'4"	Weight	20,000#
Length WL	31'10"	Fuel	300 gals.
Beam	12'6"	Water	100 gals.
Draft	3'0"	Hull Type	Modified-V
Clearance	NA	Deadrise Aft	NA

PT 42 Cockpit MY

1984–90

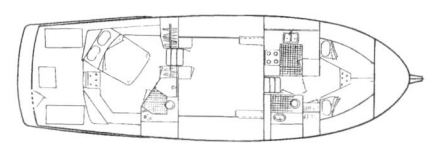

Versatile 1980s cockpit yacht with contemporary lines, traditional teak interior combined roomy accommodations with low-maintenance ownership. Conventional two-stateroom floorplan with galley down features expansive salon with built-in dinette, lower helm, twin deck doors. Galley is on the small side, but storage is excellent. Cockpit makes boarding easy; full-width aft deck is a good entertainment platform. Transom door was standard. Twin 225hp diesels cruise at 14–15 knots (about 17 knots top).

Prices Not Provided for Pre-1995 Models

Length Overall	42'0"	Clearance	NA
Length WL	38'3"	Fuel	300 gals.
Beam	13'6"	Water	150 gals.
Draft	3'6"	Hull Type	Modified-V
Weight	25,000#	Deadrise Aft	NA

Ranger R-27

2011–Current

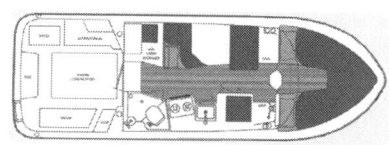

Trailerable coastal cruiser with trailerable 8'6" beam packs impressive living space in a relatively small package. Cozy midcabin interior boasts space-efficient layout with raised dinette, full-service galley, lower helm, V-berth forward. Back of passenger seat folds forward to extend dinette area. Second cabin is best suited for kids or storage. Cockpit provides adequate space for lounging or fishing. Note very slender side decks. Bow/stern thrusters are standard. Cruise economically at 10 knots (16–18 top) with single Yanmar 180hp diesel.

Insufficient Resale Data to Assign Values

Length	27'1"	Fuel	100 gals.
Beam	8'6"	Water	40 gals.
Draft	2'2"	Waste	30 gals.
Dry Weight	6,200#	Hull Type	Modified-V
Clearance	NA	Deadrise Aft	NA

Trawlers & Motoryachts

Ranger R-29

2009–Current

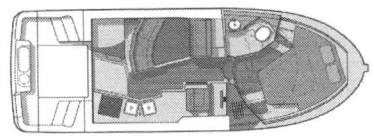

Sturdy coastal cruiser with classic tugboat lines is salty, roomy, easy on the fuel. Highlights include nicely-appointed interior with two staterooms, roomy cockpit with transom door, bow and stern thrusters, seaworthy semi-displacement hull. Midship berth, beneath raised dinette, has privacy door. Note large cabin windows, opening hatches over helm and companion seats. Slender side decks aren't for use under way—foredeck is best accessed via sliding pilothouse door. Cruise at 15 knots (20+ top) with single 260hp Yanmar diesel.

See Page 537 For Value Estimates

Length	29'0"	Fuel	150 gals.
Beam	10'0"	Water	70 gals.
Draft	2'4"	Waste	40 gals.
Weight	9,250#	Hull Type	Seemi-Disp.
Clearance	NA	Deadrise Aft	NA

Sabre 34 Sedan

1991–2002

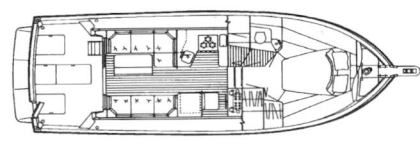

Sought-after performance trawler with many quality features makes the cut with boaters focused on timeless styling, luxury-class amenities. Traditional teak (or cherry) interior with U-shaped galley, lower helm offers near ideal accommodations for the cruising couple. Highlights include large cabin windows, convertible dinette, separate stall shower, teak-and-holly cabin sole. Wide side decks make getting around easy. Transom door, radar mast were standard. Twin Cummins 220hp diesels cruise at 15–16 knots (about 20 knots top).

See Page 539 For Value Estimates

Length w/Pulpit	37'6"	Fuel	250 gals.
Hull Length	34'0"	Water	160 gals.
Beam	12'6"	Waste	25 gals.
Draft	3'3"	Hull Type	Modified-V
Weight	17,800#	Deadrise Aft	14°

Sabre 36 Aft Cabin

1989–98

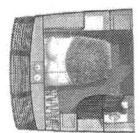

Quality double-cabin cruiser combines traditional trawler styling with luxury-class accommodations, spirited performance. Deluxe interior with teak or cherry joinery features expansive galley, twin salon deck doors, large cabin windows, teak-and-holly salon sole. Aft stateroom offered choice of twin berths (one double, one single) or optional double berth. Wide side decks, well-placed handrails make getting around easy. Underwater exhaust is a plus. Cat 255hp diesels cruise at 16 knots (20 top); 300hp Cats cruise at 18 knots (23–24 top).

See Page 539 For Value Estimates

Length w/Pulpit	40'1"	Fuel	300 gals.
Hull Length	36'0"	Water	225 gals.
Beam	12'6"	Waste	40 gals.
Draft	4'3"	Hull Type	Modified-V
Weight	20,000#	Deadrise Aft	14°

Sabre 36 Sedan

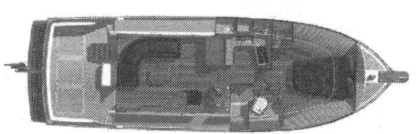

2002–07

Quality-built flybridge cruiser set class standards in her day for comfort, craftsmanship, performance. Spacious single-stateroom interior with cherrywood joinery, expansive salon is finely finished, tastefully appointed. Highlights include spacious stateroom, sliding salon deck door, teak-and-holly cabin sole, large salon windows. Cockpit wet bar, transom door, radar mast, swim platform are standard. Wide side decks, large engine room are a plus. Expect a cruising speed of 25–26 knots with optional 370hp Yanmar diesels (about 30 knots top).

See Page 539 For Value Estimates

Length	36'0"	Fuel	300 gals.
Beam	12'6"	Water	100 gals.
Draft	3'4"	Waste	30 gals.
Weight	19,500#	Hull Type	Modified-V
Clearance, Mast	19'0"	Deadrise Aft	18°

Sabre 42 Sedan

2001–Current

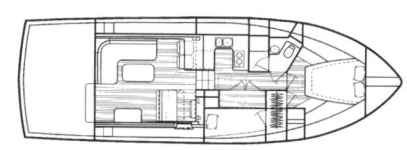

Stately Downeast sedan with beautifully appointed interior defines cruising elegance, traditional Maine craftsmanship. Lavish cherrywood interior with wide-open salon features standard lower helm, teak-and-holly cabin sole, two large staterooms, generous storage. Note that guest cabin is fitted with double French doors. Additional features include cockpit wet bar, radar mast, Subzero galley refrigeration, spacious engine room, wide side decks, swim platform. Yanmar 465hp diesels cruise at 24 knots (28–29 knots top).

See Page 539 For Value Estimates

Length	42'3"	Fuel	450 gals.
Beam	14'4"	Water	160 gals.
Draft	3'9"	Waste	60 gals.
Weight	30,000#	Hull Type	Modified-V
Headroom	6'6"	Deadrise Aft	16°

Sabre 43 Aft Cabin

1996–2005

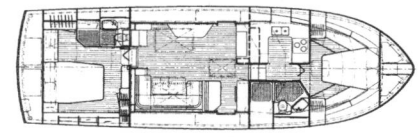

2-Stateroom Floorplan

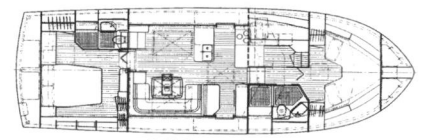

3-Stateroom Layout

See Page 539 For Value Estimates

Spacious double-cabin cruising yacht courted affluent buyers with classic styling, lavish accommodations, excellent performance. Offered with two- or three-stateroom interiors, both with lower helm, salon deck doors, large master cabin, two full heads. Features include teak interior cabinetry, full walkaround decks, foredeck storage lockers, radar mast, roomy flybridge. Note convenient cockpit access door in master stateroom. Twin 370hp Yanmar diesels cruise at 15–16 knots (about 20 knots top).

Length w/Pulpit	48'1"	Clearance, Mast	17'9"
Hull Length	43'6"	Fuel	520 gals.
Beam	15'0"	Water	250 gals.
Draft	4'0"	Hull Type	Modified-V
Weight	38,500#	Deadrise Aft	14°

Trawlers & Motoryachts

Sabre 47 Aft Cabin

1997–2007

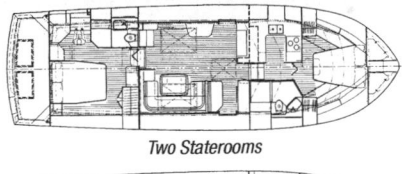

Two Staterooms

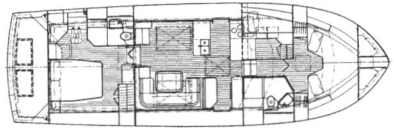

Three Staterooms

See Page 539 For Value Estimates

Lengthened version of popular Sabre 43 Aft Cabin (previous entry) boasts enlarged aft stateroom, bigger cockpit. Offered with two- or three-stateroom floorplans, both with lower helm, home-size galley, two full heads. Teak interior cabinetry is beautifully finished. Topside features include full walkaround decks, folding radar mast, spacious bridge with L-shaped dinette aft. Note side exhausts, cockpit door in master stateroom. Cabintop can stow a dinghy. Yanmar 500hp diesels cruise at 18 knots (about 22 top).

Length w/Pulpit	52'1"	Clearance, Mast	23'4"
Hull Length	47'6"	Fuel	605 gals.
Beam	15'0"	Water	300 gals.
Draft	4'5"	Hull Type	Modified-V
Weight	43,000#	Deadrise Aft	14°

Sea Ranger 45 Aft Cabin

1982–89

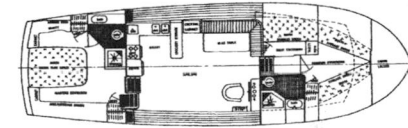

Three Staterooms

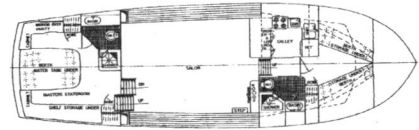

Two Staterooms

Prices Not Provided for Pre-1995 Models

Well-regarded 1980s sundeck yacht (also sold as the C&L 45) pairs heavy-duty construction with roomy accommodations, timeless styling. While a galley-down floorplan was available, most were delivered with a three-stateroom layout—rare in a 45-foot boat. Highlights include expansive salon with standard lower helm, spacious owner's stateroom, two full heads, large engine room. Afterdeck is among the largest in her class. Cruise at 12 knots with 255hp Volvo diesels (15–16 top); 16–18 knots with 375hp Cats (20+ top).

Length	45'0"	Headroom	6'5"
Beam	15'3"	Fuel	850 gals.
Draft	4'0"	Water	350 gals.
Weight	37,400#	Waste	60 gals.
Clearance	NA	Hull Type	Semi-Disp.

Sea Ranger 46 Sundeck

1985–89

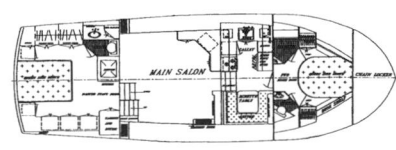

Prices Not Provided for Pre-1995 Models

Heavily built Taiwan import from late 1980s offered compelling mix of space, comfort, affordability. Standard two-stateroom, galley-down interior includes fore, aft double berths, roomy salon with entertainment center, large aft deck with wing doors, party-sized flybridge. Note split forward head with shower stall to port. Additional features include generous storage, large engine room, lower helm deck door, wide side decks. Volvo 255hp engines cruise efficiently at 12–14 knots (around 18 knots top).

Length	46'0"	Fuel	850 gals.
Beam	15'4"	Water	350 gals.
Draft	4'0"	Waste	45 gals.
Weight	40,000#	Headroom	6'5"
Clearance	NA	Hull Type	Semi-Disp.

Trawlers & Motoryachts

Sea Ranger 47 Pilothouse

1980–87

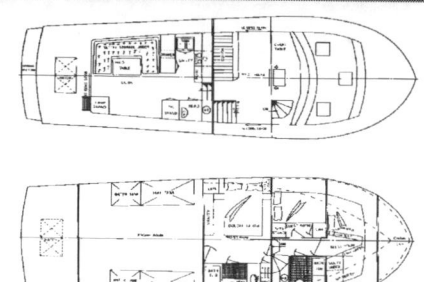

Appealing pilothouse yacht (built by C&L in Taiwan) blurs the line between sturdy coastal cruiser, feature-packed liveaboard. Roomy interior with three staterooms, two full heads boasts roomy salon with galley forward, raised pilothouse with watch berth. Note spacious walk-in engine room. Topside highlights include protected side decks, teak swim platform, cabintop dinghy platform. Salon day head was optional. Solid fiberglass hull has long, prop-protecting keel. Lehman 135hp—or GM 175hp—diesels cruise at 7–8 knots.

Prices Not Provided for Pre-1995 Models

Length Overall	47'3"	Clearance	20'7"
Length WL	43'0"	Fuel	720 gals.
Beam	15'2"	Water	360 gals.
Draft	4'4"	Waste	50 gals.
Weight	43,000#	Hull Type	Semi-Disp.

Sea Ranger 51 Motor Yacht

1983–89

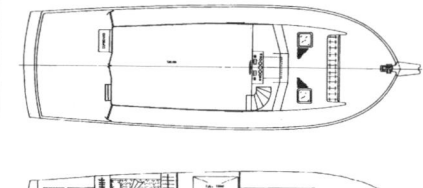

Asian-built motoryacht from late 1980s offered affordable alternative to more expensive choices from Hatteras, Viking, Ocean, etc. Highlights include full teak interior, walk-through engine room, walkaround side decks, commanding flybridge. Lower helm is open to salon for good aft visibility. Side decks are sheltered with bridge overhangs. Teak decks are a plus. Note molded bow seating. Cat 260hp diesels cruise at 12 knots (14 knots top); GM 650hp 8V92s cruise at 15–16 knots (18+ knots top).

Prices Not Provided for Pre-1995 Models

Length Overall	51'0"	Clearance	NA
Length WL	45'0"	Fuel	1,000 gals.
Beam	16'8"	Water	420 gals.
Draft	4'3"	Headroom	6'6"
Weight	55,000#	Hull Type	Semi-Disp.

Sea Ranger 52 Cockpit Motor Yacht

1985–89

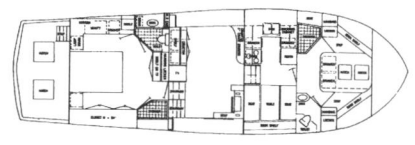

Versatile 1980s cockpit yacht (built by C&L in Taiwan) made good on Sea Ranger promise of versatility, comfort, owner satisfaction. Standard two-stateroom interior boasts huge owner's suite (with cockpit door), booth-style dinette, home-sized galley. Note good lower-helm visibility, handcrafted teak woodwork. Full-width aft deck, roomy bridge can entertain a small crowd. Most were delivered with optional wing doors, hardtop. Among several engine options, Volvo 255hp diesels cruise at 13–14 knots (16–18 top).

Prices Not Provided for Pre-1995 Models

Length	52'0"	Fuel	850 gals.
Beam	15'4"	Water	350 gals.
Draft	4'0"	Waste	50 gals.
Weight	44,000#	Headroom	6'5"
Clearance	NA	Hull Type	Semi-Disp.

Sea Ray 360 Aft Cabin

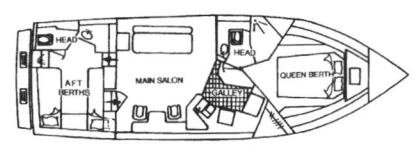

1983–87

Popular aft-cabin cruiser with innovative cabin layout offered rakish 1980s styling with comfortable accommodations, competitive price. Teak-trimmed interior is uniquely arranged with master stateroom forward, guest cabin with single berths aft—very unusual indeed. Large galley boasts upright refrigerator, teak parquet floor. Lower helm was a popular option. Aft head is tiny; forward head has separate stall shower. Good lower helm visibility. Standard 260hp gas engines (or optional 200hp Perkins diesels) cruise at 15–16 knots.

Prices Not Provided for Pre-1995 Models

Length	36'3"	Fuel	270 gals.
Beam	12'6"	Water	120 gals.
Draft	2'11"	Waste	40 gals.
Weight	15,100#	Hull Type	Modified-V
Clearance	NA	Deadrise Aft	9°

Sea Ray 370/380 Aft Cabin

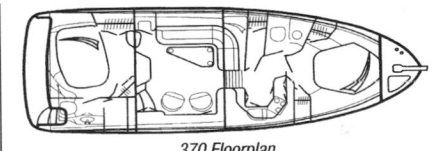
370 Floorplan

1997–2001

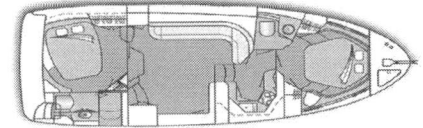
380 Layout

See Page 540 For Value Estimates

Beamy aft-cabin cruiser made the cut with late 1990s Sea Ray buyers seeking condo-style accommodations in a compact, well-built motoryacht. Richly appointed interior boasts expansive salon with L-shaped sofa, two roomy staterooms, generous storage. Mini-stateroom opposite galley can be configured as utility room. Aft deck has wet bar and wing doors. Engine room is a tight fit. Hull is fully cored. MerCruiser 380hp gas inboards cruise at 20 knots (about 30 knots top); 340hp Cat diesels cruise at 20 knots (22–23 knots top).

Length	38'2"	Fuel	300 gals.
Beam	14'3"	Water	100 gals.
Draft	3'1"	Waste	55 gals.
Weight	23,800#	Hull Type	Deep-V
Clearance, Arch	16'4"	Deadrise Aft	19.5°

Sea Ray 380 Aft Cabin

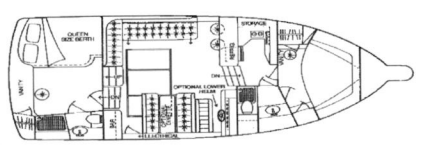

1989–91

Roomy aft-cabin cruiser with wide 13'11" beam combined sporty styling with feature-packed layout, competitive price. Space-efficient floorplan with L-shaped salon sofa, U-shaped galley includes convenient breakfast bar, optional lower helm, two double staterooms. Salon dinette was a popular option. Wide side decks afford secure bow access. Radar arch, bow pulpit, hardtop were standard. Deep-V hull has prop pockets to reduce draft. Standard 340hp gas inboards cruise at 16 knots (mid 20s top); optional 330hp Cummins diesels cruise at 20 knots.

Prices Not Provided for Pre-1995 Models

Length w/Pulpit	42'7"	Fuel	300 gals.
Hull Length	37'9"	Water	100 gals.
Beam	13'11"	Waste	40 gals.
Draft	2'7"	Hull Type	Deep-V
Weight	20,000#	Deadrise Aft	19°

Trawlers & Motoryachts

Sea Ray 390 Motoryacht; 40 MY

2003–07

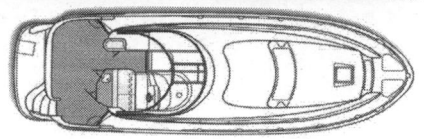

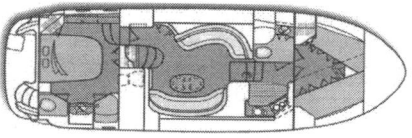

Distinctive hardtop motoryacht (called Sea Ray 390 MY in 2003–05; 40 MY in 2006–07) blends traditional flushdeck design with sleek styling, maxivolume accommodations. Deluxe interior with cherry cabinets boasts expansive salon with facing settees, well-appointed staterooms, space for optional washer/dryer. Galley enjoys good natural lighting from window above. Flushdeck layout keeps the skipper with guests rather than isolated on the flybridge. Gas 370hp engines cruise at 18 knots; Cummins 446hp diesels cruise at 20 knots.

See Page 541 For Value Estimates

Length w/Platform	41'9"	Fuel	300 gals.
Beam	14'3"	Water	100 gals.
Draft	3'0"	Waste	54 gals.
Weight	26,500#	Hull Type	Modified-V
Clearance	13'8"	Deadrise Aft	15°

Sea Ray 410/415/440 Aft Cabin

1986–91

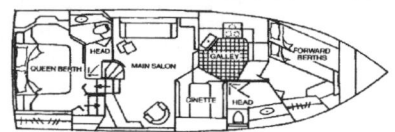

410 Floorplan (1986–87)

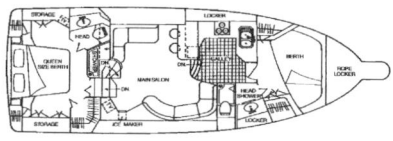

415/440 Floorplan (1989–89)

Prices Not Provided for Pre-1995 Models

Popular Sea Ray motoryacht (called 410 Aft Cabin in 1986–87; 415 Aft Cabin in 1988; 440 Aft Cabin in 1989–91) combined rakish styling with quality amenities, competitive price. Original galley-down interior with booth dinette was replaced in 1989 with more open layout featuring curved settee, portside breakfast bar. Salon dimensions are big for a 41-footer. Note salon entertainment center, vanity in aft stateroom. Washer/dryer was optional. Standard 330hp gas engines cruise at 15 knots; 375hp Cat diesels cruise at 20 knots.

Length w/Pulpit	45'11"	Fuel	400 gals.
Hull Length	43'6"	Water	130 gals.
Beam	13'11"	Waste	40 gals.
Draft	3'2"	Hull Type	Modified-V
Weight	23,000#	Deadrise Aft	17°

Sea Ray 420 Aft Cabin

1996–2002

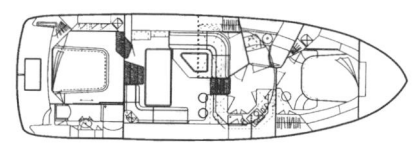

Sporty styling, spirited performance, innovative interior set this stylish aft-cabin yacht a step ahead of her late 1990s competitors. Upscale interior with large staterooms, home-size galley includes mini-stateroom—or optional laundry room—extending under salon sole. Topside features include aft-deck wing doors, transom storage locker, extended swim platform. Wide walkways provide good bow access. Hull is fully cored. Twin 420hp Cat (or 430hp Cummins) diesels cruise in the mid 20s (27–28 knots top).

See Page 541 For Value Estimates

Length	45'5"	Fuel	350 gals.
Beam	14'3"	Water	120 gals.
Draft	3'1"	Waste	55 gals.
Weight	27,000#	Hull Type	Deep-V
Clearance	15'6"	Deadrise Aft	18.5°

Sea Ray 420/44 Sedan Bridge

2004–09

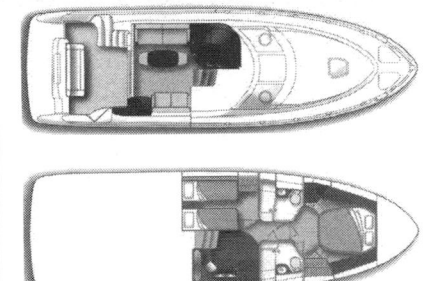

Handsome flybridge yacht with best-in-class styling (called 420 Sedan Bridge in 2004–05; 44 SB in 2006–09) met Sea Ray promise of yacht-class accommodations, versatile layout, quality construction. Posh two-stateroom interior with cherry cabinets includes raised salon dinette with panoramic outside views, large master stateroom, guest cabin with twin berths, two full heads. Large flybridge with excellent helm position. Note washer/dryer under galley steps. Cummins 480hp diesels cruise in the mid 20s (about 30 knots top).

See Page 541 For Value Estimates

Length Overall	45'5"	Fuel	350 gals.
Beam	14'3"	Water	120 gals.
Draft	3'6"	Waste	42 gals.
Weight	28,500#	Hull Type	Modified-V
Clearance	NA	Deadrise Aft	18°

Sea Ray 450 Express Bridge

1998–2004

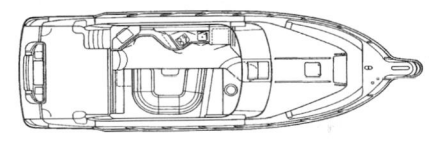

Main Deck

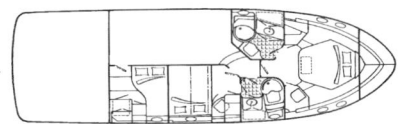

Lower Level

Rakish sedan yacht with walk-through bridge, huge interior offers luxury-class comforts, amenities of a larger yacht. Raised dinette in full-beam salon provides space below for second stateroom with washer/dryer combo. Spacious bridge boasts centerline helm, wet bar, lounge seating aft. Note twin transom doors, foldaway cockpit seat, molded bridge steps. Deep well creates secure foredeck area for passengers and guests. Twin 420hp V-drive Cat (or 430hp Cummins) diesels cruise at 20 knots (mid 20s top).

See Page 541 For Value Estimates

Length Overall	51'4"	Fuel	400 gals.
Hull Length	45'6"	Water	100 gals.
Beam	14'8"	Waste	60 gals.
Draft	3'5"	Hull Type	Modified-V
Weight	29,500#	Deadrise Aft	15°

Sea Ray 47 Sedan Bridge

2008–Current

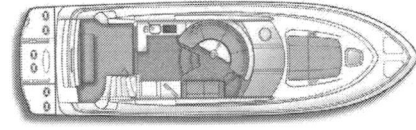

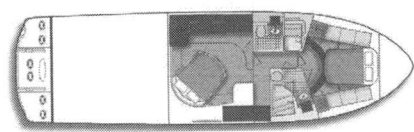

Luxurious Sea Ray flybridge yacht with sweeping lines, executive-class amenities is spacious, versatile, easy on the eye. Innovative floorplan with split-level salon has the galley aft, raised dinette and settee forward. Flip-up window in salon bulkhead provides easy pass-thru to cockpit. Party-time flybridge—accessed via wide bridge steps—includes wet bar, lounge seating. Premium decor with cherry woodwork, leather seating is state of the art. Hardtop is standard. Standard Cummins 600hp V-drive diesels cruise at 25 knots (about 28–30 top).

See Page 541 For Value Estimates

Length	50'8"	Fuel	530 gals.
Beam	14'8"	Water	117 gals.
Draft	4'2"	Waste	60 gals.
Weight	37,500#	Hull Type	Modified-V
Clearance	NA	Deadrise Aft	19°

Trawlers & Motoryachts

Sea Ray 480 Motor Yacht

2002–05

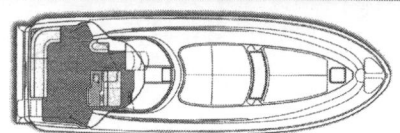

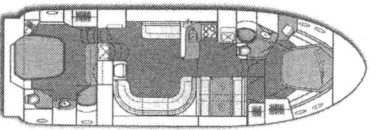

Innovative Sea Ray motoryacht with unusual flushdeck layout is rich in thoughtful features, luxurious amenities. Combined helm/aft-deck platform allows owner and guests lots of room to move around. Open-plan salon with cherry cabinets features curved Ultraleather lounge, booth-style dinette, two large double staterooms. Cozy midcabin space beneath salon sole has twin berths. Note washer/dryer combo under galley steps. Engine room is a tight fit. Cummins 535hp diesels cruise in the low 20s; optional 640hp Cats cruise in the mid 20s.

See Page 541 For Value Estimates

Length w/Platform	50'5"	Fuel	500 gals.
Beam	15'3"	Water	120 gals.
Draft	3'11"	Waste	60 gals.
Weight	38,500#	Hull Type	Modified-V
Clearance	15'0"	Deadrise Aft	15°

Sea Ray 480 Sedan Bridge

1998–2004

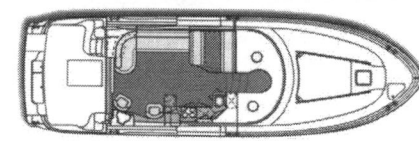

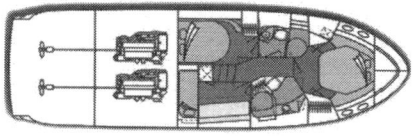

Best-selling flybridge yacht with spacious three-stateroom interior combined sporty Sea Ray styling with deluxe accommodations, competitive price. Appealing cherrywood interior boasts open-plan salon with raised dinette to port, gourmet galley opposite, full entertainment center. Second guest stateroom has built-in washer/dryer. Note roomy flybridge with centerline helm, bow sun pads, extended swim platform. Prop pockets reduce hull draft. Detroit 535hp diesels cruise in the low 20s; 660hp Cats cruise in the high 20s.

See Page 541 For Value Estimates

Length w/Platform	51'2"	Fuel	500 gals.
Beam	15'3"	Water	140 gals.
Draft	3'9"	Waste	68 gals.
Weight	40,400#	Hull Type	Modified-V
Clearance	NA	Deadrise Aft	15°

Sea Ray 500 Sedan Bridge

1990–94

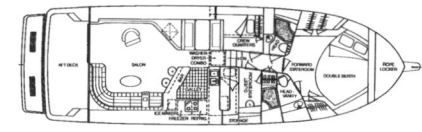

Dinette Floorplan

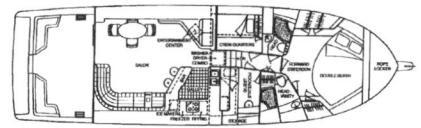

Optional Entertainment Center

One-time Sea Ray flagship (when she was introduced in 1990) offered thoughtful mix of bold styling, mini-motoryacht accommodations. Standard three-stateroom layout with wide-open salon boasts home-size galley with breakfast counter, wraparound settee, built-in entertainment center, large master stateroom, two full heads. Washer/dryer is concealed beneath salon floor. Small cockpit was a turn-off for many. Transom door, radar arch, bow pulpit were standard. GM 550hp 6V92 diesels cruise at 20–22 knots. Not a great-selling model.

Prices Not Provided for Pre-1995 Models

Length w/Platform	55'4"	Fuel	600 gals.
Hull length	49'11"	Water	200 gals.
Beam	15'0"	Waste	40 gals.
Draft	4'2"	Hull Type	Modified-V
Weight	40,000#	Deadrise Aft	17°

Sea Ray 500/52 Sedan Bridge

2005–Current

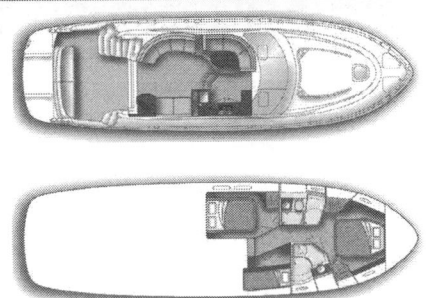

Graceful hardtop sedan (called 500 Sedan Bridge in 2005; 52 SB in 2006–09; 520 SB starting in 2010) combines best-in-class styling with executive-class accommodations, yacht-grade construction. Luxurious three-stateroom cherrywood interior features wood flooring, deluxe master and VIP staterooms with flatscreen TVs, two full heads with separate shall showers. Utility room under galley sole houses washer/dryer. Extended swim platform supports a small tender. Cruise at 24–26 knots with 640hp Cummins diesels.

See Page 542 For Value Estimates

Length w/Platform	52'3"	Fuel	500 gals.
Beam	15'3"	Water	140 gals.
Draft	4'3"	Waste	68 gals.
Weight	42,000#	Hull Type	Modified-V
Clearance	15'8"	Deadrise Aft	15°

Sea Ray 540 Cockpit MY

2001–02

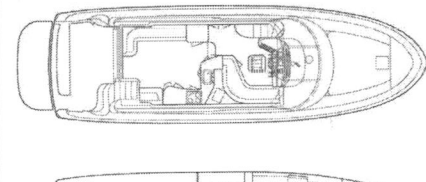

Limited production motoryacht with posh three-stateroom interior combined European lines with American versatility. Spacious bi-level salon features wraparound dinette (or optional lower helm) forward, galley with under-counter refrigeration, posh leather seating. Note inside bridge access ladder; washer/dryer in master stateroom. Flybridge dinette converts electrically into double sun pad. Extended swim platform was optional. Enormous flybridge can seat a small crowd. Standard 640hp Cat diesels cruise at 20 knots (around 25 knots top).

See Page 542 For Value Estimates

Length w/Platform	54'0"	Fuel	800 gals.
Hull Length	50'6"	Water	200 gals.
Beam	15'6"	Waste	68 gals.
Draft	4'9"	Hull Type	Modified-V
Weight	49,000#	Deadrise Aft	18°

Sea Ray 550 Sedan Bridge

1992–98

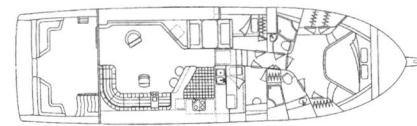

Dinette Floorplan

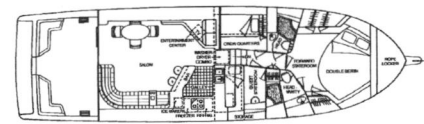

Lower Helm Floorplan

See Page 542 For Value Estimates

Stretched version of Sea Ray 500 Sedan Bridge (1989–95) adds much-needed cockpit space to an otherwise well-rounded yacht. Standard three-stateroom layout includes large owner's stateroom, dinette, breakfast bar, under-counter refrigeration, washer/dryer. Huge flybridge seats a small crowd. Transom door, radar arch, bow pulpit were standard. One of Sea Ray's most popular models. Portside lower helm was optional. Hull is fully cored. Twin 635hp Detroits cruise in the mid 20s; 776hp Cats cruise in the high 20s.

Length Overall	57'10"	Fuel	700 gals.
Hull Length	54'10"	Water	200 gals.
Beam	15'0"	Waste	40 gals.
Draft	4'2"	Hull Type	Modified-V
Weight	45,000#	Deadrise Aft	17°

Trawlers & Motoryachts

Sea Ray 560 Sedan Bridge

1998–2004

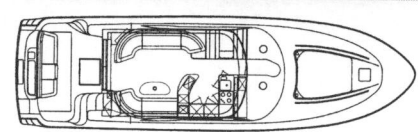

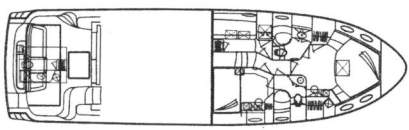

Handsome sedan yacht with seemingly endless list of amenities matched the best European imports of the era for luxury, comfort, performance. Highlights include spacious three-stateroom, two-head cherry interior, large cockpit with foldaway seating, party-time flybridge with wraparound helm and hardtop. Extended swim platform can hold PWC or dinghy. Cockpit has livewell, fish box. Marketed as the 550 Sedan Bridge in 2006. Hull is fully cored. Cat 640hp diesels cruise at 22–23 knots; 1,050hp MANs cruise at 28–30 knots.

See Page 542 For Value Estimates

Length	58'6"	Fuel	800 gals.
Beam	16'0"	Water	200 gals.
Draft	4'6"	Waste	68 gals.
Weight	50,000#	Hull Type	Modified-V
Clearance	NA	Deadrise Aft	15°

Sea Ray 58/580 Sedan Bridge

2006–Current

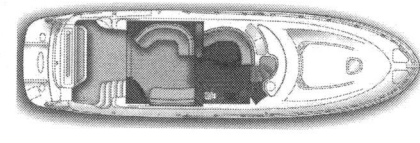

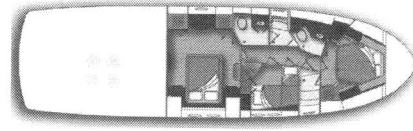

Beautifully styled flybridge yacht (called 58 Sedan Bridge in 2005–09; 580 SB thereafter) showcased Sea Ray's considerable design, engineering skills. Elegant three-stateroom interior with cherry cabinetry, salon sofa with pull-out bed features elevated galley and dinette, full-beam master stateroom with flat-screen TV. Flybridge comes standard with refrigerator, air-conditioning. Bow thruster is standard. Extended swim platform can be fitted with optional launching davit. Cruise at 25–26 knots with 900hp MAN diesels (30+ knots top).

See Page 542 For Value Estimates

Length w/Platform	58'7"	Fuel	700 gals.
Beam	16'0"	Water	150 gals.
Draft	4'3"	Waste	68 gals.
Weight	51,500#	Hull Type	Modified-V
Clearance	18'8"	Deadrise Aft	17°

Sea Ray 650 Cockpit Motor Yacht

1992–96

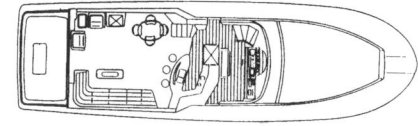

Deckhouse Layout

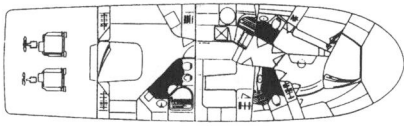

Lower Level Floorplan

Insufficient Resale Data to Assign Values

Maxi-volume cockpit motoryacht with wide 18' beam, yacht-class accommodations was the flagship of Sea Ray's 1990s-era fleet. Spacious four-stateroom interior features enormous salon with U-lounge seating and full entertainment center, raised pilothouse with centerline helm and watch berth, full-beam owner's suite with king bed. Note utility room with washer/dryer. Aft engine room is unusual in a motoryacht. Hull was fully cored. Total of 12 were built. GM 1,040hp V-drive diesels cruise at 20 knots (24–26 knots top).

Length	64'6"	Fuel	1,000 gals.
Beam	18'1"	Water	275 gals.
Draft	4'10"	Waste	264 gals.
Weight	76,000#	Hull Type	Modified-V
Clearance	25'3"	Deadrise Aft	18°

Trawlers & Motoryachts

Sealine F-42/5 Flybridge

2002–Current

Two Staterooms

Three Staterooms

Insufficient Resale Data to Assign Values

Voluminous flybridge cruiser with extendable cockpit was one of the more innovative yachts of her era. Offered with optional three-stateroom interior (rare in a boat this size), more popular two-stateroom layout offers additional salon, galley space. Good lower-helm visibility is a plus; expandable cockpit adds extra entertaining space. Large flybridge has enormous sun pad aft. Note narrow side decks, huge cockpit lazarette, compact engine room. Volvo 480hp diesels cruise in the mid-to-high 20s (30+ knots top).

Length	42'4"	Fuel	372 gals.
Beam	13'10"	Water	165 gals.
Draft	3'4"	Waste	60 gals.
Weight	27,600#	Hull Type	Modified-V
Clearance, Mast	14'3"	Deadrise Aft	16°

Sealine F-44 Flybridge

1994–2001

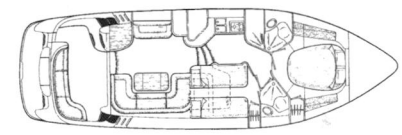

1994–98

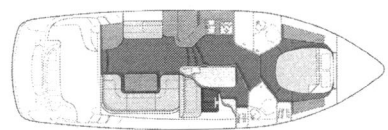

1999–2001

Insufficient Resale Data to Assign Values

Sporty flybridge yacht (called the 420 Statesman until 1998 when swim platform was extended) matched rakish styling with deluxe accommodations, good performance. Elegant two-stateroom floorplan was upgraded in 1999 when guest cabin berths were rearranged. Cockpit came standard with a built-in lounge seat, overhead storage locker. Molded steps lead to roomy bridge with large sun pad. Note big cockpit lazarette, tight engine room. Volvo 370hp diesels cruise at 22–23 knots; Cummins 450hp engines cruise in the mid-to-high 20s.

Length	44'0"	Fuel	350 gals.
Beam	13'8"	Water	120 gals.
Draft	3'6"	Waste	40 gals.
Weight	26,500#	Hull Type	Modified-V
Clearance	15'6"	Deadrise Aft	16°

Sealine T47 Motor Yacht

2000–05

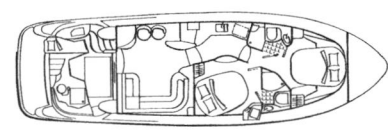

Insufficient Resale Data to Assign Values

Aggressive styling, good performance, innovative features made this U.K.-built cruiser a good boating value. Comfortable interior features spacious salon with high-gloss woodwork, large amidships galley, two full-size en suite staterooms. Lower helm visibility is excellent. Note clever storage compartment beneath galley sole. Crew cabin—accessed from beneath cockpit settee—contains single berth, toilet, washer/dryer. Engine room is a tight fit. Built on deep-V hull with prop pockets, Volvo 480hp diesels cruise at 25 knots (28–30 knots top).

Length Overall	46'9"	Fuel	514 gals.
Beam	14'2"	Water	160 gals.
Draft	3'10"	Headroom	6'6"
Weight	28,650#	Hull Type	Deep-V
Clearance	15'6"	Deadrise Aft	18.5°

Trawlers & Motoryachts

Sealine T-51 Motor Yacht

1998–2004

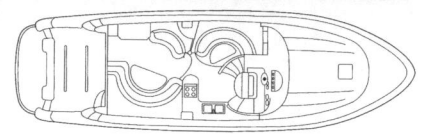

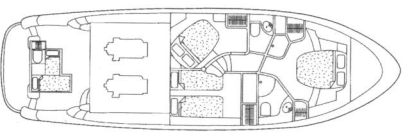

Compelling U.K. luxury yacht combines sleek Mediterranean lines with yacht-grade finish, spirited performance. Expansive three-stateroom floorplan features huge salon with facing settees, raised dinette, galley and helm forward. Note electric salon windows, limited galley storage. Huge cockpit lazarette provides entry to compact engine room. Additional features include spacious flybridge with barbecue, bow thruster, teak decks, washer/dryer. A good performer, twin 635hp Cummins diesels cruise at 25 knots (28–30 knots top).

Insufficient Resale Data to Assign Values

Length Overall	50'11"	Fuel	540 gals.
Beam	14'11"	Water	168 gals.
Draft	4'7"	Waste	60 gals.
Weight	44,000#	Hull Type	Deep-V
Clearance	12'6"	Deadrise Aft	21°

Selene 36/38 Trawler

2003–Current

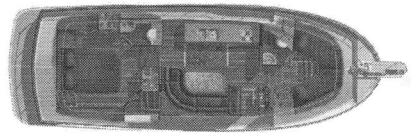

Seaworthy displacement cruiser with walkaround deck combines timeless design with solid construction, all-weather capability. Well-appointed interior with deckhouse galley features two large staterooms, comfortable salon with twin deck doors, teak-planked flooring, Corian counters. Note engine room access door in aft stateroom. Reverse front windows reduce glare. Note folding mast, transom door, hullside boarding gates. Bow thruster is standard. Single 220hp Cummins diesel delivers 7–8 knot cruising speed (about 10 knots top).

See Page 542 For Value Estimates

Length Overall	41'9"	Clearance, Mast	21'2"
Length WL	36'6"	Fuel	500 gals.
Beam	14'6"	Water	180 gals.
Draft	4'8"	Waste	55 gals.
Weight	35,700#	Hull Type	Displacement

Selene 43/45 Pilothouse

2001–Current

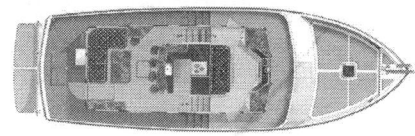

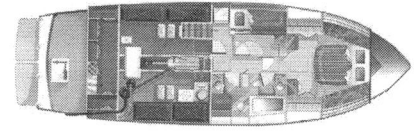

Heavy-weather displacement trawler hull pairs handsome lines with top-shelf accommodations, long-range versatility. Traditional interior with teak-planked flooring (offered in several configurations) includes two large staterooms, expansive salon, U-shaped galley with serving counter, washer/dryer, raised pilothouse with settee. Note hullside boarding gates, huge "commissary" area between engine room and lazarette. Sold as the Selene 45 since 2010. Cruise at 8 knots with 2,000-mile range with Cummins 210hp diesel.

See Page 542 For Value Estimates

Length Overall	48'5"	Ballast	3,000#
Length WL	43'11"	Fuel	1,000 gals.
Beam	15'8"	Water	230 gals.
Draft	5'0"	Waste	60 gals.
Weight	58,000#	Hull Type	Displacement

Selene 47 Pilothouse

1999–Current

Stretched version of Selene 43/45 with enlarged salon, expanded aft deck, offers a compelling mix of cruising comfort, offshore security. Spacious teak interior includes two large staterooms, two full heads, well-appointed salon with galley forward, washer/dryer, raised pilothouse with settee. Hardtop covers entire flybridge. Note protected side decks, hullside boarding gates, standard bow thruster, huge lazarette storage area. Wraparound Portuguese bridge protects against breaking waves. Cruise efficiently at 8–10 knots with 330hp Cummins diesel.

See Page 542 For Value Estimates

Length Overall	50'1"	Ballast	4,000#
Length WL	46'1"	Fuel	1,000 gals.
Beam	15'8"	Water	210 gals.
Draft	5'1"	Waste	60 gals.
Weight	64,200#	Hull Type	Displacement

Selene 48/49 Pilothouse

2003–Current

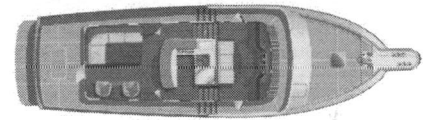

Long-range passagemaker with ballasted, full-displacement hull takes cruising comfort to the next level. Opulent pilothouse interior with traditional teak joinery, spacious salon with galley forward, boasts two large staterooms, each with ensuite head. Cockpit lazarette is huge. Note wraparound Portuguese bridge, fiberglass hardtop, protected side decks, integral swim platform. Reverse pilothouse windshield reduces glare. Marketed as the Selene 49 since 2010. Single Cummins 330hp diesel will cruise at 9–10 knots (about 12 knots top).

See Page 542 For Value Estimates

Length Overall	53'11"	Ballast	4,500#
Length WL	46'10"	Fuel	1,200 gals.
Beam	15'8"	Water	300 gals.
Draft	5'5"	Waste	60 gals.
Weight	68,800#	Hull Type	Displacement

Selene 53/54 Pilothouse

2001–Current

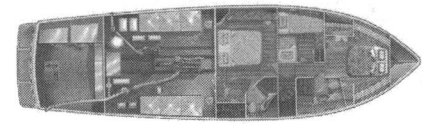

Luxury-class pilothouse yacht—Selene's most popular model—combines liveaboard comfort with solid construction, fuel-efficient operation. Versatile three-stateroom interior includes two en-suite heads, expansive salon with galley forward, walk-in engine room (with standing headroom), large pilothouse with L-shaped settee. Note protected side decks, bow and stern thrusters, copious lazarette storage. Note inside/outside flybridge access. Called the Selene 54 since 2010. Single 430hp Cummins diesel will cruise efficiently at 9–10 knots.

See Page 542 For Value Estimates

Length Overall	59'10"	Ballast	6,000#
Length WL	50'10"	Fuel	1,300 gals.
Beam	16'8"	Water	400 gals.
Draft	5'10"	Waste	120 gals.
Weight	95,000#	Hull Type	Displacement

Trawlers & Motoryachts

Senator (Chien Hwa) 35 Sundeck

1984–87

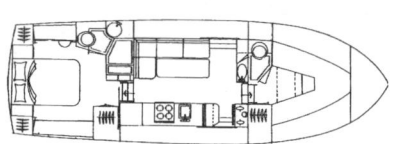

Sturdy double-cabin import built by Chien Hwa in the mid 1980s combines classic trawler profile with traditional teak interior, economical operation. Several floorplans were available, all with full-beam aft cabin, port/starboard salon deck doors, lower helm with deck door. Surprisingly roomy aft deck with hardtop; flybridge seating for four. Bow pulpit, swim platform, radar arch were standard. Long keel protects running gear from grounding. Cruise at 7 knots with single 135hp diesel; 8–10 knots with twin 85hp diesels.

Prices Not Provided for Pre-1995 Models

Length Overall	34'4"	Clearance	NA
Length WL	31'6"	Fuel	300 gals.
Beam	12'0"	Water	200 gals.
Draft	4'2"	Waste	30 gals.
Weight	18,700#	Hull Type	Semi-Disp.

Shannon 36 Voyager

1991–2005

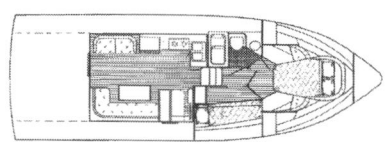

Handsome New England cruiser combines iconic trawler styling with yacht-grade finish, spirited performance. Elegant teak interior with two staterooms, roomy salon is ideal for comfortable cruising. Highlights include lower helm station with sliding deck door, convertible salon dinette, large cabin windows, teak parquet floors. Note opening center windshield section. Large cockpit has transom door for boarding, swimming. Flybridge with wet bar, cocktail table seats six. Among several engine choices, twin 300hp Cat diesels cruise at 16–18 knots (20+ top).

See Page 542 For Value Estimates

Length w/Pulpit	38'3"	Clearance	12'6"
Hull Length	35'7"	Fuel	350 gals.
Beam	13'3"	Water	150 gals.
Draft	3'0"	Hull Type	Modified-V
Weight	17,500#	Deadrise Aft	13°

Silverton 322 Motor Yacht

1989–2001

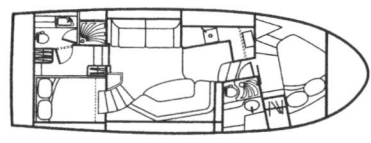

Innovative mini-motoryacht with home-sized interior meets family needs for living, storage space. Top-heavy profile conceals truly impressive interior featuring large salon with convertible dinette, full-service galley, two double staterooms, two full heads. Silverton's signature "SideWalk" deck layout permits cavernous full-beam salon. Note very small aft deck. Curved swim platform staircase makes boarding easy. Definitely not meant for offshore use. MerCruiser 300hp gas engines cruise at 16–17 knots (mid-to-high 20s top).

See Page 542 For Value Estimates

Length Overall	37'0"	Fuel	200 gals.
Beam	12'4"	Water	72 gals.
Draft	2'11"	Waste	49 gals.
Weight	19,716#	Hull Type	Modified-V
Clearance	13'6"	Deadrise Aft	16°

Silverton 34 Motor Yacht

1993–96

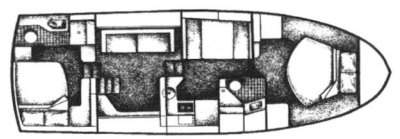

Durable aft-cabin yacht meets cruiser's need for solid construction, roomy accommodations, enduring styling. Well-appointed interior with open front windshield, light oak trim interior consists of open-plan salon with galley and dinette down, two double staterooms, two full heads. Small aft deck has space for a couple of deck chairs. Compact flybridge has guest seating forward of helm. Hardtop, radar arch, bow pulpit, swim platform were standard. Crusader 320hp gas engines cruise at 17–18 knots (about 28 knots top).

See Page 543 For Value Estimates

Length w/Pulpit	39'10"	Fuel	260 gals.
Hull Length	34'6"	Water	74 gals.
Beam	12'10"	Waste	45 gals.
Draft	3'0"	Hull Type	Modified-V
Weight	16,368#	Deadrise Aft	17°

Silverton 35 Motor Yacht

2003–Current

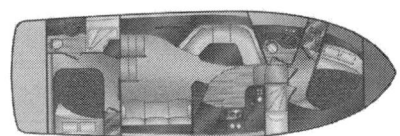

Deluxe mini-motoryacht with edgy Silverton styling delivers vast accommodations at a budget price. Wide-open interior is dominated by lavish, full-beam salon with convertible settee, four-person dinette. Small staterooms have berths positioned athwartships to save space. Note split forward head, hardwood galley sole, raised side decks. Hardtop, bow pulpit, underwater exhausts are standard. Prop pockets reduce hull draft. Not the prettiest boat at the dock. Crusader 385hp gas engines cruise in the low 20s (26–27 knots top).

See Page 543 For Value Estimates

Length Overall	40'2"	Fuel	286 gals.
Beam	13'4"	Water	94 gals.
Draft	2'11"	Waste	55 gals.
Weight	22,618#	Hull Type	Modified-V
Clearance	16'0"	Deadrise Aft	12.5°

Silverton 352 Motor Yacht

1997–2002

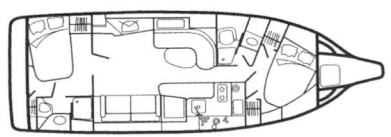

High-sided motoryacht with signature Silverton styling provides the interior space of many 40-footers. Highlights include expansive full-beam salon with dinette forward, full-service galley with upright refrigerator, two double staterooms, two full heads. Compact staterooms have berths positioned athwartships to save space. Curved staircase from swim platform to aft deck makes boarding easy. Standard 385hp gas engines cruise at 16 knots (26–27 knots top); optional 315hp Cummins diesels cruise at 18–19 knots.

See Page 543 For Value Estimates

Length Overall	41'4"	Fuel	286 gals.
Beam	13'0"	Water	100 gals.
Draft	3'3"	Waste	68 gals.
Weight	20,809#	Hull Type	Modified-V
Clearance	16'2"	Deadrise Aft	16°

Trawlers & Motoryachts

Silverton 37 Aft Cabin Motor Yacht

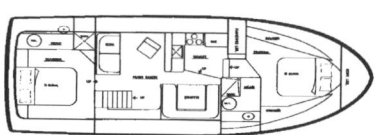

1988–89

Maxi-volume cruising with innovative interior took Silverton concept of 1980s design, value to the next level. Aft-cabin floorplan features surprisingly spacious forward stateroom, U-shaped dinette, large galley. Note light oak interior woodwork, stall showers in both heads. Lack of cockpit or small afterdeck makes docking—especially shorthanded—a tedious process. Additional features include radar arch, swim platform, bow pulpit. Standard 350hp Crusaders cruise at 15 knots (23–24 knots top). Lasted just two years in production.

Prices Not Provided for Pre-1995 Models

Length	37'6"	Fuel	300 gals.
Beam	13'9"	Water	100 gals.
Draft	3'8"	Headroom	6'4"
Weight	22,000#	Hull Type	Modified-V
Clearance	16'0"	Deadrise Aft	NA

Silverton 372/392 Motor Yacht

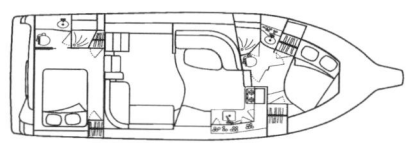

1996–2001

Innovative aft-cabin cruising yacht (called Silverton 372 MY in 1996–98; 392 in 1999–2001) took midsize motoryacht design to the next level. Enormous full-beam salon rivals most 45-footers in size, comfort. Highlights include stall showers in both heads, fully equipped galley with hardwood floor, extended swim platform (optional), foredeck sun pad. Huge bridge can seat a small crowd. Low-deadrise hull isn't too fond of a chop. Gas 320hp inboards cruise at 14 knots (low 20s top). A huge success, over 600 were sold.

See Page 543 For Value Estimates

Length	43'9"	Fuel	286 gals.
Beam	14'1"	Water	100 gals.
Draft	3'3"	Waste	60 gals.
Weight	23,577#	Hull Type	Modified-V
Clearance	16'5"	Deadrise Aft	15°

Silverton 39 Motor Yacht

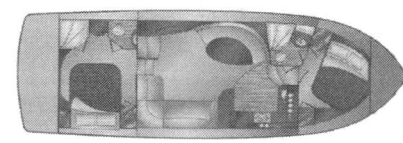

2002–Current

Maxi-volume motoryacht with portly profile favors interior volume, comfort over styling elegance. Raised walkways from bow to bridge permit expansive, full-beam deckhouse with truly expansive dimensions, generous headroom. Both staterooms are fitted with queen beds; both heads have separate stall showers. Highlights include cherry interior woodwork, extended swim platform, aft-deck hardtop, bridge seating for eight. Cruise at a modest 15–16 knots with standard 385hp gas engines (low 20s top); 20 knots with 355hp diesels.

See Page 543 For Value Estimates

Length w/Pulpit	43'7"	Fuel	334 gals.
Hull Length	41'5"	Water	100 gals.
Beam	14'0"	Waste	60 gals.
Draft	3'11"	Hull Type	Modified-V
Weight	24,900#	Deadrise Aft	17°

Silverton 40 Aft Cabin

1982–90

Practical double-cabin motoryacht from the 1980s meets boater's need for space, comfort, versatility. Standard two-stateroom interior with convertible salon settee, convertible dinette can sleep up to eight. Note separate stall showers in both heads, generous galley storage. Light oak interior trim replaced original teak cabinets in 1985. Well-proportioned flybridge and aft deck can seat several guests. Awkward two-piece entryway door from aft deck into cabin is a tight fit. Cruise at 16–17 knots with 350hp gas inboards (mid 20s top).

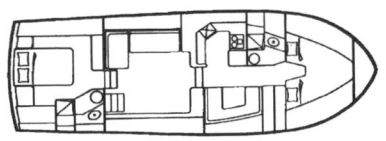

Prices Not Provided for Pre-1995 Models

Length	40'0"	Fuel	300 gals.
Beam	14'0"	Water	100 gals.
Draft	3'0"	Headroom	6'4"
Weight	24,000#	Hull Type	Modified-V
Clearance	13'6"	Deadrise Aft	14°

Silverton 402/422 Motor Yacht

1996–2000

Contemporary aft-cabin yacht (called 402 Motor Yacht in 1996–98; 422 MY in 1999–2000) is roomy, versatile, built to last. Two-stateroom floorplan with full dinette, big U-shaped galley (with lots of counter space), roomy salon is a model of space efficiency. Master stateroom was rearranged in 1999 with unusual aft-facing bed. Note roomy flybridge, wide side decks, aft-deck wet bar. Extended swim platform was a popular option. Engine room is a tight fit. Standard 320hp gas engines cruise at 14 knots (low 20s top).

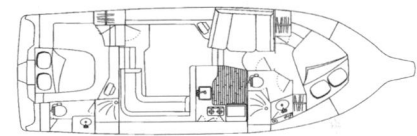

402 Floorplan, 1996–98

422 Floorplan, 1999–2001

See Page 543 For Value Estimates

Length Overall	45'11	Fuel	375 gals.
Beam	14'2"	Water	132 gals.
Draft	3'6"	Waste	58 gals.
Weight	23,826#	Hull Type	Modified-V
Clearance	17'11"	Deadrise Aft	12°

Silverton 41 Motor Yacht

1991–95

Traditional double-cabin motoryacht from early 1990s made good on Silverton promise of space, comfort at a competitive price. Well-appointed interior with roomy salon, booth-style dinette, two large staterooms sleeps six. Both heads have separate stall showers; full-service galley has plenty of storage. Roomy aft deck with hardtop, wet bar can accommodate several guests. Note side-dumping exhausts, wide side decks, integral bow pulpit. Cruise at 15 knots with big-block gas engines; 20 knots with optional 375hp Cat diesels.

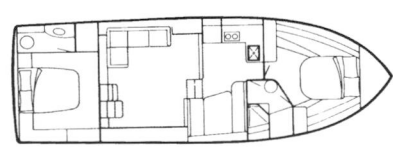

See Page 543 For Value Estimates

Length w/Pulpit	46'3"	Fuel	408 gals.
Hull Length	41'3"	Water	200 gals.
Beam	14'10"	Waste	68 gals.
Draft	3'7"	Hull Type	Modified-V
Weight	28,000#	Deadrise Aft	17°

Silverton 410 Sport Bridge

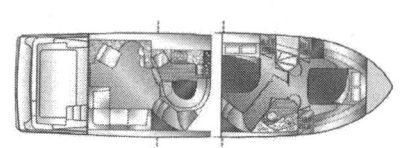

2001–04

Condo-style accommodations made this roomy sportcruiser popular with buyers willing to overlook her portly profile. Distinctive "SideWalk" deck configuration with elevated side decks results in cavernous—and innovative—full-beam salon with raised galley/dinette platform forward, two large staterooms, split head compartment. Huge bridge can entertain a small crowd. Note foredeck sun pad, extended swim platform. Cruise at 15 knots with standard gas engines; 20 knots with optional 420hp Cat diesels.

See Page 543 For Value Estimates

Length Overall	46'3"	Fuel	450 gals.
Beam	14'3"	Water	200 gals.
Draft	3'10"	Waste	40 gals.
Weight	28,495#	Hull Type	Modified-V
Clearance	15'4"	Deadrise Aft	16°

Silverton 43 Motor Yacht

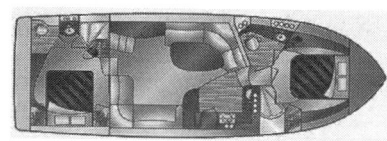

2001–07

Feature-rich motoryacht with huge interior suits livaboards and cruisers alike. Raised walkways from bow to bridge permit cavernous, full-beam salon the equal of much larger boats. Interior highlights include appealing cherry cabinetry, home-size galley, posh Ultraleather salon seating. Note divided head compartments fore and aft. Master stateroom is on the small side for a 41-footer. Curved staircase from swim platform to aft deck makes boarding easy. Volvo 480hp (or Cummins 430hp) diesels cruise at 18–19 knots (low 20s top).

See Page 543 For Value Estimates

Length w/Pulpit	47'7"	Fuel	386 gals.
Beam	14'11"	Water	150 gals.
Draft	3'8"	Waste	80 gals.
Weight	29,000#	Hull Type	Modified-V
Clearance, Arch	17'0"	Deadrise Aft	17°

Silverton 43 Sport Bridge

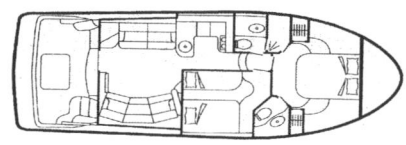

2006–Current

Popular sportcruiser combines leading-edge styling with vast accommodations, competitive price. Raised side decks maximize interior space, permit easy bow access from bridge. Full-beam main cabin offers comfortable seating for several guests. Interior highlights include Ultraleather upholstery, cherry cabinetry, retractable salon TV. Note split head with shower to starboard. Frameless windows eliminate leaks. Standard 425hp gas engines cruise at 16–18 knots; Volvo 370hp diesels with IPS drives cruise at 20–22 knots (about 28 top).

See Page 544 For Value Estimates

Length	43'5"	Fuel	430 gals.
Beam	14'4"	Water	118 gals.
Draft	3'10"	Waste	40 gals.
Weight	28,000#	Hull Type	Modified-V
Clearance	14'5"	Deadrise Aft	12°

Silverton 442 Cockpit MY

1996–2001

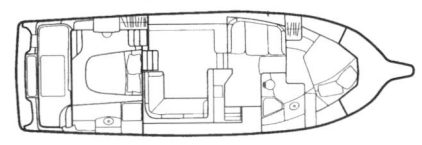

Thoughtfully conceived cockpit yacht met the demands of boaters looking for motoryacht comfort at an affordable price. Expansive two-stateroom interior includes home-size galley, full dinette, stall showers in both heads. Sliding glass door provides cockpit access from master stateroom. Weatherboards, molded seating, wet bar were standard on aft deck; storage locker is built into swim platform. Note secure side decks, centerline flybridge helm. Standard gas engines cruise at 14–15 knots (low 20s top); Cummins 355hp diesels cruise at close to 20 knots.

See Page 544 For Value Estimates

Length	45'11"	Fuel	375 gals.
Beam	14'3"	Water	132 gals.
Draft	3'6"	Waste	58 gals.
Weight	23,826#	Hull Type	Modified-V
Clearance	18'3"	Deadrise Aft	15°

Silverton 453 Motor Yacht

1999–2003

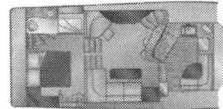 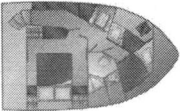

Motoryacht Floorplan

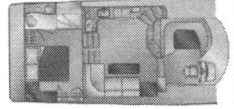 

Pilothouse Floorplan

See Page 544 For Value Estimates

Tall-freeboard cruiser with Silverton's trademark "SideWalk" deck design raised the bar for space, comfort in a mid 40' motoryacht. Cavernous interior boasts vast full-beam salon with entertainment center, fully equipped galley with Corian counters, three double staterooms. Note cherry cabin woodwork, twin recliners built into salon sofa. Tall cabin headroom is a plus. Topside features include molded boarding steps, foredeck sun pad, pilothouse deck door. Cummins 450hp diesels cruise at 18 knots (low 20s top). Definitely not the prettiest boat on the water.

Length	47'8"	Fuel	500 gals.
Beam	15'4"	Water	190 gals.
Draft	4'0"	Waste	66 gals.
Weight	35,530#	Hull Type	Modified-V
Clearance	19'5"	Deadrise Aft	16°

Silverton 46 Aft Cabin

1990–97

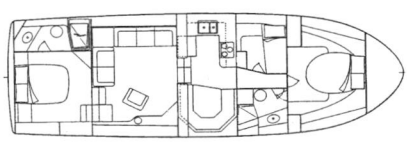

Durable 1990s motoryacht balanced spacious accommodations with rugged construction, affordable price. Space-efficient interior with three private staterooms boasts large galley with full-size refrigerator, big U-shaped dinette, two full heads. Second guest cabin has foldaway berth that converts to lounge. Note trash compactor in galley, standard washer/dryer. Aft deck came with hardtop, wet bar. Large flybridge is arranged with bench seating aft of the helm. GM 485hp diesels cruise at 22 knots (mid 20s top).

See Page 544 For Value Estimates

Length w/Pulpit	51'6"	Fuel	580 gals.
Hull Length	46'8"	Water	200 gals.
Beam	16'2"	Waste	56 gals.
Draft	3'9"	Hull Type	Modified-V
Weight	33,874#	Deadrise Aft	17°

Trawlers & Motoryachts

Silverton 52 Ovation

2008–Current

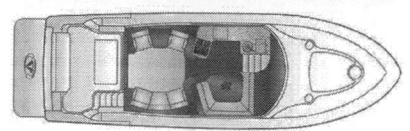
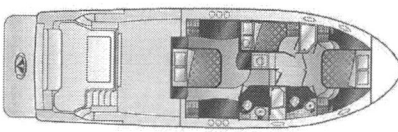

Eurostyle flybridge cruiser designed for triple IPS power is spacious, comfortable, beautifully styled. Expansive layout features raised galley and dinette forward, lavish master stateroom with flanking night stands, queen beds in both guest cabins. (Note that VIP stateroom has split head.) Well-equipped galley has plenty of storage. Cockpit can be ordered with optional hydraulic davit or hydraulic swim platform. Large engine room, wide side decks are a plus. Triple 435hp Volvo IPS diesels cruise at 24–25 knots (about 28 top).

Insufficient Resale Data to Assign Values

Length	52'0"	Fuel	610 gals.
Beam	16'4"	Water	200 gals.
Draft	4'0"	Waste	80 gals.
Weight	52,000#	Hull Type	Modified-V
Clearance	17'9"	Deadrise Aft	13°

Sundowner 30 Pilothouse Tug

1982–89

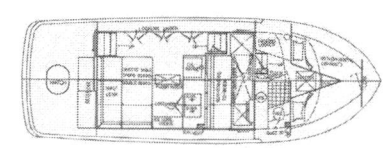

Salty pocket trawler designed for coastal cruising is affordable, stable, economical to operate. Space-efficient layout offers combined salon/galley with dining nook aft, roomy pilothouse, head-plus-V-berths forward. Excellent storage for a boat this size. Large windows, good cabin ventilation are a plus. No cockpit transom door. Lots of teak trim inside and out. Original 30-foot model ran from 1982–87; enlarged Sundowner 32 was built in 1988–89. Runs efficiently at 6–7 knots with single 85hp Perkins diesel.

Prices Not Provided for Pre-1995 Models

Length	29'6"	Headroom	6'4"
Beam	11'4"	Fuel	100 gals.
Draft	2'10"	Water	50 gals.
Weight	9,600#	Waste	20 gals.
Clearance	NA	Hull Type	Semi-Disp.

Sunseeker 46/48 Manhattan

1995–99

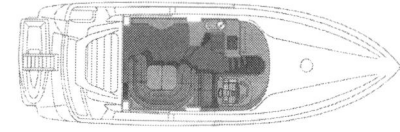
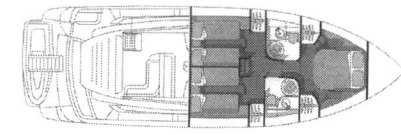

Graceful 1990s flybridge yacht (called 46 Manhattan in 1995) delivered sleek styling with top-notch construction, spirited performance. Lavish three-stateroom interior features two full heads, roomy galley, elevated lower helm, exquisite high-gloss cabinetry. Note premium galley hardware, top-shelf furnishings. Flybridge has seating for six plus sunbathing area aft. Deep swim platform can accommodate PWC, optional hydraulic davit. Typical European engine room is a tight fit. Cat 430hp V-drive diesels cruise at 22 knots (25–26 knots top).

See Page 545 For Value Estimates

Length	48'0"	Fuel	378 gals.
Beam	14'5"	Water	115 gals.
Draft	2'11"	Headroom	6'6"
Weight	41,000#	Hull Type	Deep-V
Clearance	15'5"	Deadrise Aft	20°

Sunseeker 50 Manhattan

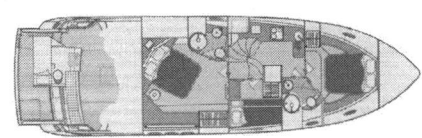

2006–08

World-class Euroyacht with extravagant three-stateroom interior raised the bar for motoryacht style, luxury, comfort. Ultra-posh interior is arranged in typical European fashion with sunken galley forward, state-of-the-art lower helm, open salon with facing settees. Huge salon windows offer panoramic outside views; full-beam owner's cabin with vertical hull ports exceeds all expectations. Note generous galley storage, surprisingly spacious engine room. MAN 800hp diesels cruise at 26 knots (30+ knots top).

Insufficient Resale Data to Assign Values

Length Overall	52'6"	Fuel	660 gals.
Beam	15'1"	Water	132 gals.
Draft	4'0"	Waste	50 gals.
Weight	50,600#	Hull Type	Deep-V
Clearance	16'2"	Deadrise Aft	19°

Sunseeker 56 Manhattan

2001–04

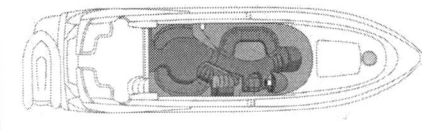

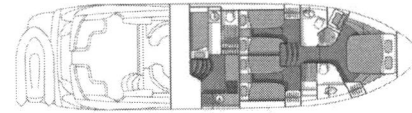

Sleek Mediterranean flybridge yacht raised the bar for motoryacht luxury, quality when she was introduced in 2001. Stunning three-stateroom, two-head interior features beautifully appointed split-level salon with leather seating, wraparound dinette, sunken galley. Inside bridge access is a plus; each cabin has flat-screen TV. Topside highlights include teak decks, bow thruster, hydraulic swim platform, extended bridge with seating for ten. Note crew quarters off galley. Cat 800hp diesels cruise in the mid 20s with a top speed of just over 30 knots.

See Page 545 For Value Estimates

Length	61'2"	Fuel	661 gals.
Beam	15'1"	Water	198 gals.
Draft	4'3"	Headroom	6'6"
Weight	58,200#	Hull Type	Deep-V
Clearance	16'11"	Deadrise Aft	19°

Sunseeker 62 Manhattan

1997–2000

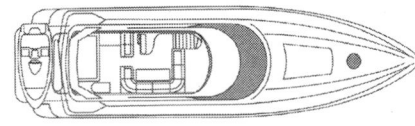

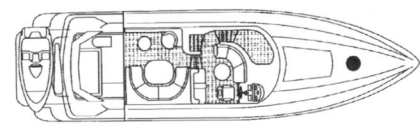

Retooled version of earlier Sunseeker 58 Manhattan (1994–96) with lavish multi-level interior, extended swim platform made an elegant yacht even better. Sleeping arrangements for six include dramatic master suite, side-by-side guest cabins. From spacious salon, sliding glass doors open to expansive aft deck. Note lower helm deck door, aft crew quarters, exquisite cherry joinery. Flybridge has seating for six with sunbathing space aft. Large engine room is plus. MTU 800hp V-drive engines cruise at 25 knots (28–29 knots top). Very popular model.

Insufficient Resale Data to Assign Values

Length	62'0"	Headroom	6'6"
Beam	15'6"	Fuel	909 gals.
Draft	4'1"	Water	172 gals.
Weight	50,600#	Hull Type	Deep-V
Clearance	14'6"	Deadrise Aft	20°

Trawlers & Motoryachts

Sunseeker 64 Manhattan

2001–05

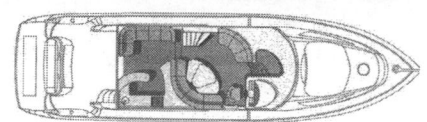

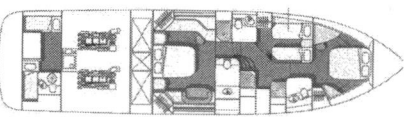

Imposing Mediterranean motoryacht combined dramatic styling (note tiered salon windows) with lavish accommodations, world-class performance. Beautifully appointed interior with split-level salon has galley aft, dining/conversation area forward—a reversal of most salon layouts. Crew quarters are aft, accessed from cockpit. Huge flybridge features wet bar, dinette, sun lounge. Note full-beam master suite, lower-helm deck door, hydraulic passerelle. MAN 800hp engines cruise at 25 knots (30 knots top).

Insufficient Resale Data to Assign Values

Length Overall	71'6"	Headroom	6'5"
Beam	17'1"	Fuel	878 gals.
Draft	4'9"	Water	259 gals.
Weight	65,920#	Hull Type	Deep-V
Clearance	18'1"	Deadrise Aft	19°

Sunseeker 66 Manhattan

2005–08

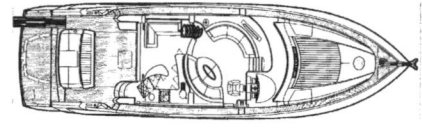

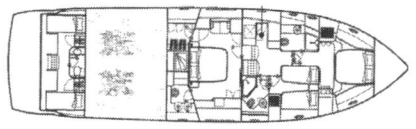

Striking U.K. motoryacht with state-of-the-art styling redefined motoryacht luxury, performance when she came out in 2005. Opulent cherry interior boasts huge master suite with walk-in closet, lavish split-level salon, top-shelf furnishings. Hydraulic-lift swim platform makes it easy to launch/retrieve tender. Additional features include lower helm deck door, inside flybridge access, aft crew quarters, teak cockpit sole. Big engine room is a plus. Exemplary finish is second to none. MAN 1,100hp diesels cruise at 25–26 knots (about 30 knots top).

Insufficient Resale Data to Assign Values

Length Overall	72'6"	Headroom	6'5"
Beam	17'1"	Fuel	898 gals.
Draft	5'0"	Water	251 gals.
Weight	77,000#	Hull Type	Deep-V
Clearance	18'8"	Deadrise Aft	19°

Sunseeker 74 Manhattan

1999–2005

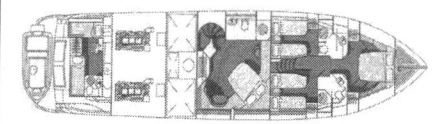

Stunning U.K.-built flybridge yacht introduced in 1999 offered standards of comfort, performance seldom encountered in large production yachts. Highlights include extravagant four-stateroom interior with full-beam salon, hydraulic swim/tender platform, huge flybridge with food-prep center. Crew quarters for two—with cockpit access—are aft of engine room. Lower-helm deck door is a plus. Note teak-laid cockpit, roomy engine compartment. Deep-V hull delivers terrific big-water ride. MAN 1,300hp engines cruise at 26 knots (30+ knots top).

Insufficient Resale Data to Assign Values

Length Overall	74'2"	Fuel	1,321 gals.
Beam	17'10"	Water	243 gals.
Draft	4'11"	Waste	75 gals.
Weight	81,600#	Hull Type	Deep-V
Clearance	15'7"	Deadrise Aft	20°

Symbol 44 MK II Sundeck

1984–89

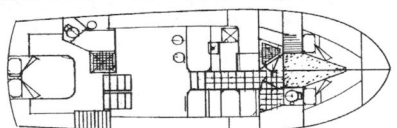

Standard Interior

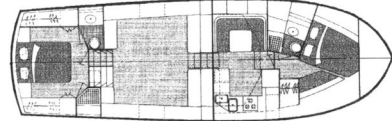

Alternate Interior

Affordable 1980s sundeck yacht with roomy aft deck, full teak interior delivered good value for the money. Standard galley-down floorplan features two large staterooms, roomy salon with breakfast bar, lower helm station with sliding deck door. Note split forward head, classy teak-and-holly cabin sole. Dinette steps lift for engine room access. Aft-deck wet bar, radar arch, hardtop, swim platform were standard. Decent finish for an inexpensive boat. Cat 375hp diesels cruise at 16 knots and reach a top speed of about 20 knots.

Prices Not Provided for Pre-1995 Models

Length	44'2"	Headroom	6'5"
Beam	14'9"	Fuel	530 gals.
Draft	3'10"	Water	250 gals.
Weight	31,000#	Hull Type	Modified-V
Clearance, Windshield	13'6"	Deadrise Aft	NA

Symbol 50 Pilothouse

1997–2002

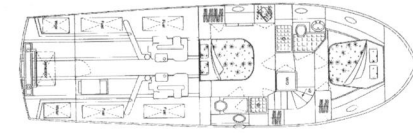

Two Staterooms

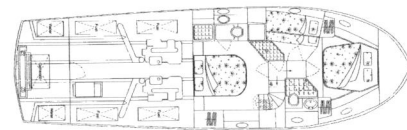

Three Staterooms

Well-styled pilothouse yacht introduced in 1997 offered an affordable alternative to higher-priced European imports. Two- or three-stateroom layouts were available, both with full-beam master, spacious salon with U-shaped galley forward. Raised pilothouse includes dinette in addition to deck access door, inside flybridge access. Hardwood interior joinery shows superior craftsmanship throughout. Cockpit engine room access is a plus, but cockpit dimensions are modest. Twin 450hp Cat (or Cummins) diesels cruise at 16 knots (18–20 top).

Insufficient Resale Data to Assign Values

Length	51'2"	Fuel	600 gals.
Beam	15'7"	Water	230 gals.
Draft	4'2"	Waste	70 gals.
Weight	38,000#	Hull Type	Modified-V
Clearance	NA	Deadrise Aft	10°

Symbol 51 Yachtfisher

1985–88

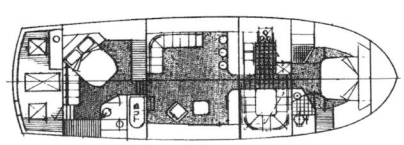

Popular 1980s import impressed owners with modest price, rakish styling, spacious accommodations. Standard two-stateroom interior with acres of teak cabinetry and paneling features roomy salon with lower helm, large galley, built-in dinette, generous storage. Note tub/shower in aft head, sliding deck door next to lower helm. Exterior highlights include radar arch, aft-deck hardtop, bow pulpit, cockpit transom door. Twin 375hp Cat diesels cruise at 17–18 knots and reach a top speed of about 20 knots.

Prices Not Provided for Pre-1995 Models

Length	50'4"	Fuel	600 gals.
Beam	15'0"	Water	250 gals.
Draft	4'0"	Headroom	6'4"
Weight	45,000#	Hull Type	Modified-V
Clearance	13'8"	Deadrise Aft	NA

Symbol 54/58 Pilothouse

2002–05

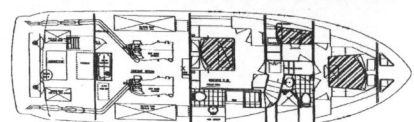

Lower Level, 54

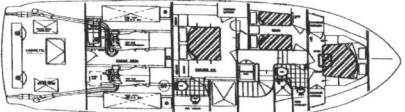

Lower Level, 58

Insufficient Resale Data to Assign Values

Deluxe pilothouse yacht (available in lengths of 54 or 58 feet) couples leading-edge styling with luxury-class accommodations. Wide 17'6" beam allows for spacious interior with three large staterooms, expansive pilothouse with gourmet galley and L-shaped dinette. Second guest cabin could be converted to office. Choice of teak or cherry interior joinery. Note large engine room, spacious flybridge, deep side decks. Hardtop was a popular option. Prop pockets reduce draft. Cat 700hp diesels cruise at 17–18 knots (20+ knots top).

Length	56'6"/59'6"	Fuel, 54	750 gals.
Beam	17'6"	Fuel, 58	850 gals.
Draft	4'6"	Water	250 gals.
Weight, 54	76,700#	Hull Type	Modified-V
Weight, 58	79,700#	Deadrise Aft	10°

Symbol 55 Pilothouse

1994–2003

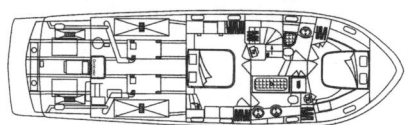

Two Staterooms

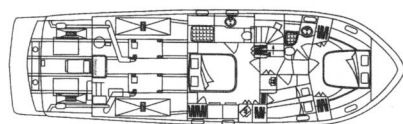

Three Staterooms

Insufficient Resale Data to Assign Values

Well-received pilothouse yacht designed by Jack Sarin combined classic lines with upscale accommodations, versatile layout. Offered with two- or three-stateroom floorplans, both with spacious salon, pilothouse-level galley and dinette, full-beam master. Large windows provide panoramic outside views. Walk-in engineroom with workbench is accessed via cockpit hatch. Note spacious lazarette, inside bridge access. Cat 435hp diesels cruise at 16–17 knots (about 20 knots top). Later models with 660hp Cats cruise at 19–20 (20+ top).

Length	57'3"	Fuel	850 gals.
Beam	16'9"	Water	230 gals.
Draft	4'3"	Waste	70 gals.
Weight	57,000#	Hull Type	Modified-V
Clearance	NA	Deadrise Aft	11°

Symbol 62 Pilothouse

2001–04

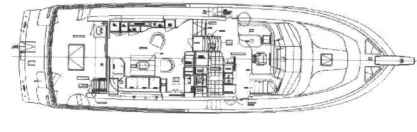

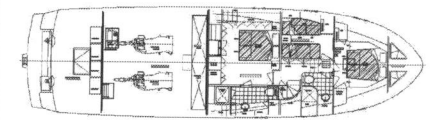

Insufficient Resale Data to Assign Values

Appealing cruising yacht with sleek lines delivers on Symbol promise of deluxe accommodations, sophisticated construction. Wide 18'6" beam results in spacious interior with opulent owner's suite, huge salon with full entertainment center, expansive pilothouse with home-sized galley, full dinette. Huge flybridge with dinghy platform can entertain a small crowd. Additional features include wide side decks, cherry interior joinery, engineroom work center, hull prop pockets. Cat 800hp diesels cruise at 18 knots (20+ knots top).

Length Overall	62'3"	Headroom	6'6"
Beam	18'6"	Fuel	1,000 gals.
Draft	4'8"	Water	350 gals.
Weight	85,000#	Waste	100 gals.
Clearance, Arch	17'4"	Hull Type	Modified-V

Trawlers & Motoryachts

Tollycraft 34 Sundeck

1986–88

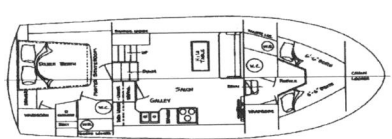

Sturdy aft-cabin motoryacht combined roomy accommodations with top-shelf construction, leading-edge amenities. Interior highlights include well-appointed salon, expansive galley, standard lower helm. Both staterooms have private head access. Large cabin windows, generous cabin storage are a plus. Topside features include full-width aft deck, radar arch, bow pulpit, roomy bridge with seating for six. Note fuel increase to 296 gallons in 1988. Twin 350hp gas engines cruise at 18 knots (high 20s top).

Prices Not Provided for Pre-1995 Models

Length	34'0"	Fuel	200/296 gals.
Beam	12'6"	Water	77 gals.
Draft	2'10"	Waste	35 gals.
Weight	17,000#	Hull Type	Modified-V
Clearance	12'0"	Deadrise Aft	13°

Tollycraft 40 Sundeck

1985–94

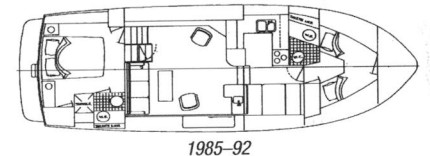

1985–92

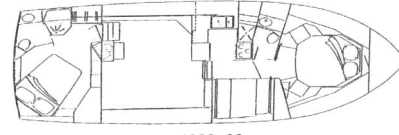

1992–93

Handsome sundeck motoryacht introduced in 1985 combined modern styling with spacious interior, quality amenities. Deluxe two-stateroom interior with booth dinette, home-size galley was offered with or without a lower helm. Large salon windows combine with teak woodwork to create a very comfortable decor. Aft cabin features walkaround queen berth. Wide side decks make getting around easy. Note fuel increase in 1991. Twin 350hp gas engines cruise at 17–18 knots (mid 20s top); 375hp Cat diesels cruise in the low 20s (25–26 knots top).

Prices Not Provided for Pre-1995 Models

Length	40'2"	Fuel	300/398 gals.
Beam	14'8"	Water	140 gals.
Draft	3'0"	Waste	40 gals.
Weight	26,000#	Hull Type	Modified-V
Clearance	12'0"	Deadrise Aft	10°

Tollycraft 43 Motor Yacht

1980–85

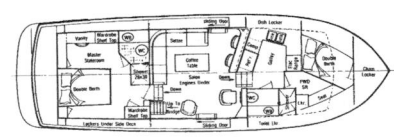

Highly regarded Northwest cruiser appeals to experienced boaters who value substance over style. Accommodations are well organized with double berths in each stateroom, and a serving bar separating the salon from the lower-level galley. Inside helm and deck access door were standard. Small cockpit with transom door makes boarding easy. Semi-displacement hull with long keel delivers superior heavy-weather performance. This boat is always—repeat, always—in demand. Cat 210hp diesels cruise efficiently at 15 knots (about 18 knots top).

Prices Not Provided for Pre-1995 Models

Length Overall	43'4"	Clearance	13'9"
Length WL	39'5"	Fuel	400 gals.
Beam	14'2"	Water	140 gals.
Draft	3'5"	Headroom	6'4"
Weight	30,000#	Hull Type	Semi-Disp.

Trawlers & Motoryachts

Tollycraft 44/45 Cockpit MY

1986–96

44 Interior

45 Interior

See Page 546 For Value Estimates

Cockpit version of popular Tollycraft 40 Sundeck combines versatile layout with classic Tollycraft lines, deluxe accommodations. Twin-stateroom floorplan was updated in mid-1992 when forward stateroom, salon were enlarged at expense of smaller aft cabin. Interior highlights include solid teak joinery, sliding salon deck door, entertainment center. Note fuel increase in 1991. Twin 350hp gas engines cruise at 17–18 knots (about 25 top); optional 375hp Cat diesels cruise in the low 20s (mid 20s top). Called the 45 Cockpit MY in 1994–96.

Length, 44 CMY	44'2"	Clearance	14'9"
Length, 45 CMY	45'3"	Fuel	300/398 gals.
Beam	14'8"	Water	140 gals.
Draft	3'0"	Hull Type	Modified-V
Weight	28,000#	Deadrise Aft	10°

Tollycraft 48 Motor Yacht

1976–98

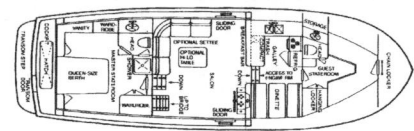

1976–94

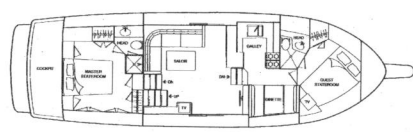

1995–98

See Page 546 For Value Estimates

Iconic Tollycraft cruiser enjoyed one of longest production runs of any modern motoryacht. Traditional galley-down interior—slightly updated in 1995—offers unsurpassed comfort, livability. Highlights include standard lower helm, huge aft stateroom (with space for washer/dryer), full walkaround decks, transom door. Early models with 320hp Cats cruise at 15 knots; later models with 400hp GMs cruise at 17–18 knots. Out of production in 1986, reintroduced in 1991. Total of 125 were built. Used models are always in demand.

Length w/Pulpit	52'10"	Clearance, Mast	17'0"
Hull Length	48'2"	Fuel	600 gals.
Beam	15'2"	Water	188 gals.
Draft	3'8"	Waste	98 gals.
Weight	42,000#	Hull Type	Semi-Disp.

Tollycraft 53 Motor Yacht

1988–94

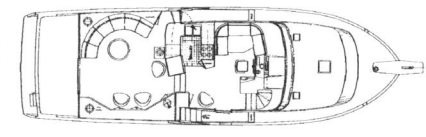

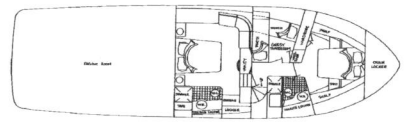

Prices Not Provided for Pre-1995 Models

Sought-after pilothouse yacht with wide 16'11" beam combines striking lines with serious cruising comfort. Spacious interior with full-beam salon rivals many larger boats in size, amenities. Highlights include salon entertainment center, home-size galley with dishwasher, opulent master suite. Note portside wing door in salon, washer/dryer in second guest stateroom. Flybridge is huge but cockpit is on the small side. Early models with 550hp GM diesels cruise at 16–17 knots. Later models with twin 735hp GMs cruise at 22–23 knots.

Length w/Pulpit	59'6"	Fuel	800 gals.
Hull Length	52'11"	Water	280 gals.
Beam	16'11"	Waste	80 gals.
Draft	3'6"	Hull Type	Modified-V
Weight	52,000#	Deadrise Aft	11°

Tollycraft 57 Cockpit Motor Yacht

1989–96

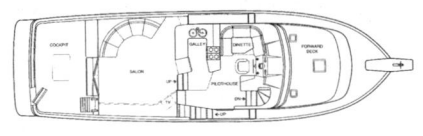

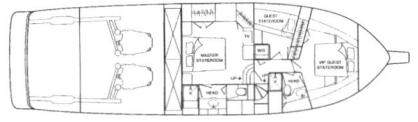

Stretched version of popular Tollycraft 53 MY (1988–94) boasts enlarged cockpit, increased fuel, maximum comfort. Spacious interior has dinette, galley on pilothouse level; full-width salon has portside wing door for easy deck access. Note huge full-beam master suite, washer/dryer in second guest stateroom. Cockpit engine room access is a plus. Walkaround model with full side decks introduced in 1996. GM 735hp, Cat 800hp, or MAN 820hp engines cruise at 20 knots (22–24 knots top). Over 30 of these quality yachts were built.

See Page 546 For Value Estimates

Length w/Pulpit...............63'7"	Fuel.......................1,200 gals.
Hull Length ....57'0"	Water.......................280 gals.
Beam...............................17'3"	Waste ....120 gals.
Draft.................................3'6"	Hull Type.................Modified-V
Weight ....58,000#	Deadrise Aft ....11°

Tollycraft 61 Pilothouse

1983–93

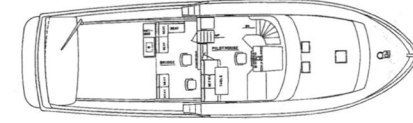

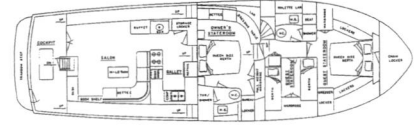

Acclaimed pilothouse yacht delivers unsurpassed blend of classic styling, luxury-class accommodations. Well-appointed interior features wide-open salon with U-shaped galley, roomy pilothouse with bridge access, full-beam master suite. Additional highlights include huge flybridge, sheltered side decks, well-organized engine room with cockpit access, deep prop-protecting keel. Early models with GM 485hp diesels cruise at 15–16 knots. Later models with GM 735hp GM engines cruise at 20–22 knots. Total of 39 were built.

Insufficient Resale Data to Assign Values

Length w/Pulpit...............67'8"	Fuel.......................1,160 gals.
Hull Length ....61'2"	Water.......................400 gals.
Beam...............................17'8"	Waste ....50 gals.
Draft.................................4'0"	Hull Type.................Modified-V
Weight ....65,000#	Deadrise Aft ....10°

Tollycraft 65 Pilothouse Cockpit MY

1993–98

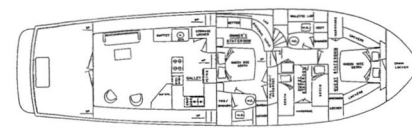

1993–94

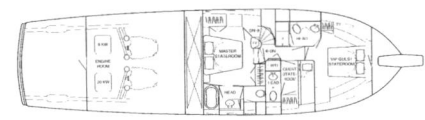

1995–98

See Page 546 For Value Estimates

Enlarged version of venerable Tollycraft 61 (1983–92) offers restyled interior, upgraded amenities, enlarged cockpit. Original three-stateroom, three-head interior was redesigned in 1995 to provide larger guest cabins, one less head. Highlights include opulent full-beam master suite, expansive salon with home-size galley, roomy pilothouse with superb visibility. Note covered side decks, massive bridge, cockpit engine room access. Twin 820hp MANs—or 800hp Cats—cruise at 22 knots (23–24 knots top). Total of 13 were built.

Length w/Pulpit...............67'10"	Fuel.......................1,160 gals.
Hull Length ....65'2"	Water.......................400 gals.
Beam...............................17'11"	Waste ....120 gals.
Draft.................................4'9"	Hull Type.................Modified-V
Weight ....68,000#	Deadrise Aft ....10°

Trawlers & Motoryachts

Tradewinds 43 Motor Yacht

1987–91

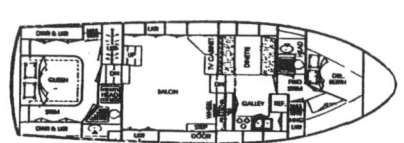

Good-selling Taiwan motoryacht delivered a compelling mix of practical deck layout, spacious accommodations, durable construction. Full teak interior features large U-shaped galley, convertible dinette, standard lower helm, two comfortable staterooms. Wraparound windows provide good natural salon lighting. Wet bar, wing doors complement full-beam aft deck. Hardtop, radar arch, swim platform, bow pulpit were standard. Note wide side decks. Cummins 210hp diesels cruise at 14 knots; 275hp Lehmans cruise at 16–17 knots.

Prices Not Provided for Pre-1995 Models

Length	42'6"	Fuel	500 gals.
Beam	14'11"	Water	320 gals.
Draft	3'10"	Headroom	6'4"
Weight	27,500#	Hull Type	Modified-V
Clearance	NA	Deadrise Aft	NA

Tradewinds 47 Motor Yacht

1986–88

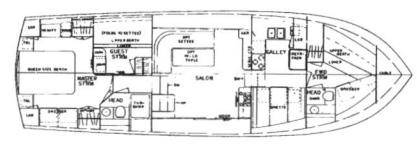

Generic sundeck yacht introduced in 1986 hit the sweet spot with boaters seeking big-boat space, amenities at a competitive price. Spacious three-stateroom interior features second guest cabin aft, which can be configured as office/den. Double-entry aft head means no private head for master stateroom. Aft deck is probably the largest to be found on a boat this size. Semi-displacement hull with relatively wide beam has shallow keel for enhanced directional stability. Volvo 200hp diesels cruise at 12 knots and reach a top speed of about 15 knots.

Prices Not Provided for Pre-1995 Models

Length	46'6"	Fuel	600 gals.
Beam	14'6"	Water	200 gals.
Draft	3'10"	Waste	60 gals.
Weight	30,000#	Hull Type	Semi-Disp
Clearance	NA	Deadrise Aft	10°

Tradewinds 47 Motor Yacht

1989–95

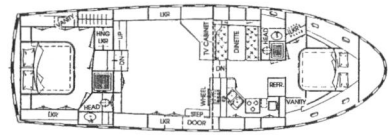

Two-Stateroom Interior

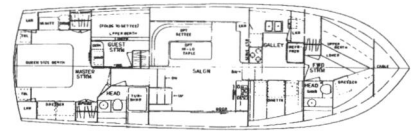

Three-Stateroom Interior

See Page 546 For Value Estimates

Durable aft-cabin motoryacht imported by Marine Trader made good on promise of maximum accommodations, solid construction, low price. Highlights include hand-crafted teak interior, large salon with sliding deck access door, protected aft deck with wing doors, spacious flybridge with U-lounge seating. Available with two or three staterooms. Lower helm was standard. Radar arch, hardtop, swim platform were standard. Twin 275hp Lehman diesels cruise at 12 knots; Volvo 305hp diesels cruise at 14–15 knots (about 18 knots top).

Length	46'6"	Fuel	500 gals.
Beam	14'11"	Water	320 gals.
Draft	3'6"	Waste	60 gals.
Weight	30,500#	Hull Type	Modified-V
Clearance	NA	Deadrise Aft	15°

Trojan 36 Tri-Cabin

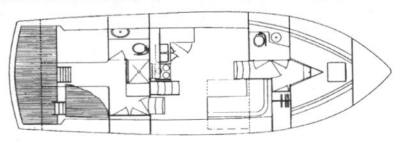

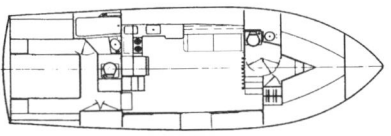

1970–87

Venerable aft-cabin cruiser from 1970s, 1980s set class standards in her day for interior comfort, user versatility. Offered with several layouts over the years, most with double bed in aft stateroom and galley aft in the salon. Design highlights include walkaround decks, combined helm/aft-deck area, molded bow seating, bow pulpit. Early models (called the 36 Sea Raider) had teak decks and cockpit. Note tall bridge windshield, good helm visibility. Many gas or diesel engine options were offered over the years.

Prices Not Provided for Pre-1995 Models

Length	36'0"	Fuel	150/220/300 gals.
Beam	13'0"	Water	65/85 gals.
Draft	2'11"	Waste	40 gals.
Weight	17,500#	Hull Type	Modified-V
Clearance	12'3"	Deadrise Aft	9°

Trojan 12 Meter Motor Yacht

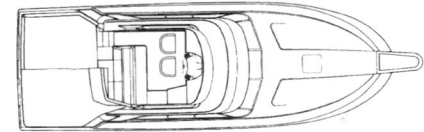

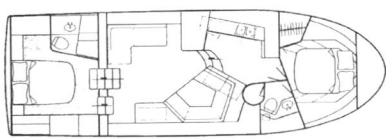

1987–92

Graceful aft-cabin motoryacht delivered on Trojan promise of comfortable accommodations, luxury-class appointments. Wide-open interior boasts spacious salon with wraparound dinette, home-sized galley with upright refrigerator, two double staterooms. Note washer/dryer space under dinette. Salon cabinet conceals pop-up entertainment center. Aft deck has weatherboards, wing doors. Side decks are none too wide. Cat 375hp diesels cruise at 19–20 knots (20+ knots top); 450hp GM diesels cruise at 22–23 knots (mid-to-high 20s top).

Prices Not Provided for Pre-1995 Models

Length	39'9"	Fuel	400 gals.
Beam	14'3"	Water	150 gals.
Draft	3'8"	Waste	55 gals.
Weight	19,000#	Hull Type	Modified-V
Clearance	NA	Deadrise Aft	12°

Vantare 64 Cockpit Motor Yacht

Amidships Engineroom

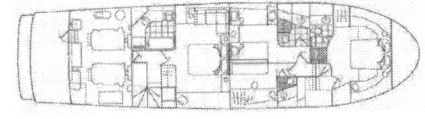

Aft Engineroom

1987–92

Cockpit version of Vantare 58 Pilothouse offered big-boat versatility, comfort at a competitive price. Available in two versions: standard three-stateroom layout with amidships engine room, or alternate aft-engine room (V-drive) model with enlarged master suite. "Cab-forward" design, wide-body salon/pilothouse results in truly spacious interior. Semi-enclosed aft deck with flybridge staircase seats eight. Note amidships crew quarters cabin with desk. Built by CHB in Taiwan. Detroit 735hp diesels cruise at 16–18 knots (about 20 knots top).

Prices Not Provided for Pre-1995 Models

Length	64'0"	Headroom	6'6"
Beam	17'6"	Fuel	1,000 gals.
Draft	4'2"	Water	390 gals.
Weight	60,000#	Waste	150 gals.
Clearance	NA	Hull Type	Semi-Disp.

Trawlers & Motoryachts

Viking 44 Motor Yacht

1982–90

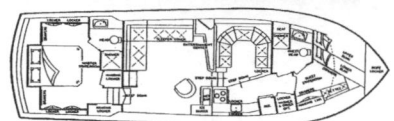

Standard Layout, 1982–88

Standard Layout, 1989–90

Prices Not Provided for Pre-1995 Models

Quality-built 1980s motoryacht with rakish lines took midsize motoryacht styling, luxury to the next level. Well-appointed teak interior boasts salon entertainment center, home-sized galley, two large staterooms. Open aft deck with wet bar seats several guests. Engine room is on the small side. Front salon windows were eliminated in 1987; flybridge was updated in 1989. Popular model is always in demand. Cruise at 23–24 knots with GM 485hp diesels (high 20s top). Cockpit version, the Viking 50 Cockpit MY, was built in 1983–87.

Length	44'0"	Fuel	460 gals.
Beam	15'0"	Water	180 gals.
Draft	4'0"	Waste	50 gals.
Weight	40,000#	Hull Type	Modified-V
Clearance	14'6"	Deadrise Aft	15.5°

Viking 48 Motor Yacht

1986–88

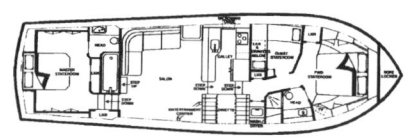

Appealing 1980s motoryacht with fully enclosed aft deck, classic Viking styling is versatile, spacious, built to last. Standard three-stateroom interior features well-appointed salon with built-in entertainment center, home-sized galley with generous storage, booth-style dinette, very spacious owner's stateroom. Note full tub in master head, washer/dryer center, salon serving counter. Enclosed aft deck—complete with wing doors and wet bar—serves as a second salon. A good performer, GM 735hp diesels cruise at 24–25 knots.

Prices Not Provided for Pre-1995 Models

Length w/Pulpit	52'7"	Clearance	12'5"
Hull Length	48'7"	Fuel	645 gals.
Beam	16'0"	Water	200 gals.
Draft	4'7"	Hull Type	Modified-V
Weight	48,500#	Deadrise Aft	15.5°

Viking 50 Motor Yacht

1990–92

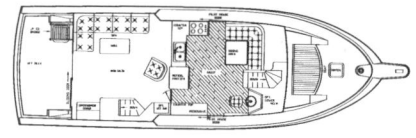

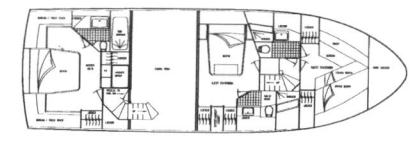

Portly twin-deck motoryacht introduced in 1990 offers the interior volume, passenger comforts of most 55-footers. Expansive floorplan with full-beam salon, country-kitchen galley includes private master suite with salon entry, two large guest staterooms forward, three full heads. Curved steps ascend from covered aft deck to huge, full-length bridge with dinghy platform. Lower helm was optional. Note stand-up engine room, sliding galley deck doors, cushioned foredeck seating. GM 735hp diesels cruise at 18–20 knots, top out in the low 20s.

Prices Not Provided for Pre-1995 Models

Length	50'6"	Fuel, Std.	600 gals.
Beam	16'4"	Fuel, Opt.	770 gals.
Draft	4'3"	Water	250 gals.
Weight	54,000#	Hull Type	Modified-V
Clearance	20'0"	Deadrise Aft	14°

Trawlers & Motoryachts

Viking 54 Sports Yacht

1992–2001

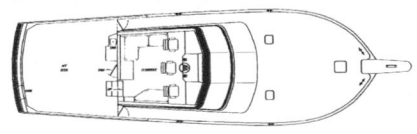

Appealing aft-cabin motoryacht made good on Viking promise of executive-class luxury, yacht-grade quality. Three-stateroom floorplan is dominated by spacious salon/galley/dinette with teak paneling, quality fabrics and furnishings. Palatial master suite has centerline king bed, walk-in closet. Additional features include large, semi-enclosed aft deck, standard washer/dryer, walk-in engine room. Enclosed bridge became standard in 1998. MAN 820hp diesels cruise at 24 knots (28 knots top); 1,050 MANs cruise at 26 knots (about 30 knots top).

See Page 548 For Value Estimates

Length	54'1"	Fuel	900 gals.
Beam	17'5"	Water	200 gals.
Draft	4'10"	Headroom	6'6"
Weight	72,000#	Hull Type	Modified-V
Clearance	16'6"	Deadrise Aft	15.5°

Viking 55 Motor Yacht

1987–90

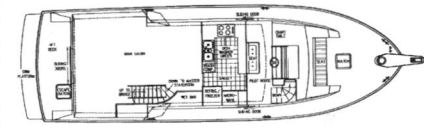

Compelling twin-deck motoryacht (originally called the Gulfstar 55) combined spacious accommodations with leading-edge construction (by 1980's standards), impressive big-boat performance. Four-stateroom interior—rare in any 55-footer—features extended, luxury-class salon with flybridge staircase, home-sized U-shaped galley, enclosed wheelhouse, private-access master suite, utility room with washer/dryer, walk-in engine room. Full-width salon became standard in 1989. Hull is fully cored. GM 735hp 8V92s cruise at a brisk 19–20 knots.

Prices Not Provided for Pre-1995 Models

Length	55'7"	Fuel	770 gals.
Beam	17'4"	Water	350 gals.
Draft	4'5"	Waste	100 gals.
Weight	56,000#	Hull Type	Modified-V
Clearance	21'5"	Deadrise Aft	15°

Viking 57 Motor Yacht

1991–95

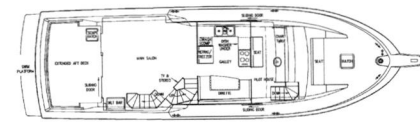

Lengthened version of original Gulfstar/Viking 55 MY (1987–91) raised the bar for 1990s engineering excellence, design innovation. Expansive four-stateroom interior features full-beam salon, separate eat-in galley, enclosed wheelhouse, private-entry master suite, walk-in engine room. Extended bridge offers seating for a small crowd. Note all-glass salon bulkhead, utility room with washer/dryer, inside flybridge stairs. Hull is fully cored to reduce weight. Twin 820hp MAN engines cruise at 19–20 knots (23 knots top).

See Page 548 For Value Estimates

Length	57'7"	Fuel	750 gals.
Beam	17'4"	Water	350 gals.
Draft	4'5"	Headroom	6'6"
Weight	78,000#	Hull Type	Modified-V
Clearance	21'2"	Deadrise Aft	15°

Viking 60 Cockpit Sport Yacht

1994–2001

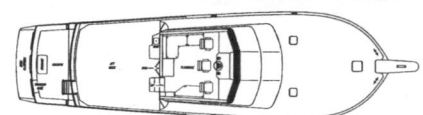

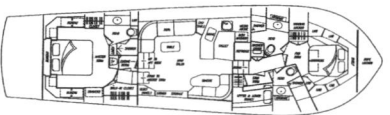

Stretched version of popular Viking 54 Motor Yacht (1992–2001) added a 6' cockpit extension for swimming, diving, fishing. Three-stateroom layout boasts fully enclosed aft deck, spacious salon/galley/dinette with teak paneling, three full heads, posh master suite with king bed, walk-in closet. Additional highlights include big walk-in engine room, wide side decks, cockpit transom door. Bridge enclosure became standard in 1998. MAN 1,050hp diesels cruise at 25 knots (30 knots top); optional 1,200hp MANs cruise at 28 knots (low 30s top).

See Page 548 For Value Estimates

Length Overall	60'1"	Fuel	1,300 gals.
Beam	17'5"	Water	200 gals.
Draft	4'10"	Headroom	6'5"
Weight	78,000#	Hull Type	Modified-V
Clearance	16'6"	Deadrise Aft	15.5°

Viking 63 Widebody MY

1987–91

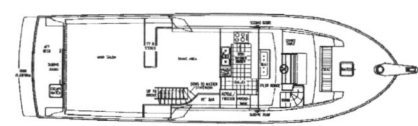

Popular widebody motoryacht defined cutting-edge luxury, sophistication in the late 1980s. Extravagant four-stateroom interior features cavernous salon with formal dining area forward, opulent master suite with walk-in closet, gourmet galley with salon pass-thru, utility room with washer/dryer and workbench. Note spacious stand-up engine room, enormous flybridge with wraparound seating. Extended Aft Deck model with walkaround decks, smaller salon was also available. GM 900hp diesels cruise at 20 knots (22–23 knots top).

Prices Not Provided for Pre-1995 Models

Length	62'6"	Fuel	1,080 gals.
Beam	17'4"	Water	350 gals.
Draft	4'9"	Headroom	6'5"
Weight	61,500#	Hull Type	Modified-V
Clearance	21'5"	Deadrise Aft	15°

Viking 65 Cockpit MY

1991–94

Appealing 1990s cockpit yacht combined bold styling with richly appointed accommodations, state-of-the-art construction. Spacious four-stateroom interior features massive full-beam salon with day head, country-kitchen galley with dinette, utility room with washer/dryer, walk-in engine room. Note crew cabin (opposite second guest stateroom), aft deck enclosure, pass-through window from galley to salon. Large cockpit with storage lockers, transom door makes boarding easy. Hull is fully cored. Standard 1,050hp MANs cruise at 20 knots.

Prices Not Provided for Pre-1995 Models

Length	64'7"	Fuel	1,030 gals.
Beam	17'4"	Water	300 gals.
Draft	4'9"	Headroom	6'5"
Weight	91,000#	Hull Type	Modified-V
Clearance	20'8"	Deadrise Aft	15°

Viking 65 Motor Yacht

1991–95

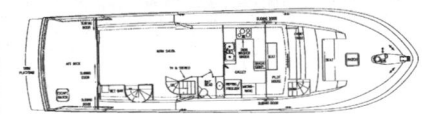

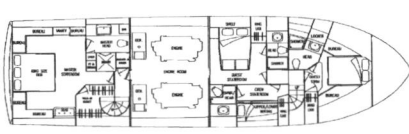

Bold Viking motoryacht introduced in 1991 combined condo-size interior accommodations with dramatic styling, top-shelf amenities. Highlights include sprawling salon with spiral bridge staircase, main deck day head, eat-in galley, opulent master suite with home-size head, enclosed aft deck with sliding—not hinged—wing doors. Note galley pass-through to dining area and wheelhouse, full walkaround decks. Extended flybridge has seating for a dozen guests. MAN 1,050hp engines cruise at 20 knots (22–23 knots wide open).

See Page 548 For Value Estimates

Length	64'7"	Fuel	1,030 gals.
Beam	17'4"	Water	300 gals.
Draft	4'9"	Headroom	6'5"
Weight	94,000#	Hull Type	Modified-V
Clearance	20'8"	Deadrise Aft	15°

Viking 72 Cockpit Motor Yacht

1990–94

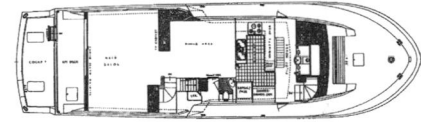

Main Deck Layout, 1990–91

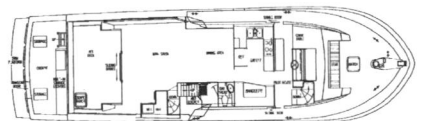

Main Deck Layout, 1992–94

Striking twin-deck motoryacht from early 1990s incorporated mega-yacht accommodations with graceful lines, impressive performance. Expansive four-stateroom interior features sprawling salon with formal dining area, enclosed U-shaped galley, opulent full-beam master with walk-in closet. Revised 1992 layout has enlarged aft deck, reduced salon dimensions, eat-in galley. Note deckhouse day head, utility room with washer/dryer, roomy cockpit with transom door. Optional 1,050hp GM engines cruise at a brisk 22 knots (mid 20s top).

Prices Not Provided for Pre-1995 Models

Length	72'0"	Fuel	1,470 gals.
Beam	17'5"	Water	350 gals.
Draft	4'10"	Cockpit	92 sq. ft.
Weight	105,000#	Hull Type	Modified-V
Clearance	21'2"	Deadrise Aft	15°

Viking 72 Motor Yacht

1989–94

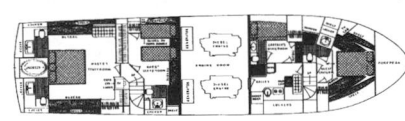

Lower Deck Layout, 1989–93

Lower Deck Layout, 1993–94

Supersize Viking cruising yacht introduced in 1989 raised the bar for American motoryacht comfort, styling, performance. Highlights include spacious full-beam salon with formal dining area, deckhouse day head, home-size galley, enclosed wheelhouse, lavish master suite. Original four-stateroom interior was completely revised in mid-1993 when engine room was moved aft. Massive flybridge can entertain a small crowd. A good performer by the standards of her day, 1,040hp GM engines cruise at 22 knots (mid 20s top).

Prices Not Provided for Pre-1995 Models

Length	72'0"	Fuel	1,470 gals.
Beam	17'5"	Water	280 gals.
Draft	4'10"	Headroom	6'5"
Weight	107,000#	Hull Type	Modified-V
Clearance	21'2"	Deadrise Aft	15°

Trawlers & Motoryachts

Viking Sport Cruisers 43 Flybridge

1995–99

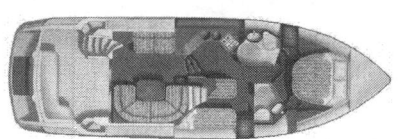

Stylish UK import (called Viking 42 Flybridge until the swim platform was stretched in 1997) made the cut with U.S. buyers looking for rakish Med styling, spirited performance. Interior highlights include wide-open salon with facing settees, elevated lower helm position, beautifully crafted woodwork. Roomy cockpit—protected by bridge overhang—has L-shaped seating with storage under, engine room access hatch. Note curved bridge steps, wide side decks. Cat 420hp (or 370hp Volvo) diesels cruise at 23 knots (high 20s knots).

Insufficient Resale Data to Assign Values

Length Overall	43'6"	Water	128 gals.
Beam	13'11"	Waste	42 gals.
Draft	3'3"	Clearance	11'6"
Weight	23,520#	Hull Type	Deep-V
Fuel	360 gals.	Deadrise Aft	19°

Viking Sport Cruisers 45 Flybridge

1999–2004

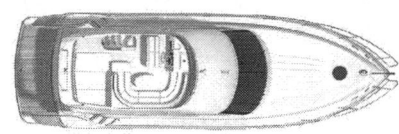

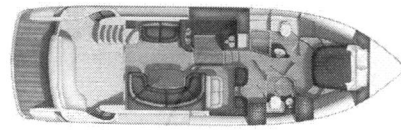

Sought-after flybridge yacht raised styling, performance bar for midsize cruisers of her era. Upscale interior with lacquered cherry cabinetry features spacious salon, twin-seat lower helm, large galley with generous counter space, two roomy staterooms. Note companionway washer/dryer, stall shower in owner's head. Hatches in cockpit sole access lazarette and small engine room; molded steps lead to bridge with U-lounge, aft sun pad. Volvo 480hp diesels cruise at 25 knots (about 30 knots top).

See Page 547 For Value Estimates

Length Overall	45'0"	Water	152 gals.
Beam	14'3"	Waste	42 gals.
Draft	3'7"	Clearance	13'7"
Weight	28,000#	Hull Type	Deep-V
Fuel	383 gals.	Deadrise Aft	19°

Viking Sport Cruisers 45/46 Flybridge

1995–2000

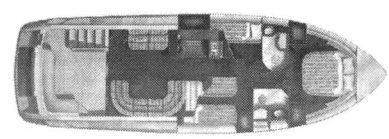

Feature-rich Med cruising yacht (called Viking 45 Flybridge until 1998 when her swim platform was extended) delivered world-class mix of luxury, performance. Three-stateroom interior—rare in a boat this size—includes well-appointed salon with U-shaped dinette, fully equipped galley, raised lower helm, two heads. Cockpit with built-in seating, molded steps is sheltered by bridge overhang. Note compact engine room, wide side decks, spacious bridge with aft sun pad. Cruise at 24–25 knots (30 knots top) with Volvo 430hp diesels.

See Page 547 For Value Estimates

Length Overall	46'9"	Water	128 gals.
Beam	13'10"	Clearance	12'1"
Draft	3'4"	Headroom	6'5"
Weight	28,000#	Hull Type	Deep-V
Fuel	370 gals.	Deadrise Aft	19°

Viking Sport Cruisers 48/50 Flybridge

1994–99

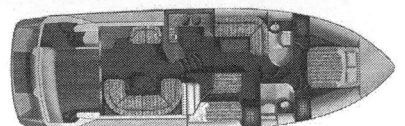

Standard Two-Stateroom Layout

Optional Three-Stateroom Layout

See Page 547 For Value Estimates

Sleek European cruising yacht (called Viking 48 Flybridge until swim her platform was extended in 1998) delivered impressive mix of style, luxury, performance. Standard twin-stateroom interior displays British craftsmanship at its best. Highlights include sliding cabin windows, generous galley storage, L-shaped lower-level dinette. Cockpit features molded bridge steps, built-in seating, transom door. Note so-so lower helm visibility, small engine room. Volvo 380hp diesels cruise at 22 knots; Volvo 430s cruise in the mid 20s.

Length Overall	51'0"	Water	187 gals.
Beam	14'2"	Clearance	12'6"
Draft	3'9"	Headroom	6'4"
Weight	33,600#	Hull Type	Deep-V
Fuel	428 gals.	Deadrise Aft	19°

Viking Sport Cruisers 50 Flybridge

2001–10

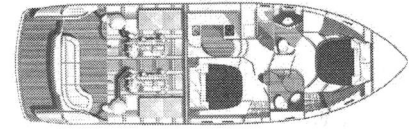

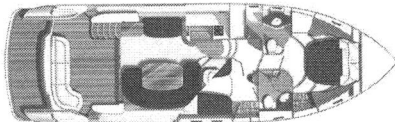

See Page 547 For Value Estimates

Richly appointed sportcruiser combines leading-edge styling with polished accommodations, sporty performance. Richly furnished interior features wide-open salon with facing settees, compact galley, two roomy staterooms, each with private head access. Additional highlights include teak-laid cockpit, extended swim platform, excellent lower helm/dash layout, washer/dryer. Note huge full-beam lazarette forward of crew cabin. Volvo 480hp diesels cruise at 22 knots (26–27 knots top); 675hp Volvos cruise at 26 knots (31–32 knots top).

Length Overall	50'3"	Water	160 gals.
Beam	14'8"	Clearance	13'1"
Draft	3'8"	Headroom	6'4"
Weight	33,600#	Hull Type	Deep-V
Fuel	540 gals.	Deadrise Aft	19°

Viking Sport Cruisers 52 Flybridge

1997–2002

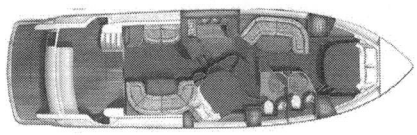

See Page 547 For Value Estimates

World-class sportcruiser from the late 1990s delivered a high-powered blend of sleek European styling, leading-edge accommodations. Offered with several two- and three-stateroom layouts, all with step-down galley, full lower helm, aft crew quarters. Notable features include high-gloss cherry woodwork, teak-laid cockpit, extended swim platform, roomy bridge with sun pad aft. Prop pockets reduce draft, improve efficiency. Bow thruster was standard. Volvo 480hp diesels cruise at 24 knots (28–29 knots top); 610hp Volvos cruise at 27 knots (30+ knots top).

Length Overall	51'8"	Fuel	504 gals.
Beam	15'0"	Water	187 gals.
Draft	3'8"	Headroom	6'3"
Weight	44,800#	Hull Type	Deep-V
Clearance, Arch	12'8"	Deadrise Aft	19°

Trawlers & Motoryachts

Viking Sport Cruisers 56 Flybridge

1997–2002

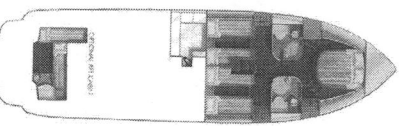

Striking UK import offered American buyers a high-octane mix of European styling, luxury, performance. Expansive three-stateroom interior boasts large salon with U-shaped settee, sunken galley (with attached laundry center), twin-seat lower helm, identical guest cabins, aft crew quarters. Teak-laid cockpit combines roomy storage lazarette, engine room entryway. Note internal bridge stairs, extended swim platform, wide side decks, spacious bridge. Volvo 610hp diesels cruise at 25 knots and reach about 28 knots top.

See Page 548 For Value Estimates

Length Overall	55'7"	Fuel	576 gals.
Beam	15'6"	Water	199 gals.
Draft	3'9"	Headroom	6'6"
Weight	47,040#	Hull Type	Deep-V
Clearance	12'10"	Deadrise Aft	19°

Viking Sport Cruisers 57 Flybridge

2005–08

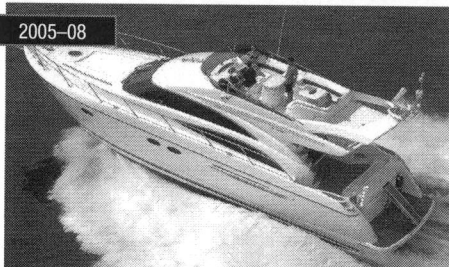

Feature-rich cruising yacht combines acclaimed Mediterranean styling with posh accommodations, exceptional quality. Lush three-stateroom interior has sunken galley forward of spacious salon, twin-seat lower helm, full dinette. Large salon windows offer panoramic outside views; utility room off galley has freezer, washer/dryer. Note interior bridge steps, storage lazarette under cockpit sole, electric side windows. Extended swim platform can stow PWC or dinghy. Volvo 715hp diesels cruise at 25 knots (30 knots top).

See Page 548 For Value Estimates

Length Overall	57'6"	Headroom	6'5"
Beam	16'1"	Fuel	745 gals.
Draft	4'2"	Water	185 gals.
Weight	50,400#	Hull Type	Deep-V
Clearance	14'0"	Deadrise Aft	19°

Viking Sport Cruisers 60 Flybridge

1996–2001

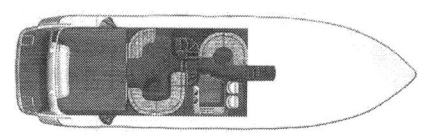
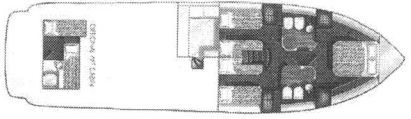

Imposing UK-built luxury yacht combines signature Viking styling with deluxe accommodations, spirited performance. Posh interior with spacious salon, sunken galley features raised dinette opposite helm, three large staterooms, two full heads. Note utility room off galley, interior bridge stairs, high-gloss cherry joinery. Large hatch in cockpit sole provides access to crew quarters. Swim platform can stow tender, PWC. Engine room is a tight fit. Volvo 610hp diesels cruise at 26 knots (29–30 knots top); optional 800 MANs cruise at 28 knots (30+ top).

See Page 548 For Value Estimates

Length Overall	59'11"	Fuel	756 gals.
Beam	16'1"	Water	199 gals.
Draft	3'11"	Headroom	6'5"
Weight	50,400#	Hull Type	Deep-V
Clearance	13'7"	Deadrise Aft	19°

Viking Sport Cruisers 61 Flybridge

2003–05

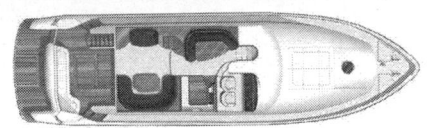

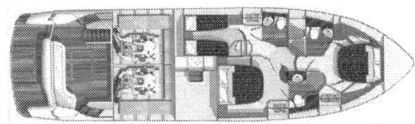

Gold-plated sportyacht delivers a sophisticated blend of European styling, American luxury, Mediterranean performance. Beautifully appointed three-stateroom interior with spacious salon features sunken galley, amidships owner's suite, three full heads. Note apartment-size galley, utility room with washer/dryer, high-gloss cherry joinery. Extended flybridge can be reached via cockpit or salon stairs; teak swim platform can stow PWC. Engine room is a tight fit. MAN 6800hp engines cruise at 25–26 knots (about 30 knots top).

Insufficient Resale Data to Assign Values

Length Overall	61'7"	Fuel	790 gals.
Beam	16'0"	Water	185 gals.
Draft	4'4"	Headroom	6'6"
Weight	58,240#	Hull Type	Deep-V
Clearance	NA	Deadrise Aft	19°

Viking Sport Cruisers 65 Motoryacht

1999–2004

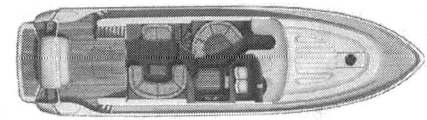

Seductive Viking motoryacht combines world-class styling with executive-class accommodations, yacht-grade amenities. Highlights include extravagant cherrywood interior, roomy cockpit with twin transom doors, extended flybridge with radar mast, hideaway electronics console. Concealed davit disappears into transom; swim platform can support tender or PWC. Note power lower-helm deck door, inside/outside bridge access, wide side decks. Engine room is a tight fit. MAN 1,050hp engines cruise at 30 knots (33–34 knots wide open).

Insufficient Resale Data to Assign Values

Length Overall	64'10"	Fuel	959 gals.
Beam	16'9"	Water	198 gals.
Draft	4'6"	Headroom	6'6"
Weight	66,774#	Hull Type	Deep-V
Clearance	13'6"	Deadrise Aft	19°

Vista 43 Motoryacht

1987–94

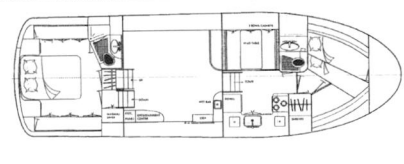

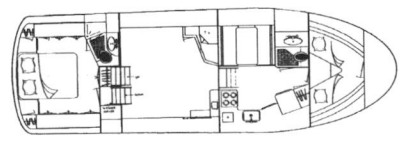

Popular sundeck motoryacht with contemporary lines delivers impressive mix of solid construction, common-sense accommodations. Wide 15-foot beam allows for spacious galley-down interior with comfortable salon, full-size dinette, two large staterooms. Many were fitted with washer/dryer in aft cabin. Wing doors enclose large afterdeck; side decks are wide enough for easy bow access. Note light oak cabinetry (rather than teak), aft-stateroom engine room access, wide side decks. Cat 375hp diesels cruise at 18 knots (20+ knots top).

Prices Not Provided for Pre-1995 Models

Length Overall	42'10"	Fuel	465 gals.
Hull Length	35'7"	Water	200 gals.
Beam	15'0"	Headroom	6'5"
Draft	3'6"	Hull Type	Modified-V
Weight	32,000#	Deadrise Aft	14°

Trawlers & Motoryachts

Wellcraft 43 San Remo

1988–90

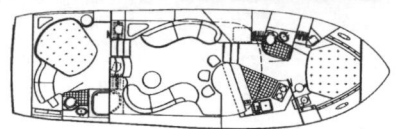

Standard Interioir

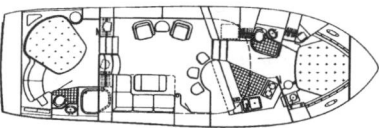

Alternate Layout

Prices Not Provided for Pre-1995 Models

Sporty double-cabin cruiser paired aggressive styling with spacious accommodations, durable construction. Offered with choice of standard "Eurostyle" interior with curved salon sofas, or more conventional (toned-down) floorplan with L-shaped sofa. Highlights include breakfast bar with storage cabinet, spacious galley with generous storage, two large staterooms with queen beds. Note transom picture window, large flybridge with seating for eight, integral bow pulpit. Cat 375hp diesels cruise at 20 knots (low 20s top).

Length	42'10"	Fuel, Gas	300 gals.
Beam	14'6"	Fuel, Diesel	400 gals.
Draft	3'2"	Water	100 gals.
Weight	26,100#	Hull Type	Modified-V
Clearance	12'6"	Deadrise Aft	14°

Wellcraft 46 Cockpit MY

1990–95

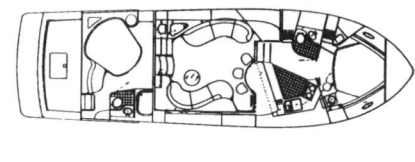

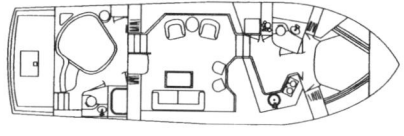

See Page 549 For Value Estimates

Cockpit version of Wellcraft 43 San Remo (1988–90) combined aggressive styling with versatile layout, spacious accommodations. Offered with choice of standard "Eurostyle" interior with curved salon sofas, or more conventional (toned-down) floorplan with L-shaped sofa. Note aft picture window, cockpit access door in aft stateroom. Topside highlights include roomy flybridge with seating for six, cockpit transom door, aft deck hardtop. Big engine room is a plus. Cruise at 18–20 knots (low 20s top) with Cat 375hp diesels.

Length	46'3"	Fuel	400 gals.
Beam	14'6"	Water	120 gals.
Draft	3'2"	Cockpit	46 sq. ft.
Weight	27,000#	Hull Type	Modified-V
Clearance	14'0"	Deadrise Aft	14°

West Bay 4500 Pilothouse

1985–91

Two Staterooms

Three Staterooms

Prices Not Provided for Pre-1995 Models

Sturdy pilothouse cruiser from late 1980s combined bold styling with roomy accommodations, quality construction. Offered with two- or three-stateroom floorplans, both with expansive full-beam salon, two full heads. (Twin-cabin layout enlarged master, space for washer/dryer.) Excellent visibility from raised pilothouse. Flybridge can stow small tender. Note cockpit engine room access, large salon windows. Among several engine options, twin 300hp Cummins—or 320hp Cat—diesels cruise at 18 knots (20+ top). About 15 were built.

Length Overall	45'0"	Headroom	6'5"
Length WL	NA	Fuel	540 gals.
Beam	14'10"	Water	206 gals.
Draft	3'0"	Hull Type	Modified-V
Weight	32,000#	Deadrise Aft	NA

West Bay 58 SonShip

1992–2005

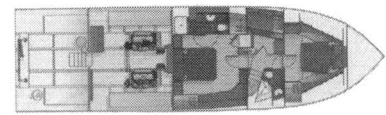

Classic Pacific Northwest cruiser—West Bay's most popular model—offers an impressive mix of sleek styling, luxury-class accommodations. Spacious pilothouse interior with three staterooms boasts huge salon with entertainment center, lavish full-beam master suite, premium systems and furnishings. Large bridge with dinghy stowage aft seats eight. Cockpit hatches access huge lazarette, well-finished engine room. Note wide side decks, good lower helm visibility. Cruise at 20 knots with 660hp Cats; 24 knots with 820hp MANs.

See Page 549 For Value Estimates

Length w/Pulpit	63'6"	Fuel	1,000 gals.
Hull Length	59'6"	Water	260 gals.
Beam	17'1"	Waste	95 gals.
Draft	4'10"	Clearance	14'0"
Weight	62,000#	Hull Type	Modified-V

West Bay 78 SonShip

2000–06

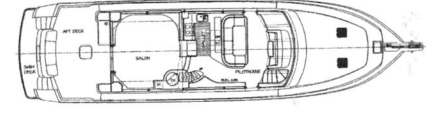

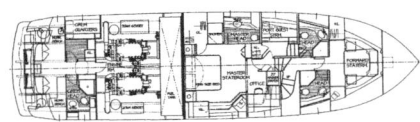

Semicustom pilothouse yacht introduced in 2000 matched traditional Northwest styling with top-tier build quality, luxury-class accomodations. Generous 20-foot beam allows for spacious three-stateroom interior with elegant salon, home-sized galley, opulent full-beam master with king bed. Crew quarters are aft, accessed from watertight door on swim platform. Note huge engine room with workbench. Large cockpit can entertain small crowd in comfort. MTU 1,480hp engines cruise at 22 knots (26–28 knots wide open).

Insufficient Resale Data to Assign Values

Length w/Pulpit	81'6"	Fuel	2,750 gals.
Hull Length	78'0"	Water	600 gals.
Beam	20'0"	Waste	100 gals.
Draft	5'0"	Hull Type	Modified-V
Weight	110,000#	Deadrise Aft	16°

Trawlers & Motoryachts

Section 2
Sportfishing Boats

See index for complete list of models.

Albemarle 27/280 Express

1984–2007

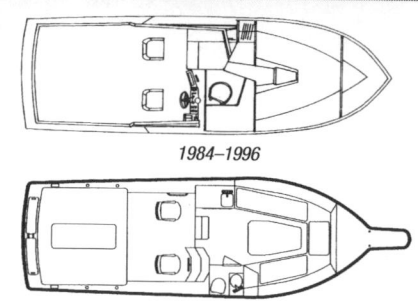

1984–1996

1997–2008

See Page 511 For Value Estimates

Best-selling fisherman with wide 9'6" beam (called 27 Express in 1984–96; 280 Express in 1997–2007) makes the cut with serious anglers. Spacious cockpit includes transom and in-floor fishboxes, double companion seat with livewell. Well-finished cabin with full galley, enclosed head sleeps two. Bridgedeck lifts for engine access. Facelift in 1997 included redesigned helm, improved cabin headroom. Jackshaft power became available in 1986. Good rough-water performer. Over 650 sold. Offered with several gas or diesel engine options.

Length w/Pulpit	29'1"	Fuel, Twin I/B	260 gals.
Hull Length	27'1"	Fuel, Single JS	172 gals.
Beam	9'6"	Water	14 gals.
Draft	3'0"	Hull Type	Deep-V
Weight	9,500#	Deadrise Aft	24°

Albemarle 290 XF

2008–Current

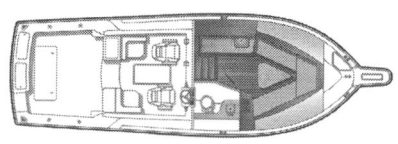

See Page 511 For Value Estimates

Heavily-built express meets high Albemarle standards for construction, seaworthiness, fishability. Elevated helmdeck with seating for four overlooks expansive cockpit with in-floor fishbox, transom fishbox, 21-gallon livewell, tackle drawers. Forward deck section lifts for engine access. Note pop-up electronics pod at helm. Cozy interior with full galley, convertible dinette, fold-down single berth sleeps four. Good range with 265-gallon fuel capacity. Shallow draft thanks to prop pockets. Yanmar 315hp diesels cruise efficiently at 25 knots (about 30 top).

Length w/Pulpit	30'6"	Fuel	265 gals.
Hull Length	28'6"	Water	28 gals.
Beam	10'9"	Clearance	8'2"
Draft	2'8"	Hull Type	Deep-V
Weight	12,500#	Deadrise Aft	21°

Albemarle 305/310 XF

1995–Current

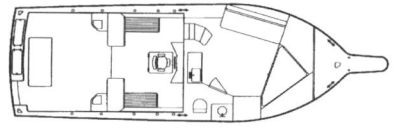

1995–2003

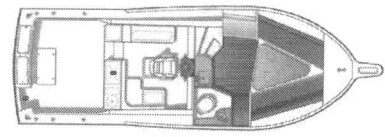

2004–Current

See Page 511 For Value Estimates

Hard-charging fishing machine with wide beam (called the 305 Express in 1995–2003; 310 Express since 2004) is stylish, versatile, built to last. Best-in-class deck layout with centerline helm includes deluxe rigging station with 30-gallon livewell, transom fishbox, dual washdowns. Roomy interior with teak trim, galley with microwave sleeps four. Bridgedeck lifts for engine access. Fuel increased, cabin and bridgedeck updated in 2004. A heavy boat for her size. Cat 350hp diesels cruise in the high 20s (about 30 knots top).

Length w/Pulpit	32'2"	Fuel	300/325 gals.
Hull Length	30'6"	Water	30 gals.
Beam	11'0"	Waste	15 gals.
Draft	2'10"	Hull Type	Deep-V
Weight	15,500#	Deadrise Aft	18°

Sportfishing Boats

Albemarle 320 Express

1990–2006

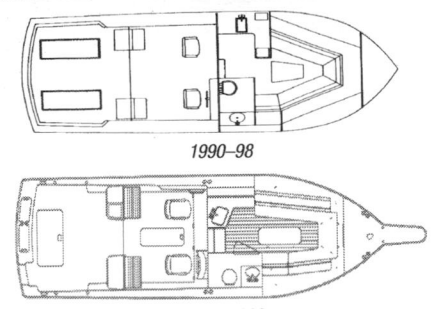

1990–98

1998–2006

Performance-driven express delivers tournament-level fishing experience with express-boat comforts, amenities. Cockpit with in-deck fishboxes, rigging station is big for a boat this size. Upscale interior has berths for four, full galley, classy teak-and-holly sole, stand-up head with shower. Updates in 2000 included raised deck for more cabin headroom, transom fishbox, improved engine room, cockpit transom door. Good fit and finish. Yanmar 370hp diesels cruise at 27–28 knots and top out at close to 30 knots.

See Page 511 For Value Estimates

Length w/Pulpit	34'9"	Fuel	300 gals.
Hull Length	32'2"	Water	30 gals.
Beam	11'0"	Waste	NA
Draft	3'0"	Hull Type	Deep-V
Weight	17,000#	Deadrise Aft	18°

Albemarle 325 Convertible

1988–2003

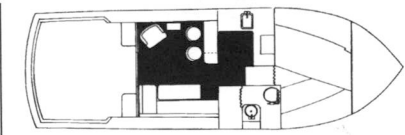

Layout, 1988–92

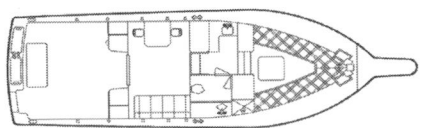

Layout, 1993–2002

Quality pocket convertible with big fishing cockpit is stylish, versatile, built to last. Galley-down interior (updated in 1993) is surprisingly spacious for a 32-footer with well-appointed salon, fully equipped galley, large head with separate stall shower. To address concerns about a harsh ride, major redesign in 1999 moved the engines forward 10" and replaced the original three-tank configuration with a single fuel tank. Transom door also became standard in 1999. Volvo 330hp gas engines cruise at 20–22 knots; 350hp Cat diesels cruise in mid/high 20s.

See Page 511 For Value Estimates

Length w/Pulpit	34'9"	Fuel	300 gals.
Hull Length	32'2"	Water	30 gals.
Beam	11'0"	Waste	25 gals.
Draft	3'0"	Hull Type	Deep-V
Weight	18,000#	Deadrise Aft	18°

Albemarle 330 XF

2007–Current

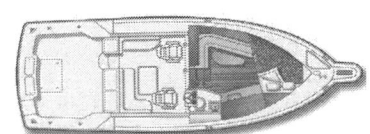

Top-of-the-line express fisherman with generous 13'5" beam is stylish, spacious, loaded with amenities. Large cockpit comes standard with full compliment of tournament-ready features including removable in-deck fishbox, transom livewell, plenty of tackle stowage. Stand-out interior with teak-and-holly cabin sole, Corian counters offers remarkable elegance and comfort. Note premium Pompanette helm chairs, super-large engine compartment, copious rod storage. No lightweight, 425hp Cummins diesels cruise at 26–28 knots (30+ top).

See Page 511 For Value Estimates

Length w/Pulpit	35'0"	Fuel	450 gals.
Hull Length	33'0"	Water	52 gals.
Beam	13'5"	Waste	20 gals.
Draft	4'0"	Hull Type	Deep-V
Dry Weight	19,500#	Deadrise Aft	24°

Sportfishing Boats

Albemarle 360 XF

2006–Current

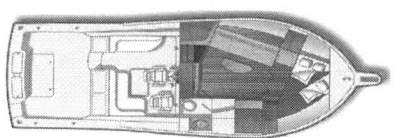

Hardcore fishing machine with wide beam measures up to Albemarle reputation for top-shelf engineering, premium build quality. Spacious cockpit boasts bait-prep station with sink, 25-gallon livewell, transom fishbox, in-deck fishbox. Centerline helm with flanking settees provides excellent visibility. Upscale interior with leather settee, split head, sleeps three. Hull running surface redesigned in 2010 for pod drives. Note generous fuel capacity. Cat 575hp diesels cruise at 30 knots; 435hp IPS Volvos cruise efficiently at 30 knots.

See Page 511 For Value Estimates

Length w/Pulpit	38'6"	Clearance	9'2"
Hull Length	36'3"	Fuel	535 gals.
Beam	13'11"	Water	95 gals.
Draft	4'0"	Hull Type	Modified-V
Weight	25,000#	Deadrise Aft	16°

Albemarle 410 Convertible

2005–Current

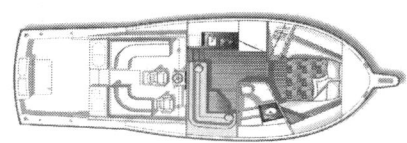

Extended-range tournament machine with wide beam, classic convertible styling hits all the right buttons. Upscale interior with cherry trim, quality appointments boasts surprisingly spacious salon with facing L-shaped settees, large galley with Sub-Zero refrigeration, comfortable staterooms. Cockpit comes with 30-gallon livewell/cooler, bait-prep center, beefy tuna door, cockpit and transom fishboxes. Note spacious bridge with pod-style center helm, large engine room. No lightweight, 710hp Cat diesels cruise at 30 knots (low 30s top).

See Page 511 For Value Estimates

Length w/Pulpit	43'6"	Fuel	600 gals.
Hull Length	41'0"	Water	100 gals.
Beam	15'9"	Clearance	13'4"
Draft	4'0"	Hull Type	Modified-V
Weight	36,000#	Deadrise Aft	15°

Albemarle 410 XF

2002–Current

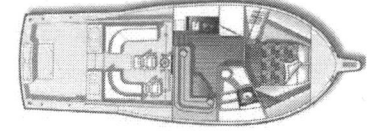

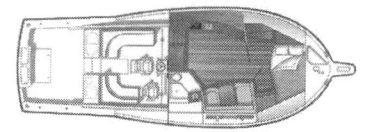

Performance-driven express combines striking lines with large cockpit, upscale accommodations. Standard fishing features include livewell, rigging station, transom fishbox, transom door. Center helm position with single-lever controls provides maximum visibility and control. Bridgedeck with facing settees lifts for engine access. Comfortable single-stateroom interior with L-shaped lounge includes full galley, large head with separate stall shower. Note well-flared bow, tall windshield. Cat 710hp diesels cruise at a fast 30 knots.

See Page 511 For Value Estimates

Length w/Pulpit	43'6"	Fuel	600 gals.
Hull Length	41'0"	Water	100 gals.
Beam	15'9"	Waste	25 gals.
Draft	4'0"	Hull Type	Modified-V
Weight	32,000#	Deadrise Aft	15°

Albin 28 Tournament Express

1993–2007

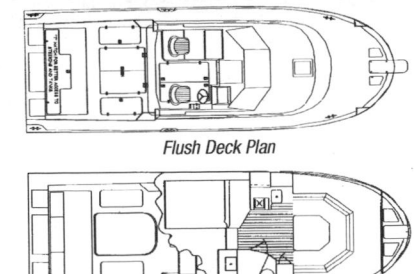

Flush Deck Plan

Enginebox Plan

Versatile fishboat/family cruiser with Downeast styling made good on Albin promise of rugged construction, good open-water performance. Features include extended hardtop, swim platform, transom door, livewell, fishboxes, tackle storage, bow thruster. Well-appointed interior with teak-and-holly sole, quarter berth sleeps three. Flush-deck option (no engine box) in 2003 moved engine forward resulting in larger cockpit. Cruise at 18 knots with single 315hp Yanmar diesel. Cummins 370hp engine (low 20s cruise) available only with enginebox version.

See Page 512 For Value Estimates

Length	29'11"	Fuel	132 gals.
Beam	10'0"	Water	36 gals.
Draft	3'2"	Waste	20 gals.
Weight	7,500#	Hull Type	Modified-V
Clearance	7'9"	Deadrise Aft	16°

Albin 32+2 Command Bridge

1989–2003

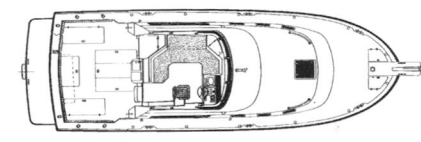

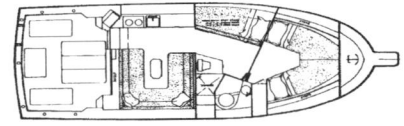

Versatile sportfisher with space-efficient deck layout combines sturdy construction with comfortable cabin accommodations, economical operation. Cockpit amenities include in-floor fish/storage boxes (3), transom door, livewell, sink, tackle storage. Original interior has convertible dinette forward, private stateroom aft; tri-cabin layout became available in 1996. Full-length keel protects running gear. Very wide side decks. Bow thruster was standard in later models. Cruise at 16 knots (low 20s top) with single 370hp Yanmar diesel.

See Page 512 For Value Estimates

Length Overall	36'9"	Fuel	260 gals.
Hull Length	34'11"	Water	117 gals.
Beam	12'2"	Waste	20 gals.
Draft	3'10"	Hull Type	Modified-V
Weight	15,000#	Deadrise Aft	13°

Albin 35 Command Bridge

2004–07

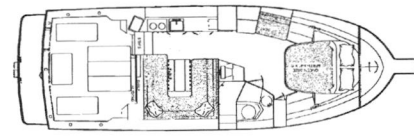

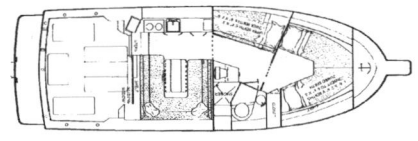

Stretched version of Albin 32+2 (1989–2003) boasts enlarged cockpit, minor cabin updates. Popular model receives high marks for surprisingly spacious interior, efficient bridge layout, solid construction. Choice of single- or twin-stateroom interiors, both with stall shower in the head. Good engine access is a plus. Note wide side decks, transom door, integral swim platform. Livewell, bow thruster were standard. Long keel protects prop in event of grounding. Cruise in the low 20s with single 370hp Cummins diesel.

See Page 512 For Value Estimates

Length w/Pulpit	36'9"	Fuel	260 gals.
Beam	12'4"	Water	117 gals.
Draft	3'10"	Headroom	6'4"
Weight	18,000#	Hull Type	Modified-V
Clearance	8'10"	Deadrise Aft	13°

Sportfishing Boats

Sportfishing Boats

Albin 35 Tournament Express

1995–2007

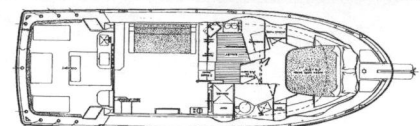

Single Stateroom Layout

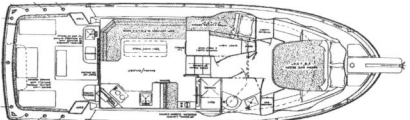

Two Stateroom Floorplan

See Page 512 For Value Estimates

Sturdy hardtop fisherman with enclosed pilothouse, protective skeg keel combines cruise-friendly interior with roomy cockpit, all-weather versatility. Highlights include spacious salon with opening windows, good helm visibility, generous galley storage, wide side decks. Offered with galley-up or galley-down floorplans, single or twin engine options. Cockpit fender storage is a nice touch. Flybridge, bow thruster were optional. Twin 370hp Cummins diesels will cruise in the mid 20s (about 30 knots top).

Length w/Pulpit	36'11"	Fuel	370 gals.
Hull Length	34'11"	Water	160 gals.
Beam	12'4"	Waste	27 gals.
Draft	3'0"	Hull Type	Modified-V
Weight	18,000#	Deadrise Aft	13°

Aquasport 275 Explorer

1999–2005

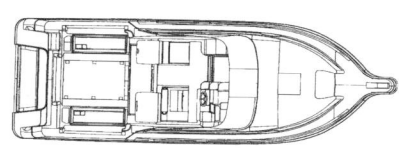

See Page 512 For Value Estimates

Maxi-beam express with roomy midcabin interior combines family-size accommodations with sporty styling, maximum cockpit space. Fishing amenities include two large in-deck fishboxes, cockpit bolsters, lighted livewell, transom door, bait-prep center, in-deck storage locker. Foldaway transom seat frees up cockpit space. Spacious cabin with galley cabinet, quarter berth, enclosed head with shower boasts near-standing headroom. Hardtop was a popular option. Walk-thru windshield is rare in a fishing boat. About 45 knots top with twin 225s.

Length w/Pulpit	28'3"	Water	27 gals.
Beam	9'8"	Clearance, Hardtop	9'3"
Draft, Drives Down	2'10"	Max HP	500
Weight	7,000#	Hull Type	Deep-V
Fuel	188 gals.	Deadrise Aft	21°

Aquasport 286/290 Express Fisherman

1982–90

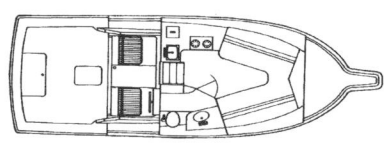

Prices Not Provided for Pre-1995 Models

Big-water express (called the 286 Express in 1982–83; 290 thereafter) ranked among the more popular 29-footers of her era. Fishing amenities include in-deck fish box, livewell, tackle center, transom door, rod holders, fresh and saltwater washdowns. Wide side decks provide secure bow access. Teak-trimmed interior with full galley, enclosed head with shower sleeps four. Excellent range. Tournament Master package included tackle station, tower. Twin 270hp gas inboards cruise at 18 knots (26–28 knots wide open).

Length w/Pulpit	31'0"	Clearance	8'0"
Hull Length	28'6"	Fuel	300 gals.
Beam	11'0"	Water	32 gals.
Draft	2'6"	Hull Type	Modified-V
Weight	9,500#	Deadrise Aft	15°

Atlantic 34 Express

1988–92

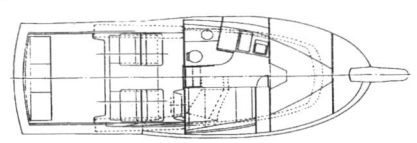

Midsize express fisherman was a surprise hit for a company better known for its trawlers and motoryachts. Large bi-level cockpit was offered in several configurations. Centerline bridgedeck hatch provides trouble-free access to motors. Roomy cabin is arranged with V-berths forward, enclosed head with shower, small galley, full dinette. Standard 350hp gas engines cruise at 25 knots (30+ knots top); optional 300hp GM 8.2 diesels cruise around 27 knots. Total of 77 were built during 5-year production run.

Prices Not Provided for Pre-1995 Models

Length	34'0"	Fuel	300 gals.
Beam	12'0"	Water	40 gals.
Draft	3'0"	Waste	15 gals.
Weight	13,500#	Hull Type	Modified-V
Clearance	8'0"	Deadrise Aft	16°

Bertram 28 Bahia Mar

1985–92

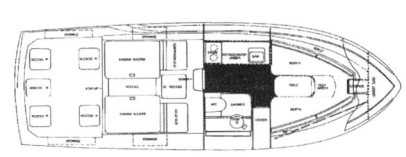

Classy 1980s express with wide 11-foot beam is spacious above, comfortable below. Expansive cockpit came standard with raw-water washdown rod storage lockers. Well-appointed cabin boasts convertible dinette, full galley, head with shower. Visibility through curved windshield is poor. Engine boxes eliminated in 1986 in favor of flush cockpit floor with more fishing space. Fiberglass fuel tanks are a problem with today's ethanol-blend gas. MerCruiser 260hp gas engines cruise at 20 knots (about 30 knots top).

Prices Not Provided for Pre-1995 Models

Length	28'6"	Fuel	185/240 gals.
Beam	11'0"	Water	48 gals.
Draft	2'11"	Waste	40 gals.
Weight	11,700#	Hull Type	Deep-V
Clearance	7'10"	Deadrise Aft	23°

Bertram 28 Flybridge Cruiser

1971–94

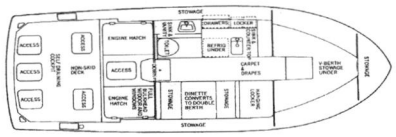

Original Floorplan, 1971–83

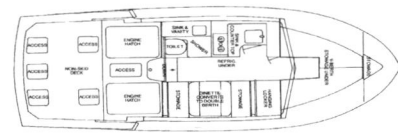

28 II Floorplan, 1983–89

Versatile flybridge cruiser with mega-wide beam, legendary deep-V hull remains the best 28-footer ever built. Huge bi-level cockpit is great for fishing, diving or socializing. Step-down interior with convertible dinette, enclosed head with shower sleeps four adults. Cabin bulkhead extended into cockpit in 1982; fuel capacity increased in 1985; flybridge updated in 1990. Fiberglass fuel tanks are a problem with ethanol-blend gas. Excellent engine access. Twin 230hp gas inboards cruise at 18 knots; 260hp MerCruisers cruise at 20 knots.

Prices Not Provided for Pre-1995 Models

Length	28'6"	Fuel	185/240 gals.
Beam	11'0"	Water	54 gals.
Draft	2'8"	Waste	40 gals.
Weight	12,060#	Hull Type	Deep-V
Clearance	9'4"	Deadrise Aft	23°

Sportfishing Boats

Bertram 28 Moppie

1987–94

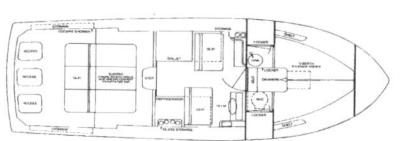

Beamy deep-V express set high standards in her day for engineering excellence, efficient deck layout, outstanding build quality. Huge cockpit for a 28-footer has concealed on-deck galley, convenient engine access. Roomy cabin includes marine head with foldaway cover, sink, V-berth, storage. Excellent rough-water ride. Fit and finish is well above average. Fiberglass fuel tanks are a problem with ethanol-blend gas. MerCruiser 260hp gas engines cruise at 24 knots (30+ knots top).

Prices Not Provided for Pre-1995 Models

Length	28'6"	Fuel	234 gals.
Beam	11'0"	Water	27 gals.
Draft	2'7"	Cockpit	85 sq. ft.
Weight	10,400#	Hull Type	Deep-V
Clearance	7'1"	Deadrise Aft	23°

Bertram 30 Flybridge Cruiser

1984–85

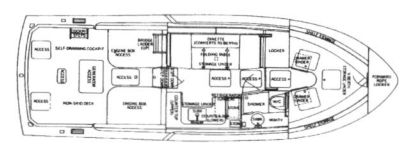

Short-lived cruiser designed to replace the classic Bertram 31 failed to catch on with buyers. Same length as the Bertram 31 but with slightly smaller cockpit dimensions, less transom deadrise (18.5° vs. 23°), improved trolling stability, and a drier ride. Well-appointed cabin offered luxuries undreamed of in the old Bertram 31. Cockpit motor boxes provide convenient seating. Too glitzy for most hardcore anglers; too expensive for others. MerCruiser 340hp gas engines cruise at 22 knots (about 30 knots top).

Prices Not Provided for Pre-1995 Models

Length	30'7"	Fuel	220 gals.
Beam	11'4"	Water	61 gals.
Draft	3'0"	Cockpit	101 sq. ft.
Weight	16,500#	Hull Type	Deep-V
Clearance	8'5"	Deadrise Aft	18.5°

Bertram 30 Moppie

1994–97

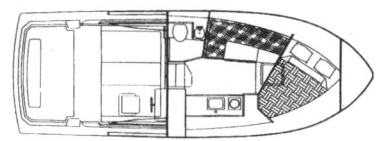

Standard Deck Layout

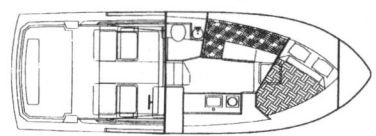

Sportfish Layout

See Page 513 For Value Estimates

Polished 1990s express delivers high-octane mix of great styling, versatile layout, quality construction. Clean lines exude sex appeal even without benefit of integrated swim platform. Three deck plans offered for fishing, cruising, daytime activities. Interior has double berth forward, small galley, convertible dinette, stand-up head. Note good engine access. Transom door and in-deck fishbox were standard. MerCruiser 310hp gas engines cruise at 22 knots (30+ knots top); 300hp Cummins (or Cat) diesels cruise at 26–27 knots.

Length	30'6"	Fuel	275 gals.
Beam	11'3"	Water	30 gals.
Draft	3'1"	Cockpit	64 sq. ft.
Weight	13,200#	Hull Type	Deep-V
Clearance	7'3"	Deadrise Aft	18.5°

Sportfishing Boats

Bertram 33 Sport Fisherman

1979–92

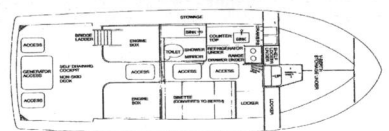

Original Floorplan, 1979–85

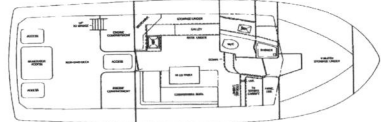

33 II Floorplan, 1986-92

Prices Not Provided for Pre-1995 Models

Popular deep-V sportfisherman combined legendary Bertram construction with big fishing cockpit, well-appointed interior. Highlights include large cockpit with engine boxes, compact flybridge with bench seating forward of helm, roomy interior with teak trim, convertible dinette, optional lower helm. Original floorplan modified in 1986 when salon bulkhead was moved aft several inches to increase cabin space. About 350 were built. Standard 350hp gas engines cruise at 20 knots; 260hp Cat diesels cruise at 23 knots.

Length	33'0"	Fuel, Gas	250/310 gals.
Beam	12'6"	Fuel, Diesel	250 gals.
Draft	3'0"	Water	70 gals.
Weight, Gas	19,603#	Hull Type	Deep-V
Weight, Diesel	21,565#	Deadrise Aft	17°

Bertram 35 Convertible

1970–86

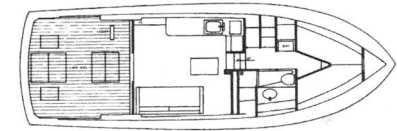

Original Floorplan, 1970–80

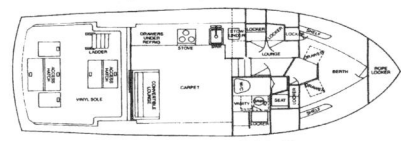

MK II Floorplan, 1981–86

Prices Not Provided for Pre-1995 Models

Classic Bertram convertible with distinctive profile ranks among the best 35-footers ever produced. Large cockpit has space for two anglers and their gear. Single-stateroom/galley-up interior boasts comfortable salon with convertible sofa, head with stall shower, lower-level day berth, copious storage. Teak interior replaced original mica decor in 1984. Original vinyl-over-plywood cockpit sole updated in 1982 with fiberglass sole. Cruise at 20 knots with standard gas engines; 22 knots with optional 320hp Cat diesels.

Length	35'4"	Fuel	285/273 gals.
Beam	13'3"	Water	50/75 gals.
Draft	3'2"	Waste	25 gals.
Weight	22,500#	Hull Type	Deep-V
Clearance	12'6"	Deadrise Aft	19°

Bertram 37 Convertible

1986–93

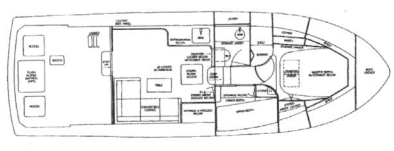

Prices Not Provided for Pre-1995 Models

Feature-rich tournament fisherman is widely viewed as one of the best midsize convertibles of her era. Upscale interior with oak woodwork boasts roomy salon with galley to port, built-in entertainment center, overhead rod storage. Guest cabin has over/under bunks; master stateroom has island berth. Cockpit is fitted with in-sole baitwell, tackle center, freezer. Big flybridge has guest seating forward of helm. Exceptional quality, outstanding handling. Cruise at 22 knots with 375hp Cat diesels; 27 knots with 450hp Detroits.

Length	37'9"	Fuel	473 gals.
Beam	13'3"	Water	100 gals.
Draft	3'9"	Waste	50 gals.
Weight	32,410#	Hull Type	Deep-V
Clearance	12'11"	Deadrise Aft	18°

Sportfishing Boats

Bertram 390 Convertible

2000–06

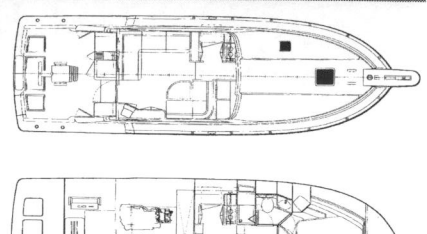

Leading-edge convertible with "new-look" Bertram styling set class standards in her day for performance, luxury. Spacious two-stateroom interior with salon dinette, cherry-wood cabinets compares well with many larger boats. Highlights include large head compartment, built-in entertainment center, roomy guest cabin with twin berths, overhead rod storage in salon. Engineroom—with cockpit access—is on the small side thanks to large forward fuel tank. Volvo 480hp V-drive diesels cruise at 24–25 knots (about 30 knots top).

See Page 514 For Value Estimates

Length w/Pulpit	41'8"	Fuel	459 gals.
Hull Length	39'0"	Water	106 gals.
Beam	13'4"	Waste	37 gals.
Draft	4'0"	Hull Type	Deep-V
Weight	34,398#	Deadrise Aft	18°

Bertram 42 Convertible

1976–87

Standard Floorplan, 1976–80

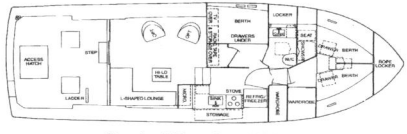

Standard Floorplan, 1983–87

Proven tournament fishing machine with large cockpit, spacious interior needs no introduction to experienced anglers. Two-stateroom floorplan went through several updates over the years—sliding salon doors were replaced with single door in 1981; teak replaced original mica trim in 1982; queen berth became standard in master stateroom in 1983. Note that flybridge was redesigned in 1986. Deep-V hull is noted for exceptional seakeeping abilities. Cruise at 22 knots with 420hp Cummins (or 435hp GM) diesels. Total of 329 were built.

Prices Not Provided for Pre-1995 Models

Length	42'6"	Fuel	488 gals.
Beam	14'10"	Water	150 gals.
Draft	4'0"	Cockpit	108 sq. ft.
Weight	39,400#	Hull Type	Deep-V
Clearance	14'11"	Deadrise Aft	17°

Bertram 43 Convertible

1988–96

Galley-Up Layout, 1988–92

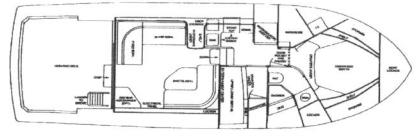

Galley-Down Layout, 1988–92

See Page 514 For Value Estimates

Strong-selling convertible earned solid reputation for top-shelf construction, superb fishability. Offered with several floorplans over the years—two-stateroom, galley-up configurations proved most popular. Huge cockpit, reinforced for fighting chair, features transom door, tackle centers, direct engine room access. Genset was relocated to engine room, cabin windows were slightly restyled in 1994. GM 535hp 6V92s cruise at 23–24 knots (28 knots top); 655hp MTUs (1995–96) will cruise at 26 knots (30+ knots top).

Length	43'4"	Fuel	546 gals.
Beam	14'11"	Water	160 gals.
Draft	4'4"	Cockpit	120 sq. ft.
Weight	41,890#	Hull Type	Deep-V
Clearance	13'5"	Deadrise Aft	17°

Bertram 450 Convertible

2000–09

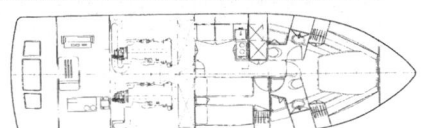
2-Stateroom Floorplan

3-Stateroom Floorplan

Quality-built convertible combines graceful styling with luxury accommodations, excellent performance. Standard two-stateroom interior features space-saving under-counter galley refrigeration, side-by-side berths (rather than over/under bunks) in guest cabin. Three-stateroom, galley-up floorplan became available in 2005. Salon is large for a 45-footer, but cockpit is smaller than competitors. U-shaped settee forward of helm converts to huge sun pad. Cruise at 26 knots with 660hp Cats (30 knots top); 28 knots (32 top) with 800hp MANs.

See Page 514 For Value Estimates

Length w/Pulpit	48'3"	Clearance	13'5"
Hull Length	45'3"	Fuel	618 gals.
Beam	14'11"	Water	159 gals.
Draft	4'4"	Hull Type	Deep-V
Weight	46,305#	Deadrise Aft	18°

Bertram 46 Convertible

1971–87

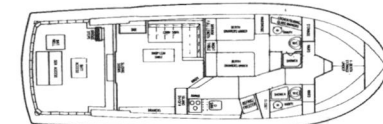
Original Two- Stateroom Layout, 1971–82

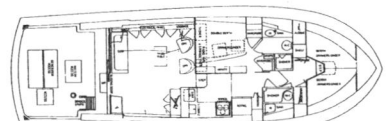
46 II Galley-Down Layout, 1983–85

Legendary fishing machine—dominant in 1970s, early 1980s—is one of the most popular convertible designs ever produced. Principal features include huge fishing cockpit, roomy interior, large bridge, sea-kindly deep-V hull. Sliding salon door replaced double doors in 1981. Fiberglass cockpit sole replaced original Nautilex liner in 1982, same year that teak interior became standard. The 46 III model (1986–87) featured a restyled interior with queen berth forward. GM 435hp engines cruise at 20 knots; 600hp GMs cruise at 25 knots.

Prices Not Provided for Pre-1995 Models

Length	46'6"	Fuel	620/720 gals.
Beam	16'0"	Water	230/246 gals.
Draft	4'6"	Cockpit	117/130 sq. ft.
Weight	44,900#	Hull Type	Deep-V
Clearance	15'6"	Deadrise Aft	19°

Bertram 46 Convertible

1995–97

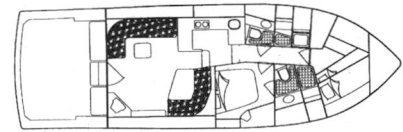
Standard Two-Stateroom Floorplan

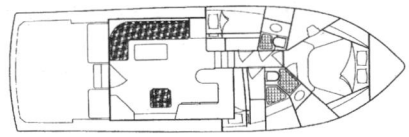
Optional Three-Stateroom Floorplan

Powerful big-game sportfisherman is sleek, luxurious, fast across the water. Drier ride than original Bertram 46 thanks to altered keel, widened chine flats. Standard two-stateroom floorplan features mid-level galley, salon dinette, amidships owner's suite, stall showers in both heads. Three-stateroom layout was optional. Additional features include light oak interior, spacious cockpit with bait-prep center, huge flybridge. Note compact engine room. Cruise at 26 knots (30+ knots top) with GM 735hp engines.

See Page 514 For Value Estimates

Length	46'3"	Water	175 gals.
Beam	15'1"	Cockpit	120 sq. ft.
Draft	4'10"	Clearance	13'5"
Weight	46,100#	Hull Type	Deep-V
Fuel	800 gals.	Deadrise Aft	17.5°

Sportfishing Boats

Bertram 50 Convertible

1987–97

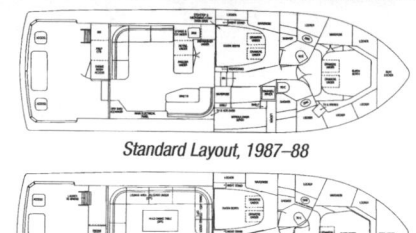

Standard Layout, 1987–88

Standard Layout, 1989–93

See Page 514 For Value Estimates

Legendary tournament machine combined muscular styling with state-of-the-art construction, executive-class accommodations. Several two- and three-stateroom floorplans were offered over the years, each with lavish salon, amidships master with queen berth. Cockpit is among the largest in her class. Updated in 1994 with larger salon windows, restyled flybridge. Considered among the best big-game sportfishing yachts ever built. Cruise at 24 knots with 735hp 8V92s; 26–27 knots with MAN 820hp diesels.

Length	50'0"	Fuel	1,046 gals.
Beam	16'2"	Water	175 gals.
Draft	5'0"	Waste	60 gals.
Weight	56,531#	Hull Type	Deep-V
Clearance	15'9"	Deadrise Aft	17°

Bertram 510 Convertible

2000–Current

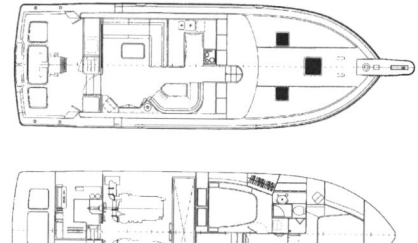

See Page 514 For Value Estimates

Premium sportfishing machine combines Bertram quality with sleek styling, luxurious accommodations. Three-stateroom interior is an impressive display of high-gloss cabinetry, top-shelf furnishings. Large cockpit can accommodate several anglers. Helm is well aft on the bridge to permit inclusion of U-shaped settee/dinette forward. Note control room aft of engine room (for generator, washer/dryer); retractable electronics panel; overhead rod storage in salon. MAN 1,050hp diesels cruise at 30 knots (33 knots top); 1,300 MANs top out at nearly 40 knots.

Length w/Pulpit	54'10"	Clearance	15'6"
Hull Length	51'5"	Fuel	1,040 gals.
Beam	16'2"	Water	185 gals.
Draft	5'0"	Hull Type	Deep-V
Weight	65,489#	Deadrise Aft	18°

Bertram 54 Convertible

1981–92

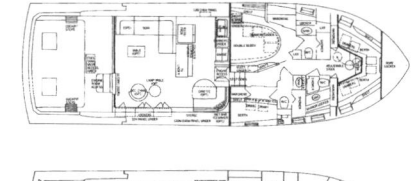

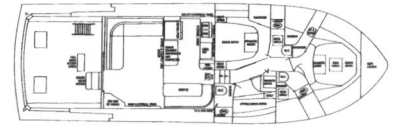

Prices Not Provided for Pre-1995 Models

Proven tournament winner is widely regarded as among best sportfishing yachts of her era. Near perfect blend of design and construction—few production (or custom) boats her size compare when it comes to heavy-weather handling. Deckhouse windshield eliminated in 1986; flybridge restyled and fuel capacity increased in 1987. Several three-stateroom floorplans were offered over the years. Huge cockpit for a 54-footer. Cruise at 24 knots with 800hp 12V71s; 29–30 knots with 1,100hp 12V92s. Total of 177 were built.

Length	54'0"	Fuel	1,200/1,450 gals.
Beam	16'11"	Water	250 gals.
Draft	5'2"	Waste	40 gals.
Weight	74,500#	Hull Type	Deep-V
Clearance	16'8"	Deadrise Aft	17°

Bertram 54 Convertible

1995–2003

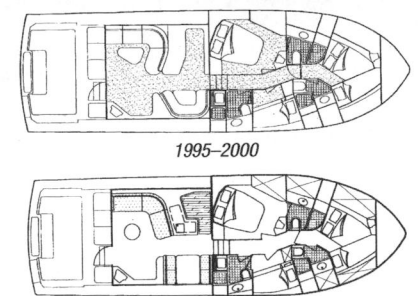

1995–2000

2001–03

See Page 514 For Value Estimates

Updated version of original Bertram 54 Convertible is faster, sleeker, far more luxurious. Three-stateroom interior (updated in 2001) is an impressive display of design and workmanship. Galley and dinette are forward in huge salon; all three heads have separate stall showers. Note that single fuel tank replaced saddle tanks found in original Bertram 54. Full-featured cockpit is ready for tournament-level anglers. Superb open-water performer. GM 1,100hp—or 1,250hp Cat—diesels cruise at 28 knots (32–33 knots top).

Length	54'0"	Fuel	1,453 gals.
Beam	16'11"	Water	250 gals.
Draft	5'2"	Cockpit	144 sq. ft.
Weight	75,400#	Hull Type	Deep-V
Clearance	16'8"	Deadrise Aft	17°

Bertram 570 Convertible

2002–Current

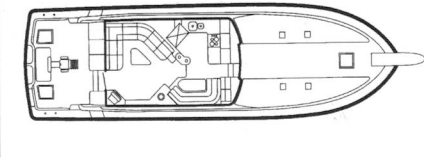

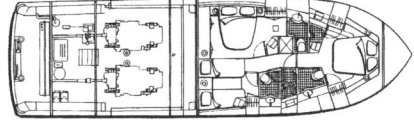

See Page 514 For Value Estimates

State-of-the-art convertible combines sleek styling with great performance, luxurious accommodations. Built on stretched version of the legendary Bertram 54 hull. Three-stateroom, three-head floorplan is arranged with galley and dinette forward on deckhouse level, one step up from spacious salon. Expansive engine room is expertly laid out with good access to all systems. Salon rod locker, washer/dryer are standard. Note huge flybridge with U-shaped lounge seating. Cruise at 30 knots with 1,300hp MANs.

Length w/Pulpit	60'6"	Fuel	1,585 gals.
Hull Length	57'0"	Water	250 gals.
Beam	16'11"	Clearance	15'4"
Draft	5'3"	Hull Type	Deep-V
Weight	84,452#	Deadrise Aft	17°

Bertram 60 Convertible

1990–2005

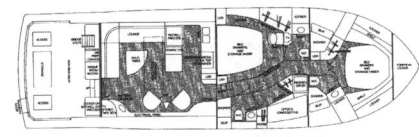

Standard Floorplan, 1990–94

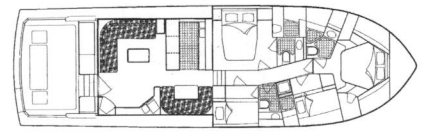

1999–2005

See Page 514 For Value Estimates

Powerful tournament fisherman blends classic Bertram styling with luxury interior, blistering performance. Offered with several floorplans over the years—later models reflect European styling influence of Ferretti Group, Bertram's corporate owner since 1998. Note state-of-the-art helm console, wide-open salon/galley/dinette area, spacious engine room. GM 1,400hp 16V92 diesels cruise at 31 knots; 1,400hp Cats cruise at fast 32 knots (about 36 knots top). Enclosed Bridge model introduced in late 1995.

Length	60'0"	Fuel	1,630 gals.
Beam	16'11"	Water	250 gals.
Draft	5'6"	Cockpit	148 sq. ft.
Weight	93,500#	Hull Type	Modified-V
Clearance	16'8"	Deadrise Aft	17°

Sportfishing Boats

Bertram 630 Convertible

2004–Current

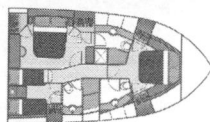

3 Staterooms

4 Staterooms

See Page XXX For Value Estimates514

Fast-action sportfisherman with open or enclosed bridge stays true to Bertram tradition for product excellence. Choice of three or four staterooms and two distinct salon layouts, both with galley, dinette forward. Circular stairway in cockpit is easier to navigate than traditional bridge ladder. (Note inside bridge access in Enclosed Bridge model.) Huge flybridge has state-of-the-art helm, seating for a small crowd. Cockpit is massive; engine room is meticulous. MTU 2,000hp engines cruise at 35 knots (40 knots top).

Length w/Pulpit	66'9"	Fuel	1,849 gals.
Beam	18'1"	Water	251 gals.
Draft	5'3"	Cockpit	160 sq. ft.
Weight	95,609#	Hull Type	Modified-V
Clearance	NA	Deadrise Aft	16°

Black Watch 30 Flybridge

1989–96

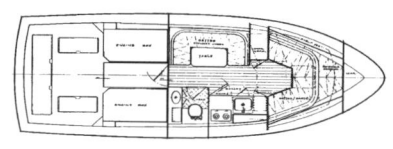

Solid construction, good seakeeping abilities made this compact convertible popular with many East Coast anglers. Cabin is surprisingly roomy for a 30-footer with V-berths forward, convertible dinette, small galley, generous storage. Note well-crafted teak interior trim, teak-and-holly cabin sole. Unique roll-back motorboxes provide good access to engines. Big cockpit lacks transom door. Standard gas engines cruise in the low 20s (30+ knots top); optional 300hp Cummins diesels cruise at 27 knots.

See Page 514 For Value Estimates

Length	30'1"	Fuel	270 gals.
Beam	10'11"	Water	40 gals.
Draft	3'0"	Cockpit	80 sq. ft.
Weight	12,000#	Hull Type	Deep-V
Clearance	9'6"	Deadrise Aft	18°

Black Watch 30 Sportfisherman

1986–95

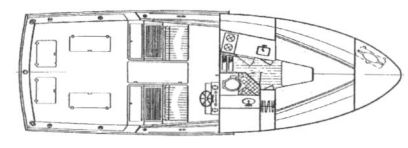

Sporty deep-V fisherman with wide beam gets high marks for solid construction, efficient deck layout. Cockpit is big for a 30-footer with room for a full-size fighting chair. Engine boxes provide easy access to engines while serving as convenient bait-watching seats. Compact cabin contains basic galley with sink and storage, enclosed head with shower, classy teak-and-holly cabin sole, berths for four. Above-average fit and finish. Optional 250hp Cummins (or GM) diesels cruise at 20–22 knots (mid 20s top).

See Page 514 For Value Estimates

Length	30'1"	Fuel	240 gals.
Beam	10'11"	Water	50 gals.
Draft	2'10"	Waste	20 gals.
Weight	9,000#	Hull Type	Deep-V
Clearance	7'0"	Deadrise Aft	18°

Sportfishing Boats

Blackfin 27 Combi

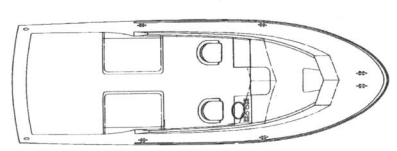

1985–91

Fast-action fishing machine made good on Blackfin promise of bulletproof construction, impressive rough-water performance. Cockpit in outboard models is fitted with raised fish box on starboard side, livewell and small fish box on port side —both with seat cushions. Inboard models have cushioned engine boxes. Well-appointed cuddy with teak trim has marine head with holding tank, sink, V-berth. Most 27 Combis were outboard powered. Twin 270hp gas inboards cruise at 25 knots; 225hp outboards max out at 40 knots.

Prices Not Provided for Pre-1995 Models

Length	27'8"	Fuel	230 gals.
Beam	10'0"	Water	30 gals.
Draft	2'5"	Cockpit	61 sq. ft.
Weight	8,780#	Hull Type	Deep-V
Clearance	7'10"	Deadrise Aft	24°

Blackfin 27 Fisherman

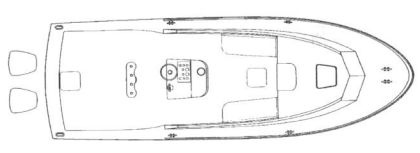

1985–91

Fast-action center console with wide 10-foot beam is stable, fast, built to last. Room at the helm for two pedestal seats or wide leaning post; enough cockpit space for a full-size fishing chair. Large 230-gallon fuel capacity provides true offshore capability. Cuddy cabin features adult-size V-berth, sink, storage shelves, marine toilet. Note twin seats forward of helm console. Deep-V hull delivers one of the best small-boat rides in the business. Twin 200hp Yamahas cruise at 25 knots (about 35 knots top).

Prices Not Provided for Pre-1995 Models

Length	27'9"	Weight, Outboard	7,840#
Beam	10'0"	Fuel	230 gals.
Draft, Inboard	2'5"	Water	30 gals.
Draft, Outboard	2'10"	Hull Type	Deep-V
Weight, Inboard	8,780#	Deadrise Aft	24°

Blackfin 27 Sportsman

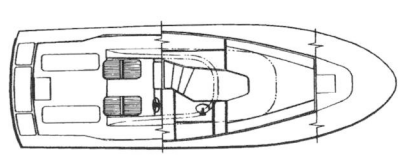

1995–98

Handsome deep-V center console from late 1990s has the look, feel of a custom boat. Spacious bi-level cockpit came standard with large in-deck fishboxes, 35-gallon livewell, centerline transom fishbox. Space at the helm for an array of flush-mounted electronics. No transom door. Originally introduced as outboard-only model, Blackfin offered inboard power beginning in 1996. Yamaha 250hp outboards cruise at 26 knots (36–38 knots top); optional Yanmar 230hp diesel inboards cruise 26–27 knots.

See Page 514 For Value Estimates

Length	27'9"	Weight, Diesel	10,980#
Beam	10'0"	Fuel	240 gals.
Draft, Outboard	1'11"	Water	30 gals.
Draft, Inboard	2'10"	Hull Type	Deep-V
Weight, Gas	9,850#	Deadrise Aft	24°

Sportfishing Boats

Blackfin 29 Combi

1983–98

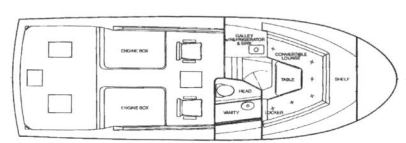

Classic fishing machine combines muscular profile with efficient deck plan, legendary rough-water ride. Teak-trimmed cabin with enclosed head, full galley is perfect for overnighting. Cushioned motorboxes double as bait-watching seats. Cabin hatch is offset to port leaving room at the helm for electronics. Low center of gravity makes for a stable trolling platform. Updated in 1995 with restyled bridgedeck, curved windshield, integral bow pulpit. Twin 320hp gas inboards—or 230hp Volvo diesels—cruise at 24–25 knots.

See Page 514 For Value Estimates

Length w/Pulpit	32'6"	Fuel	250 gals.
Beam	10'6"	Water	30 gals.
Draft	2'10"	Waste	20 gals.
Weight, Dsl	12,120#	Hull Type	Deep-V
Weight, Gas	10,025#	Deadrise Aft	22°

Blackfin 29 Flybridge

1986–99

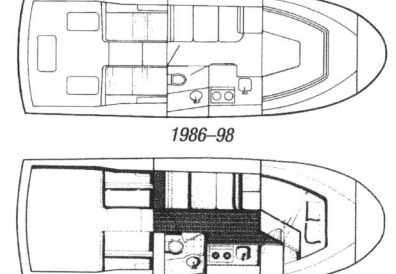

1986–98

1999

Versatile cruiser is among the smallest flybridge models built in recent years. Spacious cockpit has plenty of room for two anglers and their gear. Motorboxes provide excellent engine access, also double as bait-watching seats. Step-down cabin with convertible dinette, enclosed head with shower is surprisingly spacious, well-finished and comfortable. Deep-V hull can take on very rough water. Flybridge updated in 1995 with new seating. Twin 320hp gas inboards cruise at 22 knots; 315hp Cummins diesels cruise at 25 knots.

See Page 514 For Value Estimates

Length w/Pulpit	32'6"	Weight, Diesel	13,604#
Hull Length	29'4"	Fuel	250/263 gals.
Beam	10'6"	Water	50 gals.
Draft	2'6"	Hull Type	Deep-V
Weight, Gas	11,109#	Deadrise Aft	22°

Blackfin 31 Combi

1993–97

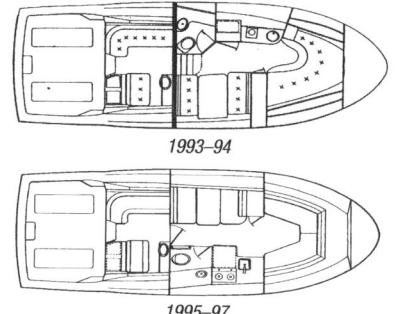

1993–94

1995–97

Proven fishing machine based on popular North Coast 31 (1988–90) meets anglers expectations for stability, fishability, dependability. Roomy cockpit includes lift-out fish/storage boxes, transom door, tackle cabinet, fresh/saltwater washdowns. Entire bridgedeck rises electrically for engine access. Well-appointed ash interior with convertible dinette, full galley, is surprisingly spacious for a 31-footer. Note wide side decks. Standard 320hp gas engines cruise at 20–21 knots (30 knots top); optional 300hp Cat diesels cruise at 23–25 knots.

See Page 514 For Value Estimates

Length w/Pulpit	33'10"	Weight, Diesel	15,500#
Hull Length	30'8"	Fuel	300 gals.
Beam	11'10"	Water	70 gals.
Draft	2'11"	Hull Type	Deep-V
Weight, Gas	13,300#	Deadrise Aft	21°

Sportfishing Boats

Blackfin 33 Combi

1993–98

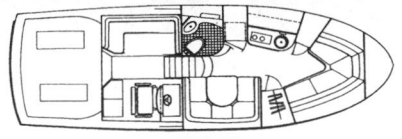

1994–95

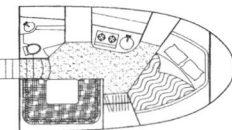

1996–97

Handsome 1990s express with versatile deck plan led the pack in her day among midsize open fisherman. Transom door with gate, insulated in-floor fish/storage boxes, raw-water washdown, power-lift bridgedeck, tackle centers, deluxe L-shaped companion seat, two-person helm seat with icemaker under. Upscale interior with convertible dinette, full galley, head with shower, sleeps four. Note tall windshield, wide side decks. Good engine access. Most were diesel-powered. Volvo 430hp diesels cruise at 28 knots (30+ knots top).

See Page 514 For Value Estimates

Length	32'11"	Fuel	340 gals.
Beam	12'0"	Water	80 gals.
Draft	2'11"	Waste	12 gals.
Weight	19,132#	Hull Type	Deep-V
Clearance	NA	Deadrise Aft	22°

Blackfin 33 Convertible

1990–99

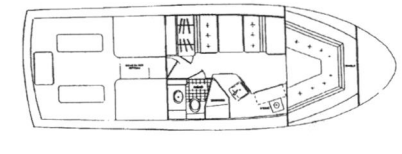

Hard-charging fishboat runs as well as she looks. Deep-V hull delivers exceptional offshore ride; wide 12-foot beam provides trolling-speed stability. Several floorplans were offered over the years, all with berths for four, head with separate stall shower. Flybridge is big for a 33-footer with dash space for extra electronics. Motor boxes provide easy engine access. Lift-out fishboxes, transom door were standard. Crusader 320hp gas engines cruise at 22 knots (30+ knots top); 375hp Cat diesels cruise at 26–27 knots (about 30 top).

See Page 514 For Value Estimates

Length w/Pulpit	36'0"	Weight, Diesel	20,169#
Hull Length	32'11"	Fuel	340 gals.
Beam	12'0"	Water	80 gals.
Draft	2'11"	Hull Type	Deep-V
Weight, Gas	17,645#	Deadrise Aft	22°

Blackfin 38 Combi

1989–98

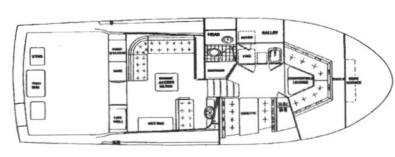

Smooth-running fisherman with wide 14'5" beam offers superior offshore fishability, impressive big-water performance. Bi-level deck layout includes L-shaped lounge on bridgedeck, wide-open cockpit with lift-out fishbox, bait-prep center with sink, livewell, transom door with gate. Comfy, well-finished interior with convertible dinette, stand-up head with shower sleeps four. Most were sold with hardtop. Roomy engine compartment, good range. Detroit 485hp diesels cruise at 25 knots; 550hp Detroits cruise at 26–27 knots.

See Page 514 For Value Estimates

Length	38'3"	Fuel	514 gals.
Beam	14'5"	Water	100 gals.
Draft	3'9"	Waste	25 gals.
Weight	34,170#	Hull Type	Deep-V
Clearance	8'9"	Deadrise Aft	18°

Sportfishing Boats

Blackfin 38 Convertible

1989–98

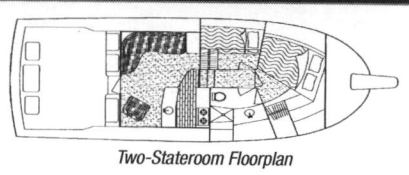

Two-Stateroom Floorplan

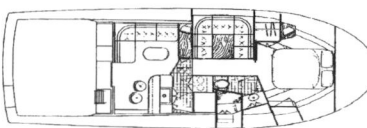

Single Stateroom w/Dinette

See Page 514 For Value Estimates

Heavy-duty convertible made the cut with hardcore anglers willing to pay for Blackfin quality, durability. Big fishing cockpit came standard with in-deck fishbox, bait-rigging center, dual washdowns, tackle drawers, transom door. Offered with two floorplans; standard two-stateroom layout, or alternate single-stateroom plan with full-size dinette in lieu of guest cabin. Wide side decks are a plus. Big engine compartment for a boat this size. Performance: Detroit 550hp (or 565hp) diesels cruise at 25 knots (30+ knots top).

Length w/o Pulpit	38'3"	Fuel	514 gals.
Beam	14'5"	Water	135 gals.
Draft	4'0"	Waste	40 gals.
Weight	35,970#	Hull Type	Deep-V
Clearance	13'0"	Deadrise Aft	18°

Boston Whaler 27 Full Cabin

1984–90

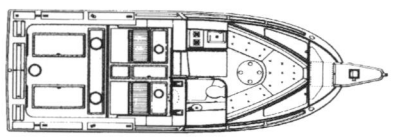

Popular 1980s express with extra-wide beam combines space, fishability in a seaworthy hull. Roomy cockpit came standard with in-deck fishboxes, rod storage, 30-gallon transom livewell. Well-finished cabin with removable dinette, compact galley, full-size head sleeps two. Signature cathedral-sponson hull design insures outstanding trolling-speed stability. Side decks are somewhat narrow. Note unsinkable hull construction. Offered with choice of OMC Sea Drives, various gas inboards or bracket-mounted outboards.

Prices Not Provided for Pre-1995 Models

Length	26'7"	Fuel	170 gals.
Beam	10'0"	Water	30 gals.
Hull Draft	1'9"	Max HP	600
Dry Weight	7,640#	Hull Type	Modified-V
Clearance	NA	Deadrise Aft	18°

Boston Whaler 27 Offshore

1991–98

Floorplan Not Available

Hard-nosed fishboat with workboat profile is tough, roomy, built to last. Highlights include hardtop, in-deck fish/storage boxes, prep-station with cutting boards, tackle storage, livewell, lockable rod lockers. Roomy walk-around cabin houses a full array of galley amenities, two berths, marine head. Additional features include bow pulpit, cockpit bolsters, opening cabin ports, bow seating for three. Note wide walkways, well-placed grabrails, fold-down splashwell, unsinkable construction. Excellent helm visibility. Over 40 knots top with twin 225s.

See Page 514 For Value Estimates

Length	26'7"	Fuel	243 gals.
Beam	10'0"	Water	30 gals.
Draft	1'9"	Max HP	500
Weight	5,800#	Hull Type	Modified-V
Clearance	NA	Deadrise Aft	20°

Boston Whaler 270 Outrage

2003–08

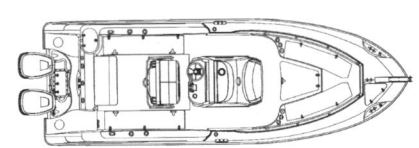

Top-notch fishing machine is unsinkable, trailerable, offshore capable. Standard features include leaning post with cooler, three in-deck storage/fishboxes, lockable head compartment with sink, lighted 23-gallon livewell, bait-prep station with cutting board. Versatile seating includes two bow bench seats, console seat, foldaway transom seat. More rod holders than a 40-footer. Big 200-gallon fuel capacity allows for long cruises. Note flawless finish, unsinkable construction. Twin 225hp Mercury outboards deliver a top speed of about 45 knots.

See Page 514 For Value Estimates

Length	27'0"	Fuel	200 gals.
Beam	8'6"	Water	20 gals.
Hull Draft	1'8"	Max HP	450
Dry Weight	5,160#	Hull Type	Deep-V
Clearance, Top	8'9"	Deadrise Aft	22°

Boston Whaler 275 Conquest

2001–05

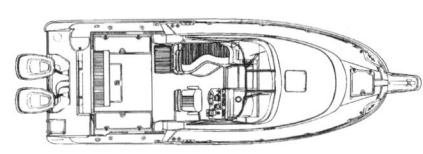

Good-looking Whaler express blurs the line between capable fishing boat, comfortable family cruiser. Lighted livewell, transom door, two in-deck fishboxes, tackle station, removable cooler, folding stern seat, fresh/salt washdowns, cockpit bolsters, transom shower, opening cabin ports, bow pulpit. Well-appointed cabin with midcabin berth, convertible dinette sleeps four. Most were sold with hardtop. Unsinkable hull construction. An expensive boat during her production years. About 40 knots max with 225 Mercs.

See Page 514 For Value Estimates

Length w/Pulpit	28'8"	Fuel	192 gals.
Beam	9'7"	Water	30 gals.
Hull Draft	1'6"	Max HP	500
Dry Weight	6,200#	Hull Type	Deep-V
Clearance w/Hardtop	8'9"	Deadrise Aft	20°

Boston Whaler 28/290 Outrage

1999–2003

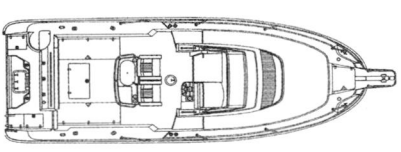

Quality walkaround fisherman combines efficient deck layout with roomy interior, top-notch finish. Fishing amenities include 30-gallon livewell, two in-deck fishboxes, bait-prep station with two sinks, underseat storage/tackle drawers, fresh/salt washdowns, transom door. Well-finished interior with enclosed head, refrigerator sleeps three. Called the 28 Outrage in 1998–2001; 290 Outrage in 2002–03. Unsinkable hull construction. Outstanding range with 296-gallon fuel capacity. About 40 knots top with 225 Mercs.

See Page 514 For Value Estimates

Length w/Pulpit	30'8"	Fuel	296 gals.
Beam	10'4"	Water	40 gals.
Draft, Up	1'8"	Max HP	500
Draft, Down	3'0"	Hull Type	Deep-V
Weight	7,000#	Deadrise Aft	20°

Sportfishing Boats

Boston Whaler 28/295 Conquest

1999–2003

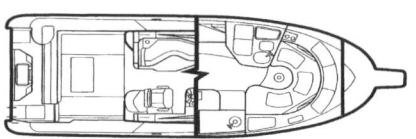

Sturdy offshore express introduced in 1999 pairs durable construction with best-in-class amenities, legendary Whaler quality. Fishing features include 30-gallon livewell, rod racks, coaming bolsters, two in-deck fishboxes, rod holders, built-in tackle drawers. Stern seat folds into transom to free up cockpit space. Well-appointed cabin with dinette/V-berth, teak-and-holly sole, midcabin berth sleeps four. Called 28 Conquest in 1998–2001; 290 Conquest in 2002–03. Excellent range. Unsinkable. Nearly 40 knots top with 225 Mercs.

See Page 514 For Value Estimates

Length w/Pulpit	30'8"	Fuel	296 gals.
Hull Length	28'5"	Water	40 gals.
Beam	10'4"	Max HP	500
Hull Draft	1'8"	Hull Type	Deep-V
Dry Weight	8,500#	Deadrise Aft	20°

Boston Whaler 280 Outrage

2009–Current

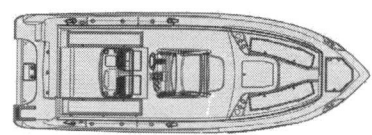

Hardcore center console with integrated hardtop/windshield targets demanding anglers with big checkbooks. Highlights include foldaway transom seat, foldaway, aft-facing amidships seats, lockable rod storage, 40-gallon livewell, two mascerated fishboxes, power windshield vent, 20 rodholders. Note through-stem anchor system and recessed windlass. Slide-out cooler doubles as sun pad filler. Steep transom deadrise makes this the deepest-V Whaler yet. Foam-filled hull is unsinkable. Twin 300hp Mercs top out at close to 50 knots.

See Page 514 For Value Estimates

Length	27'7"	Fuel	200 gals.
Beam	9'4"	Water	28 gals.
Hull Draft	1'8"	Max HP	600
Dry Weight	6,100#	Hull Type	Deep-V
Clearance w/Hardtop	8'10"	Deadrise Aft	23°

Boston Whaler 285 Conquest

2006–Current

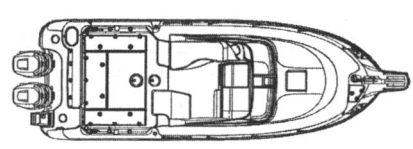

Top-shelf cruiser with graceful lines outclasses most competitors for versatility, comfort, performance. Features include hardtop with rod holders, in-deck fishboxes, dual washdowns, 20-gallon lighted livewell, foldaway stern seat, coaming bolsters, transom shower, bait-prep station with sink, tackle storage. Room at helm for mounting big-screen electronics. Roomy cabin with midcabin aft, enclosed head with shower, convertible dinette sleeps four in comfort. Foam-filled hull is unsinkable. About 40 knots max with 225 Mercs.

See Page 514 For Value Estimates

Length w/Pulpit	30'2"	Fuel	207 gals.
Beam	9'8"	Water	30 gals.
Draft, Drives Up	1'8"	Max HP	450
Draft, Drives Down	3'2"	Hull Type	Deep-V
Hull Weight	6,200#	Deadrise Aft	20°

Sportfishing Boats

Boston Whaler 305 Conquest

2004–Current

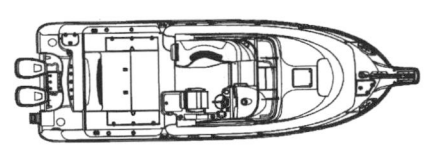

Heavily-built cruiser with executive-class amenities takes express-boat comfort, versatility to the next level. Standard features include hardtop with rod holders, 24-gallon livewell, foldaway stern seat, in-deck fishboxes with pump-outs, bait-prep center, cockpit shower, raw-water washdown, coaming bolsters, flip-up helm seat. Upscale interior with midcabin berth, cherry trim boasts surprisingly large galley, full head with VacuFlush toilet, Corian countertop. Unsinkable hull construction. Popular model. Low 30s top with 225 Mercs.

See Page 514 For Value Estimates

Length w/Pulpit	32'1"	Fuel	300 gals.
Hull Length	30'1"	Water	40 gals.
Beam	10'7"	Max HP	600
Hull Draft	1'8"	Hull Type	Deep-V
Dry Weight	8,500#	Deadrise Aft	20°

Boston Whaler 31 Sportfisherman

1988–91

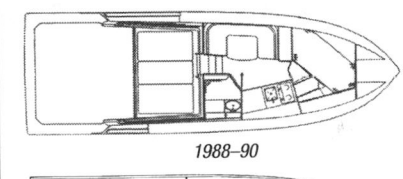

1988–90

1991–92

Popular diesel express introduced in 1988 was a rare departure from Boston Whaler's history of building outboard-only products. Fishing amenities include large insulated fishbox, transom door, livewell, fresh and saltwater washdowns. Cockpit is large enough for full-size chair. Modified-V hull with wide sponsons is stable at trolling speeds, dry in a chop. Cockpit and interior were redesigned in 1991. Bridge lifts electrically for engine access. Cummins 250hp diesels cruise at 20 knots; Cummins 300hp engines cruise at 25 knots.

Prices Not Provided for Pre-1995 Models

Length	31'9"	Fuel	313 gals.
Beam	11'10"	Water	40 gals.
Draft	2'8"	Waste	15 gals.
Weight	13,000#	Hull Type	Modified-V
Clearance	7'6"	Deadrise Aft	20°

Boston Whaler 320 Outrage

2003–Current

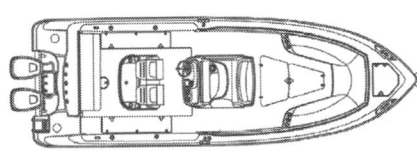

Big-water fishing machine makes the cut with serious anglers demanding the best in quality, fishability. Features include T-top with electronics box, foldaway stern seat, in-deck fishboxes, deluxe helm/passenger seats with flip-up bolsters, anchor windlass. Deluxe bait-prep station includes sink, tackle boxes, cutting board, 45-gallon livewell. Console head has standing headroom, pull-out shower, vertical rod storage. Updates in 2009 include redesigned cockpit, integrated hardtop. Keel pad improves low-speed lift. Over 40 knots top with 250hp Mercs.

See Page 514 For Value Estimates

Length	32'2"	Fuel	300 gals.
Beam	10'2"	Water	40 gals.
Hull Draft	1'10"	Max HP	600
Dry Weight	8,500#	Hull Type	Deep-V
Clearance, Top	9'11"	Deadrise Aft	23°

Sportfishing Boats

Boston Whaler 320 Outrage Cuddy

2006–Current

Classy fish-fighter combines efficient deck layout with forward guest seating, twin-berth cuddy. Highlights include standard hardtop with electronics box, bait-prep station with 45-gallon livewell, in-floor fishboxes, lockable rod storage. Console head compartment boasts standing headroom, vertical rod storage. Well-finished cuddy with rod racks, teak flooring sleeps two. Foam-filled hull is unsinkable. Optional deck suspension system softens the ride in rough seas. Keel pad improves low-speed lift. Over 40 knots top with 250hp Mercs.

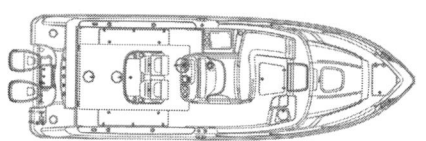

See Page 515 For Value Estimates

Length	32'2"	Fuel	300 gals.
Beam	10'2"	Water	40 gals.
Hull Draft	1'10"	Max HP	600
Dry Weight	9,000#	Hull Type	Deep-V
Clearance, Top	9'10"	Deadrise Aft	20°

Boston Whaler 34 Defiance

1999–2002

Smooth-running inboard express looks good, runs well, sold poorly. Standard features include transom livewell, bait-prep station with sink, tackle drawers, transom door, insulated in-deck fishboxes, centerline helm with flanking settees, underwater exhaust. Well-appointed interior with Corian counters, leather seating sleeps four. Traditional stringer-type hull construction differed from Whaler's signature foam-sandwich construction process. Called the 350 Defiance in 2002. Cat 350 diesels cruise at 24 knots; 420hp Yanmars cruise at 25–26 knots.

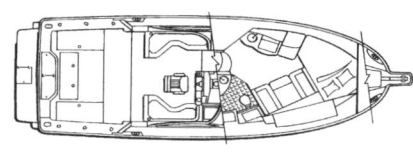

See Page 515 For Value Estimates

Length w/Pulpit	37'6"	Clearance, Top	8'2"
Hull Length	34'6"	Fuel	384 gals.
Beam	13'3"	Water	72 gals.
Draft	2'11"	Hull Type	Deep-V
Weight	19,000#	Deadrise Aft	20°

Boston Whaler 345 Conquest

2007–Current

Premium Whaler express is packed with top-shelf fishing amenities, luxury-class cabin accommodations. Highlights include stylish integrated windshield/hardtop with floodlights, uncluttered cockpit with 40-gallon livewell, bait-prep station, deluxe interior with superb galley, berths for six. Air conditioning, bow thruster, 8kw genset are standard. Note foldaway stern bench seat, macerated in-sole fishboxes. Huge center hatch provides access to tanks, pumps, etc. Triple 250hp Mercury Verados deliver 40+ knots wide open. Unsinkable construction.

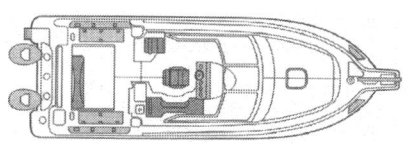

See Page 515 For Value Estimates

Length w/Pulpit	35'11"	Fuel	421 gals.
Beam	11'8"	Water	64 gals.
Hull Draft	1'10"	Max HP	750
Hull Weight	14,200#	Hull Type	Modified-V
Weight w/Engines	20,000#	Deadrise Aft	15°

Boston Whaler 370 Outrage

2010–Current

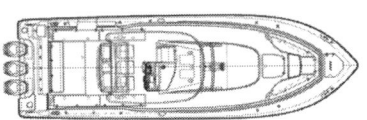

Whaler's largest boat ever delivers high-powered mix of quality construction, versatile layout, stylish design. Highlights include well-designed cockpit with five fishboxes, deluxe leaning post with large livewell, integrated hardtop/windshield with retractable sun shade, full-height cabin with berths for two. Note forward horseshoe-shaped lounge with huge storage locker below. Power helm seat, bow thruster are standard. Foam-filled hull is unsinkable. Triple 300hp Verado outboards cruise easily at 30 knots (40+ top).

Insufficient Resale Data to Assign Values

Length	37'6"	Fuel	450 gals.
Beam	11'6"	Water	60 gals.
Draft, Up	2'0"	Max HP	750
Draft, Down	3'4"	Hull Type	Deep-V
Dry Weight	13,500#	Deadrise Aft	23.5°

Cabo 31 Express

1995–2004

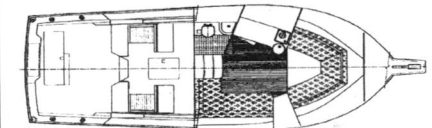

Standard Interior

Offset Double Berth

Premium West Coast express with top-level amenities blends cutting-edge quality with handsome design, unsurpassed fishability. Well-appointed cabin is spacious for a 31-footer with berths for four, full galley, teak-and-holly sole, enclosed head with shower. Cockpit amenities include bait-prep center, transom fishbox, dual washdowns, transom door with gate. Bridgedeck lifts hydraulically for engine access. Attention to detail is as good as it gets. Cat 350hp diesels cruise at 26–27 knots; 420hp Cats cruise at 29–30 knots.

See Page 515 For Value Estimates

Length w/Pulpit	33'2"	Fuel	350 gals.
Hull Length	31'0"	Water	50 gals.
Beam	12'5"	Headroom	6'5"
Draft	3'2"	Hull Type	Modified-V
Weight	15,000#	Deadrise Aft	17.5°

Cabo 32 Express

2005–Current

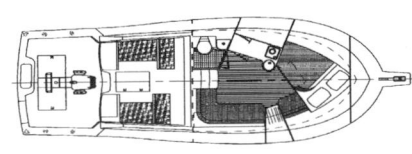

Fast-action battlewagon meets legendary Cabo standards for bold design, premium construction, unsurpassed fishability. Highlights include bait-prep center with tackle storage, 45-gallon transom livewell, transom door with gate, dual washdowns, deluxe helm/passenger seats, large-capacity in-deck fishbox. Bridgedeck lifts for access to meticulous engine room. Upscale interior with offset double berth, convertible lounge sleeps four. A great fishing boat in a small package. Cruise at 28 knots with 480 Yanmar diesels (30+ wide open).

See Page 515 For Value Estimates

Length w/Pulpit	35'0"	Fuel	350 gals.
Hull Length	32'10"	Water	50 gals.
Beam	13'3"	Waste	12 gals.
Draft	2'8"	Hull Type	Modified-V
Weight	19,100#	Deadrise Aft	17.5°

Sportfishing Boats

Cabo 35 Express

1994–Current

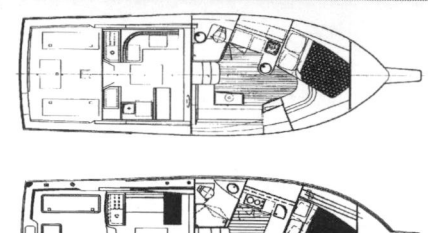

Superior construction, intelligent deck layout, meticulous finish have made this muscular express a modern sportfishing classic. Uncluttered cockpit includes bait-prep center, transom door, two in-deck fish boxes, dual washdowns. Bridgedeck lifts hydraulically for excellent engine access. Single-stateroom floorplan has seen several updates over the years. Hull bottom updated in 2000 with finer entry for softer ride, improved head-sea performance. Cat 375hp diesels cruise in the high 20s; 461hp Cats cruise at 28 knots.

See Page 515 For Value Estimates

Length w/Pulpit	37'6"	Fuel	400 gals.
Hull Length	34'6"	Water	100 gals.
Beam	13'0"	Waste	16 gals.
Draft	2'10"	Hull Type	Modified-V
Weight	20,000#	Deadrise Aft	16°

Cabo 35 Flybridge

1992–Current

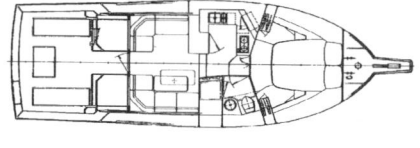

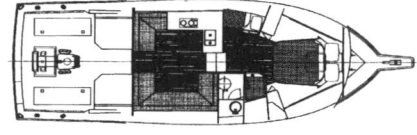

Gold-plated convertible is widely considered among the best small flybridge boats on the market. Features include insulated in-deck fishboxes, 40-gallon transom livewell, tackle center, transom door with gate, dual washdowns. Upscale interior with one or two staterooms is surprisingly open and well-appointed. Large flybridge includes bench seating, single-level controls. Hull modified in 2000 with finer entry for softer ride, improved head-sea performance. Cat 375hp diesels cruise in the mid 20s; 450hp Cats cruise at 28 knots (30+ knots top).

See Page 515 For Value Estimates

Length w/Pulpit	37'6"	Fuel	400 gals.
Hull Length	34'6"	Water	100 gals.
Beam	13'0"	Waste	16 gals.
Draft	2'6"	Hull Type	Modified-V
Weight	20,000#	Deadrise Aft	16°

Cabo 38 Express

2008–Current

No-compromise express combines leading-edge construction with unmatched fishability, deluxe accommodations. Full-size cockpit with 48-gallon transom livewell, bait-prep center, comes standard with reinforcing plate for fighting chair. Upscale interior with recessed halogen lighting, teak cabinetry sleeps 4–6 in comfort. Note horizontal rod storage in stateroom, premium galley appliances, teak-and-holly cabin sole. Entire helm deck lifts for unobstructed access to (gelcoated) engine room. Cruise at 30 knots with 700hp Cat diesels (35 knots top).

See Page 515 For Value Estimates

Length w/Pulpit	40'8"	Fuel	500 gals.
Hull Length	38'0"	Water	95 gals.
Beam	15'1"	Headroom	6'3"
Draft	3'8"	Hull Type	Modified-V
Weight	26,000#	Deadrise Aft	17°

Cabo 38 Flybridge

2008–Current

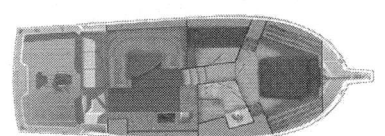

Tournament-class flybridge yacht offers the speed, range, maneuverability hardcore anglers demand. Cockpit is fitted with top-shelf amenities including deluxe bait-prep center, 48-gallon transom livewell, insulated in-deck fish boxes (2), transom door with gate. Posh interior features spacious salon with extended starboard-side galley, satin-finished teak cabinetry, wraparound lounge seating, oversized shower enclosure. Note rod storage locker in guest stateroom. Engine room is a tight fit. Cruise at 30 knots with 800hp MAN diesels.

See Page 515 For Value Estimates

Length w/Pulpit	40'8"	Fuel	475 gals.
Hull Length	38'0"	Water	95 gals.
Beam	15'1"	Headroom	6'3"
Draft	3'9"	Hull Type	Modified-V
Weight	28,000#	Deadrise Aft	17°

Cabo 40 Express

2003–Current

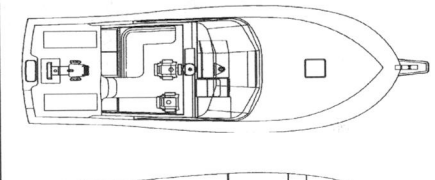

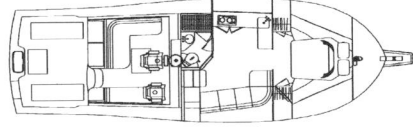

Gold-plated sportfishing machine with impressive feature list is second to none with serious anglers. Best-in-class layout includes spacious bridgedeck with centerline helm, huge cockpit with 45-gallon transom livewell, maxi-volume interior with very large stateroom, premium hardware and furnishings. Note single-lever helm controls, large-capacity fishboxes, tremendous rod storage. Engineroom is a work of art. Cruise at 28–30 knots with 715hp Cats; low to mid 30s with 788hp MANs. Newer models available with Zeus pod drives.

See Page 515 For Value Estimates

Length w/Pulpit	42'10"	Headroom	6'3"
Beam	15'9"	Fuel	550 gals.
Draft	3'5"	Water	95 gals.
Weight	28,000#	Hull Type	Modified-V
Clearance	14'2"	Deadrise Aft	16.5°

Cabo 40 Flybridge

2004–Current

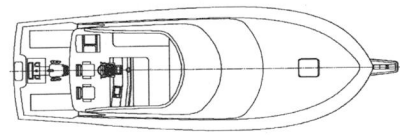

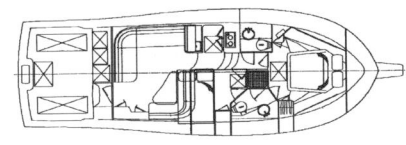

Premium midsize convertible scores with deep-pocket anglers willing to pay for Cabo quality, performance. Cockpit amenities include bait-prep center with sink, 48-gallon transom livewell, large-capacity in-deck fishboxes, transom door with gate. Handsome two-stateroom interior with teak cabinets, leather seating strikes a balance between cruising comfort, sportfish practicality. Good fore and aft sightlines from center helm position. Excellent engine room layout. Cruise at 28–30 knots with 715hp Cats; low to mid 30s with 800hp MANs.

See Page 515 For Value Estimates

Length w/Pulpit	42'10"	Fuel	550 gals.
Hull Length	40'2"	Water	95 gals.
Beam	15'9"	Waste	22 gals.
Draft	3'5"	Hull Type	Modified-V
Weight	32,000#	Deadrise Aft	16.5°

Sportfishing Boats

Cabo 43 Flybridge

2002–Current

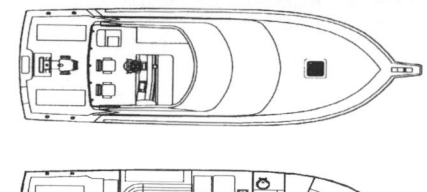

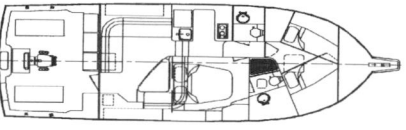

See Page 515 For Value Estimates

Spirited flybridge sportfisher for serious anglers combines small-boat maneuverability, big-boat ride. Large cockpit has all the features expected in a pocket battlewagon. Rich two-stateroom, two-head interior with Corian counters, teak-and-holly sole includes washer/dryer space. Bridge is fitted with large instrument console for big-screen electronics. Note single-lever helm controls, spacious engineroom, near perfect fit and finish. Deep-V hull delivers super-soft ride. Cruise at 30 knots with 800hp MANs (35 knots top).

Length w/Pulpit	46'0"	Clearance	15'9"
Hull Length	43'2"	Fuel	700 gals.
Beam	15'1"	Water	100 gals.
Draft	4'4"	Hull Type	Deep-V
Weight	33,500#	Deadrise Aft	18.5°

Cabo 45 Express

1997–Current

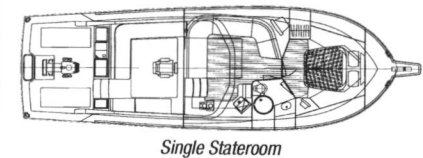

Single Stateroom

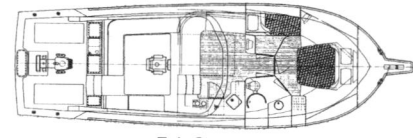

Twin Staterooms

See Page 515 For Value Estimates

Powerful open fishing machine is expensive, fast, loaded with features. Highlights include huge bridgedeck with centerline helm, spacious fish-equipped cockpit, elegant two-stateroom interior with U-shaped salon seating. Note massive, well-finished engine room. Notable features include storage for over 20 rods, electric windshield vent, teak-and-holly cabin sole. Cat 660hp diesels cruise at 25 knots (about 30 knots top); 800hp Cats cruise at 28 knots (32–33 top). Popular boat—over 100 built to date.

Length w/Pulpit	48'1"	Fuel	800 gals.
Hull Length	45'1"	Water	100 gals.
Beam	15'8"	Headroom	6'6"
Draft	4'0"	Hull Type	Modified-V
Weight	33,000#	Deadrise Aft	11.5°

Cabo 47/48 Flybridge

2000–Current

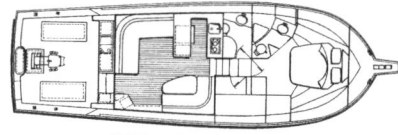

47 Floorplan (2 Staterooms)

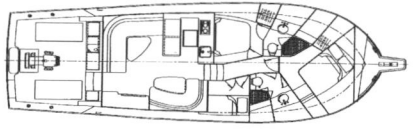

48 Floorplan (3 Staterooms)

See Page 515 For Value Estimates

World-class flybridge fisherman (called Cabo 47 until 2003) is impressive blend of modern design, quality construction, leading-edge performance. Two-stateroom interior of original Cabo 47 left space for a huge cockpit; three-stateroom, two-head layout of Cabo 48 has slightly smaller—but still massive—cockpit. Highlights include state-of-the-art helm layout, teak-and-holly salon floor, spacious engine room. Fit and finish is as good as it gets. Cruise at 28 knots with 800hp MAN engines; 32–33 knots with 1,050hp MANs.

Length w/Pulpit	50'7"	Clearance	16'0"
Hull Length	47'7"	Fuel	1,020 gals.
Beam	15'8"	Water	100 gals.
Draft	4'0"	Hull Type	Modified-V
Weight	45,000#	Deadrise Aft	11.5°

Cabo 52 Express

2006–Current

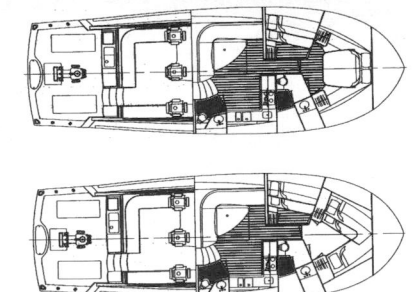

Muscular offshore express introduced in 2006 took Cabo reputation for design, engineering excellence to the next level. Topside highlights include spaciousfishing 110-square-foot cockpit, big 75-gallon transom livewell, deluxe bait-prep center, centerline helm position. Cavernous twin-cabin interior features home-size galley, day head, bulkhead-mounted plasma TV. Walk-in engineroom boasts full 6'8" headroom. Note premium Stidd helm chairs. Cat 1,550hp MAN engines cruise at 33–35 knots (about 40 knots wide open).

See Page 515 For Value Estimates

Length w/Pulpit	54'11"	Fuel	1,400 gals.
Hull Length	52'1"	Water	200 gals.
Beam	17'9"	Headroom	6'8"
Draft	4'11"	Hull Type	Modified-V
Weight	55,950#	Deadrise Aft	16°

Cape Dory 28 Flybridge

1985–94

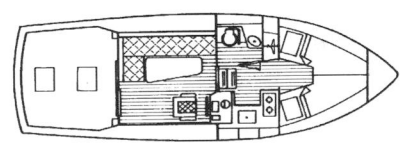

Salty Downeast cruiser with full keel is easily driven, inexpensive to operate, loaded with eye appeal. Space-efficient interior with classy teak-and-holly flooring, teak cabinets includes convertible salon dinette, standard lower helm. Tall flybridge provides great 360-degree visibility. Wide side decks allow secure bow access. Deep keel protects prop from grounding. Excellent engine access. Very popular model. Good fit and finish. Single Volvo 200hp diesel cruises economically at 14 knots (16–17 knots top).

Prices Not Provided for Pre-1995 Models

Length	27'11"	Headroom	6'3"
Beam	9'11"	Fuel	120 gals.
Draft	2'9"	Water	71 gals.
Weight	9,500#	Waste	25 gals.
Clearance	11'2"	Hull Type	Semi-Disp.

Cape Dory 28 Open

1985–94

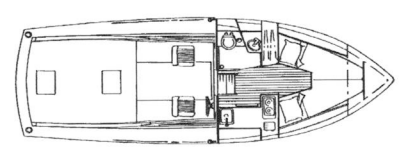

Classic Downeast bass fisherman with full-keel hull combines simple elegance with spacious cockpit, comfortable cabin accommodations. Uncluttered cockpit with flush engine hatch offers lots of room for tackle boxes and rods. Very roomy interior for a 28-foot boat with quality teak joiner work, full galley, generous storage. Note good helm visibility, wide side decks, unusually tall windshield. Truly excellent fit and finish throughout. Cruise at 12–14 knots with single 200hp Volvo diesel (about 16 knots top).

Prices Not Provided for Pre-1995 Models

Length	27'11"	Headroom	6'0"
Beam	9'11"	Fuel	120 gals.
Draft	2'9"	Water	31 gals.
Weight	8,000#	Cockpit	93 sq. ft.
Clearance	8'0"	Hull Type	Semi-Disp.

Sportfishing Boats

Sportfishing Boats

Carolina Classic 28

1994–Current

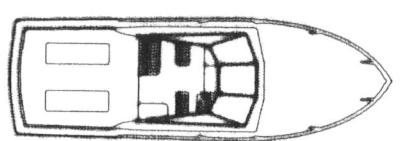

Hard-charging inboard express with wide 10'6" beam is roomy, stable, loaded with big-boat features. Well-appointed cabin with teak trim includes compact galley, large V-berths, enclosed head with shower. Spacious cockpit is fitted with full tackle center, in-deck fishboxes, dual washdowns, transom livewell. Bridgedeck lifts for engine access. Wide side decks are a plus. Terrific rough-water ride. Offered with inboard or jackshaft power. Yanmar 315hp diesels cruise at 28 knots. Volvo 260hp diesels cruise at 25 knots. Impressive resale values.

See Page 515 For Value Estimates

Length	28'5"	Fuel, Diesel	220 gals.
Beam	10'6"	Water	55 gals.
Draft	2'6"	Waste	15 gals.
Weight	15,000#	Hull Type	Deep-V
Fuel, Gas	260 gals.	Deadrise Aft	24°

Carolina Classic 32

2004–Current

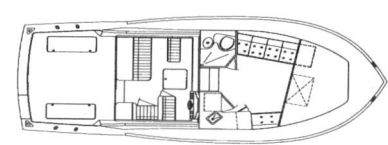

Tournament-class fishing machine with wide 13' beam competes with the big boys in the offshore fishing wars. Flush cockpit includes in-deck fishboxes, full-beam tackle station, secure rod storage, transom door, icebox. Bridgedeck—with seating for six—lifts electrically for full access to large engine compartment. Roomy cabin with teak-and-holly sole features standup head and shower, double berth, seven-foot bunk. Excellent range. About as good as it gets in a midsize fisherman. Cruise in the high 20s (30+ knots top) with Yanmar 440hp diesels.

See Page 516 For Value Estimates

Length	32'0"	Fuel	355 gals.
Beam	13'0"	Water	50 gals.
Draft	3'6"	Cockpit	80 sq. ft.
Weight	26,000#	Hull Type	Deep-V
Clearance	NA	Deadrise Aft	20°

Carolina Classic 35

1998–Current

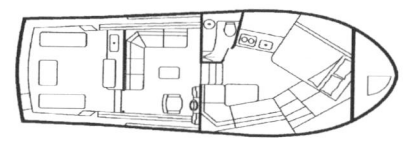

Tournament-grade express with spacious cockpit, upscale cabin appeals to experienced anglers able to afford a top-shelf fishboat. Topside highlights include full-beam rigging center, bait station with sink and icebox, cockpit toerail, in-deck fishboxes. Well-appointed interior—upscale accommodations indeed for a dedicated fishing boat—sleeps four adults. Bridgedeck lifts electrically for engine access. Truly outstanding rough-water ride. Cruise in the mid 20s with 480hp Cummins or Volvo diesels (30+ knots wide open).

See Page 516 For Value Estimates

Length	34'9"	Water	55 gals.
Beam	13'6"	Headroom	6'4"
Draft	3'0"	Clearance	NA
Weight	25,000#	Hull Type	Deep-V
Fuel	435 gals.	Deadrise Aft	18°

Cavileer 48 Convertible

2002–07

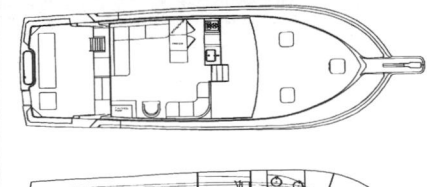

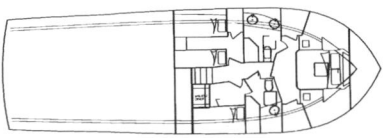

Quality East Coast convertible with graceful styling couples luxury-class accommodations with spirited performance. Three-stateroom interior is arranged with galley and dinette up, two full heads, large owner's suite forward. Well-equipped cockpit comes with huge fishbox, livewell, rigging station, bait freezer. Note spacious, well-finished engineroom. Excellent sightlines from centerline helm position. Modified-V hull incorporates prop pockets to reduce draft. Cruise at 30 knots (mid 30s top) with 800hp Cat—or 700hp GM—diesels.

Insufficient Resale Data to Assign Values

Length w/Pulpit	51'11"	Fuel	850 gals.
Hull Length	48'5"	Water	200 gals.
Beam	16'1"	Waste	55 gals.
Draft	3'8"	Hull Type	Modified-V
Weight	48,500#	Deadrise Aft	12°

Cavileer 53 Convertible

2001–06

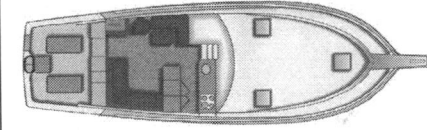

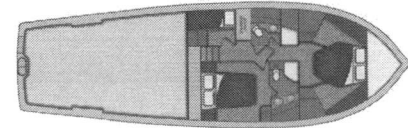

Hard-charging convertible with classic Jersey styling meets class standards for feature-rich accommodations, durable construction. Upscale three-stateroom, three-head interior is an inviting blend of high-gloss woodwork, top-quality furnishings, designer fabrics. Washer/dryer is standard. Cockpit came standard with all the goodies including bait freezer. Massive flybridge is as big as it gets in a 53-footer. Note that bottom was redesigned in 2005 for improved head-sea performance. MTU 825hp diesels cruise in the high 20s (32–33 knots top).

Insufficient Resale Data to Assign Values

Length w/Pulpit	55'6"	Fuel	900 gals.
Hull Length	53'0"	Water	150 gals.
Beam	16'6"	Waste	84 gals.
Draft	4'6"	Hull Type	Modified-V
Weight	52,500#	Deadrise Aft	10°

Century 2900 Walkaround

2001–04

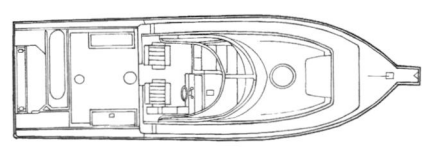

Brawny walkaround fisherman with handsome lines combines space-efficient deck layout with family-friendly cabin, sturdy construction. Roomy mid-berth interior with fully equipped galley, convertible dinette, enclosed head with shower sleeps four. Cockpit amenities include two in-deck fishboxes, 45-gallon transom livewell, rigging station with sink, coaming bolsters, foldaway rear seat, transom door. Cockpit dimensions are on the small side compared with many other 29-footers. Over 40 knots top with Yamaha 250s.

See Page 517 For Value Estimates

Length w/Pulpit	29'4"	Fuel	250 gals.
Beam	9'6"	Water	20 gals.
Draft, Down	2'7"	Max HP	500
Dry Weight	5,300#	Hull Type	Deep-V
Clearance	6'10"	Deadrise Aft	23°

Sportfishing Boats

Century 2900/2901 Center Console

2000–08

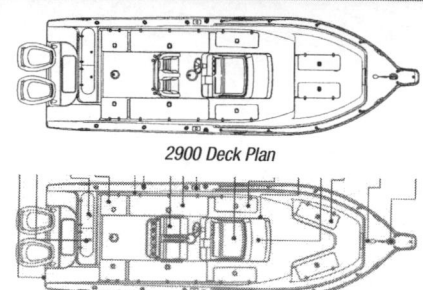

2900 Deck Plan

2901 Deck Plan

See Page 517 For Value Estimates

Well-rigged offshore fishing machine (called 2900 in 2000–06; 2901 in 2007–08) is roomy, fast, built to last. Moderate beam combines generous cockpit space with good stability. Pressure water system, deluxe leaning post, lockable electronics box, insulated fishboxes are standard. Rear seat conceals transom sink with cutting board. Enclosed head has bunk, sink, electric head. Super range with 300-gallon fuel capacity. Twin Yamaha 250hp outboards top out at over 40 knots.

Length	29'4"	Water	22 gals.
Beam	9'6"	Waste	7 gals.
Hull Draft	1'10"	Max HP	600
Hull Weight	7,000#	Hull Type	Deep-V
Fuel	300 gals.	Deadrise Aft	23°

Century 3000 Center Console

1994–99

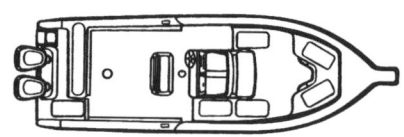

See Page 517 For Value Estimates

Weight-efficient center console with integrated transom meets angler's need for speed, range, durability. Highlights include 32-gallon transom livewell, transom sink with cutting board, bow casting platform, three in-deck fishboxes, pressure water system with shower. Tall windshield offers good protection from wind and spray. Lockable head compartment includes sleeping berth, sink, and shower. Cockpit floor isn't flush—watch the step while going forward. Light boat for her size. Twin 250 Yamahas reach 40+ knots.

Length w/Pulpit	30'11"	Fuel	270 gals.
Hull Length	29'2"	Water	20 gals.
Beam	9'8"	Max HP	500
Draft	2'11"	Hull Type	Deep-V
Dry Weight	5,500#	Deadrise Aft	20°

Century 3000 Sport Cabin

1987–2002

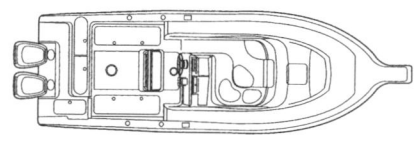

See Page 517 For Value Estimates

Innovative offshore cruiser blends center-console fishability with express-boat amenities, dayboat versatility. Guest-friendly deck layout has L-shaped settee, table and wet bar forward of helm console. Rod lockers, fishboxes, transom sink with cutting board, bow pulpit were standard. Cabin contains dinette/V-berth forward, small galley, enclosed head with shower, amidships double berth aft. Generous fuel capacity affords excellent range. Not much fishing space aft of leaning post. Yamaha 240s deliver 40+ knots max.

Length w/Pulpit	30'11"	Fuel	270 gals.
Hull Length	29'2"	Water	20 gals.
Beam	9'10"	Max HP	500
Draft	2'11"	Hull Type	Deep-V
Dry Weight	6,800#	Deadrise Aft	20°

Sportfishing Boats

Century 3100/3200 Center Console

1999–2009

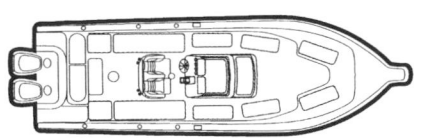

Big center console combines agile handling with excellent range, impressive rough-water performance. Cockpit is among the largest in class. Forward seating converts to optional dinette. Standard features include huge 62-gallon baitwell, in-floor fishboxes (4), lockable electronics box, leaning post with backrest & cooler, lockable rod storage, sink with cutting board. Head compartment has bunk, sink, storage. Marketed as 3100 Center Console in 1999–2000. Biggest center console ever built by Century. Tops 40 knots with 250hp Yamahas.

See Page 517 For Value Estimates

Length w/Pulpit	32'6"	Fuel	300 gals.
Beam	10'6"	Water	30 gals.
Draft, Up	1'8"	Max HP	700
Dry Weight	8,500#	Hull Type	Deep-V
Clearance, Top	9'6"	Deadrise Aft	23°

Century 3200 Walkaround

2001–07

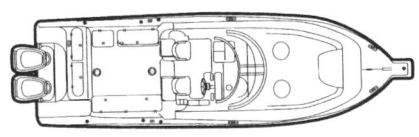

Multipurpose walkaround with deluxe cabin accommodations is ideal for extended fishing trips. Roomy midcabin interior features full galley with pullout pantry and microwave, enclosed stand-up head with shower, convertible dinette. Transom sink with cutting board, cockpit bolsters, fresh/saltwater washdowns, tilt steering were standard. Rear seat conceals 62-gallon aerated livewell. Note slick lift-out tackle box, port/starboard fuel fills, bow seating. A seriously versatile boat. Over 40 knots top with Yamaha 250s.

See Page 517 For Value Estimates

Length w/Pulpit	32'6"	Water	30 gals.
Beam	10'6"	Waste	8 gals.
Draft, Engines Down	3'4"	Max HP	600
Dry Weight	9,400#	Hull Type	Deep-V
Fuel	300 gals.	Deadrise Aft	23°

Cheoy Lee 50 Sportfisherman

1987–90

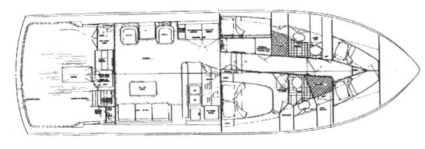

Replacement model for Cheoy Lee 48 Sport Yacht (1980–86) features greater beam, a third stateroom, much improved styling. Teak-paneled interior boasts well-planned galley area, two large heads, comfortable (if Spartan) salon with fixed table. Large fishing cockpit came standard with tackle center, freezer. Airex cored hull results in a surprisingly weight-efficient boat. Flybridge is large for a 50-footer with seating for eight. Twin 735hp 8V92 diesels cruise at 25–26 knots; later models with twin 800hp Cats cruise at 26–28 knots.

Prices Not Provided for Pre-1995 Models

Length	50'8"	Fuel	1,000 gals.
Beam	16'1"	Water	200 gals.
Draft	3'2"	Cockpit	115 sq. ft.
Weight	36,000#	Hull Type	Modified-V
Clearance	14'0"	Deadrise Aft	NA

Sportfishing Boats

Cheoy Lee 58 Sportfisherman

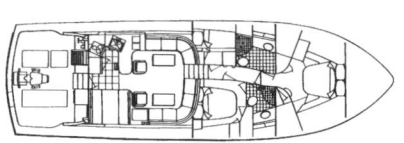

1986–91

Luxury-class convertible with fully cored hull lured 1980s anglers with an eye for cutting-edge styling. Wide beam allows for very expansive interior with three double staterooms, two large heads. Innovative salon layout has wraparound seating forward, galley and dinette aft. Additional features include well-equipped fishing cockpit, roomy bridge with circular lounge seating forward of helm, side-dumping exhausts. Offered with choice of teak or ash interior woodwork. GM 900hp 12V71 diesels cruise at 25 knots (about 28 knots top).

Prices Not Provided for Pre-1995 Models

Length	58'5"	Fuel	1,000 gals.
Beam	17'10"	Water	150 gals.
Draft	4'3"	Cockpit	138 sq. ft.
Weight	58,500#	Hull Type	Modified-V
Clearance	15'10"	Deadrise Aft	NA

Chris Craft 315 Commander

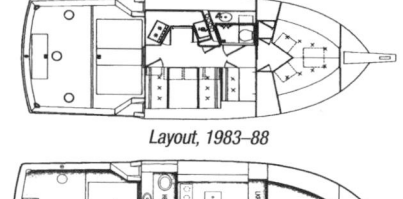

1983–90

Layout, 1983–88

Layout, 1989–90

Practical flybridge fisherman combines spacious cockpit with all-purpose interior, rugged construction. Wide 11'10" beam allows for roomy interior with convertible dinette, complete galley, overhead rod storage, two hanging lockers. Update in 1988 replaced bi-level cockpit with engine boxes to allow full-height cabin door. Forward windows were eliminated in late models. Note wide side decks, roomy flybridge. Twin 330hp gas engines cruise at 20 knots (about 28 knots top). Low-deadrise hull can be a stiff ride in a chop.

Prices Not Provided for Pre-1995 Models

Length	30'7"	Fuel	250 gals.
Beam	11'10"	Water	40 gals.
Draft	2'8"	Waste	20 gals.
Weight	11,400#	Hull Type	Modified-V
Clearance	9'6"	Deadrise Aft	5°

Chris Craft 360 Commander

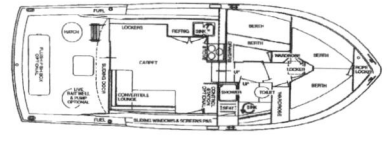

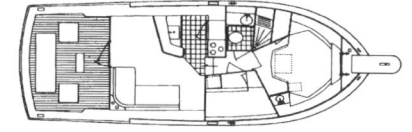

1973–86

Best-selling convertible matched Chris Craft promise of solid construction, comfortable accommodations, big-water fishability. Several two-stateroom interiors were offered over the years; lower helm was a popular option. Flush cockpit came with in-deck fishbox, rod storage, but no transom door. Increased fuel capacity in 1983, restyled deckhouse in 1985. Low-deadrise hull can be a stiff ride in a chop. Cruise at 16 knots with 330hp gas engines; 20+ with 300 Cat (or 320 Cummins) diesels.

Prices Not Provided for Pre-1995 Models

Length	36'0"	Fuel	300/400 gals.
Beam	13'0"	Water	75/100 gals.
Draft	3'2"	Waste	25 gals.
Weight	22,600#	Hull Type	Modified-V
Clearance	11'11"	Deadrise Aft	NA

Chris Craft 382/392 Convertible

1985–90

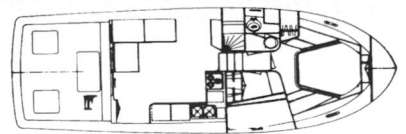

Two-Stateroom Plan

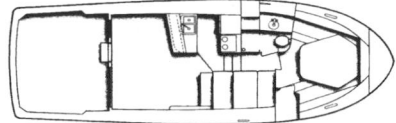

Single-Stateroom Plan

Sporty 1980s convertible is an updated version of the old Uniflite 38 Convertible (1977–84) with subtle styling, decor updates. Offered with single-stateroom/dinette floorplan or two-stateroom layout, both with teak trim, large head with stall shower, island bed in master stateroom. Lower helm was a popular option. Cockpit includes tackle centers, transom door, rod storage. Big flybridge for a 38-footer. A popular model for Chris Craft. Cruise at 17–18 knots with 340hp gas engines; 23–24 knots with 375hp Cat diesels.

Prices Not Provided for Pre-1995 Models

Length Overall	38'0"	Fuel	350 gals.
Length WL	33'0"	Water	100 gals.
Beam	13'11"	Waste	40 gals.
Draft	3'9"	Hull Type	Modified-V
Weight	28,000#	Deadrise Aft	12°

Chris Craft 422 Commander

1973–90

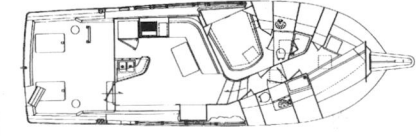

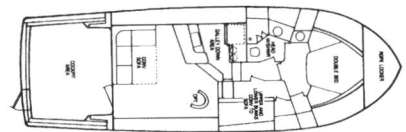

Classic Chris Craft convertible introduced in mid-1970s hit the right buttons with cruisers and anglers alike. Numerous updates over the years including complete exterior redesign in 1985. Principal features include large fishing cockpit with transom door, roomy cabin accommodations, stable modified-V hull. Noted for speed (back when 25 knots was fast) and toughness. Offered with several interior floorplans. GM 425 8V71s—or later models with 485hp 6-71s—cruise in the mid 20s (26–27 knots top).

Prices Not Provided for Pre-1995 Models

Length	42'4"	Fuel	400/525 gals.
Beam	14'0"	Water	125 gals.
Draft	3'11"	Cockpit	110 sq. ft.
Weight	34,000#	Hull Type	Modified-V
Clearance	13'7"	Deadrise Aft	8°

Chris Craft 482 Convertible

1985–88

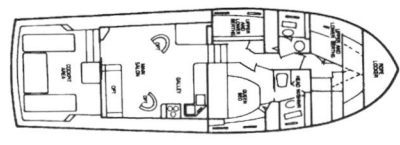

Revised version of earlier Uniflite 48 Convertible (1980–84) offered numerous exterior styling changes, interior decor upgrades. Spacious three-stateroom, two-head layout features built-in salon entertainment center, rich teak joinery, large master suite with walkaround queen bed. Most were sold with solid front windshield. Washer/dryer can be fitted in bow stateroom. Note wide side decks, uncluttered cockpit, spacious flybridge. Considered a fast boat in her day, standard 600hp GM diesels cruise at 25 knots (about 28 knots top).

Prices Not Provided for Pre-1995 Models

Length	48'10"	Fuel	780 gals.
Beam	15'9"	Water	200 gals.
Draft	4'9"	Cockpit	133 sq. ft.
Weight	28,000#	Hull Type	Modified-V
Clearance	13'9"	Deadrise Aft	14°

Sportfishing Boats

Cobia 250/260/270 Walkaround

1997–2007

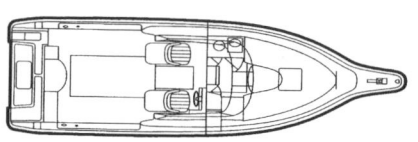

Affordably priced trailerable fisherman with efficient deck layout, compact cabin was a Cobia best-seller for several years. Roomy cockpit came standard with 25-gallon livewell, insulated fishbox, aft cutting boards, rod storage. Generic cabin with near standing headroom includes V-berth, dinette table, mini-galley, rod storage, head with portable toilet. Sold as the Cobia 250 Walkaround in 1997; 260 Walkaround in 1998–2000; 270 Walkaround in 2001–07. Twin 150hp Yamaha outboards top out at close to 40 knots.

See Page 518 For Value Estimates

Length w/Pulpit	27'6"	Fuel	175 gals.
Beam	8'6"	Water	12 gals.
Hull Draft	1'8"	Max HP	400
Dry Weight	5,000#	Hull Type	Deep-V
Clearance	8'8"	Deadrise Aft	20°

Cobia 254/264/274 Center Console

1997–2002

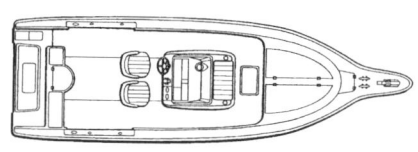

Well-mannered center console with trailerable 8'6" beam gave savvy anglers good value for the money. Highlights include single-level cockpit with transom livewell, four insulated fishboxes, cockpit bolsters, console head compartment, lockable electronics box, bow pulpit, anchor locker. Compact helm has limited space for electronics. Marketed as Cobia 254 in 1997; 264 in 1998–2000; 274 in 2001–02. Note that all-new Cobia 274 model was introduced in 2003. Over 40 knots top with Yamaha 200s.

See Page 518 For Value Estimates

Length w/Pulpit	27'6"	Fuel	175 gals.
Beam	8'6"	Water	7 gals.
Hull Draft	1'3"	Max HP	450
Dry Weight	3,900#	Hull Type	Deep-V
Clearance, T-Top	8'10"	Deadrise Aft	20°

Cobia 274 Center Console

2003–07

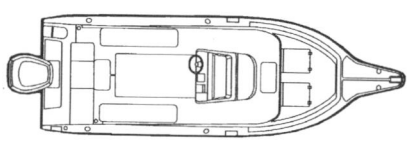

Updated version of earlier Cobia 274 Center Console (2001–02) offers improved deck layout, better range, redesigned helm. Standard fishing amenities include oval 42-gallon transom livewell, in-deck fishboxes (2), leaning post, rear cutting boards (2), cockpit bolsters, raw-water washdown, transom door, bow casting deck. Console head compartment has opening port for ventilation. Cockpit toerail is a plus. Rear seat must be removed to use livewell. Tops out around 40 knots with 200hp outboards.

See Page 518 For Value Estimates

Length w/Pulpit	27'6"	Fuel	200 gals.
Beam	8'6"	Water	7 gals.
Hull Draft	1'6"	Max HP	500
Dry Weight	4,500#	Hull Type	Deep-V
Load Capacity	3,900#	Deadrise Aft	20°

Cobia 312 Sport Cabin

2003–07

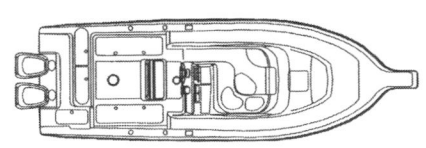

Dual-purpose family fisherman combines center-console versatility with express-boat comfort, walkaround practicality. Wide-open deck layout has lounge seating forward of helm, bench seating aft. Highlights include console head compartment with shower, 28-gallon transom livewell, in-deck fish/storage boxes, leaning post with cooler, transom sink with cutting board, raw-water washdown. Compact cabin has lounge seating forward, sink, refrigerator. Limited fishing space aft of helm seat. Over 40 knots top with Yamaha 225s.

See Page 518 For Value Estimates

Length w/Pulpit	30'11"	Fuel	270 gals.
Beam	9'10"	Water	20 gals.
Hull Draft	17"	Max HP	600
Dry Weight	7,300#	Hull Type	Deep-V
Clearance, Top	8'5"	Deadrise Aft	20°

Cobia 314 Center Console

2003–07

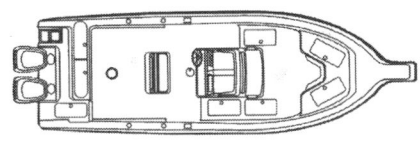

Muscular sportfishing machine—Cobia's largest boat ever—delivers enticing mix of brawny construction, big-water fishability. Features include leaning post with rod holders, cockpit bolsters, forward console seat, bow storage lockers, tackle storage, transom shower. Rear seat lifts to reveal 32-gallon livewell, bait-prep station with sink & cutting board. Walk-in console has marine head, sink, sleeping berth, opening port. Hull was modified in 2006 to carry heavier 4-stroke outboards. Yamaha 250s top out at 45 knots.

See Page 518 For Value Estimates

Length w/Pulpit	30'11"	Fuel	270 gals.
Beam	9'10"	Water	20 gals.
Draft, Engnes Up	1'5"	Max HP	600
Draft, Engines Down	2'10"	Hull Type	Deep-V
Dry Weight	7,300#	Deadrise Aft	20°

Contender 27 Open

1995–2007

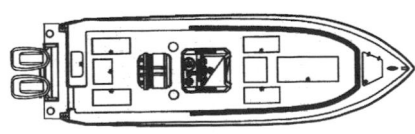

Semicustom fishing machine outguns most competitors for quality, performance, resale values. Highlights include 50-gallon round livewell, 140-gal. forward fish box, 76-gal. aft fish box, in-floor rod lockers, center storage locker, lockable electronics box, walk-in head compartment, transom door. Recessed bow rail prevents snagged lines. Slender deep-V hull delivers legendary big-water ride. Exemplary finish. Expensive. Twin 200hp Yamaha outboards reach a top speed of around 45 knots.

See Page 518 For Value Estimates

Length Overall	30'0"	Fuel	210 gals.
Beam	8'10"	Water	15 gals.
Hull Draft	18"	MaxHP	500
Dry Weight	4,950#	Hull Type	Deep-V
Clearance	NA	Deadrise Aft	24.5°

Sportfishing Boats

Contender 27T

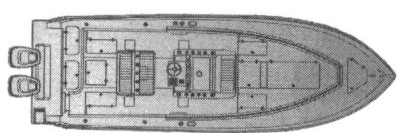

2008–Current

Next-generation Contender 27-footer with wide beam, increased fuel capacity blends quality construction with spirited performance, tournament-class fishability. Expansive single-level cockpit features four insulated in-deck fish boxes (two forward, two aft) forward in-floor rod storage, twin 40-gallon transom livewells, walk-in console with head compartment, built-in forward seat. Note recessed bow handrail, standard K-Plane trim tabs. Designed to handle the weight of today's 4-stroke outboards. No lightweight, construction and finish are to very high standards.

Insufficient Resale Data to Assign Values

Length Overall	29'8"	Fuel	265 gals.
Beam	9'6"	Water	15 gals.
Hull Draft	23"	MaxHP	600
Dry Weight	5,450#	Hull Type	Deep-V
Clearance	NA	Deadrise Aft	24.5°

Contender 31 Fish Around

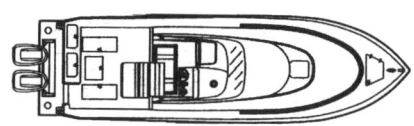

1998–Current

Compelling center console/walkaround hybrid combines 360-degree fishability with well-appointed cabin, top-shelf amenities. Features include insulated in-deck fish-boxes, 40-gallon transom livewell, bait-prep station, forward in-deck rod lockers (port & stbd), bow seat, transom door, fold-away rear seat, recessed bow rail, integral dive platform, anchor locker. Wide walkways make getting around easy. Exemplary finish, near flawless gelcoat. Outstanding open-water performance. About 50 knots top with twin 250s.

Insufficient Resale Data to Assign Values

Length	32'6"	Fuel	245 gals.
Beam	9'4"	Water	40 gals.
Hull Draft	1'6"	Max HP	600
Dry Weight	6,000#	Hull Type	Deep-V
Clearance	NA	Deadrise Aft	24.5°

Contender 31 Open

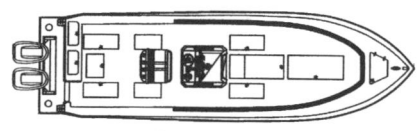

1995–2007

Semicustom fishing machine with high-performance hull, best-in-class construction puts upscale anglers in the winner's circle. Standard fishing features include raised livewell, walk-thru transom, leaning post with tackle center, two large-capacity forward fishboxes, two aft fishboxes. Single-level cockpit is easier to navigate than competitive boats with bow casting platforms. Slender deep-V hull delivers a legendary rough-water ride. As good as it gets in a 31-foot center console. Over 50 knots top with 250hp Yamahas.

See Page 518 For Value Estimates

Length	31'3"	Fuel	240 gals.
Beam	9'4"	Water	NA
Hull Draft	1'6"	Max HP	500
Dry Weight	3,500#	Hull Type	Deep-V
Weight w/Engines	5,500#	Deadrise Aft	24.5°

Contender 31T

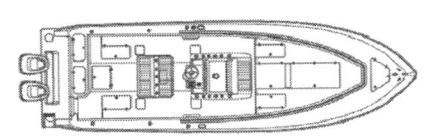

2008–Current

Hard-hitting thoroughbred couples premium construction with cutting-edge, full-bore performance. Design highlights include single-level deck, beefy console with walk-in head, in-deck fishboxes fore and aft, twin 40-gallon transom livewells, lockable rod storage, lockable electronics storage, removable rear bench seat, K-plane trim tabs. More storage than many boats her size. Note cushioned console seat, over-built T-top, mirror-glass gelcoat. About 50 knots max with twin Yamaha 250s.

Insufficient Resale Data to Assign Values

Length	32'7"	Fuel	310 gals.
Beam	9'8"	Water	NA
Hull Draft	23"	Max HP	700
Dry Weight	5,850#	Hull Type	Deep-V
Weight, Loaded	11,560#	Deadrise Aft	24.5°

Contender 33T

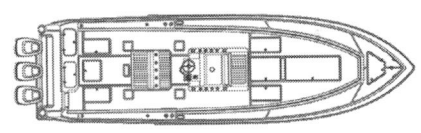

2006–Current

Deluxe tournament fisherman capable of handling triple 350s is slim, sleek, built for speed. High-performance hull with walk-in console boasts spacious, single-level deck layout with twin transom livewells. Tremendous storage capacity including 208-gallon insulated fishbox forward, 115-gallon box aft. Note clever lift-up console seat, stylish helm pod. Optional below-deck livewells make it possible to house a total of four wells. More freeboard than previous Contender models. Triple 250s deliver 50+ knots wide open.

v

Length	34'5"	Fuel	400 gals.
Beam	9'8"	Water	NA
Hull Draft	24"	Max HP	1,050
Dry Weight	6,600#	Hull Type	Deep-V
Weight, Loaded	13,500#	Deadrise Aft	24.5°

Contender 35 Side Console

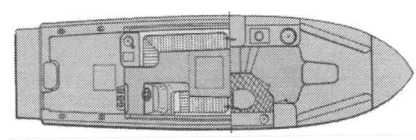

1993–Current

Sleek tournament winner with offset console, raised cuddy combines signature Contender quality with spirited performance, proven fishability. Notable features include 38-gallon transom livewell, fully integrated transom, lift-out fishbox, lounge seating opposite helm, forward console seat. Well-appointed cabin with full galley, enclosed head and shower, sleeps four. With full-width bridgedeck, bow access is a matter of climbing over the windshield—not so easy. Twin Yamaha 250s top out around 45 knots.

Insufficient Resale Data to Assign Values

Length	35'2"	Fuel	340 gals.
Beam	10'0"	Water	40 gals.
Hull Draft	24"	Max HP	750
Dry Weight	7,500#	Hull Type	Deep-V
Clearance	NA	Deadrise Aft	24.5°

Sportfishing Boats

Contender 35 Express

1989–06

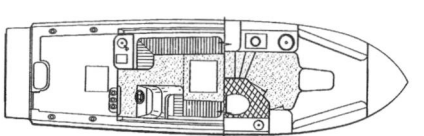

Fast-action express with integrated transom, side-console deck layout combines hardcore fishability with signature Contender ride. Raised 38 gallon livewell, spacious cockpit with lift-out in-deck fishbox, lockable electronics storage, aft-facing jump seats, L-shaped settee with bait and tackle station, transom door. Well-appointed cabin with full galley, stand-up head with shower, teak and holly sole, sleeps four. Note cavernous storage area below helm and guest seating area. Outstanding finish. Over 50 knots top with triple 250s.

Insufficient Resale Data to Assign Values

Length	35'0'	Fuel	340 gals.
Beam	10'0"	Water	45 gals.
Hull Draft	2'0"	Max HP	750
Dry Weight	5,500#	Hull Type	Deep-V
Clearance	NA	Deadrise Aft	24.5°

Contender 36 Cuddy

2003–Current

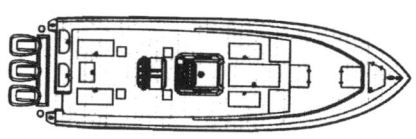

Leading-edge fishing machine with triple-outboard power takes Contender performance to the next level. Essentially a custom boat—no two are alike. Standard features include dual 50-gallon livewells, generous fishbox capacity, transom livewell, generous rod storage. Cabin has oversized V-berth, storage locker. Additional features include Kiekhaefer trim tabs, dual hydraulic steering, recessed bow rail. Superb finish, near-flawless gelcoat. Triple Yamaha 250 outboards deliver a top speed in the neighborhood of 50 knots.

Insufficient Resale Data to Assign Values

Length Overall	36'3"	Fuel, Opt.	600 gals.
Beam	10'0"	Water	45 gals.
Hull Draft	24"	Max HP	1,050
Dry Weight	7,050#	Hull Type	Deep-V
Fuel, Std.	410 gals.	Deadrise Aft	24.5

Contender 36 Open

2001–07

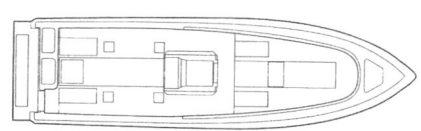

Feature-rich center console designed for triple-engine power delivers high-octane performance, no-excuses fishability. Notable features include dual 50-gallon transom livewells, transom door, step-down storage/head compartment, belowdecks rod lockers, four insulated fishboxes. Optional coffin box forward can be raised electrically for access to huge storage area beneath. Exemplary finish, flawless gelcoat. Deep-V can endure serious offshore punishment. Triple 250hp Yamaha outboards top out at close to 50 knots.

See Page 518 For Value Estimates

Length	36'2"	Fuel, Opt.	600 gals.
Beam	10'0"	Water	45 gals.
Hull Draft	1'6"	Max HP	1050
Dry Weight	6,000#	Hull Type	Deep-V
Fuel, Std.	420 gals.	Deadrise Aft	24.5

Sportfishing Boats

Davis 47 Flybridge SF

1986–91

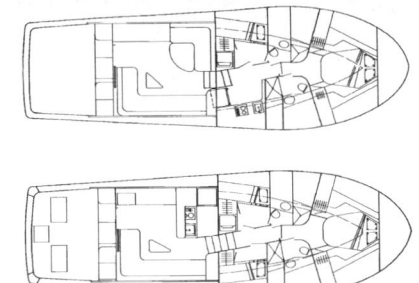

High-end Carolina convertible made good on promise of semicustom quality, tournament-class performance, big-water capability. Offered with several two- and three-stateroom floorplans, all with handcrafted teak cabinetry, premium furnishings, exceptional fit and finish. Notable features include roomy cockpit with engine room access, single-lever helm controls, wide side decks. GM 735hp diesels cruise at 24 knots; 820hp MANs cruise at 27–28 knots. Note 1990 fuel increase. Total of 88 built, the first 6 with fully cored hulls.

Prices Not Provided for Pre-1995 Models

Length	47'0"	Fuel	750/840 gals.
Beam	16'0"	Water	150 gals.
Draft	4'0"	Waste	50 gals.
Weight	45,000#	Hull Type	Modified-V
Clearance	12'10"	Deadrise Aft	14°

Davis 61 Flybridge SF

1985–93

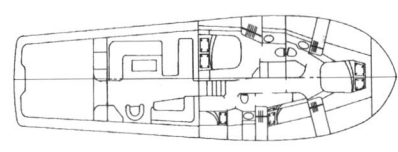

Proven big-water sportfisherman boasts world-class reputation for quality construction, exceptional head-sea performance. Standard four-stateroom interior with combined salon/galley/dinette features amidships owner's suite, premium furnishings, handcrafted teak joinery. Massive 185-square-foot fishing cockpit with teak sole is among the largest in her class. Note huge bridge with Panish controls, pop-up electronics display. Cruise at 25 knots with GM 1,040hp engines; 30 knots with GM 1,400hp diesels. Total of 35 were built.

Prices Not Provided for Pre-1995 Models

Length	61'4"	Fuel	1,500 gals.
Beam	17'6"	Water	250 gals.
Draft	5'8"	Cockpit	185 sq. ft.
Weight	80,000#	Hull Type	Modified-V
Clearance	18'0"	Deadrise Aft	16°

Dawson 38 Convertible

1987–94

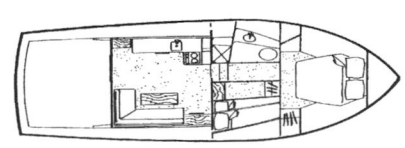

Midsize convertible with big fishing cockpit, roomy interior blurs the line between hardcore fisherman, comfortable family cruiser. Generous beam permits spacious two-stateroom, galley-up interior with extensive teak cabinetry, large head with stall shower, expansive salon with entertainment center. Flush cockpit with lift-out fishbox lacks transom door. Note well-arranged engine room, large flybridge. Deep-V hull can be a wet ride. Standard 375hp Cats cruise at 25 knots; GM 485hp engines cruise at a fast 30 knots.

Prices Not Provided for Pre-1995 Models

Length	38'0"	Fuel	400 gals.
Beam	13'8"	Water	90 gals.
Draft	3'6"	Waste	18 gals.
Weight	28,000#	Hull Type	Deep-V
Clearance	NA	Deadrise Aft	24°

Sportfishing Boats

Sportfishing Boats

Deep Impact 36 FS

2003–Current

Floorplan Not Available

Custom sportfishing machine with double-stepped hull set market standards for sophisticated design, eye-popping craftsmanship. Highlights include deluxe 3-person helm with tackle station, custom T-top, dual sliding transom doors, livewell, three fishboxes. Forward Seating model pictured above; Cabin model includes full galley, V-berth, large head. Great helm layout with Gaffrig controls. Flawless gelcoat, near perfect finish. Expensive—each is built to customer specs. Triple 225hp Mercury outboards top out at close to 55 knots.

Insufficient Resale Data to Assign Values

Length	36'0"	Fuel	320 gals.
Beam	10'0"	Water	55 gals.
Draft, Up	1'10"	Max HP	900
Draft, Down	2'10"	Hull Type	Deep-V
Dry Weight	9,500#	Deadrise Aft	24°

Donzi 29 ZF Open

2003–09

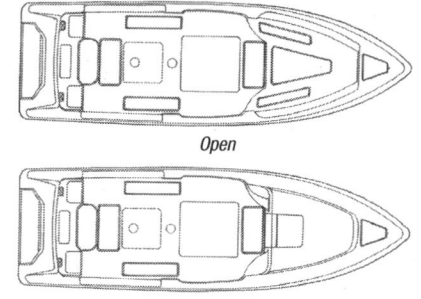

Open

Cuddy

See Page 520 For Value Estimates

High-performance sportfishing machine with lightweight stepped hull is trailerable (with a permit), stylish, fast across the water. Highlights include ready-to-fish cockpit with big 50-gallon transom livewell, deluxe leaning post, console tackle box, in-deck fishboxes, lockable electronics box, console head compartment, raw-water washdown, transom door. Slender 9-foot beam results in modest cockpit dimensions compared with most 29-footers. Also offered in Cuddy version. Yamaha 250s reach 45+ knots top.

Length Overall	28'7"	Fuel	180 gals.
Beam	9'0"	Water	7 gals.
Hull Draft	1'9"	Max HP	550
Draft, Engines Down	3'1"	Hull Type	Deep-V
Dry Weight	6,200#	Deadrise Aft	22°

Donzi 32 ZF Open

2000–07

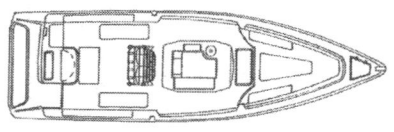

See Page 520 For Value Estimates

Race-bred speedster with lightweight twin-step hull, slender beam outguns most everything in her class. Standard features include insulated fishboxes, transom bait-prep station with sink, 50-gallon livewell, walk-in head compartment, recessed bow rails, console cooler, leaning post with drop-down bolsters, K-Planes, console tackle box, pop-up cleats, transom rod holders (5). Storage for 8 rods. Hull is fully cored. Good fit and finish. Twin 250hp outboards cruise at 35 knots and reach a top speed in excess of 50 knots.

Length Overall	32'1"	Fuel	290 gals.
Beam	9'2"	Water	20 gals.
Hull Draft	2'4"	Max HP	600
Dry Weight	7,600#	Hull Type	Deep-V
Clearance, T-Top	8'8"	Deadrise Aft	22°

Donzi 35 ZF Open

1998–Current

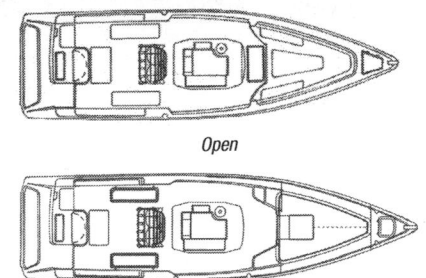

Open

Cuddy

Iigh-performance center console with stepped hull gets anglers to fishing grounds ahead of the pack. Standard features include 28-gallon transom livewell and sink, leaning post with rod holders, cockpit shower, removable cooler, console tackle box, deluxe helm seats with flip-up bolsters, console head compartment with sink & shower, transom door. Cuddy version also available. Narrow beam means less cockpit space than many 35-footers. Twin 225hp outboards deliver 40+ knots top; triple 225hps reach close to 55 knots top.

See Page 520 For Value Estimates

Length Overall	33'4"	Fuel	269 gals.
Beam	9'2"	Water	15 gals.
Hull Draft	2'6"	Max HP	750
Weight	7,950#	Hull Type	Deep-V
Clearance, T-Top	8'10"	Deadrise Aft	22°

Donzi 38 ZF Cuddy

2005–Current

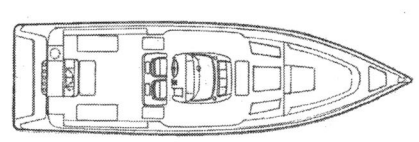

Hardcore fishing machine with triple-outboard power takes big center console performance, excitement to the next level. Standard features include fiberglass T-top, bait-prep station w/lighted baitwell, two removable coolers, lockable tackle storage, insulated fishboxes, K-Planes, locking electronics box, console tackle box, casting deck storage, console head with sink & shower. Cuddy has large V-berth, storage beneath. Stepped hull is very quick to accelerate. Max 55 knots w/triple 275 outboards.

See Page 520 For Value Estimates

Length	38'6"	Fuel	318 gals.
Beam	9'5"	Water	28 gals.
Hull Draft	3'0"	Max HP	900
Hull Weight	9,800#	Hull Type	Deep-V
Clearance, Hardtop	5'5"	Deadrise Aft	22°

Donzi 38 ZFX

2006–Current

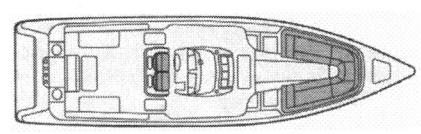

High-impact sportster built on Donzi's signature high-performance stepped hull combines hardcore fishing cockpit with comfortable wraparound seating forward. Fishing amenities include transom bait-prep center, 28-gallon livewell, raw-water washdown, in-deck fishboxes, bolster pads, transom rod holders (5), drop-down helm seat, transom door. Hardtop with electronics locker, folding rear seat, K-planes, forward wet bar, removable bow table are standard. Fast, versatile and innovative. About 60 knots top with triple 250s.

See Page 520 For Value Estimates

Length	38'6"	Fuel	318 gals.
Beam	9'5"	Water	28 gals.
Hull Draft	2'1"	Max HP	900
Dry Weight	10,200#	Hull Type	Deep-V
Clearance, Hardtop	5'5"	Deadrise Aft	22°

Sportfishing Boats

Donzi 38 ZSF

2004–Current

Feature-rich sportfisherman with double-stepped hull, well-appointed interior appeals to the dayboat crowd set as well as serious anglers. Expansive cockpit boasts 40-gallon livewell under rear bench seat, in-deck fishboxes, rod storage racks, facing lounge seats (with coolers under) forward, wet bar with sink. Comfortable interior with full galley, head with shower, twin settees, sleeps two. Note wide side decks, bow sun pad with headrest and drink holders. Fast, agile, very well finished. About 55 knots top with triple 250s.

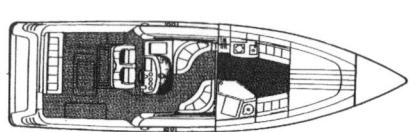

See Page 520 For Value Estimates

Length	38'6"	Fuel	420 gals.
Beam	10'6"	Water	55 gals.
Hull Draft	2'0"	Max HP	900
Dry Weight	15,000#	Hull Type	Deep-V
Clearance, Hardtop	6'6"	Deadrise Aft	22°

Donzi 54 Convertible

1989–95

Polished 1990s convertible (built by Lauderdale-based Roscioli Yachts) combines bold styling, semicustom accommodations. Spacious interior with combined salon/galley/dinette is highlighted by high-gloss cabinetry, premium furnishings, designer-style fabrics. Tournament-size cockpit includes full array of high-end fishing amenities. Note roomy bridge, wide side decks, beefy transom door. Engineroom is reached by lifting steps at salon door. Superb open-water ride. Cruise at 25 knots (30 top) with GM 1,150hp engines.

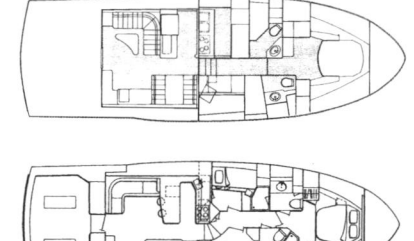

See Page 520 For Value Estimates

Length	54'0"	Fuel	1,000 gals.
Beam	17'4"	Water	240 gals.
Draft	4'4"	Headroom	6'5"
Weight	51,000#	Hull Type	Modified-V
Clearance	13'3"	Deadrise Aft	14°

Donzi 65 Convertible

1987–2003

Tournament-tested convertible from Lauderdale-based Roscioli Yachts gets high marks for handsome styling, luxury accommodations, many custom amenities. Opulent interior with three en suite staterooms boasts exquisite teak woodwork, premium fabrics and furnishings. Note spacious engine room, massive cockpit, huge bridge with seating for eight. Outstanding finish from bow to stern. Enclosed bridge is optional. One of the best heavy-weather rides in the business. Cat 1,450hp engines cruise at 24–26 knots (about 30 knots top).

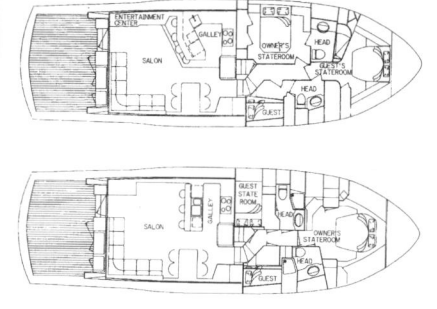

Insufficient Resale Data to Assign Values

Length	65'0"	Fuel	2,100 gals.
Beam	18'7"	Water	350 gals.
Draft	5'9"	Waste	50 gals.
Weight	72,000#	Hull Type	Modified-V
Clearance	14'4"	Deadrise Aft	12°

Dorado 30 Center Console

1992–2006

Floorplan Not Available

Distinctive, well-built offshore fishing boat with jackshaft power offers superior I/O performance without the need of an engine box. Features include insulated fishboxes, transom livewell, canvas spray hood, anchor locker, hinged console/engine box, coaming pads, raw-water washdown, forward seating, cuddy with V-berth. Trailerable—only 5,000 lbs. with engine. Low-deadrise hull is fuel efficient but a hard ride in heavy seas. Outboard model also available. Single 230hp Volvo diesel will cruise efficiently at 25 knots burning just 6 gph.

See Page 520 For Value Estimates

Length	30'0"	Fuel	85/180 gals.
Beam	8'8"	Water	23 gals.
Hull Draft	18"	Max HP	300
Dry Weight	4,900#	Hull Type	Modified-V
Clearance, T-top	6'5"	Deadrise Aft	4°

Dyer 29

1955–2003

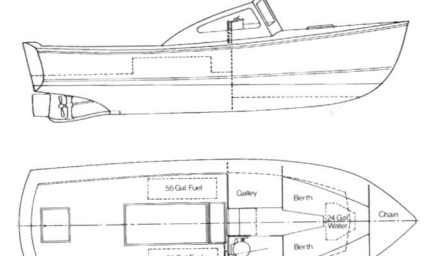

Classic Downeast cruiser with iconic lines, legendary seakeeping qualities turns heads everywhere she goes. Offered in several configurations over the years including Trunk Cabin, Hardtop, and several workboat versions. Recent models have the engine under bridgedeck eliminating cockpit engine box of early models. Many interiors were designed to owner specs. Easily driven hull with protected prop offers outstanding fuel efficiency. Single 200hp Yanmar diesel will cruise at 16–17 knots. Over 350 built. Custom models are still available.

See Page 520 For Value Estimates

Length Overall	28'6"	Clearance	6'0"
Length WL	26'0"	Water	24 gals.
Beam	9'5"	Fuel	110 gals.
Draft	2'6"	Clearance	NA
Weight	7,400#	Hull Type	Semi-Disp.

Edgewater 318 Center Console

2006–Current

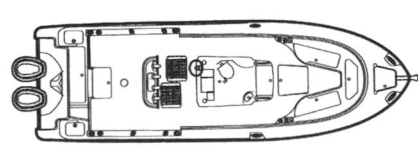

Premium fishing machine sets class standards for sophisticated engineering, leading-edge construction, unsurpassed performance. Spacious layout includes large indeck fishbox forward, bow seating with electric high/low table, lockable rod storage, deluxe leaning post with tackle storage, transom sink with pull-out shower. Two livewells—28-gallon unit at the transom and a 66-gallon well next to it. Walk-in console houses marine head with sink, shower. Foam-filled hull is unsinkable. Superb finish. Max 45 knots with Yamaha 250s.

See Page 521 For Value Estimates

Length	31'10"	Fuel	300 gals.
Beam	10'2"	Water	31 gals.
Draft, Up	1'10"	Max HP	600
Draft, Down	2'10"	Hull Type	Deep-V
Hull Weight	6,500#	Deadrise Aft	24°

Sportfishing Boats

Sportfishing Boats

Egg Harbor 33 Sedan

1982–89

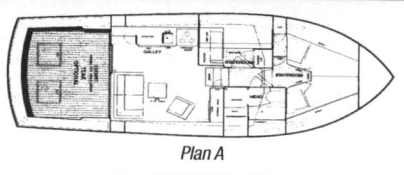

Plan A

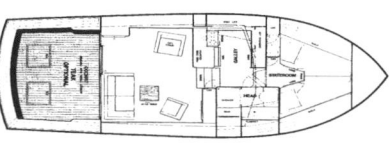

Plan B

Prices Not Provided for Pre-1995 Models

Updated version of classic Egg Harbor 33 (1971–80) boasts restyled deckhouse, increased fuel capacity, updated interior plans. Choice of single- or twin-stateroom floorplans. Teak cockpit sole was a popular option. Low-deadrise hull is quick to accelerate but a stiff ride in a chop. Narrow side decks, small cockpit. Large bridge for an older 33-foot boat. Originally marketed as the Pacemaker 33 SF before Pacemaker went bankrupt in 1980. Twin 340hp gas engines cruise at 18 knots; Cat 320hp diesels cruise in the low 20s.

Length	33'0"	Fuel	320 gals.
Beam	13'2"	Water	50 gals.
Draft	2'5"	Waste	20 gals.
Weight	16,500#	Hull Type	Modified-V
Clearance	NA	Deadrise Aft	8°

Egg Harbor 34 Convertible

1993–96

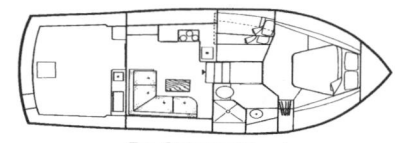

Two-Stateroom Layout

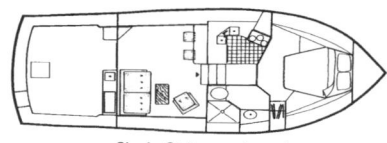

Single-Stateroom Layout

See Page 521 For Value Estimates

Classy mid-size convertible with rich teak interior couples luxury-class accommodations with handsome lines, secure performance. Full teak interior was offered with single or twin staterooms. Large cockpit includes bulkhead tackle center, in-deck fishbox, transom door. Front windshield was eliminated in order to provide space for salon entertainment center. Restyled—and rebranded as the Egg Harbor 35—in 1997. Performance: Cruise at 18 knots with 380hp gas engines; low 20s with 350hp Cat diesels.

Length w/Pulpit	37'8"	Fuel	400 gals.
Hull Length	34'6"	Water	70 gals.
Beam	13'2"	Waste	28 gals.
Draft	3'2"	Hull Type	Modified-V
Weight	17,500#	Deadrise Aft	8°

Egg Harbor 35 Convertible

1997–98

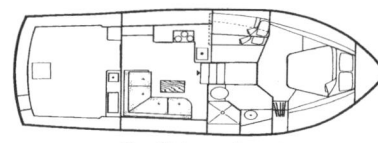

Two-Stateroom Layout

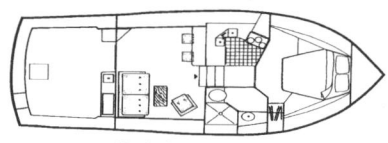

Single-Stateroom Layout

See Page 521 For Value Estimates

Sure-footed convertible—an updated version of the popular Egg Harbor 34 (1993–96)—ranked among class leaders for quality construction, leading-edge styling. Full teak interior was offered with single or twin staterooms. Large cockpit includes bulkhead tackle center, in-deck fishbox, transom door. Front windshield was eliminated in favor of salon entertainment center. Note well-arranged engine room, roomy bridge with bench seating forward. Cruise at 18 knots with 380hp gas engines; low 20s with 350hp Cat diesels.

Length w/Pulpit	37'8"	Fuel	406 gals.
Hull Length	34'6"	Water	75 gals.
Beam	13'2"	Waste	28 gals.
Draft	3'2"	Hull Type	Modified-V
Weight	20,925#	Deadrise Aft	8°

Egg Harbor 35 Predator

2000–Current

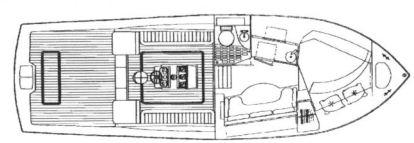

High-tech express fisherman was originally built by Predator Yachts in Sarasota, Florida. Egg Harbor acquired the tooling in 2002, reduced costs by replacing Kevlar construction with fiberglass, but upgraded previously basic interior with high-gloss teak joinery, Ultraleather upholstery. Centerline helm with flanking lounge seats provides excellent 360-degree visibility; large cockpit has transom livewell, rigging station, tackle lockers. Sea chest is unusual on a boat this size. Cruise at 30+ knots with 440hp Yanmar diesels.

See Page 521 For Value Estimates

Length	35'0"	Fuel	350 gals.
Beam	12'0"	Water	60 gals.
Draft	3'1"	Waste	15 gals.
Weight	16,000#	Hull Type	Deep-V
Clearance	6'11"	Deadrise Aft	20°

Egg Harbor 35 Sport Fisherman

1987–89

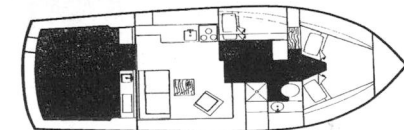
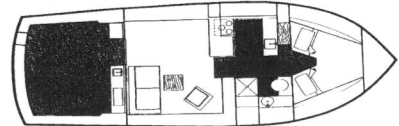

Lengthened version of popular Egg Harbor 33 Convertible (1982–89) used the extra length to create larger fishing cockpit. Well-appointed interior with quality teak joinery, open front windshield was offered with one or two staterooms. Large cockpit came standard with transom door, tackle center, bait-prep center, fish box, raw-water washdown. Teak covering boards were a popular option. Still a handsome, well-styled boat. Standard 350hp gas engines cruise at 18 knots; 320hp Cat diesels cruise in the low 20s.

Prices Not Provided for Pre-1995 Models

Length w/Pulpit	38'2"	Fuel	400 gals.
Hull Length	35'0"	Water	50 gals.
Beam	13'2"	Waste	25 gals.
Draft	3'2"	Hull Type	Modified-V
Weight	17,000#	Deadrise Aft	8°

Egg Harbor 36 Sedan

1976–85

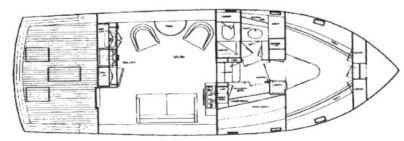

Classic flybridge convertible introduced in 1976 made the grade with boaters impressed with graceful Egg Harbor styling, seductive teak interior, large fishing cockpit. Offered with several one- or two-stateroom floorplans, all with quality teak or mahogany woodwork. Open front windshield makes salon seem larger than modern convertibles with closed windshield. Early models have mahogany deckhouse; construction became all-fiberglass in 1978. Standard 350hp gas engines cruise at 18–20 knots (high 20s top).

Prices Not Provided for Pre-1995 Models

Length	36'0"	Fuel	260/320 gals.
Beam	13'3"	Water	75 gals.
Draft	2'9"	Waste	25 gals.
Weight	17,000#	Hull Type	Modified-V
Clearance	NA	Deadrise Aft	6°

Sportfishing Boats

Egg Harbor 37 Convertible

1985–89

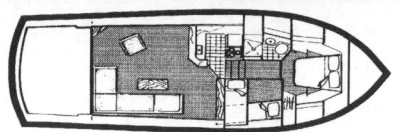

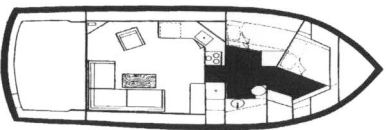

Slimmed-down version of Egg Harbor 41 SF (1984–89) is more cruiser than serious fishing machine. Wide 14'5" beam provides interior space of a larger boat. Two-stateroom interior was offered with galley up or down, choice of mahogany or teak joinery. Lower helm was optional. Wide side decks, roomy flybridge. Bigger engine room than many 37-footers. Small cockpit lacks fishing space. Fuel was increased in 1986 to 400 gallons. Cruise at 18 knots with 340hp gas inboards; low 20s with 375hp Cat diesels.

Prices Not Provided for Pre-1995 Models

Length	37'5"	Fuel	340/400 gals.
Beam	14'5"	Water	80 gals.
Draft	3'0"	Waste	30 gals.
Weight	24,000#	Hull Type	Modified-V
Clearance	NA	Deadrise Aft	9°

Egg Harbor 37 Sport Yacht

2001–Current

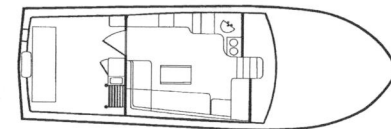

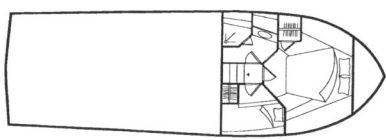

Handsome convertible with signature Egg Harbor styling impresses anglers, cruisers alike with luxury interior, top-shelf workmanship. Luxurious two-stateroom layout is an impressive display of varnished teak woodwork, designer fabrics, top-shelf furnishings. Big cockpit is fitted with transom door, tackle center, direct engine room access, transom livewell. Flybridge is large for a 37-footer with room to walk behind both helm chairs. Standard Cat 420hp diesels cruise at 27–28 knots (30+ knots top).

See Page 521 For Value Estimates

Length w/Pulpit	40'8"	Fuel	400 gals.
Hull Length	37'6"	Water	80 gals.
Beam	13'6"	Waste	40 gals.
Draft	3'4"	Hull Type	Modified-V
Weight	25,800#	Deadrise Aft	12°

Egg Harbor 38 Convertible

1990–94

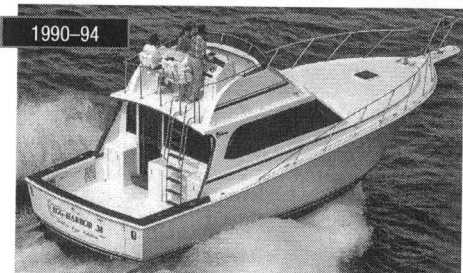

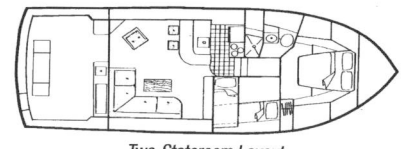

Two-Stateroom Layout

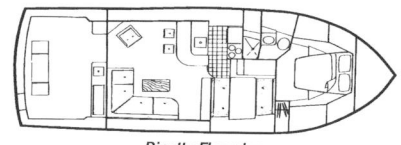

Dinette Floorplan

Broad-shouldered 1990s convertible delivers big-boat accommodations on the inside, too-small cockpit dimensions topside. Maxi-volume interior with varnished teak cabinets, built-in salon entertainment center came with choice of two-stateroom floorplan or (less popular) single-stateroom plan with dinette. Cockpit features include tackle center, livewell, transom door, fishbox. Standard gas engines cruise at 15–16 knots; Cat 375hp—or GM 400hp—diesels cruise in the low 20s. Replaced in 1995 with updated model.

Prices Not Provided for Pre-1995 Models

Length w/Pulpit	41'8"	Fuel, Gas	436 gals.
Hull Length	38'6"	Fuel, Diesel	506 gals.
Beam	15'0"	Water	120 gals.
Draft	3'10"	Hull Type	Modified-V
Weight	30,900#	Deadrise Aft	8°

Egg Harbor 38 Convertible

1995–97

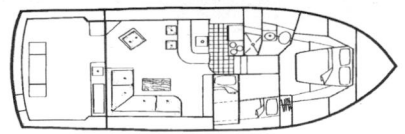

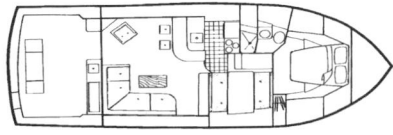

See Page 521 For Value Estimates

Restyled version of previous Egg Harbor 38 (1990–94) combined all-new profile, improved bridge layout, increased cockpit dimensions. Spacious interior with varnished teak joinery was offered with two-stateroom layout or less popular single-stateroom plan with dinette. Cockpit came standard with tackle center, livewell, transom door, fishbox. Eliminating front windshield provides space for salon entertainment center. Gas engines cruise at 15 knots, top out in the mid 20s. Cat 400hp diesels cruise at 25 knots (27–28 knots top).

Length w/Pulpit	41'8"	Fuel, Diesel	506 gals.
Hull Length	38'6"	Fuel, Gas	406 gals.
Beam	15'0"	Water	115 gals.
Draft	3'10"	Hull Type	Modified-V
Weight	30,600#	Deadrise Aft	8°

Egg Harbor 41 Convertible

1984–89

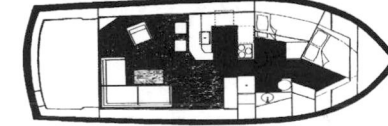

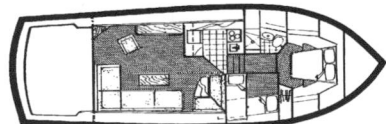

Prices Not Provided for Pre-1995 Models

Luxury-class convertible is an updated version of original Pacemaker 38 whose molds were acquired by Egg Harbor in 1980. Introduced in 1984 in both Sport Fisherman and Convertible Sedan versions, the difference being the larger salon, smaller cockpit of Convertible. Several floorplans were offered, all with quality teak joinery, upscale decor package. This boat has always been noted for her graceful styling, good seakeeping qualities. Cat 375hp cruise at 22 knots (26 knots top); 6-71 Detroits cruise at 26 knots (about 30 knots top).

Length	40'10"	Water	80 gals.
Beam	14'5"	Fuel	500 gals.
Draft	3'0"	Headroom	6'4"
Weight	28,000#	Hull Type	Modified-V
Clearance	13'0"	Deadrise Aft	8°

Egg Harbor 42 Convertible

1990–94

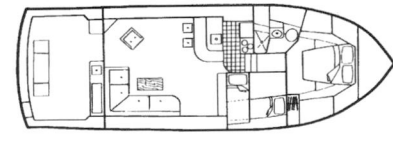

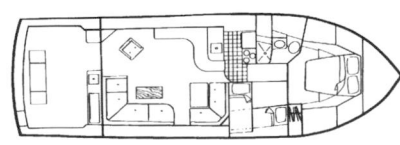

Prices Not Provided for Pre-1995 Models

Feature-rich fishing machine from early 1990s offered style, fishability, performance at a reasonable price. Large cockpit with tackle center, in-deck fishbox, livewell, transom door can accommodate full-size fighting chair with room to spare. Well-appointed interior was available with or without dinette. Tournament flybridge has good fore, aft sightlines. Note big engine room, teak trim and cover boards. Cat 375hp cruise in the low 20s (about 25 top); later models with twin 485hp 6-71 Detroits cruise at 25 knots (high 20s top).

Length w/Pulpit	45'4"	Cockpit	100 sq. ft.
Hull Length	42'2"	Fuel	600 gals.
Beam	15'0"	Water	120 gals.
Draft	3'10"	Hull Type	Modified-V
Weight	36,300#	Deadrise Aft	8°

Sportfishing Boats

Egg Harbor 42 Convertible

1995–97

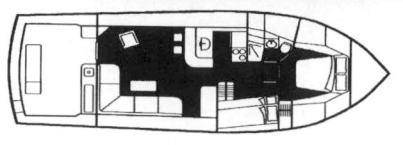

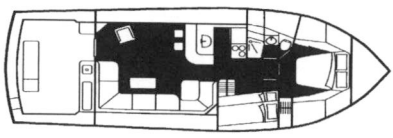

Restyled version of Egg Harbor 42 Convertible (1990–94) with redesigned bridge, revised interior compared well with best midsize convertibles of her day. Large cockpit with tackle center, in-deck fishbox can accommodate full-size fighting chair with room to spare. Well-appointed teak interior with roomy salon, comfortable staterooms was available with or without dinette. Engineroom—accessed from salon—is on the small side. Good overall finish. GM 550hp 6V92 diesels cruise at 26 knots and reach 30+ knots wide open.

See Page 521 For Value Estimates

Length w/Pulpit	45'4"	Fuel	600 gals.
Hull Length	42'2"	Water	115 gals.
Beam	15'0"	Waste	40 gals.
Draft	3'10"	Hull Type	Modified-V
Weight	36,300#	Deadrise Aft	8°

Egg Harbor 43 Sport Fisherman

1986–89

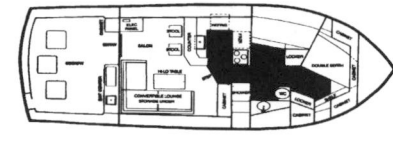

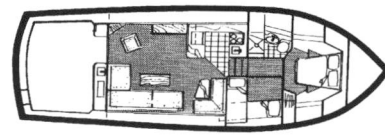

Muscular offshore fishing machine is basically a stretched version of Egg Harbor 41 Convertible (1984–89) with enlarged salon, increased fuel capacity. Two interior options were available, both with two staterooms. Eliminating front windshield allows for built-in entertainment center forward in salon. Large 120-square-foot cockpit features sink, freezer, transom door. Note teak cockpit sole, teak covering boards. Cat 375hp engines cruise in the low 20s (25 top); 485hp Detroits cruise in the mid 20s and reach 27–28 knots top.

Prices Not Provided for Pre-1995 Models

Length	43'0"	Fuel	600 gals.
Beam	14'5"	Water	80 gals.
Draft	3'0"	Headroom	6'4"
Weight	32,000#	Hull Type	Modified-V
Cockpit	120 sq. ft.	Deadrise Aft	8°

Egg Harbor 43 Sport Yacht

2004–Current

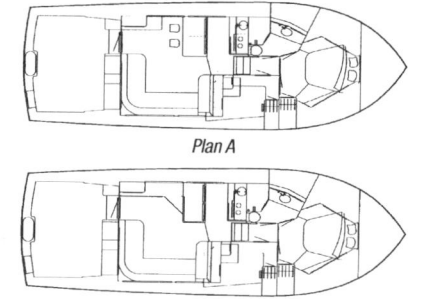

Plan A

Plan B

Updated version of Egg Harbor 42 Sport Yacht (2001–03) boasts redesigned hull with greater deadrise, prop pockets for improved performance. Several two-stateroom floorplans available, all with high-gloss cherry woodwork, designer decor package. Centerline helm with retractable electronics console offers good sightlines fore and aft. Note large cockpit with tackle center and livewell, engine room sea chest. Above-average fit and finish. Cat 700hp diesels cruise in the mid 20s (30+ knots top).

See Page 521 For Value Estimates

Length w/Pulpit	45'8"	Fuel	650 gals.
Hull Length	42'6"	Water	115 gals.
Beam	15'0"	Waste	40 gals.
Draft	3'6"	Hull Type	Modified-V
Weight	38,500#	Deadrise Aft	16°

Egg Harbor 48 Golden Egg

1978–86

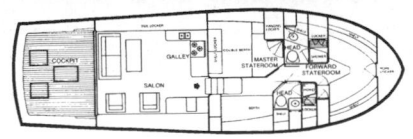

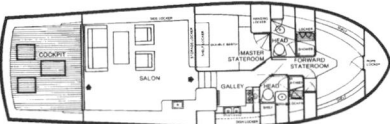

Muscular tournament sportfisherman was considered the last word in convertible style, performance in her era. Offered with several two- and three-stateroom floorplans over the years, all with rich hand-rubbed mahogany woodwork, wraparound salon windows. Teak cockpit with transom door, side lockers accommodates several anglers. Note large flybridge, wide side decks, big engine room. Late-model 48s have solid front windshield. A fast boat in her day, GM 550hp 8V92s cruise at 24–25 knots (high 20s top).

Prices Not Provided for Pre-1995 Models

Length	48'2"	Fuel	788 gals.
Beam	15'0"	Water	110/210 gals.
Draft	4'4"	Cockpit	NA
Weight	44,000#	Hull Type	Modified-V
Clearance	13'1"	Deadrise Aft	2°

Egg Harbor 54 Convertible

1988–89

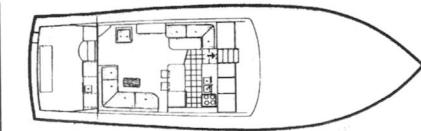

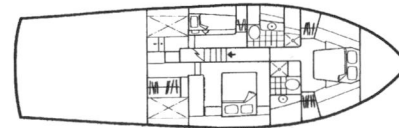

Scaled-down version of Egg Harbor 60 Convertible (1986–89) offered big-boat luxury, tournament-level fishability. Spacious 120-square-foot cockpit came loaded with standard fishing features. Huge bridge was considered state-of-the-art in her day. Elegant three-stateroom interior boasts expansive salon, amidships owner's stateroom (with unique step-down dressing room aft), large VIP guest cabin forward. Engineroom is on the small side. Cruise at 25 knots (27–28 top) with standard 735hp Detroit 8V92s.

Prices Not Provided for Pre-1995 Models

Length w/Pulpit	57'8"	Clearance	15'10"
Hull Length	54'6"	Fuel	1,000 gals.
Beam	17'6"	Water	220 gals.
Draft	5'3"	Hull Type	Modified-V
Weight	72,600#	Deadrise Aft	7°

Egg Harbor 60 Convertible

1986–89

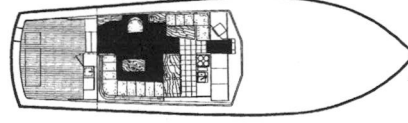

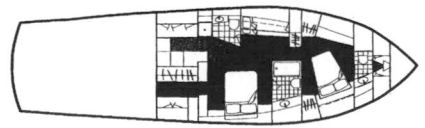

Hard-hitting tournament sportfisherman was considered state of the art in construction, size, performance in the late 1980s. Opulent three-stateroom, three-head interior features unique step-down dressing area aft of master suite, small utility room opposite. Vast salon can entertain a small crowd; apartment-sized galley will satisfy a gourmet cook. Roomy cockpit includes full array of fishing amenities. Note compact engine room, spacious bridge with extra rod storage. GM 1,080hp 12V92 diesels cruise at 27 knots (30 knots top).

Prices Not Provided for Pre-1995 Models

Length	59'6"	Fuel	1,200/1,500 gals.
Beam	17'6"	Water	300 gals.
Draft	5'3"	Cockpit	111 sq. ft.
Weight	72,000#	Hull Type	Modified-V
Clearance	18'5"	Deadrise Aft	8°

Sportfishing Boats

Sportfishing Boats

Everglades 260/270 Center Console

2006–Current

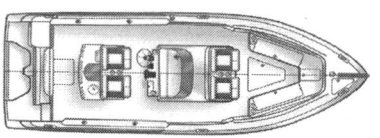

Top-shelf center console with semi-enclosed helm is distinctive, versatile, built to last. Combined T-top/console with wraparound windshield offers outstanding helm protection. Standard features include leaning post/bolster seat with 55-gallon livewell, bait rigging station, lockable rod storage, fold-down transom seat, docking lights, deluxe forward seating, powder-coated railings. Foam-filled hull is unsinkable. Slide-out cooler is a neat touch. Called the 260 CC in 2006–07; 270 in 2008–10. About 45 knots with Yamaha 250s.

See Page 521 For Value Estimates

Length	26'7"	Fuel	200 gals.
Beam	9'9"	Water	25 gals.
Draft, Up	1'8"	Max HP	500
Draft, Down	3'0"	Hull Type	Deep-V
Hull Weight	6,000#	Deadrise Aft	21°

Everglades 290 Center Console

2005–Current

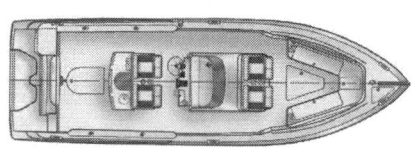

Versatile center console with integrated hardtop/windshield combines all-weather versatility with executive-class amenities, state-of-the-art construction. Highlights include standard leaning post/helm seat with 66-gallon livewell, console head with sink & shower, lockable rod storage, foldaway transom seat, slide-out cooler, tackle lockers (2), deluxe bow seating, 120-gallon fish box, foldaway transom seat. Exceptional fit & finish. Power-coated railings are a classy touch. Foam-filled hull is unsinkable. About 45 knots with Yamaha 250s.

See Page 521 For Value Estimates

Length	28'7"	Fuel	200 gals.
Beam	9'9"	Water	25 gals.
Hull Draft	1'8"	MaxHP	700
Hull Weight	6,300#	Hull Type	Deep-V
Clearance	7'8"	Deadrise Aft	21°

Everglades 350 Center Console

2007–Current

Floorplan Not Available

Premium center console designed for triple 350hp engines is innovative, fast, loaded with high-end amenities. Combined T-top/console module with wraparound windshield offers superb helm protection. Standard features include triple helm seats with flip-up bolsters, electric high-low bow table, foldaway stern seating, two livewells, enclosed head with berth. Unique foldaway seat on rear of baitwell doubles as fighting chair. Awesome helm layout. Foam-filled hull is unsinkable. This kind of quality doesn't come cheap. Triple 300hp Suzukis top out at over 40 knots.

See Page 521 For Value Estimates

Length	35'4"	Fuel	411 gals.
Beam	10'8"	Water	35 gals.
Draft, Up	2'0"	Max HP	1050
Draft, Down	3'2"	Hull Type	Deep-V
Hull Weight	9,260#	Deadrise Aft	25°

Everglades 350 LX

2008–Current

Floorplan Not Available

Luxury-class express makes good on promise of unsurpassed passenger comfort, state-of-the-art innovations. Expensive boat comes with lots of standards: hardtop with tinted skylights, generator, air-conditioning, windlass, flatscreen TV, electric grill, power helm seats with flip-up bolsters. Upscale cabin sleeps four; electric helm deck table coverts to additional berth. Note foldaway stern seats, thru-stem anchor system. Fit and finish is the best in the business. Triple 300hp Suzukis top out at over 40 knots.

See Page 521 For Value Estimates

Length	35'4"	Fuel	356 gals.
Beam	10'8"	Water	35 gals.
Draft, Up	2'0"	Max HP	1050
Draft, Down	3'5"	Hull Type	Deep-V
Hull Weight	10,800#	Deadrise Aft	25°

Grady-White 263/273 Chase

1994–Current

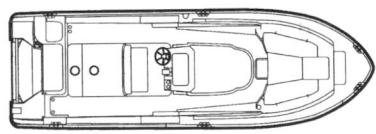

Trailerable center console in production since 1994 ranks high with anglers for quality, dependability. Standard features include 32-gallon lighted livewell, lockable rod storage, aft fishbox, deluxe leaning post, transom door, pop-up electronics enclosure, foldaway transom seat, cushioned forward seating, low-profile bow rails. Fiberglass insert fits between forward fish boxes to create raised casting deck. Marketed as Grady-White 263 Chase until 2002 when the console was redesigned. Around 45 knots top with Yamaha 225s.

See Page 523 For Value Estimates

Length	26'11"	Fuel	205 gals.
Beam	8'6"	Water	10 gals.
Hull Draft	1'3"	Max HP	500
Dry Weight	4,843#	Hull Type	Modified-V
Clearance, Top	8'3"	Deadrise Aft	18.5°

Grady-White 270 Islander

2002–05

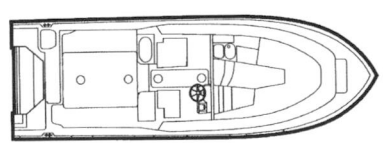

Big trailerable walkaround with roomy cockpit combines top-shelf construction with premium amenities, agile handling. Foldaway rear seat, 34-gallon livewell, transom door, insulated fishbox, deluxe helm and companion seats, lockable electronics box, bow pulpit. Well-finished cabin has galley (with slide-away butane stove), enclosed head with shower, removable dinette table, rod holders. Excellent visibility from raised helm position. Walkways around cabin are narrow. Over 40 knots max with twin 225s.

See Page 523 For Value Estimates

Length w/Pulpit	29'4"	Fuel	150 gals.
Hull Length	26'11"	Water	32 gals.
Beam	8'6"	Max HP	500
Hull Draft	1'5"	Hull Type	Modified-V
Dry Weight	5,594#	Deadrise Aft	18°

Sportfishing Boats

Sportfishing Boats

Grady-White 272 Sailfish

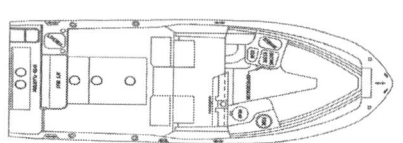

1994–2000

Updated version of popular Grady-White 25 Sailfish (1978–1993) with integrated transom, redesigned bottom, ranks with the best walkarounds ever produced. Standard features include 20-gallon livewell, aft bench seat, insulated fishboxes, cockpit bolsters, deluxe helm and companion seats, raw-water washdown, cockpit shower. Roomy cabin with fully equipped galley, enclosed head with shower, athwartships aft berth, V-berth. Most were sold with factory hardtop. Became 282 Sailfish in 2001. About 45 knots with Yamaha 250s.

See Page 523 For Value Estimates

Length w/Pulpit	27'10"	Fuel	202 gals.
Beam	9'6"	Water	32 gals.
Hull Draft	1'6"	Max HP	500
Dry Weight	5,500#	Hull Type	Deep-V
Clearance, Hardtop	9'4"	Deadrise Aft	20°

Grady-White 275 Tournament

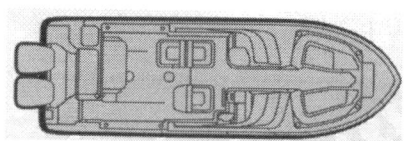

2007–Current

Top-level fishing boat/family runabout takes dual-console versatility to the next level. Notable features include 22-gallon and 46-gallon insulated transom fish boxes, cutting board, freshwater shower, padded coaming, cockpit toe rails. Note deluxe bow seating with removable table. Port console head compartment contains clever full-length rod storage—very cool. Foldaway transom seat, 32-gallon livewell are popular options. One of the largest dual console designs available. Over 40 knots top with Yamaha 200s.

See Page 523 For Value Estimates

Length	26'11"	Fuel	200 gals.
Beam	8'6"	Water	20 gals.
Hull Draft	20"	Max HP	500
Dry Weight	4,972#	Hull Type	Deep-V
Clearance, Hardtop	8'6"	Deadrise Aft	19°

Grady-White 280 Marlin

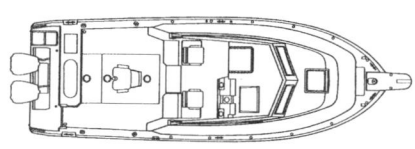

1989–94

Broad-beam fishing machine with large cockpit, spacious cabin is among the biggest 28-foot walkarounds in the business. Insulated fishbox, 40-gallon livewell, tackle drawers, bait station with sink, raw-water washdown, lockable electronics box, bow pulpit. Well-finished cabin has large V-berth, quarter berth, enclosed head with shower, fully equipped galley. Cockpit can handle full-size fighting chair. Became Grady-White 300 Marline in 1995. Most were sold with optional hardtop. About 40 knots max with twin 225s.

Prices Not Provided for Pre-1995 Models

Length w/Pulpit	32'7"	Fuel	306 gals.
Hull Length	28'0"	Water	35 gals.
Beam	10'7"	Max HP	600
Hull Draft	1'7"	Hull Type	Deep-V
Dry Weight	7,000#	Deadrise Aft	20°

Grady-White 282 Sailfish

2001–08

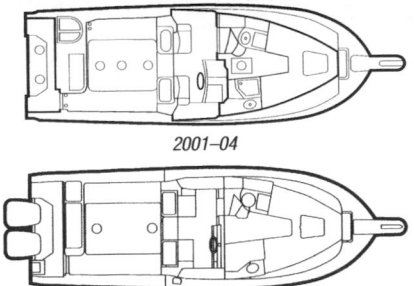

2001–04

2005–08

Updated version of best-selling 272 Sailfish (1994–2000) boasts restyled cabin windows, minor helm and cockpit revisions. Originally designed with aft bench seat and transom rigging station, cockpit was redesigned in 2005 with aft fishbox, foldaway rear bench seat. Large 40-gallon lighted livewell, cushioned fishboxes are standard. Upscale cabin with enclosed head, full galley, midcabin berth sleeps three. Note heavy-duty transom door, wide walkways. Unsurpassed fit and finish. About 40 knots max with twin 250s.

See Page 523 For Value Estimates

Length w/Pulpit	30'2"	Fuel	207 gals.
Hull Length	28'0"	Water	32 gals.
Beam	9'6"	Max HP	600
Hull Draft	1'6"	Hull Type	Deep-V
Dry Weight	6,781#	Deadrise Aft	20°

Grady-White 283 Release

2002–Current

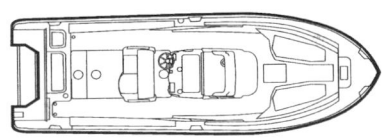

High-end center console provides the leading-edge quality, long-term satisfaction anglers expect in a Grady product. Standard features include combined leaning bar/rigging station with 45-gallon lighted livewell & tackle storage, lockable rod storage, electric pop-up electronics enclosure, sink with pull-out shower, two insulated bow fish boxes, transom fish box, lockable head enclosure. Fold-away transom seat frees up cockpit space. Superior fit and finish throughout. About 40 knots with Yamaha 225s.

See Page 523 For Value Estimates

Length	28'0"	Fuel, Std.	205 gals.
Beam	9'6"	Water	20 gals.
Hull Draft	1'6"	Max HP	600
Dry Weight	5,864#	Hull Type	Deep-V
Clearance, Top	8'5"	Deadrise Aft	20°

Grady-White 290 Chesapeake

2009–Current

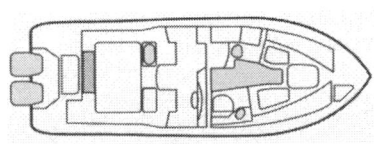

Sure-footed walkaround cabin blends signature Grady-White quality with proven deck layout, roomy cabin accommodations. Standard features include hardtop with radio box, 35-gallon livewell, foldaway transom seat, tackle storage, transom fishbox, cushioned cockpit storage boxes, cockpit bolsters. Dash space for flush-mounting twin 10" video displays. Well-appointed cabin with mini-galley, enclosed head with shower, teak and holly sole sleeps two. No lightweight, Yamaha 250s reach close to 40 knots wide open.

See Page 523 For Value Estimates

Length	28'6"	Fuel	206 gals.
Beam	9'11"	Water	32 gals.
Hull Draft	24"	Max HP	600
Dry Weight	7,650#	Hull Type	Deep-V
Clearance, Hardtop	9'9"	Deadrise Aft	20°

Sportfishing Boats

Grady-White 300 Marlin

1995–Current

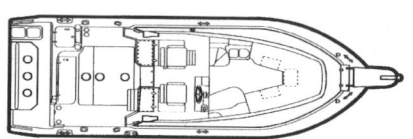

Updated version of popular Grady-White 280 Marlin (1989–94) boasts revised hull bottom, reworked cockpit. Stand-up 32-gallon livewell, tackle station, insulated fishbox, aft-facing jump seat, transom door, cockpit bolsters, bow pulpit. Well-appointed cabin has small galley with fridge, stand-up head, crawl-in aft berth. Teardrop cabin windows replaced rectangular windows in 1999. Transom redesign in 2004 added larger fishbox, folding bench seat. Yamaha 225hp outboards top out around 40 knots.

See Page 523 For Value Estimates

Length w/Pulpit	32'7"	Fuel	306 gals.
Hull Length	30'6"	Water	35 gals.
Beam	10'7"	Max HP	700
Hull Draft	1'7"	Hull Type	Deep-V
Dry Weight	8,221#	Deadrise Aft	19.5°

Grady-White 305 Express

2007–Current

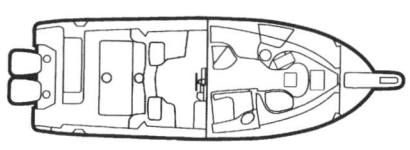

Premium big-water express combines spacious deck layout with comfortable ride, unsurpassed build quality. Fishing amenities include 32-gallon livewell, transom fishbox, fresh/saltwater washdowns, tackle trays, rocket launchers on each hardtop leg. Well-appointed cabin with midship berth, full galley, stand-up head, entertainment center sleeps four. Note centerline helm position, foldaway transom seat, power electronics box, twin cockpit showers. Bow thruster is a nice touch. Nearly 40 knots top with twin 225s.

See Page 523 For Value Estimates

Length w/Pulpit	32'7"	Fuel	290 gals.
Hull Length	30'6"	Water	32 gals.
Beam	10'7"	Max HP	700
Hull Draft	1'7"	Hull Type	Modified-V
Dry Weight	8,850#	Deadrise Aft	17°

Grady-White 306 Bimini

1998–Current

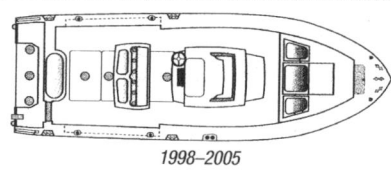

1998–2005

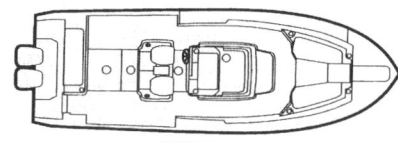

2006–Current

Premium 30-footer makes the cut with anglers willing to pay Grady quality. Highlights include 40-gallon transom livewell, console head with shower, three forward fishboxes, transom door, lockable rod storage. Leaning bar has rigging station with lockable storage. Helm came with electric pop-up electronics enclosure. Excellent cockpit nonskid. Updates in 2006 included twin fishboxes forward (replacing casting platform), combined helm seat/livewell, new transom with folding rear seat. About 40 knots top with twin 250s.

See Page 523 For Value Estimates

Length	30'6"	Fuel	290 gals.
Beam	10'7"	Water	20 gals.
Hull Draft	21"	Max HP	700
Dry Weight	6,500#	Hull Type	Deep-V
Clearance	9'4"	Deadrise Aft	19.5°

Grady-White 307 Tournament

2009–Current

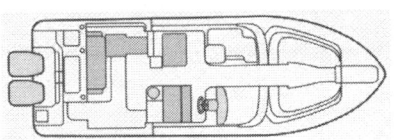

King-size dual console with luxury-class features is tough enough for anglers, roomy enough for families. Huge cockpit with deluxe wet bar (refrigerator/grill optional) includes power 2-man helm seat, double companion seat, foldaway rear seat, two fishboxes. Electric extendable portside lounge seat is a nice touch. Large head compartment in port console extends under bow seating, features lockable rod storage, fold-out 5-foot child berth. Note plush seating, top-quality hardware. Twin Yamaha 250s max out at nearly 40 knots.

See Page 523 For Value Estimates

Length	30'5"	Fuel	206 gals.
Beam	10'7"	Water	32 gals.
Hull Draft	22"	Max HP	700
Dry Weight	7,850#	Hull Type	Deep-V
Clearance, Hardtop	8'10"	Deadrise Aft	20°

Grady-White 330 Express

2001–Current

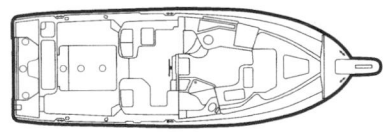

Gold-plated express with signature Grady-White quality is a sold performer in all conditions. Fishing features include large-capacity transom fishbox, 45-gallon livewell, rigging station with sink. Note aft-facing cockpit seats, pop-up electronics console. Spacious midcabin interior boasts classy teak-and-holly sole, built-in entertainment center, luxury-class amenities. Air-conditioning, hardtop, generator are standard. Yamaha 250s reach 35+ knots top. Transom was beefed up in 2009 to handle bigger Yamaha 350s (40+ knots max).

See Page 523 For Value Estimates

Length w/Pulpit	35'10"	Fuel	350 gals.
Hull Length	33'6"	Water	50 gals.
Beam	11'7"	Max HP	700
Hull Draft	1'9"	Hull Type	Deep-V
Dry Weight	10,840#	Deadrise Aft	20.5°

Grady-White 336 Canyon

2008–Current

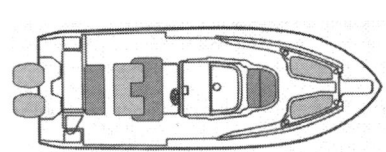

Leading-edge 33-footer with huge cockpit, leading edge components ups the ante on center-console innovation, performance. Deluxe leaning post/tackle center with 45-gallon livewell, foldaway rear seat, large-capacity transom fishbox, forward fish/storage boxes, transom door. Centerline helm with pop-up electronics module accommodates several large displays. Console interior sports full marine head, shower and sink, rod storage, twin berths forward. Big, powerful, sure to impress. About 40 knots top with twin 350s.

See Page 523 For Value Estimates

Length	33'6"	Fuel	350 gals.
Beam	11'7"	Water	44 gals.
Hull Draft	2'1"	Max HP	700
Dry Weight	9,200#	Hull Type	Deep-V
Clearance, Top	9'0"	Deadrise Aft	21°

Sportfishing Boats

Grady-White 360 Express

2005–Current

Premium (expensive) triple-outboard express takes Grady-White luxury, fishability to the next level. Standard features include transom fishbox with refrigerator/freezer, 48-gallon livewell, refrigerator/freezer (in cockpit module), foldaway rear seat. State-of-the-art center helm has electronic controls, innovative slide-out table. Upscale cabin with teak-and-holly sole, entertainment center, aft berth sleeps four adults, two kids. Bow thruster, air-conditioning, generator are standard. The ultimate outboard express. Over 35 knots with triple 250s.

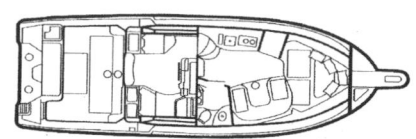

See Page 523 For Value Estimates

Length w/Pulpit	39'3"	Fuel	370 gals.
Hull Length	36'7"	Water	65 gals.
Beam	10'6"	Max HP	1,050
Hull Draft	2'5"	Hull Type	Deep-V
Dry Weight	14,919#	Deadrise Aft	21°

Grady-White 366 Canyon

2010–Current

Supersize center console with semi-enclosed helm, cruise-ready cabin splits the difference between hardcore fishing machine, versatile family boat. Features include roomy 85-sq.-ft. cockpit, two livewells, fold-away transom seat, solid glass helm enclosure, cushioned forward seating, massive T-top. Console cabin includes galley, head, double berth. Note pop-up electronics pod, wide gunwales, tinted cabin skylight. Generous freeboard insures a dry, secure cockpit. Twin Yamaha 350s reach 40–42 knots top; triple 350s top out at close to 50.

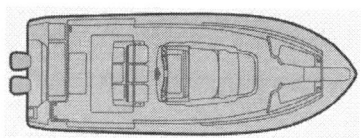

Insufficient Resale Data to Assign Values

Length	36'7"	Fuel	420 gals.
Beam	13'2"	Water	65 gals.
Hull Draft	2'5"	Max HP	1,050
Dry Weight	12,850#	Hull Type	Deep-V
Clearance	9'0"	Deadrise Aft	21°

Hatteras 32 Flybridge Fisherman

1982–88

Conservative 1980s convertible combines large cockpit with comfortable cabin layout, roomy flybridge. Step-down interior with galley to port, booth-style dinette, roomy head/shower sleeps four. Deck area between engine boxes is below cockpit level to allow standing headroom when entering cabin. Wide 12-foot beam provides cockpit space for a fighting chair. Prop pockets reduce draft, improve hull efficiency. Good engine access. Cruise at 18 knots with 300hp gas engines; about 20 knots with 320hp Cat diesels.

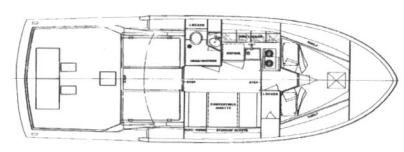

Prices Not Provided for Pre-1995 Models

Length	32'8"	Fuel	265 gals.
Beam	12'0"	Water	50 gals.
Draft	3'0"	Waste	30 gals.
Weight	18,000#	Hull Type	Modified-V
Clearance	10'6"	Deadrise Aft	18°

Hatteras 32 Sport Fisherman

1982–86

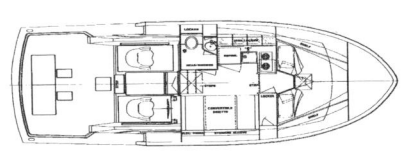

Well-built 1980s express fisherman combined efficient deck layout with upscale cabin accommodations, legendary Hatteras engineering and construction. Classy teak-trimmed interior with compact galley, convertible dinette, stand-up head with shower sleeps four. Uncluttered cockpit is big enough for six anglers, lacks transom door. Good helm visibility, but not much space for extra electronics. Prop pockets reduce draft, improve efficiency. Cruise at 18 knots with 300hp gas engines; around 20 knots with 320hp Cat diesels.

Prices Not Provided for Pre-1995 Models

Length	32'8"	Fuel	265 gals.
Beam	12'0"	Water	50 gals.
Draft	3'2"	Cockpit	95 sq. ft.
Weight	17,200#	Hull Type	Modified-V
Clearance, Windshield	8'8"	Deadrise Aft	18°

Hatteras 36 Convertible

1983–87

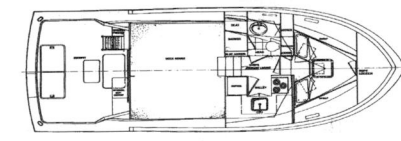

One Stateroom

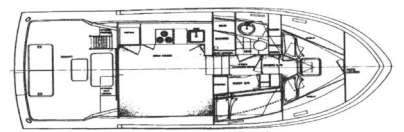

Two Staterooms

Polished 1980s convertible with wide 13'7" beam, efficient prop-pocket hull is more family cruiser than hard-nosed fishboat. Deluxe interior with spacious salon, solid teak cabinets was available with one or two staterooms. Highlights include wraparound salon windows, wide side decks, transom door, molded bow pulpit, roomy flybridge with seating for five. Hatches in cockpit sole provide access to generator. Well-appointed boat has aged well. Standard gas engines cruise at 14–16 knots; 390hp GM diesels cruise at 20 knots.

Prices Not Provided for Pre-1995 Models

Length	36'6"	Fuel	355 gals.
Beam	13'7"	Water	115 gals.
Draft	3'9"	Waste	40 gals.
Weight	26,500#	Hull Type	Modified-V
Clearance	12'6"	Deadrise Aft	18°

Hatteras 38 Convertible

1988–93

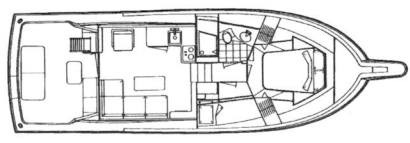

Handsome styling, executive-class accommodations, quality construction set this high-end convertible apart from competitive models. Deluxe two-stateroom interior with teak trim includes big owner's stateroom and large head, but deckhouse galley is too small with little counter, storage space. Roomy cockpit came standard with molded tackle center, in-deck fishbox, transom door. Note wide side decks, engine room air intakes under cockpit coaming. Modest performance, too-small galley. GM 485hp diesels cruise at 22 knots.

Prices Not Provided for Pre-1995 Models

Length	38'10"	Fuel	490 gals.
Beam	13'5"	Water	117 gals.
Draft	4'8"	Waste	60 gals.
Weight	28,800#	Hull Type	Modified-V
Clearance	12'6"	Deadrise Aft	9°

Sportfishing Boats

Hatteras 39 Convertible

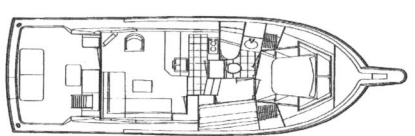

1994–98

Updated version of Hatteras 38 Convertible (1988–93) offered "new-look" 1990s styling, improved floor plan. Spacious, teak-trimmed interior features convenient salon serving counter overlooking galley. Guest cabin doubles as open day lounge or private sleeping area with lower berth, fold-down upper berth. Large flybridge overlooks cockpit with standard tackle centers, removable fishbox, transom door. Avoid models with small 314hp diesels. Optional Detroit 465hp 6-71 diesels cruise at 22–24 knots; 26+ knots wide open.

See Page 524 For Value Estimates

Length	39'0"	Fuel	490 gals.
Beam	13'7"	Water	120 gals.
Draft	4'8"	Waste	50 gals.
Weight	32,000#	Hull Type	Modified-V
Clearance	12'6"	Deadrise Aft	9°

Hatteras 39 Sport Express

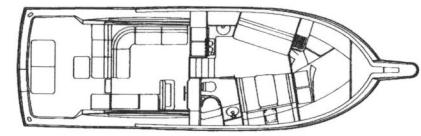

1995–98

Standard Cockpit Layout

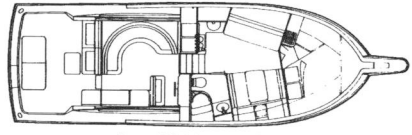

Curved Bridgedeck Seating

Graceful big-water express delivers quality Hatteras construction, versatile layout, solid performance. Spacious cockpit came standard with in-deck fishbox, bait-prep station with sink, livewell, transom door, direct engine room access. Small-but-elegant interior boasts full galley, convertible dinette, head with stall shower, teak or oak woodwork. Spacious bridgedeck came with several seating options. Offered in Cruiser or Sportfish versions. Twin 435hp Cats cruise at 22 knots; 465hp Detroit 6-71s cruise in the mid 20s.

See Page 524 For Value Estimates

Length	39'0"	Fuel	458 gals.
Beam	13'7"	Water	120 gals.
Draft	4'8"	Waste	50 gals.
Weight	30,500#	Hull Type	Modified-V
Clearance	8'10"	Deadrise Aft	9°

Hatteras 41 Convertible

1986–91

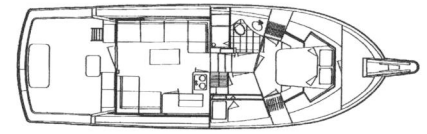

Rock-solid convertible with "new-look" Hatteras styling (note stepped sheer, rakish bridge) was forerunner of company's late 1990s convertible lineup. Offered with several interior plans, all with roomy bow stateroom, top-shelf fixtures and furnishings. Light ash woodwork became available in 1987. Spacious 120-square-foot cockpit is among largest in class. Hull was fully cored in early models. Note fuel increase in 1987. Standard 465hp 6-71 diesels cruise at 22–23 knots; optional 535hp 6V92s cruise at 25 knots (27–28 knots top).

Prices Not Provided for Pre-1995 Models

Length	41'9"	Fuel	400/500 gals.
Beam	14'3"	Water	150 gals.
Draft	4'4"	Cockpit	120 sq. ft.
Weight	35,400#	Hull Type	Modified-V
Clearance	13'9"	Deadrise Aft	NA

Sportfishing Boats

Hatteras 43 Convertible

1991–98

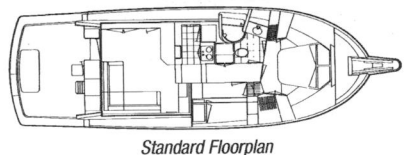

Standard Floorplan

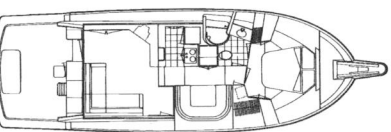

Optional Arrangement

See Page 525 For Value Estimates

Rakish 43-footer with "new-look" Hatteras styling set quality and performance standards for midsize convertibles of her era. Large 120-square-foot cockpit boasts direct engine room access, wide transom door, removable fishbox, bait and tackle center. Offered with choice of two-stateroom or dinette interior, both with large master stateroom but compact salon. Note light ash woodwork, washer/dryer space in forward passageway. Cockpit engine room access is a plus. Twin 535hp 6V92 GM diesels cruise at 24 knots (27–28 knots top).

Length	43'2"	Fuel	500 gals.
Beam	14'3"	Water	154 gals.
Draft	4'8"	Cockpit	120 sq. ft.
Weight	40,000#	Hull Type	Modified-V
Clearance	12'4"	Deadrise Aft	10°

Hatteras 43 Sport Express

1996–98

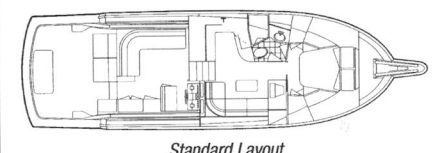

Standard Layout

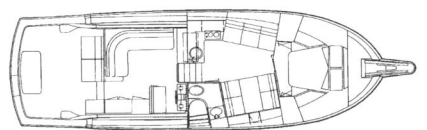

Optional Arrangement

See Page 525 For Value Estimates

Powerful offshore express—among the largest available during the late 1990s—was stylish, fast, expensive. Standard interior with U-shaped galley, stall shower in head sleeps four; alternate layout with smaller head and galley sleeps six. Rigging station, lift-out fishboxes, livewell were standard. Aft-facing bench seat in cockpit lifts for engine room access. Additional features include light oak interior woodwork, radar arch, side exhausts, bow pulpit. First-rate finish throughout. Twin 535hp GM diesels cruise at 27 knots (30+ knots top).

Length	43'2"	Fuel	530 gals.
Beam	14'3"	Water	154 gals.
Draft	4'5"	Headroom	6'6"
Weight	38,000#	Hull Type	Modified-V
Clearance	9'8"	Deadrise Aft	9°

Hatteras 45 Convertible

1984–88

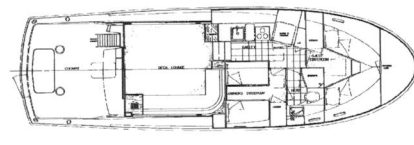

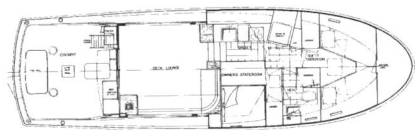

Prices Not Provided for Pre-1995 Models

Venerable Hatteras sportfisherman was everything many anglers were looking for in a 1980s-era fishing machine. Highlights include cavernous 132-square-foot cockpit, upscale two-stateroom interior with amidships owner's cabin, large flybridge with excellent cockpit visibility. Note teak interior joinery, beefy transom door. Agile performance for a big boat. One of Hatteras's most popular models for several years. Standard GM 535hp diesels cruise at 23 knots (26–27 knots wide open). Completely restyled in 1989—see next entry.

Length	45'8"	Fuel	590 gals.
Beam	14'6"	Water	165 gals.
Draft	4'6"	Cockpit	132 sq. ft.
Weight	39,000#	Hull Type	Modified-V
Clearance	14'3"	Deadrise Aft	NA

Sportfishing Boats

Sportfishing Boats

Hatteras 45 Convertible

1989–91

Restyled version of one of Hatteras's most popular models made a good boat even more desirable. Major updates included rearranged helm console with electronics enclosure, new bait-and-tackle center, redesigned interior with increased salon seating, walkaround queen bed in owner's stateroom. Huge 132-square-foot cockpit with transom door, coaming gate, molded tackle center is among largest in class. Engineroom is accessed from rear of salon. Standard GM 535hp diesels cruise at 23 knots (26–27 knots wide open).

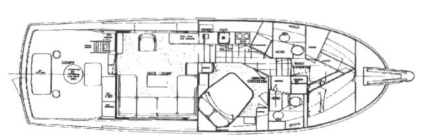

Prices Not Provided for Pre-1995 Models

Length	45'8"	Headroom	6'7"
Beam	14'6"	Fuel	590 gals.
Draft	4'7"	Water	165 gals.
Weight	43,800#	Hull Type	Modified-V
Clearance	14'3"	Deadrise Aft	NA

Hatteras 46 Convertible

1974–85

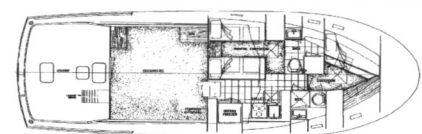

Galley Down, 1974–1981

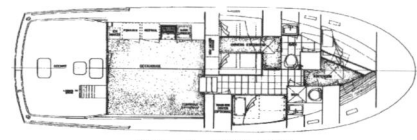

Galley Up, 1974–1981

Classic Hatteras convertible with bold 1970s styling delivered lasting blend of upscale accommodations, tournament-grade fishability. Several two-stateroom floorplans were available over the years, all with handcrafted teak woodwork. Cockpit, flybridge were considered state-of-the-art in her era. Sliding door replaced original hinged salon door in 1982. One of last Hatteras convertibles with front windshield. Updated 46 model introduced in 1986. GM 425hp diesels cruise at 19–20 knots; 650hp GMs (1982–85) cruise at 25 knots.

Prices Not Provided for Pre-1995 Models

Length	46'2"	Fuel	650/710 gals.
Beam	14'9"	Water	180 gals.
Draft	4'2"	Cockpit	125 sq. ft.
Weight	41,000#	Hull Type	Modified-V
Clearance	13'8"	Deadrise Aft	NA

Hatteras 46 Convertible

1992–95

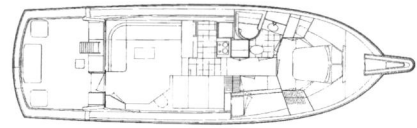

Standard Floorplan

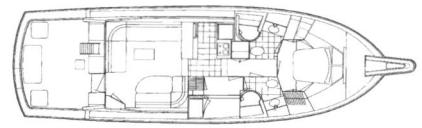

Optional Arrangement

Leading-edge mix of hardcore fishability, cruising elegance set class standards in early 1990s. Luxurious two-stateroom interior with full dinette was available with one or two heads. Spacious cockpit came with tackle centers, in-deck fishbox, transom door, direct access to stand-up engine room. Note standard washer/dryer, underwater exhaust system. A good-running boat, 735hp 8V92s cruise at 24–25 knots and reach 28 knots wide open. Optional 780hp MANs reach an honest 30 knots.

See Page 525 For Value Estimates

Length	46'10"	Fuel	775 gals.
Beam	15'7"	Water	188 gals.
Draft	4'6"	Cockpit	121 sq. ft.
Weight	52,000#	Hull Type	Modified-V
Clearance	13'9"	Deadrise Aft	7°

Hatteras 48 Convertible

1987–91

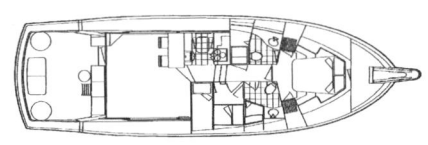

Muscular sportfishing machine impressed 1980s buyers with huge cockpit, luxury accommodations, near 30-knot performance. Two-stateroom teak interior features expansive salon with entertainment center, wet bar. Serving counter overlooks mid-level galley, but layout lacks built-in dinette found in most 48-footers. Cockpit features molded tackle center, beefy transom door, engine room access door. Note solid front windshield panels. Standard 720hp GM diesels cruise at 24 knots (27–28 knots top).

Prices Not Provided for Pre-1995 Models

Length	48'8"	Fuel	812 gals.
Beam	16'0"	Water	184 gals.
Draft	5'5"	Cockpit	135 sq. ft.
Weight	51,500#	Hull Type	Modified-V
Clearance	14'0"	Deadrise Aft	8°

Hatteras 50 Convertible

1991–98

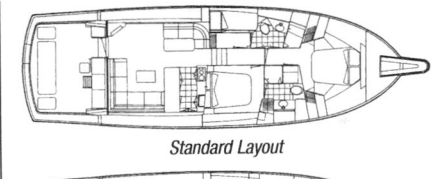

Standard Layout

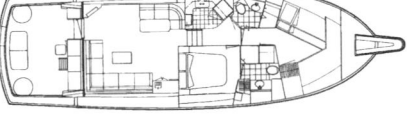

Optional Layout

Heavyweight sportfishing machine hit the sweet spot with deep-pocket anglers looking for leading-edge comfort, exhilarating performance. Lavish three-stateroom, two-head interior with deckhouse galley was standard; optional two-stateroom, galley-down floorplan boasts huge salon with seating for a crowd. Posh designer decor set convertible standards in the 1990s. Massive cockpit for a 50-footer. Restyled Hatteras 50 was introduced in 1999. GM 870hp 12-cylinder diesels cruise at 26 knots (about 30 knots top).

See Page 525 For Value Estimates

Length	50'10"	Fuel	890 gals.
Beam	16'1"	Water	184 gals.
Draft	5'4"	Waste	85 gals.
Weight	60,000#	Hull Type	Modified-V
Clearance	13'8"	Deadrise Aft	8°

Hatteras 50 Convertible

1999–2006

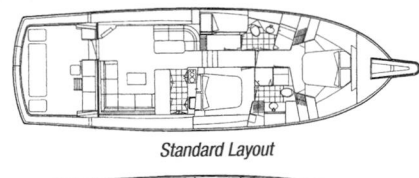

Standard Layout

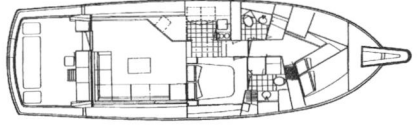

Optional Layout

Restyled version of previous Hatteras 50 provides the right mix of comfort, fishability, performance. Three-stateroom interior with deckhouse galley is standard; optional two-stateroom, galley-down floorplan boasts huge salon with seating for a crowd. Note washer/dryer in bow stateroom. Oversized bridge with single-lever controls, recessed electronics box seats captain and six guests. Huge cockpit comes standard with large bait freezer, bait and tackle center. Note fuel increase in 2001. Cat 1,400hp engines cruise at a fast 35 knots.

See Page 525 For Value Estimates

Length	50'10"	Fuel	890/1,060 gals.
Beam	16'1"	Water	184 gals.
Draft	5'4"	Waste	85 gals.
Weight	60,000#	Hull Type	Modified-V
Clearance	13'8"	Deadrise Aft	8°

Sportfishing Boats

Sportfishing Boats

Hatteras 52 Convertible

1984–87

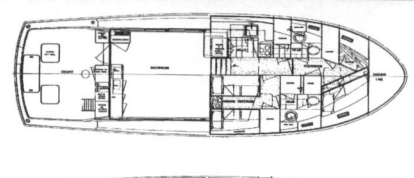

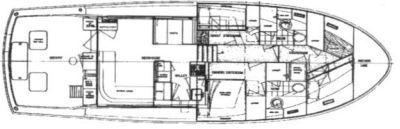

Stretched version of Hatteras 50 Convertible (1980–83) used the extra length to provide massive fishing cockpit—something her predecessor sorely lacked. Standard two-stateroom, galley-down and optional three-stateroom, galley-up floorplans are identical to 50 Convertible. Deep cockpit features molded bait and tackle center, transom door with gate, direct engine room access. A good seaboat, GM 675hp diesels cruise at 22 knots (about 26 knots top). Popular model was completely restyled for 1988—see next entry.

Prices Not Provided for Pre-1995 Models

Length	52'0"	Fuel	1,065 gals.
Beam	16'4"	Water	185 gals.
Draft	5'0"	Cockpit	153 sq. ft.
Weight	56,000#	Hull Type	Modified-V
Clearance	15'10"	Deadrise Aft	NA

Hatteras 52 Convertible

1988–91

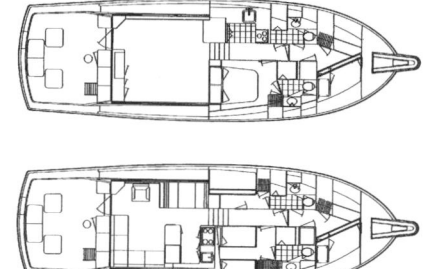

Updated version of good-selling Hatteras 52 Convertible (1984–87) boasts restyled exterior, redesigned accommodations, increased power. Available with two-stateroom, galley-down interior, or more popular three-stateroom layout with galley and dinette up. Big 153-square-foot cockpit includes bait and tackle center, removable fishbox, in-sole baitwell, direct access to engine room. Note wide side decks, 30" transom gate, massive flybridge. GM 720-hp diesels cruise in the low-to-mid 20s (26–27 knots wide open).

Prices Not Provided for Pre-1995 Models

Length	52'0"	Headroom	6'6"
Beam	16'4"	Fuel	1,068 gals.
Draft	5'0"	Water	188 gals.
Weight	55,400#	Hull Type	Modified-V
Clearance	15'10"	Deadrise Aft	NA

Hatteras 54 Convertible

1991–98

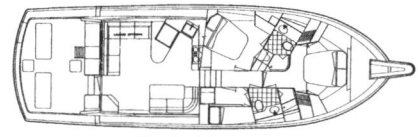

Standard Arrangement

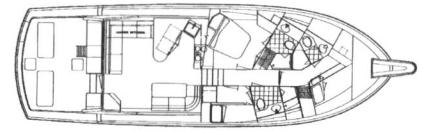

Optional Arrangement

Compelling 1990s tournament yacht met Hatteras standards for world-class construction, exceptional open-water performance. Spacious three-stateroom interior with ash cabinetry boasts huge salon with galley and dinette area, lavish master suite, standard washer/dryer in companionway. Huge flybridge included state-of-the-art helm console. Walk-in engine room is a mechanic's dream. Optional 1,040hp Detroit (or 1,020hp MAN) diesels cruise at 25 knots; later models with 1,300hp Cats cruise at 28 knots (32–33 knots top).

See Page 525 For Value Estimates

Length	54'11"	Fuel	1,320 gals.
Beam	17'4"	Water	200 gals.
Draft	5'4"	Waste	75 gals.
Weight	70,000#	Hull Type	Modified-V
Clearance	14'8"	Deadrise Aft	7°

Hatteras 54 Convertible

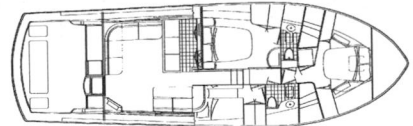

2002–Current

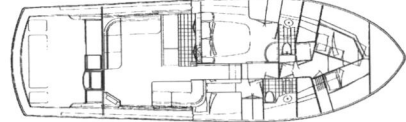

Standard Arrangement

Optional Arrangement

See Page 525 For Value Estimates

High-impact convertible combines "new-look" Hatteras styling with lavish accommodations, impressive performance. Lavish interior with three staterooms, home-size galley includes expansive salon with custom L-shaped sofa, deluxe entertainment center, two full heads. Additional features include large cockpit with mezzanine seating, state-of-the-art flybridge with pop-up console, stand-up engine room with cockpit access. Deep prop tunnels permit shallow-water operation. Cruise at 30 knots with 1,400hp Cats (35 knots top); 1,550hp Cats reach 38–40 knots.

Length	54'0"	Fuel	1,050 gals.
Beam	17'3"	Water	200 gals.
Draft	4'2"	Waste	100 gals.
Weight	67,000#	Hull Type	Modified-V
Clearance	13'10"	Deadrise Aft	2°

Hatteras 55 Convertible

1980–86

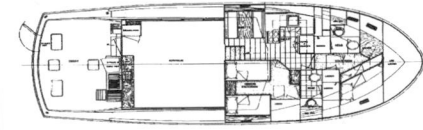

Two Staterooms

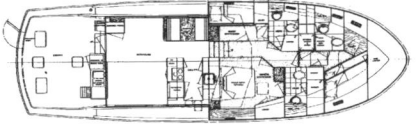

Three Staterooms

Prices Not Provided for Pre-1995 Models

Muscular, good-selling sportfishing yacht replaced iconic Hatteras 53 Convertible in 1980. Most were delivered with three-stateroom, galley-up interior with three full heads. Huge cockpit came with molded tackle center, transom door, direct access to stand-up engine room. Flybridge is huge with efficient helm layout, plenty of guest seating. No lightweight, standard 650hp GM diesels cruise at 19–20 knots (23 knots top); 870hp GMs—available from 1982—cruise at 23 knots (about 26 knots top). Updated in 1987—see following entry.

Length	55'8"	Fuel	1,285 gals.
Beam	17'6"	Water	380 gals.
Draft	4'10"	Cockpit	158 sq. ft.
Weight	70,000#	Hull Type	Modified-V
Clearance	16'8"	Deadrise Aft	NA

Hatteras 55 Convertible

1987–89

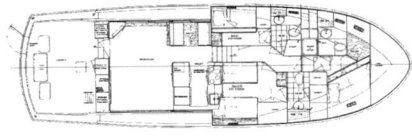

Three Staterooms

Two Staterooms

Prices Not Provided for Pre-1995 Models

Updated version of popular Hatteras 55 Convertible (1980–86) boasts restyled windows, more aggressive flybridge profile, minor interior upgrades. Most were delivered with three-stateroom, galley-up interior with amidships owner's suite, three full heads. Huge cockpit came with molded tackle center, transom door, direct access to stand-up engine room. Flybridge is huge. A heavy boat, GM 870hp diesels cruise at 23 knots (about 26 knots top); optional 1,040 GMs cruise at 25 knots (high 20s top). Note that all-new Hatteras 55 came out in 1999.

Length	55'8"	Headroom	6'6"
Beam	17'6"	Fuel	1,287 gals.
Draft	4'10"	Water	381 gals.
Weight	70,000#	Hull Type	Modified-V
Clearance	15'8"	Deadrise Aft	NA

Sportfishing Boats

Hatteras 55 Convertible

1999–2002

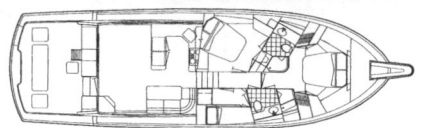

Standard Layout

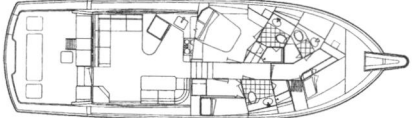

Optional Floorplan

See Page 525 For Value Estimates

Tournament-class 55-footer is an updated version of popular Hatteras 54 Convertible (1991–98) with restyled superstructure, slightly modified cockpit, increased power. Standard three-stateroom floorplan with expansive salon is identical to older 54; huge cockpit was redesigned with transom fishbox in place of in-deck units of the 54. Note pod-style helm console, newly styled tackle center. Standard 1,450hp 12-cylinder Cat diesels deliver a cruising speed of 28–29 knots and a top speed of about 33 knots.

Length	55'2"	Fuel	1,320 gals.
Beam	17'4"	Water	200 gals.
Draft	5'4"	Waste	100 gals.
Weight	74,000#	Hull Type	Modified-V
Clearance	14'8"	Deadrise Aft	6°

Hatteras 58 Convertible

1990–94

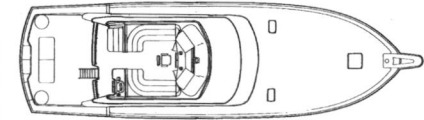

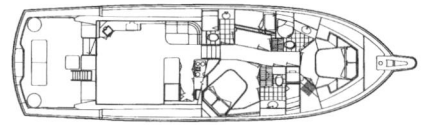

Prices Not Provided for Pre-1995 Models

Hard-charging tournament machine from early 1990s provided motoryacht luxury with sportfishing performance. Massive 175-square-foot cockpit with oversize transom door can accommodate several anglers; two-station flybridge allows helmsman to coordinate with cockpit activity. (Fully enclosed, air-conditioned bridge was optional.) Note huge walk-in engine room. No lightweight, standard 1,040hp GMs cruise at 22 knots (25–26 knots top). Popular GM 1,350hp engines cruise at 27–28 knots (30+ knots top).

Length	58'10"	Fuel	1,660 gals.
Beam	17'9"	Water	250 gals.
Draft	5'11"	Cockpit	175 sq. ft.
Weight	92,000#	Hull Type	Modified-V
Clearance	22'4"	Deadrise Aft	10°

Hatteras 60 Convertible

1977–86

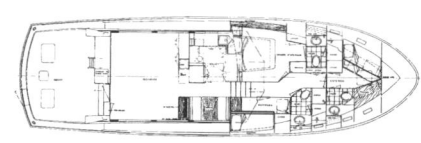

Prices Not Provided for Pre-1995 Models

Hard-nosed tournament fisherman ranks among bestselling big convertibles ever produced. Highlights include three-stateroom, three-head interior with combined salon/galley/dinette, separate utility room forward of engine room, massive 175-square-foot cockpit, optional enclosed flybridge. Early models with GM 650hp engines cruise at 17–18 knots (20 knots top). High-performance 825hp model introduced in 1986 (with beefed-up stringers, cored hullsides) will cruise at 20 knots (low 20s top). Over 125 were built.

Length	60'11"	Fuel	1,555 gals.
Beam	18'0"	Water	490 gals.
Draft	4'11"	Cockpit	175 sq. ft.
Weight	82,000#	Hull Type	Modified-V
Clearance	17'1"	Deadrise Aft	NA

Sportfishing Boats

Hatteras 60 Convertible

1998–2006

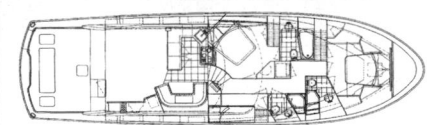

Standard Plan, 1998–2002

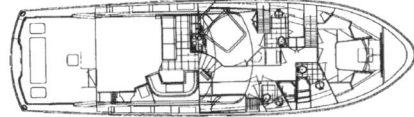

Standard Plan, 2003–06

See Page 525 For Value Estimates

World-class convertible set class standards in late 1990s for styling, luxury, flat-out performance. Three-stateroom layout with open salon/dinette/galley offers comfort equal to a Hatteras motoryacht. Huge cockpit comes with a full array of top-quality fishing features. Enclosed flybridge is optional. Note generous fuel capacity, walk-in engine room, state-of-the-art helm. Prop pockets reduce draft requirements. Standard 1,480hp Cat diesels cruise at 27–28 knots (30+ top). Replaced in 2007 with all-new 60 Convertible.

Length	60'2"	Fuel	1,622 gals.
Beam	17'4"	Water	200 gals.
Draft	5'4"	Waste	100 gals.
Weight	74,500#	Hull Type	Modified-V
Clearance, Windshield	14'8"	Deadrise Aft	5°

Hatteras 60 Convertible

2007–Current

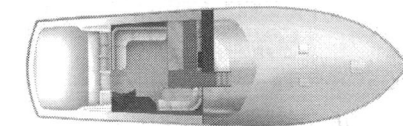

See Page 525 For Value Estimates

Broad-beamed tournament convertible with serious sex appeal targets performance-driven anglers. Design features include professional-grade mezzanine cockpit, rounded "tumblehome" hull sides, curved bridge stairs, wraparound windshield look. Standard three-stateroom interior offers true motoryacht luxuries including gourmet galley, designer decor. Flybridge electronics display is hydraulically concealed. High-strength resin infused hull (with prop pockets) is a Hatteras first. Optional Cat 1,800hp diesels cruise at a fast 33–34 knots (40 top).

Length	59'10"	Fuel	1,800 gals.
Beam	19'0"	Water	200 gals.
Draft	4'9"	Waste	100 gals.
Weight	90,000#	Hull Type	Modified-V
Clearance	13'3"	Deadrise Aft	2°

Hatteras 64 Convertible

2006–Current

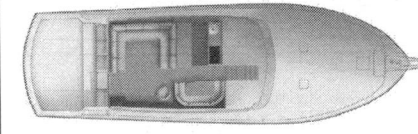

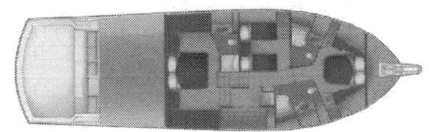

Insufficient Resale Data to Assign Values

Heavyweight convertible with broad 19'6" beam delivers sportfishing muscle, cruising elegance, engineering excellence. Standard three-stateroom, three-head interior features extravagant full-beam master with king bed, huge salon with enormous U-shaped settee. Note unique opening ports in master stateroom. Small mezzanine deck overlooks massive fishing cockpit. Engineroom is a work of art. Enclosed flybridge is optional. Deep prop pockets reduce draft, improve efficiency. Cat 1,800hp C-32 engines cruise at 28–30 knots (mid 30s top).

Length	63'10"	Fuel	1,950 gals.
Beam	19'6"	Water	343 gals.
Draft	4'10"	Waste	105 gals.
Weight	100,000#	Hull Type	Modified-V
Clearance	15'3"	Deadrise Aft	2°

Sportfishing Boats

Hatteras 65 Convertible

1987–99

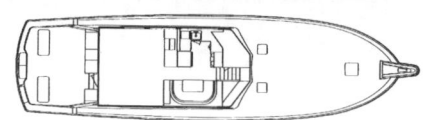

Powerful enclosed-bridge convertible remains one of the most successful Hatteras designs ever. Standard three-stateroom, galley-up layout is highlighted by spacious, beautifully appointed salon. Alternate floorplan with enlarged owner's stateroom, low-profile galley became available in 1996. Massive cockpit is largest to be found in any 65-footer. Prop pockets reduce draft, improve running efficiency. Detroit 1,035hp engines cruise at 21 knots; 1,235hp MTUs—or 1,350hp GMs—cruise at 25 knots. Total of 120 were built.

See Page 525 For Value Estimates

Length	65'5"	Fuel	1,674 gals.
Beam	18'0"	Water	460 gals.
Draft	5'4"	Waste	60 gals.
Weight	102,000#	Cockpit	183 sq. ft.
Clearance	21'11"	Hull Type	Modified-V

Hatteras 65 Convertible

2000–03

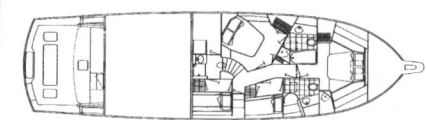

Standard 4-Stateroom Interior

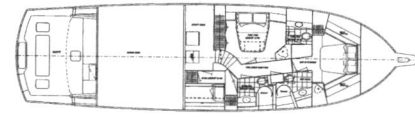

Optional 3-Stateroom Layout

Restyled version of top-selling Hatteras 65 Conv. (1987–99) boasts all-new superstructure while retaining the proven prop-pocket hull of her predecessor. Standard layout has four staterooms, three heads with tub in master. Optional three-stateroom plan replaces guest cabin with larger heads, increased storage. Note frameless cabin windows, huge engine room. Enclosed bridge model has outside control station overlooking cockpit, inside bridge access. Twin 1,400hp Cats cruise at 22–23 knots; optional 1,800hp Detroits cruise at 28 knots (30+ knots top).

See Page 525 For Value Estimates

Length	65'5"	Fuel	1,800 gals.
Beam	18'0"	Water	445 gals.
Draft	6'0"	Waste	90 gals.
Weight	103,000#	Cockpit	183 sq. ft.
Clearance	18'2"	Hull Type	Modified-V

Hatteras 68 Convertible

2005–Current

Heavyweight convertible with whopping 21'6" beam dwarfs the competition in cockpit size, interior volume. Four-stateroom, four-head interior boasts lavish full-beam master with king bed, walk-in closet. Vast salon with giant U-shaped lounge, 42" plasma TV rivals most motoryachts in size, luxury. Massive 192-square-foot cockpit—largest in her class—is overlooked by mezzanine deck with freezer, livewell. Open flybridge is standard; enclosed bridge with rounded, one-piece windshield is optional. Cruise at 28 knots (30+ top) with 1,550hp Cat diesels.

Insufficient Resale Data to Assign Values

Length	68'6"	Fuel	2,100 gals.
Beam	21'6"	Water	400 gals.
Draft	5'3"	Waste	125 gals.
Weight	140,000#	Hull Type	Modified-V
Cockpit	192 sq. ft.	Deadrise Aft	2°

Hatteras 70 Convertible

1998–2003

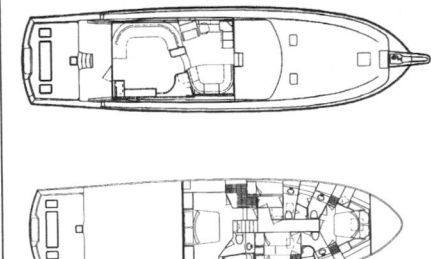

Elegant sportfishing yacht with enclosed bridge offers convertible fishability, motoryacht luxury. Wide 18-foot beam allows spacious four-stateroom, four-head interior with full-width master suite, crew quarters to port, combined salon/galley/dinette area. Mezzanine deck overlooks massive 160-square-foot cockpit; enclosed bridge is dominated by state-of-the-art helm. Note outside controls aft on bridge, frameless salon windows. Large engine room offers outstanding access. GM 1,800hp 16-cylinder diesels cruise at 28 knots (32–33 knots top).

Insufficient Resale Data to Assign Values

Length	70'3"	Fuel	2,000 gals.
Beam	18'0"	Water	365 gals.
Draft	5'4"	Waste	60 gals.
Weight	118,000#	Headroom	6'6"
Clearance	22'1"	Hull Type	Modified-V

Hydra-Sports 2800 Walkaround

2001–05

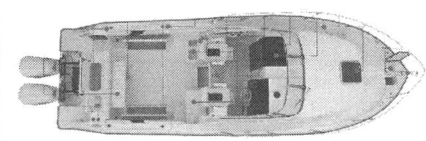

Head-turning walkaround splits the difference between hardcore fishing boat, weekend family cruiser. Features include in-deck fish boxes, transom door, 35-gallon lighted livewell, foldaway rear seat, fresh/raw-water wash-downs, bait-prep center with sink, cockpit bolsters, tackle storage (under helm seats), aft-facing jump seats, in-deck storage. Cabin amenities include galley with microwave, midcabin berth, enclosed head with VacuFlush toilet, standard air-conditioning. Impressive finish. Over 40 knots top with Yamaha 225s.

See Page 526 For Value Estimates

Length	28'2"	Fuel	284 gals.
Beam	9'8"	Water	29 gals.
Hull Draft	18"	Max HP	500
Weight w/OBs	7,225#	Hull Type	Deep-V
Clearance, Hardtop	9'0"	Deadrise Aft	23°

Hydra-Sports 2900 Vector Center Console

2006–Current

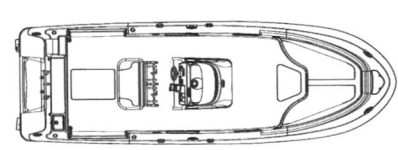

Big-water center console with tournament-tested layout targets serious anglers who recognize quality. Cockpit features include transom rigging station with sink, foldaway rear seat, lighted 55-gallon livewell, three fishboxes, lockable rod storage. Helm has space for flush-mounting two 10" video screens. Standard hardtop comes with electronics box, spreader lights. Walk-in console has portable toilet, sink with hand-held shower. Excellent range. Windshield surrounds entire helm—sweet. Yamaha 250s top out at 45 knots.

See Page 526 For Value Estimates

Length	29'8"	Fuel	300 gals.
Beam	9'8"	Water	23 gals.
Hull Draft	1'10"	Max HP	600
Dry Weight	7,904#	Hull Type	Deep-V
Clearance	8'9"	Deadrise Aft	23°

Sportfishing Boats

Hydra-Sports 2900 VX Express

2006–Current

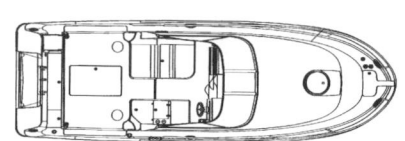

Leading-edge express combines handsome styling with top-shelf amenities, no-excuses performance. Cockpit highlights include foldaway rear seat, 35-gallon livewell, insulated fishboxes, bait-prep station, padded bolsters. Portside lounge seat converts to sun pad. Well-appointed interior with midcabin berth, pilot berths is ideal for overnight trips. Note walk-thru windshield, pop-up cleats, tackle drawers. Generous 300-gallon fuel capacity delivers impressive 400-mile cruising range. Yamaha 250s reach 45+ knots top.

See Page 526 For Value Estimates

Length	29'8"	Fuel	300 gals.
Beam	9'8"	Water	27 gals.
Hull Draft	1'10"	Max HP	600
Dry Weight	8,396#	Hull Type	Deep-V
Clearance	8'9"	Deadrise Aft	23°

Hydra-Sports 3000 Vector Center Console

1997–2000

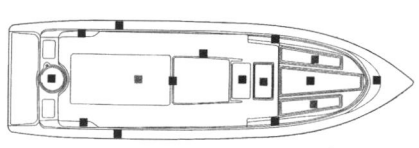

Tournament-ready fishing machine with high-performance deep-V hull combines brawn, speed, fishability. Features include walk-in console with portable head, 50-gallon transom livewell, insulated forward fishbox, pop-up cleats, rear jump seats, fresh/raw-water washdowns, lockable rod storage, leaning post, cockpit bolsters, forward console seat, bow storage lockers. Note under-gunwale tackle boxes in aft corners. One of the few trailerable 30-footers ever built. Exceptional range. Over 45 knots top with twin 225s.

See Page 526 For Value Estimates

Length	29'5"	Fuel	300 gals.
Beam	8'7"	Water	27 gals.
Draft, Engines Up	2'0"	Max HP	750
Draft, Engines Down	2'8"	Hull Type	Deep-V
Dry Weight	7,100#	Deadrise Aft	24°

Hydra-Sports 3300 Sport Fisherman

1989–92

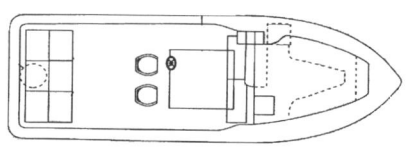

High-performance offshore fisherman from early 1990s was based on go-fast hull previously used for Donzi 33. Large 75-square-foot cockpit with padded coaming, full-height transom features aerated livewell, 6-foot-long insulated fishbox, rod storage, fold-down transom bench seat. Small cuddy with compact galley sleeps two. Additional features include enclosed head with sink and shower, double helm seat with rocket launchers, aft-facing cockpit seat, folding tower. Twin 275hp outboards deliver a top speed of 40+ knots.

Prices Not Provided for Pre-1995 Models

Length	32'11"	Fuel	270 gals.
Beam	9'6"	Water	42 gals.
Hull Draft	1'6"	Max HP	600
Dry Weight (Approx.)	10,500#	Hull Type	Deep-V
Clearance	5'6"	Deadrise Aft	24°

Sportfishing Boats

Hydra-Sports 3300 Vector Center Console

2003–10

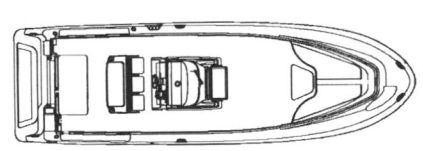

High-impact fishing machine with Kevlar-reinforced hull, triple-outboard power is strong, fast, built for the offshore tournament wars. Highlights include drop-out 3-person bolster seat with 55-gallon livewell & bait station, two forward fishboxes, lockable rod storage, foldaway rear seat, T-top with electronics box & spreader lights, pop-up cleats, washdowns, cockpit bolsters. Console head has sink, rod storage, battery access. Note cast net storage in forward floor. An impressive rough-water performer. 50+ knots with triple Yamaha 250s.

See Page 526 For Value Estimates

Length	33'5"	Fuel	352 gals.
Beam	10'4"	Water	29 gals.
Draft, Engines Down	2'10"	Max HP	900
Hull Weight	8,620#	Hull Type	Deep-V
Clearance	7'9"	Deadrise Aft	23°

Hydra-Sports 3300 VX Express

2004–07

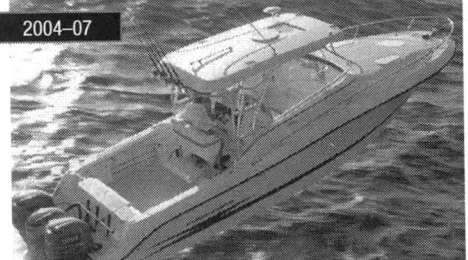
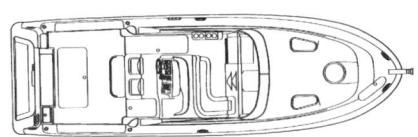

No-compromise cuddy express offers anglers tournament-grade fishability with proven big-water performance, quality construction. Roomy deck layout includes L-lounge seating forward of helm, foldaway rear seat, 55-gallon Kodiak livewell, two fishboxes, cockpit bolsters. Hardtop with sliding hatch was standard. Helm flat has room for two 10" video screens. Well-appointed cabin with enclosed head/shower, convertible dinette, midcabin berth sleeps four. Well-built boat can take a punch. About 50 knots max with triple 250s.

See Page 526 For Value Estimates

Length	33'5"	Fuel	352 gals.
Beam	10'4"	Water	35 gals.
Draft, Down	2'10"	Max HP	900
Hull Weight	10,500#	Hull Type	Deep-V
Clearance	9'3"	Deadrise Aft	23°

Hydra-Sports 3500 VX Express

2008–Current

Floorplan Not Available

Graceful hardtop express delivers luxury-class amenities seldom found in a hard-charging fishing boat. Highlights include large center console helm with tall windscreen, deluxe mid-berth cabin with stand-up head and bunks for six, standard air-conditioning (with helm vent), wraparound cockpit settee, fold-away transom seat. Cockpit may be on the small side for hardcore anglers. Comfort has a price—this is one of the more expensive outboard-powered boats on the planet. Twin 350hp Yamaha reach 40+ knots wide open.

See Page 526 For Value Estimates

Length	34'10"	Fuel	372 gals.
Beam	11'6"	Water	40 gals.
Hull Draft	2'2"	Max HP	900
Dry Weight (Approx.)	16,000#	Hull Type	Deep-V
Clearance	10'5"	Deadrise Aft	23°

Sportfishing Boats

Intrepid 289 Center Console

1987–2003

Stepped-hull center console introduced in 1987 combined solid construction with efficient deck layout, good performance. Highlights include removable rear bench seat, in-deck fishbox, leaning post with livewell, transom livewells (2), dive platform, raw-water washdown, tilt-away helm, console seat/cooler, remote oil fills. Note unusual bow head compartment. Kevlar-reinforced laminates make the 289 a strong, relatively lightweight boat for her size. A good-selling model for Intrepid. Up to 45 knots with Yamaha 225s.

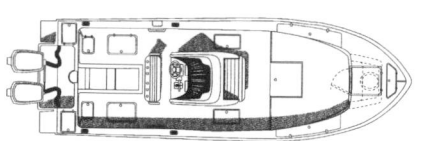

See Page 526 For Value Estimates

Length w/Bracket	28'9"	Fuel	193 gals.
Beam	9'1"	Water	20 gals.
Hull Draft	2'0"	Max HP	450
Dry Weight	3,200#	Hull Type	Deep-V
Clearance	5'2"	Deadrise Aft	22.5°

Intrepid 289 Walkaround

1997–2003

Deluxe open express with high-performance stepped hull is one part fishing boat, one part family cruiser. Guest-friendly deck layout boasts lounge seating forward of helm. Fishing amenities include insulated fishboxes, livewells, rod storage. Compact cabin has enclosed head with shower, U-shaped seating, mini-galley. Additional features include bow pulpit, anchor locker, deep walkways, small dive platform. A well-finished boat. Twin 200hp Mercury outboards cruise at 30 knots (about 45 knots top).

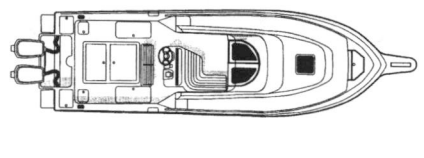

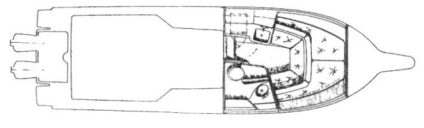

See Page 526 For Value Estimates

Length w/Bracket	28'9"	Fuel	193 gals.
Beam	9'1"	Water	15 gals.
Hull Draft	2'0"	Max HP	450
Dry Weight	3,400#	Hull Type	Deep-V
Clearance	5'2"	Deadrise Aft	22.5°

Intrepid 30 Console Cuddy

1984–93

Original Intrepid model with trailerable 8'6" beam is fast, agile, built to last. Highlights included double helm seat with rod holders, cushioned console seat, dive platform with ladder, rod storage, insulated fish box, livewell, raw-water washdown, removable rear bench seat, tackle cabinet. No-frills cuddy with portable head, rod storage sleeps two. Slender beam results in limited cockpit space for a 30-footer. Alternate version of this model with open layout (no cuddy) was also available. Max 50+ knots with 250hp Mercs.

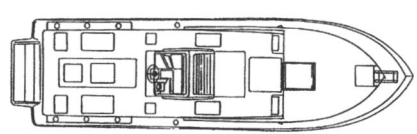

Prices Not Provided for Pre-1995 Models

Length w/Bracket	32'1"	Fuel	170 gals.
Beam	8'6"	Water	30 gals.
Draft	2'0"	Max HP	500
Weight	3,250#	Hull Type	Deep-V
Clearance	NA	Deadrise Aft	22°

Intrepid 300 Center Console

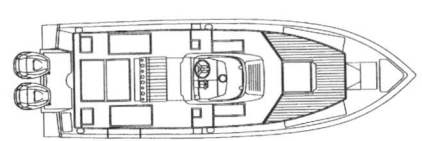

2004–Current

Hard-hitting 30-footer with performance-focused stepped hull can be customized for fishing, diving, entertaining. Standard features include transom door, deluxe forward seating, insulated forward fishbox, rod storage locker, lockable bow storage compartment. Forward console seat glides aside for entry into enclosed head with shower. Hullside dive door, removable rear seat, transom livewell, bow thruster are popular options. Quality doesn't come cheap. No bow rails. Max 50+ knots with 250hp Yamahas.

See Page 526 For Value Estimates

Length	30'0"	Fuel, Opt.	214 gals.
Beam	9'6"	Water	30 gals.
Draft, Up	1'10"	Max HP	500
Draft, Down	3'0"	Hull Type	Deep-V
Fuel, Std.	180 gals.	Deadrise Aft	22°

Intrepid 310 Walkaround

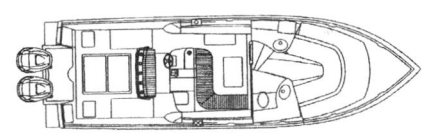

2004–Current

Sophisticated sport express with agile stepped hull, sociable deck layout takes Intrepid innovation to the next level. Bow pulpit, insulated fishbox, transom door, trim tabs are standard; everything else is optional including removable rear bench seat, Intrepid's signature hullside dive door. L-shaped lounge forward of helm seats three. Posh cabin with near standing headroom boasts full galley, wraparound seating, stand-up head with shower. More luxury cruiser than fishboat. Yamaha 250s reach 45+ knots top.

See Page 526 For Value Estimates

Length w/Pulpit	32'8"	Fuel	180 gals.
Hull Length	31'0"	Water	30 gals.
Beam	9'8"	Max HP	600
Hull Draft	2'0"	Hull Type	Deep-V
Weight	9,000#	Deadrise Aft	22.5°

Intrepid 322 Console Cuddy

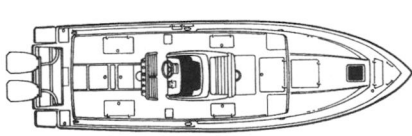

1996–2003

Versatile cuddy console with notched hull is part sportfisherman, part day cruiser, full-time fun machine. Semicustom boat offered several seating options. Standard features included in-floor storage lockers, lockable electronics box, dive platforms, anchor locker. Most were sold with Intrepid's signature hullside dive door. No-frills cuddy with V-berth is great for storage, lacks ventilation. Fishing amenities—livewells, washdowns, etc.—were optional. Exemplary fit and finish. Tops 50 knots with Yamaha 250s.

See Page 526 For Value Estimates

Length	32'2"	Fuel, Opt.	300 gals.
Beam	9'1"	Water	22 gals.
Hull Draft	2'0"	Max HP	500
Dry Weight	3,300#	Hull Type	Deep-V
Fuel, Std.	240 gals.	Deadrise Aft	22.5°

Sportfishing Boats

Intrepid 323 Center Console

2004–Current

Good-selling center console with best-in-class finish targets upmarket boat buffs with an eye for yacht-class quality. Standard features include removable rear bench seat, insulated forward fishbox, deluxe double helm seat, deck storage/rod lockers forward, cockpit bolsters, transom door, dive platforms. Several custom livewell and helm console options to choose from. Power console seat slides aside for access to head with sink and shower. This kind of quality doesn't come cheap. About 50 knots top with twin 300s.

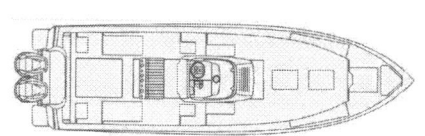

See Page 526 For Value Estimates

Length Overall	32'2"	Clearance	NA
Beam	9'6"	Water	20 gals.
Draft	2'6"	Max HP	600
Dry Weight	9,000#	Hull Type	Deep-V
Fuel	208 gals.	Deadrise Aft	22.5°

Intrepid 339 Center Console

1996–2002

Seductive center console introduced in 1996 blends semi-custom quality with quality amenities, hardcore fishability. Race-proven stepped hull reduces drag by breaking water's grip on the hull. Single-level cockpit features in-deck fish/storage boxes, lockable rod lockers; forepeak head with privacy tent is unique (if perhaps a little curious). Helm console has space for flush-mounting electronics. Forward seating folds away for fishing. Anchor locker, trim tabs, dive platform were standard. Twin 250hp outboards top out at 45+ knots.

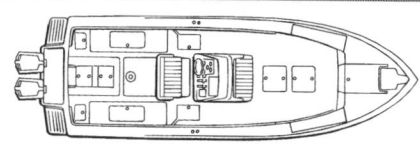
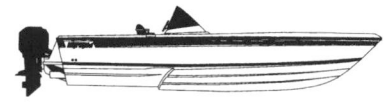

See Page 526 For Value Estimates

Length w/Bracket	33'9"	Fuel, Opt.	295 gals.
Beam	10'0"	Water	22 gals.
Hull Draft	2'0"	Max HP	500
Dry Weight	5,000#	Hull Type	Deep-V
Fuel, Std.	245 gals.	Deadrise Aft	20.5°

Intrepid 348 Walkaround

2002–04

Luxury dayboat/fishing machine with social deck plan offers speed, comfort, unabashed sex appeal. Highlights include factory hardtop, custom leaning post, forward L-lounge seating, cockpit bolsters, in-deck fishboxes, fresh/raw-water washdowns, transom door. Hull side dive door was a popular option. Note bow anchor chute. Sleek interior with full galley, enclosed head has V-berth that lifts electrically to access storage beneath. Lightweight stepped hull offers exceptional speed, agility. Near-flawless fit and finish. About 45 knots top with twin 250s.

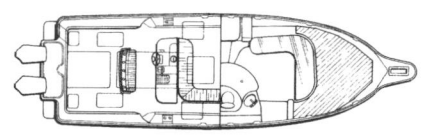

See Page 526 For Value Estimates

Length	34'8"	Fuel	258 gals.
Beam	10'6"	Water	40 gals.
Hull Draft	24"	Max HP	600
Dry Weight	7,000#	Hull Type	Deep-V
Clearance w/Top	8'7"	Deadrise Aft	22.5°

Intrepid 350 Walkaround

2005–Current

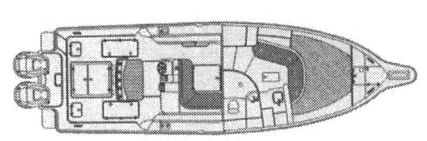

Re-tooled version of Intrepid 348 Walkaround (2002–04) boasts slightly lengthened cockpit, all-new reverse transom design with integral motor well and transom door. Super-quality boat (each built to owner specs) comes standard with dive platforms, macerated fishbox, anchor chute, deluxe console with L-shaped seating forward. Well-appointed cabin has convertible seating, compact galley, enclosed head with shower. Single-stepped hull offers exceptional speed, agility. Twin 250 Verados deliver 40+ knots top.

See Page 526 For Value Estimates

Length	35'0"	Fuel, Opt.	312 gals.
Beam	10'6"	Water	40 gals.
Hull Draft	24"	Max HP	600
Dry Weight	7,500#	Hull Type	Deep-V
Fuel, Std.	258 gals.	Deadrise Aft	22.5°

Intrepid 356 Cuddy

1994–2001

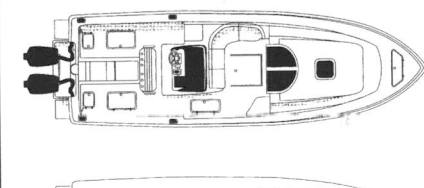

Sporty notched-bottom speedster took 1990s engineering to the next level. Versatile deck layout with forward seating is suitable for fishing, diving, cruising. Removable rear bench seat, in-deck fish box, recirculating livewell, transom door, dive platforms, two-person helm seat were standard. Upscale cabin came with galley, dinette/V-berth, enclosed head. Cabin height slightly increased in 1998. No windscreen for front seat passengers. Intrepid 366 is the same boat with a lengthened cockpit. Max 45 knots with 250hp outboards.

See Page 526 For Value Estimates

Length Overall	35'6"	Fuel, Opt.	285 gals.
Beam	10'6"	Water	50 gals.
Hull Draft	2'0"	Max HP	600
Dry Weight	6,500#	Hull Type	Deep-V
Fuel, Std.	235 gals.	Deadrise Aft	22.5°

Intrepid 366 Cuddy

1999–2003

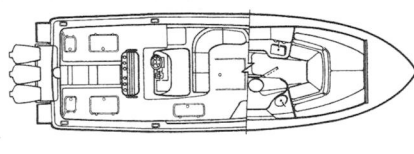

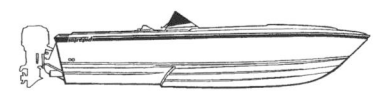

Updated version of popular Intrepid 356 Cuddy boasts enlarged cockpit, optional triple-outboard power. Versatile layout with forward seating is great for fishing, diving, cruising. Removable rear seat, in-deck fish box, recirculating livewell, transom door, dive platforms, two-person helm seat were standard. Cuddy came with galley cabinet, dinette/V-berth, enclosed head. Stepped hull is agile, fast. One of Intrepid's best-selling models. Triple 225hp Mercury outboards reach top speed of close to 50 knots.

See Page 526 For Value Estimates

Length Overall	36'6"	Fuel, Opt.	400 gals.
Beam	10'6"	Water	30 gals.
Hull Draft	2'0"	Max HP	675
Dry Weight	6,500#	Hull Type	Deep-V
Fuel, Std.	300 gals.	Deadrise Aft	22.5°

Sportfishing Boats

Intrepid 370 Cuddy

2003–Current

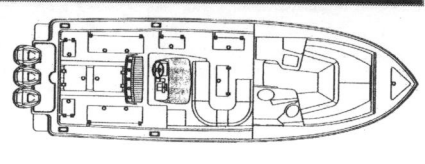
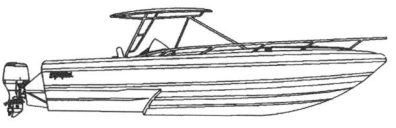

Premium semicustom sportboat with stepped hull, triple-outboard power combines unabashed luxury, high-octane performance. Removable transom seat, console cooler, tackle storage, deluxe helm seat, forward lounge seating, insulated fishbox, hullside dive door. Upscale cabin includes adult-size V-berth, portside galley, enclosed head with shower. No windshield protection for front-seat passengers. Transom door available with twin engines only. Good selling model for Intrepid. Tops out at 50+ knots with triple 250s.

See Page 526 For Value Estimates

Length	37'0"	Fuel	300 gals.
Beam	10'6"	Water	40 gals.
Draft, Up	2'0"	Max HP	600
Draft, Down	3'2"	Hull Type	Deep-V
Weight	11,000#	Deadrise Aft	22.5°

Intrepid 377 Walkaround

2000–08

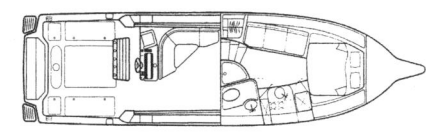

Executive-class offshore cruiser with triple-outboard power defines sportfishing luxury in the fast lane. Features include factory hardtop, in-deck fishboxes, L-lounge seating forward of helm, pop-up cleats, transom door, custom leaning post, cockpit bolsters, bow pulpit. Hull side dive door, removable rear bench seat were popular options. Well-appointed interior with galley, convertible settee, enclosed head with stall shower sleeps four. Note huge, state-of-the-art helm console. Popular, beautifully finished cruiser. Triple 275 Mercs reach 50+ knots.

See Page 526 For Value Estimates

Length w/o Pulpit	38'3"	Fuel	400 gals.
Beam	11'6"	Water	60 gals.
Hull Draft	2'4"	Max HP	900
Dry Weight	10,000#	Hull Type	Deep-V
Clearance	9'0"	Deadrise Aft	22.5°

Island Runner 31

1997–Current

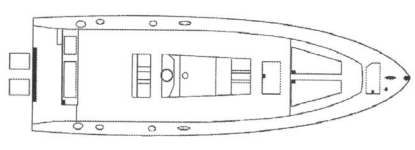

Popular South Florida fisherman with trailerable 8'6" beam combines big-boat features with small-boat agility, economy. Standard features include T-top with rod holders, above-deck 50-gallon livewell, walk-in console with marine head, insulated 380-qt fishbox, raw-water washdown. Well-designed helm has space for flush-mounting electronics. Note pop-up cleats, large in-floor storage box forward of the console. Slender deep-V hull is quick to accelerate, fast across the water. Tops out at over 50 knots with twin 225 Mercs.

See Page 527 For Value Estimates

Length	31'4"	Fuel	220 gals.
Beam	8'6"	Water	30 gals.
Draft, Up	1'8"	Max HP	500
Draft, Down	2'8"	Hull Type	Deep-V
Dry Weight	4,000#	Deadrise Aft	24°

Sportfishing Boats

Jefferson 35 Marlago Cuddy

1994–Current

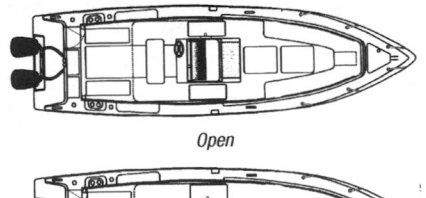

Open

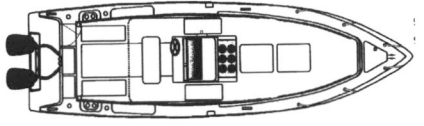

Cuddy

See Page 527 For Value Estimates

Narrow-beam center console with high-performance hull, low-profile cuddy is agile, fast, priced right. Removable rear seat, in-deck fish boxes, console seat with cooler, flip-up helm seat, fresh- and saltwater washdowns, pop-up cleats, enclosed head with pull-out shower. Offered with two transom configurations, one with transom door, bait-prep station & livewell, or "Full Transom" option with additional sink but no transom door. Open-bow model available since 2004. Yamaha 250s deliver 45+ knots top; 300 Verados can hit 50 knots.

Length	35'0"	Fuel, Std.	245 gals.
Beam	9'2"	Water	31 gals.
Draft, Up	1'8"	Max HP	600
Draft, Down	2'3"	Hull Type	Deep-V
Dry Weight	6,000#	Deadrise Aft	24°

Jupiter 27 Open

1998–2006

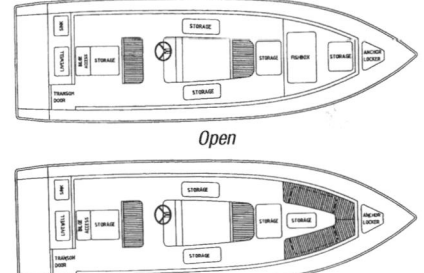

Open

Cuddy

See Page 527 For Value Estimates

Top-quality center console with full array of premium fishing amenities sets class standards for performance, fishability. Features include 40-gallon livewell, 90-gallon fish box, pop-up cleats, bait-rigging station, two electronics boxes. Console head compartment has standing headroom and V-berth. Available in Open and Cuddy configurations. Running surface extended all the way aft for increased lift in 2002. Impressive owner satisfaction. Tops out at over 45 knots with twin Yamaha 225s.

Length	27'4"	Fuel	204 gals.
Beam	8'6"	Water	37 gals.
Draft, Up	1'7"	Max HP	450
Draft, Down	2'2"	Hull Type	Deep-V
Weight w/Engines	5,820#	Deadrise Aft	24°

Jupiter 29 Forward Seating

2006–Current

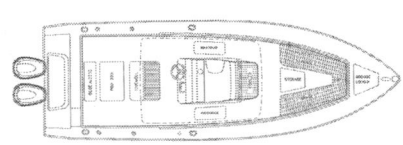

See Page 527 For Value Estimates

Hard-hitting canyon runner with roomy cockpit, cushioned bow seating makes the cut with hardcore anglers. Standard features include bait-prep center with 45-gallon livewell, 120-gallon macerated fishbox, leaning post, fresh/saltwater washdowns, lockable in-deck rod storage, tackle storage, low-profile bow rails. Space at the helm for twin big-screen displays. All hatches are gasketed and dogged. Plenty of fuel for a 29-footer. Yamaha 250hp outboards reach close to 45 knots wide open.

Length	29'6"	Fuel	285 gals.
Beam	9'4"	Water	35 gals.
Hull Draft	2'9"	Max HP	600
Weight w/Engines	9,200#	Hull Type	Deep-V
Clearance	8'10"	Deadrise Aft	24°

Sportfishing Boats

Jupiter 31 Open

1989–Current

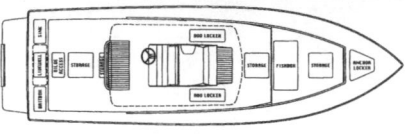

Open Deck Plan

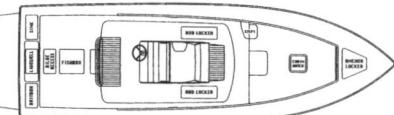

Cuddy Deck Plan

See Page 527 For Value Estimates

World-class offshore center console delivers a convincing blend of quality, features, fishability. Standard fishing gear includes transom rigging station, 30-gallon stand-up livewell, rod storage lockers, dual washdowns, large-capacity fishboxes fore and aft. Oversized console permits expansive helm layout, spacious head compartment. Hull pad provides extra low-speed lift. Extraordinary finish throughout. Available in Cuddy or Forward Seating models. One of the most popular 31-footers ever. Over 45 knots with Yamaha 250s.

Length w/Bracket	33'2"	Fuel	260 gals.
Hull Length	30'8"	Water	60 gals.
Beam	9'6"	Max HP	600
Draft, Down	2'7"	Hull Type	Deep-V
Weight	10,500#	Deadrise Aft	24°

Jupiter 34 Forward Seating

2008–Current

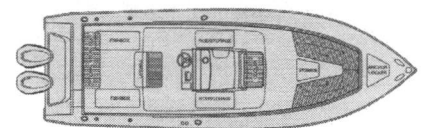

Forward Seating

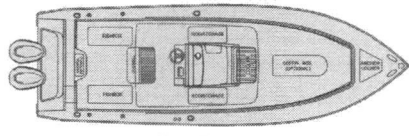

Flush Floor Plan

See Page 528 For Value Estimates

Leading-edge center console introduced in 2008 was specifically designed to accommodate newer (heavier) Yamaha 350s. Available with standard forward seating/lounge area or optional Tournament model with flush cockpit floor and over-sized coffin fish box. Standard features include deluxe leaning post/tackle center with 45-gallon livewell, fresh/saltwater washdowns, foldaway transom seat, rod storage lockers, insulated fish boxes. Walk-in head has sink and shower. Hull pad improves low-speed performance. Over 50 knots with twin 350s.

Length	33'9"	Fuel	325 gals.
Beam	10'5"	Water	50 gals.
Draft, Up	2'0"	Max HP	700
Draft, Down	3'0"	Hull Type	Deep-V
Weight w/Engines	9,880#	Deadrise Aft	23°

Jupiter 38 Forward Seating

2005–Current

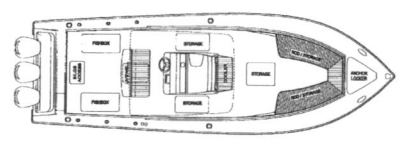

See Page 528 For Value Estimates

Feature-packed center console takes big-water fishability to the next level. Highlights include cushioned bow seating, leaning post with 50-gallon livewell, foldout stern seat, two macerated fish boxes, two six-foot storage boxes, two lockable rod storage boxes under forward seating area. Side lockers offer storage for life jackets. Console head includes shower, rod storage. Bow area is designed for optional concealed windlass. All hatches are gasketed, dogged. Twin Yamaha 250s top out in the low 40s; triple 250s hit 50+ knots.

Length	38'2"	Fuel, Std/Opt	320/480 gals.
Beam	10'7"	Water	60 gals.
Draft, Up	24"	Max HP	900
Draft, Down	36"	Hull Type	Deep-V
Weight w/Engines	8,970#	Deadrise Aft	24°

Luhrs 28 Open

2005–09

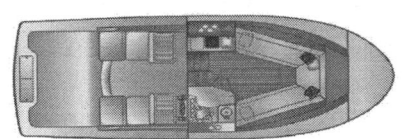

Classy inboard express with best-in-class styling is ready to fish, equipped to cruise, fun to drive. Spacious cockpit has transom fishbox, livewell, bait-prep center with cutting board, tackle drawers, fresh/raw-water washdowns. Roomy cabin with full galley, teak-and-holly sole, overhead rod storage sleeps four. Bridgedeck lifts for engine access. Note generous fuel capacity, tall fiberglass-framed windshield. Great styling, lots of cockpit space. Twin 330hp gas engines cruise at 20 knots; Yanmar 260hp diesels cruise at 24 knots.

See Page 528 For Value Estimates

Length w/Pulpit	31'10"	Fuel	300 gals.
Hull Length	29'10"	Water	55 gals.
Beam	11'6"	Waste	15 gals.
Draft	2'8"	Hull Type	Modified-V
Weight	10,000#	Deadrise Aft	19°

Luhrs Tournament 290

1989–90

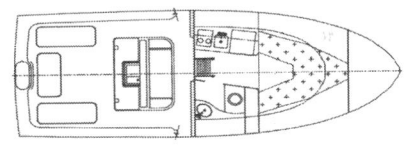

Sturdy inboard fisherman with plain-Jane personna is one part center console, one part walkaround cabin. Deep, unobstructed fishing cockpit came standard with in-deck fishboxes, transom livewell, bait-prep station, raw-water washdown. Double helm seat doubles as engine box. Teak-trimmed cabin has enclosed head with shower, full galley, convertible dinette, berths for four. Marlin tower with controls was standard. No windscreen. Not a big seller. Cruise at 20 knots with 240hp gas engines (around 28 knots wide open).

Prices Not Provided for Pre-1995 Models

Length	29'6"	Fuel	250 gals.
Beam	10'9"	Water	40 gals.
Draft	2'5"	Waste	20 gals.
Weight	7,840#	Hull Type	Modified-V
Clearance	NA	Deadrise Aft	17°

Luhrs 290 Open

1992–2002

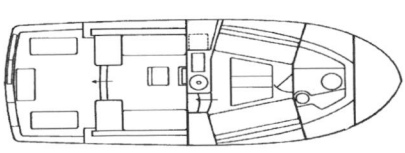

Best-selling inboard express introduced in 1992 offered great styling, proven fishability, versatile cabin accommodations. Roomy cockpit with centerline helm has two in-deck fishboxes, livewell, transom door, raw-water washdown, transom fish/storage box. Bridgedeck lifts electrically for engine access. Unique cabin layout with forward head, facing settees sleeps four. Marlin tower was standard. A great-looking boat with wide appeal. Cruise at 16–18 knots with 270hp gas engines; 20 knots with Yanmar 230hp diesels.

See Page 528 For Value Estimates

Length w/Pulpit	31'10"	Fuel	302 gals.
Hull Length	29'10"	Water	55 gals.
Beam	11'6"	Waste	20 gals.
Draft	2'0"	Hull Type	Modified-V
Weight	10,000#	Deadrise Aft	16°

Sportfishing Boats

Luhrs 30 Alura

1987–90

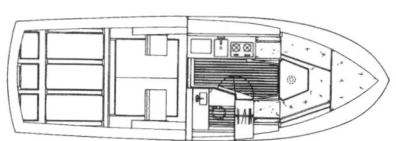

Single-inboard fishing boat with efficient semi-displacement hull is versatile enough for fishing, diving, cruising. Deep cockpit with high gunwales, in-deck fishboxes has over 100 square feet of space. Large bridgedeck hatches provide good engine access. Note tall windshield, wide side decks, standard swim platform. Roomy, well-appointed interior sleeps four. Keel was redesigned in 1988 to reduce vibration problems. Very fuel-efficient boat. Single 270hp gas inboard will cruise at 14–15 knots (low 20s top).

Prices Not Provided for Pre-1995 Models

Length Overall	30'0"	Fuel	196 gals.
Length WL	28'0"	Water	38 gals.
Beam	10'3"	Waste	15 gals.
Draft	2'11"	Hull Type	Semi-Disp.
Weight	7,800#	Deadrise Aft	NA

Luhrs 300 Tournament

1991–96

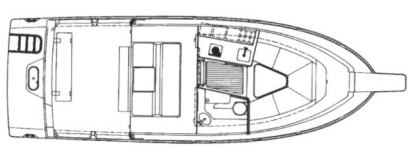

Updated version of the earlier 290 Tournament (1989–90) combines walkaround fishability with dayboat versatility. Fishing amenities include in-deck fishbox, tackle drawers, bait-prep center. Note baitwell location on transom platform—very unusual. Helm seats lift for access to tight engine compartment. Cozy cabin boasts convertible dinette, small galley, stand-up head with shower. Great for fishing, diving or overnighting. Twin 270hp gas inboards cruise at 18 knots; 170hp Yanmar diesels cruise at 18– 20 knots.

See Page 528 For Value Estimates

Length w/Pulpit	34'6"	Fuel	250 gals.
Hull Length	31'6"	Water	40 gals.
Beam	10'9"	Waste	20 gals.
Draft	2'6"	Hull Type	Modified-V
Weight	12,000#	Deadrise Aft	18°

Luhrs 30/31 Open

2004–09

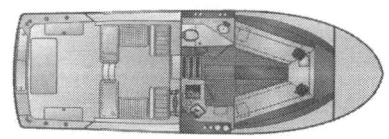

Entry-level fishing boat (called the Luhrs 30 Open in 2004–05; 31 Open in 2006–09) with rakish styling delivers signature Luhrs value at an affordable price. Standard features include hardtop, bait-prep center with sink, livewell, tackle drawers, washdowns, in-deck fishboxes, transom door. Well-appointed cabin with teak trim, convertible dinette sleeps four. Bridgedeck lifts for engine access. Twin 320hp gas inboards—or 315 Yanmar diesels—cruise at 23–24 knots. Newer models with Volvo 260hp IPS drives cruise at 22 knots.

See Page 528 For Value Estimates

Length Overall	34'4"	Fuel	300 gals.
Hull Length	31'5"	Water	50 gals.
Beam	11'10"	Waste	25 gals.
Draft	2'6"	Hull Type	Deep-V
Weight	13,500#	Deadrise Aft	20°

Luhrs 320 Convertible

1988–99

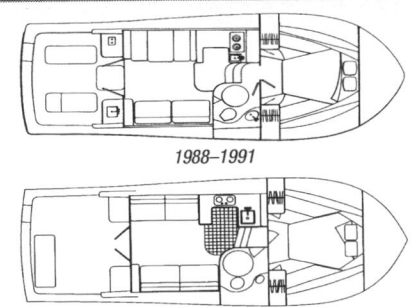

1988–1991

1992–1999

Popular midsize convertible hit the sweet spot with anglers looking for graceful styling, upscale accommodations, no-excuses fishability. In-deck fishbox, transom door, fresh/raw-water washdowns, bait-prep station with sink, bow pulpit. Roomy interior with expansive salon features private stateroom with island berth, complete galley, large head with shower. Original dinette layout was replaced in 1992 with facing salon settees. Twin 320hp gas inboards—or optional 300hp Yanmar diesels—cruise at 20–22 knots.

See Page 528 For Value Estimates

Length w/Pulpit	34'8"	Fuel	272 gals.
Hull Length	31'6"	Water	60 gals.
Beam	13'0"	Waste	30 gals.
Draft	3'1"	Hull Type	Modified-V
Weight	15,000#	Deadrise Aft	18°

Luhrs 32 Convertible

2001–02

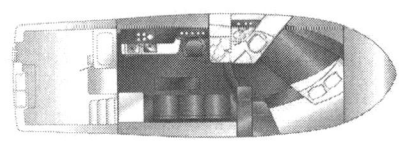

Affordable small convertible with sporty styling, well-appointed interior packed a lot of features in relatively small hull. Salon is compact but offers efficient portside galley, convertible settee, attractive teak cabinetry. Note stall shower in head. Cockpit amenities include transom door, transom fishbox, bait-prep center with livewell, washdowns. Molded bridge steps are a plus. Flybridge—with standard hardtop—seats up to six. Cruise at 20 knots with 310hp gas inboards (about 30 knots top). Production for this model lasted only two years.

See Page 528 For Value Estimates

Length w/Pulpit	34'11"	Clearance, Hardtop	16'4"
Hull Length	32'3"	Fuel	270 gals.
Beam	11'8"	Water	60 gals.
Draft	3'4"	Hull Type	Modified-V
Weight	16,250#	Deadrise Aft	18°

Luhrs 32 Open

1994–2008

Value-packed express combines graceful Palm Beach styling with large fishing cockpit, classy cabin accommodations. Cockpit amenities include livewell, dual washdowns, bait-prep center, fishbox, tackle drawers. Center helm position offers excellent 360-degree visibility. Teak-trimmed interior with dinette forward, slide-out settee sleeps five. Tower is standard; windshield is optional. Cruise at 20 knots with 320hp gas inboards (high 20s top). Optional 315hp Yanmar diesels cruise at 26–27 knots (30+ knots top).

See Page 528 For Value Estimates

Length w/Pulpit	34'8"	Fuel	340 gals.
Hull Length	31'6"	Water	60 gals.
Beam	13'0"	Waste	30 gals.
Draft	3'1"	Hull Type	Modified-V
Weight	15,000#	Deadrise Aft	18°

Sportfishing Boats

Luhrs 34 Convertible

2000–03

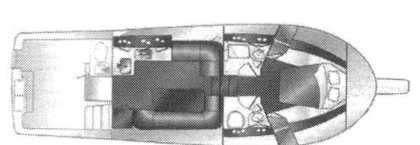

Good-looking convertible blurs the lines between well-bred fisherman, feature-rich family cruiser. Roomy interior boasts wide-open salon with facing settees, separate head/shower compartments, large stateroom. Salon settee slides out to create double berth. Transom door, bait-prep center, transom fishbox were standard. Note molded steps to flybridge. Engine room is a tight fit, but convenient cockpit access is rare in a boat this size. Twin 375hp gas engines cruise at 20 knots; 350hp Yanmar diesels cruise in the low 20s.

See Page 528 For Value Estimates

Length w/Pulpit	36'10"	Fuel	300 gals.
Beam	13'1"	Water	90 gals.
Draft	3'4"	Waste	40 gals.
Weight	18,000#	Hull Type	Modified-V
Clearance	16'5"	Deadrise Aft	18°

Luhrs 340 Sport Fisherman

1983–87

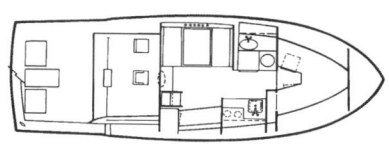

Value-priced sportfisherman from 1980s combined raised-bridgedeck styling with roomy interior, large fishing cockpit. Marketed as fully equipped fishing boat with standard marlin tower, fishboxes, washdowns, cabin rod storage. Simple interior with convertible dinette, small galley sleeps four. Note centerline helm position, roomy engine compartment, wide side decks. No transom door. Standard 340hp gas inboards cruise at 16 knots (25–26 knots top). Optional 300hp diesels cruise in the low 20s (24–25 knots top).

Prices Not Provided for Pre-1995 Models

Length	34'0"	Fuel	260 gals.
Beam	12'6"	Water	60 gals.
Draft	3'0"	Waste	40 gals.
Weight	12,300#	Hull Type	Modified-V
Clearance	11'5"	Deadrise Aft	16°

Luhrs 342 Convertible

1986–89

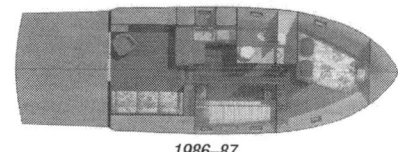

1986–87

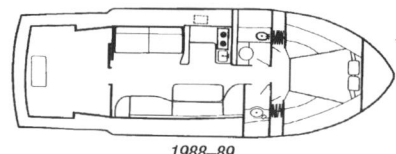

1988–89

Appealing 1980s convertible with rakish styling offered sportfish versatility at an affordable price. Large flybridge has seating forward of helm. Cockpit is large enough for two anglers and their gear but lacks transom door. Original two-stateroom floorplan was replaced in 1988 with single-stateroom layout with more spacious salon, updated decor. Note unique cabin ventilation system with air intakes beneath forward bridge overhang. Standard 320hp gas inboards cruise at 16 knots; GM 500hp diesels cruise at 18 knots.

Prices Not Provided for Pre-1995 Models

Length	34'0"	Fuel	300 gals.
Beam	12'6"	Water	60 gals.
Draft	3'2"	Waste	40 gals.
Weight	13,500#	Hull Type	Modified-V
Clearance	11'5"	Deadrise Aft	15°

Sportfishing Boats

Luhrs 350 Convertible

1990–96

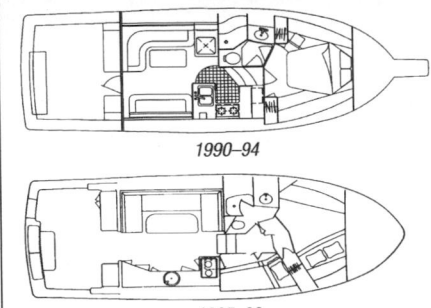

1990–94

1995–96

Muscular sportfisherman with signature Luhrs styling targets savvy anglers with an eye for value. Roomy cockpit came standard with transom door, tackle drawers, insulated fishbox, transom door, livewell. Original single-stateroom floorplan with mid-galley was replaced in 1995 with new two-stateroom, galley-up layout. Hardtop was standard. Flybridge redesigned in 1995 with improved seating. A seriously good-looking boat. Standard gas engines cruise at 17 knots; optional 350hp Cats cruise at 23–24 knots.

See Page 528 For Value Estimates

Length w/Pulpit	38'6"	Fuel	390 gals.
Hull Length	35'0"	Water	93 gals.
Beam	12'10"	Waste	40 gals.
Draft	3'4"	Hull Type	Modified-V
Weight	20,000#	Deadrise Aft	18°

Luhrs 35 Convertible

2008–09

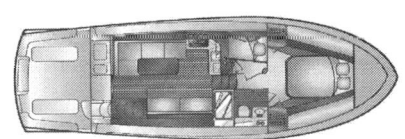

Handsome 35-footer with megawide beam provides the cockpit, cabin space of a much larger boat. Highlights include open salon with full windshield, cherry interior cabinets, oversized head with separate stall shower, two large staterooms. Lower helm is optional. Note molded bridge steps, flybridge cooler storage. Engine room is unusually spacious for a boat this size. Hardtop, generator, bait prep center are standard. Cruise at 26–28 knots with 380hp Yanmar inboard diesels; about 28 knots with 370hp Volvo IPS drives.

See Page 528 For Value Estimates

Length w/Pulpit	38'10"	Fuel	400 gals.
Hull Length	35'8"	Water	100 gals.
Beam	14'6"	Waste	26 gals.
Draft	3'0"	Hull Type	Modified-V
Weight	23,500#	Deadrise Aft	15°

Luhrs 36 Convertible

1998–2007

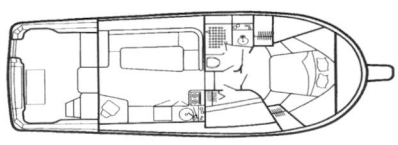

Deluxe convertible with molded flybridge steps (a new concept in 1998) is stylish, spacious, ready to cruise. Upscale two-stateroom interior with teak trim includes posh U-shaped settee/dinette in salon, big master, large head with stall shower. Engine room is accessed via hatch in salon sole. Fishing features include transom door, fishbox, bait-prep center, tackle drawers, livewell. Half-tower was standard. Bridge steps reduce cockpit space. Yanmar 440hp diesels cruise at 22 knots (26–28 knots top).

See Page 529 For Value Estimates

Length w/Pulpit	38'11"	Fuel	400 gals.
Hull Length	36'2"	Water	94 gals.
Beam	13'10"	Waste	30 gals.
Draft	3'3"	Hull Type	Modified-V
Weight	22,000#	Deadrise Aft	18°

Sportfishing Boats

Luhrs 36 Open; 36 SX

1997–2007

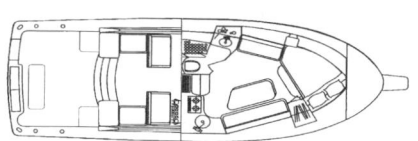

Bold tournament express with high-impact styling (called the Luhrs 36 SX in 1997–2001) personifies traditional Luhrs appeal to value-conscious anglers. Wide 13'10" beam allows for spacious cockpit with transom fishbox, bait-prep center with sink, tackle drawers, wide transom door. Bridgedeck lifts electrically for engine access. Maxi-volume interior with full galley and berths for four is roomy enough for extended family cruising. Twin 420hp gas engines cruise in the low 20s; 420hp Cat diesels cruise at 26–27 knots.

See Page 529 For Value Estimates

Length w/Pulpit	38'11"	Headroom	6'4"
Hull Length	36'2"	Fuel	400 gals.
Beam	13'10"	Water	94 gals.
Draft	3'5"	Hull Type	Modified-V
Weight	22,000#	Deadrise Aft	18°

Luhrs 37 Open (IPS)

2009–Current

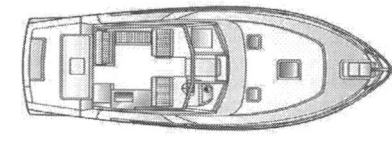

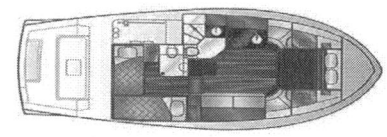

Tournament-grade sportfisherman designed for IPS pod drives combines fuel-efficient operation with innovative cabin layout. Standard-feature list includes half tower with controls, 35-gallon livewell, bait-prep center with sink, washdowns, genset, removable fishbox, 20" flat-screen TV. Two-stateroom, two-head interior is unique in a boat this size. Note cavernous step-down storage room beneath helm lounge. Around 32 knots top with Volvo 435hp IPS power. Outboard version with triple Yamaha 350s delivers 40+ knots wide open.

See Page 529 For Value Estimates

Length	38'7"	Fuel	380 gals.
Beam	14'10"	Water	100 gals.
Draft	2'8"	Waste	30 gals.
Weight	22,500#	Hull Type	Modified-V
Clearance, Top	16'0"	Deadrise Aft	14.5°

Luhrs 380/40/38 Convertible

1989–2007

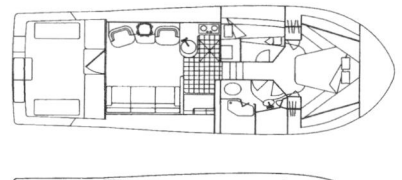

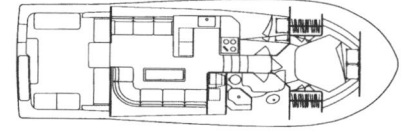

Well-bred convertible with classic Luhrs styling delivers heavyweight canyon potential at moderate price. Offered with several two-stateroom floorplans, all with spacious salon, large head with stall shower, generous galley storage. Half-tower was standard. Tournament-size cockpit features bait-prep station, livewell, fishbox, transom door. Note large flybridge. Called Luhrs 380 in 1989–98; Luhrs 40 in 1999–2003; Luhrs 38 in 2004–08. Cruise in the low-to-mid 20s with GM 485hp, Cat 420hp, or Yanmar 440hp diesels.

See Page 529 For Value Estimates

Length w/Pulpit	40'10"	Fuel	423 gals.
Hull Length	37'9"	Water	94 gals.
Beam	14'11"	Waste	36 gals.
Draft	3'7"	Hull Type	Modified-V
Weight	30,000#	Deadrise Aft	18°

Sportfishing Boats

Luhrs 380/40/38 Open

1991–2007

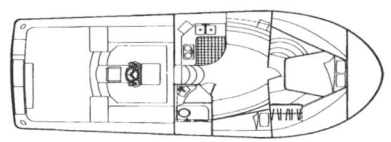

Feature-packed express with wide beam is spacious, agile, handsome. Highlights include centerline helm with flanking settees (with rod storage under), well-appointed cockpit with transom fishbox, bait-prep center, transom door. Single-stateroom interior with convertible salon settee sleeps four. Bridgedeck lifts for engine access. Note standard tuna tower. Called Luhrs 380 Open in 1991–98; 40 Open in 1999–2004; 38 Open in 2004–07. Cruise at 24–25 knots with 420hp Cat (or 440hp Yanmar) diesels.

See Page 529 For Value Estimates

Length w/Pulpit	40'10"	Fuel	563 gals.
Hull Length	37'9"	Water	80 gals.
Beam	14'11"	Waste	36 gals.
Draft	3'7"	Hull Type	Modified-V
Weight	30,000#	Transom Deadrise	18°

Luhrs Tournament 400

1987–90

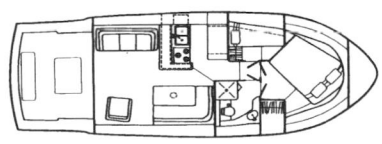

Versatile 1990s flybridge cruiser mixed fishing, cruising attributes in a practical, well-priced package. Spacious twin-stateroom interior boasts expansive salon with L-shaped dinette, complete galley with microwave, large head with shower stall. Fishing accessories include dual washdowns, in-deck fishbox, transom door, rod storage. Half-tower with controls was standard. Flybridge is large for an older 40-footer. Twin 320hp gas engines cruise at 15–16 knots; optional 375hp Cats cruise around 22 knots (mid 20s top).

Prices Not Provided for Pre-1995 Models

Length	40'0"	Fuel	400 gals.
Beam	14'0"	Water	100 gals.
Draft	3'2"	Waste	30 gals.
Weight	25,500#	Hull Type	Modified-V
Clearance	14'0"	Deadrise Aft	14°

Luhrs 41 Convertible

2004–09

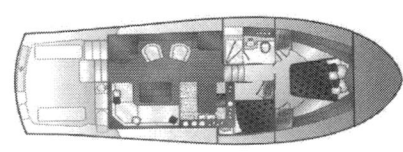

Compelling midsize convertible with flared bow is stylish, roomy, built to last. Broad 15'9" beam allows vast interior with wide-open salon, Ultraleather seating, home-size galley with under-counter refrigeration, two large staterooms. Washer/dryer can be installed in salon cabinet. Additional highlights include standard hardtop, cherrywood joinery, teak-and-holly cabin sole, electric salon sofa bed. Prop pockets reduce draft, improve efficiency. Cruise at 26–27 knots with Cummins 580hp diesels (about 30 knots top).

See Page 529 For Value Estimates

Length w/Pulpit	44'6"	Fuel	600 gals.
Hull Length	42'3"	Water	130 gals.
Beam	15'9"	Waste	40 gals.
Draft	3'6"	Hull Type	Modified-V
Weight	33,000#	Deadrise Aft	18°

Sportfishing Boats

Luhrs 41 Hardtop

2007–08

Feature-rich hardtop cruiser blends all-weather versatility with family-style comforts, angler-centric cockpit. Enclosed helm deck with teak-and-holly sole, entertainment center offers panoramic outside views. Cabin layout with private bow stateroom, convertible settee sleeps four. Fishing amenities include 50-gallon transom livewell, bait prep center, in-sole fishboxes. Note that hardtop overhangs provide partial sun protection for windshield, cockpit. Cummins 540hp diesels cruise at 25 knots; 645hp Yanmars cruise at 28–29 knots.

See Page 529 For Value Estimates

Length w/Pulpit	44'6"	Fuel	600 gals.
Hull Length	42'3"	Water	130 gals.
Beam	15'9"	Waste	40 gals.
Draft	3'6"	Hull Type	Modified-V
Weight	32,000#	Deadrise Aft	18°

Luhrs 41 Open

2006–09

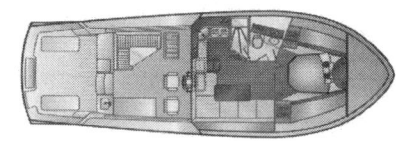

Powerful deepwater express gives anglers impressive blend of hardcore fishability, luxurious accommodations. Vast cockpit with 50-gallon livewell, bait-prep station offers plenty of fish-fighting space. Note separate pump room aft of engine room. Raised helm has watertight windshield sealed to hardtop. Upscale interior with cherry joinery, leather upholstery, uses galley counter as first step into cabin—not good. Prop pockets reduce draft, improve efficiency. Cruise at 26–27 knots with Cummins 580hp diesels (about 30 knots top).

See Page 529 For Value Estimates

Length w/Pulpit	44'6"	Clearance	22'0"
Hull Length	42'3"	Fuel	600 gals.
Beam	15'9"	Water	130 gals.
Draft	3'6"	Hull Type	Modified-V
Weight	33,000#	Deadrise Aft	18°

Luhrs 44 Convertible

2003–05

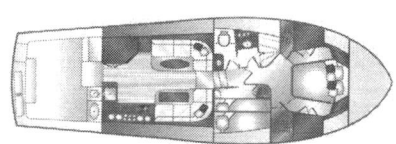

Stylish sportfisherman with innovative layout is part hardcore fishing machine, part family cruiser. Unusual salon layout has galley, entertainment center aft, seating areas forward. Long foredeck results in somewhat modest salon dimensions for boat this size; staterooms, however, are large. Note space in corridor for optional washer/dryer. Molded steps make bridge access easy, but at the expense of valuable cockpit space. Note standard hardtops. Cruise at 25 knots with 635hp Cummins diesels (28–30 knots top).

See Page 529 For Value Estimates

Length w/Pulpit	46'4"	Clearance	18'4"
Hull Length	43'2"	Fuel	700 gals.
Beam	16'0"	Water	125 gals.
Draft	4'6"	Hull Type	Modified-V
Weight	33,500#	Deadrise Aft	12°

Luhrs 50 Convertible

1999–2003

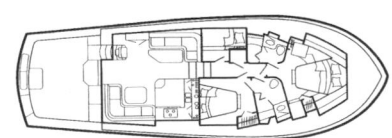

Executive-class tournament fisherman with super-wide 18-foot beam delivered comfort, luxury on a grand scale. Spacious interior features three large staterooms, two heads, dinette, salon entertainment center. Huge galley puts many home kitchens to shame. Molded bridge steps are convenient, but result in slightly awkward flybridge layout. Note massive cockpit, cavernous engine room, cherry interior joinery. Cat 800hp diesels cruise at 26–27 knots (30+ top); 1,350hp Cats cruise at 30 knots (33–34 knots wide open).

See Page 529 For Value Estimates

Length	50'10"	Fuel	1,000 gals.
Beam	18'0"	Water	200 gals.
Draft	5'0"	Headroom	6'5"
Weight	48,000#	Hull Type	Modified-V
Clearance	18'0"	Deadrise Aft	12°

Mako 282 Center Console

1998–2003

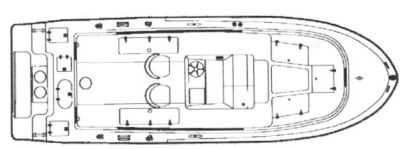

Rugged 28-footer with integrated transom, deep cockpit made the cut with anglers looking for a trailerable center console built tough. Highlights included big 42-gallon transom livewell, two in-deck fishboxes, bow casting platform, removable rear seat, recessed rod lockers, console head compartment, lockable bow storage, console seat, bow pulpit. Big fuel capacity means excellent range. Transom door, foldaway transom seat were added in 1998. Heavily built boat can take a pounding. About 45 knots with twin 225s.

See Page 530 For Value Estimates

Length w/Pulpit	31'1"	Fuel	235 gals.
Hull Length	28'1"	Water	10 gals.
Beam	8'6"	Max HP	450
Hull Draft	16"	Hull Type	Deep-V
Dry Weight	4,500#	Deadrise Aft	23°

Mako 284 Center Console

2005–Current

Maxi-volume fisherman introduced in 2005 gave seasoned anglers reason to take a fresh look at Mako boats. Wide 9'10" beam provides generous cockpit space with room for several anglers. Amenities include standard T-top with rod holders, bait station with tackle storage, big 50-gallon livewell, leaning post with sink & tackle storage, cushioned forward seating, freshwater system. Space at helm for flush-mounting electronics. Deep-V hull handles a chop without pounding; high freeboard contributes to dry ride. About 45 knots with twin 250s.

See Page 530 For Value Estimates

Length	28'4"	Fuel	235 gals.
Beam	9'10"	Water	14 gals.
Draft, Up	1'9"	Max HP	600
Draft, Down	3'2"	Hull Type	Deep-V
Dry Weight	6,000#	Deadrise Aft	21°

Sportfishing Boats

Mako 293 Walkaround

1994–2003

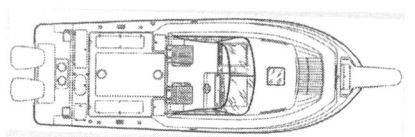

Popular 29-foot walkaround with generous 9'6" beam strikes a balance between hardcore fishing machine, family-friendly cruiser. Stand-up livewell, transom door, in-floor fishboxes, tackle center, fresh/raw-water washdowns, deluxe helm seats, rod storage, bow seating, anchor locker, bow pulpit. Roomy cabin with mid-berth aft, full galley, enclosed head with shower, convertible dinette sleeps four. Wide, deep walkarounds are a big plus. Called the 263 Walkaround in 1994. About 40 knots with 250 outboards.

See Page 530 For Value Estimates

Length w/Pulpit	30'10"	Fuel	240 gals.
Hull Length	28'7"	Water	40 gals.
Beam	9'6"	Max HP	500
Hull Draft	1'7"	Hull Type	Deep-V
Weight	6,100#	Deadrise Aft	23°

Mako 333 Center Console Cuddy

1997–2000

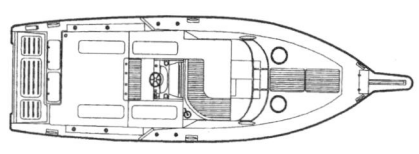

Versatile console express with comfortable interior, leading-edge styling offered something different for Mako enthusiasts. Features include foldaway rear seat, four in-deck fish/storage boxes, 60-gallon transom livewell, leaning post with rod holders, coaming bolsters, rod storage, transom door, fresh/raw-water washdowns, bow pulpit. Note L-shaped lounge seating forward of helm. Well-appointed cabin with V-berth, midcabin berth, enclosed head with shower, sleeps four. Helmdeck lifts for generator access. Over 35 knots with twin 250s.

See Page 530 For Value Estimates

Length w/Pulpit	36'0"	Fuel	350 gals.
Hull Length	33'9"	Water	35 gals.
Beam	10'6"	Max HP	750
Hull Draft	1'9"	Hull Type	Deep-V
Weight	11,500#	Deadrise Aft	24.5°

Marlin 350 Cuddy

1991–2002

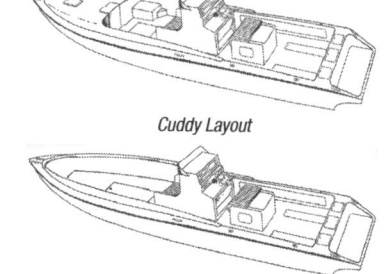

Cuddy Layout

Open Bow Layout

Feature-rich cuddy built to high standards is agile, fast, ready for action. Semicustom boat can be factory-built to customer specs. Standard version features V-berth, cushioned bow seating, 50-gallon livewell, bait-prep center, deluxe two-person helm seat, in-deck fishboxes, pop-up cleats, forward console seat, walk-in console head compartment. Large dash can handle several big-screen electronics displays. Wide walkways provide excellent 360-degree fishability. Twin 250hp outboards deliver 45 knots max.

See Page 530 For Value Estimates

Length	35'6"	Fuel	250 gals.
Beam	9'4"	Water	40 gals.
Hull Draft	1'6"	Max HP	600
Weight w/Engines	9,000#	Hull Type	Deep-V
Clearance	8'0"	Deadrise Aft	24°

Mediterranean 38 Convertible

1985–2007

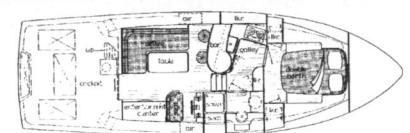

Single Stateroom

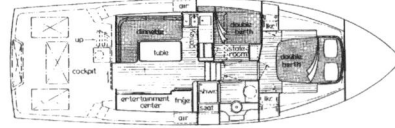

Two Staterooms

Economy-class west coast convertible sold factory-direct appealed to buyers with an eye for versatility, value. No-frills interior was available with one or two staterooms, both with queen berth in master, salon entertainment center, large head with stall shower. Uncluttered cockpit is shaded by flybridge overhang. Note molded bridge steps, wide side decks. Lower helm was optional in single-stateroom layout. So-so fit and finish. Cruise at 18 knots with 300hp gas engines; 20+ knots with 330hp Cummins diesels.

See Page 531 For Value Estimates

Length w/Pulpit	43'6"	Fuel	390 gals.
Hull Length	38'4"	Water	100 gals.
Beam	12'8"	Waste	25 gals.
Draft	3'4"	Hull Type	Modified-V
Weight	28,000#	Deadrise Aft	18°

Midnight Express 39 Cuddy

2000–Current

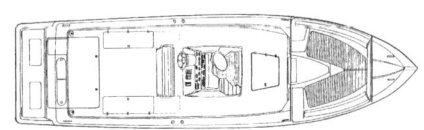

Sleek triple-engine speedster delivers high-octane dose of luxury-class amenities, bold performance. Efficient deck layout is arranged with small cuddy forward, console head compartment, 45-gallon transom livewell aft, two in-deck fishboxes. Radar arch with T-top, cockpit bolsters, transom door, Kiekhaefer trim tabs, leaning post are standard. Stylish dash has space for big-screen electronics. Built on reworked Cigarette 36 racing hull with higher hullsides, slightly reduced deadrise. Over 50 knots top with triple 275hp outboards.

See Page 532 For Value Estimates

Length	39'2"	Fuel	325 gals.
Beam	9'6"	Water	45 gals.
Hull Draft	1'10"	Max HP	900
Dry Weight	13,000#	Hull Type	Deep-V
Headroom	6'2"	Deadrise Aft	22°

Mikelson 43 Sportfisher

1997–Current

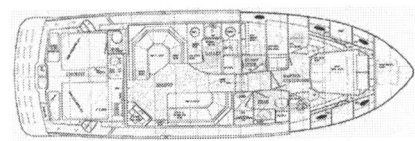

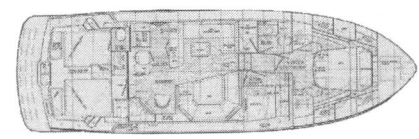

Rakish sedan fisherman with efficient, Fexas-designed hull combines versatile accommodations with quality construction, outstanding range. Original two-stateroom floorplan has galley forward in salon; aft-galley layout became available in 2006. Salon dinette is a nice touch—few boats this size have one. Engines are aft, under elevated cockpit sole. Note circular bridge settee, quality cherry interior joinery. Cummins 450hp diesels cruise in mid 20s. Newer models are offered with 480hp Zeus pod drives. Over 60 sold to date.

See Page 532 For Value Estimates

Length w/Pulpit	48'8"	Fuel	600 gals.
Hull Length	43'10"	Water	200 gals.
Beam	15'10"	Waste	60 gals.
Draft	3'10"	Hull Type	Modified-V
Weight	35,000#	Deadrise Aft	14.5°

Sportfishing Boats

Mikelson 50 Sportfisher

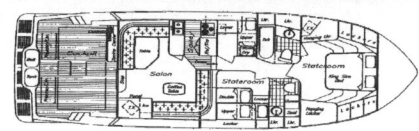

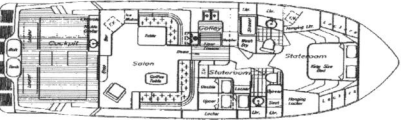

1992–Current

See Page 532 For Value Estimates

Popular West Coast convertible with appealing lines, exceptional range blurs the line between hard-hitting fishing machine, executive-class cruising yacht. Wide 16'8" beam permits truly expansive interior with wide-open salon, large staterooms. Cockpit is big for a 50-footer. Huge flybridge boasts circular settee forward, second control station aft. Weight-efficient (fully cored) hull delivers impressive performance with relatively small engines. Cummins 540hp V-drive diesels cruise at 22 knots (26–27 knots top).

Length	50'5"	Fuel	1,000 gals.
Beam	16'8"	Water	250 gals.
Draft	3'10"	Waste	80 gals.
Weight	45,000#	Hull Type	Modified-V
Clearance	NA	Deadrise Aft	12°

Mikelson 59 Nomad

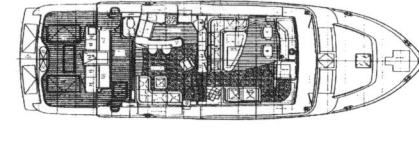

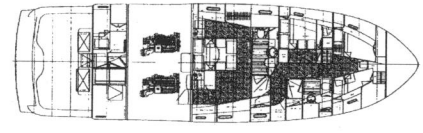

2004–Current

Insufficient Resale Data to Assign Values

Rugged pilothouse sportfisher is spacious, efficient, completely unique. Semicustom interior boasts cavernous master suite with private access, spacious salon with breakfast bar, huge pilothouse with superb helm visibility, aft crew quarters. Small afterdeck overlooks teak-planked cockpit with twin livewells, large-capacity fishboxes. Note spacious engine room, varnished cherry cabinets, unusual rooftop seating over pilothouse. Built on efficient hull with super-wide beam. Cruise at 12–15 knots with Cummins 635hp diesels.

Length Overall	61'4"	Fuel	2,000 gals.
Beam	18'6"	Water	350 gals.
Draft	5'6"	Waste	150 gals.
Weight	80,000#	Hull Type	Modified-V
Clearance	NA	Deadrise Aft	11°

Mikelson 60 Sportfisher

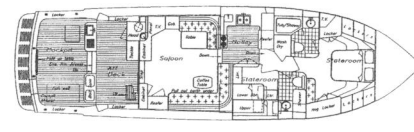

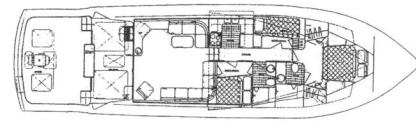

1992–99

See Page 532 For Value Estimates

Luxury sportfisher from 1990s offers top-shelf construction, long-range fishability. Several floorplans were available—standard galley-down layout has three staterooms; alternate arrangements had two staterooms with enlarged galley. Spacious salon came with built-in settees, furniture-quality teak woodwork. Small mezzanine deck overlooks huge cockpit with direct engine room access. Note enormous bridge with circular settee forward. Fully cored hull is efficient, easily driven. Cruise in the low 20s (26–27 top) with GM 735hp diesels.

Length	59'1"	Fuel	1,000 gals.
Beam	17'2"	Water	300 gals.
Draft	4'4"	Headroom	6'5"
Weight	55,000#	Hull Type	Modified-V
Clearance	NA	Deadrise Aft	14.5°

Mikelson 61 Pilothouse Sportfisher

2000–08

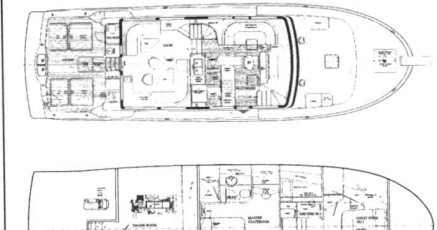

Quality-built pilothouse sportfisher with rakish profile, luxury accommodations offers space, comfort, exceptional range. Super-wide 18'11" beam provides unusually spacious interior with full-beam owner's suite, expansive salon with high-gloss joinery. Raised pilothouse hosts home-sized galley, full dinette, bridge access. Massive fishing cockpit has convenient day head—very clever. Flybridge (with aft controls) can accommodate a small crowd. Note huge engine room, fiberglass hardtop. Cruise at 20 knots with 800hp Cat diesels.

Insufficient Resale Data to Assign Values

Length	61'0"	Fuel	1,600 gals.
Beam	18'11"	Water	250 gals.
Draft	4'9"	Cockpit	165 sq. ft.
Weight	66,650#	Hull Type	Modified-V
Clearance	NA	Deadrise Aft	NA

Mikelson 64 Sportfisher

1997–2001

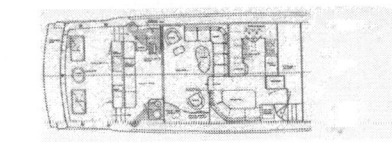

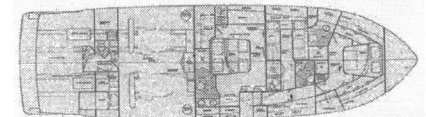

Quality-built long-range fisherman with mega-wide 19'5" beam dwarfs similar-sized boats inside and out. Broad beam translates into unusually spacious interior, massive 210-square-foot cockpit, huge flybridge with circular settee, wraparound helm, aft controls. Notable features include opulent master suite with king bed, exquisite teak cabin joinery, crew quarters, monster engine room. Note mezzanine deck with day head overlooking cockpit. Low-deadrise (fully cored) hull is notably fuel efficient. Cat 1,300hp diesels cruise at 25 knots (30+ top).

See Page 532 For Value Estimates

Length	64'9"	Fuel	1,500 gals.
Beam	19'5"	Water	350 gals.
Draft	5'0"	Headroom	6'5"
Weight	87,000#	Hull Type	Modified-V
Clearance	NA	Deadrise Aft	6°

Mikelson 70 Sportfisher

2001–Current

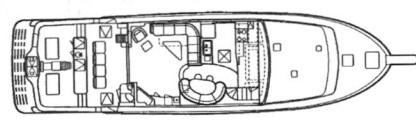

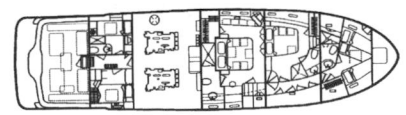

All-weather sportfisher with rakish profile, spacious interior gets high marks for luxury, range, performance. Spacious five-stateroom layout includes enormous salon, opulent full-beam master suite, twin crew cabins aft. Mezzanine deck overlooks massive fishing cockpit. Flybridge with wraparound settee, aft controls is well-suited for socializing or fishing. Note spacious engine room, teak cockpit sole. Semi-V hull with wide beam, prop pockets is fully cored to reduce weight. Cruise in mid 20s with 1,400hp Cats (28–29 knots top).

Insufficient Resale Data to Assign Values

Length	69'10"	Fuel	2,200#
Beam	19'10"	Water	350 gals.
Draft	5'0"	Headroom	6'6"
Weight	95,000#	Hull Type	Modified-V
Clearance	NA	Deadrise Aft	NA

Mikelson 72/78 Sportfisher

1994–2001

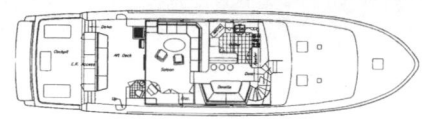

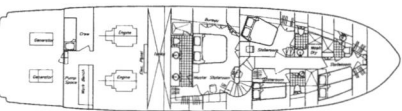

Semicustom sportfisherman with mega-wide 20'6" beam bridges the gap between fishing boat, luxury cruising yacht. Highlights include enormous salon with L-lounge seating, massive cockpit with observation deck above, stand-up engine room, exquisite teak joinery. Four-stateroom interior boasts extravagant master suite, crew quarters aft. Note huge bridge with wraparound settee, aft controls. Called Mikelson 72 until 1996 when cockpit was lengthened. Cruise at 20 knots with 1,100hp MTU engines (about 24–25 top).

Insufficient Resale Data to Assign Values

Length, 72	72'6"	Weight, 78	105,000#
Length, 78	77'6"	Fuel, 72	3,000 gals.
Beam	20'6"	Fuel, 78	3,700 gals.
Draft	5'6"	Water	420 gals.
Weight, 72	95,000#	Hull Type	Modified-V

Ocean 29 Super Sport

1990–92

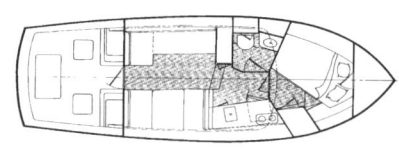

Classy 1990s convertible remains among the smallest flybridge boats ever offered by a major builder. Space-efficient teak interior boasts private bow stateroom with angled double berth, full galley, convertible salon dinette. Note unique shower enclosure in head. Central vacuum system, air-conditioning, entertainment center were standard. Athwartships bridge ladder frees up considerable cockpit space. Sleek styling still looks good today. Twin 320hp gas engines cruise at 20–22 knots; 250hp Cummins diesels cruise in the mid 20s.

Prices Not Provided for Pre-1995 Models

Length	29'0"	Fuel	215 gals.
Beam	11'6"	Water	35 gals.
Draft	2'5"	Waste	20 gals.
Weight	13,500#	Hull Type	Modified-V
Clearance	10'6"	Deadrise Aft	14°

Ocean 32 Super Sport

1989–92

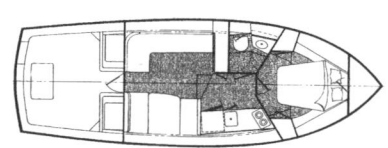

Rakish 32-footer with classic Ocean styling delivered mid-size convertible comfort, performance at an affordable price. Elegant teak interior with booth-style dinette, convertible salon settee, TV/VCR came standard with air, microwave, central vacuum system. Cockpit amenities include in-deck fish-box, bait-prep center, tackle storage, transom door, teak covering boards. Engine room is a tight fit. Athwartships bridge ladder frees up considerable cockpit space. Cruise at 22 knots with 320 gas engines; mid 20s with 300hp Cummins diesels.

Prices Not Provided for Pre-1995 Models

Length	32'0"	Fuel	280 gals.
Beam	12'4"	Water	60 gals.
Draft	2'6"	Waste	25 gals.
Weight	17,043#	Hull Type	Modified-V
Clearance	11'1"	Deadrise Aft	13°

Ocean 35 Super Sport

1988–94

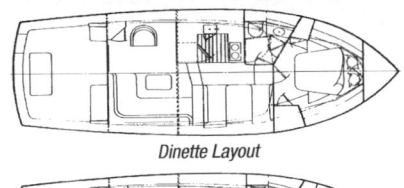

Dinette Layout

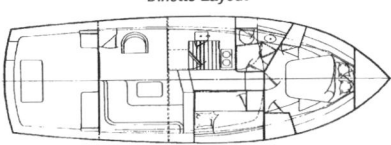

Two-Stateroom Layout

Sleek 35-footer was one of Ocean's best-selling models during her production years. Both standard single-stateroom interior and optional twin-stateroom layout were extremely well-appointed by standards of her era. Cockpit is fitted with fishbox, transom door, tackle storage, cooler/freezer, teak covering boards. Impressive equipment list included generator, air-conditioning, central vacuum system. Engine room is a tight fit. Athwartships flybridge ladder preserves cockpit space. Cruise at 22 knots with 320hp gas engines; mid 20s with 300hp Cummins diesels.

Prices Not Provided for Pre-1995 Models

Length	35'0"	Fuel	320 gals.
Beam	13'0"	Water	70 gals.
Draft	2'5"	Waste	30 gals.
Weight	19,800#	Hull Type	Modified-V
Clearance	11'9"	Deadrise Aft	13°

Ocean 37 Billfish

2008–Current

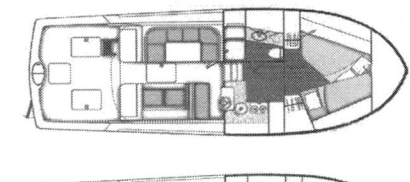

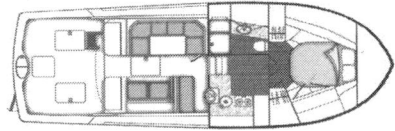

Nimble sportfisherman with vintage Palm Beach styling takes the retro look to the next level. Traditional fishing-boat layout has semi-enclosed helm deck with dinette, large cockpit with livewell, bait-prep center, two fishboxes. Upscale cabin with cherry cabinetry, head with stall shower sleeps three. Engine room is surprisingly large. Compact flybridge with center helm offers good cockpit view. Prop pockets reduce draft to just 2'6". Volvo 435hp IPS pod drives cruise at 30 knots. Early models with Yanmar 480hp diesels cruise at 24–26 knots.

See Page 534 For Value Estimates

Length	37'8"	Fuel	400 gals.
Beam	13'10"	Water	75 gals.
Draft	2'6"	Waste	35 gals.
Weight	23,500#	Hull Type	Modified-V
Clearance	15'5"	Deadrise Aft	13°

Ocean 38 Super Sport

1984–91

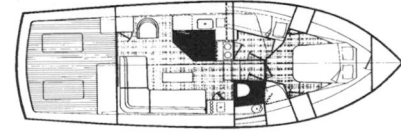

Two-Stateroom Interior

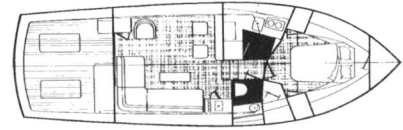

Single-Stateroom Interior

Leading-edge 1980s convertible with still-handsome lines became one of Ocean's best-selling models ever. Inviting teak interior with spacious salon was available with one or two staterooms. Cockpit with teak sole came standard with tackle center, bait freezer, in-deck fishbox, transom door, teak covering boards. Very serviceable engine room. Low-deadrise hull can be a stiff ride in a chop. Total of 158 built. Replaced in 1992 with new 38 SS model. Caterpillar 375hp diesels cruise at 24–24 knots (about 30 knots top).

Prices Not Provided for Pre-1995 Models

Length	38'4"	Fuel	354 gals.
Beam	13'8"	Water	80 gals.
Draft	3'2"	Waste	35 gals.
Weight	23,000#	Hull Type	Modified-V
Clearance	13'1"	Deadrise Aft	12°

Sportfishing Boats

Ocean 38 Super Sport

1992–95

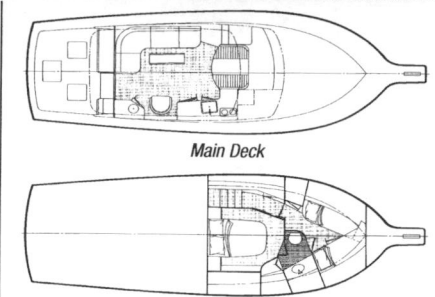

Main Deck

Lower Deck

See Page 534 For Value Estimates

Updated version of original Ocean 38 SS (1984–91) with creative interior is roomy, quick, easy on the eye. Innovative two-stateroom floorplan boasts full-beam amidships master with walkaround queen berth—a unique layout in a boat this size. Cockpit with standard tackle center, bait freezer, fishbox, transom door is on the small side for a 38-footer. Hardtop, generator, air-conditioning were standard. Engine room is a tight fit. Cat 425hp diesels (or Volvo 430s) cruise in the low 20s and reach 28–29 knots top.

Length	38'9"	Fuel	400 gals.
Beam	14'2"	Water	80 gals.
Draft	3'8"	Waste	35 gals.
Weight	27,000#	Hull Type	Modified-V
Clearance	15'4"	Deadrise Aft	12°

Ocean 40 Sport Fish

1999–2005

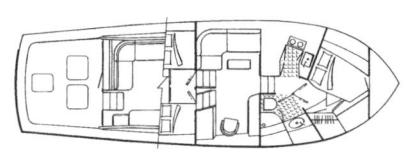

Innovative express with highly elevated bridgedeck blurs the line between hardcore sportfishing boat, capable family cruiser. Mid-stateroom layout is completely unique in an express boat this size. Transom baitwell, tackle lockers, transom door are standard; compact engine room has near-standing headroom. Bridgedeck—6 steps up from cockpit level—boasts centerline helm, lounge seating aft. Great visibility from raised helm position. Cat 420hp Cat (or 440hp Yanmar) diesels reach 30+ knots wide open.

Insufficient Resale Data to Assign Values

Length	40'4"	Fuel	390 gals.
Beam	14'2"	Water	90 gals.
Draft	3'8"	Waste	40 gals.
Weight	26,500#	Hull Type	Modified-V
Clearance	12'6"	Deadrise Aft	14°

Ocean 40 Super Sport

1997–2005

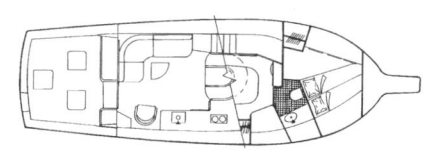

See Page 534 For Value Estimates

Best-selling convertible offers signature Ocean Yacht styling with innovative interior layout, leading-edge performance. Well-appointed two-stateroom, galley-up interior features unusual raised dinette forward in salon, amidships master stateroom with tall headroom. Cockpit highlights include engine room access, deluxe tackle center, saltwater washdown, transom door. Athwartships bridge ladder preserves cockpit space. Cat 420hp—or Yanmar 440hp—diesels cruise at 24–25 knots and reach a top speed of 30+ knots.

Length	40'4"	Fuel	408 gals.
Beam	14'2"	Water	90 gals.
Draft	3'8"	Cockpit	80 sq. ft.
Weight	27,500#	Hull Type	Modified-V
Clearance	15'5"	Deadrise Aft	14°

Sportfishing Boats

Ocean 42 Super Sport

1991–95

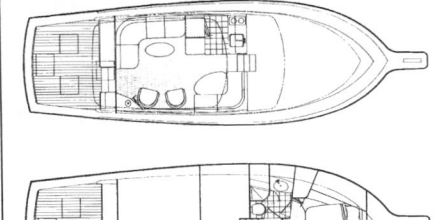

Second-generation 42 Super Sport (an earlier 42 SS model ran from 1980–83) combined leading-edge performance with iconic styling, appealing price. Well-appointed interior with L-shaped dinette features walkaround queen berth forward, double (and slide-out single) berth in guest cabin. Hatch in galley sole leads to large storage area. Expansive fishing cockpit has transom gate and door, large fishbox, tackle center, bait freezer. Cat 425hp diesels cruise at 24 knots cruise (26–27 top); GM 485hp 6-71s cruise at 26 knots (30 knots top).

See Page 534 For Value Estimates

Length	42'0"	Fuel	466 gals.
Beam	15'0"	Water	100 gals.
Draft	3'7"	Cockpit	100 sq. ft.
Weight	35,466#	Hull Type	Modified-V
Clearance	15'4"	Deadrise Aft	5°

Ocean 42 Super Sport

2006–Current

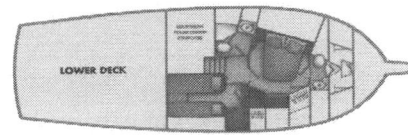

Polished sportfishing machine with handsome lines meets anglers need for space, comfort, performance. Clever two-stateroom interior boasts luxurious salon, L-shaped dinette, two full heads (most 42-footers have one), huge storage area under galley. Galley is on the small side. Note washer/dryer in guest stateroom. Roomy cockpit includes transom livewell, in-deck fishboxes, direct engine room access. Underwater exhaust system reduces noise, cockpit fumes. Cat 510hp diesels cruise at 25–26 knots (30 knots top).

See Page 534 For Value Estimates

Length	42'1"	Fuel	430 gals.
Beam	15'4"	Water	100 gals.
Draft	3'11"	Headroom	6'6"
Weight	34,151#	Hull Type	Modified-V
Clearance	15'5"	Deadrise Aft	NA

Ocean 43 Super Sport

2000–05

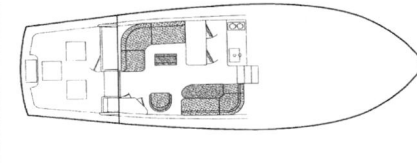

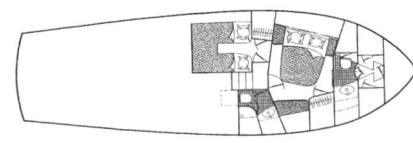

Well-received 43-footer with leading-edge styling delivers on Ocean promise of no-compromise fishability, top-shelf accommodations. Innovative two-stateroom, two-head floorplan with deckhouse galley is arranged with master suite forward, guest stateroom with twin berths (and partial standing headroom) aft. Note unusual forepeak head. Large cockpit with engine room access comes standard with freezer, livewell, huge fishbox. Very good performer: Volvo 480hp—or 500hp Yanmar—diesels cruise around 25 knots (30+ top).

See Page 534 For Value Estimates

Length	43'10"	Fuel	438 gals.
Beam	15'2"	Water	94 gals.
Draft	3'7"	Headroom	6'6"
Weight	37,000#	Hull Type	Modified-V
Clearance, Hardtop	15'5"	Deadrise Aft	7°

Sportfishing Boats

Sportfishing Boats

Ocean 44 Super Sport

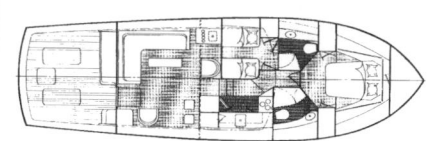

1985–91

Fast-action convertible with classic Ocean styling raised the bar in her era for sportfishing luxury, performance, affordability. Two-stateroom interior with galley down, two full heads is ideal for a boat this size. Roomy galley is large enough for optional dishwasher and trash compactor. Note built-in clothes dryer in guest stateroom. Cockpit came standard with tackle center, teak sole, engine controls. Large engine room offers good service access. GM 485hp 6-71 diesels cruise at 27 knots (30+ top). Total of 111 were built.

Prices Not Provided for Pre-1995 Models

Length	44'0"	Fuel	480 gals.
Beam	15'2"	Water	100 gals.
Draft	3'6"	Cockpit	130 sq. ft.
Weight	36,000#	Hull Type	Modified-V
Clearance	13'3"	Deadrise Aft	1.5°

Ocean 45 Super Sport

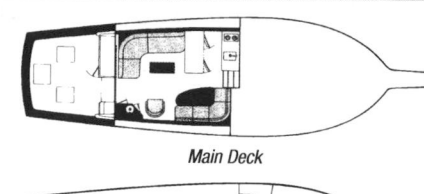

1996–99

Main Deck

Lower Deck

See Page 534 For Value Estimates

Rakish 1990s convertible delivered high-octane blend of Ocean luxury, performance at an attractive price. Innovative two-stateroom interior with combined salon/galley/dinette features big master suite with walkaround queen berth, roomy guest cabin with double bed and slide-out single berth. Note large engine room with cockpit access, standard washer/dryer, spacious flybridge with lounge seating, rod storage. Athwartships bridge ladder saves cockpit space. Cruise at 25 knots with GM 485hp 6-71s (30+ knots wide open).

Length	44'8"	Fuel	466 gals.
Beam	15'2"	Water	100 gals.
Draft	3'7"	Headroom	6'6"
Weight	37,000#	Hull Type	Modified-V
Clearance	15'4"	Deadrise Aft	1.5°

Ocean 46 Super Sport

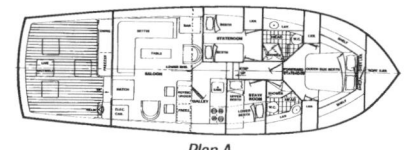

Plan A

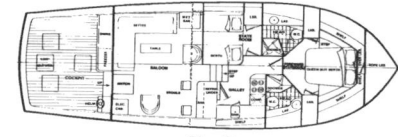

Plan B

1983–85

Best-selling 1990s canyon runner combined sleek Jersey styling with quality amenities, exhilarating performance. Three-stateroom interior is rare in a 46-footer—most boats this size have only two. Large fishing cockpit included standard livewell, helm controls, transom gate, tackle locker, freezer. Most were delivered with optional factory hardtop. Note small engine room. Cruise at 25 knots with GM 450hp diesels (about 28 knots top); 27–28 knots with 475hp 6V92s (30 knots top). Very popular model—total of 160 were built.

Prices Not Provided for Pre-1995 Models

Length	46'0"	Fuel	580 gals.
Beam	15'2"	Water	150 gals.
Draft	3'6"	Cockpit	NA
Weight	40,000#	Hull Type	Modified-V
Clearance	13'3"	Deadrise Aft	1.5°

Ocean 46 Super Sport

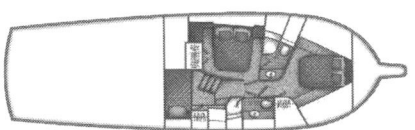

2005–Current

Handsome convertible styling, deluxe accommodations, spirited performance make this luxurious 46-footer a stand-out boating value. Creative space management permits a spacious three-stateroom interior layout—rare in a 46-foot boat. Offered with full-size double berth or crossover berths in forward stateroom. Note that small aft stateroom contains only a single berth. Expansive cockpit features twin fishboxes, livewell, engine room access. A fast ride, MTU 825hp diesels cruise at an honest 30 knots (34–35 knots top).

See Page 534 For Value Estimates

Length	46'6"	Fuel	620 gals.
Beam	15'10"	Water	125 gals.
Draft	4'2"	Headroom	6'5"
Weight	42,561#	Hull Type	Modified-V
Clearance	16'4"	Deadrise Aft	14°

Ocean 48 Sport Fish

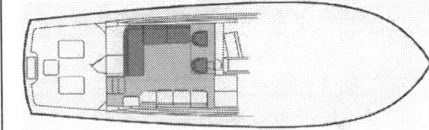

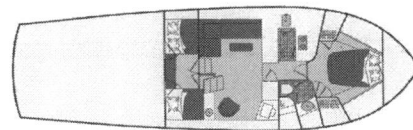

1997–2001

Fast-action express with rakish lines, roomy interior has the right stuff for serious offshore anglers. Unusual cabin layout offers large aft stateroom with single and double berths, compact salon, step-down galley and head, private forward stateroom with walkaround queen. Huge bridgedeck with centerline helm has seating for several guests. Stand-up engine room provides excellent service access. Note huge fishboxes, generous rod storage, easy-to-work cockpit. Cruise in the high 20s with GM 625 diesels (34–35 knots top).

See Page 534 For Value Estimates

Length	48'8"	Fuel	685 gals.
Beam	16'0"	Water	150 gals.
Draft	4'0"	Headroom	6'6"
Weight	42,500#	Hull Type	Modified-V
Clearance, Hardtop	15'6"	Deadrise Aft	NA

Ocean 48 Super Sport

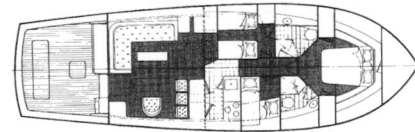

Three-Stateroom Floorplan

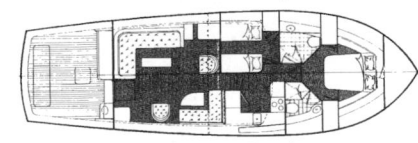

Two-Stateroom Floorplan

1986–90

Best-selling 48-footer introduced in 1986 combined signature Ocean amenities, performance in an affordably priced package. Offered with expansive three-stateroom, mid-galley interior, or conventional (less popular) two-stateroom, galley-down floorplan with enlarged salon. Roomy cockpit has full control station, bait center with freezer, livewell, wide transom door. Note teak cockpit sole, teak covering boards. Tops out at 30 knots with relatively small GM 485hp 6-71 diesels. Total of 167 of these distinctive yachts were built.

Prices Not Provided for Pre-1995 Models

Length	48'0"	Fuel	580 gals.
Beam	15'2"	Water	150 gals.
Draft	3'6"	Waste	NA
Weight	40,000#	Hull Type	Modified-V
Clearance	13'3"	Deadrise Aft	2°

Sportfishing Boats

Ocean 48 Super Sport

1991–93

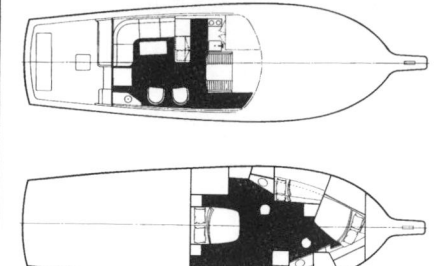

Updated version of previous Ocean 48 SS (1986–90) incorporates fresh styling, more standard features, less exterior teak. Innovative three-stateroom interior features combined salon/galley area, amidships owner's suite, two full heads. Note salon entertainment center, unusual centerline dinette. Newly configured cockpit includes recessed controls, baitwell, tackle lockers, built-in fishboxes, direct engine room access. Teak cockpit sole was a popular option. Cruise in the mid 20s (about 30 knots top) with GM 485hp 6-71 diesels.

Prices Not Provided for Pre-1995 Models

Length	48'0"	Fuel	580 gals.
Beam	15'2"	Water	150 gals.
Draft	3'6"	Waste	NA
Weight	40,000#	Hull Type	Modified-V
Clearance	13'3"	Deadrise Aft	2°

Ocean 48 Super Sport

1995–2003

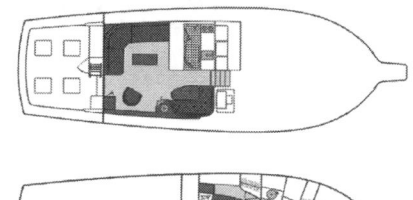

Strong-selling convertible—third in a series of Ocean 48 SS models—appealed to upscale anglers with an eye for leading-edge luxury, exceptional fishability. Well-appointed three-stateroom, two-head interior boasts combined salon/galley/dinette with entertainment center and wet bar. Two-stateroom, galley-down layout was optional. Cockpit has bait-prep station, freezer, engine controls, transom door. Angled bridge ladder saves cockpit space. GM 535hp diesels cruise at 24 knots; later models with 680hp MANs cruise at 28 knots.

See Page 534 For Value Estimates

Length	48'8"	Fuel	685 gals.
Beam	16'0"	Water	150 gals.
Draft	4'2"	Waste	60 gals.
Weight	45,000#	Hull Type	Modified-V
Clearance	15'6"	Deadrise Aft	2°

Ocean 50 Super Sport

1982–85

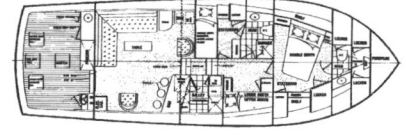

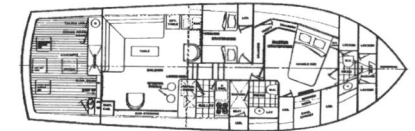

Scaled-down version of popular Ocean 55 SS (1981–90) failed to attain the popularity of her larger sibling. Two- and three-stateroom floorplans were offered—twin-cabin version is notable for huge master stateroom dimensions. Both layouts feature expansive main salon with serving counter overlooking salon. Cockpit with freezer, tackle locker is small for a 50-footer. Note poor engine room access. Low-deadrise hull is a stiff ride in a chop. GM 675hp 8V92s cruise at 25 knots and reach a top speed of 28–29 knots.

Prices Not Provided for Pre-1995 Models

Length	50'0"	Fuel	750 gals.
Beam	16'0"	Water	200 gals.
Draft	4'2"	Cockpit	NA
Weight	50,000#	Hull Type	Modified-V
Clearance	14'2"	Deadrise Aft	5°

Ocean 50 Super Sport

2004–Current

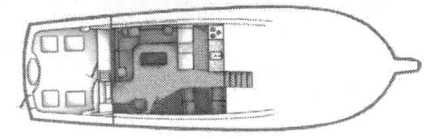

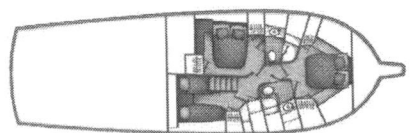

Well-styled convertible offers high-end luxury, hardcore fishability in a modern, high-performance package. Elegant three-stateroom interior is dominated by spacious salon/galley/dinette area with extended L-lounge, full entertainment center. Washer/dryer is located in companionway; forward guest stateroom is available with island berth or over/under bunks. Cockpit comes with stand-up livewell, bait-prep center, in-deck fishbox. Note spacious engine room, large helm console. MTU 825hp diesels cruise at 28–30 knots (about 33 knots top).

See Page 534 For Value Estimates

Length	50'6"	Cockpit	123 sq. ft.
Beam	16'9"	Fuel	780 gals.
Draft	4'5"	Water	150 gals.
Weight	54,038#	Hull Type	Modified-V
Clearance	18'0"	Deadrise Aft	14°

Ocean 52 Super Sport

2001–06

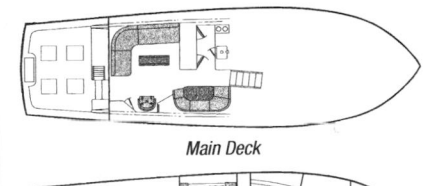

Main Deck

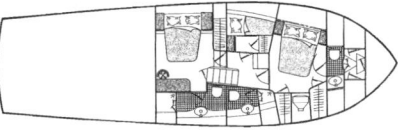

Lower Deck

Powerful tournament fisherman was smartly styled, lavishly appointed, surprisingly well priced. Spacious interior includes three staterooms and three full heads—a big floorplan for a 52-footer. Note opulent full-beam master suite beneath raised galley and dinette. Large cockpit boasts full array of fishing amenities; massive bridge features state-of-the-art helm console. Engine room is smaller than expected. Washer/dryer, factory hardtop are standard. Twin 800hp Cats—or 825hp MTUs—cruise in the high 20s (32–33 knots top).

See Page 534 For Value Estimates

Length	52'7"	Fuel	860 gals.
Beam	16'4"	Water	150 gals.
Draft	4'4"	Headroom	6'5"
Weight	56,000#	Hull Type	Modified-V
Clearance, Hardtop	17'4"	Deadrise Aft	8°

Ocean 53 Super Sport

1991–99

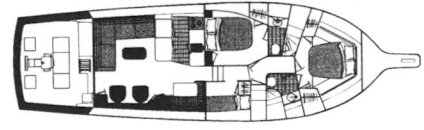

Plan A

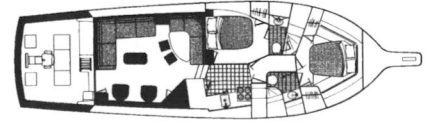

Plan B

Replacement model for popular Ocean 55 SS (1981–90) offered the same proven blend of modern styling, posh interior with improved head sea performance. Standard three-stateroom interior includes full compliment of top-shelf appliances, designer decor, teak cabinetry. Cockpit boasts full controls, tackle lockers, direct engine room access. Twin-stateroom, galley-down layout with larger salon was optional. Factory hardtop, dishwasher were standard. GM 760hp diesels cruise at 24–26 knots; 820hp MANs cruise at a fast 30 knots.

See Page 534 For Value Estimates

Length	53'0"	Fuel	860 gals.
Beam	16'4"	Water	200 gals.
Draft	4'4"	Cockpit	118 sq. ft.
Weight	52,000#	Hull Type	Modified-V
Clearance	16'3"	Deadrise Aft	8°

Sportfishing Boats

Ocean 54 Super Sport

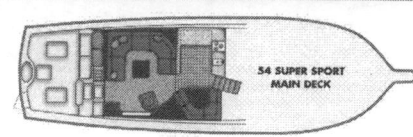

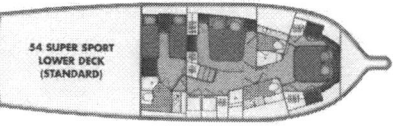

2007–Current

Hard-charging convertible with sleek lines, executive-class interior makes good on Ocean promise luxury, performance at a seriously competitive price. Innovative three-stateroom floorplan boasts spacious salon, high-gloss cherry cabinetry, standard washer/dryer, three full heads. Cockpit mezzanine with lounge seating, refrigerator/freezer is unusual in a boat this size. Note roomy flybridge with center helm position. Prop pockets reduce draft, improve efficiency. MAN 10500hp engines cruise at 25 knots (about 30 knots top).

See Page 534 For Value Estimates

Length	54'6"	Fuel	1,000 gals.
Beam	16'10"	Water	200 gals.
Draft	4'0"	Waste	50 gals.
Weight	61,000#	Hull Type	Modified-V
Clearance	17'5"	Deadrise Aft	13.5°

Ocean 55 Super Sport

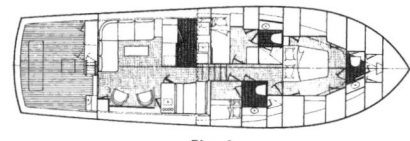

Plan A

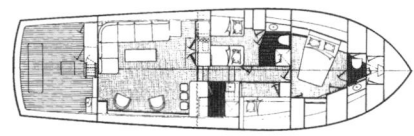

Plan B

1981–90

Best-selling tournament machine dominated the 1980s with her potent blend of bold styling, unsurpassed performance, appealing price. Highlights include expansive three-stateroom, three-head interior (note bow master suite), tournament-class fishing cockpit, impressive list of standard equipment. Weight-efficient hull performs well with relatively small engines. Restyled in 1986 with new flybridge, solid front windshield. Total of 170 were built. Tops out at an honest 30 knots (26–27 knots cruise) with 735hp GM diesels.

Prices Not Provided for Pre-1995 Models

Length	55'8"	Fuel	1,000 gals.
Beam	16'4"	Water	200 gals.
Draft	4'4"	Cockpit	130 sq. ft.
Weight	58,000#	Hull Type	Modified-V
Clearance	14'6"	Deadrise Aft	4°

Ocean 56 Super Sport

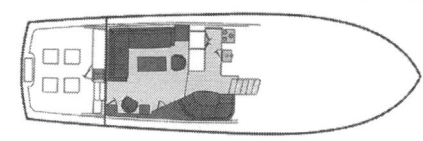

Main Deck

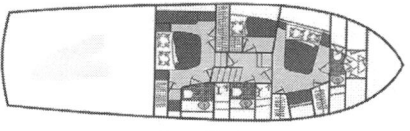

Lower Deck

1999–2002

Fast sportfisherman is a downsized version of Ocean 60 Super Sport (1996–2001) with slightly reduced cockpit dimensions. Lush three-stateroom interior—identical to the 60 SS—boasts spacious salon/galley/dinette area, posh amidships master suite, equally luxurious VIP bow stateroom with forepeak head. Washer/dryer, trash compactor were standard in galley. Easy-to-fish cockpit came with full array of premium fishing features. Note large wraparound helm console. Cruise at 30+ knots (35–36 top) with 1,050hp MAN diesels.

See Page 534 For Value Estimates

Length	56'0"	Fuel	900 gals.
Beam	16'10"	Water	220 gals.
Draft	4'5"	Headroom	6'5"
Weight	63,000#	Hull Type	Modified-V
Clearance, Hardtop	16'8"	Deadrise Aft	10°

Sportfishing Boats

Ocean 57 Super Sport

2003–07

Main Deck

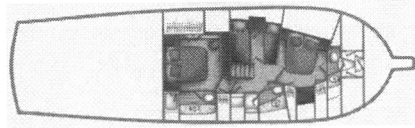

Lower Level

See Page 534 For Value Estimates

U pdated version of Ocean 56 SS (1999–2002) with reworked running surface, additional transom deadrise, redesigned interior made a good boat even better. Elegant three-stateroom interior with open salon/galley/dinette compares well with more expensive competitors in features, amenities. Note excellent engine room access, fully equipped cockpit, massive flybridge with hardtop and wraparound seating. (Enclosed bridge was optional.) Cat 1,015hp engines cruise at 28–30 knots; 1,300hp Cats cruise in the low 30s (35+ wide open).

Length	57'0"	Headroom	6'8"
Beam	16'10"	Fuel	1,047 gals.
Draft	4'10"	Water	200 gals.
Weight	66,269#	Hull Type	Modified-V
Clearance	17'5"	Deadrise Aft	14°

Ocean 58 Super Sport

1990–93

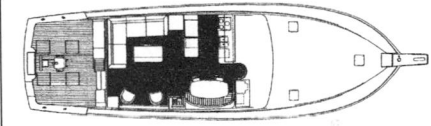

Main Deck

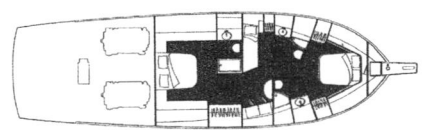

Lower Deck

Prices Not Provided for Pre-1995 Models

M uscular 1990s fishing machine impressed anglers with aggressive styling, luxurious accommodations, exceptional big-boat performance. Innovative three-stateroom, three-head interior with full-beam master was a giant departure from conventional convertible floorplans of her era. Tournament-sized cockpit features molded tackle centers, cockpit controls, transom door, engine room door. Enclosed flybridge was optional. Unique layout, good speed, comfortable accommodations. Cruise at a fast 28 knots with 1,080hp 12-cylinder GM diesels (32–33 knots top).

Length	58'0"	Fuel	1,100 gals.
Beam	17'6"	Water	250 gals.
Draft	4'10"	Cockpit	131 sq. ft.
Weight	72,215#	Hull Type	Modified-V
Clearance	14'11"	Deadrise Aft	NA

Ocean 58 Super Sport

2008–Current

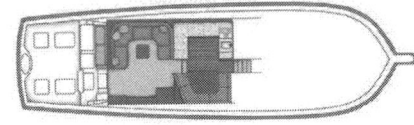

Main Deck

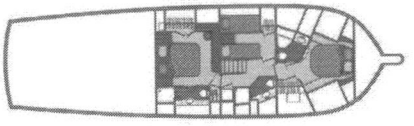

Lower Deck

Insufficient Resale Data to Assign Values

G old-plated sportfishing machine pairs classic Ocean styling with tournament-class fishability, leading-edge performance. Opulent three-stateroom interior features homesize U-shaped galley, huge dinette, palatial full-beam master with copious storage. Mezzanine with bait-prep center overlooks massive cockpit with transom livewell, in-sole fishboxes. Innovative flybridge has center-console-style helm station aft of giant wraparound settee. Hardtop is standard; enclosed flybridge is optional. MAN 1,550hp diesels cruise at nearly 35 knots.

Length	57'11"	Fuel	1,150 gals.
Beam	16'10"	Water	200 gals.
Draft	4'4"	Waste	42 gals.
Weight	67,469#	Hull Type	Modified-V
Clearance	17'5"	Deadrise Aft	14°

Sportfishing Boats

Sportfishing Boats

Ocean 60 Super Sport

1996–2001

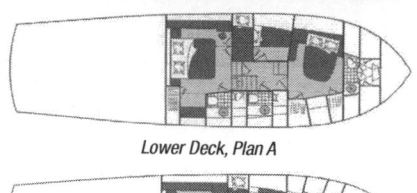

Lower Deck, Plan A

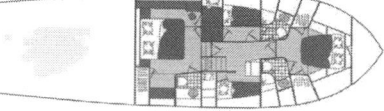

Lower Deck, Plan B

See Page 534 For Value Estimates

World-class tournament machine popular in late 1990s appealed to anglers demanding big-boat comfort, performance at a moderate price. Available with three- or four-stateroom floorplans, both with top-quality amenities, full-beam master suite, home-sized galley. Spacious cockpit came with full array of top-shelf fishing features; massive flybridge with wraparound lounge seating boasts refrigerator, standard hardtop. MAN 1,350hp engines cruise at an impressive 32 knots and reach a top speed of 35+ knots.

Length	60'0"	Fuel	1,140 gals.
Beam	17'0"	Water	240 gals.
Draft	4'8"	Headroom	6'6"
Weight	72,000#	Hull Type	Modified-V
Clearance	17'0"	Deadrise Aft	10°

Ocean 62 Super Sport

2002–08

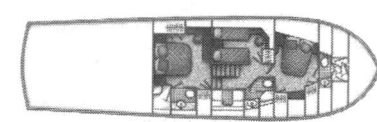

Three Stateroom Layout

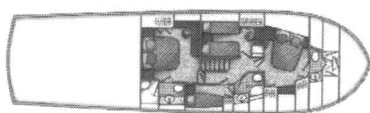

Four Stateroom Layout

See Page 535 For Value Estimates

Handsome sportfisherman offers Ocean's signature blend of aggressive styling, eye-popping luxury, exhilarating performance. Opulent interior offers several high-end decor packages with choice of three or four staterooms. (Laundry room replaces starboard guest cabin in three-stateroom layout.) Salon staircase in Enclosed Bridge model provides direct bridge access. Cockpit dimensions are modest for a 62-footer. Cat 1,400hp diesels cruise at a fast 32 knots (about 35 knots top). Optional 1500hp MTUs will hit 38 knots wide open.

Length	62'0"	Headroom	6'5"
Beam	17'5"	Fuel	1,450 gals.
Draft	5'0"	Water	255 gals.
Weight	82,000#	Hull Type	Modified-V
Clearance	17'11"	Deadrise Aft	14°

Ocean 63 Super Sport

1986–91

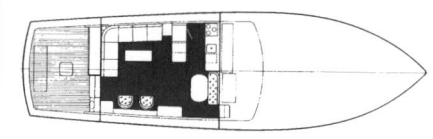

Main Deck

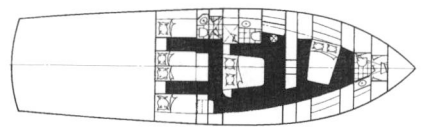

Lower Deck

Prices Not Provided for Pre-1995 Models

High-impact battlewagon made good on Ocean promise of speed, luxury, hardcore fishability. Opulent interior is arranged with four staterooms (two extending beneath the salon sole), expansive salon/galley/dinette area, amidships master, spacious VIP bow stateroom. Note glass-enclosed rod locker in hallway. Cockpit is on the small side for a 63-footer, but flybridge is huge. Standard GM 900hp 12V71s cruise at 25 knots (about 28 knots top); 1,050hp GM engines cruise at 27–28 knots (30+ top). Total of 32 were built.

Length	63'0"	Fuel	1,200 gals.
Beam	17'8"	Water	300 gals.
Draft	4'8"	Cockpit	150 sq. ft.
Weight	74,000#	Hull Type	Modified-V
Clearance	14'9"	Deadrise Aft	3°

Ocean 66 Super Sport

1993–99

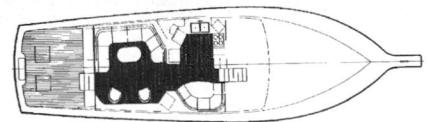

Main Deck

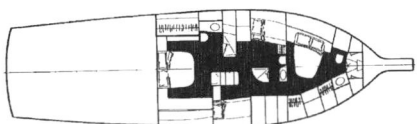

Lower Deck

See Page 535 For Value Estimates

Big-league 1990s fishing machine offered cutting-edge luxury, performance on a grand scale. Basically an improved (and easier riding) version of Ocean 63 SS (1986–91) with reworked hull bottom, additional fuel, newly configured flybridge. Highlights include extravagant four-stateroom interior with laundry center, fully equipped cockpit, massive flybridge with wet bar, wraparound lounge seating. Note huge galley/dinette area, king bed in master stateroom. Standard 1,150hp 12V-92s cruise at 25 knots (high 20s wide open).

Length	66'0"	Fuel	1,400 gals.
Beam	17'8"	Water	300 gals.
Draft	5'0"	Cockpit	135 sq. ft.
Weight	80,000#	Hull Type	Modified-V
Clearance	17'10"	Deadrise Aft	3°

Ocean 70 Super Sport

2000–04

Main Deck (Closed Bridge)

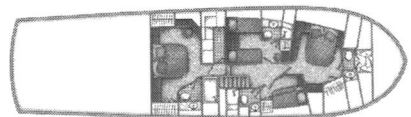

Lower Deck

Insufficient Resale Data to Assign Values

Sleek 70-footer was largest, most luxurious model in Ocean history when she was introduced in 2000. Lavish four-stateroom interior features full-beam master stateroom, huge salon, expansive galley/dinette area, utility room with washer/dryer. Enclosed bridge was standard, open bridge was optional. Modified-V hull with prop pockets has more transom deadrise than previous Ocean models for a softer ride. An excellent performer, 1,500hp Cats cruise at 28 knots (32–33 knots top); optional 1,800hp MTUs cruise at over 30 knots.

Length	70'0"	Fuel	1,865 gals.
Beam	19'8"	Water	370 gals.
Draft	5'0"	Headroom	6'6"
Weight	112,000#	Hull Type	Modified-V
Clearance, Hardtop	18'4"	Deadrise Aft	14°

Ocean 73 Super Sport

2005–08

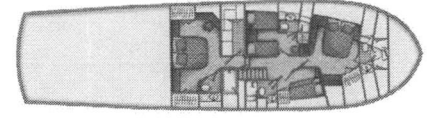

Heavy-weather battlewagon with opulent interior, enormous cockpit gives sportfishing luxury new meaning. Elegant four-stateroom layout boasts full-beam master, unique split-level deckhouse with salon aft, galley/dinette forward. Mezzanine deck overlooking cockpit provides rod storage, guest seating, in-deck freezer. Enclosed-bridge version features inside bridge access, outside steering station. Engine room is massive. Prop pockets reduce draft, improve efficiency. Cruise at 30+ knots with 2,000hp MTUs (36–38 knots top).

Insufficient Resale Data to Assign Values

Length	72'6"	Fuel	1,800 gals.
Beam	19'8"	Water	330 gals.
Draft	5'0"	Headroom	6'6"
Weight	129,223#	Hull Type	Modified-V
Clearance, Hardtop	18'3"	Deadrise Aft	14°

Sportfishing Boats

Ocean Master 27 Center Console

1987–Current

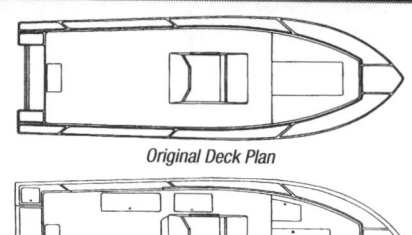

Original Deck Plan

Revised Deck Plan

Beefy 27-footer with bracket-mounted outboards makes good on factory claim of efficient deck layout, bulletproof hull construction. Console storage compartment, huge 130-gallon forward fishbox, 50-gallon aft fishboxes, recirculating gallon livewell. Revised deck plan (with full inner liner) introduced in 2000 added more storage, increased freeboard. Excellent range with 200-gallon fuel capacity. Full-transom design results in very roomy cockpit. Terrific rough-water ride. Over 40 knots with twin 225s.

Insufficient Resale Data to Assign Values

Length	26'11"	Fuel, Opt.	200 gals.
Beam	8'6"	Cockpit	68 sq. ft.
Hull Draft	1'4"	Max HP	500
Running Weight	6,500#	Hull Type	Deep-V
Fuel, Std.	160 gals.	Deadrise Aft	20°

Osprey 30

1999–2004

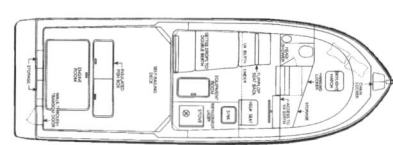

Tough pilothouse fisherman with sterndrive power offers exceptional heavy-weather performance, economical operation. Enclosed pilothouse, uncluttered cockpit will appeal to cold-weather anglers. Efficient cabin layout boasts extended galley area, convertible dinette, enclosed head with shower, but no stateroom privacy door. High freeboard results in a deep cockpit. Wide side decks and sturdy railings are a plus. Note heavy-duty window frames, watertight cabin door. Good engine access. Twin 188hp Volvo diesel I/Os cruise at 28 knots (low 30s top).

See Page 535 For Value Estimates

Length	30'4"	Water	36 gals.
Beam	10'0"	Waste	21 gals.
Draft	2'8"	Headroom	6'4"
Weight	11,000#	Cockpit	64 sq. ft.
Fuel	230/280 gals.	Hull Type	Deep-V

Pearson 38 Convertible

1987–91

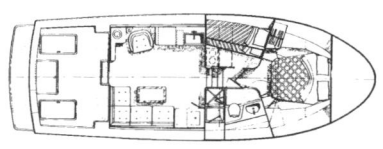

Classy flybridge cruiser introduced in 1987 was Pearson's first-ever convertible model. Rakish styling has held up well over the years. Two-stateroom interior with deckhouse galley, head with stall shower, sleeps six. Note satin-finished oak trim, salon entertainment center. Additional features included bow pulpit, transom door, swim platform. Above-average fit and finish. Deep-V hull performs well in rough seas. No racehorse, Cat 375hp diesels cruise at 22–23 knots and deliver a top speed in the neighborhood of 26 knots.

Prices Not Provided for Pre-1995 Models

Length	37'6"	Fuel	410 gals.
Beam	13'10"	Water	120 gals.
Draft	3'9"	Cockpit	NA
Weight	24,000#	Hull Type	Deep-V
Clearance	NA	Deadrise Aft	19°

Sportfishing Boats

Phoenix 27 Tournament

1990–99

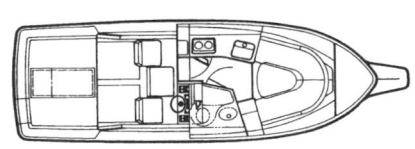

Rugged raised-deck express with inboard power combines clean lines with uncluttered fishing layout, full-feature cuddy. Topside amenities include lockable rod storage, in-deck fishbox, transom door, wide side decks. Note well-arranged helm with lockable electronics box. Commonsense cabin includes stand-up head with shower, mini-galley, convertible dinette/lounge. Deep-V hull with prop pockets delivers a good offshore ride. Cruise in the low 20s with 260hp gas inboards (28–30 knots top); Volvo 200hp diesels cruise at 22–24 knots.

See Page 535 For Value Estimates

Length w/Pulpit	30'3"	Clearance	7'6"
Hull Length	27'3"	Fuel	220 gals.
Beam	9'10"	Water	24 gals.
Draft	2'0"	Hull Type	Deep-V
Weight	8,200#	Deadrise Aft	20°

Phoenix 29 Convertible

1977–87

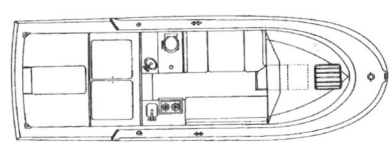

Very popular Phoenix convertible introduced in 1977 combined sporty lines with versatile layout, sturdy construction. Large bi-level cockpit, strong-running deep-V hull (with prop pockets) made this boat a favorite with offshore anglers. Modest cabin with compact galley, stand-up head with shower, convertible dinette sleeps four. Available with or without cabin bulkhead. Note small bridge, slender side decks. Volvo 124hp diesels cruise at 18 knots (22 knots top). Later models with 165hp Volvos cruise at 20–21 knots. Total of 750 were built.

Prices Not Provided for Pre-1995 Models

Length	28'10"	Fuel	160/260 gals.
Beam	10'0"	Water	50 gals.
Draft	2'4"	Cockpit	75 sq. ft.
Weight	8,500#	Hull Type	Deep-V
Clearance	9'6"	Deadrise Aft	21°

Phoenix 29 SFX Convertible

1988–99

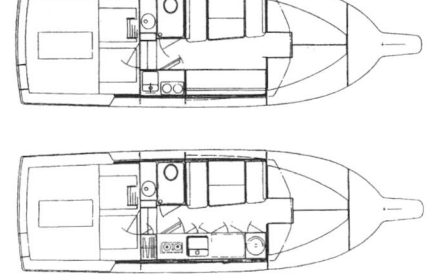

Restyled version of earlier Phoenix 29 (1977–87) matched Phoenix claim of versatile layout, solid construction, good performance. Large fishing cockpit with transom door accommodates two anglers and their gear. Cabin sleeps four or six depending on layout. Flybridge is huge for a boat this size. Unique air duct system rids cockpit of exhaust fumes. Prop pockets reduce draft, improve fuel efficiency. Twin 270hp gas engines cruise at 22 knots (29–30 knots top). Volvo 200hp diesels cruise at 25 knots (around 30 knots top).

See Page 535 For Value Estimates

Length w/Pulpit	31'11"	Clearance	9'6"
Hull Length	29'0"	Fuel	180 gals.
Beam	10'0"	Water	50 gals.
Draft	2'4"	Hull Type	Deep-V
Weight	9,450#	Deadrise Aft	22°

Sportfishing Boats

Sportfishing Boats

Phoenix 32 Tournament

1997–99

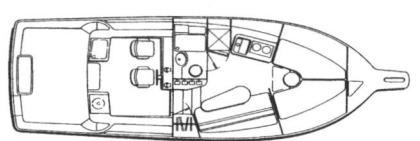

Versatile open fisherman with distinctive styling was the last Phoenix introduction before the company closed in 1999. Centerline helm puts driver in the most comfortable spot on the boat. Cockpit amenities include bait-prep center, freezer, broad transom door with gate. Comfortable cabin boasts head with stall shower, upright rod storage, full galley, berths for four. Note flared bow, small windshield. Above-average fit and finish. Optional Cat 350hp—or Volvo 370hp—diesels cruise at 25 knots (28–29 knots wide open).

See Page 535 For Value Estimates

Length w/Pulpit	34'8"	Weight, Diesel	19,320#
Hull Length	32'1"	Fuel	320 gals.
Beam	12'0"	Water	76 gals.
Draft	2'9"	Hull Type	Modified-V
Weight, Gas	16,360#	Deadrise Aft	17°

Phoenix 33 Convertible; 33/34 SFX

1987–99

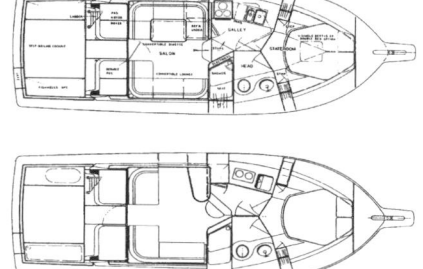

Well-appointed convertible (called Phoenix 33 Conv. in 1987–94; 33 SFX in 1992–94; 34 SFX in 1995–99) with wide 13' beam is stylish, roomy, built to last. Large cockpit with transom door, cushioned engine boxes has room for full-size chair. Offered with several cabin layouts over the years, all with galley down, stall shower in head. Flybridge is big for a 34-footer with seating for five, lockable rod storage. Note low cockpit freeboard. Standard gas engines cruise at 19 knots (high 20s top); optional 350hp Cat diesels cruise at 22 knots (30+ top).

See Page 535 For Value Estimates

Length w/Pulpit	36'9"	Weight, Diesel	23,600#
Hull Length	33'9"	Fuel	300 gals.
Beam	13'0"	Water	70 gals.
Draft	2'9"	Hull Type	Modified-V
Weight, Gas	20,810#	Deadrise Aft	17°

Post 42 Sport Fisherman

1997–2009

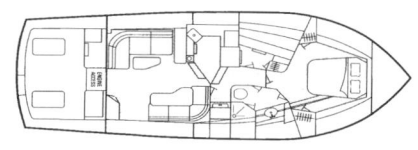

Gold-plated sportfisherman strikes near perfect balance of signature Post elegance, comfort, power. Richly appointed interior features spacious salon with L-shaped dinette, big master stateroom, guest cabin with over/under bunks. Washer/dryer installs in alcove abaft head. Extended flybridge is bigger than it looks with seating for eight, rod storage, well-arranged helm. Meticulous engine room is accessed from under cockpit step. Cruise at 24–25 knots (28 top) with Volvo 430hp diesels. Cummins 480hp diesels cruise in high 20s (30+ knots top).

See Page 535 For Value Estimates

Length	42'10"	Fuel	529 gals.
Beam	15'9"	Water	114 gals.
Draft	4'0"	Waste	31 gals.
Weight	42,996#	Hull Type	Modified-V
Clearance, Hardtop	16'11"	Deadrise Aft	7°

Post 43 Sport Fisherman

1984–89

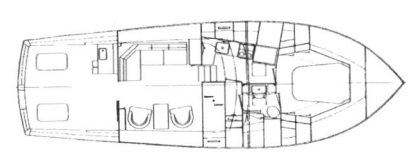

Updated version of classic Post 42 SF (1975–83) made a good boat even better. Second spray rail, increased transom deadrise improved head-sea performance. Spacious interior has large master stateroom forward, guest cabin with single berths to port. Note solid teak cabinetry, salon entertainment center, overhead rod storage. Post 43 III model introduced in 1989 included several standard-equipment updates. Twin GM 485hp engines cruise in the mid 20s (27–28 knots top). Optional 550hp GMs run a couple of knots faster.

Prices Not Provided for Pre-1995 Models

Length	43'8"	Fuel	500/550 gals.
Beam	15'9"	Water	120 gals.
Draft	3'6"	Cockpit	125 sq. ft.
Weight	33,000#	Hull Type	Modified-V
Clearance	13'7"	Deadrise Aft	8°

Post 43 Sport Fisherman

1995–96

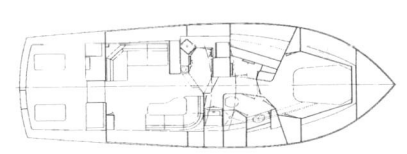

Updated version of popular Post 44 SF (1990–94) combines hardcore fishability with plush accommodations, spirited performance. Expansive salon—much larger than earlier 44—includes built-in dinette, full entertainment center. Island berth dominates large master stateroom; solid teak cabinets, plush furnishings highlight interior. Roomy engine compartment with cockpit access is a plus. Topside helm layout was state-of-the-art in her era. GM 535hp diesels cruise in the high 20s and reach a top speed of about 30 knots.

See Page 535 For Value Estimates

Length	43'9"	Water	120 gals.
Beam	15'9"	Clearance	13'7"
Draft	3'6"	Cockpit	125 sq. ft.
Weight	40,000#	Hull Type	Modified-V
Fuel	543 gals.	Deadrise Aft	7°

Post 44 Sport Fisherman

1990–94

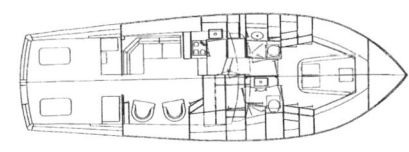

Premium sportfishing yacht from early 1990s delivered a timeless blend of Post quality, luxury, performance. Two-stateroom interior includes two heads—most boats this size have just one—resulting in relatively compact salon. Rich teak woodwork, quality furnishings are typical of Post's sophisticated interiors. Note excellent helm visibility, superb helm console. Large cockpit has tackle center, in-deck fishboxes, transom door. Cockpit engine room access became standard in 1992. Cruise at 27–28 knots (30+ top) with GM 550hp diesels.

Prices Not Provided for Pre-1995 Models

Length	43'9"	Fuel	570 gals.
Beam	15'9"	Water	120 gals.
Draft	3'6"	Cockpit	125 sq. ft.
Weight	33,000#	Hull Type	Modified-V
Clearance	13'7"	Deadrise Aft	7°

Sportfishing Boats

Post 46 Sport Fisherman

1978–96

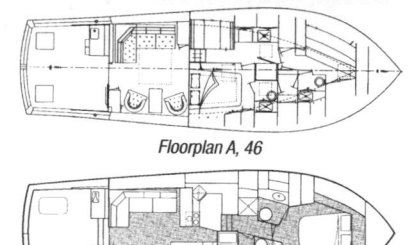

Floorplan A, 46

Floorplan A, 46 II

See Page 535 For Value Estimates

Classic Jersey-bred convertible with graceful lines, easy-riding hull led the field in her era for beauty, workmanship, owner appeal. Several two-stateroom layouts were offered, all with handcrafted teak woodwork, top-quality appliances and furnishings. Updated 46 II model (1988–96) features cockpit engine room door, stand-up engine room. Early models with 410hp 6-71 Detroit diesels cruise at 20 knots. Later 46 II models with 485hp 6-71s cruise at 23–24 knots; 625hp 6V92 diesels cruise at 25–26 knots.

Length	46'9"	Fuel	620 gals.
Beam	15'9"	Water	120 gals.
Draft	3'10"	Waste	31 gals.
Weight	44,000#	Hull Type	Modified-V
Clearance, Windshield	13'7"	Deadrise Aft	3°/7°

Post 47 Sport Fisherman

1997–2009

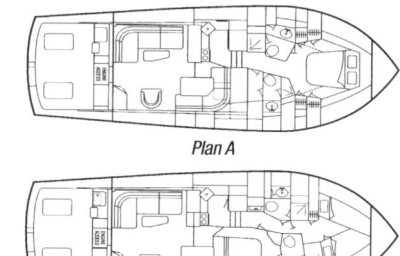

Plan A

Plan B

See Page 535 For Value Estimates

Refined version of venerable Post 46 SF (1978–96) is beautifully styled, luxuriously appointed, competitively priced. Offered with choice of two-stateroom interiors: Plan A has master forward, Plan B has amidships master. Washer/dryer is standard. Highlights include high-gloss interior joinery, huge bridge with centerline helm, meticulous engine room. Cockpit is among the largest in her class. Detroit 625hp diesels cruise at 25 knots (29–30 knots top); 680hp MANs cruise at 28 knots (around 32 knots top).

Length	46'9"	Fuel	635 gals.
Beam	15'9"	Water	120 gals.
Draft	4'2"	Waste	31 gals.
Weight	49,668#	Hull Type	Modified-V
Clearance, Hardtop	16'11"	Deadrise Aft	7°

Post 50 Convertible

1989–2009

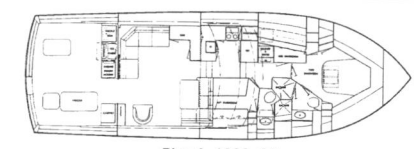

Plan A, 1989–96

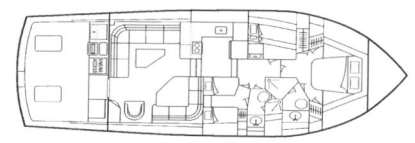

Plan A, 1997–09

See Page 535 For Value Estimates

Muscular tournament machine with signature Post styling delivers high-octane mix of quality construction, lush accommodations, world-class performance. Wide 16'11" beam results in truly expansive interior for a 50-footer. Highlights include spacious master suite, standard washer/dryer, massive 150-sq. ft. cockpit with controls, huge flybridge. Engine room headroom increased in 1995 when fuel tanks were moved aft. Over 100 built. GM 735hp diesels cruise 27–28 knots; later models with 860hp MANs cruise at 30+ knots.

Length	50'7"	Fuel	870 gals.
Beam	16'11"	Water	240 gals.
Draft	4'6"	Waste	42 gals.
Weight	57,122#	Hull Type	Modified-V
Clearance, Hardtop	17'2"	Deadrise Aft	7°

Sportfishing Boats

Post 53 Convertible

2005–09

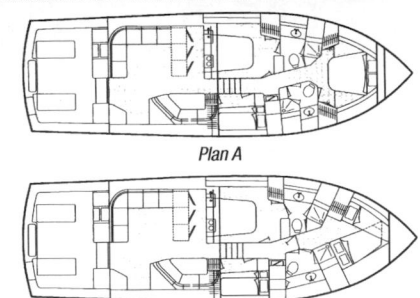

Plan A

Plan B

Premium fishing machine targets deep-pocket anglers with an eye for the beauty, amenities of a fine cruising yacht. Opulent three-stateroom interior with combined salon/galley/dinette offers unsurpassed luxury, exemplary fit and finish. Note high-gloss teak cabinetry, frameless windows, companionway washer/dryer. Additional highlights include large, tournament-ready cockpit with wide transom door, meticulous engine room, huge flybridge with seating for a small crowd. MTU 1,200hp engines cruise at 30 knots (about 35 knots top).

See Page 535 For Value Estimates

Length	52'10"	Fuel	926 gals.
Beam	16'11"	Water	240 gals.
Draft	5'0"	Waste	80 gals.
Weight	59,000#	Hull Type	Modified-V
Clearance	NA	Deadrise Aft	7°

Post 56 Convertible

2002–09

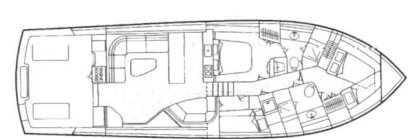

World-class convertible from one of America's premier builders is fast, luxurious, built for fishing. Lavish three-stateroom interior with lacquered teak joinery is notable for meticulous finish, top-quality furnishings. Under-counter refrigeration maximizes counter space in galley; washer/dryer is located in hallway. Tournament-ready cockpit is one of the largest of any boat this size. Flybridge boasts state-of-the-art helm, generous guest seating, rod storage. MAN 1,300hp engines cruise at 31–32 knots (35+ knots top).

See Page 535 For Value Estimates

Length	55'11"	Fuel	1,200 gals.
Beam	16'11"	Water	250 gals.
Draft	5'6"	Waste	80 gals.
Weight	66,830#	Hull Type	Deep-V
Clearance, Hardtop	17'6"	Deadrise Aft	7°

Pro-Line 27/29 Sport

2000–06

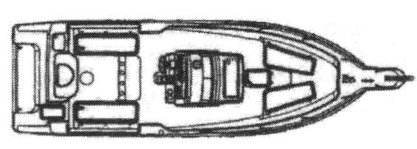

Tough center console with wide 9'10" beam, impressive standard equipment was a lot of boat for the money. Spacious cockpit with bow casting platform offers more fishing space than most boats her size. Standard features include 35-gallon livewell, in-deck fishboxes, transom door, tackle box, pop-up cleats, leaning post with rocket launcher, console cooler. Large console houses roomy stand-up head compartment. Called the Pro-Line 27 Sport in 2000–04; 29 Sport in 2005–06. About 40 knots top with twin 225s.

See Page 536 For Value Estimates

Length w/Pulpit	29'1"	Fuel	200 gals.
Beam	9'10"	Water	15 gals.
Hull Draft	1'8"	Max HP	500
Dry Weight	5,200#	Hull Type	Deep-V
Clearance	NA	Deadrise Aft	19°

Sportfishing Boats

Sportfishing Boats

Pro-Line 2810 Walkaround

1997–2000

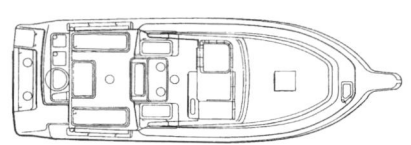

Popular family fisherman with center helm position delivers traditional Pro-Line mix of rugged construction, large fishing cockpit, comfortable accommodations. Amenities include large 42-gallon livewell, in-deck fishboxes, raw-water washdown, tackle storage drawers, bait-prep station, rod storage. Cozy cabin includes removable table, galley cabinet, rod storage locker, enclosed head with shower. Note large electronics box, tilt-out dash panel. Called the Pro-Line 28 Walk in 2000. About 40 knots top with 225 Mercs.

See Page 536 For Value Estimates

Length w/Pulpit	29'6"	Fuel	200 gals.
Beam	10'2"	Water	21 gals.
Hull Draft	2'1"	Max HP	500
Hull Weight	6,500#	Hull Type	Deep-V
Cockpit	72 sq. ft.	Deadrise Aft	21°

Pro-Line 2950 Mid Cabin

1992–2000

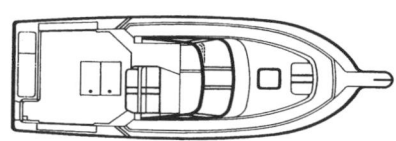

Best-selling Pro-Line express available with outboard or sterndrive power offered impressive versatility, features at an attractive price. Highlights include bait station with livewell, built-in tackle box, transom door, raw-water washdown, insulated fishboxes, cockpit bolsters, rear bench seat. Mid-cabin interior with enclosed head/shower, full galley, rod storage, removable dinette sleeps three. Most were sold with optional hardtop. Very popular model for Pro-Line. Cruise at 20 knots with single 260hp MerCruiser I/O; 25 knots with twin 225 Merc outboards.

See Page 536 For Value Estimates

Length	30'0"	Fuel	220 gals.
Beam	10'9"	Water	42 gals.
Hull Draft	1'10"	Max HP	500
Hull Weight	7,500#	Hull Type	Deep-V
Cockpit	80 sq. ft.	Deadrise Aft	19°

Pro-Line 30 Walkaround

2000–05

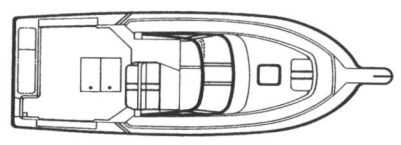

Restyled version of earlier Pro-Line 2950 (1992–2000) with integrated transom added new life to popular design. Versatile layout offers proven fishability with room for entertaining. Standard features included 45-gallon livewell, built-in tackle box, insulated fishboxes, freshwater sink, transom door. Well-appointed cabin with full galley, enclosed head with shower, midcabin berth sleeps three. Note deep walkways. Tops out around 40 knots with 225hp outboards. (Called Pro-Line 31 Walk in 2005.)

See Page 536 For Value Estimates

Length	32'6"	Fuel	300 gals.
Beam	10'10"	Water	39 gals.
Hull Draft	1'10"	Max HP	600
Hull Weight	7,600#	Hull Type	Deep-V
Cockpit	84 sq. ft.	Deadrise Aft	19°

Pro-Line 30 Express

2000–05

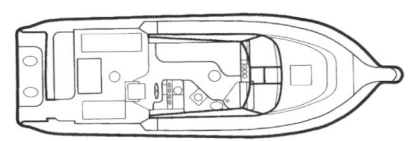

Good-looking express with innovative layout is more family dayboat than hardcore fishing machine. Expansive deck plan with open-air galley, forward lounge seating is uniquely suited for entertaining. Standard features include livewell, in-deck fishboxes, integrated tackle box, transom door, bow pulpit. Compact cabin is arranged with double berth forward, standup head with shower, storage bin aft with wine rack. Helm is well aft, reducing cockpit fishing space. Called 31 Express in 2005. About 40 knots top with twin 225s.

See Page 536 For Value Estimates

Length	32'6"	Fuel	312 gals.
Beam	10'10"	Water	30 gals.
Hull Draft	1'10"	Max HP	500
Hull Weight	7,700#	Hull Type	Deep-V
Cockpit	102 sq. ft.	Deadrise Aft	19°

Pro-Line 32 Express

2005–Current

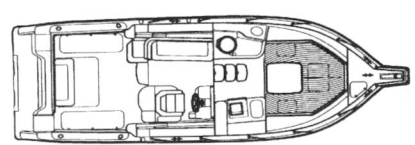

Versatile express combines durable Pro-Line construction with value-priced amenities, feature-rich accommodations. Standard fishing gear includes two in-deck fishboxes, 35-gallon livewell, tackle drawers, fresh/raw-water washdowns. Note aft-facing cockpit seat, foldaway stern seat. Roomy midcabin interior with full galley, enclosed head/shower sleeps four. Large lazarette can accommodate optional generator. Good range with generous 300-gallon fuel capacity. About 40 knots top with twin Mercury 250s.

See Page 536 For Value Estimates

Length	32'4"	Fuel	300 gals.
Beam	10'10"	Water	39 gals.
Hull Draft	1'11"	Max HP	600
Hull Weight	9,500#	Hull Type	Deep-V
Clearance, Top	10'2"	Deadrise Aft	22°

Pro-Line 3250/32 Express

1997–2002

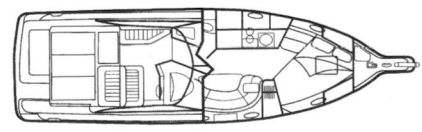

Sporty sterndrive express (called 3250 Express in 1997–99; 32 Express thereafter) combined large cockpit with no-frills interior, reasonable price. Cockpit amenities included bait station with 35-gallon livewell, cockpit bolsters, tackle drawers, lockable rod storage, transom door. Small-but-efficient cabin offers convertible U-shaped dinette forward, mid-berth aft, mini-galley, stand-up head with shower. Folding privacy door separates aft berth from salon. Twin 310hp MerCruiser (or Volvo) I/Os cruise in the high 20s (38–40 knots top).

See Page 536 For Value Estimates

Length	33'8"	Fuel	250 gals.
Beam	11'0"	Water	35 gals.
Hull Draft	2'1"	Waste	15 gals.
Weight	12,000#	Hull Type	Deep-V
Clearance	7'4"	Deadrise Aft	19°

Sportfishing Boats

Pro-Line 33 Express

1999–2006

Appealing inboard fishing machine with broad beam holds her own against more expensive competitors. Cockpit came standard with bait-prep center, 35-gallon livewell, dual washdowns, transom fishbox, raw-water washdown, transom door. Teak-trimmed cabin with full galley, convertible dinette, rod storage, enclosed head/shower sleeps four. Entire bridgedeck lifts for engine access. Excellent engine access. Yanmar 315hp diesels cruise at 24–26 knots (about 30 knots top); Yanmar 370 top out at 32–34 knots.

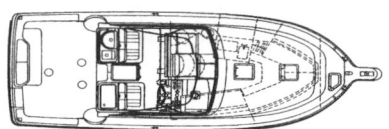

See Page 536 For Value Estimates

Length	33'0"	Fuel	300 gals.
Beam	12'6"	Water	40 gals.
Draft	3'5"	Waste	20 gals.
Weight	11,200#	Hull Type	Deep-V
Clearance	7'8"	Deadrise Aft	19°

Pro-Line 33 Walkaround

2003–05

Well-rounded express (called Pro-Line 34 Walkaround in 2005) delivers signature Pro-Line fishability, comfort without breaking the bank account. Roomy cockpit came standard with two in-deck fishboxes, raw-water washdown, padded bolsters, lockable rod storage, transom door, tackle station with sink. Forty-gallon oval livewell resides under lift-up transom seat. No-frills cabin with convertible dinette, midcabin berth sleeps four adults, two kids. Windlass, bow pulpit were standard. Nearly 40 knots top with twin 225s.

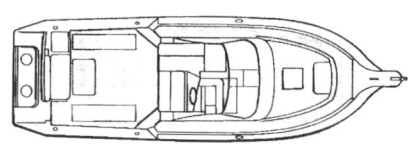

See Page 536 For Value Estimates

Length	33'8"	Fuel	285 gals.
Beam	11'0"	Water	39 gals.
Hull Draft	2'1"	Max HP	600
Dry Weight	12,000#	Hull Type	Deep-V
Clearance	6'10"	Deadrise Aft	19°

Pro-Line 35 Express

2006–Current

Hard-charging fishboat/cruiser rated for triple-outboard power blends modern styling with upmarket amenities, versatile layout. Highlights include large 45-gallon livewell, in-deck fishboxes, tackle storage center, dual washdowns, pop-up cleats, foldaway stern seat, L-shaped bridgedeck seating. Well-appointed interior with midship berth, enclosed head/shower, dinette sleeps four. Note easy access to pumps, generator. Good helm visibility. Twin 250hp outboards top out at 40 knots; triple 225s reach close to 50 knots top.

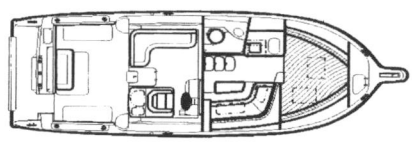

See Page 536 For Value Estimates

Length	35'6"	Water	60 gals.
Beam	12'6"	Waste	21 gals.
Hull Draft	2'1"	Max HP	900
Hull Weight	11,200#	Hull Type	Deep-V
Fuel	320 gals.	Deadrise Aft	19°

Pursuit 2700 Open

1983–93

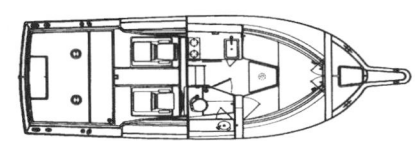

Iconic inboard express—essentially a Tiara 2700 Open (1988–93) with additional fishing features—has a well-earned reputation for proven reliability, long-term owner satisfaction. Spacious 12-foot cockpit is large enough for a mounted chair. Well-appointed cabin features V-berth/dinette forward, full galley, stand-up head with shower. Motor boxes provide good engine access. Note sturdy windshield, aggressive cockpit non-skid. Deep-V hull delivers good open-water ride. Standard 270hp gas engines cruise in the low 20s (about 30 knots top).

Prices Not Provided for Pre-1995 Models

Length w/Pulpit	29'5"	Fuel	240 gals.
Hull Length	27'0"	Water	30 gals.
Beam	10'0"	Waste	20 gals.
Hull Draft	2'2"	Hull Type	Deep-V
Dry Weight	7,500#	Deadrise Aft	22°

Pursuit 2800 Open

1989–92

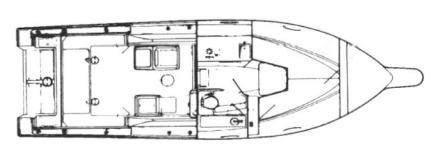

Dual-purpose express with many standard features blurs the line between hardcore fishing boat, comfortable weekend cruiser. Wide 10-foot beam provides stability required to handle topside weight of a small tower. Uncluttered cockpit features aft-facing jump seat with livewell under, in-floor fishbox, rod holders. Classy cabin with enclosed head, complete galley, generous storage sleeps two. Note very wide side decks, sturdy windshield, integral bow pulpit. Twin 225hp outboards cruise at 25 knots (about 40 knots wide open).

Prices Not Provided for Pre-1995 Models

Length w/Pulpit	30'4"	Clearance	6'9"
Hull Length	28'2"	Fuel	290 gals.
Beam	10'0"	Water	22 gals.
Hull Draft	1'9"	Hull Type	Deep-V
Weight	5,500#	Deadrise Aft	20°

Pursuit 2870 Offshore CC

1996–2002

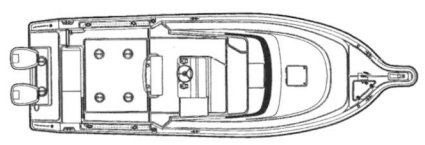

Innovative offshore cruiser with centerline helm splits the difference between capable fishing boat, deluxe family cruiser. Cockpit comes with large in-floor fishbox, rod holders, transom rigging station with cutting board and sink. Leaning post houses 26-gallon livewell. Aft-facing jump seat next to helm sits atop a five-drawer tackle center. Upscale cabin with removable table, mini-galley sleeps two. Huge in-deck compartment aft of console provides access to batteries, oil reservoirs. Yamaha 225s cruise at 25 knots (40+ knots wide open).

See Page 536 For Value Estimates

Length w/Pulpit	30'0"	Fuel	234 gals.
Hull Length	28'0"	Water	20 gals.
Beam	9'6"	Max HP	450
Hull Draft	1'8"	Hull Type	Deep-V
Hull Weight	5,950#	Deadrise Aft	22°

Sportfishing Boats

Pursuit 2870 Walkaround

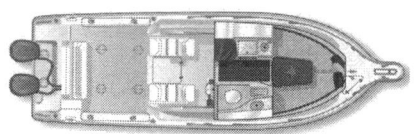

1996–2006

Premium fishing machine with full array of cruising comforts is rigged for tournament-level action. Topside highlights include hinged aft seat with fishbox/cooler under, hardtop with spreader lights, cockpit bolsters, aft-facing cockpit seats, tilt-away helm console. Deep cockpit, aggressive nonskid enhance safety. Well-appointed cabin—big for a 28-footer—includes convertible dinette, teak-and-holly sole, galley with sink, enclosed head. Note athwartships single berth under helmdeck. Yamaha 225hp outboards top out at 40+ knots.

See Page 536 For Value Estimates

Length w/Pulpit	30'0"	Fuel	234 gals.
Hull Length	28'0"	Water	20 gals.
Beam	9'6"	Max HP	500
Hull Draft	1'8"	Hull Type	Deep-V
Dry Weight	7,570#	Deadrise Aft	22°

Pursuit OS 285

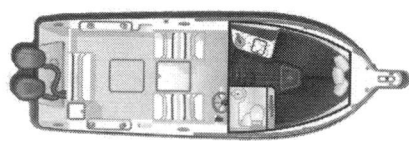

2008–Current

Deluxe offshore express matches signature Pursuit quality with multipurpose layout. Topside features include deluxe helm and companion seats with armrests, fiberglass hardtop with PFD storage, aft-facing cockpit seats with backrests, 32-gallon livewell, hinged rear seat with macerated fish box. Tall windshield (with vents) protects helm from high-rpm wind blast. Note hot/cold shower at swim platform. Compact cabin with mini-galley, midcabin berth, enclosed head sleeps three. Twin Yamaha 250s top out at 40+ knots.

See Page 536 For Value Estimates

Length w/Pulpit	30'8"	Fuel	232 gals.
Beam	9'6"	Water	30 gals.
Hull Draft	1'9"	Max HP	600
Weight w/T250s	7,570#	Hull Type	Deep-V
Clearance, Top	8'4"	Deadrise Aft	22°

Pursuit C 280

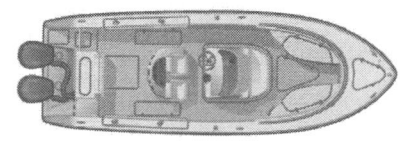

2009–Current

Premium offshore fishing machine with classic center console lines takes legendary Pursuit quality, fishability to the next level. Single-level cockpit with forward seating comes standard with transom fishbox, large in-floor fishbox with macerator, transom bait station, custom leaning post with tackle trays and 52-gallon oval livewell. Deluxe console has space for two big-screen video displays. Bow anchor chute is a nice touch. Yamaha 250s max out around 45 knots. Note that previous C 280 model ran from 2007–08.

See Page 536 For Value Estimates

Length	28'0"	Fuel	220 gals.
Beam	9'6"	Water	20 gals.
Draft, Up	1'7"	Max HP	500
Draft, Down	2'10"	Hull Type	Deep-V
Weight w/250s	7,300#	Deadrise Aft	24°

Sportfishing Boats

Pursuit 3000 Express

1998–2003

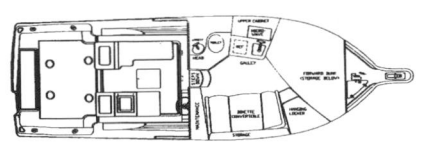

Classy open-cockpit fisherman with semicustom looks gets high marks for styling, finish, versatility. Cockpit came with full array of fishing amenities including centerline bait station, cushioned storage boxes, transom fishbox. Bridgedeck lifts for engine access. Super-comfortable cabin with full galley, pilot berths sleeps four. Visibility is excellent from raised helm. Twin 375hp gas inboards cruise at 25 knots (mid 30s top); 230hp Volvo diesels cruise at 23–24 knots (28–29 knots top).

See Page 536 For Value Estimates

Length w/Pulpit	32'8"	Fuel	210 gals.
Hull Length	30'10"	Water	30 gals.
Beam	10'6"	Waste	18 gals.
Draft	2'10"	Hull Type	Deep-V
Weight	10,600#	Deadrise Aft	21°

Pursuit 3000 Offshore

1995–2004

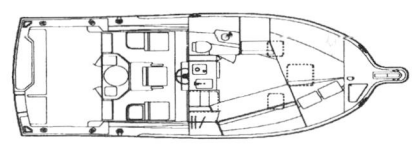

Enduring inboard fisherman with classic Palm Beach styling, top-notch finish gets high marks for performance, versatility. Cockpit came with full array of fishing amenities including centerline bait station, cushioned storage boxes, transom fishbox. Bridgedeck lifts for easy engine access. Surprisingly spacious cabin with full galley, pilot berths, backlit rod storage display, sleeps four. Visibility is excellent from raised helm. Gas 375hp inboards cruise at 25 knots; 230hp Volvo diesels cruise at 23–24 knots.

See Page 536 For Value Estimates

Length w/Pulpit	31'2"	Fuel	250 gals.
Hull Length	29'1"	Water	40 gals.
Beam	12'0"	Waste	20 gals.
Draft	2'9"	Hull Type	Modified-V
Weight	11,500#	Deadrise Aft	19°

Pursuit 3070 Center Console

2001–07

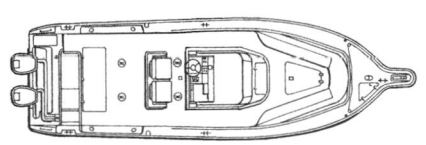

High-end fishing machine (called Pursuit C 300 in 2007) combines quality construction with first-rate amenities, agile performance. Single-level cockpit layout includes 40-gallon livewell, leaning post with rocket launchers, tackle drawers, lockable rod storage, transom rigging center with cutting board, insulated in-floor fishbox with macerator, bow storage lockers, raw-water washdown. Helm space for big-screen electronics. Big console houses marine head with sink, opening port. About 40 knots top with Yamaha 25s.

See Page 536 For Value Estimates

Length w/Pulpit	32'8"	Fuel	310 gals.
Hull Length	30'10"	Water	30 gals.
Beam	10'6"	Max HP	500
Draft, Down	3'3"	Hull Type	Deep-V
Dry Weight	8,945#	Deadrise Aft	21°

Sportfishing Boats

Pursuit 3070 Offshore Center Console

1999–2006

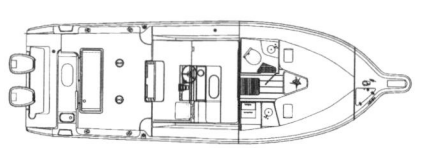

Luxury-class sportfisherman combines walkaround versatility with efficient center-console deck layout, compact cabin with family-style amenities. Highlights include 44-gallon livewell, bait-prep center with sink, tackle storage, large in-floor fishbox. Electric leaning post tilts open to expose lighted storage for up to 12 rods. Well-appointed cuddy with midcabin berth, enclosed head sleeps three–four. Full wraparound windshield replaced original cut-down windscreen in 2003. Yamaha 250s deliver 40 knots top.

See Page 536 For Value Estimates

Length w/Pulpit	32'8"	Fuel	310 gals.
Hull Length	30'10"	Water	30 gals.
Beam	10'6"	Max HP	500
Draft, Down	3'3"	Hull Type	Deep-V
Dry Weight	8,100#	Deadrise Aft	21°

Pursuit 3070 Offshore Express

2002–07

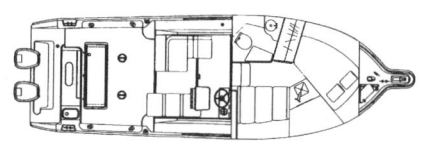

Deluxe offshore express (called OS 305 Offshore in 2007) appeals to serious anglers who appreciate top-shelf construction, yacht-class amenities. Deck layout is highlighted by expansive bridgedeck with posh L-lounge, ladder-back helm seat. Roomy cockpit includes 30-gallon livewell, aft-facing jump seat, transom bait-prep center. Bridgedeck lifts to reveal cavernous storage compartment. Note standard hardtop. Upscale cabin with full galley, head with shower features handy aft bunk, classy teak-and-holly flooring. About 40 knots top with Yamaha 250s.

See Page 536 For Value Estimates

Length w/Pulpit	32'8"	Fuel	310 gals.
Hull Length	30'10"	Water	30 gals.
Beam	10'6"	Max HP	500
Hull Draft	1'6"	Hull Type	Deep-V
Dry Weight	9,640#	Deadrise Aft	21°

Pursuit 3100 Express

1993–97

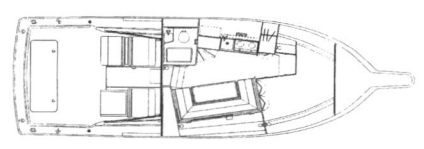

Popular big-water express—essentially a Tiara 3100 Open (1979–91) with extra fishing features—meets the needs of anglers and cruisers alike. Single-level cockpit is big enough for a mounted chair. Tackle center fits behind helm seat; livewell was popular option. Roomy cabin with teak-and-holly sole, U-shaped dinette, private stateroom sleeps four. Tall windshield provides superior weather protection. Not the softest rough-water ride. Standard 300hp gas inboards cruise at 20–21 knots (around 30 knots top).

See Page 537 For Value Estimates

Length w/Pulpit	33'9"	Fuel, Std.	206 gals.
Hull Length	31'1"	Fuel, Opt.	276 gals.
Beam	12'0"	Water	36 gals.
Draft	2'9"	Hull Type	Modified-V
Weight	11,000#	Deadrise Aft	16°

Pursuit C 310

2007–Current

Tournament-bred center console with top-shelf amenities, superb finish makes the cut with hardcore anglers. Fishing features include big 52-gallon lighted livewell, five fishboxes (two forward, two in the deck, one at the transom), 12 rod holders, bait-prep station. Lockable rod rack under forward seat swings out for use. Deluxe helm seats with flip-up bolsters, folding transom seat, pop-up cleats, recessed bow rails are standard. Space at the helm for two 12-inch displays. Heavily-built hull can take a pounding. Yamaha 250s top out at 45 knots.

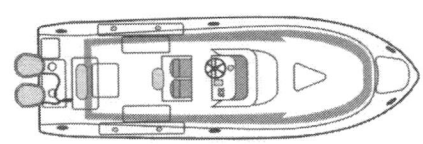

See Page 537 For Value Estimates

Length	31'2"	Fuel	260 gals.
Beam	9'6"	Water	20 gals.
Draft, Up	1'10"	Max HP	500
Draft, Down	2'8"	Hull Type	Deep-V
Weight w/T250s	8,500#	Deadrise Aft	24°

Pursuit OS 315

2008–Current

Luxury-class express from top-tier builder delivers great mix of leading-edge styling, upscale amenities, secure handling. Versatile deck layout appeals to anglers and cruisers alike. Topside features include L-shaped bridgedeck seating, lighted 32-gallon livewell, twin in-deck fishboxes, swivel helm seat, power windshield vent, raw-water washdowns. Well-appointed midcabin interior with teak flooring, quality fabrics sleeps four. Good range with 284-gallon fuel capacity. Yamaha 250hp outboards max out at 36–38 knots.

See Page 537 For Value Estimates

Length w/Pulpit	32'8"	Fuel	284 gals.
Beam	10'8"	Water	30 gals.
Hull Draft	1'6"	Max HP	600
Weight w/T250s	11,000#	Hull Type	Deep-V
Clearance, Top	9'3"	Deadrise Aft	20°

Pursuit 3100 Offshore

2004–05

Stylish inboard express combines top-shelf construction, superb performance. Single-piece windshield with epoxy frame is completely distinctive. Fishing features include removable fishbox, circulating livewell, tackle center. Aft bridgedeck raises on electronic rams for engine access. Teak-and-holly sole adds upscale tone to plush cabin with convertible dinette, enclosed head, large double berth forward. Standard 320hp gas inboards cruise in the mid 20s; optional 315hp Yanmar diesels cruise at 30 knots.

See Page 537 For Value Estimates

Length w/Pulpit	34'6"	Fuel	192 gals.
Hull Length	32'4"	Water	30 gals.
Beam	10'6"	Waste	18 gals.
Draft	3'3"	Hull Type	Deep-V
Weight	10,322#	Deadrise Aft	21°

Sportfishing Boats

Sportfishing Boats

Pursuit 3370 Offshore; OS 335

2004–08

Handsome express (called 3370 Offshore in 2004–06; OS 335 in 2007–08) took Pursuit styling, value to the next level. Distinctive one-piece windshield, expensive vacuum-bagged construction help set this quality canyon runner apart from the competition. Notable features include fold-down transom seat, hardtop with radio box, removable in-floor fishbox, 45-gallon livewell. Richly appointed interior with leather seating, teak-and-holly sole, full-service galley sleeps four. Twin 300hp Mercs max out around 40 knots.

See Page 537 For Value Estimates

Length w/Pulpit	35'1"	Fuel	310 gals.
Beam	10'6"	Water	30 gals.
Draft	2'4"	Max HP	600
Weight w/T250s	10,670#	Hull Type	Deep-V
Clearance	9'7"	Deadrise Aft	21°

Pursuit 3400 Express

1997–2003

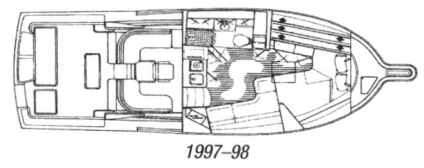

1997–98

1999–2003

Hard-hitting fishing machine targets big-water anglers with an appreciation for legendary Tiara luxury, quality. Original model with centerline helm, offset companionway was updated in 1999 with all-new deck design featuring starboard-side helm, rearranged tackle center and livewell, enlarged interior with centerline entry, full dinette, stall shower in head. Entire bridgedeck lifts for access to engines. Side exhausts keep cockpit free of fumes. Cummins 370hp diesels cruise in the mid 20s (30+ knots top).

See Page 537 For Value Estimates

Length w/Pulpit	36'4"	Fuel	350 gals.
Hull Length	33'9"	Water	60 gals.
Beam	12'9"	Waste	30 gals.
Draft	2'2"	Hull Type	Modified-V
Weight	14,000#	Deadrise Aft	18°

Pursuit 3480 Center Console; C 340

2005–Current

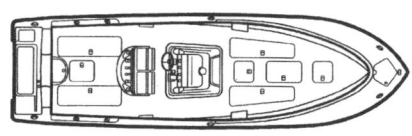

Hard core sportfishing machine (called Pursuit 3480 CC in 2006; C 340 thereafter) makes the cut with demanding, quality-focused anglers. World-class layout boasts custom leaning post with circulating 52-gallon livewell, four insulated in-floor fishboxes, cockpit bolsters, transom bait-prep station, enclosed head compartment with forward door, pop-up cleats. Transom livewell, bow seating, folding rear seat, factory T-top are popular options. Slender deep-V hull is quick to accelerate. Over 40 knots top with Yamaha 250s.

See Page 537 For Value Estimates

Length	34'5"	Fuel	375 gals.
Beam	9'6"	Water	30 gals.
Hull Draft	1'10"	Max HP	600
Weight w/T250s	9,300#	Hull Type	Deep-V
Clearance, Top	9'4"	Deadrise Aft	24.5°

Pursuit OS 375

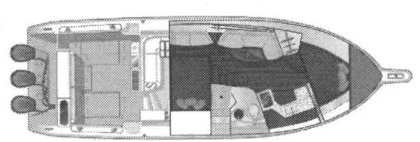

2008–Current

Feature-rich fishing boat with broad 13-foot beam strikes a balance between yacht-class amenities, big-water fishability. Highlights include factory hardtop, 50-gallon livewell, tackle stowage, refrigerated fishboxes, bow thruster, cockpit grill, windlass. Plush midcabin interior with huge galley, teak-and-maple sole features clever forward berth that allows a couple to sleep fore and aft or athwartships. Bridge air-conditioning is standard. Impressive fit and finish throughout. Triple Yamaha 350s deliver 45+ knots wide open.

See Page 537 For Value Estimates

Length w/Pulpit	39'2"	Fuel	370 gals.
Hull Length	36'11"	Water	65 gals.
Beam	13'0"	Max HP	1,050
Hull Draft	3'6"	Hull Type	Modified-V
Weight, 3/350	18,450#	Deadrise Aft	18°

Pursuit 3800 Express

2002–04

Handsome offshore express combines semicustom styling with spacious layout, best-in-class construction. Posh teak-trimmed interior offers luxury accommodations for four; large cockpit with foldaway transom seat is big enough for several anglers without bumping shoulders. Highlights include L-shaped bridgedeck seating, 50-gallon livewell, bait-prep station, teak-and-holly cabin sole. Note lighted rod locker, stand-up engine room, stylish epoxy-framed windshield. Cummins 450hp—or Volvo 480hp—diesels cruise in the mid 20s (30+ knots top).

See Page 537 For Value Estimates

Length w/Pulpit	40'11"	Headroom	6'2"
Hull Length	38'6"	Fuel	438 gals.
Beam	14'2"	Water	110 gals.
Draft	3'11"	Waste	40 gals.
Weight	21,800#	Hull Type	Modified-V

Rampage 28 Sportsman

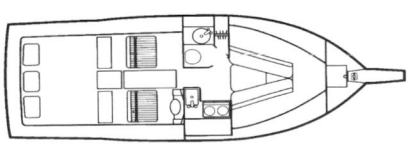

1986–93

Beefy 28-footer with wide 11-foot beam offers more cockpit, cabin space than most boats her size. Topside highlights include lockable rod storage, in-floor livewell, bow pulpit, aft-facing cockpit seats. Teak-trimmed interior with full galley, stand-up head, sleeps three. Motorboxes beneath helm, companion seats provide good access to engines. Transom door was a popular option. Note fully cored hull construction, lockable electronics storage. Twin 260hp gas inboards cruise at 22–24 knots (about 30 knots top).

Prices Not Provided for Pre-1995 Models

Length w/Pulpit	29'6"	Fuel	240 gals.
Hull Length	28'0"	Water	25 gals.
Beam	11'0"	Cockpit	80 sq. ft.
Draft	2'6"	Hull Type	Modified-V
Weight	8,200#	Deadrise Aft	10°

Sportfishing Boats

Rampage 30 Express

1999–Current

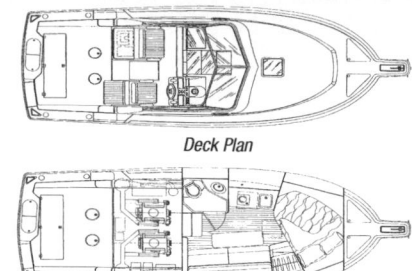

Deck Plan

Interior

See Page 537 For Value Estimates

Well-rigged midsize express with handsome lines delivers impressive mix of top-shelf amenities, proven big-water performance. Unobstructed cockpit includes 38-gallon lighted livewell, large in-deck fishbox, dual washdowns, bait-prep center, lockable tackle storage. Cherrywood interior with Corian counters, leather seating sleeps four. Tilt-away helm, lighted engine compartment, transom door are standard. Weight-efficient hull is fully cored. Twin 315hp Yanmar diesels cruise in the mid 20s with top speed of 30+ knots.

Length w/Pulpit	31'0"	Fuel	250 gals.
Beam	11'3"	Water	31 gals.
Draft	2'10"	Waste	20 gals.
Weight	12,000#	Hull Type	Modified-V
Clearance	7'0"	Deadrise Aft	19°

Rampage 30 Offshore

2002–06

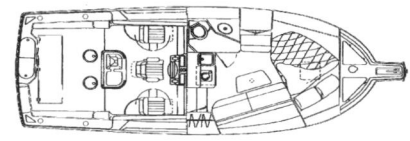

Handsome midsize express (originally called Rampage 30 Open) with appealing Palm Beach styling combines top-shelf amenities, agile performance. Spacious cockpit features 38-gallon lighted livewell, large in-deck fishbox, dual washdowns, bait-prep center with sink, lockable tackle storage. Upscale cherry-trimmed interior with convertible dinette, angled berth sleeps four. Additional features include centerline helm position, transom door and gate, fully cored hull. Twin 315hp Yanmar diesels cruise in the mid 20s (30+ top).

See Page 537 For Value Estimates

Length w/Pulpit	31'0"	Fuel	250 gals.
Hull Length	28'9"	Water	31 gals.
Beam	11'3"	Waste	20 gals.
Draft	2'10"	Hull Type	Modified-V
Weight	12,000#	Deadrise Aft	19°

Rampage 31 Sportfisherman

1985–93

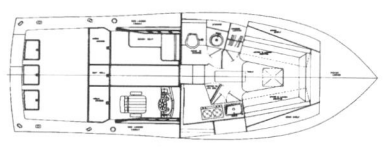

Wide-beam express introduced in 1985 packed big-boat features in modest 31-foot hull. Huge cockpit dwarfs anything in her class. Highlights include huge in-floor livewell, extra-wide transom door, lockable rod storage, bow pulpit, wide side decks. Well-appointed cabin with teak trim, full galley, enclosed head with shower sleeps four. Slide-back engine hatches allow excellent engine access. Note tall windshield, fully cored hull construction. Definitely a stiff ride in a chop. Standard 330hp gas inboards cruise at 22–24 knots (30+ top).

Prices Not Provided for Pre-1995 Models

Length w/Pulpit	31'10"	Fuel	256 gals.
Hull Length	30'10"	Water	50 gals.
Beam	11'11"	Cockpit	114 sq. ft.
Draft	2'9"	Hull Type	Modified-V
Weight	12,000#	Deadrise Aft	10°

Rampage 33 Express

2005–08

Versatile offshore fishing boat with centerline helm matches agile handling, wide-beam accommodations. Spacious cockpit can be configured with 45-gallon livewell/bait-prep center for fishing, or wet bar and foldaway stern seating for cruising. Classy cherry-trimmed interior with Corian counters, flip-up backrests, sleeps six. Note huge engine compartment, cabin rod storage, large fishbox, wide side decks. Prop-pocket hull draws very little water. Cruise in the mid 20s with 460hp Cat C7 diesels (30+ knots top).

See Page 537 For Value Estimates

Length w/Pulpit	35'6"	Fuel	367 gals.
Hull Length	33'0"	Water	60 gals.
Beam	13'0"	Waste	45 gals.
Draft	2'5"	Hull Type	Modified-V
Weight	17,200#	Deadrise Aft	18°

Rampage 33 Sportfisherman

1990–93

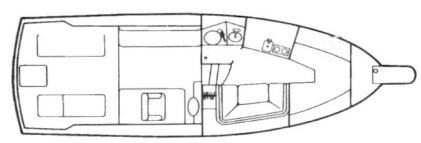

Rugged 1990s express with handsome lines made good on Rampage promise of dependable construction, top-level amenities. Large cockpit with in-deck fishboxes, wide transom door, lockable rod storage is big enough for several anglers. Ergonomic helm has space for electronic add-ons. Well-finished cabin—plain but comfortable—sleeps four. Note wide side decks, excellent engine access. Fully cored hull with flared bow, generous beam is dry, stable. Cummins 300hp diesels cruise at 24–25 knots; Cat 320hp diesels run a knot or two faster.

Prices Not Provided for Pre-1995 Models

Length w/Pulpit	34'10"	Clearance	11'2"
Hull Length	32'4"	Fuel	300 gals.
Beam	12'4"	Water	58 gals.
Draft	2'7"	Hull Type	Modified-V
Weight	14,500#	Deadrise Aft	18°

Rampage 36 Sportfisherman

1989–93

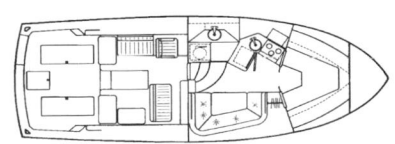

Polished 1990s canyon runner offered impressive blend of distinctive styling, agile performance. Beamy, fully cored hull provides big bi-level fishing cockpit without cutting into cabin space. Highlights include oversized transom door, large in-deck fishboxes, concealed rod storage, well-arranged helm, good engine access. Upscale interior with cherry trim sleeps four. Note tall windshield. Cummins 300hp diesels cruise at 20 knots (around 25 knots top); 425hp Cats cruise at 25 knots and deliver 29–30 knots wide open.

Prices Not Provided for Pre-1995 Models

Length w/Pulpit	37'8"	Clearance	8'10"
Hull Length	35'6"	Fuel	435 gals.
Beam	13'9"	Water	70 gals.
Draft	2'9"	Hull Type	Modified-V
Weight	19,000#	Deadrise Aft	17°

Sportfishing Boats

Sportfishing Boats

Rampage 45 Convertible

2002–Current

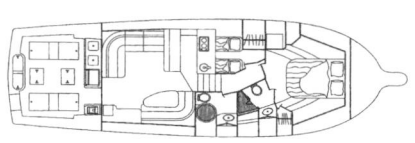

High-end tournament machine delivers impressive blend of rakish styling, state-of-the-art construction. Highlights include massive 130-square-foot cockpit, stand-up engine room, huge bridge with lockable rod storage, luxurious two-stateroom, two-head interior with cherry cabinetry, leather upholstery. Note hidden salon rod storage, wraparound helm display, single-lever controls. Low-deadrise hull with solid fiberglass bottom has prop pockets to reduce draft, improve efficiency. Cruise at 26–28 knots (mid 30s top) with 800hp Cats.

See Page 537 For Value Estimates

Length w/Pulpit	48'8"	Fuel	700 gals.
Hull Length	45'10"	Water	100 gals.
Beam	16'0"	Waste	60 gals.
Draft	4'0"	Hull Type	Modified-V
Weight	36,000#	Deadrise Aft	10°

Regulator 28 FS

2010–Current

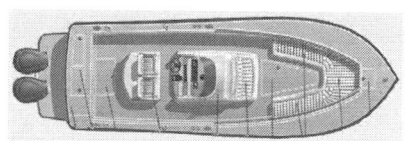

Focused, no-frills center console with bracket-mounted outboards is sure to catch the eye of hardcore fisherman. Principal features include cushioned forward seating with insulated fishboxes under, in-floor fishbox/rod storage, insulated cooler seat, integrated leaning post/livewell/tackle center, transom fishbox, transom door. Flush deck means no cockpit obstructions when fighting a fish. Walk-in console contains marine head, opening port for ventilation. Note fold-away rear seat, wide forward gunwales. Twin 300hp Yamahas reach 50+ knots.

Insufficient Resale Data to Assign Values

Length	27'7"	Fuel	235 gals.
Beam	9'5"	Water	33 gals.
Draft, Up	2'0"	Max HP	600
Draft, Down	2'8"	Hull Type	Deep-V
Dry Weight	8,260#	Deadrise Aft	24°

Regulator 29 FS

2006–Current

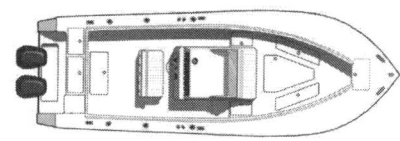

Open Deck Plan

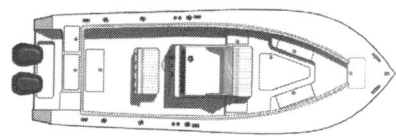

Forward Seating Deck Plan

Top-shelf fisherman meets angler demands for superior craftsmanship, no-excuses fishability. Standard features include combined leaning post/tackle center, transom and in-floor fishboxes, 30-gallon livewell, pop-up cleats, insulated cooler, fresh/saltwater washdowns, cushioned bow seating, console head with marine toilet. Helm offers lots of space for flush-mounting electronics. Forward fishbox doubles as lockable rod locker. Excellent range. Forward Seating model available since 2006. Yamaha 250s reach 45 knots.

See Page 538 For Value Estimates

Length	29'0"	Fuel	285 gals.
Beam	9'6"	Water	20 gals.
Draft, Up	2'0"	Max HP	500
Draft, Down	2'7"	Hull Type	Deep-V
Hull Weight	6,900#	Deadrise Aft	24°

Regulator 32 FS

1999–Current

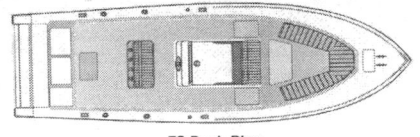

FS Deck Plan

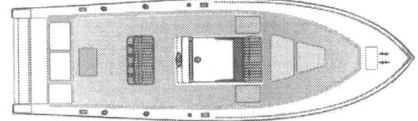

Open Deck Plan

Smooth-running center console with forward seating ranks with class leaders for quality, performance, long-term owner satisfaction. Standard fishing features include deluxe leaning post/tackle center with flip-up bolsters, 50-gallon transom baitwell, transom fishbox, lockable in-deck rod storage, bait-rigging station. Console compartment houses marine toilet with sink, hand-held shower. Popular boat enjoys strong resale values. Open model (no bow seating) also available. Over 40 knots with Yamaha 200s.

See Page 538 For Value Estimates

Length	32'0"	Fuel	310 gals.
Beam	10'5"	Water	38 gals.
Draft, Up	2'0"	Max HP	700
Draft, Down	2'8"	Hull Type	Deep-V
Dry Weight	7,400#	Deadrise Aft	24°

Regulator 34 SS

2009–Current

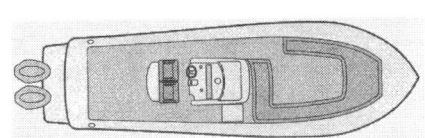

Blue-chip center console with circular starboard seating (hence the "SS"), oversized console with galley and berths for two, takes center-console comfort to the next level. Large cockpit boasts 85-gallon transom fishbox, deluxe folding rear seat, transom door, 360-degree coaming pads. Dash is big enough for two 15" video displays; standard leaning post comes with flip-up bolsters. Unique bow seating design means access aft is to port only. Note flush deck, fishboxes under bow cushions. Twin 350hp Yamahas reach 45+ knots top.

Insufficient Resale Data to Assign Values

Length w/Bracket	38'6"	Fuel	380 gals.
Beam	10'11"	Water	35 gals.
Draft, Up	2'3"	Max HP	700
Draft, Down	2'7"	Hull Type	Deep-V
Weight	11,115#	Deadrise Aft	24°

Riviera 33 Convertible

1992–97

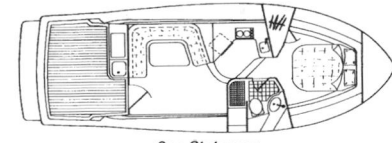

One Stateroom

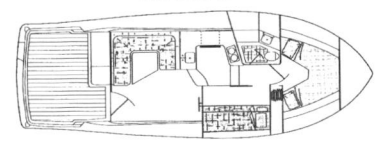

Two Staterooms

Classy 1990s convertible with Bertram-like styling combined low price with solid construction, well-planned accommodations. Offered with single- and twin-stateroom floorplans, both with teak trim, convertible dinette, step-down galley, lower helm station. Large fishing cockpit came standard with transom door, fish box, tackle center. Flybridge is huge for a 33-footer. Note forward collision bulkhead. Cockpit engine room entry is completely unique for a boat this size. Cummins 333hp diesels cruise in the low 20s (27–28 knots top).

See Page 538 For Value Estimates

Length	33'0"	Fuel	296 gals.
Beam	12'6"	Water	84 gals.
Draft	2'7"	Waste	25 gals.
Weight	20,500#	Hull Type	Modified-V
Cockpit	NA	Deadrise Aft	16°

Sportfishing Boats

Riviera 33 Convertible

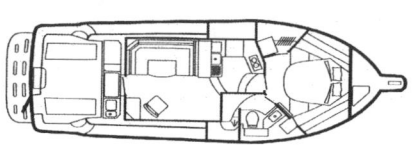

2005–08

Aussie-built pocket convertible offered smart styling, roomy accommodations at a surprisingly affordable price. Single-stateroom interior with convertible dinette is available with or without lower helm. Cockpit features tackle station with freshwater sink, top-loading refrigerator cabinet to port, in-deck fishbox, bait-prep center. Cockpit engine room entry is unique for a boat this size. Solid fiberglass hull with prop pockets, underwater exhausts boasts forward collision bulkhead. Volvo 370hp diesels cruise in the mid 20s (30+ knots top).

See Page 538 For Value Estimates

Length w/Pulpit	37'3"	Fuel	264 gals.
Beam	12'7"	Water	103 gals.
Draft	3'3"	Waste	18 gals.
Weight	19,800#	Hull Type	Modified-V
Clearance	14'5"	Deadrise Aft	15°

Riviera 34 Convertible

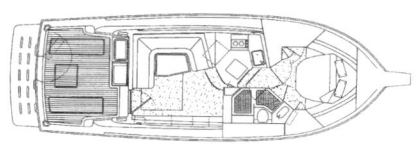

1997–2002

Good-selling, affordably priced cruiser with timeless convertible styling is one part sportfishing boat, one part family cruiser. No-frills interior boasts surprisingly spacious salon with U-shaped dinette, step-down galley, optional lower helm. Note in-floor galley storage compartment. Cockpit came standard with bait-prep station (with freezer), transom door, engine room access hatch. Tournament-style bridge has bench seating forward of helm. Cummins 330hp diesels cruise in the mid 20s (28–30 knots top).

See Page 538 For Value Estimates

Length	34'0"	Water	84 gals.
Beam	13'4"	Clearance	NA
Draft	2'7"	Headroom	6'4"
Weight	19,400#	Hull Type	Modified-V
Fuel	296 gals.	Deadrise Aft	17°

Riviera 36 Convertible

1993–2002

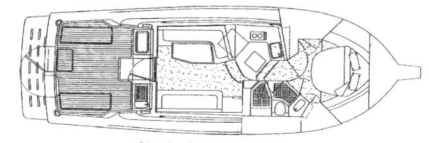

Single-Stateroom Layout

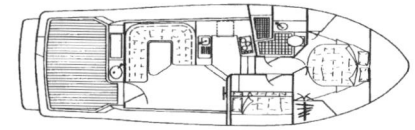

Two-Stateroom Floorplan

Popular Australian import with Bertram-like styling is handsome, sturdy, built to last. Available with choice of single- or twin-stateroom interiors, both with optional lower helm, step-down galley, separate stall shower in head. Transom door, tackle center, engine room access hatch were standard in the cockpit. Tournament-style bridge has bench seating forward of simple helm console. Note wide side decks, forward collision bulkhead. Cummins 315hp diesels cruise at 23–24 knots; 350hp Cats cruise at 27–28 knots.

See Page 539 For Value Estimates

Length	36'0"	Water	119 gals.
Beam	13'5"	Clearance	NA
Draft	3'5"	Headroom	6'4"
Weight	22,800#	Hull Type	Modified-V
Fuel	324 gals.	Deadrise Aft	16°

Sportfishing Boats

Riviera 37 Convertible

2001–08

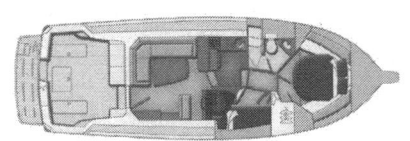

Australian-built convertible with rakish styling, roomy interior splits the difference between capable fishing boat, comfortable family cruiser. Well-appointed interior features surprisingly spacious salon, open-plan galley, two comfortable staterooms. Big cockpit with engine room access includes transom door, insulated fishbox, molded tackle center. Cruising-style bridge has helm forward, guest seating aft. Bow pulpit, swim platform, generator, collision bulkhead are standard. Note wide side decks. Volvo 370hp diesels cruise at 25 knots (28–29 knots top).

See Page 539 For Value Estimates

Length w/Pulpit	42'11"	Fuel	370 gals.
Hull Length	37'11"	Water	122 gals.
Beam	13'10"	Waste	18 gals.
Draft	3'5"	Hull Type	Modified-V
Weight	24,000#	Deadrise Aft	18°

Riviera 39 Convertible

1994–99

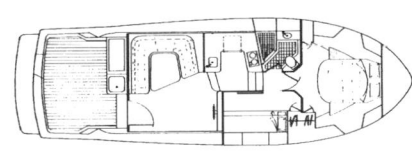

Spirited 1990s convertible offered clean styling, good speed, well-placed fishing amenities. Conservative twin-stateroom interior with step-down galley features spacious salon with 360-degree visibility, lower helm station, teak joinery. Unique double bed in guest cabin converts to upper/lower berths. Cockpit with tackle center, transom door, engine room access door has room for mounted chair. Cat 350hp diesels cruise in the low 20s; 420hp Cummins diesels cruise at 25 knots and reach a top speed of 31–32 knots.

See Page 539 For Value Estimates

Length	39'4"	Water	100 gals.
Beam	14'6"	Clearance	NA
Draft	3'7"	Headroom	6'5"
Weight	28,400#	Hull Type	Modified-V
Fuel	400 gals.	Deadrise Aft	15°

Riviera 40 Convertible

2001–06

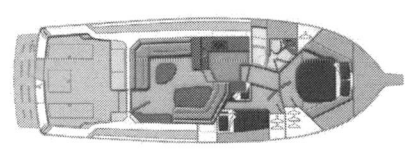

Popular, well-priced 40-footer from Down Under ranked among the best boating vales of her era. Unpretentious two-stateroom interior includes L-shaped dinette forward in salon. Front salon windows are rare in a modern convertible. Lower helm layout is optional. Note three single berths, washer/dryer space in guest stateroom. Exterior highlights include well-equipped cockpit with engine room access, spacious bridge, wide side decks, swim platform. Cruise in the mid 20s (28–29 knots top) with 450hp Cummins or 460hp Cat diesels.

See Page 539 For Value Estimates

Length w/Pulpit	46'4"	Fuel	473 gals.
Hull Length	42'11"	Water	122 gals.
Beam	14'11"	Waste	18 gals.
Draft	4'1"	Hull Type	Modified-V
Weight	29,800#	Deadrise Aft	15°

Sportfishing Boats

Riviera 42 Convertible

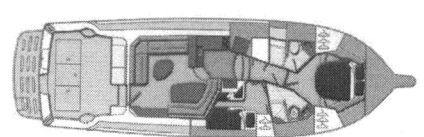

2004–06

Appealing 42-foot convertible with rakish styling, solid construction was designed for serious fishing, sociable cruising. Practical two-stateroom, two-head interior features spacious salon with leather lounge, L-shaped dinette, home-size galley with slide-out dishwasher, triple-bunk guest cabin. Note salon entertainment center, high-gloss teak joinery. Bait-prep center, in-sole fishbox, cooler/freezer, trash receptacle are standard in cockpit. Engine room is a little tight. Cruise at 22–23 knots with 480hp Cummins diesels (26–28 knots top).

See Page 539 For Value Estimates

Length w/Pulpit	50'10"	Fuel	476 gals.
Hull Length	42'11"	Water	122 gals.
Beam	14'11"	Waste	40 gals.
Draft	4'2"	Hull Type	Modified-V
Weight	30,900#	Deadrise Aft	15°

Riviera 43 Convertible

1996–2003

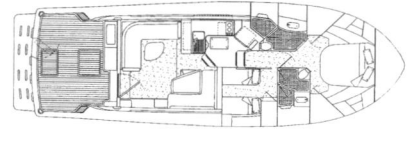
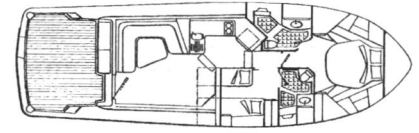

Rugged Down Under convertible splits the difference between fishing machine, comfortable family cruiser. Standard two-stateroom interior (available with or without lower helm) features mid-level galley, stall showers in both heads, well-appointed salon with leather seating, teak trim. Cockpit came with freezer, storage cabinets, direct access to spacious engine room. Flybridge is large for a 43-footer with L-lounge seating, removable table forward of helm. Twin 420hp Cats—or 430hp Cummins—cruise in the low 20s (26–28 knots top).

See Page 539 For Value Estimates

Length w/Pulpit	48'6"	Water	164 gals.
Beam	15'8"	Clearance	16'8"
Draft	4'2"	Headroom	6'6"
Weight	35,300#	Hull Type	Modified-V
Fuel	580/832 gals.	Deadrise Aft	16°

Riviera 47 Convertible

2003–07

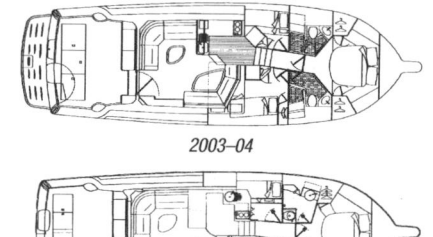

2003–04

2005–07

Blue-chip convertible with loads of standard features combines spacious accommodations with handsome lines, bulletproof construction. One of just a few boats this size to offer three private staterooms. Note that Series II model introduced in 2005 features redesigned interior with larger salon, double berth in master, underwater exhausts, prop pockets. Highlights include high-gloss cherry joinery, huge cockpit, forward collision bulkhead, bridge seating for eight. Engine room is a tight fit. Cummins 660hp diesels cruise at 28 knots (30+ top).

See Page 539 For Value Estimates

Length w/Pulpit	53'1"	Fuel	977 gals.
Hull Length	49'10"	Water	164 gals.
Beam	16'1"	Waste	40 gals.
Draft	4'5"	Hull Type	Modified-V
Weight	43,200#	Deadrise Aft	16°

Riviera 48 Convertible

1993–2002

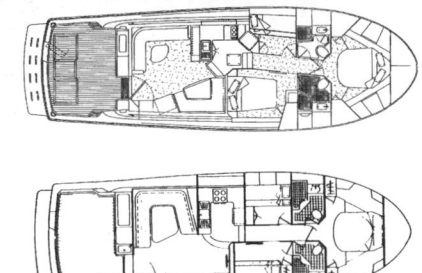

High-end convertible from Australia delivered impressive blend of styling, comfort, performance. Offered with several three-stateroom interiors—lower helm was standard in early years; later models have dinette in place of helm. Highlights include large fishing cockpit, expansive bridge with dinette forward of helm console, well-planned bridge. (Optional enclosed bridge was introduced in 1989.) Note forward collision bulkhead, watertight engine room bulkheads. Cat 660hp diesels cruise in the mid 20s; 800hp Cats cruise at 27–28 knots.

See Page 539 For Value Estimates

Length w/Pulpit	54'0"	Water	227 gals.
Beam	16'0"	Clearance	16'6"
Draft	4'7"	Headroom	6'5"
Weight	39,600#	Hull Type	Modified-V
Fuel	650/940 gals.	Deadrise Aft	18°

Riviera 51 Convertible

2004–Current

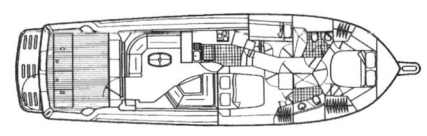

Muscular Aussie convertible combines solid construction with efficient layout, serious eye appeal. Upscale three-stateroom interior with combined salon/dinette/galley features leather settees, varnished cherry joinery, washer/dryer space, salon entertainment center. Additional highlights include spacious flybridge, teak-laid cockpit, well-finished engine room. Note overhead rod storage in salon, forward collision bulkhead, bow thruster. Enclosed bridge version available beginning in 2007. MTU 825hp engines cruise at 26–28 knots (30+ knots top).

Insufficient Resale Data to Assign Values

Length w/Pulpit	58'2"	Fuel	977 gals.
Hull Length	54'8"	Water	227 gals.
Beam	16'2"	Waste	40 gals.
Draft	4'6"	Hull Type	Modified-V
Weight	48,060#	Deadrise Aft	14°

Riviera 60 Enclosed Bridge Conv.

2006–07

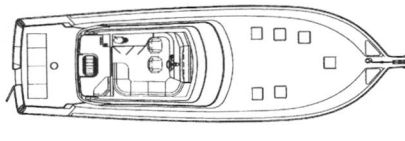

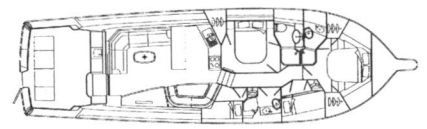

Bold closed-bridge convertible delivers spacious accommodations, tournament-class fishability. Highlights include four-stateroom interior with combined salon/galley/dinette, roomy cockpit with bait-prep center, expansive engine room with excellent service access. Enclosed flybridge with seating for 10 serves as second salon. Note steering station on after bridgedeck, generous fuel capacity, wide transom door. Bridge access is via cockpit ladder only—no interior stairway. Twin 1,520hp MTUs cruise at 30+ knots (mid 30s top).

Insufficient Resale Data to Assign Values

Length w/Platform	64'5"	Clearance	NA
Hull Length	61'0"	Fuel	1,506 gals.
Beam	17'9"	Water	264 gals.
Draft	5'2"	Hull Type	Modified-V
Weight	67,200#	Deadrise Aft	10°

Sportfishing Boats

Robalo 300 Center Console

2007–Current

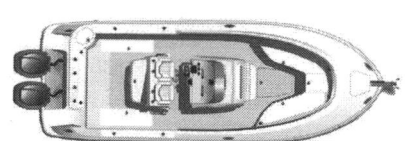

Hardcore center console with yacht-class finish takes Robalo engineering, quality to the next level. Broad 10'6" beam allows plenty of fishing space for two anglers. Single-level cockpit with wide walkways makes getting around easy. Dash has space for twin big-screen displays. Note upright rod rack in head compartment, lockable cockpit rod storage, recessed bow rails. Tilt helm access is a plus. Two livewells, both with blue LED lighting, are standard. Good range with 300-gallon fuel capacity. Yamaha 250hp outboards top out at 40+ knots.

See Page 539 For Value Estimates

Length	29'2"	Fuel	300 gals.
Beam	10'6"	Water	30 gals.
Draft, Up	1'8"	Max HP	600
Draft, Down	2'10"	Hull Type	Deep-V
Dry Weight	7,500#	Deadrise Aft	21°

Robalo 305 Walkaround

2007–Current

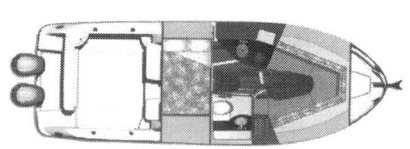

Top-quality express with serious eye appeal is proof again that you get what you pay for. Bridge deck is two steps up from cockpit for improved helm visibility. Uncluttered cockpit with bait-prep center, twin livewells. Foldaway transom seat is as good as it gets in a 30-foot express. L-shaped lounge seat opposite helm has clever 3-position back rest. Freshwater washdown at bow is way cool. Upscale cabin can sleep six (in a pinch). Note pull-up cleats, standard hardtop with spreader lights. Yamaha 250hp outboards top out at close to 40 knots.

See Page 539 For Value Estimates

Length	29'2"	Fuel	296 gals.
Beam	10'6"	Water	40 gals.
Draft, Up	1'8"	Max HP	600
Draft, Down	2'10"	Hull Type	Deep-V
Dry Weight	9,300#	Deadrise Aft	21°

Scout 280 Sportfish

2001–06

Beamy center console with sleek profile gets high marks for tough construction, roomy deck layout. Standard features include factory T-top, spreader lights, 30-gallon transom livewell, leaning post with full tackle center, in-floor fishboxes, console head with opening port, cockpit bolsters, fresh/saltwater washdowns, cushioned bow seating. Lockable rod storage in cockpit sole. Unique outboard mounting system makes brackets part of stringer system. No transom door. Over 40 knots with Yamaha 200s.

See Page 539 For Value Estimates

Length w/Pulpit	28'6"	Fuel	210 gals.
Beam	9'5"	Water	20 gals.
Hull Draft	20"	Max HP	600
Dry Weight	4,300#	Hull Type	Deep-V
Clearance, T-Top	8'0"	Deadrise Aft	21°

Sportfishing Boats

Scout 282 Sportfish

2006–Current

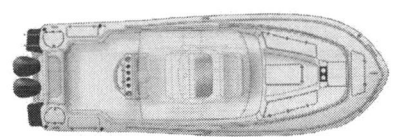

Feature-rich fishboat with distinctive styling, bracket-mounted outboards takes center-console aesthetics, quality to the next level. Highlights include standard T-top with electronics box, bait-prep station with sink & tackle storage, port and starboard 35-gallon livewells, forward fishboxes, console head with sink, fresh/raw-water washdowns, cushioned bow seating. Deluxe leaning post has backrest, foldaway footrest. Recessed bow rails, pop-up cleats mean no snagged lines. Yamaha 250s reach close to 50 knots wide open.

See Page 539 For Value Estimates

Length	28'2"	Fuel	205 gals.
Beam	9'6"	Water	20 gals.
Draft, Up	1'6"	Max HP	600
Draft, Down	3'0"	Hull Type	Deep-V
Dry Weight	5,100#	Deadrise Aft	22°

Sea Ray 270 Amberjack

1986–90

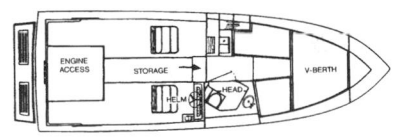

Versatile 1980s express with spacious single-level cockpit is just right for fishing, cruising or diving. Highlights include walk-through transom door, swim platform with ladder, tinted windshield with side vents, back-to-back companion seat, teak bow pulpit. Big cockpit hatch provides good engine access. Cabin with full galley, enclosed head, sleeps two. Ten-foot beam is wide for a 27-footer. Great range with 200-gal. fuel capacity. MerCruiser 260hp sterndrives reach a top speed of over 30 knots.

Prices Not Provided for Pre-1995 Models

Length w/Pulpit	29'3"	Weight	7,000#
Hull Length	27'7"	Fuel	200 gals.
Beam	10'0"	Water	28 gals.
Draft, Up	1'3"	Hull Type	Deep-V
Draft, Down	2'8"	Deadrise Aft	22°

Sea Ray 270 Amberjack

2005–09

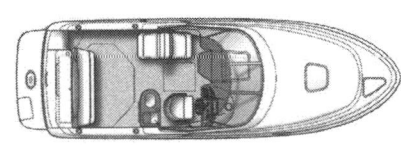

Shapely sterndrive express with trailerable 8'6" beam combined sporty styling with versatile layout, top-notch quality. Roomy single-level cockpit with foldaway rear seat can be fitted with optional fishing package with bait-prep station, livewell, raw-water washdown. Deluxe interior with cherry cabinetry, full galley, enclosed head sleeps two. Note transom storage locker, big swim platform. Easy-lift hatch provides quick engine access. Modest fuel capacity limits range. Single 320hp MerCruiser I/O delivers a top speed in excess of 30 knots.

See Page 539 For Value Estimates

Length	30'0"	Fuel	100 gals.
Beam	8'6"	Water	28 gals.
Draft, Up	15"	Waste	28 gals.
Draft, Down	3'8"	Hull Type	Deep-V
Weight	7,325#	Deadrise Aft	21°

Sportfishing Boats

Sea Ray 290 Amberjack

2000–09

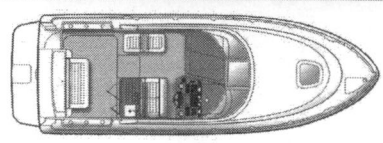

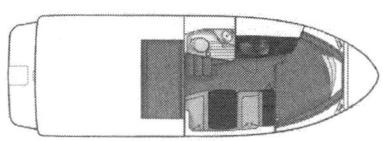

Dual-purpose express split the difference between practical weekend cruiser, capable family fisherman. Fishing amenities include molded bait-prep station (with livewell) behind helm seat, cockpit rod storage, tiered dash with space for big-screen electronics. Well-finished interior with full galley, convertible dinette, enclosed head, sleeps six—four adults, two children. More fuel capacity than most 28-footers. Twin 260hp MerCruiser I/Os cruise at 22 knots (35 knots top); twin 300hp V-drive inboards cruise at 25 knots (40 knots wide open).

See Page 540 For Value Estimates

Length w/Platform	31'4"	Fuel	250 gals.
Beam	10'6"	Water	30 gals.
Draft, Up	2'5"	Waste	28 gals.
Draft, Down	2'10"	Hull Type	Deep-V
Weight	12,215#	Deadrise Aft	21°

Sea Ray 310 Amberjack

1992–94

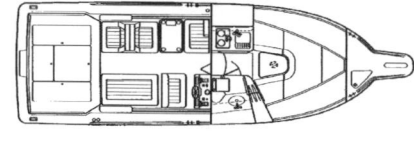

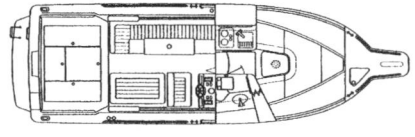

Good-looking express with multi-purpose personality splits the difference between light-tackle family fisherman, comfortable weekend cruiser. Topside features include extended helmdeck with dinette, roomy cockpit with transom door, insulated fish boxes. Oak-trimmed cabin with convertible dinette, enclosed head with shower provides overnight accommodations for two. Excellent engine access. Huge fuel capacity for a boat this size. Prop pockets reduce draft. Cruise at 25 knots with 310hp MerCruiser inboards (30+ knots wide open).

Prices Not Provided for Pre-1995 Models

Length	31'2"	Clearance	NA
Beam	11'5"	Fuel	296 gals.
Draft	3'1"	Water	40 gals.
Weight	10,500#	Hull Type	Modified-V
Cockpit	57 sq. ft.	Deadrise Aft	18°

Sea Ray 340 Amberjack

2001–03

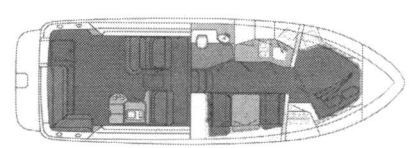

Multipurpose family cruiser combines spacious cockpit with roomy interior, dependable inboard power. Wide 13'5" beam results in spacious cabin layout with booth-style dinette, fully equipped galley, private bow stateroom. Cockpit features include aft-facing settee, fold-away transom seat, in-deck livewell and fish box, combined bait-prep center/wet bar. Bridgedeck lifts electrically for engine access. Wide side decks are a plus. Fully cored hull has prop pockets to reduce draft. Twin 370hp MerCruiser inboards cruise at 20 knots (about 30 knots top).

See Page 540 For Value Estimates

Length w/Platform	38'0"	Fuel	275 gals.
Hull Length	33'6"	Water	50 gals.
Beam	13'5"	Waste	28 gals.
Draft	3'0"	Hull Type	Deep-V
Weight	16,500#	Deadrise Aft	19.5°

Sea Ray 340 Sport Fisherman

1984–87

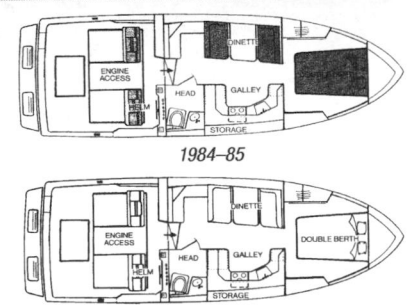

1984–85

1986–87

Good-running 1980s sedan targeted family-focused anglers seeking a compelling mix of cruising amenities, offshore fishability. Semi-enclosed lower helm is open to large, uncluttered cockpit. Offered with two cabin layouts, both with convertible dinette, fully equipped galley, open bow stateroom. Topside features include double helm and companion seats, transom door, removable stern seat, swim platform, side-dumping exhausts. Modest fuel capacity for a fishing boat. Cruise at 20 knots (30+ top) with standard 340hp MerCruiser gas inboards.

Prices Not Provided for Pre-1995 Models

Length	33'7"	Fuel	250 gals.
Beam	11'11"	Water	52 gals.
Draft	2'5"	Headroom	6'4"
Weight	10,600#	Hull Type	Deep-V
Clearance	NA	Deadrise Aft	21°

Sea Ray 390 Sedan Sportfish

1983–86

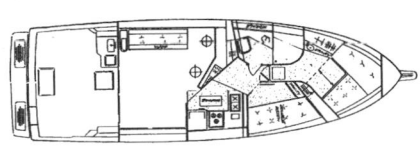

Versatile 1980s convertible is essentially a stretched version of the Sea Ray 360 Sedan with additional cockpit space. Spacious interior includes private master stateroom with slide-out double berth, guest stateroom with upper/lower berths, fully equipped galley, carpeted salon with convertible sofa. Uncluttered cockpit with transom door has room for several anglers. Lower helm was optional. Flybridge is small compared with a modern 39-footer. Standard 350hp gas inboards cruise at 17 knots; 320hp Cat diesels cruise at 20+ knots.

Prices Not Provided for Pre-1995 Models

Length w/Pulpit	40'6"	Fuel	400 gals.
Hull Length	39'0"	Water	100 gals.
Beam	13'11"	Waste	40 gals.
Draft	2'7"	Hull Type	Deep-V
Weight	18,400#	Deadrise Aft	19°

Sea Vee 290B Open

2000–04

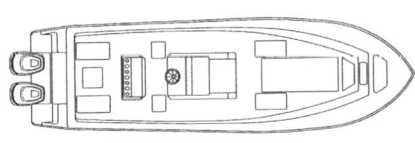

High-performance fishing machine with narrow 8'3" beam is seriously fast, built to last. Single-level cockpit features huge fishbox forward, six in-deck storage boxes, console head compartment, 35-gallon in-floor livewell, pop-up cleats, deluxe leaning post. Space at the helm for plenty of electronics. Uncluttered deck provides full 360-degree fishability. Slender beam results in modest cockpit space compared with most other 29-footers. Replaced in 2005 with new Sea Vee 290B model. Nearly 50 knots top with twin 225s.

See Page 542 For Value Estimates

Length	29'6"	Fuel, Std.	180 gals.
Beam	8'3"	Fuel, Opt.	240 gals.
Draft, Up	1'6"	Max HP	500
Draft, Down	3'0"	Hull Type	Deep-V
Hull Weight	3,400#	Deadrise Aft	25°

Sportfishing Boats

Sea Vee 290B Open

2005–Current

Updated version of original Sea Vee 290B (2000–04) with greater beam, increased range made a good boat even better. Expansive single-level cockpit comes standard with massive in-deck fishbox forward, 50-gallon transom livewell, transom door, freshwater washdown, pop-up cleats, walk-in head with forward entry. Tremendous rod storage. Unique cooler slides out on track from under leaning post. Deep-V hull delivers outstanding rough-water ride. Designed for today's heavy 4-stroke engines. Over 50 knots with twin 250s.

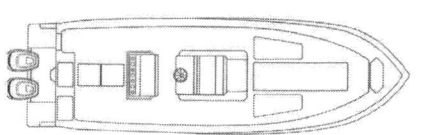

See Page 542 For Value Estimates

Length	29'6"	Fuel	235 gals.
Beam	9'0"	Water	40 gals.
Draft, Up	1'6"	Max HP	500
Draft, Down	3'2"	Hull Type	Deep-V
Hull Weght	4,850#	Deadrise Aft	25°

Sea Vee 340B Open

2001–Current

Tournament-ready 34-footer with triple-outboard potential combines quality construction with agile performance, hardcore fishability. Single-level cockpit features huge 60-gallon transom livewell, lockable in-deck rod storage, three insulated fishboxes, pop-up cleats, tackle lockers. Roomy head compartment (with forward entry) has electric toilet, sink, shower. Plenty of space at the helm for electronics. This kind of quality isn't cheap. Cuddy and diesel inboard models also available. Yamaha 250s deliver 40+ knots top.

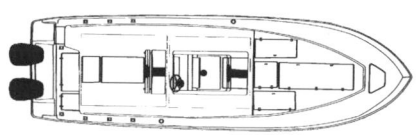

See Page 542 For Value Estimates

Length	34'9"	Fuel	350 gals.
Beam	10'0"	Water	50 gals.
Draft, Up	1'8"	Max HP	1,050
Draft, Down	3'0"	Hull Type	Deep-V
Hull Weight	6,500#	Deadrise Aft	23.5°

Shamrock 270 Mackinaw

2000–09

All-weather hardtop fisherman with inboard power, pocket-type hull is tough, versatile, built to last. Enclosed pilothouse contains small galley, removable table, fully equipped helm, berths for two. Head is very small with only sitting headroom. Cockpit has aft-facing bench seating, transom door, in-deck fishbox, transom livewell. Note opening cabin windows, bow pulpit. Finish is average, but construction is tough. Cruise at 18 knots with single 320hp gas engine (high 20s top); 22–23 knots with optional Yanmar 315hp diesel.

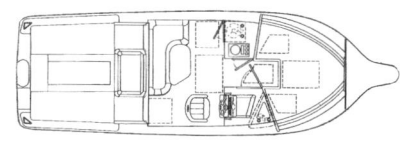

See Page 542 For Value Estimates

Length w/Pulpit	30'6"	Weight	7,525#
Hull Length	28'10"	Fuel	156 gals.
Beam	9'3"	Water	20 gals.
Draft	2'5"	Hull Type	Modified-V
Clearance	8'2"	Deadrise Aft	14°

Sportfishing Boats

Shamrock 270 Open

2000–09

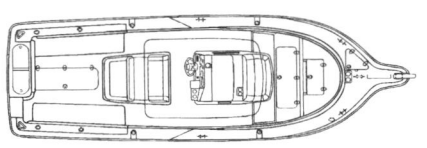

Rock-solid fisherman with inboard power combines space, versatility, economy. Highlights include large console with space for electronics, enclosed head with sink and shower, removable in-deck fishboxes, transom bait-prep center, 32-gallon livewell. Note wide transom door with gate. Relatively heavy boat delivers a good open-water ride; modified-V hull has prop pocket to reduce draft, improve efficiency. Cruise at 18 knots with single 320hp gas engine (high 20s top); 22–23 knots with popular Yanmar 315hp diesel.

See Page 542 For Value Estimates

Length w/Pulpit	30'6"	Weight	6,276#
Hull Length	28'10"	Fuel	160 gals.
Beam	9'3"	Water	20 gals.
Draft	2'5"	Hull Type	Modified-V
Clearance, Top	8'8"	Deadrise Aft	14°

Shamrock 290 Walkaround

1999–2003

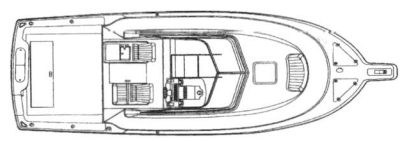

Heavily built walkaround cabin with smooth-riding deep-V hull is one part fishing boat, one part family cruiser. Standard features include 38-gallon livewell, bait-rigging station behind passenger seat, big in-deck fishbox, fresh- and salt-water washdowns, transom door. Surprisingly large cabin with galley, enclosed head with shower, sleeps four. Note tilt-away helm, deep cockpit, wide side decks. Entire bridgedeck lifts for engine access. Twin 300hp gas inboards cruise in the low 20s and top out at over 30 knots.

See Page 542 For Value Estimates

Length w/Pulpit	30'10"	Clearance, Top	10'5"
Hull Length	28'10"	Fuel	250 gals.
Beam	11'3"	Water	30 gals.
Draft	2'10"	Hull Type	Deep-V
Weight	10,500#	Deadrise Aft	19°

Shamrock 31 Grand Slam

1987–94

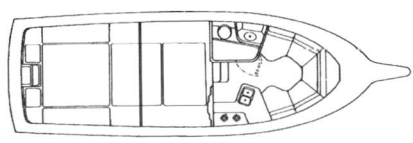

Deep-V express introduced in 1987 was a notable departure from Shamrock's signature "Keel-Drive" single-inboard hull design. Well-arranged cockpit with tackle center, 30-gallon livewell has room for full-size fighting chair. Helm seat pivots up to serve as leaning post. Cozy cabin with convertible dinette, enclosed head with shower, pipe berths sleeps four. Unique service bay houses mechanical, electrical systems. Popular boat—total of 160 built. Cummins 250hp diesels cruise at 28 knots; Cummins 300hp diesels cruise at 30 knots.

Prices Not Provided for Pre-1995 Models

Length	31'0"	Fuel, Std.	290 gals.
Beam	11'4"	Fuel, Opt.	340 gals.
Draft	3'4"	Water	40 gals.
Weight	10,800#	Hull Type	Deep-V
Clearance	18'0"	Deadrise Aft	19°

Sportfishing Boats

Skipjack 30 Flybridge

1997–2006

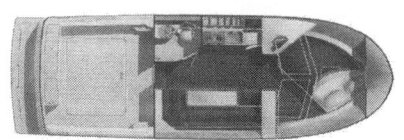

Rugged California-built fisherman matches solid construction with no-frills accommodations, dependable performance. Large cockpit, sturdy rails, wide side decks appeal to experienced anglers. Efficient single-level interior with oak trim, convertible dinette, angled double berth sleeps four. Note wraparound cabin windows, generous storage. Transom fishbox, 30-gallon livewell, transom door are standard. Cockpit hatch lifts electrically for engine access. Yanmar 315hp V-drive diesels cruise at 22–24 knots (about 30 top).

See Page 544 For Value Estimates

Length w/Pulpit	34'10"	Fuel	300 gals.
Hull Length	30'0"	Water	75 gals.
Beam	11'2"	Waste	40 gals.
Draft	3'4"	Hull Type	Modified-V
Weight	16,000#	Deadrise Aft	16°

Southport 28 Center Console

2005–Current

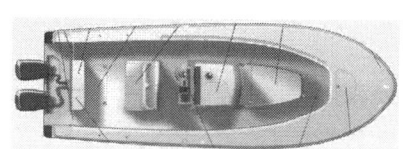

No-nonsense fishing machine appeals to hardcore anglers with an eye for superior engineering, leading-edge quality. Leaning post with backrest, deluxe helm seat with 45-gallon livewell, fore/aft coaming pads, transom rigging station with sink, lift-out aft fishbox, console head compartment with lockable rod storage. Insulated coffin box forward doubles as lounge seating. Single-level cockpit means no stubbed toes. Very impressive finish. Deep-V hull can take a pounding. Max 40+ knots with 225hp Hondas.

See Page 544 For Value Estimates

Length	28'6"	Fuel	250 gals.
Beam	10'6"	Water	NA
Draft, Up	1'7"	Max HP	700
Draft, Down	2'10"	Hull Type	Deep-V
Hull Weight	5,800#	Deadrise Aft	22°

Stamas 270 Express

1997–Current

Floorplan Not Available

Dual-purpose family fisherman combines roomy cockpit with space-efficient cabin, durable construction. Standard fishing features include 18-gallon transom livewell, transom fishbox, tackle drawers, rod storage, raw-water washdown. Note aft-facing cockpit seats with insulated fish/storage boxes under. Full-featured cabin with stand-up head, midcabin berth, compact galley sleeps four. Wide side decks add extra level of security. Note excellent helm layout, generous storage capacity. Twin 200hp outboards deliver a top speed of close to 40 knots.

See Page 544 For Value Estimates

Length w/Pulpit	28'9"	Fuel	204 gals.
Hull Length	27'1"	Water	20 gals.
Beam	9'7"	Max HP	450
Hull Draft	1'6"	Hull Type	Modified-V
Weight w/Engine	5,800#	Deadrise Aft	18°

Sportfishing Boats

Stamas 288 Liberty/Family Fisherman

1987–94

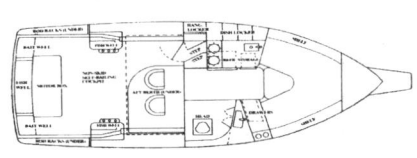

Well built express (called the 288 Fisherman in 1993–94; 288 Family Fisherman in 1995–94) with large cockpit gave anglers and cruisers a lot to like. Deep, single-level cockpit came standard with two forward fishboxes, two livewells, insulated icebox. Cozy cabin with stand-up head, mini-galley, mid-berth sleeps four adults. Broad 11'2" beam made this one of the bigger 28-footers in her class. Offered with sterndrive or bracket-mounted outboard power. Twin 205hp I/Os cruise at 20 knots (30+ knots top); twin 225hp outboards reach 40 knots top.

Prices Not Provided for Pre-1995 Models

Length w/Pulpit	30'2"	Fuel	196 gals.
Hull Length	28'4"	Water	20 gals.
Beam	11'2"	Max HP	500
Draft	1'6"	Hull Type	Modified-V
Weight	9,500#	Deadrise Aft	18°

Stamas 290 Express

1992–Current

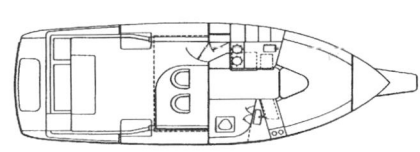

Durable outboard express with appealing lines is one part fishing boat, one part family cruiser. Deep, single-level cockpit comes standard with 20-gallon baitwell, transom door, insulated fishbox, tackle box. Comfortable interior with mid-berth, compact galley, enclosed head with shower, sleeps four. Original double-helm seating was replaced in 1998 with separate helm, companion seats. Tall windshield offers good wind protection. Twin 225hp Yamahas cruise at 40+ knots top. Also available with sterndrive power.

See Page 544 For Value Estimates

Length w/Pulpit	31'7"	Fuel	250 gals.
Hull Length	29'3"	Water	27 gals.
Beam	10'4"	Max HP	500
Hull Draft	1'5"	Hull Type	Modified-V
Weight	6,550#	Deadrise Aft	18°

Stamas 290 Tarpon

1995–Current

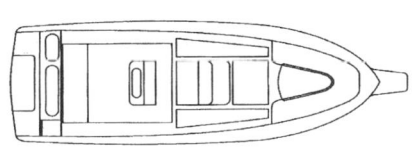

Thoughtfully conceived center console with excellent range, U-shaped bow seating is easy on the eye, built to last. Un-cluttered deck layout with low-freeboard gunwales boasts in-floor rod storage, transom fishbox, two forward fishboxes, built-in tackle box, transom door, removable aft storage box, raw-water washdown, lockable head compartment, electronic box. Leaning post incorporates rigging station, sink, 50-gallon livewell. Casting platform converts to dinette. Also available with sterndrive power. Yamaha 225s reach 40+ knots top.

See Page 544 For Value Estimates

Length w/Pulpit	31'7"	Fuel	302 gals.
Hull Length	29'3"	Water	20 gals.
Beam	10'4"	Max HP	500
Hull Draft	1'5"	Hull Type	Modified-V
Weight	6,000#	Deadrise Aft	18°

Sportfishing Boats

Stamas 310 Express

1993–Current

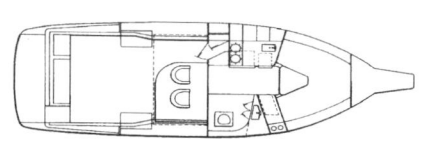

Classy midsize express gets high marks for common-sense layout, solid construction, comfortable ride. More fishboat than cruiser, well-appointed midcabin interior has all the amenities required for comfortable weekends away from home. Spacious cockpit comes standard with full array of fishing features including bait-prep station with sink, cutting board, tackle storage drawers, livewell, transom door. Note efficient helm layout with space for electronics. Twin 225hp Yamahas top out at close to 40 knots. Also available with inboard power.

See Page 544 For Value Estimates

Length w/Pulpit	32'6"	Fuel	300 gals.
Hull Length	30'9"	Water	40 gals.
Beam	11'2"	Max HP	500
Hull Draft	1'8"	Hull Type	Modified-V
Weight w/OB	9,800#	Deadrise Aft	18°

Sportfishing Boats

Stamas 310 Tarpon

1999–Current

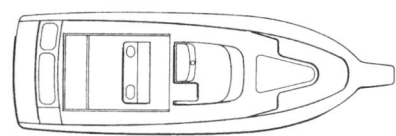

Full-size center console delivers on Stamas promise of common-sense deck layout, practical amenities, traditional construction. Spacious deck layout with forward seating features standard leaning post with rigging station, 50-gallon circulating livewell, rear bench seat, transom door, forward fish boxes (2), raw-water washdown. Huge console houses roomy head with unique entry door next to helm. Excellent range. Modified-V hull delivers stable rough-water ride. Sterndrive diesel is optional. About 40 knots top with twin 250s.

See Page 544 For Value Estimates

Length w/Pulpit	32'6"	Fuel	400 gals.
Hull Length	30'9"	Water	20 gals.
Beam	11'2"	Max HP	500
Hull Draft	1'6"	Hull Type	Modified-V
Weight w/OB	9,250#	Deadrise Aft	18°

Stamas 320 Express

2004–Current

Floorplan Not Available

Spirited midsize express offered with inboard or outboard power combines appealing lines with roomy accommodations, durable construction. Large cockpit comes standard with full array of fishing amenities including transom livewell, insulated transom fishbox, wide transom door. Engine access is via hydraulic deck hatch. Teak-trimmed interior with midcabin berth, convertible dinette, teak-and-holly sole sleeps six. Twin 320hp MerCruiser gas inboards cruise at 22 knots (30 top). Outboard version with 225hp Yamahas tops out at close to 35 knots.

See Page 544 For Value Estimates

Length w/Pulpit	34'5"	Fuel, IB	240 gals.
Hull Length	32'3"	Fuel, OB	316 gals.
Beam	11'2"	Water	40 gals.
Draft	2'20"	Hull Type	Modified-V
Weight	13,200#	Deadrise Aft	18°

Stamas 340 Express

2003–Current

Floorplan Not Available

Dual-purpose offshore express splits the difference between hardcore fishboat, comfortable family cruiser. Uncluttered cockpit comes standard with full array of fishing amenities including transom livewell, insulated fishbox, wide transom door. Engine access is via hydraulic deck hatch. Well-appointed interior with midcabin berth sleeps six. Prop pockets reduce draft, improve efficiency. MerCruiser 370hp gas inboards cruise at 22 knots (30+ top); Yanmar 370hp diesels cruise at 25 knots (30 top). Outboard version also available.

See Page 544 For Value Estimates

Length w/Pulpit	36'2"	Clearance	7'3"
Hull Length	34'0"	Fuel	350 gals.
Beam	12'6"	Water	84 gals.
Draft	2'4"	Hull Type	Modified-V
Weight	14,000#	Deadrise Aft	18°

Stamas 360 Express

1992–99

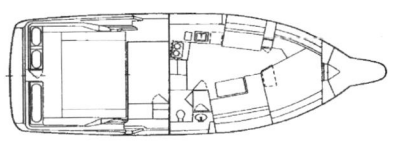

Conservative inboard express with midcabin interior appealed to 1990s boaters drawn to versatile layout, solid construction, comfortable open-water ride. Fishing amenities include livewell, raw-water washdown, insulated fishboxes, rod storage. Elevated helm affords excellent visibility. Tasteful midcabin interior with convertible dinette, full galley, sleeps four adults, two kids. Note reverse transom with centerline door. Prop pockets reduce draft, improve efficiency. Standard 310hp MerCruiser gas inboards cruise at 18 knots (high 20s top).

See Page 544 For Value Estimates

Length w/Pulpit	38'6"	Clearance	8'3"
Hull Length	36'0"	Fuel	372 gals.
Beam	13'2"	Water	90 gals.
Draft	2'4"	Hull Type	Modified-V
Weight	16,975#	Deadrise Aft	18°

Stamas 370 Express

2000–09

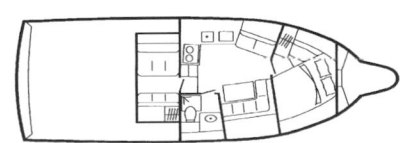

Revised version of Stamas 360 Express (1992–99) combined redesigned hull (no more reverse transom) with improved cockpit layout. Midcabin interior is rare in a dedicated fishing boat. Sizable cockpit has built-in livewell, insulated fishbox, bait-prep station, tackle drawers. Well-designed helm has space for flush-mounting electronics. Note wide side decks. Power engine hatch provides outstanding service access. Deep keel, prop pockets protect running gear in event of grounding. Yanmar 420hp diesels cruise at 24–26 knots (30+ knots wide open).

See Page 545 For Value Estimates

Length w/Pulpit	39'2"	Headroom	6'4"
Hull Length	36'8"	Fuel	400 gals.
Beam	13'2"	Water	84 gals.
Draft	2'4"	Hull Type	Modified-V
Weight	16,975#	Deadrise Aft	18°

Sportfishing Boats

Strike 29 Sportfisherman

1985–89; 96–06

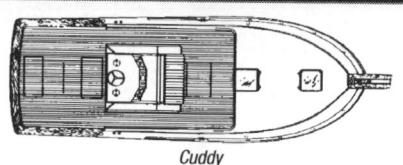

Cuddy

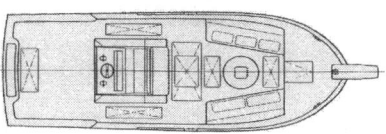

Open

Semicustom center console with twin diesel inboards, super-wide 10'11" beam, meets the demands of many traditional anglers. Efficient deck plan combines the utility of a small cuddy and the walkaround attributes of a center console. Total of 35 were built through 1989; reintroduced in 1995 with molded pulpit, full inner liner, new deck tooling. Early models with 240hp Perkins diesels cruise at 25 knots (high 20s top). Newer models with 330hp Cummins diesels cruise at 30 knots (35+ knots top).

See Page 545 For Value Estimates

Length w/Pulpit	31'7"	Clearance	7'6"
Hull Length	29'0"	Fuel	200 gals.
Beam	10'11"	Water	20 gals.
Draft	2'6"	Hull Type	Deep-V
Weight	12,000#	Deadrise Aft	23"

Sunseeker 37 Sportfisher

2004–07

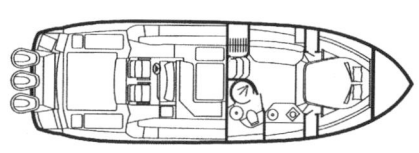

English-built fishing boat combines spirited performance with top-shelf construction, uncommon luxury. Center-console deck layout with seating forward results in relatively small aft cockpit. Beautifully finished interior features high-gloss cherry cabinetry, premium furnishings. Livewell, bait-prep center, fishboxes are standard. Side-boarding ladder keeps swimmers away from props. Note high-performance stepped hull. Volvo 310hp diesel I/Os top out at 35 knots; triple 250hp Yamaha outboards reach top speed of 40+ knots.

See Page 545 For Value Estimates

Length w/Pulpit	39'8"	Fuel	396 gals.
Hull Length	37'1"	Water	60 gals.
Beam	11'7"	Waste	10 gals.
Draft, Drives Down	3'9"	Hull Type	Deep-V
Weight	17,420#	Deadrise Aft	19°

Tiara 2700 Open

1987–93

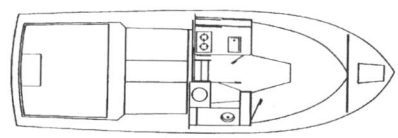

Iconic inboard express supplies enduring mix of spacious cockpit, upscale interior, quality construction. Teak-trimmed cabin with full-service galley, stand-up head with shower, sleeps two. Single-level cockpit with back-to-back seating is large enough for mounted chair. Wide side decks, sturdy rails provide secure foredeck access. Note commercial-quality windshield, easy-access motorboxes, deep-V hull. Many updates/improvements over the years. Crusader 270hp gas engines cruise in the low 20s (28–30 knots wide open).

Prices Not Provided for Pre-1995 Models

Length w/Pulpit	29'5"	Clearance	7'0"
Hull Length	27'0"	Fuel	240 gals.
Beam	10'0"	Water	20 gals.
Draft	2'0"	Hull Type	Deep-V
Weight	7,500#	Deadrise Aft	22°

Sportfishing Boats

Tiara 2900 Open

1993–2006

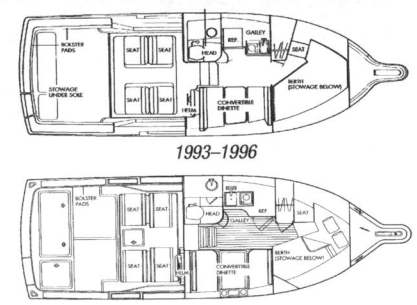

1993–1996

1997–2006

See Page 545 For Value Estimates

Multi-purpose Tiara cruiser set the gold standard in her class for sophisticated express-boat design, top-shelf engineering and construction. Uncluttered cockpit features double helm and companion seats forward, twin aft-facing seats, wide transom door. Well-appointed cabin with full galley, convertible dinette sleeps four. Wide beam for a 29-footer. Entire bridgedeck lifts electrically for engine access. Used models are always in demand. Twin 320hp inboard gas engines cruise at 20 knots (close to 30 knots top).

Length w/Pulpit	30'9"	Fuel	200 gals.
Hull Length	28'9"	Water	30 gals.
Beam	11'4"	Waste	20 gals.
Draft	2'8"	Hull Type	Modified-V
Weight	10,700#	Deadrise Aft	19°

Tiara 3000 Open

2007–Current

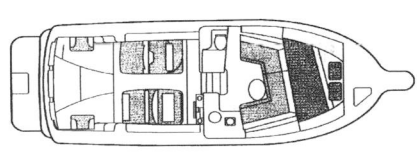

See Page 545 For Value Estimates

Premium hardtop express with innovative interior couples graceful styling with efficient deck plan, signature Tiara quality. Wide beam creates large cockpit with jump seat, workstation/wet bar with insulated storage, sprayer, cutting board. Elegant teak cabin with hardwood sole, forward side berth features posh aft-facing lounge that converts to double berth. Note tall windshield, tilt-away helm, opening hardtop vents. Bridgedeck lifts electrically for engine access. Cruise at 22–24 knots with 385hp gas inboards (low-to-mid 30s top).

Length w/Pulpit	33'0"	Fuel	210 gals.
Hull Length	30'6"	Water	32 gals.
Beam	12'6"	Waste	20 gals.
Draft	2'8"	Hull Type	Modified-V
Weight	13,225#	Deadrise Aft	14°

Tiara 3100 Open

1979–91

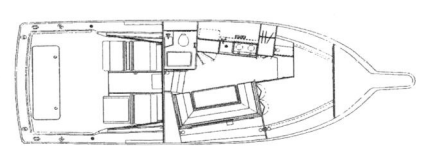

Prices Not Provided for Pre-1995 Models

Classic 1980s express did much to establish Tiara reputation for superior engineering, durable construction. Versatile layout—equally well-suited for fishing or cruising—boasts appealing teak-trimmed interior with big U-shaped dinette, large cockpit with removable bench seat, roomy engine compartment with good service access. Note tall, commercial-quality windshield, aft-facing cockpit seats. Modified-V hull can be a wet ride. Standard 350hp gas inboards cruise in the low 20s (32–33 knots top). Replaced with all-new 3100 Open in 1992.

Length w/Pulpit	33'9"	Clearance, Arch	7'6"
Hull Length	31'3"	Fuel	196 gals.
Beam	12'0"	Water	36 gals.
Draft	2'9"	Hull Type	Modified-V
Weight	10,500#	Deadrise Aft	14°

Sportfishing Boats

Tiara 3100 Open

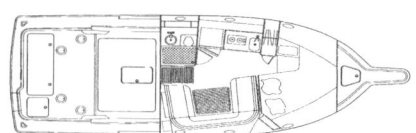

Updated version of original 3100 Open (1979–91) with major modifications made a great boat even better. Reworked hull with prop pockets, increased deadrise, delivers better head-sea ride than her predecessor. Bi-level cockpit allows installation of diesels in larger engine compartment. Luxury-class interior with U-shaped dinette, full galley sleeps four. Cockpit came with in-deck fishbox, livewell, foldaway rear seat. Transom door became standard in 1994. Cruise at 20 knots with 320hp gas engines; 22–23 knots with 330hp Cummins diesels.

See Page 545 For Value Estimates

Length w/Pulpit	33'10"	Fuel	246 gals.
Hull Length	31'6"	Water	38 gals.
Beam	12'0"	Waste	20 gals.
Draft	3'0"	Hull Type	Modified-V
Weight	12,300#	Deadrise Aft	18°

Tiara 3200 Open

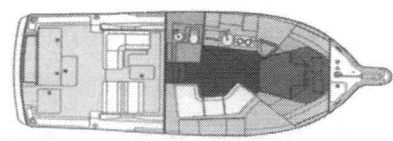

Graceful styling, quality construction and many luxury appointments have made this versatile express a class leader with savvy buyers. Bi-level cockpit with in-deck fishbox, transom door is large enough for several anglers. Upscale interior with solid teak cabinetry, Ultraleather seating sleeps four. Bridgedeck rises electrically for engine access. Optional livewell replaces standard fold-down transom seat. Hardtop is a popular option. Note prop-pocket hull bottom. Cruise at 22 knots with 385hp gas engines; mid 20ss with Volvo 310hp diesels.

See Page 545 For Value Estimates

Length w/Pulpit	35'1"	Fuel	256 gals.
Hull Length	32'7"	Water	38 gals.
Beam	13'0"	Waste	20 gals.
Draft	3'0"	Hull Type	Modified-V
Weight	15,950#	Deadrise Aft	18°

Tiara 3300 Open

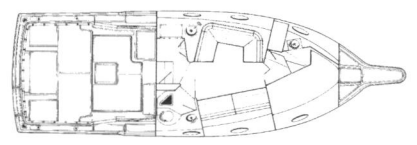

Feature-rich express with conservative lines, superior finish delivers exceptional cruising comfort, owner satisfaction. Elegant teak-trimmed interior with U-shaped dinette, convertible settee sleeps six in genuine comfort. Tournament-grade cockpit with transom door, fishbox is big enough for serious fishing pursuits. Wide side decks, good engine access, well-designed helm layout. Low-deadrise hull can be a stiff ride. Cruise at 20 knots with standard gas engines; 24 knots with 315hp Cummins diesels.

See Page 545 For Value Estimates

Length w/Pulpit	35'8"	Fuel	295 gals.
Hull Length	32'10"	Water	46 gals.
Beam	12'6"	Waste	20 gals.
Draft	2'3"	Hull Type	Modified-V
Weight	13,500#	Deadrise Aft	14°

Sportfishing Boats

Tiara 3500 Open

1998–2004

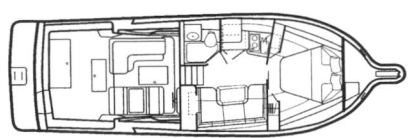

Top-ranked express combines traditional Tiara styling with high-end construction, uncommon luxury. Spacious single-stateroom interior features solid teak joinery, leather upholstery, beautiful teak-and-holly cabin sole. Crowd-friendly cockpit with foldaway rear seat serves anglers, cruisers alike. Entire bridgedeck rises for engine access. Note wide side decks, power windshield vent, ergonomic helm layout. Standard gas inboards cruise at 16–18 knots; optional 370hp Cummins diesels cruise at 25–26 knots.

See Page 546 For Value Estimates

Length w/Pulpit	40'8"	Fuel	360 gals.
Hull Length	35'6"	Water	70 gals.
Beam	13'3"	Waste	30 gals.
Draft	3'3"	Hull Type	Modified-V
Weight	14,000#	Deadrise Aft	18°

Tiara 3600 Convertible

1987–95

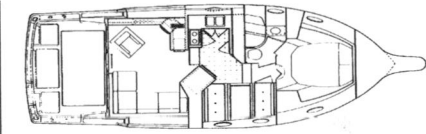

Two-Stateroom Interior

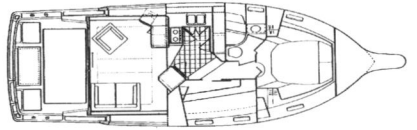

Single-Stateroom Interior

Polished flybridge sedan introduced in 1987 is one part fishing boat, two parts coastal cruiser. Offered with original two-stateroom interior or less popular single-stateroom layout with dinette in place of guest cabin. Sliding glass door leads into roomy salon whose open front windshield allowed for optional lower helm position. Modest cockpit dimensions preclude installation of tackle center. Standard 350hp gas engines cruise at 19–20 knots; optional Cat 375hp diesels cruise at 25 knots and post a top speed of 29–30 knots.

See Page 546 For Value Estimates

Length w/Pulpit	39'8"	Clearance	12'6"
Hull Length	36'8"	Fuel	396 gals.
Beam	13'9"	Water	85 gals.
Draft	3'0"	Hull Type	Modified-V
Weight	18,300#	Deadrise Aft	14°

Tiara 3600 Open

1987–96

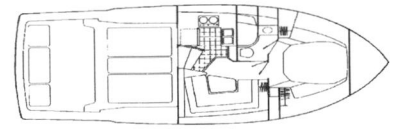

Standard Floorplan

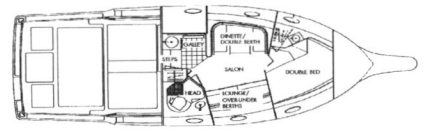

Alternate Floorplan

Strong-selling express set class standards in her era for unsurpassed mix of hard-nosed fishability, family-style accommodations. Highlights include well-appointed interior with solid teak joinery, expansive bi-level cockpit, top-quality construction. Original cabin layout with island berth forward sleeps four; alternate layout introduced in 1989 sleeps six. Entire bridgedeck lifts on hydraulic rams for engine access. Conservative lines still look good today. Standard 350hp gas engines cruise at 18 knots; 375hp Cats cruise at 24–25 knots.

See Page 546 For Value Estimates

Length w/Pulpit	36'8"	Headroom	6'2"
Beam	13'9"	Fuel	396 gals.
Draft	2'11"	Water	85 gals.
Weight	16,500#	Hull Type	Modified-V
Clearance	9'7"	Deadrise Aft	14°

Sportfishing Boats

Sportfishing Boats

Tiara 3600 Open

2005–Current

Handsome dual-purpose express with signature Tiara styling blurs the line between hard-core fishing boat, deluxe family cruiser. Posh interior with solid teak joinery, Ultraleather dinette (with flip-up backrest) sleeps five. Professional-grade cockpit features aft-facing seats, in-deck fishboxes, transom livewell, fold-down transom seat. Bridgedeck lifts for engine access. Note aggressive nonskid, tilt-away dash, sturdy windshield. Cummins 380hp diesels cruise at 26–28 knots. Newer models with 370hp Volvo IPS drives cruise efficiently at 28 knots.

See Page 546 For Value Estimates

Length	36'5"	Fuel	400 gals.
Beam	13'3"	Water	70 gals.
Draft	3'5"	Waste	30 gals.
Weight	19,100#	Hull Type	Modified-V
Clearance	9'10"	Deadrise Aft	18°

Tiara 3700 Open

1995–2000

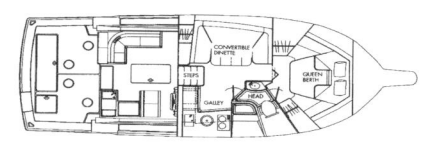

Well-built sport express with handsome lines matched Tiara promise of leading-edge versatility, quality amenities, durable construction. Upscale cabin with solid teak joinery, leather upholstery features huge U-shaped dinette, surprisingly roomy galley, private bow stateroom. Topside amenities include L-shaped companion seat with aft-facing double seat, cockpit fishboxes, cooler. Radar arch, foldaway rear cockpit seat were popular options. Note wide side decks. Bridgedeck lifts for engine access. Cat 435hp diesels cruise in the mid 20s (30+ top).

See Page 546 For Value Estimates

Length w/Pulpit	39'8"	Fuel	411 gals.
Hull Length	37'1"	water	98 gals.
Beam	14'2"	Waste	40 gals.
Draft	3'9"	Hull Type	Modified-V
Weight	21,800#	Deadrise Aft	18°

Tiara 3800 Open

2001–08

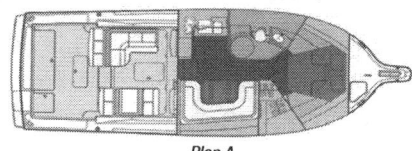

Plan A

Plan B

Dual-purpose express splits the difference between luxury sportcruiser, tournament-class fishing machine. Beautifully finished interior features posh seating, solid teak cabinetry, first-rate galley appliances. Note appealing teak-and-holly cabin sole, hideaway salon TV. Topside highlights include cockpit wet bar, foldaway transom seat, wide transom door. Note stylish reverse transom. Bridgedeck lifts for engine access. Hardtop with overhead hatches was optional. Cummins 480hp diesels cruise at 25–26 knots (about 30 knots top).

See Page 546 For Value Estimates

Length Overall	40'9"	Fuel	411 gals.
Beam	14'2"	Water	110 gals.
Draft	3'6"	Waste	40 gals.
Weight	22,600#	Hull Type	Modified-V
Clearance	9'7"	Deadrise Aft	18°

Tiara 3900 Convertible

2006–Current

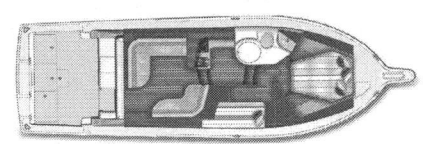

Capable—but not hardcore—fishing boat loaded with features courts high-end buyers with an eye for beauty, quality. Elegant two-stateroom interior boasts comfortable salon with facing settees, satin-finished teak joinery, traditional teak-and-holly cabin sole. Optional front salon window will appeal to cruisers, but not anglers. Note generous galley storage, posh Ultraleather bulkheads. Hardtop is standard. Cockpit—with engine room door—is on the small side. Cummins 540hp diesels cruise in the mid 20s (29–30 wide open).

See Page 546 For Value Estimates

Length w/Pulpit	41'7"	Fuel	470 gals.
Hull Length	39'0"	Water	110 gals.
Beam	14'5"	Waste	38 gals.
Draft	3'6"	Hull Type	Modified-V
Weight	30,125#	Deadrise Aft	14°

Tiara 3900 Open

2009–Current

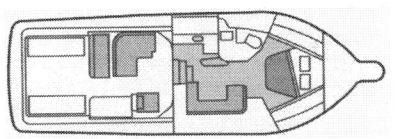

Quality dual-purpose express with wide 15' beam turns up the volume on features important to anglers and cruisers alike. Highlights include elegant single-stateroom interior with teak-and-holly sole, big 95-sq.ft. fishing cockpit with in-deck fishboxes, swivel L-shaped companion lounge, meticulous engine compartment. Note raised 3-person mezzanine seating aft of helm deck. Fishing package includes 55-gallon transom livewell, deluxe tackle center. Hardtop is optional. Cummins 600hp diesels cruise at 30 knots (low 30s top).

See Page 546 For Value Estimates

Length w/Pulpit	41'11"	Fuel	535 gals.
Beam	15'0"	Water	120 gals.
Draft	3'6"	Waste	38 gals.
Weight	24,500#	Hull Type	Modified-V
Clearance, Top	10'4"	Deadrise Aft	18°

Tiara 4100 Open

1996–2002

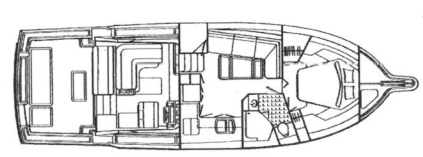

Muscular big-water express with spacious cockpit, upscale interior blurs the line between tournament-grade fishing machine, executive-class sportcruiser. Classy single-stateroom interior includes big U-shaped dinette, open galley with plenty of storage, very roomy head. Raised bridgedeck, three steps above cockpit, provides exceptional helm visibility. Large cockpit boasts beefy transom door, engine room entry door. Wide side decks are always a plus. Cat 435hp diesels cruise at 22 knots (26–27 knots top).

See Page 546 For Value Estimates

Length w/Pulpit	43'6"	Fuel	524 gals.
Hull Length	41'3"	Water	130 gals.
Beam	14'8"	Waste	50 gals.
Draft	3'6"	Hull Type	Modified-V
Weight	27,500#	Deadrise Aft	18°

Sportfishing Boats

Tiara 4200 Open

2003–09

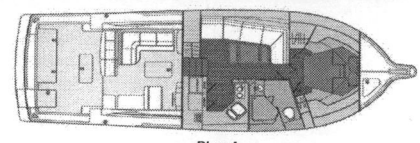

Plan A

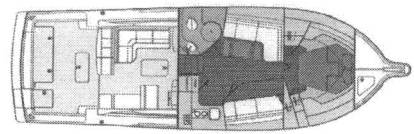

Plan B

See Page 546 For Value Estimates

Bold Tiara sportcruiser with world-class styling, deluxe accommodations combines sportfishing muscle with cruising elegance. Plan A interior has portside lounge/dinette with galley and head opposite; Plan B adds starboard lounge with curtain or solid enclosure, creating second stateroom. Big 85-sq.ft. cockpit—with engine room entry, foldaway rear seat—can be configured for fishing, diving, or cruising. Note fiberglass windshield frame, superb helm layout. Hardtop was optional. Cummins 670hp diesels cruise at 28 knots (32–33 knots top).

Length w/Pulpit	44'10"	Fuel	520 gals.
Hull Length	42'6"	Water	130 gals.
Beam	14'11"	Waste	50 gals.
Draft	4'2"	Hull Type	Modified-V
Weight	28,600#	Deadrise Aft	17.5°

Tiara 4300 Convertible

1990–2002

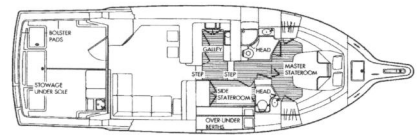

Standard Interior

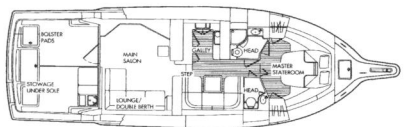

Optional Dinette Floorplan

See Page 546 For Value Estimates

Enduring 1990s convertible coupled cruising comfort with handsome styling, hardcore fishability. Original two-stateroom interior has serving counter overlooking galley; optional single-stateroom layout replaced guest cabin with U-shaped dinette. Note overhead rod storage, built-in entertainment center in salon. Roomy cockpit features beefy transom door, bait-prep center with freezer. (Cockpit engine room access became standard in 1994.) GM 550hp diesels cruise at 22–24 knots; Cat 660hp diesels cruise in the high 20s.

Length w/Pulpit	46'7"	Fuel	640 gals.
Hull Length	43'2"	Water	160 gals.
Beam	15'2"	Waste	60 gals.
Draft	4'0"	Hull Type	Modified-V
Weight	31,500#	Deadrise Aft	16°

Tiara 4300 Open

1991–2002

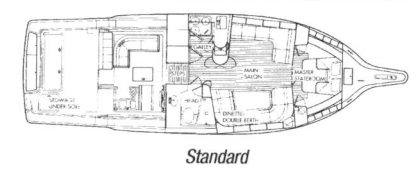

Standard

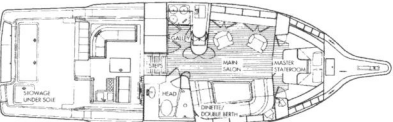

Optional

See Page 546 For Value Estimates

Big multipurpose express with fishboat cockpit, luxury-class accommodations set Tiara's 1990 standards for engineering excellence, state-of-the-art construction. Standard interior with convertible L-shaped lounge, convertible dinette sleeps six; optional layout with enlarged salon sleeps four. Note hydraulic salon operated dinette, elegant teak-and-holly sole. Cockpit redesign in 1999 added fold-down rear seat, direct access to engine room. Cruise at 25 knots with 550hp GM 6V92s; 26–27 knots with 660hp Cats.

Length w/Pulpit	46'7"	Fuel	526 gals.
Hull Length	43'2"	Water	150 gals.
Beam	15'2"	Waste	62 gals.
Draft	4'0"	Hull Type	Modified-V
Weight	29,500#	Deadrise Aft	16°

Tollycraft 34 Convertible Sedan

1981–86

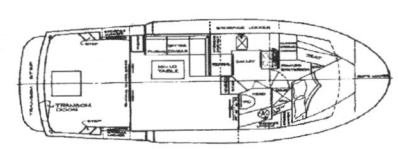

Popular 1980s convertible with distinctive lines met Tollycraft claim of practical layout, sea-kindly hull design, solid construction. Broad 12'6" beam permits surprisingly spacious interior for a boat this size with accommodations for four. Extra-large cabin windows provide exceptional visibility from standard lower helm. Flybridge could be ordered with helm forward or aft. Deep cockpit features transom door, molded corner steps to wide side decks. Note sturdy bow rails. Twin 270hp gas engines cruise at 18 knots (26–27 knots top).

Prices Not Provided for Pre-1995 Models

Length	34'0"	Fuel	200 gals.
Beam	12'6"	Water	100 gals.
Draft	2'10"	Cockpit	72 sq. ft.
Weight	17,000#	Hull Type	Modified-V
Clearance	12'2"	Deadrise Aft	12°

Tollycraft 37 Convertible

1974–85

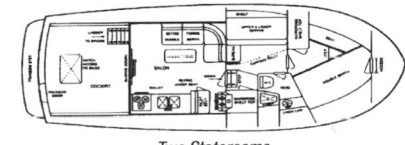

Two Staterooms

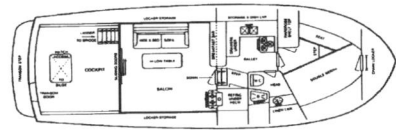

Single Stateroom

Prices Not Provided for Pre-1995 Models

Seaworthy West Coast convertible built a well-earned reputation for versatile layout, rock-solid construction. Offered with single- or twin-stateroom interiors, both featuring standard lower helm, roomy salon with convertible sofa. Original Formica interior was updated to teak in 1977. Extra-large cabin windows provide plenty of natural lighting, good helm visibility. Cockpit is large enough for serious fishing. Twin 350hp gas engines cruise at 20 knots (high 20s top); 210hp Cat diesels cruise at 16–17 knots (around 20 knots top).

Length	37'4"	Fuel	300 gals.
Beam	13'2"	Water	140 gals.
Draft	3'0"	Cockpit	89 sq. ft.
Weight	22,000#	Hull Type	Modified-V
Clearance	12'6"	Deadrise Aft	8°

Topaz 29 Sportfisherman

1983–88

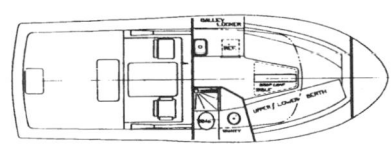

Popular 1980s express with large, uncluttered fishing cockpit is fast, stable, built to last. Efficient layout with raised helm deck includes in-sole fishbox, transom door, teak covering boards, pedestal helm and companion seats. Cockpit is large enough for a mounted chair. Full-feature cabin with enclosed head, V-berth, upper/lower berth sleeps three. Most were sold with factory tower. Large bridgedeck hatch provides good engine access. Note tall windshield. Twin 200hp Volvo inboard diesels cruise in the mid 20s (around 30 knots top).

Prices Not Provided for Pre-1995 Models

Length	29'0"	Fuel	225 gals.
Beam	10'3"	Water	30 gals.
Draft	2'6"	Cockpit	65 sq. ft.
Weight	8,100#	Hull Type	Modified-V
Clearance	NA	Deadrise Aft	NA

Sportfishing Boats

Topaz 32 Sportfisherman

1986–91

Iconic East Coast express from the late 1980s combines classic good looks with proven fishability, spirited performance. Highlights include roomy fishing cockpit with in-deck storage, raised bridgedeck with centerline engine hatch, snug-but-useful interior with forward V-berth, convertible dinette. Tall windshield provides good high-rpm wind protection. Sea-kindly hull with generous beam, flared bow is known for dry, slightly bow-high ride. Volvo 306hp diesels—or Cat 320s—cruise in the mid 20s (about 30 knots top).

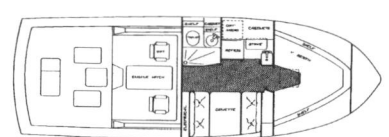

Prices Not Provided for Pre-1995 Models

Length	32'8"	Fuel	300 gals.
Beam	12'2"	Water	40 gals.
Draft	2'1"	Waste	25 gals.
Weight	16,500#	Hull Type	Modified-V
Clearance	NA	Deadrise Aft	18°

Topaz 32/33 Express

2004–Current

Updated version of classic Topaz 32 SF (1986–91) brings a popular, time-tested design up to current sportfish standards. Cockpit space is maximized by locating livewell, rigging station forward and placing split-lid fishbox in deck. Efficient helm console has display space for big-screen electronics. Teak-trimmed cabin with convertible dinette, full galley, stand-up head, rod storage sleeps four. Bridgedeck lifts for engine access. Cruise at 25–26 knots with 370hp Cummins diesels (about 30 knots top). Called 32 Express in 2004–06.

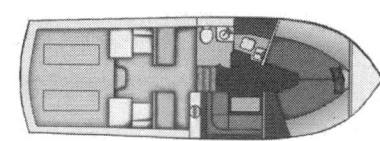

See Page 546 For Value Estimates

Length	32'8"	Headroom	6'3"
Beam	12'2"	Fuel	400 gals.
Draft	3'1"	Water	40 gals.
Weight	20,500#	Hull Type	Modified-V
Clearance	NA	Deadrise Aft	18°

Topaz 36 Sportfisherman

1980–85

Durable sportfishing machine with distinctive styling established the Topaz name with hardcore anglers in the early 1980s. Spacious cockpit with in-deck fishboxes has room for full-size mounted chair. Belowdecks accommodations include convertible dinette, full galley, adult-sized V-berth, large head with separate stall shower. Note tight engine access. Beamy hull is very stable, but flat after-sections make for stiff rough-water ride. Among several engine options, Cat 355hp diesels cruise in the low 20s (26–27 knots top).

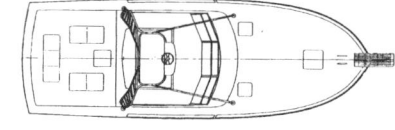
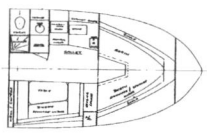

Prices Not Provided for Pre-1995 Models

Length	36'2"	Fuel	300 gals.
Beam	13'0"	Water	50 gals.
Draft	2'5"	Cockpit	NA
Weight	17,800#	Hull Type	Modified-V
Clearance	NA	Deadrise Aft	NA

Topaz 37 Sportfisherman

1986–91

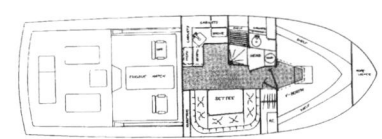

Reworked version of best-selling Topaz 36 Sportfisherman (1980–85) boasts additional fuel, larger interior, improved engine access. Highlights include big fishing cockpit with in-deck storage, well-arranged helm with lockable electronics locker, roomy interior with U-shaped dinette, head with stall shower. Entire bridgedeck lifts for engine access. Solid fiberglass hull is heavily built, dry, stable. Handsome boat has aged well over the years. Cat 375hp diesels cruise at 25 knots (28–29 knots wide open).

Prices Not Provided for Pre-1995 Models

Length	37'6"	Fuel	350 gals.
Beam	13'0"	Water	60 gals.
Draft	3'4"	Cockpit	81 sq. ft.
Weight	19,800#	Hull Type	Modified-V
Clearance	NA	Deadrise Aft	17°

Topaz 39 Royale

1988–91

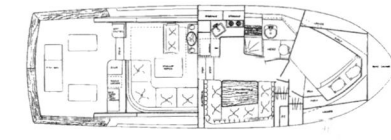

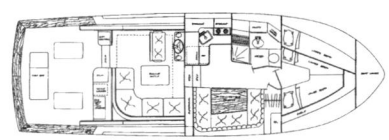

Popular Topaz express with rakish styling combined hardcore fishability with luxury-class amenities, agile performance. Well-appointed interior boasts spacious head with separate stall shower, full-featured galley, generous storage, U-shaped dinette. Raised bridgedeck features L-shaped settee; cockpit came standard with tackle center with freezer, lift-out fishbox. Note unusual portside helm position. Modified-V hull with moderate beam, generous bow flare delivers good low-speed stability. Cruise at a fast 28 knots with GM 485hp diesels (low 30s top).

Prices Not Provided for Pre-1995 Models

Length	39'1"	Fuel	400 gals.
Beam	13'0"	Water	60 gals.
Draft	3'1"	Headroom	6'4"
Weight	21,900#	Hull Type	Modified-V
Clearance, Windshield	7'7"	Deadrise Aft	17°

Triton 2895 Center Console

2004–07

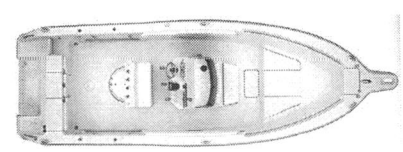

Muscular sportfishing machine with efficient deck layout, heavy-duty construction, makes the cut with hard core anglers. Highlights include two-person helm seat with built-in 50-gallon livewell, raised casting platform, 21-gallon transom livewell, tackle locker, forward console seat, pop-up cleats, raw-water washdown, transom door, console head compartment with sink. Recessed bow rails mean no snagged lines. More storage space than many 28-footers. Deep-V hull can take a serious pounding. Over 45 knots top with Honda 225s.

See Page 546 For Value Estimates

Length w/Pulpit	29'10"	Fuel	204 gals.
Beam	9'5"	Water	18 gals.
Draft, Up	1'9"	Max HP	500
Draft, Down	3'0"	Hull Type	Deep-V
Hull Weight	5,300#	Deadrise Aft	20°

Sportfishing Boats

Triton 351 Center Console

2005–Current

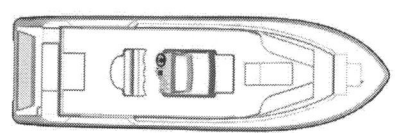

Heavily built battlewagon designed to handle triple-outboard power takes sportfishing excitement, fishability to the next level. Highlights include triple helm seat with 50-gallon livewell, 21-gallon transom livewell, transom storage box, lockable rod lockers (2), folding rear seat, forward fender storage box, forward fishbox with macerator, walk-in head with sink. Tilt-up console has space for twin 15" displays. Cockpit hatch provides easy access to bilge. No lightweight compared with boats her size. Over 50 knots with triple 275 Mercs.

See Page 546 For Value Estimates

Length	34'10"	Fuel	355 gals.
Beam	10'0"	Water	20 gals.
Draft, Up	2'0"	Max HP	1,050
Draft, Down	3'0"	Hull Type	Deep-V
Hull Weight	8,352#	Deadrise Aft	24°

Trojan 32 Sedan

1973–91

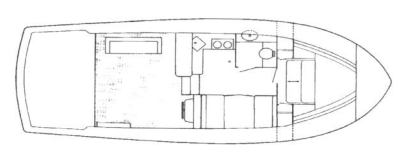

Classic flybridge sedan with large cockpit, semi-enclosed lower helm remains among the most popular boats of her type ever produced. Offered with or without a flybridge, the appeal of this boat rested with her roomy accommodations, handsome lines, affordable price. Well-planned interior with convertible dinette, stand-up head, full galley sleeps four. Early models had teak decks; once-optional 220-gallon fuel capacity became standard in 1984. Cruise at 18 knots with 250hp Chrysler gas engines; 20 knots with 270hp Crusaders.

Prices Not Provided for Pre-1995 Models

Length	32'0"	Water	40 gals.
Beam	13'0"	Fuel	120/220 gals.
Draft	2'6"	Cockpit	60 sq. ft.
Weight	12,000#	Hull Type	Modified-V
Clearance	12'6"	Deadrise Aft	8°

Trojan 36 Convertible

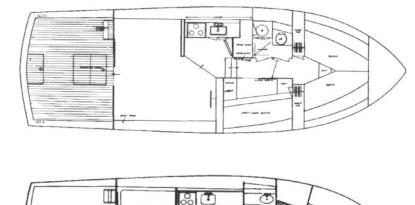

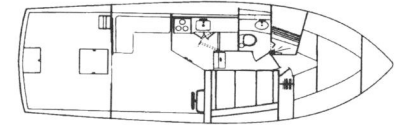

1972–89

Well-priced, well-styled convertible introduced in 1972 turned out to be one of the most popular production boats ever designed. Several single- and twin-stateroom floorplans were available during her long production run, all with standard lower helm. Teak cockpit sole was standard through 1976—a potential source of problems. Uncluttered cockpit lacks transom door, fishbox, or livewell. Note wide side decks. Among many engine choices, twin 350hp gas engines cruise at 18 knots (24–25 knots top).

Prices Not Provided for Pre-1995 Models

Length	36'0"	Water	80 gals.
Beam	13'0"	Fuel	250/350 gals.
Draft	2'11"	Cockpit	75 sq. ft.
Weight	16,000#	Hull Type	Modified-V
Clearance	13'0"	Deadrise Aft	9°

Sportfishing Boats

Trojan 11 Meter Sedan

1985–88

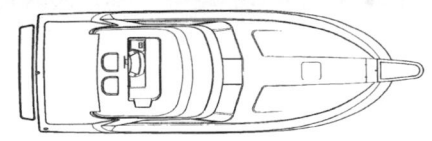

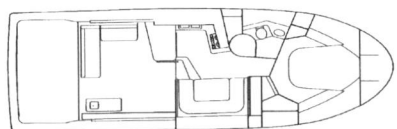

Rakish 1980s sedan with wide 14' beam combined bold styling with maxi-volume accommodations, spirited performance. Spacious interior with wide-open salon features large dinette, head with circular stall shower, U-shaped galley with generous stowage. Cockpit design is compromised by intrusive bridge ladder. Roomy flybridge has guest seating forward of helm. Note wide side decks, glass salon bulkhead, salon wet bar. Standard 350hp gas engines cruise at 18 knots (high 20s top); 375hp Cat diesels cruise at 22 knots (26–27 top).

Prices Not Provided for Pre-1995 Models

Length	37'6"	Water	100 gals.
Beam	14'0"	Fuel	350 gals.
Draft	3'5"	Headroom	6'5"
Weight	18,000#	Hull Type	Modified-V
Clearance	12'6"	Deadrise Aft	14°

Trophy 2802 Walkaround

1997–2001

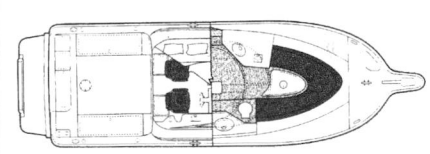

Durable family fisherman with bracket-mounted outboards is well-equipped, built tough, priced right. Fishing amenities include 34-gallon livewell, bait-prep station, two in-deck fishboxes, fresh/saltwater washdowns, fold-down jump seats, cockpit bolsters, transom door. Wide 9'9" beam results in spacious cockpit, wide walkways. Well-arranged cabin with mini-galley, enclosed head with shower, aft mid-berth sleeps 3–4. Excellent helm visibility. Deep cockpit provides an extra level of passenger security. About 40 knots top with twin 200s.

See Page 547 For Value Estimates

Length	31'0"	Fuel	240 gals.
Beam	9'9"	Water	30 gals.
Draft, Up	1'3"	Max HP	450
Draft, Down	2'6"	Hull Type	Modified-V
Dry Weight	7,394#	Deadrise Aft	19°

Trophy 2902 Walkaround

2003–09

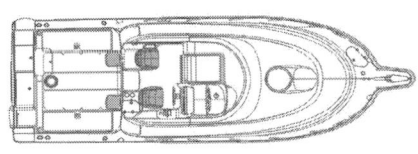

Stylish coastal fisherman with many standard features appeals to family anglers with an eye for versatility, value. Armstrong outboard bracket, 30-gallon transom livewell, aft bait-prep station, two in-deck fishboxes, fold-down jump seats, raw-water washdown, storage lockers, transom door, bow pulpit. Efficient cabin with galley cabinet, enclosed head with shower, aft mid-berth sleeps 3 to 4. Note sink behind helm seat. Deep cockpit, wide walkways are a plus. Trophy's largest model. Over 40 knots top with twin 225s.

See Page 547 For Value Estimates

Length w/Pulpit	31'5"	Fuel	218 gals.
Beam	9'9"	Water	30 gals.
Draft, Up	2'0"	Max HP	500
Draft, Down	2'10"	Hull Type	Modified-V
Weight w/OB	8,200#	Deadrise Aft	19°

Sportfishing Boats

True World TE288

2002–07

Floorplan Not Available

Single-diesel fishing boat with super-wide side decks, protected helm is practical, versatile, unusually fuel efficient. Highlights include deep cockpit with in-deck fishboxes, sturdy hardtop, leaning post with backrest, transom livewell. No-frills cabin offers cozy dinette/V-berth, mini-galley, enclosed head. Amidships engine location lowers center of gravity for improved balance, low-speed stability. Pilothouse superstructure impairs helm visibility. Yanmar 315hp diesel with jackshaft drive cruises at 22–23 knots (burning just 7 gph).

See Page 547 For Value Estimates

Length w/Pulpit	29'6"	Clearance	8'8"
Hull Length	28'0"	Fuel	130 gals.
Beam	9'3"	Water	15 gals.
Draft	1'8"	Hull Type	Modified-V
Weight	6,800#	Deadrise Aft	18°

Venture 27 Open

2007–Current

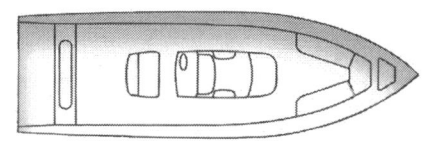

Hard-hitting open fisherman with Kevlar reinforced hull lives up to Venture reputation for quality construction, impressive performance. Generous 9' beam results in roomy cockpit layout for a 27-footer. Highlights include fore and aft in-floor fish boxes, 44-gallon transom livewell, bait-prep station with sink, leaning post with tackle storage. Walk-in console has 6-foot headroom. Fiberglass hardtop, pop-up deck hardware are standard. Note recessed bow rail. Twin 200hp Mercury outboards top out at close to 45 knots.

See Page 547 For Value Estimates

Length	27'0"	Fuel	200 gals.
Beam	9'0"	Water	20 gals.
Draft, Up	1'8"	Max HP	500
Draft, Down	2'2"	Hull Type	Deep-V
Hull Weight	5,500#	Deadrise Aft	24°

Venture 34 Open

1997–Current

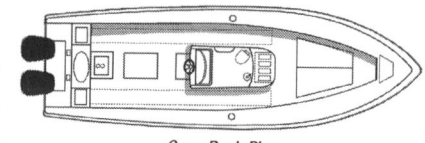

Open Deck Plan

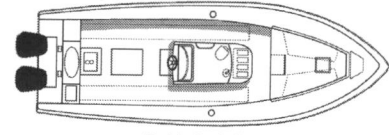

Cuddy Deck Plan

Legendary tournament fishing machine couples sleek lines with top-shelf construction, exceptional open-water performance. Notable features include factory hardtop, leaning post/tackle center, 55-gallon transom livewell, lockable electronics storage, bait-prep station with sink, three fishboxes, fresh/saltwater washdowns, in-deck storage boxes, walk-in head with sink and shower. Exemplary workmanship throughout. Also offered in Cuddy, Forward Seating models. About 45 knots top with twin 250s; 50+ top with triple 300s.

See Page 547 For Value Estimates

Length	34'0"	Fuel	300 gals.
Beam	10'0"	Water	55 gals.
Draft, Up	1'9"	Max HP	600
Draft, Down	2'4"	Hull Type	Deep-V
Weight	6,400#	Deadrise Aft	24°

Sportfishing Boats

Venture 39 Open

2005–Current

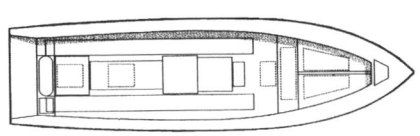

Full-throttle center console is easy on the eye, fun to fish, expensive to buy. Generous 10'8" beam allows for large cockpit with fishing space for several anglers. Highlights include vacuum-bagged construction, big 55-gallon transom livewell, walk-in console with 6-foot headroom, oversized (lighted!) anchor locker with space for hundreds of feet of line. Note tremendous dry storage, huge 550-gallon fuel capacity. Advanced technology, sophisticated engineering rank at top of her class. Tops out at over 45 knots with triple 275hp Mercury outboards.

See Page 547 For Value Estimates

Length	39'6"	Fuel	550 gals.
Beam	10'8"	Water	50 gals.
Draft, Up	1'8"	Max HP	900
Draft, Down	2'7"	Hull Type	Deep-V
Dry Weight	8,000#	Deadrise Aft	24°

Viking 35 Convertible

1985–92

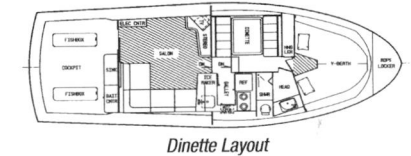

Dinette Layout

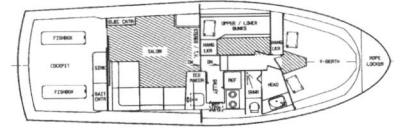

Two-Stateroom Layout

Prices Not Provided for Pre-1995 Models

Handsome midsize convertible blurs the line between serious sportfishing boat, deluxe family cruiser. Well-appointed teak interior was offered in several dinette or twin-stateroom configurations. Highlights include large fishing cockpit with bait-prep center and two in-deck fish boxes, huge flybridge (for a 35-footer) with seating for six, open-plan salon with built-in entertainment center. Note solid front windshield. No transom door. Standard 350hp gas engines cruise at 18 knots; 375hp Cat diesels cruise in the low 20s (26–28 knots top).

Length w/Pulpit	38'6"	Fuel	300 gals.
Hull Length	35'0"	Water	75 gals.
Beam	13'1"	Waste	30 gals.
Draft	4'1"	Hull Type	Modified-V
Weight	20,000#	Deadrise Aft	15.5°

Viking 38 Convertible

1990–95

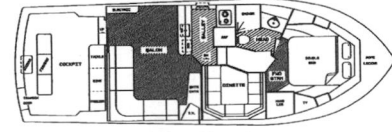

Dinette Floorplan

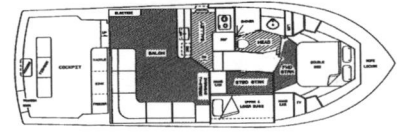

Two Staterooms

See Page 547 For Value Estimates

Polished midsized convertible from the 1990s made good on Viking promise of hardcore fishability, luxury-class accommodations. Expansive interior with rich teak paneling was available with choice of dinette or twin-stateroom layouts, both with mid-level galley. Large cockpit came standard with in-deck fishbox, transom door, molded tackle center with freezer. Note well-finished engine room, central vacuum system. Standard gas engines cruise at 15–16 knots; optional 485hp GM diesels cruise at 22 knots (25 knots wide open).

Length	39'4"	Fuel	430 gals.
Beam	14'2"	Water	110 gals.
Draft	4'1"	Waste	40 gals.
Weight	32,890#	Hull Type	Modified-V
Clearance	11'10"	Deadrise Aft	15.5°

Sportfishing Boats

Viking 41 Convertible

1983–89

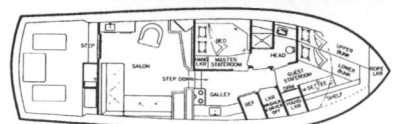

2-Stateroom Layout, 1983–86

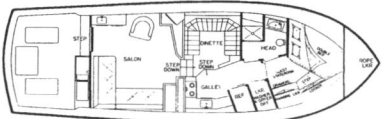

Dinette Layout, 1983–88

Prices Not Provided for Pre-1995 Models

Top-selling Viking convertible delivered a winning blend of handsome styling, deluxe accommodations, excellent performance. Offered with several single- or (more popular) twin-stateroom interiors over the years, all with matched teak joinerwork, decorator fabrics, open front windshield. Uncluttered cockpit came standard with in-deck fishboxes, molded tackle center with sink. Note spacious flybridge, wide side decks. Used models are always in demand. Cruise at 25–26 knots with GM 485hp diesels (about 30 knots wide open).

Length	41'2"	Fuel	380/430 gals.
Beam	14'10"	Water	125 gals.
Draft	4'3"	Waste	40 gals.
Weight	32,000#	Hull Type	Modified-V
Clearance	12'0"	Deadrise Aft	15.5°

Viking 43 Convertible

1990–2002

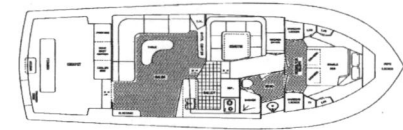

Dinette Floorplan

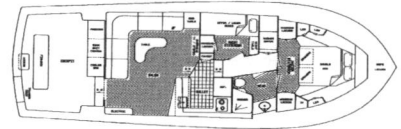

Two Staterooms

See Page 547 For Value Estimates

Versatile 1990s convertible with best-in-class styling set class standards in her era for leading-edge accommodations, muscular construction. Features include big tournament-ready cockpit with engine room access, luxury-class interior with choice of dinette or twin-stateroom layouts, huge flybridge (extended in 1997) with seating for eight. Many updates/refinements over the years including fuel increase in 1996. Cruise at 22–23 knots with 485hp GM diesels; 25–26 knots with GM 625hp engines; 30 knots with 680 MANs (standard after 1999).

Length	43'0"	Fuel	525/600 gals.
Beam	15'3"	Water	115 gals.
Draft	4'3"	Waste	40 gals.
Weight	38,595#	Hull Type	Modified-V
Clearance	15'10"	Deadrise Aft	15.5°

Viking 43 Open Sportfish

1994–2002

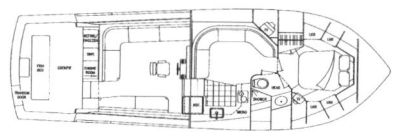

Single Stateroom

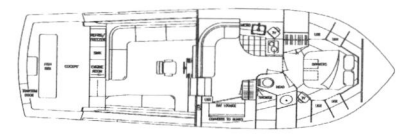

Two Staterooms

See Page 547 For Value Estimates

Powerful sportfishing machine with striking lines, exemplary finish delivers high-octane blast of luxury, fishability, performance. Choice of one- or two-stateroom interiors, both with large galley, exquisite teak woodwork, premium decor. Spacious helmdeck—three steps above cockpit—features wraparound lounge seating, centerline helm with best-in-class dash layout. Cockpit engine room access is a plus. Popular model—over 70 were built. GM 550hp diesels cruise at 25 knots; later models with 680hp MANs cruise at 30 knots.

Length	43'0"	Fuel	525/600 gals.
Beam	15'3"	Water	115 gals.
Draft	4'3"	Waste	40 gals.
Weight	34,500#	Hull Type	Modified-V
Clearance, Hardtop	9'11"	Deadrise Aft	15.5°

Sportfishing Boats

Viking 45 Convertible

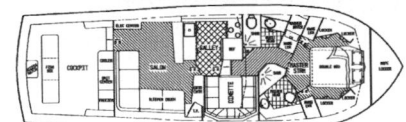

1987–93

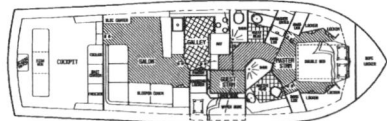

Plan A, Dinette Layout

Plan B, Two Staterooms

Prices Not Provided for Pre-1995 Models

Acclaimed tournament convertible with leading-edge styling, luxury-class accommodations remains one of Viking's best-selling yachts ever. Well-crafted interior—offered with or without dinette—features open-plan salon with serving counter, two large heads, quality appliances and furnishings. Spacious cockpit came with tackle center, transom door, recessed fishboxes. Engine room can be reached from salon or cockpit. About 250 were built. GM 485hp diesels cruise at 23–24 knots; GM 550hp diesels cruise in the high 20s.

Length	45'5"	Fuel	600 gals.
Beam	15'0"	Water	160 gals.
Draft	4'0"	Waste	50 gals.
Weight	44,400#	Hull Type	Modified-V
Clearance	12'5"	Deadrise Aft	15.5°

Viking 45 Convertible

2003–09

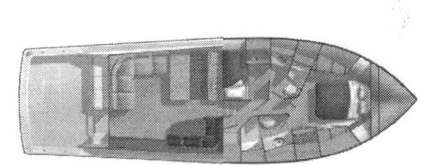

See Page 547 For Value Estimates

Sought-after convertible introduced in 2003 combined signature Viking styling with yacht-grade accommodations. Lavish twin-stateroom interior with spacious salon features open-plan galley with under-counter refrigeration, L-shaped dinette, large master cabin. Best-in-class cockpit includes tackle storage, bait freezer, cooler under salon step. Note space-saving offset bridge ladder, rod storage under salon settee, beautifully detailed engine room with excellent outboard access. MAN 900hp diesels cruise at an honest 30 knots (33–34 knots top).

Length	45'10"	Fuel	848 gals.
Beam	16'4"	Water	150 gals.
Draft	4'6"	Waste	50 gals.
Weight	49,750#	Hull Type	Modified-V
Clearance	16'4"	Deadrise Aft	15.5°

Viking 45 Open Sportfish

2004–09

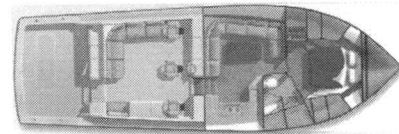

Single Stateroom

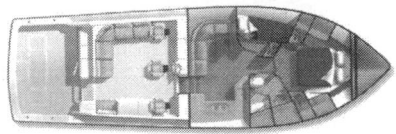

Two Staterooms

See Page 547 For Value Estimates

Muscular dual-purpose express blends sportfishing excellence, cruising luxury. Huge bridgedeck features centerline helm position, three Murray chairs, L-shaped lounge (with rod storage under), full wet bar. Available with one or two staterooms, both with open-plan galley, solid teak cabinetry, Ultraleather seating. Insulated fishboxes, rigging station, tackle storage are standard in large cockpit. Note well-arranged engine room, wide side decks. Superior open-water handling. MANs 900hp diesels cruise at 30 knots (33–34 knots top).

Length	45'10"	Fuel	848 gals.
Beam	16'4"	Water	150 gals.
Draft	4'6"	Waste	50 gals.
Weight	49,760#	Hull Type	Modified-V
Clearance	NA	Deadrise Aft	15.5°

Sportfishing Boats

Viking 46 Convertible

1981–85

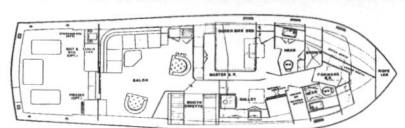

Two Staterooms

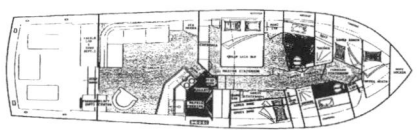

Three Staterooms

Prices Not Provided for Pre-1995 Models

Handsome East Coast convertible delivered the speed, agility, and muscle of a serious 1980s canyon runner. Well-appointed two-stateroom interior has dinette forward in salon; alternate three-stateroom layout—rare in a boat this size—has serving counter, step-down galley. Note front salon windows, solid teak joinery, standard washer/dryer. Cockpit with in-deck fishboxes, tackle locker is conservative in size, but flybridge is huge. GM 500hp engines cruise at 23–24 knots cruise (26 top); 8V92 GMs cruise at 27–28 knots (30 knots top).

Length	46'6"	Fuel	620/750 gals.
Beam	16'0"	Water	200 gals.
Draft	4'0"	Cockpit	120 sq. ft.
Weight	44,000#	Hull Type	Modified-V
Clearance	NA	Deadrise Aft	15.5°

Viking 46 Convertible

2009–Current

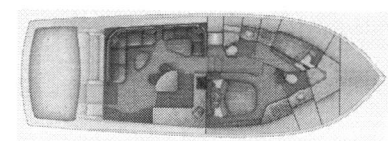

Insufficient Resale Data to Assign Values

Tournament-grade sportfishing yacht combines leading-edge design with unsurpassed luxury, exceptional open-water performance. Lavish two-stateroom, two-head interior with spacious salon, amidships master suite boasts social walk-thru galley with island countertop and twin bar stools. Note companionway laundry center, beautiful high-gloss teak joinery. Mezzanine seat overlooking cockpit houses bait freezer, stowage compartments, direct engine room access. Optional 1,100hp MAN diesels cruise at a fast 35 knots.

Length	46'11"	Fuel	870 gals.
Beam	16'6"	Water	150 gals.
Draft	4'5"	Cockpit	121 Sq. Ft.
Weight	54,120#	Hull Type	Modified-V
Clearance	NA	Deadrise Aft	12°

Viking 47 Convertible

1994–2002

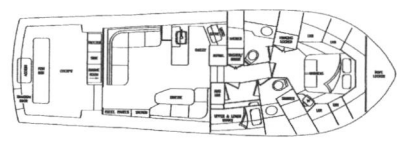

See Page 547 For Value Estimates

Hard-charging tournament machine with classic Viking styling raised the bar in her day for executive-class accommodations, world-class performance. Two-stateroom layout with combined salon/galley/dinette is unusually spacious, well-appointed. Note lavish teak cabinetry, premium galley appliances, standard washer/dryer. Roomy fishing cockpit with huge in-floor fishbox features direct access to meticulous engine room. MAN 680hp diesels cruise at 26 knots (30 knots top); 800hp MANs cruise at 28–30 knots (low 30s top).

Length	47'2"	Fuel	700 gals.
Beam	15'6"	Water	160 gals.
Draft	4'5"	Cockpit	135 sq. ft.
Weight	46,300#	Hull Type	Modified-V
Clearance	16'10"	Deadrise Aft	15.5°

Viking 48 Convertible

1985–90

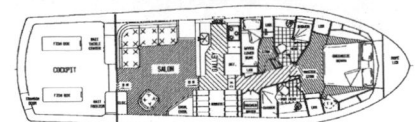

Two Staterooms

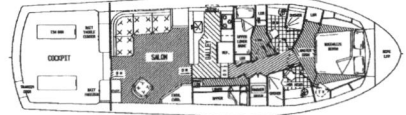

Three Staterooms

Prices Not Provided for Pre-1995 Models

Popular 1980s Viking convertible with huge fishing cockpit coupled spacious accommodations with quality construction, excellent performance. Highlights include well-appointed teak interior with choice of two- or three-stateroom floorplans, massive 144-sq.-ft. fishing cockpit, state-of-the-art flybridge, spacious engine room with cockpit access. Not the softest ride when the seas pick up. Cruise at 23–24 knots with GM 550hp engines (about 26 knots top). GM 735hp diesels cruise at 27–28 knots (30 knots wide open).

Length	48'7"	Fuel	680 gals.
Beam	16'0"	Water	200 gals.
Draft	4'7"	Cockpit	144 sq. ft.
Weight	45,500#	Hull Type	Modified-V
Clearance	12'5"	Deadrise Aft	15.5°

Viking 48 Convertible

2002–09

Two-Stateroom Layout

Three-Stateroom Layout

See Page 547 For Value Estimates

Purebred Viking convertible with leading-edge styling balanced executive-class luxury with muscular construction, exceptional performance. Highlights include sumptuous teak interior with choice of two or three staterooms, companionway laundry center, enormous 130-sq.-ft. fishing cockpit, state-of-the-art helm with huge electronics space, best-in-class engine room. Note that bridge ladder is positioned over salon steps to save cockpit space. A terrific performer, 1,100hp MANs (or 1,015hp Cats) cruise at 30 knots (34–35 top).

Length	48'10"	Fuel	1,012 gals.
Beam	16'6"	Water	175 gals.
Draft	4'9"	Waste	50 gals.
Weight	56,450#	Hull Type	Modified-V
Clearance	NA	Deadrise Aft	15°

Viking 50 Convertible

1991–2001

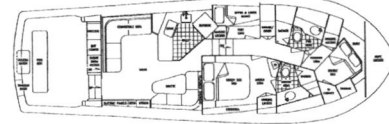

Three-Stateroom Layout

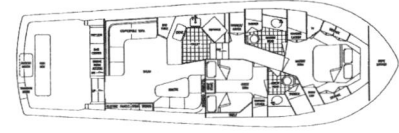

Two-Stateroom Layout

See Page 547 For Value Estimates

Scaled-down version of popular Viking 53 Convertible (1990–98) defined 1990s standards for sportfishing quality, luxury, performance. Spacious three-stateroom interior with amidships master boasts beautifully appointed salon/galley/dinette with entertainment center, standard washer/dryer, under-counter refrigeration. Note huge fishing cockpit, walk-in engine room, massive flybridge. No lightweight, 820hp MANs cruise at 24–25 knots. Optional 1,200hp MANs at 30+ knots (high 30s top). Over 120 were built.

Length	50'7"	Fuel	805 gals.
Beam	16'4"	Water	208 gals.
Draft	4'9"	Cockpit	144 sq. ft.
Weight	58,814#	Hull Type	Modified-V
Clearance	16'5"	Deadrise Aft	15.5°

Sportfishing Boats

Sportfishing Boats

Viking 50 Convertible

2009–Current

Broad-beamed convertible with muscular Viking styling takes modern sportfishing luxury, performance to the next level. Opulent three-stateroom, two-head interior with combined salon/dinette/galley features posh UltraLeather seating, deluxe entertainment center, standard washer/dryer. Note huge flybridge with pod-style helm console. Mezzanine seat overlooking massive cockpit houses bait freezer, stowage compartments, engine room access. MAN 1,350hp engines cruise at a fast 35 knots (nearly 40 knots top).

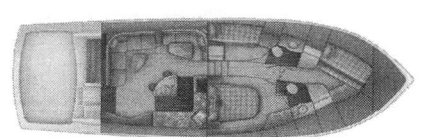

See Page 547 For Value Estimates

Length	50'6"	Fuel	1,000 gals.
Beam	17'0"	Water	175 gals.
Draft	4'10"	Cockpit	132 Sq. Ft.
Weight	66,500#	Hull Type	Modified-V
Clearance	NA	Deadrise Aft	12°

Viking 50 Open

1999–2003

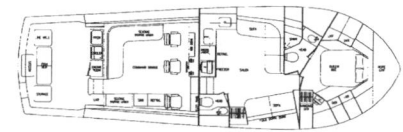

One Stateroom

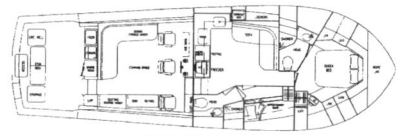

Twin Staterooms

Hard-hitting sportfisherman with powerful lines, exceptional performance remains a formidable tournament contender. Wide 16'4" beam permits huge cockpit, expansive accommodations. Highlights include beautifully appointed interior with choice of layouts, huge bridgedeck with centerline helm, fully equipped cockpit with custom tackle center. Note unique salon day head, beefy transom door. Engine room is as good as it gets. Standard 800hp MANs cruise at 30 knots (33–34 knots top); optional 1200hp MANs cruise at 35 knots (38–40 top).

See Page 547 For Value Estimates

Length	50'7"	Fuel	805 gals.
Beam	16'4"	Water	208 gals.
Draft	4'9"	Cockpit	140 sq. ft.
Weight	55,700#	Hull Type	Modified-V
Clearance, Hardtop	11'5"	Deadrise Aft	15.5°

Viking 52 Convertible

2002–09

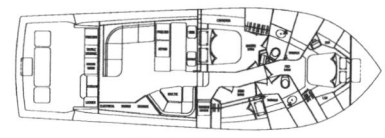

Standard Floorplan

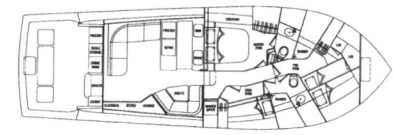

Optional Floorplan

World-class convertible with huge fishing cockpit embodies classic Viking styling, comfort, performance. Opulent three-stateroom floorplan with combined salon/galley/dinette features amidships master suite, choice of queen or single berths forward. Note triple-entry guest head, premium Subzero galley refrigeration, washer/dryer compartment, exquisite teak joinery. Helm layout was state-of-the-art in her day; meticulous engine room is a work of art. Optional 1,360hp MANs cruise at an honest 33 knots (36–37 knots top).

See Page 547 For Value Estimates

Length w/Pulpit	56'11"	Fuel	1,200 gals.
Hull Length	52'10"	Water	205 gals.
Beam	17'5"	Waste	52 gals.
Draft	5'1"	Hull Type	Modified-V
Weight	62,000#	Deadrise Aft	15.5°

Viking 52 Open

2007–Current

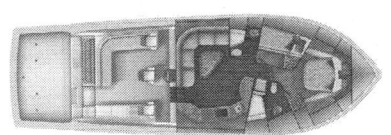

Broad-beamed express with luxury-class accommodations splits the difference between hardcore fishing boat, deluxe family cruiser. Tournament-level cockpit provides vast 145 square feet of fishing space overlooked by mezzanine deck. Lush twin-stateroom, twin-head cabin layout features walkaround queen berth forward, salon rod storage, home-size galley with Corian countertop. Visibility from center helm position is as good as it gets in a big express. Walk-in engine room is cavernous. MAN 1,360 V-12 diesels cruise at a fast 35 knots.

Insufficient Resale Data to Assign Values

Length	52'10"	Fuel	1,200 gals.
Beam	17'3"	Water	200 gals.
Draft	5'0"	Waste	NA
Weight	57,040#	Hull Type	Modified-V
Cockpit	145 sq. ft.	Deadrise Aft	15°

Viking 53 Convertible

1990–98

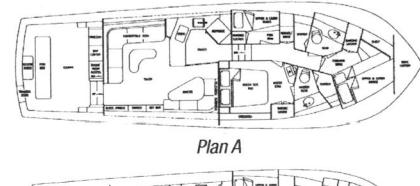

Plan A

Plan B

See Page 547 For Value Estimates

Iconic 1990s Viking convertible with huge cockpit, honest 30-knot performance became one of the best-selling big sportfishing yachts ever built. Lavish three-stateroom interior with amidships master boasts spacious salon with built-in dinette, home-size galley with serving counter, large VIP cabin. Cockpit amenities include full tackle center with freezer, big in-deck fishbox, direct engine room access. Frameless windows became standard in 1997. Over 100 were built. MAN 1,000hp diesels cruise at 30 knots; 1,200hp MANs cruise at 33 knots.

Length	53'7"	Fuel	900/1,100 gals.
Beam	16'7"	Water	200 gals.
Draft	4'10"	Cockpit	150 sq. ft.
Weight	63,500#	Hull Type	Modified-V
Clearance	13'4"	Deadrise Aft	15°

Viking 54 Convertible

2008–Current

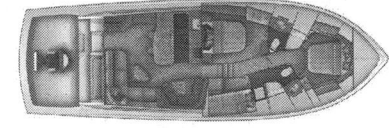

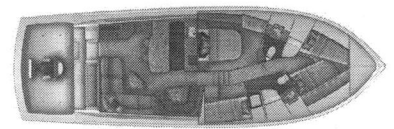

Blue-chip convertible with signature Viking styling takes modern sportfishing elegance, luxury to the next level. Roomy 160-square-foot cockpit features mezzanine deck—shaded by bridge overhang—with lounge seating, engine room access. Posh three-stateroom, twin-head interior boasts master suite to port with walkaround queen, U-shaped galley with Sub-Zero refrigeration. Meticulous engine room, world-class helm are reminders of Viking's production-boat excellence. MAN 1,550hp V12 engines cruise at 34–35 knots (40 top).

Insufficient Resale Data to Assign Values

Length	54'8"	Fuel	1,445 gals.
Beam	17'9"	Water	225 gals.
Draft	5'2"	Waste	100 gals.
Weight	77,900#	Hull Type	Modified-V
Cockpit	160 sq. ft.	Deadrise Aft	15°

Sportfishing Boats

Viking 55 Convertible

1998–2002

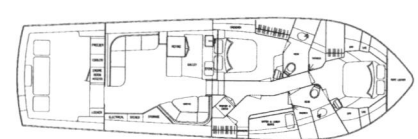

Hard-hitting Viking convertible introduced in 1998 combined luxury accommodations with remarkable performance, world-class quality. Posh three-stateroom interior with amidships master features opulent salon/galley/dinette with high-gloss cabinetry, full entertainment center. Additional highlights include huge 153-square-foot cockpit, meticulous engine room, massive bridge with wraparound helm. MAN 1,200hp diesels cruise at 32 knots (35–36 knots top)—impressive performance for a 55-footer. Total of 115 were built in just five years.

See Page 548 For Value Estimates

Length	55'10"	Fuel	1,250 gals.
Beam	17'4"	Water	250 gals.
Draft	4'10"	Cockpit	153 sq. ft.
Weight	68,800#	Hull Type	Modified-V
Clearance	17'1"	Deadrise Aft	15°

Viking 56 Convertible

2004–10

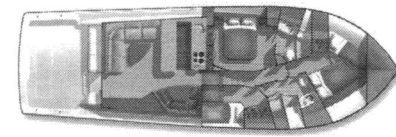

Strong-selling tournament fisherman combines classic Viking styling with luxury-class accommodations, best-in-class performance. Lavish three-stateroom interior is an impressive display of high-gloss teak joinery, designer fabrics, top-quality furnishings. Highlights include spacious open-plan salon with dinette and home-size galley, massive cockpit with mezzanine deck, meticulous engine room with cockpit access door. Prop pockets reduce hull draft, improve efficiency. MAN 1,550hp diesels cruise at a blistering 34 knots (37–38 knots top).

See Page 548 For Value Estimates

Length	57'6"	Fuel	1,500 gals.
Beam	18'2"	Water	240 gals.
Draft	4'10"	Cockpit	157 sq. ft.
Weight	80,800#	Hull Type	Modified-V
Clearance	20'3"	Deadrise Aft	15°

Viking 57 Convertible

1989–91

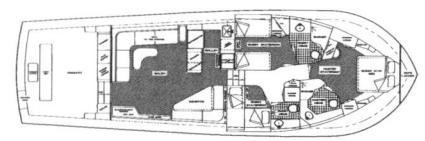

Sportfishing battlewagon introduced in 1989 offered anglers an unsurpassed blend of fishability, comfort, performance. Elegant interior with combined salon/galley/dinette includes spacious master suite forward, twin guest cabins with single berths, standard washer/dryer, three heads. Highlights include huge fishing cockpit, stand-up engine room, wide side decks, spacious flybridge with well-designed helm. Note teak cover boards, wide transom door. Cruise at 28 knots (30+ knots top) with 1,080hp GM diesels. A total of 29 were built.

Prices Not Provided for Pre-1995 Models

Length	57'2"	Fuel	1,500 gals.
Beam	18'0"	Water	250 gals.
Draft	5'3"	Cockpit	165 sq. ft.
Weight	69,000#	Hull Type	Modified-V
Clearance	14'6"	Deadrise Aft	15.5°

Sportfishing Boats

Viking 58 Convertible

1991–2000

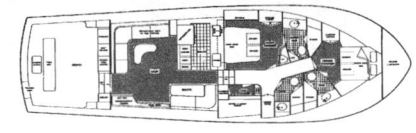

1991–95

1996–97

See Page 548 For Value Estimates

Updated version of Viking 57 Convertible (1989–91) with reworked hull made an already good Viking design even better. Opulent three-stateroom interior features open salon/galley/dinette with entertainment center, three full heads, amidships master suite. Spacious cockpit offers unmatched fishing space; engine room ranks among the best to be found in a boat this size. Note huge flybridge, generous bow flare. MAN 1,100hp engines cruise at 28 knots (31–32 knots top); 1,200hp MANs cruise 30 knots (33–34 knots top). Over 110 were built.

Length	58'11"	Fuel	1,500 gals.
Beam	18'0"	Water	260 gals.
Draft	5'3"	Cockpit	168 sq. ft.
Weight	81,500#	Hull Type	Modified-V
Clearance	17'7"	Deadrise Aft	15.5°

Viking 60 Convertible

2008–Current

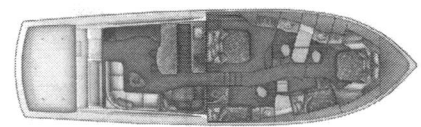

Insufficient Resale Data to Assign Values

Blue-chip convertible pairs legendary Viking quality with executive-level accommodations, awesome big-water performance. Sprawling 170-square-foot cockpit features mezzanine deck—shaded by bridge overhang—with lounge seating, engine room access. Lavish three-stateroom, three-head interior boasts master suite to port with walkaround queen, U-shaped galley with Sub-Zero refrigeration. Note meticulous engine room, state-of-the-art center helm position. Cat 1,825hp V12 diesels cruise at 34–35 knots (40 top).

Length	60'8"	Fuel	1,620 gals.
Beam	18'9"	Water	300 gals.
Draft	5'1"	Waste	135 gals.
Weight	91,300#	Hull Type	Modified-V
Cockpit	170 sq. ft.	Deadrise Aft	15°

Viking 61 Convertible

2001–06

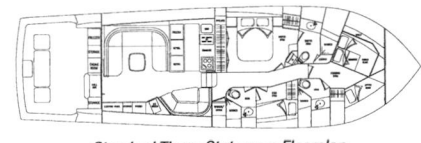

Standard Three-Stateroom Floorplan

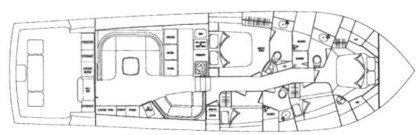

Alternate Four-Stateroom Layout

See Page 548 For Value Estimates

World-class tournament machine introduced in 2001 set design, performance standards in her day for class competitors. Offered with three- or four-stateroom interiors, both with spacious salon, home-size galley, built-in dinette. Massive cockpit is fitted with full array of fishing amenities. Flybridge features centerline helm with huge console. Note standard washer/dryer, meticulous engine room, pump room for A/C compressors. Prop pockets added in 2003 for improved performance. Cruise at over 30 knots with 1,520hp MANs (35+ top).

Length w/Pulpit	65'11"	Clearance, Hardtop	18'3"
Hull Length	61'9"	Fuel	1,700 gals.
Beam	18'2"	Water	310 gals.
Draft	5'4"	Cockpit	170 sq. ft.
Weight	82,000#	Hull Type	Modified-V

Viking 64 Convertible

2006–Current

Three-Stateroom Layout

Four-Stateroom Layout

Gold-plated sportfishing machine with classic Viking styling takes modern convertible design, performance to the next level. Enormous interior (note wide 19'2" beam) with choice of three or four staterooms rivals most motoryachts for unabashed luxury, comfort. Highlights include home-size galley with serving counter, three full heads, 40" plasma TV, electric salon door. Huge cockpit has mezzanine deck with cushioned bench seat. Engine room is a work of art. Cat 1,825hp engines cruise at 32 knots (high 30s top). Enclosed bridge model also available.

See Page 548 For Value Estimates

Length	63'9"	Fuel	1,930 gals.
Beam	19'2"	Water	325 gals.
Draft	5'2"	Waste	200 gals.
Weight	105,000#	Hull Type	Modified-V
Clearance	18'6"	Deadrise Aft	15°

Viking 65 Convertible

1999–2005

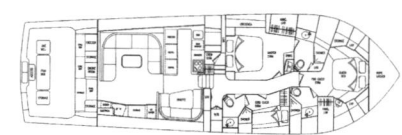

Original 4-Stateroom Interior

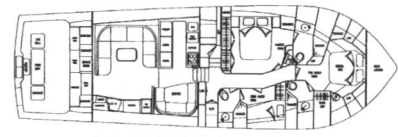

Late-Model 4-Stateroom Interior

Powerful Viking convertible introduced in 1999 made good on Viking promise of best-in-class styling, luxury, performance. Lavish four-stateroom interior with beautifully appointed salon, huge galley, includes posh amidships master, crew quarters, hand-finished joinery. Optional closed-bridge model with aft steering station, salon access, provides all-weather versatility. Massive cockpit came with full array of tournament-class fishing amenities. Prop pockets were added to hull in 2002. MAN or GM 1,800hp engines cruise at 32–33 knots (high 30s top).

See Page 548 For Value Estimates

Length w/Pulpit	69'10"	Fuel	2,000 gals.
Hull Length	65'10"	Water	360 gals.
Beam	18'9"	Cockpit	179 sq. ft.
Draft	6'1"	Hull Type	Modified-V
Weight	96,000#	Deadrise Aft	15.5°

Viking 68 Convertible

2006–09

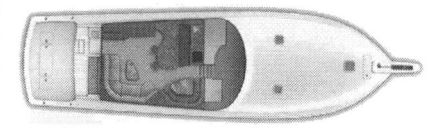

Compelling Viking convertible with leading-edge styling outguns the competition from start to finish. Sprawling 186-square-foot cockpit is overlooked by mezzanine deck with freezer, fishbox, storage cabinets. Lavish four-stateroom interior features exquisite teak joinery, granite countertops, electrically operated salon door, top-of-the-line galley appliances. Frameless windows eliminate leaks; entertainment center includes 42" plasma TV. Offered with open or closed bridge. Optional 2,400hp MTUs cruise at an honest 35 knots (40+ top).

Insufficient Resale Data to Assign Values

Length	68'8"	Fuel	2,060 gals.
Beam	19'4"	Water	355 gals.
Draft	5'5"	Cockpit	186 sq. ft.
Weight	115,000#	Hull Type	Modified-V
Clearance	NA	Deadrise Aft	15°

Viking 72 Convertible

1996–2002

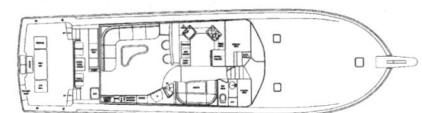

Sportfishing mega-yacht introduced in 1996 remains among largest production convertibles ever offered. Extravagant four-stateroom interior features opulent salon/galley area, full-beam master, four heads. Enclosed bridge has wet bar, seating for a small crowd. Note walk-in storage room forward of galley, inside bridge access, second helm station on bridgedeck overlooking cockpit. Massive cockpit includes full array of tournament fishing features. Standard 1,800hp diesels cruise at 25 knots (28–30 knots top).

Insufficient Resale Data to Assign Values

Length	71'7"	Fuel	2,500 gals.
Beam	19'4"	Water	252 gals.
Draft	5'10"	Cockpit	216 sq. ft.
Weight	120,000#	Hull Type	Modified-V
Clearance	20'0"	Deadrise Aft	15.5°

Viking 74 Convertible

2006–10

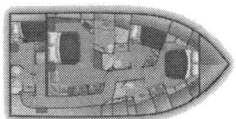

World-class tournament yacht—available with open or closed bridge—splits the difference between sportfishing excellence, cruising opulence. Sprawling 218-square-foot cockpit is overlooked by mezzanine deck with aft-facing seats, freezer, storage cabinets. Lavish four-stateroom interior features exquisite teak joinery, granite counters, power salon door, top-of-the-line galley appliances. Entertainment center includes 50" plasma TV. Note frameless windows, massive flybridge. MTU 2,000hp engines cruise at 30 knots (mid 30s top).

Insufficient Resale Data to Assign Values

Length	74'0"	Fuel	2,416 gals.
Beam	19'9"	Water	385 gals.
Draft	5'7"	Cockpit	218 sq. ft.
Weight	135,000#	Hull Type	Modified-V
Clearance	NA	Deadrise Aft	15°

Vista 48/50 Sportfisherman

1986–94

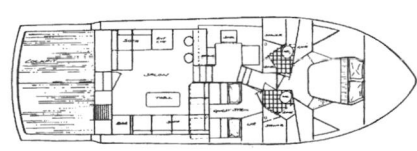

Rakish Fexas-designed sportfishing yacht with fully cored hull combines graceful styling with comfortable accommodations, immense cockpit. Standard two-stateroom layout features expansive salon with entertainment center, breakfast bar, two full heads, extensive teak cabinetry. Huge cockpit came equipped with livewell, fishboxes, teak cover boards, direct engine room access. Note that Vista 50 (1988–94) has slightly larger salon than original Vista 48 (1986–87). GM 550hp diesels cruise at 20 knots (low 20s top).

Prices Not Provided for Pre-1995 Models

Length	48'0"	Fuel	700 gals.
Beam	16'0"	Water	180 gals.
Draft	3'1"	Headroom	6'4"
Weight	36,000#	Hull Type	Modified-V
Clearance	13'10"	Deadrise Aft	3°

Wellcraft 270 Coastal

2001–04; 07–08

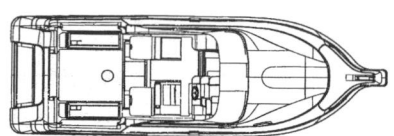

Popular coastal express—re-introduced in 2007—splits the difference between capable family fisherman, comfortable weekend cruiser. Standard fishing features include insulated fishboxes, full-height transom door, lighted livewell, raw-water washdown. Space-efficient cabin with convertible dinette, midcabin berth, enclosed head with shower, sleeps four. Hardtop became standard in 2007. Wide beam results in very roomy cockpit. Tops out at 40+ knots with Yamaha 225 outboards. Sterndrive models with 330hp Merc reach 35 knots top.

See Page 548 For Value Estimates

Length w/Pulpit	28'3"	Fuel	188 gals.
Beam	9'9"	Water	27 gals.
Draft, Up	1'10"	Max HP	500
Draft, Down	2'10"	Hull Type	Deep-V
Hull Weight	7,225#	Deadrise Aft	21°

Wellcraft 2800 Coastal

1986–94

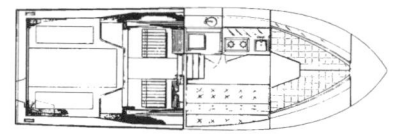

1986–93

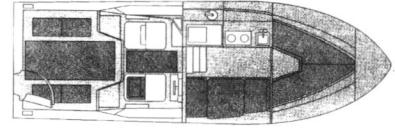

1994

Roomy inboard fisherman with thoughtfully conceived layout offered budget-minded boaters good value for the money. Topside highlights include raised bridgedeck with swivel helm/companion seats, deep walkaround decks, big cockpit with in-floor fishboxes. Open interior with convertible settee, full galley, sleeps four. Transom door is a plus—many 28-footers don't have one. Factory hardtop was a popular option. Early models (1986–1990) had quality-control issues. Twin 260hp gas inboards cruise in the low 20s (high 20s top).

Prices Not Provided for Pre-1995 Models

Length w/Pulpit	29'8"	Clearance	7'6"
Hull Length	27'7"	Fuel	182 gals.
Beam	9'11"	Water	20 gals.
Draft	2'4"	Hull Type	Modified-V
Weight	8,200#	Deadrise Aft	16°

Wellcraft 290 Coastal

1999–2009

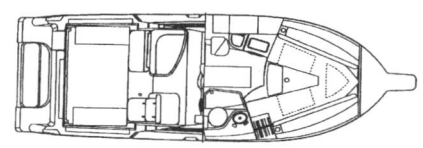

Hard-hitting fisherman with handsome lines offers a class-competitive mix of space, comfort, fishability. Well-planned cockpit comes standard with two in-deck fish-boxes, fold-out rear seat, coaming bolsters, transom door. Helm seating module contains 42-gallon livewell (with Lucite window), sink with pressure water, cutting board. Midcabin interior with convertible dinette, stand-up head, sleeps four. V-berth back-rests double as pilot berths. A lot of boat for the money. Twin 225hp outboards cruise in the mid 20s (35+ knots top).

See Page 548 For Value Estimates

Length w/Pulpit	30'2"	Fuel	225 gals.
Hull Length	27'10"	Water	42 gals.
Beam	10'5"	Max HP	600
Draft	2'9"	Hull Type	Modified-V
Weight	8,735#	Deadrise Aft	18°

Sportfishing Boats

Wellcraft 29 Scarab Sport; 29 CCF

2001–04

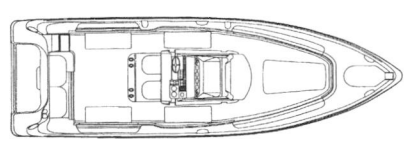

Fast-action center console with high-performance hull keeps on going when the going gets rough. Flush-level cockpit with wide walkways provides excellent 360-degree fishability. Standard features include four insulated fishboxes, 39-gallon livewell, rigging station with sink, dual washdowns, pop-up cleats, recessed bow rails, foldaway transom seat. Walk-in console houses marine head, tackle storage. Called 29 Scarab Sport in 2001–02; 29 CCF in 2003–04. Hull has keel pad for increased lift. Max 50 knots with twin 250s.

See Page 548 For Value Estimates

Length	28'6"	Fuel	214 gals.
Beam	8'10"	Water	8 gals.
Draft, Up	1'9"	Max HP	500
Draft, Down	2'5"	Hull Type	Deep-V
Hull Weight	6,345#	Deadrise Aft	24°

Wellcraft 30 Scarab Sport

1979–93

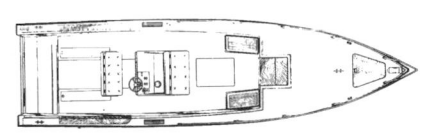

Go-fast center console with narrow 8' beam evolved from Wellcraft's offshore racing program of the early 1970s. Standard features include under-gunnel rod racks, removable rear seat, in-deck fishbox, livewell, rod holders, forward jump seats, anchor locker, low-profile bow rails. Porta-Potti stows between V-berths in cuddy cabin. Offered with several cockpit seating options. Narrow beam results in fast acceleration and high top speed, but cockpit is small compared with competitive 30-footers. About 50 knots top with twin 225s.

Prices Not Provided for Pre-1995 Models

Length	29'9"	Fuel	150 gals.
Beam	8'0"	Water	None
Draft, Up	2'0"	Max HP	500
Draft, Down	3'0"	Hull Type	Deep-V
Dry Weight	4,000#	Deadrise Aft	24°

Wellcraft 30 Scarab Tournament

2007–09

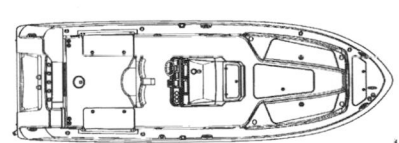

Sleek center console has what serious anglers demand in a high-performance offshore fishing rig. Efficient deck layout features large fore and aft fish boxes, 18 rod holders, optional livewell/leaning post, transom rigging station. Fold-down transom seat frees up cockpit space when necessary. Space at the helm for flush-mounting two big-screen electronics. T-top with rocket launchers, cockpit bolsters were standard. Slender deep-V hull delivers superior rough-water ride. Yamaha 250hp outboards max out at nearly 45 knots.

See Page 548 For Value Estimates

Length	30'2"	Fuel	288 gals.
Beam	9'2"	Water	13 gals.
Draft, Up	1'8"	Max HP	600
Draft, Down	2'6"	Hull Type	Deep-V
Dry Weight	6,635#	Deadrise Aft	23°

Sportfishing Boats

Wellcraft 302 Scarab Sport

1995–2000

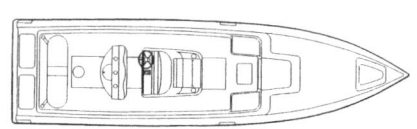

Updated version of original 30 Scarab Sport (1979–93) with bracket-mounted power targets hard core anglers with a need for speed. Standard fishing goodies include large transom fishbox, dual leaning post with 40-gallon livewell, raw-water washdown, lockable rod storage. Compact bow cuddy contains V-berth, storage lockers, space for portable head. Helm console includes lockable electronics storage, forward-opening storage compartment. Slender beam means limited cockpit space. About 50 knots top with twin 225s.

See Page 548 For Value Estimates

Length	29'6"	Fuel	238 gals.
Beam	8'0"	Water	9 gals.
Draft, Up	2'0"	Max HP	600
Draft, Down	3'0"	Hull Type	Deep-V
Dry Weight	5,000#	Deadrise Aft	24°

Wellcraft 32 Scarab Sport; 32 CCF

2001–06

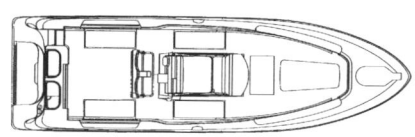

Notched-bottom speedster with roomy fishing cockpit, premium amenities is sexy, fast, built to last. Standard features included T-top with rod holders, in-deck fishboxes (4), 37-gallon lighted livewell, central rigging station with sink, leaning post with cooler, folding rear seat, pop-up cleats, glove box, dual washdowns, forward storage boxes, console head compartment with opening port. Deep-V hull is quick out of the hole. Called 32 Scarab Sport in 2001–04; 32 CCF in 2005–06. Yamaha 250s top out at 45+ knots.

See Page 548 For Value Estimates

Length	31'1"	Fuel	281 gals.
Beam	9'2"	Water	8 gals.
Draft, Up	1'11"	Max HP	600
Draft, Down	2'5"	Hull Type	Deep-V
Hull Weight	7,865#	Deadrise Aft	24°

Wellcraft 3200 Coastal

1984–86

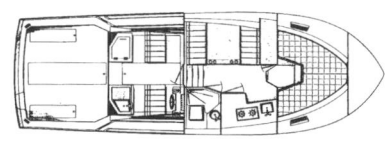

Heavily built Wellcraft express impressed 1980s anglers with her practical deck layout, agile handling, competitive. Bi-level cockpit with unusual inward-opening transom door has enough space for three anglers and their gear. Teak-paneled cabin sleeps four, includes full galley, convertible dinette, stand-up head with shower. Note tall windshield, good helm visibility, wide side decks. So-so finish, but the price was right. Twin 350hp gas engines cruise at 20–22 knots with a top speed of around 30 knots.

Prices Not Provided for Pre-1995 Models

Length	32'0"	Fuel, Std.	290 gals.
Beam	11'6"	Fuel, Opt.	350 gals.
Draft	3'0"	Water	80 gals.
Weight	13,200#	Hull Type	Modified-V
Clearance	8'3"	Deadrise Aft	14°

Wellcraft 330 Coastal

1989–2009

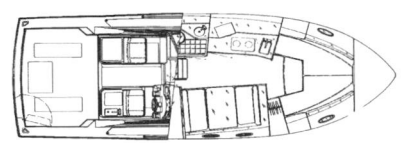

Dual-purpose coastal express with broad beam hit the sweet spot with Wellcraft buyers looking for space, comfort, value. Well-appointed interior with large galley, convertible dinette sleeps four. Roomy cockpit came standard with livewell, insulated fishboxes, tackle center, transom door. Many updates over the years—oval ports replaced original cabin windows in 1998, fuel was increased in 2005. Early models with 310hp gas inboards cruise at 18–20 knots. Later models with 375hp Volvo gas engines cruise in low 20s.

See Page 548 For Value Estimates

Length w/Pulpit	38'5"	Fuel	288/370 gals.
Hull Length	33'3"	Water	52 gals.
Beam	12'5"	Waste	20 gals.
Draft	3'0"	Hull Type	Modified-V
Weight	16,000#	Deadrise Aft	16°

Wellcraft 34 Scarab Super Sport

1987–92

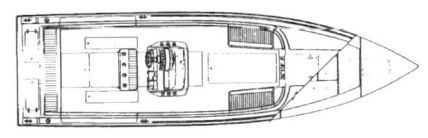

Fast-action center console with bracket-mounted outboards, narrow 8'4" beam gets offshore anglers to the fishing grounds fast. Principal features include in-sole livewell, insulated transom fishboxes, rear bench seat with storage under, forward tackle center, lockable rod storage. Compact cuddy with V-berth, Porta-Potti provides generous dry storage. Far less cockpit space than other 34-footers. Deep-V hull handles rough water with ease. Slender hull is legally trailerable in all states. Over 45 knots max with twin 250s.

Prices Not Provided for Pre-1995 Models

Length	33'10"	Clearance	6'8"
Beam	8'4"	Fuel	250 gals.
Draft, Up	2'0"	Max HP	500
Draft, Down	3'6"	Hull Type	Deep-V
Dry Weight	5,100#	Deadrise Aft	23°

Wellcraft 35 Scarab Sport

2007–09

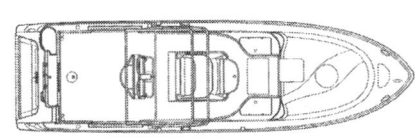

Sleek console cuddy combines time-tested deck layout with deep-V performance, quality amenities. Highlights include deluxe helm seat with flip-up bolsters, aft livewell, folding rear seat, T-top with electronics box, tilt-out tackle box, cockpit bolsters, dual washdowns, forward jump seats, enclosed head with sink & shower. Helm space for big-screen electronics. Compact cuddy with V-berth sleeps two. Good-looking boat is very well finished. Twin 225hp outboards top out at 40+ knots; triple 250s reach speeds of 50+ knots.

See Page 548 For Value Estimates

Length	35'4"	Fuel	400 gals.
Beam	9'11"	Water	13 gals.
Draft, Up	1'11"	Max HP	900
Draft, Down	3'3"	Hull Type	Deep-V
Dry Weight	8,600#	Deadrise Aft	23°

Sportfishing Boats

Wellcraft 35 Scarab Sport; 35 CCF

2001–05

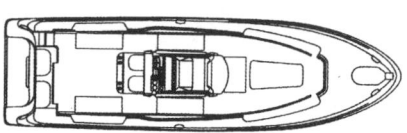

High-speed fishing rig with stepped hull ranked among the biggest, baddest fastest fishing machines of her era. Highlights include T-top with electronics box, 37-gallon lighted livewell, transom bait-prep station, foldaway rear seat, dual washdowns, leaning post with tackle storage, console cooler, enclosed head with sink. Space at helm for big-screen electronics. Called 35 Scarab Sport in 2001–02; Wellcraft 35 CCF in 2003–5. Great rough-water ride. Twin 225hp outboards top out at 40+ knots; triple 250s reach speeds of 50+ knots.

See Page 548 For Value Estimates

Length	34'10"	Fuel	300 gals.
Beam	9'11"	Water	29 gals.
Draft, Up	1'11"	Max HP	900
Draft, Down	2'9"	Hull Type	Deep-V
Weight w/OBs	10,000#	Deadrise Aft	23°

Wellcraft 350 Coastal

2000–03

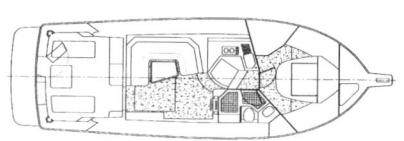

Classy sports sedan (built for Wellcraft by Aussie-based Riviera Marine) took small-convertible styling, personality to next level. Roomy single-stateroom interior with standard lower helm is well-suited to needs of family cruisers. Fishing amenities include large insulated fishbox, lighted baitwell (with viewing window), cockpit coaming, reinforced deck with plate for fighting chair. Engine room access, via cockpit hatch, is a tight fit. Among several engine options, twin 370hp Volvo diesels cruise at 25 knots (about 30 knots top).

See Page 549 For Value Estimates

Length w/Pulpit	37'6"	Fuel	227 gals.
Hull Length	33'2"	Water	81 gals.
Beam	12'6"	Waste	20 gals.
Draft	3'4"	Hull Type	Modified-V
Weight	19,900#	Deadrise Aft	15°

Wellcraft 360 Coastal

2006–09

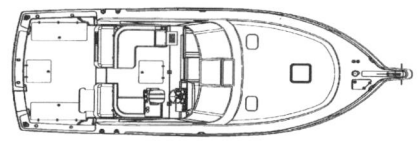

Handsome offshore express blends hardcore fishability with feature-rich interior, long-range capability. Topside highlights include huge bridgedeck with wraparound lounge seating, wide side decks, well-equipped cockpit with 37-gallon livewell, insulated fishboxes, bait-prep center. Upscale cabin with cherry trim, Corian counters, sleeps four. Note standard hardtop, single-level electronic controls. Hunt-designed hull delivers steady open-water performance. Volvo 370hp diesels cruise at 25–26 knots (about 30 knots wide open).

See Page 549 For Value Estimates

Length w/Pulpit	39'6"	Fuel	400 gals.
Hull Length	36'6"	Water	107 gals.
Beam	13'8"	Waste	18 gals.
Draft	3'4"	Hull Type	Deep-V
Weight	20,000#	Deadrise Aft	18°

Wellcraft 3700 Cozumel

1988–89

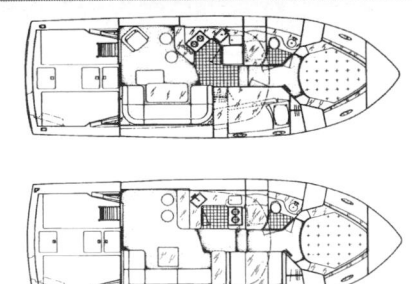

Value-priced convertible combined rakish lines with un-cluttered cockpit, family-style accommodations. Available with one or two staterooms, Eurostyle interior is a blend of cheap Formica, vinyl, chrome—too glitzy for most anglers of her era. Large cockpit came equipped with lockable rod storage, transom door, cockpit bolsters, insulated fishbox. Bridge is big for a 37-footer with guest seating forward of helm. Wide side decks are a plus. Twin 340hp gas engines cruise at 18 knots; optional 375hp Cat diesels cruise at 22–24 knots.

Prices Not Provided for Pre-1995 Models

Length	36'11"	Fuel	400 gals.
Beam	13'6"	Water	90 gals.
Draft	3'3"	Cockpit	90 sq. ft.
Weight	21,000#	Hull Type	Modified-V
Clearance	12'3"	Deadrise Aft	16.5°

Wellcraft 400 Coastal

1999–2003

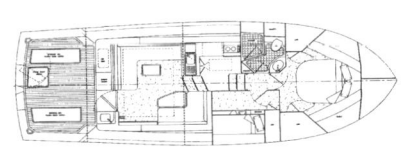

Handsome sport sedan (built for Wellcraft by Riviera Marine in Australia) offers boaters comfort, fishability, performance in a stylish package. Unpretentious two-stateroom interior with leather seating, beechwood cabinetry is comfortable, simple, easy to clean. Large cockpit features 12 rod holders, rigging station with freezer, 37-gallon livewell, fishbox. Retractable sunshade extends out from bridge overhang; access to the engine room is via hatch in cockpit sole. Note standard hardtop. Volvo 480hp diesels cruise at 26 knots (about 30 knots top).

See Page 548 For Value Estimates

Length w/Pulpit	44'7"	Cockpit	94 sq. ft.
Hull Length	39'1"	Fuel	469 gals.
Beam	14'4"	Water	121 gals
Draft	4'1"	Hull Type	Modified-V
Weight	23,400#	Deadrise Aft	15°

Yellowfin 34

2005–Current

Floorplan Not Available

Hard-nosed fishing machine matches class standards for quality, fishability, open-water performance. Highlights include 55-gallon transom livewell, cockpit coaming pads, flush-mounted cleats, leaning post with backrest, T-top, removable rear bench seat, cockpit bolsters, forward seating, recessed bow rails, dual washdowns, high-performance K-Planes. Second 70-gallon in-sole livewell is available with twin-engine models. Very well-finished boat. Twin Mercury 275s max out at 45 knots; triple 275s reach 55+ knots wide open.

See Page 549 For Value Estimates

Length	34'8"	Fuel, Std.	300 gals.
Beam	10'0"	Water	20 gals.
Draft, Up	1'8"	Max HP	1,050
Draft, Down	2'10"	Hull Type	Deep-V
Hull Weight	8,800#	Deadrise Aft	22°

Sportfishing Boats

Yellowfin 36

2003–Current

Floorplan Not Available

World-class center console rated for triple-engine power runs fast, fishes hard, turns heads. Highlights include T-top with rod holders, leaning post with livewell, 50-gallon transom livewell, K-Plane trim tabs, pop-up cleats, saltwater washdown, console seat, 9-foot rod storage boxes. Optional coffin box tilts back to reveal big in-floor fishbox. High-performance stepped hull, stern lifting pad delivers exceptional high-speed handling. Twin Mercury 300 4-strokes top 45 knots; triple 300 Mercs reach 55+ knots wide open.

See Page 549 For Value Estimates

Length	36'8"	Fuel, Std.	330 gals.
Beam	10'0"	Fuel, Opt.	525 gals.
Draft, Up	1'8"	Max HP	1,400
Draft, Down	3'6"	Hull Type	Deep-V
Hull Weight	9,500#	Deadrise Aft	22°

Sportfishing Boats

Section 3
Cruisers & Sedans

See index for complete list of models.

Cruisers & Sedans

Albin 27 Family Cruiser

1983–95

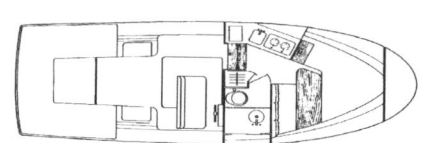

Practical twin-cabin cruiser with very distinctive profile combines comfort, efficiency in one of the more popular small boats ever produced. Shallow draft is ideal for cruising intercoastal or inland lake waters. Forward cabin includes double berth, galley, dinette, enclosed head; aft cabin has twin berths. Center-cockpit layout boasts inboard seating, semi-enclosed helm. Bow thruster was standard in later models. Engine access is a pain. Fuel consumption averages 2 gallons per hour at 10–12 knots with single Perkins diesel.

See Page 511 For Value Estimates

Length Overall	26'9"	Fuel	72 gals.
Length WL	24'4"	Water	40 gals.
Beam	9'8"	Waste	25 gals.
Draft	2'6"	Hull Type	Semi-Disp.
Weight	6,500#	Deadrise Aft	NA

Albin 30 Family Cruiser

2004–07

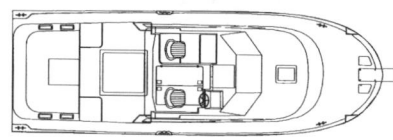

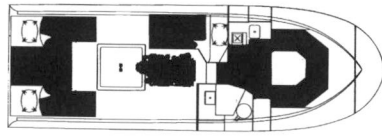

Practical family cruiser—successor to best-selling Albin 27 Family Cruiser (1983–95)—combines economical operation with easy handling, space-efficient layout. Unique aft-cabin layout sleeps five adults in two separate cabins. Visibility from semi-enclosed helm is excellent. Deep cockpit keeps kids and guests safe, secure. Solid, well-built boat requires little maintenance. Wide side decks, good engine access, ten opening ports. Good helm visibility. Cruise at 16–17 knots (about 20 top) with single 300hp diesel.

See Page 512 For Value Estimates

Length Overall	31'5"	Fuel	126 gals.
Length WL	26'8"	Water	26 gals.
Beam	10'0"	Waste	18 gals.
Draft	3'2"	Hull Type	Modified-V
Weight	9,800#	Deadrise Aft	19°

Azimut 62S

2006–Current

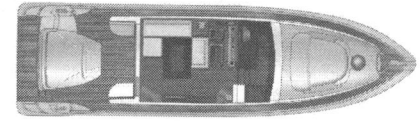

Stunning sportcruiser with square-shaped portholes, shark-fin sidescreens, sliding sunroof is in a styling class of her own. Lavish two-stateroom interior includes expansive deckhouse salon, versatile lower salon with self-contained galley, truly amazing full-beam owner's cabin. Airy cockpit with sunpad can seat a small crowd. Tender garagefits a 9-foot RIB launched on rollers. Note wide side decks, well-designed engine compartment. Meticulous finish is hard to believe. Cat 1,015hp V-drive diesels cruise at 28 knots (low 30s wide open).

Insufficient Resale Data to Assign Values

Length	62'6"	Headroom	6'4"
Beam	16'1"	Fuel	713 gals.
Draft	5'0"	Water	238 gals.
Weight	56,800#	Hull Type	Deep-V
Clearance	NA	Deadrise Aft	19°

Cruisers & Sedans

Azimut 68S

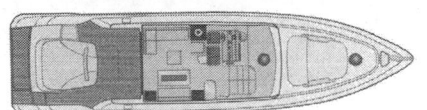

2005–Current

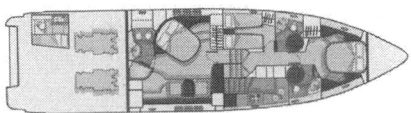

Sleek sportcruiser gained instant fame in 2005 for novel hardtop design, innovative interior layout. Where most European sportyachts use the main deck for open-air lounging, the 68S offers true, fully furnished salon with luxury-class decor. Full-beam master stateroom is rare in a boat this size. Highlights include tender garage, joystick engine controls, sunroof, small crew cabin, washer/dryer, huge cockpit sun pad. Dash layout is superb; galley is small. MTU 1,300hp V-drive diesels cruise at a fast 30 knots (35–36 knots top).

Insufficient Resale Data to Assign Values

Length	68'0"	Fuel	845 gals.
Beam	17'1"	Water	251 gals.
Draft	5'2"	Waste	NA
Weight	69,440#	Hull Type	Modified-V
Clearance	NA	Deadrise Aft	15°

Back Cove 26

2005–09

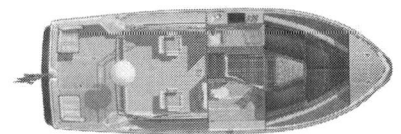

Widely acclaimed inboard express takes small-boat elegance, sophistication to the next level. Wide 9'4" beam results in more cabin, cockpit space than any boat in her class. Well-appointed interior boasts cherry woodwork, teak and holly sole, enclosed head, near-standing headroom. Tall windshield provides super protection from wind, spray. Rear cockpit seats are a plus; entire helm deck lifts on gas struts to expose engine compartment. Cruise efficiently at 22 knots (mid 20s top) with single 260hp Yanmar diesel.

See Page 512 For Value Estimates

Length	26'6"	Water	30 gals.
Beam	9'4"	Waste	30 gals.
Draft	2'6"	Headroom	5'7"
Weight	8,500#	Hull Type	Modified-V
Fuel	100 gals.	Deadrise Aft	14°

Back Cove 29

2004–09

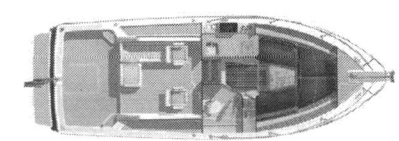

Popular hardtop cruiser with classic lines blends leading-edge construction with practical layout, fuel-efficient operation. Warm cherry interior boasts traditional teak-and-holly sole, ash ceiling strips, adult-size berths, full galley. Semi-enclosed pilothouse has opening center windshield, sliding side windows. Bridgedeck lifts electrically for engine access. Note wide side decks, sturdy bow rails. Prop pocket reduces draft for shallow-water exploring. Single Yanmar 315hp diesel will cruise efficiently at 20 knots (26–27 knots top).

See Page 512 For Value Estimates

Length	29'5"	Fuel	150 gals.
Beam	10'5"	Water	30 gals.
Draft	2'6"	Waste	30 gals.
Weight	10,000#	Hull Type	Modified-V
Clearance	8'4"	Deadrise Aft	16°

Cruisers & Sedans

Back Cove 30

2011–Current

Good-looking pocket cruiser delivers on Back Cove promise of quality construction, social accommodations, impressive single-diesel performance. Space-efficient layout features well-appointed interior with wraparound bow seating, roomy bridgedeck with facing settees, roomy cockpit with built-in seating. Note cockpit transom door, premium Stidd helm seat, standard bow thruster. Deck lifts electrically for engine access. Prop pocket improves efficiency, reduces draft. Cruise at 18 knots with Yanmar 315hp diesel (about 25 knots top).

Insufficient Resale Data to Assign Values

Length	30'6"	Fiel	160 gals.
Beam	11'2"	Water	60 gals.
Draft	2'6"	Waste	30 gals.
Weight	12,000#	Hull Type	Modified-V
Clearance	NA	Deadrise Aft	16°

Back Cove 33

2007–Current

Tasteful Downeast cruiser combines single-diesel efficiency with state-of-the-art construction, luxury-class accommodations. Semi-enclosed pilothouse with dinette, in-line galley offers excellent helm visibility. Surprisingly large head has separate stall shower. Stidd helm chair is a quality touch; helm deck sole lifts electrically for engine access. Upscale cabin with teak and holly sole, quality appliances, sleeps four. Prop pocket reduces draft, improves efficiency. Cruise at 20 knots with 435hp Cummins diesel (mid 20s top).

See Page 512 For Value Estimates

Length	34'4"	Fuel	185 gals.
Beam	12'0"	Water	60 gals.
Draft	3'1"	Waste	60 gals.
Weight	16,000#	Hull Type	Modified-V
Clearance	NA	Deadrise Aft	14°

Bayliner 2655 Ciera Sunbridge

1994–99

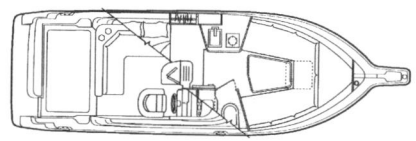

Updated version of earlier Bayliner 2655 Ciera Sunbridge (1990–93) is wider, sleeker, better equipped. Tastefully appointed interior sleeps four with standing headroom, large dinette, good storage. Midcabin berth is no place for claustrophobics. Roomy cockpit has L-shaped seating opposite helm, optional pullout bench seat aft, walk-thru transom. Gas-assist engine hatch in cockpit sole provides good service access. Note narrow side decks. Cruise at 22–23 knots with single 250hp MerCruiser sterndrive power (about 30 knots top).

Insufficient Resale Data to Assign Values

Length w/Pulpit	27'9"	Fuel	70 gals.
Beam	8'5"	Water	27 gals.
Draft, Up	1'4"	Waste	13 gals.
Draft, Down	3'1"	Hull Type	Modified-V
Weight	5,175#	Deadrise Aft	16°

Cruisers & Sedans

Bayliner 275 SB Cruiser

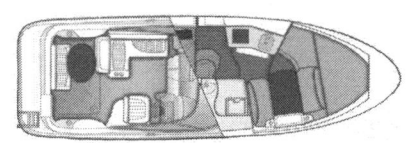

2005–07

Value-priced cruiser with wide 9'5" beam delivers more cockpit, cabin space than most 27-footers. Midcabin floorplan with convertible dinette, full galley sleeps four adults and two kids. Roomy head compartment offers enough elbow room to be comfortable. Standard features include convertible lounge opposite helm, transom seat, carry-on cooler, radio/CD player, removable cockpit table. Good finish belies her low price. Small fuel capacity. Tops out in the high 30s/low 40s with optional 320hp MerCruiser power.

See Page 512 For Value Estimates

Length	26'7"	Fuel	77 gals.
Beam	9'5"	Water	31 gals.
Draft, Up	1'9"	Waste	20 gals.
Draft, Down	3'2"	Hull Type	Modified-V
Weight	6,485#	Deadrise Aft	15°

Bayliner 2755 Ciera Sunbridge

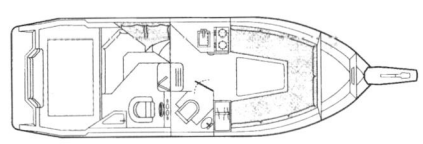

1989–93

Big trailerable cruiser with lots of standard equipment offered budget-minded buyers good value for the money. Narrow midcabin interior sleeps four (two adults, two kids), includes removable dinette table, small galley, stand-up head with sink, shower. Cockpit features L-shaped lounge forward, transom seat, sink. Good helm visibility. Additional features include four opening ports, walk-through windshield, radar arch, bow pulpit. Lots of rough edges in the finish department. Cruise at 25 knots with single 300hp gas engine.

Prices Not Provided for Pre-1995 Models

Length	27'0"	Fuel	78 gals.
Beam	8'6"	Water	28 gals.
Draft, Up	1'8"	Waste	13 gals.
Draft, Down	3'3"	Hull Type	Deep-V
Weight	5,200#	Deadrise Aft	20°

Bayliner 2850/2855 Sunbridge

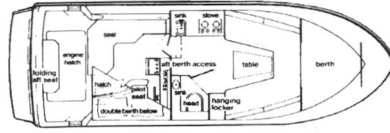

1983–89

Contessa Floorplan (1983–87)

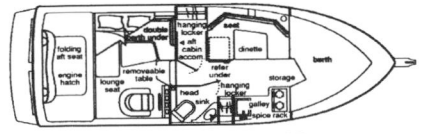

Ciera Floorplan (1988–89)

Lightweight, value-priced family cruiser became one of Bayliner's best-selling models during the 1980s. Roomy interior sleeps six with stand-up head compartment, convertible dinette, full-size galley, generous storage. Large cockpit offers seating for five. Good helm visibility. Standard features included radar arch, teak interior trim, transom platform, bow pulpit, dockside power. Called 2850 Contessa SB in 1983–87; 2855 Ciera SB in 1988–89. Floorplan revised in 1988. Single 260hp Volvo I/O will cruise at 20 knots.

Prices Not Provided for Pre-1995 Models

Length	27'5"	Clearance	6'8"
Beam	10'0"	Fuel	120 gals.
Draft, Up	1'11"	Water	30 gals.
Draft, Down	3'3"	Hull Type	Modified-V
Weight	5,775#	Deadrise Aft	NA

Cruisers & Sedans

Bayliner 2850/2858 Command Bridge

1983–89

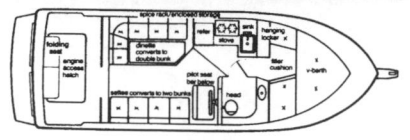

1983–85

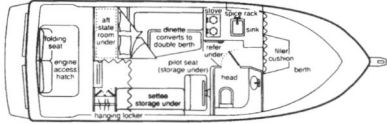

1986–89

Compact flybridge cruiser for coastal, inland cruising proved popular with entry-level buyers. Space-efficient interior includes amidships stateroom under salon dinette, compact galley, enclosed head with sink and shower. Lower helm position permits all-weather operation. Swim platform, bow pulpit, teak exterior trim, and swim ladder were standard. One of the few 28-foot flybridge boats ever produced. Called 2850 Contessa CB in 1983–87; 2855 Ciera CB in 1988–89. Floorplan updated in 1986. Single 260hp Volvo I/O will cruise at 18 knots (mid 20s top).

Prices Not Provided for Pre-1995 Models

Length	27'7"	Clearance	6'8"
Beam	10'0"	Fuel	120 gals.
Draft, Up	1'11"	Water	30 gals.
Draft, Down	3'3"	Hull Type	Modified-V
Weight	5,775#	Deadrise Aft	NA

Cruisers & Sedans

Bayliner 2855 Ciera Sunbridge

1991–93

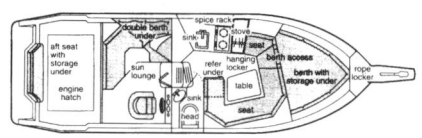

Strong-selling 1990s cruiser delivered traditional Bayliner value in a stylish package. Roomy interior boasts wraparound dinette with seating for six. Midcabin berth comes with headboard storage, privacy curtain. Small galley lacks counter, storage space. Cockpit includes U-shaped lounge seating opposite helm, rear bench seat, removable table, transom shower. Modest fuel capacity, poor finish. Single 230hp MerCruiser I/O will cruise at 16–18 knots; optional 300hp I/O will cruise at 20 knots. Replaced in 1994 with all-new 2855 Sunbridge model.

Prices Not Provided for Pre-1995 Models

Length	28'1"	Fuel	102 gals.
Beam	9'6"	Water	35 gals.
Draft, Up	1'8"	Waste	13 gals.
Draft, Down	3'3"	Hull Type	Modified-V
Weight	6,510#	Deadrise Aft	18°

Bayliner 2855 Ciera Sunbridge

1994–99

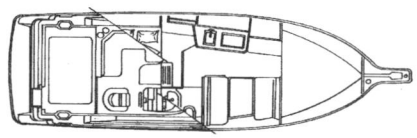

Updated version of earlier 2855 Ciera Sunbridge model combined freshened styling with larger galley, improved head sea performance. Midcabin layout is arranged with double berths fore and aft, convertible dinette, stand-up head with sink, shower. Privacy curtains separate sleeping areas from salon. Good engine access; well-designed helm with space for electronics. Note slide-out jump seats behind companion lounge. Hugely popular model for Bayliner with over 1,000 sold. Cruise at 20 knots (30+ top) with single 300hp I/O.

See Page 512 For Value Estimates

Length w/Pulpit	30'3"	Clearance	8'6"
Beam	9'7"	Fuel	109 gals.
Draft, Up	1'8"	Water	33 gals.
Draft, Down	3'4"	Hull Type	Deep-V
Weight	6,510#	Deadrise Aft	22°

Bayliner 2859 Ciera Express

1993–2002

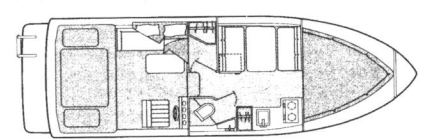

Popular hardtop cruiser (called 2859 Classic in 1993–95) is practical, affordable, exceptionally versatile. Roomy interior comes complete with galley, convertible dinette, private head, aft double berth. Excellent visibility from semi-enclosed helm position. Deep cockpit offers great security for kids and guests. Note narrow side decks. Additional features include transom door, swim platform, fold-down helm seats, swim ladder. Single 310hp MerCruiser will cruise at 22 knots and top out at close to 30 knots. Note modest fuel capacity.

See Page 513 For Value Estimates

Length	27'9"	Fuel	102 gals.
Beam	9'9"	Water	36 gals.
Draft, Up	1'7"	Waste	30 gals.
Draft, Down	3'0"	Hull Type	Modified-V
Weight	7,597#	Deadrise Aft	15°

Bayliner 285 SB Cruiser

2000–Current

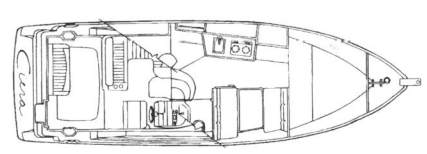

Stylish single-engine cruiser (called the 2855 Ciera Sunbridge in 2000–02) makes good on Bayliner promise of space, comfort at a reasonable price. Sleeping quarters for six is rare on a boat this size. Midcabin privacy door is a nice touch—most 28-footers have curtains. Cockpit with fold-down transom seat, removable cockpit table seats six. Note walk-through windshield, transom shower. Roomy engine compartment thanks to single-engine design. Cruise economically at 22 knots (30+ top) with 300hp MerCruiser power.

See Page 513 For Value Estimates

Length	28'7"	Fuel	89 gals.
Beam	9'11"	Water	28 gals.
Draft, Up	2'1"	Waste	30 gals.
Draft, Down	3'5"	Hull Type	Modified-V
Weight	8,056#	Deadrise Aft	17°

Bayliner 288 Classic Cruiser

1996–2005

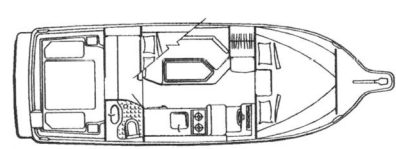

Sporty flybridge cruiser (called Bayliner 2858 Ciera Command Bridge in 1996–2002) is versatile, roomy, inexpensive to operate. Impressive accommodations for a 28-footer include private midcabin berth below salon sole, convertible dinette, enclosed head with shower, full galley. Good visibility from lower helm. Note narrow side decks. Bow pulpit, radar arch, swim platform are standard. Decent finish considering her super-low price. Single 310hp MerCruiser sterndrive engine will cruise at 22 knots (32–33 knots top).

See Page 513 For Value Estimates

Length w/Pulpit	30'7"	Fuel	113 gals.
Beam	10'0"	Water	34 gals.
Draft, Up	1'8"	Waste	26 gals.
Draft, Down	3'2"	Hull Type	Modified-V
Weight	6,100#	Deadrise Aft	18°

Cruisers & Sedans

Cruisers & Sedans

Bayliner 2950/2958 Command Bridge

1988–90

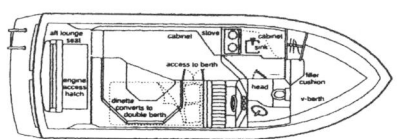

Inexpensive flybridge cruiser combined sporty styling with traditional Bayliner value. Efficient midcabin floorplan includes mini-stateroom beneath salon settee. Privacy curtain separates V-berth from galley. Visibility from lower helm—with its double seat—is very good. Note small cockpit. Lounge seating on flybridge seats several guests. Bow pulpit, radar arch, sliding cabin windows, transom door, swim platform were standard. Engine compartment is small. Twin 230hp sterndrive engines cruise at 20 knots (28–30 knots top).

Prices Not Provided for Pre-1995 Models

Length	28'8"	Fuel	121 gals.
Beam	10'6"	Water	29 gals.
Draft, Up	2'0"	Waste	13 gals.
Draft, Down	3'6"	Hull Type	Deep-V
Weight	8,750#	Deadrise Aft	20°

Bayliner 2955 Avanti Sunbridge

1988–90

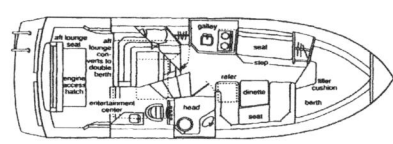

Generic family express with sleek styling defined Bayliner concept of value, affordability in a 1980s cruiser. Wide 10'6" beam permits spacious interior dimensions. Midcabin floorplan includes two private sleeping areas, stand-up head with shower, efficient galley, convertible dinette, generous storage. Note multi-colored hull graphics. Unimpressive fit and finish. Engine compartment is a tight fit with twin engines. Single 340hp sterndrive will cruise at 16 knots (mid 20s top); twin 260hp engines cruise at 22 knots (30+ knots top).

Prices Not Provided for Pre-1995 Models

Length	28'8"	Fuel	120 gals.
Beam	10'6"	Water	30 gals.
Draft, Up	2'0"	Waste	13 gals.
Draft, Down	3'6"	Hull Type	Deep-V
Weight	7,400#	Deadrise Aft	20°

Bayliner 315 SB Cruiser

2008–Current

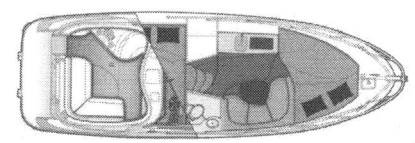

Sleek twin-engine cruiser (called 300 SB Cruiser in 2009) takes express-boat affordability, value to the next level. Roomy single-level cockpit with L-shaped lounge, small refreshment center seats six without being crowded. Note dual helm seat with flip-up bolster, optional power engine compartment hatch. Cabin, with large side windows, screened companionway door, is well lit and ventilated. Midcabin berth has fixed doorway rather than a curtain—definitely a plus. Twin 260hp MerCruiser I/Os cruise at 25 knots (around 35 knots top).

See Page 513 For Value Estimates

Length	30'6"	Fuel	120 gals.
Beam	10'0"	Water	33 gals.
Draft, Up	2'1"	Waste	30 gals.
Draft, Down	3'4"	Hull Type	Modified-V
Weight	9,098#	Deadrise Aft	18°

Bayliner 3055 Ciera Sunbridge

1991–94

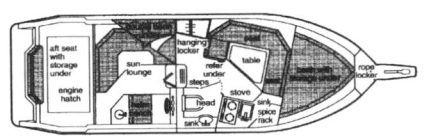

Early 1990s express cruiser delivered roomy accommodations, decent performance at rock-bottom price. Midcabin floorplan features convertible dinette, full galley (refrigerator is under dinette seat), enclosed head with shower. Both staterooms have curtains for nighttime privacy. Bi-level cockpit includes lounge seating forward, wet bar, storage cabinet, transom seat. Reverse arch is a sporty touch. Low-deadrise hull is not fond of a chop. Single 300hp sterndrive will cruise at 17 knots (mid 20s knots top).

Prices Not Provided for Pre-1995 Models

Length	30'7"	Clearance	8'9"
Beam	10'0"	Fuel	125 gals.
Draft, Up	1'6"	Water	36 gals.
Draft, Down	3'0"	Hull Type	Modified-V
Weight	8,000#	Deadrise Aft	14°

Bayliner 305 SB Cruiser

1999–2007

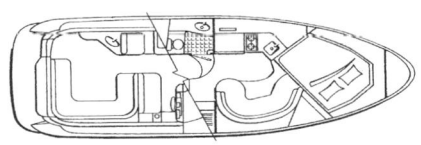

Portly family cruiser (called 3055 Ciera Sunbridge in 1999–2002) with wide 11-foot beam has much to offer in comfort, versatility. Expansive midcabin interior boasts full 6'5" headroom, two double berths, fully equipped galley, roomy head compartment. Cockpit has removable table, fill-in sun pad. Walk-through windshield provides easy bow access. Long list of standard equipment included cockpit wet bar, tilt wheel, radar arch, trim tabs, transom shower. Cruise at 25 knots (high 30s top) with twin 300hp MerCruiser I/Os.

See Page 513 For Value Estimates

Length Overall	31'6"	Fuel	148 gals.
Beam	11'0"	Water	35 gals.
Draft, Up	1'9"	Waste	30 gals.
Draft, Down	2'9"	Hull Type	Modified-V
Weight	11,857#	Deadrise Aft	17°

Bayliner 320/335 SB Cruiser

2008–Current

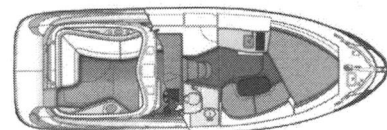

Standard Fixed Berth

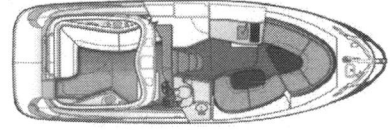

Optional Open Lounge

Value-priced express (called the Bayliner 335 SB Cruiser since 2010) delivers the goods without causing sticker shock. Generic cabin offered with standard fixed berth or open lounge boasts private midcabin berth, fully equipped galley, good lighting, plenty of storage. Innovative cockpit design with extended portside lounge is unusual. Swivel helm seat with flip-up bolster, windlass, cockpit refreshment center, foredeck sun pads are standard. Cruise at 25 knots with twin 300hp MerCruiser I/Os (high 30s top).

See Page 513 For Value Estimates

Length	32'6"	Fuel	160 gals.
Beam	11'0"	Water	35 gals.
Draft, Up	2'1"	Waste	30 gals.
Draft, Down	3'2"	Hull Type	Modified-V
Weight	12,000#	Deadrise Aft	NA

Cruisers & Sedans

Bayliner 325 SB Cruiser

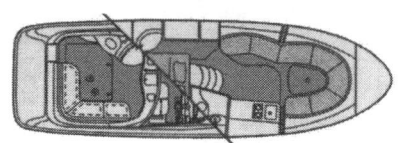

2005–07

Family-friendly cruiser with spacious midcabin interior delivers plenty of bang for the buck. Wide-open cabin with generous headroom is surprisingly roomy for 32-footer. Full-featured galley includes microwave, coffeemaker; aft cabin has privacy door rather than curtain—a real plus. Swivel helm seat rotates to face the cockpit. Additional features include non-glare helm, walk-through windshield, extended swim platform, radar arch, tilt steering, windlass. Cruise at 26–28 knots (40+ top) with twin 320hp MerCruiser I/Os.

See Page 513 For Value Estimates

Length	35'0"	Fuel	175 gals.
Beam	11'6"	Water	31 gals.
Draft, Up	1'9"	Waste	30 gals.
Draft, Down	3'4"	Hull Type	Modified-V
Weight	11,319#	Deadrise Aft	18°

Bayliner 3255 Avanti Sunbridge

1995–99

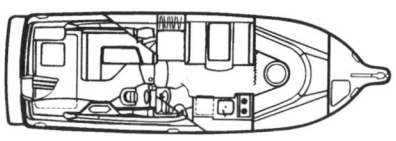

Sporty family express from late 1990s combined roomy interior with large cockpit, affordable price. Midcabin floorplan features double berths fore and aft, complete galley, enclosed head with shower, convertible dinette, large hanging locker. Pocket door—not a curtain—separates forward stateroom from salon. Cockpit wet bar, transom door, bow pulpit, swim platform, foredeck sun pad were standard. Note stylish reverse radar arch. Cruise at 20 knots (mid 30s top) with twin 310hp MerCruiser sterndrives.

See Page 513 For Value Estimates

Length w/Pulpit	35'0"	Fuel	180 gals.
Hull Length	32'11"	Water	35 gals.
Beam	11'0"	Waste	30 gals.
Draft	3'0"	Hull Type	Modified-V
Weight	11,000#	Deadrise Aft	16°

Bayliner 3258 Command Bridge

1995–2000

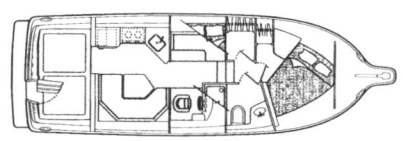

Good styling, spacious accommodations made this commonsense cruiser attractive to budget-minded buyers in late 1990s. Innovative two-stateroom interior is arranged with lounge, head forward in salon, U-shaped dinette, large galley aft. Stall shower in head is a useful feature. Lower helm visibility is good forward, poor to the sides. Bow pulpit, radar arch, swim platform, transom door, trim tabs were standard. Note small cockpit. Twin 250hp Merc I/Os cruise at 20 knots; 310hp Mercs cruise at 25 knots (about 35 knots top).

See Page 513 For Value Estimates

Length w/Platform	35'2"	Weight	10,230#
Hull Length	32'11"	Fuel	180 gals.
Beam	11'0"	Water	52 gals.
Draft, Up	2'0"	Hull Type	Modified-V
Draft, Down	3'3"	Deadrise Aft	17°

Bayliner 3388 Motor Yacht

1996–2000

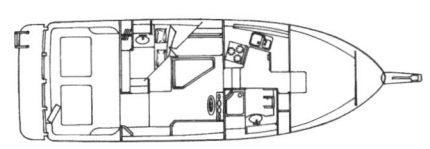

Affordable twin-diesel family cruiser was basically an up-dated version of previous Bayliner 3288 MY (1981–95) with fresh exterior styling, rearranged floorplan, numerous hull refinements. Midcabin floorplan with galley down includes standard lower helm, head with separate stall shower, raised salon settee, large cabin windows. Additional features include teak interior trim, radar arch, midcabin vanity and sink, swim platform, bow pulpit. Prop pockets reduce hull draft. Standard 260hp gas inboards will cruise at 16 knots (around 25 knots top).

See Page 513 For Value Estimates

Length	32'11"	Fuel	200 gals.
Beam	11'6"	Water	90 gals.
Draft	2'8"	Waste	30 gals.
Weight	15,500#	Hull Type	Modified-V
Clearance	13'6"	Deadrise Aft	6°

Bayliner 340 SB Cruiser

2008–09

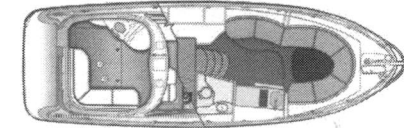

Standard Open Lounge

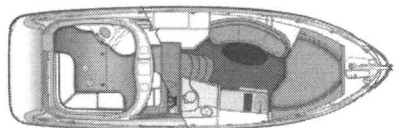

Optional Fixed Berth

Contemporary sterndrive express raised the bar for Bay-liner styling, versatility in a low-priced cruiser. Uncluttered single-level cockpit with portside lounge, L-shaped rear seat has more space than most 34-footers. Comfortable cabin—available with fixed berth forward or wraparound lounge seat—features private midcabin berth, fully equipped galley, generous storage. Six opening ports and three deck hatches provide good cabin ventilation. Good engine access. MerCruiser 300hp Bravo III engines cruise easily at 25–26 knots (low 40s top).

See Page 513 For Value Estimates

Length	35'0"	Fuel	175 gals.
Beam	11'6"	Water	40 gals.
Draft, Up	2'2"	Waste	30 gals.
Draft, Down	3'5"	Hull Type	Modified-V
Weight	11,226#	Deadrise At	NA

Bayliner 3488 Avanti Command Bridge

1996–99

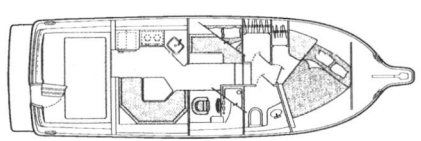

Spacious flybridge cruiser with contemporary styling, roomy interior offered exceptional value to 1990s buyers. Interior is arranged with private midcabin below salon settee. Note separate stall shower in head compartment. L-shaped galley provides plenty of counter, storage space. Good visibility from lower helm. Additional features include bow pulpit, radar arch, transom door, swim platform. MerCruiser 310hp gas inboards (with V-drives) cruise at 18 knots (26–28 knots max). Replaced with all-new 3488 Command Bridge model in 2001.

See Page 513 For Value Estimates

Length Overall	36'7"	Fuel	180 gals.
Hull Length	34'4"	Water	52 gals.
Beam	11'0"	Waste	52 gals.
Draft	3'5"	Hull Type	Modified-V
Weight	12,549#	Deadrise Aft	17°

Cruisers & Sedans

Bayliner 3488 Command Bridge

2001–02

Sporty, strong-selling Bayliner cruiser was one of the most affordable 35-footers of her era. Midcabin interior includes spacious galley with plenty of counter and storage space, two private staterooms, head with separate stall shower, large cabin windows. Lower helm was a popular option. Note roomy cockpit, molded flybridge stairs. Bow pulpit, radar arch, transom door, swim platform were standard. Low-deadrise hull is a stiff ride in a chop. Standard 260hp gas inboards cruise at 14 knots (about 20 knots top).

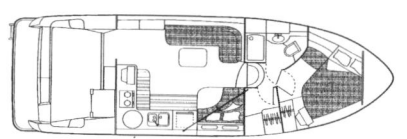

See Page 513 For Value Estimates

Length	35'0"	Fuel	224 gals.
Beam	11'8"	Water	92 gals.
Draft	3'2"	Waste	30 gals.
Weight	17,000#	Hull Type	Modified-V
Clearance, Arch	13'6"	Deadrise Aft	7.5°

Bayliner 3450/3485/3785 Sunbridge

1987–90

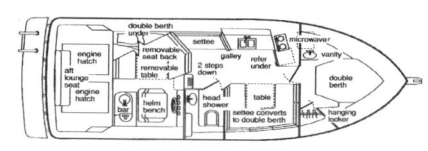

Maxi-volume express (called the 3450 Avanti SB in 1987; 3485 in 1988–89; 3785 in 1990) has little to recommend in today's market other than low price. Styling can only be described as tacky; poor finish is typical of late 1980s Bayliner boats. Generic midcabin interior includes full galley, convertible dinette, roomy master stateroom with vanity, sink, privacy door. Bow pulpit, radar arch, transom door were standard. Integral swim platform became standard in 1990. Twin 330hp V-drive gas engines cruise at 20 knots (27–28 knots top).

Prices Not Provided for Pre-1995 Models

Length w/Pulpit	36'7"	Clearance	9'6"
Hull Length	33'9"	Fuel	205 gals.
Beam	12'10"	Water	50 gals.
Draft	3'0"	Waste	34 gals.
Weight	13,150#	Hull Type	Modified-V

Bayliner 3555 Ciera Sunbridge

1988–94

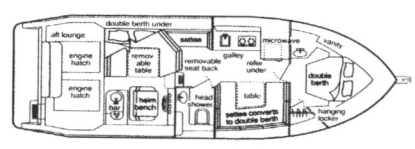

Rakish family express combined signature Bayliner value with roomy cockpit, versatile interior. Generic midcabin layout includes convertible dinette, full galley, forward stateroom with privacy door and vanity. Midcabin space isn't as cramped as some. Roomy cockpit is fitted with wraparound lounge, wet bar, removable table. Bow pulpit, radar arch, transom door, extended swim platform were standard. Twin 250hp MerCruiser sterndrives cruise at 20 knots (28–29 knots wide open). Called the Bayliner 3250 Sunbridge in 1988; 3255 Sunbridge in 1989.

Prices Not Provided for Pre-1995 Models

Length	34'7"	Fuel	205 gals.
Beam	11'5"	Water	50 gals.
Draft, Drives Up	2'4"	Waste	34 gals.
Draft, Drives Down	3'8"	Hull Type	Modified-V
Weight	10,200#	Deadrise Aft	19°

Cruisers & Sedans

Bayliner 3685 Avanti Sunbridge

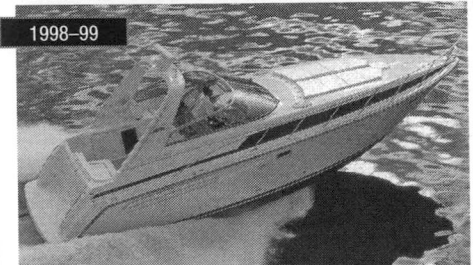

1998–99

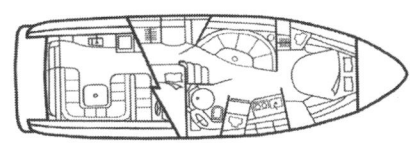

Value-priced inboard express with long equipment list delivered a lot of bang for the buck. Conventional midcabin floorplan has double staterooms fore and aft, full galley, convertible dinette, head with shower. Sliding doors ensure real privacy in forward stateroom. Removable cocktail table stores beneath cockpit sole. Large gas-assist hatch provides good access to engine compartment. Note narrow side decks, foredeck sun pad. So-so fit and finish. Twin 310hp V-drive gas engines cruise at 18 knots (26–28 knots wide open).

See Page 513 For Value Estimates

Length Overall	39'4"	Fuel	244 gals.
Beam	13'0"	Water	65 gals.
Draft	3'7"	Waste	48 gals.
Weight	21,000#	Hull Type	Modified-V
Clearance, Arch	12'11"	Deadrise Aft	15°

Bayliner 4085 Avanti Sunbridge

1997–99

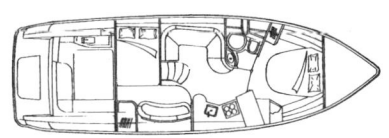

Maxi-volume express cruiser with roomy interior, large cockpit was stylish, practical, very affordable. Contemporary midcabin interior has pocket doors for both cabins—a real plus where privacy is concerned. Features include ash interior trim, large galley, enclosed stall shower, double-wide helm seat, radar arch, side exhausts, foredeck sun pad. Extended swim platform can store PWC. MerCruiser 310hp gas (V-drive) inboards cruise at a modest 15–16 knots (25 knots top); Cummins 315hp diesels cruise at 25 knots.

See Page 513 For Value Estimates

Length	42'0"	Fuel	330 gals.
Beam	13'5"	Water	77 gals.
Draft	3'5"	Waste	45 gals.
Weight	22,100#	Hull Type	Modified-V
Clearance, Arch	12'11"	Deadrise Aft	16°

Bertram 33 Flybridge Cruiser

1977–92

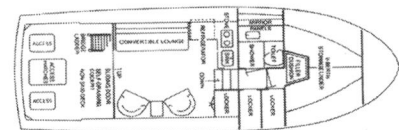

Single-Stateroom Layout, 1977–79

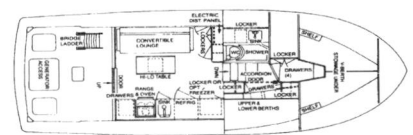

Two-Stateroom Layout, 1980–87

Prices Not Provided for Pre-1995 Models

Premium flybridge cruiser with classic Bertram profile took small-convertible comfort, versatility to the next level. Enormous interior rivals most 35-footers in size. Several floorplans were offered over the years—two-stateroom layout became standard in 1980. Teak cabinetry replaced mica in 1984. Small cockpit is okay for light-tackle anglers. Lower helm was optional. Bertram 33 II, introduced in 1988, has restyled flybridge, light oak interior. Standard 340hp gas engines cruise at 18 knots; 260hp Cat diesels cruise at 22 knots.

Length	33'0"	Fuel, Gas	250/315 gals.
Beam	12'6"	Fuel, Diesel	255 gals.
Draft	3'0"	Water	70 gals.
Weight	22,800#	Hull Type	Deep-V
Clearance	12'6"	Deadrise Aft	17°

Cruisers & Sedans

Californian 30 LRC

1978–81

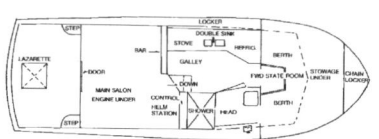

This small Californian sedan combines a versatile layout with handsome styling and very economical operation. Single-stateroom mahogany interior features a cozy salon with lower helm and convertible settee, enclosed head with shower stall, fully equipped galley with double sink and serving counter. Note sliding window next to lower helm. Cockpit is large enough for fishing. Easy engine access is a plus. Excellent lower helm visibility. Good fit and finish. Cruise (about 12 knots top) at 8 knots with single 135hp Perkins diesel.

Prices Not Provided for Pre-1995 Models

Length	29'6"	Fuel	120 gals.
Beam	10'3"	Water	38 gals.
Draft	1'10"	Waste	20 gals.
Weight	9,200#	Hull Type	Modified-V
Clearance	NA	Deadrise Aft	NA

Californian 35 Convertible

1985–87

Sporty flybridge convertible from 1980s doubles as family cruiser, light-tackle fisherman. Single-stateroom, galley-down interior features wide-open salon, good storage, enclosed shower in head. Roomy flybridge has bench seating forward of helm. Additional features include mahogany interior cabinetry, wide side decks, molded bow pulpit, good-sized engine room. No cockpit transom door or tackle centers. Crusader 270hp gas engines cruise at 16 knots (22–24 knots top); 210hp Cat diesels cruise efficiently at 16 knots.

Prices Not Provided for Pre-1995 Models

Length	34'11"	Fuel	300 gals.
Beam	12'4"	Water	75 gals.
Draft	3'2"	Waste	35 gals.
Weight	18,000#	Hull Type	Modified-V
Clearance	10'8"	Deadrise Aft	15°

Californian 39 SL

1999–2003

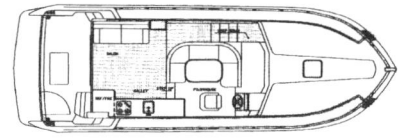

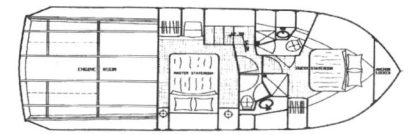

Sturdy west coast cruiser (built by Navigator Yachts) combines conservative styling with comfortable ride, competitive price. Innovative interior plan has dinette centered on pilothouse level, next to the helm. Bi-level galley extends into the pilothouse making it somewhat awkward to use. Both staterooms are fitted with double berths, both heads have enclosed showers. Lower helm visibility is excellent. Note flybridge dinghy stowage. Radar arch, transom door were standard. Volvo 318hp diesels cruise at 20 knots (23–24 knots wide open).

See Page 515 For Value Estimates

Length	39'0"	Headroom	6'5"
Beam	15'0"	Fuel	250 gals.
Draft	4'4"	Water	100 gals.
Weight	27,500#	Cockpit	60 sq. ft.
Clearance	NA	Hull Type	Modified-V

Californian 44 Veneti

1988–89

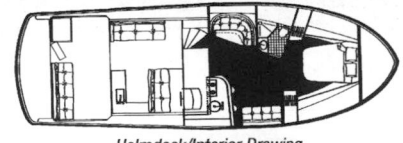

Helmdeck/Interior Drawing

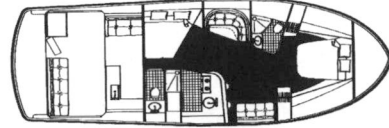

Full Interior Drawing

Rakish styling made this late 1980s express one of the more distinctive boats of her era. Unusual two-head interior resulted in compact salon dimensions. Features include big engine room, wide side decks, radar arch, good cabin storage. Original hull was a wet ride until spray rails were added early in 1989. Slightly confusing dash layout. One of first American sportcruisers to employ integrated swim platform. Twin 375hp Cat diesels will cruise at 20–21 knots (about 24 knots top). Popular model for Californian.

Prices Not Provided for Pre-1995 Models

Length w/Pulpit	47'10"	Clearance	10'0"
Hull Length	44'0"	Fuel	400 gals.
Beam	15'2"	Water	190 gals.
Draft	4'0"	Hull Type	Modified-V
Weight	30,000#	Deadrise Aft	15°

Cape Dory 28 Flybridge

1985–94

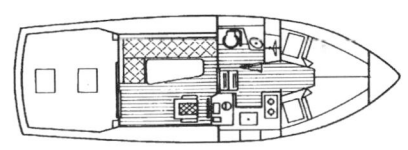

Salty Downeast cruiser with full keel is easily driven, inexpensive to operate, loaded with eye appeal. Space-efficient interior with classy teak-and-holly flooring, teak cabinets includes convertible salon dinette, standard lower helm. Tall flybridge provides great 360-degree visibility. Wide side decks allow secure bow access. Deep keel protects prop from grounding. Excellent engine access. Very popular model. Good fit and finish. Single Volvo 200hp diesel cruises economically at 14 knots (16–17 knots top).

Prices Not Provided for Pre-1995 Models

Length	27'11"	Headroom	6'3"
Beam	9'11"	Fuel	120 gals.
Draft	2'9"	Water	71 gals.
Weight	9,500#	Waste	25 gals.
Clearance	11'2"	Hull Type	Semi-Disp.

Cape Dory 28 Open

1985–94

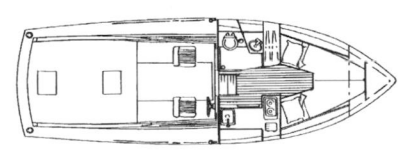

Classic Downeast bass fisherman with full-keel hull combines simple elegance with spacious cockpit, comfortable cabin accommodations. Uncluttered cockpit with flush engine hatch offers lots of room for tackle boxes and rods. Very roomy interior for a 28-foot boat with quality teak joiner work, full galley, generous storage. Note good helm visibility, wide side decks, unusually tall windshield. Truly excellent fit and finish throughout. Cruise at 12–14 knots with single 200hp Volvo diesel (about 16 knots top).

Prices Not Provided for Pre-1995 Models

Length	27'11"	Headroom	6'0"
Beam	9'11"	Fuel	120 gals.
Draft	2'9"	Water	31 gals.
Weight	8,000#	Cockpit	93 sq. ft.
Clearance	8'0"	Hull Type	Semi-Disp.

Cruisers & Sedans

Cruisers & Sedans

Carver 27/530 Montego

1986–93

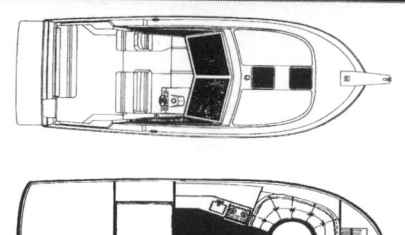

Maxi-volume cruiser packs impressive living space into modest 27-foot hull. Midcabin floorplan features unusual circular dinette/double berth forward in addition to compact galley, double-entry head compartment. Note stand-up dressing area in midcabin entryway. Swim platform was replaced in 1990 with more elaborate bolt-on unit. Unimpressive fit and finish; stiff ride in a chop. Cruise at 20 knots with 205hp sterndrive gas engines. Called Carver 27 Montego in 1986–90, 530 Montego in 1991–92, 300 Montego in 1993.

Prices Not Provided for Pre-1995 Models

Length w/Platform	29'2"	Clearance	9'0"
Hull Length	27'3"	Fuel	120 gals.
Beam	10'0"	Water	41 gals.
Draft	2'10"	Hull Type	Modified-V
Weight	6,900#	Deadrise Aft	8°

Carver 27/630/300 Santego

1988–93

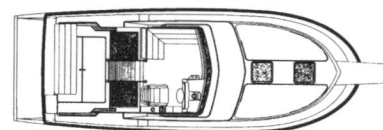

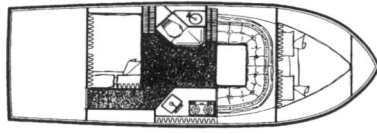

Good-selling family cruiser with full-beam interior (called 27 Santego in 1988–90; 630 Santego in 1991–92; 300 Santego in 1993) appealed to entry-level buyers on a budget. Spacious midcabin floorplan with V-berth, convertible dinette sleeps four adults, two kids. Hatch in cockpit sole provides good access to engines. Note foredeck sun lounge, built-in cockpit seating. Low-deadrise hull is a hard ride in a chop. Finish is less than impressive. Twin 205hp gas sterndrives cruise at 19–20 knots (around 30 knots top).

Prices Not Provided for Pre-1995 Models

Length Overall	31'2"	Clearance	9'2"
Hull Length	27'3"	Fuel	100 gals.
Beam	10'0"	Water	41 gals.
Draft	2'8"	Hull Type	Modified-V
Weight	8,400#	Deadrise Aft	8°

Carver 28 Mariner/Voyager

1983–90

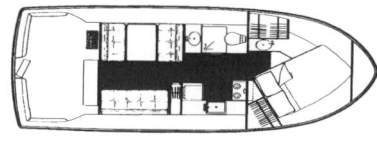

Mariner Interior

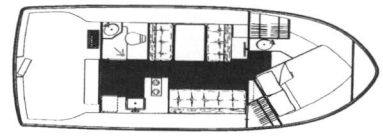

Voyager Interior

Popular 1980s flybridge sedan offered space, comfort at very competitive price. Mariner layout has galley and head forward; Voyager interior has galley and head aft with standard lower helm station. Both layouts have small private stateroom with hanging locker, vanity. Huge flybridge has seating for six with table that converts into full-width sun pad. Stiff ride when the seas pick up. Standard 220hp gas engines (with V-drives) cruise at 18 knots (26–27 knots wide open). One of just a few production 28-foot flybridge boats ever built.

Prices Not Provided for Pre-1995 Models

Length	28'0"	Fuel	150 gals.
Beam	11'1"	Water	51 gals.
Draft	2'10"	Waste	20 gals.
Weight	10,300#	Hull Type	Modified-V
Clearance	9'11"	Deadrise Aft	10°

Carver 28 Riviera

1983–89

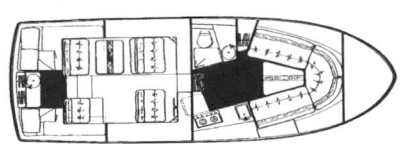

Durable family cruiser with unique aft-cabin layout makes good on promise of small-boat comfort, versatility. Open-air center cockpit with wraparound windshield, seating for six is the focal point of the boat. Forward cabin features convertible U-shaped dinette, enclosed head, compact galley. Small aft cabin with twin berths has four opening ports for ventilation. Note good engine access, wide side decks, standard bow pulpit. Low-deadrise hull is a stiff ride in a chop. Twin 220hp gas engines cruise at 18 knots (25–26 knots top).

Prices Not Provided for Pre-1995 Models

Length	28'0"	Cockpit	NA
Beam	11'1"	Fuel	160 gals.
Draft	2'10"	Water	52 gals.
Weight	8,900#	Hull Type	Modified-V
Clearance	9'3"	Deadrise Aft	10°

Carver 280 MidCabin Express

1988–98

25 Montego Interior, 1988–92

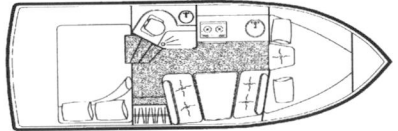

280 Interior, 1993–98

See Page 516 For Value Estimates

Lightweight express (called the Carver 25 Montego in 1988–91; 528 Montego in 1991–92) squeezed lots of living space into beamy, 28-foot hull. Original Montego interior was completely redesigned in 1993 when Carver reintroduced this model as 280 MidCabin Express. Where the original 25 Montego slept four, the 280 MidCabin interior sleeps six. Notable features include double-wide helm seat, removable cockpit table, bow pulpit, swim platform. Cruise at 22 knots with standard 300hp gas sterndrive (30+ knots top).

Length	29'10"	Fuel	100 gals.
Beam	9'6"	Water	25 gals.
Draft	3'3"	Waste	18 gals.
Weight	5,900#	Hull Type	Modified-V
Clearance	NA	Deadrise Aft	19°

Carver 280 Sedan

1991–98

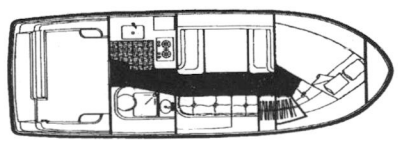

Compact coastal cruiser (called the Carver 26 Sedan in 1991–92) is among the smallest flybridge boats ever produced. Wide beam creates roomy interior with standing headroom. Cabin extends well forward on deck to maximize interior space. Layout includes convertible dinette aft, U-shaped galley, enclosed head. Lower helm was a popular option. Compact flybridge seats two guests aft of the helm. Modified-V hull isn't fond of a chop. Twin MerCruiser (or Volvo) V-6 sterndrives cruise at 18–20 knots (about 30 knots top).

See Page 516 For Value Estimates

Length w/Pulpit	29'11"	Fuel	112 gals.
Hull Length	27'9"	Water	45 gals.
Beam	9'6"	Waste	20 gals.
Draft	2'4"	Hull Type	Modified-V
Weight	9,778#	Deadrise Aft	15°

Cruisers & Sedans

Carver 28 Sedan; 300 Sedan

1991–93

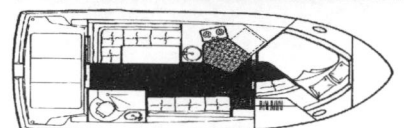

Lower Helm Floorplan

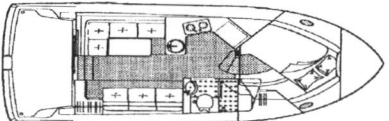

No Lower Helm

Prices Not Provided for Pre-1995 Models

Beamy small sedan (called the 28 Sedan in 1991–92; 300 Sedan in 1993) remains among the "biggest" 28-footers ever built. Offered with two floorplans, one with standard lower helm and small head, the other—less popular—with large forward head but no lower helm. Berths are provided for six in either layout, and a solid door (rather than a curtain) provides stateroom privacy. Flybridge is huge for a boat this size with seating that converts into a sun lounge. Very small cockpit. Crusader 260hp gas engines cruise at 18 knots (25–26 knots top).

Length Overall	32'4"	Clearance	9'1"
Length w/Platform	30'6"	Fuel	150 gals.
Beam	11'10"	Water	51 gals.
Draft	2'11"	Hull Type	Modified-V
Weight	12,500#	Deadrise Aft	16°

Carver 29 Monterey

1985–86

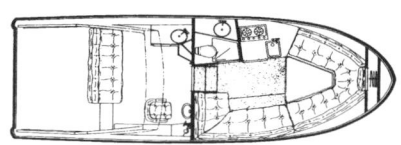

Inexpensive cruiser from 1980s appealed to entry-level buyers with an eye for value. Inboard power is rare in a boat this size—most express boats feature sterndrive power. Full-beam interior with wraparound lounge seating, compact galley, convertible dinette sleeps four. Large cockpit is perfect for entertaining, big enough for fishing. Note walk-through windshield, reverse radar arch, bow pulpit. Roomy engine compartment is a plus. Cruise at 18 knots with twin 270hp gas engines (26–28 knots top).

Prices Not Provided for Pre-1995 Models

Length w/Pulpit	32'9"	Clearance	10'8"
Hull Length	28'8"	Fuel	200 gals.
Beam	11'1"	Water	52 gals.
Draft	2'10"	Hull Type	Modified-V
Weight	10,000#	Deadrise Aft	10°

Carver 30 Allegra

1989–90

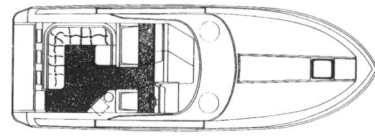

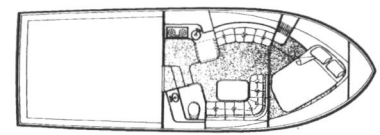

Value-priced sportcruiser designed for entry-level buyers lasted only two years in production. Highlights include color-coordinated hull graphics, reverse radar arch, bolt-on swim platform, large cockpit with seating for a small crowd. Roomy interior boasts bow stateroom with double berth and privacy door, fully equipped galley, enclosed head with sink and shower. Note transom door and foredeck sun lounge. Uneven fit and finish. Cruise at 20 knots (30 knots top) with twin 235hp gas sterndrives.

Prices Not Provided for Pre-1995 Models

Length Overall	34'0"	Fuel	150 gals.
Hull Length	30'8"	Water	51 gals.
Beam	11'0"	Waste	37 gals.
Draft	3'1"	Hull Type	Modified-V
Weight	10,950#	Deadrise Aft	18°

Cruisers & Sedans

Carver 30/634/340 Santego

1988–94

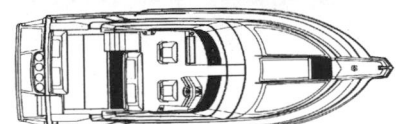

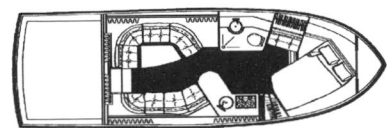

Spacious party boat (called the Carver 30 Santego in 1988–90, 634 Santego in 1991–92, 340 Santego in 1993–94) has more interior volume than just about any other 30-footer on the market. Full-beam cabin is laid out on a single level with facing salon settees, complete galley. Large forward stateroom has angled double berth, bi-fold privacy doors. Flybridge was redesigned in 1991 with walk-through to foredeck. Note cheap-looking bolt-on swim platform. Available with V-drive inboards or sterndrive power.

Prices Not Provided for Pre-1995 Models

Length	33'7"	Headroom	6'4"
Beam	11'0"	Fuel	150 gals.
Draft	3'1"	Water	48 gals.
Weight	11,150#	Hull Type	Deep-V
Clearance	14'10"	Deadrise Aft	19°

Carver 310 Mid-Cabin Express

1995–97

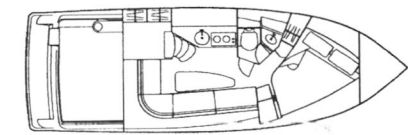

Standard Floorplan

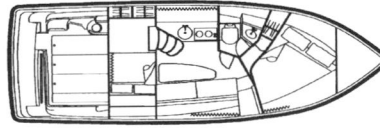

Alternate Floorplan

See Page 516 For Value Estimates

Curvaceous 1990s express with large cockpit, roomy interior gives cruising families plenty of breathing space. Standard layout has spacious salon with L-shaped lounge aft that converts to double berth; alternate floorplan offered conventional midcabin berth at expense of smaller salon. Wraparound cockpit seating converts to sun lounge. Additional features include foredeck sun pad, walk-through windshield, bow pulpit, side exhausts, radar arch. Offered with inboard or sterndrive power.

Length	31'3"	Fuel	180 gals.
Beam	10'10"	Water	56 gals.
Draft	2'8"	Waste	28 gals.
Weight	11,400#	Hull Type	Modified-V
Clearance, Arch	10'11"	Deadrise Aft	12°

Carver 310 Santego

1994–98

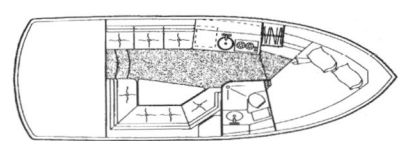

See Page 516 For Value Estimates

Maxi-volume 1990s cruiser with amenities of small apartment had great appeal to entry-level boaters. Full-beam interior is arranged on a single level with double stateroom forward, compact galley, head with shower. U-shaped salon dinette converts to double berth; portside lounge converts to upper and lower bunk and includes privacy curtain. Center-console flybridge offers seating for five and full walkaround accessibility. Offered with inboard or sterndrive power. Note fuel increase in 1997 to 164 gallons.

Length w/Pulpit	33'5"	Clearance	9'10"
Hull Length	31'3"	Fuel	130/164 gals.
Beam	11'0"	Water	66 gals.
Draft	2'9"	Waste	30 gals.
Weight	12,500#	Hull Type	Modified-V

Cruisers & Sedans

Carver 32 Convertible

1984–93

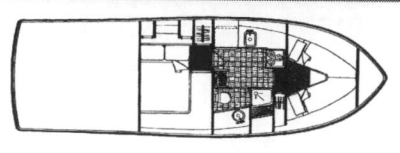

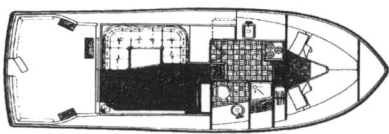

Popular family convertible became one of Carver's best-selling boats in the 1980s. Innovative two-stateroom floorplan is made possible by locating engines under cockpit sole. Highlights include full-size galley refrigerator, standard lower helm, roomy cockpit with centerline transom door, stall shower in head. Cockpit is large enough for two anglers and their gear. Compact flybridge seats four. Bow pulpit and swim platform were standard. Cruise at 16 knots with Crusader 270hp V-drive gas inboards (mid 20s top).

Prices Not Provided for Pre-1995 Models

Length	32'0"	Fuel	220 gals.
Beam	11'7"	Water	84 gals.
Draft	2'10"	Waste	20 gals.
Weight	12,600#	Hull Type	Modified-V
Clearance	11'6"	Deadrise Aft	10°

Carver 32 Montego

1987–91

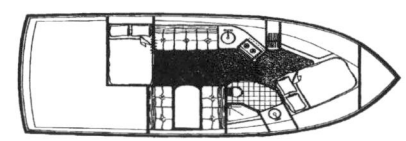

Affordable sportcruiser introduced in 1987 combined sporty styling with family friendly layout, affordable price. Full-beam interior sleeps six, boasts private forward stateroom, four-person convertible dinette, compact galley with under-counter refrigerator, double-entry head with stall shower. Roomy bi-level cockpit has generic L-shaped companion seat, numerous stowage compartments, walk-through transom. Twin 270hp V-drive gas engines will cruise at 18–20 knots (just under 30 knots top).

Prices Not Provided for Pre-1995 Models

Length	32'3"	Fuel	192 gals.
Beam	12'4"	Water	92 gals.
Draft	2'9"	Waste	20 gals.
Weight	13,000#	Hull Type	Modified-V
Clearance	9'0"	Deadrise Aft	6°

Carver 320 Voyager

1994–99

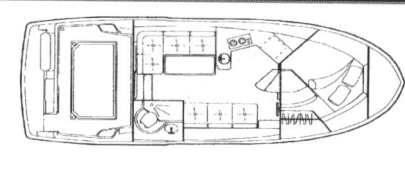

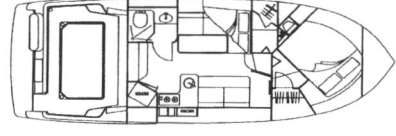

Sporty family sedan with oversized flybridge is stylish, versatile, fun to drive. Roomy interior—available with one or two staterooms—includes compact galley, head with sink and shower, private master stateroom. More cabin storage than most 32-footers. Lower helm was a popular option. Cockpit is large enough for light-tackle fishing. Note integral swim platform with fender stowage, hidden boarding ladder. Narrow side decks make bow access a bit tricky. Twin 265hp gas inboards cruise at 16 knots (27–28 knots top).

See Page 516 For Value Estimates

Length	35'0"	Fuel	188 gals.
Beam	11'10"	Water	56 gals.
Draft	2'11"	Waste	20 gals.
Weight	15,200#	Hull Type	Modified-V
Clearance	NA	Deadrise Aft	16°

Cruisers & Sedans

Carver 32 Mariner; 330 Mariner

1985–96

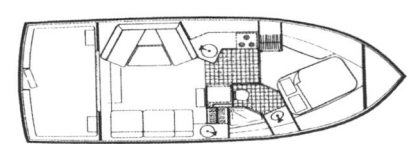

Roomy condo-boat from the late 1980s, early '90s scored with entry-level buyers for expansive accommodations, party-time bridge. Enormous full-beam, single-level interior boasts expansive salon with facing settees, full galley (with upright refrigerator), roomy head with stall shower. Unique salon ladder provides easy access to massive flybridge with walk-through gate to bow. Low-deadrise hull will knock your fillings out in choppy water. Cruise at 16 knots with 260hp gas inboards. Called Carver 330 Mariner in 1994–96.

See Page 516 For Value Estimates

Length w/Pulpit	35'5"	Clearance	10'10"
Hull Length	32'3"	Fuel	192 gals.
Beam	12'4"	Water	92 gals.
Draft	2'9"	Hull Type	Modified-V
Weight	12,000#	Deadrise Aft	6°

Carver 33/35/36 Super Sport

2005–08

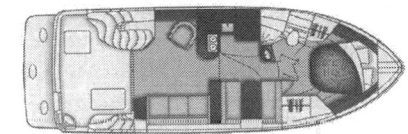

Standard Interior

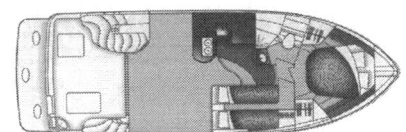

Mid-Cabin Interior

Stylish Carver cruiser (called the 33 SS in 2005–06; 35 SS in 2007; 36 SS in 2008) delivers features buyers demand in a midsize flybridge yacht. Highlights include spacious, full-beam salon, full galley with upright refrigerator, convertible dinette, private bow stateroom, head with separate stall shower. Lots of cabin storage. Wide side decks, molded bridge steps make getting around easy. Large engine room is a plus. Midcabin layout became optional in 2007. Crusader 320hp gas engines cruise at 18 knots (26–28 knots top.)

See Page 561 For Value Estimates

Length	37'3"	Fuel	311 gals.
Beam	13'1"	Water	78 gals.
Draft	3'1"	Waste	37 gals.
Weight	21,753#	Hull Type	Modified-V
Clearance	14'8"	Deadrise Aft	11.5°

Carver 350 Mariner

1997–2003

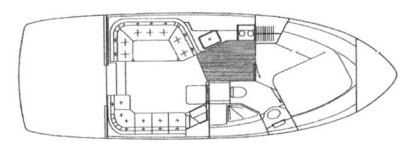

Hugely popular sportcruiser combines enormous, full-beam interior with massive flybridge in what boating purists might describe as a styling train wreck. Spacious cabin floorplan boasts wide-open salon with facing settees, good-size galley, double-entry head with stall shower, private stateroom with offset double berth. Note handy bridge access ladder forward in salon. Party-time bridge seats eight. Foredeck bench seat converts into sun pad. Twin 320hp V-drive gas engines cruise at 14–15 knots (around 20 knots top).

See Page 516 For Value Estimates

Length	36'7"	Fuel	246 gals.
Beam	12'9"	Water	75 gals.
Draft	3'1"	Waste	20 gals.
Weight	18,800#	Headroom	6'3"
Clearance, Arch	14'2"	Hull Type	Modified-V

Cruisers & Sedans

Cruisers & Sedans

Carver 350 Voyager

1993–94

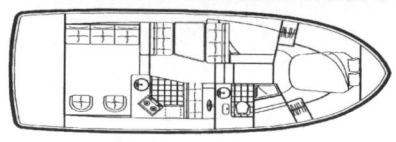

With Optional Lower Helm

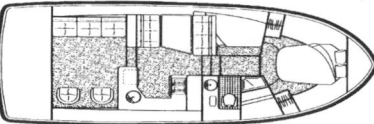

Standard Floorplan

Prices Not Provided for Pre-1995 Models

Length w/Pulpit	39'0"	Fuel	280 gals.
Hull Length	33'10"	Water	101 gals.
Beam	13'3"	Waste	35 gals.
Draft	2'7"	Hull Type	Modified-V
Weight	17,000#	Deadrise Aft	11°

Versatile 1990s sedan is ideally suited for entry-level boaters with growing families. Super-spacious interior includes two double staterooms, head with separate stall shower, split-level salon/galley with booth dinette. Lower helm station was a popular option. Flybridge is one of the largest to be found on a 35-footer, but cockpit is very small. Note handy pass-through from galley to bridge. Bow pulpit, transom door and swim platform were standard. Standard 300hp gas engines cruise at 18–19 knots (about 28 knots top).

Carver 538 Montego/380 Express

1990–94

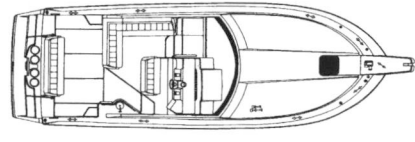

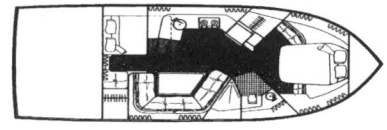

Prices Not Provided for Pre-1995 Models

Length w/Pulpit	41'3"	Fuel	250 gals.
Beam	13'2"	Water	91 gals.
Draft	3'4"	Waste	35 gals.
Weight	16,000#	Hull Type	Modified-V
Clearance	15'11"	Deadrise Aft	19°

Sporty 1990s express with roomy interior offered full array of amenities at very affordable price. Highlights include privacy doors for both staterooms (very unusual), head with separate stall shower, large galley with generous storage and counter space. Radar arch, bow pulpit, fender racks, cockpit wet bar were standard. Bolt-on swim platform looks cheap. Twin 350hp gas inboards cruise at 16–17 knots and reach a top speed of 25 knots. Called Carver 35 Montego in 1990; 538 Montego in 1991–92; 380 Express in 1993–94.

Carver 36 Mariner

1984–88

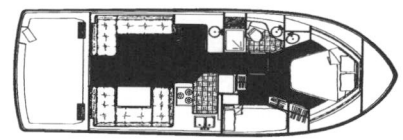

Prices Not Provided for Pre-1995 Models

Length Overall	35'7"	Clearance	13'6"
Length WL	31'4"	Fuel	274 gals.
Beam	12'6"	Water	103 gals.
Draft	3'2"	Hull Type	Modified-V
Weight	19,500#	Deadrise Aft	8°

Mega-volume cruiser with zero eye appeal offers big-boat accommodations in modest 36-foot hull. Enormous full-beam, single-level interior features facing salon settees, large galley with upright refrigerator, head with stall shower, private bow stateroom with double berth and sink. Massive bridge—accessed from cockpit or salon—seats a small crowd with huge sun lounge aft. Note wide side decks, foredeck sun pad, radar arch, cockpit transom door. Cruise at 16 knots with 350hp gas inboards (mid 20s top).

Carver 36 Mariner

2004–Current

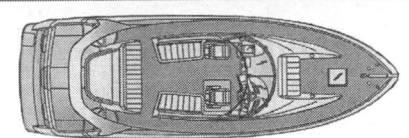

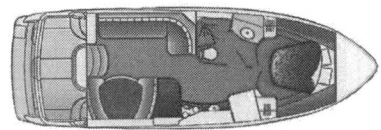

Updated version of Carver's original 36 Mariner (1984–88) with spacious single-level interior is designed for entertaining on a grand scale. Full-beam salon features posh Ultraleather seating, large dinette, high-gloss cherry woodwork, full entertainment center, large galley area. Extra-large head contains separate stall shower. Party-time flybridge can accommodate a small crowd. Low-deadrise hull can be a stiff ride in a chop. Portly profile is hard on the eye. Cruise at 20 knots (28 top) with 375hp gas inboards.

See Page 516 For Value Estimates

Length	36'7"	Fuel	250 gals.
Beam	12'9"	Water	75 gals.
Draft	37"	Waste	31 gals.
Weight	19,500#	Hull Type	Modified-V
Clearance, Arch	14'2"	Deadrise Aft	4°

Carver 360 Sport Sedan

2003–06

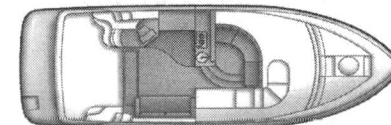

Main Deck Plan

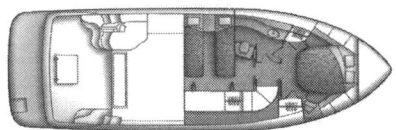

Lower Level Plan

Versatile, high-freeboard cruising yacht with condo-style accommodations is a true home away from home. Spacious two-stateroom interior includes raised dinette/lounge area forward of salon, expansive galley, large head compartment, glossy cherry trim. Tiered salon windows admit plenty of natural lighting. Hardwood floor in galley area is a nice touch. Note molded cockpit steps to bridge and side decks. Engineroom is a tight fit. Twin 320hp gas inboards cruise at 18 knots and top out in the low 20s.

See Page 561 For Value Estimates

Length	37'8"	Fuel	280 gals.
Beam	13'2"	Water	75 gals.
Draft	2'7"	Waste	25 gals.
Weight	24,746#	Hull Type	Modified-V
Clearance, Arch	14'6"	Deadrise Aft	14°

Carver 34/638/380 Santego

1989–2002

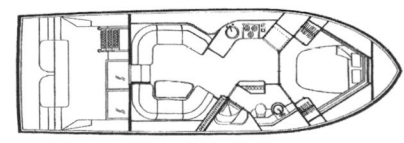

Strong buyer demand kept this maxi-volume sportcruiser (called Carver 34 Santego in 1989–90; Carver 638 Santego in 1991–92) in production for well over a decade. Expansive full-beam salon with facing settees, large galley creates guest-friendly layout seldom encountered in a boat this size. Notable features include private bow stateroom, large head with stall shower, huge flybridge with foredeck access gate. Bolt-on swim platform looks cheap, but roomy cockpit is a plus. Twin 300hp V-drive gas inboards cruise at 18 knots.

See Page 516 For Value Estimates

Length w/Pulpit	41'8"	Fuel	216 gals.
Beam	13'2"	Water	90 gals.
Draft	3'4"	Waste	37 gals.
Weight	19,300#	Hull Type	Modified-V
Clearance	NA	Deadrise Aft	19°

Cruisers & Sedans

Carver 38 Santego

1988–90

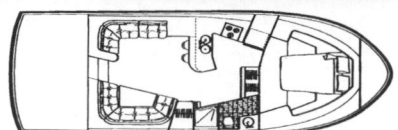
Single-Stateroom Floorplan

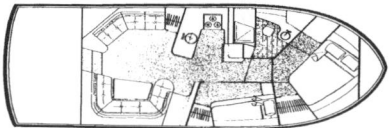
Optional 2-Stateroom Layout (1990 Only)

Prices Not Provided for Pre-1995 Models

Versatile family cruiser from the late 1980s appealed to entry-level buyers with an eye for value. Full-beam interior provides far more entertaining space than most 38-footers. Highlights include large stateroom with privacy door, well-equipped galley, cavernous, full-beam salon with facing settees, built-in cockpit seating. Flybridge cutout reveals a set of molded steps leading to the foredeck. Bolt-on swim platform looks cheap. Twin 330hp gas inboards cruise at 14–15 knots (low 20s top).

Length w/Pulpit	37'6"	Fuel	265 gals.
Beam	14'0"	Water	92 gals.
Draft	3'5"	Waste	40 gals.
Weight	19,000#	Hull Type	Modified-V
Clearance	NA	Deadrise Aft	12°

Carver 38 Super Sport

2005–Current

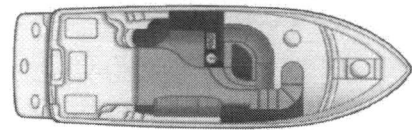

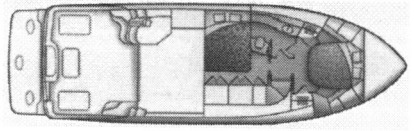

See Page 516 For Value Estimates

Rakish sport sedan combines European styling with American-bred comfort, versatile layout. Well-appointed interior with cherry trim features spacious, full-beam salon with raised dinette, expansive galley with hardwood floor, two double staterooms. Extended swim platform can carry a small dinghy. Optional sport package adds rod holders, livewell, in-deck fishboxes. Note sizeable cockpit, small foredeck, slender side decks. Low-deadrise hull isn't too fond of a chop. MerCruiser 375hp gas engines cruise at 20 knots (28–29 knots top).

Length	39'11"	Fuel	334 gals.
Beam	13'5"	Water	86 gals.
Draft	2'4"	Waste	45 gals.
Weight	25,000#	Hull Type	Modified-V
Clearance	14'1"	Deadrise Aft	14°

Carver 42/43 Super Sport

2006–Current

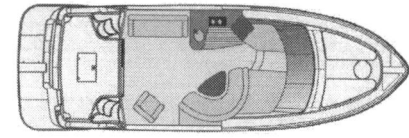
Upper Level

Lower Level

See Page 517 For Value Estimates

Feature-rich sport sedan with expansive, full-beam interior couples big-boat luxury with traditional Carver quality, value. Combined salon/galley/dinette with cherry paneling offers spacious accommodations with room for nonstop entertaining. Both staterooms feature queen berths—unusual in a boat this size. Note washer/dryer beneath galley sole, low galley counters. Party-time bridge can seat a small crowd. Bridge overhang shades large cockpit. Optional Volvo 370hp diesels with IPS drives cruise at 24 knots (about 28 knots top).

Length	43'7"	Fuel	400 gals.
Beam	13'11"	Water	90 gals.
Draft	3'10"	Waste	50 gals.
Weight	33,650#	Hull Type	Modified-V
Clearance, Arch	19'7"	Deadrise Aft	NA

Chaparral 26/27/270 Signature

1992–2000

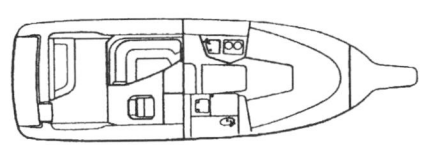

Good-running 1990s sportcruiser (called Signature 26 in 1992; Signature 27 in 1993–99; Signature 270 in 2000) delivered impressive mix of modern styling, roomy accommodations, excellent open-water performance. Highlights include well-appointed interior with sliding windows, woodgrain dash, flip-up helm seat, cockpit dinette with removable table, transom door, molded bow pulpit. Above-average fit and finish. Single 300hp 7.4L MerCruiser I/O will cruise in the mid 20s and reach a top speed of 34–35 knots.

See Page 517 For Value Estimates

Length w/Pulpit	28'5"	Fuel	105 gals.
Beam	9'0"	Water	25 gals.
Draft, Drive Up	2'1"	Waste	25 gals.
Draft, Drive Down	2'9"	Hull Type	Modified-V
Weight	6,249#	Deadrise Aft	20°

Chaparral 270 Signature

2007–Current

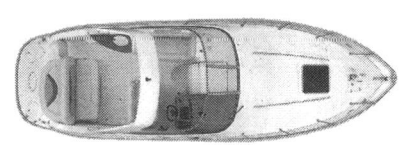

Sporty 27-footer with generic midcabin interior couples signature Chaparral quality with aggressive styling, first-rate amenities. Cockpit features include full-length rear sun pad, portside lounge seat, double helm seat with flip-up bolsters, wet bar with portable ice chest. Like most trailerable cruisers this size, cabin accommodations are a bit claustrophobic due to slender 8'6" beam. Note power engine compartment hatch, transom storage bin under sun pad. Single 320hp MerCruiser I/O tops out at close to 40 knots.

See Page 517 For Value Estimates

Length	28'11"	Fuel	87 gals.
Beam	8'6"	Water	29 gals.
Draft, Up	1'5"	Waste	28 gals.
Draft, Down	2'9"	Hull Type	Modified-V
Weight	7,450#	Deadrise Aft	18°

Chaparral 270/280 Signature

2003–09

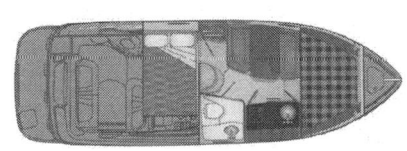

Stylish family cruiser (called Signature 270 in 2003–05; Signature 280 in 2006–09) offers proven mix of quality construction, practical accommodations. Well-appointed cabin features fixed dinette, full-size galley, premium hardware and fabrics. Guest-friendly cockpit includes wet bar, dual helm seat with flip-up cushions, removable table, portable ice chest. Walk-through windshield make bow access easy. Note transom storage locker, extended swim platform. Cruise at 26–28 knots with 225hp Volvo sterndrives (around 40 knots top).

See Page 518 For Value Estimates

Length w/Platform	29'3"	Fuel	100 gals.
Beam	9'6"	Water	29 gals.
Draft, Up	1'5"	Waste	28 gals.
Draft, Down	2'9"	Hull Type	Modified-V
Weight	9,100#	Deadrise Aft	20°

Cruisers & Sedans

Chaparral 28/29 Signature

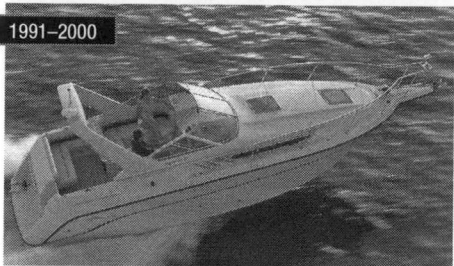

1991–2000

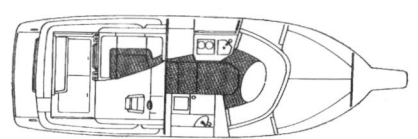

Popular family cruiser (called Signature 28 in 1991–92; 29 Signature in 1993–2000) hit the sweet spot with savvy buyers focused on quality, durability. Carpeted cabin boasts wraparound sofa, full galley, convertible dinette, spacious aft cabin with privacy door. Super-practical cockpit design has settee/dinette opposite helm. Note narrow side decks, foldaway stern seat. Good engine access. Bow pulpit, radar arch, cockpit wet bar were standard. Twin 190hp MerCruiser I/Os cruise in the mid 20s (about 35 knots top).

See Page 518 For Value Estimates

Length w/Pulpit	31'11"	Weight	8,200#
Hull Length	29'3"	Fuel	121 gals.
Beam	9'9"	Water	30 gals.
Draft, Up	1'11"	Hull Type	Modified-V
Draft, Down	2'9"	Deadrise Aft	20°

Chaparral 280/290 Signature

2001–09

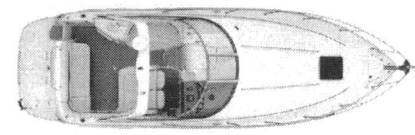

Popular sportcruiser (marketed as Signature 280 in 2001–03; Signature 290 since 2004) combines customary Chaparral quality with posh accommodations, impressive open-water performance. Highlights include well-appointed interior with cherry cabinets, well-planned cockpit with wraparound lounge seating, cockpit wet bar, extended swim platform. Note roomy engine compartment, walk-through windshield. Transom storage trunk can stow dive tank and fenders. Twin 270hp Volvo I/Os top out at 42–44 knots. Replaced with all-new 290 model in 2010.

See Page 518 For Value Estimates

Length w/Platform	30'8"	Fuel	115 gals.
Beam	10'0"	Water	25 gals.
Draft, Up	2'1"	Waste	28 gals.
Draft, Down	2'9"	Hull Type	Modified-V
Weight	9,700#	Deadrise Aft	18°

Chaparral 300 Signature

1998–2003

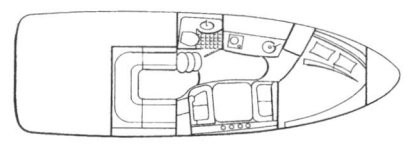

Smooth-running express with graceful styling matched Chaparral promise of leading-edge design, upscale accommodations. Open-plan interior with teak trim boasts full-size galley with generous storage, roomy midcabin with U-shaped settee, Corian counters. Cockpit seats six with double-wide helm seat, companion lounge, U-shaped settee aft. Note foldaway stern seat, walk-through windshield. Gas-assist hatch provides easy access to engine compartment. Volvo 250hp sterndrives cruise in the mid-to-high 20s (around 40 knots top).

See Page 518 For Value Estimates

Length w/Platform	31'3"	Clearance, Arch	11'0"
Beam	10'3"	Fuel	153 gals.
Draft, Up	2'1"	Water	30 gals.
Draft, Down	2'9"	Hull Type	Modified-V
Weight	9,800#	Deadrise Aft	20°

Cruisers & Sedans

Chaparral 30/31 Signature

1990–97

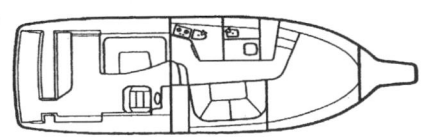

Full-bodied sportcruiser (called 30 Signature in 1990–92; 31 Signature in 1993–97)) set high standards for expressboat design, comfort. Well-finished midcabin interior sleeps six, includes roomy aft cabin, wraparound salon sofa/dinette. Curtains separate fore and aft double berths from main cabin. Galley is on the small side with modest storage and counter space. Single-level cockpit features lounge seating forward, foldaway bench seating aft. Helm console updated in 1993. Cruise at 18 knots (30+ knots top) with 230hp sterndrive power.

See Page 518 For Value Estimates

Length w/Pulpit	33'2"	Weight	9,750#
Hull Length	30'6"	Fuel	150 gals.
Beam	10'9"	Water	40 gals.
Draft, Up	1'11"	Hull Type	Modified-V
Draft, Down	2'9"	Deadrise Aft	17°

Chaparral 310 Signature

2004–09

Luxurious family cruiser introduced in 2004 took Chaparral reputation for quality, owner satisfaction to the next level. Posh interior with high-gloss cherry cabinets, hardwood flooring, designer furnishings sleeps six. Cockpit highlights include sun lounge opposite helm, mini-galley with sink, well-designed helm, U-shaped aft seating. Electric hatch offers good access to engine compartment. Note walk-through windshield, transom storage locker. Cruise at 25 knots (high 30s top) with twin 270hp Volvo gas I/Os. Replaced with new 310 Signature model in 2010.

See Page 518 For Value Estimates

Length w/Platform	33'4"	Fuel	147 gals.
Beam	10'7"	Water	29 gals.
Draft, Up	2'1"	waste	28 gals.
Draft, Down	2'9"	Hull Type	Modified-V
Weight	11,375#	Deadrise Aft	17°

Chaparral 330 Signature

2003–09

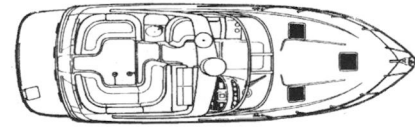

Polished big-water cruiser with innovative interior, thoughtful cockpit design offers something different in modern express-boat design. Unique cabin layout with circular seating forward, dual dinettes, private aft cabin is versatile, comfortable, luxurious. Partial standing headroom in midcabin entryway is a plus. Centerline transom door provides easy access to integral swim platform. Note twin transom storage lockers, walk-through windshield. Twin 300hp I/Os deliver top speed in the range of 40 knots. Replaced with new 330 Signature model in 2011.

See Page 518 For Value Estimates

Length w/Platform	35'0"	Fuel	170 gals.
Beam	11'3"	Water	45 gals.
Draft, Up	2'1"	Waste	28 gals.
Draft, Down	3'2"	Hull Type	Modified-V
Weight	13,400#	Deadrise Aft	19°

Cruisers & Sedans

Chaparral 350 Signature

2001–09

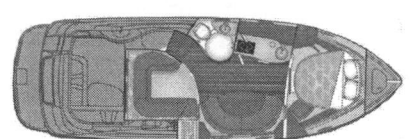

Quality construction, luxurious accommodations, solid performance make this midsize express a tough act to follow. Highlights include spacious cabin with cherry cabinetry and large aft cabin, ergonomic helm layout with tiered gauges, cockpit galley, transom storage trunk, generous fuel capacity. Pocket door offers privacy for forward stateroom. Electric hatch provides easy access to engines. Exceptionally well-finished boat isn't inexpensive. Twin 375hp gas I/Os cruise in the low 30s (40+ knots top). Replaced with updated 350 Signature model in 2010.

See Page 518 For Value Estimates

Length w/Platform	37'0"	Fuel	240 gals.
Beam	11'10"	Water	40 gals.
Draft, Up	2'1"	Waste	28 gals.
Draft, Down	2'9"	Hull Type	Modified-V
Weight	15,000#	Deadrise Aft	18°

Chris Craft 272/282/30 Crowne

1991–97

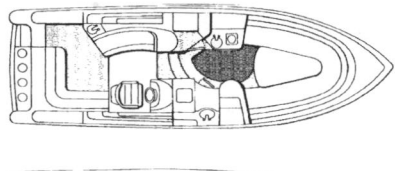

Economy-class express (called 272 Crowne in 1991–92; 282 Crowne in 1993–94; 30 Crowne in 1995–97) targets entry-level buyers with an eye for value. Generic midcabin interior with full galley, enclosed head with shower, sleeps four. Aft stateroom privacy door is a nice touch. Roomy cockpit features companion lounge, double-wide helm seat, foldaway rear bench, sink with stowage under. Note walk-through windshield, bow pulpit, radar arch. Twin 190hp sterndrives top out in the 30- to 35-knot range.

See Page 518 For Value Estimates

Length w/Pulpit	31'6"	Weight	8,400#
Hull Length	29'5"	Fuel	100 gals.
Beam	10'0"	Water	25 gals.
Draft, Up	1'10"	Hull Type	Modified-V
Draft, Down	3'2"	Deadrise Aft	16°

Chris Craft 28 Corsair

2003–08

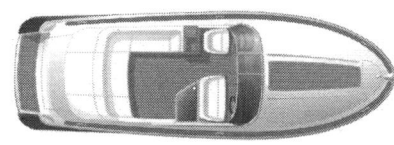

Classic Chris Craft runabout combines retro styling with quality construction, top-shelf materials. Highlights include ultra-plush cockpit seating, old-world dash layout, custom windshield, flawless gelcoat. Curved foredeck conceals useful cuddy cabin with V-berth, portable head. Electric hatch provides easy access to engine compartment. Meticulous fit and finish. Volvo 280hp sterndrives cruise in the mid 20s; optional 240hp Yanmar diesels cruise at a fast 35 knots. Premium price gives new meaning to sticker shock.

See Page 518 For Value Estimates

Length	28'0"	Clearance	5'5"
Beam	10'0"	Fuel	150 gals.
Draft, Up	1'11"	Water	35 gals.
Draft, Down	3'6"	Hull Type	Deep-V
Weight	7,500#	Deadrise Aft	20°

Cruisers & Sedans

Chris Craft 28 Launch

2003–09

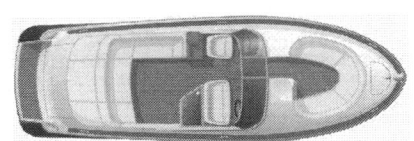

Retro-style bowrider with wide 10-foot beam delivers compelling mix of quality, elegance seldom seen in a production boat. Highlights include ultra-plush cockpit seating, old-world dash layout, custom windshield, flawless gelcoat. Electric hatch provides easy access to engine compartment. Cockpit cooler, transom shower, flip-up bucket seats are standard. Roomy head compartment; large fuel capacity. Premium price may induce a heart attack. Single 385hp gas MerCruiser tops out at 40 knots; twin 300hp Mercs reach 45+ knots.

See Page 518 For Value Estimates

Length	28'0"	Clearance	5'5"
Beam	10'0"	Fuel	150 gals.
Draft, Up	1'11"	Water	35 gals.
Draft, Down	3'6"	Hull Type	Deep-V
Weight	7,500#	Deadrise Aft	20°

Chris Craft 280/284 Amerosport

1987–90

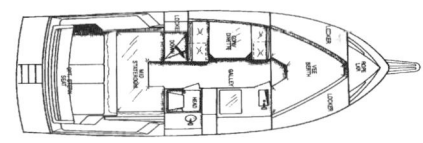

Gaudy express cruiser with overdone graphics, cheap bolt-on swim platform is a good example of why Chris Craft lost serious market share in the late 1980s, early 1990s. Tall freeboard conceals roomy midcabin interior with stand-up head compartment, full galley, convertible dinette. Topside features include double-wide helm seat, stern cockpit seats, bow pulpit, good engine access. Note high bow rail, so-so fit and finish. Twin Volvo 271hp Duoprop sterndrives cruise at 25–26 knots and deliver a top speed of over 35 knots.

Prices Not Provided for Pre-1995 Models

Length w/Pulpit	31'3"	Clearance	9'0"
Hull Length	27'9"	Fuel	150 gals.
Beam	10'2"	Water	25 gals.
Draft	2'9"	Hull Type	Deep-V
Weight	8,214#	Deadrise Aft	NA

Chris Craft 280/281 Catalina

1977–86

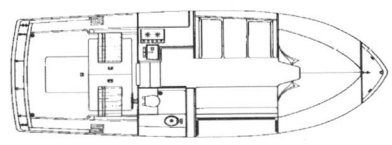

Classic Chris Craft express achieved great popularity throughout the 1980s for practical cabin and cockpit design, rugged construction. Surprisingly open interior with convertible dinette, convertible settee sleeps six. Simple, uncluttered cockpit has plenty of room for anglers. Additional features include wide side decks, wraparound cabin windows, cockpit railings, good engine access. Single 230hp gas inboard will cruise at 15–16 knots; twin gas engines cruise at 20 knots. (Note that 280 model has single engine, 281 has twins.)

Prices Not Provided for Pre-1995 Models

Length	28'11"	Fuel, Single	100 gals.
Beam	10'9"	Fuel, Twin	125 gals.
Draft	2'5"	Water	25 gals.
Weight	7,000#	Hull Type	Modified-V
Clearance	8'6"	Deadrise Aft	15°

Cruisers & Sedans

Chris Craft 292 Sunbridge

1986–89

Sporty family sedan paired solid construction with common-sense layout, modest price. Wide-open interior with wraparound cabin windows, convertible settee sleeps four adults, two kids. Roomy, uncluttered cockpit is well suited for fishing, swimming, lounging. Twin cockpit hatches provide good access to the engines. Additional features include wide side decks, bridge seating for five, bow pulpit, swim platform. So-so fit and finish. Twin 220hp gas inboards cruise at 18 knots and top out in the high 20s.

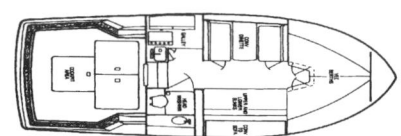

Prices Not Provided for Pre-1995 Models

Length	28'11"	Fuel	125 gals.
Beam	10'9"	Water	25 gals.
Draft	2'3"	Cockpit	NA
Weight	7,800#	Hull Type	Modified-V
Clearance	9'4"	Deadrise Aft	NA

Chris Craft 300/308 Express Cruiser

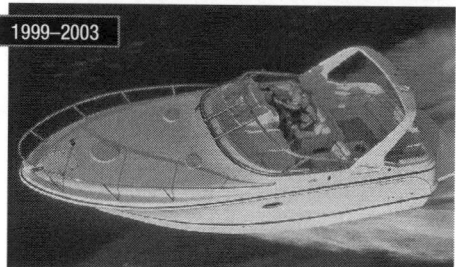

1999–2003

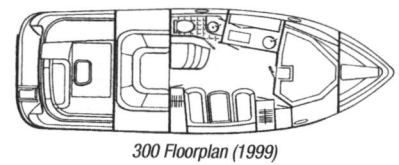

300 Floorplan (1999)

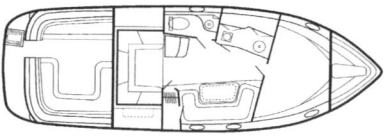

308 Layout (2000–03)

See Page 518 For Value Estimates

Generic family cruiser with smooth-running deep-V hull delivers mediocre blend of styling, comfort, performance. Original interior of the 300 Express—a poorly designed layout with refrigerator under forward berth—was updated in 2000 (eliminating side decks in favor of larger cabin dimensions) when she was reintroduced as the Chris 308 Express. Standard features included radar arch, doublewide helm seat, cockpit wet bar. Note walk-through windshield in 308 model. Twin 250hp sterndrive engines cruise at 25 knots (high 30s top).

Length	32'10"	Fuel	150 gals.
Beam	10'6"	Water	41 gals.
Draft	2'6"	Waste	35 gals.
Weight	10,000#	Hull Type	Deep-V
Clearance	7'3"	Deadrise Aft	21°

Chris Craft 320 Amerosport Sedan

1987–90

Plain-Jane 1980s sedan offered comfortable accommodations, good turn of speed at a low price. Midcabin floorplan is arranged with second stateroom under elevated dinette. Wide beam, wraparound cabin windows create spacious, wide-open interior. Original teak interior joinery was updated in 1990 to light oak. Cockpit includes bench seating at the transom; flybridge is arranged with helm forward, guest seating aft. Bolt-on swim platform looks cheap. Twin 270hp gas inboards cruise at 18 knots (25–26 knots wide open).

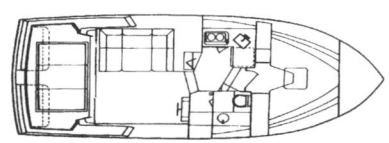

Prices Not Provided for Pre-1995 Models

Length	31'11"	Fuel	200 gals.
Beam	11'11"	Water	50 gals.
Draft	2'8"	Waste	18 gals.
Weight	12,000#	Hull Type	Modified-V
Clearance	10'9"	Deadrise Aft	NA

Cruisers & Sedans

Chris Craft 320/322 Amerosport Express

1987–90

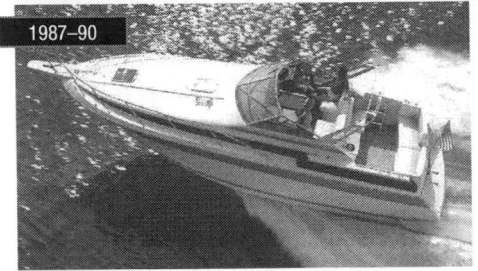

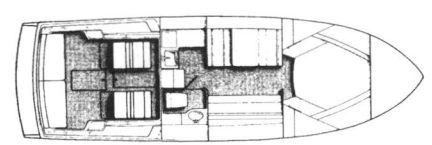

Poorly styled express introduced in 1987 reflected the problems Chris Craft was having in this era. Wide 11'11" beam permits large interior with convertible dinette, full galley, stand-up head with sink, shower. Single-level cockpit features double-wide helm and companion seats, bench seating aft. Radar arch, cockpit lighting, bow pulpit were standard. Note disappointing fit and finish. Twin 270hp inboard gas engines cruise at 18 knots (high 20s top); optional 350hp engines cruise at 22 knots (33–34 knots wide open).

Prices Not Provided for Pre-1995 Models

Length w/Pulpit	34'7"	Fuel	200 gals.
Hull Length	31'11"	Water	50 gals.
Beam	11'11"	Waste	30 gals.
Draft	2'7"	Hull Type	Deep-V
Weight	12,000#	Deadrise Aft	NA

Chris Craft 320/328 Express Cruiser

1997–2003

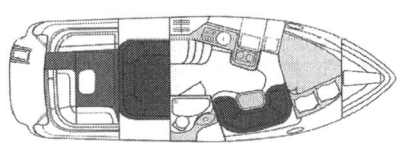

Good-selling express with contemporary midcabin interior appealed to entry-level buyers on a budget. Expansive layout is typical of most modern cruisers with double berths fore and aft, small galley, head with shower. Large cockpit includes wraparound lounge seating, triple helm seat, transom door. Note power engine room hatch, unusual centerline helm position. Trim tabs, transom shower, sport arch, cockpit lights were standard. Twin Volvo 280hp sterndrives cruise at 30 knots (40+ knots wide open).

See Page 518 For Value Estimates

Length	32'0"	Fuel	210 gals.
Beam	11'10"	Water	41 gals.
Draft	3'2"	Waste	35 gals.
Weight	12,000#	Hull Type	Deep-V
Clearance	9'7"	Deadrise Aft	21°

Chris Craft 33 Corsair

2006–Current

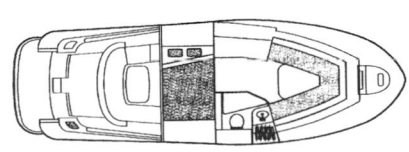

Head-turning speedster blends classic sportboat lines, express-cruiser amenities. Roomy cockpit features double-wide helm/companion seats with flip-up bolsters, U-shaped lounge seating, hot/cold shower. Stowaway top storage is a nice touch. Note classic retro-style helm. Upscale cabin with generous galley, aft berth, cherry cabinetry, sleeps two adults, two kids. Near-flawless gelcoat, trademark Chris Craft tumblehome. Twin 320hp MerCruiser I/Os max out at close to 40 knots. Expensive.

See Page 518 For Value Estimates

Length	34'11"	Fuel	207 gals.
Beam	12'3"	Water	37 gals.
Draft	3'0"	Waste	20 gals.
Weight	13,200#	Hull Type	Deep-V
Clearance	NA	Deadrise Aft	20°

Cruisers & Sedans

Chris Craft 332 Express

1981–87

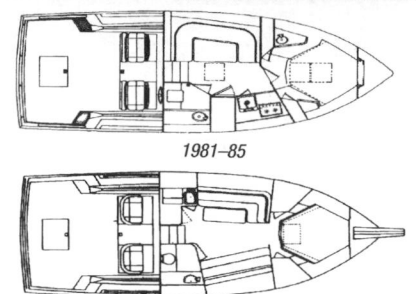

1981–85

1986 Plan

Prices Not Provided for Pre-1995 Models

Popular inboard express from 1980s combined versatile cabin accommodations with expansive, wide-open cockpit. Generous 12'1" beam permits spacious interior—updated in 1986—with convertible dinette, full-size galley, double berth forward. Single-level cockpit is suitable for fishing. Note wide side decks, windshield vents, good engine access. Bolt-on swim platform became standard in 1986. Deep-V hull can handle a pretty good chop. Twin 350hp gas inboards will cruise at 20 knots (close to 30 knots top).

Length	33'0"	Fuel	250 gals.
Beam	12'1"	Water	50 gals.
Draft	2'9"	Headroom	6'2"
Weight	11,560#	Hull Type	Deep-V
Clearance	7'11"	Deadrise Aft	18°

Chris Craft 333 Sedan

1981–87

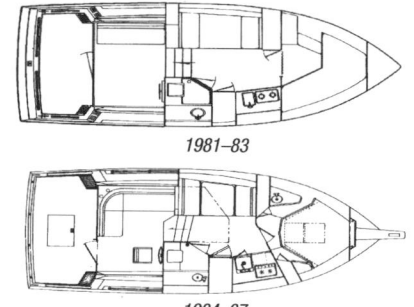

1981–83

1984–87

Prices Not Provided for Pre-1995 Models

Good-selling 1980s sedan offered buyers impressive blend of family-friendly accommodations, good open-water performance. Roomy interior with wraparound windows (slightly updated in 1984) features private bow stateroom, convertible dinette, compact salon with lower helm. Cockpit is too small for any serious fishing pursuits. New flybridge design in 1986 located helm aft with bench seating forward of console. Standard 350hp gas engines cruise at 20 knots and deliver a top speed of close to 30 knots.

Length	33'0"	Fuel	250 gals.
Beam	12'1"	Water	50 gals.
Draft	2'9"	Headroom	6'4"
Weight, Gas	13,000#	Hull Type	Deep-V
Weight, Diesel	14,940#	Deadrise Aft	18°

Chris Craft 336 Mid-Cabin Express

1983–87

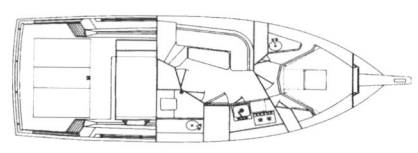

Prices Not Provided for Pre-1995 Models

Sporty 1980s express offered contemporary styling, dependable inboard power at an affordable price. Conventional midcabin interior came with full galley, convertible dinette, private bow stateroom. Roomy cockpit can accommodate several guests. Additional features include wide side decks, bow pulpit, large head with sink and shower. Deep-V hull provides good offshore performance. Twin 340hp gas engines cruise at 20 knots and reach a top speed of 28 knots. Note that she was called the 336 Amerosport in 1987.

Length	33'0"	Cockpit	NA
Beam	12'1"	Fuel	250 gals.
Draft	2'9"	Water	50 gals.
Weight	12,360#	Hull Type	Deep-V
Clearance	7'11"	Deadrise Aft	18°

Chris Craft 33/34 Crowne

1993–97

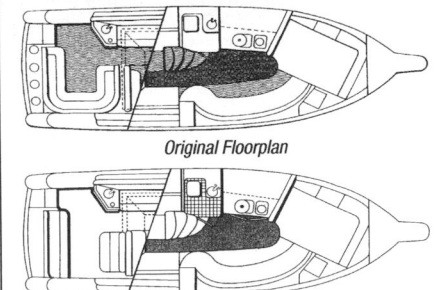

Original Floorplan

Updated Layout

Popular 1990s express—available with sterndrive or inboard power—made good on promise of affordability, performance. Extended settee dominates main cabin; both sleeping areas have privacy curtains. Cockpit redesign in 1996 replaced U-shaped aft lounge with bench seat. Standard features included wet bar, radar arch, transom door, power engine hatch. Twin 235hp I/Os cruise in the low 20s; twin 300hp V-drive inboards cruise at 25 knots. (Note that 33 Crowne has sterndrive power, 34 Crowne is inboard-powered.)

See Page 518 For Value Estimates

Length w/Pulpit	34'10"	Weight	10,000#
Hull Length	32'8"	Fuel	180 gals.
Beam	11'0"	Water	35 gals.
Draft, 34	2'11"	Hull Type	Deep-V
Draft, 33	3'2"	Deadrise Aft	18°

Chris Craft 370 Amerosport; 360 Express

1988–92

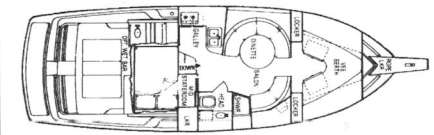

1988–89

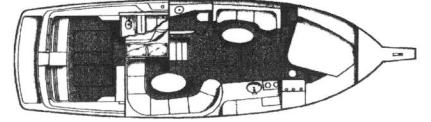

1990–92

Prices Not Provided for Pre-1995 Models

Widebody express cruiser (called 370 Amerosport in 1988–89) embodied bold 1980s styling with spacious floorplan, wide-open cockpit. Two floorplans were used in this boat—the first lasted just a year before being replaced in 1989 by a new layout where the midcabin lounge extends right into the salon. Bi-level cockpit with transom door, double-wide helm seat, wet bar seats six in comfort. Radar arch, bow pulpit were standard. Note cheap materials, poor finish. Twin 300hp gas inboards cruise at 18 knots with a top speed of 25+ knots.

Length	38'7"	Fuel	300 gals.
Beam	13'0"	Water	50 gals.
Draft	3'0"	Cockpit	NA
Weight	15,000#	Hull Type	Deep-V
Clearance	NA	Deadrise Aft	18°

Chris Craft 380 Continental

1993–97

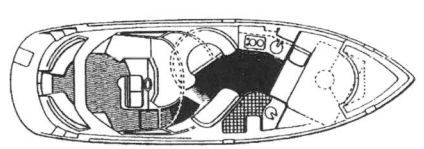

Poor-selling Chris Craft express took 1990s styling, design to unacceptable lengths. Unorthodox floorplan boasts roomy bow stateroom, circular dinette, double-entry head, full galley with generous storage. Circular cockpit is arranged with facing settees aft, centerline helm, centerline transom door. Note walk-through windshield, sunken bow area. Wraparound swim platform has storage lockers, hot/cold shower. A heavy boat, standard 330hp V-drive gas inboards cruise at 15 knots and reach a top speed in the mid 20s.

See Page 518 For Value Estimates

Length Overall	39'7"	Fuel	300 gals.
Hull Length	35'5"	Water	77 gals.
Beam	12'6"	Waste	20 gals.
Draft	3'1"	Hull Type	Modified-V
Weight	15,000#	Deadrise Aft	15°

Cruisers & Sedans

Chris Craft 40 Roamer

2003–08

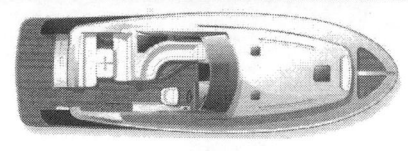

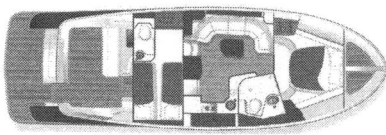

High-end express (called 43 Roamer in 2003–04) delivers unabashed blast of gorgeous styling, luxury amenities, top-tier quality. Upscale interior with wraparound dinette, full-size galley boasts two private staterooms, two heads. Salon is very roomy. Topside highlights include posh cockpit seating, wide side decks, extended swim platform, foredeck seating. Engineroom is a tight fit. Seriously expensive. Cruise at 25 knots with Volvo 480hp diesels (mid 30s top). Volvo IPS gas or diesel engines (with joystick control) available since 2006.

See Page 518 For Value Estimates

Length	43'6"	Water	95 gals.
Beam	14'0"	Waste	35 gals.
Draft	3'2"	Headroom	6'4"
Weight	25,200#	Hull Type	Deep-V
Fuel	400 gals.	Deadrise Aft	20°

Chris Craft 412 Amerosport Express

1987–90

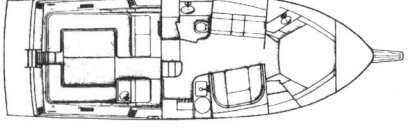

Sporty 1990s express made the cut with Chris Craft buyers looking for eye-catching styling, family-friendly accommodations. Cheap decor, so-so finish compared poorly with other boats of her era. Privacy curtains separate fore, aft sleeping areas from salon; large head stands in contrast to compact galley. Roomy cockpit with wraparound lounge seating, double-wide helm seat can entertain a small crowd. Standard 350hp gas engines cruise at 17–18 knots and top out in the high 20s. Called the Chris Craft 400 Express in 1990.

Prices Not Provided for Pre-1995 Models

Length	38'9"	Fuel	380 gals.
Beam	14'0"	Water	100 gals.
Draft	3'2"	Cockpit	80 sq. ft.
Weight	15,000#	Hull Type	Modified-V
Clearance	9'5"	Deadrise Aft	NA

Crownline 270 CR

2004–09

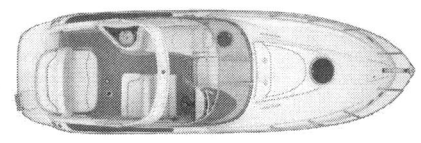

Sporty trailerable cruiser with sleek styling, leading-edge amenities offers big-boat comfort, performance at a reasonable price. Traditional midcabin interior with cherry cabinets includes convertible dinette forward, galley with ceramic cooktop, stand-up head with shower. Flip-up double pilot's seat provides good visibility for docking or close maneuvering. Stern lounge seat—which lifts electrically for engine access—converts to large sun pad. Single 300hp Volvo sterndrive tops out around 35 knots.

See Page 518 For Value Estimates

Length w/Platform	28'8"	Fuel	75 gals.
Beam	8'6"	Water	25 gals.
Draft, Up	1'9"	Waste	25 gals.
Draft, Down	2'10"	Hull Type	Modified-V
Weight	7,400#	Deadrise Aft	18°

Crownline 290 CR

1999–2004

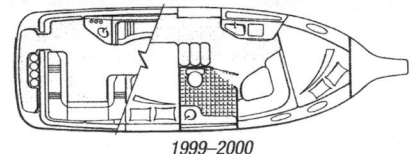

1999–2000

2001–04

Sporty 29-footer introduced in 1999 offered a compelling mix of practical accommodations, spirited performance, attractive price. Original midcabin floorplan had canted forward berth coupled with L-shaped dinette/lounge, spacious head. Updated interior in 2001 has U-shaped dinette/double berth forward, smaller head. Four opening ports, three deck hatches allow excellent cabin ventilation. Note flip-up helm seat, windshield vents, removable rear bench seat. Among several engine choices, twin 250hp MerCruisers top out at 35+ knots.

See Page 519 For Value Estimates

Length w/Pulpit	31'2"	Clearance	8'6"
Hull Length	28'11"	Fuel	146 gals.
Beam	10'4"	Water	20 gals.
Draft, Down	2'11"	Hull Type	Modified-V
Weight	9,000#	Deadrise Aft	16°

Crownline 330 CR

1996–2000

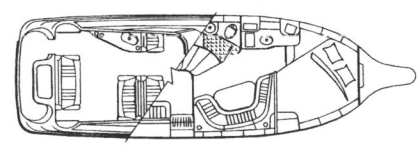

Stylish family express from late 1990s combined comfort, performance at a very competitive price. Spacious mid-cabin interior benefits from wide 11'7" beam. Privacy curtains separate both sleeping areas from salon; large U-shaped dinette, extended galley offer added comfort and convenience. Cockpit with built-in wet bar, removable dinette seats seven. Note power engine hatch, walk-through windshield, bolt-on swim platform, transom storage locker. Cruise at 18 knots (30 top) with 310hp MerCruiser sterndrive engines.

See Page 519 For Value Estimates

Length w/Pulpit	33'7"	Fuel	225 gals.
Beam	11'7"	Water	51 gals.
Draft, Up	1'5"	Waste	30 gals.
Draft, Down	2'11"	Hull Type	Modified-V
Weight	13,800#	Deadrise Aft	16°

Crownline 340/350 CR

2007–Current

Floorplan Not Available

Versatile sterndrive cruiser (called the 340 CR in 2007–09) delivers signature Crownline value in a sporty, well-equipped package. Standard features include hardtop with hatch, deluxe cockpit wet bar with refrigerator, genset, entertainment center with flatscreen TV, anchor windlass. Spacious interior with mahogany flooring, high-gloss cherry cabinets includes large hanging locker, plenty of overhead storage. Teak inlaid swim platform is a nice touch. No lightweight, twin 300hp MerCruiser I/Os cruise at 25 knots (around 35 knots wide open).

See Page 519 For Value Estimates

Length w/Pulpit	36'0"	Fuel	193 gals.
Beam	11'11"	Water	38 gals.
Draft, Up	2'7"	Waste	30 gals.
Draft, Down	3'5"	Hull Type	Modified-V
Weight	16,300#	Deadrise Aft	18°

Cruisers & Sedans

Cruisers 2870 Express; 280 CXi

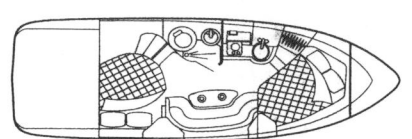

1998–2007

Polished midcabin express (called 2870 Express in 1998–2003) makes good on promise of comfort, performance. Open-plan interior with crescent-shaped dinette/sofa, full-featured galley has double berths fore and aft, each with privacy curtain. Double-wide helm seat, facing cockpit settees seat six. Helm has space for electronic add-ons. Note full-width extended swim platform, walk-through windshield. Single 375hp MerCruiser sterndrive will cruise at 22–23 knots (30+ top); twin 225hp Volvo I/Os cruise in the mid 20s (35+ top).

See Page 519 For Value Estimates

Length w/Platform	31'0"	Fuel	100 gals.
Hull Length	28'6"	Water	25 gals.
Beam	10'0"	Waste	20 gals.
Draft, Down	2'11"	Hull Type	Modified-V
Weight	10,000#	Deadrise Aft	16°

Cruisers 2870 Rogue

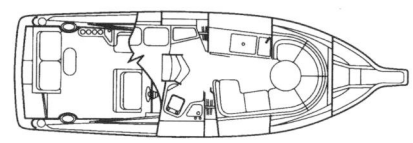

1990–95

Maxi-volume cruiser (called Cruisers 2870 Holiday in 1990; 2870 Rogue in 1991–94; 2970 Rogue in 1995) put emphasis on comfort, performance. Wide 9'6" beam allows for roomy interior with wraparound V-berth/dinette forward, fully equipped galley, stand-up head with shower, mid-cabin berth. Well-planned cockpit with double-wide helm seat features integrated ice chest, drink holders, transom door. Note narrow side decks, roomy engine compartment. Twin 235hp gas sterndrives top out at over 35 knots.

See Page 519 For Value Estimates

Length w/Pulpit	28'8"	Clearance	8'8"
Hull Length	26'0"	Fuel	120 gals.
Beam	9'6"	Water	30 gals.
Draft	3'2"	Hull Type	Modified-V
Weight	7,800#	Deadrise Aft	NA

Cruisers 288/298 Villa Vee; 2980 Esprit

1978–90

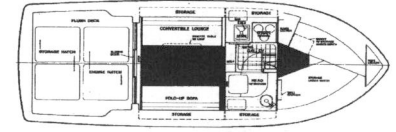

Original Floorplan

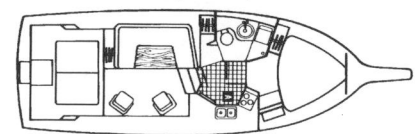

Mid-1980s Floorplan

Compact flybridge cruiser (called 288 Villa Vee in 1978–83; 298 Villa Vee in 1984–87; 2980 Esprit in 1988–90) enjoyed lasting popularity with loyal owners. Wide 10'8" beam allows for surprisingly spacious interior. Several single-stateroom floorplans were offered, all with fully equipped galley, convertible dinette, roomy head with shower. Lower helm was optional. Note slender side decks. Small bridge seats for four. Twin 230hp gas inboards cruise at 18 knots (25 knots top); 260hp engines cruise at 20 knots (28–29 knots top).

Prices Not Provided for Pre-1995 Models

Length Overall	28'8"	Clearance	9'5"
Length WL	24'11"	Fuel	150/180 gals.
Beam	10'8"	Water	45 gals.
Draft	2'9"	Hull Type	Modified-V
Weight	9,500#	Deadrise Aft	17°

Cruisers & Sedans

Cruisers 286/2860/3000 Rogue

1987–89

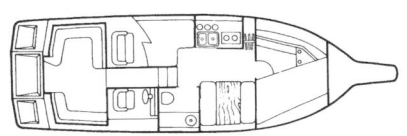

Portly family express (called 286 Rogue in 1987; 2860 Rogue in 1988; 3000 Rogue in 1989) fails to impress. Fairly stylish boat in her day with dramatic hull graphics, integrated swim platform, elongated bow pulpit. Midcabin floorplan with private forward stateroom, convertible dinette sleeps six. Note narrow side decks, modest cabin headroom. Bold hull graphics tend to fade after time. Radar arch was standard on 286 and 2860 models. Among several engine options, twin 260hp I/Os cruise at 23 knots (33–34 knots top).

Prices Not Provided for Pre-1995 Models

Length w/Pulpit	32'11"	Headroom	6'1"
Hull Length	27'4"	Fuel	120 gals.
Beam	10'0"	Water	31 gals.
Draft, Drives Down	3'0"	Hull Type	Modified-V
Weight	7,900#	Deadrise Aft	17°

Cruisers 296 Avanti Vee

1984–87

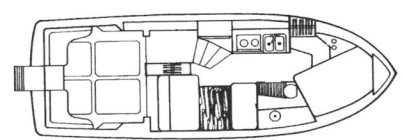

Beamy family express—obviously dated by today's sportboat standards—offered mid-1980s buyers good value for the money. Built on solid fiberglass hull with positive flotation, prop pockets to reduce draft. Roomy midcabin interior differs from most in that dinette is positioned well aft in salon. Privacy curtains separate sleeping areas from main cabin. Raised helm position offers good visibility. Note good engine access. Twin 260hp gas engines cruise at 19–20 knots and reach a top speed of around 30 knots.

Prices Not Provided for Pre-1995 Models

Length Overall	28'8"	Clearance	7'5"
Length WL	24'11"	Fuel	200/250 gals.
Beam	10'8"	Water	45 gals.
Draft	2'9"	Hull Type	Modified-V
Weight	9,000#	Deadrise Aft	17°

Cruisers 2970 Esprit

1986–91

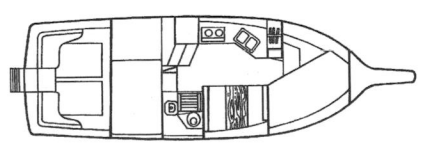

Durable family cruiser introduced in 1986 combined interior comfort with sporty handling, affordable price. Generic midcabin floorplan boasts exceptional headroom, good-quality fixtures and furnishings. Prop-pocket hull is filled with foam flotation—a safety feature seldom found in boats this size. Good visibility from raised helm position. Radar arch, bow pulpit, swim platform were standard. Note that hull graphics tend to fade over time. Twin 260/270hp gas engines cruise at 20 knots (29–30 knots top).

Prices Not Provided for Pre-1995 Models

Length Overall	28'8"	Clearance	7'5"
Length WL	24'11"	Fuel	200/250 gals.
Beam	10'8"	Water	45 gals.
Draft	2'9"	Hull Type	Deep-V
Weight	9,000#	Deadrise Aft	17°

Cruisers 300 CXi/300 Express

2007–Current

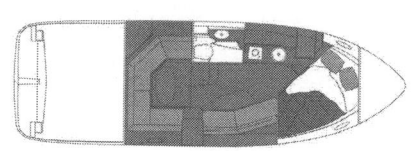

No-frills weekend cruiser (called 300 CXi in 2007–08) delivers all the essentials without breaking the bank. Efficient cockpit layout with double helm seat, wet bar with cooler, companion lounge, rear seating is as good as it gets in a boat this size. Generic interior with aft settee, crescent-shaped dinette, roomy head, boasts 6'3" headroom throughout salon. Easy engine access is plus. Note walk-through windshield, extended swim platform. Twin 225hp Volvo gas I/Os cruise at 18–20 knots (30 knots top).

See Page 519 For Value Estimates

Length	31'3"	Fuel	125 gals.
Beam	10'0"	Water	30 gals.
Draft, Up	2'0"	Waste	23 gals.
Draft, Down	3'0"	Hull Type	Modified-V
Weight	10,300#	Deadrise Aft	16°

Cruisers 300/310 Express

2005–07

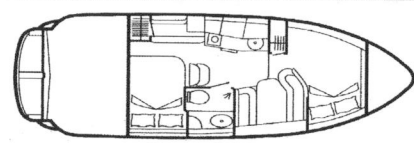

Original Floorplan

2007 Floorplan

Stylish 30-footer with forward-facing arch, extended swim platform blends cruising comfort with agile handling. Original cabin layout with booth-style dinette, double berth aft replaced in 2007 with more open floorplan. Highlights include cherrywood cabinets, walk-through windshield, cockpit wet bar, standard windlass. Molded steps to opening windshield are quite narrow. Screen cabin door inside main door is a nice touch. Optional 320hp Volvo gas I/Os cruise at 30 knots (about 40 knots top). Marketed as Cruisers 310 Express in 2007.

See Page 519 For Value Estimates

Length	32'3"	Fuel	150 gals.
Beam	10'6"	Water	30 gals.
Draft, Drives Up	21"	Waste	25 gals.
Draft, Drives Down	36"	Hull Type	Modified-V
Weight	11,500#	Deadrise Aft	18°

Cruisers 3070 Rogue

1990–94

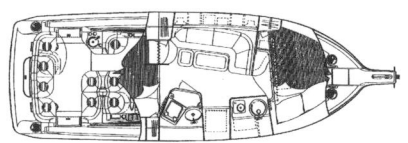

Appealing 1990s express combined practical layout with solid performance, good build quality. Wide-open interior with convertible dinette, fully equipped galley, sleeps six in comfort. Note compact head compartment. Cabin ventilation is excellent thanks to six opening ports, three deck hatches. Topside features include radar arch, bow pulpit, circular foredeck sun pad, fore and aft fender wells. Standard 230hp gas I/Os cruise at 20 knots (32–33 knots top); optional 300hp engines cruise at 24 knots (40+ knots wide open).

Prices Not Provided for Pre-1995 Models

Length w/Pulpit	30'8"	Weight	9,800#
Hull Length	28'8"	Fuel	170 gals.
Beam	10'6"	Water	35 gals.
Draft, Drives Down	3'0"	Hull Type	Deep-V
Draft, Drives Up	2'1"	Deadrise Aft	20°

Cruisers & Sedans

Cruisers 3075 Express

1997–2003

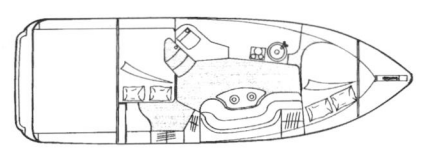

Shapely family express delivered style, performance at budget-friendly price. Well-finished interior with mid-berth aft, small galley, convertible dinette sleeps six. Head compartment—next to companionway steps—is easily accessed from cockpit. U-shaped cockpit settee converts to large sun pad. Note clever integrated anchor platform, good engine access, walk-through windshield. MerCruiser 260hp sterndrives cruise at 25 knots and reach 35+ knots wide open. Inboard power was optional.

See Page 519 For Value Estimates

Length w/Pulpit	33'4"	Fuel	150 gals.
Hull Length	32'1"	Water	30 gals.
Beam	10'4"	Headroom	6'3"
Draft, Down	2'9"	Hull Type	Modified-V
Weight	9,500#	Deadrise Aft	16°

Cruisers 3020/3120 Aria

1992–97

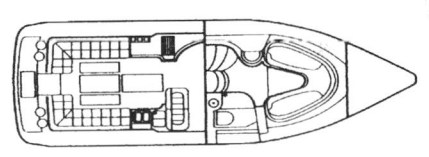

Feature-rich express (called 3020 Aria in 1992–94; 3120 Aria in 1995–97) trades cabin volume for expansive cockpit. Clever rear seat folds out to create sun lounge, or folds into transom pocket to leave cockpit open. Compact cabin has dinette/V-berth forward, mini-galley, enclosed head with sit-down shower. Midcabin berth was optional; otherwise that space is used for storage. Note cockpit wet bar, big in-floor storage bin. Twin 250hp I/Os cruise at 20 knots (35 top); optional 330hp engines cruise at 25 knots (about 40 knots top).

See Page 519 For Value Estimates

Length w/Pulpit	30'8"	Weight	8,800#
Hull Length	28'8"	Fuel	200 gals.
Beam	10'6"	Water	32 gals.
Draft, Down	3'0"	Hull Type	Deep-V
Draft, Up	2'1"	Deadrise Aft	20°

Cruisers 3175 Rogue

1995–98

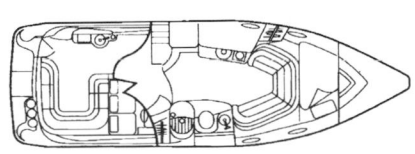

Generic 1990s sterndrive cruiser with rakish styling, mid-cabin interior, gave entry-level buyers a lot of boat for the money. Wide-open cabin with compact galley, wrap-around dinette, features unique raised forepeak berth for kids. Note large head with stall shower, three overhead hatches. Helm has space for flush-mounted electrics. Additional highlights include cockpit wet bar, foredeck sun pad, trim tabs, walk-through windshield. Hull is fully cored to reduce weight. Twin 250hp gas I/Os cruise at 22–23 knots (high 30s top).

See Page 519 For Value Estimates

Length w/Pulpit	32'8"	Weight	9,300#
Hull Length	30'8"	Fuel	163 gals.
Beam	10'6"	Water	32 gals.
Draft, Up	2'1"	Hull Type	Deep-V
Draft, Down	3'0"	Deadrise Aft	20°

Cruisers & Sedans

Cruisers 320 Express

2002–06

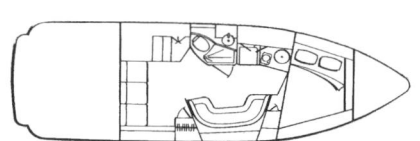

Well-bred midrange cruiser (called 3275 Express in 2002–03) offers leading-edge comfort, performance, in a sporty package. Wide-open interior with aft sofa/sleeper, crescent-shaped dinette, cherry woodwork is unusually spacious for a boat this size. Topside features include radar arch, walk-through windshield, double foredeck sun pad (with headrest), anchor chute. Extended swim platform is a popular option. Cockpit sole lifts for engine access. Twin 320hp MerCruiser I/Os cruise at 20 knots and top out in the mid 30s.

See Page 519 For Value Estimates

Length w/Platform	35'9"	Fuel	200 gals.
Beam	11'3"	Water	40 gals.
Draft, Up	2'0"	Waste	30 gals.
Draft, Down	2'11"	Hull Type	Modified-V
Weight	13,500#	Deadrise Aft	16°

Cruisers 3270 Esprit

1988–94

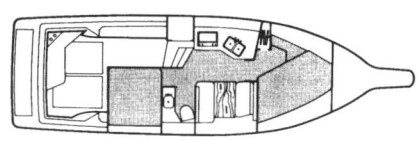

Contemporary family express introduced in 1988 offered bold styling, top-shelf accommodations. Wide 10'10" hull allows spacious midcabin interior with large galley, head with shower, generous storage, berths for six. Well-arranged cockpit features elevated helm position, L-shaped companion lounge, rear bench seat. Hatches in cockpit sole provide good engine access. Hull graphics tend to fade over time. Radar arch, bow pulpit were standard. Twin 250hp V-drive gas inboards cruise at 18–20 knots (high 20s top).

Prices Not Provided for Pre-1995 Models

Length	30'10"	Fuel	200 gals.
Beam	10'10"	Water	45 gals.
Draft	2'10"	Waste	20 gals.
Weight	10,500#	Hull Type	Modified-V
Clearance	7'0"	Deadrise Aft	18°

Cruisers 330 Express

2008–Current

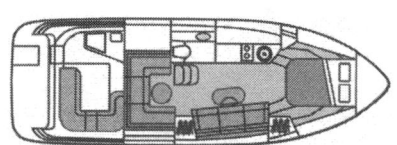

Good-looking family express with wide beam sets high standards for comfort, livability. No side decks means interior makes full use of the beam. Roomy cockpit includes large double-wide helm seat, portside chaise lounge, aft U-shaped settee that converts into sun pad. Busy-but-comfortable cabin with vertical hull ports, cherry cabinetry is big for a 33-footer. Note cushioned master berth headboard, space-saving rectangular dinette. Volvo 375hp V-drive gas inboards cruise at 25 knots (low 30s top).

See Page 519 For Value Estimates

Length	35'6"	Fuel	232 gals.
Beam	11'8"	Water	40 gals.
Draft, Up	2'10"	Waste	30 gals.
Draft, Down	3'8"	Hull Type	Modified-V
Clearance	10'1"	Deadrise Aft	16°

Cruisers 336 Ultra Vee

1983–88

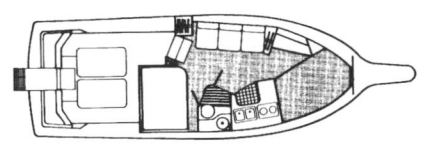

Well-rounded 1980s cruiser combined unique interior with sturdy construction, comfortable ride. Aft cabin—with partial standing headroom, privacy door—serves as master stateroom rather than guest quarters. Double-entry head offers access from both salon and aft stateroom. Hatches in cockpit sole provide good engine access. Visibility from raised helm seat is excellent. Note fuel increase in 1985. Prop-pocket hull delivers good turn of speed: 20 knots cruise, about 30 knots top with 350hp inboard gas engines.

Prices Not Provided for Pre-1995 Models

Length	32'10"	Fuel	250/300 gals.
Beam	11'10"	Water	70 gals.
Draft	2'9"	Headroom	6'3"
Weight	11,500#	Hull Type	Modified-V
Clearance	8'6"	Deadrise Aft	18°

Cruisers 3370 Esprit

1986–94

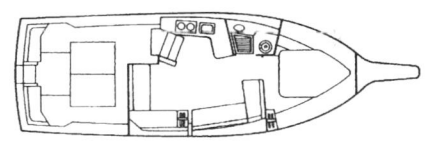

Tall-freeboard express introduced in 1986 combined rakish styling, roomy accommodations. Well-appointed interior is surprisingly spacious. Aft sleeper/sofa (with privacy curtain) is open to salon; forward stateroom has bi-fold privacy door. Full-feature galley has generous counter, storage space. Single-level cockpit features double-wide helm seat, aft bench seats, engine room access hatches. Prop-pocket hull delivers good turn of speed: 20 knots cruise, about 30 knots top with 350hp inboard gas engines.

Prices Not Provided for Pre-1995 Models

Length	32'10"	Fuel	300 gals.
Beam	11'10"	Water	70 gals.
Draft	2'9"	Headroom	6'3"
Weight	11,500#	Hull Type	Modified-V
Clearance	8'6"	Deadrise Aft	18°

Cruisers 3380 Esprit

1985–94

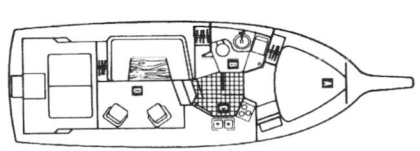

Popular flybridge cruiser (called 338 Chateau Vee in 1985–87) with rakish lines, innovative interior enjoyed decade-long production run. Twin-stateroom floorplan features private midcabin berth beneath salon dinette, generous storage, head with stall shower, step-down galley with upright refrigerator. Hatches in cockpit sole provide good access to engines; oversized bridge has helm forward, wraparound seating aft. Note prop-pocket hull bottom. Crusader 340hp gas inboards cruise at 20 knots (about 30 knots wide open).

Prices Not Provided for Pre-1995 Models

Length	32'10"	Fuel	300 gals.
Beam	11'10"	Water	70 gals.
Draft	2'10"	Headroom	6'4"
Weight	13,000#	Hull Type	Modified-V
Clearance	11'6"	Deadrise Aft	18°

Cruisers & Sedans

Cruisers 340 Express

2001–07

Standard Layout

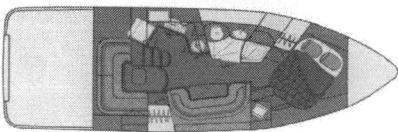

Alternate Layout

See Page 519 For Value Estimates

Quality-built midcabin express combined unusually spacious layout with choice of inboard, sterndrive power. Standard interior has fixed midcabin berth, dinette with facing seats; alternate floorplan has aft sleeper/sofa open to salon, U-shaped dinette. Privacy curtains separate sleeping areas from salon. Note stall shower in head. Topside features include cockpit wet bar, transom door, forward-facing arch, foredeck sun pad. Twin 370hp V-drive inboards top out at 30 knots; 375hp MerCruiser sterndrives top out in the high 30s.

Length	36'6"	Fuel	232 gals.
Beam	11'8"	Water	40 gals.
Draft	3'0"	Waste	30 gals.
Weight, Gas	15,500#	Hull Type	Modified-V
Weight, Diesel	16,500#	Deadrise Aft	16°

Cruisers 3570/3575 Esprit; 3572 Express

1995–2002

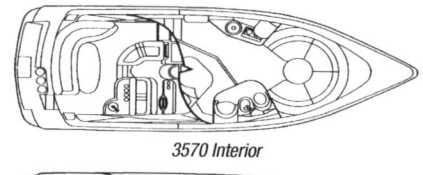

3570 Interior

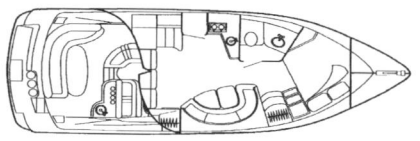

3575 Interior

See Page 519 For Value Estimates

Innovative 1990s cruiser offered two very different floorplans in the same express-boat package. Original 3570 layout features private amidships master stateroom with queen berth. Alternate interior—introduced in 1996—has traditional midcabin floorplan similar to most express cruisers. Unique cockpit layout has double-wide helm and companion seats leading aft into cockpit. Note fully cored hull with prop pockets. Twin 310hp V-drive gas engines reach 28–30 knots top. Marketed as the Cruisers 3572 Express in 2001–02.

Length	39'3"	Fuel	300 gals.
Beam	13'0"	Water	70 gals.
Draft	3'5"	Waste	50 gals.
Weight	16,000#	Hull Type	Modified-V
Clearance, Arch	10'10"	Deadrise Aft	17°

Cruisers 3580/3585 Flybridge

1996–99

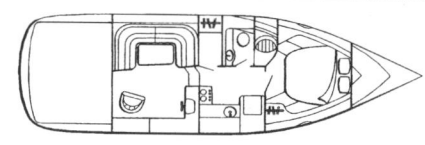

3580 Floorplan

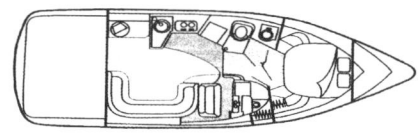

3585 Floorplan

See Page 519 For Value Estimates

Appealing 1990s flybridge cruiser offered choice of two very different interiors. Original 3580 floorplan has galley down with optional lower helm (with poor outside visibility); newer 3585 floorplan introduced in 1998 has elevated lower helm, galley forward in salon. Both layouts have small midcabin under salon, separate stall shower in head. Note molded bridge steps, narrow side decks, compact engine room, prop-pocket hull bottom. Standard 320hp V-drive gas inboards cruise at 18 knots (26–27 knots wide open).

Length Overall	39'3"	Fuel	300 gals.
Hull Length	37'4"	Water	70 gals.
Beam	13'0"	Waste	40 gals.
Draft	3'5"	Hull Type	Modified-V
Weight	18,200#	Deadrise Aft	16°

Cruisers 360 Express

2008–Current

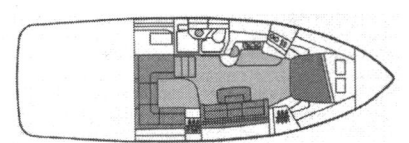

Contemporary express gets thumbs-up for luxury-class accommodations, very competitive price. No side decks permits the interior to make full use of the beam. Guest-friendly cockpit includes double-wide helm seat, portside chaise lounge, rear U-shaped settee that converts into sun pad. Well-appointed cabin with cherry cabinetry is big for a 36-footer. Note cushioned master berth headboard, space-saving rectangular dinette. Fiberglass hardtop is standard. Volvo 375hp V-drive gas inboards cruise at 24 knots (30+ top).

See Page 519 For Value Estimates

Length	38'0"	Fuel	300 gals.
Beam	12'6"	Water	64 gals.
Draft, V-Drive	3'0"	Waste	40 gals.
Draft, I/O	3'5"	Hull Type	Modified-V
Clearance, Hardtop	11'0"	Deadrise Aft	16°

Cruisers 3670 Esprit

1989–92

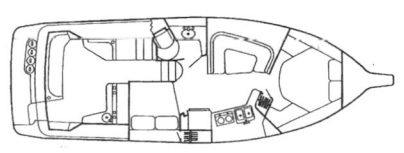

Maxi-volume cruiser introduced in 1989 delivered express-boat style, comfort at a competitive price. Well-appointed interior with 6'5" headroom features convertible U-shaped dinette, fully equipped galley, double berths fore and aft. Roomy cockpit has elevated double helm seat forward, aft bench seating, wet bar. Hatches in cockpit sole provide good engine access. Note stainless-steel arch, fender storage, cockpit shower, foredeck sun pad. Twin 310hp V-drive gas engines cruise at 18 knots (high 20s top).

Prices Not Provided for Pre-1995 Models

Length Overall	39'5"	Clearance	9'7"
Hull Length	35'3"	Fuel	300 gals.
Beam	13'0"	Water	110 gals.
Draft	3'5"	Hull Type	Modified-V
Weight	16,400#	Deadrise Aft	17°

Cruisers 3670/3675/3775 Esprit

1991–96

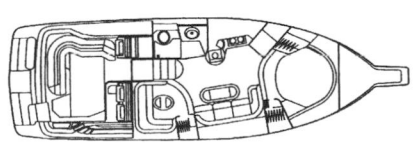

Handsome inboard express (called Cruisers 3670 in 1991–92; 3675 in 1993–94; 3775 in 1997–96) offered buyers luxury, performance at a reasonable price. Spacious interior with overhead skylights features open galley with full-size refrigerator, head with separate stall shower. Aft seating area with privacy enclosure converts to sleeping berth. Large cockpit includes wraparound aft seating, transom door, wet bar. Note spacious helm, bow pulpit, foredeck sun pad. Twin 310hp V-drive gas engines cruise at 18 knots (26–28 knots top).

See Page 519 For Value Estimates

Length Overall	39'5"	Weight, Diesel	17,500#
Hull Length	35'3"	Fuel	300 gals.
Beam	13'0"	Water	93 gals.
Draft	3'5"	Hull Type	Modified-V
Weight, Gas	16,400#	Deadrise Aft	17°

Cruisers 3672/3772/370 Express

2000–07

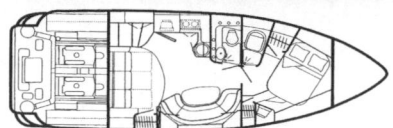

Single Stateroom Layout

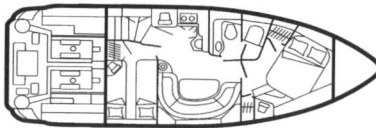

Twin Stateroom Floorplan

See Page 519 For Value Estimates

S tylish inboard cruiser (called 3672 Express in 2000–02; 3772 Express in 2003; 370 in 2004–07) blends upscale accommodations with quality construction, posh amenities. Offered with choice of floorplans: expansive single-stateroom layout has aft sleeper/sofa open to salon; alternate mid-cabin interior has private aft stateroom. Note high-gloss cherry woodwork, walk-through windshield, extended swim platform. Standard 370hp V-drive gas engines cruise at 16 knots; optional 370hp Cummins diesels cruise in the low 20s.

Length	40'2"	Fuel	300 gals.
Beam	13'0"	Water	70 gals.
Draft	3'0"	Waste	55 gals.
Weight, Gas	18,000#	Hull Type	Modified-V
Weight, Diesel	19,000#	Deadrise Aft	16°

Cruisers 3870 Express

1998–2003

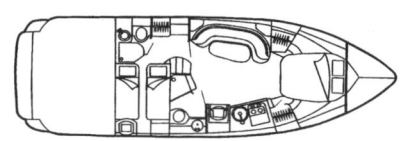

See Page 519 For Value Estimates

G ood-looking express introduced in 1997 offered upmarket mix of style, luxury, performance. Spacious interior with two heads, full-service galley features unique amidships stateroom with stand-up dressing area, built-in TV, private head with shower. Cockpit has L-lounge opposite helm, wet bar, U-shaped seating aft. Note walk-through windshield, easy-access engine compartment. Extended swim platform supports dinghy, PWC. Twin 370hp gas V-drive inboards cruise at 20 knots (about 30 knots top).

Length Overall	43'3"	Fuel	300 gals.
Hull Length	40'8"	Water	75 gals.
Beam	13'6"	Waste	50 gals.
Draft	3'0"	Hull Type	Modified-V
Weight	19,500#	Deadrise Aft	16°

Cruisers 390 Sports Coupe

2007–Current

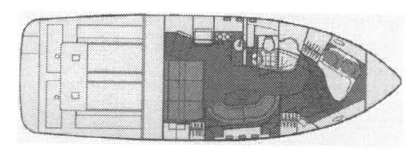

See Page 519 For Value Estimates

F eature-rich express with semi-enclosed bridgedeck offers passengers maximum protection from the elements. Roomy open-plan salon with single stateroom forward boasts aft sofa that converts to midcabin berth, cherry-veneer cabinetry, large head with separate stall shower. Note limited galley storage. Unique companion seat converts to dinette. Cockpit floor lifts electrically for engine access. Available with V-drive inboard or Volvo IPS Drive System. Cruise at 28 knots with Yanmar 380hp V-drive diesel inboards (30+ top).

Length	40'2"	Fuel	300 gals.
Beam	13'0"	Water	75 gals.
Draft	3'9"	Waste	55 gals.
Weight	22,000#	Hull Type	Modified-V
Clearance	11'3"	Deadrise Aft	16°

Cruisers & Sedans

Cruisers 3970/400/420 Express

2003–Current

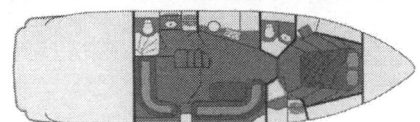

Standard Layout, 2003–04

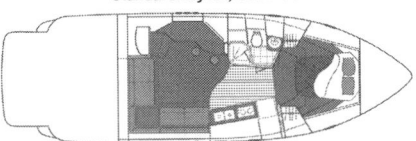

Standard Layout, 2005–Current

See Page 519 For Value Estimates

Upscale sportcruiser (called 3970 Exp. in 2003; 400 Exp. in 2004–05; 420 Exp. since 2006) combines smart styling with brisk performance, quality amenities. Original mid-cabin interior updated in 2005 with more spacious single-stateroom layout with vertical hull ports. Cockpit—also redesigned in 2005—replaced original centerline companionway with portside entry, pod-style helm/companion seats. Twin 420hp V-drive gas engines cruise at 20 knots; Yanmar 370hp diesels cruise in the low 20s. Recent models with 370hp IPS drives cruise at 26 knots.

Length	43'0"	Fuel	300 gals.
Beam	13'6"	Water	70 gals.
Draft	3'8"	Waste	50 gals.
Weight, Gas	22,000#	Hull Type	Modified-V
Weight, Diesel	23,500#	Deadrise Aft	16°

Cruisers 420 Sports Coupe

2009–Current

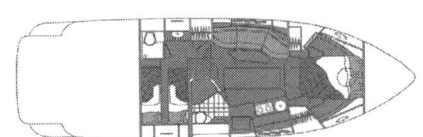

Shapely hardtop express with seductive profile takes cruising comfort to the next level. Elegant two-stateroom, cherrywood interior with near 7-foot headroom includes nifty salon liquor cabinet, 26" flatscreen TV, Corian counters, vertical hull ports. Cockpit amenities include U-shaped lounge seating with storage under, power engine room hatch, deluxe wet bar. Note sunroof, foredeck chaise lounge, walk-through windshield, extended swim platform. Cruise at 24–25 knots with Volvo 370hp IPS diesels.

Insufficient Resale Data to Assign Values

Length w/Platform	43'0"	Fuel	300 gals.
Beam	13'6"	Water	80 gals.
Draft	38"	Waste	50 gals.
Weight, Gas	23,000#	Hull Type	Modified-V
Weight, Diesel	23,500#	Deadrise Aft	16°

Cruisers 4270 Express

1997–2003

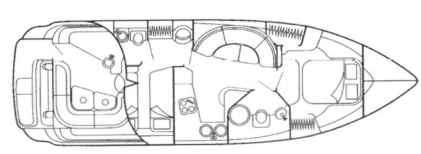

Full-bodied express with extended swim platform, forward-facing arch gets high marks for aggressive styling, spirited performance. Upscale interior features wide-open salon with contoured settee, huge U-shaped galley, unique midcabin suite with twin berths, private head, stand-up dressing area. Cockpit includes removable aft seats—very practical. Note walk-through windshield, transom storage locker, concealed windlass. Space at helm for extra electronics. Cat 420hp V-drive diesels cruise at 26–28 knots (30+ knots top).

See Page 519 For Value Estimates

Length	46'6"	Fuel	400 gals.
Beam	14'0"	Water	100 gals.
Draft	3'6"	Waste	50 gals.
Weight, Gas	22,000#	Hull Type	Modified-V
Weight, Diesel	23,500#	Deadrise Aft	16°

Cruisers & Sedans

Cruisers 4285 Express Bridge

1990–95

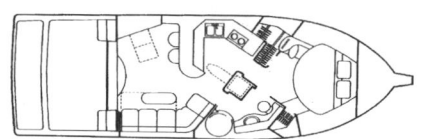

Spacious family cruiser with party-time accommodations delivers impressive comfort, versatility. Single-stateroom interior features huge full-beam salon with entertainment center, open galley with serving counter, large master cabin. Massive flybridge can seat a small crowd. Bridge steps in cockpit are a nice touch. Fully cored hull has prop pockets to reduce shaft angles. Cat 375hp diesels cruise at 20 knots (around 24 knots top). Note that Cruisers 4280 Express Bridge is same boat with two-stateroom interior.

See Page 519 For Value Estimates

Length	46'6"	Headroom	6'5"
Beam	14'6"	Fuel	400 gals.
Draft	3'6"	Water	160 gals.
Weight, Gas	23,700#	Hull Type	Modified-V
Weight, Diesel	25,200#	Deadrise Aft	16°

Cruisers 440 Express

2003–05

Standard Layout

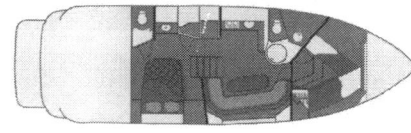

Optional Layout

Luxury sportcruiser with maxi-volume interior offers express-boat versatility, motoryacht comforts. Opulent cabin accommodations include full-size master stateroom (with private head, shower), vast salon with crescent-shaped dinette/sofa, open-plan galley with Corian counters, generous storage. Note high-gloss cherry cabinetry, posh upholstery. Extended swim platform can support PWC. Bi-level cockpit seats 8–10 guests in comfort. Fiberglass hardtop was optional. Yanmar 440hp V-drive diesels cruise at 25 knots (high 20s top).

See Page 520 For Value Estimates

Length	46'9"	Fuel	400 gals.
Beam	14'0"	Water	95 gals.
Draft	42"	Waste	50 gals.
Weight, Gas	24,300#	Hull Type	Modified-V
Weight, Diesel	25,900#	Deadrise Aft	16°

Cruisers 520 Express

2006–Current

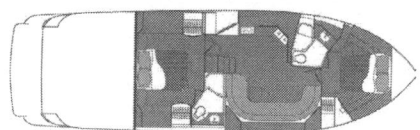

Standard Layout

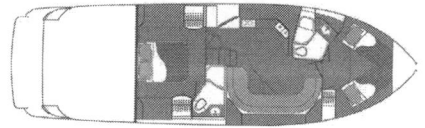

Optional Layout

Posh accommodations, aggressive styling, impressive performance make this maxi-volume cruiser a standout entry in today's premium sportyacht market. Enormous twin-stateroom interior boasts full-beam master with en suite head, huge galley, opulent main salon with 12-foot Ultraleather sectional. Feature-rich cockpit seats a small crowd in comfort. Note walk-through windshield, cherry interior cabinetry, optional hardtop. Volvo 715hp V-drive diesels deliver a top speed in excess of 30 knots.

See Page 520 For Value Estimates

Length	52'3"	Fuel	500 gals.
Beam	15'6"	Water	150 gals.
Draft	3'8"	Waste	75 gals.
Weight	42,000#	Hull Type	Modified-V
Headroom	6'6"	Deadrise Aft	15°

Cruisers & Sedans

Cruisers 540/560 Express

2001–Current

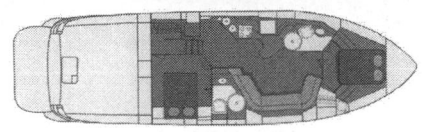

Standard Plan

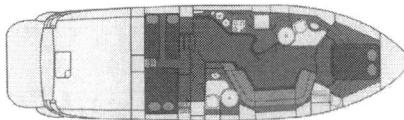

Alternate Plan

See Page 520 For Value Estimates

Head-turning sportyacht (called 5370 Express in 2001–02; 540 Express in 2003–06) with bold styling, deluxe accommodations defines luxury in the nautical fast lane. Spacious interior with two (or three) staterooms features two full heads, enormous salon with leather sofa, home-size galley. Circular cockpit lounge converts electrically into huge sun pad. Retractable dinette table in salon is way cool. Hardtop is optional. Hull is fully cored. Volvo 715hp V-drive diesels top out at 30+ knots.

Length	58'0"	Fuel	650 gals.
Beam	16'0"	Water	150 gals.
Draft	3'10"	Waste	100 gals.
Weight	46,000#	Hull Type	Modified-V
Clearance	12'7"	Deadrise Aft	15°

Donzi 275 Express

1995–2000

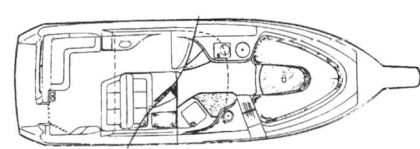

See Page 520 For Value Estimates

Entry-level family cruiser with plenty of standard features gave 1990s buyers good value for the money. Generic midcabin interior includes full galley, enclosed head with shower, dinette/V-berth forward. Cockpit layout with aft bench seat (convertible to sun lounge) is comfortable for six adults. Cockpit wet bar, integrated swim platform, Dino steering wheel, radar arch, integral bow pulpit were all standard. Good cabin headroom; so-so fit and finish. Single 310hp MerCruiser sterndrive will cruise at 25 knots (35+ knots wide open.)

Length Overall	29'3"	Clearance	7'0"
Beam	8'6"	Fuel	103 gals.
Draft, Drives Up	1'9"	Water	20 gals.
Draft, Drives Down	3'5"	Hull Type	Modified-V
Weight	6,500#	Deadrise Aft	19°

Donzi 3250 Express

1996–2000

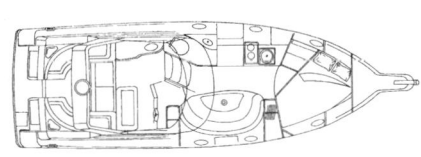

See Page 520 For Value Estimates

Sporty sterndrive express combined signature Donzi performance with bold styling, practical cabin accommodations. Maxi-volume interior with berths for six includes private forward stateroom, circular salon dinette, fully equipped galley. Flashy 1990s cabin decor may not be for everyone. Innovative cockpit design with centerline transom door, doublewide helm seat boasts lounge seating for a small crowd. Note wide side decks. Faster than many so-called sportboats, twin 310hp I/Os cruise at close to 30 knots (40+ top).

Length Overall	33'8"	Clearance	NA
Beam	11'0"	Fuel	198 gals.
Draft, Drives Up	2'4"	Water	35 gals.
Draft, Drives Down	3'1"	Hull Type	Modified-V
Weight	11,500#	Deadrise Aft	19°

Cruisers & Sedans

Dyer 29

1955–2003

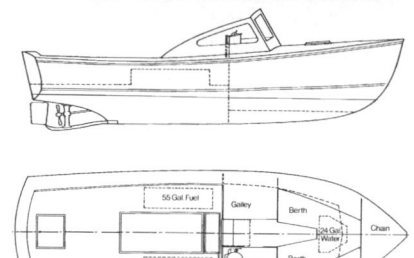

Classic Downeast cruiser with iconic lines, legendary sea-keeping qualities turns heads everywhere she goes. Offered in several configurations over the years including Trunk Cabin, Hardtop, and several workboat versions. Recent models have the engine under bridgedeck eliminating cockpit engine box of early models. Many interiors were designed to owner specs. Easily driven hull with protected prop offers outstanding fuel efficiency. Single 200hp Yanmar diesel will cruise at 16–17 knots. Over 350 built. Custom models are still available.

See Page 520 For Value Estimates

Length Overall	28'6"	Clearance	6'0"
Length WL	26'0"	Water	24 gals.
Beam	9'5"	Fuel	110 gals.
Draft	2'6"	Clearance	NA
Weight	7,400#	Hull Type	Semi-Disp.

Ellis 36

1998–2003

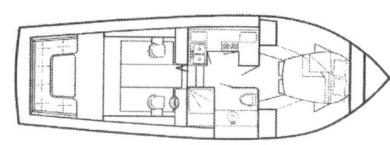

Semicustom Downeast cruiser offers extended cruising in comfort, elegance, security. Highlights include full teak interior with private stateroom, large head with stall shower, excellent engine access, generous storage. Cockpit seating converts to additional berths on canvass-enclosed bridge deck. Hardtop was a popular option. Exemplary fit and finish throughout. Refined version of original Ellis full-keel hull delivers remarkable ride comfort. Cruise efficiently at 18 knots (low 20s top) with single 440 Yanmar diesel. Twin waterjet propulsion was also available.

See Page 521 For Value Estimates

Length	35'10"	Headroom	6'3"
Beam	13'2"	Fuel	200 gals.
Draft	3'10"	Water	100 gals.
Weight	15,500#	Hull Type	Modified-V
Clearance	NA	Deadrise Aft	0°

Fairline 40 Targa

2000–07

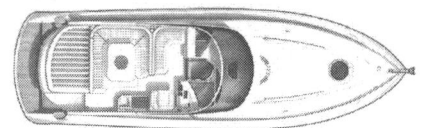

Spirited sportcruiser with transom garage built an impressive sales record during her production years. Impeccably detailed cockpit has food-prep center with barbecue across from U-lounge. Midcabin interior with private staterooms boasts posh furnishings, stunning cherry woodwork. Aft sun pad rises hydraulically for access to tender; engine room, beneath garage, can only be accessed if dinghy is removed. Bow thruster is standard. Note narrow side decks. Volvo 285hp diesel I/Os cruise at 27–28 knots (low 30s top).

See Page 521 For Value Estimates

Length Overall	41'10"	Water	79 gals.
Beam	12'1"	Clearance	13'2"
Draft, Down	3'0"	Headroom	6'4"
Weight	16,000#	Hull	Deep-V
Fuel	197 gals.	Deadrise Aft	17°

Fairline 43 Targa

1998–2004

Best-selling U.K. express yacht with rakish lines was designed as much for socializing as she was for speed. Highlights include lavish two-stateroom, two-head interior with lacquered cherry cabinets, teak-and-holly cabin sole, luxury-class cockpit with wraparound seating, deluxe wet bar, teak-laid swim platform, flip-up helm seat, fore and aft sun pads. Deep-V hull delivers exceptional open-water performance. Transom garage is a convenient big-boat touch. Twin 480hp Volvo diesels cruise at 28 knots (mid 30s top).

See Page 521 For Value Estimates

Length Overall	45'1"	Fuel	280 gals.
Beam	12'6"	Water	74 gals.
Draft	3'3	Waste	NA
Weight	20,723#	Hull Type	Deep-V
Clearance	13'3"	Deadrise Aft	18°

Fairline 48 Targa

1998–2002

Best-selling U.K. express with eye-catching elliptical windshield raised the bar in her era for sportboat styling, nautical sex appeal. Three-stateroom interior has matching guest cabins aft, posh salon, top-shelf galley appliances. Forward head is small; doors to aft cabins are narrow. Cockpit is divided into three areas: command bridge forward, settee and wet bar in the middle, tender garage aft. Engineroom is shoehorn tight. Volvo 430hp diesels top out at 30+ knots; low 30s with Volvo 480s.

See Page 521 For Value Estimates

Length	49'10"	Fuel	360 gals.
Beam	12'11"	Water	120 gals.
Draft	3'3"	Waste	40 gals.
Weight	24,600#	Hull Type	Deep-V
Clearance	NA	Deadrise Aft	19°

Fairline 52 Targa

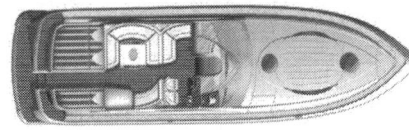

2003–Current

Muscular, big-water express introduced in 2003 took sportyacht styling, performance to the next level. Luxury-class interior with high-gloss cabinets boasts three private staterooms, two full heads, opulent salon with home-size galley. Note king bed in master stateroom. Optional den/office can replace port guest cabin. Transom garage is big enough to handle a 12-foot tender. Additional features include impressive stowage, easy engine room access, teak cockpit sole. Cruise in the high 20s with 715hp Volvo diesels (about 35 knots top).

See Page 521 For Value Estimates

Length Overall	52'5"	Headroom	6'6"
Beam	14'0"	Fuel	480 gals.
Draft	3'7"	Water	120 gals.
Weight	35,200#	Hull Type	Deep-V
Clearance	15'10"	Deadrise Aft	19°

Cruisers & Sedans

Cruisers & Sedans

Formula 27 PC

1994–Current

Wide-beam sportcruiser produced since 1994 is a proven blend of solid construction, versatile accommodations. Upscale interior with wraparound dinette forward includes full galley with Corian counter, aft private berth with privacy enclosure. Roomy cockpit comes with double-wide helm seat, wet bar, foldaway aft lounge, sun pad insert. Note power engine compartment hatch, walk-through windshield. Single 310hp MerCruiser will cruise at 22 knots (34–35 knots top); twin 310hp MerCruisers cruise at 26–28 knots (mid 40s knots top).

See Page 522 For Value Estimates

Length Overall	29'5"	Fuel	107 gals.
Hull Length	27'0"	Water	26 gals.
Beam	9'7"	Waste	30 gals.
Draft	3'1"	Hull Type	Modified-V
Weight	9,500#	Deadrise Aft	18°

Formula 28 PC

1985–87

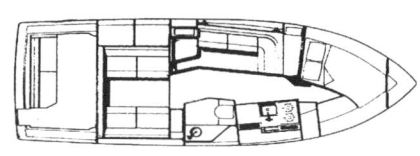

Quality-built 1980s express is roomy, quick, agile. Considered an upscale boat during her production years—rugged construction, stylish hull graphics allowed her to age gracefully well into the 1990s. Conventional midcabin interior has sliding panel forward for stateroom privacy, large settee, stand-up head with sink and shower. Open cockpit features L-shaped lounge next to helm, wet bar, foldaway stern seat. Note bow pulpit, spacious engine compartment. Twin 260hp sterndrives cruise at 23–25 knots (mid 30s top).

Prices Not Provided for Pre-1995 Models

Length Overall	30'6"	Clearance	8'4"
Hull Length	28'0"	Fuel	160 gals.
Beam	10'0"	Water	39 gals.
Draft	2'10"	Hull Type	Deep-V
Weight	7,850#	Deadrise Aft	24°

Formula 29 PC

1988–92

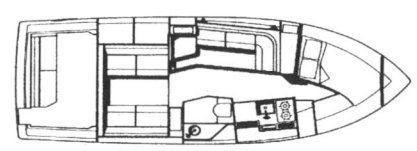

Maxi-volume family cruiser introduced in 1988 targeted upscale boaters focused on sporty performance, top-shelf accommodations. Tastefully furnished interior with full-featured galley, stand-up head with shower sleeps six. Cabin entry is wide, headroom is generous. Wraparound seating opposite helm keeps skipper close to guests. Note large engine compartment, swivel helm seat, foldaway stern seat. Excellent high-speed handling, above-average finish. Twin MerCruiser 5.7-liter sterndrives cruise at 20 knots (low 30s top).

Prices Not Provided for Pre-1995 Models

Length Overall	33'9"	Clearance	8'9"
Hull Length	29'0"	Fuel	165 gals.
Beam	10'7"	Water	50 gals.
Draft	2'6"	Hull Type	Deep-V
Weight	9,700#	Deadrise Aft	20°

Formula 31 PC

1993–2004

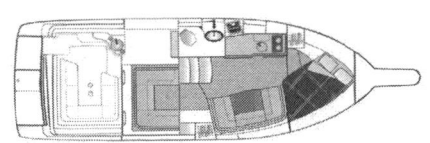

Best-selling express hit the right buttons with Formula buyers for over a decade. Topside amenities include roomy cockpit with wraparound lounge seating, wet bar, portside lounger, well-designed helm with double-wide seat. Entire aft lounge becomes large sun pad when tables are lowered. Wide-open cabin with U-shaped dinette, full-featured galley sleeps six. Hardware, furnishings, appliances are first rate. MerCruiser 320hp engines cruise at 25 knots (high 30s top). Note that all-new Formula 31 PC was introduced in 2005.

See Page 522 For Value Estimates

Length Overall	34'0"	Fuel	180 gals.
Hull Length	31'0"	Water	50 gals.
Beam	11'0"	Waste	40 gals.
Draft	3'2"	Hull Type	Modified-V
Weight	11,730#	Deadrise Aft	18°

Formula 31 PC

2005–Current

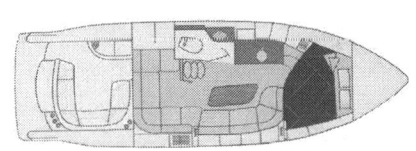

Updated version of original Formula 31 PC (1993–2004) adds stylish sport arch, extended swim platform, revised interior with Ultraleather upholstery. Cabin highlights include Corian galley and head counters, cherrywood dinette table, top-quality galley appliances. Foredeck sun pads are reached via opening windshield with molded steps, hand railing. Standard features include windlass, transom shower, flat-screen TV/DVD, power engine hatch. Not inexpensive, twin 320hp MerCruiser sterndrives top out at 35+ knots.

See Page 522 For Value Estimates

Length Overall	33'1"	Fuel	180 gals.
Beam	11'0"	Water	50 gals.
Draft, Up	2'6"	Waste	40 gals.
Draft, Down	3'4"	Hull Type	Modified-V
Weight	14,100#	Deadrise Aft	18°

Formula 34 PC

1991–2002

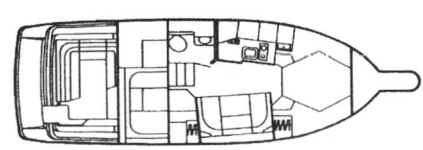

Polished midcabin express racked up impressive sales numbers for Formula throughout the 1990s. Cockpit amenities include U-shaped aft lounge with removable table, double-wide companion seat, flip-up helm seat, wet bar. Portside floor compartment holds small cooler. Smartly appointed cabin with Ultraleather settee, large galley, contoured aft lounge sleeps six. Bow pulpit, radar arch, transom shower, foredeck sun pads were standard. Twin MerCruiser 310hp sterndrives cruise at 23–24 knots (mid 30s top).

See Page 522 For Value Estimates

Length Overall	37'0"	Clearance w/Arch	10'0"
Hull Length	34'0"	Fuel	222 gals.
Beam	12'0"	Water	60 gals.
Draft	2'6"	Hull Type	Modified-V
Weight	13,500#	Deadrise Aft	18°

Cruisers & Sedans

Cruisers & Sedans

Formula 34 PC

2004–Current

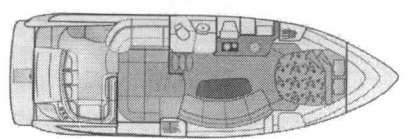

Restyled version of previous Formula 34 PC (1991–2002) inherits best features of her predecessor in restyled, updated package. Topside amenities include wraparound cockpit seating with removable table, double-wide helm seat with flip-up bolsters, twin foredeck sun pads, extended swim platform, transom storage. Spacious cabin with Ultraleather seating, Corian counters, cherry woodwork is as good as it gets in a family cruiser. Note walk-through windshield, power engine compartment hatch. MerCruiser 320hp I/Os top out at 35+ knots.

See Page 522 For Value Estimates

Length Overall	35'7"	Fuel	206 gals.
Beam	11'6"	Water	55 gals.
Draft	3'0"	Waste	40 gals.
Weight	15,710#	Hull Type	Modified-V
Clearance	11'4"	Deadrise Aft	18°

Formula 35 PC

1986–89

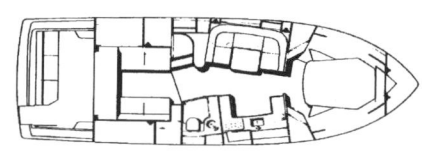

Late 1980s inboard express delivered bold styling, classy accommodations, good open-water performance at a competitive price. Common-sense interior boasts large U-shaped galley, full dinette, facing aft settees. Cabin fabrics, furnishings, and appliances were considered first rate in their day. Cockpit seating includes L-shaped companion lounge, foldaway stern seat. Note windshield vents, side-dumping exhausts, roomy dash, power engine hatch. Twin 340hp V-drive engines cruise at 20 knots and top out at 28–30 knots.

Prices Not Provided for Pre-1995 Models

Length Overall	40'0"	Clearance	10'2"
Hull Length	35'0"	Fuel	275 gals.
Beam	12'0"	Water	50 gals.
Draft	2'8"	Hull Type	Deep-V
Weight	13,750#	Deadrise Aft	20°

Formula 36 PC

1990–95

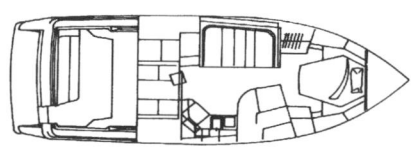

Well-crafted family cruiser with straight inboard power set high standards in early 1990s for style, quality, performance. Roomy midcabin interior with private forward stateroom gets high marks for quality materials, excellent workmanship. Entertainment center on aft bulkhead is an innovative touch. Cockpit seating includes L-shaped companion lounge, foldaway stern seat. Note windshield vents, side exhausts, power engine hatch, generous fuel capacity. Standard 340hp gas engines cruise at 17 knots (26–27 knots top).

See Page 522 For Value Estimates

Length Overall	38'3"	Clearance	10'9"
Hull Length	36'0"	Fuel	300 gals.
Beam	13'3"	Water	60 gals.
Draft	2'8"	Hull Type	Modified-V
Weight	17,600#	Deadrise Aft	18°

Formula 37 PC

2000–Current

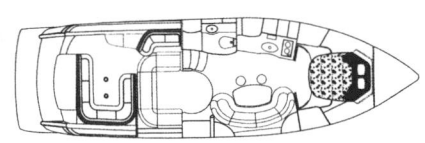

Leading-edge sportcruiser is well built, beautifully finished, easy on the eye. Luxurious interior with Ultraleather seating, furniture-quality woodwork should satisfy the most demanding buyers. Note large head compartment, standard central vacuum system. Topside features include wraparound cockpit seating, double-wide helm seat, walk-through windshield (with handrail), foredeck sun pads, transom storage locker. Power cockpit seat provides good engine room access. Volvo 375hp sterndrives top out at just over 40 knots.

See Page 522 For Value Estimates

Length Overall	38'5"	Fuel	236 gals.
Beam	11'11"	Water	55 gals.
Draft	2'6"	Waste	57 gals.
Weight	16,500#	Hull Type	Modified-V
Clearance	14'4"	Deadrise Aft	18°

Formula 40 PC

2003–Current

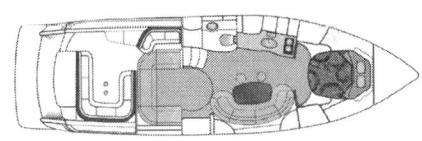

Smooth-riding express competes with the best in luxury amenities, upscale accommodations, long-term owner satisfaction. Posh midcabin interior with private bow stateroom is a tasteful blend of high-gloss cherry cabinetry, Ultraleather upholstery, designer fabrics and furnishings. Topside features include walk-through windshield, flip-up helm seat, transom storage locker, foredeck sun pads. Outstanding finish, near flawless gelcoat. Yanmar 420hp V-drive diesels cruise at 24 knots. Volvo IPS power optional in late models.

See Page 522 For Value Estimates

Length	42'7"	Fuel	250 gals.
Beam	12'8"	Water	55 gals.
Draft	2'11"	Waste	57 gals.
Weight	21,550#	Hull Type	Modified-V
Clearance	16'8"	Deadrise Aft	18°

Formula 41 PC

1996–2004

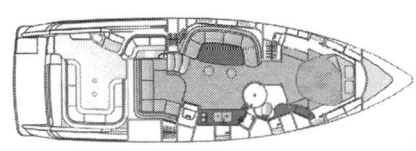

Luxury sportyacht introduced in 1996 met Formula standards for quality, performance, nautical sex appeal. Elegant interior with private forward stateroom, home-sized galley boasts comforts of a small motoryacht. Deep cockpit has huge U-lounge aft, full wet bar, double helm seat, portside lounger. Note walk-through windshield. Entire cockpit sole lifts for engine access. Beamy deep-V hull has prop pockets to reduce draft. Standard gas engines cruise at 16–17 knots; 450hp Cummins diesels cruise at 24–25 knots (about 30 knots top).

See Page 522 For Value Estimates

Length Overall	43'1"	Fuel, Gas	300 gals.
Hull Length	41'0"	Fuel, Diesel	350 gals.
Beam	13'6"	Water	81 gals.
Draft	2'9"	Hull Type	Modified-V
Weight	18,520#	Deadrise Aft	18°

Cruisers & Sedans

Formula 45 Yacht

2007–Current

High-end luxury yacht combines signature Formula styling with spirited performance, executive-class amenities. Highlights include enclosed bridgedeck with excellent visibility, outdoor galley/wet bar, luxurious two-stateroom, two-head interior, convenient walk-through windshield. Optional hydraulic swim platform can stow PWC. Entire aft cockpit rises for engine access. Note power sunroof. Side decks are narrow. Slender beam delivers good heavy-weather handling. Volvo 575hp V-drive diesels cruise at 25–26 knots (about 30 knots top).

See Page 522 For Value Estimates

Length Overall	48'2"	Fuel	350 gals.
Beam	13'11"	Water	100 gals.
Draft	3'5"	Waste	75 gals.
Weight	33,500#	Hull Type	Modified-V
Clearance	15'5"	Deadrise Aft	18°

Formula 48 Yacht

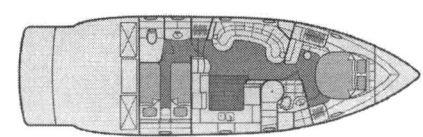

2004–07

Performance, luxury, engineering are combined in this powerful, state-of-the-art cruising yacht. Lavish interior with home-sized galley, high-gloss woodwork boasts second head compartment in aft stateroom. Elegant cockpit seats ten with room to spare. Note superb helm layout, walk-through windshield, spacious engine room with power hatch. Extended swim platform supports PWC. Twin 660hp Cummins diesels cruise in the mid 20s (32–33 knots top). Called the Formula 47 Yacht in 2004. Impressive and expensive.

See Page 522 For Value Estimates

Length	51'0"	Fuel	400 gals.
Beam	14'0"	Water	100 gals.
Draft	3'8"	Waste	75 gals.
Weight	35,750#	Hull Type	Modified-V
Clearance	14'0"	Deadrise Aft	18°

Four Winns 278 Vista

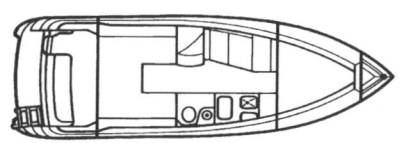

1994–98

Maxi-cube 1990s cruiser combines widebody comforts with versatile layout, spirited performance. Generic mid-cabin interior with full galley, enclosed head, convertible dinette sleeps four adults, two kids. Note generous galley storage. Topside highlights include stylish helm layout, walk-through windshield, foldaway stern seat, double-wide helm seat. Oval cabin ports replaced original sliding cabin windows in 1996. Permit required for trailering. Single 310hp I/O tops out at 30 knots; twin 190hp I/Os reach a top speed of 32–34 knots.

See Page 522 For Value Estimates

Length	27'2"	Fuel	110 gals.
Beam	9'4"	Water	38 gals.
Draft	3'3"	Waste	30 gals.
Weight	6,650#	Hull	Modified-V
Clearance	8'6"	Deadrise Aft	17°

Four Winns 278/285 Vista

2006–Current

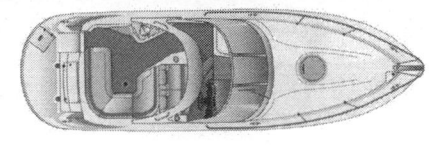

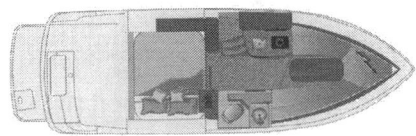

Graceful sport express (called 278 Vista in 2006–09; V285 beginning in 2010) delivers a compelling blend of top-shelf construction, feature-rich accommodations. Topside highlights include deluxe cockpit seating, double-wide helm seat with flip-up bolsters, refreshment center with removable cooler. Luxury-class interior with cherry cabinets, top-shelf amenities is as good as it gets in a boat of this type. Note transom storage locker, sporty dash. Radar arch is a popular option. Single 375hp Volvo sterndrive tops out at 30+ knots.

See Page 522 For Value Estimates

Length	28'4"	Fuel	85 gals.
Beam	8'6"	Water	21 gals.
Draft, Up	1'8"	Waste	21 gals.
Draft, Down	3'3"	Hull Type	Modified-V
Weight	7,100#	Deadrise Aft	17°

Four Winns 285 Express

1991–93

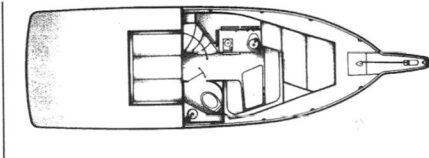

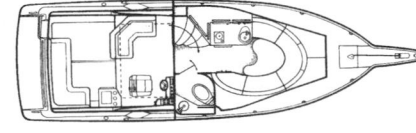

Affordable 1990s express made good on Four Winns promise of solid construction, common-sense cabin accommodations. Offered with choice of two midcabin layouts—standard (more popular) interior has wraparound dinette/V-berth with seating for six. Alternate layout had separate dinette, double berth forward. Companion seat opposite helm rotates to face cockpit. Additional features include foldaway stern seat, good engine access, bow pulpit, swim ladder with handrail. Twin 230hp OMC I/Os top out at over 35 knots.

Prices Not Provided for Pre-1995 Models

Length	28'11"	Headroom	6'2"
Beam	10'2"	Fuel	140 gals.
Draft	3'3"	Water	35 gals.
Weight	9,060#	Hull	Modified-V
Clearance	8'6"	Deadrise Aft	19°

Four Winns 285 Vista

1988–90

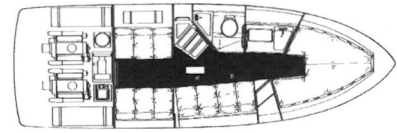

Standard 285 Floorplan

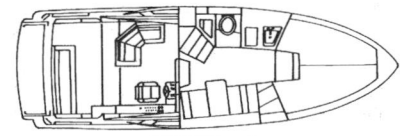

285 SE Floorplan

Vintage 1980s express paired sporty styling with versatile layout, sturdy construction. Relatively wide beam results in roomy interior with stand-up head, full galley, berths for four adults, two kids. Cockpit is arranged with an L-shaped lounge to port (that pivots fore and aft), bench seating aft. Circular foredeck hatches provide good cabin ventilation. Note that 285 SE model (introduced in 1990) has slightly revised interior, lower cost. Single 340hp sterndrive will cruise at 20 knots (about 30 knots top); twin 260hp I/Os run a few knots faster.

Prices Not Provided for Pre-1995 Models

Length w/Pulpit	28'11"	Fuel	150 gals.
Hull Length	27'5"	Water	35 gals.
Beam	10'0"	Clearance	NA
Draft	2'9"	Hull Type	Modified-V
Weight	9,670#	Deadrise Aft	19°

Cruisers & Sedans

Four Winns 288 Vista

2004–09

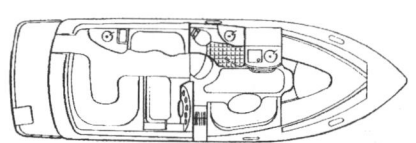

Good-looking Four Winns cruiser strikes the right balance of comfort, price, performance. Expansive interior features upscale decor package with vinyl overheads, Ultraleather seating, high-gloss cherry cabinetry. Midcabin area is a tight fit, but head is large. Note that refrigerator is above galley counter for easy access. Topside highlights include power motor hatch, extended swim platform, cockpit refreshment center, freshwater shower, double helm seat with flip-up bolsters. Volvo 270hp I/Os top out at close to 40 knots.

See Page 522 For Value Estimates

Length w/Platform	30'0"	Fuel	120 gals.
Beam	9'8"	Water	25 gals.
Draft, Down	3'3"	Waste	25 gals.
Weight	10,380#	Hull Type	Modified-V
Clearance, Arch	9'0"	Deadrise Aft	18°

Four Winns 298 Vista

1999–2005

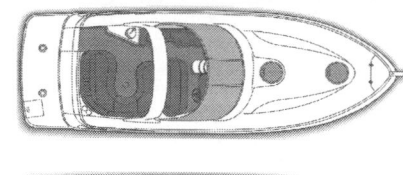

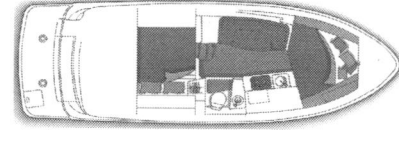

Feature-rich express paired signature Four Winns quality with deluxe accommodations, no-excuses performance. Roomy cockpit with U-shaped seating, double helm seat, refreshment center seats six to eight. Surprisingly spacious interior boasts comfortable salon, plenty of galley storage, top-quality furnishings. Good visibility from raised helm position. Transom locker provides storage for fenders, shore power connections. Note walk-through windshield, bolt-on platform, flip-up helm seat. Volvo 270hp I/Os top out at close to 40 knots.

See Page 522 For Value Estimates

Length w/Platform	30'11"	Clearance, Arch	9'2"
Hull Length	28'0"	Fuel	140 gals.
Beam	10'6"	Water	31 gals.
Draft	3'3"	Hull Type	Modified-V
Weight	10,650#	Deadrise Aft	19°

Four Winns 318/335 Vista

2006–Current

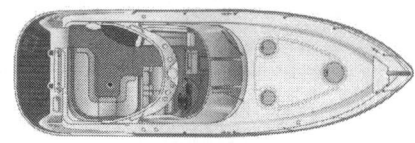

Spirited high-end express (called 318 Vista in 2006–09; V335 beginning in 2010) is graceful, luxurious, built to last. Ergonomic helm is surrounded by spacious cockpit with U-shaped seating, portside lounger, refreshment center with sink, ice-maker. Expansive interior features roomy midcabin layout with table, pullout galley storage, cherrywood cabinetry, large head with shower. Screened companionway door is a plus, but steps are steep. Note transom locker for fenders, shore cord. Twin Volvo 280hp I/Os deliver a top speed of 38–40 knots.

See Page 522 For Value Estimates

Length w/Platform	33'0"	Clearance	11'2"
Beam	10'9"	Fuel	170 gals.
Draft, Up	1'6"	Water	35 gals.
Draft, Down	3'2"	Hull Type	Modified-V
Weight	11,200#	Deadrise Aft	19°

Four Winns 315/325 Express

1988–93

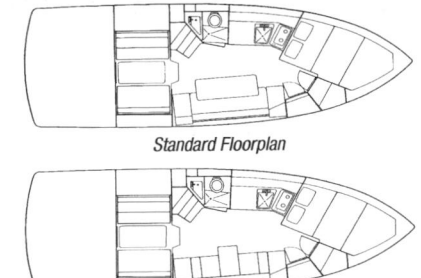

Standard Floorplan

Alternate Floorplan

Prices Not Provided for Pre-1995 Models

Versatile express introduced in 1988 with sterndrive power (315 Express) was joined in 1991 with inboard-powered sibling, the 325 Express. Both shared identical midcabin interiors with double berths fore and aft, convertible dinette, full galley, compact head with shower. (Note that two dinette configurations were available.) Roomy cockpit seats six in comfort. Note fuel increase in 1991. Twin 260hp I/Os cruise 315 Express at 23 knots (about 35 knots top); 270hp inboards cruise the 325 at 18 knots (26–28 top).

Length w/Pulpit	30'6"	Max Headroom	6'3"
Beam	11'0"	Fuel	150/180 gals.
Draft	3'4"	Water	35 gals.
Weight	10,600#	Hull	Modified-V
Clearance	9'0"	Deadrise Aft	19°

Four Winns 328 Vista

1999–2006

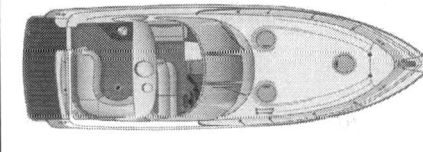

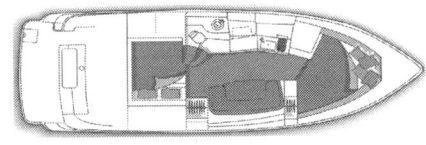

See Page 522 For Value Estimates

Rakish Four Winns cruiser struck an ideal balance between sleek styling, spacious cabin, versatile deck layout. Wide 11'9" beam affords plenty of cabin, cockpit space. Well-finished interior with tasteful decor, high-gloss cherry woodwork features home-size galley, convertible dinette, roomy head compartment. U-shaped cockpit lounge converts to big sun pad; refreshment center comes with ice-maker, sink. Note walk-through windshield, power engine compartment hatch. Volvo 280hp I/Os deliver a top speed of about 35 knots.

Length w/Platform	35'7"	Fuel	220 gals.
Hull Length	33'5"	Water	45 gals.
Beam	11'9"	Waste	30 gals.
Draft	3'2"	Hull Type	Modified-V
Weight	12,600#	Deadrise Aft	19°

Four Winns 338/358 Vista

2007–09

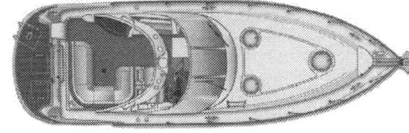

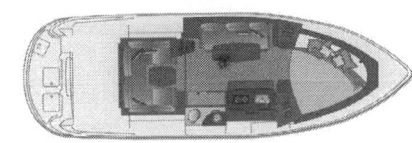

See Page 522 For Value Estimates

Sleek sportcruiser available with sterndrive (338 Vista) or inboard (358 Vista) power offered impressive mix of modern styling, upscale decor, good performance. Interior highlights include high-gloss cherry cabinets, 20" flat-screen TV, teak-and-holly galley sole, central vacuum system. Bow access is via narrow side decks or walk-through windshield. Note unique fold-down, aft-facing swim platform seat, power engine compartment hatch. MerCruiser 300hp gas I/Os reach nearly 40 knots top. Twin 320hp inboards run a few knots slower.

Length	35'0"	Fuel	200 gals.
Beam	11'6"	Water	45 gals.
Draft, Up	2'6"	Waste	30 gals.
Draft, Down	3'4"	Hull Type	Modified-V
Weight	12,090#	Deadrise Aft	19°

Cruisers & Sedans

Four Winns 348 Vista

2001–04

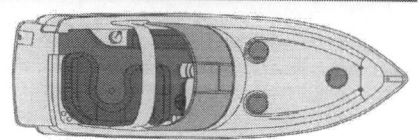

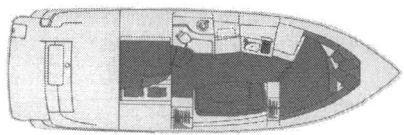

Top-level express (called 338 Vista in 2001) combines inboard dependability with appealing styling, upscale amenities. Well-finished interior with tasteful decor, high-gloss cherry woodwork features home-size galley, midcabin dinette, roomy head compartment. U-shaped cockpit lounge converts to sun pad. Note walk-through windshield, power engine hatch, transom locker, companionway screen door. Above-average fit and finish. MerCruiser 320hp inboards top out at close to 30 knots. Replaced in 2005 with all-new 348 Vista.

See Page 522 For Value Estimates

Length w/Platform	35'7"	Fuel	220 gals.
Beam	11'9"	Water	44 gals.
Draft	2'11"	Waste	30 gals.
Weight	13,100#	Hull Type	Modified-V
Clearance, Arch	9'2"	Deadrise Aft	19°

Four Winns 348/358/375 Vista

2005–Current

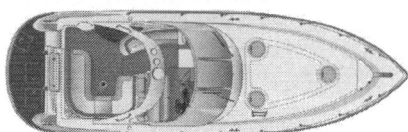

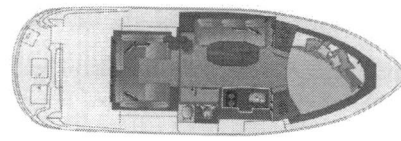

Updated version of earlier 348 Vista (2001–04) appeals to savvy buyers with an eye for quality. Posh midcabin interior offered with open floorplan or with stateroom bulkhead door for privacy. Topside highlights include sporty helm layout with space for electronics, double helm seat with flip-up bolsters, extended swim platform, transom storage locker, power engine hatch, wet bar with ice-maker. Inboard 320hp engines top out at 30 knots; 320hp I/Os reach about 35 knots. Called 348 Vista in 2005–07; V358 in 2008–09; V375 in 2010

See Page 522 For Value Estimates

Length w/Platform	37'0"	Fuel	230 gals.
Beam	12'0"	Water	51 gals.
Draft	3'4"	Waste	30 gals.
Weight	14,600#	Hull Type	Modified-V
Clearance	11'2"	Deadrise Aft	19°

Four Winns 378 Vista

2002–09

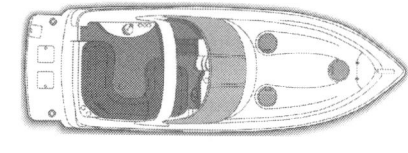

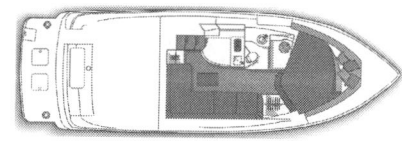

Luxury-class sportcruiser with roomy salon, huge cockpit is as good as it gets in a modern family express. Wide-open interior features expansive salon with two convertible sofas, well-appointed galley, elegant high-gloss cherry cabinetry. Bow-stateroom privacy door is optional. Cockpit—with huge wraparound settee and wet bar—is one of the largest offered in a boat this size. Bow anchor chute is better than a pulpit. Finish is well above average. Twin 375hp gas inboards cruise in the low 20s (30+ knots top).

See Page 523 For Value Estimates

Length w/Platform	41'3"	Fuel	300 gals.
Hull Length	37'9"	Water	66 gals.
Beam	12'9"	Waste	42 gals.
Draft	3'6"	Hull Type	Modified-V
Weight	21,300#	Deadrise Aft	19°

Four Winns V458/V475

2008–Current

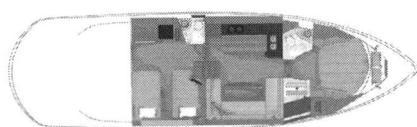

All-weather express with pod drives couples spirited performance with sporty styling, executive-level comforts. Topside highlights include hardtop with triple skylights, wide-open cockpit layout with seating for ten, huge extended swim platform. Well-finished interior boasts two private staterooms, two heads, big home-size galley. Aft deck rises for engine access. Cockpit AC is standard. Note narrow side decks. Joystick control system makes handling easy. Cruise efficiently at 25 knots (low-to-mid 30s top) with 435hp Volvo IPS diesel inboards.

See Page 523 For Value Estimates

Length w/Platform	49'4"	Fuel	380 gals.
Hull Length	44'6"	Water	101 gals.
Beam	14'0"	Waste	57 gals.
Draft	3'7"	Hull Type	Modified Deep-V
Weight	30,000#	Deadrise Aft	19°

Grand Banks 38 Eastbay Express

1994–2004

Standard Floorplan

Optional Layout

Original Eastbay model introduced in 1994 launched Grand Banks in a completely new direction. Single-stateroom teak interior was designed for the cruising couple. User-friendly cockpit has built-in seating. Teak swim platform, radar mast, foredeck storage lockers were standard. Popular hardtop model became available in 2002. Good engine access via hydraulic-opening hatch. Hunt-designed deep-V hull delivers outstanding open-water comfort, performance. Cat 375hp diesels cruise at 22 knots (high 20s top). Over 130 were built.

See Page 523 For Value Estimates

Length Overall	38'0"	Fuel	344 gals.
Length WL	34'5"	Water	95 gals.
Beam	13'2"	Clearance	9'3"
Draft	3'4"	Hull Type	Deep-V
Weight	28,500#	Deadrise Aft	18°

Grand Banks 39 Eastbay SX/HX

2006–Current

SX Layout

HX Layout

Graceful hardtop cruiser—successor to the original 38 Express that launched the Eastbay series—blends classic Downeast beauty with exceptional performance, unsurpassed luxury. Deluxe single-stateroom interior is perfect for the cruising couple. Expansive, teak-laid cockpit has built-in seating, large lazarette. Note frameless windows, immaculate engine room, wide side decks. SX model has fully enclosed salon; HX version has semi-enclosed helmdeck. Yanmar 480hp diesels cruise at 24–26 knots (about 30 knots top).

See Page 523 For Value Estimates

Length w/Platform	42'4"	Fuel	352 gals.
Hull Length	39'2"	Water	100 gals.
Beam	13'3"	Waste	28 gals.
Draft	3'4"	Hull Type	Deep-V
Weight	28,494#	Deadrise Aft	18°

Cruisers & Sedans

Grand Banks 43 Eastbay Flybridge

1998–2004

Standard Floorplan

Optional Layout

See Page 524 For Value Estimates

Gold-plated flybridge yacht (called Eastbay 40 until 1998 when cockpit was lengthened) with timeless Downeast styling delivers impressive blend of luxury, craftsmanship, performance. Elegant two-stateroom interior with lower helm, deluxe galley, features handcrafted teak cabinetry, top-quality hardware and furnishings. Spacious cockpit with transom door can entertain a small crowd. Note wide side decks. Twin 300hp Cat diesels cruise at 18–20 knots (about 22 knots top); 375hp Cats cruise at 22–24 knots (high 20s top).

Length	43'0"	Fuel	450 gals.
Beam	13'4"	Water	110 gals.
Draft	3'8"	Headroom	6'6"
Weight	31,970#	Hull Type	Deep-V
Clearance	16'6"	Deadrise Aft	18°

Grand Banks 43 Eastbay Express

2000–04

Standard Layout

Optional Layout

See Page 524 For Value Estimates

Classic open express delivers sophisticated blend of style, comfort, performance. Lavish two-stateroom interior with hand-rubbed teak woodwork, leather seating is impressive display of old-world nautical elegance. Highlights include spacious helmdeck with facing settees, large cockpit, teak decking, Corian galley counters. Modified-V hull has prop pockets to reduce draft, shaft angles. Hardtop model became available in 2002. Standard 435hp Cats cruise at 24 knots with a top speed of 27–28 knots. Not cheap, but quality never is.

Length	43'0"	Fuel	450 gals.
Beam	13'2"	Water	110 gals.
Draft	3'8"	Headroom	6'4"
Weight	33,000#	Hull Type	Modified-V
Clearance	16'6"	Deadrise Aft	14°

Grand Banks 43 Eastbay SX/HX

2002–2007

Standard HX Layout

Alternate HX Layout

See Page 524 For Value Estimates

Hardtop cruising yacht with semi-enclosed helm combines classic Downeast styling with meticulous finish, seakindly hull. Two-stateroom interior with hand-rubbed teak woodwork, leather seating is an impressive display of boatbuilding excellence. Highlights include spacious helmdeck with facing settees, teak-laid cockpit, wide side decks, roomy engine compartment. SX model has fully enclosed helm. Prop pockets to reduce draft, shaft angles. Twin 440hp Yanmar diesels cruise at 25 knots (28–29 knots top).

Length Overall	43'0"	Clearance, Mast	14'0"
Length WL	39'5"	Fuel	450 gals.
Beam	13'2"	Water	110 gals.
Draft	3'7"	Hull Type	Modified-V
Weight	29,760#	Deadrise Aft	14°

Cruisers & Sedans

Grand Banks 47 Eastbay Flybridge

2005–Current

Standard Floorplan

Optional Layout

See Page 524 For Value Estimates

Elegant Downeast flybridge yacht boasts top-drawer build quality with spacious accommodations, luxury amenities. Available with standard two-cabin layout or optional single-cabin floorplan with two heads, open-plan "office" with sofa bed in place of second stateroom. Highlights include Burmese teak interior, wide side decks, unique spiral bridge staircase, large cockpit with built-in seating. Note teak cockpit sole, fold-down radar mast, spacious engine room. Cruise at 25 knots (about 30 knots top) with 720hp Caterpillar diesels.

Length Overall	52'4"	Fuel	700 gals.
Length WL	43'3"	Water	206 gals.
Beam	15'0"	Waste	75 gals.
Draft	3'10"	Hull Type	Deep-V
Weight	47,900#	Deadrise Aft	18°

Grand Banks 49 Eastbay SX/HX

1999–Current

SX Layout

HX Layout

See Page 524 For Value Estimates

Premium hardtop express sets the gold standard for seductive Downeast styling, lush accommodations, sophisticated construction. Rich two-stateroom, two-head interior with home-size galley, huge master stateroom is long on luxury, short on salon space. SX model has fully enclosed salon; HX version has semi-enclosed helm. Note wide side decks, power-assisted center windshield panel, spacious engine room. Exemplary fit and finish. Deep-V hull delivers superb big-water performance. Cruise at 25–26 knots (30 top) with 670hp Cat diesels.

Length Overall	54'7"	Clearance	NA
Length WL	45'8"	Fuel	775 gals.
Beam	16'0"	Water	176 gals.
Draft	4'4"	Hull Type	Deep-V
Weight	48,000#	Deadrise Aft	18°

Grand Banks 54 Eastbay SX

2003–07

Standard 2-Stateroom Plan

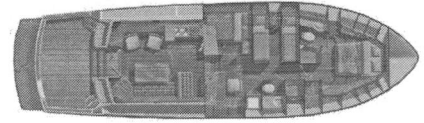

Optional 3-Stateroom Plan

See Page 524 For Value Estimates

Exquisitely detailed hardtop cruiser with enclosed helm/salon combines classic Downeast styling with sumptuous accommodations, agile performance. Standard galley-down, two-stateroom floorplan is notable for spacious staterooms, huge galley; optional three-cabin layout has deckhouse galley. Office area with desk, washer/dryer is standard in either layout. Cockpit has built-in seating, teak sole, engine room access. Outstanding finish, near perfect gelcoat. Cat 800hp diesels cruise in the mid 20s (28–29 knots top).

Length Overall	53'9"	Clearance	16'3"
Length WL	49'6"	Fuel	935 gals.
Beam	16'0"	Water	200 gals.
Draft	4'4"	Hull Type	Deep-V
Weight	56,500#	Deadrise Aft	18°

Cruisers & Sedans

Grand Banks 58 Eastbay Flybridge

2004–07

Standard Layout

Optional Layout

See Page 524 For Value Estimates

Prestigious flybridge yacht with gorgeous Downeast styling sets class standard for cruising elegance. Opulent three-stateroom, galley-down interior boasts wide-open salon; optional galley-up layout provides fourth cabin that may also serve as an office. Highlights include lower-helm deck door, holding-plate refrigeration, stand-up engine room, wide side decks. Note curved bridge staircase, teak cockpit sole. Stidd helm seats, cockpit wet bar, bow thruster are standard. Cat 1,400hp diesels deliver a top speed of over 30 knots.

Length w/Platform	63'5"	Clearance	18'9"
Hull Length	58'8"	Fuel	1,175 gals.
Beam	17'8"	Water	280 gals.
Draft	5'4"	Hull Type	Deep-V
Weight	91,000#	Deadrise Aft	21°

Hatteras 36 Sedan

1986–87

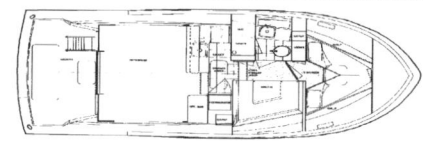

One Stateroom

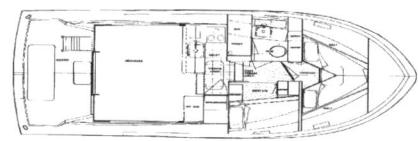

Two Staterooms

Prices Not Provided for Pre-1995 Models

Classy sport sedan with very expansive interior but too-small cockpit is more family cruiser than hardcore fishing machine. Very well-appointed interior (by 1980s standards) with wide-open salon was offered with choice of dinette or second stateroom. Features include large head compartment with separate stall shower, teak interior cabinetry, large cabin windows, bow pulpit, wide side decks. Tiny cockpit is practically useless for serious fishing activities. Prop pockets reduce draft. Twin gas engines cruise at 15 knots (mid 20s top).

Length	36'6"	Fuel	355 gals.
Beam	13'7"	Water	115 gals.
Draft	3'9"	Cockpit	72 sq. ft.
Weight	25,500#	Hull Type	Modified-V
Clearance	12'6"	Deadrise Aft	18°

Hatteras 43 Sport Express

1996–98

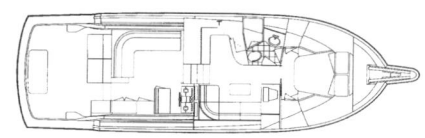

Standard Layout

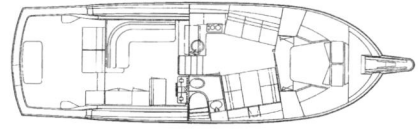

Optional Arrangement

See Page 525 For Value Estimates

Powerful offshore express—among the largest available during the late 1990s—was stylish, fast, expensive. Standard interior with U-shaped galley, stall shower in head sleeps four; alternate layout with smaller head and galley sleeps six. Rigging station, lift-out fishboxes, livewell were standard. Aft-facing bench seat in cockpit lifts for engine room access. Additional features include light oak interior woodwork, radar arch, side exhausts, bow pulpit. First-rate finish throughout. Twin 535hp GM diesels cruise at 27 knots (30+ knots top).

Length	43'2"	Fuel	530 gals.
Beam	14'3"	Water	154 gals.
Draft	4'5"	Headroom	6'6"
Weight	38,000#	Hull Type	Modified-V
Clearance	9'8"	Deadrise Aft	9°

Hi-Star Star 44 Convertible

1986–92

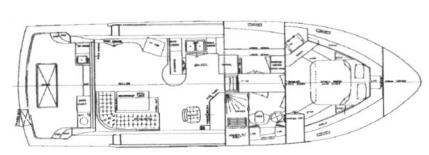

Durable Taiwan import with Bertram-like styling is long on interior volume, short on cockpit space. Two-stateroom interior dwarfs most 44-footers for interior volume. Note exceptionally well-crafted teak joinery, spacious salon with built-in settee, standard lower helm station. Well-arranged engine room is accessed by lifting steps forward of galley. Cockpit is too small for any serious fishing. Additional features include wide side decks, transom door, flybridge seating for six. Cat 375hp diesels cruise at 18 knots and reach 22–23 knots top.

Prices Not Provided for Pre-1995 Models

Length	43'9"	Fuel	500 gals.
Beam	15'2"	Water	250 gals.
Draft	3'6"	Cockpit	65 sq. ft.
Weight	33,000#	Hull Type	Modified-V
Clearance	NA	Deadrise Aft	16°

Hi-Star Star 48 Convertible

1986–92

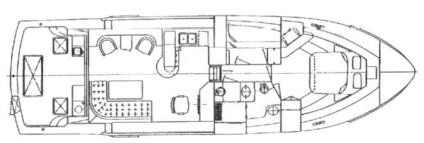

Versatile 1990s convertible with Bertram-like styling is more family cruiser than hard-core fishing machine. Two-stateroom interior with spacious salon features standard lower helm, huge master stateroom, copious storage. Note double-entry stall shower. Small cockpit is best suited for swimming or diving. Engineroom is very well finished. Additional features include wide side decks, transom door, bow pulpit, bridge seating for six. One of the few Asian-built convertibles imported into the US. Cat 375hp diesels cruise at 18 knots (22–23 knots top).

Prices Not Provided for Pre-1995 Models

Length	47'9"	Fuel	500 gals.
Beam	15'2"	Water	250 gals.
Draft	3'8"	Cockpit	108 sq. ft.
Weight	37,000#	Hull Type	Modified-V
Clearance	13'6"	Deadrise Aft	16°

Hinckley T29R

2003–Current

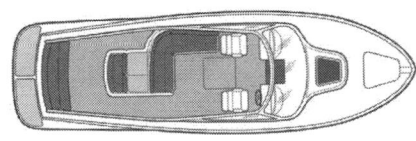

Seductive retro-runabout with jet-drive power stops traffic everywhere she goes. Composite Kevlar-reinforced construction is state of the art. Cockpit—with teak console, custom Nardi wheel—resembles a classic sports car. Engine box doubles as aft-facing passenger seat, conceals sink and cooler. Cuddy is fitted with V-berth, VacuFlush head. Additional features include power engine box, joystick steering, teak swim platform, bow thruster. Meticulous finish. Single Yanmar 440hp diesel will cruise in the high 20s (30+ knots top).

See Page 525 For Value Estimates

Length Overall	29'2"	Clearance	5'6"
Length WL	26'8"	Fuel	100 gals.
Beam	9'1"	Water	20 gals.
Draft	1'9"	Hull	Modified-V
Weight	8,200#	Deadrise Aft	19°

Cruisers & Sedans

Hinckley 36 Picnic Boat

1994–2007

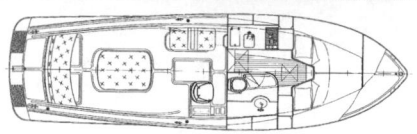

Standard Version

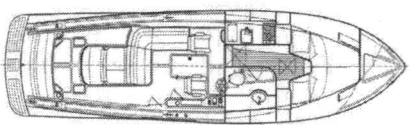

Extended Pilothouse Version

See Page 525 For Value Estimates

Iconic jet-powered weekender with Downeast look is elegant, expensive, built to last. Comfortable cockpit layout (engine box doubles as seat or table), semi-enclosed helm, deluxe mahogany interior with compact galley, large head compartment. Truly outstanding fit and finish. Extended pilothouse model with additional seating came out in 2001. A seriously popular boat—over 400 were built. Replaced in 2008 with all-new Picnic Boat model. Cruise at 20 knots with 350hp Yanmar diesel; 22–23 knots with 440hp Yanmar.

Length Overall	36'5"	Fuel	160 gals.
Length WL	33'7"	Water	35 gals.
Beam	10'0"	Clearance	11'4"
Draft	1'6"	Hull	Modified-V
Weight	11,850#	Deadrise Aft	15°

Hinckley Talaria 40

2002–Current

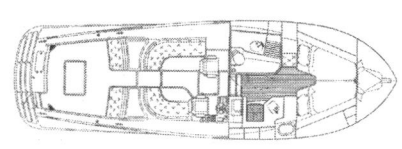

See Page 525 For Value Estimates

Sophisticated jet-powered cruiser with distinctive Downeast profile bears strong resemblance to Hinckley's great-selling 36 Picnic Boat. Fully cored, shallow-draft hull is notable for high-tech construction, generous transom tumblehome. Elegant cockpit with extended hardtop features weather-protected seating and helm. Note feature-rich interior with teak-and-holly sole. Aft-facing cockpit settees lift electrically for engine access. Yanmar 440hp diesels matched to Hamilton waterjets cruise at 28 knots (32–33 knots top).

Length Overall	40'1"	Clearance	8'7"
Length WL	37'1"	Fuel	340 gals.
Beam	12'5"	Water	80 gals.
Draft	2'3"	Hull Type	Modified-V
Weight	26,000#	Deadrise Aft	16°

Hinckley Talaria 44 Express

1999–2008

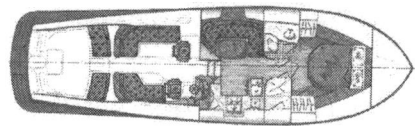

Single Stateroom

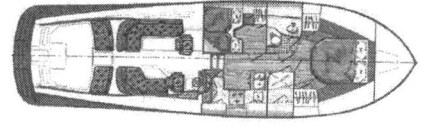

Two Staterooms

See Page 525 For Value Estimates

Stately jet-powered cruiser personifies Hinckley legendary commitment to timeless design, top-quality construction. Highlights include semi-enclosed pilothouse with facing settees, varnished teak interior with choice of one or two staterooms, wide side decks (but no bow rails). Extended hardtop protects much of the cockpit; aft-facing seats hinge forward for easy engine access. Waterjet drives can safely cruise in very shallow water. JetStick control system makes docking easy. Yanmar 440hp diesels cruise at 25–26 knots (30+ knots top).

Length Overall	44'10"	Fuel	500 gals.
Length WL	41'0"	Water	100 gals.
Beam	13'6"	Waste	35 gals.
Draft	2'3"	Hull	Modified-V
Weight	29,000#	Deadrise Aft	16.5°

Hunt 29 Surfhunter

2004–Current

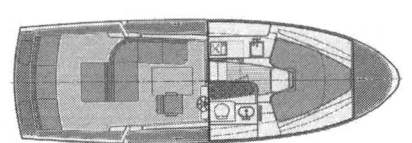

Popular (and practical) dayboat with luxury-class amenities combines seaworthy deep-V performance with classic lines, premium construction. Standard features include deluxe helmseat, L-shaped settee, custom teak bridgedeck table. Engine box doubles as extra seating. Yacht-grade interior with teak-and-holly sole boasts compact galley, enclosed head, V-berth/dinette. Note built-in transom seat, wide side decks. Hardtop is a popular option. Cruise at 25 knots (30+ top) with single Volvo 370hp Duoprop diesel.

See Page 525 For Value Estimates

Length	29'6"	Fuel	150 gals.
Beam	10'6"	Water	28 gals.
Draft	3'0"	Waste	15 gals.
Weight	8,000#	Hull Type	Deep-V
Clearance	5'9"	Deadrise Aft	22°

Hunt 33 Express

1999–2004

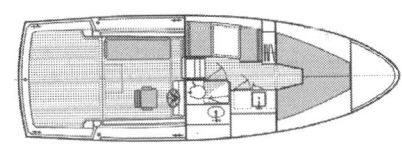

Feature-rich cruising yacht with enduring lines offers luxurious—but not glitzy—accommodations, top-shelf construction. Available in express, hardtop sedan (pictured above) versions. Features include fully cored hull with propeller tunnel, large cockpit, underwater exhaust system. Upscale interior boasts varnished mahogany trim, teak-and-holly sole. Note flawless gelcoat. Bridgedeck lifts electrically for engine access. Single 370hp Cummins diesel will cruise at 24–25 knots; Yanmar 440hp cruises at 26–28 knots.

See Page 525 For Value Estimates

Length	32'9"	Fuel	125 gals.
Beam	10'10"	Water	30 gals.
Draft	3'0"	Headroom	6'1"
Weight	10,000#	Hull Type	Deep-V
Clearance	15'0"	Deadrise Aft	20°

Hunt 33 Surfhunter

2005–Current

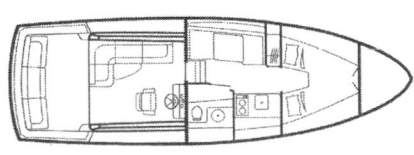

Elegant deep-V express offers extraordinary comfort, security for the cruising couple. Highlights include beautifully finished cabin with varnished teak joinery, roomy cockpit with removable transom seating, 7-foot-long bridgedeck with L-shaped settee. Entire bridgedeck lifts for excellent engine access. Note standard bow thruster, tall windshield with side vents, deep chain locker. Exemplary workmanship, flawless gelcoat justifies high price. Brisk cruising speed of 22–24 knots (about 28 top) with single 380hp Cummins (or 370hp Yanmar) diesel is remarkable.

See Page 525 For Value Estimates

Length	33'0"	Headroom	6'2"
Beam	11'4"	Fuel	125 gals.
Draft	3'0"	Water	28 gals.
Weight	11,000#	Hull Type	Deep-V
Clearance	NA	Deadrise Aft	20°

Cruisers & Sedans

Cruisers & Sedans

Hunt 36 Harrier

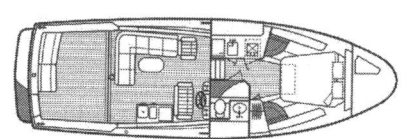

2003–Current

Gold-plated express delivers acclaimed blend of rich styling, superb build quality, impressive big-water performance. Elegant open-plan interior with full galley, large head boasts varnished cherry cabinetry, classy teak-and-holly sole. Bridgedeck settee extends by lowering forward passenger seat; cockpit can be left open for fishing or fitted with extra seating for cruising. Fully cored deep-V hull with slender beam is designed to handle seriously rough water. Yanmar 370hp diesels cruise at 30 knots (about 35 knots top).

See Page 525 For Value Estimates

Length	36'6"	Fuel	250 gals.
Beam	11'0"	Water	50 gals.
Draft	3'0"	Waste	20 gals.
Weight	13,500#	Hull Type	Deep-V
Clearance	8'0"	Deadrise Aft	22°

Hylas 47 Convertible

1987–93

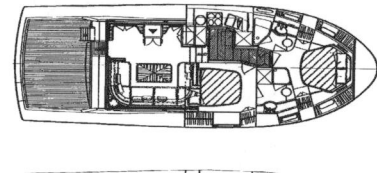

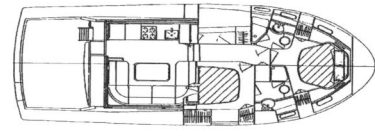

Taiwan import with a rakish lines combines very wide beam with sea-kindly hull, family-friendly layout. Hull was drawn by Jim Wynne, features balsa-cored hullsides, prop pockets, plenty of freeboard all around. The interior is very spacious thanks to broad beam. One of the few boats her size to have walkaround queens in both staterooms. (Three-stateroom layout was optional.) Both heads have separate stall showers. High cockpit gunwales are not well-suited to fishing. Note cockpit engine room access door. Twin 450-hp 6-71 diesels cruise in the low 20s, optional 550-hp 6V92s cruise at 24–25 knots.

Prices Not Provided for Pre-1995 Models

Length	46'6"	Fuel	600 gals.
Beam	16'9"	Water	160 gals.
Draft	3'10"	Waste	50 gals.
Weight	38,000#	Hull Type	Modified-V
Clearance	13'4"	Deadrise Aft	14°

Intrepid 390 Sport Yacht

2007–Current

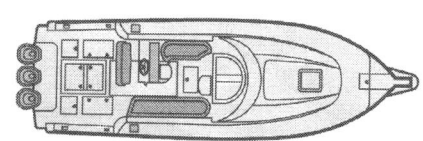

Custom-produced luxury sportyacht with triple-outboard power delivers high-octane mix of yacht-class comfort, speedboat performance. Expansive cockpit with lounge seating forward (with electric backrests) comes standard with fishboxes, livewell, removable rear bench seat. Posh interior with queen and convertible guest berths includes head with separate shower, teak-and-holly sole. Note power helm seat, distinctive shark-fin cabin windows. Hullside dive door is a popular option. Over 50 knots max with triple 300hp Verados.

See Page 526 For Value Estimates

Length	41'10"	Fuel	400 gals.
Beam	12'0"	Water	60 gals.
Hull Draft	24"	Max HP	1,150
Dry Weight	15,500#	Hull Type	Deep-V
Clearance	9'0"	Deadrise Aft	20°

Intrepid 475 Sport Yacht

2006–Current

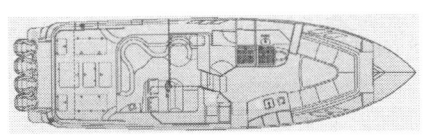

Purebred performance cruiser with stepped hull, quad outboard power takes Intrepid luxury, engineering to the next level. Surprisingly spacious interior with two private staterooms, large head with separate stall shower is beautifully appointed, tastefully finished. Expansive deck layout with state-of-the-art helm features wraparound lounge seating for six. Note hullside windows, wide side decks. Outboard power results in more living, storage space than most comparably sized inboards. Four 275hp Verado outboards reach 40+ knots wide open.

Insufficient Resale Data to Assign Values

Length	47'6"	Fuel	480 gals.
Beam	13'8"	Water	100 gals.
Hull Draft	3'2"	Max HP	1,100
Weight	28,500#	Hull Type	Deep-V
Clearance	12'4"	Deadrise Aft	24°

Island Gypsy 40 Sedan

1986–94

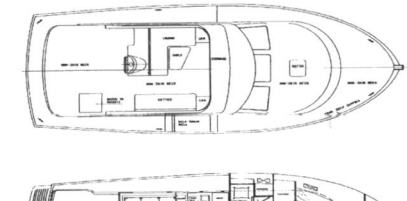

Popular sedan cruiser lured buyers with spacious interior, rugged construction, attractive price. Highlights include standard lower helm with deck door, wide side decks, large engine room, enormous flybridge with L-shaped settee forward of helm. Note solid teak interior cabinetry. Combined salon/cockpit area offers expansive entertaining platform. Extended bridge shades cockpit. No transom door. Twin 135hp diesels cruise economically at 8 knots. Later models with 375hp Cats cruise at 18 knots (20+ knots top).

Prices Not Provided for Pre-1995 Models

Length Overall	40'0"	Clearance	13'3"
Length WL	35'3"	Fuel	400 gals.
Beam	14'3"	Water	200 gals.
Draft	3'6"	Headroom	6'4"
Weight	33,500#	Hull Type	Semi-Disp.

Legacy 28 Express

1999–2006

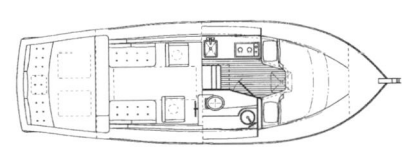

Sought-after New England express combines traditional styling, stem-to-stern quality, elegant practicality. Generous 9'6" beam permits roomy cabin with complete galley, enclosed head with shower, berths for two. Notable features include full-width transom seat, underwater exhaust system, well-arranged helm console, wide side decks. Tall windshield offers excellent wind, spray protection. Low-deadrise hull isn't the softest ride in rough water. Single Yanmar 315hp diesel will cruise at 22–24 knots (high 20s top).

See Page 528 For Value Estimates

Length	28'0"	Water	30 gals.
Beam	9'6"	Waste	25 gals.
Draft	2'2"	Headroom	6'0"
Weight	6,500#	Hull Type	Modified-V
Fuel	120 gals.	Deadrise Aft	5°

Cruisers & Sedans

Legacy 32 Express

2007–08

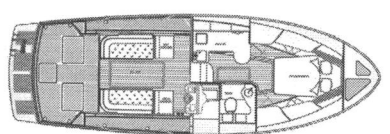

Beamy 32-footer with polished profile offers dayboat luxury, cruising comfort at its best. Extended semi-enclosed bridge deck with large windows, facing settees can entertain several guests. (Note that helm and companion seats can be electrically lowered to extend settees.) High-gloss cherry cabin with leather seating, teak-and-holly sole has the feel of a custom yacht. Additional features include underwater exhaust system, cockpit seating, wide side decks, spacious engine room. Cruise efficiently at 16 knots (22 top) with single 380hp Cummins diesel.

See Page 528 For Value Estimates

Length	32'6"	Fuel	200 gals.
Beam	12'4"	Water	60 gals.
Draft	3'10"	Waste	35 gals.
Weight	14,500#	Hull Type	Modified-V
Clearance	NA	Deadrise Aft	NA

Legacy 34 Express

1996–2006

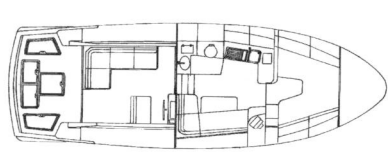

Quality Downeast cruiser delivers leading-edge comfort, elegance in a 34-foot boat. Versatile cockpit is large enough for fishing or entertaining; well-appointed interior with mahogany cabinetry, teak-and-holly sole drips luxury. Note wide side decks, excellent helm visibility. Fully cored hull has short keel for directional stability and—in single-screw version—prop, rudder protection. Engine room is tight with twin engines. Cruise at 16–18 knots with single 440hp Cummins diesel; mid 20s with twin 440hp Cummins.

See Page 528 For Value Estimates

Length	34'0"	Water	94 gals.
Beam	12'5"	Waste	35 gals.
Draft	3'6"	Headroom	6'5"
Weight	15,800#	Hull Type	Modified-V
Fuel	251 gals.	Deadrise Aft	17°

Legacy 34 Sedan

1997–2006

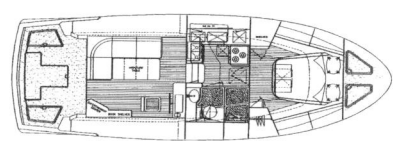

Appealing hardtop cruiser with Downeast profile met signature Legacy standards for midsize luxury, superior craftsmanship. Upscale interior features spacious master stateroom, head with stall shower, varnished teak-and-holly cabin sole. Large ports, generous storage are a plus. Roomy pilothouse seats several guests in comfort. Note wide side decks, excellent helm visibility. Short keel offers prop, rudder protection in single-screw models. Cruise at 16–18 knots with single 440hp Cummins diesel; mid 20s with twin 440hp Cummins.

See Page 528 For Value Estimates

Length	34'0"	Fuel	251 gals.
Beam	12'5"	Water	94 gals.
Draft	3'6"	Waste	35 gals.
Weight	17,500#	Hull Type	Modified-V
Clearance	NA	Deadrise Aft	17°

Cruisers & Sedans

Legacy 40 Express

1995–2006

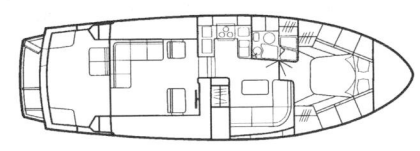

Graceful semicustom cruiser with tremendous eye appeal enjoys a gold-plated reputation for top-notch construction, sea-kindly ride, luxury-class amenities. Finely crafted interior with semi-enclosed deckhouse, modest salon is well-finished, tasteful, comfortable. Stateroom is roomier than expected. Large windows provide outstanding 360° helm visibility. Wide side decks are a plus. Easily-driven hull delivers a superb open-water ride. Cruise at 16–18 knots with single 440hp Yanmar diesel; low 20s with twin 370hp Cummins diesels.

Insufficient Resale Data to Assign Values

Length Overall	39'4"	Fuel	410 gals.
Length WL	36'0"	Water	120 gals.
Beam	13'7"	Waste	40 gals.
Draft	3'8"	Hull Type	Modified-V
Weight	22,000#	Deadrise Aft	17°

Legacy 40 Sedan

1995–2006

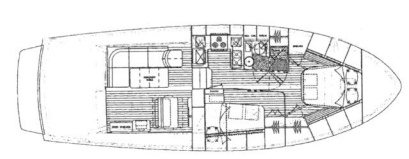

Purebred Downeast sedan introduced in 1995 was Legacy's first-ever powerboat model. Luxurious galley-down, two-stateroom floorplan boasts comfortable pilothouse/salon area with L-shaped settee, teak-and-holly sole, deck access doors. Wide side decks make getting around easy. Note attractive teak exterior trim. Shallow keel protects running gear in single-engine installations. Exceptional craftsmanship throughout. Single 420hp Cat diesel will cruise at 17–18 knots; twin 370hp Cummins cruise at 22–23 knots. Flybridge was optional.

Insufficient Resale Data to Assign Values

Length Overall	39'4"	Fuel	410 gals.
Length WL	36'0"	Water	120 gals.
Beam	13'7"	Waste	40 gals.
Draft	3'8"	Hull Type	Modified-V
Weight	22,000#	Deadrise Aft	17°

Luhrs 3400 Motor Yacht

1990–92

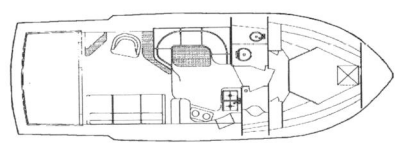

Versatile family cruiser from early 1990s was a departure from Luhr's fishing-boat tradition. Single-stateroom interior features expansive salon wide open to U-shaped dinette to port, mid-level galley opposite. Note split head/shower compartments, oak parquet galley floor, numerous storage bins. Cockpit is too small for much fishing. Huge flybridge has convenient walk-through passage to foredeck. Swim platform, bow pulpit were standard. Standard 320hp gas inboards cruise at 16 knots and reach 26–27 knots wide open.

Prices Not Provided for Pre-1995 Models

Length	34'0"	Fuel	300 gals.
Beam	12'6"	Water	60 gals.
Draft	3'2"	Headroom	6'3"
Weight	13,500#	Hull Type	Modified-V
Clearance	22'0"	Deadrise Aft	16°

Cruisers & Sedans

Luhrs 3420 Motor Yacht

1991–93

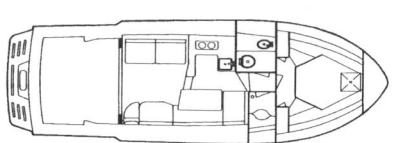

Durable flybridge sedan from early 1990s gets high marks for well-planned accommodations, roomy cockpit. Expansive single-stateroom interior includes built-in dinette, big U-shaped galley, generous storage. Note split head/shower compartments, hardwood galley floor. Uncluttered cockpit—without transom door or fishboxes—is big enough for two anglers. Baitwell is inconveniently located on swim platform. Radar arch, bow pulpit, swim platform were standard. Twin 340hp gas engines cruise at 16–17 knots (mid 20s top).

Prices Not Provided for Pre-1995 Models

Length	34'0"	Fuel	300 gals.
Beam	12'6"	Water	60 gals.
Draft	3'2"	Headroom	6'2"
Weight	13,500#	Hull Type	Modified-V
Clearance	22'0"	Deadrise Aft	15°

Luhrs 35 Alura

1987–89

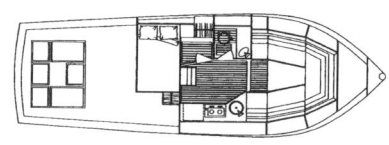

Distinctive 1980s express impressed savvy buyers with an eye for versatility, value. Spacious cockpit with bait-prep center, in-deck fishbox has room for several anglers without bumping elbows. Simple interior with standing headroom boasts private aft stateroom, stand-up shower, teak-and-holly cabin sole. Tall windshield offers good wind, spray protection. Swim platform was standard, but transom door wasn't. Note wide side decks, bow pulpit. Twin 270hp gas inboards cruise at 16–17 knots with a top speed in the mid 20s.

Prices Not Provided for Pre-1995 Models

Length	35'5"	Fuel	260 gals.
Beam	12'2"	Water	55 gals.
Draft	2'11"	Headroom	6'2"
Weight	12,800#	Hull Type	Modified-V
Clearance	NA	Deadrise Aft	15°

Mainship 30 Pilot

1998–2007

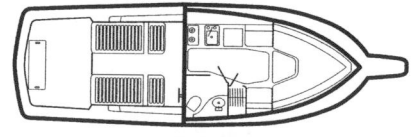

1998–2002

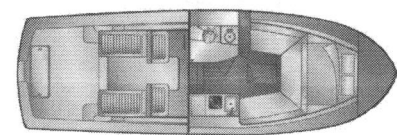

2003–07

See Page 529 For Value Estimates

Best-selling diesel express with handsome Downeast styling makes good on promise of economical operation, common-sense accommodations. Compact cabin with U-shaped settee, full galley, stand-up head with shower sleeps two. Updated Pilot II model (introduced in 2003) boasts revised cabin layout with folding V-berth, shortened keel, prop pocket. Note good engine access, tall windshield, wide decks. Early models with 170hp Yanmar cruise at 13–14 knots; Pilot II models with 315hp Yanmar cruise at 16–18 knots.

Length w/Pulpit	33'1"	Weight	10,000#
Hull Length	30'0"	Fuel	175 gals.
Beam	10'3"	Water	40 gals.
Draft, Original Hull	2'11"	Waste	13 gals.
Draft, Series II	2'3"	Hull Type	Semi-Disp.

Cruisers & Sedans

Mainship 30 Pilot Sedan

2000–07

1998–2002

2003–07

See Page 529 For Value Estimates

Hardtop version of popular Mainship 30 Express combines semi-enclosed helm with roomy cockpit, efficient cabin layout. Well-appointed interior with U-shaped settee, full galley, stand-up head with shower sleeps two. Updated Pilot II model (introduced in 2003) boasts revised interior plan with folding V-berth, shortened keel section, hull prop pocket. Note good engine access, tall windshield, wide side decks. Early models with 170hp Yanmar cruise at 13–14 knots; Pilot II models with 315hp Yanmar cruise at 16–18 knots.

Length w/Pulpit	33'1"	Weight	11,000#
Hull Length	30'0"	Fuel	175 gals.
Beam	10'3"	Water	40 gals.
Draft, Original Hull	2'11"	Waste	13 gals.
Draft, Series II	2'3"	Hull Type	Semi-Disp.

Mainship 31 Pilot

2008–Current

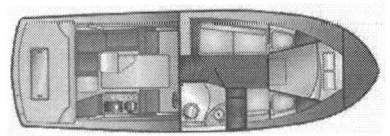

See Page 529 For Value Estimates

All-weather hardtop cruiser balances versatile cockpit design with solid construction, low-cost operation. Cherrywood interior with cherry-planked sole includes convertible sofa (expandable into full-size upper/lower berths), queen size island berth, roomy head. Semi-enclosed helm with large side windows provides good helm visibility. Transom door, bow thruster are standard. Wide side decks are a plus. Note open-air galley with electric grill. Exceptional engine access. Cruise at 14 knots (about 20 top) with single 315hp Yanmar diesel.

Length w/Platform	35'5"	Clearance	9'6"
Hull Length	33'5"	Fuel	180 gals.
Beam	10'2"	Water	40 gals.
Draft	2'6"	Waste	30 gals.
Weight	11,750#	Hull Type	Semi-Disp.

Mainship 31 Sedan Bridge

1994–99

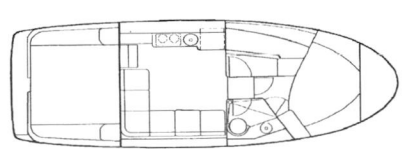

See Page 529 For Value Estimates

Affordable 1990s sedan with full-beam interior took small-boat space, comfort to the next level. Highlights include spacious salon, double-entry head compartment, two private staterooms (rare in a boat this size). Small galley lacks storage, counter space. Flybridge has walk-through forward gate for bow access. Entire cockpit sole lifts for engine access. Radar arch, transom door, bow pulpit, swim platform were standard. Molded steps make bridge access easy. Cruise at 18 knots with 340hp V-drive gas engines (about 30 knots top).

Length Overall	33'3"	Clearance	14'4"
Hull Length	31'3"	Fuel	200 gals.
Beam	11'10"	Water	50 gals.
Draft	2'10"	Hull Type	Modified-V
Weight	16,000#	Deadrise Aft	13°

Cruisers & Sedans

Mainship 34 Pilot

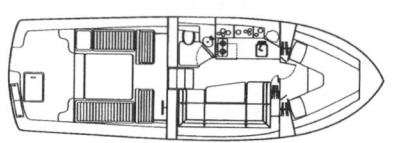

1999–2008

Popular open-water express offers conservative styling with practical cabin layout, versatile cockpit seating. Topside highlights include spacious cockpit with lounge seating, easy-access engine compartment, transom door. Comfortable interior with U-shaped dinette, bow stateroom with bi-fold door, sleeps four. Bow thruster, bow pulpit, teak-planked cabin sole were standard. Long keel protects running gear from grounding. Single 350hp Yanmar diesel will cruise 14 knots (16–17 knots top). Twin 240hp Yanmars cruise at 18 knots (20+ top).

See Page 529 For Value Estimates

Length w/Pulpit	36'1"	Clearance	9'0"
Hull Length	34'0"	Fuel	250 gals.
Beam	12'3"	Water	70 gals.
Draft	3'3"	Waste	20 gals.
Weight	15,000#	Hull Type	Semi-Disp.

Mainship 34 Pilot Sedan

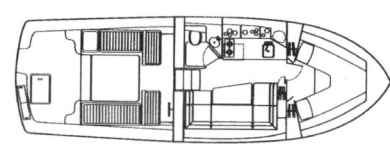

2001–09

Downeast-style hardtop with handsome lines is classy, comfortable, built to last. Generous 12-foot beam affords plenty of cockpit, cabin space. Topside highlights include deep cockpit with lounge seating, easy-access engine compartment, efficient helm layout. Well-planned cabin with big U-shaped dinette, teak-and-holly sole sleeps four. Bow thruster, tilt-away helm, transom door were standard. Single 350hp Yanmar diesel will cruise 14 knots (16–17 knots top). Twin 240hp Yanmars cruise at 18 knots (20+ top).

See Page 529 For Value Estimates

Length w/Pulpit	36'1"	Clearance	9'0"
Hull Length	34'0"	Fuel	250 gals.
Beam	12'3"	Water	70 gals.
Draft	3'3"	Waste	20 gals.
Weight	16,000#	Hull Type	Semi-Disp.

Mainship 35 Convertible

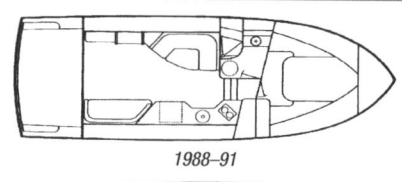

1988–91

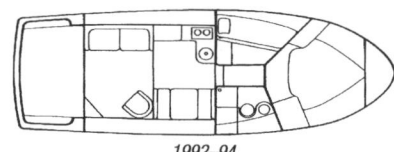

1992–94

1988–94

Value-priced sedan introduced in 1988 boasts one of the largest interiors in her class. Original single-stateroom floorplan was replaced with a two-stateroom dinette layout in 1992 when the boat was also slightly restyled. Expansive salon is wide open to L-shaped galley, booth-style dinette. Cockpit is small with transom door, engine compartment hatches. Note molded bridge steps, Eurostyle bow rails, spacious flybridge, narrow side decks. Standard 320hp Crusader gas engines cruise at 17–18 knots (mid 20s top).

Prices Not Provided for Pre-1995 Models

Length	34'11"	Fuel	250 gals.
Beam	12'8"	Water	80 gals.
Draft	2'10"	Cockpit	80 sq. ft.
Weight	16,000#	Hull Type	Modified-V
Clearance	15'0"	Deadrise Aft	12°

Mainship 35 Open Bridge

1990–92

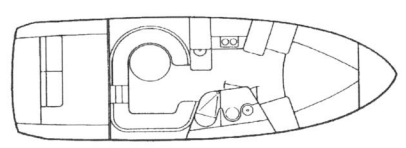

Generic family cruiser (called Mainship 36 Sedan Bridge in 1992) with spacious interior never won any beauty, quality awards. Cavernous full-beam salon with facing settees, tall headroom seats eight for cocktails; full-size galley features upright refrigerator. Small cabin windows reduce natural lighting. Note cockpit bridge steps, center bridge walk-through to foredeck. Additional features include radar arch, integrated swim platform, cockpit seating. Standard 320hp gas engines cruise at 17–18 knots (mid 20s top).

Prices Not Provided for Pre-1995 Models

Length	36'0"	Fuel	250 gals.
Beam	12'5"	Water	85 gals.
Draft	2'8"	Headroom	6'6"
Weight	13,500#	Hull Type	Modified-V
Clearance	10'0"	Deadrise Aft	12°

Mainship 35 Open; 36 Express

1990–93

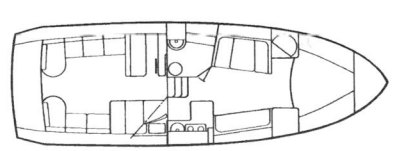

Hard-riding express (called Mainship 35 Open in 1990–91; 36 Express in 1992–93) was designed for entry-level buyers more concerned with price than styling or finish. Large cockpit is a plus, but portside helm position is awkward. Generic midcabin interior is arranged with double berths in both staterooms, compact galley, head with stall shower. Interior was restyled in 1991 for brighter, more open look. Twin Crusader gas engines cruise at 19 knots and reach a top speed in the neighborhood of 27–28 knots.

Prices Not Provided for Pre-1995 Models

Length Overall	36'5"	Clearance	10'6"
Length WL	NA	Fuel	250 gals.
Beam	12'5"	Water	75 gals.
Draft	2'8"	Hull Type	Modified-V
Weight	13,500#	Deadrise Aft	12°

Mainship 36 Nantucket

1986–88

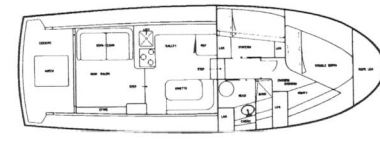

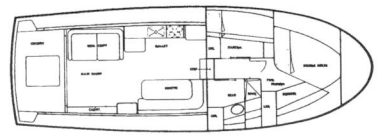

Family-oriented sedan (called Mainship 36 Sedan in 1986) combined low cost with spacious interior, economical operation. Extended salon is big for a 36-footer because bulkhead is well aft, vastly increasing interior at the expense of cockpit space. Lower helm was optional; light oak woodwork was standard. Note compact engine room. Large flybridge seats several guests aft of helm. Transom door eases boarding. Relatively small 270hp gas engines cruise at 14–15 knots (low 20s top). About 50 were built.

Prices Not Provided for Pre-1995 Models

Length	36'2"	Fuel	240 gals.
Beam	13'0"	Water	100 gals.
Draft	3'0"	Headroom	6'5"
Weight	20,000#	Hull Type	Semi-Disp.
Clearance	11'3"	Deadrise Aft	NA

Cruisers & Sedans

Mainship 39 Express

1989–93

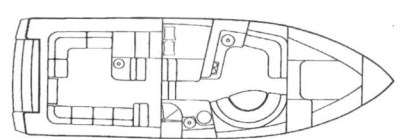

Beefy inboard express with rakish 1990s styling offered signature Mainship value at an affordable price. Wide 14-foot beam permits very spacious cockpit, expansive two-stateroom interior. Topside features include wraparound cockpit seating, transom door, foredeck sun pad, radar arch. Note unusual portside helm position. Plain-Jane interior contains two staterooms, full-size galley, large head with separate stall shower. Swim platform is tiny, side decks are narrow, finish is not great. Twin big-block Crusader gas engines cruise at 20 knots and top out at 28 knots.

Prices Not Provided for Pre-1995 Models

Length	39'2"	Fuel	320 gals.
Beam	14'1"	Water	80 gals.
Draft	3'4"	Headroom	6'3"
Weight	15,000#	Hull Type	Modified-V
Clearance	8'0"	Deadrise Aft	12°

Mainship 40 Sedan Bridge

1993–99

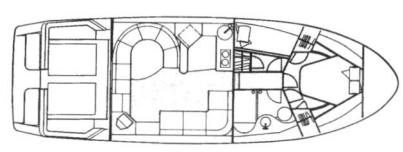

Conservative 1990s sedan with spacious interior combined cruising comfort with versatile layout, economical price. Expansive interior—one step down from cockpit level—includes two large staterooms, full-beam salon with open galley, lounge seating for eight. Small cockpit has built-in bench seating, centerline transom door, twin engine hatches. Note walk-through door in forward flybridge coaming. Unimpressive fit and finish. Standard 320hp V-drive gas engines cruise at a sedate 16 knots and deliver a top speed in the mid 20s.

See Page 529 For Value Estimates

Length	40'7"	Fuel	310 gals.
Beam	13'6"	Water	93 gals.
Draft	3'5"	Headroom	6'4"
Weight	20,000#	Hull Type	Modified-V
Clearance	17'0"	Deadrise Aft	18°

Mainship 45 Pilot Sedan

2008–09

Seductive coastal cruiser with generous beam is smart, practical, loaded with features. Highlights include twin-stateroom cabin with two heads, spacious cockpit with lounge seating, fantastic engine access, opening hardtop skylights. Vertical ceiling pole between helm seat and dining table is a plus; sliding side windows, opening windshield provide excellent ventilation. Hardtop overhang partially shades windshield, cockpit. Large bow locker stows windlass, anchor and chain. Yanmar 440hp diesels cruise at 17 knots (20–21 knots top).

See Page 530 For Value Estimates

Length w/Pulpit	47'9"	Clearance	10'7"
Hull Length	43'0"	Fuel	777 gals.
Beam	15'6"	Water	200 gals.
Draft	3'8"	Waste	56 gals.
Weight	38,000#	Hull Type	Semi-Disp.

Cruisers & Sedans

Marlow 375 Prowler

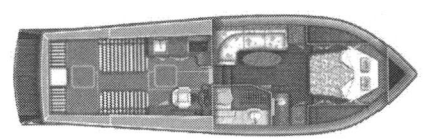

2005–Current

Stylish retro cruiser blends vintage runabout styling with versatile deck plan, impressive performance. Open deck layout with bridgedeck galley offers seating for several guests. Note sporty dash, sturdy three-section windshield. Varnished teak interior with queen berth forward provides comfortable retreat for two. Additional features include cockpit engine boxes, teak-and-holly cabin sole, windshield vents, hidden windlass. Great price compared with domestic picnic-style boats. Optional 440hp Yanmar diesels cruise at 30 knots (mid 30s top).

Insufficient Resale Data to Assign Values

Length Overall	37'6"	Fuel	350 gals.
Beam	12'0"	Water	60 gals.
Draft	2'3"	Waste	30 gals.
Weight	17,000#	Hull Type	Modified-V
Clearance, Hardtop	7'5"	Deadrise Aft	NA

Marquis 50 Sport Coupe

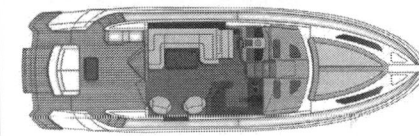

2008–Current

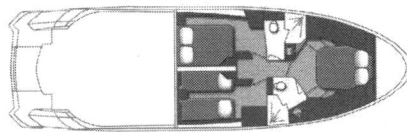

Striking American sportyacht with triple IPS drives is an exceptional blend of bold Italian styling, top-quality construction, leading-edge performance. Appealing three-stateroom interior with designer furnishings has cockpit, salon, helm station and galley on the same level. Joystick control makes docking easy. Note expansive electric sunroof, cherrywood salon flooring, power helm seat. Transom lounge extends aft to expand cockpit size. Engine room is a tight fit. Triple 435hp Volvo diesels reach 35+ knots wide open.

See Page 530 For Value Estimates

Length	49'6"	Fuel	506 gals.
Beam	15'7"	Water	160 gals.
Draft	3'9"	Waste	90 gals.
Weight	44,500#	Hull Type	Modified-V
Clearance	16'0"	Deadrise Aft	16.5

Maxum 2600/2700 SE

2006–09

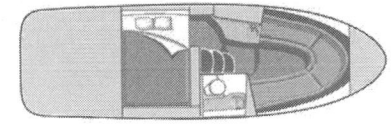

Affordable express (called 2600 SE in 2006–07; 2700 SE in 2008–09) with trailerable 8'6" beam is stylish, versatile, sporty. Very roomy cockpit—largest in her class—offers choice of rear seating in addition to wet bar with refrigerator, flip-up helm seat. Midcabin interior with pullout galley counter, convertible dinette sleeps four. Open transom design makes boarding easy; optional sport arch folds down for trailering. Good engine access. Note swivel double helm seat with flip-up bolster. Single 320hp MerCruiser I/O tops out at 35 knots.

See Page 530 For Value Estimates

Length	27'0"	Fuel	85 gals.
Beam	8'6"	Water	20 gals.
Draft, Up	1'11"	Waste	20 gals.
Draft, Down	3'4"	Hull Type	Modified-V
Weight	6,784#	Deadrise Aft	17°

Cruisers & Sedans

Maxum 2700 SCR

1993–96

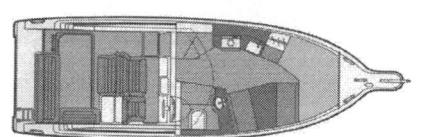

Durable 1990s cruiser combined leading-edge styling with wide-body interior, entry-level price tag. Roomy cockpit with triple helm seat, facing cockpit lounges has room for eight. Open-plan cabin with offset forward berth, booth-style dinette, aft double berth sleeps four adults, two kids. Good-sized head has shower, generous storage. Note walk-through windshield. Strut-supported engine hatch affords good access to engines. Twin 205hp MerCruiser I/Os cruise at 22 knots (about 35 knots top).

See Page 530 For Value Estimates

Length	28'9"	Fuel	102 gals.
Beam	9'8"	Water	30 gals.
Draft, Up	1'10"	Waste	16 gals.
Draft, Down	3'3"	Hull Type	Modified-V
Weight	6,450#	Deadrise Aft	18°

Maxum 2700 SE

2001–07

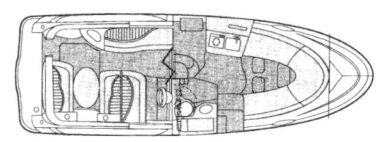

Maxi-volume express with generous 9'5" beam offers more space, amenities than most 27-footers. Topside features include double helm seat, companion sun lounge, cockpit U-lounge with table, wet bar. Roomy cabin with standing headroom holds dinette/V-berth, midcabin double berth, full galley, head with shower. Note walk-through windshield, four opening ports. Good engine access. Stereo/CD, cooler, transom shower are standard. Single 320hp MerCruiser sterndrive will cruise at 20 knots and reach 30+ knots top.

See Page 530 For Value Estimates

Length	28'1"	Fuel	84 gals.
Beam	9'5"	Water	30 gals.
Draft, Up	1'10"	Waste	20 gals.
Draft, Down	3'3"	Hull Type	Modified-V
Weight	7,400#	Deadrise Aft	16°

Maxum 2800/2900 SCR; 2900 SE

1993–2006

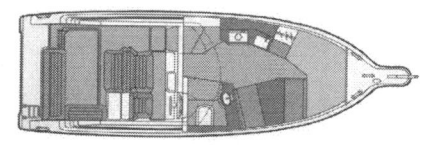

Popular midcabin cruiser (called 2800 SCR in 1997–2000; 2900 SCR in 2001–02; 2900 SE in 2003–06) delivered affordable mix of contemporary styling, versatile accommodations. Roomy cockpit with triple helm seat, wraparound lounge has room for eight. Open-plan cabin with offset forward berth, booth-style dinette, aft double berth sleeps four adults, two kids. Note walk-through windshield, molded bow pulpit. Large engine hatch affords good access to engines. Twin 220hp MerCruiser I/Os cruise at 22 knots (mid 30s top).

See Page 530 For Value Estimates

Length	29'10"	Fuel	102 gals.
Beam	9'9"	Water	30 gals.
Draft, Up	1'10"	Waste	16 gals.
Draft, Down	3'3"	Hull Type	Modified-V
Weight	9,100#	Deadrise Aft	18°

Cruisers & Sedans

Maxum 2900 SE

2008–09

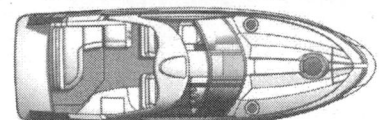

Well-rounded family express with contemporary styling took Maxum affordability, value to the next level. Practical cockpit design has bench seats forward, L-shaped lounge aft plus aft bench seat that converts to sun pad. Both forward seats rotate to face aft; dash has space for mounting big-screen video display. Generic midcabin interior with open-plan layout, teak-and-holly galley sole sleeps five. Walk-thru windshield is accessed via steps molded into cabin door. Twin 300-hp MerCruiser I/Os cruise at 25 knots (low 30s top).

See Page 530 For Value Estimates

Length	30'0"	Fuel	125 gals.
Beam	9'11"	Water	30 gals.
Draft, Up	2'3"	Waste	30 gals.
Draft, Down	3'3"	Hull Type	Modified-V
Weight	10,187#	Deadrise Aft	18°

Maxum 3000 SCR

1997–2001

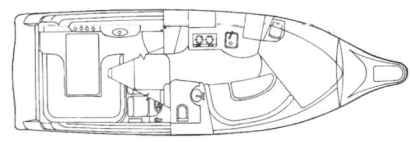

Popular 1990s express took entry-level value, comfort to the next level. Spacious cabin with Ultraleather dinette, offset forward berth boasts fully equipped galley with Avonite counter, generous storage. Note forward accordion privacy door, excellent headroom. Center-facing U-lounge in cockpit converts to sun lounge. Additional features include walk-through windshield, radar arch, transom shower, tiered dash with burlwood tilt wheel. Twin 220hp MerCruiser sterndrives cruise at 22 knots (about 35 knots top).

See Page 530 For Value Estimates

Length	32'9"	Fuel	150 gals.
Beam	9'11"	Water	40 gals.
Draft, Up	1'10"	Waste	30 gals.
Draft, Down	3'7"	Hull Type	Modified-V
Weight	11,500#	Deadrise Aft	18°

Maxum 3100 SE

2002–08

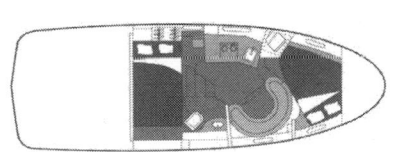

Sporty family express combines sleek styling with upscale interior, spirited performance. Topside highlights include sporty burled dash, companion L-lounge, U-shaped aft seating, wet bar with integrated cooler. Well-appointed cabin with full galley, Ultraleather dinette, faux maple cabinetry sleeps six. Note generous galley storage, roomy head. Additional features include foredeck sun pads, transom shower, large anchor locker. Twin 260hp MerCruiser sterndrives cruise in the mid 20s and reach 33–34 knots top.

See Page 530 For Value Estimates

Length	30'9"	Fuel	150 gals.
Beam	10'6"	Water	35 gals.
Draft, Up	2'1"	Waste	30 gals.
Draft, Down	3'5"	Hull Type	Modified-V
Weight	11,000#	Deadrise Aft	18°

Cruisers & Sedans

Maxum 3200 SCR

1994–98

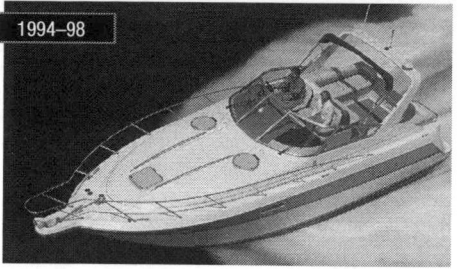

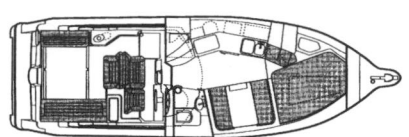

Generic 1990s midcabin express appealed to entry-level buyers looking for comfort, space at an affordable price. Wide 11-foot beam results in roomy cockpit, spacious interior. Cabin features include full 6'6" headroom, hardwood galley sole, midcabin accordion door, three overhead deck hatches. Expansive cockpit with centerline transom door has facing lounge seats aft, wet bar. Note that companion helm seat converts to sun lounge. Twin 250hp MerCruiser sterndrives cruise at 20 knots (30+ knots top).

See Page 530 For Value Estimates

Length	34'9"	Fuel	186 gals.
Beam	11'0"	Water	36 gals.
Draft, Up	2'3"	Waste	30 gals.
Draft, Down	3'8"	Hull Type	Modified-V
Weight	10,800#	Deadrise Aft	17°

Maxum 3300 SE

1999–2007

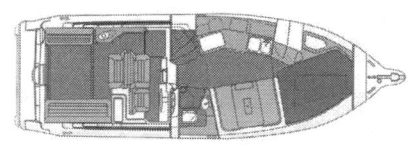

Stylish sportcruiser with many standard features gets high marks for comfort, performance, affordability. Topside highlights include wide-open cockpit with facing aft settees, fold-down companion seat, sporty burled dash, wet bar, foredeck sun pad. Well-appointed interior with roomy galley, Ultraleather dinette sleeps four adults, two kids. Note relatively small head compartment, narrow side decks, huge engine room. Twin 320hp MerCruiser sterndrive engines cruise in the low-to-mid 20s and reach a top speed of 35+ knots.

See Page 530 For Value Estimates

Length	35'7"	Fuel	179 gals.
Beam	11'5"	Water	36 gals.
Draft	3'6"	Waste	30 gals.
Weight	11,300#	Hull Type	Modified-V
Clearance	10'6"	Deadrise Aft	17°

Maxum 3500 SY

2001–08

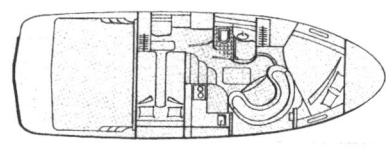

Feature-rich sportcruiser with classic express-boat styling set industry standard for low-price value, affordability. Well-appointed interior includes two large staterooms with privacy curtain forward, solid door aft. Full-size head boasts VacuFlush toilet, separate stall shower. Bridgedeck hatch provides good engine access. Transom shower, walk-through windshield, wet bar are standard. Early models with 310hp V-drive inboards cruise at 20 knots (30 knots top); later models with 300hp I/Os cruise in the low 20s (mid 30s top).

See Page 531 For Value Estimates

Length	34'11"	Fuel	240 gals.
Beam	12'2"	Water	40 gals.
Draft, Up	2'2"	Waste	40 gals.
Draft, Down	3'1"	Hull Type	Modified-V
Weight	15,510#	Deadrise Aft	15°

Cruisers & Sedans

Maxum 3700 SCR

1998–2001

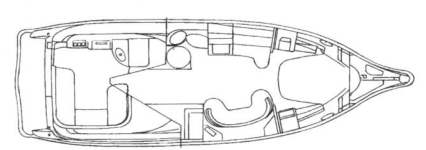

Roomy family cruiser introduced in 1998 paired low price with smart styling, sturdy construction. Open-plan interior with Avonite counters, earth-tone fabrics features home-sized galley with hardwood floor, large head with circular stall shower, cozy aft cabin with twin berths that quickly convert to queen bed. Note that accordion door—not a curtain—provides midcabin privacy. Twin 380hp V-drive gas inboards cruise at 18 knots (26–27 knots top); 370hp Cummins diesels cruise in the mid 20s (28–30 top).

See Page 531 For Value Estimates

Length	39'3"	Fuel	244 gals.
Beam	13'0"	Water	65 gals.
Draft	3'7"	Waste	50 gals.
Weight	20,700#	Hull Type	Modified-V
Clearance	12'11"	Deadrise Aft	15°

Maxum 3700 SY

2003–09

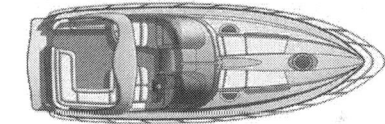

Smooth-riding sportcruiser offered Maxum's signature blend of space, comfort, value. Wide 13-foot beam allows for expansive interior as well as large cockpit area. Cabin highlights include full-size galley with plenty of storage, roomy master stateroom with island berth and privacy door, well-appointed head with stall shower. Note hardwood galley floor, generous headroom. U-shaped cockpit lounge converts to huge sun pad. Standard 320hp gas V-drives cruise at 18 knots (mid-20s top); optional 370hp gas engines reach 28–30 knots top.

See Page 531 For Value Estimates

Length	37'2"	Fuel	300 gals.
Beam	13'0"	Water	80 gals.
Draft, Up	2'4"	Waste	45 gals.
Draft, Down	3'6"	Hull Type	Modified-V
Weight	17,800#	Deadrise Aft	15°

Maxum 4100 SCR

1996–99

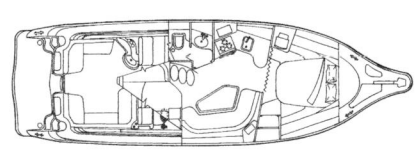

Conservative 1990s sportboat priced at the lower end of the market delivered lots of bang for the buck. Wide 13'6" beam affords spacious interior with home-size galley, private forward stateroom, convertible aft settee. Huge cockpit has U-lounge seating aft, two removable tables, centerline transom door. Unusual port/starboard transom steps access side decks. Called Maxum 3900 SCR in 1996. Twin 400hp V-drive gas inboards cruise at 20 knots (26–27 knots top); 370hp Cummins diesels cruise at 20 knots (low 20s top).

See Page 531 For Value Estimates

Length	43'7"	Fuel	330 gals.
Beam	13'6"	Water	77 gals.
Draft	3'2"	Waste	45 gals.
Weight	18,800#	Hull Type	Modified-V
Clearance	13'4"	Deadrise Aft	16°

Cruisers & Sedans

Cruisers & Sedans

Maxum 4200 SY

2002–08

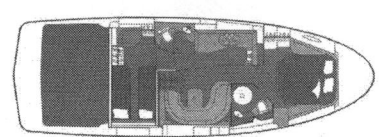

Maxi-volume express with unusual "floating" hardtop, arching side windows offered luxury-class amenities at an affordable price. Expansive midcabin interior with high-gloss cherry cabinetry, Ultraleather upholstery features full-size galley with wine storage, two heads, big U-shaped settee with adjustable table. Molded steps in transom corners lead to wide side decks; aft cockpit section lifts for engine access. Lots of boat for the money. Twin 450hp Cummins V-drive diesels cruise in the low-to-mid 20s (27–28 knots top).

See Page 531 For Value Estimates

Length	42'9"	Fuel	480 gals.
Beam	13'10"	Water	130 gals.
Draft	3'8"	Waste	70 gals.
Weight	35,700#	Hull Type	Modified-V
Clearance, Hardtop	12'0"	Deadrise Aft	18°

Meridian 341 Sedan

2003–04

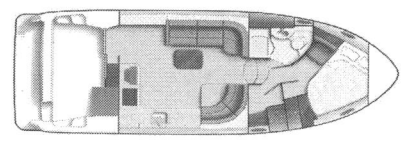

Entry-level sedan (called the Bayliner 3488 Command Bridge in 2001–02) combined rakish styling with expansive accommodations, low price. Roomy two-stateroom interior is nicely highlighted with cherry joinery, leather upholstery. Wraparound cabin windows provide plenty of natural lighting. Salon has two incliners facing full entertainment center. Note cockpit bridge steps, extended flybridge, narrow side decks. Twin 300hp gas inboards cruise at 20 knots (26–28 knots top). All-new Meridian 341 Sedan was introduced in 2005.

See Page 531 For Value Estimates

Length	35'3"	Fuel	224 gals.
Beam	11'8"	Water	92 gals.
Draft	3'2"	Waste	30 gals.
Weight	17,000#	Hull Type	Modified-V
Clearance	13'6"	Deadrise Aft	7.5°

Meridian 341 Sedan

2005–09

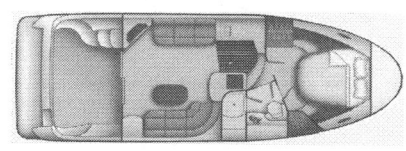

Roomy sport sedan with rakish lines couples tasteful accommodations with spirited performance, attractive price. Expansive salon with panoramic windows, port and starboard lounge seating is wide open to large galley with cherrywood cabinets, faux-granite countertops. Forward master stateroom has island berth; guest cabin has twin single berths. Note molded bridge steps in cockpit, narrow side decks. Transom door, underwater exhaust are standard. Lower helm was optional. Cruise at 18 knots with 320hp gas inboards (26–27 knots top).

See Page 531 For Value Estimates

Length	35'10"	Fuel	250 gals.
Beam	12'6"	Water	90 gals.
Draft	4'0"	Waste	35 gals.
Weight	18,254#	Hull Type	Modified-V
Clearance	14'1"	Deadrise Aft	11°

Meridian 381 Sedan

2003–05

Updated version of Bayliner 3788 MY (2001–02) became the Meridian 381 in 2003 when Bayliner got out of the big-boat business and Meridian Yachts was formed. Spacious two-stateroom interior boasts home-size galley, two full heads, faux-leather upholstery. Island berth is located in master stateroom; guest stateroom is partially tucked under salon floor. Additional features include molded bridge steps, radar arch, transom door. Twin 320hp gas inboards cruise at 15–16 knots and top out in the mid 20s.

See Page 531 For Value Estimates

Length	38'6"	Fuel	300 gals.
Beam	13'7"	Water	125 gals.
Draft	3'4"	Waste	37 gals.
Weight	22,275#	Hull Type	Modified-V
Clearance	14'1"	Deadrise Aft	10°

Meridian 391 Sedan

2006–Current

Sleek flybridge yacht delivers on promise of liveaboard comfort, feature-rich accommodations. Enormous salon/galley/dinette offers spacious living area made even larger by panoramic windows, generous headroom. Guest cabin with queen berth extends under raised dinette. Bridge steps—while convenient—consume valuable cockpit space. Huge bridge seats a small crowd. Note split head, big engine room, narrow side decks. Standard 370hp gas engines cruise at 18 knots; optional 380hp Cummins diesels cruise at 20+ knots.

See Page 531 For Value Estimates

Length	40'11	Fuel	350 gals.
Beam	13'11"	Water	125 gals.
Draft	3'3"	Waste	40 gals.
Weight	25,000#	Hull Type	Modified-V
Clearance	14'0"	Deadrise Aft	10°

Midnight Express 37 Cuddy

2006–Current

Sleek full-cabin express with high-performance, double-stepped hull offers genuine luxury cruising in the fast lane. Space-efficient layout (mandated by slender 11'6" beam) features richly appointed interior with full galley, convertible settee, island berth forward, stand-up head with shower. Extended hardtop, Kiekhaefer trim tabs are standard. Rear cockpit lounge lifts on hydraulic rams for genset access. High-tech construction results in a strong, lightweight hull. Over 50 knots top with triple 275hp Mercury outboards.

See Page 531 For Value Estimates

Length	37'2"	Fuel	365 gals.
Beam	11'6"	Water	70 gals.
Hull Draft	1'8"	Max HP	900
Dry Weight	15,000#	Hull Type	Deep-V
Headroom	6'2"	Deadrise Aft	22°

Cruisers & Sedans

Mikelson 42 Sedan

1986–90

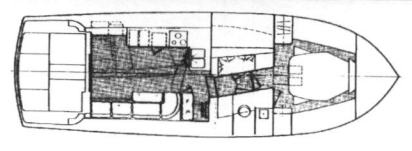

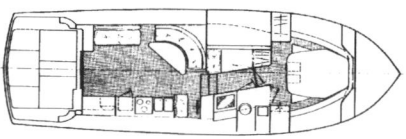

Sporty Fexas-designed sedan with distinctive styling (note long foredeck, large cabin windows) put Mikelson in the sportfish business back in 1986. Most were delivered with two-stateroom, galley-up interior with single head, standard lower helm. Interior is completely finished with handcrafted teak cabinetry. Large flybridge for a 42-footer. Cockpit came with transom door, teak sole, tackle center. Low-deadrise (fully cored) hull with rounded chines is fuel efficient, easily driven. Cruise at 16–17 knots with 260hp GM diesels (about 20 knots top).

Prices Not Provided for Pre-1995 Models

Length Overall	41'9"	Fuel	400 gals.
Beam	13'0"	Water	200 gals.
Draft	3'0"	Waste	35 gals.
Weight	24,000#	Hull Type	Modified-V
Clearance	10'4"	Deadrise Aft	5°

MJM 29Z

2007–Current

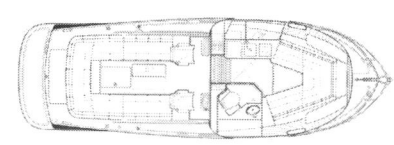

Yacht-grade weekender with sterndrive power combines remarkable fuel efficiency with beautiful lines, exceptional craftsmanship. Well-appointed interior with teak-and-holly sole includes stand-up head, small galley, convertible dinette. Roomy cockpit features U-shaped seating for eight. Note teak cockpit table, ergonomic helm position, sturdy bow rail. Aft cockpit seat lifts for engine access. Cruise at a brisk 22 knots (at close to 3 mpg!) with single four-cylinder 260hp Volvo Duoprop diesel. Did we say expensive?

See Page 532 For Value Estimates

Length	32'6"	Fuel	125 gals.
Beam	10'2"	Water	30 gals.
Hull Draft	1'4"	Waste	20 gals.
Weight	8,000#	Hull Type	Modified-V
Clearance	8'5"	Deadrise Aft	17°

MJM 34Z

2004–Current

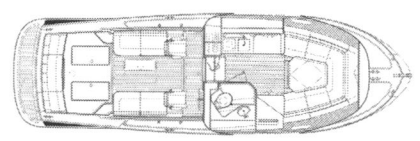

Well conceived Downeast cruiser with slender hull, single-diesel power takes fuel-efficient elegance to the next level. Practical layout includes comfortable cabin with Ultraleather seating and teak-and-holly sole, semi-enclosed pilothouse with facing lounge seats. Note wide side decks, fold-out windshield panels. Bridgedeck deck lifts on power rams for engine access. Lightweight composite hull contributes to exceptional fuel efficiency (about 2 mpg at 22 knots) with single 440hp Yanmar diesel. Easily trailerable with a permit.

See Page 532 For Value Estimates

Length	34'0"	Fuel	148 gals.
Beam	11'0"	Water	60 gals.
Draft	2'4"	Waste	20 gals.
Weight	10,600	Hull Type	Modified-V
Clearance	9'6"	Deadrise Aft	18°

Cruisers & Sedans

Monterey 265/276 Cruiser

1993–99

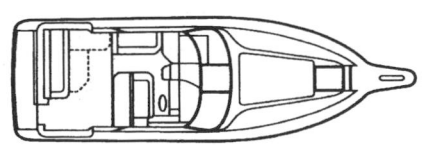

Good-looking overnighter (called Monterey 265 Cruiser in 1993–94; 276 Cruiser in 1995–99) packs a lot of space in a relatively small hull. Midcabin interior includes full galley, stand-up head with shower, wraparound dinette forward. Foldaway stern seat frees up cockpit space for swimming, diving. Additional features include walk-through windshield, foredeck sun pad, wet bar with sink, woodgrain dash. Single 310hp MerCruiser sterndrive tops out at 35+ knots; twin 190hp engines will reach 40+ knots wide open.

See Page 532 For Value Estimates

Length w/Pulpit	29'0"	Fuel	100 gals.
Hull Length	26'10"	Water	32 gals.
Beam	9'6"	Waste	21 gals.
Draft, Down	3'0"	Hull Type	Deep-V
Weight	6,500#	Deadrise Aft	20°

Monterey 270 Cruiser

2006–08

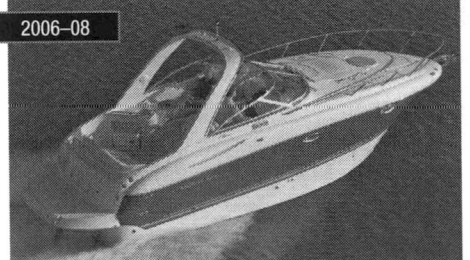

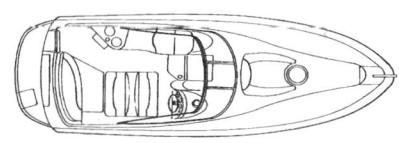

Clean-cut sportcruiser offers family comfort, space in a trailerable package. Well-planned cockpit includes portside sun lounge, removable transom seat, sporty dash layout, walk-through windshield. Double helm seat converts to lounge for sunning. Generic midcabin interior with standing headroom, compact galley accommodates four in comfort. Note transom stowage locker, foredeck sun pad, extended swim platform. Triple-axle trailer required for trailering. Single Volvo 320hp gas I/O will cruise at 20+ knots (low 30s top).

See Page 532 For Value Estimates

Length	29'0"	Fuel	89 gals.
Beam	8'6"	Water	21 gals.
Draft, Up	1'10"	Waste	21 gals.
Draft, Down	3'4"	Hull Type	Modified-V
Weight	7,400#	Deadrise Aft	18°

Monterey 282 Cruiser

2001–06

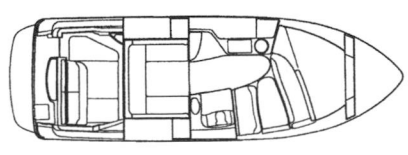

Classy sportcruiser has everything families need to enjoy weekends afloat. Innovative interior has booth-style dinette in addition to large midcabin lounge, angled forward berth. Head has hinged seat over toilet, which makes changing clothes (or taking a shower) easy. Cockpit amenities include double-wide helm seat with flip-up bolster, foldaway stern seat, full wet bar. Note walk-through windshield, foredeck sun pad, transom storage box. Cruise at 30 knots (45+ top) with optional 300hp sterndrive engines.

See Page 532 For Value Estimates

Length w/Platform	30'10"	Fuel	142 gals.
Hull Length	28'9"	Water	38 gals.
Beam	10'0"	Waste	18 gals.
Draft, Down	3'1"	Hull Type	Modified-V
Weight	10,000#	Deadrise Aft	19°

Cruisers & Sedans

Monterey 290 Cruiser; 300 SCR

2006–Current

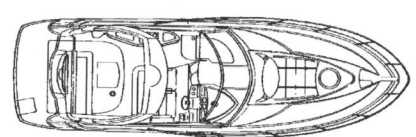

Value-priced weekender (called 290 Cruiser in 2006–08) gets high marks for comfort, performance. Sporty helm design boasts heads-up instrument panel, tilt wheel, stereo remote. Extended swim platform provides easy water access; roomy cockpit can seat six without crowding. Removable aft lounge seat frees up cockpit space. Well-appointed cabin with complete galley, roomy head sleeps four, seats six. Good engine access. Note standard bow sun pad, transom shower, radar arch. Twin 270hp Volvo gas engines reach close to 40 knots wide open.

See Page 532 For Value Estimates

Length	31'4"	Fuel	142 gals.
Beam	10'3"	Water	38 gals.
Draft, Up	1'9"	Waste	18 gals.
Draft, Down	3'1"	Hull Type	Modified-V
Weight	10,000#	Deadrise Aft	19°

Monterey 296 Cruiser

1993–2000

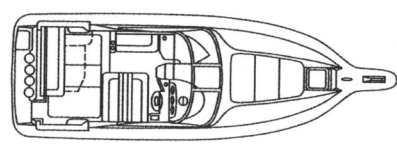

Feature-rich 1990s express was Monterey's first entry into highly competitive 30-foot sterndrive cruiser market. Called the 286 Cruiser in 1993–94, the cockpit was revised in 1995 when she became the 296 Cruiser. Roomy midcabin interior is arranged in the usual fashion with double berths fore and aft, convertible dinette, enclosed head with shower, generous storage. Note walk-through windshield, foldaway stern seat, transom fender racks, foredeck sun pad. Twin 250hp Volvo I/Os top out at 40+ knots.

See Page 532 For Value Estimates

Length w/Pulpit	31'6"	Fuel	140 gals.
Hull Length	28'10"	Water	44 gals.
Beam	10'0"	Waste	21 gals.
Draft, Down	3'1"	Hull Type	Modified-V
Weight	8,000#	Deadrise Aft	19°

Monterey 302 Cruiser

2000–06

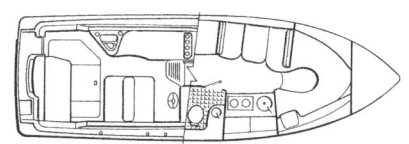

Handsome midcabin weekender combines sleek lines, brisk performance with impressive feature list. Well-appointed interior with booth-style dinette, fully equipped galley has aft-cabin privacy door rather than just a curtain. Well-planned cockpit with double-wide helm seat, removable transom seat can entertain a small crowd. Note walk-through windshield, reverse arch, transom storage locker, foredeck sun pad. A good performer, twin 280hp MerCruiser sterndrives deliver a top speed of about 38 knots.

See Page 532 For Value Estimates

Length w/Platform	32'1"	Fuel	160 gals.
Hull Length	30'5"	Water	45 gals.
Beam	10'6"	Waste	28 gals.
Draft, Down	3'1"	Hull Type	Modified-V
Weight	10,700#	Deadrise Aft	19°

Monterey 322 Cruiser

1998–07

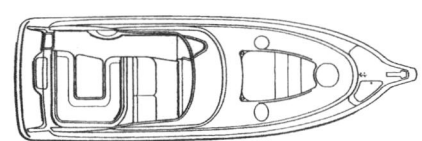

Value-priced sportcruiser matched class standards in her day for comfort, styling, performance. Open-plan cabin boats large L-shaped dinette/sofa, spacious forward berth, full-service galley with microwave, coffeemaker. Three overhead hatches, five opening ports provide good cabin ventilation. Well-designed cockpit has wraparound lounge seating aft, wet bar, double-wide helm seat. Note walk-through windshield, fender storage rack. MerCruiser 320hp gas sterndrives cruise in the mid 20s and reach a top speed of about 40 knots.

See Page 532 For Value Estimates

Length w/Platform	36'3"	Fuel	210 gals.
Hull Length	32'8"	Water	44 gals.
Beam	10'10"	Waste	30 gals.
Draft, Down	3'4"	Hull Type	Modified-V
Weight	12,000#	Deadrise Aft	18°

Monterey 330/340 Sport Yacht

2007–Current

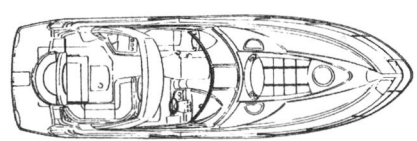

Appealing sportcruiser with muscular profile (called 330 SY in 2007–08) meets market demand for style, comfort, performance. Topside highlights include six-person cockpit lounge, daybed companion lounge, double helm seat with dual bolsters, walk-through windshield, extended swim platform. Cabin is richly appointed with cherry mica woodwork, quality fabrics, synthetic wood floor. Flat-screen TV is standard. Sporty dash layout is a real attention-getter. Cruise at 25 knots with twin 320hp Volvo sterndrive engines (high 30s top).

See Page 532 For Value Estimates

Length	35'3"	Fuel	210 gals.
Beam	11'3"	Water	42 gals.
Draft, Up	2'1"	Waste	28 gals.
Draft, Down	3'4"	Hull Type	Modified-V
Weight	14,200#	Deadrise Aft	17°

Monterey 350/360 Sport Yacht

2005–Current

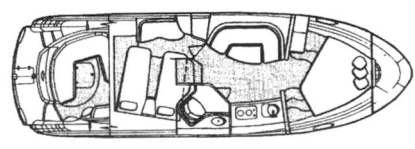

Stylish open-water cruiser (called the 350 SY in 2005–08) is sexy, fast, loaded with family-friendly features. Topside amenities include big U-shape cockpit lounge (which converts into a sun pad), extended swim platform, wide side decks, foredeck sun cushion. Well-appointed cabin with hardwood cabinetry, Ultraleather upholstery boasts aft stateroom with standing headroom, large galley, private bow stateroom. Power engine compartment hatch is a plus. Hardtop became optional in 2008. Mercury 375hp gas I/Os cruise at 25 knots (40+ knots top).

See Page 532 For Value Estimates

Length Overall	37'0"	Fuel	230 gals.
Beam	11'6"	Water	48 gals.
Draft, Up	2'4"	Waste	38 gals.
Draft, Down	3'6"	Hull Type	Modified-V
Weight	16,500#	Deadrise Aft	17°

Cruisers & Sedans

Cruisers & Sedans

Monterey 400 Sport Yacht

2008–Current

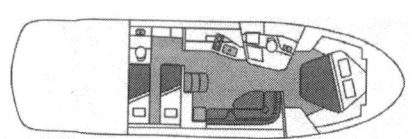

High-impact express with Volvo IPS drives pairs modern styling with upscale amenities, excellent performance. Twin-stateroom interior with two heads is notable—many express models this size have just one head. Sociable cockpit layout with wraparound settee, portside lounge includes full wet bar, doublewide helm seat, transom shower. Hardtop, windlass are standard; note fantastic engine access. Joystick control permits precise slow-speed control. Cruise efficiently at 26–28 knots (35 top) with 370hp Volvo diesels.

See Page 532 For Value Estimates

Length w/Platform	41'0"	Fuel	330 gals.
Beam	12'6"	Water	75 gals.
Draft	3'9"	Waste	36 gals.
Weight	22,000#	Hull Type	Modified-V
Clearance	10'7"	Deadrise Aft	17°

Navigator 42 Classic

1996–99

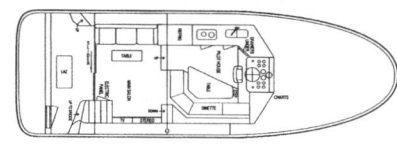

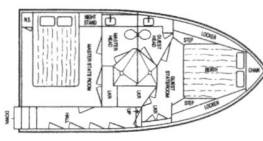

Popular midsize motorcruiser with wide 15-foot beam has the interior volume of a much larger boat. Spacious floorplan includes two double staterooms with en suite heads (each with stall shower), roomy salon with entertainment center, raised pilothouse with dinette and galley. Large cabin windows provide panoramic outside views. Note cockpit bridge steps, standard radar arch, transom door. Flybridge offers exceptional helm visibility. Twin 318hp Volvo diesels will cruise at 20 knots with a top speed in the neighborhood of 25 knots.

See Page 532 For Value Estimates

Length Overall	42'0"	Fuel	400 gals.
Beam	15'0"	Water	130 gals.
Draft	4'4"	Waste	40 gals.
Weight	30,000#	Hull Type	Modified-V
Clearance	NA	Deadrise Aft	15°

Navigator 4300 Flybridge Sedan

1990–94

Good-looking sedan from early 1990s delivered comfort, performance at a reasonable price. At least two floorplans were offered during her production run, both two-stateroom, galley-up affairs with fully equipped galley, stall showers in both heads. While accommodations are spacious for a boat this size, no-frills interior is fairly Spartan. Exterior features include radar arch, bow pulpit, transom door. Lower helm was optional. Among several engine options, twin 330hp Volvos cruise at 21–22 knots (about 25 knots top).

Prices Not Provided for Pre-1995 Models

Length Overall	43'3"	Fuel	400/600 gals.
Beam	14'11"	Water	200 gals.
Draft	4'3"	Waste	NA
Weight	30,000#	Hull Type	Modified-V
Headroom	6'5"	Deadrise Aft	15°

Neptunus 54 Express

1998–2000

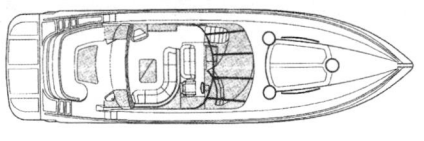

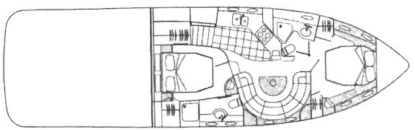

Head-turning express from Canadian arm of Dutch builder Neptunus conceals big-boat accommodations within seductive, powerful-looking lines. Hardtop (with electric sunroof) forms fully enclosed pilothouse/upper salon—a cutting-edge design in the late 1990s. Second salon with wraparound settee lies below along with L-shaped galley, two private staterooms, two full heads. Sliding glass door opens to large cockpit with cushioned lounge seating, deluxe wet bar. Prop pockets reduce draft. Cruise at 25–26 knots with 660hp Cat diesels.

Insufficient Resale Data to Assign Values

Length	56'5"	Fuel	680 gals.
Beam	15'7"	Water	130 gals.
Draft	4'10"	Waste	65 gals.
Weight	40,000#	Hull Type	Deep-V
Clearance	NA	Deadrise Aft	21°

Ocean Alexander 42 Sedan

1987–93

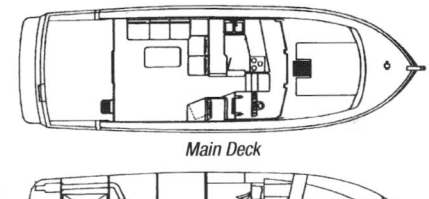

Main Deck

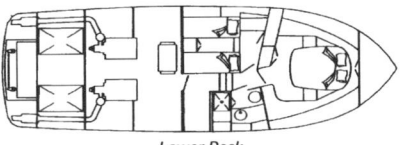

Lower Deck

Popular cockpit yacht with sporty lines made good on Alexander promise of top-level construction, practical accommodations. Appealing two-stateroom teak interior includes standard lower helm, step-up galley forward with serving counter, large master stateroom with walkaround queen, guest cabin with single berths. Small cabin adjacent to head can serve as storage area, laundry center. Roomy cockpit is a plus. Cummins 250hp diesels cruise at 14 knots; Cat 375hp diesels cruise at 20–21 knots. Over 140 were sold.

Prices Not Provided for Pre-1995 Models

Length	42'0"	Fuel	500 gals.
Beam	14'4"	Water	150 gals.
Draft	3'2"	Waste	40 gals.
Weight	23,000#	Hull Type	Modified-V
Clearance	11'6"	Deadrise Aft	NA

Ocean Alexander 420/422 Sport Sedan

1994–2001

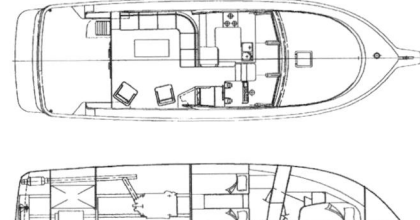

Stylish flybridge sedan (called 420 Sedan in 1994–95; 422 Sedan thereafter) offered Alexander buyers impressive blend of smart styling, tasteful accommodations. Appealing two-stateroom teak interior includes standard lower helm, step-up galley forward with serving counter, large master stateroom with walkaround queen, guest cabin with single berths. Small cabin adjacent to head can serve as storage area, laundry center. Roomy cockpit is a plus. Cat 375 diesels cruise at 22 knots (25 top); 420hp Cats run a knot or two faster.

See Page 533 For Value Estimates

Length	42'0"	Fuel	500 gals.
Beam	14'4"	Water	150 gals.
Draft	3'3"	Headroom	6'4"
Weight	33,100#	Hull Type	Modified-V
Clearance	NA	Deadrise Aft	NA

Cruisers & Sedans

Pearson True North 33

2004–08

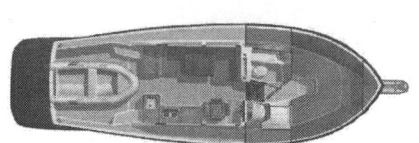

Scaled-down version of popular True North 38 invokes visions of classic New England lobster boats. Galley and dinette are on pilothouse level, wide open to cockpit. Dinette seat converts electrically into forward-facing bench seat. Note glossy cherrywood trim, sliding cabin windows. Twin transom doors allow dinghy to be easily stowed in cockpit—very clever. Impressive fit and finish. Tapered hull carries beam well forward; rudder and prop are fully protected by integral skeg. Cruise at 20 knots with single 440hp Yanmar diesel (mid 20s top).

See Page 535 For Value Estimates

Length	36'2"	Fuel	200 gals.
Beam	12'4"	Water	80 gals.
Draft	3'4"	Waste	25 gals.
Weight	12,500#	Hull Type	Modified-V
Clearance, Mast	11'7"	Deadrise Aft	18°

Pearson 34 Convertible

1989–91

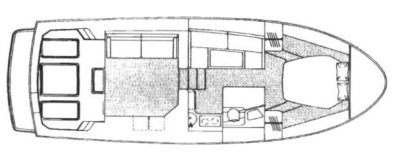

Rugged deep-V convertible with wide 13-foot beam offers spacious accommodations, impressive rough-water handling. Teak-trimmed interior boasts roomy salon with sofa/bed, convertible dinette, owner stateroom with island queen berth. Compact galley is short on storage, counter space. Large windows admit plenty of natural lighting. Additional features include well-finished engine room, transom door, bow pulpit, swim platform. Cockpit is small for a 34-footer. Cat 320hp diesels cruise at 22–23 knots (high 20s top).

Prices Not Provided for Pre-1995 Models

Length	33'9"	Fuel	310 gals.
Beam	13'0"	Water	70 gals.
Draft	3'4"	Headroom	6'4"
Weight	19,000#	Hull Type	Deep-V
Clearance	NA	Deadrise Aft	19°

Pearson True North 38

2002–08

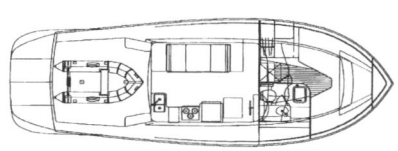

Distinctive hardtop express with reverse transom gets high marks for innovative design, top-shelf construction. "Sleeping loft" for kids is located above V-berth; galley is positioned aft in semi-enclosed pilothouse where it's convenient to cockpit. (Pilothouse can be fully enclosed with optional bulkhead.) Twin transom doors allow dinghy to be stowed in cockpit. Bow thruster is standard. High-tech hull boasts deep forefoot, skeg-mounted rudder. Single 440hp Yanmar diesel will cruise at 20 knots (25–26 knots top). Over 100 built to date.

See Page 535 For Value Estimates

Length	38'6"	Fuel	220 gals.
Beam	13'6"	Water	100 gals.
Draft	3'6"	Waste	35 gals.
Weight	15,000#	Hull Type	Modified-V
Clearance	15'5"	Deadrise Aft	12°

Cruisers & Sedans

Phoenix 27 Weekender

1979–94

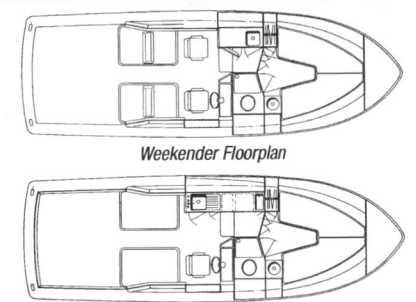

Weekender Floorplan

Fishbuster Floorplan

Prices Not Provided for Pre-1995 Models

Versatile 27-footer with expansive single-level cockpit is great for fishing, diving, daytime entertaining. Highlights include tackle storage locker, bait-prep center, compact cabin with V-berths, stand-up head with shower. "Fishbuster" version (1979–89) has galley forward in cockpit. Engine boxes double as back-to-back seats. Deep-V hull with prop pockets delivers good rough-water performance. Inboard 270hp gas engines cruise at 22–23 knots (about 30 knots top); optional 200hp Volvo diesels cruise around 25 knots (high 20s top).

Length Overall	27'3"	Clearance	6'9"
Length WL	23'6"	Fuel	200 gals.
Beam	9'10"	Water	24 gals.
Draft	1'10"	Hull Type	Deep-V
Weight	7,200#	Deadrise Aft	20°

Pursuit 2860/2865 Denali

1997–2004

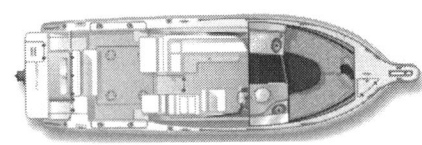

See Page 536 For Value Estimates

Beautifully finished daycruiser is well adapted to fishing, swimming, occasional overnighting. Highlights include spacious bridgedeck with L-lounge seating, roomy cockpit with foldaway rear seat, upscale cabin with enclosed head, berths for two. Eye-catching reverse transom contains freshwater sink, insulated fishbox/cooler, raw-water washdown. Note stylish helm layout. Updated 2865 model introduced in 2003 features curved windshield, added cockpit seating, cabin revisions. Single Volvo 375hp gas I/O engine tops out at close to 35 knots.

Length w/Pulpit	32'10"	Fuel	148 gals.
Hull Length	28'0"	Water	30 gals.
Beam	9'6"	Waste	20 gals.
Draft, Drives Down	3'0"	Hull Type	Deep-V
Weight	7,600#	Deadrise Aft	21°

Pursuit LS 345 Drummond Runner

2006–08

Standard Plan

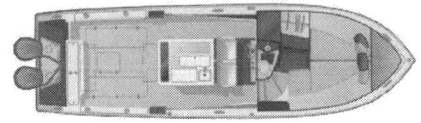

Sportfish Plan

See Page 537 For Value Estimates

Multi-purpose express with innovative center-island galley/wet bar sets class standards for comfort, practicality, luxury. Highlights include electric helm seat, windlass, flat-screen TV, fiberglass top with canvas enclosure. Relatively small cabin with stand-up head is beautifully finished. Available in cruising and sportfish deck layouts. Deep-V hull can handle serious weather. Note sturdy single-piece windshield. Beautifully finished boat drips quality, elegance. Cruise at 30 knots with Yamaha 250s (around 40 knots top). Expensive.

Length	34'5"	Fuel	300 gals.
Beam	9'6"	Water	30 gals.
Hull Draft	1'10"	Max HP	600
Weight w/T250s	10,395#	Hull Type	Deep-V
Clearance, Top	8'0"	Deadrise Aft	24.5°

Cruisers & Sedans

Regal 260 Valenti; 272 Commodore

1991–96

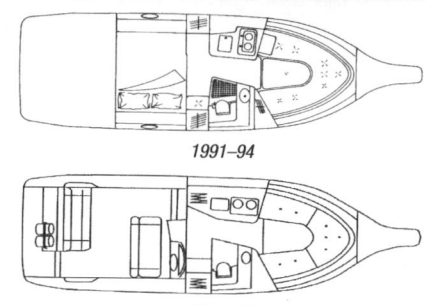

1991–94

1995–96

See Page 537 For Value Estimates

Portly 1990s express (called Valenti 260 in 1991–92; 272 Commodore in 1993–96) combines time-tested layout with spirited performance, durable construction. Midcabin interior with convertible dinette, stand-up head—slightly updated in 1995—sleeps four. Topside features include double-wide helm seat, walk-through windshield, transom locker, stern seat, power engine hatch. Note fully cored hull construction. Twin Volvo 180hp engines cruise at 22 knots (high 30s top); single 300hp engine will cruise at 20 knots (30+ top).

Length w/Pulpit	28'6"	Fuel	105 gals.
Beam	9'2"	Water	27 gals.
Draft, Up	1'6"	Waste	17 gals.
Draft, Down	3'6"	Hull Type	Deep-V
Weight	6,800#	Deadrise Aft	21°

Regal 2660/2765 Commodore

1999–2005

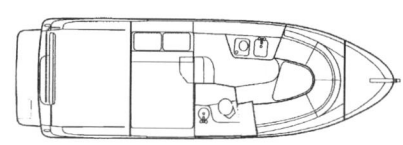

See Page 537 For Value Estimates

Well-built cruiser with notched hull delivers good mix of passenger comfort, good performance at a reasonable price. Topside highlights include removable rear bench seat, refreshment center with cooler, walk-through windshield, sliding screen door, extended swim platform. Comfortable interior with upscale decor sleeps four. Called 2660 Commodore in 1999–2001. Modest fuel capacity for a 27-footer. Not many trailerable boats offer twin-engine option. Single 310hp MerCruiser I/O tops out at 35 knots; twin 220hp Mercs reach 40+ knots top.

Length	29'10"	Fuel	76 gals.
Beam	8'6"	Water	28 gals.
Draft, Down	2'9"	Waste	28 gals.
Weight	6,950#	Hull Type	Deep-V
Clearance	7'2"	Deadrise Aft	21°

Regal 277XL/280 Commodore

1982–89

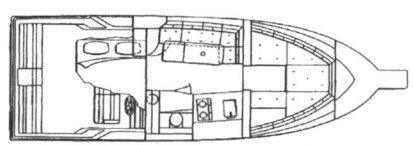

Prices Not Provided for Pre-1995 Models

Contemporary 1980s express with family-friendly layout was one of Regal's better-selling models during her production years. Belowdecks comforts include enclosed head with shower, full galley, convertible dinette, aft cabin with double berth. Note teak cabin trim, generous headroom. Cockpit amenities include aft bench seats, double-wide helm seat, tilt steering wheel. Updated 280 model introduced in 1988 featured integrated radar arch. Twin 260hp MerCruiser I/Os cruise at 26–28 knots and reach over 40 knots wide open.

Length	27'1"	Fuel	140 gals.
Beam	10'0"	Water	35 gals.
Draft, Down	3'2"	Waste	21 gals.
Weight	8,200#	Hull Type	Modified-V
Headroom	6'3"	Deadrise Aft	16°

Cruisers & Sedans

Regal 2760/2860 Commodore

1998–2005

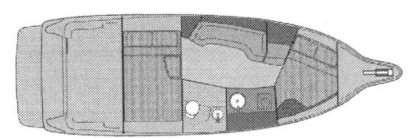

Maxi-volume express cruiser with innovative topside seating is versatile, stylish, agile. Broad 9'11" beam allows for spacious interior with large head, cherry cabinetry, berths for six. Refrigerator under forward berth allows storage space under galley counter. Pivoting helm seat, aft L-shaped lounge with removable table, foldaway aft settee maximize cockpit space. Note walk-through windshield, performance-enhancing stepped hull. Twin 220hp MerCruiser I/Os cruise at 22–23 knots and top out in the mid-to-high 30s.

See Page 537 For Value Estimates

Length w/Pulpit	31'0"	Fuel	103 gals.
Beam	9'11"	Water	27 gals.
Draft, Down	3'3"	Waste	17 gals.
Weight	8,350#	Hull Type	Deep-V
Clearance	8'10"	Deadrise Aft	21°

Regal 2860 Window Express

2006–Current

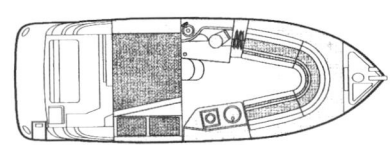

Stylish family express with unique foredeck windows packs luxury amenities into trailerable hull. Roomy midcabin interior with dinette forward, compact galley, stand-up head with shower, sleeps four. Seat backs convert dinette for sleeping. Vinyl fabrics, cherry trim presents very upscale decor. Large aft-cockpit seating area has removable table, refreshment center. Note pull-up swim-platform cleats. Modified-V hull with keel pad delivers comfortable ride. Twin 220hp MerCruiser I/Os cruise at 25 knots (38–40 knots top).

See Page 537 For Value Estimates

Length	29'5"	Headroom	6'3"
Beam	9'6"	Fuel	100 gals.
Draft, Down	3'3"	Water	35 gals.
Weight	9,000#	Hull Type	Modified-V
Clearance	10'2"	Deadrise Aft	18°

Regal 290/300 Commodore

1990–94

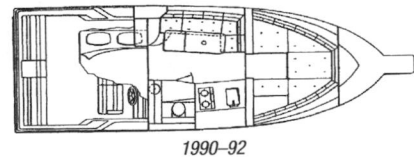

1990–92

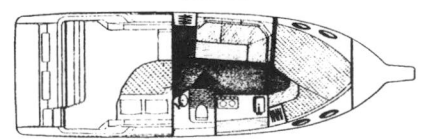

1993–94

Prices Not Provided for Pre-1995 Models

Completely updated version of Regal's popular 277/280 Commodore (1982–89) paired smart styling with upscale interior, sure-footed performance. Topside highlights include big single-level cockpit with reversible helm seat, integrated swim platform with storage lockers, foredeck sun pad, wide side decks, curved windshield. Midcabin interior with convertible dinette, fully equipped galley was updated in 1993. Among several engine options, twin 260hp MerCruiser I/Os cruise at 26–28 knots (40+ knots wide open).

Length w/Pulpit	32'5"	Fuel	140 gals.
Hull length	30'0"	Water	35 gals.
Beam	10'0"	Waste	21 gals.
Draft, Down	3'2"	Hull Type	Modified-V
Weight	9,200#	Deadrise Aft	16°

Regal 292/2960/3060 Commodore

1995–2003

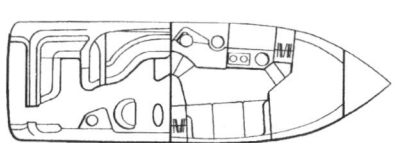

Quality-built express (called 292 Commodore in 1995–99; 2960 Commodore in 2000–01; 3060 Commodore in 2002–03) blends crisp styling, excellent performance. Plush interior with Corian counters, cherrywood trim, convertible dinette sleeps four adults, two kids. Removable settee opens up cockpit for entertaining, fishing. Transom door, wet bar were standard. Note walk-through windshield, stylish helm. Twin 260hp MerCruiser I/Os cruise at 22 knots (high 30s top); 280hp Volvos cruise at 24 knots (about 40 knots top).

See Page 537 For Value Estimates

Length Overall	31'10"	Fuel	150 gals.
Beam	10'4"	Water	35 gals.
Draft, Up	1'8"	Waste	30 gals.
Draft, Down	3'2"	Hull Type	Deep-V
Weight	9,500#	Deadrise Aft	18°

Regal 3060 Window Express

2004–Current

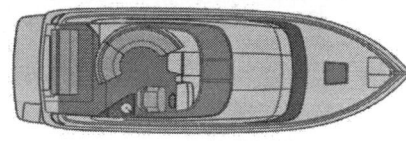

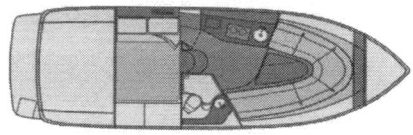

Sporty family cruiser with foredeck windows combines distinctive Regal styling with spacious interior, exemplary finish. Upscale cabin with wraparound dining area, fully equipped galley boasts glossy cherry cabinetry, outstanding headroom. Note roomy midcabin berth, Corian galley counter. Well-designed cockpit has foldaway transom seat, swivel helm seat, walk-through windshield. Companionway screen door, extended swim platform, transom shower are standard. Twin 270hp Volvo I/Os cruise at 25–26 knots (about 42 knots wide open).

See Page 537 For Value Estimates

Length	30'10"	Fuel	151 gals.
Beam	10'6"	Water	30 gals.
Draft, Up	1'8"	Waste	28 gals.
Draft, Down	3'2"	Hull Type	Modified-V
Weight	11,000#	Deadrise Aft	18°

Regal 320 Commodore

1988–92

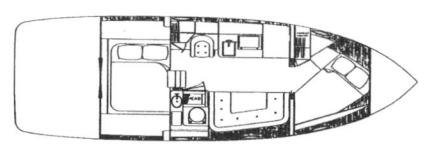

Widebody sportcruiser introduced in 1988 appealed to owners willing to pay for quality construction, top-tier amenities. Interior sports oversized double berth forward, U-shaped dinette with drop-down table, large midcabin berth. Note generous storage, good cabin lighting and headroom. Well-planned cockpit with wet bar, electric engine hatch, seats seven. Note slender side decks. Modified-V hull delivers comfortable big-water ride. Twin 260hp I/Os top out at 35 knots; twin 340hp engines reach about 40 knots top.

Prices Not Provided for Pre-1995 Models

Length	31'10"	Clearance	9'4"
Beam	11'2"	Fuel	178 gals.
Draft, Up	1'8"	Water	50 gals.
Draft, Down	2'11"	Hull Type	Modified-V
Weight	11,000#	Deadrise Aft	19°

Cruisers & Sedans

Regal Ventura 9.8; 322/3260 Commodore

1993–2004

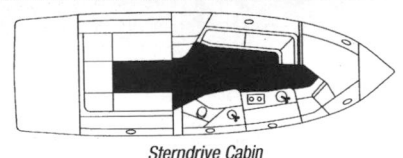

Sterndrive Cabin

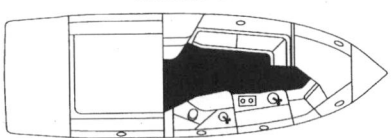

Inboard Cabin

Popular express cruiser (called Ventura 9.8 in 1993–94; 322 Commodore 1995–99; 3260 Commodore in 2000–04) delivered quality, comfort at competitive price. Richly appointed interior is accented with posh Ultraleather upholstery, glossy cherry trim, Corian countertops. Cockpit table converts into sun pad; aft seating group can be removed for fishing. Note walk-through windshield, transom storage lockers. Inboard models with 300hp MerCruiser V-drives top out at 35 knots; twin 300hp I/Os reach 40+ knots top.

See Page 537 For Value Estimates

Hull Length	32'0"	Fuel	172 gals.
Beam	11'2"	Water	50 gals.
Draft	3'2"	Waste	30 gals.
Weight	11,800#	Hull Type	Modified-V
Clearance, Arch	10'1"	Deadrise Aft	19°

Regal 3360 Express

2006–Current

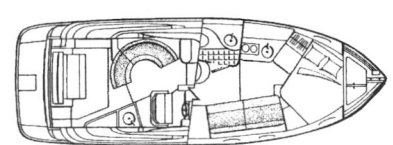

Classy sterndrive express with rakish lines gets high marks for comfort, quality, performance. Well-appointed salon with large foldout sleeper offers plenty of storage, lots of elbow room. Forward window inserts, side windows provide plenty of natural lighting. Note cherrywood cabinetry, posh upholstery, hardwood salon floor. Topside amenities include wet bar, transom shower, electric engine hatch. Extended swim platform, radar arch, transom storage are standard. Volvo 320hp I/Os cruise at 25 knots and reach 36–38 knots top.

See Page 537 For Value Estimates

Length	34'8"	Fuel	180 gals.
Beam	11'4"	Water	52 gals.
Draft, Down	2'11"	Waste	28 gals.
Weight	12,120#	Hull Type	Deep-V
Headroom	6'4"	Deadrise Aft	19°

Regal 3560/3760 Commodore

2003–Current

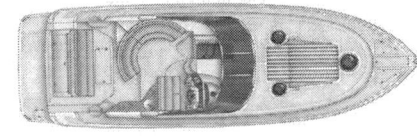

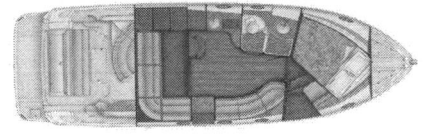

Luxury sportcruiser (called 3560 Commodore in 2003–06) ranks near the top of her class in quality, luxury, performance. Spacious interior with cherry cabinetry, leather upholstery offers unsurpassed comfort, elegance. Highlights include private forward stateroom, large galley with chest-level refrigerator, hardwood salon flooring. Cockpit is arranged with horseshoe lounge opposite helm, wet bar, foldaway rear seat. Volvo 420hp I/Os cruise at 28–30 knots (40+ knots top); 420hp gas inboards cruise in the low-to-mid 20s (around 35 knots top).

See Page 537 For Value Estimates

Length Overall	38'0"	Fuel	276 gals.
Hull Length	34'8"	Water	67 gals.
Beam	12'2"	Waste	30 gals.
Draft	3'0"	Hull Type	Deep-V
Weight	15,200#	Deadrise Aft	19°

Cruisers & Sedans

Regal 360 Commodore

1985–90

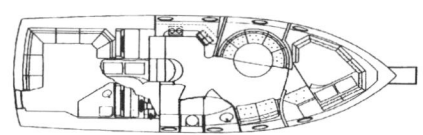

Sporty midcabin cruiser—flagship of Regal's late 1980s fleet—was among most popular midsize express boats of her era. Accommodations include roomy salon with circular dining area, private forward stateroom, full galley with refrigerator/freezer, large head with stall shower. Topside features include cockpit seating for six (note foldaway transom bench), foredeck sun pad, bow pulpit. Solid fiberglass hull has prop pockets to reduce draft, increase efficiency. Twin 340hp gas inboards cruise at 18–20 knots (high 20s top).

Price Not Provided for Pre-1995 Models

Length	36'1"	Fuel	280 gals.
Beam	13'1"	Water	125 gals.
Draft	2'10"	Waste	65 gals.
Weight	17,000#	Hull Type	Modified-V
Clearance	9'7"	Deadrise Aft	17°

Regal 3860/4060 Commodore

2002–Current

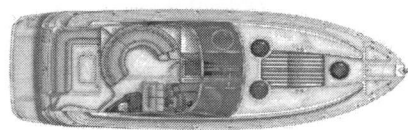

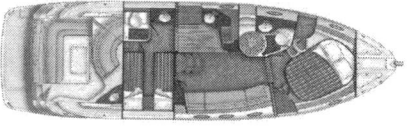

Full-bodied sportyacht (called 3860 Commodore in 2002–06) successfully blends comfort, luxury, performance. Posh interior with two private cabins boasts second head in aft stateroom—a rare luxury in boats this size. Expansive cockpit with circular bridgedeck lounge accommodates a small crowd. Rear cockpit deck lifts for walk-in access to engine compartment from swim platform. Note power windshield vent. Standard 420hp gas engines cruise at 18 knots (30+ knots top); 370hp Cummins diesels cruise at 22 knots (30 knots top).

See Page 538 For Value Estimates

Length w/Platform	40'1"	Fuel	277 gals.
Beam	13'0"	Water	75 gals.
Draft	3'3"	Waste	40 gals.
Weight	19,000#	Hull Type	Modified-V
Clearance, Arch	11'9"	Deadrise Aft	18°

Regal 3880/4080 Commodore

2001–Current

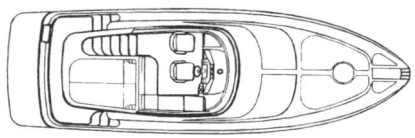

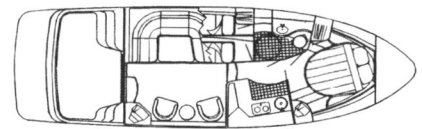

High-style flybridge yacht (called 3880 Commodore in 2001–06) delivers yacht-class comfort on a grand scale. Luxurious two-stateroom interior offers spacious full-beam salon with oversized dinette, large galley with side-by-side refrigerator. Note storage compartments under salon sole. Topside amenities include cockpit engine room access, foredeck sun pads, foldout cockpit seat. Note overhead cockpit storage. Gas 420hp V-drive engines cruise at 20 knots; 370hp Cummins diesels cruise at 22–23 knots. IPS pod drives available since 2010.

See Page 538 For Value Estimates

Length Overall	40'1"	Fuel	252 gals.
Beam	13'0"	Water	80 gals.
Draft	3'3"	Waste	40 gals.
Weight	19,300#	Hull Type	Modified-V
Clearance, Arch	16'9"	Deadrise Aft	18°

Regal 380/400/402 Commodore

1991–99

380/400 Layout

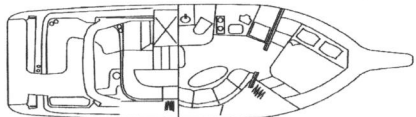

402 Layout

See Page 538 For Value Estimates

Popular 1990s cruiser (called Regal 380 Commodore in 1991–92; 400 Commodore in 1993–94; 402 Commodore in 1995–99) ranked among the largest express boats of her era. Roomy interior—updated in 1995—boasts privacy doors for both staterooms, fully equipped galley, rich leather seating. Note standing aft-cabin headroom. Large cockpit seats eight. Power engine hatch, bow pulpit were standard. Twin 310hp gas engines cruise at 18–19 knots (27–28 knots top); optional Cummins 330hp diesels cruise at 26 knots (30 knots top).

Length w/Pulpit	42'0"	Fuel	265 gals.
Hull Length	39'5"	Water	125 gals.
Beam	13'11"	Waste	65 gals.
Draft	3'0"	Hull Type	Modified-V
Weight	16,000#	Deadrise Aft	17°

Regal 4160/4260/4460 Commodore

2000–Current

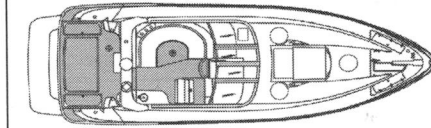

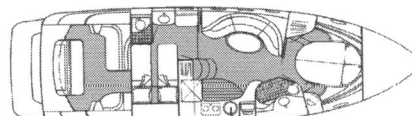

See Page 538 For Value Estimates

Bold American sportyacht (called 4160 Commodore in 2000–01; 4260 Commodore in 2002–05) delivers compelling mix of modern styling, posh accommodations, spirited performance. Wide-open salon with leather seating, home-sized galley with hardwood floor, two private staterooms, two heads. Huge bridgedeck boasts circular lounge seating. Transom storage locker, power engine hatch are standard. Fiberglass hardtop is a popular option. Cummins 450hp-or Volvo 480hp-diesels cruise at 28 knots (30+ knots top).

Length w/Platform	44'4"	Fuel	328 gals.
Hull Length	40'10"	Water	101 gals.
Beam	14'0"	Waste	48 gals.
Draft	2'11"	Hull Type	Deep-V
Weight	20,375#	Deadrise Aft	20°

Regal 52 Sport Coupe

2008–Current

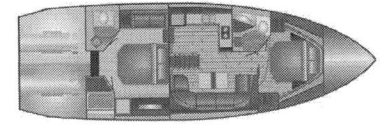

See Page 538 For Value Estimates

Bold Eurostyle express with luxury-class accommodations, Volvo IPS drive system makes Regal a player in large sportyacht market. Integral hardtop with electric sunroof, wraparound widows protect most of the cockpit. Versatile design gives buyers choice of four interior layouts, two cockpit configurations. Enormous full-beam master stateroom dwarfs anything in its class. Huge engine room is a plus; vertical hull ports provide plenty of natural lighting. Cruise at 25 knots (30 top) with fuel-efficient 435hp Volvo IPS diesels.

Length	53'0"	Fuel	450 gals.
Beam	15'4"	Water	125 gals.
Draft	3'10"	Waste	65 gals.
Weight	34,400#	Hull Type	Modified-V
Clearance	12'0"	Deadrise Aft	15°

Cruisers & Sedans

Cruisers & Sedans

Rinker 270 Fiesta Vee

1999–2006

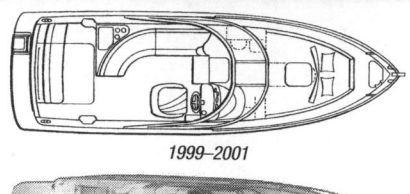

1999–2001

2002–06

Value-priced express blends traditional styling with roomy accommodations, solid construction. Carpeted midcabin interior with attractive cherry trim sleeps four, includes convertible dinette forward, enclosed head, full galley. Single-level cockpit sole means no step to trip over. Standard features include walk-through windshield, radar arch, burlwood dash, electric engine hatch/rear seat, transom shower. Note cockpit redesign in 2002. Single 320hp MerCruiser I/O will cruise in the low 20s (35+ knots top).

See Page 538 For Value Estimates

Length w/Platform	30'4"	Fuel	100 gals.
Hull Length	27'10"	Water	33 gals.
Beam	9'1"	Waste	27 gals.
Draft, Drives Down	3'0"	Hull Type	Modified-V
Weight	7,350#	Deadrise Aft	18°

Rinker 280 Fiesta Vee

1993–99

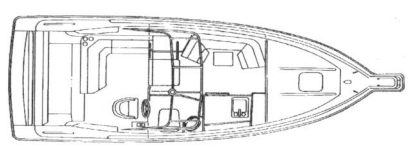

Sturdy Rinker express with generous 10' beam offered 1990s boaters space, comfort at a competitive price. Generic midcabin interior has double berths fore and aft, convertible dinette, full galley, stand-up head with shower. Privacy curtains separate sleeping areas from salon. Note 6'6" cabin headroom, numerous storage cabinets. Roomy cockpit with L-shaped settee, rear lounge seats eight. Side decks are narrow; fuel capacity is modest. Twin 190hp MerCruiser I/Os cruise at 20 knots (about 30 knots wide open).

See Page 538 For Value Estimates

Length w/Pulpit	30'2"	Fuel	120 gals.
Beam	10'0"	Water	33 gals.
Draft, Drives Up	1'10"	Waste	27 gals.
Draft, Drives Down	3'0"	Hull Type	Deep-V
Weight	8,680#	Deadrise Aft	20°

Rinker 280 Express Cruiser

2008–Current

Single-engine express with many standard features targets budget-focused boaters with an eye for value. Cockpit with U-shaped rear seating, portside lounger, double helm seat can accommodate a small crowd. Well-appointed cabin is more compact than many other 28-footers with greater beam. Rear-facing transom seat is a nice touch; hot/cold transom shower is standard. Unusually high cockpit freeboard keeps passengers safe underway. Single 375hp MerCruiser I/O will cruise at 24–25 knots (mid 30s top).

See Page 538 For Value Estimates

Length	31'8"	Fuel	100 gals.
Beam	9'1"	Water	33 gals.
Draft, Up	2'0"	Waste	27 gals.
Draft, Down	3'0"	Hull Type	Modified-V
Weight	7,640#	Deadrise Aft	18°

Rinker 290 Fiesta Vee; 300 Express Cruiser

2003–09

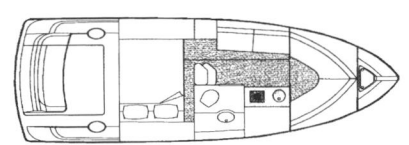

Stylish family express (called 290 Fiesta Vee in 2003–04; 300 EC in 2005–09) combines spacious accommodations, nimble performance. So-called "price boat" delivers features generally found in more expensive boats. Highlights include roomy cabin with berths for six, anchor windlass, electric engine hatch, extended swim platform. Original floorplan with too-small forward berth (not shown) was replaced in 2004 with revised dinette-forward layout. MerCruiser 260hp I/Os cruise in the mid 20s (35+ knots top).

See Page 538 For Value Estimates

Length	33'2"	Fuel	150 gals.
Beam	10'6"	Water	33 gals.
Draft, Up	1'10"	Waste	47 gals.
Draft, Down	3'0"	Hull Type	Modified-V
Weight	11,100#	Deadrise Aft	18°

Rinker 300 Fiesta Vee

1990–97

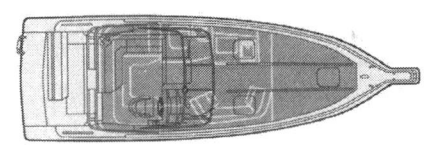

Popular 30-footer from 1990s offered big-time value in a midsize boat. Generous 10'6" beam results in spacious cabin layout well-suited for entertaining, cruising. Six opening ports, three deck hatches provide good ventilation. Storage—including aircraft-style overhead lockers in salon—is excellent. Lounge cockpit seating can accommodate six adults. Note narrow side decks, large bridgedeck. Twin 260hp MerCruiser I/Os cruise in the low 20s and reach a top speed of about 35 knots. About 150 were built.

See Page 538 For Value Estimates

Length w/Pulpit	33'11"	Fuel	140 gals.
Beam	10'6"	Water	34 gals.
Draft, Drives Up	1'8"	Waste	25 gals.
Draft, Drives Down	2'10"	Hull Type	Modified-V
Weight	10,000#	Deadrise Aft	18°

Rinker 310/312 Fiesta Vee; 320 Express

2000–09

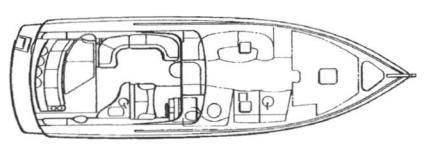

Affordable sportcruiser (called 310 Fiesta Vee in 2000–02; 312 Fiesta Vee in 2003–04; 320 EC in 2005–09) combines modern styling with roomy interior, comfortable ride. Generous 11'4" beam is among widest in her class. Highlights include forward-facing radar arch, extended swim platform, U-shaped cockpit seating, transom storage. Helm was redesigned in 2003 with more space for electronics. Generator, air-conditioning, power engine hatch are standard. Twin 260hp MerCruiser I/Os cruise at 20 knots (mid 30s top).

See Page 538 For Value Estimates

Length	34'8"	Fuel	165 gals.
Beam	11'4"	Water	39 gals.
Draft, Up	1'10"	Waste	45 gals.
Draft, Down	3'0"	Hull Type	Modified-V
Weight	12,360#	Deadrise Aft	18°

Cruisers & Sedans

Rinker 330/340 Express Cruiser

2008–Current

Roomy family express (called 330 EC in 2008; 340 EC since 2010) takes signature Rinker value, affordability to the next level. Uncluttered cockpit with big U-shaped lounge makes socializing easy. Attractive midcabin interior with lots of storage is well arranged, not flashy. Dash has space for installing single 12" video screen. Aft-facing transom seat is a plus. Air-conditioning, generator, windlass are standard. Flip-up helm bolster seat isn't split between skipper, mate. Cruise at 24–25 knots (about 35 top) with twin 280hp Volvo I/Os.

See Page 538 For Value Estimates

Length	35'8"	Fuel	168 gals.
Beam	11'4"	Water	40 gals.
Draft, Up	1'10"	Waste	47 gals.
Draft, Down	3'0"	Hull Type	Modified-V
Weight	14,100#	Deadrise Aft	18°

Rinker 330/340/342 Fiesta Vee

1998–2006

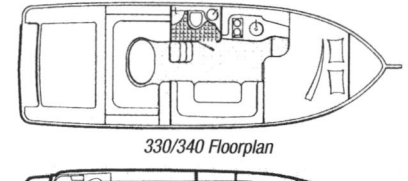

330/340 Floorplan

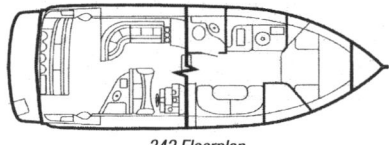

342 Floorplan

Appealing weekend retreat (called 330 Fiesta Vee in 1998–99; 340 Fiesta Vee in 2000–2001) is proof that good boats don't have to cost a fortune. Many standard features—windlass, generator, air-conditioning—cost extra on other boats. Update in 2000 lowered salon floor and raised foredeck for increased cabin headroom. Changes in 2002 included new floorplan, extended swim platform, increased fuel. Note walk-through windshield, electric engine hatch. Twin 280hp Volvo gas I/Os cruise in the low-to-mid 20s (around 35 knots top).

See Page 538 For Value Estimates

Length w/Platform	37'0"	Fuel	200/235 gals.
Beam	12'0"	Water	51 gals.
Draft, Drives Down	2'11"	Waste	45 gals.
Weight	14,280#	Hull Type	Modified-V
Clearance	9'8"	Deadrise Aft	18°

Rinker 350/360 Express Cruiser

2008–Current

Conservative midsize express (called 350 EC in 2008) with impressive feature list raised the bar for value-based pricing. Open-plan interior with pullout galley stowage, Ultra-Leather seating sleeps six. Well-appointed cockpit with wet bar (with refrigerator) offers all the comforts, amenities of more expensive competitors. Generator, air-conditioning, windlass are standard. Note walk-through windshield, clever rear-facing transom seat, good engine access. MerCruiser 300hp engines cruise at 22–23 knots (mid 30s top).

See Page 538 For Value Estimates

Length	37'11"	Fuel	235 gals.
Beam	12'0"	Water	51 gals.
Draft, Up	1'10"	Waste	45 gals.
Draft, Down	3'0"	Hull Type	Modified-V
Weight	15,550#	Deadrise Aft	18°

Cruisers & Sedans

Rinker 360/370/380 Express Cruiser

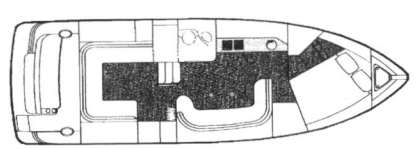

2005–Current

Durable family express (called 360 EC in 2005–06; 370 EC in 2007–08; 380 EC in 2009) holds her own against more expensive competitors. Impressive standard-equipment list belied her very affordable price. Well-appointed interior with cherry trim features private forward stateroom, spacious midcabin, large galley with lots of counter space. Twin cockpit lounges, double-wide helm seat up to ten. Note walk-through windshield, extended swim platform, transom storage. Cruise at 28–30 knots with 375hp MerCruiser I/Os

See Page 538 For Value Estimates

Length	39'4"	Fuel	235 gals.
Beam	12'3"	Water	51 gals.
Draft, Up	2'0"	Waste	45 gals.
Draft, Down	3'0"	Hull Type	Modified-V
Weight	18,400#	Deadrise Aft	18°

Rinker 390/400 Express Cruiser

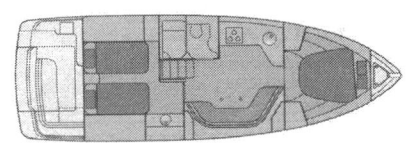

2006–Current

Maxi-volume sterndrive cruiser (called 390 EC in 2006) makes the cut with boaters looking for space, performance, affordability. Huge interior with 7-foot headroom features private forward stateroom, super-size aft cabin (with twin berths, sink, privacy door), spacious salon/galley area with teak-and-holly cabin sole. Elevated bridgedeck provides comfortable seating, excellent helm visibility. Note walk-through windshield, cockpit wet bar. Power hatch provides easy engine access. Twin 375hp Mercury I/Os cruise at 25 knots (35+ top).

See Page 538 For Value Estimates

Length Overall	41'6"	Fuel	300 gals.
Beam	13'0"	Water	69 gals.
Draft, Drives Up	1'10"	Waste	45 gals.
Draft, Drives Down	3'2"	Hull Type	Modified-V
Weight	19,680#	Deadrise Aft	18°

Rinker 390/410/420 Express Cruiser

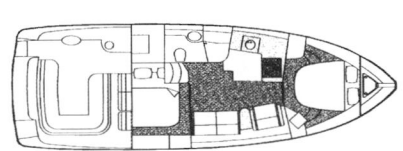

2004–07

Well-balanced sportcruiser (called 390 Fiesta Vee in 2004; 410 EC in 2005–06; 420 EC in 2007) delivers serious value in a big express-boat package. Spacious interior with 7-foot headroom, home-size galley features two private staterooms, each with built-in TVs. Note washer/dryer space next to head, separate child berth in aft cabin. Huge cockpit with hideaway gas grill seats a crowd. Hardtop became available in 2005. Standard 425hp V-drive gas inboards cruise at 22–25 knots; Cummins 380hp diesels cruise at 25 knots.

See Page 538 For Value Estimates

Length w/Platform	43'6"	Fuel	300 gals.
Beam	13'10"	Water	100 gals.
Draft	3'2"	Waste	88 gals.
Weight	24,500#	Hull Type	Modified-V
Clearance	12'10"	Deadrise Aft	18°

Cruisers & Sedans

Riviera 3600 Sport Yacht

2007–Current

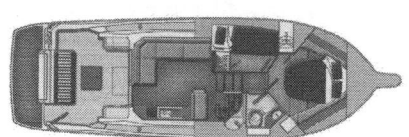

Well-bred express with fully enclosed hardtop takes cruising comfort to the next level. Unique stainless-steel–framed bulkhead swings up to expose galley/salon to cockpit with built-in settee, teak dining table. Good cabin ventilation with overhead hatches, sliding salon windows. Cherry panel conceals galley when not in use. Engine room, reached via cockpit hatch, is very tight. Prop pockets reduce draft, improve efficiency. Note quiet underwater exhaust system. Cruise in the mid 20s with 370hp Volvo diesels (about 30 knots top).

See Page 539 For Value Estimates

Length w/Pulpit	38'6"	Fuel	212 gals.
Beam	12'7"	Water	103 gals.
Draft	3'3"	Waste	18 gals.
Weight	20,300#	Hull Type	Modified-V
Clearance	NA	Deadrise Aft	15°

Riviera 4000 Offshore

1998–2003

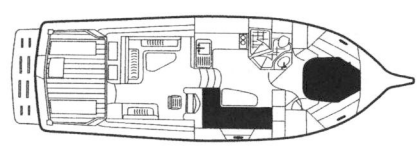

Conservative express cruiser introduced in 1998 gave budget-minded boaters exceptional boating value for the money. Versatile layout boasts large cockpit for fishing or entertaining, roomy single-stateroom interior with convertible dinette for weekend cruising. Highlights include oak interior trim, L-shaped cockpit dinette, radar arch, swim platform, spacious engine room, well-designed helm position. Factory hardtop was optional. Cummins 450hp—or Cat 435hp—diesels cruise in the mid 20s and reach a top speed of close to 30 knots.

See Page 539 For Value Estimates

Length w/Pulpit	44'7"	Fuel	394 gals.
Hull Length	41'0"	Water	119 gals.
Beam	14'4"	Headroom	6'4"
Draft	3'11"	Hull Type	Modified-V
Weight	25,353#	Deadrise Aft	15°

Sabre 34 Sedan

1991–2002

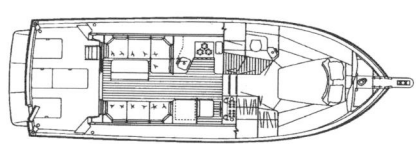

Sought-after performance trawler with many quality features makes the cut with boaters focused on timeless styling, luxury-class amenities. Traditional teak (or cherry) interior with U-shaped galley, lower helm offers near ideal accommodations for the cruising couple. Highlights include large cabin windows, convertible dinette, separate stall shower, teak-and-holly cabin sole. Wide side decks make getting around easy. Transom door, radar mast were standard. Twin Cummins 220hp diesels cruise at 15–16 knots (about 20 knots top).

See Page 539 For Value Estimates

Length w/Pulpit	37'6"	Fuel	250 gals.
Hull Length	34'0"	Water	160 gals.
Beam	12'6"	Waste	25 gals.
Draft	3'3"	Hull Type	Modified-V
Weight	17,800#	Deadrise Aft	14°

Sabre 34 Hardtop Express

2006–2010

Blue-chip express blends hardtop versatility with yacht-class interior, timeless Downeast styling. Space-efficient layout is arranged with galley up (rather than down as with most boats of this type) resulting in more living space below. Posh cabin with convertible dinette, stall shower in head is perfect for the cruising couple. Note excellent helm visibility, opening side windows, wide side decks. Engine compartment is a little tight. This boat drips quality. Cruise at 22 knots (high 20s top) with twin 310hp Volvo inboard diesels.

See Page 539 For Value Estimates

Length	34'6"	Fuel	275 gals.
Beam	13'3"	Water	80 gals.
Draft	3'0"	Waste	30 gals.
Weight	19,000#	Hull Type	Modified-V
Clearance, Mast	12'8"	Deadrise Aft	16°

Sabre 36 Express

1996–2003

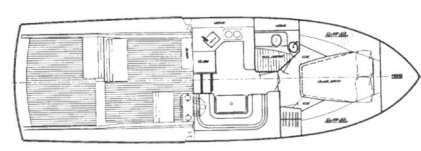

Handsome, exceptionally well-finished Downeast cruiser turns heads wherever she goes. Traditional teak interior with U-shaped galley, convertible dinette sleeps four in elegant surroundings. Deep cockpit is big enough for fishing, entertaining. Note wide side decks, radar mast. No shower stall in head. Cored hull was redesigned in 2000 (MKII version), increasing transom deadrise from 14 to 18 degrees, eliminating skeg. Hardtop model also available. Cat 300hp engines cruise at 20 knots; MKII models with 370hp Yanmars cruise in mid 20s.

See Page 539 For Value Estimates

Length w/Pulpit	40'1"	Clearance, Mast	12'0"
Hull Length	36'0"	Fuel	300 gals.
Beam	12'6"	Water	100 gals.
Draft	3'4"	Hull Type	Modified-V
Weight	18,500#	Deadrise Aft	14°/18°

Sabre 36 Sedan

2002–07

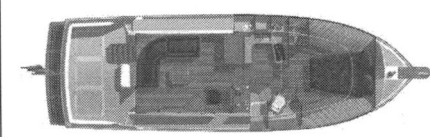

Quality-built flybridge cruiser set class standards in her day for comfort, craftsmanship, performance. Spacious single-stateroom interior with cherrywood joinery, expansive salon is finely finished, tastefully appointed. Highlights include spacious stateroom, sliding salon deck door, teak-and-holly cabin sole, large salon windows. Cockpit wet bar, transom door, radar mast, swim platform are standard. Wide side decks, large engine room are a plus. Expect a cruising speed of 25–26 knots with optional 370hp Yanmar diesels (about 30 knots top).

See Page 539 For Value Estimates

Length	36'0"	Fuel	300 gals.
Beam	12'6"	Water	100 gals.
Draft	3'4"	Waste	30 gals.
Weight	19,500#	Hull Type	Modified-V
Clearance, Mast	19'0"	Deadrise Aft	18°

Cruisers & Sedans

Sabre 38 Express

2005–10

Compelling hardtop express combines exceptional beauty with yacht-class accommodations, exceptional seakeeping abilities. Semi-enclosed pilothouse with swivel helm and companion seats, folding teak table, full wet bar provides unmatched open-air luxury. Luxurious single-stateroom interior with high-gloss cherry cabinets boasts teak-and-holly sole, posh leather settee, full-service galley, roomy head with stall shower. Note overhead hardtop hatches, wide side decks, excellent helm visibility. Yanmar 440hp diesels cruise at 25–26 knots.

See Page 539 For Value Estimates

Length	36'8"	Fuel	350 gals.
Beam	13'8"	Water	100 gals.
Draft	3'4"	Waste	30 gals.
Weight	21,500#	Hull Type	Modified-V
Clearance, Mast	13'5"	Deadrise Aft	18°

Sabre 42 Express

2004–Current

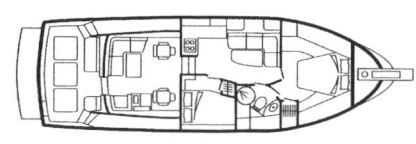

Sophisticated Downeast express introduced in 2004 embodies the graceful styling, high-quality construction common to all Sabre yachts. Semi-enclosed pilothouse with swivel helm and companion seats, well-positioned lounge seating provides extraordinary cruising luxury. Posh two-stateroom interior is highlighted with varnished cherry joinery, leather upholstery, impressive furnishings. Prop pockets reduce draft. Yanmar 440hp inboard diesels cruise at 22–23 knots. Newer models with 850hp Zeus pod drives cruise efficiently at 28 knots.

See Page 539 For Value Estimates

Length	42'3"	Fuel	450 gals.
Beam	14'4"	Water	160 gals.
Draft	3'9"	Waste	60 gals.
Weight	29,000#	Hull Type	Modified-V
Clearance, Mast	13'3"	Deadrise Aft	16°

Sabre 52 Salon Express

2007–Current

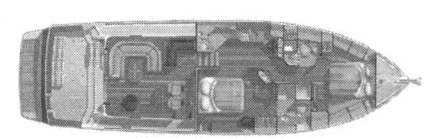

Executive-class cruising yacht with timeless Downeast styling takes yachting elegance, sophistication to the next level. Roomy cherrywood interior—designed for two couples—features richly-appointed pilothouse with posh leather seating, two large staterooms, two full heads. Power sunroof, 360-degree windows bathe pilothouse/salon in natural lighting. Note stand-up engine room, distinctive reverse transom. Prop pockets reduce draft, improve efficiency. Cruise at 26–28 knots with 865hp Cat diesels. Offered with 700hp Volvo IPS drives since 2010.

See Page 539 For Value Estimates

Length	53'2"	Fuel	800 gals.
Beam	16'0"	Water	200 gals.
Draft	4'3"	Waste	80 gals.
Weight	46,000#	Hull Type	Modified-V
Clearance	11'5"	Deadrise Aft	15°

Cruisers & Sedans

San Juan 38

2000–Current

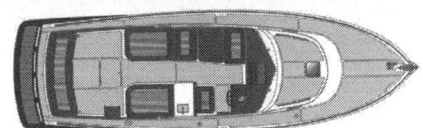

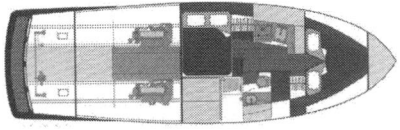

Top-quality "gentleman's yacht" boasts impressive mix of graceful styling, lavish accommodations, high-tech construction. Highlights include semi-enclosed pilothouse with convertible dinette, richly appointed two-stateroom interior with varnished teak cabinetry, faux granite counters, teak-and-holly sole. Large cockpit with built-in transom seat is suitable for entertaining, fishing. Note fine teak instrument console, retractable sunroof. Yanmar 350hp diesel inboards cruise in the mid 20s (about 30 knots top).

See Page 539 For Value Estimates

Length Overall	40'7"	Fuel	300 gals.
Beam	12'2"	Waste	80 gals.
Draft	2'2"	Waste	15 gals.
Weight	15,800#	Hull Type	Modified-V
Clearance	9'11"	Deadrise Aft	14°

Sea Ray 270 Sundancer

1982–88

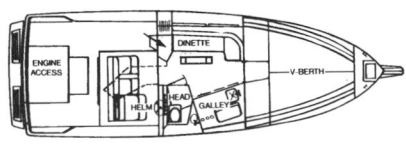

Durable 1980s-era express with generous 10-foot beam gave Sea Ray buyers a lot of boat for the money in her day. Spacious midcabin interior with full galley, enclosed head with shower, sleeps six. Roomy cockpit boasts adjustable helm seat, foldaway stern seat, transom door. Teak swim platform, bow pulpit were standard. Most were sold with optional radar arch. Narrow side decks make going forward a dicey proposition. Very popular model. Twin 260hp MerCruiser sterndrives will cruise at 25 knots (high 30s top).

Prices Not Provided for Pre-1995 Models

Length w/Pulpit	29'2"	Fuel	120 gals.
Beam	10'0"	Water	28 gals.
Draft, Up	1'10"	Headroom	6'2"
Draft, Down	2'8"	Hull Type	Deep-V
Weight	6,700#	Deadrise Aft	22°

Sea Ray 270 Sundancer

1992–93

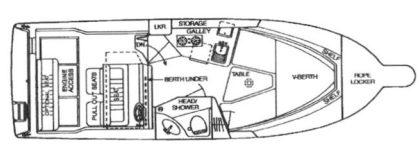

Sporty Sea Ray express—second in a series of Sea Ray 270 Sundancer models—was among the biggest trailerable cruisers of her era. Generic midcabin floorplan is arranged with V-berth forward, removable dinette table, efficient galley, stand-up head with shower. Double berth in aft cabin is a tight fit for adults. Cockpit layout includes double-wide helm seat, pull-out jump seats, transom seat. Bow pulpit, swim platform were standard. Restyled in 2004 both inside and out. Cruise at 20 knots (mid 30s top) with single 330hp MerCruiser sterndrive.

Prices Not Provided for Pre-1995 Models

Length w/Pulpit	28'6"	Fuel	100 gals.
Beam	8'6"	Water	24 gals.
Draft, Up	1'8"	Waste	20 gals.
Draft, Down	3'0"	Hull Type	Deep-V
Weight	5,600#	Deadrise Aft	20°

Cruisers & Sedans

Cruisers & Sedans

Sea Ray 270 Sundancer

1994-97; 1999

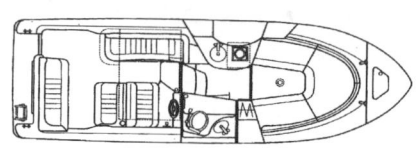

Updated version of previous Sea Ray 270 Sundance model (1992–93) packed big-boat accommodations in a trailerable hull. Well-appointed cabin with compact galley, convertible dinette sleeps four. Surprisingly roomy cockpit features include double back-to-back helm seat, portside lounger, aft bench seat, transom door. Deep-V hull delivers stable open-water ride. Out of production in 1997; produced again in 1999 as the 270 Sundancer "Special Edition." Cruise at 22 knots with single 330hp MerCruiser I/O (about 35 knots top).

See Page 540 For Value Estimates

Length w/Pulpit	29'11"	Fuel	100 gals.
Beam	8'6"	Water	24 gals.
Draft, Up	1'11"	Waste	20 gals.
Draft, Down	3'0"	Hull Type	Deep-V
Weight	6,400#	Deadrise Aft	20°

Sea Ray 270 Sundancer

1998–2001

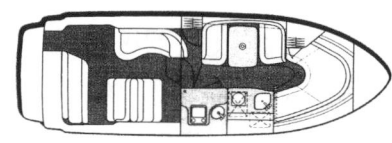

Strong-selling express with broad 9'2" beam delivers traditional Sea Ray comfort, performance in a well-crafted package. Spacious interior with booth-style dinette, full galley, sleeps six. Aft stateroom has curved sliding window for ventilation. Space-efficient cockpit includes wet bar, cooler and stereo. Additional features include transom storage, cockpit shower, extended swim platform, gas-assist engine hatch. Cruise at 20 knots with single 310hp I/O (30+ top); mid 20s with twin 190hp engines (40+ knots top).

See Page 540 For Value Estimates

Length w/Platform	29'10"	Fuel	100 gals.
Beam	9'2"	Water	28 gals.
Draft, Up	1'11"	Waste	28 gals.
Draft, Down	3'5"	Hull Type	Deep-V
Weight	7,500#	Deadrise Aft	21°

Sea Ray 270 Weekender

1992–93

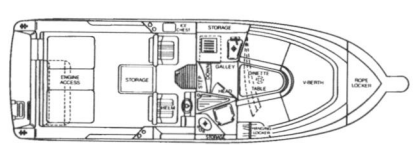

Dual-purpose trailerable express with large cockpit, barebones interior is great for fishing, diving, overnighting. Single-level cockpit with foldaway stern seat, in-floor storage can accommodate several guests or anglers. Cozy cabin with mini-galley, enclosed head with shower, removable dinette table, sleeps two adults. Note built-in ice chest next to companion seat. Bow pulpit, swim ladder were standard. Solid fiberglass, deep-V hull can take a punch. Single 300hp MerCruiser I/O reaches a top speed of 30+ knots.

Prices Not Provided for Pre-1995 Models

Length w/Pulpit	28'6"	Clearance	NA
Beam	8'6"	Fuel	100 gals.
Draft, Up	1'8"	Water	24 gals.
Draft, Down	3'0"	Hull Type	Deep-V
Weight	5,600#	Deadrise Aft	20°

Sea Ray 270/290 Sundancer

1990–93

1990–92 Floorplan

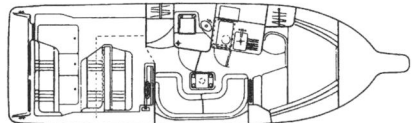

1993 Floorplan

Prices Not Provided for Pre-1995 Models

Spirited 1990s express set class standards in her day for aggressive sportboat styling, leading-edge amenities. Open-plan interior with full galley, convertible dinette sleeps six. Privacy curtains separate forward berth from salon—useful for cruising with friends. Cockpit came standard with foldaway stern seat, wet bar, triple-wide helm seat. Called 270 Sundancer in 1990–91; 290 Sundancer in 1992–93. Floorplan undated in 1993. Cruise at 20 knots with single 300hp Mercury I/O; mid 20s with twin 205hp Mercs.

Length w/Pulpit	30'6"	Fuel	100 gals.
Beam	9'0"	Water	24 gals.
Draft, Up	1'10"	Waste	20 gals.
Draft, Down	3'1"	Hull Type	Deep-V
Weight	5,800#	Deadrise Aft	20°

Sea Ray 280 Sundancer

1989–91

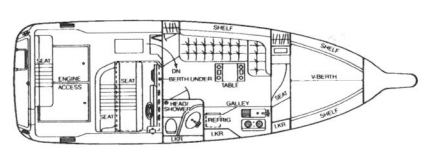

See Page 540 For Value Estimates

Good-selling express introduced in 1989 met Sea Ray promise of family-friendly accommodations, brisk performance, durable construction. Generic midcabin interior with large galley, convertible dinette sleeps six. Space-efficient cockpit features double helm seat with aft-facing seat, foldaway rear seat, transom door. Bow pulpit, cockpit bolsters, ice chest, were standard. Privacy curtains separate forward berth from salon—great for cruising with friends. Twin 260hp MerCruiser sterndrives cruise in the mid 20s (about 35 knots top).

Length w/Pulpit	31'11"	Clearance	9'0"
Beam	10'6"	Fuel	120 gals.
Draft, Up	1'10"	Water	35 gals.
Draft	2'8"	Hull Type	Deep-V
Weight	8,000#	Deadrise Aft	20°

Sea Ray 280 Sundancer

2001–09

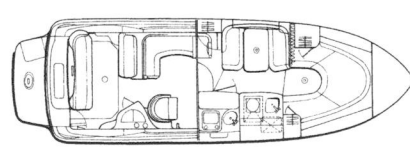

See Page 540 For Value Estimates

Polished Sea Ray express introduced in 2001 combined leading-edge styling with luxury-class accommodations, sporty performance. Well-appointed interior with cherry cabinetry, posh decor sleeps four adults, two kids in comfort. Cockpit has wet bar with built-in cooler, portside lounger, fold-down sun pad. Sporty helm layout includes flip-up seat, wood-grain dash, tilt wheel. Note extended swim platform, sport arch with overhead lighting. Near-flawless gelcoat. Cruise at 30 knots with twin 260hp MerCruiser sterndrive power (mid 40s top).

Length w/Platform	31'1"	Fuel	100 gals.
Beam	9'5"	Water	28 gals.
Draft, Up	1'10"	Waste	28 gals.
Draft, Down	3'3"	Hull Type	Deep-V
Weight	8,630#	Deadrise Aft	21°

Cruisers & Sedans

Sea Ray 280 Sundancer

2010–Current

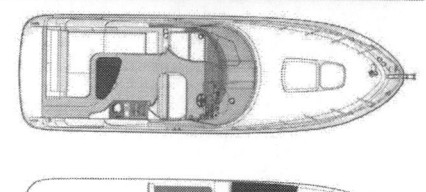

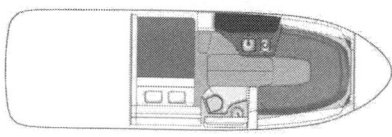

Next-generation 280 Sundancer (note two previous 280 Sundancer models) delivers single-engine economy with sleek styling, signature Sea Ray quality. Standard features include curved cockpit seating with storage under, removable cooler, power engine hatch, cockpit wet bar with Corian counter. Stern backrest folds flat into a large sun pad. Comfy midcabin interior includes full galley with fridge, butane stove, microwave. Towable with the right tow vehicle and an overwide permit. Cruise at 25 knots (35 top) with single 320hp MerCruiser I/O.

See Page 540 For Value Estimates

Length w/Platform	28'8"	Fuel	84 gals.
Beam	8'10"	Water	28 gals.
Draft, Up	2'0"	Waste	28 gals.
Draft, Down	3'5"	Hull Type	Deep-V
Weight	8,211#	Deadrise Aft	19°

Sea Ray 290 Sundancer

1994–97

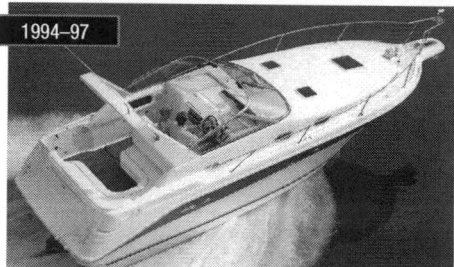

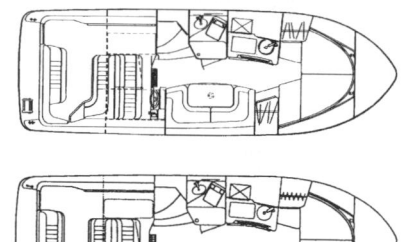

Bold 1990s cruiser with deluxe accommodations took express-boat comfort, styling to the next level. Very spacious interior with double berths fore and aft features large galley, convertible dinette, two hanging lockers. Cockpit highlights include U-shaped lounge seating, double helm seat with flip-up bolsters, very large dash with chart flat. Engine compartment is a tight fit with twin engines. No cockpit wet bar. Replaced in 1998 with all-new 290 Sundancer model. Cruise at 20 knots with single 300hp MerCruiser; 24–25 knots with twin 190hp Mercs.

See Page 540 For Value Estimates

Length w/Pulpit	32'1"	Fuel	130 gals.
Beam	9'8"	Water	24 gals.
Draft, Up	2'0"	Waste	24 gals.
Draft, Down	3'9"	Hull Type	Deep-V
Weight	8,500#	Deadrise Aft	21°

Sea Ray 290 Sundancer

1998–2001

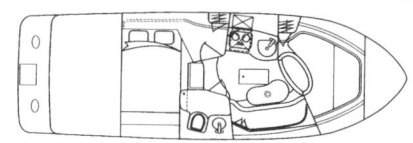

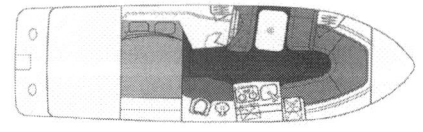

Redesigned version of previous 290 Sundancer (1994–97) boasts enlarged cockpit, updated styling, all-new interior. Topside highlights include extended swim platform, portside lounge seat (opposite helm), wet bar, flip-up helm seat. Rear bench seat can be removed to free up cockpit space. Offered with three interior layouts. Side decks are narrow. Engine compartment is a tight fit with twins. Heavy boat for her size. Cruise at 20 knots with single 310hp Merc I/O; twin 260hp Mercs cruise in the mid 20s.

See Page 540 For Value Estimates

Length	29'8"	Fuel	130 gals.
Beam	10'2"	Water	28 gals.
Draft, Up	2'3"	Waste	28 gals.
Draft, Down	3'1"	Hull Type	Deep-V
Weight	10,500#	Deadrise Aft	21°

Cruisers & Sedans

Sea Ray 290 Sundancer

2006–08

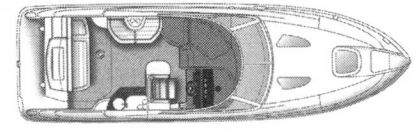

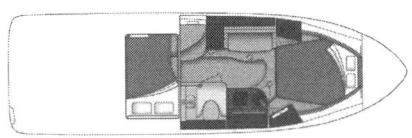

Blue-chip express combines world-class styling with luxury amenities, no-excuses performance. Stylish interior with cherry cabinets, leather seating gets high marks for premium furnishings, excellent finish. Island berth converts to aft-facing seat with storage under. Topside features include wet bar with Corian counter, power engine hatch, transom shower, walk-through windshield. One of the best-looking boats in her class. Twin 260hp MerCruiser sterndrives cruise at 25 knots (about 40 knots wide open).

See Page 540 For Value Estimates

Length Overall	31'1"	Fuel	125 gals.
Beam	9'6"	Water	28 gals.
Draft, Drives Up	2'4"	Waste	28 gals.
Draft, Drives Down	3'3"	Hull Type	Deep-V
Weight	9,250#	Deadrise Aft	21°

Sea Ray 300 Sedan Bridge

1985–87

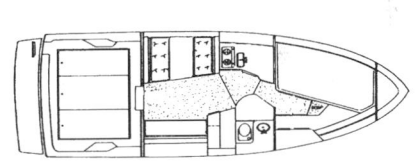

Popular Sea Ray sedan offered 1980s boaters a practical blend of comfort, versatility in a well-styled package. Teak-trimmed interior with large galley, convertible dinette and sofa, lower helm, head with shower sleeps six. Angled berth in forward cabin preserves cabin space; compact galley is short on storage. Cockpit hatches provide good engine access. Side decks are very narrow. Side-dumping exhausts keep noxious fumes out of the cockpit. Twin 260hp MerCruiser inboards cruise at 18 knots and top out in the high 20s.

Prices Not Provided for Pre-1995 Models

Length	29'1"	Fuel	140 gals.
Beam	11'0"	Water	40 gals.
Draft	2'5"	Cockpit	60 sq. ft.
Weight	10,500#	Hull Type	Deep-V
Clearance	NA	Deadrise Aft	21°

Sea Ray 300 Sundancer

1985–89

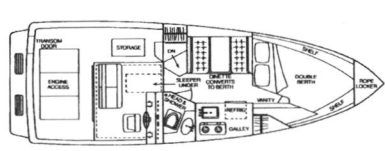

Top-selling 1980s express made the cut with buyers drawn to bold styling, roomy accommodations, spirited performance. Carpeted interior with teak trim includes fully equipped galley, stand-up head with shower, convertible dinette, double berths fore and aft. Uncluttered cockpit is arranged with elevated helm seat and companion seats, foldaway aft-facing jump seats, transom door. Radar arch, generator were popular options. One of Sea Ray's most popular models ever. Twin 260hp I/Os cruise at 22 knots (about 35 knots wide open).

Prices Not Provided for Pre-1995 Models

Length w/Pulpit	31'4"	Weight	9,800#
Hull Length	29'8"	Fuel	140 gals.
Beam	11'0"	Water	40 gals.
Draft, Up	1'6"	Hull Type	Deep-V
Draft, Down	2'11"	Deadrise Aft	21°

Cruisers & Sedans

Sea Ray 300 Sundancer

1992–93

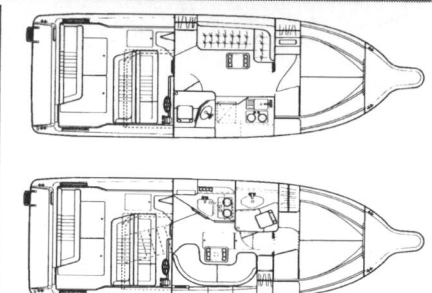

Contemporary 1990s express with integral swim platform delivered crisp styling with common-sense layout, quality construction. Generic midcabin interior with convertible dinette sleeps six. Triple-wide helm seat, aft-facing bench seat, wet bar, foldaway rear seat were standard in cockpit. Integral swim platform, vented windshield, good engine access. Small fuel capacity limits range. Replaced in 1994 with new 300 Sundancer model. Cruise at 20 knots with 230hp V-drive inboards; 22–24 knots with 230hp sterndrives.

Prices Not Provided for Pre-1995 Models

Length w/Pulpit	31'11"	Clearance	8'8"
Hull Length	29'9"	Fuel	120 gals.
Beam	10'6"	Water	35 gals.
Draft	2'8"	Hull Type	Deep-V
Weight	8,300#	Deadrise Aft	21°

Sea Ray 300 Sundancer

1994–97

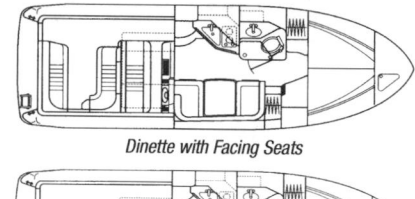

Dinette with Facing Seats

Circular Dinette

See Page 540 For Value Estimates

Good-selling express from the mid 1990s offered Sea Ray owners state-of-the-art comfort, styling at a reasonable price. Cockpit with facing bench seats, triple helm seat is larger than most 30-foot express cruisers. Traditional midcabin interior with teak trim, stand-up head, full galley, sleeps six. Chart flat in dash is a nice touch. Offered with inboard or sterndrive power. Twin 250hp V-drive inboards cruise at 20 knots (30 top); sterndrive versions of the same engines cruise in the low 20s (about 35 knots top).

Length w/Pulpit	33'1"	Fuel	200 gals.
Hull Length	30'6"	Water	35 gals.
Beam	10'6"	Waste	28 gals.
Draft	2'11"	Hull Type	Deep-V
Weight	10,200#	Deadrise Aft	21°

Sea Ray 300 Sundancer

2002–07

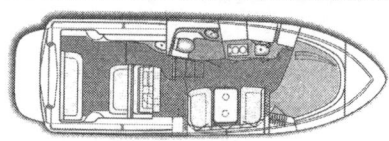

Standard Floorplan

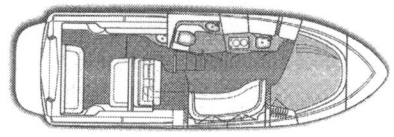

Optional Floorplan

See Page 540 For Value Estimates

Sophisticated sportcruiser combined graceful styling with best-in-class accommodations, spirited open-water performance. Highlights include upscale interior with cherry-wood cabinetry, extended swim platform, versatile cockpit with foldaway rear seat, sporty helm with flip-up bolster seat. Salon was offered with choice of dinette or curved settee. More galley stowage than many 30-footers. Cockpit sole lifts electrically for engine access. Twin 260hp MerCruiser sterndrive engines cruise at 20 knots (around 35 knots top).

Length w/Platform	33'4"	Fuel	170 gals.
Beam	10'5"	Water	35 gals.
Draft, Up	2'0"	Waste	28 gals.
Draft, Down	3'4"	Hull Type	Deep-V
Weight	12,000#	Deadrise Aft	21°

Sea Ray 305/300 Sedan Bridge

1988–89

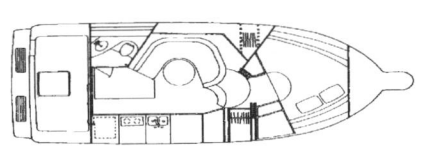

Portly flybridge cruiser with slightly unorthodox styling is long on interior space, short on eye appeal. Spacious interior includes cozy mid-stateroom under salon dinette. Extended galley with double sink boasts copious storage, abundant counter space—rare luxuries in any 30-foot boat. Tiny cockpit is shaded by bridge overhang. Transom door is standard. Short production run. Called the 305 Sedan Bridge in 1988; 300 Sedan Bridge in 1999. Standard 260hp MerCruiser inboards cruise in the low 20s (28–29 knots top).

Prices Not Provided for Pre-1995 Models

Length	29'10"	Fuel	200 gals.
Beam	12'0"	Water	60 gals.
Draft	2'6"	Cockpit	40 sq. ft.
Weight	11,500#	Hull Type	Modified-V
Clearance	NA	Deadrise Aft	18°

Sea Ray 300 Weekender

1985–89

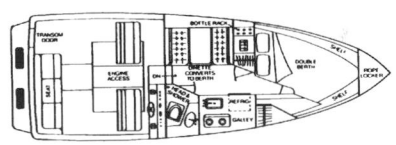

Iconic Sea Ray express with inboard power took 1980's styling, cruising standards to the next level. Topside features include roomy single-level cockpit with double helm and companion seats, removable rear seat, transom door, swim platform, side exhausts. Open-plan interior with convertible dinette, enclosed head with shower sleeps four. Cockpit hatches provide good engine access. Updated 300 Weekender model came out in 1991. Twin 260hp gas engines cruise at 22–24 knots with a top speed of 30+ knots.

Prices Not Provided for Pre-1995 Models

Length w/Pulpit	31'4"	Clearance	NA
Hull Length	29'8"	Fuel	200 gals.
Beam	11'0"	Water	40 gals.
Draft	2'5"	Hull Type	Deep-V
Weight	9,500	Deadrise Aft	21°

Sea Ray 300 Weekender

1991–95

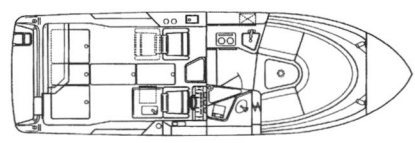

Versatile 1990s express with large cockpit is the ideal platform for fishing, diving, daytime entertaining. Cockpit highlights include back-to-back companion seat, cockpit cooler, transom door, wet bar, folding stern seat. Efficient cabin layout with mini-galley, convertible dinette, enclosed head sleeps two. Good engine access via removable cockpit hatches. Inboard models have prop pockets. Twin 250hp MerCruiser V-drive inboards cruise in the mid 20s (30+ knots top); 250hp sterndrives reach close to 40 knots top.

See Page 540 For Value Estimates

Length w/Pulpit	31'11"	Fuel	200 gals.
Hull Length	29'9"	Water	28 gals.
Beam	10'6"	Waste	28 gals.
Draft	2'8"	Hull Type	Deep-V
Weight	7,800#	Deadrise Aft	21°

Cruisers & Sedans

Cruisers & Sedans

Sea Ray 310/330 Express Cruiser

1990–95

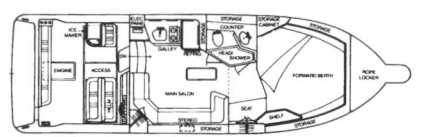

Richly appointed express (called the 310 Express Cruiser in 1990–91; 330 Express Cruiser in 1992–95) combined signature Sea Ray styling with surprisingly spacious interior, state-of-the-art engineering and construction. Versatile midcabin floorplan with U-shaped dinette sleeps six adults in comfort. Smallish cockpit has unusual triple-wide helm seat in addition to aft-facing seat, wet bar. Inboard models have prop pockets, side-dumping exhausts. Twin 310hp Mercury inboards cruise at 20 knots; twin 300hp Merc I/Os cruise in the mid 20s.

See Page 540 For Value Estimates

Length w/Pulpit	35'4"	Weight	10,000#
Hull Length	32'10"	Fuel	200 gals.
Beam	11'5"	Water	40 gals.
Draft, Inboard	2'3"	Hull Type	Deep-V
Draft, I/Os	3'0"	Deadrise Aft	21°

Sea Ray 310/330 Sundancer

1990–94

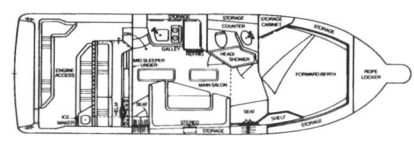

Top-selling Sea Ray cruiser from the early 1990s offered modern express-boat styling with spacious interior, wide-open cockpit. Comfortable midcabin floorplan with U-shaped dinette, fully equipped galley, sleeps six adults in comfort. Cockpit includes unusual triple-wide helm seat in addition to aft-facing seat, wet bar. Called 310 Sundancer in 1990–92; 330 Sundancer in 1992–94. Inboard models have prop pockets, side-dumping exhausts. Twin 310hp Merc inboards cruise at 20 knots; twin 300hp I/Os cruise in the mid 20s.

Prices Not Provided for Pre-1995 Models

Length w/Pulpit	35'4"	Weight	10,000#
Hull Length	32'10"	Fuel	180 gals.
Beam	11'5"	Water	40 gals.
Draft, Inboards	2'3"	Hull Type	Deep-V
Draft, I/Os	3'0"	Deadrise Aft	21°

Sea Ray 310/330 Sundancer

2007–Current

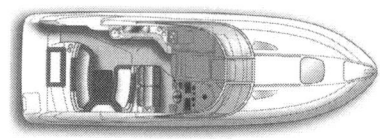

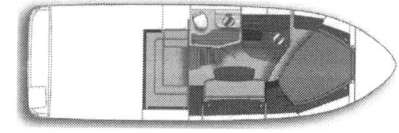

Popular Sea Ray express (called 310 Sundancer in 2007–09; 330 Sundancer starting in 2010) combines graceful styling with luxury-class amenities, sporty performance. Deluxe interior with high-gloss cherry cabinets, Ultraleather seating gets high marks for premium furnishings, hardwood flooring, generous storage. Foldaway transom seat creates aft-facing seating on swim platform. Axius drive system standard in late 2009. Twin Mercruiser 300hp V-drive inboards (gas) cruise at 25 knots; 320hp Merc I/Os cruise at 28+ knots.

See Page 540 For Value Estimates

Length	33'4"	Fuel	200 gals.
Beam	10'5"	Water	35 gals.
Draft, Up	2'5"	Waste	28 gals.
Draft, Down	3'3"	Hull Type	Deep-V
Weight	14,000#	Deadrise Aft	21°

Sea Ray 310 Sundancer

1998–2002

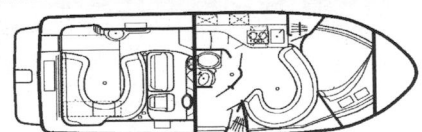

1998 Floorplan

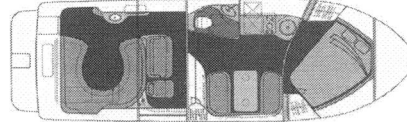

1999–2002

Compelling family express introduced in 1998 matched eye-catching styling with luxury-class accommodations, cutting-edge amenities. Very spacious cockpit with U-shaped rear seating boasts double companion seat next to helm—very unusual. Original midcabin floorplan with horseshoe seating was replaced in 1999 with more conventional (and spacious) dinette layout with enlarged bow stateroom. Twin 260hp V-drive inboards cruise at 18 knots (high 20s knots top); 260hp MerCruiser sterndrives top out in the mid 30s.

See Page 540 For Value Estimates

Length w/Platform	33'10"	Weight	12,000#
Hull Length	31'6"	Fuel	200 gals.
Beam	11'2"	Water	35 gals.
Draft, Drives Up	1'11"	Hull Type	Deep-V
Draft, Drives Down	3'7"	Deadrise Aft	23°

Sea Ray 310 Sundancer

2010–Current

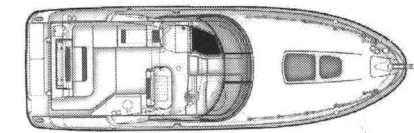

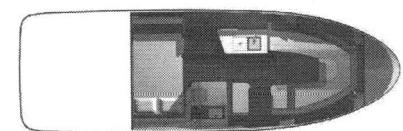

Sporty midsize cruiser—latest in a series of 310 Sundancer models—delivers an impressive mix of upscale accommodations, competitive price. Highlights include well-appointed cabin with mid-berth aft, cockpit wet bar with optional grill, walk-through windshield, power engine compartment hatch. Fold-down transom seat converts to sun pad. Modest 10-foot beam results in less living space than many 30-footers. Choice of twin sterndrives or Axius drives with joystick control. Cruise at 25 knots (high 30s top) with twin 260hp Mercury Bravo Three drives.

See Page 540 For Value Estimates

Length	31'0"	Fuel	125 gals.
Beam	10'0"	Water	28 gals.
Draft, Up	2'6"	Waste	28 gals.
Draft, Down	3'5"	Hull Type	Deep-V
Weight	11,630#	Deadrise Aft	21°

Sea Ray 320 Sundancer

2003–07

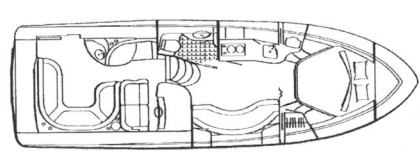

Mega-popular express introduced in 2003 set high standards for bold styling, lush accommodations, solid resale vale. Highlights include roomy, open-plan interior with lacquered cherry cabinets, expansive cockpit with U-shaped lounge seating, double helm seat with flip-up bolsters, burled dash, extended swim platform, power engine room hatch. Side decks are narrow; engine access is a little tight. Offered with inboard or sterndrive bower. Cruise in mid 20s with twin Mercury 300hp V-drive inboards or twin 260hp I/Os.

See Page 540 For Value Estimates

Length w/Platform	35'6"	Fuel	200 gals.
Beam	11'5"	Water	40 gals.
Draft	2'9"	Waste	28 gals.
Weight	13,200#	Hull Type	Deep-V
Clearance	10'2"	Deadrise Aft	21°

Cruisers & Sedans

Sea Ray 330 Express Cruiser

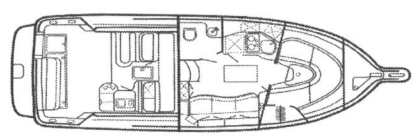

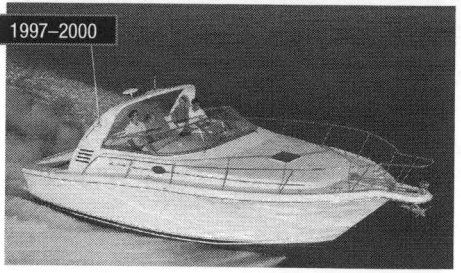

1997–2000

Enduring Sea Ray express with wide 13'5" beam combines spacious cockpit with maxi-volume cabin accommodations. Wide-open interior with private bow stateroom, built-in TV/VCR, convertible settee sleeps four. Cockpit amenities include foldaway transom seat, in-deck livewell and fish box, combined bait-prep station/wet bar. Entire bridgedeck lifts electrically for engine access. Power windshield vent is a useful touch. Cored hull has prop pockets to reduce draft. Twin 380hp MerCruiser inboards cruise at 20 knots (about 30 knots top).

See Page 540 For Value Estimates

Length w/Platform	38'0"	Fuel	275 gals.
Hull Length	33'6"	Water	50 gals.
Beam	13'5"	Waste	28 gals.
Draft	3'0"	Hull Type	Deep-V
Weight	16,500#	Deadrise Aft	19.5°

Sea Ray 330 Sundancer

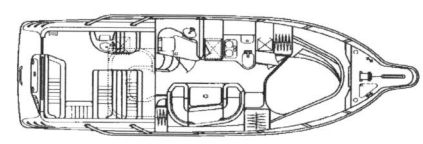

1995–99

Sought-after Sea Ray express from the late 1990s combined bold styling with roomy accommodations, first-rate features and amenities. Open-plan interior with convertible mid-berth aft boasts Ultraleather salon seating, fully equipped galley, large head with shower. Ergonomic helm came with sporty burlwood dash, tilt steering, room for extra electronics. Transom storage locker is a plus. Slender side decks require caution. Twin 310hp MerCruiser V-drive inboards cruise at 22 knots (30+ knots top). MerCruiser 300hp I/Os run a few knots faster.

See Page 540 For Value Estimates

Length w/Pulpit	35'10"	Weight	11,200#
Hull Length	33'6"	Fuel	225 gals.
Beam	11'5"	Water	40 gals.
Draft, Inboards	2'1"	Hull Type	Modified-V
Draft, I/Os	3'0"	Deadrise Aft	17°

Sea Ray 330/350 Sundancer

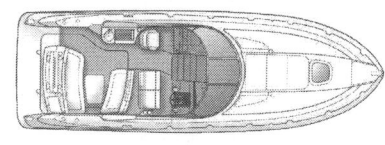

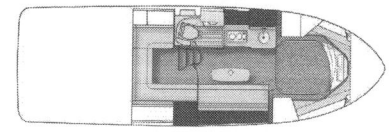

2008–Current

Sporty midsize express (called 330 Sundancer in 2008–09; 350 Sundancer starting in 2010) takes American sporty-acht styling, quality to European levels. Expansive cockpit boasts aft-facing transom seat, full-service wet bar with refrigerator, power engine access hatch. Luxurious interior with cherry cabinets, hardwood flooring includes built-in TV/DVD, home-size galley, abundant storage. Note classy helm layout. Offered with sterndrive or V-drive inboard power. Twin 370hp MerCruiser gas inboards cruise at 25 knots (mid 30s top).

See Page 540 For Value Estimates

Length	35'6"	Fuel	225 gals.
Beam	11'6"	Water	40 gals.
Draft, Up	2'9"	Waste	28 gals.
Draft, Down	3'6"	Hull Type	Deep-V
Weight	15,400#	Deadrise Aft	21°

Cruisers & Sedans

Sea Ray 340 Express Cruiser

1984–89

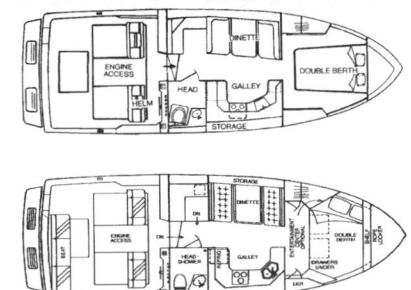

Classic 1980s express sold well in her day thanks to aggressive styling, feature-rich accommodations, competitive price. Roomy interior—dated by today's sportboat standards—combines large forward stateroom with full-size galley, convertible dinette, generous storage. Big single-level cockpit includes double helm and companion seats, transom door, removable stern seat. Cockpit hatches provide good engine access. Radar arch was a popular option. Cruise at 20 knots (30+ top) with standard 340hp straight-drive gas inboards.

Prices Not Provided for Pre-1995 Models

Length w/Platform	35'11"	Clearance	NA
Hull Length	33'7"	Fuel	250 gals.
Beam	11'11"	Water	52 gals.
Draft	2'5"	Hull Type	Deep-V
Weight	12,100#	Deadrise Aft	21°

Sea Ray 340 Sedan Bridge

1983–87

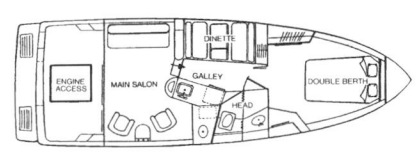

Popular 1980s sedan hit the mark with boaters looking for space, versatility at a competitive price. Single-stateroom interior—large for a 34-footer—includes convertible salon settee, convertible dinette, large stateroom with privacy door. Salon is dominated by distinctive bottle-and-glass cabinet with sliding tambour doors. Lower helm was a popular option. Transom door, swim platform were standard. Cockpit is small for a sedan this size. Twin 350hp V-drive gas inboards cruise at 20 knots (28–30 knots top).

Prices Not Provided for Pre-1995 Models

Length	33'7"	Fuel	204 gals.
Beam	11'11"	Water	80 gals.
Draft	2'6"	Headroom	6'3"
Weight	11,400#	Hull Type	Deep-V
Clearance	NA	Deadrise Aft	21°

Sea Ray 340 Sundancer

1984–89

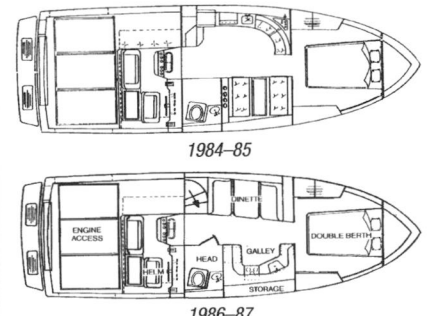

1984–85

1986–87

Widebody 34-footer from the 1980s set class standards in her day for modern styling, deluxe accommodations, durable construction. Offered with several floorplans during her production years, all with teak cabin trim, convertible dinette, double berths fore and aft. Large cockpit with double-wide helm seat, removable rear bench seat, has more elbow space than many express boats her size. Modest fuel capacity limits range. Standard 340hp MerCruiser V-drive gas inboards cruise in the low 20s (30 knots top).

Prices Not Provided for Pre-1995 Models

Length w/Platform	35'11"	Clearance	NA
Hull Length	33'7"	Fuel	172 gals.
Beam	11'11"	Water	52 gals.
Draft	2'5"	Hull Type	Deep-V
Weight	12,500#	Deadrise Aft	21°

Cruisers & Sedans

Sea Ray 340 Sundancer

1999–2002

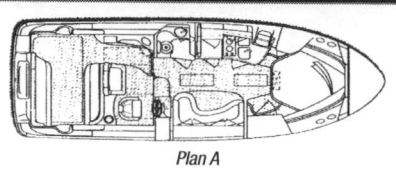

Plan A

Plan B

See Page 540 For Value Estimates

Top-selling express—among Sea Ray's most popular Sundancer models ever—delivers an enviable blend of sophisticated design, luxury accommodations. Highlights include spacious cherry interior with premium furnishings, central vacuum system, cockpit wet bar with fridge, double-wide companion seat, transom shower, hydraulic lift engine room access. Note pull-out wall-mounted TV viewable from anywhere in the cabin. Offered with inboard or sterndrive power. Twin 320hp V-drive gas inboards cruise at 22 knots (30+ wide open).

Length w/Platform	33'6"	Fuel	225 gals.
Beam	11'5"	Water	40 gals.
Draft	2'5"	Waste	28 gals.
Weight	13,000#	Hull Type	Modified-V
Clearance	NA	Deadrise Aft	17°

Sea Ray 340 Sundancer

2003–08

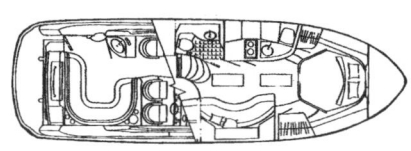

See Page 540 For Value Estimates

Graceful Sea Ray express with curvaceous lines, lush accommodations led the way for midsize American sporty-achts of her era. Polished midcabin interior with cherry cabinetry gets high marks for quality appliances, exceptional fit and finish. Topside highlights include wraparound cockpit seating, transom storage locker, extended swim platform. Twin-seat helm has dash space for flush-mounting electronics. Power hatch makes engine access easy. MerCruiser 370hp V-drive inboards cruise at 25 knots (low 30s top).

Length	37'6"	Fuel	225 gals.
Beam	12'0"	Water	45 gals.
Draft, Up	2'3"	Waste	28 gals.
Draft, Down	3'1"	Hull Type	Deep-V
Weight	15,500#	Deadrise Aft	21°

Sea Ray 350 Express Bridge

1992–94

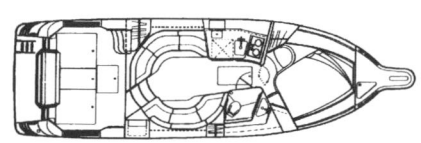

Prices Not Provided for Pre-1995 Models

Low-profile sedan with step-down interior offers more useable cabin space than most 35-footers, before or since. Vast, condo-sized interior with full-beam salon, private bow stateroom can seat a small crowd. Walk-through flybridge gate with molded steps provides convenient access to foredeck seat. Radar arch, transom door, bow pulpit were standard. No stall shower in head compartment. Hatches in cockpit sole provide good engine access. Twin 310hp V-drive gas inboards cruise in the low 20s (30+ knots wide open).

Length	35'4"	Fuel	200 gals.
Beam	11'5"	Water	60 gals.
Draft	3'1"	Headroom	6'5"
Weight	11,500#	Hull Type	Modified-V
Clearance	NA	Deadrise Aft	18°

Sea Ray 350/370 Sundancer

2008–Current

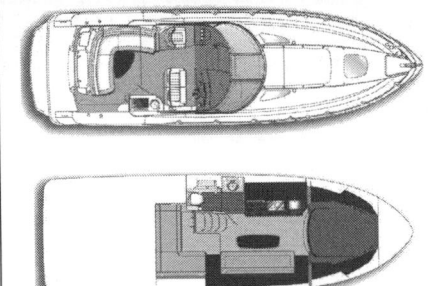

Sleek hardtop express (called 350 Sundancer in 2008–09; 370 Sundancer starting in 2010) takes signature Sea Ray styling, luxury to the next level. Beautifully finished interior provides yacht-class accommodations for six. Large hull windows admit good natural lighting. Power engine access hatch, aft-facing transom seat, pivoting helm/companion seats are standard. Hydraulic swim platform is optional. Cruise at 24–26 knots with 375hp gas I/Os; about 20 knots with V-drive inboards. Axius power with joystick control also available.

See Page 540 For Value Estimates

Length	37'6"	Fuel	225 gals.
Beam	12'0"	Water	50 gals.
Draft, Up	2'3"	Waste	28 gals.
Draft, Down	3'3"	Hull Type	Deep-V
Weight	18,064#	Deadrise Aft	21°

Sea Ray 350/370 Express Cruiser

1990–95

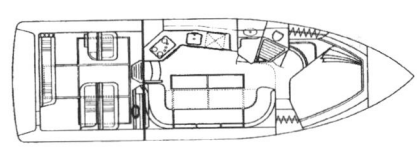

Popular 1990s express (marketed as the Sea Ray 350 Express Cruiser in 1990–92; 370 Express Cruiser in 1993–95) combined cutting-edge styling with comfortable accommodations, party-size cockpit. Roomy interior with private stateroom, king-size galley is dominated by 10-foot salon sofa, large mid-cabin area with removable dinette. Optional TV/VCR swivels out for easy viewing. Cockpit came standard with double helm seat, wet bar, foldaway transom seat. MerCruiser 310hp gas inboards cruise at 20–22 knots (about 30 knots top).

See Page 540 For Value Estimates

Length w/Pulpit	39'5"	Fuel	250 gals.
Hull Length	36'10"	Water	70 gals.
Beam	12'4"	Waste	20 gals.
Draft	2'5"	Hull Type	Deep-V
Weight	13,100#	Deadrise Aft	21°

Sea Ray 350/370 Sundancer

1990–94

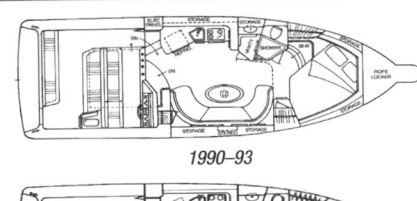

1990–93

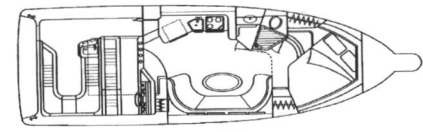

1994

Prices Not Provided for Pre-1995 Models

Appealing styling, lush accommodations, sporty performance made this 1990s cruiser yet another sales success for Sea Ray. Expansive midcabin interior with private bow stateroom, home-size galley is dominated by huge 10-foot semi-circular sofa. Triple-wide helm seat is unusual. Roomy engine compartment makes service access easy. Note folding stern seat, cockpit wet bar with fridge. Called Sea Ray 350 Sundancer in 1990–91; 370 Sundancer in 1992–94. Twin 310hp MerCruiser V-drive inboards cruise at 20 knots (high 20s top).

Length w/Platform	39'5"	Fuel	250 gals.
Hull Length	36'10"	Water	70 gals.
Beam	12'4"	Waste	20 gals.
Draft	2'5"	Hull Type	Deep-V
Weight	13,500#	Deadrise Aft	21°

Cruisers & Sedans

Sea Ray 360 Sundancer

2002–06

Versatile family cruiser with best-in-class styling combined traditional Sea Ray luxury with deluxe accommodations, no-excuses performance. Upscale interior with cherry cabinets, Ultraleather seating gets high marks for superior furnishings, top-shelf hardware and appliances. Cockpit floor lifts on hydraulic rams for engine access. Extended swim platform, underwater exhaust, transom locker were standard. Stateroom door is a rare luxury these days. MerCruiser 370hp V-drive gas engines cruise at 18 knots (30+ knots wide open).

See Page 540 For Value Estimates

Length w/Platform	39'0"	Fuel	250 gals.
Beam	12'6"	Water	55 gals.
Draft	3'1"	Waste	35 gals.
Weight	18,500#	Hull Type	Deep-V
Clearance	11'4"	Deadrise Aft	21°

Sea Ray 36 Sedan Bridge

2007–09

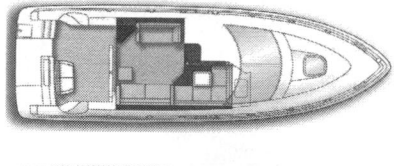

Good-looking sport sedan made good on Sea Ray claim of advanced styling, luxury-class accommodations. High-style interior with compact salon boasts roomy owner's stateroom with generous storage, small guest cabin with twin berths, divided head compartments with separate stall shower. In-floor galley compartment offers much-needed storage space. Centerline helm console has room for big-screen electronics. Engine room is a tight fit. Gas 370hp inboards cruise at 20 knots; 380hp Cummins diesels cruise at 22+knots.

See Page 540 For Value Estimates

Length	38'4"	Fuel	300 gals.
Beam	13'0"	Water	75 gals.
Draft	3'4"	Waste	35 gals.
Weight	22,000#	Hull Type	Modified-V
Clearance	18'0"	Deadrise Aft	17°

Sea Ray 370 Express Cruiser

1997–2000

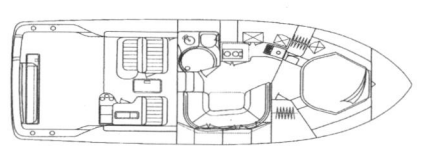

Stylish 1990s express with huge cockpit made the cut with Sea Ray buyers focused on versatile layout, feature-rich accommodations. Well-appointed interior with rare private bow stateroom sleeps four. Cockpit fishing features include insole rod storage, freshwater washdown, lift-out fish boxes. Entire helmdeck lifts electrically for engine access. Foldaway transom seat frees up cockpit space. Moderately wide side decks are a plus. Deep-V hull is fully cored. Twin 310hp gas inboards cruise at 16 knots; optional 340hp Cat diesels cruise at 25 knots.

See Page 540 For Value Estimates

Length w/Platform	41'4"	Fuel	350 gals.
Hull Length	37'0"	Water	70 gals.
Beam	14'2"	Waste	28 gals.
Draft	3'3"	Hull Type	Deep-V
Weight	18,000#	Deadrise Aft	19.5°

Sea Ray 370 Sedan Bridge

1991–97

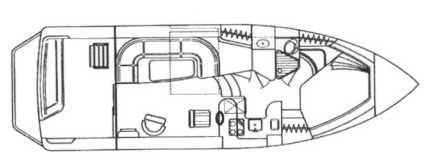

Versatile 1990s sport sedan delivered a winning mix of rakish Sea Ray styling, roomy accommodations, spirited performance. Well-appointed interior with oak cabinets, large cabin windows includes two private staterooms, huge U-shaped salon dinette, built-in entertainment center, choice of breakfast bar or optional lower helm station. Radar arch, swim platform, transom door, bow pulpit were standard. Side decks are on the narrow side. Standard 340hp MerCruiser gas inboards cruise at 18 knots (mid 20s top).

See Page 540 For Value Estimates

Length w/Platform	40'10"	Fuel	250 gals.
Hull Length	36'10"	Water	70 gals.
Beam	12'4"	Waste	20 gals.
Draft	2'7"	Hull Type	Deep-V
Weight	14,600#	Deadrise Aft	21°

Sea Ray 370 Sundancer

1995–99

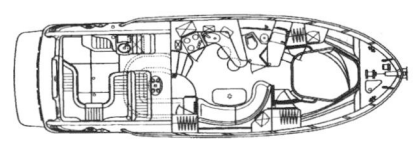

Bold 1990s sportcruiser delivered a compelling blend of aggressive styling, luxury-class accommodations. Lavish interior boasts spacious salon with U-shaped settee, large galley with granite bar, convertible rear dinette. Forward stateroom has privacy door—a plus for cruising with friends. Roomy cockpit with entertainment center seats a small crowd. Note stylish woodgrain helm, big transom storage locker. Underwater exhausts reduce noise, fumes. Twin 310hp gas inboards cruise at 18 knots; 292hp Cat diesels cruise in the low 20s.

See Page 540 For Value Estimates

Length w/Pulpit	40'1"	Fuel	275 gals.
Hull Length	37'6"	Water	70 gals.
Beam	12'7"	Waste	28 gals.
Draft	2'8"	Hull Type	Deep-V
Weight	17,000#	Deadrise Aft	20°

Sea Ray 380 Sundancer

1999–2003

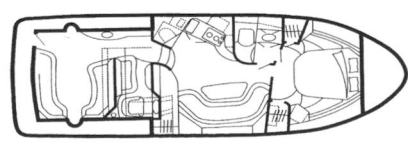

Blue-chip Sea Ray introduced in 1999 combined aggressive styling with quality construction, first-rate accommodations. Well-appointed interior with cherry cabinetry, upscale decor features private bow stateroom, built-in entertainment center, 10-foot salon sofa. Mid-stateroom lounge converts electrically to double berth. Spacious cockpit with wraparound seating has full wet bar, fender storage. New 38 Sundancer model came out in 2006. Standard 370hp V-drive inboards cruise at 18 knots; 340hp Cat diesels cruise at 25 knots.

See Page 541 For Value Estimates

Length w/Platform	42'0"	Fuel	275 gals.
Hull Length	38'0"	Water	70 gals.
Beam	13'0"	Waste	42 gals.
Draft	2'8"	Hull Type	Deep-V
Weight	20,000#	Deadrise Aft	19.5°

Cruisers & Sedans

Cruisers & Sedans

Sea Ray 38/390 Sundancer

2006–Current

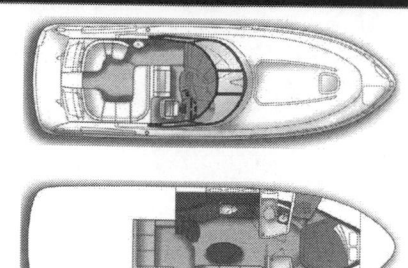

Feature-packed sportcruiser (called 38 Sundancer in 2006–09; 390 Sundancer starting in 2010) delivers traditional Sea Ray blend of sleek styling, lush accommodations. Upscale interior with cherry cabinets boasts roomy salon with leather settee, large galley, drop-down TV, private bow stateroom. Split head/shower will appeal to cruisers. Transom storage, power engine room hatch, underwater exhausts are standard. Anchor washdown system is a nice touch. MerCruiser 420hp gas inboards cruise at 20 knots; 380hp Cummins diesels cruise at 25–26 knots.

See Page 541 For Value Estimates

Length Overall	39'0"	Fuel	250 gals.
Beam	12'6"	Water	55 gals.
Draft	3'1"	Waste	35 gals.
Weight	19,400#	Hull Type	Deep-V
Clearance	12'1"	Deadrise Aft	21°

Sea Ray 390 Express Cruiser

1984–91

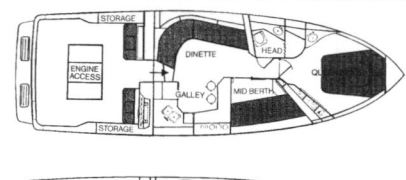

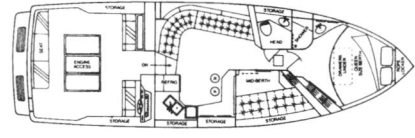

Maxivolume 1980s express took American sportyacht styling, comfort to the next level. Spacious interior boasts big U-shaped galley with serving counter, curved salon settee, large head with stall shower, private bow stateroom. Guest cabin is separated from salon by retractable mirrored bulkhead. Flush cockpit can accommodate a small crowd. Note removable stern bench seat. First of the big U.S. express boats when she came out in 1984. Twin 340hp gas inboards cruise at 16–18 knots; 375hp Cats cruise in the mid 20s.

Prices Not Provided for Pre-1995 Models

Length	39'0"	Fuel	300 gals.
Beam	13'11"	Water	100 gals.
Draft	2'4"	Waste	40 gals.
Weight	16,400#	Hull Type	Deep-V
Clearance	NA	Deadrise Aft	19°

Sea Ray 390/40 Sundancer

2004–09

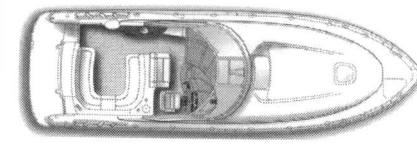

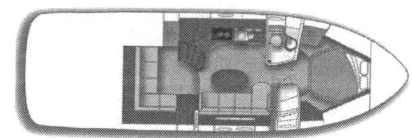

Head-turning express (called 390 Sundancer in 2004–05; 40 Sundancer in 2006–09) appeals to upscale boaters with a taste for world-class styling, premium accommodations. Lavish interior with two heads, huge galley, drop-down TV gets high marks for tasteful decor, well-placed amenities. Large cockpit with U-lounge seating, full wet bar, Euro-style helm is as good as it gets. Hardtop with full enclosure was optional. Entire cockpit sole lifts for engine access. Twin 370hp V-drive gas engines cruise in the low 20s (about 30 knots top).

See Page 541 For Value Estimates

Length w/Platform	41'0"	Fuel	275 gals.
Beam	13'2"	Water	70 gals.
Draft	3'4"	Waste	42 gals.
Weight	19,300#	Hull Type	Deep-V
Clearance	13'3"	Deadrise Aft	19°

Sea Ray 400 Express Cruiser

1992–99

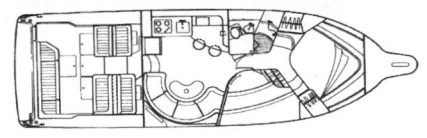

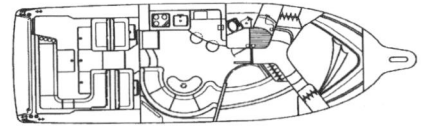

Bold 1990s sportyacht combined muscular styling with best-in-class luxury, state-of-the-art engineering. Upscale interior with top-shelf appliances boasts home-size galley with breakfast bar, posh U-shaped dinette, private bow stateroom with TV/VCR. Pocket door converts salon sitting room into private stateroom with full-size bed, convertible upper bunk. Extended swim platform was a popular option. Big cockpit seats a small crowd. Twin 340hp gas inboards cruise at 18 knots; Cat 340hp diesels cruise in the mid 20s.

See Page 541 For Value Estimates

Length w/Pulpit	45'7"	Fuel	300 gals.
Hull Length	40'4"	Water	100 gals.
Beam	13'0"	Waste	30 gals.
Draft	3'3"	Hull Type	Deep-V
Weight	18,000#	Deadrise Aft	19°

Sea Ray 400 Sedan Bridge

1996–2003

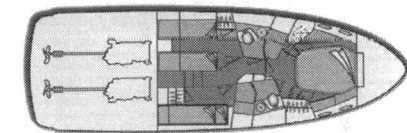

Plan A

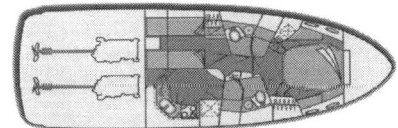

Plan B

Popular Sea Ray sedan introduced in 1996 combined contemporary sportyacht styling with versatile layout, deluxe accommodations. Available with three-stateroom, galley-up floorplan or two-stateroom, galley down layout with lower helm. Interior highlights include high-gloss cherry woodwork, hardwood galley sole, Ultraleather upholstery, designer furnishings and appliances. Engine room is a tight fit. Fully cored hull has prop pockets to reduce draft. Twin 370hp gas inboards cruise at 20 knots; 340hp Cat diesels cruise at 22–23 knots.

See Page 541 For Value Estimates

Length w/Platform	44'0"	Fuel	350 gals.
Hull Length	41'6"	Water	120 gals.
Beam	14'3"	Waste	28 gals.
Draft	3'4"	Hull Type	Modified-V
Weight	22,000#	Deadrise Aft	18.5°

Sea Ray 400 Sundancer

1997–99

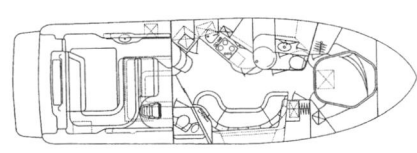

Muscular 1990s express had the space, amenities boaters sought in a Sea Ray sportyacht of her era. Sumptuous cherry interior features mid-cabin stateroom with privacy door, two heads, fully equipped galley with generous storage. Huge cockpit with wraparound seating can entertain a small crowd. Tiered instrument panel has room for extra electronics. Cockpit sole lifts for engine access. Twin 340hp V-drive gas inboards cruise at 16 knots (mid 20s top); Cat 340hp diesels cruise in the mid 20s (close to 30 knots top).

See Page 541 For Value Estimates

Length w/Platform	44'4"	Fuel	330 gals.
Hull Length	41'6"	Water	100 gals.
Beam	13'8"	Waste	28 gals.
Draft	3'4"	Hull Type	Deep-V
Weight	22,500#	Deadrise Aft	19°

Cruisers & Sedans

Sea Ray 410 Express Cruiser

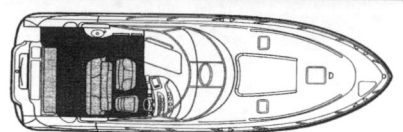

2000–2003

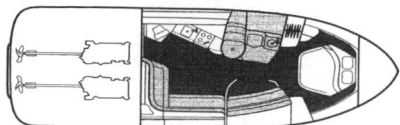

Deck Layout

Interior Floorplan

See Page 541 For Value Estimates

Luxury-class sportyacht with powerful lines is sleek, roomy, built to last. Posh open-plan salon with leather seating, cherry cabinets includes semi-enclosed sitting room (opposite head) that converts into private guest stateroom. Topside features include stylish burlwood dash, transom storage locker, foredeck sun pad, extended swim platform. Aft cockpit sole lifts electrically for engine access. Hull is fully cored. Hardtop was optional. Cummins 417hp diesels cruise in the mid 20s and reach a top speed of close to 30 knots.

Length w/Platform	45'6"	Fuel	335 gals.
Hull Length	41'6"	Water	100 gals.
Beam	13'10"	Waste	42 gals.
Draft	3'4"	Hull Type	Deep-V
Weight	21,000#	Deadrise Aft	19°

Sea Ray 410 Sundancer

2000–03

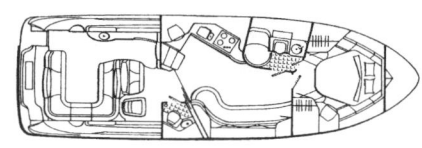

See Page 541 For Value Estimates

World-class express gave European sportcruisers a serious run for the money in the early 2000s. Lavish interior with high-gloss cherry cabinetry boasts two heads, electrically powered midcabin sleeper/sofa, huge galley with full-size refrigerator. Topside features include superb helm position with double companion seat, posh U-shaped cockpit seating, transom storage locker. Very good engine access. Hull with prop pockets is fully cored. Cat 420hp diesels cruise in the mid 20s and reach a top speed of 28–30 knots.

Length w/Platform	45'6"	Fuel	335 gals.
Hull Length	41'6"	Water	100 gals.
Beam	13'10"	Waste	42 gals.
Draft	3'2"	Hull Type	Deep-V
Weight	21,000#	Deadrise Aft	19°

Sea Ray 420/44 Sundancer

2003–08

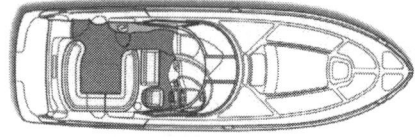

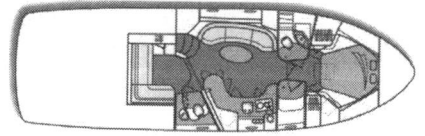

See Page 541 For Value Estimates

Seductive hardtop sportyacht (called 420 Sundancer in 2003–05; 44 Sundancer in 2006–08) combines signature Sea Ray styling with yacht-class accommodations, state-of-the-art construction. Opulent midcabin interior with cherrywood cabinetry boasts two private staterooms, deluxe gourmet galley with serving counter, two heads, copious storage. Feature-loaded cockpit with posh U-lounge seating is among the largest in her class. Cockpit floor lifts for engine access. Cummins 480hp diesels cruise in the mid 20s (30+ top).

Length Overall	45'0"	Fuel	335 gals.
Beam	14'0"	Water	100 gals.
Draft	3'6"	Waste	42 gals.
Weight	22,500#	Hull Type	Deep-V
Clearance	11'3"	Deadrise Aft	19°

Cruisers & Sedans

Sea Ray 420/440 Sundancer

1990–95

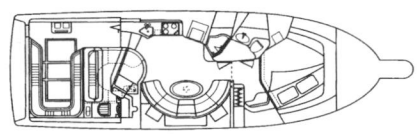

Purebred sportcruiser (called 420 Sundancer in 1990–91; 440 in 1993–95) was state-of-the-art in luxury, design in the early 1990s. Posh midcabin interior with two heads features 9-foot salon sofa, full entertainment center, large galley with upright refrigerator. Salon extends aft into midcabin with convertible sofa, sliding privacy door. Huge cockpit has triple companion seat at the helm, U-shaped aft seating. Note that 440 model has hull pockets, 420 does not. Standard gas inboards cruise at 15–16 knots; 364hp Cat diesel cruise in the low 20s.

See Page 541 For Value Estimates

Length w/Pulpit	47'1"	Fuel	400 gals.
Hull Length	44'0"	Water	100 gals.
Beam	13'11"	Waste	28 gals.
Draft	3'3"	Hull Type	Deep-V
Weight	20,000#	Deadrise Aft	19°

Sea Ray 440 Express Bridge

1993–98

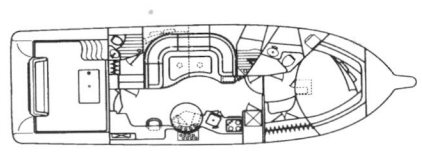

Wide-beam cruising yacht with innovative walk-through bridge has the interior volume of many 50-footers. Enormous two-stateroom floorplan boasts full-beam salon with big U-shaped settee, two heads, galley with upright refrigerator. Party-time bridge with centerline helm, wet bar seats up to ten. Additional highlights include twin transom doors, built-in cockpit seat, foredeck seating, generous storage. Hull is fully cored. Prop pockets reduce draft. Cat 340hp diesels cruise at 20 knots and deliver a top speed of 23–24 knots.

See Page 541 For Value Estimates

Length w/Pulpit	47'1"	Fuel	400 gals.
Hull Length	44'0"	Water	100 gals.
Beam	13'11"	Waste	60 gals.
Draft	3'3"	Hull Type	Modified-V
Weight	28,000#	Deadrise Aft	19°

Sea Ray 450 Sundancer

1995–99

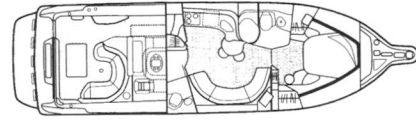

1995–97

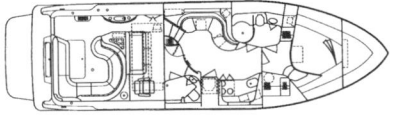

1998–99

High-impact sportyacht introduced in 1995 showcased Sea Ray's industry-leading design, cutting-edge construction, world-class luxury. Enormous two-stateroom, two-head interior boasts home-size galley with copious storage, huge head compartment, top-shelf furnishings and hardware. Spacious cockpit with circular aft seating; superb helm position. Big transom locker is a useful touch. Hull is fully cored. Twin 340hp Cat diesels cruise in the low 20s; optional 407hp Cats cruise at 24–25 (about 30 knots top).

See Page 541 For Value Estimates

Length w/Pulpit	48'1"	Fuel	400 gals.
Hull Length	45'6"	Water	100 gals.
Beam	13'11"	Waste	60 gals.
Draft	3'7"	Hull Type	Deep-V
Weight	23,500#	Deadrise Aft	20°

Cruisers & Sedans

Cruisers & Sedans

Sea Ray 460 Express Cruiser

1985–89

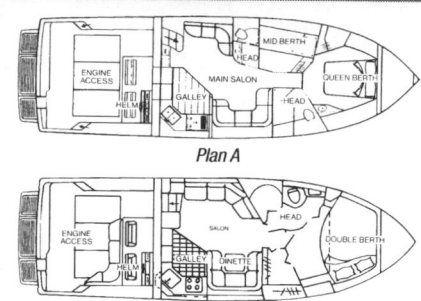

Plan A

Plan B

Prices Not Provided for Pre-1995 Models

Broad-shouldered sportyacht from the late 1980s combined innovative Sea Ray styling with spacious accommodations, big-water security. Original two-stateroom interior with two heads was replaced in 1988 with more expansive single-stateroom layout boasting much larger salon. Huge bi-level cockpit with transom door has room for a crowd. Good engine access. Side-dumping exhausts were standard. Biggest U.S.-built express available in 1985. Cat 375hp diesels cruise at 20 knots; optional 550hp 6V92 Detroits cruise in the mid 20s.

Length	45'6"	Fuel	420 gals.
Beam	14'11"	Water	150 gals.
Draft	3'2"	Waste	40 gals.
Weight	27,500#	Hull Type	Modified-V
Clearance	9'9"	Deadrise Aft	17°

Sea Ray 460 Sundancer

1999–2003

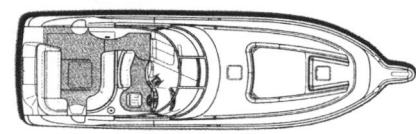

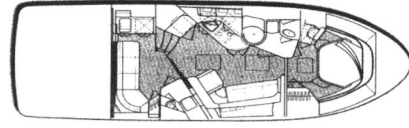

See Page 541 For Value Estimates

Seductive Sea Ray sportcruiser introduced in 1999 was an impressive display of advanced styling, yacht-class accommodations. Expansive interior matches the finest European imports in comfort, amenities. Midcabin stateroom with washer/dryer combo has privacy behind two sliding doors. Facing cockpit settees convert electrically to sun pad. Original cored hull bottom was upgraded in late 1999 to solid fiberglass. Slightly underpowered with 340hp Cats (25–26 knots top), larger 480hp Cummins diesels cruise in the low 20s (28–30 knots wide open).

Length Overall	51'4"	Fuel	400 gals.
Hull Length	45'6"	Water	100 gals.
Beam	14'8"	Waste	60 gals.
Draft	3'7"	Hull Type	Modified-V
Weight	28,000#	Deadrise Aft	15°

Sea Ray 43/470 Sundancer

2009–Current

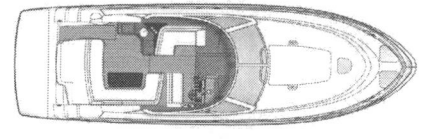

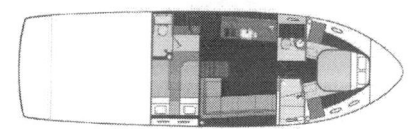

See Page 541 For Value Estimates

Innovative American-bred sportyacht designed specifically for Zeus pod drives sets class standards for dramatic styling, yacht-class accommodations, spirited performance. Highlights include posh two-stateroom/two-head interior with hardwood floors, huge cockpit with Euro-style sun pad aft, dual power sunroofs, power windows, extended swim platform. Note L-shaped cockpit galley, built-in chart table under helm seat. Joystick control makes docking a breeze. Cruise economically at 22 knots (30+ top) with 425hp Cummins diesels.

Length Overall	47'3"	Fuel	350 gals.
Beam	14'0"	Water	100 gals.
Draft (Zeus)	4'0"	Waste	42 gals.
Weight	28,500#	Hull Type	Deep-V
Clearance	14'2"	Deadrise Aft	19°

Sea Ray 48 Sundancer

2005–09

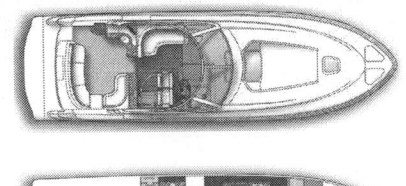

Stunning hardtop express with sweeping lines took American sportyacht styling to the next level. Helm deck, with distinctively shaped side windows, includes standard hardtop with overhead lighting, two opening sunroof hatches. Posh twin-head interior with cherry joinery, hardwood flooring features elegant salon with leather settee, spacious U-shaped galley, complete entertainment center. Optional hydraulic swim platform can support a 10' dinghy. Cruise in the low 20s with standard 526hp Cummins V-drive diesels (28–29 knots top).

See Page 541 For Value Estimates

Length w/Platform	50'8"	Fuel	400 gals.
Beam	14'8"	Water	110 gals.
Draft	4'0"	Waste	60 gals.
Weight	33,600#	Hull Type	Deep-V
Clearance	NA	Deadrise Aft	19°

Sea Ray 480/500 Sundancer

1990–99

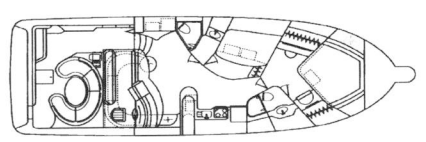

High-impact Sea Ray express (called 480 Sundancer in 1990–91; 500 Sundancer in 1992–99) set class standards in her day for powerful styling, feature-rich accommodations. Vast interior with enormous salon, upscale furnishings rivals that of a small motoryacht for space, amenities. Highlights include huge cockpit with pit-style seating, spacious engine room, wide side decks. Oval ports replaced sliding cabin windows in 1994. Early models with GM 485hp diesels cruise in the low 20s; later models with optional 735hp GMs cruise at 28–30 knots.

See Page 541 For Value Estimates

Length w/Platform	55'8"	Fuel	500 gals.
Hull Length	50'1"	Water	150 gals.
Beam	15'0"	Waste	68 gals.
Draft	4'0"	Hull Type	Modified-V
Weight	34,500#	Deadrise Aft	17°

Sea Ray 510 Sundancer

2000–03

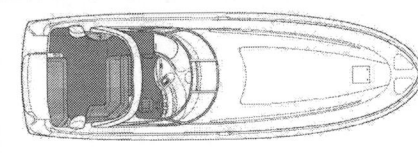

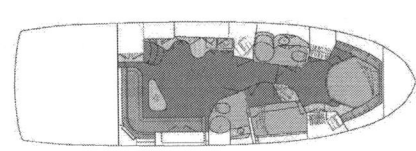

World-class sportcruiser with wide 15'8" beam delivers more luxury, comfort than same-size European sportyachts of her era. Posh two-stateroom interior with cherry cabinets, Ultraleather seating includes two full heads, home-size galley with pull-out bar, salon entertainment center, central vacuum system, hardwood flooring. Retractable sun pad, hardtop, wraparound helm were standard. Underwater exhausts reduce cockpit fumes. Cat 660hp V-drive diesels cruise at 25 knots; 770hp Cats will cruise in the high 20s.

See Page 542 For Value Estimates

Length w/Platform	53'6"	Fuel	600 gals.
Hull Length	50'6"	Water	150 gals.
Beam	15'8"	Waste	68 gals.
Draft	4'3"	Hull Type	Deep-V
Weight	38,500#	Deadrise Aft	18°

Cruisers & Sedans

Sea Ray 500/52 Sundancer

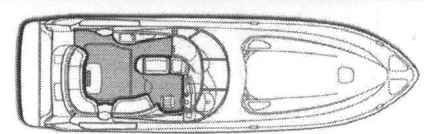

2003–09

Blue-chip American sportyacht (called the 500 Sundancer in 2003–05; 52 Sundancer in 2006–09) matched top-ranked European imports for sex appeal, luxury, state-of-the-art construction. Opulent cherry interior boasts expansive salon with Ultraleather lounge, gourmet galley with under-counter refrigeration, two large heads, well-appointed staterooms. Semi-sheltered cockpit offers vast entertainment potential. Good engine access; superb helm. Cummins 640hp V-drive diesels cruise at a quick 26–28 knots (30+ knots top).

See Page 541 For Value Estimates

Length	53'4"	Fuel	560 gals.
Beam	15'3"	water	150 gals.
Draft	4'2"	Waste	68 gals.
Weight	40,015#	Hull Type	Deep-V
Clearance	14'0"	Deadrise Aft	19°

Sea Ray 540 Sundancer

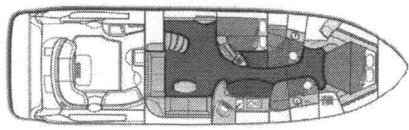

1998–2001

Good-selling Sea Ray sportyacht outpaced late 1990s competitors for space, comfort, outright sex appeal. Posh two-stateroom interior with cherry woodwork is dominated by 10' leather sofa with electric slide-out bed. Full-service galley features copious storage, condo-size refrigerator. Cockpit settees convert electrically into huge sun pad. Hydraulic swim platform makes launching a tender easy. Note washer/dryer cabinet in bow stateroom. Cat 640hp diesels cruise in the mid 20s; 776hp Cats cruise in the high 20s.

See Page 542 For Value Estimates

Length w/Platform	57'8"	Fuel	600 gals.
Hull Length	54'11"	Water	150 gals.
Beam	15'11"	Waste	68 gals.
Draft	3'11"	Hull Type	Modified-V
Weight	39,000#	Deadrise Aft	17°

Sea Ray 540 Sundancer

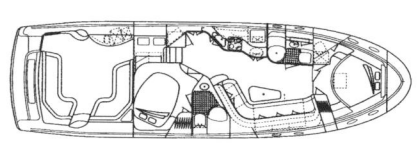

2010–Current

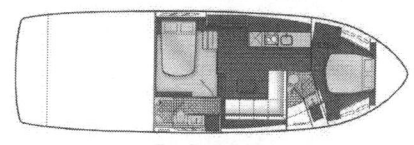

Two Staterooms

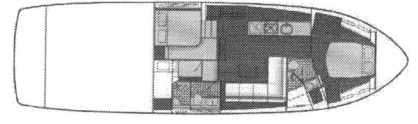

Three Staterooms

Insufficient Resale Data to Assign Values

Exciting deep-V express yacht couples Sea Ray styling with the exceptional handling, efficiency of Zeus pod drives. Highlights include palatial cherrywood interior with choice of two or three staterooms, fiberglass hardtop with retractable sunroof, giant cockpit with circular 10-seat lounge, deluxe wet bar, convertible sun pad aft. Note hardwood cabin flooring, generous salon headroom. Hullside windows provide significant natural lighting below. Joystick control makes docking easy. Cruise at 25 knots (30+) with 715hp Cummins diesels.

Length w/Platform	54'9"	Fuel	600 gals.
Beam	15'3"	Water	150 gals.
Draft	4'2"	Waste	68 gals.
Weight	50,000#	Hull Type	Deep-V
Clearance	16'4"	Deadrise Aft	21°

Cruisers & Sedans

Sea Ray 550 Sundancer

2002–04

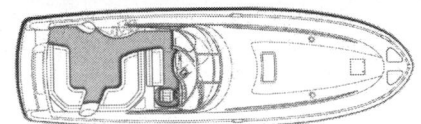

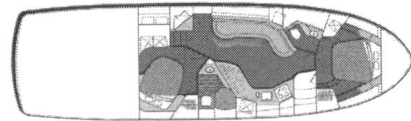

Updated version of popular 540 Sundancer (1998–2001) with revised interior, redesigned hardtop made a great boat even better. Posh two-stateroom layout with cherry woodwork includes curved salon sofa (which converts electrically into slide-out bed), gourmet galley, space for washer/dryer. Bow thruster was standard. Power cockpit settees convert into huge sun pad. Hydraulic high-low swim platform makes launching a tender easy. Engine room is a tight fit. Twin 640hp Cat diesels cruise in the mid 20s; 765hp MANs cruise at 26–28 knots.

See Page 542 For Value Estimates

Length	57'8"	Fuel	600 gals.
Beam	15'11"	Water	150 gals.
Draft	4'0"	Waste	68 gals.
Weight	39,000#	Hull Type	Modified-V
Clearance	13'4"	Deadrise Aft	17°

Sea Ray 55/580 Sundancer

2008–Current

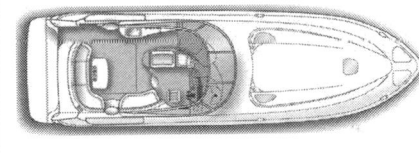

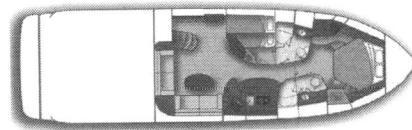

Supersize sportcruiser (called 55 Sundancer in 2008–09; 580 Sundancer starting in 2010) takes Sundancer styling, comfort to the next level. Lavish two-stateroom interior boasts home-size galley with serving counter, full-beam owner's suite, teak salon flooring, two full heads. Twin-section cockpit lounge slides around on circular tracks—very cool. Note massive engine room, cockpit galley with wet bar & grill, premium entertainment center. Hardtop has retractable sunroofs. Man 900hp V-drive diesels cruise at 25–26 knots (about 30 knots top).

See Page 542 For Value Estimates

Length Overall	60'0"	Fuel	825 gals.
Beam	15'11"	Water	200 gals.
Draft	4'6"	Waste	70 gals.
Weight	53,500#	Hull Type	Modified-V
Clearance	17'9"	Deadrise Aft	17°

Sea Ray 580 Super Sun Sport

1997–2002

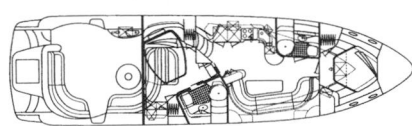

Standard Floorplan

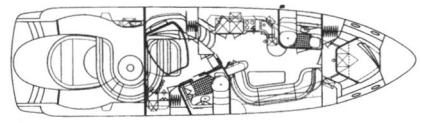

Alternate Floorplan

High-powered sportcruiser with transom garage, optional hardtop heightened Sea Ray reputation for cutting-edge styling, world-class luxury. Lavish interior features two private staterooms, home-size galley with concealed appliances, electric Ultraleather salon sofa bed, premium entertainment system. Massive cockpit with wraparound seating boasts custom wet bar, sun pad atop jet-bike garage. Hull is fully cored. Foldout boarding steps are a nice touch. Cat 776hp—or 735hp GM—diesels cruise at 26–28 knots (low 30s top).

See Page 542 For Value Estimates

Length w/Platform	60'10"	Fuel	700 gals.
Hull Length	58'11"	Water	200 gals.
Beam	15'9"	Waste	68 gals.
Draft	4'1"	Hull Type	Modified-V
Weight	48,000#	Deadrise Aft	17°

Cruisers & Sedans

Sea Ray 60/610 Sundancer

2006–Current

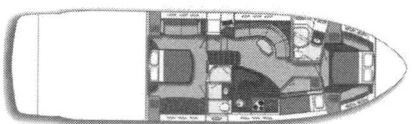

Compelling American sportyacht—flagship of today's Sea Ray fleet—combines unsurpassed luxury with bold styling, top-shelf construction. Opulent three-stateroom interior includes full-beam owner's suite, enclosed pilothouse, state-of-the-art helm. Small crew cabin with transom entry is optional. Swim platform can stow tender, PWC. Bow/stern thrusters, twin sunroofs, cockpit grill are standard. Exemplary fit and finish justifies high price. MAN 1,100hp V-drive diesels cruise at a fast 28 knots (33–34 knots top). Called 610 DA beginning in 2010.

Insufficient Resale Data to Assign Values

Length	61'6"	Fuel	900 gals.
Beam	16'9"	Water	200 gals.
Draft	4'2"	Waste	70 gals.
Weight	55,700#	Hull Type	Modified-V
Clearance	NA	Deadrise Aft	17°

Sea Ray 630 Super Sun Sport

1991–2000

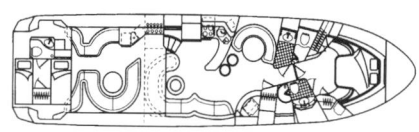

Big American-bred sportyacht set class standards in her era for luxurious accommodations, cutting-edge styling. Enormous single-stateroom, two-head interior boasts massive salon with electric sofa/bed, home-sized galley with breakfast bar, lavish master stateroom with his-and-her heads. Huge cockpit offers seating for twelve. Crew quarters aft were optional. Look-alike sibling, the Sea Ray 630 Sundancer, is powered with Arneson Surface Drives. Detroit 1,100hp diesels will cruise at 30 knots (32–33 knots top).

Insufficient Resale Data to Assign Values

Length w/Platform	64'6"	Fuel	800 gals.
Hull Length	62'6"	Water	200 gals.
Beam	15'9"	Waste	70 gals.
Draft	5'0"	Hull Type	Deep-V
Weight	54,500#	Deadrise Aft	19°

Silverton 271 Express

1995–97

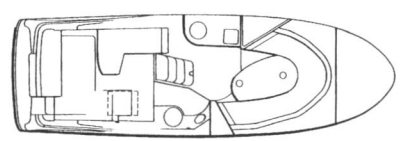

Roomy 1990s express with trailerable 8'6" beam delivered interior comfort, cockpit versatility at an affordable price. Generic midcabin floorplan includes double berths fore and aft, full-size galley, removable dinette, enclosed head with sink and shower. High freeboard permits generous cabin headroom; opening ports provide modest ventilation. Cockpit seating includes wraparound companion seat, full-length stern seat. Note walk-through windshield. Cruise at 18 knots with single 300hp MerCruiser I/O (mid 20s top).

See Page 542 For Value Estimates

Length w/Pulpit	29'9"	Weight	7,643#
Hull Length	27'10"	Fuel	109 gals.
Beam	8'6"	Water	30 gals.
Draft, Drive Up	1'8"	Hull Type	Modified-V
Draft, Drive Down	3'1"	Deadrise Aft	14°

Cruisers & Sedans

Silverton 29 Sportcruiser

1985–87

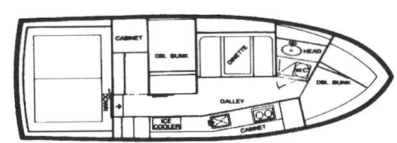

Popular 1990s cruiser with straight-inboard power combined unique floorplan arrangement with rugged construction, affordable price. Uncommon interior with two full-height private staterooms sacrifices salon dimensions (i.e., entertainment space) for sleeping comfort. Head, forward of salon, is not easily reached from the cockpit. Low-profile flybridge with tall windshield seats five. Cockpit hatches provide good engine access. Deep cockpit offers extra security for kids. Twin 195hp gas engines cruise at 15–16 knots (mid 20s top).

Prices Not Provided for Pre-1995 Models

Length	29'2"	Fuel	150 gals.
Beam	10'10"	Water	40 gals.
Draft	1'7"	Cockpit	50 sq. ft.
Weight	7,800#	Hull Type	Modified-V
Clearance	8'2"	Deadrise Aft	NA

Silverton 30X Express

1988–89

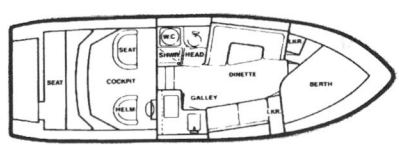

Sporty 1980s express matched appealing price with tasteful accommodations, spirited performance. Topside features include roomy bi-level cockpit with seating for six, foredeck sun pad, large helm console, radar arch with stereo speakers. No-frills interior with private bow stateroom, convertible dinette, convertible settee sleeps six. Additional features include four opening ports, integral bow pulpit, transom door. Inconsistent finish reflects low price. Standard 270hp V-drive gas engines cruise in the low 20s (about 30 knots top).

Prices Not Provided for Pre-1995 Models

Length	30'8"	Fuel	185 gals.
Beam	10'10"	Water	37 gals.
Draft	3'0"	Headroom	6'2"
Weight	9,100#	Hull Type	Modified-V
Clearance	8'5"	Designer	NA

Silverton 31 Convertible

1983–87

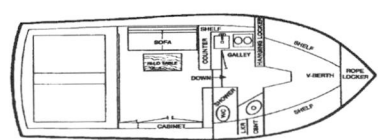

Practical pocket convertible with pleasing lines appealed to entry-level boaters looking for versatility, comfort in an affordable package. Oak-trimmed interior with private bow stateroom, convertible sofa, boasts a surprisingly roomy salon for a boat this size. Lower helm was a popular option. Note large head compartment, small but well-equipped galley. Deep cockpit keeps passengers safe, but lacks a transom door. Flybridge with helm forward seats three. Twin 220hp V-drive gas inboards will cruise at 17–18 knots (mid 20s wide open).

Prices Not Provided for Pre-1995 Models

Length	31'0"	Fuel	220 gals.
Beam	11'11"	Water	40 gals.
Draft	2'11"	Cockpit	82 sq. ft.
Weight	11,400#	Hull Type	Modified-V
Clearance	10'8"	Deadrise Aft	NA

Cruisers & Sedans

Silverton 31 Convertible

1991–95

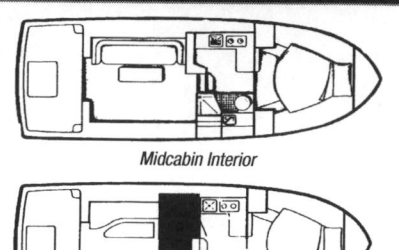

Midcabin Interior

Single-Stateroom Interior

See Page 542 For Value Estimates

Updated version of earlier Silverton 31 Convertible (1983–87) boasts all-new styling, redesigned hull, more standard equipment. Originally offered with midcabin interior, in 1992 Silverton offered a single-stateroom option with an enlarged galley, more spacious salon. Open front windshield bathes salon in natural lighting. Cockpit is on the small side compared with most 34-foot convertibles. Note steep flybridge ladder. Swim platform, bow pulpit were standard. Twin 235hp gas engines cruise at 17–18 knots (mid 20s top).

Length	31'2"	Cockpit	48 sq. ft.
Beam	11'8"	Fuel	250 gals.
Draft	3'0"	Water	84 gals.
Weight	11,000#	Hull Type	Modified-V
Clearance	11'9"	Deadrise Aft	NA

Silverton 31 Gulfstream

1979–86

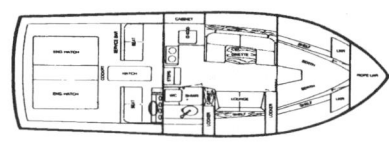

Durable 1980s express with wide 11'11" beam built on Silverton reputation for value, practicality, affordability. Roomy, well-planned interior with convertible dinette, stand-up head with shower, full galley sleeps four. Big single-level cockpit with doublewide helm and companion seats is large enough for a small crowd. Good engine access, so-so fit and finish. Note slender side decks. Twin 270hp inboard gas engines cruise at 18–19 knots (high 20ss top); optional 350hp gas engines cruise at 24 knots (30+ top).

Prices Not Provided for Pre-1995 Models

Length	31'0"	Fuel	250 gals.
Beam	11'11"	Water	40 gals.
Draft	2'11"	Waste	25 gals.
Weight	9,500#	Hull Type	Modified-V
Clearance	NA	Deadrise Aft	NA

Silverton 310 Express

1994–2000

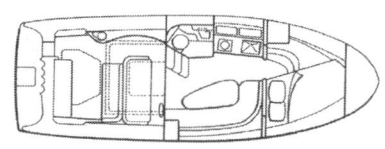

Appealing 1990s express with wide-open interior took Silverton value, practicality to the next level. Entry steps to cabin are suspended from aluminum weldment making interior seem unusually spacious. Lounge and cocktail table in aft cabin convert to double berth. Seven opening ports, two deck hatches provide good ventilation. Removable cockpit table drops to form sun pad. Transom door, cockpit wet bar, bow pulpit, walk-through windshield were standard. Cruise at 25 knots (35+ top) with optional 300hp MerCruiser sterndrive engines.

See Page 542 For Value Estimates

Length	32'0"	Fuel	150 gals.
Beam	11'6"	Water	54 gals.
Draft	2'2"	Waste	35 gals.
Weight	9,202#	Hull Type	Modified-V
Clearance	10'5"	Deadrise Aft	14°

Silverton 312 Sedan Cruiser

1994–99

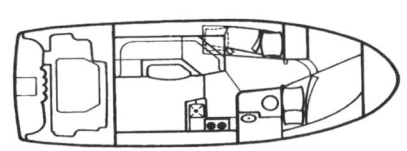

Popular family convertible with rakish lines is roomy, sporty, fun to drive. Space-efficient interior with raised dinette, step-down galley, includes curtained-off area opposite the head with upper/lower bunks, double berth forward with privacy curtain. Sliding glass door opens to small cockpit with transom door, molded flybridge stairs. Note extended swim platform with built-in fender racks. Very modest fuel capacity. Choice of inboard or sterndrive power. MerCruiser 235hp 5.7-liter I/Os cruise at 20 knots (about 30+ knots top).

See Page 542 For Value Estimates

Length Overall	32'0"	Fuel	160 gals.
Hull Length	28'0"	Water	54 gals.
Beam	11'6"	Waste	28 gals.
Draft	2'8"	Hull Type	Modified-V
Weight	9,937#	Deadrise Aft	14°

Silverton 33 Convertible

2007–Current

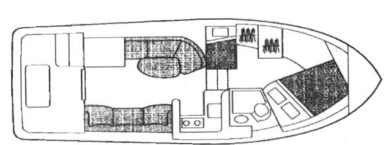

Entry-level flybridge cruiser couples family-size accommodations with good performance, very low price. Wide 12'8" beam permits expansive two-stateroom interior with open salon, small galley, decent storage—impressive accommodations for a boat this size. Sliding windows provide good ventilation. Molded steps make bridge access easy. So-so fit and finish is good enough considering the price. Additional features include radar arch, transom door, swim platform. Cruise at 20 knots with 375hp gas inboards (high 20s top).

See Page 543 For Value Estimates

Length	32'7"	Fuel	208 gals.
Beam	12'8"	Water	82 gals.
Draft	2'5"	Waste	30 gals.
Weight	16,800#	Hull Type	Modified-V
Clearance	15'6"	Deadrise Aft	14°

Silverton 33 Sports Coupe

2008–Current

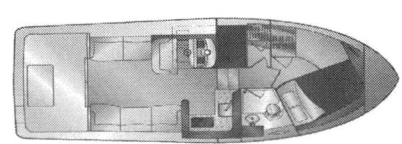

Beamy hardtop sedan with enclosed pilothouse/salon targets cruising couples with an eye for value. Highlights include comfortable salon with huge power-activated sunroof, large master stateroom with angled berth, guest cabin with athwartships berth, sliding glass cockpit doors. Helm visibility is excellent thanks to large salon windows. Starboard salon lounge converts to double berth. Cockpit with transom door, storage lazarette is shaded by hardtop overhang. Cruise at 20 knots (29–30 top) with twin 375hp Crusader gas engines.

See Page 543 For Value Estimates

Length	32'7"	Fuel	208 gals.
Beam	12'8"	Water	82 gals.
Draft	2'6"	Waste	30 gals.
Weight	16,300#	Hull Type	Modified-V
Clearance	12'1"	Deadrise Aft	14°

Cruisers & Sedans

Cruisers & Sedans

Silverton 330 Sport Bridge

1999–2007

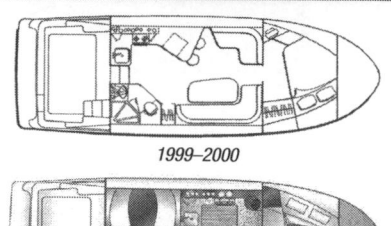

1999–2000

2001–07

See Page 543 For Value Estimates

Feature-packed Silverton sedan combines spacious interior with sporty styling, solid construction. Signature "Side-Walk" deck layout permits expansive full-beam salon with tremendous headroom. Floorplan was updated in 2001 with improved decor, galley design. Note opening salon windows—very unusual. Oversized flybridge with wet bar seats six in comfort. Early models with 300hp gas inboards cruise at 18 knots (25–26 knots top); later models with 385hp gas engines will cruise at 20 knots (around 30 knots top).

Length Overall	35'4"	Fuel	214 gals.
Beam	12'4"	Water	104 gals.
Draft	2'11"	Waste	30 gals.
Weight	15,685#	Hull Type	Modified-V
Clearance	11'0"	Deadrise Aft	16°

Silverton 34 Convertible

1984–88

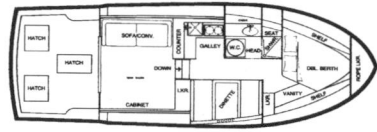

Double Berth Forward

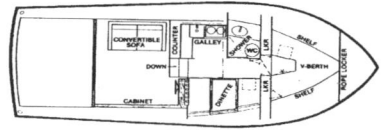

V-Berths Forward

Prices Not Provided for Pre-1995 Models

Restyled version of original Silverton 34 Convertible (1978–83) gave entry-level buyers exceptional value for the money. Single-stateroom, galley-down floorplan—offered with double berth or V-berth forward—sleeps six. Lower helm was optional. Topside features include deep cockpit, wide side decks, bow pulpit, roomy flybridge with good helm visibility. Modified-V hull delivers comfortable big-water ride. Note large engine room. Twin 270hp gas engines cruise at 18–19 knots and top out in the high 20s.

Length	34'0"	Fuel	250 gals.
Beam	12'6"	Water	40 gals.
Draft	3'1"	Cockpit	70 sq. ft.
Weight	12,500#	Hull Type	Modified-V
Clearance	13'3"	Deadrise Aft	15°

Silverton 34 Convertible

1989–90

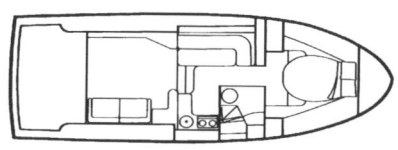

Prices Not Provided for Pre-1995 Models

Well-received 34-footer combined affordable price with roomy interior, plenty of standard equipment. Galley-down floorplan features roomy stateroom with island berth, head with enclosed stall shower, L-shaped dinette, expansive salon with convertible sofa. Note light-oak interior woodwork, cockpit transom door, large bridge with seating for five. Tiny galley leaves a lot to be desired. Lower helm station was optional. Twin 350hp gas engines cruise at 19–20 knots (high 20s top). Lasted only two years in production.

Length	34'6"	Fuel	300 gals.
Beam	12'7"	Water	40 gals.
Draft	3'2"	Waste	28 gals.
Weight	13,500#	Hull Type	Modified-V
Clearance	13'5"	Deadrise Aft	17°

Silverton 34 Convertible

1991–95

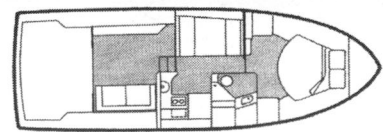

Single-Stateroom Interior

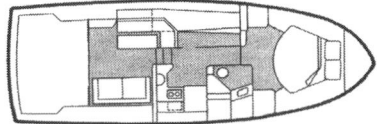

Two-Stateroom Interior

See Page 543 For Value Estimates

Rakish 1990s convertible combined sporty styling with tasteful accommodations, roomy cockpit. Standard single-stateroom, oak-trimmed interior features booth-style dinette opposite galley. Optional two-stateroom layout with small guest cabin fits the dinette into an already-small salon. Note full-size galley refrigerator. Topside highlights include deep cockpit, wide side decks, bow pulpit, swim platform. Flybridge was slightly restyled in 1995. Crusader 350hp gas inboards cruise at 18 knots (high 20s wide open).

Length	34'6"	Fuel	300 gals.
Beam	12'11"	Water	84 gals.
Draft	2'11"	Waste	28 gals.
Weight	18,000#	Hull Type	Modified-V
Clearance	14'11"	Deadrise Aft	17°

Silverton 34 Convertible

2004–06

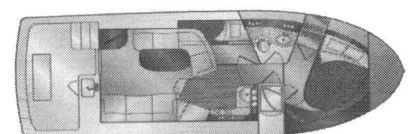

Good-looking convertible with graceful lines is one part coastal cruiser, one part family fisherman. Efficient two-stateroom interior boasts roomy salon with wraparound windows, huge galley with Corian counters, guest cabin with over/under berths, split head compartment. Note attractive cherry woodwork, hardwood galley floor. Transom door, in-deck fishbox were standard in the cockpit. Molded bridge steps are a plus. Standard 330hp gas inboards cruise at 16 knots; optional 385hp gas engines cruise at 20 knots (high 20s top).

See Page 543 For Value Estimates

Length	37'7"	Fuel	286 gals.
Beam	13'10"	Water	94 gals.
Draft	3'3"	Waste	37 gals.
Weight	18,550#	Hull Type	Modified-V
Clearance	12'7"	Deadrise Aft	12°

Silverton 34 Express

1987–89

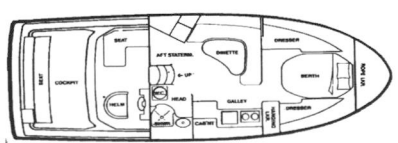

Generic 1980s express with inboard power offered entry-level buyers space, comfort at budget-friendly price. Mid-cabin floorplan with convertible dinette, double berths fore and aft sleeps four adults, two kids. Stall shower in the head is a plus; aft-cabin privacy door is a rare luxury. Topside features include standard bow pulpit, expansive cockpit with seating for six, radar arch, bolt-on swim platform. Styling is way dated by today's standards. Twin 350hp V-drive gas engines cruise at 20 knots (28–30 knots top).

Prices Not Provided for Pre-1995 Models

Length	34'6"	Fuel	250 gals.
Beam	12'7"	Water	40 gals.
Draft	3'8"	Cockpit	62 sq. ft.
Weight	11,000#	Hull Type	Modified-V
Clearance	NA	Deadrise Aft	17°

Cruisers & Sedans

Silverton 34 Express

1990–94

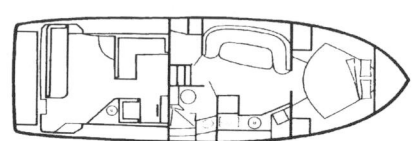

Value-priced express from early 1990s delivered sporty styling, upmarket amenities without breaking the bank. Expansive midcabin interior with six overhead hatches boasts big U-shaped dinette, fully equipped galley with generous storage, large head with separate stall shower. Exterior features include power engine room hatch, foredeck sun pad, radar arch, fender storage racks, bow pulpit. So-so fit and finish. Twin 300hp gas engines (with V-drives) cruise at 20 knots and deliver a top speed of 27–28 knots.

Prices Not Provided for Pre-1995 Models

Length	34'3"	Fuel	254 gals.
Beam	12'8"	Water	47 gals.
Draft	3'1"	Waste	28 gals.
Weight	16,500#	Hull Type	Modified-V
Clearance	9'3"	Deadrise Aft	17°

Silverton 351 Sedan

1997–2000

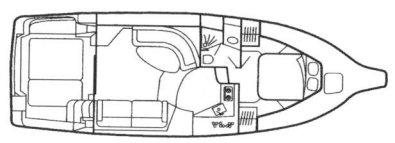

Spacious sedan cruiser with Silverton's signature "Side-Walk" deck design offered more interior space than anything in her class. Expansive floorplan features full-beam salon with convertible dinette and settee, large galley with hardwood floor, roomy stateroom. Molded steps make bridge access easy and safe. V-drives allow engines to be positioned beneath cockpit sole to further increase interior volume. Prop pockets reduce hull draft, improve efficiency. No racehorse, 320hp gas engines cruise at 14–15 knots (mid 20s top).

See Page 543 For Value Estimates

Length	38'10"	Fuel	300 gals.
Beam	13'0"	Water	94 gals.
Draft	2'5"	Waste	37 gals.
Weight	16,094#	Hull Type	Modified-V
Clearance	12'0"	Deadrise Aft	12°

Silverton 361/360 Express

1995–2000

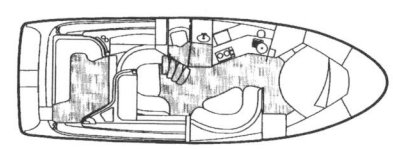

Bold inboard express (called Silverton 361 Express in 1995–96; 360 Express in 1997–2000) delivered comfort, performance at a low price. Roomy midcabin floorplan has double berths fore and aft, full galley, circular salon dinette. Note privacy doors for both staterooms—a convenience seldom found in modern midcabin cruisers. Walk-through windshield provides easy bow access. Solid fiberglass hull has prop pockets to reduce draft, improve efficiency. Crusader 320hp V-drive inboards cruise at 18–19 knots (high 20s top).

See Page 543 For Value Estimates

Length	36'1"	Water	100 gals.
Beam	12'11"	Waste	40 gals.
Draft	2'6"	Clearance	9'10"
Weight	16,032#	Hull Type	Modified-V
Fuel	286 gals.	Deadrise Aft	12°

Cruisers & Sedans

Silverton 362 Sedan Cruiser

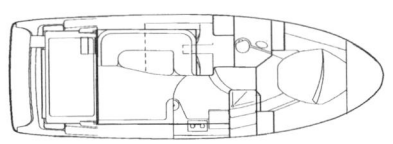

1994–98

Multipurpose family convertible with large flybridge scored with 1990s buyers sold on traditional Silverton value. Well-appointed interior with expansive salon features private midcabin stateroom with twin berths, bow stateroom with island berth, well-positioned galley with generous storage. Split head/shower is especially convenient when cruising with guests. Roomy cockpit with transom door has molded steps to flybridge. Note integrated swim platform, foredeck sun pad. Cruise at 18 knots with 320hp V-drive gas engines (mid 20s top).

See Page 543 For Value Estimates

Length	36'1"	Fuel	300 gals.
Beam	12'11"	Water	100 gals.
Draft	3'0"	Waste	40 gals.
Weight	15,058#	Hull Type	Modified-V
Clearance	13'0"	Deadrise Aft	17°

Silverton 37 Convertible

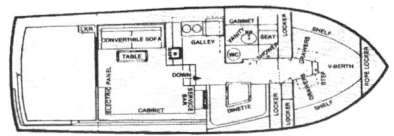

1980–89

Smooth-running convertible enjoyed great popularity in the 1980s thanks to smart styling, user-friendly accommodations, good open-water performance. Space-efficient interior with convertible sofa and dinette, head with stall shower sleeps six. Original teak joinery was updated in 1985 to light oak. Small flybridge seats four. Deep cockpit is large enough for fishing but lacks transom door. Note that straight-drive inboards replaced V-drive power in 1981. Cruise at 18–19 knots with 350hp gas inboards (mid 20s top).

Prices Not Provided for Pre-1995 Models

Length	37'0"	Fuel	300 gals.
Beam	14'0"	Water	100 gals.
Draft	3'7"	Cockpit	75 sq. ft.
Weight	20,000#	Hull Type	Modified-V
Clearance	12'6"	Deadrise Aft	14°

Silverton 37 Convertible

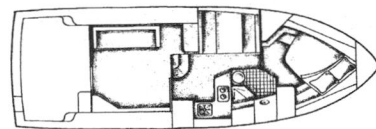

1990–2000

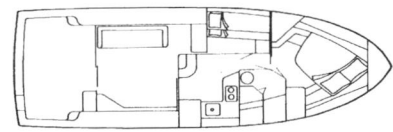

Dinette Interior, 1993–2001

Midcabin Interior, 1993–2001

See Page 543 For Value Estimates

Updated version of original Silverton 37 Convertible (1980–89) hit the mark with rakish styling, family-friendly accommodations, affordable price. Offered with choice of one or two staterooms, both with spacious open-plan salon, roomy head with stall shower, fully equipped galley. Fish, swim, or dive from deep cockpit with in-deck fishbox, transom door. Note side exhausts, large engine room. Prop pockets reduce draft, improve running efficiency. Standard 320hp gas engines cruise at 15–16 knots (mid 20s wide open).

Length w/Pulpit	41'3"	Fuel	375 gals.
Hull Length	37'4"	Water	100 gals.
Beam	13'11"	Waste	40 gals.
Draft	3'7"	Hull Type	Modified-V
Weight	21,852#	Deadrise Aft	17°

Cruisers & Sedans

Silverton 38 Convertible

2003–09

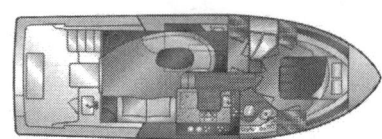

Versatile flybridge convertible delivered big-boat comfort, performance at a reasonable price. Twin-stateroom interior—highlighted by plush Ultraleather upholstery, glossy cherry cabinetry—gets high marks for tasteful decor, full-feature galley with hardwood floor, space for washer/dryer. Note split head/shower compartments forward. Relatively small cockpit has twin in-deck fishboxes, transom door, optional bait-prep center, engine room access. Standard 385hp gas inboards cruise at 18 knots and top out in the mid 20s.

See Page 543 For Value Estimates

Length w/Pulpit	41'1"	Fuel	360 gals.
Beam	14'3"	Water	100 gals.
Draft	3'7"	Waste	40 gals.
Weight	26,450#	Hull Type	Modified-V
Clearance	16'8"	Deadrise Aft	17°

Silverton 38 Express

1990–94

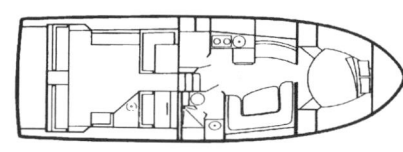

Beamy 1990s express made good on Silverton promise of family-friendly layout, economy-class price. Midcabin interior boasts double berths in both staterooms, head with stall shower, big U-shaped dinette. Note Plexiglas window/wall separating forward stateroom from salon. Cluster of six overhead skylights provide the only natural cabin lighting. Privacy door for aft stateroom is a nice touch. Bi-level cockpit can seat six. Twin 355hp V-drive gas engines cruise at 20 knots and deliver a top speed in the high 20s.

Prices Not Provided for Pre-1995 Models

Length	37'7"	Fuel	300 gals.
Beam	13'11"	Water	110 gals.
Draft	3'7"	Cockpit	NA
Weight	21,000#	Hull Type	Modified-V
Clearance	9'9"	Deadrise Aft	17°

Silverton 38 Sport Bridge

2005–Current

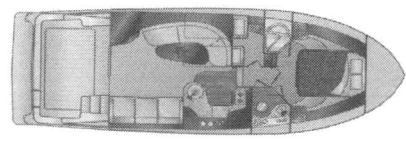

Top-selling family sedan with big two-stateroom floorplan gets high marks for versatility, comfort. Elevated walkways permit expansive salon whose dimensions rival those of a larger boat. Dinette is a step up from salon floor to make room for midcabin below. Note split head with toilet to starboard, shower to port. Molded bridge steps, extended swim platform, transom storage locker are standard. Engine room is tight; flybridge is huge. Cruise in low 20s with 425hp gas engines; 24–25 knots with optional 355hp Cummins diesels.

See Page 543 For Value Estimates

Length	39'11"	Fuel	372 gals.
Beam	14'4"	Water	110 gals.
Draft	2'11"	Waste	40 gals.
Weight	26,900#	Hull Type	Modified-V
Clearance	14'11"	Deadrise Aft	12°

Silverton 40 Convertible

1985–90

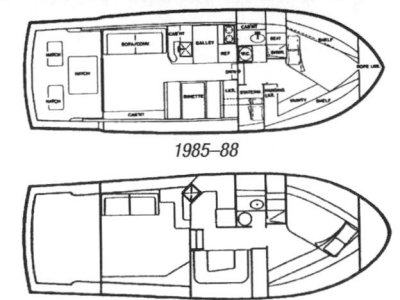

1985–88

1989–90

Prices Not Provided for Pre-1995 Models

Economy-class 40-footer with appealing lines offered 1980s convertible buyers a lot of boat for the money. Original twin-stateroom, mid-galley interior gave way to more open single-stateroom, galley-down floorplan in 1989. Most were sold with light oak interior trim. Cockpit is large enough for fishing, but this boat proved far more popular as a family cruiser. Lower helm was never offered. Note wide side decks, roomy flybridge, spacious engine room. Cruise at 15–16 knots with standard 350hp gas engines (mid 20s top).

Length	40'0"	Fuel	300 gals.
Beam	14'0"	Water	100 gals.
Draft	3'0"	Cockpit	75 sq. ft.
Weight	23,000#	Hull Type	Modified-V
Clearance	13'6"	Deadrise Aft	14°

Silverton 41 Convertible

1991–99

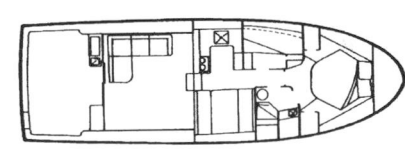

See Page 543 For Value Estimates

Well-built 1990s sedan with plenty of standard equipment made the cut with value-conscious buyers. Standard galley-down interior with open front windshield features wide-open salon with convertible sofa, big 6-person dinette, two comfortable staterooms. Offered with choice of oak or cherry interior trim. Deep cockpit with in-deck fishboxes, transom door is big enough for several anglers. Standard 385hp gas engines cruise at 19–20 knots (high 20s top); optional 425hp Cat diesels cruise at 24–25 knots (high 20s wide open).

Length w/Pulpit	46'3"	Fuel	524 gals.
Hull Length	41'3"	Water	200 gals.
Beam	14'10"	Waste	60 gals.
Draft	3'7"	Hull Type	Modified-V
Weight	24,975#	Deadrise Aft	17°

Silverton 42 Convertible

2000–Current

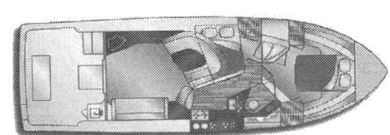

See Page 543 For Value Estimates

Stylish family convertible with wide 14'11" beam is sporty on the outside, comfortable on the inside. Classy galley-down interior incorporates unique raised dinette forward in salon, two double staterooms, home-sized galley with generous storage. Note split head/shower arrangement, overhead rod locker in salon. Uncluttered cockpit has engine room access door, tackle center, molded bridge steps, transom door. Fiberglass hardtop, power windows are optional. Cruise at 20 knots with 440hp Cummins diesels (mid 20s wide open).

Length Overall	44'6"	Fuel	524 gals.
Beam	14'11"	Water	200 gals.
Draft	3'7"	Waste	40 gals.
Weight	26,300#	Hull Type	Modified-V
Clearance	16'8"	Deadrise Aft	17°

Cruisers & Sedans

Silverton 45 Convertible

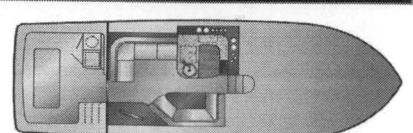

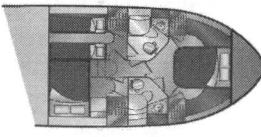

2006–Current

Feature-rich sports convertible signature Silverton styling is sporty, spacious, seaworthy. Space-efficient layout combines roomy three-stateroom interior (most 45-footers have two) with big 80-square-foot cockpit. Entertainment center with retractable TV is standard in salon. Washer/dryer can be fitted in second guest cabin. Additional features include standard hardtop, Ultraleather upholstery, cherry cabinets, molded bridge steps, cockpit engine room access. Volvo 500hp diesels cruise at 22–24 knots (high 20s top).

See Page 544 For Value Estimates

Length	47'8"	Fuel	607 gals.
Beam	15'4"	Water	120 gals.
Draft	3'8"	Waste	72 gals.
Weight	42,048#	Hull Type	Modified-V
Clearance	16'10"	Deadrise Aft	13°

Silverton 48/50 Convertible

2004–Current

Conservative family convertible (called Silverton 48 in 2004–06) offers style, substance at a competitive price. Upscale three-stateroom interior boasts modern blend of high-gloss cherry cabinetry, deep-pile carpeting, quality furnishings. Washer/dryer is standard; master stateroom is fitted with foldaway flat-screen TV. Cockpit is on the small side, but flybridge is among the largest to be found on a 48-footer. Prop pockets reduce hull draft, improve efficiency. Note standard hardtop. Volvo 715hp diesels cruise in the high 20s (about 30 knots top).

See Page 544 For Value Estimates

Length w/Pulpit	51'7"	Fuel	793 gals.
Beam	16'4"	Water	200 gals.
Draft	4'0"	Waste	80 gals.
Weight	47,600#	Hull Type	Modified-V
Clearance	17'6"	Deadrise Aft	12°

Stamas 320 Express

2004–Current

Floorplan Not Available

Spirited midsize express offered with inboard or outboard power combines appealing lines with roomy accommodations, durable construction. Large cockpit comes standard with full array of fishing amenities including transom livewell, insulated transom fishbox, wide transom door. Engine access is via hydraulic deck hatch. Teak-trimmed interior with midcabin berth, convertible dinette, teak-and-holly sole sleeps six. Twin 320hp MerCruiser gas inboards cruise at 22 knots (30 top). Outboard version with 225hp Yamahas tops out at close to 35 knots.

See Page 544 For Value Estimates

Length w/Pulpit	34'5"	Fuel, IB	240 gals.
Hull Length	32'3"	Fuel, OB	316 gals.
Beam	11'2"	Water	40 gals.
Draft	2'20"	Hull Type	Modified-V
Weight	13,200#	Deadrise Aft	18°

Stamas 340 Express

2003–Current

Dual-purpose offshore express splits the difference between hardcore fishboat, comfortable family cruiser. Uncluttered cockpit comes standard with full array of fishing amenities including transom livewell, insulated fishbox, wide transom door. Engine access is via hydraulic deck hatch. Well-appointed interior with midcabin berth sleeps six. Prop pockets reduce draft, improve efficiency. MerCruiser 370hp gas inboards cruise at 22 knots (30+ top); Yanmar 370hp diesels cruise at 25 knots (30 top). Outboard version also available.

Floorplan Not Available

See Page 544 For Value Estimates

Length w/Pulpit	36'2"	Clearance	7'3"
Hull Length	34'0"	Fuel	350 gals.
Beam	12'6"	Water	84 gals.
Draft	2'4"	Hull Type	Modified-V
Weight	14,000#	Deadrise Aft	18°

Stamas 360 Express

1992–99

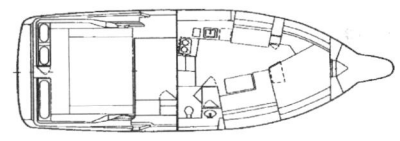

Conservative inboard express with midcabin interior appealed to 1990s boaters drawn to versatile layout, solid construction, comfortable open-water ride. Fishing amenities include livewell, raw-water washdown, insulated fishboxes, rod storage. Elevated helm affords excellent visibility. Tasteful midcabin interior with convertible dinette, full galley, sleeps four adults, two kids. Note reverse transom with centerline door. Prop pockets reduce draft, improve efficiency. Standard 310hp MerCruiser gas inboards cruise at 18 knots (high 20s top).

See Page 544 For Value Estimates

Length w/Pulpit	38'6"	Clearance	8'3"
Hull Length	36'0"	Fuel	372 gals.
Beam	13'2"	Water	90 gals.
Draft	2'4"	Hull Type	Modified-V
Weight	16,975#	Deadrise Aft	18°

Stamas 370 Express

2000–09

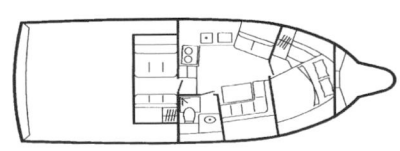

Revised version of Stamas 360 Express (1992–99) combined redesigned hull (no more reverse transom) with improved cockpit layout. Midcabin interior is rare in a dedicated fishing boat. Sizable cockpit has built-in livewell, insulated fishbox, bait-prep station, tackle drawers. Well-designed helm has space for flush-mounting electronics. Note wide side decks. Power engine hatch provides outstanding service access. Deep keel, prop pockets protect running gear in event of grounding. Yanmar 420hp diesels cruise at 24–26 knots (30+ knots wide open).

See Page 545 For Value Estimates

Length w/Pulpit	39'2"	Headroom	6'4"
Hull Length	36'8"	Fuel	400 gals.
Beam	13'2"	Water	84 gals.
Draft	2'4"	Hull Type	Modified-V
Weight	16,975#	Deadrise Aft	18°

Sunseeker 34 Superhawk

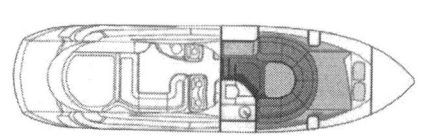

1997–2003

Fast-action sportcruiser combines extraordinary handling with dramatic styling, first-rate build quality. Posh cockpit seats several guests in comfort. Compact interior with double berth forward is beautifully finished but lacks headroom. Small head is nearly worthless for showers; galley is fine as long as you stick to sandwiches. Power engine hatch reveals neat (but tight) engine room. Terrific open-water performer still outguns most competitors. Volvo 285hp diesel I/Os hit close to 45 knots wide open. Total of 160 were built.

See Page 545 For Value Estimates

Length	37'2"	Clearance	NA
Beam	10'2"	Fuel	185 gals.
Draft, Drives Up	2'2"	Water	18 gals.
Draft, Drives Down	3'9"	Hull Type	Deep-V
Weight	12,800#	Deadrise Aft	21°

Sunseeker 44 Camargue

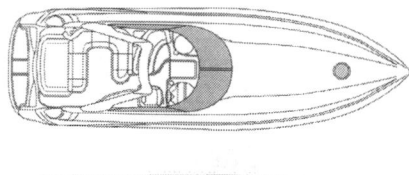

1998–2002

Strong-selling U.K. import introduced in 1998 delivered best-in-class blend of luxury, finish, performance. Curvaceous cockpit includes full-size sun lounge, folding dining table with seating for eight. Upscale interior with roomy salon, two heads boasts high-gloss cherry woodwork, top-quality appliances, designer furnishings. Extended swim platform, foredeck fender storage, teak cockpit sole, bow thruster were standard. Windlass is stored inside anchor locker. Twin 420hp Cat diesels cruise in the mid 20s, top out at 30+ knots.

See Page 545 For Value Estimates

Length	44'0"	Fuel	265 gals.
Beam	13'6"	Water	80 gals.
Draft	3'5"	Headroom	6'4"
Weight	29,000#	Hull Type	Deep-V
Clearance	9'10"	Deadrise Aft	20°

Sunseeker 46 Portofino

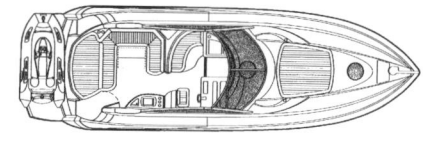

2003–05

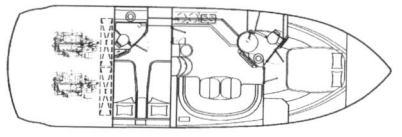

Compelling English sportyacht with seductive styling lives up to Sunseeker promise of state-of-the-art construction, luxury-class amenities. Posh interior with high-gloss cherry cabinetry, UltraLeather seating offers two private staterooms, hidden galley appliances, two heads, generous cabinet storage. Topside highlights include hydraulic swim platform, foredeck sun pad, deluxe cockpit galley with refrigerator and barbeque. Engine access is no picnic. Cruise at 28 knots (32–33 top) with 480hp Volvo diesels.

See Page 545 For Value Estimates

Length Overall	48'5"	Headroom	6'3"
Beam	13'9"	Fuel	346 gals.
Draft	3'10"	Water	99 gals.
Weight	32,300#	Hull Type	Deep-V
Clearance	13'1"	Deadrise Aft	19°

Sunseeker 47 Camargue

1996–99

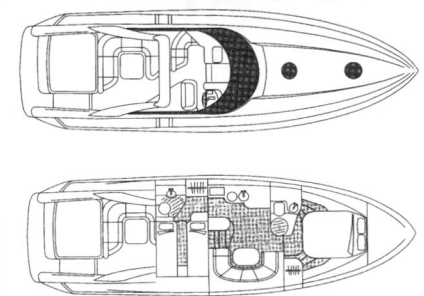

Blue-chip sportcruiser imported in the late 1990s offered cutting-edge European styling, exceptional build quality. Opulent midcabin interior contains two heads, large galley with hidden appliances, premium hardware and furnishings. Single-level cockpit is a full-feature entertainment center with wraparound seating, deluxe wet bar, foldaway dining table. Note chart flat with light, transom shower. Aft sun pad conceals transom garage. Cat 435hp diesel inboards cruise at 25–26 knots (30 knots top); 625hp GMs cruise at 30 knots (34–35 top).

See Page 545 For Value Estimates

Length	46'9"	Fuel	365 gals.
Beam	13'5"	Water	100 gals.
Draft	3'3"	Headroom	6'5"
Weight	30,644#	Hull Type	Deep-V
Clearance	9'4"	Deadrise Aft	23°

Sunseeker 48 Superhawk

1996–2005

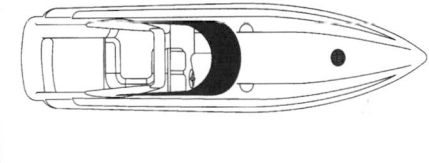

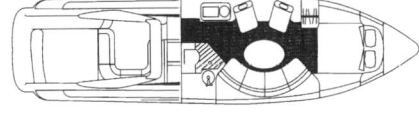

Powerful triple-engine UK express blows past most everything on the water except a fuel dock. Standard topside goodies include twin racing bolsters, cockpit seating for six, sun pad, wet bar. Elegant single-stateroom interior features plush lounge seating, head with shower, small galley, built-in entertainment system. Deep-V hull has keel pad for enhanced acceleration. Note standard bow thruster. Triple 415hp gas MerCruisers (with surface drives) reach 50 knots; triple 260hp Volvo diesel I/Os hit 40+ knots. Total of 247 were built.

See Page 545 For Value Estimates

Length Overall	50'2"	Headroom	6'1"
Beam	10'8"	Fuel	280 gals.
Draft	2'6"	Water	58 gals.
Weight	22,100#	Hull Type	Deep-V
Clearance	10'4"	Deadrise Aft	22°

Cruisers & Sedans

Sunseeker 50 Camargue

2000–03

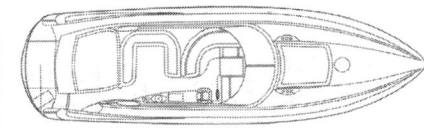

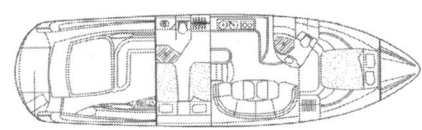

Inspired Mediterranean cruiser with seductive lines took signature Sunseeker styling, luxury, performance to the next level. Highlights include huge cockpit seating for eight, exceptionally comfortable twin-stateroom interior with elegant salon, private en suite heads. Aft deck lifts electrically to expose large transom garage for dinghy, PWC. Hardtop was optional. Note fore and aft sun pads, excellent helm layout. Large engine room is a plus. Twin 660hp Cats—straight inboards, not V-drives—cruise in the mid 20s (about 30 knots top).

See Page 545 For Value Estimates

Length	52'11"	Fuel	528 gals.
Beam	14'7"	Water	112 gals.
Draft	4'7"	Headroom	6'3"
Weight	41,400#	Hull Type	Deep-V
Clearance	12'6"	Deadrise Aft	22.5°

Sunseeker 51 Camargue

1995–97

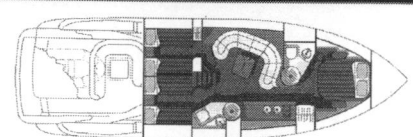

Three-Stateroom Interior

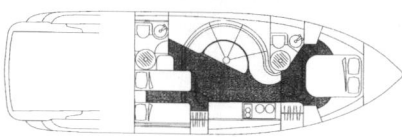

Two-Stateroom Interior

See Page 545 For Value Estimates

Elegant English sportyacht yacht introduced to American market in 1995 delivered a compelling blend of sleek styling, deluxe amenities, flawless joinery. Originally offered with opulent twin-cabin interior, updated three-stateroom layout became available in 1996. Expansive cockpit with teak sole has comfortable seating for ten. Aft-deck sun lounge sits atop hydraulically operated storage garage with electric launch/recovery winch. Note telescoping gangway. Engine room is a very tight fit. Cat 600hp (or GM 625hp) V-drive diesels reach 30+ knots.

Length	49'0"	Fuel	465 gals.
Beam	14'5"	Water	130 gals.
Draft	3'8"	Headroom	6'2"
Weight	42,460#	Hull Type	Deep-V
Clearance	12'9"	Deadrise Aft	19°

Sunseeker 53 Portofino

2004–09

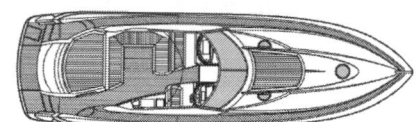

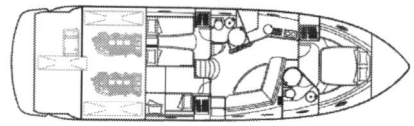

See Page 545 For Value Estimates

High-impact sportyacht combines the lush accommodations, spirited performance buyers have come to expect of a Sunseeker product. Opulent three-stateroom interior is an impressive display of handcrafted cherry cabinetry, leather upholstery, top-shelf hardware and appliances. Roomy cockpit with U-shaped seating, teak sole, boasts slick foldaway table. Power sun pad lifts to reveal tender garage. First-rate engine compartment, near-flawless gelcoat. Expect 30+ knots top with 715hp Cat or Volvo diesels.

Length	56'11"	Fuel	486 gals.
Beam	15'1"	Water	88 gals.
Draft	4'0"	Waste	24 gals.
Weight	42,500#	Hull Type	Deep-V
Clearance	14'5"	Deadrise Aft	19°

Sunseeker 55 Camargue

1994–96

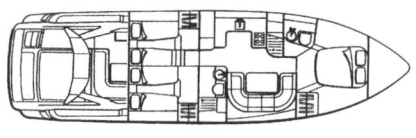

1994

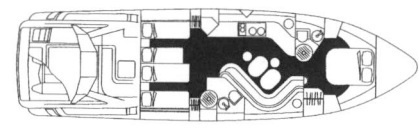

1995–96

See Page 545 For Value Estimates

Early Sunseeker import gave U.S. buyers a taste of English luxury, quality. Extravagant three-stateroom, two-head interior—completely updated in 1995—is an impressive display of high-gloss woodwork, posh seating, premium fixtures and furnishings. Exterior highlights include well-appointed cockpit with seating for ten, tender garage with launch/recovery winch, teak cockpit sole, bow storage locker. Note ergonomic helm position. Tight engine room space is typical of European yachts. GM 760hp diesels reach 30+ knots top.

Length	55'0"	Fuel	753 gals.
Beam	14'7"	Water	150 gals.
Draft	4'1"	Headroom	6'3"
Weight	39,970#	Hull Type	Deep-V
Clearance	11'2"	Deadrise Aft	23°

Sunseeker 56 Predator

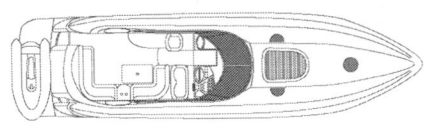

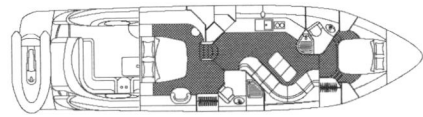

2000–04

Muscular sportcruiser introduced to US market in 2000 combined dramatic styling with palatial owner's cabin, state-of-the-art construction. Lavish interior boasts opulent main salon with leather seating, extra-large galley with built-in washer/dryer, two large staterooms with en suite heads, exquisite cherry joinery. Raised bridgedeck offers seating for eight; adjoining aft cockpit seating has retractable sun lounge. Electro-hydraulic high-low bathing platform handles a tender. Cat 800hp diesels cruise in the mid-to-high 20s (32–33 knots top).

Insufficient Resale Data to Assign Values

Length	60'2"	Fuel	621 gals.
Beam	15'1"	Water	172 gals.
Draft	4'5"	Headroom	6'5"
Weight	52,030#	Hull Type	Deep-V
Clearance	12'9"	Deadrise Aft	19°

Sunseeker 58/60 Predator

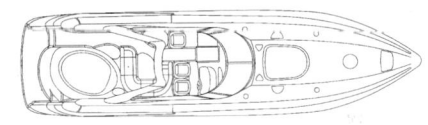

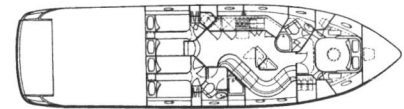

1997–2002

High-impact express (called Predator 58 in 1997–99; 60 Predator in 2000–02) made good on Sunseeker promise of leading-edge performance, world-class construction. Lush interior with warm, club-like atmosphere features spacious salon with sweeping settee, extended galley, three private cabins. Cockpit is dominated by oval sun pad over dinghy/PWC garage with a built-in launch/retrieval winch. Note stylish helm layout, wide side decks. Hardtop with sunroof was a popular option. Cruise at 26–27 knots with 800hp Cat diesels (30+ knots top).

See Page 545 For Value Estimates

Length	57'11"	Fuel	753 gals.
Beam	15'1"	Water	170 gals.
Draft	4'5"	Headroom	6'8"
Weight	48,400#	Hull Type	Deep-V
Clearance	10'8"	Deadrise Aft	22.5°

Sunseeker 61 Predator

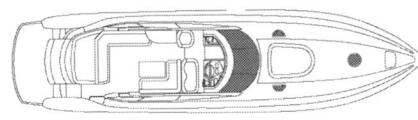

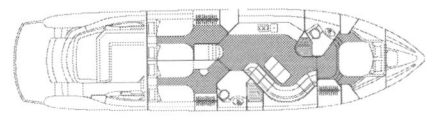

2002–05

Blue-chip hardtop cruiser with retractable sunroof combines exotic Med styling with plush accommodations, powerful performance. Beautifully crafted interior is enhanced by high-gloss cherry joinery, leather seating, hidden galley appliances. Master stateroom with en suite head is forward; twin aft cabins share day head in salon. Super-lush cockpit layout. Hydraulic swim platform makes launching/retrieving tender from aft garage simple, easy. Cruise at an honest 30 knots with MAN 1,050hp diesels (about 35 knots top).

Insufficient Resale Data to Assign Values

Length	61'0"	Fuel	779 gals.
Beam	15'1"	Water	165 gals.
Draft	4'5"	Headroom	6'6"
Weight	57,320#	Hull Type	Deep-V
Clearance	16'1"	Deadrise Aft	19°

Cruisers & Sedans

Sunseeker 63 Predator

1995–99

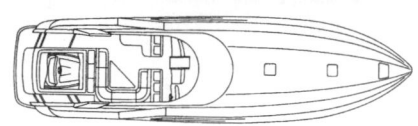

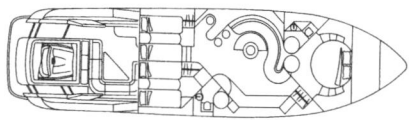

Gold-plated 63-footer imported in late 1990s was among largest production yachts of her era. Enormous cockpit has retractable soft top for weather protection. Massive aft sun lounge conceals garage capable of storing—and launching—a 13-foot jet boat. Palatial interior with wide-open salon, designer furnishings sleeps six in three staterooms. Note dual transom gates, wraparound cockpit seating, excellent helm layout. Twin 1,100hp MAN diesels (jammed into a tight engine room) cruise at a fast 32 knots (36–38 knots top).

Insufficient Resale Data to Assign Values

Length Overall	63'0"	Headroom	6'3"
Beam	15'6"	Fuel	798 gals.
Draft	4'1"	Water	185 gals.
Weight	48,400#	Hull Type	Deep-V
Clearance	14'5"	Deadrise Aft	21°

Sunseeker 68 Predator

2002–06

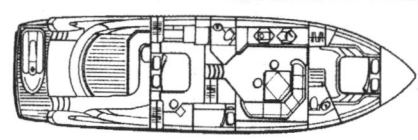

Master Suite Aft

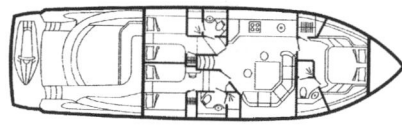

Master Suite Forward

Handsome Med-style cruiser with retractable hardtop, state-of-the-art amenities raised the bar for sportyacht luxury, performance. Lavish interior with three staterooms, three heads is dominated by cavernous salon, elegant master suite. Topside highlights include spacious cockpit with executive-class amenities, enormous foredeck sun pad with flanking skylights, hydraulic swim platform, tender garage. Note full walkaround decks, large engine room, cockpit barbecue. A seriously fast ride, MAN 1,300hp engines top out at 36–37 knots.

Insufficient Resale Data to Assign Values

Length	66'9"	Fuel	1,030 gals.
Beam	17'1"	Water	185 gals.
Draft	4'8"	Waste	60 gals.
Weight	66,140#	Hull Type	Deep-V
Clearance	11'6"	Deadrise Aft	19°

Sunseeker 75 Predator

1999–2004

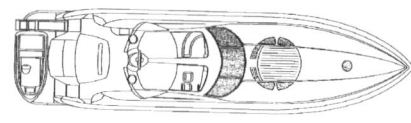

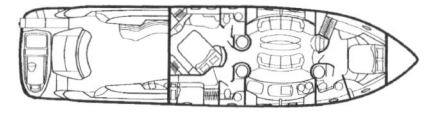

Imposing 75-foot Med yacht pushed the limits of late 1990s engineering, design excellence. Enclosed bridgedeck features five helm chairs, opening side windows, twin sunroofs, massive stainless-and-glass sliding cockpit doors. Extravagant triple-cabin interior is dominated by ultra-luxurious salon with exquisite cherry joinery, full-length galley, leather upholstery. Huge sun pad sits atop tender garage. Note hydraulic swim platform, aft crew quarters, teak cockpit sole. MAN 1,200hp engines reach a top speed of just over 30 knots.

Insufficient Resale Data to Assign Values

Length Overall	75'0"	Fuel	1,321 gals.
Beam	17'10"	Water	300 gals.
Draft	4'11"	Waste	60 gals.
Weight	75,000#	Hull Type	Deep-V
Clearance	16'8"	Deadrise Aft	20°

Cruisers & Sedans

Tiara 2700 Continental

1982–86

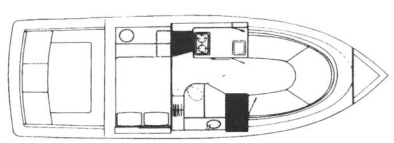

Well-finished express offered 1980s buyers exceptional small-boat quality, versatility. Space-efficient deck layout boasts roomy cockpit, wide side decks, well-arranged helm with tall windshield. Teak-trimmed cabin with U-shaped dinette, full galley, midcabin berth sleeps six in comfort. Swim, dive, or fish from large single-level cockpit. Note excellent nonskid, sturdy bow rails. Hatches in cockpit sole provide good access to engine room. Twin 260hp MerCruiser sterndrives cruise at 24–26 knots (close to 40 knots top).

Prices Not Provided for Pre-1995 Models

Length	27'6"	Water	24 gals.
Beam	9'10"	Clearance	7'0"
Hull Draft	2'8"	Cockpit Length	11'0"
Weight	7,400#	Hull Type	Deep-V
Fuel	137 gals.	Deadrise Aft	20°

Tiara 2700 Open

1987–93

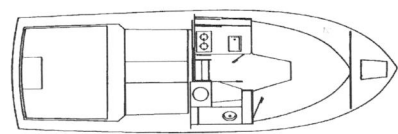

Iconic inboard express supplies enduring mix of spacious cockpit, upscale interior, quality construction. Teak-trimmed cabin with full-service galley, stand-up head with shower, sleeps two. Single-level cockpit with back-to-back seating is large enough for mounted chair. Wide side decks, sturdy rails provide secure foredeck access. Note commercial-quality windshield, easy-access motorboxes, deep-V hull. Many updates/improvements over the years. Crusader 270hp gas engines cruise in the low 20s (28–30 knots wide open).

Prices Not Provided for Pre-1995 Models

Length w/Pulpit	29'5"	Clearance	7'0"
Hull Length	27'0"	Fuel	240 gals.
Beam	10'0"	Water	20 gals.
Draft	2'0"	Hull Type	Deep-V
Weight	7,500#	Deadrise Aft	22°

Tiara 2900 Coronet

1997–2007

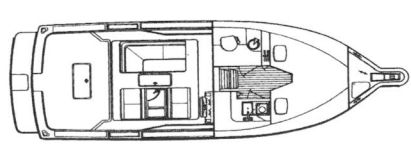

Graceful sportcruiser with inboard power delivers impressive blend of sophisticated styling, top-shelf construction. Single-level cockpit has double helm seat, L-lounge forward, removable bench seats aft. Entire forward section of deck lifts for engine access. Compact interior with enclosed head, mini-galley, teak-and-holly cabin sole sleeps two. Note centerline transom door, cockpit wet bar. Tall windshield has reverse-angle spray guard along top. Exemplary finish throughout. Cruise at 21–22 knots with 320hp gas inboards (30+ knots top).

See Page 545 For Value Estimates

Length w/Pulpit	31'7"	Fuel	200 gals.
Hull Length	28'2"	Water	30 gals.
Beam	11'4"	Waste	20 gals.
Draft	2'8"	Hull Type	Modified-V
Weight	10,000#	Deadrise Aft	19°

Cruisers & Sedans

Tiara 2900 Open

1993–2006

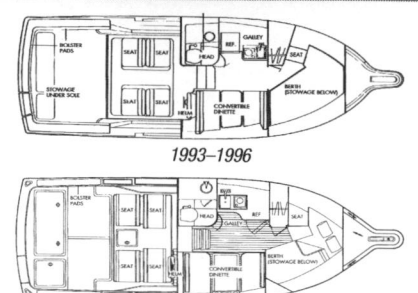

1993–1996

1997–2006

Multi-purpose Tiara cruiser set the gold standard in her class for sophisticated express-boat design, top-shelf engineering and construction. Uncluttered cockpit features double helm and companion seats forward, twin aft-facing seats, wide transom door. Well-appointed cabin with full galley, convertible dinette sleeps four. Wide beam for a 29-footer. Entire bridgedeck lifts electrically for engine access. Used models are always in demand. Twin 320hp inboard gas engines cruise at 20 knots (close to 30 knots top).

See Page 545 For Value Estimates

Length w/Pulpit	30'9"	Fuel	200 gals.
Hull Length	28'9"	Water	30 gals.
Beam	11'4"	Waste	20 gals.
Draft	2'8"	Hull Type	Modified-V
Weight	10,700#	Deadrise Aft	19°

Tiara 3000 Open

2007–Current

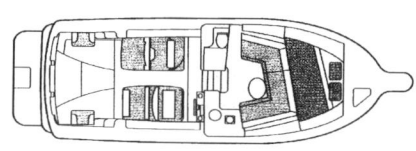

Premium hardtop express with innovative interior couples graceful styling with efficient deck plan, signature Tiara quality. Wide beam creates large cockpit with jump seat, workstation/wet bar with insulated storage, sprayer, cutting board. Elegant teak cabin with hardwood sole, forward side berth features posh aft-facing lounge that converts to double berth. Note tall windshield, tilt-away helm, opening hardtop vents. Bridgedeck lifts electrically for engine access. Cruise at 22–24 knots with 385hp gas inboards (low-to-mid 30s top).

See Page 545 For Value Estimates

Length w/Pulpit	33'0"	Fuel	210 gals.
Hull Length	30'6"	Water	32 gals.
Beam	12'6"	Waste	20 gals.
Draft	2'8"	Hull Type	Modified-V
Weight	13,225#	Deadrise Aft	14°

Tiara 3100 Open

1979–91

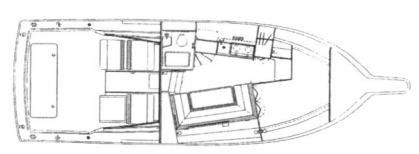

Classic 1980s express did much to establish Tiara reputation for superior engineering, durable construction. Versatile layout—equally well-suited for fishing or cruising—boasts appealing teak-trimmed interior with big U-shaped dinette, large cockpit with removable bench seat, roomy engine compartment with good service access. Note tall, commercial-quality windshield, aft-facing cockpit seats. Modified-V hull can be a wet ride. Standard 350hp gas inboards cruise in the low 20s (32–33 knots top). Replaced with all-new 3100 Open in 1992.

Prices Not Provided for Pre-1995 Models

Length w/Pulpit	33'9"	Clearance, Arch	7'6"
Hull Length	31'3"	Fuel	196 gals.
Beam	12'0"	Water	36 gals.
Draft	2'9"	Hull Type	Modified-V
Weight	10,500#	Deadrise Aft	14°

Tiara 3100 Open

1992–2004

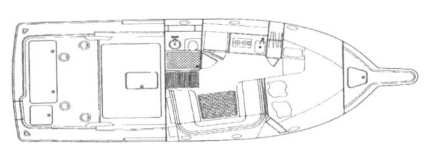

Updated version of original 3100 Open (1979–91) with major modifications made a great boat even better. Reworked hull with prop pockets, increased deadrise, delivers better head-sea ride than her predecessor. Bi-level cockpit allows installation of diesels in larger engine compartment. Luxury-class interior with U-shaped dinette, full galley sleeps four. Cockpit came with in-deck fishbox, livewell, foldaway rear seat. Transom door became standard in 1994. Cruise at 20 knots with 320hp gas engines; 22–23 knots with 330hp Cummins diesels.

See Page 545 For Value Estimates

Length w/Pulpit	33'10"	Fuel	246 gals.
Hull Length	31'6"	Water	38 gals.
Beam	12'0"	Waste	20 gals.
Draft	3'0"	Hull Type	Modified-V
Weight	12,300#	Deadrise Aft	18°

Tiara 3200 Open

2004–Current

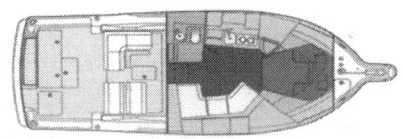

Graceful styling, quality construction and many luxury appointments have made this versatile express a class leader with savvy buyers. Bi-level cockpit with in-deck fishbox, transom door is large enough for several anglers. Upscale interior with solid teak cabinetry, Ultraleather seating sleeps four. Bridgedeck rises electrically for engine access. Optional livewell replaces standard fold-down transom seat. Hardtop is a popular option. Note prop-pocket hull bottom. Cruise at 22 knots with 385hp gas engines; mid 20ss with Volvo 310hp diesels.

See Page 545 For Value Estimates

Length w/Pulpit	35'1"	Fuel	256 gals.
Hull Length	32'7"	Water	38 gals.
Beam	13'0"	Waste	20 gals.
Draft	3'0"	Hull Type	Modified-V
Weight	15,950#	Deadrise Aft	18°

Tiara 3300 Open

1988–97

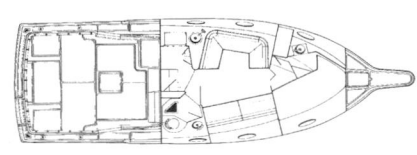

Feature-rich express with conservative lines, superior finish delivers exceptional cruising comfort, owner satisfaction. Elegant teak-trimmed interior with U-shaped dinette, convertible settee sleeps six in genuine comfort. Tournament-grade cockpit with transom door, fishbox is big enough for serious fishing pursuits. Wide side decks, good engine access, well-designed helm layout. Low-deadrise hull can be a stiff ride. Cruise at 20 knots with standard gas engines; 24 knots with 315hp Cummins diesels.

See Page 545 For Value Estimates

Length w/Pulpit	35'8"	Fuel	295 gals.
Hull Length	32'10"	Water	46 gals.
Beam	12'6"	Waste	20 gals.
Draft	2'3"	Hull Type	Modified-V
Weight	13,500#	Deadrise Aft	14°

Cruisers & Sedans

Tiara 3500 Express

1995–2003

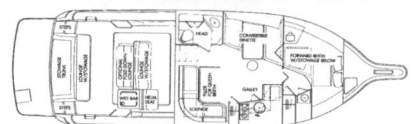

Standard Floorplan

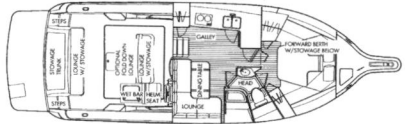

Optional Layout

Luxury-class cruiser from late 1990s surpassed the competition for tasteful accommodations, premium amenities, spirited performance. Interior is huge for a 35-footer thanks to wide 13'9" beam. Salon lounge converts into second stateroom at night. Huge cockpit with foldaway rear seat, twin transom doors is among largest in her class. Extended swim platform can stow inflatable or PWC. Note huge transom storage trunk. Cummins 370hp V-drive diesels top out in the high 20s; 435hp Cats reach 30 knots wide open.

See Page 545 For Value Estimates

Length w/Pulpit	38'10"	Weight, Diesel	21,500#
Hull Length	35'8"	Fuel	354 gals.
Beam	13'9"	Water	124 gals.
Draft	2'10"	Hull Type	Modified-V
Weight, Gas	18,600#	Deadrise Aft	18°

Tiara 3500 Open

1998–2004

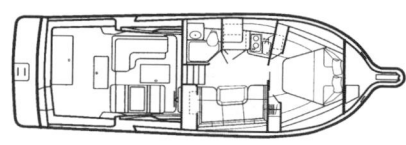

Top-ranked express combines traditional Tiara styling with high-end construction, uncommon luxury. Spacious single-stateroom interior features solid teak joinery, leather upholstery, beautiful teak-and-holly cabin sole. Crowd-friendly cockpit with foldaway rear seat serves anglers, cruisers alike. Entire bridgedeck rises for engine access. Note wide side decks, power windshield vent, ergonomic helm layout. Standard gas inboards cruise at 16–18 knots; optional 370hp Cummins diesels cruise at 25–26 knots.

See Page 546 For Value Estimates

Length w/Pulpit	40'8"	Fuel	360 gals.
Hull Length	35'6"	Water	70 gals.
Beam	13'3"	Waste	30 gals.
Draft	3'3"	Hull Type	Modified-V
Weight	14,000#	Deadrise Aft	18°

Tiara 3500 Sovran

2008–Current

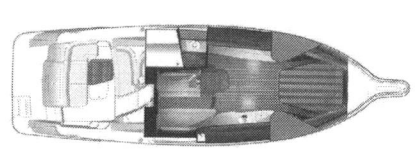

Beautifully finished hardtop express with efficient Volvo IPS power provides uncommon luxury for the cruising couple. Wide beam results in considerably more cockpit/cabin space than most 35-footers. Elegant open-plan interior boasts unusually spacious midcabin area with facing settees, wall-mounted flat-screen TV. Split-level cockpit seats eight in comfort. Note that hardtop lacks opening sunroof. Cockpit sole lifts electrically for access to engine compartment. Cruise at 25–26 knots (30+ top) with Volvo 300hp IPS diesels.

See Page 546 For Value Estimates

Length Overall	37'9"	Fuel	250 gals.
Beam	12'11"	Water	70 gals.
Draft	3'1"	Waste	30 gals.
Weight	17,600#	Hull Type	Modified-V
Clearance	9'8"	Deadrise Aft	15°

Cruisers & Sedans

Tiara 3600 Open

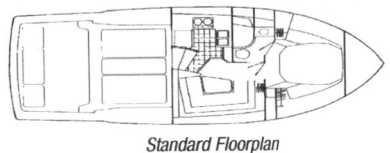

1987–96

Standard Floorplan

Alternate Floorplan

Strong-selling express set class standards in her era for unsurpassed mix of hard-nosed fishability, family-style accommodations. Highlights include well-appointed interior with solid teak joinery, expansive bi-level cockpit, top-quality construction. Original cabin layout with island berth forward sleeps four; alternate layout introduced in 1989 sleeps six. Entire bridgedeck lifts on hydraulic rams for engine access. Conservative lines still look good today. Standard 350hp gas engines cruise at 18 knots; 375hp Cats cruise at 24–25 knots.

See Page 546 For Value Estimates

Length w/Pulpit	36'8"	Headroom	6'2"
Beam	13'9"	Fuel	396 gals.
Draft	2'11"	Water	85 gals.
Weight	16,500#	Hull Type	Modified-V
Clearance	9'7"	Deadrise Aft	14°

Tiara 3600 Open

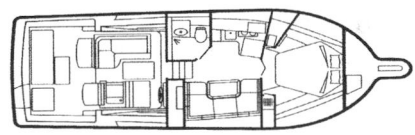

2005 Current

Handsome dual-purpose express with signature Tiara styling blurs the line between hard-core fishing boat, deluxe family cruiser. Posh interior with solid teak joinery, Ultraleather dinette (with flip-up backrest) sleeps five. Professional-grade cockpit features aft-facing seats, in-deck fishboxes, transom livewell, fold-down transom seat. Bridgedeck lifts for engine access. Note aggressive nonskid, tilt-away dash, sturdy windshield. Cummins 380hp diesels cruise at 26–28 knots. Newer models with 370hp Volvo IPS drives cruise efficiently at 28 knots.

See Page 564 For Value Estimates

Length	36'5"	Fuel	400 gals.
Beam	13'3"	Water	70 gals.
Draft	3'5"	Waste	30 gals.
Weight	19,100#	Hull Type	Modified-V
Clearance	9'10"	Deadrise Aft	18°

Tiara 3600 Sovran

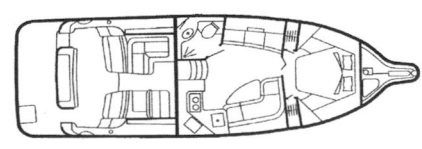

2004–06

Premium sportcruiser with semi-enclosed helm combines sleek styling with luxury-class accommodations. Sumptuous interior with wide-open salon is highlighted by solid teak cabinetry, Corian counters, leather upholstery. Bi-level cockpit features L-lounge opposite helm, aft-facing seats, foldaway rear seat, full wet bar. Hardtop with opening hatches was standard. Bridgedeck lifts for engine access. Note large transom locker, extended swim platform. Standard 385hp V-drive gas engines cruise 22–23 knots; 380hp Cummins diesels cruise at 24 knots.

See Page 546 For Value Estimates

Length w/Pulpit	41'8"	Fuel	326 gals.
Hull Length	36'4"	Water	105 gals.
Beam	13'0"	Waste	40 gals.
Draft	3'8"	Hull Type	Modified-V
Weight	18,000#	Deadrise Aft	19°

Cruisers & Sedans

Tiara 3700 Open

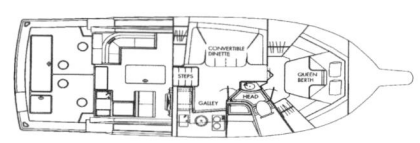

1995–2000

Well-built sport express with handsome lines matched Tiara promise of leading-edge versatility, quality amenities, durable construction. Upscale cabin with solid teak joinery, leather upholstery features huge U-shaped dinette, surprisingly roomy galley, private bow stateroom. Topside amenities include L-shaped companion seat with aft-facing double seat, cockpit fishboxes, cooler. Radar arch, foldaway rear cockpit seat were popular options. Note wide side decks. Bridgedeck lifts for engine access. Cat 435hp diesels cruise in the mid 20s (30+ top).

See Page 546 For Value Estimates

Length w/Pulpit	39'8"	Fuel	411 gals.
Hull Length	37'1"	water	98 gals.
Beam	14'2"	Waste	40 gals.
Draft	3'9"	Hull Type	Modified-V
Weight	21,800#	Deadrise Aft	18°

Tiara 3800 Open

2001–08

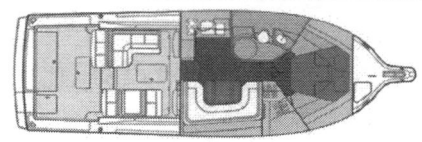

Plan A

Plan B

Dual-purpose express splits the difference between luxury sportcruiser, tournament-class fishing machine. Beautifully finished interior features posh seating, solid teak cabinetry, first-rate galley appliances. Note appealing teak-and-holly cabin sole, hideaway salon TV. Topside highlights include cockpit wet bar, foldaway transom seat, wide transom door. Note stylish reverse transom. Bridgedeck lifts for engine access. Hardtop with overhead hatches was optional. Cummins 480hp diesels cruise at 25–26 knots (about 30 knots top).

See Page 564 For Value Estimates

Length Overall	40'9"	Fuel	411 gals.
Beam	14'2"	Water	110 gals.
Draft	3'6"	Waste	40 gals.
Weight	22,600#	Hull Type	Modified-V
Clearance	9'7"	Deadrise Aft	18°

Tiara 3900 Open

2009–Current

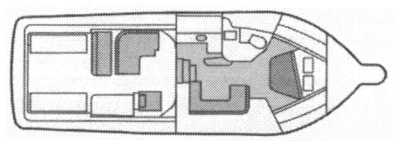

Quality dual-purpose express with wide 15' beam turns up the volume on features important to anglers and cruisers alike. Highlights include elegant single-stateroom interior with teak-and-holly sole, big 95-sq.ft. fishing cockpit with in-deck fishboxes, swivel L-shaped companion lounge, meticulous engine compartment. Note raised 3-person mezzanine seating aft of helm deck. Fishing package includes 55-gallon transom livewell, deluxe tackle center. Hardtop is optional. Cummins 600hp diesels cruise at 30 knots (low 30s top).

See Page 546 For Value Estimates

Length w/Pulpit	41'11"	Fuel	535 gals.
Beam	15'0"	Water	120 gals.
Draft	3'6"	Waste	38 gals.
Weight	24,500#	Hull Type	Modified-V
Clearance, Top	10'4"	Deadrise Aft	18°

Tiara 3900 Sovran

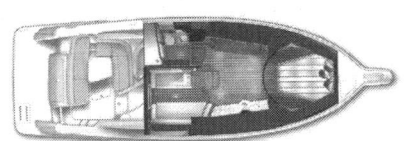

2007–Current

Bold hardtop express designed around Volvo's IPS pod drives makes good on Tiara promise of cutting-edge engineering, exceptional build quality. Very spacious interior with quality teak joinery, large galley has unique lounge area aft complete with facing leather settees, flat-screen TV. Cockpit and bridgedeck seating are protected by standard hardtop. Note extended swim platform, transom storage locker. IPS joystick control provides truly precise handling. Volvo 370hp diesels cruise economically at 26 knots (30+ knots wide open).

See Page 546 For Value Estimates

Length	39'3"	Fuel	300 gals.
Beam	13'3"	Water	102 gals.
Draft	3'5"	Waste	38 gals.
Weight	23,000#	Hull Type	Modified-V
Clearance	10'3"	Deadrise Aft	14.5°

Tiara 4000 Express

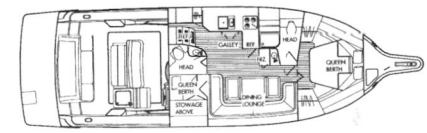

1994–2003

Standard Floorplan

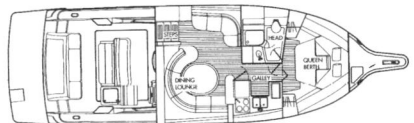

Optional Layout

Blue-chip Tiara express introduced in 1994 earned a reputation for timeless styling, yacht-grade accommodations, impressive owner satisfaction. Standard midcabin interior with two heads, open galley sleeps six; alternate floorplan offers greatly expanded salon but no aft cabin. Twin transom doors open to extended swim platform; transom trunk stows bikes, dive equipment. Center section of cockpit sole lifts for engine access. Hardtop was a popular option. Cruise at 23–34 knots with 450hp Cummins or Cat diesels (high 20s top).

See Page 546 For Value Estimates

Length w/Pulpit	43'6"	Fuel	444 gals.
Hull Length	40'6"	Water	160 gals.
Beam	14'6"	Waste	57 gals.
Draft	4'0"	Hull Type	Modified-V
Weight	26,500#	Deadrise Aft	18°

Tiara 4100 Open

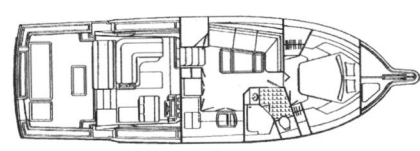

1996–2002

Muscular big-water express with spacious cockpit, upscale interior blurs the line between tournament-grade fishing machine, executive-class sportcruiser. Classy single-stateroom interior includes big U-shaped dinette, open galley with plenty of storage, very roomy head. Raised bridgedeck, three steps above cockpit, provides exceptional helm visibility. Large cockpit boasts beefy transom door, engine room entry door. Wide side decks are always a plus. Cat 435hp diesels cruise at 22 knots (26–27 knots top).

See Page 546 For Value Estimates

Length w/Pulpit	43'6"	Fuel	524 gals.
Hull Length	41'3"	Water	130 gals.
Beam	14'8"	Waste	50 gals.
Draft	3'6"	Hull Type	Modified-V
Weight	27,500#	Deadrise Aft	18°

Cruisers & Sedans

Tiara 4200 Open

2003–09

Plan A

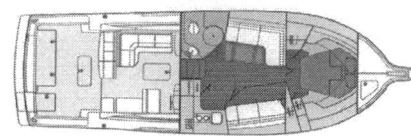

Plan B

See Page 546 For Value Estimates

Bold Tiara sportcruiser with world-class styling, deluxe accommodations combines sportfishing muscle with cruising elegance. Plan A interior has portside lounge/dinette with galley and head opposite; Plan B adds starboard lounge with curtain or solid enclosure, creating second stateroom. Big 85-sq.ft. cockpit—with engine room entry, foldaway rear seat—can be configured for fishing, diving, or cruising. Note fiberglass windshield frame, superb helm layout. Hardtop was optional. Cummins 670hp diesels cruise at 28 knots (32–33 knots top).

Length w/Pulpit	44'10"	Fuel	520 gals.
Hull Length	42'6"	Water	130 gals.
Beam	14'11"	Waste	50 gals.
Draft	4'2"	Hull Type	Modified-V
Weight	28,600#	Deadrise Aft	17.5°

Tiara 4300 Open

1991–2002

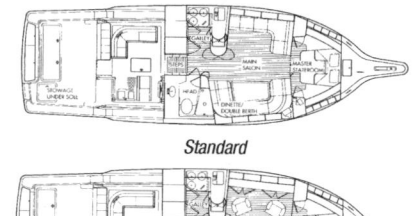

Standard

Optional

See Page 546 For Value Estimates

Big multipurpose express with fishboat cockpit, luxury-class accommodations set Tiara's 1990 standards for engineering excellence, state-of-the-art construction. Standard interior with convertible L-shaped lounge, convertible dinette sleeps six; optional layout with enlarged salon sleeps four. Note hydraulic salon operated dinette, elegant teak-and-holly sole. Cockpit redesign in 1999 added fold-down rear seat, direct access to engine room. Cruise at 25 knots with 550hp GM 6V92s; 26–27 knots with 660hp Cats.

Length w/Pulpit	46'7"	Fuel	526 gals.
Hull Length	43'2"	Water	150 gals.
Beam	15'2"	Waste	62 gals.
Draft	4'0"	Hull Type	Modified-V
Weight	29,500#	Deadrise Aft	16°

Tiara 4300 Sovran

2006–10

See Page 546 For Value Estimates

Luxury-class sportyacht was the first American boat designed specifically for Volvo's then new IPS pod-drive system. Posh interior is big for a 40-footer—since IPS permits smaller engine room, designers were able to include second stateroom with head. Note TV built into salon bulkhead. Above-deck layout features raised helmdeck seating, state-of-the-art helm, wraparound cockpit settee. Volvo 370hp diesels cruise at 22–23 knots; optional 425hp Volvos cruise in the high 20s. One of Tiara's best-selling models ever with over 100 sold.

Length w/Pulpit	45'3"	Fuel	375 gals.
Hull Length	40'2"	Water	110 gals.
Beam	14'9"	Waste	50 gals.
Draft	3'7"	Hull Type	Modified-V
Weight	26,800#	Deadrise Aft	17°

Cruisers & Sedans

Tiara 4400/4700 Sovran

2003–08

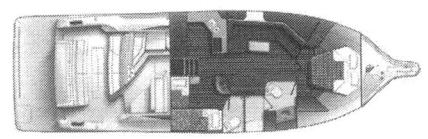

World-class sportcruiser (called 4400 Sovran in 2003–06, 4700 Sovran in 2007–08) with semi-enclosed helm-deck boasts heightened levels of Tiara luxury, comfort, finish. Expansive twin-stateroom interior with solid teak wood-work, Corian counters, Ultraleather seating sleeps five. Note washer/dryer concealed in aft stateroom. No salon access to ei-ther head. Additional features include power helm seat, hydraulic cockpit tables. Engine room is a tight fit. Cummins 670hp diesels cruise at 26–28 knots; 715hp Cummins cruise in the low 30s.

See Page 546 For Value Estimates

Length w/Pulpit	50'4"	Fuel	526 gals.
Hull Length	43'8"	Water	150 gals.
Beam	14'6"	Waste	50 gals.
Draft	4'5"	Hull Type	Modified-V
Weight	33,150#	Deadrise Aft	17°

Tiara 5000 Express

1999–2003

Std. Two-Stateroom

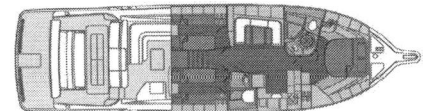

Opt. Three-Stateroom

See Page 546 For Value Estimates

Sophisticated sportcruiser (called 5200 Express in 2003) combines powerful styling with yacht-grade accommoda-tions, top-tier build quality. Richly appointed interior boasts beautifully crafted teak cabinetry, Ultraleather upholstery, top-quality furnishings. Plan A features two-stateroom layout with huge salon; Plan B has three staterooms, smaller salon. Electric cockpit tables rise for dining, lower for use as sun pad. Swim platform supports dinghy or PWC. Note huge transom locker. Cat 800hp V-drive diesels cruise at 26–28 knots.

Length w/Pulpit	55'0"	Fuel	700 gals.
Hull Length	50'9"	Water	200 gals.
Beam	15'11"	Waste	80 gals.
Draft	5'1"	Hull Type	Modified-V
Weight	38,600#	Deadrise Aft	17°

Tiara 5200 Sovran Salon

2003–06

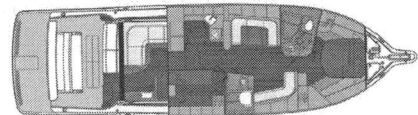

Plan A

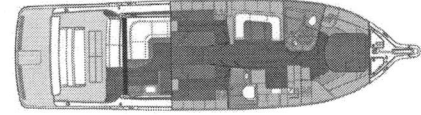

Plan A

See Page 546 For Value Estimates

Distinctly American sportcruiser with fully enclosed com-mand bridge is stylish, luxurious, expensive. Posh interior blends solid teak cabinetry, premium furnishings, Ultra-leather upholstery. Standard two-stateroom layout boasts huge salon, aft galley; optional three-stateroom floorplan has galley forward in salon. Highlights include electric cockpit table, cockpit engine room access, salon wet bar, power sunroof in hardtop. Exemplary finish. Swim platform is designed to carry PWC. Cat 865hp diesels cruise at 26–28 knots (30+ top).

Length w/Pulpit	58'3"	Fuel	700 gals.
Hull Length	50'9"	Water	200 gals.
Beam	15'11"	Waste	80 gals.
Draft	5'1"	Hull Type	Modified-V
Weight	49,000#	Deadrise Aft	17°

Cruisers & Sedans

Cruisers & Sedans

Tollycraft 30 Sport Cruiser

1985–92

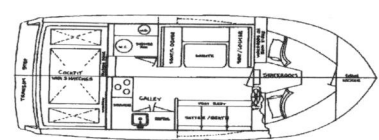

Good-looking small cruiser with step-down interior combines quality construction with common-sense layout. Wide 11'6" beam allows for extremely roomy cabin with private V-berth, enclosed head/shower, convertible dinette, complete galley. Large cockpit with integral swim platform doubles as entertainment center or fishing platform. Flybridge—big for a 30-footer—seats six adults. Note fuel increase to 198 gallons in 1988. Transom door, radar arch, bow pulpit were standard. Twin 260hp gas engines cruise at 20 knots (around 28 knots top).

Prices Not Provided for Pre-1995 Models

Length	30'6"	Water	42 gals.
Beam	11'6"	Fuel	150/198 gals.
Draft	2'7"	Cockpit	45 sq. ft.
Weight	11,500#	Hull Type	Modified-V
Clearance	11'8"	Deadrise Aft	10°

Tollycraft 34 Sport Sedan

1987–93

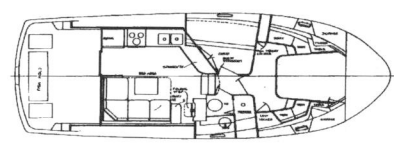

Feature-packed sedan hits the right buttons with Tollycraft enthusiasts focused on quality construction, versatile accommodations. Well-appointed interior with solid teak cabinetry boasts two private staterooms—no small achievement in a 34-foot boat. Transom door, in-deck fishbox were standard in small cockpit. Flybridge was offered with helm aft for East Coast buyers, helm forward for Pacific market. Wide side decks are a plus. Note fuel increase beginning with 1988 models. Twin 340hp gas engines cruise at 20 knots (high 20s top).

Prices Not Provided for Pre-1995 Models

Length	34'0"	Cockpit	72 sq. ft.
Beam	12'6"	Fuel	200/296 gals.
Draft	2'10"	Water	116 gals.
Weight	17,000#	Hull Type	Modified-V
Clearance	13'11"	Deadrise Aft	13°

Tollycraft 40 Sport Sedan

1987–95

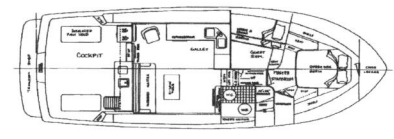

1987–88

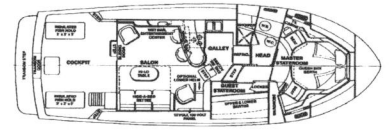

1989–1995

See Page 546 For Value Estimates

Appealing sports convertible with signature Tollycraft styling combines large fishing cockpit with roomy cabin accommodations. Two-stateroom interior—completely updated in 1989—is notable for upscale appointments, large windows, generous storage. Lower helm was optional. Cockpit amenities include two in-deck fishboxes, centerline transom door. Big fuel capacity delivers excellent range. Flybridge was offered with helm forward or aft. Cat 375hp diesels cruise at 22 knots (25 knots top); 485hp GMs cruise in the mid 20s (30 knots wide open).

Length	40'2"	Fuel	500 gals.
Beam	14'8"	Water	140 gals.
Draft	3'0"	Cockpit	100 sq. ft.
Weight	26,000#	Hull Type	Modified-V
Clearance	12'4"	Deadrise Aft	10°

Trojan 8.6 Meter Mid-Cabin

1987–90

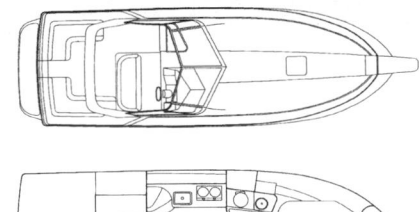

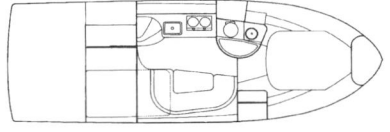

Sporty 1980s express combined sporty styling with large, open-air cockpit, roomy accommodations. Eurostyle interior features private bow stateroom, complete galley, large U-shaped dinette, compact double berth aft. Single-level cockpit has triple-wide elevated helm seat, removable bench seating at the transom, centerline transom gate. Helm was updated in 1989. Radar arch was a popular option. Note narrow side decks, sturdy bow rails. Standard 260hp gas sterndrives cruise at 25 knots and reach a top speed in the mid 30s.

Prices Not Provided for Pre-1995 Models

Length	28'8"	Water	40 gals.
Beam	10'6"	Fuel	140 gals.
Draft	2'2"	Cockpit	NA
Weight	9,500#	Hull Type	Modified-V
Clearance	8'7"	Deadrise Aft	14°

Trojan 10 Meter Express

1981–89

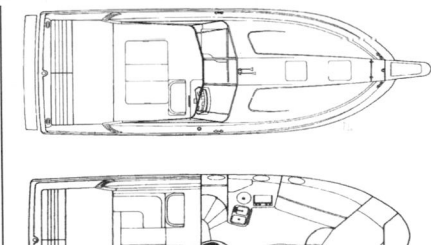

Bold 1980s express with mega-wide 13' beam, Eurostyle interior was considered a breakthrough design for Trojan. Huge cockpit offers plenty of room for fishing, diving, entertaining. Wide-open interior with curved bulkheads features electrically operated doors to master stateroom and head, convertible dinette, convertible settee. Note curved companionway steps, excellent engine access, plentiful stowage. Standard 350hp gas engines cruise at 19–20 knots with a top speed in the high 20s. Over 600 were built.

Prices Not Provided for Pre-1995 Models

Length	33'0"	Water	40 gals.
Beam	13'0"	Fuel	242 gals.
Draft	2'0"	Waste	40 gals.
Weight	11,250#	Hull Type	Modified-V
Clearance	9'4"	Deadrise Aft	9°

Trojan 10 Meter Mid-Cabin

1986–92

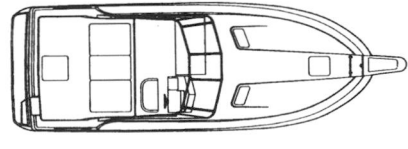

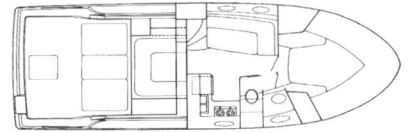

Bold Trojan express with broad 13' beam offers the cockpit, cabin dimensions of much larger boat. Expansive interior with private bow stateroom, home-sized galley, head with separate stall shower, sleeps six. Big cockpit with double-wide helm seats provides plenty of entertaining, fishing space. Additional features include radar arch, bow pulpit, good engine access. Updates in 1989 included bolt-on swim platform, powdercoated deck rails. Cruise at 17–18 knots with standard 350hp gas engines (mid 20s wide open).

Prices Not Provided for Pre-1995 Models

Length	33'0"	Water	55 gals.
Beam	13'0"	Fuel	250 gals.
Draft	2'0"	Waste	40 gals.
Weight	12,500#	Hull Type	Modified-V
Clearance	9'4"	Deadrise Aft	9°

Cruisers & Sedans

Trojan 10 Meter Sedan

1982–89

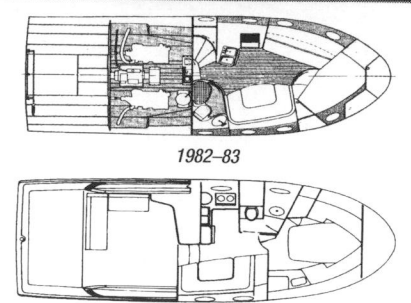

1982–83

1984–89

Prices Not Provided for Pre-1995 Models

Rakish sedan cruiser from the 1980s packs surprising living space into a modest 33-foot length. Original Eurostyle interior with curved bulkheads was poorly received—an offset companionway (rare in any convertible) isolated the salon from lower-level dinette and galley. Revised layout in 1984 proved much more popular. Note that lower helm was standard in pre-1987 models. Flybridge is small for a boat this size. No cockpit transom door. Standard 350hp gas engines cruise at 18 knots (mid 20s top).

Length	33'0"	Water	40/55 gals.
Beam	13'0"	Fuel	242 gals.
Draft	2'0"	Cockpit	60 sq. ft.
Weight	14,250#	Hull Type	Modified-V
Clearance	12'2"	Deadrise Aft	9°

Trojan 10.8 Meter Express

1991–92

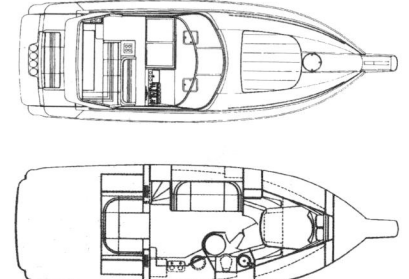

Prices Not Provided for Pre-1995 Models

Sporty express cruiser was introduced by Trojan just before the company declared bankruptcy in 1992. Spacious mid-cabin interior with private bow stateroom boasts full galley, convertible dinette, stand-up head with separate stall shower. Entire deck aft of helm can be raised at the push of a button for engine access. Note twin transom gates, foredeck sun pad, sport-style dash design. Deep-V hull delivers good open-water ride. Twin 355hp V-drive gas engines cruise at 18 knots and reach 26–28 knots wide open.

Length w/Pulpit	39'4"	Fuel	280 gals.
Hull Length	35'5"	Water	70 gals.
Beam	13'2"	Waste	40 gals.
Draft	3'7"	Hull Type	Deep-V
Weight	19,572#	Deadrise Aft	20°

Trojan 10.8 Meter Sedan

1986–92

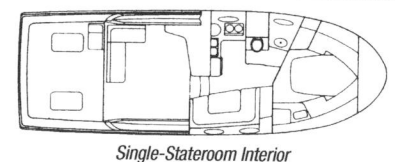

Single-Stateroom Interior

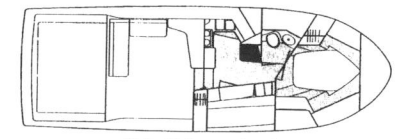

Twin-Stateroom Interior

Prices Not Provided for Pre-1995 Models

Stretched version of Trojan's earlier 10 Meter Sedan (1982–89) boasts larger cockpit, increased fuel capacity. Standard single-stateroom interior with expansive salon was updated in 1989 to include a stall shower in the head—a modification that took some elbow space out of the bow stateroom. Two-stateroom floorplan also became available in 1989. Note compact engine room, narrow side decks. No transom door. Standard 350hp gas engines cruise at 17–18 knots and reach a top speed in the mid 20s.

Length	35'4"	Fuel	325 gals.
Beam	13'0"	Water	55 gals.
Draft	2'4"	Cockpit	87 sq. ft.
Weight	15,000#	Hull Type	Modified-V
Clearance	12'2"	Deadrise Aft	9°

Trojan 350/360 Express

1995–2001

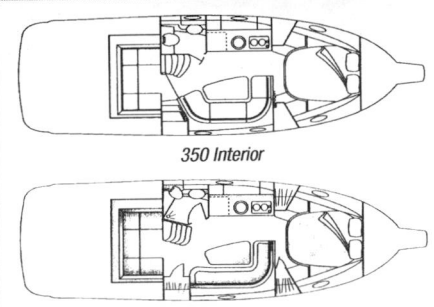

350 Interior

360 Layout

See Page 546 For Value Estimates

Inboard power distinguishes this otherwise-generic express from her contemporary, sterndrive-powered competitors. Roomy midcabin interior is arranged with double berths fore and aft, convertible dinette, roomy head with sink and shower. Sliding door (instead of a curtain) provides forward stateroom privacy. Bridgedeck has triple-wide helm seat, wet bar, wrap-around lounge seating. Twin 320hp V-drive gas inboards cruise at 15–16 knots (mid 20s top). Marketed as the Trojan 350 Express in 1995–98; 360 Express in 1999–2002.

Length w/Pulpit	37'8"	Fuel	220 gals.
Beam	12'0"	Water	60 gals.
Draft	2'10"	Waste	30 gals.
Weight	16,500#	Hull Type	Modified-V
Clearance	9'8"	Deadrise Aft	16.5°

Trojan 11 Meter Express

1983–89

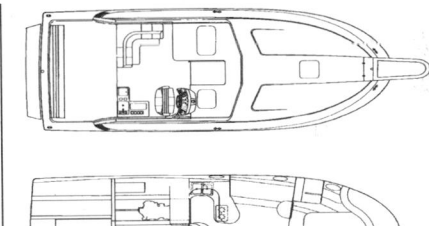

Prices Not Provided for Pre-1995 Models

Bold 1980s express with mega-wide beam, signature Delta-Conic hull design, took Trojan styling, luxury to the next level. So-called Eurostyle interior—dated by modern sportboat standards—is a blend of curved bulkheads, indirect lighting, off-white laminates. Note owner's stateroom vanity, privacy door. L-shaped galley extends well into the salon, which interrupts traffic flow. Bow pulpit, radar arch, swim platform were standard. Twin 350hp gas engines cruise at 18 knots (26–27 knots top); 375hp Cat diesels cruise at 24 knots (about 27 knots top).

Length	37'6"	Fuel	350 gals.
Beam	14'0"	Water	100 gals.
Draft	3'3"	Headroom	6'3"
Weight	16,800#	Hull Type	Modified-V
Clearance	9'4"	Deadrise Aft	14°

Trojan 11 Meter Express

1990–92

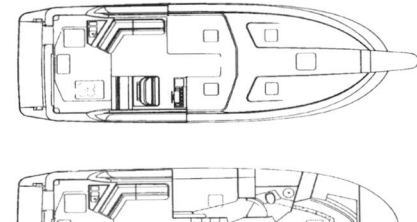

Prices Not Provided for Pre-1995 Models

Updated version of original Trojan 11 Meter Express (1983–89) set class standards in early 1990s for leading-edge styling, luxury-class accommodations. Unusual cabin layout has portside stateroom with double berth, forward dinette area, huge head compartment. Cockpit is arranged with L-shaped lounge seating forward, wet bar, bench seating aft. Radar arch, bow pulpit, transom door were standard. Note wide side decks. Twin 360hp gas engines cruise at 18 knots; optional 425hp Cat diesels cruise at 24–25 knots.

Length w/Pulpit	39'0"	Fuel	350 gals.
Beam	14'0"	Water	100 gals.
Draft	3'3"	Headroom	6'4"
Weight	16,800#	Hull Type	Modified-V
Clearance	9'4"	Deadrise Aft	14°

Cruisers & Sedans

Trojan 370/390/400 Express

1993–2002

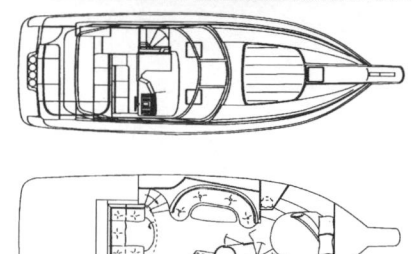

Deluxe family express (called Trojan 370 Express in 1993–94; 390 Express in 1995–97; 400 Express in 1998–2002) offered comfort, performance at economy-class price. Generic midcabin interior features large galley, head with stall shower, good-sized bow stateroom with private head access. Aft cockpit sole lifts for access to engine compartment. Update in 1998 added extended swim platform. Twin 320hp V-drive gas inboards cruise at 18 knots (26–27 knots top); optional 330hp Cummins diesels cruise in the mid 20s.

See Page 547 For Value Estimates

Length w/Pulpit	41'2"	Fuel	280 gals.
Hull Length	35'5"	Water	91 gals.
Beam	13'6"	Waste	52 gals.
Draft	3'7"	Hull Type	Modified-V
Weight	19,500#	Deadrise Aft	17°

Trojan 12 Meter Convertible

1986–92

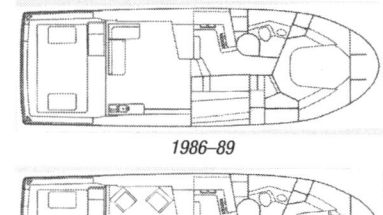

1986–89

1990–92

Prices Not Provided for Pre-1995 Models

Sporty 1990s convertible combined posh accommodations with bold hull graphics, unusually wide beam. Expansive two-stateroom, galley-down layout features spacious salon with breakfast bar, home-sized galley, island berth in forward stateroom. Large 110-sq.-ft. cockpit has two in-deck fishboxes, dual washdowns, wide transom door, tackle center. Note wraparound salon windows. Flybridge is small for a 40-footer. Cat 375hp diesels cruise at 22 knots (mid 20s top); 485hp Detroits cruise at 25 knots (about 30 knots top).

Length	39'9"	Water	100 gals.
Beam	14'3"	Fuel	400 gals.
Draft	3'6"	Cockpit	110 sq. ft.
Weight	19,000#	Hull Type	Modified-V
Clearance	12'6"	Deadrise Aft	12°

Trojan 12 Meter Express

1989–92

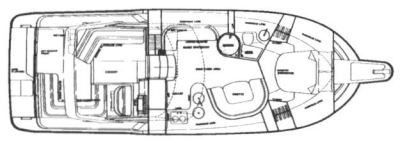

Handsome 40-foot express introduced in 1989 raised the bar in her day for bold styling, deluxe accommodations, leading-edge amenities. Highlights include huge cockpit with fore and aft seating, full wraparound windshield, high-style helm, molded boarding steps, wide-open interior with berths for six. Hidden privacy curtain converts portside settee into a unique stateroom with over/under berths. Note wide side decks, in-deck storage well for inflatable. Optional 485hp GM diesels cruise at 26–27 knots (about 30 knots top).

Prices Not Provided for Pre-1995 Models

Length	39'9"	Water	95 gals.
Beam	14'3"	Fuel	325 gals.
Draft	3'8"	Headroom	6'4"
Weight	18,000#	Hull Type	Modified-V
Clearance	NA	Deadrise Aft	12°

Cruisers & Sedans

Trojan 13 Meter Express

1984–90

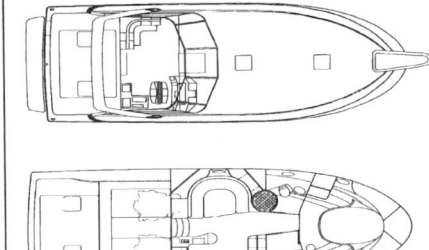

Compelling 1980s sportcruiser offered signature Trojan styling, comfort in one of the largest express cruisers of her era. Super-wide 16'3" beam blew away the competition; colorful hull graphics of early models was very distinctive. Enormous interior features two private staterooms, huge U-shaped dinette, king-sized galley. Note push-button bow stateroom door, circular stall shower, power high/low dinette table, power windshield vent. Lack of cockpit transom door is truly puzzling. Detroit 735hp diesels cruise at a fast 30 knots (32+ knots top).

Prices Not Provided for Pre-1995 Models

Length	43'0"	Fuel	510 gals.
Beam	16'3"	Water	175 gals.
Draft	3'2"	Waste	75 gals.
Weight	24,000#	Hull Type	Modified-V
Clearance	10'1"	Deadrise Aft	12°

Trojan 440 Express

1995–2002

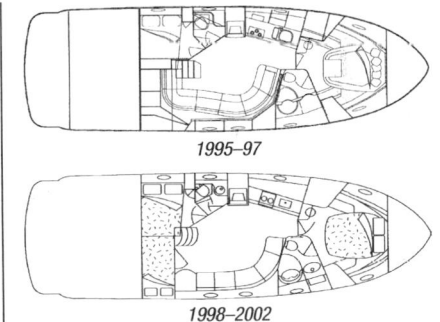

1995–97

1998–2002

See Page 547 For Value Estimates

Head-turning express yacht with rakish lines, luxury interior offered late 1990s buyers an impressive mix of sportboat styling, competitive price. Well-finished two-stateroom interior (updated in 1998 with third stateroom) includes wraparound salon seating, home-size galley. Aft cockpit seating converts into huge sun pad. Choice of hydraulic high/low swim platform (for PWC) or standard extended platform. Good engine access. Cummins 450hp V-drive diesels cruise at 22 knots (25–26 knots top).

Length	44'7"	Fuel	432 gals.
Beam	15'0"	Water	104 gals.
Draft	4'0"	Waste	88 gals.
Weight	30,000#	Hull Type	Modified-V
Clearance	10'11"	Deadrise Aft	16.5°

Viking Sport Cruisers V50 Express

1999–2005

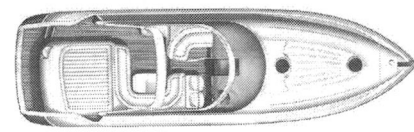

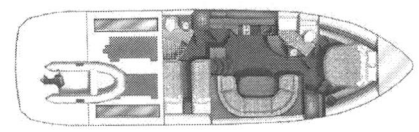

See Page 547 For Value Estimates

Finely crafted Eurocruiser with classic Med styling splits the difference between hard-charging sportboat, luxurious coastal cruiser. Elegant cherrywood interior features two private cabins with en suite heads, concealed galley, leather U-shaped salon sofa. Large cockpit with wet bar, contoured seating accommodates several guests. Good helm ergonomics. Transom garage is concealed under aft sun pad. Note teak cockpit sole, good engine room access. Cruise at 28 knots (32–33 knots wide open) with Volvo 610hp inboards.

Length Overall	51'0"	Water	105 gals.
Beam	14'1"	Clearance	11'5"
Draft	3'6"	Headroom	6'3"
Weight	35,840#	Hull Type	Deep-V
Fuel	490 gals.	Deadrise Aft	21°

Cruisers & Sedans

Viking Sport Cruisers V58 Express

2003–10

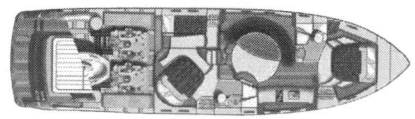

High-impact Eurocruiser with folding sunroof, tender garage makes good on Viking promise of unrivaled luxury, unsurpassed performance. Teak-planked cockpit boasts U-shaped seating and dining area, wet bar with refrigerator, electric grill. Double helm seat converts to leaning post for stand-up driving. Opulent interior sleeps six in three staterooms. Note sub-floor galley storage. Additional features include spacious engine room, hidden galley appliances, parquet salon floor. MAN 860hp engines cruise at 30 knots (34–35 knots top).

See Page 548 For Value Estimates

Length	58'11"	Fuel	660 gals.
Beam	15'5"	Water	125 gals.
Draft	3'6"	Waste	54 gals.
Weight	44,800#	Hull Type	Deep-V
Clearance	16'6"	Deadrise Aft	19°

Viking Sport Cruisers V65 Express

2000–04

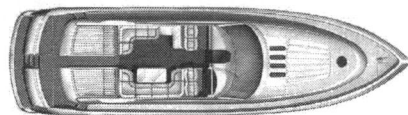

High-performance sportcruiser with aggressive styling, retractable sunroof is easy to praise, hard to fault. Standard hardtop offers security of a protected helm and—with sunroof retracted—the enjoyment of an open express. Principal features include luxurious cherrywood interior, twin transom garages (one for small tender, one for PWC), superb helm layout, large galley with serving counter and concealed appliances. Note compact engine room, wide side decks, teak-laid cockpit. MAN 1,300hp engines top out at a fast 36–38 knots.

Insufficient Resale Data to Assign Values

Length Overall	65'2"	Fuel	960 gals.
Beam	16'11"	Water	180 gals.
Draft	4'5"	Headroom	6'6"
Weight	64,752#	Hull Type	Deep-V
Clearance	14'3"	Deadrise Aft	21°

Wellcraft 2700 Martinique

1994–95

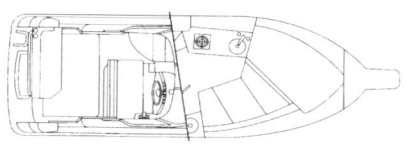

Generic 27-foot family express from the 1990s offered rakish styling, impressive space at an affordable price. Highlights include expansive cockpit with seating for six, walkthrough windshield, spacious midcabin interior with convertible dinette, complete galley, enclosed head with shower. Note excellent cabin headroom, generous storage. Space at helm for extra electronics. Bow pulpit, transom shower were standard. Not the prettiest boat on the water. Single 300hp Volvo I/O will cruise at 22 knots (mid 30s top).

See Page 548 For Value Estimates

Length w/Pulpit	28'4"	Fuel	100 gals.
Hull Length	26'6"	Water	22 gals.
Beam	9'6"	Waste	15 gals.
Draft	3'0"	Hull Type	Modified-V
Weight	6,950#	Deadrise Aft	17°

Wellcraft 2800 Martinique

1997–99

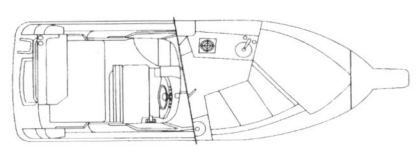

Restyled version of earlier Wellcraft 2700 Martinique (1994–95) offered express-boat space, versatility at a competitive price. Highlights include roomy cockpit with seating for six, walk-through windshield, comfortable midcabin interior with convertible dinette, full-service galley, enclosed head with shower. Note generous cabin headroom, space at helm for extra electronics. Radar arch, transom shower were standard. Single 310hp sterndrive will cruise at 22 knots (low 30s top); twin 190hp I/Os cruise at 25 knots (40 knots top).

See Page 548 For Value Estimates

Length w/Pulpit	28'4"	Fuel	100 gals.
Hull Length	26'6"	Water	22 gals.
Beam	9'6"	Waste	15 gals.
Draft	3'0"	Hull Type	Modified-V
Weight	7,100#	Deadrise Aft	17°

Wellcraft 2800 Martinique

2001 02

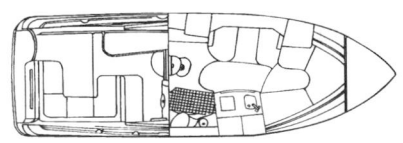

Generic sterndrive express with roomy midcabin interior combined durable construction with entry-level price. Cockpit amenities include double-wide helm seat with flip-up bolster, aft U-shaped lounge seating, power engine compartment hatch. Well-designed galley makes good use of limited space. Tilt wheel was standard; walk-through windshield provides easy bow access. Open-plan interior sleeps four adults, two kids. Twin 190hp MerCruiser I/Os cruise in the low 20s (35–36 knots top). Note that production lasted only two years.

See Page 548 For Value Estimates

Length	27'10"	Clearance w/Arch	8'6"
Beam	9'6"	Fuel	100 gals.
Draft, Up	2'0"	Water	28 gals.
Draft, Down	3'6"	Hull Type	Modified-V
Weight	6,600#	Deadrise Aft	20°

Wellcraft 2800 Monte Carlo

1986–89

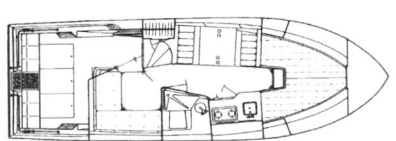

Entry-level 1980s sportboat lived up to Wellcraft promise of versatile layout, spirited performance at an affordable price. Roomy single-level cockpit with fold-down jump seat, removable transom seat is great for fishing, swimming, diving. Visibility from raised helm is very good. Open-plan interior with convertible dinette, complete galley, sleeps six. Note tall windshield, good engine access, standard bow pulpit. Beamy modified-V hull delivers stable, dry ride. Twin 260hp MerCruiser sterndrives cruise at 25 knots (35+ knots top).

Prices Not Provided for Pre-1995 Models

Length	27'7"	Clearance	NA
Beam	9'11"	Fuel	115 gals.
Draft, Up	1'9"	Water	28 gals.
Draft, Down	2'9"	Hull Type	Modified-V
Weight	7,200#	Deadrise Aft	16°

Cruisers & Sedans

Wellcraft 288 Suncruiser; 2900 Express

1981–87

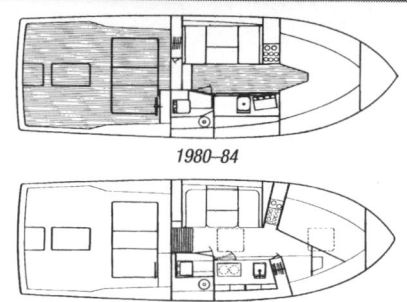

1980–84

1985–87

Prices Not Provided for Pre-1995 Models

Conservative family cruiser (called 288 Suncruiser in 1981–82; 2900 Express in 1983–87) gets high marks for spacious, uncluttered cockpit, dependable inboard power. Broad 10'8" beam makes this one of the roomiest boats in her class. Single-level cockpit with fold-out seats is great for fishing, diving, swimming. Simple interior, obviously dated by modern decor standards, offers the amenities required for comfortable cruising. Note limited fuel capacity. Twin 230hp MerCruiser gas engines cruise at 19–20 knots (high 20s top).

Length	28'8"	Fuel	120 gals.
Beam	10'8"	Water	28 gals.
Draft	2'6"	Cockpit	NA
Weight	9,000#	Hull Type	Modified-V
Clearance	7'4"	Deadrise Aft	16°

Wellcraft 3000 Martinique

1998–2002

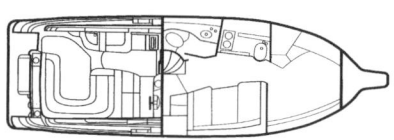

See Page 548 For Value Estimates

Sporty family cruiser introduced in 1998 delivered versatility, performance at an entry-level price. Wide 10'6" beam results in plenty of cockpit, cabin space. Roomy interior provides large salon, open midcabin area, roomy head with shower. Galley storage is increased by locating refrigerator under forward dinette seat. Well-planned cockpit with wraparound lounge, portside lounger seats eight. Note power engine compartment hatch, walk-through windshield. Twin 260hp MerCruiser I/Os cruise at 25 knots (about 40 knots top).

Length w/Pulpit	32'4"	Clearance	8'7"
Beam	10'6"	Fuel	160 gals.
Draft, Drives Up	2'3"	Water	41 gals.
Draft, Drives Down	3'1"	Hull Type	Modified-V
Weight	11,000#	Deadrise Aft	16°

Wellcraft 3200 Martinique

1994–2000

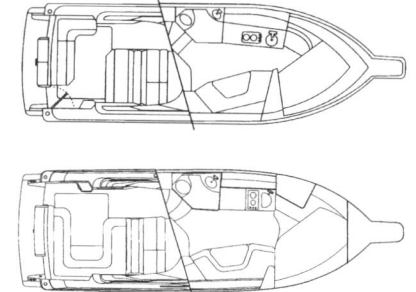

See Page 548 For Value Estimates

Maxi-volume express with generic midcabin layout appealed to entry-level boaters with an eye for value. Tasteful interior with U-shaped dinette boasts surprisingly large galley, spacious midcabin area, generous storage. Several cockpit seating schemes were offered over the years. Ergonomic helm layout has room for extra electronics. Note that oval hull ports replaced sliding cabin windows in 1997. Twin Volvo 310hp I/Os cruise at 25 knots (high 30s top). Inboard models with 320hp MerCruisers cruise at 22–23 knots (low 30s top).

Length w/Pulpit	34'5"	Fuel	162 gals.
Hull Length	32'0"	Water	43 gals.
Beam	11'2"	Waste	20 gals.
Draft	3'1"	Hull Type	Modified-V
Weight	10,300#	Deadrise Aft	16°

Cruisers & Sedans

Wellcraft 3200 St. Tropez

1985–93

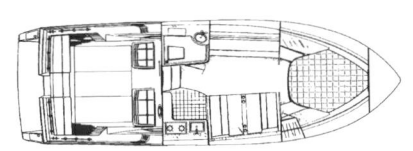

Hugely popular inboard express ranks among Wellcraft's best-selling family boats ever produced. Eurostyle decor with mauve-colored fabrics, brushed aluminum accents differed from traditional teak-trimmed interiors of her era. Several updates over the years—the most significant modification came in 1988 with addition of integral swim platform. Single-level cockpit is well-suited for fishing, entertaining. Engine room is a tight fit. Standard 260hp V-drive gas engines cruise at 20 knots (high 20s top). Over 1,700 were built.

Prices Not Provided for Pre-1995 Models

Length	31'8"	Fuel	180 gals.
Beam	11'8"	Water	40 gals.
Draft	2'10"	Waste	20 gals.
Weight	10,300#	Hull Type	Modified-V
Clearance	8'5"	Deadrise Aft	16°

Wellcraft 3300 Martinique

2001 02

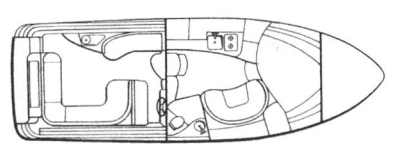

Stylish inboard cruiser with roomy accommodations, many standard features delivered the goods without breaking the bank. Generic midcabin interior with open-plan layout sleeps six. Well-planned cockpit features portside lounge forward, double helm seat, wraparound seating aft. Power hatch provides access to very well-organized engine compartment. Note walk-through windshield. Among several engine options, twin 310hp MerCruiser V-drive inboards cruise at 20 knots and reach a top speed of close to 30 knots.

See Page 548 For Value Estimates

Length	33'2"	Fuel	226 gals.
Beam	11'7"	Water	40 gals.
Draft	2'11"	Waste	35 gals.
Weight	11,000#	Hull Type	Deep-V
Clearance, Arch	9'0"	Deadrise Aft	22°

Wellcraft 34 Triumph Express

1991–93

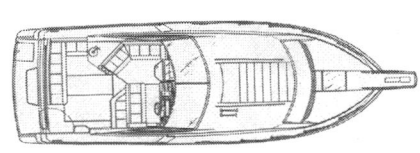

Roomy midcabin express from the early 90s offered family-size accommodations, comfort at a competitive price. Elevated helm deck permits expansive, single-level interior with private owner's stateroom, double-entry head, salon/galley area with convertible dinette. Midcabin berth is a tight fit for two adults. Note large cabin windows, storage boxes under cabin sole. Bi-level cockpit boasts sun lounge, aft wet bar, L-shaped rear seat. Three cockpit hatches provide good engine access. Cruise at 18–20 knots (high 20s top) with 330hp gas inboards.

Prices Not Provided for Pre-1995 Models

Length w/Pulpit	36'9"	Clearance	9'2"
Hull Length	34'0"	Fuel	226 gals.
Beam	12'6"	Water	46 gals.
Draft	3'0"	Hull Type	Modified-V
Weight	15,000#	Deadrise Aft	14°

Cruisers & Sedans

Wellcraft 34 Triumph Sedan

1990–93

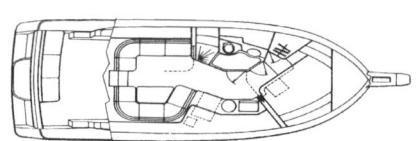

Maxi-volume 34-footer made good on Wellcraft promise of space, comfort, value. Single-level interior features wide-open salon with facing settees (both of which convert to double berths), huge head with separate stall shower, full-size galley, private forward stateroom. Pass-through from galley to flybridge is a nice touch. Note narrow side decks, roomy bridge, molded foredeck seating. So-so fit and finish. No race-horse, Crusader 300hp V-drive gas engines cruise at a sedate 15–16 knots (about 25 knots top).

Prices Not Provided for Pre-1995 Models

Length w/Pulpit	36'9"	Clearance	9'9"
Hull Length	34'0"	Fuel	256 gals.
Beam	12'6"	Water	60 gals.
Draft	3'0"	Hull Type	Modified-V
Weight	15,700#	Deadrise Aft	14°

Wellcraft 3400 Gran Sport

1984–92

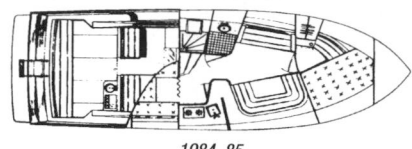

1984–85

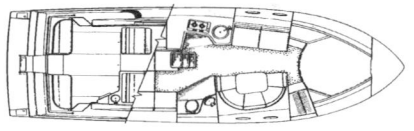

1986–92

Prices Not Provided for Pre-1995 Models

Beamy 1980s express with inboard power lived up to Wellcraft reputation for sporty styling, solid construction. Bulkhead-free interior allows for expansive salon with full-service galley, two-sleeper aft cabin, island double berth forward. Large single-level cockpit with wet bar can seat a small crowd without bumping elbows. Updates included new bolt-on reverse swim platform in 1988, white-on-white dash in 1990. So-so fit and finish. Standard 340hp gas engines cruise at 18 knots and reach a top speed of 26–28 knots.

Length w/Pulpit	35'5"	Clearance	9'4"
Length	33'7"	Fuel	270 gals.
Beam	12'6"	Water	75 gals.
Draft	3'0"	Hull Type	Modified-V
Weight	13,400#	Deadrise Aft	16°

Wellcraft 3500 Corsair; 3600 St. Tropez

1992–93

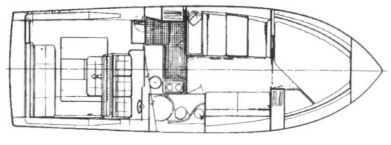

Contemporary 1990s cruiser with large cockpit, expansive interior delivered space, comfort at a competitive price. Considered a rakish boat by standards of her day with integrated swim platform, tall arch, sporty wraparound windshield. Cabin highlights include private forward stateroom, large head with separate stall shower, well-equipped galley, berths for six. Walk-through windshield provides easy bow access. Twin 400hp MerCruiser gas inboards (with V-drives) cruise at 18 knots (28–29 knots top). Note brief two-year production run.

Prices Not Provided for Pre-1995 Models

Length w/Pulpit	38'7"	Fuel	270 gals.
Hull Length	33'10"	Water	76 gals.
Beam	12'6"	Clearance, Arch	9'9"
Draft	2'9"	Hull Type	Modified-V
Weight	14,400#	Deadrise Aft	16°

Wellcraft 3600 Martinique

1994–2000

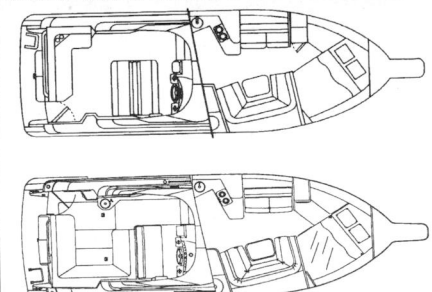

Popular 1990s sportcruiser delivered the space, amenities of more expensive competitors at a surprisingly affordable price. Conventional midcabin interior offers expansive salon with U-shaped dinette, well-equipped galley, separate stall shower in head. Several cockpit plans were offered over the years, all with wet bar, walk-through windshield. Additional features include radar arch, bow pulpit, well-arranged engine room. Prop pockets reduce draft, improve hull efficiency. MerCruiser 310hp V-drive inboards cruise at 18 knots (high 20s top).

See Page 549 For Value Estimates

Length w/Pulpit	38'0"	Clearance, Arch	9'10"
Hull Length	35'6"	Fuel	264 gals.
Beam	12'6"	Water	47 gals.
Draft	3'0"	Hull Type	Modified-V
Weight	15,000#	Deadrise Aft	16°

Wellcraft 3700 Corsica

1989–91

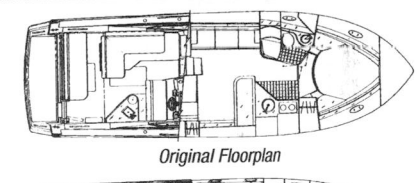

Original Floorplan

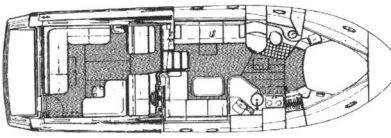

Revised Layout

Durable family express introduced in 1989 matched contemporary styling with spacious accommodations. Original midcabin interior with diminutive dinette—judged too confining—was replaced by all-new floorplan with combined breakfast bar/galley counter after hull #15. Bi-fold privacy door for owner's stateroom (instead of just a curtain) is a plus. Expansive single-level cockpit came with double-wide helm seat, wet bar, L-shaped lounge. So-so fit and finish. MerCruiser 380hp gas inboards cruise at 20 knots (high 20s top).

Prices Not Provided for Pre-1995 Models

Length	36'11"	Fuel	300 gals.
Beam	13'6"	Water	100 gals.
Draft	3'1"	Headroom	6'3"
Weight	16,800#	Hull Type	Modified-V
Clearance	9'9"	Deadrise Aft	16°

Wellcraft 3700 Martinique

2001–02

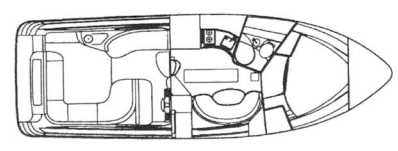

Stylish family cruiser introduced in 2001 matched Wellcraft claim of luxury-boat comfort at an affordable price. Big open-plan interior with cherry trim is arranged with double berths fore and aft, convertible dinette, private bow stateroom. Galley is on small side but storage is excellent. Inviting cockpit with double-wide helm seat, wet bar, portside lounger, seats eight. Note walk-through windshield, power engine-compartment hatch, transom shower. Twin 380hp MerCruiser V-drive gas engines cruise at 20 knots (about 30 knots top).

See Page 549 For Value Estimates

Length	36'11"	Fuel	288 gals.
Beam	13'0"	Water	57 gals.
Draft	3'4"	Waste	35 gals.
Weight	16,400#	Hull Type	Deep-V
Clearance	9'5"	Deadrise Aft	22°

Cruisers & Sedans

Wellcraft 38 Excalibur

1996–2002

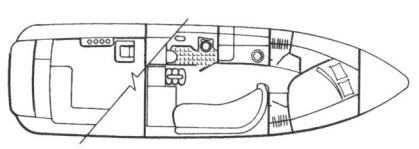

Sleek 38-foot sportster (built for Wellcraft by Aussie-based Riviera Marine) is part performance boat, part family cruiser. Chief attributes include smooth-riding deep-V hull, well-appointed interior, ergonomic helm, roomy cockpit with wet bar. Master stateroom has privacy door rather than curtain; helm seat can be adjusted electrically. Engine access—under aft cockpit seat—is very good, but side decks are narrow. Above-average fit and finish. MerCruiser 385hp gas sterndrives cruise at 30–32 knots and reach 40+ knots wide open.

See Page 549 For Value Estimates

Length	37'11"	Clearance	7'5"
Beam	10'8"	Fuel	240 gals.
Draft, Drive Up	2'3"	Water	60 gals.
Draft, Drive Down	3'2"	Hull Type	Deep-V
Weight	13,200#	Deadrise Aft	21°

Wellcraft 43 Portofino

1987–97

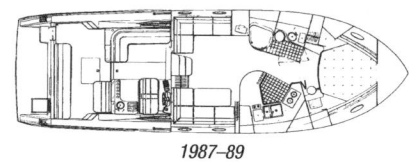

1987–89

1990–97

Popular big-water express set class standards in the late 1980s for bold styling, deluxe accommodations. Originally offered with expansive single-stateroom interior; revised two-stateroom layout became standard in 1990. Huge bi-level cockpit provides seating for a dozen guests. Bridgedeck hatch provides good engine access. Helm was redesigned in 1990. Prop pockets reduce draft, improve efficiency. Standard 340hp gas engines cruise at 15 knots (24–25 knots top); optional 375hp Cat diesels cruise at 20–22 knots (mid 20s top).

See Page 549 For Value Estimates

Length w/Pulpit	45'7"	Fuel	436 gals.
Hull Length	42'10"	Water	100 gals.
Beam	14'6"	Waste	20 gals.
Draft	3'0"	Hull Type	Modified-V
Weight	20,000#	Deadrise Aft	14°

Wellcraft 45 Excalibur

1995–2001

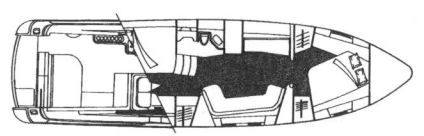

Sleek 45-footer (built by Riviera Marine in Australia) is one part performance boat, one part family cruiser. Highlights include well-appointed interior with premium furnishings, roomy cockpit with U-shaped lounge seating, excellent helm layout. Privacy doors (rather than curtains) separate both sleeping areas from main salon. Engine access—under aft cockpit seat—is very good. Side decks are quite narrow. Slender deep-V hull is agile, quick to accelerate. Big-block 415hp gas I/Os cruise at 28 knots (low 40s top).

See Page 549 For Value Estimates

Length	44'6"	Fuel	274 gals.
Beam	11'8"	Water	70 gals.
Draft	3'3"	Headroom	6'5"
Weight	15,000#	Hull Type	Deep-V
Clearance	8'6"	Deadrise Aft	21°

Cruisers & Sedans

About These Prices

Retail high-low values are provided for boats built since 1995 except in those cases where limited resale activity makes it impossible to come up with a reliable estimate. Prices are intended to provide readers with general price estimates only and are not meant to represent precise market values. Boat depreciation depends on local and national market conditions whose fluctuations are impossible to predict. The prices are intended for use from November, 2011 until November, 2012.

The *Retail High* is the estimated selling price of a clean, well-maintained boat with average equipment. The *Retail Low* is the estimated selling price of a boat showing below-average maintenance, limited equipment, and high-hour engines.

The prices quoted in the price pages apply to boats found in the Florida, Atlantic East Coast, and Gulf Coast markets. Prices for boats located in other regions must be adjusted as follows:

Great Lakes	Add 10 to 15%
Pacific Northwest	Add 5 to 10%
California	Add 5 to 10%
Inland Rivers & Lakes	Add 5 to 10%

Note that a series of six asterisks (******) means that pricing data is unavailable.

Year	Power	Retail Low	Retail High
Albemarle 27/280 Express (Inboard)			
2007	T280G	63,000	73,000
2007	T225D	86,000	99,000
2006	T280G	58,000	66,000
2006	T225D	78,000	90,000
2005	T280G	52,000	60,000
2005	T210D	71,000	82,000
2003	T300G	48,000	55,000
2003	T210D	65,000	74,000
2002	T300G	43,000	50,000
2002	T210D	59,000	68,000
2001	T300G	39,000	45,000
2001	T210D	53,000	62,000
2000	T300G	36,000	41,000
2000	T210D	49,000	56,000
1999	T300G	33,000	37,000
1999	T230D	44,000	51,000
1998	T300G	30,000	34,000
1998	T230D	41,000	47,000
1997	T290G	27,000	32,000
1997	T230D	37,000	43,000
1996	T290G	25,000	29,000
1996	T230D	34,000	40,000
1995	T290G	23,000	27,000
1995	T230D	32,000	36,000
Albemarle 290 XF			
2010	T315D	******	******
2009	T315D	193,000	225,000
2008	T315D	177,000	207,000
Albemarle 305/310 XF			
2010	T330D	******	******
2009	T330D	******	******

Year	Power	Retail Low	Retail High
2008	T330D	174,000	201,000
2007	T330D	159,000	182,000
2006	T330D	144,000	166,000
2005	T315D	131,000	151,000
2004	T315D	119,000	137,000
2003	T315D	109,000	125,000
2002	T300D	99,000	114,000
2001	T300D	90,000	103,000
2000	T300D	82,000	94,000
1999	T300D	75,000	86,000
1998	T300D	69,000	80,000
1997	T300D	64,000	73,000
1996	T300D	58,000	67,000
1995	T300D	54,000	62,000
Albemarle 320 Express			
2006	T350D	158,000	182,000
2005	T350D	144,000	165,000
2004	T350D	131,000	150,000
2003	T350D	119,000	137,000
2002	T350D	108,000	124,000
2001	T350D	98,000	113,000
2000	T350D	89,000	103,000
1999	T350D	81,000	94,000
1998	T350D	75,000	86,000
1997	T350D	69,000	79,000
1996	T300D	63,000	73,000
1995	T300D	58,000	67,000
Albemarle 325 Convertible			
2003	T350D	147,000	169,000
2002	T350D	134,000	154,000
2001	T350D	122,000	140,000
2000	T350D	111,000	128,000
1999	T300D	101,000	116,000

Year	Power	Retail Low	Retail High
1998	T300D	92,000	106,000
1997	T300D	83,000	96,000
1996	T300D	76,000	87,000
1995	T300D	69,000	79,000
Albemarle 330 XF			
2010	T425D	******	******
2009	T425D	280,000	330,000
2008	T425D	260,000	307,000
Albemarle 360 XF			
2009	T540D	******	******
2008	T575D	286,000	329,000
2007	T575D	263,000	302,000
2006	T575D	242,000	278,000
Albemarle 410 Convertible			
2009	T710D	******	******
2008	T725D	516,000	578,000
2007	T700D	470,000	526,000
2006	T700D	427,000	479,000
2005	T700D	389,000	436,000
Albemarle 410 XF			
2009	T710D	******	******
2008	T725D	477,000	534,000
2007	T700D	434,000	486,000
2006	T700D	395,000	442,000
2005	T700D	359,000	402,000
2004	T700D	327,000	366,000
2003	T660D	297,000	333,000
2002	T660D	271,000	303,000
Albin 27 Family Cruiser			
1995	216D	24,000	29,000

Year	Power	Retail Low	Retail High

Albin 28 Tournament Express

Year	Power	Retail Low	Retail High
2007	S315D	91,000	105,000
2006	S315D	88,000	101,000
2005	S370D	80,000	92,000
2004	S370D	73,000	84,000
2003	S370D	66,000	76,000
2002	S370D	61,000	70,000
2001	S370D	56,000	64,000
2000	S370D	51,000	59,000
1999	S370D	47,000	54,000
1998	S300D	43,000	50,000
1997	S300D	40,000	46,000
1996	S300D	37,000	43,000
1995	S280D	34,000	40,000

Albin 30 Family Cruiser

Year	Power	Retail Low	Retail High
2007	S315D	91,000	105,000
2006	S315D	85,000	97,000
2005	S315D	79,000	91,000
2004	S315D	73,000	84,000

Albin 32+2 Command Bridge

Year	Power	Retail Low	Retail High
2003	370D	149,000	171,000
2002	370D	138,000	159,000
2001	370D	129,000	148,000
2000	370D	119,000	137,000
1999	350D	111,000	128,000
1998	300D	103,000	119,000
1997	300D	97,000	112,000
1996	300D	91,000	105,000
1995	300D	86,000	99,000

Albin 35 Command Bridge

Year	Power	Retail Low	Retail High
2007	S370D	141,000	162,000
2006	S370D	129,000	149,000
2005	S370D	119,000	137,000
2004	S370D	110,000	126,000

Albin 35 Tournament Express

Year	Power	Retail Low	Retail High
2007	T370D	175,000	201,000
2006	T370D	159,000	183,000
2005	T370D	147,000	169,000
2004	T370D	135,000	155,000
2003	T370D	125,000	144,000
2002	T370D	116,000	134,000
2001	T370D	108,000	125,000
2000	T370D	101,000	116,000
1999	T350D	94,000	108,000
1998	T350D	88,000	101,000
1997	T350D	83,000	95,000
1996	T350D	78,000	89,000
1995	T350D	73,000	84,000

Albin 36 Express Trawler

Year	Power	Retail Low	Retail High
2004	S450D	128,000	147,000
2003	S450D	119,000	137,000
2002	S450D	111,000	127,000
2001	S450D	103,000	118,000
2000	S420D	97,000	111,000
1999	S420D	91,000	105,000

Albin 40 North Sea Cutter

Year	Power	Retail Low	Retail High
2007	T315D	******	******
2006	T315D	181,000	204,000
2005	T315D	170,000	192,000

Albin 45 Command Bridge

Year	Power	Retail Low	Retail High
2007	T480D	******	******
2006	T480D	******	******
2005	T480D	261,000	294,000
2004	T450D	242,000	274,000
2003	T450D	225,000	255,000

American 34 Tug

Year	Power	Retail Low	Retail High
2010	380D	******	******
2009	380D	332,000	381,000
2008	380D	308,000	355,000
2007	380D	287,000	330,000
2006	380D	267,000	307,000
2005	380D	248,000	285,000
2004	380D	230,000	265,000
2003	380D	214,000	247,000
2002	370D	199,000	229,000
2001	370D	185,000	213,000

American 41 Tug

Year	Power	Retail Low	Retail High
2010	575D	******	******
2009	575D	545,000	610,000
2008	575D	506,000	567,000
2007	575D	471,000	527,000
2006	575D	438,000	490,000
2005	575D	407,000	456,000

Aquasport 275 Explorer

Year	Power	Retail Low	Retail High
2005	T225 O/B	57,000	65,000
2004	T225 O/B	52,000	60,000
2003	T225 O/B	48,000	55,000
2002	T225 O/B	44,000	51,000
2001	T225 O/B	41,000	47,000
2000	T225 O/B	38,000	44,000
1999	T225 O/B	35,000	41,000

Azimut 39

Year	Power	Retail Low	Retail High
2005	T350D	******	******
2004	T350D	******	******
2003	T355D	******	******
2002	T350D	******	******
2001	T350D	171,000	197,000
2000	T325D	163,000	187,000
1999	T325D	155,000	178,000

Azimut 42

Year	Power	Retail Low	Retail High
2005	T385D	274,000	315,000
2004	T390D	252,000	290,000
2003	T390D	232,000	267,000
2002	T375D	213,000	245,000
2001	T375D	198,000	228,000
2000	T375D	184,000	212,000
1999	T375D	171,000	197,000

Azimut 43

Year	Power	Retail Low	Retail High
2010	T480D	******	******
2011	T480D	******	******
2008	T480D	395,000	454,000
2007	T425D	363,000	417,000

Azimut 43S

Year	Power	Retail Low	Retail High
2010	T435 IPS	******	******
2009	T435 IPS	******	******
2008	T435 IPS	425,000	488,000
2007	T370 IPS	395,000	454,000

Azimut 46

Year	Power	Retail Low	Retail High
2004	T505D	351,000	404,000
2003	T435D	327,000	376,000
2002	T435D	304,000	349,000
2001	T435D	282,000	325,000
2000	T435D	263,000	302,000
1999	T435D	244,000	281,000
1998	T435D	227,000	261,000
1997	T435D	211,000	243,000

Azimut 50

Year	Power	Retail Low	Retail High
2010	T715D	******	******
2009	T715D	******	******
2008	T715D	******	******
2007	T715D	******	******
2006	T715D	440,000	506,000
2005	T700D	413,000	475,000
2004	T700D	388,000	447,000

Azimut 50/52

Year	Power	Retail Low	Retail High
2002	T600D	******	******
2001	T600D	******	******
2000	T600D	******	******
1999	T600D	300,000	345,000
1998	T600D	285,000	327,000
1997	T600D	270,000	311,000
1996	T600D	257,000	295,000

Azimut 54/58

Year	Power	Retail Low	Retail High
2001	T765D	424,000	487,000
2000	T765D	398,000	458,000
1999	T765D	374,000	430,000
1998	T765D	352,000	404,000
1997	T765D	331,000	380,000
1996	T765D	311,000	357,000
1995	T765D	292,000	336,000
1994	T765D	274,000	316,000
1993	T765D	258,000	297,000

Azimut 55

Year	Power	Retail Low	Retail High
2005	T710D	******	******
2004	T710D	******	******
2003	T660D	490,000	563,000
2002	T660D	456,000	524,000
2001	T660D	424,000	487,000

Azimut 62 Flybridge

Year	Power	Retail Low	Retail High
2006	T1015D	978,000	1,124,000
2005	T1015D	938,000	1,079,000
2004	T910D	901,000	1,036,000
2003	T910D	865,000	995,000

Azimut 68 Plus

Year	Power	Retail Low	Retail High
2007	1150D	******	******
2006	1150D	******	******
2005	1150D	******	******
2004	1150D	900,000	1,008,000
2003	1150D	855,000	957,000
2002	1150D	812,000	909,000
2001	1150D	771,000	864,000

Back Cove 26

Year	Power	Retail Low	Retail High
2010	260D	******	******
2009	260D	******	******
2008	260D	82,000	96,000
2007	260D	75,000	89,000
2006	260D	70,000	82,000
2005	260D	65,000	76,000

Back Cove 29

Year	Power	Retail Low	Retail High
2009	260D	145,000	166,000
2008	260D	134,000	155,000
2007	260D	125,000	144,000
2006	260D	116,000	134,000
2005	260D	108,000	124,000
2004	260D	100,000	116,000

Back Cove 33

Year	Power	Retail Low	Retail High
2010	380D	******	******
2009	380D	247,000	284,000
2008	380D	232,000	267,000
2007	380D	218,000	250,000

Bayliner 275 SB Cruiser

Year	Power	Retail Low	Retail High
2007	250 I/O	40,000	48,000
2006	250 I/O	36,000	43,000
2005	250 I/O	33,000	40,000

Bayliner 2855 Ciera SB (1994-99)

Year	Power	Retail Low	Retail High
1999	310 I/O	19,000	23,000
1998	310 I/O	18,000	21,000
1997	310 I/O	17,000	20,000
1996	300 I/O	16,000	19,000
1995	300 I/O	15,000	18,000

Year	Power	Retail Low	Retail High
Bayliner 2859 Ciera Express			
2002	300 I/O	24,000	28,000
2001	300 I/O	22,000	26,000
2000	300 I/O	21,000	24,000
1999	310 I/O	19,000	22,000
1998	310 I/O	18,000	21,000
1997	310 I/O	16,000	19,000
1996	310 I/O	15,000	18,000
1995	310 I/O	14,000	17,000
Bayliner 285 SB Cruiser			
2010	300 I/O	70,000	83,000
2009	300 I/O	63,000	74,000
2008	300 I/O	56,000	67,000
2007	300 I/O	51,000	60,000
2006	300 I/O	46,000	55,000
2005	300 I/O	42,000	50,000
2004	320 I/O	38,000	45,000
2003	320 I/O	34,000	41,000
2002	320 I/O	31,000	37,000
2001	320 I/O	28,000	34,000
2000	320 I/O	26,000	31,000
Bayliner 288 Classic Cruiser			
2005	300 I/O	33,000	40,000
2004	300 I/O	30,000	36,000
2003	300 I/O	28,000	33,000
2002	300 I/O	25,000	30,000
2001	300 I/O	23,000	28,000
2000	300 I/O	21,000	26,000
1999	330 I/O	20,000	24,000
1998	330 I/O	18,000	22,000
1997	330 I/O	17,000	21,000
1996	330 I/O	16,000	19,000
Bayliner 305 SB Cruiser			
2007	T300G I/O	67,000	78,000
2006	T300G I/O	61,000	71,000
2005	T300G I/O	56,000	65,000
2004	T260G I/O	52,000	60,000
2003	T260G I/O	48,000	55,000
2002	T260G I/O	44,000	51,000
2001	T260G I/O	40,000	47,000
2000	T260G I/O	37,000	43,000
1999	T260G I/O	35,000	40,000
Bayliner 315 SB Cruiser			
2010	T220 I/O	108,000	124,000
2009	T220 I/O	97,000	111,000
2008	T220 I/O	87,000	100,000
Bayliner 320/335 SB Cruiser			
2010	T260 I/O	122,000	140,000
2009	T260 I/O	109,000	126,000
2008	T260 I/O	98,000	113,000
Bayliner 325 SB Cruiser			
2007	T260 I/O	80,000	92,000
2006	T260 I/O	72,000	83,000
2005	T260 I/O	66,000	76,000
Bayliner 3255 Avanti SB			
1999	T300G I/O	31,000	36,000
1998	T300G I/O	29,000	33,000
1997	T300G I/O	27,000	31,000
1996	T300G I/O	25,000	29,000
1995	T300G I/O	24,000	27,000
Bayliner 3258 Command Bridge			
2001	T300G I/O	43,000	50,000
2000	T310G I/O	40,000	46,000
1999	T310G I/O	37,000	43,000
1998	T310G I/O	35,000	40,000
1997	T300G I/O	33,000	38,000
1996	T300G I/O	31,000	35,000
1995	T300G I/O	29,000	33,000
Bayliner 3270/3288 MY			
1995	T150D	42,000	48,000
Bayliner 3388 Motor Yacht			
2000	T260G	58,000	66,000
2000	T250D	67,000	77,000
1999	T260G	52,000	60,000
1999	T250D	57,000	65,000
1988	T260G	47,000	54,000
1998	T250D	53,000	61,000
1997	T260G	43,000	50,000
1997	T250D	49,000	56,000
1996	T260G	40,000	46,000
1996	T210D	46,000	52,000
Bayliner 340 SB Cruiser			
2009	T260 I/O	116,000	139,000
2008	T300 I/O	104,000	102,000
Bayliner 3488 Avanti CB (1996-99)			
1999	T310G	52,000	60,000
1998	T310G	48,000	55,000
1997	T310G	45,000	52,000
1996	T310G	42,000	48,000
Bayliner 3488 CB (2001-02)			
2002	T260G	66,000	76,000
2001	T260G	61,000	70,000
Bayliner 3587 Motor Yacht			
1999	T310G	72,000	82,000
1999	T330D	84,000	96,000
1998	T310G	67,000	77,000
1998	T330D	78,000	90,000
1997	T310G	63,000	73,000
1997	T315D	74,000	85,000
1996	T310G	59,000	68,000
1996	T315D	69,000	80,000
1995	T310G	56,000	64,000
1995	T315D	65,000	75,000
Bayliner 3685 Avanti Sunbridge			
1999	T310G	64,000	74,000
1998	T310G	58,000	67,000
Bayliner 3788 MY (1996-99)			
1999	T310G	75,000	86,000
1999	T330D	93,000	107,000
1998	T310G	70,000	81,000
1998	T330D	88,000	101,000
1997	T310G	66,000	76,000
1997	T250D	82,000	95,000
1996	T310G	62,000	71,000
1996	T250D	77,000	89,000
Bayliner 3788 MY (2001-02)			
2002	T310G	101,000	116,000
2002	T330D	123,000	142,000
2001	T310G	94,000	108,000
2001	T330D	115,000	132,000
Bayliner 3988 MY			
2002	T320G	120,000	
2002	T330D	141,000	138,000
2001	T320G	112,000	162,000
2001	T330D	131,000	129,000
2000	T320G	104,000	151,000
2000	T330D	122,000	120,000
1999	T310G	97,000	140,000
1999	T330D	113,000	111,000
1998	T310G	91,000	130,000
1998	T330D	106,000	104,000
1997	T310G	85,000	122,000
1997	T315D	100,000	98,000
1996	T310G	80,000	115,000
1996	T315D	94,000	92,000
1995	T310G	75,000	108,000
1995	T315D	88,000	87,000
Bayliner 4085 Avanti SB			
1999	T310G	72,000	82,000
1999	T330D	89,000	101,000
1998	T310G	68,000	77,000
1998	T330D	83,000	95,000
1997	T310G	63,000	72,000
1997	T-Diesel	78,000	89,000
Bayliner 4087 Cockpit MY			
2001	T320G	103,000	117,000
2001	T330D	127,000	144,000
2000	T320G	95,000	109,000
2000	T330D	118,000	134,000
1999	T310G	89,000	101,000
1999	T330D	109,000	125,000
1998	T310G	82,000	94,000
1998	T330D	102,000	116,000
1997	T310G	77,000	87,000
1997	T330D	95,000	108,000
Bayliner 4587 Cockpit MY			
1995	T300G	80,000	92,000
1995	T310D	92,000	105,000
Bayliner 4788 Pilothouse MY			
2002	T370D	226,000	256,000
2001	T370D	211,000	238,000
2000	T370D	196,000	221,000
1999	T315D	182,000	206,000
1998	T315D	171,000	193,000
1997	T315D	161,000	182,000
1996	T315D	151,000	171,000
1995	T310D	142,000	161,000
Bayliner 5288 Pilothouse MY			
2002	T610D	364,000	415,000
2001	T610D	342,000	390,000
2000	T610D	322,000	367,000
1999	T600D	302,000	345,000
Bayliner 5788 Motor Yacht			
2002	T610D	480,000	552,000
2001	T610D	446,000	513,000
2000	T610D	415,000	477,000
1999	T600D	390,000	449,000
1998	T600D	367,000	422,000
1997	T600D	345,000	396,000
Beneteau 42 Trawler			
2009	T370D	*****	*****
2008	T370D	*****	*****
2007	T370D	273,000	314,000
2006	T370D	254,000	292,000
2005	T370D	236,000	272,000
2004	T370D	220,000	253,000
Bertram 30 Moppie			
1997	T320G	55,000	66,000
1997	T300G	69,000	83,000
1996	T320G	51,000	62,000
1996	T300D	65,000	78,000
1995	T320G	48,000	58,000
1995	T300D	61,000	74,000
Bertram 36 Moppie			
2000	T430D	184,000	212,000
1999	T430D	173,000	199,000
1998	T430D	163,000	187,000
1997	T330D	153,000	176,000
1996	T315D	144,000	165,000

Bertram 390 Convertible

Year	Power	Retail Low	Retail High
2006	460D	385,000	442,000
2005	480D	358,000	411,000
2004	480D	332,000	382,000
2003	480D	313,000	359,000
2002	480D	294,000	338,000
2001	480D	276,000	318,000
2000	480D	259,000	298,000

Bertram 43 Convertible

Year	Power	Retail Low	Retail High
1996	625D	216,000	249,000
1995	600D	203,000	234,000

Bertram 450 Convertible

Year	Power	Retail Low	Retail High
2009	900D	******	******
2008	900D	******	******
2007	900D	******	******
2006	900D	659,000	757,000
2005	900D	612,000	704,000
2004	660D	569,000	655,000
2003	660D	530,000	609,000
2002	660D	492,000	566,000
2001	660D	458,000	527,000
2000	660D	426,000	490,000

Bertram 46 Convertible

Year	Power	Retail Low	Retail High
1997	760D	298,000	352,000
1996	760D	280,000	331,000
1995	735D	264,000	311,000

Bertram 50 Convertible

Year	Power	Retail Low	Retail High
1997	820D	520,000	608,000
1996	820D	494,000	577,000
1995	735D	469,000	549,000

Bertram 510 Convertible

Year	Power	Retail Low	Retail High
2010	1360D	******	******
2009	1360D	******	******
2008	1000D	985,000	1,113,000
2007	800D	925,000	1,046,000
2006	800D	870,000	983,000
2005	800D	818,000	924,000
2004	800D	777,000	878,000
2003	800D	738,000	834,000
2002	800D	701,000	792,000
2001	800D	666,000	752,000
2000	800D	633,000	715,000

Bertram 54 Convertible

Year	Power	Retail Low	Retail High
2003	1200D	******	******
2002	1200D	1,062,000	1,211,000
2001	1400D	988,000	1,126,000
2000	1400D	919,000	1,047,000
2000	1350D	854,000	974,000
1999	1350D	794,000	906,000
1998	1350D	739,000	842,000
1997	1350D	687,000	783,000
1996	1100D	639,000	728,000
1995	1100D	594,000	677,000

Bertram 570 Convertible

Year	Power	Retail Low	Retail High
2010	1360D	******	******
2009	1300D	******	******
2008	1300D	******	******
2007	1300D	******	******
2006	1300D	1,020,000	1,152,000
2005	1300D	969,000	1,094,000
2004	1300D	920,000	1,040,000
2003	1300D	874,000	988,000
2002	1300D	830,000	938,000

Bertram 60 Conv. (Open Bridge)

Year	Power	Retail Low	Retail High
2005	1400D	******	******
2004	1400D	******	******
2003	1400D	******	******
2002	1400D	1,237,000	1,398,000
2001	1400D	1,150,000	1,300,000
2000	1400D	1,070,000	1,209,000
1999	1400D	995,000	1,124,000
1998	1450D	925,000	1,045,000
1997	1450D	860,000	972,000
1996	1400D	800,000	904,000
1995	1400D	752,000	850,000

Bertram 630 Conv. (Open Bridge)

Year	Power	Retail Low	Retail High
2010	2000D	******	******
2009	2000D	******	******
2008	2000D	******	******
2007	2000D	******	******
2006	2000D	1,629,000	1,841,000
2005	2000D	1,531,000	1,730,000
2004	2000D	1,439,000	1,626,000

Black Watch 30 Flybridge

Year	Power	Retail Low	Retail High
1996	T250G	43,000	51,000
1996	T300D	52,000	62,000
1995	T250G	40,000	48,000
1995	T300D	48,000	58,000

Black Watch 30 SF

Year	Power	Retail Low	Retail High
1995	T250G	37,000	44,000
1995	T300D	46,000	55,000

Blackfin 27 Sportsman

Year	Power	Retail Low	Retail High
1998	T270G	35,000	42,000
1998	T230D	44,000	52,000
1997	T270G	32,000	39,000
1997	T230D	41,000	49,000
1996	T270G	30,000	37,000
1996	T230D	38,000	46,000
1995	T270G	29,000	34,000
1995	T230D	36,000	43,000

Blackfin 29 Combi

Year	Power	Retail Low	Retail High
1998	T320G	45,000	54,000
1998	T330D	56,000	68,000
1997	T320G	42,000	50,000
1997	T330D	52,000	63,000
1996	T320G	39,000	47,000
1996	T330D	49,000	59,000
1995	T320G	36,000	43,000
1995	T330D	45,000	54,000

Blackfin 29 Flybridge

Year	Power	Retail Low	Retail High
1998	T-Gas	51,000	61,000
1998	T330D	62,000	75,000
1997	T-Gas	47,000	56,000
1997	T330D	58,000	70,000
1996	T-Gas	44,000	53,000
1996	T330D	54,000	65,000
1995	T-Gas	41,000	49,000
1995	T330D	50,000	60,000

Blackfin 31 Combi

Year	Power	Retail Low	Retail High
1997	T320G	58,000	70,000
1997	T300D	75,000	90,000
1996	T320G	53,000	64,000
1996	T300D	69,000	82,000
1995	T320G	49,000	59,000
1995	T300D	63,000	76,000

Blackfin 33 Combi

Year	Power	Retail Low	Retail High
1998	T375D	92,000	110,000
1997	T375D	86,000	103,000
1996	T375D	81,000	97,000
1995	T375D	76,000	91,000

Blackfin 33 Convertible

Year	Power	Retail Low	Retail High
1999	T435D	102,000	123,000
1998	T375D	96,000	116,000
1997	T375D	90,000	109,000
1996	T-Gas	70,000	84,000
1996	T375D	85,000	102,000
1995	T-Gas	66,000	79,000
1995	T375D	80,000	96,000

Blackfin 38 Combi

Year	Power	Retail Low	Retail High
1998	435D	142,000	171,000
1997	450D	134,000	160,000
1996	450D	126,000	151,000
1995	450D	118,000	142,000
1994	450D	111,000	133,000

Blackfin 38 Convertible

Year	Power	Retail Low	Retail High
1998	550D	168,000	201,000
1997	550D	158,000	189,000
1996	485D	148,000	178,000
1995	485D	139,000	167,000

Boston Whaler 27 Offshore

Year	Power	Retail Low	Retail High
1998	T225 O/B	31,000	37,000
1997	T225 O/B	29,000	35,000
1996	T225 O/B	28,000	34,000
1995	T225 O/B	27,000	32,000

Boston Whaler 270 Outrage

Year	Power	Retail Low	Retail High
2008	T225 O/B	78,000	94,000
2007	T225 O/B	70,000	84,000
2006	T225 O/B	64,000	77,000
2005	T225 O/B	59,000	71,000
2004	T225 O/B	54,000	65,000
2003	T225 O/B	50,000	60,000

Boston Whaler 275 Conquest

Year	Power	Retail Low	Retail High
2005	T225 O/B	73,000	88,000
2004	T225 O/B	67,000	81,000
2003	T225 O/B	62,000	75,000
2002	T225 O/B	58,000	70,000
2001	T225 O/B	54,000	65,000

Boston Whaler 28/290 Outrage

Year	Power	Retail Low	Retail High
2003	T225 O/B	69,000	82,000
2002	T225 O/B	64,000	77,000
2001	T225 O/B	59,000	71,000
2000	T225 O/B	55,000	66,000
1999	T225 O/B	51,000	61,000

Boston Whaler 28/295 Conquest

Year	Power	Retail Low	Retail High
2003	T225 O/B	75,000	90,000
2002	T225 O/B	70,000	84,000
2001	T225 O/B	65,000	78,000
2000	T225 O/B	60,000	72,000
1999	T225 O/B	56,000	67,000

Boston Whaler 280 Outrage

Year	Power	Retail Low	Retail High
2010	T225 O/B	145,000	171,000
2009	T225 O/B	133,000	157,000

Boston Whaler 285 Conquest

Year	Power	Retail Low	Retail High
2010	T225 O/B	******	******
2009	T225 O/B	135,000	159,000
2008	T225 O/B	124,000	146,000
2007	T225 O/B	114,000	134,000
2006	T225 O/B	105,000	124,000

Boston Whaler 305 Conquest

Year	Power	Retail Low	Retail High
2010	T225 O/B	******	******
2009	T225 O/B	175,000	206,000
2008	T225 O/B	161,000	189,000
2007	T225 O/B	148,000	174,000
2006	T225 O/B	136,000	160,000
2005	T225 O/B	126,000	149,000
2004	T225 O/B	117,000	139,000

Boston Whaler 320 Outrage

Year	Power	Retail Low	Retail High
2010	T250 O/B	******	******

Year	Power	Retail Low	Retail High	Year	Power	Retail Low	Retail High	Year	Power	Retail Low	Retail High
2009	T250 O/B	150,000	172,000	2005	461D	270,000	311,000	2006	800D	530,000	599,000
2008	T250 O/B	138,000	158,000	2004	450D	248,000	286,000	2005	800D	488,000	551,000
2007	T250 O/B	126,000	146,000	2003	450D	229,000	263,000	2004	800D	449,000	507,000
2006	T250 O/B	116,000	134,000	2002	435D	210,000	242,000	2003	800D	413,000	467,000
2005	T250 O/B	107,000	123,000	2001	435D	193,000	222,000	2002	800D	384,000	434,000
2004	T250 O/B	99,000	114,000	2000	435D	180,000	207,000	2001	800D	357,000	404,000
2003	T250 O/B	92,000	106,000	1999	435D	167,000	192,000	2000	800D	332,000	375,000
Boston Whaler 320 Outrage Cuddy				1998	435D	157,000	181,000	**Cabo 52 Express**			
2010	T250 O/B	******	******	1997	435D	148,000	170,000	2010	1550D	******	******
2009	T250 O/B	166,000	190,000	1996	435D	139,000	160,000	2009	1550D	******	******
2008	T250 O/B	152,000	175,000	1995	375D	130,000	150,000	2008	1550D	1,040,000	1,175,000
2007	T250 O/B	140,000	161,000	**Cabo 38 Express**				2007	1550D	967,000	1,093,000
2006	T250 O/B	129,000	148,000	2010	715D	******	******	2006	1550D	899,000	1,016,000
Boston Whaler 34 Defiance				2009	715D	******	******	**Californian 39 SL**			
2002	T355D	168,000	193,000	2008	715D	435,000	491,000	2003	T318D	172,000	197,000
2001	T355D	154,000	178,000	**Cabo 38 Flybridge**				2002	T318D	160,000	183,000
2000	T355D	142,000	163,000	2010	715D	******	******	2001	T318D	149,000	170,000
1999	T355D	131,000	150,000	2009	715D	******	******	2000	T318D	139,000	158,000
Boston Whaler 345 Conquest				2008	715D	525,000	593,000	1999	T318D	129,000	147,000
2010	3/225 O/B	******	******	**Cabo 40 Express**				**Camano 28/31**			
2009	3/225 O/B	******	******	2010	720D	******	******	2007	S-Diesel	137,000	160,000
2008	3/225 O/B	244,000	280,000	2009	720D	544,000	615,000	2006	S-Diesel	128,000	148,000
2007	3/225 O/B	226,000	260,000	2008	720D	499,000	564,000	2005	S-Diesel	119,000	138,000
Cabo 31 Express				2007	710D	459,000	519,000	2004	S-Diesel	112,000	130,000
2004	T385D	******	******	2006	710D	427,000	483,000	2003	S-Diesel	105,000	122,000
2003	T385D	137,000	158,000	2005	710D	397,000	449,000	2002	S-Diesel	99,000	114,000
2002	T385D	126,000	145,000	2004	700D	369,000	418,000	2001	S-Diesel	93,000	108,000
2001	T385D	116,000	134,000	2003	700D	344,000	388,000	2000	S-Diesel	87,000	101,000
2000	T385D	107,000	123,000	**Cabo 40 Flybridge**				1999	S-Diesel	82,000	95,000
1999	T350D	100,000	115,000	2010	710D	******	******	1998	S-Diesel	78,000	90,000
1998	T350D	94,000	108,000	2009	710D	******	******	1997	S-Diesel	74,000	86,000
1997	T350D	89,000	102,000	2008	710D	******	******	1996	S-Diesel	70,000	81,000
1996	T350D	83,000	96,000	2007	710D	516,000	583,000	1995	S-Diesel	67,000	77,000
1995	T350D	78,000	90,000	2006	710D	475,000	536,000	**Camano 41**			
Cabo 32 Express				2005	710D	441,000	499,000	2007	440D	******	******
2010	T425D	******	******	2004	700D	410,000	464,000	2006	440D	320,000	368,000
2009	T425D	******	******	**Cabo 43 Flybridge**				**Carolina Classic 28**			
2009	T425D	******	******	2010	720D	******	******	2010	T275G	******	******
2008	T425D	244,000	278,000	2009	720D	******	******	2010	T300D	******	******
2007	T425D	224,000	256,000	2008	720D	617,000	697,000	2009	T375G	******	******
2006	T461D	206,000	235,000	2007	710D	567,000	641,000	2009	T315D	******	******
2005	T461D	192,000	219,000	2006	710D	522,000	590,000	2008	T375G	130,000	149,000
Cabo 35 Express				2005	710D	480,000	543,000	2008	T315D	158,000	181,000
2010	T425D	******	******	2004	680D	442,000	499,000	2007	T375G	120,000	139,000
2009	T425D	******	******	2003	680D	411,000	464,000	2007	T315D	146,000	168,000
2008	T425D	******	******	2002	680D	382,000	432,000	2006	T375G	112,000	129,000
2007	T425D	******	******	**Cabo 45 Express**				2006	T315D	136,000	157,000
2006	T461D	237,000	272,000	2010	800D	******	******	2005	T375G	104,000	120,000
2005	T461D	218,000	251,000	2009	800D	850,000	960,000	2005	T300D	127,000	146,000
2004	T450D	200,000	230,000	2008	800D	765,000	864,000	2004	T375G	97,000	111,000
2003	T450D	184,000	212,000	2007	800D	688,000	778,000	2004	T300D	118,000	135,000
2002	T435D	171,000	197,000	2006	800D	619,000	700,000	2003	T375G	90,000	104,000
2001	T435D	159,000	183,000	2005	800D	557,000	630,000	2003	T300D	109,000	126,000
2000	T435D	148,000	170,000	2004	800D	501,000	567,000	2002	T375G	84,000	96,000
1999	T435D	138,000	158,000	2003	800D	451,000	510,000	2002	T250D	102,000	117,000
1998	T435D	128,000	147,000	2002	800D	406,000	459,000	2001	T375G	78,000	89,000
1997	T435D	120,000	138,000	2001	800D	365,000	413,000	2001	T250D	95,000	109,000
1996	T435D	113,000	130,000	2000	800D	329,000	372,000	2000	T300G	72,000	83,000
1995	T375D	106,000	122,000	1999	800D	296,000	334,000	2000	T250D	89,000	102,000
1994	T375D			1998	800D	266,000	301,000	1999	T300G	68,000	78,000
Cabo 35 Flybridge				1997	800D	240,000	271,000	1999	T250D	84,000	96,000
2010	425D	******	******	**Cabo 47/48 Flybridge**				1998	T300G	64,000	73,000
2009	425D	******	******	2010	800D	******	******	1998	T230D	78,000	90,000
2008	425D	******	******	2009	800D	******	******	1997	T300G	60,000	69,000
2007	425D	323,000	371,000	2008	800D	******	******	1997	T230D	74,000	85,000
2006	461D	294,000	338,000	2007	800D	577,000	652,000				

Year	Power	Retail Low	Retail High
1996	T300G	56,000	65,000
1996	T230D	69,000	80,000
1995	T300G	53,000	61,000
1995	T230D	65,000	75,000

Carolina Classic 32

Year	Power	Retail Low	Retail High
2010	T480D	******	******
2009	T480D	******	******
2008	T425D	******	******
2007	T425D	218,000	250,000
2006	T500D	204,000	235,000
2005	T500D	192,000	221,000
2004	T440D	181,000	208,000

Carolina Classic 35

Year	Power	Retail Low	Retail High
2010	T550D	******	******
2009	T600D	******	******
2008	T540D	260,000	291,000
2007	T540D	244,000	273,000
2006	T500D	229,000	257,000
2005	T480D	215,000	241,000
2004	T480D	202,000	227,000
2003	T480D	190,000	213,000
2002	T480D	179,000	200,000
2001	T450D	168,000	188,000
2000	T450D	158,000	177,000
1999	T450D	148,000	166,000
1998	T450D	140,000	156,000

Carver 280 Mid Cabin Express

Year	Power	Retail Low	Retail High
1998	T205G	22,000	26,000
1997	T205G	20,000	24,000
1996	T205G	19,000	22,000
1995	T205G	17,000	21,000

Carver 280 Sedan

Year	Power	Retail Low	Retail High
1998	T205G	25,000	30,000
1997	T205G	23,000	27,000
1996	T205G	21,000	25,000
1995	T205G	20,000	24,000

Carver 310 Mid-Cabin Express

Year	Power	Retail Low	Retail High
1997	T220 I/O	27,000	32,000
1996	T220 I/O	25,000	30,000
1995	T220 I/O	23,000	28,000

Carver 310 Santego

Year	Power	Retail Low	Retail High
1998	T220 I/O	37,000	44,000
1997	T220 I/O	34,000	41,000
1996	T220 I/O	32,000	38,000
1995	T220 I/O	29,000	35,000

Carver 320 Voyager

Year	Power	Retail Low	Retail High
1999	T300G	61,000	71,000
1998	T300G	56,000	66,000
1997	T260G	52,000	61,000
1996	T260G	49,000	57,000
1995	T260G	45,000	53,000

Carver 325/326 Aft Cabin

Year	Power	Retail Low	Retail High
2001	T300G	63,000	73,000
2000	T300G	58,000	68,000
1999	T300G	54,000	63,000
1998	T260G	50,000	59,000
1997	T260G	47,000	55,000
1996	T260G	43,000	51,000
1995	T260G	40,000	47,000

Carver 32/330 Mariner

Year	Power	Retail Low	Retail High
1996	T260G	42,000	49,000
1995	T260G	39,000	46,000

Carver 33/35/36 Super Sport

Year	Power	Retail Low	Retail High
2008	T375G	225,000	261,000
2007	T320G	207,000	240,000
2006	T320G	190,000	220,000
2005	T320G	175,000	203,000

Carver 350 Mariner

Year	Power	Retail Low	Retail High
2003	T300G	85,000	98,000
2002	T300G	78,000	90,000
2001	T300G	71,000	83,000
2000	T300G	66,000	76,000
1999	T260G	61,000	71,000
1998	T260G	57,000	66,000
1997	T260G	53,000	61,000

Carver 355/356 Motor Yacht

Year	Power	Retail Low	Retail High
2003	T320G	97,000	113,000
2002	T320G	88,000	103,000
2001	T320G	80,000	93,000
2000	T310G	73,000	85,000
1999	T310G	67,000	77,000
1998	T310G	60,000	70,000
1997	T310G	56,000	65,000
1996	T320G	51,000	59,000
1995	T320G	47,000	55,000

Carver 36 Mariner

Year	Power	Retail Low	Retail High
2010	T320G	******	******
2009	T320G	******	******
2008	T320G	175,000	203,000
2007	T320G	161,000	186,000
2006	T320G	148,000	171,000
2005	T320G	137,000	159,000
2004	T320G	128,000	148,000

Carver 36 Motor Yacht

Year	Power	Retail Low	Retail High
2007	T375G	220,000	257,000
2007	T315D	243,000	284,000
2006	T320G	202,000	236,000
2006	T315D	223,000	261,000
2006	T320G	186,000	217,000
2006	T315D	205,000	240,000
2005	T320G	173,000	202,000
2005	T280D	191,000	223,000
2004	T320G	161,000	188,000
2004	T280D	177,000	208,000
2003	T320G	149,000	175,000
2003	T280D	165,000	193,000
2002	T320G	139,000	162,000
2002	T280D	153,000	180,000

Carver 360 Sport Sedan

Year	Power	Retail Low	Retail High
2006	T375G	168,000	196,000
2005	T375G	156,000	182,000
2004	T375G	145,000	170,000
2003	T320G	135,000	158,000

Carver 36/370 Aft Cabin MY

Year	Power	Retail Low	Retail High
1996	T300G	81,000	93,000
1996	T300D	100,000	116,000
1995	T300G	76,000	88,000
1995	T300D	94,000	109,000

Carver 370/374 Voyager

Year	Power	Retail Low	Retail High
2002	T320G	110,000	126,000
2002	T330D	125,000	143,000
2001	T320G	101,000	116,000
2001	T330D	115,000	132,000
2000	T320G	94,000	108,000
2000	T330D	106,000	122,000
1999	T320G	87,000	100,000
1999	T315D	99,000	114,000
1998	T300G	81,000	93,000
1998	T315D	92,000	106,000
1997	T300G	75,000	87,000
1997	T315D	86,000	98,000
1996	T300G	70,000	80,000
1996	T315D	80,000	92,000

Year	Power	Retail Low	Retail High
1995	T300G	65,000	75,000
1995	T315D	74,000	85,000

Carver 34/638/380 Santego

Year	Power	Retail Low	Retail High
2002	T320G	107,000	125,000
2001	T320G	99,000	116,000
2000	T310G	92,000	108,000
1999	T310G	86,000	100,000
1998	T300G	80,000	93,000
1997	T320G	74,000	87,000
1996	T320G	69,000	80,000
1995	T320G	64,000	75,000

Carver 38 Super Sport

Year	Power	Retail Low	Retail High
2010	T315D	******	******
2010	T385G	******	******
2009	T315D	******	******
2009	T385G	******	******
2008	T375G	225,000	261,000
2007	T375G	207,000	240,000
2006	T375G	190,000	220,000
2005	T375G	175,000	203,000

Carver 38/390 Aft Cabin

Year	Power	Retail Low	Retail High
1995	T330G	88,000	102,000
1995	T-Diesel	107,000	124,000

Carver 396/39/40 Motor Yacht

Year	Power	Retail Low	Retail High
2007	T385G	247,000	289,000
2007	T370D	284,000	332,000
2006	T385G	227,000	266,000
2006	T370D	261,000	306,000
2005	T385G	207,000	242,000
2005	T370D	238,000	278,000
2004	T385G	188,000	220,000
2004	T370D	216,000	253,000
2003	T370D	173,000	202,000
2003	T370D	199,000	233,000
2002	T370D	161,000	188,000
2002	T370D	185,000	217,000
2001	T370D	149,000	175,000
2001	T330D	172,000	201,000
2000	T380D	139,000	163,000
2000	T330D	160,000	187,000

Carver 390/400/404 Cockpit MY

Year	Power	Retail Low	Retail High
2003	T320G	146,000	171,000
2003	T370D	177,000	207,000
2002	T320G	134,000	157,000
2002	T370D	163,000	191,000
2001	T320G	123,000	144,000
2001	T370D	150,000	175,000
2000	T310G	113,000	133,000
2000	T370D	138,000	161,000
1999	T310G	105,000	123,000
1999	T370D	128,000	150,000
1998	T310G	98,000	115,000
1998	T370D	119,000	139,000
1997	T310G	91,000	107,000
1997	T370D	111,000	130,000
1996	T310G	85,000	99,000
1996	T370D	103,000	121,000
1995	T310G	80,000	93,000
1995	T315D	97,000	113,000

Carver 405/406 Aft Cabin MY

Year	Power	Retail Low	Retail High
2002	T320G	140,000	162,000
2002	T330D	167,000	194,000
2001	T320G	130,000	151,000
2001	T330D	155,000	180,000
2000	T320G	121,000	140,000
2000	T330D	144,000	168,000
1999	T310G	112,000	130,000
1999	T330D	134,000	156,000

Year	Power	Retail Low	Retail High
1998	T310G	104,000	121,000
1998	T330D	125,000	145,000
1997	T310G	97,000	113,000
1997	T315D	116,000	135,000

Carver 41 Cockpit MY

Year	Power	Retail Low	Retail High
2007	T375G	232,000	255,000
2007	T370D	259,000	300,000
2006	T375G	211000	245,000
2006	T370D	236,000	273,000
2005	T385G	194,000	225,000
2005	T370D	217,000	252,000

Carver 410 Sport Sedan

Year	Power	Retail Low	Retail High
2003	T375G	165,000	191,000
2003	T370D	191,000	222,000
2002	T375G	153,000	177,000
2002	T370D	177,000	206,000

Carver 42 Mariner

Year	Power	Retail Low	Retail High
2006	T385G	201,000	233,000
2006	T370D	234,000	271,000
2005	T385G	184,000	214,000
2005	T370D	215,000	249,000
2004	T385G	170,000	197,000
2004	T330D	198,000	229,000

Carver 42/43 Super Sport

Year	Power	Retail Low	Retail High
2010	T385G	******	******
2010	T370D	******	******
2009	T385G	******	******
2009	T370D	******	******
2008	T375G	255,000	296,000
2008	T370D	289,000	335,000
2007	T375G	232,000	269,000
2007	T370D	263,000	305,000
2006	T375G	211,000	245,000
2006	T370D	239,000	277,000

Carver 430 Cockpit MY

Year	Power	Retail Low	Retail High
1997	T380G	105,000	122,000
1997	T315D	122,000	142,000
1996	T380G	99,000	114,000
1996	T315D	115,000	133,000
1995	T380G	93,000	108,000
1995	T315D	108,000	125,000

Carver 43/47 Motor Yacht

Year	Power	Retail Low	Retail High
2010	T385G	******	******
2010	T370D	******	******
2009	T385G	******	******
2009	T370D	******	******
2008	T375G	292,000	336,000
2008	T370D	334,000	385,000
2007	T375G	266,000	306,000
2007	T370D	304,000	350,000
2006	T375G	242,000	278,000
2006	T370D	277,000	318,000

Carver 440/445 Aft Cabin

Year	Power	Retail Low	Retail High
1999	T450D	172,000	199,000
1998	T320G	154,000	179,000
1998	T420D	160,000	185,000
1997	T320G	142,000	165,000
1997	T420D	149,000	172,000
1996	T320G	130,000	151,000
1996	T420D	138,000	160,000
1995	T320G	120,000	139,000
1995	T420D	128,000	149,000

Carver 444 Cockpit MY

Year	Power	Retail Low	Retail High
2006	T370D	220,000	253,000
2005	T370D	204,000	235,000
2004	T330D	190,000	218,000
2003	T330D	176,000	203,000

Year	Power	Retail Low	Retail High
2002	T330D	164,000	189,000
2001	T330D	153,000	176,000

Carver 450 Voyager

Year	Power	Retail Low	Retail High
2004	T450D	245,000	281,000
2003	T450D	222,000	256,000
2002	T450D	202,000	233,000
2001	T450D	184,000	212,000
2000	T450D	168,000	193,000
1999	T450D	152,000	175,000

Carver 455/456 Aft Cabin MY

Year	Power	Retail Low	Retail High
2000	T430D	220,000	253,000
1999	T340D	204,000	235,000
1998	T340D	190,000	218,000
1997	T340D	176,000	203,000
1996	T340D	164,000	189,000

Carver 466 Motor Yacht

Year	Power	Retail Low	Retail High
2007	T480D	321,000	369,000
2006	T480D	295,000	340,000
2005	T480D	272,000	312,000
2004	T480D	252,000	290,000
2003	T480D	235,000	270,000
2002	T480D	218,000	251,000
2001	T480D	203,000	234,000

Carver 460/46 Voyager

Year	Power	Retail Low	Retail High
2010	T370D	******	******
2009	T370D	******	******
2008	T370D	******	******
2007	T370D	******	******
2006	T370D	320,000	368,000
2005	T370D	297,000	342,000
2004	T370D	276,000	318,000
2003	T370D	257,000	296,000

Carver 500/504 Cockpit MY

Year	Power	Retail Low	Retail High
2000	T400D	212,000	246,000
1999	T400D	199,000	231,000
1998	T420D	187,000	217,000
1997	T420D	176,000	204,000
1996	T420D	165,000	192,000

Carver 506 Motoryacht

Year	Power	Retail Low	Retail High
2004	T480D	******	******
2003	T480D	******	******
2002	T480D	******	******
2001	T480D	259,000	292,000
2000	T480D	240,000	272,000

Carver 530 Voyager PH

Year	Power	Retail Low	Retail High
2005	T480D	335,000	392,000
2004	T480D	330,000	386,000
2003	T480D	307,000	359,000
2002	T480D	289,000	338,000
2001	T480D	268,000	314,000
2000	T480D	249,000	292,000
1999	T480D	232,000	271,000
1998	T480D	216,000	252,000

Carver 564 Cockpit MY

Year	Power	Retail Low	Retail High
2006	T480D	******	******
2005	T480D	******	******
2004	T480D	435,000	495,000
2003	T480D	404,000	461,000
2002	T480D	376,000	428,000

Carver 570/56 Voyager Sedan

Year	Power	Retail Low	Retail High
2010	T500D	******	******
2009	T500D	******	******
2008	T500D	******	******
2007	T500D	******	******
2006	T675D	******	******
2005	T675D	******	******

Year	Power	Retail Low	Retail High
2004	T660D	490,000	553,000
2003	T635D	455,000	514,000
2002	T635D	423,000	478,000
2001	T635D	394,000	445,000

Century 2900 Walkaround

Year	Power	Retail Low	Retail High
2004	T250 O/B	58,000	67,000
2003	T250 O/B	52,000	61,000
2002	T250 O/B	48,000	56,000
2001	T250 O/B	43,000	51,000

Century 2900/2901 Center Console

Year	Power	Retail Low	Retail High
2008	T250 O/B	100,000	117,000
2007	T250 O/B	91,000	106,000
2006	T250 O/B	82,000	96,000
2005	T250 O/B	76,000	89,000
2004	T250 O/B	70,000	82,000
2003	T250 O/B	64,000	75,000
2002	T250 O/B	59,000	69,000
2001	T250 O/B	54,000	63,000
2000	T250 O/B	50,000	58,000

Century 3000 Center Console

Year	Power	Retail Low	Retail High
1999	T250 O/B	28,000	32,000
1998	T250 O/B	26,000	30,000
1997	T250 O/B	24,000	28,000
1996	T250 O/B	22,000	26,000
1995	T250 O/B	20,000	24,000
1994	T250 O/B	19,000	22,000

Century 3000 Sport Cabin

Year	Power	Retail Low	Retail High
2002	T250 O/B	33,000	38,000
2001	T250 O/B	30,000	35,000
2000	T250 O/B	27,000	32,000
1999	T250 O/B	25,000	30,000
1998	T250 O/B	23,000	27,000
1997	T250 O/B	21,000	25,000

Century 3100/3200 Center Console

Year	Power	Retail Low	Retail High
2009	T250 O/B	141,000	164,000
2008	T250 O/B	128,000	150,000
2007	T250 O/B	116,000	136,000
2006	T250 O/B	106,000	124,000
2005	T250 O/B	96,000	113,000
2004	T250 O/B	88,000	104,000
2003	T250 O/B	81,000	95,000
2002	T250 O/B	75,000	88,000
2001	T250 O/B	69,000	81,000
2000	T250 O/B	63,000	74,000
1999	T250 O/B	58,000	68,000

Century 3200 Walkaround

Year	Power	Retail Low	Retail High
2007	T250 O/B	121,000	141,000
2006	T250 O/B	110,000	128,000
2005	T250 O/B	100,000	117,000
2004	T250 O/B	91,000	106,000
2003	T250 O/B	83,000	98,000
2002	T250 O/B	77,000	90,000
2001	T250 O/B	71,000	83,000
2000	T250 O/B	65,000	76,000

Chaparral Signature 26/27/270

Year	Power	Retail Low	Retail High
2000	310 I/0	31,000	35,000
1999	310 I/0	28,000	33,000
1998	310 I/0	26,000	30,000
1997	310 I/0	24,000	28,000
1996	310 I/0	23,000	26,000
1995	310 I/0	21,000	24,000

Charappal Signature 270

Year	Power	Retail Low	Retail High
2010	320 I/0	******	******
2009	320 I/0	******	******
2008	300 I/0	67,000	78,000
2007	300 I/0	61,000	72,000

See Page 511 For Price Adjustments

Chaparral Signature 270/280

Year	Power	Retail Low	Retail High
2009	T270 I/O	92,000	107,000
2008	T270 I/O	83,000	97,000
2007	T270 I/O	76,000	89,000
2006	T270 I/O	69,000	81,000
2005	T260 I/O	63,000	73,000
2004	T260 I/O	57,000	67,000
2003	T260 I/O	52,000	61,000

Charappal 28/29 Signature

Year	Power	Retail Low	Retail High
2000	T190 I/O	36,000	42,000
1999	T190 I/O	33,000	39,000
1998	T190 I/O	31,000	37,000
1997	T190 I/O	29,000	34,000
1996	T190 I/O	28,000	32,000
1995	T190 I/O	26,000	30,000
2009	T220 I/O	111,000	129,000
2008	T220 I/O	101,000	118,000
2007	T220 I/O	91,000	107,000
2006	T220 I/O	83,000	97,000
2005	T220 I/O	76,000	90,000
2004	T220 I/O	70,000	82,000
2003	T220 I/O	65,000	76,000
2002	T190 I/O	59,000	70,000
2001	T190 I/O	55,000	64,000

Chaparral Signature 300

Year	Power	Retail Low	Retail High
2003	T260 I/O	65,000	76,000
2002	T260 I/O	59,000	69,000
2001	T260 I/O	55,000	64,000
2000	T260 I/O	50,000	59,000
1999	T260 I/O	46,000	54,000
1998	T260 I/O	42,000	50,000

Chaparral Signature 30/31

Year	Power	Retail Low	Retail High
1997	T260 I/O	26,000	30,000
1996	T260 I/O	24,000	28,000
1995	T260 I/O	22,000	26,000

Chaparral Signarure 310

Year	Power	Retail Low	Retail High
2009	T300 I/O	140,000	163,000
2008	T300 I/O	128,000	150,000
2007	T300 I/O	118,000	138,000
2006	T300 I/O	109,000	127,000
2005	T300 I/O	100,000	117,000
2004	T300 I/O	92,000	107,000

Chaparral Signature 330

Year	Power	Retail Low	Retail High
2009	T300 I/O	165,000	193,000
2008	T300 I/O	151,000	177,000
2007	T300 I/O	139,000	163,000
2006	T300 I/O	128,000	150,000
2005	T300 I/O	118,000	138,000
2004	T300 I/O	108,000	127,000
2003	T300 I/O	100,000	117,000

Chaparral Signature 350

Year	Power	Retail Low	Retail High
2009	T320	221,000	254,000
2008	T320	201,000	231,000
2007	T320	183,000	210,000
2006	T320	166,000	191,000
2005	T300	151,000	174,000
2004	T300	139,000	160,000
2003	T300	128,000	147,000
2002	T300	118,000	135,000
2001	T300	108,000	124,000

Chris Craft 272/282/30 Crowne

Year	Power	Retail Low	Retail High
1997	T215 I/O	22,000	25,000
1996	T215 I/O	20,000	24,000
1995	T215 I/O	19,000	23,000

Chris Craft 28 Corsair

Year	Power	Retail Low	Retail High
2008	T280 I/O	105,000	123,000
2007	T320 I/O	96,000	113,000
2006	T320 I/O	89,000	104,000
2005	T320 I/O	82,000	95,000
2004	T375 I/O	75,000	88,000
2003	T375 I/O	69,000	81,000

Chris Craft 28 Launch

Year	Power	Retail Low	Retail High
2009	T320 I/O	******	******
2008	T320 I/O	72,000	84,000
2007	T320 I/O	66,000	78,000
2006	T320 I/O	61,000	71,000
2005	T320 I/O	56,000	66,000
2004	T375 I/O	52,000	60,000
2003	T375 I/O	47,000	56,000

Chris Craft 300/308 Express Cruiser

Year	Power	Retail Low	Retail High
2003	T270 I/O	52,000	61,000
2002	T270 I/O	48,000	56,000
2001	T250 I/O	43,000	51,000
2000	T250 I/O	39,000	46,000
1999	T250 I/O	36,000	42,000

Chris Craft 320/328 Express Cruiser

Year	Power	Retail Low	Retail High
2003	T270 I/O	58,000	68,000
2002	T270 I/O	53,000	62,000
2001	T280 I/O	48,000	56,000
2000	T280 I/O	44,000	51,000
1999	T280 I/O	40,000	46,000
1998	T280 I/O	36,000	43,000
1997	T280 I/O	33,000	39,000

Chris Craft 33 Corsair

Year	Power	Retail Low	Retail High
2009	T420 I/O	******	******
2008	T420 I/O	166,000	190,000
2007	T420 I/O	152,000	175,000
2006	T420 I/O	140,000	161,000

Chris Craft 33 Crowne

Year	Power	Retail Low	Retail High
1997	T250 I/O	26,000	29,000
1996	T250 I/O	23,000	27,000
1995	T250 I/O	22,000	25,000

Chris Craft 34 Crowne

Year	Power	Retail Low	Retail High
1997	T320G I/B	38,000	43,000
1996	T320G I/B	35,000	41,000
1995	T300G I/B	33,000	38,000

Chris Craft 380 Continental

Year	Power	Retail Low	Retail High
1997	T380G	70,000	81,000
1996	T330G	66,000	77,000
1995	T330G	63,000	73,000

Chris Craft 40 Roamer

Year	Power	Retail Low	Retail High
2008	T370D	******	******
2007	T370D	******	******
2006	T370D	244,000	281,000
2005	480D	224,000	258,000
2004	480D	206,000	238,000
2003	480D	190,000	218,000

Cobia 250/260/270 Walkaround

Year	Power	Retail Low	Retail High
2007	T200 O/B	50,000	58,000
2006	T200 O/B	45,000	53,000
2005	T200 O/B	41,000	48,000
2004	T200 O/B	37,000	44,000
2003	T200 O/B	34,000	40,000
2002	T200 O/B	31,000	36,000
2001	T200 O/B	29,000	33,000
2000	T200 O/B	26,000	31,000
1999	T200 O/B	24,000	28,000
1998	T200 O/B	22,000	26,000
1997	T200 O/B	20,000	24,000

Cobia 254/264/274 Center Console

Year	Power	Retail Low	Retail High
2002	T200 O/B	29,000	34,000
2001	T200 O/B	26,000	31,000
2000	T200 O/B	24,000	28,000
1999	T200 O/B	22,000	25,000
1998	T200 O/B	20,000	23,000
1997	T200 O/B	18,000	21,000

Cobia 274 Center Console

Year	Power	Retail Low	Retail High
2007	T200 O/B	49,000	57,000
2006	T200 O/B	44,000	51,000
2005	T200 O/B	39,000	46,000
2004	T200 O/B	35,000	42,000
2003	T200 O/B	32,000	37,000

Cobia 312 Sport Cabin

Year	Power	Retail Low	Retail High
2007	T250 O/B	68,000	80,000
2006	T250 O/B	62,000	73,000
2005	T250 O/B	56,000	66,000
2004	T250 O/B	51,000	60,000
2003	T250 O/B	47,000	55,000

Cobia 314 Center Console

Year	Power	Retail Low	Retail High
2007	T250 O/B	66,000	77,000
2006	T250 O/B	59,000	69,000
2005	T250 O/B	53,000	62,000
2004	T250 O/B	48,000	56,000
2004	T250 O/B	43,000	50,000
2003	T250 O/B	39,000	45,000

Contender 27 Open

Year	Power	Retail Low	Retail High
2007	T200 O/B	******	******
2006	T200 O/B	******	******
2005	T200 O/B	******	******
2004	T200 O/B	******	******
2003	T200 O/B	44,000	50,000
2002	T200 O/B	40,000	47,000
2001	T200 O/B	38,000	43,000
2000	T200 O/B	35,000	40,000
1999	T200 O/B	32,000	37,000
1998	T200 O/B	30,000	35,000
1997	T200 O/B	28,000	32,000
1996	T200 O/B	26,000	30,000
1995	T200 O/B	24,000	28,000

Contender 31 Open

Year	Power	Retail Low	Retail High
2007	T225 O/B	90,000	105,000
2006	T225 O/B	82,000	96,000
2005	T225 O/B	74,000	87,000
2004	T225 O/B	68,000	79,000
2003	T225 O/B	62,000	72,000
2002	T225 O/B	56,000	66,000
2001	T225 O/B	51,000	60,000
2000	T225 O/B	47,000	55,000
1999	T225 O/B	43,000	50,000
1998	T225 O/B	40,000	46,000
1997	T225 O/B	36,000	43,000
1996	T225 O/B	33,000	39,000
1995	T225 O/B	31,000	36,000

Contender 36 Open

Year	Power	Retail Low	Retail High
2007	3/250 O/B	88,000	102,000
2006	3/250 O/B	81,000	95,000
2005	3/250 O/B	76,000	89,000
2004	3/250 O/B	70,000	82,000
2003	3/250 O/B	65,000	77,000
2002	3/250 O/B	61,000	71,000
2001	3/250 O/B	56,000	66,000

Crownline 270 CR

Year	Power	Retail Low	Retail High
2009	300 I/O	74,000	86,000
2008	300 I/O	67,000	78,000
2007	300 I/O	61,000	71,000
2006	300 I/O	55,000	65,000
2005	300 I/O	50,000	59,000
2004	300 I/O	46,000	54,000

Year	Power	Retail Low	Retail High
Crownline 290 CR			
2004	T250G	44,000	50,000
2003	T250G	40,000	46,000
2002	T250G	36,000	42,000
2001	T250G	33,000	38,000
2000	T250G	30,000	34,000
1999	T250G	27,000	31,000
Crownline 330 CR			
2000	T310G	50,000	57,000
1999	T310G	46,000	53,000
1998	T310G	42,000	49,000
1997	T310G	39,000	45,000
1996	T310G	36,000	41,000
Crownline 340/350 CR			
2010	T300G	******	******
2009	T300G	******	******
2008	T300G	******	******
2007	T300G	125,000	143,000
Cruisers 2870 Exp; 280 CXi			
2007	T220G	51,000	60,000
2006	T220G	46,000	54,000
2005	T220G	42,000	49,000
2004	T220G	38,000	45,000
2003	T220G	35,000	41,000
2002	T220G	32,000	37,000
2001	T220G	29,000	34,000
2000	T220G	26,000	31,000
1999	T220G	24,000	28,000
1998	T220G	22,000	26,000
Cruisers 2870 Rogue			
1995	T235G	14,000	17,000
Cruisers 300 Cxi/300 Express			
2010	T225 I/O	******	******
2009	T225 I/O	95,000	111,000
2008	T225 I/O	86,000	101,000
2007	T225 I/O	78,000	92,000
2006	T225 I/O	71,000	83,000
2005	T220G	65,000	77,000
Cruisers 300/310 Express			
2007	T270G	90,000	105,000
2006	T270G	81,000	95,000
2005	T270G	74,000	87,000
Cruisers 3075 Express			
2003	T260G	61,000	71,000
2002	T260G	56,000	65,000
2001	T260G	51,000	60,000
2000	T260G	47,000	55,000
1999	T260G	44,000	51,000
1998	T260G	41,000	48,000
1997	T260G	38,000	44,000
Cruisers 3020/3120 Aria			
1997	T230G	29,000	34,000
1996	T230G	27,000	32,000
1995	T230G	25,000	29,000
Cruisers 3175 Rogue			
1998	T260G	35,000	41,000
1997	T260G	32,000	38,000
1996	T260G	30,000	35,000
1995	T260G	27,000	32,000
Cruisers 320 Express			
2006	T320G	77,000	90,000
2005	T320G	70,000	82,000
2004	T320G	64,000	75,000
2003	T320G	58,000	68,000
2002	T320G	53,000	62,000
Cruisers 330 Express			
2010	T320G	******	******
2009	T320G	162,000	186,000
2008	T375G	147,000	169,000
Cruisers 340 Express			
2007	T370G VD	131,000	151,000
2007	T375G I/O	123,000	142,000
2006	T370G VD	119,000	138,000
2006	T320G I/O	111,000	129,000
2005	T320G VD	108,000	125,000
2005	T320G I/O	101,000	118,000
2004	T320G VD	99,000	115,000
2004	T320G I/O	93,000	108,000
2003	T320G VD	91,000	106,000
2003	T320G I/O	86,000	100,000
2002	T320G VD	84,000	97,000
2002	T320G I/O	79,000	92,000
2001	T320G VD	77,000	90,000
2001	T320G I/O	72,000	84,000
Cruisers 3570/3575 Esprit; 3572 Exp.			
2002	T370G	94,000	109,000
2001	T310G	86,000	100,000
2000	T310G	79,000	92,000
1999	T310G	73,000	84,000
1998	T310G	67,000	78,000
1997	T310G	61,000	71,000
1996	T310G	56,000	66,000
1995	T310G	52,000	60,000
Cruisers 3580/3585 Flybridge			
1999	T320G	69,000	80,000
1998	T320G	63,000	73,000
1997	T320G	57,000	66,000
1996	T320G	52,000	60,000
Cruisers 360 Express			
2010	T375G	******	******
2009	T375G	242,000	278,000
2008	T375G	222,000	256,000
Cruisers 3670/3675/3775 Esprit			
1996	T310G	60,000	69,000
1995	T310G	55,000	63,000
Cruisers 3672/3772/370 Express			
2007	T375G	169,000	194,000
2006	T375G	153,000	177,000
2005	T370G	140,000	161,000
2004	T370G	127,000	146,000
2003	T370G	116,000	133,000
2002	T370G	105,000	121,000
2001	T370G	96,000	110,000
2000	T370G	87,000	100,000
Cruisers 3650/375 MY			
2005	T-Gas	172,000	197,000
2005	T310D	196,000	225,000
2004	T-Gas	156,000	179,000
2004	T370D	178,000	205,000
2003	T-Gas	142,000	163,000
2003	T370D	162,000	186,000
2002	T-Gas	129,000	149,000
2002	T370D	147,000	169,000
2001	T-Gas	117,000	135,000
2001	T370D	134,000	154,000
2000	T-Gas	108,000	124,000
2000	T370D	123,000	142,000
1999	T-Gas	99,000	114,000
1999	T370D	113,000	130,000
1998	T-Gas	91,000	105,000
1998	T-Diesel	104,000	120,000
1997	T-Gas	85,000	98,000
1997	T-Diesel	97,000	111,000
1996	T-Gas	79,000	91,000
1996	T-Diesel	90,000	104,000
1995	T-Gas	73,000	84,000
1995	T-Diesel	84,000	96,000
Cruisers 3870 Express			
2003	T370G	134,000	154,000
2002	T370G	122,000	140,000
2001	T370G	111,000	128,000
2000	T370G	101,000	116,000
1999	T380G	92,000	106,000
1998	T380G	83,000	96,000
1997	T380G	76,000	87,000
Cruisers 3850/3950 Aft Cabin MY			
1997	T310G	96,000	110,000
1997	T300D	120,000	138,000
1996	T310G	88,000	101,000
1996	T300D	110,000	127,000
1995	T310G	81,000	93,000
1995	T300D	101,000	116,000
Cruisers 390 Sports Coupe			
2010	T375G	******	******
2009	T375G	******	******
2008	T375G	208,000	239,000
2007	T375G	193,000	222,000
Cruisers 385/395 MY			
2008	T375G	274,000	315,000
2007	T370G	252,000	290,000
2006	T370G	232,000	267,000
Cruisers 3970/400/420 Express			
2010	T-Gas	******	******
2010	T-Diesel	******	******
2009	T370G	******	******
2009	T435D	******	******
2008	T375G	******	******
2008	T435D	******	******
2007	T375G	224,000	257,000
2007	T435D	260,000	300,000
2006	T375G	204,000	234,000
2006	T370D	237,000	273,000
2005	T375G	185,000	213,000
2005	T370D	216,000	248,000
2004	T375G	170,000	196,000
2004	T370D	198,000	228,000
2003	T375G	157,000	180,000
2003	T370D	182,000	210,000
Cruisers 405/415 Express MY			
2010	2010	******	******
2009	2009	******	******
2008	T435D	******	******
2007	T435D	320,000	368,000
2006	T370D	294,000	338,000
2005	T370D	270,000	311,000
2004	T370D	249,000	286,000
2003	T370D	229,000	263,000
Cruisers 4270 Express			
2003	T440D	202,000	233,000
2002	T440D	184,000	212,000
2001	T420D	167,000	192,000
2000	T420D	152,000	175,000
1999	T420D	138,000	159,000
1998	T420D	126,000	145,000
1997	T420D	115,000	132,000
Cruisers 4285 Express Bridge			
1995	T375D	85,000	97,000

Year	Power	Retail Low	Retail High
Cruisers 440 Express			
2005	T440D	215,000	247,000
2004	T440D	197,000	227,000
2003	T440D	181,000	209,000
Cruisers 4450 Express MY			
2003	T480D	269,000	309,000
2002	T480D	245,000	282,000
2001	T480D	223,000	256,000
2000	T480D	203,000	233,000
Cruisers 447 Sport Sedan			
2010	T435D	******	******
2009	T435D	******	******
2008	T435D	372,000	416,000
2007	T440D	338,000	379,000
Cruisers 455 Express MY			
2010	T480D	******	******
2009	T480D	******	******
2008	T480D	******	******
2007	T480D	405,000	454,000
2006	T480D	369,000	413,000
2005	T480D	335,000	376,000
2004	T480D	305,000	342,000
Cruisers 497 Sport Sedan			
2007	T575D	458,000	513,000
2006	T575D	417,000	467,000
Cruisers 5000 Sedan Sport			
2003	T710D	352,000	395,000
2002	T660D	320,000	359,000
2001	T660D	292,000	327,000
2000	T660D	265,000	297,000
1999	T660D	241,000	270,000
1998	T625D	220,000	246,000
Cruisers 520 Express			
2010	T715D	******	******
2009	T715D	******	******
2008	T715D	******	******
2007	T715D	495,000	554,000
2006	T715D	450,000	504,000
Cruisers 540/560 Express			
2010	T715D	******	******
2009	T715D	******	******
2008	T715D	******	******
2007	T715D	******	******
2006	T715D	578,000	648,000
2005	T715D	526,000	589,000
2004	T715D	479,000	536,000
2003	T800D	436,000	488,000
2002	T800D	396,000	444,000
2001	T800D	361,000	404,000
DeFever 44 Trawler			
2004	T-Diesel	345,000	397,000
2003	T-Diesel	321,000	369,000
2002	T-Diesel	299,000	343,000
2001	T-Diesel	278,000	319,000
2000	T135D	264,000	303,000
1999	T135D	250,000	288,000
1998	T135D	238,000	274,000
1997	T135D	226,000	260,000
1996	T135D	215,000	247,000
1995	T135D	206,000	237,000
DeFever 45 Pilothouse			
2008	T/225D	******	******
2007	T225D	******	******
2006	T150D	350,000	392,000
2005	T150D	332,000	372,000
2004	T150D	315,000	353,000
2003	T150D	300,000	336,000
2002	T150D	285,000	319,000
DeFever 49 Cockpit MY			
2007	T150D	381,000	426,000
2006	T150D	361,000	405,000
2005	T150D	343,000	385,000
2004	T150D	326,000	365,000
2003	T150D	310,000	347,000
2002	T150D	294,000	330,000
2001	T150D	280,000	313,000
2000	T150D	268,000	301,000
1999	T150D	258,000	289,000
1998	T135D	247,000	277,000
1997	T135D	237,000	266,000
1996	T135D	228,000	255,000
1995	T135D	219,000	245,000
1994	T135D	210,000	235,000
DeFever 49 PH (1977-2004)			
2004	T135D	******	******
2003	T135D	******	******
2002	T135D	301,000	337,000
2001	T135D	283,000	316,000
2000	T135D	266,000	297,000
1999	T135D	250,000	280,000
1998	T135D	235,000	263,000
1997	T135D	223,000	250,000
1996	T135D	212,000	237,000
1995	T135D	201,000	225,000
Donzi 275 Express			
2000	310 I/O	25,000	30,000
1999	310 I/O	23,000	28,000
1998	310 I/O	21,000	25,000
1997	310 I/O	19,000	23,000
1996	300 I/O	18,000	21,000
1995	300 I/O	16,000	20,000
Donzi 29 ZF Open			
2009	T250 O/B	******	******
2008	T250 O/B	86,000	101,000
2007	T250 O/B	78,000	92,000
2006	T250 O/B	71,000	84,000
2005	T250 O/B	64,000	76,000
2004	T250 O/B	58,000	69,000
2003	T250 O/B	53,000	63,000
Donzi 32 ZF			
2007	T250 O/B	89,000	105,000
2006	T250 O/B	80,000	95,000
2005	T250 O/B	73,000	86,000
2004	T250 O/B	67,000	79,000
2003	T250 O/B	61,000	72,000
2002	T250 O/B	56,000	66,000
2001	T250 O/B	52,000	61,000
2000	T250 O/B	48,000	56,000
Donzi 3250 Express			
2000	T310 I/O	58,000	68,000
1999	T310 I/O	53,000	62,000
1998	T300 I/O	49,000	57,000
1997	T300 I/O	45,000	53,000
1996	T300 I/O	41,000	49,000
Donzi 35 ZF Open			
2010	T275 O/B	******	******
2009	T275 O/B	******	******
2008	T275 O/B	******	******
2007	T275 O/B	105,000	123,000
2006	T275 O/B	95,000	112,000
2005	T275 O/B	86,000	102,000
2004	T275 O/B	79,000	93,000
2003	T275 O/B	72,000	84,000
Donzi 38 ZF Cuddy (col 3 top)			
2002	T225 O/B	65,000	77,000
2001	T225 O/B	59,000	70,000
2000	T225 O/B	54,000	64,000
1999	T225 O/B	49,000	58,000
1998	T225 O/B	44,000	53,000
Donzi 38 ZF Cuddy			
2010	3/250	******	******
2009	3/250	******	******
2008	3/250	******	******
2007	3/250	146,000	167,000
2006	3/250	134,000	154,000
2005	3/250	123,000	142,000
Donzi 38 ZFX			
2010	3/250	******	******
2009	3/250	******	******
2008	3/250	******	******
2007	3/250	150,000	174,000
2006	3/250	139,000	161,000
Donzi 38 ZSF			
2010	3/250	******	******
2009	3/250	******	******
2008	3/250	******	******
2007	3/250	167,000	192,000
2006	3/250	153,000	176,000
2005	3/250	141,000	162,000
2004	3/250	130,000	149,000
Donzi 54 Convertible			
1995	1150D	350,000	450,000
Dorado 30 Center Console			
2006	S-Diesel	62,000	74,000
2005	S-Diesel	57,000	67,000
2004	S-Diesel	52,000	61,000
2004	S-Diesel	47,000	55,000
2002	S-Diesel	43,000	50,000
2001	S-Diesel	39,000	46,000
2000	S-Diesel	36,000	42,000
1999	S-Diesel	33,000	39,000
1998	S-Diesel	30,000	36,000
1997	S-Diesel	28,000	33,000
1996	S-Diesel	25,000	30,000
Dyer 29 Trunk Cabin			
2003	S-Diesel	******	******
2002	S-Diesel	******	******
2001	S-Diesel	******	******
2000	S-Diesel	******	******
1999	S-Diesel	62,000	74,000
1998	S-Diesel	58,000	70,000
1997	S-Diesel	55,000	67,000
1996	S-Diesel	53,000	63,000
1995	S-Diesel	50,000	60,000
Eagle 32 PH Trawler			
1998	135D	95,000	118,000
1997	135D	90,000	112,000
1996	135D	85,000	107,000
1995	135D	81,000	101,000
Eagle 40 PH Trawler			
2002	S/Diesel	******	******
2001	S/Diesel	******	******
2000	S/Diesel	250,000	300,000
1999	S/Diesel	237,000	285,000
1998	S/Diesel	225,000	270,000
1997	S/Diesel	214,000	257,000
1996	S/Diesel	203,000	244,000
1995	S/Diesel	193,000	232,000

See Page 511 For Price Adjustments

Edgewater 318 Center Console

Year	Power	Retail Low	Retail High
2010	T250 O/B	******	******
2009	T250 O/B	124,000	145,000
2008	T250 O/B	114,000	133,000
2007	T250 O/B	104,000	122,000
2006	T250 O/B	96,000	112,000

Egg Harbor 34 Convertible

Year	Power	Retail Low	Retail High
1996	T320G	76,000	89,000
1996	T350D	95,000	111,000
1995	T320G	70,000	82,000
1995	T350D	88,000	102,000

Egg Harbor 35 Convertible

Year	Power	Retail Low	Retail High
1998	T320G	91,000	106,000
1998	T350D	115,000	133,000
1997	T320G	83,000	97,000
1997	T350D	105,000	121,000

Egg Harbor 35 Predator

Year	Power	Retail Low	Retail High
2010	T450D	******	******
2009	T450D	******	******
2008	T450D	******	******
2007	T440D	******	******
2006	T440D	196,000	225,000
2005	T440D	178,000	205,000
2004	T440D	162,000	186,000
2003	T440D	147,000	170,000
2002	T440D	******	******
2001	T440D	******	******
2000	T440D	******	******

Egg Harbor 37 Sport Yacht

Year	Power	Retail Low	Retail High
2010	T440D	******	******
2009	T440D	******	******
2008	T440D	******	******
2007	T440D	******	******
2006	T440D	257,000	288,000
2005	T440D	234,000	262,000
2004	T440D	213,000	239,000
2003	T440D	194,000	217,000
2002	T420D	176,000	198,000
2001	T420D	160,000	180,000

Egg Harbor 38 Convertible

Year	Power	Retail Low	Retail High
1997	T-Gas	119,000	134,000
1997	T420D	151,000	170,000
1996	T-Gas	108,000	121,000
1996	T420D	138,000	154,000
1995	T-Gas	99,000	111,000
1995	T420D	125,000	140,000

Egg Harbor 42 Convertible

Year	Power	Retail Low	Retail High
1997	420D	183,000	207,000
1996	420D	169,000	191,000
1995	420D	155,000	175,000

Egg Harbor 43 Sport Yacht

Year	Power	Retail Low	Retail High
2009	715D	******	******
2008	715D	******	******
2007	715D	400,000	460,000
2006	715D	368,000	423,000
2005	700D	338,000	389,000
2004	700D	311,000	358,000

Ellis 36 Express

Year	Power	Retail Low	Retail High
2003	440D	******	******
2002	440D	******	******
2001	440D	******	******
2000	440D	******	******
1999	440D	160,000	192,000
1998	440D	152,000	182,000

Endeavour TrawlerCat 36

Year	Power	Retail Low	Retail High
2005	T125D	******	******
2004	T125D	******	******
2003	T125D	130,000	156,000
2002	T125D	126,000	151,000
2001	T100D	122,000	146,000
2000	T100D	118,000	142,000
1999	T100D	115,000	138,000
1998	T100D	111,000	133,000

Endeavour TrawlerCat 44

Year	Power	Retail Low	Retail High
2004	T240D	215,000	258,000
2003	T240D	208,000	250,000
2002	T240D	203,000	242,000
2001	T240D	196,000	235,000

Everglades 260/270 Center Console

Year	Power	Retail Low	Retail High
2010	T250 O/B	******	******
2009	T250 O/B	92,000	110,000
2008	T250 O/B	84,000	100,000
2007	T250 O/B	76,000	91,000
2006	T250 O/B	69,000	83,000

Everglades 290 Center Console

Year	Power	Retail Low	Retail High
2010	T250 O/B	******	******
2009	T250 O/B	101,000	121,000
2008	T250 O/B	92,000	110,000
2007	T250 O/B	83,000	100,000
2006	T250 O/B	76,000	91,000
2005	T250 O/B	69,000	83,000

Everglades 350 Center Console

Year	Power	Retail Low	Retail High
2010	3/250 O/B	******	******
2009	3/250 O/B	175,000	203,000
2008	3/250 O/B	161,000	186,000
2007	3/250 O/B	148,000	171,000

Everglades 350 LX

Year	Power	Retail Low	Retail High
2010	3/250 O/B	******	******
2009	3/250 O/B	******	******
2008	3/250 O/B	185,000	216,000

Fairline 40 Targa

Year	Power	Retail Low	Retail High
2007	310D	253,000	283,000
2006	310D	233,000	261,000
2005	310D	214,000	240,000
2004	310D	197,000	221,000
2003	310D	181,000	203,000
2002	310D	167,000	187,000
2001	260D	153,000	172,000
2000	260D	141,000	158,000

Fairline 43 Phantom

Year	Power	Retail Low	Retail High
2004	480D	321,000	360,000
2003	480D	295,000	331,000
2002	480D	272,000	304,000
2001	480D	250,000	280,000
2000	480D	230,000	257,000

Fairline 43 Targa

Year	Power	Retail Low	Retail High
2004	480D	248,000	278,000
2003	480D	228,000	255,000
2002	480D	210,000	235,000
2001	480D	193,000	216,000
2000	480D	177,000	199,000
1999	480D	163,000	183,000
1998	480D	150,000	168,000

Fairline 46 Phantom

Year	Power	Retail Low	Retail High
2005	500D	418,000	469,000
2004	480D	385,000	431,000
2003	480D	354,000	397,000
2002	480D	326,000	365,000
2001	480D	300,000	336,000
2000	480D	276,000	309,000
1999	480D	254,000	284,000

Fairline 48 Targa

Year	Power	Retail Low	Retail High
2002	430D	250,000	280,000
2001	430D	232,000	260,000
2000	420D	216,000	242,000
1999	420D	201,000	225,000
1998	420D	187,000	209,000

Fairline 50 Phantom

Year	Power	Retail Low	Retail High
2006	T675D	******	******
2005	T675D	******	******
2004	T675D	480,000	537,000
2003	T675D	451,000	505,000
2002	T675D	424,000	475,000

Fairline 52 Squadron

Year	Power	Retail Low	Retail High
2002	T700D	372,000	417,000
2001	T600D	346,000	388,000
2000	T600D	322,000	361,000
1999	T600D	299,000	335,000
1998	T600D	278,000	312,000

Fairline 52 Targa

Year	Power	Retail Low	Retail High
2009	T800D	******	******
2008	T800D	******	******
2007	T800D	******	******
2006	T715D	552,000	618,000
2005	T715D	507,000	568,000
2004	T715D	467,000	523,000
2003	T715D	429,000	481,000

Fairline 55 Squadron

Year	Power	Retail Low	Retail High
2004	T715D	596,000	668,000
2003	T715D	555,000	621,000
2002	T700D	516,000	578,000
2001	T660D	480,000	537,000
2000	T660D	451,000	505,000
1999	T660D	424,000	475,000
1998	T660D	398,000	446,000
1997	T660D	374,000	419,000
1996	T660D	352,000	394,000

Fairline 58 Squadron

Year	Power	Retail Low	Retail High
2008	T715D	******	******
2007	T715D	******	******
2006	T800D	810,000	907,000
2005	T800D	753,000	843,000
2004	T800D	700,000	784,000
2003	T800D	651,000	729,000
2002	T700D	605,000	678,000
2001	T660D	563,000	631,000

Fairline 59 Squadron

Year	Power	Retail Low	Retail High
1999	T650D	410,000	459,000
1998	T650D	381,000	427,000
1997	T650D	354,000	397,000
1996	T650D	329,000	369,000

Fairline 62 Squadron

Year	Power	Retail Low	Retail High
2002	T1050D	******	******
2001	T1050D	585,000	672,000
2000	T1050D	549,000	632,000
1999	T1050D	516,000	594,000

Fairline 65 Squadron

Year	Power	Retail Low	Retail High
2003	T1400D	******	******
2002	T1400D	******	******
2001	T1400D	******	******
2000	T1400D	792,000	888,000
1999	T1000D	745,000	834,000
1998	T1000D	700,000	784,000
1997	T1000D	658,000	737,000
1996	T1000D	619,000	693,000
1995	T1000D	581,000	651,000

Fairline 74 Squadron

Year	Power	Retail Low	Retail High
2007	1550D	******	******

Year	Power	Retail Low	Retail High
2006	1550D	1,500,000	1,680,000
2005	1550D	1,395,000	1,562,000
2004	1300D	1,297,000	1,453,000
2003	1300D	1,206,000	1,351,000

Fleming 55 Pilothouse

Year	Power	Retail Low	Retail High
2010	T500D	******	******
2009	T500D	******	******
2008	T500D	1,000,000	1,120,000
2007	T450D	940,000	1,052,000
2006	T450D	883,000	989,000
2005	T450D	830,000	930,000
2004	T450D	780,000	874,000
2003	T450D	741,000	830,000
2002	T450D	704,000	789,000
2001	T450D	669,000	749,000
2000	T435D	635,000	712,000
1999	T435D	604,000	676,000
1998	T435D	573,000	642,000
1997	T435D	545,000	610,000
1996	T435D	517,000	580,000
1995	T435D	492,000	551,000

Fleming 65 Pilothouse

Year	Power	Retail Low	Retail High
2010	T800D	******	******
2009	T800D	******	******
2008	T800D	******	******
2007	T800D	1,800,000	2,070,000
2006	T800D	1,710,000	1,966,000

Fleming 75 Pilothouse MY

Year	Power	Retail Low	Retail High
2007	T800D	******	******
2006	T800D	******	******
2005	T800D	******	******
2004	T800D	******	******
2003	T800D	2,500,000	2,800,000
2002	T800D	2,350,000	2,632,000
2001	T800D	2,209,000	2,474,000

Formula 27 PC

Year	Power	Retail Low	Retail High
2010	T320G	******	******
2009	T320G	115,000	136,000
2008	T280G	105,000	124,000
2007	T280G	95,000	112,000
2006	T280G	88,000	103,000
2005	T280G	81,000	95,000
2004	T260G	74,000	87,000
2003	T260G	68,000	80,000
2002	T260G	63,000	74,000
2001	T260G	58,000	68,000
2000	T260G	53,000	63,000
1999	T260G	49,000	57,000
1998	T260G	45,000	53,000
1997	T250G	42,000	50,000
1996	T250G	39,000	46,000
1995	T250G	36,000	43,000
1994	T250G		

Formula 31 PC

Year	Power	Retail Low	Retail High
2010	T320G	******	******
2009	T320G	137,000	160,000
2008	T320G	124,000	145,000
2007	T320G	113,000	132,000
2006	T320G	104,000	122,000
2005	T320G	96,000	112,000
2004	T320G	88,000	103,000
2003	T320G	81,000	95,000
2002	T320G	74,000	87,000
2001	T320G	68,000	80,000
2000	T320G	63,000	74,000
1999	T310G	59,000	69,000
1998	T310G	55,000	64,000
1997	T310G	51,000	60,000

Year	Power	Retail Low	Retail High
1996	T330G	47,000	55,000
1995	T330G	44,000	52,000

Formula 34 PC (1991-2002)

Year	Power	Retail Low	Retail High
2002	T375G	93,000	107,000
2001	T375G	83,000	95,000
2000	T375G	76,000	88,000
1999	T375G	70,000	81,000
1998	T310G	64,000	74,000
1997	T300G	59,000	68,000
1996	T300G	54,000	63,000
1995	T300G	50,000	58,000

Formula 34 PC (2004-Current)

Year	Power	Retail Low	Retail High
2010	T375G	******	******
2009	T375G	170,000	195,000
2008	T375G	154,000	177,000
2007	T375G	140,000	161,000
2006	T375G	128,000	147,000
2005	T370G	116,000	134,000
2004	T370G	106,000	121,000

Formula 36 PC

Year	Power	Retail Low	Retail High
1995	T300G	45,000	55,000

Formula 37 PC

Year	Power	Retail Low	Retail High
2010	T375G	******	******
2009	T375G	******	******
2008	T375G	160,000	185,000
2007	T375G	147,000	170,000
2006	T375G	135,000	157,000
2005	T375G	124,000	144,000
2004	T375G	114,000	132,000
2003	T375G	106,000	123,000
2002	T375G	99,000	114,000
2001	T400G	92,000	106,000
2000	T400G	85,000	99,000
1999	T400G	79,000	92,000

Formula 40 PC

Year	Power	Retail Low	Retail High
2010	T425G	******	******
2010	T440D	******	******
2009	T425G	******	******
2009	T440D	******	******
2008	T425G	263,000	295,000
2008	T440D	298,000	334,000
2007	T425G	240,000	269,000
2007	T440D	271,000	303,000
2006	T425G	218,000	244,000
2006	T440D	246,000	276,000
2005	T425G	198,000	222,000
2005	T440D	224,000	251,000
2004	T420G	182,000	204,000
2004	T440D	206,000	231,000
2003	T420G	168,000	188,000
2003	T440D	190,000	213,000

Formula 41 PC

Year	Power	Retail Low	Retail High
2004	T480D	******	******
2003	T480D	******	******
2002	T450D	187,000	215,000
2001	T450D	170,000	196,000
2000	T450D	156,000	180,000
1999	T450D	144,000	166,000
1998	T420D	132,000	152,000
1997	T420D	122,000	140,000
1996	T420D	112,000	129,000

Formula 45 Yacht

Year	Power	Retail Low	Retail High
2010	T435D	******	******
2009	T435D	******	******
2008	T435D	439,000	497,000
2007	T435D	404,000	457,000

Formula 48

Year	Power	Retail Low	Retail High
2007	T660D	508,000	574,000
2006	T660D	462,000	522,000
2005	T660D	421,000	475,000
2004	T660D	383,000	432,000

Four Winns 278 Vista (1994-98)

Year	Power	Retail Low	Retail High
1998	T205 I/O	18,000	21,000
1997	T205 I/O	16,000	20,000
1996	T205 I/O	15,000	18,000
1995	T190 I/O	14,000	16,000

Four Winns 278/285 Vista

Year	Power	Retail Low	Retail High
2010	320 I/O	85,000	102,000
2009	300 I/O	77,000	92,000
2008	300 I/O	70,000	84,000
2007	300 I/O	64,000	76,000
2006	280 I/O	58,000	69,000

Four Winns 288 Vista

Year	Power	Retail Low	Retail High
2009	T270G	97,000	116,000
2008	T270G	88,000	106,000
2007	T270G	80,000	96,000
2006	T270G	73,000	88,000
2005	T270G	67,000	81,000
2004	T270G	62,000	74,000

Four Winns 298 Vista

Year	Power	Retail Low	Retail High
2005	T280G	69,000	83,000
2004	T280G	63,000	76,000
2003	T280G	57,000	69,000
2002	T280G	52,000	62,000
2001	T280G	47,000	57,000
2000	T280G	43,000	52,000
1999	T280G	39,000	47,000

Four Winns 318/335 Vista

Year	Power	Retail Low	Retail High
2010	T270G	150,000	180,000
2009	T270G	136,000	163,000
2008	T270G	124,000	149,000
2007	T270G	113,000	135,000
2006	T270G	102,000	123,000

Four Winns 328 Vista

Year	Power	Retail Low	Retail High
2006	T280G	115,000	138,000
2005	T280G	105,000	126,000
2004	T280G	95,000	114,000
2003	T280G	86,000	104,000
2002	T280G	79,000	94,000
2001	T280G	72,000	87,000
2000	T280G	66,000	80,000
1999	T280G	61,000	73,000

Four Winns 338/358 Vista

Year	Power	Retail Low	Retail High
2009	T300 I/O	151,000	182,000
2008	T320 I/O	138,000	165,000
2007	T320 I/O	125,000	150,000

Four Winns 348 Vista

Year	Power	Retail Low	Retail High
2004	T320 I/B	113,000	134,000
2003	T320 I/B	103,000	122,000
2002	T320 I/B	94,000	111,000
2001	T320 I/B	85,000	101,000

Four Winns 348/358/375 Vista

Year	Power	Retail Low	Retail High
2010	T320 I/B	******	******
2010	T320 I/O	******	******
2009	T320 I/B	******	******
2009	T320 I/O	******	******
2008	T320 I/B	160,000	187,000
2008	T320 I/O	153,000	179,000
2007	T320 I/B	145,000	170,000
2007	T320 I/O	139,000	163,000
2006	T320 I/B	132,000	155,000
2006	T320 I/O	127,000	148,000
2005	T320 I/B	120,000	141,000
2005	T320 I/O	115,000	135,000

See Page 511 For Price Adjustments

Four Winns 378 Vista

Year	Power	Retail Low	Retail High
2009	T400G IPS	******	******
2008	T375G	224,000	262,000
2007	T375G	204,000	238,000
2006	T370G	185,000	217,000
2005	T420G	168,000	197,000
2004	T420G	155,000	181,000
2003	T420G	142,000	167,000
2002	T420G	131,000	153,000

Four Winns V458/V475

Year	Power	Retail Low	Retail High
2010	T418D IPS	******	******
2009	T435D IPS	******	******
2008	T435D IPS	387,000	446,000

Grady-White 263/273 Chase

Year	Power	Retail Low	Retail High
2010	T200 O/B	******	******
2009	T200 O/B	******	******
2008	T200 O/B	77,000	93,000
2007	T200 O/B	70,000	84,000
2006	T200 O/B	63,000	75,000
2005	T200 O/B	56,000	68,000
2004	T200 O/B	51,000	62,000
2003	T200 O/B	47,000	56,000
2002	T200 O/B	42,000	51,000
2001	T200 O/B	38,000	46,000
2000	T200 O/B	35,000	42,000
1999	T200 O/B	32,000	38,000
1998	T200 O/B	29,000	35,000
1997	T200 O/B	26,000	32,000
1996	T200 O/B	24,000	29,000
1995	T200 O/B	22,000	26,000

Grady-White 270 Islander

Year	Power	Retail Low	Retail High
2005	T225 O/B	50,000	60,000
2004	T225 O/B	46,000	55,000
2003	T225 O/B	42,000	50,000
2002	T225 O/B	38,000	46,000

Grady-White 272 Sailfish

Year	Power	Retail Low	Retail High
2000	T225 O/B	35,000	42,000
1999	T225 O/B	32,000	38,000
1998	T225 O/B	29,000	35,000
1997	T225 O/B	26,000	32,000
1996	T225 O/B	24,000	29,000
1995	T225 O/B	22,000	26,000

Grady-White 275 Tournament

Year	Power	Retail Low	Retail High
2010	T200 O/B	******	******
2009	T200 O/B	******	******
2008	T200 O/B	75,000	90,000
2007	T200 O/B	68,000	82,000

Grady-White 282 Sailfish

Year	Power	Retail Low	Retail High
2008	T225 O/B	102,000	120,000
2007	T225 O/B	92,000	109,000
2006	T225 O/B	84,000	99,000
2005	T225 O/B	76,000	90,000
2004	T225 O/B	69,000	82,000
2003	T225 O/B	63,000	75,000
2002	T225 O/B	57,000	68,000
2001	T225 O/B	52,000	62,000

Grady-White 283 Release

Year	Power	Retail Low	Retail High
2010	T225 O/B	******	******
2009	T225 O/B	97,000	116,000
2008	T225 O/B	88,000	106,000
2007	T225 O/B	80,000	96,000
2006	T225 O/B	73,000	88,000
2005	T225 O/B	67,000	81,000
2004	T225 O/B	62,000	74,000
2003	T225 O/B	57,000	68,000
2002	T225 O/B	52,000	63,000

Grady-White 290 Chesapeake

Year	Power	Retail Low	Retail High
2010	T225 O/B	140,000	163,000
2009	T225 O/B	127,000	149,000

Grady White 300 Marlin

Year	Power	Retail Low	Retail High
2010	T225 O/B	******	******
2009	T225 O/B	******	******
2008	T225 O/B	127,000	149,000
2007	T225 O/B	115,000	135,000
2006	T225 O/B	105,000	123,000
2005	T225 O/B	97,000	113,000
2004	T225 O/B	89,000	104,000
2003	T225 O/B	82,000	96,000
2002	T225 O/B	75,000	88,000
2001	T225 O/B	69,000	81,000
2000	T225 O/B	63,000	74,000
1999	T225 O/B	58,000	68,000
1998	T225 O/B	54,000	64,000
1997	T225 O/B	50,000	59,000
1996	T225 O/B	47,000	55,000
1995	T225 O/B	44,000	51,000

Grady-White 305 Express

Year	Power	Retail Low	Retail High
2010	T250 O/B	160,000	187,000
2009	T250 O/B	145,000	170,000
2008	T250 O/B	132,000	155,000
2007	T250 O/B	120,000	141,000

Grady-White 306 Bimini

Year	Power	Retail Low	Retail High
2010	T250 I/O	138,000	161,000
2009	T250 I/O	125,000	146,000
2008	T250 I/O	114,000	133,000
2007	T250 I/O	103,000	121,000
2006	T250 I/O	94,000	110,000
2005	T250 I/O	87,000	101,000
2004	T250 I/O	80,000	93,000
2003	T250 I/O	73,000	86,000
2002	T250 I/O	67,000	79,000
2001	T250 I/O	62,000	72,000
2000	T250 I/O	57,000	67,000
1999	T250 I/O	52,000	61,000
1998	T250 I/O	48,000	56,000

Grady-White 307 Tournament

Year	Power	Retail Low	Retail High
2010	T250 O/B	141,000	166,000
2009	T250 O/B	130,000	152,000

Grady-White 330 Express

Year	Power	Retail Low	Retail High
2010	T250 O/B	251,000	291,000
2009	T250 O/B	228,000	264,000
2008	T250 O/B	207,000	241,000
2007	T250 O/B	189,000	219,000
2006	T250 O/B	172,000	199,000
2005	T250 O/B	158,000	183,000
2004	T250 O/B	145,000	168,000
2003	T250 O/B	134,000	155,000
2002	T250 O/B	123,000	143,000
2001	T250 O/B	113,000	131,000

Grady-White 336 Canyon

Year	Power	Retail Low	Retail High
2010	T250 O/B	******	******
2009	T250 O/B	155,000	179,000
2008	T250 O/B	141,000	163,000

Grady-White 360 Express

Year	Power	Retail Low	Retail High
2010	3/250 O/B	358,000	411,000
2009	3/250 O/B	325,000	374,000
2008	3/250 O/B	299,000	344,000
2007	3/250 O/B	275,000	317,000
2006	3/250 O/B	253,000	291,000
2005	3/250 O/B	233,000	268,000

Grand Alaskan 64 PH

Year	Power	Retail Low	Retail High
2006	T715D	990,000	1,188,000
2005	T715D	930,000	1,116,000
2004	T715D	874,000	1,049,000
2003	T715D	822,000	986,000
2002	T450D	772,000	927,000
2001	T435D	734,000	881,000
2000	T435D	697,000	837,000
1999	T435D	662,000	795,000
1998	T435D	629,000	755,000

Grand Banks 32 Sedan

Year	Power	Retail Low	Retail High
1995	135D	80,000	95,000

Grand Banks 36 Classic

Year	Power	Retail Low	Retail High
2004	T210D	******	******
2003	T210D	******	******
2002	T210D	******	******
2001	T210D	******	******
2000	T210D	******	******
1999	No Prod	******	******
1998	No Prod	******	******
1997	No Prod	******	******
1996	210D	130,000	156,000
1996	T210D	144,000	172,000

Grand Banks 36 Europa

Year	Power	Retail Low	Retail High
1998	210D	******	******
1997	210D	******	******
1996	210D	130,000	156,000
1996	T210D	144,000	172,000
1995	210D	123,000	148,000
1995	T210D	136,000	164,000

Grand Banks 36 Motor Yacht

Year	Power	Retail Low	Retail High
1998	T210D	200,000	230,000
1997	T210D	188,000	216,000
1996	T210D	176,000	203,000
1995	T135D	166,000	191,000

Grand Banks 36 Sedan

Year	Power	Retail Low	Retail High
1996	210D	155,000	186,000
1995	210D	147,000	176,000

Grand Banks 38 Eastbay Express

Year	Power	Retail Low	Retail High
2004	T420D	******	******
2003	T350D	******	******
2002	T375D	******	******
2001	T375D	220,000	254,000
2000	T375D	205,000	236,000
1999	T375D	191,000	219,000
1998	T375D	177,000	204,000
1997	T375D	167,000	192,000
1996	T375D	157,000	180,000
1995	T375D	147,000	169,000
1994	T375D	138,000	159,000

Grand Banks Eastbay 39 SX

Year	Power	Retail Low	Retail High
2010	T380D	******	******
2009	T500D	******	******
2008	T500D	******	******
2007	T445D	403,000	464,000
2006	T480D	379,000	436,000

Grand Banks 41 Heritage EU

Year	Power	Retail Low	Retail High
2010	T425D	850,000	952,000
2009	T425D	782,000	875,000

Grand Banks 42 Classic

Year	Power	Retail Low	Retail High
2004	T450D	274,000	324,000
2003	T450D	258,000	305,000
2002	T450D	242,000	286,000
2001	T450D	228,000	269,000
2000	T375D	216,000	256,000
1999	T350D	206,000	243,000
1998	T350D	195,000	231,000
1997	T375D	186,000	219,000

Year	Power	Retail Low	Retail High
1996	T375D	176,000	208,000
1995	T375D	167,000	198,000

Grand Banks 42 Europa

Year	Power	Retail Low	Retail High
2004	T450D	277,000	326,000
2003	T450D	260,000	307,000
2002	T450D	244,000	288,000
2001	T450D	230,000	271,000
2000	T375D	218,000	257,000
1999	T350D	207,000	245,000
1998	T350D	197,000	232,000
1997	T375D	187,000	221,000
1996	T375D	178,000	210,000
1991-95 No Prod.		******	******

Grand Banks 42 Motor Yacht

Year	Power	Retail Low	Retail High
2004	T450D	285,000	336,000
2003	T450D	267,000	316,000
2002	T450D	251,000	297,000
2001	T450D	236,000	279,000
2000	T375D	224,000	265,000
1999	T350D	213,000	252,000
1998	T350D	202,000	239,000
1997	T375D	192,000	227,000
1996	T375D	183,000	216,000
1995	T375D	174,000	205,000
1994	T300D	165,000	195,000
1993	T300D	158,000	187,000
1992	T300D	152,000	179,000
1991	T300D	146,000	172,000
1990	T300D	140,000	165,000

Grand Banks 43 Eastbay Flybridge

Year	Power	Retail Low	Retail High
2004	T420D	345,000	407,000
2003	T420D	327,000	386,000
2002	T420D	311,000	367,000
2001	T420D	295,000	349,000
2000	T420D	281,000	331,000
1999	T420D	269,000	318,000
1998	T420D	258,000	305,000

Grand Banks 43 Eastbay Express

Year	Power	Retail Low	Retail High
2004	T420D	320,000	377,000
2003	T420D	304,000	358,000
2002	T420D	288,000	340,000
2001	T420D	274,000	323,000
2000	T420D	260,000	307,000

Grand Banks 43 Eastbay HX

Year	Power	Retail Low	Retail High
2007	T455D	350,000	413,000
2006	T455D	329,000	388,000
2005	T440D	309,000	364,000
2004	T440D	290,000	343,000
2003	T440D	273,000	322,000
2002	T440D	256,000	303,000

Grand Banks 43 Eastbay SX

Year	Power	Retail Low	Retail High
2007	T455D	370,000	436,000
2006	T455D	347,000	410,000
2005	T440D	326,000	385,000
2004	T440D	307,000	362,000
2003	T440D	288,000	340,000
2002	T440D	271,000	320,000

Grand Banks 46 Classic

Year	Power	Retail Low	Retail High
2007	T455D	******	******
2006	T455D	445,000	516,000
2005	T465D	422,000	490,000
2004	T465D	401,000	465,000
2003	T420D	381,000	442,000
2002	T420D	366,000	424,000
2001	T420D	351,000	407,000
2000	T375D	337,000	391,000
1999	T375D	324,000	375,000
1998	T375D	311,000	360,000
1997	T375D	298,000	346,000
1996	T375D	286,000	332,000
1995	T375D	275,000	319,000
1994	T135D	266,000	309,000
1993	T135D	258,000	300,000
1992	T135D	251,000	291,000
1991	T135D	243,000	282,000
1990	T135D	236,000	274,000
1989	T135D	229,000	265,000
1988	T135D	222,000	257,000
1987	T135D	215,000	250,000

Grand Banks 46 Europa

Year	Power	Retail Low	Retail High
2008	T500D	******	******
2007	T500D	******	******
2006	T500D	427,000	495,000
2005	T500D	401,000	465,000
2004	T450D	377,000	437,000
2003	T420D	358,000	415,000
2002	T420D	340,000	394,000
2001	T420D	323,000	375,000
2000	T375D	307,000	356,000
1999	T375D	291,000	338,000
1998	T375D	277,000	321,000
1997	T375D	263,000	305,000
1996	T375D	252,000	293,000
1995	T375D	242,000	281,000
1994	T135D	233,000	270,000
1993	T135D	223,000	259,000

Grand Banks 46 Motor Yacht

Year	Power	Retail Low	Retail High
2001	T375D	******	******
2000	T375D	******	******
1999	T375D	******	******
1998	T375D	******	******
1997	T375D	******	******
1996	T375D	250,000	295,000
1995	T375D	237,000	280,000

Grand Banks 47 Eastbay FB

Year	Power	Retail Low	Retail High
2010	T670D	******	******
2009	T670D	******	******
2008	T720D	******	******
2007	T720D	******	******
2006	T720D	550,000	643,000
2005	T720D	522,000	611,000

Grand Banks 47 Heritage Classic

Year	Power	Retail Low	Retail High
2010	T670D	******	******
2009	T670D	******	******
2008	T567D	730,000	854,000
2007	T567D	693,000	811,000

Grand Banks 47 Heritage Europa

Year	Power	Retail Low	Retail High
2010	T670D	******	******
2009	T670D	******	******
2008	T567D	730,000	854,000
2007	T567D	693,000	811,000

Grand Banks 49 Classic

Year	Power	Retail Low	Retail High
1997	T375D	******	******
1996	T375D	******	******
1995	T375D	315,000	368,000

Grand Banks 49 Eastbay SX

Year	Power	Retail Low	Retail High
2010	T705D	******	******
2009	T705D	******	******
2008	T705D	******	******
2007	T705D	650,000	760,000
2006	T705D	611,000	714,000
2005	T700D	574,000	671,000
2004	T700D	539,000	631,000
2003	T700D	512,000	600,000
2002	T700D	487,000	570,000
2001	T700D	462,000	541,000
2000	T670D	439,000	514,000
1999	T670D	417,000	488,000

Grand Banks 49 Motor Yacht

Year	Power	Retail Low	Retail High
1999	T375D	426,000	498,000
1998	T375D	404,000	473,000
1997	T375D	384,000	449,000
1996	T375D	365,000	427,000
1995	T375D	346,000	405,000

Grand Banks 52 Europa

Year	Power	Retail Low	Retail High
2008	T660D	970,000	1,134,000
2007	T660D	921,000	1,078,000
2006	T660D	875,000	1,024,000
2005	T660D	831,000	973,000
2004	T660D	790,000	924,000
2003	T375D	750,000	878,000
2002	T375D	713,000	834,000
2001	T375D	677,000	792,000
2000	T375D	650,000	760,000
1999	T375D	624,000	730,000
1998	T375D	599,000	701,000

Grand Banks 54 Eastbay SX

Year	Power	Retail Low	Retail High
2007	T1000D	******	******
2006	T1000D	770,000	900,000
2005	T1000D	731,000	855,000
2004	T800D	694,000	813,000
2003	T800D	660,000	772,000

Grand Banks 58 Eastbay FB

Year	Power	Retail Low	Retail High
2007	T1550D	******	******
2006	T1550D	1,300,000	1,521,000
2005	T1550D	1,235,000	1,444,000
2004	T1400D	1,173,000	1,372,000
2003	T1400D	1,114,000	1,304,000

Grand Banks 58 Classic

Year	Power	Retail Low	Retail High
2002	T660D	******	******
2001	T660D	******	******
2000	T660D	******	******
1999	T660D	******	******
1998	T660D	******	******
1997	T460D	******	******
1996	T460D	550,000	649,000
1995	T460D	522,000	616,000

Grand Banks 59 Aleutian RP

Year	Power	Retail Low	Retail High
2010	T1000D	******	******
2009	T1000D	2,300,000	2,645,000
2008	T1000D	2,185,000	2,512,000
2007	T1000D	2,075,000	2,387,000

Grand Banks 72 Aleutian

Year	Power	Retail Low	Retail High
2010	T1015D	******	******
2009	T1015D	******	******
2008	T1015D	******	******
2007	T1000D	******	******
2006	T1000D	2,500,000	2,875,000

Hampton 580 PH

Year	Power	Retail Low	Retail High
2010	T720D	******	******
2009	T715D	1,700,000	1,955,000
2008	T715D	1,598,000	1,837,000

Hatteras 39 Convertible

Year	Power	Retail Low	Retail High
1998	485D	158,000	185,000
1997	485D	146,000	170,000
1996	485D	134,000	157,000
1995	485D	123,000	144,000

Hatteras 39 Sport Express

Year	Power	Retail Low	Retail High
1998	485D	149,000	175,000
1997	485D	137,000	161,000

Year	Power	Retail Low	Retail High	Year	Power	Retail Low	Retail High	Year	Power	Retail Low	Retail High
1996	485D	126,000	148,000	2004	1400D	828,000	953,000	2005	S440D	201,000	237,000
1995	485D	116,000	136,000	2003	1400D	754,000	867,000	2004	S440D	187,000	220,000
				2002	1400D	686,000	789,000	2003	S440D	173,000	205,000

Hatteras 40 Motor Yacht | **Hatteras 55 Convertible** | **Hinckley 36 Picnic Boat**

Year	Power	Retail Low	Retail High	Year	Power	Retail Low	Retail High	Year	Power	Retail Low	Retail High
1997	T340D	157,000	184,000	2002	1450D	775,000	914,000	2007	S440 Jet	******	******
1996	T340D	144,000	169,000	2001	1450D	705,000	832,000	2006	S440 Jet	******	******
1995	T340D	133,000	155,000	2000	1450D	641,000	757,000	2005	S440 Jet	288,000	346,000
				1999	1450D	584,000	689,000	2004	S440 Jet	274,000	329,000

Hatteras 42 Cockpit MY | **Hatteras 60 Convertible**

Year	Power	Retail Low	Retail High	Year	Power	Retail Low	Retail High	Year	Power	Retail Low	Retail High
1997	T364D	169,000	199,000	2010	1800D	******	******	2003	S440 Jet	260,000	312,000
1996	T364D	157,000	185,000	2009	1800D	******	******	2002	S350 Jet	250,000	300,000
1995	T340D	146,000	172,000	2008	1800D	******	******	2001	S350 Jet	240,000	288,000
				2007	1800D	******	******	2000	S350 Jet	230,000	276,000

Hatteras 43 Convertible

Year	Power	Retail Low	Retail High	Year	Power	Retail Low	Retail High	Year	Power	Retail Low	Retail High
1998	T625D	226,000	267,000	2006	1800D	******	******	1999	S350 Jet	221,000	265,000
1997	T625D	208,000	246,000	2005	1650D	1,174,000	1,350,000	1998	S350 Jet	212,000	255,000
1996	T535D	191,000	226,000	2004	1650D	1,080,000	1,242,000	1997	S350 Jet	204,000	244,000
1995	T535D	176,000	208,000	2003	1400D	994,000	1,143,000	1996	S350 Jet	195,000	235,000

Hatteras 43 Sport Express

Year	Power	Retail Low	Retail High	Year	Power	Retail Low	Retail High	Year	Power	Retail Low	Retail High
1998	T625D	207,000	245,000	2002	1400D	914,000	1,051,000	1995	S350 Jet	188,000	225,000
1997	T600D	191,000	225,000	2001	1400D	841,000	967,000				
1996	T600D	175,000	207,000	2000	1400D	782,000	899,000				

Hatteras 46 Conv. (1992-95) | | **Hinckley Talaria 40**

Year	Power	Retail Low	Retail High	Year	Power	Retail Low	Retail High	Year	Power	Retail Low	Retail High
1995	720D	250,000	292,000	1999	1400D	727,000	836,000	2010	T440D	******	******
				1998	1350D	676,000	778,000	2009	T440D	550,000	660,000

Hatteras 48 Cockpit MY | **Hatteras 60 Motor Yacht**

Year	Power	Retail Low	Retail High	Year	Power	Retail Low	Retail High	Year	Power	Retail Low	Retail High
1996	T535D	248,000	291,000	2010	T1000D	******	******	2008	T440D	522,000	627,000
1995	T535D	239,000	279,000	2009	T1000D	******	******	2007	T440D	496,000	595,000
				2008	T1000D	1,600,000	1,840,000	2006	T440D	471,000	565,000

Hatteras 48 MY (1990-96) | **Hatteras 6300 Raised Pilothouse**

Year	Power	Retail Low	Retail High	Year	Power	Retail Low	Retail High	Year	Power	Retail Low	Retail High
1996	T720D	269,000	310,000	2003	1500D	964,000	1,128,000	2005	T440D	452,000	543,000
1995	T720D	248,000	285,000	2002	1400D	896,000	1,049,000	2004	T440D	434,000	521,000
				2001	1400D	834,000	975,000	2003	T440D	417,000	500,000

Hatteras 50 Convertible

Year	Power	Retail Low	Retail High	Year	Power	Retail Low	Retail High	Year	Power	Retail Low	Retail High
2006	1000D	******	******	2000	1400D	775,000	907,000	2002	T440D	400,000	480,000

Hatteras 65 Convertible | **Hinckley Talaria 44 Express**

Year	Power	Retail Low	Retail High	Year	Power	Retail Low	Retail High	Year	Power	Retail Low	Retail High
2005	1000D	680,000	789,000	2003	1400D	1,200,000	1,404,000	2008	T440D	******	******
2004	1000D	625,000	726,000	2002	1400D	1,104,000	1,291,000	2007	T440D	******	******
2003	1000D	575,000	667,000	2001	1400D	1,015,000	1,188,000	2006	T440D	******	******
2002	800D	529,000	614,000	2000	1400D	934,000	1,093,000	2005	T440D	******	******
2001	800D	487,000	565,000	1999	1400D	859,000	1,005,000	2004	T440D	******	******
2000	800D	448,000	520,000	1998	1450D	790,000	925,000	2003	T440D	******	******
1999	800D	412,000	478,000	1997	1400D	727,000	851,000	2002	T440D	460,000	552,000
1998	900D	379,000	440,000	1996	1350D	669,000	783,000	2001	T440D	437,000	524,000
1997	870D	349,000	405,000	1995	1350D	615,000	720,000	2000	T440D	415,000	498,000
1996	870D	321,000	372,000					1999	T440D	394,000	473,000
1995	870D	295,000	342,000								

Hatteras 50 Sport Deck MY | **Hatteras 65 Motor Yacht** | **Hunt 29 Surfhunter**

Year	Power	Retail Low	Retail High	Year	Power	Retail Low	Retail High	Year	Power	Retail Low	Retail High
1998	T565D	340,000	397,000	1996	870D	680,000	795,000	2010	S315D	******	******
1997	T545D	316,000	369,000	1995	870D	632,000	739,000	2009	S315D	******	******
1996	T545D	294,000	344,000					2008	S315D	210,000	252,000

Hatteras 52 Cockpit MY | **Heritage East 36 Sundeck**

Year	Power	Retail Low	Retail High	Year	Power	Retail Low	Retail High	Year	Power	Retail Low	Retail High
1999	800D	385,000	451,000	2010	230D	******	******	2007	S315D	191,000	229,000
1998	760D	354,000	415,000	2009	230D	******	******	2006	S315D	173,000	208,000
1997	735D	326,000	381,000	2008	230D	******	******	2005	S315D	158,000	189,000
1996	720D	300,000	351,000	2007	230D	******	******	2004	S310D	144,000	172,000
1995	720D	276,000	323,000	2006	230D	******	******				

Hatteras 52 Motor Yacht | | **Hunt 33 Express**

Year	Power	Retail Low	Retail High	Year	Power	Retail Low	Retail High	Year	Power	Retail Low	Retail High
1996	720D	314,000	367,000	2005	230D	******	******	2004	S370D	154,000	184,000
1995	720D	298,000	349,000	2004	230D	******	******	2003	S370D	141,000	170,000
				2003	230D	128,000	153,000	2002	S370D	130,000	156,000

Hatteras 54 Conv. (1991-98)

Year	Power	Retail Low	Retail High	Year	Power	Retail Low	Retail High	Year	Power	Retail Low	Retail High
1998	1100D	400,000	468,000	2002	230D	121,000	145,000	2001	S370D	120,000	144,000
1997	1075D	372,000	435,000	2001	230D	115,000	138,000	2000	S370D	110,000	132,000
1996	1040D	345,000	404,000	2000	230D	109,000	131,000	1999	S370D	101,000	121,000
1995	1040D	321,000	376,000	1999	230D	104,000	125,000				

| | | | | 1998 | 230D | 99,000 | 118,000 | **Hunt 33 Surfhunter** | | | |

Hatteras 54 Conv. (Current)

Year	Power	Retail Low	Retail High	Year	Power	Retail Low	Retail High	Year	Power	Retail Low	Retail High
2009	1500D	******	******	1997	230D	94,000	112,000	2010	S370D	******	******
2008	1500D	******	******	1996	135D	89,000	107,000	2009	S370D	******	******
2007	1400D	1,100,000	1,265,000	1995	135D	84,000	101,000	2008	S370D	******	******
2006	1400D	1,001,000	1,151,000					2007	S370D	220,000	264,000

Hinckley T29R

Year	Power	Retail Low	Retail High	Year	Power	Retail Low	Retail High
2005	1400D	910,000	1,047,000	2006	S370D	202,000	242,000
				2005	S315D	186,000	223,000

Year	Power	Retail Low	Retail High
2010	S370D	******	******
2009	S370D	******	******
2008	S370D	250,000	295,000
2007	S370D	232,000	274,000
2006	S440D	216,000	255,000

Hunt 36 Harrier

Year	Power	Retail Low	Retail High
2009	T370D	******	******
2008	T370D	******	******
2007	T370D	******	******
2006	T370D	******	******
2005	T370D	******	******
2004	T370D	******	******

See Page 511 For Price Adjustments

Year	Power	Retail Low	Retail High
2003	T370D	240,000	288,000
Hydra-Sports 2796/2800 CC			
2005	T225/OB	49,000	59,000
2004	T225/OB	44,000	53,000
2003	T225/OB	40,000	48,000
2002	T225/OB	36,000	43,000
2001	T225/OB	33,000	39,000
2000	T225/OB	30,000	36,000
Hydra-Sports 2800 Walkaround			
2005	T225/OB	54,000	65,000
2004	T225/OB	50,000	60,000
2003	T225/OB	45,000	54,000
2002	T225/OB	41,000	49,000
2001	T225/OB	37,000	45,000
Hydra-Sports 2800/3100 SF			
1998	T225 O/B	34,000	40,000
1997	T225 O/B	31,000	37,000
1996	T225 O/B	28,000	33,000
1995	T225 O/B	25,000	30,000
Hydra-Sports Vector 2900 CC			
2010	T250 O/B	******	******
2009	T250 O/B	95,000	114,000
2008	T250 O/B	86,000	103,000
2007	T250 O/B	78,000	94,000
2006	T250 O/B	71,000	85,000
Hydra-Sports 2900 VX Express			
2010	T250 O/B	******	******
2009	T250 O/B	105,000	126,000
2008	T250 O/B	95,000	114,000
2007	T250 O/B	86,000	104,000
2006	T250 O/B	79,000	94,000
Hydra-Sports Vector 3000 CC			
2000	T225/OB	34,000	41,000
1999	T225/OB	31,000	37,000
1998	T225/OB	28,000	33,000
1997	T225/OB	25,000	30,000
Hydra-Sports Vector 3300 CC			
2010	3/250 O/B	******	******
2009	3/250 O/B	******	******
2008	3/250 O/B	120,000	142,000
2007	3/250 O/B	108,000	128,000
2006	3/250 O/B	97,000	115,000
2005	3/250 O/B	88,000	104,000
2004	3/250 O/B	80,000	95,000
2003	3/250 O/B	73,000	86,000
Hydra-Sports 3300 VX Express			
2007	3/250 O/B	131,000	155,000
2006	3/250 O/B	120,000	141,000
2005	3/250 O/B	109,000	128,000
2004	3/250 O/B	99,000	117,000
Hydra-Sports 3500 VX Express			
2010	3/250 O/B	******	******
2009	3/250 O/B	******	******
2008	3/250 O/B	220,000	264,000
Independence 45 Trawler			
2000	S350D	******	******
1999	S350D	******	******
1998	S350D	******	******
1997	S350D	325,000	390,000
1996	S350D	308,000	370,000
1995	S350D	293,000	351,000
Intrepid 289 Center Console			
2003	T225 O/B	49,000	58,000

Year	Power	Retail Low	Retail High
2002	T225 O/B	45,000	54,000
2001	T225 O/B	41,000	49,000
2000	T225 O/B	38,000	45,000
1999	T225 O/B	35,000	42,000
1998	T225 O/B	32,000	38,000
1997	T225 O/B	29,000	35,000
Intrepid 289 Walkaround			
2003	T225 O/B	55,000	66,000
2002	T225 O/B	50,000	60,000
2001	T225 O/B	46,000	55,000
2000	T225 O/B	42,000	50,000
1999	T225 O/B	38,000	46,000
1998	T225 O/B	35,000	43,000
1997	T225 O/B	32,000	39,000
Intrepid 300 Center Console			
2010	T250 O/B	******	******
2009	T250 O/B	******	******
2008	T250 O/B	113,000	135,000
2007	T250 O/B	102,000	123,000
2006	T250 O/B	93,000	112,000
2005	T250 O/B	85,000	102,000
2004	T250 O/B	77,000	92,000
Intrepid 310 Walkaround			
2010	T250 O/B	******	******
2009	T250 O/B	******	******
2008	T250 O/B	118,000	141,000
2007	T250 O/B	107,000	128,000
2006	T250 O/B	97,000	117,000
2005	T250 O/B	88,000	106,000
2004	T250 O/B	80,000	97,000
Intrepid 322 Console Cuddy			
2003	T250 O/B	78,000	93,000
2002	T250 O/B	71,000	86,000
2001	T250 O/B	66,000	79,000
2000	T250 O/B	60,000	72,000
1999	T250 O/B	55,000	67,000
1998	T250 O/B	51,000	61,000
1997	T250 O/B	47,000	56,000
1996	T250 O/B	43,000	52,000
Intrepid 323 Center Console			
2010	T250 O/B	******	******
2009	T250 O/B	******	******
2008	T250 O/B	156,000	187,000
2007	T250 O/B	141,000	170,000
2006	T250 O/B	129,000	155,000
2005	T250 O/B	117,000	141,000
2004	T250 O/B	106,000	128,000
Intrepid 339 Center Console			
2002	T250 O/B	60,000	72,000
2001	T250 O/B	54,000	65,000
2000	T250 O/B	49,000	59,000
1999	T250 O/B	45,000	54,000
1998	T250 O/B	41,000	49,000
1997	T250 O/B	38,000	45,000
1996	T250 O/B	35,000	42,000
Intrepid 339 Walkaround			
2002	T250 O/B	66,000	79,000
2001	T250 O/B	60,000	72,000
2000	T250 O/B	54,000	65,000
1999	T250 O/B	50,000	60,000
1998	T250 O/B	46,000	55,000
1997	T250 O/B	42,000	51,000
1996	T250 O/B	39,000	46,000
1995	T250 O/B	36,000	43,000

Year	Power	Retail Low	Retail High
Intrepid 348 Walkaround			
2004	T250 O/B	107,000	128,000
2003	T250 O/B	98,000	118,000
2002	T250 O/B	90,000	108,000
Intrepid 350 Walkaround			
2010	T250 O/B	******	******
2009	T250 O/B	220,000	259,000
2008	T250 O/B	200,000	236,000
2007	T250 O/B	182,000	214,000
2006	T250 O/B	165,000	195,000
2005	T250 O/B	150,000	178,000
Intrepid 356 Cuddy			
2001	T250 O/B	75,000	90,000
2000	T250 O/B	69,000	82,000
1999	T250 O/B	63,000	76,000
1998	T250 O/B	58,000	70,000
1997	T250 O/B	53,000	64,000
1996	T250 O/B	49,000	59,000
1995	T250 O/B	45,000	54,000
Intrepid 366 Cuddy			
2003	3/225 O/B	120,000	144,000
2002	3/225 O/B	109,000	131,000
2001	3/225 O/B	99,000	119,000
2000	3/225 O/B	90,000	108,000
1999	3/225 O/B	82,000	98,000
Intrepid 370 Cuddy			
2010	2/300 O/B	******	******
2009	3/275 O/B	255,000	300,000
2008	3/275 O/B	229,000	270,000
2007	3/275 O/B	206,000	243,000
2006	3/250 O/B	185,000	219,000
2005	3/250 O/B	169,000	199,000
2004	3/250 O/B	153,000	181,000
2003	3/250 O/B	140,000	165,000
Intrepid 377 Walkaround			
2008	3/250 O/B	******	******
2007	3/250 O/B	210,000	252,000
2006	3/250 O/B	189,000	226,000
2005	3/250 O/B	170,000	204,000
2004	3/250 O/B	154,000	185,000
2003	3/250 O/B	140,000	169,000
2002	3/250 O/B	128,000	153,000
2001	3/250 O/B	116,000	139,000
2000	3/250 O/B	106,000	127,000
Intrepid 390 Sport Yacht			
2010	3/300 O/B	******	******
2009	3/300 O/B	******	******
2008	3/300 O/B	300,000	354,000
2007	3/300 O/B	276,000	325,000
Island Gypsy 32 Sedan			
1996	220D	87,000	104,000
1995	220D	84,000	101,000
Island Gypsy 32 Europa			
2003	220D	131,000	157,000
2002	220D	118,000	142,000
2001	220D	111,000	133,000
2000	220D	104,000	125,000
1999	220D	98,000	118,000
1998	220D	92,000	111,000
1997	220D	86,000	104,000
1996	210D	81,000	98,000
1995	210D	76,000	92,000

Year	Power	Retail Low	Retail High
Island Gypsy 36 Classic			
2002	220D	******	******
2001	220D	******	******
2000	220D	******	******
1999	220D	******	******
1998	220D	110,000	132,000
1997	210D	105,000	126,000
1996	210D	101,000	121,000
1995	210D	97,000	116,000
Island Gypsy 36 Europa			
1998	210D	113,000	135,000
1997	210D	109,000	131,000
1996	210D	106,000	127,000
1995	210D	103,000	123,000
Island Gypsy 36 MY			
2002	220D	******	******
2001	220D	******	******
2000	220D	******	******
1999	220D	******	******
1998	210D	115,000	138,000
1997	210D	110,000	132,000
1996	210D	105,000	127,000
1995	210D	101,000	122,000
Island Gypsy 40 Europa			
1998	T300D	******	******
1997	T300D	******	******
1996	T210D	128,000	153,000
1995	T210D	121,000	145,000
Island Gypsy 44 Flush Aft Deck			
1996	T300D	138,000	165,000
1995	T300D	129,000	155,000
Island Gypsy 44 Motor Cruiser			
1996	T135D	133,000	159,000
1995	T135D	126,000	151,000
Island Runner 31			
2010	T225 O/B	******	******
2009	T225 O/B	69,000	82,000
2008	T225 O/B	62,000	75,000
2007	T225 O/B	57,000	68,000
2006	T225 O/B	51,000	62,000
2005	T225 O/B	47,000	56,000
2004	T225 O/B	43,000	52,000
2003	T225 O/B	40,000	48,000
2002	T225 O/B	36,000	44,000
2001	T225 O/B	33,000	40,000
2000	T225 O/B	31,000	37,000
1999	T200 O/B	29,000	35,000
1998	T200 O/B	27,000	32,000
1997	T200 O/B	25,000	30,000
Jefferson 35 Marlago Cuddy			
2010	T250 O/B	******	******
2009	T250 O/B	******	******
2008	T250 O/B	******	******
2007	T250 O/B	80,000	96,000
2006	T250 O/B	72,000	87,000
2005	T250 O/B	66,000	79,000
2004	T250 O/B	60,000	72,000
2003	T250 O/B	54,000	65,000
2002	T250 O/B	49,000	59,000
2001	T250 O/B	45,000	54,000
2000	T250 O/B	41,000	49,000
1999	T250 O/B	38,000	45,000
1998	T250 O/B	34,000	41,000
1997	T250 O/B	32,000	38,000
1996	T250 O/B	29,000	35,000
1995	T250 O/B	27,000	32,000
Jefferson 43 Marlago SD			
2001	T3305D	184,000	221,000
2000	T3305D	170,000	204,000
1999	T3305D	158,000	189,000
1998	T315D	147,000	176,000
1997	T315D	136,000	164,000
1996	T300D	127,000	152,000
1995	T300D	118,000	141,000
Jefferson 46 Marlago SD			
2001	T450D	205,000	246,000
2000	T430D	189,000	227,000
1999	T430D	174,000	209,000
1998	T430D	160,000	192,000
1997	T375D	147,000	176,000
1996	T375D	135,000	162,000
1995	T300D	124,000	149,000
Jefferson 50 Rivanna SE			
2009	500D	******	******
2008	500D	******	******
2007	500D	350,000	410,000
2006	500D	319,000	373,000
2005	480D	290,000	339,000
2004	480D	264,000	309,000
Jefferson 52 Marquessa			
2001	T600D	324,000	379,000
2000	T600D	298,000	349,000
1999	T550D	274,000	321,000
1998	T550D	252,000	295,000
1997	T550D	232,000	271,000
1996	T550D	213,000	250,000
1995	T550D	196,000	230,000
Jefferson 52 Pilothouse SE			
2010	T600D	******	******
2009	T500D	******	******
2008	T500D	550,000	649,000
2007	T500D	511,000	603,000
2006	T500D	475,000	561,000
2005	T450D	442,000	522,000
Jefferson 52 Rivanna CMY			
1999	T450D	230,000	277,000
1998	T450D	212,000	254,000
1997	T450D	195,000	234,000
1996	T450D	179,000	215,000
1995	T435D	165,000	198,000
Jefferson 56 Marquessa CMY			
2001	T600D	******	******
2000	T600D	******	******
1999	T550D	******	******
1998	T550D	******	******
1997	T550D	250,000	295,000
1996	T550D	235,000	277,000
1995	T550D	220,000	260,000
Jefferson 56 Rivanna CMY			
2009	T700D	******	******
2008	T700D	******	******
2007	T700D	******	******
2006	T700D	******	******
2005	T635D	******	******
2004	T635D	410,000	483,000
2003	T635D	385,000	454,000
2002	T635D	362,000	427,000
2001	T635D	340,000	401,000
2000	T600D	320,000	377,000
1999	T600D	304,000	358,000
1998	T600D	288,000	340,000
1997	T550D	274,000	323,000
1996	T550D	260,000	307,000
1995	T550D	247,000	292,000
Jefferson 57 Pilothouse			
2009	T700D	******	******
2008	T700D	******	******
2007	T700D	******	******
2006	T700D	******	******
2005	T635D	551,000	644,000
2004	T635D	512,000	599,000
2003	T635D	476,000	557,000
2002	T635D	443,000	518,000
2001	T600D	412,000	482,000
Jefferson 60 Marquessa CMY			
2009	T700D	******	******
2008	T700D	******	******
2007	T700D	******	******
2006	T700D	******	******
2005	T800D	445,000	520,000
2004	T800D	413,000	484,000
2003	T800D	384,000	450,000
2002	T800D	357,000	418,000
2001	T800D	332,000	389,000
2000	T800D	309,000	362,000
1999	T800D	287,000	336,000
Johnson 56/58 Motor Yacht			
2005	800D	550,000	649,000
2004	800D	511,000	603,000
2003	800D	475,000	561,000
2002	800D	442,000	522,000
2001	800D	411,000	485,000
2000	800D	382,000	451,000
1999	800D	359,000	424,000
1998	735D	338,000	398,000
1997	735D	317,000	375,000
1996	735D	298,000	352,000
1995	735D	280,000	331,000
Johnson 70 Motor Yacht			
2006	T1550D	******	******
2005	T1550D	970,000	1,134,000
2004	T1550D	902,000	1,055,000
2003	T1550D	838,000	981,000
2002	T1550D	780,000	912,000
2001	T1550D	725,000	848,000
2000	T1550D	674,000	789,000
1999	T1550D	634,000	742,000
1998	T1100D	596,000	697,000
1997	T1100D	560,000	655,000
1996	T1100D	526,000	616,000
Jupiter 27 Open			
2006	T225 O/B	56,000	68,000
2005	T225 O/B	51,000	61,000
2004	T225 O/B	45,000	55,000
2003	T225 O/B	41,000	50,000
2002	T225 O/B	38,000	45,000
2001	T225 O/B	34,000	41,000
2000	T225 O/B	31,000	37,000
1999	T225 O/B	28,000	34,000
1998	T225 O/B	26,000	31,000
Jupiter 29 Forward Seating			
2010	T250 O/B	******	******
2009	T250 O/B	114,000	136,000
2008	T250 O/B	103,000	124,000
2007	T250 O/B	94,000	113,000
2006	T250 O/B	85,000	103,000
Jupiter 31 Open			
2010	T250 O/B	******	******
2009	T250 O/B	134,000	160,000

Year	Power	Retail Low	Retail High
2008	T250 O/B	120,000	144,000
2007	T250 O/B	108,000	130,000
2006	T250 O/B	97,000	117,000
2005	T250 O/B	87,000	105,000
2004	T250 O/B	80,000	96,000
2003	T250 O/B	72,000	87,000
2002	T250 O/B	66,000	79,000
2001	T250 O/B	60,000	72,000
2000	T250 O/B	54,000	65,000
1999	T250 O/B	49,000	59,000
1998	T250 O/B	45,000	54,000
1997	T250 O/B	41,000	49,000
1996	T250 O/B	37,000	45,000
1995	T225 O/B	34,000	41,000

Jupiter 34 Forward Seating

Year	Power	Retail Low	Retail High
2010	T350 O/B	******	******
2009	T350 O/B	160,000	192,000
2008	T350 O/B	144,000	172,000

Jupiter 38 Forward Seating

Year	Power	Retail Low	Retail High
2010	3/300 O/B	******	******
2009	3/300 O/B	******	******
2008	3/300 O/B	150,000	180,000
2007	3/300 O/B	136,000	163,000
2006	3/300 O/B	124,000	149,000
2005	T300 O/B	113,000	135,000

Krogen 39 Trawler

Year	Power	Retail Low	Retail High
2010	121D	******	******
2009	121D	******	******
2008	121D	******	******
2007	121D	******	******
2006	120D	******	******
2005	120D	360,000	424,000
2004	115D	342,000	403,000
2003	115D	324,000	383,000
2002	115D	308,000	364,000
2001	80D	293,000	346,000
2000	80D	278,000	328,000
1999	80D	264,000	312,000
1998	80D	251,000	296,000

Krogen 42 Trawler

Year	Power	Retail Low	Retail High
1997	135D	275,000	324,000
1996	135D	264,000	311,000
1995	135D	253,000	299,000

Krogen 44 Trawler

Year	Power	Retail Low	Retail High
2010	S156D	*****	******
2009	S156D	*****	******
2008	S156D	600,000	708,000
2007	S156D	570,000	672,000
2006	S156D	541,000	638,000
2005	S156D	514,000	607,000
2004	S156D	488,000	576,000

Krogen 48 North Sea Trawler

Year	Power	Retail Low	Retail High
2008	S201D	******	******
2007	S201D	725,000	848,000
2006	S201D	681,000	797,000
2005	S201D	640,000	749,000
2004	S210D	602,000	704,000
2003	S210D	572,000	669,000
2002	S210D	543,000	635,000
2001	S210D	516,000	604,000
2000	S210D	490,000	573,000
1999	S210D	470,000	550,000
1998	S210D	452,000	528,000
1997	S210D	433,000	507,000
1996	S210D	416,000	487,000

Krogen 48 Whaleback

Year	Power	Retail Low	Retail High
2003	S210D	******	******
2002	S210D	550,000	649,000
2001	S210D	522,000	616,000
2000	S210D	496,000	585,000
1999	S210D	471,000	556,000
1998	S210D	447,000	528,000
1997	S210D	425,000	502,000
1996	S210D	404,000	477,000
1995	S210D	384,000	453,000

Krogen 58 Trawler

Year	Power	Retail Low	Retail High
2010	S154D	******	******
2009	S154D	******	******
2008	S154D	******	******
2007	S154D	******	******
2006	S154D	******	******
2005	S154D	1,100,000	1,100,000
2004	S154D	1,045,000	1,045,000
2003	S154D	992,000	992,000
2002	S154D	943,000	943,000
2001	S154D	895,000	895,000

Lagoon 43

Year	Power	Retail Low	Retail High
2005	T250D	300,000	360,000
2004	T250D	279,000	334,000
2003	T250D	259,000	311,000
2002	T250D	241,000	289,000
2001	T250D	224,000	269,000

Lazzara 68 MY

Year	Power	Retail Low	Retail High
2009	T1000D	1,900,000	2,280,000
2008	T1000D	1,824,000	2,188,000
2007	T1000D	1,751,000	2,101,000
2006	T1000D	1,680,000	2,017,000
2005	T1000D	1,613,000	1,936,000

Legacy 28 Express

Year	Power	Retail Low	Retail High
2006	250D	95,000	114,000
2005	250D	88,000	106,000
2004	250D	82,000	98,000
2003	250D	76,000	91,000
2002	250D	71,000	85,000
2001	250D	66,000	79,000
2000	250D	61,000	73,000
1999	250D	57,000	68,000

Legacy 32 Express

Year	Power	Retail Low	Retail High
2008	380D	240,000	288,000
2007	380D	223,000	267,000

Legacy 34 Express/Sedan

Year	Power	Retail Low	Retail High
2006	T380D	******	******
2005	T380D	210,000	252,000
2004	T380D	191,000	229,000
2003	T300D	173,000	208,000
2002	T300D	158,000	189,000
2001	T330D	144,000	172,000
2000	T330D	131,000	157,000
1999	T270D	119,000	143,000
1998	T270D	108,000	130,000
1997	T270D	98,000	118,000
1996	T270D	89,000	107,000

Lien Hwa 47 Cockpit MY

Year	Power	Retail Low	Retail High
1999	S250D	******	******
1998	T375D	******	******
1997	T375D	******	******
1996	T375D	150,000	225,000
1995	T375D	139,000	209,000

Luhrs 28 Open

Year	Power	Retail Low	Retail High
2009	T330G	******	******
2009	T260D	******	******
2008	T330G	******	******
2008	T260D	******	******
2007	T320G	93,000	111,000
2007	T260D	114,000	137,000
2006	T320G	84,000	101,000
2006	T240D	104,000	125,000
2005	T320G	77,000	92,000
2005	T240D	95,000	114,000

Luhrs 290 Open

Year	Power	Retail Low	Retail High
2002	T325G	58,000	69,000
2001	T325G	52,000	63,000
2000	T325G	48,000	57,000
1999	T320G	43,000	52,000
1998	T320G	40,000	48,000
1997	T270G	37,000	44,000
1996	T270G	34,000	40,000
1995	T270G	31,000	37,000

Luhrs 300 Tournament

Year	Power	Retail Low	Retail High
1996	T270G	30,000	36,000
1995	T270G	28,000	33,000

Luhrs 30/31 Open

Year	Power	Retail Low	Retail High
2009	T260D IPS	******	******
2008	T260D IPS	******	******
2007	T320G	112,000	135,000
2007	T315D	144,000	173,000
2006	T320G	102,000	123,000
2006	T315D	131,000	157,000
2005	T320G	93,000	112,000
2005	T315D	119,000	143,000
2004	T320G	85,000	101,000
2004	T315D	108,000	130,000

Luhrs 320 Convertible

Year	Power	Retail Low	Retail High
1999	T320G	55,000	66,000
1999	T300D	72,000	86,000
1998	T320G	50,000	60,000
1998	T300D	66,000	79,000
1997	T340G	46,000	55,000
1997	T300D	60,000	73,000
1996	T340G	42,000	51,000
1996	T300D	56,000	67,000
1995	T340G	39,000	47,000
1995	T300D	51,000	60,000

Luhrs 32 Convertible

Year	Power	Retail Low	Retail High
2002	T325G	67,000	81,000
2002	T315D	93,000	112,000
2001	T325G	61,000	74,000
2001	T300D	85,000	102,000

Luhrs 32 Open

Year	Power	Retail Low	Retail High
2008	T375G	171,000	205,000
2008	T315D	210,000	252,000
2007	T375G	155,000	186,000
2007	T315D	191,000	229,000
2006	T375G	141,000	170,000
2006	T315D	174,000	209,000
2005	T320G	129,000	154,000
2005	T315D	158,000	190,000

Luhrs 34 Convertible

Year	Power	Retail Low	Retail High
2003	T320G	120,000	144,000
2003	T315D	145,000	174,000
2002	T375G	109,000	131,000
2002	T300D	132,000	158,000
2001	T310G	99,000	119,000
2001	T300D	120,000	144,000
2000	T310G	90,000	108,000
2000	T300D	109,000	131,000

Luhrs 35 Convertible

Year	Power	Retail Low	Retail High
2009	T480D	318,000	381,000
2008	T380D	292,000	351,000

Luhrs 350 Convertible

Year	Power	Retail Low	Retail High
1996	T370G	71,000	85,000
1996	T300D	87,000	104,000
1995	T370G	65,000	78,000
1995	T300D	80,000	96,000

Luhrs 36 Convertible

Year	Power	Retail Low	Retail High
2007	T425G	218,000	262,000
2007	T440D	258,000	310,000
2006	T420G	198,000	238,000
2006	T440D	235,000	282,000
2005	T420G	180,000	217,000
2005	T440D	214,000	257,000

Luhrs 36 Open/36 SX

Year	Power	Retail Low	Retail High
2007	T425G	207,000	248,000
2007	T440D	246,000	296,000
2006	T425G	188,000	226,000
2006	T440D	224,000	269,000
2005	T420G	171,000	205,000
2005	T420D	204,000	245,000
2004	T420G	156,000	187,000
2004	T420D	186,000	223,000
2003	T420G	142,000	170,000
2003	T420D	169,000	203,000
2002	T420G	129,000	155,000
2002	T420D	154,000	184,000
2001	T420G	118,000	142,000
2001	T420D	141,000	170,000
2000	T420G	109,000	131,000
2000	T420D	130,000	156,000
1999	T420G	100,000	120,000
1999	T420D	119,000	143,000
1998	T340G	92,000	111,000
1998	T420D	110,000	132,000
1997	T340G	85,000	102,000
1997	T420D	101,000	121,000

Luhrs 37 Open

Year	Power	Retail Low	Retail High
2010	T435D IPS	******	******
2009	T435D IPS	335,000	402,000

Luhrs 380/40/38 Convertible

Year	Power	Retail Low	Retail High
2007	T440D	297,000	356,000
2006	T440D	270,000	324,000
2005	T440D	245,000	295,000
2004	T420D	223,000	268,000
2003	T420D	203,000	244,000
2002	T420D	185,000	222,000
2001	T420D	168,000	202,000
2000	T420D	155,000	186,000
1999	T420D	142,000	171,000
1998	T420D	131,000	157,000
1997	T420D	120,000	144,000
1996	T420D	111,000	133,000
1995	T420D	102,000	122,000

Luhrs 380/40/38 Open

Year	Power	Retail Low	Retail High
2007	T440D	270,000	324,000
2006	T440D	245,000	294,000
2005	T440D	223,000	268,000
2004	T420D	203,000	244,000
2003	T420D	185,000	222,000
2002	T420D	168,000	202,000
2001	T420D	153,000	183,000
2000	T420D	141,000	169,000
1999	T420D	129,000	155,000
1998	T420D	119,000	143,000
1997	T420D	109,000	131,000
1996	T420D	101,000	121,000
1995	T420D	92,000	111,000

Luhrs 41 Convertible

Year	Power	Retail Low	Retail High
2009	T665D	******	******
2008	T540D	******	******
2007	T540D	317,000	368,000
2006	T540D	289,000	335,000
2005	T535D	263,000	304,000
2004	T535D	239,000	277,000

Luhrs 41 Hardtop

Year	Power	Retail Low	Retail High
2008	T540D	******	******
2007	T540D	320,000	384,000

Luhrs 41 Open

Year	Power	Retail Low	Retail High
2009	T665D	******	******
2008	T540D	******	******
2007	T540D	315,000	371,000
2006	T540D	286,000	338,000

Luhrs 44 Convertible

Year	Power	Retail Low	Retail High
2005	T635D	******	******
2004	T500D	******	******
2003	T500D	185,000	222,000

Luhrs 50 Convertible

Year	Power	Retail Low	Retail High
2003	T900D	******	******
2002	T900D	******	******
2001	T900D	******	******
2000	T800D	450,000	540,000
1999	T800D	414,000	496,000

Mainship Pilot 30

Year	Power	Retail Low	Retail High
2007	S315D	85,000	102,000
2006	S315D	77,000	92,000
2005	S315D	70,000	84,000
2004	S315D	64,000	76,000
2003	S315D	58,000	70,000
2002	S230D	54,000	65,000
2001	S230D	49,000	59,000
2000	S230D	46,000	55,000
1999	S230D	43,000	51,000
1998	S230D	40,000	48,000

Mainship Pilot 30 Sedan

Year	Power	Retail Low	Retail High
2007	S315D	93,000	112,000
2006	S315D	85,000	102,000
2005	S315D	77,000	92,000
2004	S315D	70,000	84,000
2003	S315D	64,000	77,000
2002	S230D	59,000	71,000
2001	S230D	54,000	65,000
2000	S230D	50,000	60,000

Mainship 31 Sedan Bridge

Year	Power	Retail Low	Retail High
1999	T290G	47,000	57,000
1998	T290G	44,000	52,000
1997	T270G	40,000	48,000
1996	T270G	37,000	44,000
1995	T270G	34,000	41,000
1994	T270G	31,000	37,000

Mainship 31 Pilot

Year	Power	Retail Low	Retail High
2010	S380D	******	******
2009	S380D	170,000	204,000
2008	S315D	156,000	187,000

Mainship 34 Motor Yacht

Year	Power	Retail Low	Retail High
1998	T320G	60,000	72,000
1997	T340G	55,000	66,000
1996	T340G	50,000	61,000

Mainship 34 Pilot

Year	Power	Retail Low	Retail High
2008	S315D	157,000	189,000
2007	S315D	143,000	171,000
2006	S315D	130,000	156,000
2005	S315D	118,000	142,000
2004	S315D	108,000	129,000
2003	S315D	98,000	117,000
2002	S300D	90,000	108,000
2001	S300D	83,000	99,000
2000	S300D	76,000	91,000
1999	S300D	70,000	84,000

Mainship 34 Pilot Sedan

Year	Power	Retail Low	Retail High
2009	S315D	******	******
2008	S315D	164,000	197,000
2007	S315D	149,000	179,000
2006	S315D	136,000	163,000
2005	S315D	124,000	148,000
2004	S315D	112,000	135,000
2003	S315D	102,000	123,000
2002	S300D	94,000	113,000
2001	S300D	86,000	104,000

Mainship 34 Trawler

Year	Power	Retail Low	Retail High
2009	S380DD	270,000	324,000
2008	S380D	248,000	298,000
2007	S240D	228,000	274,000
2006	S240D	210,000	252,000
2005	S240D	193,000	232,000

Mainship 350/390 Trawler

Year	Power	Retail Low	Retail High
2005	S370D	130,000	156,000
2005	T240D	146,000	176,000
2004	S-Diesel	120,000	144,000
2004	T370D	134,000	161,000
2003	S-Diesel	110,000	132,000
2003	T-240D	124,000	149,000
2002	S-Diesel	102,000	123,000
2002	T-240D	115,000	138,000
2001	S-Diesel	95,000	114,000
2001	T-230D	107,000	128,000
2000	S-Diesel	88,000	106,000
2000	T-230D	99,000	119,000
1999	S-Diesel	82,000	99,000
1999	T-200D	92,000	111,000
1998	S-Diesel	76,000	92,000
1998	T-Diesel	86,000	103,000
1997	S-Diesel	71,000	85,000
1997	T-Diesel	80,000	96,000
1996	S-Diesel	66,000	79,000
1996	T-Diesel	74,000	89,000

Mainship 37 Motor Yacht

Year	Power	Retail Low	Retail High
1998	T320G	82,000	99,000
1997	I-320G	76,000	91,000
1996	T-340G	70,000	84,000
1995	T-340G	64,000	77,000

Mainship 40 Sedan Bridge

Year	Power	Retail Low	Retail High
1999	T320G	74,000	88,000
1998	T320G	67,000	80,000
1997	T320G	61,000	73,000
1996	T320G	55,000	67,000
1995	T320G	51,000	61,000
1994	T320G	47,000	56,000
1993	T320G	43,000	52,000

Mainship 40 Trawler; 41 Expedition

Year	Power	Retail Low	Retail High
2010	S380D	******	******
2010	T220D	******	******
2009	S380D	270,000	318,000
2009	T220D	310,000	365,000
2008	S370D	251,000	296,000
2008	T260D	251,000	296,000
2007	S370D	288,000	340,000
2007	T240D	233,000	275,000
2006	S370D	233,000	275,000
2006	T240D	268,000	316,000
2005	S370D	217,000	256,000
2005	T240D	217,000	256,000
2004	S370D	249,000	294,000
2004	T240D	201,000	238,000

Year	Power	Retail Low	Retail High
2003	S315D	201,000	238,000
2003	T240D	231,000	273,000

Mainship 430 Aft Cabin Trawler

Year	Power	Retail Low	Retail High
2006	T370D	278,000	328,000
2005	T370D	253,000	298,000
2004	T370D	230,000	271,000
2003	T315D	209,000	247,000
2002	T315D	190,000	225,000
2001	T300D	175,000	207,000
2000	T300D	161,000	190,000
1999	T300D	148,000	175,000

Mainship 43/45 Trawler

Year	Power	Retail Low	Retail High
2010	T440D	******	******
2009	T440D	******	******
2008	T440D	376,000	451,000
2007	T440D	349,000	419,000
2006	T440D	325,000	390,000

Mainship 45 Pilot

Year	Power	Retail Low	Retail High
2009	T440D	******	******
2008	T440D	360,000	432,000

Mainship 47 Motor Yacht

Year	Power	Retail Low	Retail High
1999	T485D	230,000	276,000
1998	T485D	211,000	253,000
1997	T485D	194,000	233,000
1996	T485D	179,000	214,000
1995	T485D	164,000	197,000

Mako 282 Center Console

Year	Power	Retail Low	Retail High
2003	T225 O/B	35,000	42,000
2002	T225 O/B	32,000	38,000
2001	T225 O/B	29,000	35,000
2000	T225 O/B	26,000	31,000
1999	T225 O/B	24,000	29,000
1998	T225 O/B	22,000	26,000
1997	T225 O/B	20,000	24,000
1996	T225 O/B	18,000	21,000
1995	T225 O/B	16,000	19,000

Mako 284 Center Console

Year	Power	Retail Low	Retail High
2010	T250 O/B	******	******
2009	T250 O/B	******	******
2008	T250 O/B	58,000	70,000
2007	T250 O/B	52,000	63,000
2006	T250 O/B	47,000	56,000
2005	T250 O/B	42,000	51,000

Mako 293 Walkaround

Year	Power	Retail Low	Retail High
2003	T250 O/B	40,000	49,000
2002	T250 O/B	36,000	44,000
2001	T250 O/B	33,000	39,000
2000	T250 O/B	30,000	36,000
1999	T250 O/B	27,000	32,000
1998	T250 O/B	24,000	29,000
1997	T250 O/B	22,000	27,000
1996	T250 O/B	20,000	24,000
1995	T250 O/B	18,000	22,000

Mako 333 CC Cuddy

Year	Power	Retail Low	Retail High
2000	T250 O/B	51,000	62,000
1999	T250 O/B	47,000	56,000
1998	T250 O/B	42,000	51,000
1997	T250 O/B	39,000	46,000

Marine Trader 34 DC

Year	Power	Retail Low	Retail High
2001	135D	77,000	93,000
2000	135D	73,000	87,000
1999	135D	68,000	82,000
1998	135D	64,000	77,000
1997	135D	60,000	72,000
1996	135D	57,000	68,000
1995	135D	53,000	64,000

Marine Trader 34 Sedan

Year	Power	Retail Low	Retail High
2001	135D	80,000	96,000
2000	135D	76,000	91,000
1999	135D	72,000	86,000
1998	135D	68,000	82,000
1997	135D	65,000	78,000
1996	135D	61,000	74,000
1995	135D	58,000	70,000

Marine Trader 38 Double Cabin

Year	Power	Retail Low	Retail High
2000	T135D	******	******
1999	T135D	******	******
1998	T135D	******	******
1997	T135D	100,000	120,000
1996	T135D	95,000	114,000
1995	T135D	90,000	108,000

Marine Trader 40 Sundeck

Year	Power	Retail Low	Retail High
2000	T135D	120,000	144,000
1999	T135D	111,000	133,000
1998	T135D	103,000	124,000
1997	T135D	97,000	117,000
1996	T135D	91,000	110,000
1995	T135D	86,000	103,000

Marlin 350 Cuddy

Year	Power	Retail Low	Retail High
2002	T250 O/B	54,000	64,000
2001	T250 O/B	49,000	59,000
2000	T250 O/B	45,000	54,000
1999	T250 O/B	42,000	50,000
1998	T250 O/B	38,000	46,000
1997	T250 O/B	35,000	42,000
1996	T250 O/B	32,000	39,000
1995	T250 O/B	30,000	36,000

Marquis 40 Sport Coupe

Year	Power	Retail Low	Retail High
2010	T435 IPS	******	******
2009	T435 IPS	******	******
2008	T435 IPS	540,000	648,000

Marquis 50 Sport Coupe

Year	Power	Retail Low	Retail High
2010	3/435D IPS	******	******
2009	3/435D IPS	680,000	802,000
2008	3/370D IPS	632,000	746,000

Marquis 55 LS

Year	Power	Retail Low	Retail High
2010	T715D	******	******
2009	T715D	******	******
2008	T715D	700,000	840,000
2007	T715D	644,000	772,000

Marquis 59/600 PH

Year	Power	Retail Low	Retail High
2010	715D	******	******
2009	715D	******	******
2008	715D	825,000	990,000
2007	825D	767,000	920,000
2006	825D	713,000	856,000
2005	825D	663,000	796,000
2004	825D	617,000	740,000
2003	825D	573,000	688,000

Marquis 65 PH

Year	Power	Retail Low	Retail High
2010	T1360D	******	******
2009	T1360D	******	******
2008	T1360D	1,300,000	1,534,000
2007	T1360D	1,209,000	1,426,000
2006	T1360D	1,124,000	1,326,000
2005	T1360D	1,045,000	1,233,000

Maxum 2600/2700 SE

Year	Power	Retail Low	Retail High
2009	300 I/O	47,000	56,000
2008	320 I/O	42,000	51,000
2007	320 I/O	39,000	46,000
2006	320 I/O	35,000	42,000

Maxum 2700 SCR

Year	Power	Retail Low	Retail High
1996	T190 I/O	16,000	20,000
1995	T190 I/O	15,000	18,000

Maxum 2700 SE

Year	Power	Retail Low	Retail High
2007	320 I/O	42,000	50,000
2006	320 I/O	38,000	45,000
2005	320 I/O	34,000	41,000
2004	320 I/O	31,000	37,000
2003	320 I/O	29,000	34,000
2002	320 I/O	26,000	32,000
2001	320 I/O	24,000	29,000

Maxum 2800/2900 SCR; 2900 SE

Year	Power	Retail Low	Retail High
2006	320 I/O	46,000	56,000
2006	T190 I/O	48,000	58,000
2005	320 I/O	42,000	51,000
2005	T190 I/O	44,000	53,000
2004	320 I/O	38,000	46,000
2004	T190 I/O	40,000	48,000
2003	320 I/O	35,000	42,000
2003	T190 I/O	36,000	44,000
2002	320 I/O	32,000	38,000
2002	T190 I/O	33,000	40,000
2001	310 I/O	29,000	35,000
2001	T190 I/O	30,000	36,000
2000	310 I/O	27,000	32,000
2000	T190 I/O	28,000	33,000
1999	310 I/O	25,000	30,000
1999	T190 I/O	26,000	31,000
1998	310 I/O	23,000	27,000
1998	T190 I/O	24,000	29,000
1997	310 I/O	21,000	26,000
1997	T190 I/O	22,000	27,000
1996	310 I/O	20,000	24,000
1996	T190 I/O	20,000	25,000
1995	300 I/O	18,000	22,000
1995	T180 I/O	19,000	23,000

Maxum 2900 SE

Year	Power	Retail Low	Retail High
2009	T260 I/O	90,000	108,000
2008	T260 I/O	82,000	99,000

Maxum 3000 SCR

Year	Power	Retail Low	Retail High
2001	T260 I/O	34,000	41,000
2000	T260 I/O	31,000	37,000
1999	T260 I/O	28,000	33,000
1998	T260 I/O	25,000	30,000
1997	T260 I/O	23,000	28,000

Maxum 3100 SE

Year	Power	Retail Low	Retail High
2008	T260 I/O	97,000	116,000
2007	T260 I/O	88,000	106,000
2006	T260 I/O	80,000	96,000
2005	T260 I/O	73,000	87,000
2004	T260 I/O	66,000	79,000
2003	T260 I/O	60,000	72,000
2002	T260 I/O	55,000	66,000

Maxum 3200 SCR

Year	Power	Retail Low	Retail High
1998	T260 I/O	33,000	39,000
1997	T260 I/O	30,000	36,000
1996	T260 I/O	28,000	33,000
1995	T260 I/O	25,000	31,000
1994	T260 I/O	23,000	28,000

Maxum 3300 SE

Year	Power	Retail Low	Retail High
2007	T320 I/O	102,000	122,000
2006	T320 I/O	95,000	114,000
2005	T320 I/O	86,000	103,000
2004	T320 I/O	78,000	94,000
2003	T320 I/O	71,000	86,000
2002	T320 I/O	65,000	78,000
2001	T320 I/O	59,000	71,000

See Page 511 For Price Adjustments

Year	Power	Retail Low	Retail High	Year	Power	Retail Low	Retail High	Year	Power	Retail Low	Retail High
2000	T310 I/O	54,000	65,000	1998	T370D	134,000	161,000	2007	T370G	177,000	212,000
1999	T310 I/O	50,000	60,000	1997	T370D	123,000	148,000	2007	T330D	209,000	251,000
								2006	T370G	161,000	193,000
Maxum 3500 SY				**McKinna 47/481 Sedan**				2006	T330D	190,000	228,000
2008	T370G	136,000	163,000	2006	T370D	******	******	2005	T370G	146,000	176,000
2007	T370G	124,000	148,000	2005	T370D	300,000	360,000	2005	T330D	173,000	208,000
2006	T370G	112,000	135,000	2004	T370D	273,000	327,000				
2005	T370G	102,000	123,000	2003	T370D	248,000	298,000	**Meridian 381 Sedan**			
2004	T370G	94,000	113,000	2002	T370D	226,000	271,000	2005	T320G	140,000	168,000
2003	T370G	86,000	104,000	2001	T370D	207,000	249,000	2005	T330D	156,000	187,000
2002	T380G	80,000	96,000	2000	T330D	191,000	229,000	2004	T320G	127,000	152,000
2001	T380G	73,000	88,000	1999	T330D	176,000	211,000	2004	T270D	141,000	170,000
								2003	T320G	115,000	139,000
Maxum 3700 SCR				**McKinna 48 Pilothouse**				2003	T270D	129,000	155,000
2001	T380G	94,000	113,000	2000	T450D	******	******				
2000	T380G	85,000	103,000	1999	T450D	240,000	288,000	**Meridian 391 Sedan**			
1999	T380G	78,000	93,000	1998	T450D	223,000	267,000	2009	T370G	168,000	201,000
1998	T380G	75,000	90,000	1997	T450D	207,000	249,000	2009	T370D	195,000	234,000
				1996	T450D	193,000	231,000	2008	T370G	152,000	183,000
Maxum 3700 Sport Yacht								2008	T370D	177,000	212,000
2009	T370G	195,000	234,000	**McKinna 57 Pilothouse**				2007	T370G	139,000	166,000
2008	T370G	179,000	215,000	2006	T660D	******	******	2007	T330D	161,000	193,000
2007	T370G	165,000	198,000	2005	T660D	******	******	2006	T370G	126,000	151,000
2005	T370G	151,000	182,000	2004	T635D	******	******	2006	T330D	146,000	176,000
2004	T370G	139,000	167,000	2003	T450D	******	******				
2003	T370G	128,000	154,000	2002	T450D	******	******	**Meridian 408 MY**			
				2001	T450D	365,000	431,000	2008	T380D	291,000	344,000
Maxum 4100 SCR				2000	T450D	340,000	401,000	2007	T380D	268,000	316,000
1999	T400G	82,000	98,000	1999	T450D	316,000	373,000	2006	T380D	246,000	291,000
1999	T370D	92,000	111,000	1998	T450D	294,000	347,000	2005	T370D	227,000	268,000
1998	T400G	75,000	90,000	1997	T450D	273,000	322,000	2004	T370D	209,000	246,000
1998	T370D	85,000	102,000					2003	T370D	192,000	226,000
1997	T310G	69,000	83,000	**McKinna 65 Pilothouse**							
1997	T315D	78,000	93,000	2005	T1100D	******	******	**Meridian 411 Sedan**			
1996	T310G	63,000	76,000	2004	T1100D	******	******	2007	T380D	275,000	324,000
1996	T315D	72,000	86,000	2003	T1100D	******	******	2006	T380D	253,000	298,000
				2002	T800D	650,000	767,000	2005	T370G	232,000	274,000
Maxum 4100 SCA				2001	T800D	604,000	713,000	2004	T370G	214,000	252,000
2001	T400G	104,000	125,000	2000	T800D	562,000	663,000	2003	T370D	197,000	232,000
2001	T330D	134,000	161,000								
2000	T400G	95,000	114,000	**Mediterranean 38 Convertible**				**Meridian 441 Sedan Bridge**			
2000	T330D	122,000	146,000	2007	T330D	******	******	2009	T425D	360,000	424,000
1999	T400G	86,000	104,000	2006	T330D	******	******	2008	T425D	331,000	390,000
1999	T330D	111,000	133,000	2005	T330D	******	******				
1998	T400G	79,000	95,000	2004	T330D	******	******	**Meridian 459 Cockpit MY**			
1998	T330D	102,000	122,000	2003	T330D	******	******	2008	T330D	385,000	455,000
1997	T400G	73,000	88,000	2002	T330D	115,000	138,000	2007	T330D	355,000	419,000
1997	T330D	94,000	113,000	2001	T330D	104,000	125,000	2006	T330D	326,000	385,000
				2000	T330D	96,000	115,000	2005	T370D	300,000	354,000
Maxum 4100 SCB				1999	T330D	88,000	106,000	2004	T370D	276,000	326,000
2001	T-Gas	100,000	120,000	1998	T-Diesel	81,000	97,000	2003	T370D	254,000	300,000
2001	T330D	130,000	156,000	1997	T-Diesel	74,000	89,000				
2000	T-Gas	91,000	109,000	1996	T-Diesel	68,000	82,000	**Meridian 490 PH**			
2000	T330D	118,000	142,000	1995	T-Diesel	63,000	76,000	2008	T330D	406,000	479,000
1999	T-Gas	83,000	99,000					2007	T330D	373,000	440,000
1999	T330D	107,000	129,000	**Meridian 341 Sedan**				2006	T330D	343,000	405,000
1998	T-Gas	76,000	91,000	2009	T320G	192,000	231,000	2005	T330D	316,000	373,000
1998	T330D	99,000	118,000	2009	T330D	221,000	265,000	2004	T330D	290,000	343,000
1997	T-Gas	70,000	84,000	2008	T320G	163,000	195,000				
1997	T330D	91,000	109,000	2008	T330D	190,000	229,000	**Meridian 540 Pilothouse**			
				2007	T320G	148,000	178,000	2006	T635D	******	******
Maxum 4200 Sport Yacht				2007	T330D	173,000	208,000	2005	T635D	******	******
2008	T425D	311,000	373,000	2006	T320G	135,000	162,000	2004	T635D	410,000	483,000
2007	T425D	283,000	339,000	2006	T250D	158,000	189,000	2003	T635D	381,000	449,000
2006	T450D	257,000	309,000	2005	T320G	123,000	147,000				
2005	T450D	234,000	281,000	2005	T250D	143,000	172,000	**Meridian 580 Pilothouse**			
2004	T450D	213,000	255,000	2004	T260D	111,000	134,000	2009	T715D	******	******
2003	T450D	194,000	232,000	2004	T250D	130,000	157,000	2008	T715D	660,000	772,000
2002	T450D	176,000	211,000	2003	T260G	101,000	122,000	2007	T635D	613,000	718,000
				2003	T250D	119,000	142,000	2006	T635D	570,000	667,000
Maxum 4600 SCB								2005	T635D	530,000	621,000
2001	T450D	173,000	207,000	**Meridian 368 MY**				2004	T635D	493,000	577,000
2000	T370D	159,000	191,000	2008	T370G	194,000	233,000	2003	T635D	459,000	537,000
1999	T370D	146,000	175,000	2008	T370D	230,000	276,000				
								Midnight Express 37 Cuddy			

Year	Power	Retail Low	Retail High
2010	3/275 O/B	******	******
2009	3/275 O/B	240,000	288,000
2008	3/275 O/B	218,000	262,000
2007	3/275 O/B	198,000	238,000
2006	3/275 O/B	180,000	217,000

Midnight Express 39

Year	Power	Retail Low	Retail High
2010	3/275 O/B	******	******
2009	3/275 O/B	225,000	270,000
2008	3/275 O/B	204,000	245,000
2007	3/275 O/B	186,000	223,000
2006	3/275 O/B	169,000	203,000
2005	3/275 O/B	154,000	185,000
2004	3/275 O/B	140,000	168,000
2003	3/250 O/B	127,000	153,000
2002	3/250 O/B	116,000	139,000
2001	3/250 O/B	105,000	126,000
2000	3/250 O/B	96,000	115,000

Mikelson 43 Sportfisher

Year	Power	Retail Low	Retail High
2010	T480D Zeus	******	******
2009	T480D Zeus	570,000	672,000
2008	T540D	518,000	612,000
2007	T540D	472,000	556,000
2006	T450D	429,000	506,000
2005	T450D	390,000	461,000
2004	T450D	355,000	419,000
2003	T450D	323,000	381,000
2002	T430D	297,000	351,000
2001	T430D	273,000	323,000
2000	T420D	252,000	297,000
1999	T420D	231,000	273,000
1998	T420D	213,000	251,000
1997	T420D	196,000	231,000

Mikelson 50 Sportfisher

Year	Power	Retail Low	Retail High
2010	T600D	******	******
2009	T600D	******	******
2008	T600D	******	******
2007	T540D	******	******
2006	T450D	520,000	624,000
2005	T450D	483,000	580,000
2004	T450D	449,000	539,000
2003	T450D	418,000	501,000
2002	T450D	388,000	466,000
2001	T435D	361,000	434,000
2000	T435D	336,000	403,000
1999	T435D	312,000	375,000
1998	T435D	290,000	349,000
1997	T435D	270,000	324,000
1996	T435D	251,000	302,000
1995	T435D	234,000	280,000

Mikelson 60 Sportfisher

Year	Power	Retail Low	Retail High
1999	T735D	******	******
1998	T735D	******	******
1997	T735D	360,000	425,000
1996	T735D	335,000	396,000
1995	T735D	312,000	368,000
1994	T735D	290,000	342,000
1993	T735D	269,000	318,000
1992	T735D	251,000	296,000

Mikelson 64 Sportfisher

Year	Power	Retail Low	Retail High
2001	T1400D	763,000	915,000
2000	T800D	702,000	842,000
1999	T800D	645,000	775,000
1998	T800D	594,000	713,000
1997	T800D	546,000	656,000

MJM 29Z

Year	Power	Retail Low	Retail High
2010	S260D I/O	******	******
2009	S260D I/O	235,000	282,000
2008	S260D I/O	220,000	265,000
2007	S260D I/O	207,000	249,000

MJM 34Z

Year	Power	Retail Low	Retail High
2010	S440D	******	******
2009	S440D	******	******
2008	S440D	******	******
2007	S440D	275,000	330,000
2006	S440D	261,000	313,000
2005	S440D	248,000	297,000
2004	S370D	235,000	282,000

Monk 36 Trawler

Year	Power	Retail Low	Retail High
2007	230D	210,000	252,000
2006	230D	199,000	239,000
2005	220D	189,000	227,000
2004	220D	180,000	216,000
2003	220D	171,000	205,000
2002	220D	162,000	194,000
2001	220D	155,000	187,000
2000	220D	149,000	179,000
1999	220D	143,000	172,000
1998	220D	138,000	165,000
1997	220D	132,000	158,000
1996	220D	127,000	152,000
1995	220D	122,000	146,000

Monterey 265/276 Cruiser

Year	Power	Retail Low	Retail High
1999	310 I/O	22,000	26,000
1998	310 I/O	20,000	24,000
1997	310 I/O	19,000	22,000
1996	310 I/O	17,000	21,000
1995	310 I/O	16,000	19,000

Monterey 270 Cruiser

Year	Power	Retail Low	Retail High
2008	300 I/O	60,000	72,000
2007	300 I/O	54,000	65,000
2006	320 I/O	49,000	59,000

Monterey 282 Cruiser

Year	Power	Retail Low	Retail High
2006	T220 I/O	55,000	66,000
2005	T220 I/O	50,000	60,000
2004	T220 I/O	45,000	54,000
2003	T220 I/O	41,000	49,000
2002	T220 I/O	37,000	45,000
2001	T190 I/O	34,000	41,000

Monterey 290 CR; 300 SCR

Year	Power	Retail Low	Retail High
2010	T260 I/O	******	******
2009	T260 I/O	135,000	162,000
2008	T260 I/O	122,000	147,000
2007	T260 I/O	111,000	134,000
2006	T260 I/O	101,000	122,000

Monterey 296 Cruiser

Year	Power	Retail Low	Retail High
2000	T250 I/O	33,000	39,000
1999	T250 I/O	30,000	36,000
1998	T250 I/O	27,000	33,000
1997	T250 I/O	25,000	30,000
1996	T250 I/O	23,000	28,000
1995	T250 I/O	21,000	26,000

Monterey 302 Cruiser

Year	Power	Retail Low	Retail High
2006	T320 I/O	62,000	74,000
2005	T320 I/O	56,000	67,000
2004	T320 I/O	51,000	61,000
2003	T320 I/O	46,000	56,000
2002	T320 I/O	42,000	51,000
2001	T320 I/O	38,000	46,000
2000	T320 I/O	35,000	42,000

Monterey 322 Cruiser

Year	Power	Retail Low	Retail High
2007	T300 I/O	110,000	132,000
2006	T300 I/O	100,000	120,000
2005	T300 I/O	91,000	109,000
2004	T300 I/O	82,000	99,000
2003	T320 I/O	75,000	90,000
2002	T320 I/O	68,000	82,000
2001	T320 I/O	63,000	75,000
2000	T310 I/O	58,000	69,000
1999	T310 I/O	53,000	64,000
1998	T310 I/O	49,000	59,000

Monterey 330/340 Sport Yacht

Year	Power	Retail Low	Retail High
2010	T300 I/O	******	******
2009	T300 I/O	******	******
2008	T320 I/O	135,000	162,000
2007	T300 I/O	122,000	147,000

Monterey 350/360 Sport Yacht

Year	Power	Retail Low	Retail High
2010	T375G	******	******
2009	T375G	******	******
2008	T375G	******	******
2007	T375G	150,000	180,000
2006	T375G	138,000	165,000
2005	T375G	126,000	152,000

Monterey 400 Sport Yacht

Year	Power	Retail Low	Retail High
2010	T370D	******	******
2009	T370D	******	******
2008	T370D	325,000	390,000

Navigator 42 Classic

Year	Power	Retail Low	Retail High
1999	T318D	150,000	180,000
1998	T318D	139,000	167,000
1997	T318D	129,000	155,000
1996	T318D	120,000	144,000

Navigator 44 Classic

Year	Power	Retail Low	Retail High
2007	T318D	260,000	312,000
2006	T318D	239,000	287,000
2005	T318D	220,000	264,000
2004	T318D	202,000	242,000
2003	T318D	186,000	223,000
2002	T318D	171,000	205,000

Navigator 48 Classic

Year	Power	Retail Low	Retail High
2007	T318D	******	******
2006	T318D	******	******
2005	T318D	285,000	342,000
2004	T318D	262,000	314,000
2003	T318D	241,000	289,000
2002	T318D	221,000	266,000
2001	T318D	204,000	245,000
2000	T318D	189,000	227,000
1999	T318D	176,000	211,000
1998	T318D	164,000	197,000
1997	T318D	152,000	183,000

Navigator 50 Classic

Year	Power	Retail Low	Retail High
2000	T370D	210,000	252,000
1999	T370D	193,000	231,000
1998	T370D	177,000	213,000
1997	T370D	163,000	196,000
1996	T370D	152,000	182,000
1995	T370D	141,000	169,000
1994	T370D	131,000	157,000
1993	T370D	122,000	146,000

Navigator 53 Classic

Year	Power	Retail Low	Retail High
2006	T370D	******	******
2005	T370D	******	******
2004	T370D	320,000	384,000
2003	T370D	294,000	353,000
2002	T370D	270,000	325,000
2001	T370D	249,000	299,000
2000	T370D	229,000	275,000
1999	T370D	213,000	255,000
1998	T370D	198,000	237,000
1997	T370D	184,000	221,000
1996	T370D	171,000	205,000

Year	Power	Retail Low	Retail High
1995	T370D	159,000	191,000

Navigator 56 Classic

Year	Power	Retail Low	Retail High
2005	T370D	440,000	528,000
2004	T370D	404,000	485,000
2003	T370D	372,000	446,000
2002	T370D	342,000	411,000
2001	T370D	318,000	382,000
2000	T370D	296,000	355,000

Navigator 5600

Year	Power	Retail Low	Retail High
1999	T430D	275,000	330,000
1998	T430D	256,000	307,000
1997	T430D	238,000	286,000
1996	T430D	221,000	266,000
1995	T430D	206,000	247,000

Navigator 57 Rival

Year	Power	Retail Low	Retail High
2007	T370D	******	******
2006	T370D	******	******
2005	T370D	******	******
2004	T370D	410,000	483,000
2003	T370D	377,000	445,000

Navigator 5800

Year	Power	Retail Low	Retail High
2002	T485D	******	******
2001	T485D	******	******
2000	T485D	******	******
1999	T485D	350,000	413,000

Navigator 6100

Year	Power	Retail Low	Retail High
2003	T700D	555,000	654,000
2002	T700D	510,000	602,000
2001	T700D	469,000	554,000
2000	T700D	432,000	509,000
1999	T700D	397,000	469,000

Nordhavn 35 Coastal Pilot

Year	Power	Retail Low	Retail High
2005	370D	275,000	330,000
2004	370D	266,000	320,000
2003	370D	258,000	310,000
2002	370D	250,000	301,000
2001	370D	243,000	292,000

Nordhavn 40

Year	Power	Retail Low	Retail High
2010	105D	******	******
2009	105D	******	******
2008	105D	******	******
2007	105D	450,000	526,000
2006	105D	427,000	500,000
2005	105D	406,000	475,000
2004	105D	385,000	451,000
2003	105D	366,000	428,000
2002	105D	351,000	411,000
2001	105D	337,000	395,000
2000	105D	324,000	379,000
1999	105D	311,000	364,000

Nordhavn 46

Year	Power	Retail Low	Retail High
2005	140D	******	******
2004	140D	******	******
2003	140D	******	******
2002	140D	450,000	526,000
2001	140D	432,000	505,000
2000	140D	414,000	485,000
1999	140D	398,000	465,000
1998	140D	382,000	447,000
1997	140D	366,000	429,000
1996	140D	352,000	412,000
1995	140D	338,000	395,000

Nordhavn 47

Year	Power	Retail Low	Retail High
2010	173D	******	******
2009	173D	******	******
2008	173D	******	******
2007	173D	******	******
2006	173D	775,000	914,000
2005	173D	736,000	868,000
2004	173D	699,000	825,000
2003	173D	664,000	784,000

Nordhavn 50

Year	Power	Retail Low	Retail High
2006	S/Diesel	******	*******
2005	S/Diesel	******	*******
2004	S/Diesel	720,000	849,000
2003	S/Diesel	684,000	807,000
2002	S/Diesel	649,000	766,000
2001	S/Diesel	623,000	736,000
2000	S/Diesel	598,000	706,000
1999	S/Diesel	574,000	678,000
1998	S/Diesel	551,000	651,000
1997	S/Diesel	529,000	625,000

Nordhavn 55

Year	Power	Retail Low	Retail High
2010	330D	******	******
2009	330D	******	******
2008	330D	******	******
2007	330D	1,200,000	1,404,000
2006	330D	1,140,000	1,333,000
2005	330D	1,083,000	1,267,000

Nordhavn 57

Year	Power	Retail Low	Retail High
2007	S/Diesel	******	******
2006	S/Diesel	******	******
2005	S/Diesel	******	******
2004	S/Diesel	******	******
2003	S/Diesel	******	******
2002	S/Diesel	800,000	944,000
2001	S/Diesel	768,000	906,000
2000	S/Diesel	737,000	869,000
1999	S/Diesel	707,000	835,000

Nordic 26 Tug

Year	Power	Retail Low	Retail High
1997	S/Diesel	57,000	68,000
1996	S/Diesel	54,000	65,000
1995	S/Diesel	52,000	63,000

Nordic 32 Tug

Year	Power	Retail Low	Retail High
2010	280D	******	******
2009	280D	181,000	217,000
2008	280D	172,000	206,000
2007	280D	163,000	196,000
2006	270D	155,000	186,000
2005	270D	147,000	177,000
2004	270D	140,000	168,000
2003	270D	133,000	160,000
2002	220D	126,000	152,000
2001	220D	121,000	145,000
2000	220D	116,000	140,000
1999	220D	112,000	134,000
1998	220D	107,000	129,000
1997	210D	103,000	123,000
1996	210D	100,000	120,000
1995	210D	97,000	116,000

Nordic 37 Tug

Year	Power	Retail Low	Retail High
2010	380D	******	******
2009	380D	322,000	380,000
2008	380D	305,000	361,000
2007	380D	290,000	342,000
2006	380D	276,000	325,000
2005	330D	262,000	309,000
2004	330D	249,000	294,000
2003	330D	239,000	282,000
2002	330D	229,000	270,000
2001	330D	220,000	260,000
2000	330D	211,000	249,000
1999	330D	203,000	239,000
1998	330D	195,000	230,000

Nordic 42 Tug

Year	Power	Retail Low	Retail High
2010	540D	******	******
2009	540D	******	******
2008	540D	410,000	479,000
2007	540D	385,000	450,000
2006	540D	362,000	423,000
2005	450D	340,000	398,000
2004	450D	320,000	374,000
2003	450D	304,000	355,000
2002	450D	288,000	338,000
2001	330D	274,000	321,000
2000	330D	260,000	305,000
1999	330D	247,000	289,000
1998	330D	235,000	275,000
1997	330D	223,000	261,000
1996	330D	212,000	248,000

Ocean Alexander 390 Sundeck

Year	Power	Retail Low	Retail High
1999	T220D	123,000	147,000
1998	T220D	113,000	136,000
1997	T220D	104,000	125,000
1996	T220D	96,000	115,000
1995	T220D	89,000	107,000

Ocean Alexander 420 Sundeck

Year	Power	Retail Low	Retail High
1999	T220D	139,000	189,000
1998	T220D	128,000	174,000
1997	T220D	118,000	160,000
1996	T250D	108,000	147,000
1995	T250D	100,000	135,000

Ocean Alexander 420/422 Sport Sedan

Year	Power	Retail Low	Retail High
2001	T420D	203,000	293,000
2000	T420D	186,000	269,000
1999	T420D	172,000	248,000
1998	T420D	158,000	228,000
1997	T375D	145,000	210,000
1996	T375D	135,000	195,000
1995	T375D	125,000	181,000

Ocean Alexander 423 Classico

Year	Power	Retail Low	Retail High
2002	T220D	213,000	308,000
2001	T220D	196,000	283,000
2000	T220D	180,000	261,000
1999	T220D	166,000	240,000
1998	T220D	153,000	221,000
1997	T220D	140,000	203,000
1996	T220D	129,000	187,000
1995	T220D	120,000	174,000

Ocean Alexander 426 Classico

Year	Power	Retail Low	Retail High
2002	T220D	220,000	317,000
2001	T220D	202,000	292,000
2000	T220D	186,000	268,000
1999	T220D	171,000	247,000
1998	T220D	157,000	227,000
1997	T220D	145,000	209,000
1996	T220D	133,000	192,000
1995	T220D	124,000	179,000

Ocean Alexander 430/460 Classico MKI

Year	Power	Retail Low	Retail High
2006	T220D	******	******
2005	T220D	******	******
2004	T220D	******	******
2003	T220D	216,000	398,000
2002	T220D	199,000	367,000
2001	T220D	183,000	337,000
2000	T220D	168,000	310,000

Ocean Alexander 450 Classico Sedan

Year	Power	Retail Low	Retail High
2004	T220D	******	******
2003	T220D	******	******
2002	T220D	241,000	282,000
2001	T220D	221,000	259,000

Year	Power	Retail Low	Retail High
2000	T210D	204,000	238,000

Ocean Alexander 456 Classico

Year	Power	Retail Low	Retail High
2002	T375D	248,000	290,000
2001	T375D	228,000	267,000
2000	T375D	210,000	245,000
1999	T375D	193,000	226,000
1998	T375D	177,000	208,000
1997	T375D	163,000	191,000
1996	T375D	152,000	178,000
1995	T375D	141,000	165,000

Ocean Alexander 480 Sport Sedan

Year	Power	Retail Low	Retail High
2001	T420D	238,000	278,000
2000	T420D	218,000	256,000
1999	T420D	201,000	235,000
1998	T420D	185,000	216,000
1997	T420D	170,000	199,000
1996	T375D	156,000	183,000
1995	T375D	144,000	168,000

Ocean Alexander 51/53 Sedan

Year	Power	Retail Low	Retail High
1998	T550D	260,000	306,000
1997	T550D	241,000	285,000
1996	T485D	224,000	265,000
1995	T735D	209,000	246,000

Ocean Alexander 520/540 PH

Year	Power	Retail Low	Retail High
2002	T420D	308,000	361,000
2001	T420D	287,000	335,000
2000	T420D	267,000	312,000
1999	T420D	248,000	290,000
1998	T435D	230,000	270,000
1997	T435D	214,000	251,000
1996	T435D	199,000	233,000
1995	T435D	187,000	219,000

Ocean Alexander 548 PH

Year	Power	Retail Low	Retail High
2002	T660D	462,000	540,000
2001	T660D	429,000	502,000
2000	T660D	399,000	467,000
1999	T660D	371,000	434,000
1998	T550D	349,000	408,000
1997	T550D	328,000	384,000
1996	T550D	308,000	361,000

Ocean Alexander 58 PH

Year	Power	Retail Low	Retail High
2009	T760D	******	******
2008	T760D	880,000	1,012,000
2007	T760D	818,000	941,000
2006	T760D	761,000	875,000
2005	T700D	707,000	814,000
2004	T700D	658,000	757,000

Ocean Alexander 64 MY

Year	Power	Retail Low	Retail High
2007	T825D	1,100,000	1,276,000
2006	T825D	1,023,000	1,186,000
2005	T825D	951,000	1,103,000
2004	T825D	884,000	1,026,000
2003	T825D	822,000	954,000
2002	T825D	765,000	887,000

Ocean Master 27 Center Console

Year	Power	Retail Low	Retail High
2009	T200 O/B	******	******
2008	T200 O/B	******	******
2007	T200 O/B	******	******
2006	T200 O/B	******	******
2005	T200 O/B	******	******
2004	T200 O/B	******	******
2003	T200 O/B	******	******
2002	T200 O/B	53,000	64,000
2001	T200 O/B	48,000	57,000
2000	T200 O/B	43,000	52,000
1999	T200 O/B	39,000	47,000
1998	T200 O/B	36,000	43,000

Year	Power	Retail Low	Retail High
1997	T200 O/B	33,000	39,000
1996	T200 O/B	30,000	36,000
1995	T200 O/B	27,000	33,000

Ocean 37 Billfish

Year	Power	Retail Low	Retail High
2010	T480D	******	******
2009	T480D	340,000	408,000
2008	T480D	312,000	375,000

Ocean 38 Super Sport

Year	Power	Retail Low	Retail High
1995	T420D	116,000	139,000

Ocean 40 Sport Fish

Year	Power	Retail Low	Retail High
2005	T420D	204,000	241,000
2004	T420D	186,000	219,000
2003	T420D	169,000	199,000
2002	T420D	154,000	181,000
2001	T420D	140,000	165,000
2000	T420D	127,000	150,000
1999	T420D	116,000	137,000

Ocean 40 Super Sport

Year	Power	Retail Low	Retail High
2005	T420D	223,000	264,000
2004	T420D	203,000	240,000
2003	T420D	185,000	218,000
2002	T420D	168,000	198,000
2001	T420D	153,000	181,000
2000	T420D	139,000	164,000
1999	T420D	127,000	149,000
1998	T420D	115,000	136,000
1997	T420D	105,000	124,000

Ocean 42 SS (1991-95)

Year	Power	Retail Low	Retail High
1995	T485D	146,000	173,000

Ocean 42 SS (Current)

Year	Power	Retail Low	Retail High
2010	T510D	******	******
2009	T510D	******	******
2008	T510D	******	******
2007	T510D	370,000	436,000
2006	T510D	340,000	401,000

Ocean 43 Super Sport

Year	Power	Retail Low	Retail High
2005	T480D	280,000	330,000
2004	T480D	254,000	300,000
2003	T480D	231,000	273,000
2002	T480D	211,000	248,000
2001	T480D	194,000	229,000
2000	T480D	176,000	208,000

Ocean 44 Motor Yacht

Year	Power	Retail Low	Retail High
1999	T485D	196,000	231,000
1998	T485D	180,000	213,000
1997	T485D	166,000	196,000
1996	T485D	153,000	180,000
1995	T485D	140,000	166,000

Ocean 45 Super Sport

Year	Power	Retail Low	Retail High
1999	T485D	198,000	234,000
1998	T485D	182,000	215,000
1997	T485D	168,000	198,000
1996	T485D	154,000	182,000

Ocean 46 Super Sport

Year	Power	Retail Low	Retail High
2010	T715D	******	******
2009	T715D	******	******
2008	T715D	510,000	596,000
2007	T715D	469,000	548,000
2006	T710D	431,000	505,000
2005	T710D	397,000	464,000

Ocean 48 Cockpit MY

Year	Power	Retail Low	Retail High
1999	T485D	233,000	273,000
1998	T485D	215,000	251,000
1997	T485D	197,000	231,000
1996	T485D	182,000	212,000

Year	Power	Retail Low	Retail High
1995	T485D	167,000	195,000

Ocean 48 Sport Fish

Year	Power	Retail Low	Retail High
2001	T800D	279,000	326,000
2000	T800D	254,000	297,000
1999	T660D	231,000	270,000
1998	T625D	210,000	246,000
1997	T625D	191,000	224,000

Ocean 48 Super Sport

Year	Power	Retail Low	Retail High
2003	T660D	338,000	395,000
2002	T660D	311,000	364,000
2001	T660D	286,000	334,000
2000	T660D	263,000	308,000
1999	T660D	242,000	283,000
1998	T625D	222,000	260,000
1997	T625D	205,000	239,000
1996	T625D	188,000	220,000
1995	T625D	175,000	205,000

Ocean 50 Super Sport

Year	Power	Retail Low	Retail High
2010	T825D	******	******
2009	T825D	******	******
2008	T825D	******	******
2007	T825D	568,000	665,000
2006	T800D	523,000	612,000
2005	T800D	481,000	563,000
2004	T800D	442,000	518,000

Ocean 52 Super Sport

Year	Power	Retail Low	Retail High
2006	T800D	547,000	640,000
2005	T800D	503,000	589,000
2004	T800D	463,000	542,000
2003	T800D	426,000	498,000
2002	T800D	392,000	458,000
2001	T800D	360,000	422,000

Ocean 53 Super Sport

Year	Power	Retail Low	Retail High
1999	T820D	285,000	334,000
1998	T820D	263,000	307,000
1997	T820D	242,000	283,000
1996	T820D	222,000	260,000
1995	T820D	204,000	239,000

Ocean 54 Super Sport

Year	Power	Retail Low	Retail High
2010	1015D	******	******
2009	1015D	******	******
2008	1050D	810,000	947,000
2007	1050D	745,000	871,000

Ocean 56 Super Sport

Year	Power	Retail Low	Retail High
2002	1050D	430,000	503,000
2001	1050D	395,000	462,000
2000	1050D	363,000	425,000
1999	1050D	334,000	391,000

Ocean 57 Odyssey

Year	Power	Retail Low	Retail High
2010	T1050D	******	******
2009	T1050D	******	******
2008	T1050D	******	******
2007	T1015D	710,000	830,000
2006	T1015D	653,000	764,000
2005	T1015D	600,000	703,000
2004	T1015D	552,000	646,000

Ocean 57 Super Sport

Year	Power	Retail Low	Retail High
2007	1015D	707,000	827,000
2006	1015D	650,000	761,000
2005	1015D	598,000	700,000
2004	1015D	550,000	644,000
2003	1015D	506,000	592,000

Ocean 60 Super Sport

Year	Power	Retail Low	Retail High
2001	1350D	******	******
2000	1350D	******	******
1999	1350D	552,000	640,000

Year	Power	Retail Low	Retail High
1998	1350D	513,000	595,000
1997	1350D	477,000	553,000
1996	1350D	444,000	515,000

Ocean 62 Super Sport

Year	Power	Retail Low	Retail High
2008	1500D	******	******
2007	1500D	******	******
2006	1400D	******	******
2005	1400D	******	******
2004	1400D	******	******
2003	1350D	857,000	1,003,000
2002	1350D	797,000	933,000

Ocean 66 Super Sport

Year	Power	Retail Low	Retail High
1999	1350D	606,000	703,000
1998	1350D	563,000	654,000
1997	1350D	524,000	608,000
1996	1350D	487,000	565,000
1995	1150D	453,000	526,000

Offshore 48 Yacht Fish

Year	Power	Retail Low	Retail High
1999	T435D	280,000	330,000
1998	T435D	260,000	307,000
1997	T435D	242,000	285,000
1996	T435D	225,000	265,000
1995	T375D	209,000	247,000

Offshore 48 Pilothouse

Year	Power	Retail Low	Retail High
2001	T435D	455,000	536,000
2000	T420D	423,000	499,000
1999	T420D	393,000	464,000

Offshore 48 Sedan

Year	Power	Retail Low	Retail High
2001	T435D	370,000	436,000
2000	T435D	344,000	406,000
1999	T435D	320,000	377,000
1998	T435D	297,000	351,000
1997	T435D	276,000	326,000
1996	T435D	257,000	303,000
1995	T375D	239,000	282,000

Offshore 52/54 Pilothouse

Year	Power	Retail Low	Retail High
2010	T460D	******	******
2009	T460D	******	******
2008	T460D	******	******
2007	T460D	******	******
2006	T450D	******	******
2005	T450D	740,000	865,000
2004	T450D	688,000	805,000
2003	T450D	640,000	748,000
2002	T450D	595,000	696,000
2001	T450D	553,000	647,000
2000	T450D	514,000	602,000
1999	T450D	478,000	560,000
1998	T420D	445,000	520,000

Osprey 30

Year	Power	Retail Low	Retail High
2003	T188D I/O	70,000	84,000
2002	T188D I/O	64,000	77,000
2001	T188D I/O	59,000	71,000
2000	T188D I/O	54,000	65,000
1999	T188D I/O	50,000	60,000

Pacific Mariner 65 Motor Yacht

Year	Power	Retail Low	Retail High
2008	T825D	******	******
2007	T825D	******	******
2006	T825D	1,070,000	1,262,000
2005	T825D	984,000	1,161,000
2004	T825D	905,000	1,068,000
2003	T825D	833,000	983,000
2002	T800D	766,000	904,000
2001	T800D	712,000	841,000
2000	T800D	662,000	782,000
1999	T800D	616,000	727,000
1998	T800D	573,000	676,000

Year	Power	Retail Low	Retail High
1997	T800D	533,000	629,000

Pacific Seacraft 38T Fast Trawler

Year	Power	Retail Low	Retail High
2002	350D	******	******
2001	350D	******	******
2000	350D	210,000	252,000
1999	350D	197,000	236,000

Pacific Trawler 40

Year	Power	Retail Low	Retail High
2002	220D	210,000	252,000
2001	220D	197,000	236,000
2000	220D	185,000	222,000

PDQ 34 Powercat

Year	Power	Retail Low	Retail High
2007	T100D	250,000	300,000
2006	T100D	237,000	285,000
2005	T100D	225,000	270,000
2004	T100D	214,000	257,000
2003	T100D	205,000	246,000
2002	T75D	197,000	237,000
2001	T75D	189,000	227,000
2000	T75D	182,000	218,000

Pearson True North 33

Year	Power	Retail Low	Retail High
2008	440D	******	******
2007	440D	******	******
2006	440D	145,000	174,000
2005	440D	133,000	160,000
2004	440D	122,000	147,000

Pearson True North 38

Year	Power	Retail Low	Retail High
2008	440D	******	******
2007	440D	270,000	318,000
2006	440D	251,000	296,000
2005	440D	233,000	275,000
2004	440D	217,000	256,000
2003	440D	201,000	238,000
2002	440D	187,000	221,000

Phoenix 27 Tournament

Year	Power	Retail Low	Retail High
1999	T260G	38,000	46,000
1998	T260G	35,000	42,000
1997	T260G	32,000	39,000
1996	T260G	29,000	35,000
1995	T260G	27,000	33,000

Phoenix 29 SFX Convertible

Year	Power	Retail Low	Retail High
1999	T310G	65,000	78,000
1999	T240D	85,000	102,000
1998	T310G	60,000	72,000
1998	T240D	79,000	94,000
1997	T310G	56,000	67,000
1997	T240D	73,000	88,000
1996	T310G	52,000	62,000
1996	T240D	68,000	82,000
1995	T310G	48,000	58,000
1995	T240D	63,000	76,000

Phoenix 32 Tournament

Year	Power	Retail Low	Retail High
1999	T350D	70,000	84,000
1998	T350D	63,000	76,000
1997	T350D	57,000	69,000

Phoenix 33/34 SFX Convertible

Year	Power	Retail Low	Retail High
1999	T310G	73,000	88,000
1999	T385D	94,000	113,000
1998	T310G	67,000	81,000
1998	T375D	86,000	104,000
1997	T310G	62,000	74,000
1997	T375D	79,000	95,000
1996	T310G	57,000	68,000
1996	T375D	73,000	88,000
1995	T310G	52,000	63,000
1995	T350D	67,000	81,000

Post 42 Sport Fisherman

Year	Power	Retail Low	Retail High
2009	T510D	******	******
2008	T510D	******	******
2007	T510D	420,000	491,000
2006	T510D	382,000	447,000
2005	T480D	347,000	406,000
2004	T480D	316,000	370,000
2003	T480D	288,000	336,000
2002	T480D	262,000	306,000
2001	T430D	241,000	282,000
2000	T430D	221,000	259,000
1999	T430D	204,000	238,000
1998	T430D	187,000	219,000
1997	T430D	172,000	202,000

Post 43 Sport Fisherman

Year	Power	Retail Low	Retail High
1996	T550D	220,000	257,000
1995	T550D	209,000	244,000

Post 46 Sport Fisherman

Year	Power	Retail Low	Retail High
1996	T550D	250,000	300,000
1995	T550D	230,000	276,000

Post 47 Sport Fisherman

Year	Power	Retail Low	Retail High
2009	T715D	******	******
2008	T715D	******	******
2007	T715D	******	******
2006	T715D	******	******
2005	T680D	******	******
2004	T680D	******	******
2003	T680D	******	******
2002	T680D	******	******
2001	T680D	380,000	456,000
2000	T680D	345,000	414,000
1999	T680D	314,000	377,000
1998	T680D	286,000	343,000
1997	T550D	260,000	312,000

Post 50 Sport Fisherman

Year	Power	Retail Low	Retail High
2009	T865D	******	******
2008	T865D	******	******
2007	T865D	******	******
2006	T865D	******	******
2005	T860D	******	******
2004	T860D	******	******
2003	T860D	520,000	613,000
2002	T820D	473,000	558,000
2001	T820D	430,000	508,000
2000	T820D	391,000	462,000
1999	T820D	356,000	420,000
1998	T820D	324,000	382,000
1997	T735D	295,000	348,000
1996	T735D	268,000	317,000
1995	T735D	244,000	288,000

Post 53 Convertible

Year	Power	Retail Low	Retail High
2009	T1100D	******	******
2008	T1100D	******	******
2007	T1100D	******	******
2006	T1100D	670,000	790,000
2005	T1100D	623,000	735,000

Post 56 Convertible

Year	Power	Retail Low	Retail High
2009	T1300D	******	******
2007	T1300D	******	******
2006	T1300D	******	******
2005	T1300D	******	******
2004	T1300D	700,000	819,000
2003	T1300D	651,000	761,000
2002	T1300D	605,000	708,000
2001	T1300D	563,000	658,000

Pro-Line 27 Walk

Year	Power	Retail Low	Retail High
2004	T200 O/B	36,000	43,000

Year	Power	Retail Low	Retail High
2003	T200 O/B	33,000	39,000
2002	T200 O/B	30,000	36,000
2001	T200 O/B	27,000	32,000
2000	T200 O/B	25,000	30,000
1999	T200 O/B	23,000	27,000
1998	T200 O/B	21,000	25,000

Pro-Line 27/29 Sport

Year	Power	Retail Low	Retail High
2006	T200 O/B	44,000	53,000
2005	T200 O/B	40,000	49,000
2004	T200 O/B	37,000	44,000
2003	T200 O/B	33,000	40,000
2001	T200 O/B	30,000	36,000
2000	T200 O/B	28,000	33,000

Pro-Line 2810 Walkaround

Year	Power	Retail Low	Retail High
2000	T225 O/B	30,000	36,000
1999	T225 O/B	27,000	32,000
1998	T225 O/B	24,000	29,000
1997	T225 O/B	21,000	26,000

Pro-Line 2950 Mid Cabin

Year	Power	Retail Low	Retail High
2000	T225 O/B	35,000	43,000
1999	T250 I/O	37,000	45,000
1998	T225 O/B	33,000	39,000
1998	T250 I/O	34,000	41,000
1997	T225 O/B	30,000	36,000
1997	T250 I/O	31,000	38,000
1996	T225 O/B	28,000	33,000
1996	T250 I/O	29,000	35,000
1995	T225 O/B	25,000	30,000
1995	T250 I/O	26,000	32,000

Pro-Line 30 Walkaround

Year	Power	Retail Low	Retail High
2005	T225 O/B	56,000	68,000
2004	T225 O/B	51,000	62,000
2003	T225 O/B	47,000	56,000
2002	T225 O/B	42,000	51,000
2001	T225 O/B	38,000	46,000
2000	T225 O/B	35,000	42,000

Pro-Line 30 Express

Year	Power	Retail Low	Retail High
2005	T225 O/B	55,000	67,000
2004	T225 O/B	50,000	61,000
2003	T225 O/B	46,000	55,000
2002	T225 O/B	42,000	50,000
2001	T225 O/B	38,000	46,000
2000	T225 O/B	34,000	41,000

Pro-Line 30/31 Sport

Year	Power	Retail Low	Retail High
2006	T225 O/B	54,000	65,000
2005	T225 O/B	48,000	58,000
2004	T225 O/B	43,000	52,000
2003	T225 O/B	39,000	47,000
2002	T225 O/B	35,000	42,000
2001	T225 O/B	31,000	38,000
2000	T225 O/B	28,000	34,000

Pro-Line 3250/32 Express

Year	Power	Retail Low	Retail High
2002	T320G	56,000	67,000
2001	T320G	51,000	61,000
2000	T310G	46,000	55,000
1999	T310G	42,000	50,000
1998	T310G	38,000	46,000
1997	T310G	35,000	42,000

Pro-Line 32 Express

Year	Power	Retail Low	Retail High
2009	T250 O/B	120,000	144,000
2008	T250 O/B	109,000	131,000
2007	T250 O/B	99,000	119,000
2006	T250 O/B	90,000	109,000
2005	T250 O/B	82,000	99,000

Pro-Line 33 Express

Year	Power	Retail Low	Retail High
2006	T370G I/B	******	******
2006	T315D I/B	133,000	159,000
2005	T370G I/B	******	******
2005	T315D I/B	121,000	145,000
2004	T370G I/B	96,000	116,000
2004	T315D I/B	110,000	132,000
2003	T370G I/B	88,000	105,000
2003	T315D I/B	100,000	120,000
2002	T370G I/B	80,000	96,000
2002	T315D I/B	91,000	109,000
2001	T310G I/B	72,000	87,000
2001	T350D I/B	83,000	99,000
2000	T310G I/B	66,000	79,000
2000	T350D I/B	75,000	90,000
1999	T310G I/B	60,000	72,000
1999	T350D I/B	68,000	82,000

Pro-Line 33 Walkaround

Year	Power	Retail Low	Retail High
2005	T250 O/B	76,000	91,000
2004	T250 O/B	69,000	83,000
2003	T250 O/B	62,000	75,000

Pro-Line 3400 SS Cuddy

Year	Power	Retail Low	Retail High
2001	T250 O/B	54,000	65,000
2000	T250 O/B	49,000	59,000
1999	T250 O/B	44,000	53,000
1998	T250 O/B	40,000	49,000

Pro-Line 35 Express

Year	Power	Retail Low	Retail High
2009	3/225 O/B	164,000	197,000
2008	3/225 O/B	149,000	179,000
2007	3/225 O/B	136,000	163,000
2006	3/225 O/B	123,000	148,000

Pursuit 2860/2865 Denali

Year	Power	Retail Low	Retail High
2004	375G I/O	44,000	52,000
2003	375G I/O	40,000	48,000
2002	375G I/O	37,000	44,000
2001	310G I/O	34,000	41,000
2000	310G I/O	31,000	37,000
1999	310G I/O	29,000	34,000
1998	310G I/O	26,000	32,000
1997	310G I/O	24,000	29,000

Pursuit 2870 CC; C280

Year	Power	Retail Low	Retail High
2008	T225 O/B	90,000	108,000
2007	T225 O/B	82,000	99,000
2006	T225 O/B	75,000	90,000
2005	T225 O/B	68,000	82,000
2004	T225 O/B	62,000	74,000
2003	T225 O/B	56,000	67,000
2002	T225 O/B	52,000	62,000
2001	T225 O/B	47,000	57,000
2000	T225 O/B	44,000	52,000
1999	T225 O/B	40,000	48,000
1998	T225 O/B	37,000	44,000
1997	T225 O/B	34,000	41,000

Pursuit 2870 Offshore CC

Year	Power	Retail Low	Retail High
2002	T225 O/B	44,000	53,000
2001	T225 O/B	40,000	48,000
2000	T225 O/B	36,000	43,000
1999	T225 O/B	33,000	39,000
1998	T225 O/B	30,000	36,000
1997	T225 O/B	27,000	33,000
1996	T225 O/B	25,000	30,000

Pursuit 2870 Walkaround

Year	Power	Retail Low	Retail High
2006	T225 O/B	74,000	89,000
2005	T225 O/B	67,000	81,000
2004	T225 O/B	61,000	74,000
2003	T225 O/B	56,000	67,000
2002	T225 O/B	51,000	61,000
2001	T225 O/B	46,000	56,000
2000	T225 O/B	43,000	51,000
1999	T225 O/B	39,000	47,000
1998	T225 O/B	36,000	43,000
1997	T225 O/B	33,000	40,000
1996	T225 O/B	30,000	37,000

Pursuit C 280 (2009-Current)

Year	Power	Retail Low	Retail High
2010	T250 O/B	125,000	150,000
2009	T250 O/B	112,000	135,000

Pursuit OS 285

Year	Power	Retail Low	Retail High
2010	T250 O/B	******	******
2009	T250 O/B	116,000	139,000
2008	T250 O/B	106,000	127,000

Pursuit 3000 Express

Year	Power	Retail Low	Retail High
2003	T320G	71,000	85,000
2003	T250D	84,000	101,000
2002	T320G	64,000	77,000
2002	T250D	77,000	92,000
2001	T320G	58,000	70,000
2001	T250D	70,000	84,000
2000	T320G	53,000	64,000
2000	T250D	63,000	76,000
1999	T320G	48,000	58,000
1999	T250D	58,000	69,000
1998	T320G	44,000	53,000
1998	T225D	52,000	63,000

Pursuit 3000 Offshore

Year	Power	Retail Low	Retail High
2004	T375G	83,000	99,000
2004	T285D	103,000	124,000
2003	T375G	75,000	90,000
2003	T285D	94,000	112,000
2002	T375G	68,000	82,000
2002	T260D	85,000	102,000
2001	T320G	62,000	75,000
2001	T260D	77,000	93,000
2000	T320G	57,000	69,000
2000	T260D	71,000	85,000
1999	T320G	53,000	63,000
1999	T260D	65,000	79,000
1998	T320G	48,000	58,000
1998	T260D	60,000	72,000
1997	T320G	44,000	53,000
1997	T260D	55,000	66,000
1996	T320G	41,000	49,000
1996	T260D	51,000	61,000
1995	T320G	38,000	45,000
1995	T260D	47,000	56,000

Pursuit 3070 Center Console

Year	Power	Retail Low	Retail High
2007	T250 O/B	92,000	111,000
2006	T250 O/B	83,000	100,000
2005	T250 O/B	75,000	90,000
2004	T250 O/B	67,000	81,000
2003	T250 O/B	60,000	72,000
2002	T250 O/B	54,000	65,000
2001	T250 O/B	49,000	59,000

Pursuit 3070 Offshore CC

Year	Power	Retail Low	Retail High
2006	T250 O/B	97,000	117,000
2005	T250 O/B	88,000	106,000
2004	T250 O/B	80,000	97,000
2003	T250 O/B	73,000	88,000
2002	T250 O/B	67,000	80,000
2001	T250 O/B	61,000	73,000
2000	T250 O/B	55,000	66,000
1999	T250 O/B	50,000	60,000

Pursuit 3070 Offshore Express

Year	Power	Retail Low	Retail High
2007	T250 O/B	114,000	137,000
2006	T250 O/B	103,000	124,000
2005	T250 O/B	94,000	113,000
2004	T250 O/B	86,000	103,000

Year	Power	Retail Low	Retail High
2003	T250 O/B	78,000	93,000
2002	T250 O/B	71,000	85,000
2001	T250 O/B	64,000	77,000

Pursuit 3100 Express

Year	Power	Retail Low	Retail High
1997	T300G	46,000	56,000
1996	T300G	42,000	51,000
1995	T300G	39,000	47,000

Pursuit C 310 Center Console

Year	Power	Retail Low	Retail High
2010	T250 O/B	******	******
2009	T250 O/B	114,000	137,000
2008	T250 O/B	102,000	123,000
2007	T250 O/B	93,000	112,000

Pursuit OS 315

Year	Power	Retail Low	Retail High
2010	T250 O/B	******	******
2009	T250 O/B	153,000	183,000
2008	T250 O/B	139,000	167,000

Pursuit 3100 Offshore

Year	Power	Retail Low	Retail High
2005	T330G	107,000	129,000
2005	T315D	122,000	147,000
2004	T330G	98,000	117,000
2004	T315D	111,000	134,000

Pursuit 3370 Offshore; OS 335

Year	Power	Retail Low	Retail High
2008	T250 O/B	153,000	184,000
2007	T250 O/B	139,000	167,000
2006	T250 O/B	127,000	152,000
2005	T250 O/B	115,000	138,000
2004	T250 O/B	105,000	126,000

Pursuit 3400 Express

Year	Power	Retail Low	Retail High
2003	T375G	94,000	113,000
2003	T370D	118,000	142,000
2002	T375G	85,000	102,000
2002	T370D	108,000	129,000
2001	T370G	78,000	93,000
2001	T370D	98,000	118,000
2000	T370G	71,000	85,000
2000	T370D	89,000	107,000
1999	T320G	64,000	77,000
1999	T370D	81,000	97,000
1998	T320G	58,000	70,000
1998	T370D	74,000	88,000
1997	T320G	53,000	64,000
1997	T370D	67,000	80,000

Pursuit 3480 CC; C 340

Year	Power	Retail Low	Retail High
2010	T250 O/B	******	******
2009	T250 O/B	126,000	151,000
2008	T250 O/B	113,000	136,000
2007	T250 O/B	102,000	122,000
2006	T250 O/B	92,000	110,000
2005	T250 O/B	84,000	101,000

Pursuit LS 345 Drummond Runner

Year	Power	Retail Low	Retail High
2008	T250 O/B	139,000	167,000
2007	T250 O/B	128,000	154,000
2006	T250 O/B	119,000	143,000

Pursuit OS 375

Year	Power	Retail Low	Retail High
2010	3/350 O/B	******	******
2009	3/350 O/B	325,000	391,000
2008	3/350 O/B	293,000	351,000

Pursuit 3800 Express

Year	Power	Retail Low	Retail High
2004	T480D	206,000	247,000
2003	T480D	187,000	225,000
2002	T480D	170,000	204,000

Rampage 30 Express

Year	Power	Retail Low	Retail High
2010	T375G	******	******
2010	T315D	******	******
2009	T375G	******	******
2009	T315D	******	******
2008	T375G	144,000	173,000
2008	T315D	170,000	204,000
2007	T375G	131,000	157,000
2007	T315D	155,000	186,000
2006	T375G	119,000	143,000
2006	T315D	141,000	169,000
2005	T300G	108,000	130,000
2005	T315D	128,000	154,000
2004	T300G	98,000	118,000
2004	T315D	116,000	140,000
2003	T300G	90,000	109,000
2003	T315D	107,000	128,000
2002	T300G	83,000	100,000
2002	T315D	98,000	118,000
2001	T300G	77,000	92,000
2001	T315D	90,000	109,000
2000	T300G	70,000	85,000
2000	T315D	83,000	100,000
1999	T300G	65,000	78,000
1999	T300D	77,000	92,000

Rampage 30 Offshore

Year	Power	Retail Low	Retail High
2006	T375G	91,000	109,000
2006	T315D	108,000	130,000
2005	T375G	83,000	99,000
2005	T315D	98,000	118,000
2004	T300G	75,000	90,000
2004	T315D	89,000	107,000
2003	T300G	68,000	82,000
2003	T315D	81,000	98,000
2002	T300G	62,000	75,000
2002	T315D	74,000	89,000

Rampage 33 Express

Year	Power	Retail Low	Retail High
2008	T425G	160,000	192,000
2008	T460D	205,000	246,000
2007	T425G	146,000	175,000
2007	T460D	186,000	224,000
2006	T370G	133,000	159,000
2006	T425D	169,000	203,000
2005	T370G	121,000	145,000
2005	T425D	154,000	185,000

Rampage 45 Convertible

Year	Power	Retail Low	Retail High
2010	T865D	******	******
2009	T865D	******	******
2008	T865D	******	******
2007	T865D	******	******
2006	T865D	******	******
2005	T800D	437,000	516,000
2004	T800D	402,000	475,000
2003	T800D	370,000	437,000
2002	T800D	340,000	402,000

Ranger R-29

Year	Power	Retail Low	Retail High
2010	260D	******	******
2009	260D	160,000	192,000

Regal 260 Valenti; 272 Commodore

Year	Power	Retail Low	Retail High
1996	S300 I/O	15,000	18,000
1996	T190 I/O	17,000	20,000
1995	S300 I/O	14,000	17,000
1995	T190 I/O	15,000	19,000

Regal 2660/2765 Commodore

Year	Power	Retail Low	Retail High
2005	S375 I/O	37,000	45,000
2005	T220 I/O	42,000	50,000
2004	S375 I/O	34,000	41,000
2004	T220 I/O	38,000	46,000
2003	S375 I/O	31,000	37,000
2003	T220 I/O	35,000	42,000
2002	S320 I/O	28,000	33,000
2002	T190 I/O	31,000	38,000

Year	Power	Retail Low	Retail High
2001	S310 I/O	26,000	31,000
2001	T190 I/O	29,000	35,000
2000	S310 I/O	23,000	28,000
2000	T190 I/O	26,000	32,000
1999	S310 I/O	22,000	26,000
1999	T190 I/O	24,000	29,000

Regal 2760/2860 Commodore

Year	Power	Retail Low	Retail High
2005	T225 I/O	48,000	57,000
2004	T220 I/O	43,000	52,000
2003	T220 I/O	39,000	47,000
2002	T220 I/O	36,000	43,000
2001	T210 I/O	32,000	39,000
2000	T210 I/O	30,000	36,000
1999	T210 I/O	27,000	33,000

Regal 2860 Windows Express

Year	Power	Retail Low	Retail High
2010	T220 I/O	******	******
2009	T220 I/O	82,000	98,000
2008	T220 I/O	74,000	89,000
2007	T220 I/O	68,000	81,000
2006	T220 I/O	62,000	74,000

Regal 292/2960/3060 Commodore

Year	Power	Retail Low	Retail High
2003	T260 I/O	43,000	52,000
2002	T260 I/O	39,000	47,000
2001	T260 I/O	36,000	43,000
2000	T260 I/O	33,000	39,000
1999	T260 I/O	30,000	36,000
1998	T260 I/O	28,000	33,000
1997	T260 I/O	25,000	31,000
1996	T260 I/O	23,000	28,000
1995	T260 I/O	21,000	26,000

Regal 3060 Window Express

Year	Power	Retail Low	Retail High
2010	T260 I/O	******	******
2009	T260 I/O	92,000	110,000
2008	T260 I/O	82,000	99,000
2007	T260 I/O	74,000	89,000
2006	T260 I/O	67,000	81,000
2005	T260 I/O	61,000	74,000
2004	T260 I/O	56,000	67,000

Regal Ventura 9.8; 322/3260 Commodore

Year	Power	Retail Low	Retail High
2004	T320 I/B	80,000	96,000
2004	T300 I/O	70,000	84,000
2003	T320 I/B	72,000	87,000
2003	T300 I/O	63,000	76,000
2002	T320 I/B	66,000	80,000
2002	T300 I/O	58,000	70,000
2001	T310 I/B	61,000	73,000
2001	T310 I/O	53,000	64,000
2000	T310 I/B	56,000	68,000
2000	T310 I/O	49,000	59,000
1999	T310 I/B	52,000	63,000
1999	T310 I/O	46,000	55,000
1998	T310 I/B	49,000	58,000
1998	T310 I/O	42,000	51,000
1997	T310 I/B	45,000	54,000
1997	T310 I/O	39,000	47,000
1996	T310 I/B	42,000	50,000
1996	T310 I/O	37,000	44,000
1995	T310 I/B	39,000	47,000
1995	T310 I/O	34,000	41,000

Regal 3360 Express

Year	Power	Retail Low	Retail High
2010	T300 I/O	******	******
2009	T300 I/O	129,000	154,000
2008	T300 I/O	116,000	139,000
2007	T320 I/O	104,000	125,000
2006	T320 I/O	94,000	112,000

Regal 3560/3760 Commodore

Year	Power	Retail Low	Retail High
2010	T420 VD	******	******

See Page 511 For Price Adjustments

Year	Power	Retail Low	Retail High
2010	T370 I/O	******	******
2009	T420 V/D	******	******
2009	T375 I/O	******	******
2008	T370 V/D	155,000	186,000
2008	T320 I/O	147,000	177,000
2007	T370 V/D	141,000	170,000
2007	T320 I/O	134,000	161,000
2006	T320 V/D	128,000	154,000
2006	T320 I/O	122,000	146,000
2005	T320 V/D	117,000	140,000
2005	T320 I/O	111,000	133,000
2004	T320 V/D	106,000	128,000
2004	T375 I/O	101,000	121,000
2003	T320 V/D	97,000	116,000
2003	T375 I/O	92,000	110,000

Regal 3860/4060 Commodore

Year	Power	Retail Low	Retail High
2010	T375G IPS	******	******
2010	T370D IPS	******	******
2009	T375G IPS	******	******
2009	T300D IPS	******	******
2008	T420G	255,000	306,000
2008	T370D	300,000	360,000
2007	T420G	234,000	281,000
2007	T370D	276,000	331,000
2006	T420G	215,000	258,000
2006	T370D	253,000	304,000
2005	T420G	198,000	238,000
2005	T370D	233,000	280,000
2004	T420G	184,000	221,000
2004	T370D	217,000	260,000
2003	T3420G	171,000	206,000
2003	T370D	202,000	242,000
2002	T3420G	159,000	191,000
2002	T370D	187,000	225,000

Regal 3880/4080 Commodore

Year	Power	Retail Low	Retail High
2010	T375G IPS	******	******
2010	T370D IPS	******	******
2009	T420G	******	******
2009	T370D	******	******
2008	T420G	******	******
2008	T370D	******	******
2007	T420G	215,000	258,000
2007	T370D	249,000	299,000
2006	T420G	195,000	235,000
2006	T370D	226,000	272,000
2005	T420G	178,000	213,000
2005	T370D	206,000	247,000
2004	T420G	163,000	196,000
2004	T370D	189,000	227,000
2003	T420G	150,000	181,000
2003	T370D	174,000	209,000
2002	T420G	138,000	166,000
2002	T370D	160,000	192,000
2001	T420G	127,000	153,000
2001	T330D	147,000	177,000

Regal 380/400/402 Commodore

Year	Power	Retail Low	Retail High
1999	T310G	85,000	102,000
1998	T310G	78,000	94,000
1997	T310G	72,000	86,000
1996	T310G	66,000	79,000
1995	T310G	61,000	73,000

Regal 4160/4260/4460 Commodore

Year	Power	Retail Low	Retail High
2910	T425D IPS	******	******
2010	T370G IPS	******	******
2009	T435D	******	******
2009	T420G	******	******
2008	T480D	******	******
2008	T420G	******	******
2007	T480D	298,000	355,000
2007	T420G	264,000	314,000
2006	T480D	271,000	323,000
2006	T420G	240,000	285,000
2005	T450D	249,000	297,000
2005	T420G	221,000	263,000
2004	T450D	229,000	273,000
2004	T420G	203,000	241,000
2003	T450D	211,000	251,000
2003	T420G	187,000	222,000
2002	T370D	194,000	231,000
2002	T420G	172,000	204,000
2001	T370D	179,000	213,000
2001	T380G	158,000	188,000
2000	T370D	164,000	196,000
2000	T380G	145,000	173,000

Regal 52 Sport Coupe

Year	Power	Retail Low	Retail High
2010	T435D IPS	******	******
2009	T435D IPS	550,000	649,000
2008	T435D IPS	495,000	584,000

Regulator 29 FS

Year	Power	Retail Low	Retail High
2010	T250 O/B	125,000	150,000
2009	T250 O/B	113,000	136,000
2008	T250 O/B	103,000	124,000
2007	T250 O/B	94,000	113,000
2006	T250 O/B	85,000	102,000

Regulator 32 FS

Year	Power	Retail Low	Retail High
2010	T250 O/B	******	******
2009	T250 O/B	136,000	163,000
2008	T250 O/B	123,000	148,000
2007	T250 O/B	112,000	135,000
2006	T250 O/B	102,000	122,000
2005	T250 O/B	93,000	111,000
2004	T250 O/B	85,000	102,000
2003	T250 O/B	78,000	94,000
2002	T250 O/B	72,000	87,000
2001	T250 O/B	66,000	80,000
2000	T250 O/B	61,000	73,000
1999	T250 O/B	56,000	67,000

Rinker 270 Fiesta Vee

Year	Power	Retail Low	Retail High
2006	300 I/O	34,000	40,000
2005	300 I/O	31,000	37,000
2004	250 I/O	29,000	35,000
2003	250 I/O	27,000	32,000
2002	250 I/O	25,000	30,000
2001	250 I/O	23,000	28,000
2000	250 I/O	21,000	26,000
1999	250 I/O	20,000	24,000

Rinker 280 Express Cruiser

Year	Power	Retail Low	Retail High
2010	280 I/O	******	******
2009	300 I/O	54,000	64,000
2008	300 I/O	48,000	58,000

Rinker 280 Fiesta Vee

Year	Power	Retail Low	Retail High
1999	T190 I/O	22,000	26,000
1998	T190 I/O	20,000	24,000
1997	T190 I/O	19,000	22,000
1996	T180 I/O	17,000	21,000
1995	T180 I/O	16,000	19,000

Rinker 290/300 Express

Year	Power	Retail Low	Retail High
2009	T260 I/O	95,000	114,000
2008	T260 I/O	86,000	103,000
2007	T260 I/O	78,000	94,000
2006	T260 I/O	72,000	86,000
2005	T260 I/O	66,000	79,000
2004	T260 I/O	61,000	73,000
2003	T260 I/O	56,000	67,000

Rinker 300 Fiesta Vee

Year	Power	Retail Low	Retail High
1997	T250 I/O	22,000	26,000
1996	T250 I/O	20,000	24,000
1995	T250 I/O	19,000	23,000

Rinker 310/312 Fiesta; 320 Express

Year	Power	Retail Low	Retail High
2009	T260 I/O	122,000	146,000
2008	T260 I/O	111,000	133,000
2007	T260 I/O	101,000	121,000
2006	T260 I/O	91,000	110,000
2005	T260 I/O	84,000	101,000
2004	T260 I/O	77,000	93,000
2003	T260 I/O	71,000	85,000
2002	T260 I/O	65,000	79,000
2001	T240 I/O	60,000	72,000
2000	T240 I/O	55,000	66,000

Rinker 330/340 Express Cruiser

Year	Power	Retail Low	Retail High
2010	T300 I/O	155,000	186,000
2009	T300 I/O	139,000	167,000
2008	T300 I/O	125,000	150,000

Rinker 330/340/342 Fiesta Vee

Year	Power	Retail Low	Retail High
2006	T300 I/O	110,000	132,000
2005	T300 I/O	101,000	121,000
2004	T300 I/O	93,000	111,000
2003	T300 I/O	85,000	102,000
2002	T300 I/O	78,000	94,000
2001	T260 I/O	73,000	87,000
2000	T260 I/O	68,000	81,000
1999	T260 I/O	63,000	76,000
1998	T260 I/O	58,000	70,000

Rinker 350/360 Express Cruiser

Year	Power	Retail Low	Retail High
2010	T300 I/O	******	******
2009	T300 I/O	160,000	192,000
2008	T300 I/O	145,000	174,000

Rinker 360/370/380 Express Cruiser

Year	Power	Retail Low	Retail High
2009	T320 I/O	******	******
2008	T320 I/O	165,000	198,000
2007	T320 I/O	150,000	180,000
2006	T320 I/O	136,000	163,000
2005	T320 I/O	124,000	149,000

Rinker 390/400 Express Cruiser

Year	Power	Retail Low	Retail High
2010	T375G I/O	******	******
2009	T375G I/O	******	******
2008	T375G I/O	220,000	264,000
2007	T375G I/O	202,000	242,000
2006	T375G I/O	186,000	223,000

Rinker 390/410/420 Express Cruiser

Year	Power	Retail Low	Retail High
2007	T420G	240,000	288,000
2006	T420G	220,000	264,000
2005	T420G	203,000	243,000
2004	T420G	186,000	224,000

Riviera 33 Conv. (1992-97)

Year	Power	Retail Low	Retail High
1997	T210D	100,000	120,000
1996	T210D	93,000	111,000
1995	T210D	86,000	103,000

Riviera 33 Convertible

Year	Power	Retail Low	Retail High
2008	T370D	******	******
2007	T370D	190,000	228,000
2006	T310D	176,000	212,000
2005	T310D	164,000	197,000

Riviera 34 Convertible

Year	Power	Retail Low	Retail High
2002	T370D	124,000	187,000
2001	T370D	113,000	136,000
2000	T350D	103,000	123,000
1999	T330D	94,000	113,000
1998	T315D	87,000	104,000
1997	T315D	80,000	96,000

Riviera 36 Convertible

Year	Power	Retail Low	Retail High
2002	T370D	136,000	164,000
2001	T370D	124,000	149,000
2000	T350D	114,000	137,000
1999	T330D	105,000	126,000
1998	T315D	96,000	116,000
1997	T315D	89,000	107,000
1996	T315D	82,000	98,000
1995	T315D	75,000	90,000

Riviera 3600 Sport Yacht

Year	Power	Retail Low	Retail High
2010	T301D IPS	******	******
2009	T370D	240,000	288,000
2008	T370D	220,000	264,000
2007	T370D	203,000	243,000

Riviera 37 Convertible

Year	Power	Retail Low	Retail High
2008	T370D	320,000	377,000
2007	T330D	294,000	347,000
2006	T330D	270,000	319,000
2005	T330D	249,000	294,000
2004	T330D	229,000	270,000
2003	T330D	210,000	248,000
2002	T330D	194,000	228,000
2001	T315D	178,000	210,000

Riviera 39 Convertible

Year	Power	Retail Low	Retail High
1999	T450D	137,000	161,000
1998	T420D	126,000	148,000
1997	T420D	115,000	136,000
1996	T375D	106,000	125,000
1995	T375D	98,000	115,000

Riviera 40 Convertible

Year	Power	Retail Low	Retail High
2006	T460D	286,000	338,000
2005	T455D	260,000	307,000
2004	T430D	237,000	280,000
2003	T430D	216,000	254,000
2002	T470D	196,000	231,000
2001	T470D	178,000	211,000

Riviera 4000 Offshore

Year	Power	Retail Low	Retail High
2003	T450D	177,000	209,000
2002	T450D	161,000	190,000
2001	T450D	146,000	173,000
2000	T450D	133,000	157,000
1999	T450D	121,000	143,000
1998	T435D	110,000	130,000

Riviera 42 Convertible

Year	Power	Retail Low	Retail High
2006	T480D	******	******
2005	T480D	340,000	401,000
2004	T480D	309,000	365,000

Riviera 43 Convertible

Year	Power	Retail Low	Retail High
2003	T430D	325,000	383,000
2002	T430D	295,000	348,000
2001	T430D	269,000	317,000
2000	T450D	244,000	288,000
1999	T450D	225,000	265,000
1998	T420D	207,000	244,000
1997	T420D	190,000	225,000

Riviera 47 Convertible

Year	Power	Retail Low	Retail High
2007	T660D	521,000	615,000
2006	T700D	479,000	566,000
2005	T700D	441,000	520,000
2004	T700D	406,000	479,000
2003	T660D	373,000	440,000

Riviera 48 Convertible

Year	Power	Retail Low	Retail High
2002	T800D	400,000	480,000
2001	T800D	364,000	436,000
2000	T660D	331,000	397,000
1999	T660D	301,000	361,000
1998	T660D	274,000	329,000
1997	T435D	249,000	299,000
1996	T435D	227,000	272,000
1995	T435D	206,000	248,000

Robalo 300 Center Console

Year	Power	Retail Low	Retail High
2010	T250 O/B	******	******
2009	T250 O/B	133,000	159,000
2008	T250 O/B	122,000	146,000
2007	T250 O/B	112,000	135,000

Robalo 305 Walkaround

Year	Power	Retail Low	Retail High
2010	T250 O/B	******	******
2009	T250 O/B	147,000	176,000
2008	T250 O/B	135,000	162,000
2007	T250 O/B	124,000	149,000

Sabre 34 Sedan

Year	Power	Retail Low	Retail High
2002	T220D	153,000	183,000
2001	T220D	142,000	170,000
2000	T220D	132,000	158,000
1999	T220D	123,000	147,000
1998	T220D	114,000	137,000
1997	T220D	106,000	127,000
1996	T210D	99,000	118,000
1995	T210D	93,000	111,000

Sabre 34 Hardtop Express

Year	Power	Retail Low	Retail High
2010	T310D	******	******
2009	T310D	******	******
2008	T315D	310,000	372,000
2007	T315D	288,000	345,000
2006	T315D	268,000	321,000

Sabre 36 Aft Cabin

Year	Power	Retail Low	Retail High
1998	T300D	110,000	132,000
1997	T300D	102,000	122,000
1996	T300D	95,000	114,000
1995	T255D	88,000	106,000

Sabre 36 Express

Year	Power	Retail Low	Retail High
2003	T315D	148,000	177,000
2002	T315D	137,000	165,000
2001	T315D	128,000	153,000
2000	T315D	119,000	143,000
1999	T300D	110,000	133,000
1998	T300D	103,000	123,000
1997	T300D	95,000	115,000
1996	T300D	89,000	107,000

Sabre 36 Sedan

Year	Power	Retail Low	Retail High
2007	T315D	******	******
2006	T315D	245,000	294,000
2005	T315D	228,000	274,000
2004	T315D	212,000	255,000
2003	T315D	197,000	237,000
2002	T315D	183,000	220,000

Sabre 38 Express

Year	Power	Retail Low	Retail High
2010	T380D	******	******
2009	T380D	******	******
2008	T370D	310,000	372,000
2007	T370D	291,000	349,000
2006	T370D	273,000	328,000
2005	T370D	257,000	308,000

Sabre 42 Express

Year	Power	Retail Low	Retail High
2010	T440D Zeus	******	******
2009	T440D Zeus	******	******
2008	T440D	440,000	519,000
2007	T440D	409,000	482,000
2006	T440D	380,000	449,000
2005	T440D	353,000	417,000
2004	T440D	329,000	388,000

Sabre 42 Sedan

Year	Power	Retail Low	Retail High
2009	T440D	******	******
2008	T440D	470,000	554,000
2007	T440D	437,000	515,000
2006	T440D	406,000	479,000
2005	T440D	378,000	446,000
2004	T440D	355,000	419,000
2003	T440D	334,000	394,000
2002	T420D	314,000	370,000
2001	T420D	295,000	348,000

Sabre 43 Aft Cabin

Year	Power	Retail Low	Retail High
2005	T370D	******	******
2004	T370D	******	******
2003	T370D	******	******
2002	T370D	******	******
2001	T370D	324,000	382,000
2000	T350D	301,000	355,000
1999	T350D	283,000	334,000
1998	T350D	266,000	314,000
1997	T350D	250,000	295,000
1996	T350D	235,000	277,000

Sabre 47 Aft Cabin

Year	Power	Retail Low	Retail High
2007	T465D	******	******
2006	T465D	******	******
2005	T465D	******	******
2004	T465D	360,000	421,000
2003	T465D	334,000	391,000
2002	T420D	311,000	364,000
2001	T420D	289,000	338,000
2000	T420D	269,000	315,000
1999	T420D	253,000	296,000
1998	T420D	237,000	278,000
1997	T350D	223,000	261,000

Sabre 52 Salon Express

Year	Power	Retail Low	Retail High
2010	T865D	990,000	1,168,000
2009	T865D	930,000	1,098,000
2008	T865D	874,000	1,032,000
2007	T865D	822,000	970,000

San Juan 38

Year	Power	Retail Low	Retail High
2010	T440D	******	******
2008	T440D	******	******
2007	T440D	******	******
2006	T440D	******	******
2005	T440D	345,000	414,000
2004	T440D	327,000	393,000
2003	T350D	311,000	373,000
2002	T350D	295,000	354,000
2001	T350D	281,000	337,000
2000	T350D	266,000	320,000

Scout 280 Sportfish

Year	Power	Retail Low	Retail High
2006	T200 O/B	57,000	69,000
2005	T200 O/B	52,000	62,000
2004	T200 O/B	47,000	57,000
2003	T200 O/B	43,000	52,000
2002	T200 O/B	39,000	47,000
2001	T200 O/B	35,000	43,000

Scout 282 SF

Year	Power	Retail Low	Retail High
2010	T250 O/B	******	******
2009	T250 O/B	87,000	104,000
2008	T250 O/B	78,000	94,000
2007	T250 O/B	70,000	84,000
2006	T250 O/B	65,000	78,000

Sea Ray 270 AJ (2005-09)

Year	Power	Retail Low	Retail High
2009	320 I/O	57,000	69,000
2008	320 I/O	52,000	63,000
2007	320 I/O	47,000	57,000
2006	320 I/O	43,000	52,000

See Page 511 For Price Adjustments

Year	Power	Retail Low	Retail High
2005	320 I/O	39,000	47,000

Sea Ray 270 Sundancer (8'6" Beam)

Year	Power	Retail Low	Retail High
1999	310 I/O	19,000	23,000
1998	No Prod.	******	******
1997	310 I/O	17,000	21,000
1996	310 I/O	16,000	19,000
1995	310 I/O	14,000	17,000
1994	300 I/O	13,000	16,000
1993	300 I/O	12,000	15,000
1992	300 I/O	11,000	13,000

Sea Ray 270 Sundancer (9'2" Beam)

Year	Power	Retail Low	Retail High
2001	310 I/O	29,000	35,000
2001	T190 I/O	31,000	37,000
2000	310 I/O	26,000	31,000
2000	T190 I/O	28,000	34,000
1999	300 I/O	24,000	29,000
1999	T190 I/O	25,000	31,000
1998	300 I/O	22,000	26,000
1998	T190 I/O	23,000	28,000

Sea Ray 280 Sundancer (Current)

Year	Power	Retail Low	Retail High
2010	300G I/O	95,000	114,000

Sea Ray 280 Sundancer (2001-09)

Year	Power	Retail Low	Retail High
2009	T260 I/O	117,000	141,000
2008	T260 I/O	107,000	128,000
2007	T260 I/O	97,000	117,000
2006	T260 I/O	88,000	106,000
2005	T260 I/O	80,000	96,000
2004	T260 I/O	74,000	89,000
2003	T260 I/O	68,000	82,000
2002	T260 I/O	62,000	75,000
2001	T260 I/O	57,000	69,000

Sea Ray 290 Amberjack

Year	Power	Retail Low	Retail High
2009	T260 I/O	129,000	149,000
2008	T260 I/O	116,000	140,000
2007	T260 I/O	105,000	126,000
2006	T260 I/O	94,000	113,000
2005	T260 I/O	85,000	102,000
2004	T260 I/O	76,000	91,000
2003	T260 I/O	68,000	82,000
2002	T240 I/O	62,000	74,000
2001	T240 I/O	55,000	67,000
2000	T240 I/O	50,000	60,000

Sea Ray 290 Sundancer (1994-2001)

Year	Power	Retail Low	Retail High
2001	T260 I/O	54,000	82,000
2000	T260 I/O	50,000	60,000
1999	T260 I/O	46,000	55,000
1998	T260 I/O	42,000	51,000
1997	T190 I/O	39,000	47,000
1996	T190 I/O	36,000	43,000
1995	T190 I/O	33,000	39,000
1994	T190 I/O	30,000	36,000

Sea Ray 290 Sundancer (2006-08)

Year	Power	Retail Low	Retail High
2008	T220 I/O	91,000	109,000
2007	T220 I/O	81,000	98,000
2006	T220 I/O	73,000	88,000

Sea Ray 300 Sundancer (1994-97)

Year	Power	Retail Low	Retail High
1997	T290 VD	43,000	51,000
1997	T210 I/O	39,000	47,000
1996	T250 VD	38,000	46,000
1996	T250 I/O	35,000	42,000
1995	T250 VD	35,000	42,000
1995	T250 I/O	31,000	38,000

Sea Ray 300 Sundancer (02-07)

Year	Power	Retail Low	Retail High
2007	T260 I/O	86,000	103,000
2006	T260 I/O	79,000	94,000
2005	T260 I/O	72,000	87,000
2004	T260 I/O	66,000	80,000
2003	T260 I/O	61,000	73,000
2002	T260 I/O	56,000	68,000

Sea Ray 300 Weekender (91-95)

Year	Power	Retail Low	Retail High
1995	T230 I/O	30,000	36,000
1995	T250 VD	32,000	38,000

Sea Ray 310 Sundancer (1998-2002)

Year	Power	Retail Low	Retail High
2002	T260 I/O	63,000	75,000
2001	T260 I/O	57,000	69,000
2000	T260 I/O	52,000	62,000
1999	T260 I/O	47,000	57,000
1998	T260 I/O	43,000	52,000

Sea Ray 310/330 Sundancer

Year	Power	Retail Low	Retail High
2010	T260 I/O	******	******
2009	T260 I/O	135,000	162,000
2008	T260 I/O	123,000	148,000
2007	T260 I/O	113,000	136,000

Sea Ray 320 Sundancer

Year	Power	Retail Low	Retail High
2007	T300 VD	123,000	148,000
2007	T300 I/O	113,000	136,000
2006	T320 VD	112,000	134,000
2006	T260 I/O	103,000	123,000
2005	T320 VD	102,000	122,000
2005	T260 I/O	93,000	112,000
2004	T300 VD	93,000	111,000
2004	T260 I/O	85,000	102,000
2003	T300 VD	84,000	101,000
2003	T260 I/O	77,000	93,000

Sea Ray 310/330 EC (1990-95)

Year	Power	Retail Low	Retail High
1995	T300 I/O	35,000	42,000
1995	T310 I/B	38,000	46,000

Sea Ray 330 Express Cruiser

Year	Power	Retail Low	Retail High
2000	T310G	70,000	84,000
1999	T310G	65,000	78,000
1998	T310G	59,000	71,000
1997	T310G	55,000	66,000

Sea Ray 330 Sundancer (95-99)

Year	Power	Retail Low	Retail High
1999	T300 I/O	60,000	72,000
1999	T310 VD	63,000	76,000
1998	T300 I/O	55,000	66,000
1998	T310 VD	57,000	69,000
1997	T300 I/O	50,000	60,000
1997	T310 VD	52,000	63,000
1996	T300 I/O	45,000	54,000
1996	T310 VD	47,000	57,000
1995	T300 I/O	41,000	50,000
1995	T310 VD	43,000	52,000

Sea Ray 330/350 Sundancer

Year	Power	Retail Low	Retail High
2010	T320G I/O	******	******
2010	T3700G VD	******	******
2009	T320G I/O	186,000	223,000
2009	T3700G VD	195,000	234,000
2008	T320G I/O	169,000	203,000
2008	T370G VD	177,000	212,000

Sea Ray 340 Amberjack

Year	Power	Retail Low	Retail High
2003	T370G	103,000	123,000
2002	T370G	93,000	112,000
2001	T370G	85,000	102,000

Sea Ray 340 Sundancer (2003-08)

Year	Power	Retail Low	Retail High
2008	T375 I/O	149,000	179,000
2008	T375 VD	153,000	184,000
2007	T375 I/O	136,000	163,000
2007	T370 VD	140,000	168,000
2006	T320 I/O	123,000	148,000
2006	T320 VD	127,000	153,000
2005	T320 I/O	112,000	135,000
2005	T320 VD	116,000	139,000
2004	T320 I/O	102,000	123,000
2004	T320 VD	105,000	126,000
2003	T320 I/O	93,000	112,000
2003	T320 VD	96,000	115,000

Sea Ray 340 Sundancer (1999-02)

Year	Power	Retail Low	Retail High
2002	T320 VD	82,000	98,000
2001	T320 VD	74,000	89,000
2000	T320 VD	68,000	81,000
1999	T320 VD	62,000	74,000

Sea Ray 350/370 Sundancer

Year	Power	Retail Low	Retail High
2010	T375G I/O	260,000	312,000
2010	T370G VD	265,000	318,000
2009	T375G VD	234,000	280,000
2009	T370G VD	238,000	286,000
2008	T375G I/O	210,000	252,000
2008	T370G VD	214,000	257,000

Sea Ray 350/370 EC (1990-95)

Year	Power	Retail Low	Retail High
1995	T310G	45,000	55,000

Sea Ray 360 Sundancer

Year	Power	Retail Low	Retail High
2006	T370 VD	172,000	206,000
2005	T370 VD	156,000	188,000
2004	T370 VD	142,000	171,000
2003	T370 VD	129,000	155,000
2002	T370 VD	118,000	141,000

Sea Ray 36 Sedan Bridge

Year	Power	Retail Low	Retail High
2009	T370G	317,000	381,000
2008	T370G	292,000	350,000
2008	T370D	269,000	322,000
2007	T370G	247,000	297,000
2007	T380D	227,000	273,000

Sea Ray 370 Express Cruiser

Year	Power	Retail Low	Retail High
2000	T380G	102,000	122,000
2000	T340D	123,000	147,000
1999	T380G	93,000	111,000
1999	T340D	111,000	134,000
1998	T380G	84,000	101,000
1998	T340D	101,000	122,000
1997	T380G	77,000	92,000
1997	T340D	92,000	111,000

Sea Ray 370 Sedan Bridge

Year	Power	Retail Low	Retail High
1997	T340G	79,000	95,000
1997	T292D	97,000	117,000
1996	T340G	72,000	86,000
1996	T292D	88,000	106,000
1995	T310G	65,000	78,000
1995	T292D	80,000	97,000

Sea Ray 370 Sundancer (1995-99)

Year	Power	Retail Low	Retail High
1999	T310G	103,000	124,000
1999	T292D	126,000	151,000
1998	T310G	94,000	112,000
1998	T292D	115,000	138,000
1997	T310G	85,000	102,000
1997	T292D	104,000	125,000
1996	T310G	77,000	93,000
1996	T292D	95,000	114,000
1995	T310G	70,000	85,000
1995	T292D	86,000	104,000

Sea Ray 370/380 Aft Cabin

Year	Power	Retail Low	Retail High
2001	T380G	128,000	153,000
2001	T340D	152,000	183,000
2000	T380G	116,000	139,000
2000	T340D	138,000	166,000
1999	T380G	106,000	127,000
1999	T340D	126,000	151,000
1998	T-Gas	96,000	115,000
1998	T340D	114,000	137,000

Year	Power	Retail Low	Retail High
1997	T-Gas	87,000	105,000
1997	T340D	104,000	125,000

Sea Ray 380 Sundancer

Year	Power	Retail Low	Retail High
2003	T370G	151,000	181,000
2003	T340D	177,000	213,000
2002	T370G	138,000	165,000
2002	T340D	161,000	194,000
2001	T370G	125,000	150,000
2001	T340D	147,000	176,000
2000	T310G	114,000	137,000
2000	T340D	134,000	160,000
1999	T310G	103,000	124,000
1999	T340D	122,000	146,000

Sea Ray 38/390 Sundancer

Year	Power	Retail Low	Retail High
2010	T420G	******	******
2010	T301D	******	******
2009	T375G	286,000	344,000
2009	T306D	312,000	374,000
2008	T420G	263,000	316,000
2008	T306D	287,000	344,000
2007	T420G	242,000	291,000
2007	T306D	264,000	317,000
2006	T420G	223,000	267,000
2006	T306D	243,000	291,000

Sea Ray 390 MY; 40 MY

Year	Power	Retail Low	Retail High
2007	T370G	274,000	323,000
2007	T407D	314,000	371,000
2006	T370G	249,000	294,000
2006	T446D	286,000	337,000
2005	T370G	227,000	268,000
2005	T446D	260,000	307,000
2004	T370G	206,000	244,000
2004	T446D	237,000	279,000
2003	T370G	188,000	222,000
2003	T446D	215,000	254,000

Sea Ray 390/40 Sundancer

Year	Power	Retail Low	Retail High
2009	T420G	336,000	396,000
2009	T407D	382,000	450,000
2008	T420G	309,000	364,000
2008	T407D	351,000	414,000
2007	T420G	284,000	335,000
2007	T407D	323,000	381,000
2006	T420G	261,000	308,000
2006	T364D	297,000	351,000
2005	T370G	240,000	284,000
2005	T340D	273,000	323,000
2004	T370G	221,000	261,000
2004	T340D	251,000	297,000

Sea Ray 400 Express Cruiser

Year	Power	Retail Low	Retail High
1999	T380G	108,000	128,000
1999	T340D	130,000	153,000
1998	T380G	99,000	117,000
1998	T340D	119,000	141,000
1997	T340G	91,000	108,000
1997	T340D	110,000	130,000
1996	T340G	84,000	99,000
1996	T292D	101,000	119,000
1995	T340G	77,000	91,000
1995	T292D	93,000	110,000

Sea Ray 400 Sedan Bridge

Year	Power	Retail Low	Retail High
2003	T370G	169,000	203,000
2003	T417D	203,000	244,000
2002	T370G	155,000	187,000
2002	T417D	187,000	224,000
2001	T380G	143,000	172,000
2001	T340D	172,000	206,000
2000	T380G	131,000	158,000
2000	T340D	158,000	190,000

Year	Power	Retail Low	Retail High
1999	T380G	121,000	145,000
1999	T340D	145,000	175,000
1998	T380G	111,000	134,000
1998	T340D	134,000	161,000
1997	T380G	102,000	123,000
1997	T340D	123,000	148,000
1996	T380G	94,000	113,000
1996	T340D	113,000	136,000

Sea Ray 400 Sundancer

Year	Power	Retail Low	Retail High
1999	T380G	124,000	149,000
1999	T340D	150,000	180,000
1998	T380G	113,000	135,000
1998	T340D	136,000	163,000
1997	T340G	103,000	123,000
1997	T340D	124,000	149,000

Sea Ray 410 Express Cruiser

Year	Power	Retail Low	Retail High
2003	T370G	153,000	184,000
2003	T417D	179,000	215,000
2002	T370G	140,000	168,000
2002	T417D	163,000	196,000
2001	T380G	127,000	152,000
2001	T340D	148,000	178,000
2000	T380G	115,000	139,000
2000	T340D	135,000	162,000

Sea Ray 410 Sundancer

Year	Power	Retail Low	Retail High
2003	T370G	162,000	194,000
2003	T340D	189,000	227,000
2002	T370G	147,000	177,000
2002	T340D	172,000	206,000
2001	T380G	134,000	161,000
2001	T340D	156,000	188,000
2000	T380G	122,000	146,000
2000	T340D	142,000	171,000

Sea Ray 420 Aft Cabin

Year	Power	Retail Low	Retail High
2002	T370G	187,000	225,000
2002	T417D	217,000	261,000
2001	T370G	170,000	205,000
2001	T417D	197,000	237,000
2000	T380G	155,000	186,000
2000	T407D	180,000	216,000
1999	T380G	143,000	171,000
1999	T407D	165,000	198,000
1998	T380G	131,000	158,000
1998	T407D	152,000	182,000
1997	T380G	121,000	145,000
1997	T407D	140,000	168,000
1996	T380G	111,000	133,000
1996	T407D	129,000	154,000

Sea Ray 420/44 Sundancer

Year	Power	Retail Low	Retail High
2008	T420G	302,000	363,000
2008	T478D	349,000	419,000
2007	T420G	275,000	330,000
2007	T478D	317,000	381,000
2006	T370G	250,000	300,000
2006	T417D	289,000	347,000
2005	T370G	228,000	273,000
2005	T417D	263,000	315,000
2004	T370G	207,000	248,000
2004	T417D	239,000	287,000
2003	T370G	188,000	226,000
2003	T417D	218,000	261,000

Sea Ray 420/44 Sedan Bridge

Year	Power	Retail Low	Retail High
2009	T478D	470,000	564,000
2008	T478D	423,000	507,000
2007	T478D	380,000	456,000
2006	T478D	346,000	415,000
2005	T417D	315,000	378,000
2004	T417D	286,000	344,000

Sea Ray 420/440 Sundancer

Year	Power	Retail Low	Retail High
1995	T425D	120,000	144,000

Sea Ray 440 Express Bridge

Year	Power	Retail Low	Retail High
1998	T340D	168,000	201,000
1997	T340D	154,000	185,000
1996	T340D	142,000	170,000
1995	T350D	131,000	157,000
1994	T350D	120,000	144,000
1993	T375D	110,000	133,000

Sea Ray 450 Express Bridge

Year	Power	Retail Low	Retail High
2004	T460D	288,000	346,000
2003	T450D	262,000	315,000
2002	T430D	239,000	286,000
2001	T430D	217,000	261,000
2000	T430D	198,000	237,000
1999	T420D	180,000	216,000
1998	T420D	164,000	196,000

Sea Ray 450 Sundancer

Year	Power	Retail Low	Retail High
1999	T340D	180,000	216,000
1998	T340D	164,000	197,000
1997	T340D	149,000	179,000
1996	T375D	137,000	165,000
1995	T375D	126,000	152,000

Sea Ray 460 Sundancer

Year	Power	Retail Low	Retail High
2003	T446D	293,000	352,000
2002	T446D	270,000	324,000
2001	T430D	248,000	298,000
2000	T430D	228,000	274,000
1999	T430D	210,000	252,000

Sea Ray 47 Sedan Bridge

Year	Power	Retail Low	Retail High
2010	T600D	******	******
2009	T574D	******	******
2008	T574D	430,000	516,000

Sea Ray 43/470 Sundancer

Year	Power	Retail Low	Retail High
2010	T425 Zeus	******	******
2009	T425 Zeus	500,000	600,000

Sea Ray 48 Sundancer

Year	Power	Retail Low	Retail High
2009	T526D	555,000	666,000
2008	T517D	505,000	606,000
2007	T517D	459,000	551,000
2006	T517D	418,000	501,000
2005	T446D	380,000	456,000

Sea Ray 480 Motor Yacht

Year	Power	Retail Low	Retail High
2005	T660D	394,000	473,000
2004	T640D	367,000	440,000
2003	T640D	341,000	409,000
2002	T640D	317,000	381,000

Sea Ray 480 Sedan Bridge

Year	Power	Retail Low	Retail High
2004	T640D	361,000	433,000
2003	T640D	329,000	394,000
2002	T640D	299,000	359,000
2001	T640D	272,000	326,000
2000	T640D	250,000	300,000
1999	T640D	230,000	276,000
1998	T640D	212,000	254,000

Sea Ray 480/500 Sundancer

Year	Power	Retail Low	Retail High
1999	T535D	305,000	366,000
1998	T535D	278,000	333,000
1997	T535D	253,000	303,000
1996	T535D	232,000	279,000
1995	T535D	214,000	256,000

Sea Ray 500/52 Sundancer

Year	Power	Retail Low	Retail High
2009	T765D	******	******
2008	T765D	******	******
2007	T640D	460,000	542,000

Year	Power	Retail Low	Retail High
2006	T640D	418,000	493,000
2005	T640D	380,000	449,000
2004	T640D	346,000	409,000
2003	T640D	315,000	372,000
Sea Ray 510 Sundancer			
2003	T616D	410,000	484,000
2002	T640D	373,000	440,000
2001	T640D	339,000	401,000
2000	T640D	309,000	364,000
Sea Ray 500/52 Sedan Bridge			
2010	T640D	******	******
2009	T640D	******	******
2008	T640D	******	******
2007	T640D	470,000	554,000
2006	T640D	432,000	510,000
2005	T640D	397,000	469,000
Sea Ray 540 Cockpit MY			
2002	T640D	407,000	480,000
2001	T640D	374,000	441,000
Sea Ray 540 Sundancer			
2001	T640D	379,000	447,000
2000	T640D	348,000	411,000
1999	T640D	320,000	378,000
1998	T640D	295,000	348,000
Sea Ray 550 Sedan Bridge			
1998	T776D	274,000	323,000
1997	T735D	252,000	297,000
1996	T635D	232,000	273,000
1995	T635D	213,000	252,000
Sea Ray 550 Sundancer			
2004	T765D	515,000	607,000
2003	T765D	479,000	565,000
2002	T765D	445,000	525,000
Sea Ray 55/580 Sundancer			
2010	T765D	******	******
2009	T765D	******	******
2008	T765D	800,000	960,000
Sea Ray 560 Sedan Bridge			
2004	T1000D	546,000	655,000
2003	T1000D	497,000	596,000
2002	T776D	452,000	543,000
2001	T776D	411,000	494,000
2000	T776D	374,000	449,000
1999	T776D	341,000	409,000
1998	T776D	310,000	372,000
Sea Ray 58/580 Sedan Bridge			
2010	T900D	******	******
2009	T900D	******	******
2008	T900D	740,000	873,000
2007	T900D	673,000	794,000
2006	T900D	612,000	723,000
Sea Ray 580 Super Sun Sport			
2002	T776D	******	******
2001	T776D	******	******
2000	T776D	******	******
1999	T776D	335,000	402,000
1998	T776D	311,000	373,000
1997	T776D	289,000	347,000
Sea Vee 290B Open (Current)			
2010	T250 O/B	******	******
2009	T250 O/B	******	******
2008	T250 O/B	89,000	107,000
2007	T250 O/B	81,000	97,000
2006	T250 O/B	74,000	88,000
2005	T250 O/B	67,000	80,000

Year	Power	Retail Low	Retail High
Sea Vee 290B (2000-04)			
2004	T250 O/B	62,000	74,000
2003	T250 O/B	56,000	67,000
2002	T250 O/B	50,000	60,000
2001	T250 O/B	45,000	54,000
2000	T250 O/B	40,000	49,000
Sea Vee 340B Open			
2010	T250 O/B	******	******
2009	T250 O/B	******	******
2008	T250 O/B	141,000	169,000
2007	T250 O/B	127,000	152,000
2006	T250 O/B	114,000	137,000
2005	T250 O/B	103,000	123,000
2004	T250 O/B	92,000	111,000
2003	T250 O/B	83,000	100,000
2002	T250 O/B	75,000	90,000
2001	T250 O/B	67,000	81,000
Selene 36/38 Trawler			
2010	230D	******	******
2009	230D	290,000	348,000
2008	230D	272,000	327,000
2007	230D	256,000	307,000
2006	230D	243,000	292,000
2005	230D	231,000	277,000
2004	230D	219,000	263,000
2003	230D	208,000	250,000
Selene 43/45 Pilothouse			
2010	S/Diesel	******	******
2009	S/Diesel	******	******
2008	S/Diesel	500,000	600,000
2007	S/Diesel	475,000	570,000
2006	S/Diesel	451,000	541,000
2005	S/Diesel	428,000	514,000
2004	S/Diesel	407,000	488,000
2003	S/Diesel	390,000	469,000
2002	S/Diesel	375,000	450,000
2001	S/Diesel	360,000	432,000
Selene 47 Pilothouse			
2010	330D	******	******
2009	330D	******	******
2008	330D	******	******
2007	330D	******	******
2006	330D	540,000	648,000
2005	330D	513,000	615,000
2004	330D	487,000	584,000
2003	330D	462,000	555,000
2002	330D	444,000	533,000
2001	220D	426,000	512,000
2000	220D	409,000	491,000
1999	220D	393,000	471,000
Selene 48/49 Pilothouse			
2010	330D	******	******
2009	330D	******	******
2008	330D	******	******
2007	330D	610,000	732,000
2006	330D	579,000	695,000
2005	330D	550,000	660,000
2004	330D	522,000	627,000
2003	330D	496,000	596,000
Selene 53/54 Pilothouse			
2010	S/Diesel	******	******
2009	S/Diesel	840,000	982,000
2008	S/Diesel	798,000	933,000
2007	S/Diesel	758,000	886,000
2006	S/Diesel	720,000	842,000
2005	S/Diesel	691,000	808,000
2004	S/Diesel	663,000	776,000
2003	S/Diesel	637,000	745,000

Year	Power	Retail Low	Retail High
2002	S/Diesel	611,000	715,000
2001	S/Diesel	587,000	687,000
Shamrock 270 Mackinaw			
2009	315D	******	******
2008	315D	******	******
2007	315D	75,000	90,000
2006	315D	69,000	82,000
2005	315D	63,000	76,000
2004	315D	58,000	70,000
2003	315D	53,000	64,000
2002	315D	49,000	59,000
2001	230D	46,000	55,000
2000	230D	43,000	51,000
Shamrock 270 Open			
2009	315D	******	******
2008	315D	******	******
2007	315D	65,000	78,000
2006	315D	59,000	70,000
2005	315D	53,000	64,000
2004	315D	48,000	58,000
2003	315D	44,000	53,000
2002	315D	41,000	49,000
2001	230D	37,000	45,000
2000	230D	34,000	41,000
Shamrock 290 Walkaround			
2003	T330G	52,000	62,000
2002	T300G	47,000	56,000
2001	T300G	43,000	51,000
2000	T300G	39,000	47,000
1999	T300G	35,000	42,000
Shannon 36 Voyager			
2005	T300D	******	******
2004	T300D	******	******
2003	T300D	******	******
2002	T300D	190,000	228,000
2001	T300D	178,000	214,000
2000	T300D	167,000	201,000
1999	T300D	159,000	191,000
1998	T300D	151,000	181,000
1997	T300D	143,000	172,000
1996	T300D	136,000	164,000
1995	T300D	129,000	155,000
Silverton 271 Express			
1997	250 I/O	17,000	21,000
1996	250 I/O	16,000	19,000
1995	250 I/O	15,000	18,000
Silverton 31 Convertible			
1995	T235G	30,000	36,000
Silverton 310 Express			
2000	T250 I/O	40,000	49,000
1999	T250 I/O	38,000	45,000
1998	T250 I/O	35,000	42,000
1997	T250 I/O	32,000	39,000
1996	T235 I/O	30,000	36,000
1995	T235 I/O	28,000	34,000
Silverton 312 Sedan Cruiser			
1999	T250 I/O	35,000	43,000
1998	T260 I/O	33,000	39,000
1997	T260 I/O	30,000	36,000
1996	T235 I/O	28,000	33,000
1995	T235 I/O	25,000	30,000
Silverton 322 Motor Yacht			
2001	T300G	69,000	83,000
2000	T300G	63,000	76,000
1999	T320G	58,000	70,000
1998	T320G	53,000	64,000

Silverton 33 Convertible

Year	Power	Retail Low	Retail High
2010	T275G	******	******
2009	T275G	149,000	178,000
2008	T275G	135,000	162,000
2007	T275G	124,000	149,000

Silverton 33 Sports Coupe

Year	Power	Retail Low	Retail High
2010	T275G	******	******
2009	T275G	174,000	209,000
2008	T275G	159,000	190,000

Silverton 330 Sport Bridge

Year	Power	Retail Low	Retail High
2007	T330G	129,000	155,000
2006	T330G	118,000	141,000
2005	T330G	107,000	128,000
2004	T320G	97,000	117,000
2003	T320G	88,000	106,000
2002	T320G	80,000	97,000
2001	T320G	74,000	89,000
2000	T320G	68,000	82,000
1999	T320G	63,000	75,000

Silverton 34 Conv. (1991-95)

Year	Power	Retail Low	Retail High
1995	T300G	46,000	56,000

Silverton 34 Conv. (2004-06)

Year	Power	Retail Low	Retail High
2006	T330G	144,000	173,000
2005	T330G	131,000	158,000
2004	T320G	119,000	143,000

Silverton 34 Motor Yacht

Year	Power	Retail Low	Retail High
1996	T320G	50,000	60,000
1995	T300G	46,000	55,000

Silverton 35 Motor Yacht

Year	Power	Retail Low	Retail High
2010	T385G	******	******
2010	T315D	******	******
2009	T385G	******	******
2009	T315D	******	******
2008	T385G	191,000	229,000
2008	T315D	168,000	201,000
2007	T385G	176,000	211,000
2007	T315D	154,000	185,000
2006	T385G	161,000	194,000
2006	T315D	142,000	170,000
2005	T385G	149,000	178,000
2005	T315D	130,000	157,000
2004	T385G	137,000	164,000
2004	T315D	120,000	144,000
2003	T385G	126,000	151,000
2003	T315D	110,000	133,000

Silverton 351 Sedan

Year	Power	Retail Low	Retail High
2000	T320G	66,000	79,000
1999	T320G	60,000	73,000
1998	T300G	56,000	67,000
1997	T300G	51,000	61,000

Silverton 352 Motor Yacht

Year	Power	Retail Low	Retail High
2002	T370G	91,000	109,000
2002	T250D	107,000	128,000
2001	T320G	83,000	99,000
2001	T250D	97,000	117,000
2000	T320G	75,000	90,000
2000	T250D	88,000	106,000
1999	T320G	68,000	82,000
1999	T300D	80,000	97,000
1998	T320G	62,000	75,000
1998	T300D	73,000	88,000
1997	T320G	57,000	68,000
1997	T300D	66,000	80,000

Silverton 361/360 Express

Year	Power	Retail Low	Retail High
2000	T320G	61,000	73,000
1999	T320G	56,000	67,000
1998	T320G	51,000	62,000
1997	T320G	47,000	57,000
1996	T320G	43,000	52,000
1995	T300G	40,000	48,000

Silverton 362 Sedan Cruiser

Year	Power	Retail Low	Retail High
1998	T320G	63,000	76,000
1997	T320G	58,000	70,000
1996	T320G	53,000	64,000
1995	T320G	49,000	59,000

Silverton 37 Convertible

Year	Power	Retail Low	Retail High
2000	T320G	89,000	106,000
2000	T350D	106,000	128,000
1999	T320G	81,000	98,000
1999	T350D	98,000	117,000
1998	T320G	75,000	90,000
1998	T350D	90,000	108,000
1997	T320G	69,000	83,000
1997	T350D	83,000	99,000
1996	T320G	63,000	76,000
1996	T350D	76,000	91,000
1995	T320G	58,000	70,000
1995	T350D	70,000	84,000

Silverton 372/392 Motor Yacht

Year	Power	Retail Low	Retail High
2001	T385G	111,000	134,000
2001	T350D	133,000	160,000
2000	T385G	101,000	122,000
2000	T350D	121,000	146,000
1999	T385G	92,000	111,000
1999	T350D	110,000	132,000
1998	T320G	85,000	102,000
1998	T350D	101,000	122,000
1997	T320G	78,000	94,000
1997	T350D	93,000	112,000
1996	T320G	72,000	86,000
1996	T350D	86,000	103,000

Silverton 38 Convertible

Year	Power	Retail Low	Retail High
2009	T385G	293,000	352,000
2009	T370D	340,000	408,000
2008	T385G	267,000	320,000
2008	T370D	309,000	371,000
2007	T385G	243,000	291,000
2007	T370D	281,000	338,000
2006	T385G	221,000	265,000
2006	T370D	256,000	307,000
2005	T385G	201,000	241,000
2005	T370D	233,000	280,000
2004	T385G	183,000	219,000
2004	T370D	212,000	254,000
2003	T385G	217,000	260,000
2003	T370D	170,000	204,000

Silverton 38 Sport Bridge

Year	Power	Retail Low	Retail High
2010	T385G	******	******
2010	T380D	******	******
2009	T385G	******	******
2009	T380D	******	******
2008	T385G	241,000	289,000
2008	T380D	287,000	345,000
2007	T385G	219,000	263,000
2007	T380D	262,000	314,000
2006	T385G	199,000	239,000
2006	T380D	238,000	286,000
2005	T385G	181,000	218,000
2005	T355D	216,000	260,000

Silverton 39 Motor Yacht

Year	Power	Retail Low	Retail High
2010	T385G	******	******
2010	T380D	******	******
2009	T385G	******	******
2009	T380D	******	******
2008	T385D	245,000	294,000
2008	T380D	282,000	339,000
2007	T385G	223,000	267,000
2007	T380D	257,000	309,000
2006	T385G	202,000	243,000
2006	T380D	234,000	281,000
2005	T385G	184,000	221,000
2005	T380D	213,000	255,000
2004	T385G	169,000	203,000
2004	T380D	196,000	235,000
2003	T385G	156,000	187,000
2003	T380D	180,000	216,000
2002	T385G	143,000	172,000
2002	T355D	166,000	199,000

Silverton 402/422 Motor Yacht

Year	Power	Retail Low	Retail High
2000	T380G	116,000	140,000
2000	T325D	134,000	161,000
1999	T380G	107,000	128,000
1999	T370D	123,000	148,000
1998	T380G	98,000	118,000
1998	T370D	113,000	136,000
1997	T380G	90,000	109,000
1997	T370D	104,000	125,000
1996	T380G	83,000	100,000
1996	T370D	96,000	115,000

Silverton 41 Convertible

Year	Power	Retail Low	Retail High
1999	T380G	121,000	145,000
1998	T380G	111,000	134,000
1997	T380G	102,000	123,000
1996	T380G	94,000	113,000
1995	T320G	87,000	104,000

Silverton 41 Motor Yacht

Year	Power	Retail Low	Retail High
1995	T355G	87,000	105,000
1995	T375D	111,000	133,000

Silverton 410 Sport Bridge

Year	Power	Retail Low	Retail High
2004	T425G	190,000	228,000
2004	T350D	216,000	260,000
2003	T425G	175,000	210,000
2003	T350D	199,000	239,000
2002	T425G	161,000	193,000
2002	T350D	183,000	220,000
2001	T385G	148,000	177,000
2001	T350D	168,000	202,000

Silverton 42 Convertible

Year	Power	Retail Low	Retail High
2010	T440D	******	******
2009	T425G	******	******
2009	T440D	******	******
2008	T440D	338,000	406,000
2007	T440D	308,000	369,000
2006	T380D	280,000	336,000
2005	T380D	255,000	306,000
2004	T380D	232,000	278,000
2003	T380D	213,000	256,000
2002	T-350D	196,000	235,000
2001	T-350D	180,000	217,000
2000	T350D	166,000	199,000

Silverton 43 Motor Yacht

Year	Power	Retail Low	Retail High
2007	T425G	307,000	369,000
2007	T440D	336,000	404,000
2006	T425G	283,000	339,000
2006	T440D	310,000	372,000
2005	T425G	260,000	312,000
2005	T380D	285,000	342,000
2004	T425G	239,000	287,000
2004	T380D	262,000	314,000
2003	T425G	220,000	264,000
2003	T380D	241,000	289,000

See Page 511 For Price Adjustments

Year	Power	Retail Low	Retail High	Year	Power	Retail Low	Retail High	Year	Power	Retail Low	Retail High
2002	T425G	202,000	243,000	2007	T225 O/B	82,000	99,000	2008	T225 O/B	******	******
2002	T380D	222,000	266,000	2006	T225 O/B	75,000	90,000	2007	T225 O/B	******	******
2001	T-Gas	186,000	224,000	2005	T225 O/B	68,000	82,000	2006	T225 O/B	******	******
2001	T355D	204,000	245,000	**Stamas 270 Express**				2005	T225 O/B	61,000	73,000
Silverton 43 Sport Bridge				2010	T225 O/B	******	******	2004	T225 O/B	55,000	67,000
2010	T435G IPS	******	******	2009	T225 O/B	******	******	2002	T225 O/B	50,000	60,000
2010	T370D IPS	******	******	2008	T225 O/B	79,000	95,000	2002	T225 O/B	46,000	55,000
2009	T435G IPS	******	******	2007	T225 O/B	73,000	87,000	2001	T225 O/B	42,000	51,000
2009	T370D IPS	******	******	2006	T225 O/B	65,000	78,000	2000	T225 O/B	39,000	46,000
2008	T425G	******	******	2005	T225 O/B	59,000	70,000	1999	T225 O/B	36,000	43,000
2008	T345D	******	******	2004	T225 O/B	53,000	63,000	1998	T225 O/B	33,000	39,000
2007	T425G	294,000	353,000	2003	T225 O/B	47,000	57,000	1997	T225 O/B	30,000	36,000
2007	T380D	334,000	400,000	2002	T225 O/B	43,000	51,000	1996	T225 O/B	28,000	33,000
2006	T425G	271,000	325,000	2001	T225 O/B	39,000	47,000	1995	T225 O/B	25,000	30,000
2006	T380D	307,000	368,000	2000	T225 O/B	36,000	43,000	**Stamas 310 Tarpon**			
Silverton 442 Cockpit MY				1999	T225 O/B	33,000	40,000	2010	T225 O/B	******	******
2001	T-Gas	131,000	158,000	1998	T225 O/B	30,000	37,000	2009	T225 O/B	******	******
2001	T355D	154,000	185,000	1997	T225 O/B	28,000	34,000	2008	T225 O/B	******	******
2000	T-Gas	121,000	145,000	**Stamas 270 Tarpon**				2007	T225 O/B	******	******
2000	T355D	141,000	170,000	2010	T225 O/B	******	******	2006	T225 O/B	******	******
1999	T-Gas	111,000	133,000	2009	T225 O/B	******	******	2005	T225 O/B	******	******
1999	T350D	130,000	156,000	2008	T225 O/B	74,000	89,000	2004	T225 O/B	59,000	71,000
1998	T-Gas	102,000	123,000	2007	T225 O/B	67,000	80,000	2003	T225 O/B	53,000	64,000
1998	T350D	120,000	144,000	2006	T225 O/B	60,000	72,000	2002	T225 O/B	49,000	58,000
1997	T-Gas	94,000	113,000	2005	T225 O/B	54,000	65,000	2001	T225 O/B	44,000	53,000
1997	T350D	110,000	132,000	2004	T225 O/B	49,000	58,000	2000	T225 O/B	40,000	48,000
1996	T-Gas	86,000	104,000	2003	T225 O/B	44,000	52,000	1999	T225 O/B	37,000	44,000
1996	T350D	101,000	122,000	2002	T225 O/B	40,000	48,000	**Stamas 320 Express**			
Silverton 45 Convertible				2001	T225 O/B	37,000	44,000	2010	T250 O/B	******	******
2010	T500D	******	******	2000	T225 O/B	34,000	41,000	2010	T330 I/B	******	******
2009	T500D	520,000	613,000	1999	T225 O/B	31,000	37,000	2009	T330 I/B	******	******
2008	T500D	478,000	564,000	1998	T225 O/B	29,000	34,000	2009	T250 O/B	******	******
2007	T575D	440,000	519,000	1997	T225 O/B	77,000	92,000	2008	T330 I/B	******	******
2006	T540D	404,000	477,000	**Stamas 290 Express**				2008	T250 O/B	******	******
Silverton 453 Motor Yacht				2010	T225 O/B	******	******	2007	T320 I/B	******	******
2003	T430D	249,000	294,000	2009	T225 O/B	******	******	2007	T250 O/B	******	******
2002	T350D	229,000	270,000	2008	T225 O/B	******	******	2006	T320 I/B	102,000	122,000
2001	T350D	211,000	249,000	2007	T225 O/B	******	******	2006	T250 O/B	92,000	110,000
2000	T355D	194,000	229,000	2006	T225 O/B	******	******	2005	T320 I/B	92,000	111,000
1999	T350D	178,000	211,000	2005	T225 O/B	76,000	92,000	2005	T250 O/B	83,000	100,000
Silverton 46 Aft Cabin				2004	T225 O/B	69,000	83,000	2004	T320 I/B	84,000	101,000
1997	T485D	171,000	202,000	2003	T225 O/B	63,000	76,000	2004	T250 O/B	76,000	91,000
1996	T485D	159,000	188,000	2002	T225 O/B	57,000	69,000	**Stamas 340 Express**			
1995	T485D	148,000	175,000	2001	T225 O/B	52,000	63,000	2010	T385G	******	******
Silverton 48/50 Convertible				2000	T225 O/B	48,000	58,000	2010	T380D	******	******
2010	T715D	******	******	1999	T225 O/B	44,000	53,000	2009	T385G	******	******
2009	T715D	******	******	1998	T225 O/B	40,000	49,000	2009	T380D	******	******
2008	T715D	******	******	1997	T225 O/B	37,000	45,000	2008	T385G	******	******
2007	T715D	******	******	1996	T225 O/B	34,000	41,000	2008	T380D	******	******
2006	T715D	352,000	422,000	1995	T225 O/B	31,000	38,000	2007	T320G	******	******
2005	T715D	324,000	389,000	**Stamas 290 Tarpon**				2007	T370D	******	******
2004	T715D	298,000	357,000	2010	T225 O/B	******	******	2006	T320G	128,000	153,000
Skipjack 30 Flybridge				2009	T225 O/B	******	******	2006	T370D	157,000	189,000
2006	T330D	155,000	186,000	2008	T225 O/B	******	******	2005	T320G	116,000	139,000
2005	T330D	141,000	169,000	2007	T225 O/B	******	******	2005	T370D	143,000	172,000
2004	T330D	128,000	154,000	2006	T225 O/B	73,000	87,000	2004	T320G	106,000	127,000
2003	T330D	116,000	140,000	2005	T225 O/B	66,000	79,000	2004	T370D	130,000	156,000
2002	T315D	106,000	127,000	2004	T225 O/B	60,000	72,000	2003	T320G	97,000	117,000
2001	T315D	97,000	117,000	2003	T225 O/B	55,000	66,000	2003	T370D	120,000	144,000
2000	T315D	89,000	107,000	2002	T225 O/B	50,000	60,000	2002	T320G	89,000	107,000
1999	T315D	82,000	99,000	2001	T225 O/B	45,000	54,000	2002	T370D	110,000	132,000
1998	T315D	76,000	91,000	2000	T225 O/B	41,000	50,000	**Stamas 360 Express**			
1997	T315D	70,000	84,000	1999	T225 O/B	38,000	46,000	1999	T310G	70,000	84,000
Southport 28 Center Console				1998	T225 O/B	35,000	42,000	1999	T300D	87,000	104,000
2010	T225 O/B	110,000	132,000	1997	T225 O/B	32,000	39,000	1998	T310G	64,000	77,000
2009	T225 O/B	100,000	120,000	1996	T225 O/B	30,000	36,000	1998	T300D	79,000	95,000
2008	T225 O/B	91,000	109,000	1995	T225 O/B	27,000	33,000	1997	T310G	58,000	70,000
				Stamas 310 Express				1997	T300D	72,000	86,000
				2009	T225 O/B	******	******	1996	T310G	53,000	63,000

Year	Power	Retail Low	Retail High
1996	T300D	65,000	78,000
1995	T310G	48,000	58,000
1995	T300D	60,000	72,000

Stamas 370 Express

Year	Power	Retail Low	Retail High
2009	T370G	******	******
2009	T440D	******	******
2008	T370G	******	******
2008	T440D	******	******
2007	T370G	******	******
2007	T440D	******	******
2006	T370G	******	******
2006	T440D	******	******
2005	T370G	132,000	159,000
2005	T440D	175,000	210,000
2004	T370G	120,000	145,000
2004	T440D	159,000	191,000
2003	T370G	110,000	132,000
2003	T440D	145,000	174,000
2002	T370G	100,000	120,000
2002	T440D	132,000	158,000
2001	T370G	91,000	109,000
2001	T440D	120,000	144,000
2000	T370G	82,000	99,000
2000	T440D	109,000	131,000

Strike 29 Sportfisherman

Year	Power	Retail Low	Retail High
2006	T330D	100,000	120,000
2005	T330D	91,000	109,000
2004	T330D	82,000	99,000
2003	T330D	75,000	90,000
2002	T330D	68,000	82,000
2001	T330D	62,000	74,000
2000	T330D	56,000	68,000
1999	T330D	52,000	62,000
1998	T330D	48,000	57,000
1997	T330D	44,000	53,000
1996	T330D	40,000	48,000

Sunseeker 34 Superhawk

Year	Power	Retail Low	Retail High
2003	T285D	137,000	164,000
2002	T285D	127,000	153,000
2001	T285D	118,000	142,000
2000	T230D	110,000	132,000
1999	T230D	102,000	123,000
1998	T230D	95,000	114,000
1997	T230D	88,000	106,000

Sunseeker 37 Sport Fish

Year	Power	Retail Low	Retail High
2007	3/250 O/B	******	******
2006	3/250 O/B	200,000	240,000
2005	3/250 O/B	184,000	220,000
2004	3/250 O/B	169,000	203,000

Sunseeker 44 Camargue

Year	Power	Retail Low	Retail High
2002	T480D	225,000	270,000
2001	T480D	207,000	249,000
2000	T435D	190,000	229,000
1999	T435D	175,000	210,000
1998	T435D	161,000	193,000

Sunseeker 46 Portifino

Year	Power	Retail Low	Retail High
2005	T460D	358,000	429,000
2004	T480D	333,000	399,000
2003	T480D	309,000	371,000

Sunseeker 47 Camargue

Year	Power	Retail Low	Retail High
1999	T435D	196,000	235,000
1998	T435D	182,000	218,000
1997	T435D	169,000	203,000
1996	T435D	157,000	189,000

Sunseeker 46/48 Manhattan

Year	Power	Retail Low	Retail High
1999	T435D	283,000	340,000
1998	T435D	266,000	319,000
1997	T435D	250,000	300,000
1996	T435D	235,000	282,000

Sunseeker 48 Superhawk

Year	Power	Retail Low	Retail High
2005	3/300 I/O	260,000	312,000
2004	3/300 I/O	239,000	287,000
2003	3/300 I/O	220,000	264,000
2002	3/260 I/O	202,000	242,000
2001	3/260 I/O	188,000	225,000
2000	3/260 I/O	175,000	210,000
1999	3/260 I/O	162,000	195,000
1998	3/260 I/O	151,000	181,000
1997	3/260 I/O	140,000	169,000
1996	3/260 I/O	130,000	157,000

Sunseeker 50 Camargue

Year	Power	Retail Low	Retail High
2003	T660D	335,000	402,000
2002	T660D	308,000	369,000
2001	T660D	283,000	340,000
2000	T660D	260,000	313,000

Sunseeker 51 Camargue

Year	Power	Retail Low	Retail High
1997	T600D	252,000	302,000
1996	T600D	234,000	281,000
1995	T600D	217,000	261,000

Sunseeker 53 Portofino

Year	Power	Retail Low	Retail High
2009	T800D	******	******
2008	T800D	******	******
2007	T800D	******	******
2006	T705D	500,000	600,000
2005	T705D	465,000	558,000
2004	T705D	432,000	518,000

Sunseeker 55 Camargue

Year	Power	Retail Low	Retail High
1996	T760D	265,000	318,000
1995	T760D	246,000	295,000

Sunseeker 56 Manhattan

Year	Power	Retail Low	Retail High
2004	T800D	664,000	796,000
2003	T800D	617,000	741,000
2002	T800D	574,000	689,000
2001	T800D	534,000	640,000

Sunseeker 58/60 Predator

Year	Power	Retail Low	Retail High
2002	T800D	******	******
2001	T800D	******	******
2000	T800D	******	******
1999	T800D	390,000	468,000
1998	T800D	362,000	435,000
1997	T800D	337,000	404,000

Tiara 2900 Coronet

Year	Power	Retail Low	Retail High
2007	T330G	72,000	86,000
2006	T330G	65,000	78,000
2005	T330G	59,000	71,000
2004	T320G	54,000	65,000
2003	T320G	50,000	60,000
2002	T320G	46,000	55,000
2001	T320G	42,000	50,000
2000	T320G	38,000	46,000
1999	T320G	35,000	43,000
1998	T320G	33,000	39,000
1997	T320G	30,000	36,000

Tiara 2900 Open

Year	Power	Retail Low	Retail High
2006	T330G	79,000	94,000
2005	T330G	71,000	86,000
2004	T330G	65,000	78,000
2003	T330G	59,000	71,000
2002	T320G	54,000	65,000
2001	T320G	50,000	60,000
2000	T320G	46,000	55,000
1999	T320G	42,000	51,000
1998	T320G	39,000	47,000
1997	T320G	36,000	43,000
1996	T320G	33,000	39,000
1995	T260G	30,000	37,000

Tiara 3000 Open

Year	Power	Retail Low	Retail High
2010	T385G	******	******
2010	T330D	******	******
2009	T385G	165,000	198,000
2009	T330D	198,000	238,000
2008	T385G	150,000	180,000
2008	T330D	180,000	216,000
2007	T385G	138,000	166,000
2007	T330D	166,000	199,000

Tiara 3100 Open

Year	Power	Retail Low	Retail High
2004	T385G	89,000	107,000
2004	T330D	112,000	135,000
2003	T385G	81,000	97,000
2003	T330D	102,000	122,000
2002	T320G	73,000	88,000
2002	T330D	93,000	111,000
2001	T320G	67,000	81,000
2001	T330D	85,000	102,000
2000	T320G	62,000	75,000
2000	T230D	78,000	94,000
1999	T320G	57,000	69,000
1999	T230D	72,000	87,000
1998	T320G	52,000	63,000
1998	T230D	66,000	80,000
1997	T320G	48,000	58,000
1997	T230D	61,000	73,000
1996	T320G	44,000	53,000
1996	T230D	56,000	67,000
1995	T320G	41,000	49,000
1995	T230D	52,000	63,000

Tiara 3200 Open

Year	Power	Retail Low	Retail High
2010	T385G	******	******
2010	T355D	******	******
2009	T385G	180,000	216,000
2009	T355D	225,000	271,000
2008	T385G	164,000	197,000
2008	T355D	205,000	246,000
2007	T385G	149,000	179,000
2007	T355D	187,000	224,000
2006	T330G	137,000	165,000
2006	T310D	172,000	206,000
2005	T385G	126,000	151,000
2005	T310D	158,000	189,000
2004	T385G	116,000	139,000
2004	T310D	145,000	174,000

Tiara 3300 Open

Year	Power	Retail Low	Retail High
1997	T380G	53,000	64,000
1997	T315D	70,000	84,000
1996	T380G	49,000	59,000
1996	T315D	64,000	77,000
1995	T300G	45,000	54,000
1995	T300D	60,000	72,000

Tiara 3500 Express

Year	Power	Retail Low	Retail High
2003	T385G	102,000	123,000
2003	T450D	135,000	162,000
2002	T385G	93,000	112,000
2002	T435D	122,000	147,000
2001	T385G	85,000	102,000
2001	T435D	111,000	134,000
2000	T385G	78,000	94,000
2000	T435D	102,000	123,000
1999	T320G	72,000	86,000
1999	T435D	94,000	113,000

Year	Power	Retail Low	Retail High
1998	T380G	66,000	79,000
1998	T435D	87,000	104,000
1997	T380G	61,000	73,000
1997	T435D	80,000	96,000
1996	T380G	56,000	67,000
1996	T435D	73,000	88,000
1995	T380G	51,000	61,000
1995	T435D	67,000	81,000

Tiara 3500 Open

Year	Power	Retail Low	Retail High
2004	T385G	98,000	118,000
2004	T370D	123,000	147,000
2003	T385G	89,000	107,000
2003	T370D	112,000	134,000
2002	T385G	81,000	97,000
2002	T370D	102,000	122,000
2001	T320G	74,000	89,000
2001	T370D	92,000	111,000
2000	T320G	68,000	82,000
2000	T370D	85,000	102,000
1999	T320G	62,000	75,000
1999	T370D	78,000	94,000
1998	T320G	57,000	69,000
1998	T370D	72,000	86,000

Tiara 3500 Sovran

Year	Power	Retail Low	Retail High
2010	T375G IPS	******	******
2010	T300D IPS	******	******
2009	T375G IPS	239,000	287,000
2009	T300D IPS	269,000	323,000
2008	T375G IPS	218,000	262,000
2008	T300D IPS	245,000	294,000

Tiara 3600 Convertible

Year	Power	Retail Low	Retail High
1995	T355G	80,000	96,000
1995	T375D	104,000	125,000

Tiara 3600 Open (1987-96)

Year	Power	Retail Low	Retail High
1996	T355G	77,000	93,000
1996	T375D	92,000	111,000
1995	T355G	71,000	85,000
1995	T375D	85,000	102,000

Tiara 3600 Open (Current)

Year	Power	Retail Low	Retail High
2010	T385G	******	******
2010	T380D	******	******
2009	T385G	221,000	265,000
2009	T380D	276,000	332,000
2008	T385G	201,000	241,000
2008	T380D	251,000	302,000
2007	T385G	183,000	219,000
2007	T380D	229,000	275,000
2006	T385G	166,000	200,000
2006	T380D	208,000	250,000
2005	T385G	153,000	184,000
2005	T380D	191,000	230,000

Tiara 3600 Sovran

Year	Power	Retail Low	Retail High
2006	T385G	151,000	182,000
2006	T490D	192,000	231,000
2005	T385G	138,000	165,000
2005	T480D	175,000	210,000
2004	T385G	125,000	150,000
2004	T380D	159,000	191,000

Tiara 3700 Open

Year	Power	Retail Low	Retail High
1999	T435D	110,000	133,000
1998	T435D	125,000	151,000
1997	T435D	102,000	122,000
1996	T435D	115,000	138,000
1995	T435D	93,000	112,000

Tiara 3800 Open

Year	Power	Retail Low	Retail High
2008	T490D	******	******
2007	T490D	******	******

Year	Power	Retail Low	Retail High
2006	T490D	263,000	316,000
2005	T490D	239,000	287,000
2004	T480D	218,000	261,000
2003	T480D	198,000	238,000
2002	T480D	182,000	219,000
2001	T480D	168,000	201,000

Tiara 3900 Convertible

Year	Power	Retail Low	Retail High
2009	T550D	420,000	504,000
2008	T540D	382,000	458,000
2007	T540D	347,000	417,000
2006	T540D	316,000	379,000

Tiara 3900 Open

Year	Power	Retail Low	Retail High
2010	T550D	******	******
2009	T550D	400,000	480,000

Tiara 3900 Sovran

Year	Power	Retail Low	Retail High
2010	T370D IPS	******	******
2009	T370D IPS	370,000	444,000
2008	T370D IPS	336,000	404,000
2007	T370D IPS	306,000	367,000

Tiara 4000 Express

Year	Power	Retail Low	Retail High
2003	T450D	209,000	251,000
2002	T450D	192,000	231,000
2001	T450D	192,000	231,000
2000	T435D	177,000	213,000
1999	T435D	177,000	213,000
1998	T435D	163,000	196,000
1997	T435D	163,000	196,000
1996	T435D	151,000	182,000
1995	T435D	151,000	182,000

Tiara 4100 Open

Year	Power	Retail Low	Retail High
2002	T450D	187,000	225,000
2001	T450D	172,000	207,000
2000	T435D	159,000	190,000
1999	T435D	146,000	175,000
1998	T435D	134,000	161,000
1997	T435D	123,000	148,000
1996	T435D	113,000	136,000

Tiara 4200 Open

Year	Power	Retail Low	Retail High
2009	T670D	******	******
2008	T670D	400,000	480,000
2007	T670D	364,000	437,000
2006	T670D	331,000	397,000
2005	T670D	301,000	361,000
2004	T660D	274,000	329,000
2003	T660D	249,000	299,000

Tiara 4300 Convertible

Year	Power	Retail Low	Retail High
2002	T660D	300,000	360,000
2001	T660D	276,000	331,000
2000	T660D	254,000	304,000
1999	T570D	233,000	280,000
1998	T550D	215,000	258,000
1997	T550D	197,000	237,000
1996	T550D	182,000	218,000
1995	T550D	169,000	203,000

Tiara 4300 Open

Year	Power	Retail Low	Retail High
2002	T660D	264,000	316,000
2001	T660D	242,000	291,000
2000	T660D	223,000	268,000
1999	T550D	205,000	246,000
1998	T550D	189,000	227,000
1997	T550D	174,000	208,000
1996	T550D	160,000	192,000
1995	T550D	148,000	178,000

Tiara 4300 Sovran

Year	Power	Retail Low	Retail High
2010	T435D IPS	******	******
2009	T435D IPS	******	******

Year	Power	Retail Low	Retail High
2008	T435D IPS	398,000	477,000
2007	T435D IPS	366,000	439,000
2006	T435D IPS	336,000	404,000

Tiara 4400/4700 Sovran

Year	Power	Retail Low	Retail High
2008	T670D	******	******
2007	T670D	448,000	538,000
2006	T670D	412,000	494,000
2005	T670D	379,000	455,000
2004	T660D	349,000	418,000
2003	T660D	321,000	385,000

Tiara 5000/5200 Express

Year	Power	Retail Low	Retail High
2003	T800D	******	******
2002	T800D	******	******
2001	T800D	400,000	480,000
2000	T800D	368,000	441,000
1999	T800D	338,000	406,000

Tiara 5200 Sovran Salon

Year	Power	Retail Low	Retail High
2006	T800D	******	******
2005	T800D	******	...
2004	T800D	500,000	600,000
2003	T800D	460,000	552,000

Tollycraft 40 Sport Sedan

Year	Power	Retail Low	Retail High
1995	T-Gas	109,000	131,000
1995	T400D	125,000	151,000

Tollycraft 44/45 Cockpit MY

Year	Power	Retail Low	Retail High
1996	T400D	150,000	180,000
1995	T400D	139,000	167,000

Tollycraft 48 Motor Yacht

Year	Power	Retail Low	Retail High
1998	T435D	199,000	239,000
1997	T435D	185,000	222,000
1996	T435D	172,000	207,000
1995	T435D	160,000	192,000

Tollycraft 57 Motor Yacht

Year	Power	Retail Low	Retail High
1996	T735D	449,000	539,000
1995	T735D	418,000	502,000

Tollycraft 65 Cockpit MY

Year	Power	Retail Low	Retail High
1998	T760D	615,000	738,000
1997	T760D	572,000	686,000
1996	T665D	531,000	638,000
1995	T665D	494,000	593,000

Topaz 32/33 Express

Year	Power	Retail Low	Retail High
2009	T440D	******	******
2008	T440D	******	******
2007	T440D	152,000	183,000
2006	T440D	138,000	166,000
2005	T370D	126,000	151,000
2004	T370D	127,000	153,000

Tradewinds 47 Motor Yacht

Year	Power	Retail Low	Retail High
1995	T305D	225,000	270,000

Triton 2895 Center Console

Year	Power	Retail Low	Retail High
2007	T225 O/B	63,000	76,000
2006	T225 O/B	57,000	69,000
2005	T225 O/B	52,000	63,000
2004	T225 O/B	47,000	57,000

Triton 351 Center Console

Year	Power	Retail Low	Retail High
2010	T250 O/B	******	******
2009	T250 O/B	******	******
2008	T250 O/B	110,000	132,000
2007	T250 O/B	99,000	118,000
2006	T250 O/B	83,000	100,000
2005	T250 O/B	75,000	90,000

Trojan 350/360 Express

Year	Power	Retail Low	Retail High
2001	T320G	75,000	90,000
2000	T320G	68,000	81,000

Year	Power	Retail Low	Retail High
1999	T310G	62,000	74,000
1997	T310G	56,000	67,000
1996	T310G	51,000	61,000
1995	T310G	46,000	56,000

Trojan 370/390/400 Express

Year	Power	Retail Low	Retail High
2002	T320G	103,000	124,000
2001	T320G	94,000	113,000
2000	T320G	85,000	103,000
1999	T320G	78,000	93,000
1998	T320G	71,000	85,000
1997	T320G	64,000	77,000
1996	T320G	58,000	70,000
1995	T350G	54,000	65,000

Trojan 440 Express

Year	Power	Retail Low	Retail High
2002	T450D	225,000	270,000
2001	T450D	204,000	245,000
2000	T450D	186,000	223,000
1999	T450D	169,000	203,000
1998	T450D	154,000	185,000
1997	T450D	141,000	170,000
1996	T420D	130,000	156,000
1995	T420D	120,000	144,000

Trophy 2802 Walkaround

Year	Power	Retail Low	Retail High
2001	T225/OB	36,000	43,000
2000	T225/OB	32,000	39,000
1999	T225/OB	29,000	35,000
1998	T225/OB	27,000	32,000
1997	T225/OB	24,000	29,000

Trophy 2902 Walkaround

Year	Power	Retail Low	Retail High
2009	T225 O/B	78,000	94,000
2008	T225 O/B	71,000	86,000
2007	T225 O/B	65,000	78,000
2006	T225 O/B	59,000	71,000
2005	T225 O/B	54,000	64,000
2004	T225 O/B	49,000	59,000
2003	T225 O/B	44,000	53,000

True World TE288

Year	Power	Retail Low	Retail High
2008	315D	77,000	92,000
2007	315D	70,000	84,000
2006	315D	63,000	76,000
2005	315D	58,000	69,000
2004	315D	52,000	63,000
2003	315D	48,000	57,000
2002	315D	43,000	52,000

Venture 27 Open

Year	Power	Retail Low	Retail High
2010	T200 O/B	******	******
2009	T200 O/B	77,000	92,000
2008	T200 O/B	70,000	84,000
2007	T200 O/B	63,000	76,000

Venture 34 Open

Year	Power	Retail Low	Retail High
2010	T250 O/B	******	******
2009	T250 O/B	******	******
2008	T250 O/B	114,000	137,000
2007	T250 O/B	103,000	124,000
2006	T250 O/B	93,000	111,000
2005	T250 O/B	83,000	100,000
2004	T250 O/B	75,000	90,000
2003	T250 O/B	67,000	81,000
2002	T250 O/B	61,000	74,000
2001	T250 O/B	56,000	67,000
2000	T250 O/B	51,000	61,000
1999	T250 O/B	46,000	55,000
1998	T250 O/B	42,000	50,000
1997	T250 O/B	39,000	47,000

Venture 39 Open

Year	Power	Retail Low	Retail High
2010	3/275 O/B	******	******
2009	3/275 O/B	******	******
2008	3/275 O/B	158,000	189,000
2007	3/275 O/B	142,000	170,000
2006	3/275 O/B	128,000	153,000
2005	3/275 O/B	119,000	142,000

Viking 38 Convertible

Year	Power	Retail Low	Retail High
1995	T485D	120,000	144,000

Viking Sport Cruisers 43 FB

Year	Power	Retail Low	Retail High
1999	T420D	207,000	244,000
1998	T420D	192,000	227,000
1997	T420D	179,000	211,000
1996	T420D	166,000	196,000
1995	T420D	154,000	182,000

Viking 43 Convertible

Year	Power	Retail Low	Retail High
2002	T680D	310,000	441,000
2001	T680D	285,000	406,000
2000	T680D	262,000	373,000
1999	T680D	241,000	344,000
1998	T680D	222,000	316,000
1997	T680D	204,000	291,000
1996	T600D	188,000	267,000
1995	T600D	173,000	246,000

Viking 43 Open

Year	Power	Retail Low	Retail High
2002	T680D	279,000	397,000
2001	T680D	256,000	365,000
2000	T680D	236,000	336,000
1999	T680D	217,000	309,000
1998	T680D	200,000	284,000
1997	T680D	184,000	261,000
1996	T600D	169,000	240,000
1995	T600D	155,000	221,000

Viking 45 Conv. (Current)

Year	Power	Retail Low	Retail High
2009	T900D	******	******
2008	T900D	******	******
2007	T900D	638,000	765,000
2006	T900D	580,000	696,000
2005	T900D	527,000	632,000
2004	T800D	485,000	582,000
2003	T800D	446,000	535,000

Viking 45 Open SF

Year	Power	Retail Low	Retail High
2009	T900D	******	******
2008	T900D	******	******
2007	T900D	******	******
2006	T900D	******	******
2005	T900D	504,000	605,000
2004	T800D	463,000	556,000

Viking Sport Cruisers 45 FB

Year	Power	Retail Low	Retail High
2004	T480D	487,000	584,000
2003	T480D	448,000	537,000
2002	T480D	412,000	494,000
2001	T480D	379,000	455,000
2000	T370D	348,000	418,000
1999	T370D	321,000	385,000

Viking Sport Cruisers 45/46 FB

Year	Power	Retail Low	Retail High
2000	T430D	246,000	296,000
1999	T430D	224,000	269,000
1998	T430D	204,000	245,000
1997	T430D	185,000	223,000
1996	T430D	169,000	203,000
1995	T430D	153,000	184,000

Viking 47 Convertible

Year	Power	Retail Low	Retail High
2002	T800D	396,000	476,000
2001	T680D	365,000	438,000
2000	T680D	335,000	403,000
1999	T680D	309,000	370,000
1998	T680D	284,000	341,000
1997	T680D	261,000	313,000

Year	Power	Retail Low	Retail High
1996	T680D	243,000	291,000
1995	T680D	226,000	271,000

Viking 48 Conv. (2002-09)

Year	Power	Retail Low	Retail High
2009	T1100D	******	******
2008	T1100D	******	******
2007	T1100D	800,000	944,000
2006	T1100D	736,000	868,000
2005	T1050D	677,000	799,000
2004	T1050D	622,000	735,000
2003	T860D	573,000	676,000
2002	T860D	527,000	622,000

Viking Sport Cruisers 48/50 FB

Year	Power	Retail Low	Retail High
1999	T435D	290,000	343,000
1998	T435D	270,000	319,000
1997	T435D	251,000	296,000
1996	T435D	233,000	275,000
1995	T435D	219,000	259,000

Viking 50 Convertible

Year	Power	Retail Low	Retail High
2001	1050D	495,000	585,000
2000	1050D	456,000	538,000
1999	1050D	419,000	495,000
1998	1200D	386,000	455,000
1997	1200D	355,000	419,000
1995	820D	326,000	385,000

Viking 50 Open

Year	Power	Retail Low	Retail High
2003	T820D	583,000	699,000
2002	T800D	536,000	643,000
2001	T800D	493,000	592,000
2000	T800D	454,000	544,000
1999	T800D	417,000	501,000

Viking Sport Cruisers 50 FB

Year	Power	Retail Low	Retail High
2009	T660D	******	******
2008	T660D	******	******
2007	T660D	******	******
2007	T675D	******	******
2005	T675D	628,000	741,000
2004	T700D	577,000	681,000
2003	T700D	531,000	627,000
2002	T700D	489,000	577,000
2001	T700D	449,000	530,000

Viking Sport Cruisers V50 Express

Year	Power	Retail Low	Retail High
2005	T715D	690,000	814,000
2004	T715D	634,000	749,000
2003	T700D	584,000	689,000
2002	T700D	537,000	634,000
2001	T700D	494,000	583,000
2000	T700D	454,000	536,000
1999	T700D	418,000	493,000

Viking 52 Convertible

Year	Power	Retail Low	Retail High
2009	T1360D	******	******
2008	T1360D	******	******
2007	T1360D	******	******
2006	T1300D	1,067,000	1,259,000
2005	T1300D	982,000	1,159,000
2004	T1300D	903,000	1,066,000
2003	T1050D	831,000	981,000
2002	T1050D	764,000	902,000

Viking Sport Cruisers 52 FB

Year	Power	Retail Low	Retail High
2002	T615D	534,000	630,000
2001	T615D	496,000	586,000
2000	T610D	462,000	545,000
1999	T610D	429,000	507,000
1998	T610D	399,000	471,000
1997	T610D	371,000	438,000

Viking 53 Convertible

Year	Power	Retail Low	Retail High
1998	T820D	359,000	423,000

Year	Power	Retail Low	Retail High
1997	T820D	330,000	389,000
1996	T820D	304,000	358,000
1995	T820D	279,000	330,000

Viking 54 Sports Yacht

Year	Power	Retail Low	Retail High
2001	T820D	475,000	561,000
2000	T820D	437,000	516,000
1999	T820D	402,000	475,000
1998	T820D	370,000	437,000
1997	T820D	340,000	402,000
1996	T820D	313,000	370,000
1995	T820D	288,000	340,000

Viking 55 Convertible

Year	Power	Retail Low	Retail High
2002	T1300D	616,000	727,000
2001	T1050D	567,000	669,000
2000	T1050D	521,000	615,000
1999	T1050D	480,000	566,000
1998	T1050D	441,000	521,000

Viking 56 Convertible

Year	Power	Retail Low	Retail High
2009	T1550D	******	******
2008	T1550D	******	******
2007	T1550D	1,150,000	1,345,000
2006	T1550D	1,069,000	1,251,000
2005	T1520D	994,000	1,163,000
2004	T1480D	925,000	1,082,000

Viking Sport Cruisers 56 FB

Year	Power	Retail Low	Retail High
2002	T700D	******	******
2001	T700D	560,000	649,000
2000	T700D	520,000	604,000
1999	T700D	484,000	561,000
1998	T700D	450,000	522,000
1997	T610D	418,000	485,000

Viking 57 Motor Yacht

Year	Power	Retail Low	Retail High
1995	T760D	360,000	424,000

Viking Sport Cruisers 57 FB

Year	Power	Retail Low	Retail High
2008	T715D	******	******
2007	T715D	******	******
2006	T715D	961,000	1,124,000
2005	T715D	884,000	1,034,000

Viking 58 Convertible

Year	Power	Retail Low	Retail High
2000	T1200D	592,000	698,000
1999	T1200D	544,000	642,000
1998	T1150D	501,000	591,000
1997	T1200D	461,000	544,000
1996	T1200D	424,000	500,000
1995	T1200D	390,000	460,000
1994	T1100D	362,000	428,000
1993	T1100D	337,000	398,000
1992	T1100D	313,000	370,000
1991	T1100D	291,000	344,000

Viking Sport Cruisers V58 Express

Year	Power	Retail Low	Retail High
2009	T1100D	******	******
2008	T1100D	******	******
2007	T1100D	******	******
2006	T1100D	******	******
2005	T900D	971,000	1,146,000
2004	T860D	903,000	1,065,000
2003	T860D	839,000	991,000

Viking 60 Cockpit Sport Yacht

Year	Power	Retail Low	Retail High
2001	T820D	607,000	716,000
2000	T820D	558,000	659,000
1999	T820D	513,000	606,000
1998	T820D	472,000	557,000
1997	T820D	434,000	513,000
1996	T820D	404,000	477,000
1995	T820D	376,000	443,000

Viking Sports Cruisers 60 FB

Year	Power	Retail Low	Retail High
2001	T800D	******	******
2000	T800D	******	******
1999	T800D	475,000	555,000
1998	T800D	437,000	511,000
1997	T800D	402,000	470,000
1996	T800D	369,000	432,000

Viking 61 Convertible

Year	Power	Retail Low	Retail High
2006	T1520D	1,389,000	1,853,000
2005	T1520D	1,291,000	1,723,000
2004	T1480D	1,201,000	1,602,000
2003	T1480D	1,117,000	1,490,000
2002	T1480D	1,039,000	1,386,000
2001	T1300D	966,000	1,289,000

Viking 64 Convertible

Year	Power	Retail Low	Retail High
2010	T1835D	******	******
2009	T1835D	******	******
2008	T1835D	2,000,000	2,320,000
2007	T1835D	1,860,000	2,157,000
2006	T1835D	1,729,000	2,006,000

Viking 65 Convertible

Year	Power	Retail Low	Retail High
2005	T2030D	******	******
2004	T2000 D	1,327,000	1,552,000
2003	T1800 D	1,234,000	1,443,000
2002	T1800 D	1,147,000	1,342,000
2001	T1800 D	1,067,000	1,248,000
2000	T1800 D	992,000	1,161,000
1999	T1800 D	923,000	1,080,000

Viking 65 Motor Yacht

Year	Power	Retail Low	Retail High
1995	T1000D	480,000	561,000

Wellcraft 2700 Martinique

Year	Power	Retail Low	Retail High
1995	330 I/O	15,000	22,000
1994	330 I/O	14,000	20,000

Wellcraft 270 Coastal

Year	Power	Retail Low	Retail High
2008	T225 O/B	87,000	110,000
2007	T225 O/B	79,000	100,000
2006	No Production	******	******
2005	No Producton	******	******
2004	T225 O/B	59,000	74,000
2004	S375 I/O	64,000	81,000
2003	T225 O/B	54,000	67,000
2003	S375 I/O	59,000	73,000
2002	T225 O/B	49,000	61,000
2002	S330 I/O	53,000	67,000
2001	T225 O/B	44,000	56,000
2001	S330 I/O	48,000	61,000

Wellcraft 2800 Martinique (01-02)

Year	Power	Retail Low	Retail High
2002	T190 I/O	33,000	40,000
2002	S310 I/O	31,000	38,000
2001	T190 I/O	30,000	36,000
2001	T190 I/O	29,000	34,000

Wellcraft 2800 Martinique (97-99)

Year	Power	Retail Low	Retail High
1999	T190 I/O	25,000	30,000
1999	330 I/O	23,000	27,000
1998	T190 I/O	23,000	27,000
1998	330 I/O	21,000	25,000
1997	T190 I/O	21,000	25,000
1997	330 I/O	19,000	23,000

Wellcraft 290 Coastal

Year	Power	Retail Low	Retail High
2009	T225 O/B	113,000	135,000
2008	T225 O/B	102,000	123,000
2007	T225 O/B	93,000	112,000
2006	T225 O/B	85,000	102,000
2005	T225 O/B	77,000	92,000
2004	T225 O/B	71,000	85,000
2003	T225 O/B	65,000	78,000
2002	T225 O/B	60,000	72,000

Year	Power	Retail Low	Retail High
2001	T225 O/B	55,000	66,000
2000	T225 O/B	51,000	61,000
1999	T225 O/B	46,000	56,000

Wellcraft 29 Scarab Sport; 29 CCF

Year	Power	Retail Low	Retail High
2004	T225 O/B	50,000	60,000
2003	T225 O/B	45,000	54,000
2002	T225 O/B	40,000	49,000
2001	T225 O/B	36,000	44,000

Wellcraft 30 Scarab Tourn.

Year	Power	Retail Low	Retail High
2009	T250 O/B	******	******
2008	T250 O/B	86,000	103,000
2007	T250 O/B	77,000	93,000

Wellcraft 3000 Martinique

Year	Power	Retail Low	Retail High
2002	T260 I/O	47,000	57,000
2001	T260 I/O	44,000	52,000
2000	T260 I/O	40,000	48,000
1999	T260 I/O	37,000	44,000
1998	T260 I/O	34,000	41,000

Wellcraft 302 Scarab Sport

Year	Power	Retail Low	Retail High
2000	T250 O/B	34,000	41,000
1999	T250 O/B	31,000	38,000
1998	T250 O/B	28,000	34,000
1997	T250 O/B	26,000	31,000
1996	T250 O/B	23,000	28,000
1995	T250 O/B	21,000	26,000

Wellcraft 32 Scarab Sport; 32 CCF

Year	Power	Retail Low	Retail High
2006	T250 O/B	69,000	83,000
2005	T250 O/B	62,000	74,000
2004	T250 O/B	56,000	67,000
2003	T250 O/B	50,000	60,000
2002	T250 O/B	45,000	54,000
2001	T250 O/B	40,000	49,000

Wellcraft 3200 Martinique

Year	Power	Retail Low	Retail High
2000	T310 I/O	43,000	51,000
1999	T310 I/O	39,000	47,000
1998	T310 I/O	36,000	43,000
1997	T310 I/O	33,000	40,000
1996	T300 I/O	30,000	36,000
1995	T300 I/O	28,000	34,000
1994	T300 I/O	26,000	31,000

Wellcraft 330 Coastal

Year	Power	Retail Low	Retail High
2009	T370D	******	******
2008	T370D	******	******
2007	T370D	158,000	189,000
2006	T370D	143,000	172,000
2005	T360D	131,000	157,000
2004	T360D	119,000	143,000
2003	T360D	108,000	130,000
2002	T360D	98,000	118,000
2001	T350D	89,000	107,000
2000	T350D	82,000	99,000
1999	T350D	76,000	91,000
1998	T350D	69,000	83,000
1997	T300D	64,000	77,000
1996	T300D	59,000	71,000
1995	T300D	54,000	65,000

Wellcraft 3300 Martinique

Year	Power	Retail Low	Retail High
2002	T310G	57,000	69,000
2001	T310G	52,000	63,000

Wellcraft 35 Scarab Sport

Year	Power	Retail Low	Retail High
2009	3/250 O/B	******	******
2008	3/250 O/B	106,000	127,000
2007	3/250 O/B	95,000	114,000

Wellcraft 35 Scarab Sport; 35 CCF

Year	Power	Retail Low	Retail High
2005	T250 O/B	64,000	77,000
2004	T250 O/B	58,000	69,000

Year	Power	Retail Low	Retail High
2003	T250 O/B	52,000	62,000
2002	T250 O/B	47,000	56,000
2001	T250 O/B	42,000	50,000

Wellcraft 350 Coastal

Year	Power	Retail Low	Retail High
2003	T375G	146,000	176,000
2003	T360D	174,000	209,000
2002	T375G	134,000	161,000
2002	T360D	160,000	193,000
2001	T375G	124,000	149,000
2001	T360D	148,000	177,000
2000	T375G	114,000	137,000
2000	T370D	136,000	163,000

Wellcraft 360 Coastal

Year	Power	Retail Low	Retail High
2009	T370D	******	******
2008	T370D	******	******
2007	T370D	234,000	281,000
2006	T370D	211,000	253,000

Wellcraft 3600 Martinique

Year	Power	Retail Low	Retail High
2000	T385G	59,000	71,000
1999	T385G	55,000	66,000
1998	T380G	50,000	60,000
1997	T330G	46,000	56,000
1996	T330G	42,000	51,000
1995	T330G	39,000	47,000
1994	T330G	37,000	44,000

Wellcraft 3700 Martinique

Year	Power	Retail Low	Retail High
2002	T370G	98,000	118,000
2001	T370G	91,000	109,000

Wellcraft 38 Excalibur

Year	Power	Retail Low	Retail High
2002	T425 I/O	140,000	168,000
2001	T425 I/O	129,000	155,000
2000	T385 I/O	118,000	142,000
1999	T385 I/O	109,000	131,000
1998	T385 I/O	100,000	120,000
1997	T385 I/O	93,000	112,000
1996	T385 I/O	86,000	104,000

Wellcraft 400 Coastal

Year	Power	Retail Low	Retail High
2003	T480D	244,000	293,000
2002	T480D	225,000	270,000
2001	T430D	207,000	248,000
2000	T430D	190,000	228,000
1999	T430D	175,000	210,000

Wellcraft 43 Portifino

Year	Power	Retail Low	Retail High
1997	T-Gas	100,000	120,000
1997	T420D	121,000	146,000
1996	T-Gas	92,000	111,000
1996	T420D	112,000	134,000
1995	T-Gas	85,000	102,000
1995	T350D	103,000	123,000

Wellcraft 45 Excalibur

Year	Power	Retail Low	Retail High
2001	T415G	132,000	158,000
2000	T415G	123,000	147,000
1999	T415G	114,000	137,000
1998	T415G	106,000	127,000
1997	T415G	99,000	118,000
1996	T415G	92,000	110,000
1995	T415G	85,000	102,000

Wellcraft 46 Cockpit MY

Year	Power	Retail Low	Retail High
1995	T435D	144,000	173,000

West Bay 58 Sonship

Year	Power	Retail Low	Retail High
2005	T700D	500,000	590,000

Yellowfin 34

Year	Power	Retail Low	Retail High
2010	3/250 O/B	******	******
2009	3/250 O/B	******	******
2008	3/250 O/B	137,000	164,000
2007	3/250 O/B	123,000	148,000
2006	3/250 O/B	111,000	133,000
2005	3/250 O/B	100,000	120,000

Yellowfin 36

Year	Power	Retail Low	Retail High
2010	3/275 O/B	******	******
2009	3/275 O/B	******	******
2008	3/275 O/B	155,000	186,000
2007	3/275 O/B	139,000	167,000
2006	3/275 O/B	125,000	150,000
2005	3/275 O/B	113,000	135,000
2004	3/275 O/B	101,000	122,000
2003	3/275 O/B	91,000	109,000

Index

Index

Index

Index

Index

T

Made in the USA
Lexington, KY
22 February 2012